Lecture Notes in Computer Science   13673

More information about this series at https://link.springer.com/bookseries/558

Shai Avidan · Gabriel Brostow ·
Moustapha Cissé · Giovanni Maria Farinella ·
Tal Hassner (Eds.)

Computer Vision – ECCV 2022

17th European Conference
Tel Aviv, Israel, October 23–27, 2022
Proceedings, Part XIII

 Springer

Editors
Shai Avidan
Tel Aviv University
Tel Aviv, Israel

Gabriel Brostow ⓘ
University College London
London, UK

Moustapha Cissé
Google AI
Accra, Ghana

Giovanni Maria Farinella ⓘ
University of Catania
Catania, Italy

Tal Hassner ⓘ
Facebook (United States)
Menlo Park, CA, USA

ISSN 0302-9743   ISSN 1611-3349 (electronic)
Lecture Notes in Computer Science
ISBN 978-3-031-19777-2   ISBN 978-3-031-19778-9 (eBook)
https://doi.org/10.1007/978-3-031-19778-9

This Springer imprint is published by the registered company Springer Nature Switzerland AG
The registered company address is: Gewerbestrasse 11, 6330 Cham, Switzerland

Foreword

Organizing the European Conference on Computer Vision (ECCV 2022) in Tel-Aviv during a global pandemic was no easy feat. The uncertainty level was extremely high, and decisions had to be postponed to the last minute. Still, we managed to plan things just in time for ECCV 2022 to be held in person. Participation in physical events is crucial to stimulating collaborations and nurturing the culture of the Computer Vision community.

There were many people who worked hard to ensure attendees enjoyed the best science at the 16th edition of ECCV. We are grateful to the Program Chairs Gabriel Brostow and Tal Hassner, who went above and beyond to ensure the ECCV reviewing process ran smoothly. The scientific program includes dozens of workshops and tutorials in addition to the main conference and we would like to thank Leonid Karlinsky and Tomer Michaeli for their hard work. Finally, special thanks to the web chairs Lorenzo Baraldi and Kosta Derpanis, who put in extra hours to transfer information fast and efficiently to the ECCV community.

We would like to express gratitude to our generous sponsors and the Industry Chairs, Dimosthenis Karatzas and Chen Sagiv, who oversaw industry relations and proposed new ways for academia-industry collaboration and technology transfer. It's great to see so much industrial interest in what we're doing!

Authors' draft versions of the papers appeared online with open access on both the Computer Vision Foundation (CVF) and the European Computer Vision Association (ECVA) websites as with previous ECCVs. Springer, the publisher of the proceedings, has arranged for archival publication. The final version of the papers is hosted by SpringerLink, with active references and supplementary materials. It benefits all potential readers that we offer both a free and citeable version for all researchers, as well as an authoritative, citeable version for SpringerLink readers. Our thanks go to Ronan Nugent from Springer, who helped us negotiate this agreement. Last but not least, we wish to thank Eric Mortensen, our publication chair, whose expertise made the process smooth.

October 2022

Rita Cucchiara
Jiří Matas
Amnon Shashua
Lihi Zelnik-Manor

Preface

Welcome to the proceedings of the European Conference on Computer Vision (ECCV 2022). This was a hybrid edition of ECCV as we made our way out of the COVID-19 pandemic. The conference received 5804 valid paper submissions, compared to 5150 submissions to ECCV 2020 (a 12.7% increase) and 2439 in ECCV 2018. 1645 submissions were accepted for publication (28%) and, of those, 157 (2.7% overall) as orals.

846 of the submissions were desk-rejected for various reasons. Many of them because they revealed author identity, thus violating the double-blind policy. This violation came in many forms: some had author names with the title, others added acknowledgments to specific grants, yet others had links to their github account where their name was visible. Tampering with the LaTeX template was another reason for automatic desk rejection.

ECCV 2022 used the traditional CMT system to manage the entire double-blind reviewing process. Authors did not know the names of the reviewers and vice versa. Each paper received at least 3 reviews (except 6 papers that received only 2 reviews), totalling more than 15,000 reviews.

Handling the review process at this scale was a significant challenge. To ensure that each submission received as fair and high-quality reviews as possible, we recruited more than 4719 reviewers (in the end, 4719 reviewers did at least one review). Similarly we recruited more than 276 area chairs (eventually, only 276 area chairs handled a batch of papers). The area chairs were selected based on their technical expertise and reputation, largely among people who served as area chairs in previous top computer vision and machine learning conferences (ECCV, ICCV, CVPR, NeurIPS, etc.).

Reviewers were similarly invited from previous conferences, and also from the pool of authors. We also encouraged experienced area chairs to suggest additional chairs and reviewers in the initial phase of recruiting. The median reviewer load was five papers per reviewer, while the average load was about four papers, because of the emergency reviewers. The area chair load was 35 papers, on average.

Conflicts of interest between authors, area chairs, and reviewers were handled largely automatically by the CMT platform, with some manual help from the Program Chairs. Reviewers were allowed to describe themselves as senior reviewer (load of 8 papers to review) or junior reviewers (load of 4 papers). Papers were matched to area chairs based on a subject-area affinity score computed in CMT and an affinity score computed by the Toronto Paper Matching System (TPMS). TPMS is based on the paper's full text. An area chair handling each submission would bid for preferred expert reviewers, and we balanced load and prevented conflicts.

The assignment of submissions to area chairs was relatively smooth, as was the assignment of submissions to reviewers. A small percentage of reviewers were not happy with their assignments in terms of subjects and self-reported expertise. This is an area for improvement, although it's interesting that many of these cases were reviewers handpicked by AC's. We made a later round of reviewer recruiting, targeted at the list of authors of papers submitted to the conference, and had an excellent response which helped provide enough emergency reviewers. In the end, all but six papers received at least 3 reviews.

The challenges of the reviewing process are in line with past experiences at ECCV 2020. As the community grows, and the number of submissions increases, it becomes ever more challenging to recruit enough reviewers and ensure a high enough quality of reviews. Enlisting authors by default as reviewers might be one step to address this challenge.

Authors were given a week to rebut the initial reviews, and address reviewers' concerns. Each rebuttal was limited to a single pdf page with a fixed template.

The Area Chairs then led discussions with the reviewers on the merits of each submission. The goal was to reach consensus, but, ultimately, it was up to the Area Chair to make a decision. The decision was then discussed with a buddy Area Chair to make sure decisions were fair and informative. The entire process was conducted virtually with no in-person meetings taking place.

The Program Chairs were informed in cases where the Area Chairs overturned a decisive consensus reached by the reviewers, and pushed for the meta-reviews to contain details that explained the reasoning for such decisions. Obviously these were the most contentious cases, where reviewer inexperience was the most common reported factor.

Once the list of accepted papers was finalized and released, we went through the laborious process of plagiarism (including self-plagiarism) detection. A total of 4 accepted papers were rejected because of that.

Finally, we would like to thank our Technical Program Chair, Pavel Lifshits, who did tremendous work behind the scenes, and we thank the tireless CMT team.

October 2022

Gabriel Brostow
Giovanni Maria Farinella
Moustapha Cissé
Shai Avidan
Tal Hassner

Organization

General Chairs

Rita Cucchiara	University of Modena and Reggio Emilia, Italy
Jiří Matas	Czech Technical University in Prague, Czech Republic
Amnon Shashua	Hebrew University of Jerusalem, Israel
Lihi Zelnik-Manor	Technion – Israel Institute of Technology, Israel

Program Chairs

Shai Avidan	Tel-Aviv University, Israel
Gabriel Brostow	University College London, UK
Moustapha Cissé	Google AI, Ghana
Giovanni Maria Farinella	University of Catania, Italy
Tal Hassner	Facebook AI, USA

Program Technical Chair

Pavel Lifshits	Technion – Israel Institute of Technology, Israel

Workshops Chairs

Leonid Karlinsky	IBM Research, Israel
Tomer Michaeli	Technion – Israel Institute of Technology, Israel
Ko Nishino	Kyoto University, Japan

Tutorial Chairs

Thomas Pock	Graz University of Technology, Austria
Natalia Neverova	Facebook AI Research, UK

Demo Chair

Bohyung Han	Seoul National University, Korea

Social and Student Activities Chairs

Tatiana Tommasi	Italian Institute of Technology, Italy
Sagie Benaim	University of Copenhagen, Denmark

Diversity and Inclusion Chairs

Xi Yin	Facebook AI Research, USA
Bryan Russell	Adobe, USA

Communications Chairs

Lorenzo Baraldi	University of Modena and Reggio Emilia, Italy
Kosta Derpanis	York University & Samsung AI Centre Toronto, Canada

Industrial Liaison Chairs

Dimosthenis Karatzas	Universitat Autònoma de Barcelona, Spain
Chen Sagiv	SagivTech, Israel

Finance Chair

Gerard Medioni	University of Southern California & Amazon, USA

Publication Chair

Eric Mortensen	MiCROTEC, USA

Area Chairs

Lourdes Agapito	University College London, UK
Zeynep Akata	University of Tübingen, Germany
Naveed Akhtar	University of Western Australia, Australia
Karteek Alahari	Inria Grenoble Rhône-Alpes, France
Alexandre Alahi	École polytechnique fédérale de Lausanne, Switzerland
Pablo Arbelaez	Universidad de Los Andes, Columbia
Antonis A. Argyros	University of Crete & Foundation for Research and Technology-Hellas, Crete
Yuki M. Asano	University of Amsterdam, The Netherlands
Kalle Åström	Lund University, Sweden
Hadar Averbuch-Elor	Cornell University, USA

Hossein Azizpour   KTH Royal Institute of Technology, Sweden
Vineeth N. Balasubramanian   Indian Institute of Technology, Hyderabad, India
Lamberto Ballan   University of Padova, Italy
Adrien Bartoli   Université Clermont Auvergne, France
Horst Bischof   Graz University of Technology, Austria
Matthew B. Blaschko   KU Leuven, Belgium
Federica Bogo   Meta Reality Labs Research, Switzerland
Katherine Bouman   California Institute of Technology, USA
Edmond Boyer   Inria Grenoble Rhône-Alpes, France
Michael S. Brown   York University, Canada
Vittorio Caggiano   Meta AI Research, USA
Neill Campbell   University of Bath, UK
Octavia Camps   Northeastern University, USA
Duygu Ceylan   Adobe Research, USA
Ayan Chakrabarti   Google Research, USA
Tat-Jen Cham   Nanyang Technological University, Singapore
Antoni Chan   City University of Hong Kong, Hong Kong, China
Manmohan Chandraker   NEC Labs America, USA
Xinlei Chen   Facebook AI Research, USA
Xilin Chen   Institute of Computing Technology, Chinese
                                      Academy of Sciences, China
Dongdong Chen   Microsoft Cloud AI, USA
Chen Chen   University of Central Florida, USA
Ondrej Chum   Vision Recognition Group, Czech Technical
                                      University in Prague, Czech Republic
John Collomosse   Adobe Research & University of Surrey, UK
Camille Couprie   Facebook, France
David Crandall   Indiana University, USA
Daniel Cremers   Technical University of Munich, Germany
Marco Cristani   University of Verona, Italy
Canton Cristian   Facebook AI Research, USA
Dengxin Dai   ETH Zurich, Switzerland
Dima Damen   University of Bristol, UK
Kostas Daniilidis   University of Pennsylvania, USA
Trevor Darrell   University of California, Berkeley, USA
Andrew Davison   Imperial College London, UK
Tali Dekel   Weizmann Institute of Science, Israel
Alessio Del Bue   Istituto Italiano di Tecnologia, Italy
Weihong Deng   Beijing University of Posts and
                                      Telecommunications, China
Konstantinos Derpanis   Ryerson University, Canada
Carl Doersch   DeepMind, UK

Matthijs Douze	Facebook AI Research, USA
Mohamed Elhoseiny	King Abdullah University of Science and Technology, Saudi Arabia
Sergio Escalera	University of Barcelona, Spain
Yi Fang	New York University, USA
Ryan Farrell	Brigham Young University, USA
Alireza Fathi	Google, USA
Christoph Feichtenhofer	Facebook AI Research, USA
Basura Fernando	Agency for Science, Technology and Research (A*STAR), Singapore
Vittorio Ferrari	Google Research, Switzerland
Andrew W. Fitzgibbon	Graphcore, UK
David J. Fleet	University of Toronto, Canada
David Forsyth	University of Illinois at Urbana-Champaign, USA
David Fouhey	University of Michigan, USA
Katerina Fragkiadaki	Carnegie Mellon University, USA
Friedrich Fraundorfer	Graz University of Technology, Austria
Oren Freifeld	Ben-Gurion University, Israel
Thomas Funkhouser	Google Research & Princeton University, USA
Yasutaka Furukawa	Simon Fraser University, Canada
Fabio Galasso	Sapienza University of Rome, Italy
Jürgen Gall	University of Bonn, Germany
Chuang Gan	Massachusetts Institute of Technology, USA
Zhe Gan	Microsoft, USA
Animesh Garg	University of Toronto, Vector Institute, Nvidia, Canada
Efstratios Gavves	University of Amsterdam, The Netherlands
Peter Gehler	Amazon, Germany
Theo Gevers	University of Amsterdam, The Netherlands
Bernard Ghanem	King Abdullah University of Science and Technology, Saudi Arabia
Ross B. Girshick	Facebook AI Research, USA
Georgia Gkioxari	Facebook AI Research, USA
Albert Gordo	Facebook, USA
Stephen Gould	Australian National University, Australia
Venu Madhav Govindu	Indian Institute of Science, India
Kristen Grauman	Facebook AI Research & UT Austin, USA
Abhinav Gupta	Carnegie Mellon University & Facebook AI Research, USA
Mohit Gupta	University of Wisconsin-Madison, USA
Hu Han	Institute of Computing Technology, Chinese Academy of Sciences, China

Bohyung Han	Seoul National University, Korea
Tian Han	Stevens Institute of Technology, USA
Emily Hand	University of Nevada, Reno, USA
Bharath Hariharan	Cornell University, USA
Ran He	Institute of Automation, Chinese Academy of Sciences, China
Otmar Hilliges	ETH Zurich, Switzerland
Adrian Hilton	University of Surrey, UK
Minh Hoai	Stony Brook University, USA
Yedid Hoshen	Hebrew University of Jerusalem, Israel
Timothy Hospedales	University of Edinburgh, UK
Gang Hua	Wormpex AI Research, USA
Di Huang	Beihang University, China
Jing Huang	Facebook, USA
Jia-Bin Huang	Facebook, USA
Nathan Jacobs	Washington University in St. Louis, USA
C.V. Jawahar	International Institute of Information Technology, Hyderabad, India
Herve Jegou	Facebook AI Research, France
Neel Joshi	Microsoft Research, USA
Armand Joulin	Facebook AI Research, France
Frederic Jurie	University of Caen Normandie, France
Fredrik Kahl	Chalmers University of Technology, Sweden
Yannis Kalantidis	NAVER LABS Europe, France
Evangelos Kalogerakis	University of Massachusetts, Amherst, USA
Sing Bing Kang	Zillow Group, USA
Yosi Keller	Bar Ilan University, Israel
Margret Keuper	University of Mannheim, Germany
Tae-Kyun Kim	Imperial College London, UK
Benjamin Kimia	Brown University, USA
Alexander Kirillov	Facebook AI Research, USA
Kris Kitani	Carnegie Mellon University, USA
Iasonas Kokkinos	Snap Inc. & University College London, UK
Vladlen Koltun	Apple, USA
Nikos Komodakis	University of Crete, Crete
Piotr Koniusz	Australian National University, Australia
Philipp Kraehenbuehl	University of Texas at Austin, USA
Dilip Krishnan	Google, USA
Ajay Kumar	Hong Kong Polytechnic University, Hong Kong, China
Junseok Kwon	Chung-Ang University, Korea
Jean-Francois Lalonde	Université Laval, Canada

Ivan Laptev	Inria Paris, France
Laura Leal-Taixé	Technical University of Munich, Germany
Erik Learned-Miller	University of Massachusetts, Amherst, USA
Gim Hee Lee	National University of Singapore, Singapore
Seungyong Lee	Pohang University of Science and Technology, Korea
Zhen Lei	Institute of Automation, Chinese Academy of Sciences, China
Bastian Leibe	RWTH Aachen University, Germany
Hongdong Li	Australian National University, Australia
Fuxin Li	Oregon State University, USA
Bo Li	University of Illinois at Urbana-Champaign, USA
Yin Li	University of Wisconsin-Madison, USA
Ser-Nam Lim	Meta AI Research, USA
Joseph Lim	University of Southern California, USA
Stephen Lin	Microsoft Research Asia, China
Dahua Lin	The Chinese University of Hong Kong, Hong Kong, China
Si Liu	Beihang University, China
Xiaoming Liu	Michigan State University, USA
Ce Liu	Microsoft, USA
Zicheng Liu	Microsoft, USA
Yanxi Liu	Pennsylvania State University, USA
Feng Liu	Portland State University, USA
Yebin Liu	Tsinghua University, China
Chen Change Loy	Nanyang Technological University, Singapore
Huchuan Lu	Dalian University of Technology, China
Cewu Lu	Shanghai Jiao Tong University, China
Oisin Mac Aodha	University of Edinburgh, UK
Dhruv Mahajan	Facebook, USA
Subhransu Maji	University of Massachusetts, Amherst, USA
Atsuto Maki	KTH Royal Institute of Technology, Sweden
Arun Mallya	NVIDIA, USA
R. Manmatha	Amazon, USA
Iacopo Masi	Sapienza University of Rome, Italy
Dimitris N. Metaxas	Rutgers University, USA
Ajmal Mian	University of Western Australia, Australia
Christian Micheloni	University of Udine, Italy
Krystian Mikolajczyk	Imperial College London, UK
Anurag Mittal	Indian Institute of Technology, Madras, India
Philippos Mordohai	Stevens Institute of Technology, USA
Greg Mori	Simon Fraser University & Borealis AI, Canada

Vittorio Murino	Istituto Italiano di Tecnologia, Italy
P. J. Narayanan	International Institute of Information Technology, Hyderabad, India
Ram Nevatia	University of Southern California, USA
Natalia Neverova	Facebook AI Research, UK
Richard Newcombe	Facebook, USA
Cuong V. Nguyen	Florida International University, USA
Bingbing Ni	Shanghai Jiao Tong University, China
Juan Carlos Niebles	Salesforce & Stanford University, USA
Ko Nishino	Kyoto University, Japan
Jean-Marc Odobez	Idiap Research Institute, École polytechnique fédérale de Lausanne, Switzerland
Francesca Odone	University of Genova, Italy
Takayuki Okatani	Tohoku University & RIKEN Center for Advanced Intelligence Project, Japan
Manohar Paluri	Facebook, USA
Guan Pang	Facebook, USA
Maja Pantic	Imperial College London, UK
Sylvain Paris	Adobe Research, USA
Jaesik Park	Pohang University of Science and Technology, Korea
Hyun Soo Park	The University of Minnesota, USA
Omkar M. Parkhi	Facebook, USA
Deepak Pathak	Carnegie Mellon University, USA
Georgios Pavlakos	University of California, Berkeley, USA
Marcello Pelillo	University of Venice, Italy
Marc Pollefeys	ETH Zurich & Microsoft, Switzerland
Jean Ponce	Inria, France
Gerard Pons-Moll	University of Tübingen, Germany
Fatih Porikli	Qualcomm, USA
Victor Adrian Prisacariu	University of Oxford, UK
Petia Radeva	University of Barcelona, Spain
Ravi Ramamoorthi	University of California, San Diego, USA
Deva Ramanan	Carnegie Mellon University, USA
Vignesh Ramanathan	Facebook, USA
Nalini Ratha	State University of New York at Buffalo, USA
Tammy Riklin Raviv	Ben-Gurion University, Israel
Tobias Ritschel	University College London, UK
Emanuele Rodola	Sapienza University of Rome, Italy
Amit K. Roy-Chowdhury	University of California, Riverside, USA
Michael Rubinstein	Google, USA
Olga Russakovsky	Princeton University, USA

Mathieu Salzmann	École polytechnique fédérale de Lausanne, Switzerland
Dimitris Samaras	Stony Brook University, USA
Aswin Sankaranarayanan	Carnegie Mellon University, USA
Imari Sato	National Institute of Informatics, Japan
Yoichi Sato	University of Tokyo, Japan
Shin'ichi Satoh	National Institute of Informatics, Japan
Walter Scheirer	University of Notre Dame, USA
Bernt Schiele	Max Planck Institute for Informatics, Germany
Konrad Schindler	ETH Zurich, Switzerland
Cordelia Schmid	Inria & Google, France
Alexander Schwing	University of Illinois at Urbana-Champaign, USA
Nicu Sebe	University of Trento, Italy
Greg Shakhnarovich	Toyota Technological Institute at Chicago, USA
Eli Shechtman	Adobe Research, USA
Humphrey Shi	University of Oregon & University of Illinois at Urbana-Champaign & Picsart AI Research, USA
Jianbo Shi	University of Pennsylvania, USA
Roy Shilkrot	Massachusetts Institute of Technology, USA
Mike Zheng Shou	National University of Singapore, Singapore
Kaleem Siddiqi	McGill University, Canada
Richa Singh	Indian Institute of Technology Jodhpur, India
Greg Slabaugh	Queen Mary University of London, UK
Cees Snoek	University of Amsterdam, The Netherlands
Yale Song	Facebook AI Research, USA
Yi-Zhe Song	University of Surrey, UK
Bjorn Stenger	Rakuten Institute of Technology
Abby Stylianou	Saint Louis University, USA
Akihiro Sugimoto	National Institute of Informatics, Japan
Chen Sun	Brown University, USA
Deqing Sun	Google, USA
Kalyan Sunkavalli	Adobe Research, USA
Ying Tai	Tencent YouTu Lab, China
Ayellet Tal	Technion – Israel Institute of Technology, Israel
Ping Tan	Simon Fraser University, Canada
Siyu Tang	ETH Zurich, Switzerland
Chi-Keung Tang	Hong Kong University of Science and Technology, Hong Kong, China
Radu Timofte	University of Würzburg, Germany & ETH Zurich, Switzerland
Federico Tombari	Google, Switzerland & Technical University of Munich, Germany

James Tompkin   Brown University, USA
Lorenzo Torresani   Dartmouth College, USA
Alexander Toshev   Apple, USA
Du Tran   Facebook AI Research, USA
Anh T. Tran   VinAI, Vietnam
Zhuowen Tu   University of California, San Diego, USA
Georgios Tzimiropoulos   Queen Mary University of London, UK
Jasper Uijlings   Google Research, Switzerland
Jan C. van Gemert   Delft University of Technology, The Netherlands
Gul Varol   Ecole des Ponts ParisTech, France
Nuno Vasconcelos   University of California, San Diego, USA
Mayank Vatsa   Indian Institute of Technology Jodhpur, India
Ashok Veeraraghavan   Rice University, USA
Jakob Verbeek   Facebook AI Research, France
Carl Vondrick   Columbia University, USA
Ruiping Wang   Institute of Computing Technology, Chinese
                                          Academy of Sciences, China
Xinchao Wang   National University of Singapore, Singapore
Liwei Wang   The Chinese University of Hong Kong,
                                          Hong Kong, China
Chaohui Wang   Université Paris-Est, France
Xiaolong Wang   University of California, San Diego, USA
Christian Wolf   NAVER LABS Europe, France
Tao Xiang   University of Surrey, UK
Saining Xie   Facebook AI Research, USA
Cihang Xie   University of California, Santa Cruz, USA
Zeki Yalniz   Facebook, USA
Ming-Hsuan Yang   University of California, Merced, USA
Angela Yao   National University of Singapore, Singapore
Shaodi You   University of Amsterdam, The Netherlands
Stella X. Yu   University of California, Berkeley, USA
Junsong Yuan   State University of New York at Buffalo, USA
Stefanos Zafeiriou   Imperial College London, UK
Amir Zamir   École polytechnique fédérale de Lausanne,
                                          Switzerland
Lei Zhang   Alibaba & Hong Kong Polytechnic University,
                                          Hong Kong, China
Lei Zhang   International Digital Economy Academy (IDEA),
                                          China
Pengchuan Zhang   Meta AI, USA
Bolei Zhou   University of California, Los Angeles, USA
Yuke Zhu   University of Texas at Austin, USA

Todd Zickler   Harvard University, USA
Wangmeng Zuo   Harbin Institute of Technology, China

Technical Program Committee

Davide Abati
Soroush Abbasi
  Koohpayegani
Amos L. Abbott
Rameen Abdal
Rabab Abdelfattah
Sahar Abdelnabi
Hassan Abu Alhaija
Abulikemu Abuduweili
Ron Abutbul
Hanno Ackermann
Aikaterini Adam
Kamil Adamczewski
Ehsan Adeli
Vida Adeli
Donald Adjeroh
Arman Afrasiyabi
Akshay Agarwal
Sameer Agarwal
Abhinav Agarwalla
Vaibhav Aggarwal
Sara Aghajanzadeh
Susmit Agrawal
Antonio Agudo
Touqeer Ahmad
Sk Miraj Ahmed
Chaitanya Ahuja
Nilesh A. Ahuja
Abhishek Aich
Shubhra Aich
Noam Aigerman
Arash Akbarinia
Peri Akiva
Derya Akkaynak
Emre Aksan
Arjun R. Akula
Yuval Alaluf
Stephan Alaniz
Paul Albert
Cenek Albl

Filippo Aleotti
Konstantinos P.
  Alexandridis
Motasem Alfarra
Mohsen Ali
Thiemo Alldieck
Hadi Alzayer
Liang An
Shan An
Yi An
Zhulin An
Dongsheng An
Jie An
Xiang An
Saket Anand
Cosmin Ancuti
Juan Andrade-Cetto
Alexander Andreopoulos
Bjoern Andres
Jerone T. A. Andrews
Shivangi Aneja
Anelia Angelova
Dragomir Anguelov
Rushil Anirudh
Oron Anschel
Rao Muhammad Anwer
Djamila Aouada
Evlampios Apostolidis
Srikar Appalaraju
Nikita Araslanov
Andre Araujo
Eric Arazo
Dawit Mureja Argaw
Anurag Arnab
Aditya Arora
Chetan Arora
Sunpreet S. Arora
Alexey Artemov
Muhammad Asad
Kumar Ashutosh

Sinem Aslan
Vishal Asnani
Mahmoud Assran
Amir Atapour-Abarghouei
Nikos Athanasiou
Ali Athar
ShahRukh Athar
Sara Atito
Souhaib Attaiki
Matan Atzmon
Mathieu Aubry
Nicolas Audebert
Tristan T.
  Aumentado-Armstrong
Melinos Averkiou
Yannis Avrithis
Stephane Ayache
Mehmet Aygün
Seyed Mehdi
  Ayyoubzadeh
Hossein Azizpour
George Azzopardi
Mallikarjun B. R.
Yunhao Ba
Abhishek Badki
Seung-Hwan Bae
Seung-Hwan Baek
Seungryul Baek
Piyush Nitin Bagad
Shai Bagon
Gaetan Bahl
Shikhar Bahl
Sherwin Bahmani
Haoran Bai
Lei Bai
Jiawang Bai
Haoyue Bai
Jinbin Bai
Xiang Bai
Xuyang Bai

Yang Bai
Yuanchao Bai
Ziqian Bai
Sungyong Baik
Kevin Bailly
Max Bain
Federico Baldassarre
Wele Gedara Chaminda
  Bandara
Biplab Banerjee
Pratyay Banerjee
Sandipan Banerjee
Jihwan Bang
Antyanta Bangunharcana
Aayush Bansal
Ankan Bansal
Siddhant Bansal
Wentao Bao
Zhipeng Bao
Amir Bar
Manel Baradad Jurjo
Lorenzo Baraldi
Danny Barash
Daniel Barath
Connelly Barnes
Ioan Andrei Bârsan
Steven Basart
Dina Bashkirova
Chaim Baskin
Peyman Bateni
Anil Batra
Sebastiano Battiato
Ardhendu Behera
Harkirat Behl
Jens Behley
Vasileios Belagiannis
Boulbaba Ben Amor
Emanuel Ben Baruch
Abdessamad Ben Hamza
Gil Ben-Artzi
Assia Benbihi
Fabian Benitez-Quiroz
Guy Ben-Yosef
Philipp Benz
Alexander W. Bergman

Urs Bergmann
Jesus Bermudez-Cameo
Stefano Berretti
Gedas Bertasius
Zachary Bessinger
Petra Bevandić
Matthew Beveridge
Lucas Beyer
Yash Bhalgat
Suvaansh Bhambri
Samarth Bharadwaj
Gaurav Bharaj
Aparna Bharati
Bharat Lal Bhatnagar
Uttaran Bhattacharya
Apratim Bhattacharyya
Brojeshwar Bhowmick
Ankan Kumar Bhunia
Ayan Kumar Bhunia
Qi Bi
Sai Bi
Michael Bi Mi
Gui-Bin Bian
Jia-Wang Bian
Shaojun Bian
Pia Bideau
Mario Bijelic
Hakan Bilen
Guillaume-Alexandre
  Bilodeau
Alexander Binder
Tolga Birdal
Vighnesh N. Birodkar
Sandika Biswas
Andreas Blattmann
Janusz Bobulski
Giuseppe Boccignone
Vishnu Boddeti
Navaneeth Bodla
Moritz Böhle
Aleksei Bokhovkin
Sam Bond-Taylor
Vivek Boominathan
Shubhankar Borse
Mark Boss

Andrea Bottino
Adnane Boukhayma
Fadi Boutros
Nicolas C. Boutry
Richard S. Bowen
Ivaylo Boyadzhiev
Aidan Boyd
Yuri Boykov
Aljaz Bozic
Behzad Bozorgtabar
Eric Brachmann
Samarth Brahmbhatt
Gustav Bredell
Francois Bremond
Joel Brogan
Andrew Brown
Thomas Brox
Marcus A. Brubaker
Robert-Jan Bruintjes
Yuqi Bu
Anders G. Buch
Himanshu Buckchash
Mateusz Buda
Ignas Budvytis
José M. Buenaposada
Marcel C. Bühler
Tu Bui
Adrian Bulat
Hannah Bull
Evgeny Burnaev
Andrei Bursuc
Benjamin Busam
Sergey N. Buzykanov
Wonmin Byeon
Fabian Caba
Martin Cadik
Guanyu Cai
Minjie Cai
Qing Cai
Zhongang Cai
Qi Cai
Yancheng Cai
Shen Cai
Han Cai
Jiarui Cai

Bowen Cai
Mu Cai
Qin Cai
Ruojin Cai
Weidong Cai
Weiwei Cai
Yi Cai
Yujun Cai
Zhiping Cai
Akin Caliskan
Lilian Calvet
Baris Can Cam
Necati Cihan Camgoz
Tommaso Campari
Dylan Campbell
Ziang Cao
Ang Cao
Xu Cao
Zhiwen Cao
Shengcao Cao
Song Cao
Weipeng Cao
Xiangyong Cao
Xiaochun Cao
Yue Cao
Yunhao Cao
Zhangjie Cao
Jiale Cao
Yang Cao
Jiajiong Cao
Jie Cao
Jinkun Cao
Lele Cao
Yulong Cao
Zhiguo Cao
Chen Cao
Razvan Caramalau
Marlène Careil
Gustavo Carneiro
Joao Carreira
Dan Casas
Paola Cascante-Bonilla
Angela Castillo
Francisco M. Castro
Pedro Castro

Luca Cavalli
George J. Cazenavette
Oya Celiktutan
Hakan Cevikalp
Sri Harsha C. H.
Sungmin Cha
Geonho Cha
Menglei Chai
Lucy Chai
Yuning Chai
Zenghao Chai
Anirban Chakraborty
Deep Chakraborty
Rudrasis Chakraborty
Souradeep Chakraborty
Kelvin C. K. Chan
Chee Seng Chan
Paramanand Chandramouli
Arjun Chandrasekaran
Kenneth Chaney
Dongliang Chang
Huiwen Chang
Peng Chang
Xiaojun Chang
Jia-Ren Chang
Hyung Jin Chang
Hyun Sung Chang
Ju Yong Chang
Li-Jen Chang
Qi Chang
Wei-Yi Chang
Yi Chang
Nadine Chang
Hanqing Chao
Pradyumna Chari
Dibyadip Chatterjee
Chiranjoy Chattopadhyay
Siddhartha Chaudhuri
Zhengping Che
Gal Chechik
Lianggangxu Chen
Qi Alfred Chen
Brian Chen
Bor-Chun Chen
Bo-Hao Chen

Bohong Chen
Bin Chen
Ziliang Chen
Cheng Chen
Chen Chen
Chaofeng Chen
Xi Chen
Haoyu Chen
Xuanhong Chen
Wei Chen
Qiang Chen
Shi Chen
Xianyu Chen
Chang Chen
Changhuai Chen
Hao Chen
Jie Chen
Jianbo Chen
Jingjing Chen
Jun Chen
Kejiang Chen
Mingcai Chen
Nenglun Chen
Qifeng Chen
Ruoyu Chen
Shu-Yu Chen
Weidong Chen
Weijie Chen
Weikai Chen
Xiang Chen
Xiuyi Chen
Xingyu Chen
Yaofo Chen
Yueting Chen
Yu Chen
Yunjin Chen
Yuntao Chen
Yun Chen
Zhenfang Chen
Zhuangzhuang Chen
Chu-Song Chen
Xiangyu Chen
Zhuo Chen
Chaoqi Chen
Shizhe Chen

Xiaotong Chen
Xiaozhi Chen
Dian Chen
Defang Chen
Dingfan Chen
Ding-Jie Chen
Ee Heng Chen
Tao Chen
Yixin Chen
Wei-Ting Chen
Lin Chen
Guang Chen
Guangyi Chen
Guanying Chen
Guangyao Chen
Hwann-Tzong Chen
Junwen Chen
Jiacheng Chen
Jianxu Chen
Hui Chen
Kai Chen
Kan Chen
Kevin Chen
Kuan-Wen Chen
Weihua Chen
Zhang Chen
Liang-Chieh Chen
Lele Chen
Liang Chen
Fanglin Chen
Zehui Chen
Minghui Chen
Minghao Chen
Xiaokang Chen
Qian Chen
Jun-Cheng Chen
Qi Chen
Qingcai Chen
Richard J. Chen
Runnan Chen
Rui Chen
Shuo Chen
Sentao Chen
Shaoyu Chen
Shixing Chen

Shuai Chen
Shuya Chen
Sizhe Chen
Simin Chen
Shaoxiang Chen
Zitian Chen
Tianlong Chen
Tianshui Chen
Min-Hung Chen
Xiangning Chen
Xin Chen
Xinghao Chen
Xuejin Chen
Xu Chen
Xuxi Chen
Yunlu Chen
Yanbei Chen
Yuxiao Chen
Yun-Chun Chen
Yi-Ting Chen
Yi-Wen Chen
Yinbo Chen
Yiran Chen
Yuanhong Chen
Yubei Chen
Yuefeng Chen
Yuhua Chen
Yukang Chen
Zerui Chen
Zhaoyu Chen
Zhen Chen
Zhenyu Chen
Zhi Chen
Zhiwei Chen
Zhixiang Chen
Long Chen
Bowen Cheng
Jun Cheng
Yi Cheng
Jingchun Cheng
Lechao Cheng
Xi Cheng
Yuan Cheng
Ho Kei Cheng
Kevin Ho Man Cheng

Jiacheng Cheng
Kelvin B. Cheng
Li Cheng
Mengjun Cheng
Zhen Cheng
Qingrong Cheng
Tianheng Cheng
Harry Cheng
Yihua Cheng
Yu Cheng
Ziheng Cheng
Soon Yau Cheong
Anoop Cherian
Manuela Chessa
Zhixiang Chi
Naoki Chiba
Julian Chibane
Kashyap Chitta
Tai-Yin Chiu
Hsu-kuang Chiu
Wei-Chen Chiu
Sungmin Cho
Donghyeon Cho
Hyeon Cho
Yooshin Cho
Gyusang Cho
Jang Hyun Cho
Seungju Cho
Nam Ik Cho
Sunghyun Cho
Hanbyel Cho
Jaesung Choe
Jooyoung Choi
Chiho Choi
Changwoon Choi
Jongwon Choi
Myungsub Choi
Dooseop Choi
Jonghyun Choi
Jinwoo Choi
Jun Won Choi
Min-Kook Choi
Hongsuk Choi
Janghoon Choi
Yoon-Ho Choi

Yukyung Choi
Jaegul Choo
Ayush Chopra
Siddharth Choudhary
Subhabrata Choudhury
Vasileios Choutas
Ka-Ho Chow
Pinaki Nath Chowdhury
Sammy Christen
Anders Christensen
Grigorios Chrysos
Hang Chu
Wen-Hsuan Chu
Peng Chu
Qi Chu
Ruihang Chu
Wei-Ta Chu
Yung-Yu Chuang
Sanghyuk Chun
Se Young Chun
Antonio Cinà
Ramazan Gokberk Cinbis
Javier Civera
Albert Clapés
Ronald Clark
Brian S. Clipp
Felipe Codevilla
Daniel Coelho de Castro
Niv Cohen
Forrester Cole
Maxwell D. Collins
Robert T. Collins
Marc Comino Trinidad
Runmin Cong
Wenyan Cong
Maxime Cordy
Marcella Cornia
Enric Corona
Huseyin Coskun
Luca Cosmo
Dragos Costea
Davide Cozzolino
Arun C. S. Kumar
Aiyu Cui
Qiongjie Cui

Quan Cui
Shuhao Cui
Yiming Cui
Ying Cui
Zijun Cui
Jiali Cui
Jiequan Cui
Yawen Cui
Zhen Cui
Zhaopeng Cui
Jack Culpepper
Xiaodong Cun
Ross Cutler
Adam Czajka
Ali Dabouei
Konstantinos M. Dafnis
Manuel Dahnert
Tao Dai
Yuchao Dai
Bo Dai
Mengyu Dai
Hang Dai
Haixing Dai
Peng Dai
Pingyang Dai
Qi Dai
Qiyu Dai
Yutong Dai
Naser Damer
Zhiyuan Dang
Mohamed Daoudi
Ayan Das
Abir Das
Debasmit Das
Deepayan Das
Partha Das
Sagnik Das
Soumi Das
Srijan Das
Swagatam Das
Avijit Dasgupta
Jim Davis
Adrian K. Davison
Homa Davoudi
Laura Daza

Matthias De Lange
Shalini De Mello
Marco De Nadai
Christophe De
    Vleeschouwer
Alp Dener
Boyang Deng
Congyue Deng
Bailin Deng
Yong Deng
Ye Deng
Zhuo Deng
Zhijie Deng
Xiaoming Deng
Jiankang Deng
Jinhong Deng
Jingjing Deng
Liang-Jian Deng
Siqi Deng
Xiang Deng
Xueqing Deng
Zhongying Deng
Karan Desai
Jean-Emmanuel Deschaud
Aniket Anand Deshmukh
Neel Dey
Helisa Dhamo
Prithviraj Dhar
Amaya Dharmasiri
Yan Di
Xing Di
Ousmane A. Dia
Haiwen Diao
Xiaolei Diao
Gonçalo José Dias Pais
Abdallah Dib
Anastasios Dimou
Changxing Ding
Henghui Ding
Guodong Ding
Yaqing Ding
Shuangrui Ding
Yuhang Ding
Yikang Ding
Shouhong Ding

Haisong Ding
Hui Ding
Jiahao Ding
Jian Ding
Jian-Jiun Ding
Shuxiao Ding
Tianyu Ding
Wenhao Ding
Yuqi Ding
Yi Ding
Yuzhen Ding
Zhengming Ding
Tan Minh Dinh
Vu Dinh
Christos Diou
Mandar Dixit
Bao Gia Doan
Khoa D. Doan
Dzung Anh Doan
Debi Prosad Dogra
Nehal Doiphode
Chengdong Dong
Bowen Dong
Zhenxing Dong
Hang Dong
Xiaoyi Dong
Haoye Dong
Jiangxin Dong
Shichao Dong
Xuan Dong
Zhen Dong
Shuting Dong
Jing Dong
Li Dong
Ming Dong
Nanqing Dong
Qiulei Dong
Runpei Dong
Siyan Dong
Tian Dong
Wei Dong
Xiaomeng Dong
Xin Dong
Xingbo Dong
Yuan Dong

Samuel Dooley
Gianfranco Doretto
Michael Dorkenwald
Keval Doshi
Zhaopeng Dou
Xiaotian Dou
Hazel Doughty
Ahmad Droby
Iddo Drori
Jie Du
Yong Du
Dawei Du
Dong Du
Ruoyi Du
Yuntao Du
Xuefeng Du
Yilun Du
Yuming Du
Radhika Dua
Haodong Duan
Jiafei Duan
Kaiwen Duan
Peiqi Duan
Ye Duan
Haoran Duan
Jiali Duan
Amanda Duarte
Abhimanyu Dubey
Shiv Ram Dubey
Florian Dubost
Lukasz Dudziak
Shivam Duggal
Justin M. Dulay
Matteo Dunnhofer
Chi Nhan Duong
Thibaut Durand
Mihai Dusmanu
Ujjal Kr Dutta
Debidatta Dwibedi
Isht Dwivedi
Sai Kumar Dwivedi
Takeharu Eda
Mark Edmonds
Alexei A. Efros
Thibaud Ehret

Max Ehrlich
Mahsa Ehsanpour
Iván Eichhardt
Farshad Einabadi
Marvin Eisenberger
Hazim Kemal Ekenel
Mohamed El Banani
Ismail Elezi
Moshe Eliasof
Alaa El-Nouby
Ian Endres
Francis Engelmann
Deniz Engin
Chanho Eom
Dave Epstein
Maria C. Escobar
Victor A. Escorcia
Carlos Esteves
Sungmin Eum
Bernard J. E. Evans
Ivan Evtimov
Fevziye Irem Eyiokur
    Yaman
Matteo Fabbri
Sébastien Fabbro
Gabriele Facciolo
Masud Fahim
Bin Fan
Hehe Fan
Deng-Ping Fan
Aoxiang Fan
Chen-Chen Fan
Qi Fan
Zhaoxin Fan
Haoqi Fan
Heng Fan
Hongyi Fan
Linxi Fan
Baojie Fan
Jiayuan Fan
Lei Fan
Quanfu Fan
Yonghui Fan
Yingruo Fan
Zhiwen Fan

Zicong Fan
Sean Fanello
Jiansheng Fang
Chaowei Fang
Yuming Fang
Jianwu Fang
Jin Fang
Qi Fang
Shancheng Fang
Tian Fang
Xianyong Fang
Gongfan Fang
Zhen Fang
Hui Fang
Jiemin Fang
Le Fang
Pengfei Fang
Xiaolin Fang
Yuxin Fang
Zhaoyuan Fang
Ammarah Farooq
Azade Farshad
Zhengcong Fei
Michael Felsberg
Wei Feng
Chen Feng
Fan Feng
Andrew Feng
Xin Feng
Zheyun Feng
Ruicheng Feng
Mingtao Feng
Qianyu Feng
Shangbin Feng
Chun-Mei Feng
Zunlei Feng
Zhiyong Feng
Martin Fergie
Mustansar Fiaz
Marco Fiorucci
Michael Firman
Hamed Firooz
Volker Fischer
Corneliu O. Florea
Georgios Floros

Wolfgang Foerstner
Gianni Franchi
Jean-Sebastien Franco
Simone Frintrop
Anna Fruehstueck
Changhong Fu
Chaoyou Fu
Cheng-Yang Fu
Chi-Wing Fu
Deqing Fu
Huan Fu
Jun Fu
Kexue Fu
Ying Fu
Jianlong Fu
Jingjing Fu
Qichen Fu
Tsu-Jui Fu
Xueyang Fu
Yang Fu
Yanwei Fu
Yonggan Fu
Wolfgang Fuhl
Yasuhisa Fujii
Kent Fujiwara
Marco Fumero
Takuya Funatomi
Isabel Funke
Dario Fuoli
Antonino Furnari
Matheus A. Gadelha
Akshay Gadi Patil
Adrian Galdran
Guillermo Gallego
Silvano Galliani
Orazio Gallo
Leonardo Galteri
Matteo Gamba
Yiming Gan
Sujoy Ganguly
Harald Ganster
Boyan Gao
Changxin Gao
Daiheng Gao
Difei Gao

Chen Gao
Fei Gao
Lin Gao
Wei Gao
Yiming Gao
Junyu Gao
Guangyu Ryan Gao
Haichang Gao
Hongchang Gao
Jialin Gao
Jin Gao
Jun Gao
Katelyn Gao
Mingchen Gao
Mingfei Gao
Pan Gao
Shangqian Gao
Shanghua Gao
Xitong Gao
Yunhe Gao
Zhanning Gao
Elena Garces
Nuno Cruz Garcia
Noa Garcia
Guillermo
    Garcia-Hernando
Isha Garg
Rahul Garg
Sourav Garg
Quentin Garrido
Stefano Gasperini
Kent Gauen
Chandan Gautam
Shivam Gautam
Paul Gay
Chunjiang Ge
Shiming Ge
Wenhang Ge
Yanhao Ge
Zheng Ge
Songwei Ge
Weifeng Ge
Yixiao Ge
Yuying Ge
Shijie Geng

Zhengyang Geng
Kyle A. Genova
Georgios Georgakis
Markos Georgopoulos
Marcel Geppert
Shabnam Ghadar
Mina Ghadimi Atigh
Deepti Ghadiyaram
Maani Ghaffari Jadidi
Sedigh Ghamari
Zahra Gharaee
Michaël Gharbi
Golnaz Ghiasi
Reza Ghoddoosian
Soumya Suvra Ghosal
Adhiraj Ghosh
Arthita Ghosh
Pallabi Ghosh
Soumyadeep Ghosh
Andrew Gilbert
Igor Gilitschenski
Jhony H. Giraldo
Andreu Girbau Xalabarder
Rohit Girdhar
Sharath Girish
Xavier Giro-i-Nieto
Raja Giryes
Thomas Gittings
Nikolaos Gkanatsios
Ioannis Gkioulekas
Abhiram
    Gnanasambandam
Aurele T. Gnanha
Clement L. J. C. Godard
Arushi Goel
Vidit Goel
Shubham Goel
Zan Gojcic
Aaron K. Gokaslan
Tejas Gokhale
S. Alireza Golestaneh
Thiago L. Gomes
Nuno Goncalves
Boqing Gong
Chen Gong

Yuanhao Gong
Guoqiang Gong
Jingyu Gong
Rui Gong
Yu Gong
Mingming Gong
Neil Zhenqiang Gong
Xun Gong
Yunye Gong
Yihong Gong
Cristina I. González
Nithin Gopalakrishnan
    Nair
Gaurav Goswami
Jianping Gou
Shreyank N. Gowda
Ankit Goyal
Helmut Grabner
Patrick L. Grady
Ben Graham
Eric Granger
Douglas R. Gray
Matej Grcić
David Griffiths
Jinjin Gu
Yun Gu
Shuyang Gu
Jianyang Gu
Fuqiang Gu
Jiatao Gu
Jindong Gu
Jiaqi Gu
Jinwei Gu
Jiaxin Gu
Geonmo Gu
Xiao Gu
Xinqian Gu
Xiuye Gu
Yuming Gu
Zhangxuan Gu
Dayan Guan
Junfeng Guan
Qingji Guan
Tianrui Guan
Shanyan Guan

Denis A. Gudovskiy
Ricardo Guerrero
Pierre-Louis Guhur
Jie Gui
Liangyan Gui
Liangke Gui
Benoit Guillard
Erhan Gundogdu
Manuel Günther
Jingcai Guo
Yuanfang Guo
Junfeng Guo
Chenqi Guo
Dan Guo
Hongji Guo
Jia Guo
Jie Guo
Minghao Guo
Shi Guo
Yanhui Guo
Yangyang Guo
Yuan-Chen Guo
Yilu Guo
Yiluan Guo
Yong Guo
Guangyu Guo
Haiyun Guo
Jinyang Guo
Jianyuan Guo
Pengsheng Guo
Pengfei Guo
Shuxuan Guo
Song Guo
Tianyu Guo
Qing Guo
Qiushan Guo
Wen Guo
Xiefan Guo
Xiaohu Guo
Xiaoqing Guo
Yufei Guo
Yuhui Guo
Yuliang Guo
Yunhui Guo
Yanwen Guo

Akshita Gupta
Ankush Gupta
Kamal Gupta
Kartik Gupta
Ritwik Gupta
Rohit Gupta
Siddharth Gururani
Fredrik K. Gustafsson
Abner Guzman Rivera
Vladimir Guzov
Matthew A. Gwilliam
Jung-Woo Ha
Marc Habermann
Isma Hadji
Christian Haene
Martin Hahner
Levente Hajder
Alexandros Haliassos
Emanuela Haller
Bumsub Ham
Abdullah J. Hamdi
Shreyas Hampali
Dongyoon Han
Chunrui Han
Dong-Jun Han
Dong-Sig Han
Guangxing Han
Zhizhong Han
Ruize Han
Jiaming Han
Jin Han
Ligong Han
Xian-Hua Han
Xiaoguang Han
Yizeng Han
Zhi Han
Zhenjun Han
Zhongyi Han
Jungong Han
Junlin Han
Kai Han
Kun Han
Sungwon Han
Songfang Han
Wei Han

Xiao Han
Xintong Han
Xinzhe Han
Yahong Han
Yan Han
Zongbo Han
Nicolai Hani
Rana Hanocka
Niklas Hanselmann
Nicklas A. Hansen
Hong Hanyu
Fusheng Hao
Yanbin Hao
Shijie Hao
Udith Haputhanthri
Mehrtash Harandi
Josh Harguess
Adam Harley
David M. Hart
Atsushi Hashimoto
Ali Hassani
Mohammed Hassanin
Yana Hasson
Joakim Bruslund Haurum
Bo He
Kun He
Chen He
Xin He
Fazhi He
Gaoqi He
Hao He
Haoyu He
Jiangpeng He
Hongliang He
Qian He
Xiangteng He
Xuming He
Yannan He
Yuhang He
Yang He
Xiangyu He
Nanjun He
Pan He
Sen He
Shengfeng He

Songtao He
Tao He
Tong He
Wei He
Xuehai He
Xiaoxiao He
Ying He
Yisheng He
Ziwen He
Peter Hedman
Felix Heide
Yacov Hel-Or
Paul Henderson
Philipp Henzler
Byeongho Heo
Jae-Pil Heo
Miran Heo
Sachini A. Herath
Stephane Herbin
Pedro Hermosilla Casajus
Monica Hernandez
Charles Herrmann
Roei Herzig
Mauricio Hess-Flores
Carlos Hinojosa
Tobias Hinz
Tsubasa Hirakawa
Chih-Hui Ho
Lam Si Tung Ho
Jennifer Hobbs
Derek Hoiem
Yannick Hold-Geoffroy
Aleksander Holynski
Cheeun Hong
Fa-Ting Hong
Hanbin Hong
Guan Zhe Hong
Danfeng Hong
Lanqing Hong
Xiaopeng Hong
Xin Hong
Jie Hong
Seungbum Hong
Cheng-Yao Hong
Seunghoon Hong

Yi Hong
Yuan Hong
Yuchen Hong
Anthony Hoogs
Maxwell C. Horton
Kazuhiro Hotta
Qibin Hou
Tingbo Hou
Junhui Hou
Ji Hou
Qiqi Hou
Rui Hou
Ruibing Hou
Zhi Hou
Henry Howard-Jenkins
Lukas Hoyer
Wei-Lin Hsiao
Chiou-Ting Hsu
Anthony Hu
Brian Hu
Yusong Hu
Hexiang Hu
Haoji Hu
Di Hu
Hengtong Hu
Haigen Hu
Lianyu Hu
Hanzhe Hu
Jie Hu
Junlin Hu
Shizhe Hu
Jian Hu
Zhiming Hu
Juhua Hu
Peng Hu
Ping Hu
Ronghang Hu
MengShun Hu
Tao Hu
Vincent Tao Hu
Xiaoling Hu
Xinting Hu
Xiaolin Hu
Xuefeng Hu
Xiaowei Hu

Yang Hu
Yueyu Hu
Zeyu Hu
Zhongyun Hu
Binh-Son Hua
Guoliang Hua
Yi Hua
Linzhi Huang
Qiusheng Huang
Bo Huang
Chen Huang
Hsin-Ping Huang
Ye Huang
Shuangping Huang
Zeng Huang
Buzhen Huang
Cong Huang
Heng Huang
Hao Huang
Qidong Huang
Huaibo Huang
Chaoqin Huang
Feihu Huang
Jiahui Huang
Jingjia Huang
Kun Huang
Lei Huang
Sheng Huang
Shuaiyi Huang
Siyu Huang
Xiaoshui Huang
Xiaoyang Huang
Yan Huang
Yihao Huang
Ying Huang
Ziling Huang
Xiaoke Huang
Yifei Huang
Haiyang Huang
Zhewei Huang
Jin Huang
Haibin Huang
Jiaxing Huang
Junjie Huang
Keli Huang

Lang Huang
Lin Huang
Luojie Huang
Mingzhen Huang
Shijia Huang
Shengyu Huang
Siyuan Huang
He Huang
Xiuyu Huang
Lianghua Huang
Yue Huang
Yaping Huang
Yuge Huang
Zehao Huang
Zeyi Huang
Zhiqi Huang
Zhongzhan Huang
Zilong Huang
Ziyuan Huang
Tianrui Hui
Zhuo Hui
Le Hui
Jing Huo
Junhwa Hur
Shehzeen S. Hussain
Chuong Minh Huynh
Seunghyun Hwang
Jaehui Hwang
Jyh-Jing Hwang
Sukjun Hwang
Soonmin Hwang
Wonjun Hwang
Rakib Hyder
Sangeek Hyun
Sarah Ibrahimi
Tomoki Ichikawa
Yerlan Idelbayev
A. S. M. Iftekhar
Masaaki Iiyama
Satoshi Ikehata
Sunghoon Im
Atul N. Ingle
Eldar Insafutdinov
Yani A. Ioannou
Radu Tudor Ionescu

Umar Iqbal
Go Irie
Muhammad Zubair Irshad
Ahmet Iscen
Berivan Isik
Ashraful Islam
Md Amirul Islam
Syed Islam
Mariko Isogawa
Vamsi Krishna K. Ithapu
Boris Ivanovic
Darshan Iyer
Sarah Jabbour
Ayush Jain
Nishant Jain
Samyak Jain
Vidit Jain
Vineet Jain
Priyank Jaini
Tomas Jakab
Mohammad A. A. K.
 Jalwana
Muhammad Abdullah
 Jamal
Hadi Jamali-Rad
Stuart James
Varun Jampani
Young Kyun Jang
YeongJun Jang
Yunseok Jang
Ronnachai Jaroensri
Bhavan Jasani
Krishna Murthy
 Jatavallabhula
Mojan Javaheripi
Syed A. Javed
Guillaume Jeanneret
Pranav Jeevan
Herve Jegou
Rohit Jena
Tomas Jenicek
Porter Jenkins
Simon Jenni
Hae-Gon Jeon
Sangryul Jeon

Boseung Jeong
Yoonwoo Jeong
Seong-Gyun Jeong
Jisoo Jeong
Allan D. Jepson
Ankit Jha
Sumit K. Jha
I-Hong Jhuo
Ge-Peng Ji
Chaonan Ji
Deyi Ji
Jingwei Ji
Wei Ji
Zhong Ji
Jiayi Ji
Pengliang Ji
Hui Ji
Mingi Ji
Xiaopeng Ji
Yuzhu Ji
Baoxiong Jia
Songhao Jia
Dan Jia
Shan Jia
Xiaojun Jia
Xiuyi Jia
Xu Jia
Menglin Jia
Wenqi Jia
Boyuan Jiang
Wenhao Jiang
Huaizu Jiang
Hanwen Jiang
Haiyong Jiang
Hao Jiang
Huajie Jiang
Huiqin Jiang
Haojun Jiang
Haobo Jiang
Junjun Jiang
Xingyu Jiang
Yangbangyan Jiang
Yu Jiang
Jianmin Jiang
Jiaxi Jiang

Jing Jiang
Kui Jiang
Li Jiang
Liming Jiang
Chiyu Jiang
Meirui Jiang
Chen Jiang
Peng Jiang
Tai-Xiang Jiang
Wen Jiang
Xinyang Jiang
Yifan Jiang
Yuming Jiang
Yingying Jiang
Zeren Jiang
ZhengKai Jiang
Zhenyu Jiang
Shuming Jiao
Jianbo Jiao
Licheng Jiao
Dongkwon Jin
Yeying Jin
Cheng Jin
Linyi Jin
Qing Jin
Taisong Jin
Xiao Jin
Xin Jin
Sheng Jin
Kyong Hwan Jin
Ruibing Jin
SouYoung Jin
Yueming Jin
Chenchen Jing
Longlong Jing
Taotao Jing
Yongcheng Jing
Younghyun Jo
Joakim Johnander
Jeff Johnson
Michael J. Jones
R. Kenny Jones
Rico Jonschkowski
Ameya Joshi
Sunghun Joung

Felix Juefei-Xu
Claudio R. Jung
Steffen Jung
Hari Chandana K.
Rahul Vigneswaran K.
Prajwal K. R.
Abhishek Kadian
Jhony Kaesemodel Pontes
Kumara Kahatapitiya
Anmol Kalia
Sinan Kalkan
Tarun Kalluri
Jaewon Kam
Sandesh Kamath
Meina Kan
Menelaos Kanakis
Takuhiro Kaneko
Di Kang
Guoliang Kang
Hao Kang
Jaeyeon Kang
Kyoungkook Kang
Li-Wei Kang
MinGuk Kang
Suk-Ju Kang
Zhao Kang
Yash Mukund Kant
Yueying Kao
Aupendu Kar
Konstantinos Karantzalos
Sezer Karaoglu
Navid Kardan
Sanjay Kariyappa
Leonid Karlinsky
Animesh Karnewar
Shyamgopal Karthik
Hirak J. Kashyap
Marc A. Kastner
Hirokatsu Kataoka
Angelos Katharopoulos
Hiroharu Kato
Kai Katsumata
Manuel Kaufmann
Chaitanya Kaul
Prakhar Kaushik

Yuki Kawana
Lei Ke
Lipeng Ke
Tsung-Wei Ke
Wei Ke
Petr Kellnhofer
Aniruddha Kembhavi
John Kender
Corentin Kervadec
Leonid Keselman
Daniel Keysers
Nima Khademi Kalantari
Taras Khakhulin
Samir Khaki
Muhammad Haris Khan
Qadeer Khan
Salman Khan
Subash Khanal
Vaishnavi M. Khindkar
Rawal Khirodkar
Saeed Khorram
Pirazh Khorramshahi
Kourosh Khoshelham
Ansh Khurana
Benjamin Kiefer
Jae Myung Kim
Junho Kim
Boah Kim
Hyeonseong Kim
Dong-Jin Kim
Dongwan Kim
Donghyun Kim
Doyeon Kim
Yonghyun Kim
Hyung-Il Kim
Hyunwoo Kim
Hyeongwoo Kim
Hyo Jin Kim
Hyunwoo J. Kim
Taehoon Kim
Jaeha Kim
Jiwon Kim
Jung Uk Kim
Kangyeol Kim
Eunji Kim

Daeha Kim
Dongwon Kim
Kunhee Kim
Kyungmin Kim
Junsik Kim
Min H. Kim
Namil Kim
Kookhoi Kim
Sanghyun Kim
Seongyeop Kim
Seungryong Kim
Saehoon Kim
Euyoung Kim
Guisik Kim
Sungyeon Kim
Sunnie S. Y. Kim
Taehun Kim
Tae Oh Kim
Won Hwa Kim
Seungwook Kim
YoungBin Kim
Youngeun Kim
Akisato Kimura
Furkan Osman Kınlı
Zsolt Kira
Hedvig Kjellström
Florian Kleber
Jan P. Klopp
Florian Kluger
Laurent Kneip
Byungsoo Ko
Muhammed Kocabas
A. Sophia Koepke
Kevin Koeser
Nick Kolkin
Nikos Kolotouros
Wai-Kin Adams Kong
Deying Kong
Caihua Kong
Youyong Kong
Shuyu Kong
Shu Kong
Tao Kong
Yajing Kong
Yu Kong

Zishang Kong
Theodora Kontogianni
Anton S. Konushin
Julian F. P. Kooij
Bruno Korbar
Giorgos Kordopatis-Zilos
Jari Korhonen
Adam Kortylewski
Denis Korzhenkov
Divya Kothandaraman
Suraj Kothawade
Iuliia Kotseruba
Satwik Kottur
Shashank Kotyan
Alexandros Kouris
Petros Koutras
Anna Kreshuk
Ranjay Krishna
Dilip Krishnan
Andrey Kuehlkamp
Hilde Kuehne
Jason Kuen
David Kügler
Arjan Kuijper
Anna Kukleva
Sumith Kulal
Viveka Kulharia
Akshay R. Kulkarni
Nilesh Kulkarni
Dominik Kulon
Abhinav Kumar
Akash Kumar
Suryansh Kumar
B. V. K. Vijaya Kumar
Pulkit Kumar
Ratnesh Kumar
Sateesh Kumar
Satish Kumar
Vijay Kumar B. G.
Nupur Kumari
Sudhakar Kumawat
Jogendra Nath Kundu
Hsien-Kai Kuo
Meng-Yu Jennifer Kuo
Vinod Kumar Kurmi

Yusuke Kurose
Keerthy Kusumam
Alina Kuznetsova
Henry Kvinge
Ho Man Kwan
Hyeokjun Kweon
Heeseung Kwon
Gihyun Kwon
Myung-Joon Kwon
Taesung Kwon
YoungJoong Kwon
Christos Kyrkou
Jorma Laaksonen
Yann Labbe
Zorah Laehner
Florent Lafarge
Hamid Laga
Manuel Lagunas
Shenqi Lai
Jian-Huang Lai
Zihang Lai
Mohamed I. Lakhal
Mohit Lamba
Meng Lan
Loic Landrieu
Zhiqiang Lang
Natalie Lang
Dong Lao
Yizhen Lao
Yingjie Lao
Issam Hadj Laradji
Gustav Larsson
Viktor Larsson
Zakaria Laskar
Stéphane Lathuilière
Chun Pong Lau
Rynson W. H. Lau
Hei Law
Justin Lazarow
Verica Lazova
Eric-Tuan Le
Hieu Le
Trung-Nghia Le
Mathias Lechner
Byeong-Uk Lee

Chen-Yu Lee
Che-Rung Lee
Chul Lee
Hong Joo Lee
Dongsoo Lee
Jiyoung Lee
Eugene Eu Tzuan Lee
Daeun Lee
Saehyung Lee
Jewook Lee
Hyungtae Lee
Hyunmin Lee
Jungbeom Lee
Joon-Young Lee
Jong-Seok Lee
Joonseok Lee
Junha Lee
Kibok Lee
Byung-Kwan Lee
Jangwon Lee
Jinho Lee
Jongmin Lee
Seunghyun Lee
Sohyun Lee
Minsik Lee
Dogyoon Lee
Seungmin Lee
Min Jun Lee
Sangho Lee
Sangmin Lee
Seungeun Lee
Seon-Ho Lee
Sungmin Lee
Sungho Lee
Sangyoun Lee
Vincent C. S. S. Lee
Jaeseong Lee
Yong Jae Lee
Chenyang Lei
Chenyi Lei
Jiahui Lei
Xinyu Lei
Yinjie Lei
Jiaxu Leng
Luziwei Leng

Jan E. Lenssen
Vincent Lepetit
Thomas Leung
María Leyva-Vallina
Xin Li
Yikang Li
Baoxin Li
Bin Li
Bing Li
Bowen Li
Changlin Li
Chao Li
Chongyi Li
Guanyue Li
Shuai Li
Jin Li
Dingquan Li
Dongxu Li
Yiting Li
Gang Li
Dian Li
Guohao Li
Haoang Li
Haoliang Li
Haoran Li
Hengduo Li
Huafeng Li
Xiaoming Li
Hanao Li
Hongwei Li
Ziqiang Li
Jisheng Li
Jiacheng Li
Jia Li
Jiachen Li
Jiahao Li
Jianwei Li
Jiazhi Li
Jie Li
Jing Li
Jingjing Li
Jingtao Li
Jun Li
Junxuan Li
Kai Li

Kailin Li
Kenneth Li
Kun Li
Kunpeng Li
Aoxue Li
Chenglong Li
Chenglin Li
Changsheng Li
Zhichao Li
Qiang Li
Yanyu Li
Zuoyue Li
Xiang Li
Xuelong Li
Fangda Li
Ailin Li
Liang Li
Chun-Guang Li
Daiqing Li
Dong Li
Guanbin Li
Guorong Li
Haifeng Li
Jianan Li
Jianing Li
Jiaxin Li
Ke Li
Lei Li
Lincheng Li
Liulei Li
Lujun Li
Linjie Li
Lin Li
Pengyu Li
Ping Li
Qiufu Li
Qingyong Li
Rui Li
Siyuan Li
Wei Li
Wenbin Li
Xiangyang Li
Xinyu Li
Xiujun Li
Xiu Li

Xu Li
Ya-Li Li
Yao Li
Yongjie Li
Yijun Li
Yiming Li
Yuezun Li
Yu Li
Yunheng Li
Yuqi Li
Zhe Li
Zeming Li
Zhen Li
Zhengqin Li
Zhimin Li
Jiefeng Li
Jinpeng Li
Chengze Li
Jianwu Li
Lerenhan Li
Shan Li
Suichan Li
Xiangtai Li
Yanjie Li
Yandong Li
Zhuoling Li
Zhenqiang Li
Manyi Li
Maosen Li
Ji Li
Minjun Li
Mingrui Li
Mengtian Li
Junyi Li
Nianyi Li
Bo Li
Xiao Li
Peihua Li
Peike Li
Peizhao Li
Peiliang Li
Qi Li
Ren Li
Runze Li
Shile Li

Sheng Li
Shigang Li
Shiyu Li
Shuang Li
Shasha Li
Shichao Li
Tianye Li
Yuexiang Li
Wei-Hong Li
Wanhua Li
Weihao Li
Weiming Li
Weixin Li
Wenbo Li
Wenshuo Li
Weijian Li
Yunan Li
Xirong Li
Xianhang Li
Xiaoyu Li
Xueqian Li
Xuanlin Li
Xianzhi Li
Yunqiang Li
Yanjing Li
Yansheng Li
Yawei Li
Yi Li
Yong Li
Yong-Lu Li
Yuhang Li
Yu-Jhe Li
Yuxi Li
Yunsheng Li
Yanwei Li
Zechao Li
Zejian Li
Zeju Li
Zekun Li
Zhaowen Li
Zheng Li
Zhenyu Li
Zhiheng Li
Zhi Li
Zhong Li

Zhuowei Li
Zhuowan Li
Zhuohang Li
Zizhang Li
Chen Li
Yuan-Fang Li
Dongze Lian
Xiaochen Lian
Zhouhui Lian
Long Lian
Qing Lian
Jin Lianbao
Jinxiu S. Liang
Dingkang Liang
Jiahao Liang
Jianming Liang
Jingyun Liang
Kevin J. Liang
Kaizhao Liang
Chen Liang
Jie Liang
Senwei Liang
Ding Liang
Jiajun Liang
Jian Liang
Kongming Liang
Siyuan Liang
Yuanzhi Liang
Zhengfa Liang
Mingfu Liang
Xiaodan Liang
Xuefeng Liang
Yuxuan Liang
Kang Liao
Liang Liao
Hong-Yuan Mark Liao
Wentong Liao
Haofu Liao
Yue Liao
Minghui Liao
Shengcai Liao
Ting-Hsuan Liao
Xin Liao
Yinghong Liao
Teck Yian Lim

Che-Tsung Lin
Chung-Ching Lin
Chen-Hsuan Lin
Cheng Lin
Chuming Lin
Chunyu Lin
Dahua Lin
Wei Lin
Zheng Lin
Huaijia Lin
Jason Lin
Jierui Lin
Jiaying Lin
Jie Lin
Kai-En Lin
Kevin Lin
Guangfeng Lin
Jiehong Lin
Feng Lin
Hang Lin
Kwan-Yee Lin
Ke Lin
Luojun Lin
Qinghong Lin
Xiangbo Lin
Yi Lin
Zudi Lin
Shijie Lin
Yiqun Lin
Tzu-Heng Lin
Ming Lin
Shaohui Lin
SongNan Lin
Ji Lin
Tsung-Yu Lin
Xudong Lin
Yancong Lin
Yen-Chen Lin
Yiming Lin
Yuewei Lin
Zhiqiu Lin
Zinan Lin
Zhe Lin
David B. Lindell
Zhixin Ling

Zhan Ling
Alexander Liniger
Venice Erin B. Liong
Joey Litalien
Or Litany
Roee Litman
Ron Litman
Jim Little
Dor Litvak
Shaoteng Liu
Shuaicheng Liu
Andrew Liu
Xian Liu
Shaohui Liu
Bei Liu
Bo Liu
Yong Liu
Ming Liu
Yanbin Liu
Chenxi Liu
Daqi Liu
Di Liu
Difan Liu
Dong Liu
Dongfang Liu
Daizong Liu
Xiao Liu
Fangyi Liu
Fengbei Liu
Fenglin Liu
Bin Liu
Yuang Liu
Ao Liu
Hong Liu
Hongfu Liu
Huidong Liu
Ziyi Liu
Feng Liu
Hao Liu
Jie Liu
Jialun Liu
Jiang Liu
Jing Liu
Jingya Liu
Jiaming Liu

Jun Liu
Juncheng Liu
Jiawei Liu
Hongyu Liu
Chuanbin Liu
Haotian Liu
Lingqiao Liu
Chang Liu
Han Liu
Liu Liu
Min Liu
Yingqi Liu
Aishan Liu
Bingyu Liu
Benlin Liu
Boxiao Liu
Chenchen Liu
Chuanjian Liu
Daqing Liu
Huan Liu
Haozhe Liu
Jiaheng Liu
Wei Liu
Jingzhou Liu
Jiyuan Liu
Lingbo Liu
Nian Liu
Peiye Liu
Qiankun Liu
Shenglan Liu
Shilong Liu
Wen Liu
Wenyu Liu
Weifeng Liu
Wu Liu
Xiaolong Liu
Yang Liu
Yanwei Liu
Yingcheng Liu
Yongfei Liu
Yihao Liu
Yu Liu
Yunze Liu
Ze Liu
Zhenhua Liu

Zhenguang Liu
Lin Liu
Lihao Liu
Pengju Liu
Xinhai Liu
Yunfei Liu
Meng Liu
Minghua Liu
Mingyuan Liu
Miao Liu
Peirong Liu
Ping Liu
Qingjie Liu
Ruoshi Liu
Risheng Liu
Songtao Liu
Xing Liu
Shikun Liu
Shuming Liu
Sheng Liu
Songhua Liu
Tongliang Liu
Weibo Liu
Weide Liu
Weizhe Liu
Wenxi Liu
Weiyang Liu
Xin Liu
Xiaobin Liu
Xudong Liu
Xiaoyi Liu
Xihui Liu
Xinchen Liu
Xingtong Liu
Xinpeng Liu
Xinyu Liu
Xianpeng Liu
Xu Liu
Xingyu Liu
Yongtuo Liu
Yahui Liu
Yangxin Liu
Yaoyao Liu
Yaojie Liu
Yuliang Liu

Yongcheng Liu
Yuan Liu
Yufan Liu
Yu-Lun Liu
Yun Liu
Yunfan Liu
Yuanzhong Liu
Zhuoran Liu
Zhen Liu
Zheng Liu
Zhijian Liu
Zhisong Liu
Ziquan Liu
Ziyu Liu
Zhihua Liu
Zechun Liu
Zhaoyang Liu
Zhengzhe Liu
Stephan Liwicki
Shao-Yuan Lo
Sylvain Lobry
Suhas Lohit
Vishnu Suresh Lokhande
Vincenzo Lomonaco
Chengjiang Long
Guodong Long
Fuchen Long
Shangbang Long
Yang Long
Zijun Long
Vasco Lopes
Antonio M. Lopez
Roberto Javier
   Lopez-Sastre
Tobias Lorenz
Javier Lorenzo-Navarro
Yujing Lou
Qian Lou
Xiankai Lu
Changsheng Lu
Huimin Lu
Yongxi Lu
Hao Lu
Hong Lu
Jiasen Lu

Juwei Lu
Fan Lu
Guangming Lu
Jiwen Lu
Shun Lu
Tao Lu
Xiaonan Lu
Yang Lu
Yao Lu
Yongchun Lu
Zhiwu Lu
Cheng Lu
Liying Lu
Guo Lu
Xuequan Lu
Yanye Lu
Yantao Lu
Yuhang Lu
Fujun Luan
Jonathon Luiten
Jovita Lukasik
Alan Lukezic
Jonathan Samuel Lumentut
Mayank Lunayach
Ao Luo
Canjie Luo
Chong Luo
Xu Luo
Grace Luo
Jun Luo
Katie Z. Luo
Tao Luo
Cheng Luo
Fangzhou Luo
Gen Luo
Lei Luo
Sihui Luo
Weixin Luo
Yan Luo
Xiaoyan Luo
Yong Luo
Yadan Luo
Hao Luo
Ruotian Luo
Mi Luo

Tiange Luo
Wenjie Luo
Wenhan Luo
Xiao Luo
Zhiming Luo
Zhipeng Luo
Zhengyi Luo
Diogo C. Luvizon
Zhaoyang Lv
Gengyu Lyu
Lingjuan Lyu
Jun Lyu
Yuanyuan Lyu
Youwei Lyu
Yueming Lyu
Bingpeng Ma
Chao Ma
Chongyang Ma
Congbo Ma
Chih-Yao Ma
Fan Ma
Lin Ma
Haoyu Ma
Hengbo Ma
Jianqi Ma
Jiawei Ma
Jiayi Ma
Kede Ma
Kai Ma
Lingni Ma
Lei Ma
Xu Ma
Ning Ma
Benteng Ma
Cheng Ma
Andy J. Ma
Long Ma
Zhanyu Ma
Zhiheng Ma
Qianli Ma
Shiqiang Ma
Sizhuo Ma
Shiqing Ma
Xiaolong Ma
Xinzhu Ma

Gautam B. Machiraju
Spandan Madan
Mathew Magimai-Doss
Luca Magri
Behrooz Mahasseni
Upal Mahbub
Siddharth Mahendran
Paridhi Maheshwari
Rishabh Maheshwary
Mohammed Mahmoud
Shishira R. R. Maiya
Sylwia Majchrowska
Arjun Majumdar
Puspita Majumdar
Orchid Majumder
Sagnik Majumder
Ilya Makarov
Farkhod F.
 Makhmudkhujaev
Yasushi Makihara
Ankur Mali
Mateusz Malinowski
Utkarsh Mall
Srikanth Malla
Clement Mallet
Dimitrios Mallis
Yunze Man
Dipu Manandhar
Massimiliano Mancini
Murari Mandal
Raunak Manekar
Karttikeya Mangalam
Puneet Mangla
Fabian Manhardt
Sivabalan Manivasagam
Fahim Mannan
Chengzhi Mao
Hanzi Mao
Jiayuan Mao
Junhua Mao
Zhiyuan Mao
Jiageng Mao
Yunyao Mao
Zhendong Mao
Alberto Marchisio

Diego Marcos
Riccardo Marin
Aram Markosyan
Renaud Marlet
Ricardo Marques
Miquel Martí i Rabadán
Diego Martin Arroyo
Niki Martinel
Brais Martinez
Julieta Martinez
Marc Masana
Tomohiro Mashita
Timothée Masquelier
Minesh Mathew
Tetsu Matsukawa
Marwan Mattar
Bruce A. Maxwell
Christoph Mayer
Mantas Mazeika
Pratik Mazumder
Scott McCloskey
Steven McDonagh
Ishit Mehta
Jie Mei
Kangfu Mei
Jieru Mei
Xiaoguang Mei
Givi Meishvili
Luke Melas-Kyriazi
Iaroslav Melekhov
Andres Mendez-Vazquez
Heydi Mendez-Vazquez
Matias Mendieta
Ricardo A. Mendoza-León
Chenlin Meng
Depu Meng
Rang Meng
Zibo Meng
Qingjie Meng
Qier Meng
Yanda Meng
Zihang Meng
Thomas Mensink
Fabian Mentzer
Christopher Metzler

Gregory P. Meyer
Vasileios Mezaris
Liang Mi
Lu Mi
Bo Miao
Changtao Miao
Zichen Miao
Qiguang Miao
Xin Miao
Zhongqi Miao
Frank Michel
Simone Milani
Ben Mildenhall
Roy V. Miles
Juhong Min
Kyle Min
Hyun-Seok Min
Weiqing Min
Yuecong Min
Zhixiang Min
Qi Ming
David Minnen
Aymen Mir
Deepak Mishra
Anand Mishra
Shlok K. Mishra
Niluthpol Mithun
Gaurav Mittal
Trisha Mittal
Daisuke Miyazaki
Kaichun Mo
Hong Mo
Zhipeng Mo
Davide Modolo
Abduallah A. Mohamed
Mohamed Afham
 Mohamed Aflal
Ron Mokady
Pavlo Molchanov
Davide Moltisanti
Liliane Momeni
Gianluca Monaci
Pascal Monasse
Ajoy Mondal
Tom Monnier

Aron Monszpart
Gyeongsik Moon
Suhong Moon
Taesup Moon
Sean Moran
Daniel Moreira
Pietro Morerio
Alexandre Morgand
Lia Morra
Ali Mosleh
Inbar Mosseri
Sayed Mohammad
    Mostafavi Isfahani
Saman Motamed
Ramy A. Mounir
Fangzhou Mu
Jiteng Mu
Norman Mu
Yasuhiro Mukaigawa
Ryan Mukherjee
Tanmoy Mukherjee
Yusuke Mukuta
Ravi Teja Mullapudi
Lea Müller
Matthias Müller
Martin Mundt
Nils Murrugarra-Llerena
Damien Muselet
Armin Mustafa
Muhammad Ferjad Naeem
Sauradip Nag
Hajime Nagahara
Pravin Nagar
Rajendra Nagar
Naveen Shankar Nagaraja
Varun Nagaraja
Tushar Nagarajan
Seungjun Nah
Gaku Nakano
Yuta Nakashima
Giljoo Nam
Seonghyeon Nam
Liangliang Nan
Yuesong Nan
Yeshwanth Napolean

Dinesh Reddy
    Narapureddy
Medhini Narasimhan
Supreeth
    Narasimhaswamy
Sriram Narayanan
Erickson R. Nascimento
Varun Nasery
K. L. Navaneet
Pablo Navarrete Michelini
Shant Navasardyan
Shah Nawaz
Nihal Nayak
Farhood Negin
Lukáš Neumann
Alejandro Newell
Evonne Ng
Kam Woh Ng
Tony Ng
Anh Nguyen
Tuan Anh Nguyen
Cuong Cao Nguyen
Ngoc Cuong Nguyen
Thanh Nguyen
Khoi Nguyen
Phi Le Nguyen
Phong Ha Nguyen
Tam Nguyen
Truong Nguyen
Anh Tuan Nguyen
Rang Nguyen
Thao Thi Phuong Nguyen
Van Nguyen Nguyen
Zhen-Liang Ni
Yao Ni
Shijie Nie
Xuecheng Nie
Yongwei Nie
Weizhi Nie
Ying Nie
Yinyu Nie
Kshitij N. Nikhal
Simon Niklaus
Xuefei Ning
Jifeng Ning

Yotam Nitzan
Di Niu
Shuaicheng Niu
Li Niu
Wei Niu
Yulei Niu
Zhenxing Niu
Albert No
Shohei Nobuhara
Nicoletta Noceti
Junhyug Noh
Sotiris Nousias
Slawomir Nowaczyk
Ewa M. Nowara
Valsamis Ntouskos
Gilberto Ochoa-Ruiz
Ferda Ofli
Jihyong Oh
Sangyun Oh
Youngtaek Oh
Hiroki Ohashi
Takahiro Okabe
Kemal Oksuz
Fumio Okura
Daniel Olmeda Reino
Matthew Olson
Carl Olsson
Roy Or-El
Alessandro Ortis
Guillermo Ortiz-Jimenez
Magnus Oskarsson
Ahmed A. A. Osman
Martin R. Oswald
Mayu Otani
Naima Otberdout
Cheng Ouyang
Jiahong Ouyang
Wanli Ouyang
Andrew Owens
Poojan B. Oza
Mete Ozay
A. Cengiz Oztireli
Gautam Pai
Tomas Pajdla
Umapada Pal

Simone Palazzo
Luca Palmieri
Bowen Pan
Hao Pan
Lili Pan
Tai-Yu Pan
Liang Pan
Chengwei Pan
Yingwei Pan
Xuran Pan
Jinshan Pan
Xinyu Pan
Liyuan Pan
Xingang Pan
Xingjia Pan
Zhihong Pan
Zizheng Pan
Priyadarshini Panda
Rameswar Panda
Rohit Pandey
Kaiyue Pang
Bo Pang
Guansong Pang
Jiangmiao Pang
Meng Pang
Tianyu Pang
Ziqi Pang
Omiros Pantazis
Andreas Panteli
Maja Pantic
Marina Paolanti
Joao P. Papa
Samuele Papa
Mike Papadakis
Dim P. Papadopoulos
George Papandreou
Constantin Pape
Toufiq Parag
Chethan Parameshwara
Shaifali Parashar
Alejandro Pardo
Rishubh Parihar
Sarah Parisot
JaeYoo Park
Gyeong-Moon Park

Hyojin Park
Hyoungseob Park
Jongchan Park
Jae Sung Park
Kiru Park
Chunghyun Park
Kwanyong Park
Sunghyun Park
Sungrae Park
Seongsik Park
Sanghyun Park
Sungjune Park
Taesung Park
Gaurav Parmar
Paritosh Parmar
Alvaro Parra
Despoina Paschalidou
Or Patashnik
Shivansh Patel
Pushpak Pati
Prashant W. Patil
Vaishakh Patil
Suvam Patra
Jay Patravali
Badri Narayana Patro
Angshuman Paul
Sudipta Paul
Rémi Pautrat
Nick E. Pears
Adithya Pediredla
Wenjie Pei
Shmuel Peleg
Latha Pemula
Bo Peng
Houwen Peng
Yue Peng
Liangzu Peng
Baoyun Peng
Jun Peng
Pai Peng
Sida Peng
Xi Peng
Yuxin Peng
Songyou Peng
Wei Peng

Weiqi Peng
Wen-Hsiao Peng
Pramuditha Perera
Juan C. Perez
Eduardo Pérez Pellitero
Juan-Manuel Perez-Rua
Federico Pernici
Marco Pesavento
Stavros Petridis
Ilya A. Petrov
Vladan Petrovic
Mathis Petrovich
Suzanne Petryk
Hieu Pham
Quang Pham
Khoi Pham
Tung Pham
Huy Phan
Stephen Phillips
Cheng Perng Phoo
David Picard
Marco Piccirilli
Georg Pichler
A. J. Piergiovanni
Vipin Pillai
Silvia L. Pintea
Giovanni Pintore
Robinson Piramuthu
Fiora Pirri
Theodoros Pissas
Fabio Pizzati
Benjamin Planche
Bryan Plummer
Matteo Poggi
Ashwini Pokle
Georgy E. Ponimatkin
Adrian Popescu
Stefan Popov
Nikola Popović
Ronald Poppe
Angelo Porrello
Michael Potter
Charalambos Poullis
Hadi Pouransari
Omid Poursaeed

Shraman Pramanick
Mantini Pranav
Dilip K. Prasad
Meghshyam Prasad
B. H. Pawan Prasad
Shitala Prasad
Prateek Prasanna
Ekta Prashnani
Derek S. Prijatelj
Luke Y. Prince
Véronique Prinet
Victor Adrian Prisacariu
James Pritts
Thomas Probst
Sergey Prokudin
Rita Pucci
Chi-Man Pun
Matthew Purri
Haozhi Qi
Lu Qi
Lei Qi
Xianbiao Qi
Yonggang Qi
Yuankai Qi
Siyuan Qi
Guocheng Qian
Hangwei Qian
Qi Qian
Deheng Qian
Shengsheng Qian
Wen Qian
Rui Qian
Yiming Qian
Shengju Qian
Shengyi Qian
Xuelin Qian
Zhenxing Qian
Nan Qiao
Xiaotian Qiao
Jing Qin
Can Qin
Siyang Qin
Hongwei Qin
Jie Qin
Minghai Qin

Yipeng Qin
Yongqiang Qin
Wenda Qin
Xuebin Qin
Yuzhe Qin
Yao Qin
Zhenyue Qin
Zhiwu Qing
Heqian Qiu
Jiayan Qiu
Jielin Qiu
Yue Qiu
Jiaxiong Qiu
Zhongxi Qiu
Shi Qiu
Zhaofan Qiu
Zhongnan Qu
Yanyun Qu
Kha Gia Quach
Yuhui Quan
Ruijie Quan
Mike Rabbat
Rahul Shekhar Rade
Filip Radenovic
Gorjan Radevski
Bogdan Raducanu
Francesco Ragusa
Shafin Rahman
Md Mahfuzur Rahman
  Siddiquee
Hossein Rahmani
Kiran Raja
Sivaramakrishnan
  Rajaraman
Jathushan Rajasegaran
Adnan Siraj Rakin
Michaël Ramamonjisoa
Chirag A. Raman
Shanmuganathan Raman
Vignesh Ramanathan
Vasili Ramanishka
Vikram V. Ramaswamy
Merey Ramazanova
Jason Rambach
Sai Saketh Rambhatla

Clément Rambour
Ashwin Ramesh Babu
Adín Ramírez Rivera
Arianna Rampini
Haoxi Ran
Aakanksha Rana
Aayush Jung Bahadur
  Rana
Kanchana N. Ranasinghe
Aneesh Rangnekar
Samrudhdhi B. Rangrej
Harsh Rangwani
Viresh Ranjan
Anyi Rao
Yongming Rao
Carolina Raposo
Michalis Raptis
Amir Rasouli
Vivek Rathod
Adepu Ravi Sankar
Avinash Ravichandran
Bharadwaj Ravichandran
Dripta S. Raychaudhuri
Adria Recasens
Simon Reiß
Davis Rempe
Daxuan Ren
Jiawei Ren
Jimmy Ren
Sucheng Ren
Dayong Ren
Zhile Ren
Dongwei Ren
Qibing Ren
Pengfei Ren
Zhenwen Ren
Xuqian Ren
Yixuan Ren
Zhongzheng Ren
Ambareesh Revanur
Hamed Rezazadegan
  Tavakoli
Rafael S. Rezende
Wonjong Rhee
Alexander Richard

Christian Richardt
Stephan R. Richter
Benjamin Riggan
Dominik Rivoir
Mamshad Nayeem Rizve
Joshua D. Robinson
Joseph Robinson
Chris Rockwell
Ranga Rodrigo
Andres C. Rodriguez
Carlos Rodriguez-Pardo
Marcus Rohrbach
Gemma Roig
Yu Rong
David A. Ross
Mohammad Rostami
Edward Rosten
Karsten Roth
Anirban Roy
Debaditya Roy
Shuvendu Roy
Ahana Roy Choudhury
Aruni Roy Chowdhury
Denys Rozumnyi
Shulan Ruan
Wenjie Ruan
Patrick Ruhkamp
Danila Rukhovich
Anian Ruoss
Chris Russell
Dan Ruta
Dawid Damian Rymarczyk
DongHun Ryu
Hyeonggon Ryu
Kwonyoung Ryu
Balasubramanian S.
Alexandre Sablayrolles
Mohammad Sabokrou
Arka Sadhu
Aniruddha Saha
Oindrila Saha
Pritish Sahu
Aneeshan Sain
Nirat Saini
Saurabh Saini

Takeshi Saitoh
Christos Sakaridis
Fumihiko Sakaue
Dimitrios Sakkos
Ken Sakurada
Parikshit V. Sakurikar
Rohit Saluja
Nermin Samet
Leo Sampaio Ferraz
    Ribeiro
Jorge Sanchez
Enrique Sanchez
Shengtian Sang
Anush Sankaran
Soubhik Sanyal
Nikolaos Sarafianos
Vishwanath Saragadam
István Sárándi
Saquib Sarfraz
Mert Bulent Sariyildiz
Anindya Sarkar
Pritam Sarkar
Paul-Edouard Sarlin
Hiroshi Sasaki
Takami Sato
Torsten Sattler
Ravi Kumar Satzoda
Axel Sauer
Stefano Savian
Artem Savkin
Manolis Savva
Gerald Schaefer
Simone Schaub-Meyer
Yoni Schirris
Samuel Schulter
Katja Schwarz
Jesse Scott
Sinisa Segvic
Constantin Marc Seibold
Lorenzo Seidenari
Matan Sela
Fadime Sener
Paul Hongsuck Seo
Kwanggyoon Seo
Hongje Seong

Dario Serez
Francesco Setti
Bryan Seybold
Mohamad Shahbazi
Shima Shahfar
Xinxin Shan
Caifeng Shan
Dandan Shan
Shawn Shan
Wei Shang
Jinghuan Shang
Jiaxiang Shang
Lei Shang
Sukrit Shankar
Ken Shao
Rui Shao
Jie Shao
Mingwen Shao
Aashish Sharma
Gaurav Sharma
Vivek Sharma
Abhishek Sharma
Yoli Shavit
Shashank Shekhar
Sumit Shekhar
Zhijie Shen
Fengyi Shen
Furao Shen
Jialie Shen
Jingjing Shen
Ziyi Shen
Linlin Shen
Guangyu Shen
Biluo Shen
Falong Shen
Jiajun Shen
Qiu Shen
Qiuhong Shen
Shuai Shen
Wang Shen
Yiqing Shen
Yunhang Shen
Siqi Shen
Bin Shen
Tianwei Shen

Xi Shen
Yilin Shen
Yuming Shen
Yucong Shen
Zhiqiang Shen
Lu Sheng
Yichen Sheng
Shivanand Venkanna
    Sheshappanavar
Shelly Sheynin
Baifeng Shi
Ruoxi Shi
Botian Shi
Hailin Shi
Jia Shi
Jing Shi
Shaoshuai Shi
Baoguang Shi
Boxin Shi
Hengcan Shi
Tianyang Shi
Xiaodan Shi
Yongjie Shi
Zhensheng Shi
Yinghuan Shi
Weiqi Shi
Wu Shi
Xuepeng Shi
Xiaoshuang Shi
Yujiao Shi
Zenglin Shi
Zhenmei Shi
Takashi Shibata
Meng-Li Shih
Yichang Shih
Hyunjung Shim
Dongseok Shim
Soshi Shimada
Inkyu Shin
Jinwoo Shin
Seungjoo Shin
Seungjae Shin
Koichi Shinoda
Suprosanna Shit

Palaiahnakote
    Shivakumara
Eli Shlizerman
Gaurav Shrivastava
Xiao Shu
Xiangbo Shu
Xiujun Shu
Yang Shu
Tianmin Shu
Jun Shu
Zhixin Shu
Bing Shuai
Maria Shugrina
Ivan Shugurov
Satya Narayan Shukla
Pranjay Shyam
Jianlou Si
Yawar Siddiqui
Alberto Signoroni
Pedro Silva
Jae-Young Sim
Oriane Siméoni
Martin Simon
Andrea Simonelli
Abhishek Singh
Ashish Singh
Dinesh Singh
Gurkirt Singh
Krishna Kumar Singh
Mannat Singh
Pravendra Singh
Rajat Vikram Singh
Utkarsh Singhal
Dipika Singhania
Vasu Singla
Harsh Sinha
Sudipta Sinha
Josef Sivic
Elena Sizikova
Geri Skenderi
Ivan Skorokhodov
Dmitriy Smirnov
Cameron Y. Smith
James S. Smith
Patrick Snape

Mattia Soldan
Hyeongseok Son
Sanghyun Son
Chuanbiao Song
Chen Song
Chunfeng Song
Dan Song
Dongjin Song
Hwanjun Song
Guoxian Song
Jiaming Song
Jie Song
Liangchen Song
Ran Song
Luchuan Song
Xibin Song
Li Song
Fenglong Song
Guoli Song
Guanglu Song
Zhenbo Song
Lin Song
Xinhang Song
Yang Song
Yibing Song
Rajiv Soundararajan
Hossein Souri
Cristovao Sousa
Riccardo Spezialetti
Leonidas Spinoulas
Michael W. Spratling
Deepak Sridhar
Srinath Sridhar
Gaurang Sriramanan
Vinkle Kumar Srivastav
Themos Stafylakis
Serban Stan
Anastasis Stathopoulos
Markus Steinberger
Jan Steinbrener
Sinisa Stekovic
Alexandros Stergiou
Gleb Sterkin
Rainer Stiefelhagen
Pierre Stock

Ombretta Strafforello
Julian Straub
Yannick Strümpler
Joerg Stueckler
Hang Su
Weijie Su
Jong-Chyi Su
Bing Su
Haisheng Su
Jinming Su
Yiyang Su
Yukun Su
Yuxin Su
Zhuo Su
Zhaoqi Su
Xiu Su
Yu-Chuan Su
Zhixun Su
Arulkumar Subramaniam
Akshayvarun Subramanya
A. Subramanyam
Swathikiran Sudhakaran
Yusuke Sugano
Masanori Suganuma
Yumin Suh
Yang Sui
Baochen Sun
Cheng Sun
Long Sun
Guolei Sun
Haoliang Sun
Haomiao Sun
He Sun
Hanqing Sun
Hao Sun
Lichao Sun
Jiachen Sun
Jiaming Sun
Jian Sun
Jin Sun
Jennifer J. Sun
Tiancheng Sun
Libo Sun
Peize Sun
Qianru Sun

Shanlin Sun
Yu Sun
Zhun Sun
Che Sun
Lin Sun
Tao Sun
Yiyou Sun
Chunyi Sun
Chong Sun
Weiwei Sun
Weixuan Sun
Xiuyu Sun
Yanan Sun
Zeren Sun
Zhaodong Sun
Zhiqing Sun
Minhyuk Sung
Jinli Suo
Simon Suo
Abhijit Suprem
Anshuman Suri
Saksham Suri
Joshua M. Susskind
Roman Suvorov
Gurumurthy Swaminathan
Robin Swanson
Paul Swoboda
Tabish A. Syed
Richard Szeliski
Fariborz Taherkhani
Yu-Wing Tai
Keita Takahashi
Walter Talbott
Gary Tam
Masato Tamura
Feitong Tan
Fuwen Tan
Shuhan Tan
Andong Tan
Bin Tan
Cheng Tan
Jianchao Tan
Lei Tan
Mingxing Tan
Xin Tan

Zichang Tan
Zhentao Tan
Kenichiro Tanaka
Masayuki Tanaka
Yushun Tang
Hao Tang
Jingqun Tang
Jinhui Tang
Kaihua Tang
Luming Tang
Lv Tang
Sheyang Tang
Shitao Tang
Siliang Tang
Shixiang Tang
Yansong Tang
Keke Tang
Chang Tang
Chenwei Tang
Jie Tang
Junshu Tang
Ming Tang
Peng Tang
Xu Tang
Yao Tang
Chen Tang
Fan Tang
Haoran Tang
Shengeng Tang
Yehui Tang
Zhipeng Tang
Ugo Tanielian
Chaofan Tao
Jiale Tao
Junli Tao
Renshuai Tao
An Tao
Guanhong Tao
Zhiqiang Tao
Makarand Tapaswi
Jean-Philippe G. Tarel
Juan J. Tarrio
Enzo Tartaglione
Keisuke Tateno
Zachary Teed

Ajinkya B. Tejankar
Bugra Tekin
Purva Tendulkar
Damien Teney
Minggui Teng
Chris Tensmeyer
Andrew Beng Jin Teoh
Philipp Terhörst
Kartik Thakral
Nupur Thakur
Kevin Thandiackal
Spyridon Thermos
Diego Thomas
William Thong
Yuesong Tian
Guanzhong Tian
Lin Tian
Shiqi Tian
Kai Tian
Meng Tian
Tai-Peng Tian
Zhuotao Tian
Shangxuan Tian
Tian Tian
Yapeng Tian
Yu Tian
Yuxin Tian
Leslie Ching Ow Tiong
Praveen Tirupattur
Garvita Tiwari
George Toderici
Antoine Toisoul
Aysim Toker
Tatiana Tommasi
Zhan Tong
Alessio Tonioni
Alessandro Torcinovich
Fabio Tosi
Matteo Toso
Hugo Touvron
Quan Hung Tran
Son Tran
Hung Tran
Ngoc-Trung Tran
Vinh Tran

Phong Tran
Giovanni Trappolini
Edith Tretschk
Subarna Tripathi
Shubhendu Trivedi
Eduard Trulls
Prune Truong
Thanh-Dat Truong
Tomasz Trzcinski
Sam Tsai
Yi-Hsuan Tsai
Ethan Tseng
Yu-Chee Tseng
Shahar Tsiper
Stavros Tsogkas
Shikui Tu
Zhigang Tu
Zhengzhong Tu
Richard Tucker
Sergey Tulyakov
Cigdem Turan
Daniyar Turmukhambetov
Victor G. Turrisi da Costa
Bartlomiej Twardowski
Christopher D. Twigg
Radim Tylecek
Mostofa Rafid Uddin
Md. Zasim Uddin
Kohei Uehara
Nicolas Ugrinovic
Youngjung Uh
Norimichi Ukita
Anwaar Ulhaq
Devesh Upadhyay
Paul Upchurch
Yoshitaka Ushiku
Yuzuko Utsumi
Mikaela Angelina Uy
Mohit Vaishnav
Pratik Vaishnavi
Jeya Maria Jose Valanarasu
Matias A. Valdenegro Toro
Diego Valsesia
Wouter Van Gansbeke
Nanne van Noord

Simon Vandenhende
Farshid Varno
Cristina Vasconcelos
Francisco Vasconcelos
Alex Vasilescu
Subeesh Vasu
Arun Balajee Vasudevan
Kanav Vats
Vaibhav S. Vavilala
Sagar Vaze
Javier Vazquez-Corral
Andrea Vedaldi
Olga Veksler
Andreas Velten
Sai H. Vemprala
Raviteja Vemulapalli
Shashanka
    Venkataramanan
Dor Verbin
Luisa Verdoliva
Manisha Verma
Yashaswi Verma
Constantin Vertan
Eli Verwimp
Deepak Vijaykeerthy
Pablo Villanueva
Ruben Villegas
Markus Vincze
Vibhav Vineet
Minh P. Vo
Huy V. Vo
Duc Minh Vo
Tomas Vojir
Igor Vozniak
Nicholas Vretos
Vibashan VS
Tuan-Anh Vu
Thang Vu
Mårten Wadenbäck
Neal Wadhwa
Aaron T. Walsman
Steven Walton
Jin Wan
Alvin Wan
Jia Wan

Jun Wan
Xiaoyue Wan
Fang Wan
Guowei Wan
Renjie Wan
Zhiqiang Wan
Ziyu Wan
Bastian Wandt
Dongdong Wang
Limin Wang
Haiyang Wang
Xiaobing Wang
Angtian Wang
Angelina Wang
Bing Wang
Bo Wang
Boyu Wang
Binghui Wang
Chen Wang
Chien-Yi Wang
Congli Wang
Qi Wang
Chengrui Wang
Rui Wang
Yiqun Wang
Cong Wang
Wenjing Wang
Dongkai Wang
Di Wang
Xiaogang Wang
Kai Wang
Zhizhong Wang
Fangjinhua Wang
Feng Wang
Hang Wang
Gaoang Wang
Guoqing Wang
Guangcong Wang
Guangzhi Wang
Hanqing Wang
Hao Wang
Haohan Wang
Haoran Wang
Hong Wang
Haotao Wang

Hu Wang
Huan Wang
Hua Wang
Hui-Po Wang
Hengli Wang
Hanyu Wang
Hongxing Wang
Jingwen Wang
Jialiang Wang
Jian Wang
Jianyi Wang
Jiashun Wang
Jiahao Wang
Tsun-Hsuan Wang
Xiaoqian Wang
Jinqiao Wang
Jun Wang
Jianzong Wang
Kaihong Wang
Ke Wang
Lei Wang
Lingjing Wang
Linnan Wang
Lin Wang
Liansheng Wang
Mengjiao Wang
Manning Wang
Nannan Wang
Peihao Wang
Jiayun Wang
Pu Wang
Qiang Wang
Qiufeng Wang
Qilong Wang
Qiangchang Wang
Qin Wang
Qing Wang
Ruocheng Wang
Ruibin Wang
Ruisheng Wang
Ruizhe Wang
Runqi Wang
Runzhong Wang
Wenxuan Wang
Sen Wang

Shangfei Wang
Shaofei Wang
Shijie Wang
Shiqi Wang
Zhibo Wang
Song Wang
Xinjiang Wang
Tai Wang
Tao Wang
Teng Wang
Xiang Wang
Tianren Wang
Tiantian Wang
Tianyi Wang
Fengjiao Wang
Wei Wang
Miaohui Wang
Suchen Wang
Siyue Wang
Yaoming Wang
Xiao Wang
Ze Wang
Biao Wang
Chaofei Wang
Dong Wang
Gu Wang
Guangrun Wang
Guangming Wang
Guo-Hua Wang
Haoqing Wang
Hesheng Wang
Huafeng Wang
Jinghua Wang
Jingdong Wang
Jingjing Wang
Jingya Wang
Jingkang Wang
Jiakai Wang
Junke Wang
Kuo Wang
Lichen Wang
Lizhi Wang
Longguang Wang
Mang Wang
Mei Wang

Min Wang
Peng-Shuai Wang
Run Wang
Shaoru Wang
Shuhui Wang
Tan Wang
Tiancai Wang
Tianqi Wang
Wenhai Wang
Wenzhe Wang
Xiaobo Wang
Xiudong Wang
Xu Wang
Yajie Wang
Yan Wang
Yuan-Gen Wang
Yingqian Wang
Yizhi Wang
Yulin Wang
Yu Wang
Yujie Wang
Yunhe Wang
Yuxi Wang
Yaowei Wang
Yiwei Wang
Zezheng Wang
Hongzhi Wang
Zhiqiang Wang
Ziteng Wang
Ziwei Wang
Zheng Wang
Zhenyu Wang
Binglu Wang
Zhongdao Wang
Ce Wang
Weining Wang
Weiyao Wang
Wenbin Wang
Wenguan Wang
Guangting Wang
Haolin Wang
Haiyan Wang
Huiyu Wang
Naiyan Wang
Jingbo Wang

Jinpeng Wang
Jiaqi Wang
Liyuan Wang
Lizhen Wang
Ning Wang
Wenqian Wang
Sheng-Yu Wang
Weimin Wang
Xiaohan Wang
Yifan Wang
Yi Wang
Yongtao Wang
Yizhou Wang
Zhuo Wang
Zhe Wang
Xudong Wang
Xiaofang Wang
Xinggang Wang
Xiaosen Wang
Xiaosong Wang
Xiaoyang Wang
Lijun Wang
Xinlong Wang
Xuan Wang
Xue Wang
Yangang Wang
Yaohui Wang
Yu-Chiang Frank Wang
Yida Wang
Yilin Wang
Yi Ru Wang
Yali Wang
Yinglong Wang
Yufu Wang
Yujiang Wang
Yuwang Wang
Yuting Wang
Yang Wang
Yu-Xiong Wang
Yixu Wang
Ziqi Wang
Zhicheng Wang
Zeyu Wang
Zhaowen Wang
Zhenyi Wang

Zhenzhi Wang
Zhijie Wang
Zhiyong Wang
Zhongling Wang
Zhuowei Wang
Zian Wang
Zifu Wang
Zihao Wang
Zirui Wang
Ziyan Wang
Wenxiao Wang
Zhen Wang
Zhepeng Wang
Zi Wang
Zihao W. Wang
Steven L. Waslander
Olivia Watkins
Daniel Watson
Silvan Weder
Dongyoon Wee
Dongming Wei
Tianyi Wei
Jia Wei
Dong Wei
Fangyun Wei
Longhui Wei
Mingqiang Wei
Xinyue Wei
Chen Wei
Donglai Wei
Pengxu Wei
Xing Wei
Xiu-Shen Wei
Wenqi Wei
Guoqiang Wei
Wei Wei
XingKui Wei
Xian Wei
Xingxing Wei
Yake Wei
Yuxiang Wei
Yi Wei
Luca Weihs
Michael Weinmann
Martin Weinmann

Congcong Wen
Chuan Wen
Jie Wen
Sijia Wen
Song Wen
Chao Wen
Xiang Wen
Zeyi Wen
Xin Wen
Yilin Wen
Yijia Weng
Shuchen Weng
Junwu Weng
Wenming Weng
Renliang Weng
Zhenyu Weng
Xinshuo Weng
Nicholas J. Westlake
Gordon Wetzstein
Lena M. Widin Klasén
Rick Wildes
Bryan M. Williams
Williem Williem
Ole Winther
Scott Wisdom
Alex Wong
Chau-Wai Wong
Kwan-Yee K. Wong
Yongkang Wong
Scott Workman
Marcel Worring
Michael Wray
Safwan Wshah
Xiang Wu
Aming Wu
Chongruo Wu
Cho-Ying Wu
Chunpeng Wu
Chenyan Wu
Ziyi Wu
Fuxiang Wu
Gang Wu
Haiping Wu
Huisi Wu
Jane Wu

Jialian Wu
Jing Wu
Jinjian Wu
Jianlong Wu
Xian Wu
Lifang Wu
Lifan Wu
Minye Wu
Qianyi Wu
Rongliang Wu
Rui Wu
Shiqian Wu
Shuzhe Wu
Shangzhe Wu
Tsung-Han Wu
Tz-Ying Wu
Ting-Wei Wu
Jiannan Wu
Zhiliang Wu
Yu Wu
Chenyun Wu
Dayan Wu
Dongxian Wu
Fei Wu
Hefeng Wu
Jianxin Wu
Weibin Wu
Wenxuan Wu
Wenhao Wu
Xiao Wu
Yicheng Wu
Yuanwei Wu
Yu-Huan Wu
Zhenxin Wu
Zhenyu Wu
Wei Wu
Peng Wu
Xiaohe Wu
Xindi Wu
Xinxing Wu
Xinyi Wu
Xingjiao Wu
Xiongwei Wu
Yangzheng Wu
Yanzhao Wu

Yawen Wu
Yong Wu
Yi Wu
Ying Nian Wu
Zhenyao Wu
Zhonghua Wu
Zongze Wu
Zuxuan Wu
Stefanie Wuhrer
Teng Xi
Jianing Xi
Fei Xia
Haifeng Xia
Menghan Xia
Yuanqing Xia
Zhihua Xia
Xiaobo Xia
Weihao Xia
Shihong Xia
Yan Xia
Yong Xia
Zhaoyang Xia
Zhihao Xia
Chuhua Xian
Yongqin Xian
Wangmeng Xiang
Fanbo Xiang
Tiange Xiang
Tao Xiang
Liuyu Xiang
Xiaoyu Xiang
Zhiyu Xiang
Aoran Xiao
Chunxia Xiao
Fanyi Xiao
Jimin Xiao
Jun Xiao
Taihong Xiao
Anqi Xiao
Junfei Xiao
Jing Xiao
Liang Xiao
Yang Xiao
Yuting Xiao
Yijun Xiao

Yao Xiao
Zeyu Xiao
Zhisheng Xiao
Zihao Xiao
Binhui Xie
Christopher Xie
Haozhe Xie
Jin Xie
Guo-Sen Xie
Hongtao Xie
Ming-Kun Xie
Tingting Xie
Chaohao Xie
Weicheng Xie
Xudong Xie
Jiyang Xie
Xiaohua Xie
Yuan Xie
Zhenyu Xie
Ning Xie
Xianghui Xie
Xiufeng Xie
You Xie
Yutong Xie
Fuyong Xing
Yifan Xing
Zhen Xing
Yuanjun Xiong
Jinhui Xiong
Weihua Xiong
Hongkai Xiong
Zhitong Xiong
Yuanhao Xiong
Yunyang Xiong
Yuwen Xiong
Zhiwei Xiong
Yuliang Xiu
An Xu
Chang Xu
Chenliang Xu
Chengming Xu
Chenshu Xu
Xiang Xu
Huijuan Xu
Zhe Xu

Jie Xu
Jingyi Xu
Jiarui Xu
Yinghao Xu
Kele Xu
Ke Xu
Li Xu
Linchuan Xu
Linning Xu
Mengde Xu
Mengmeng Frost Xu
Min Xu
Mingye Xu
Jun Xu
Ning Xu
Peng Xu
Runsheng Xu
Sheng Xu
Wenqiang Xu
Xiaogang Xu
Renzhe Xu
Kaidi Xu
Yi Xu
Chi Xu
Qiuling Xu
Baobei Xu
Feng Xu
Haohang Xu
Haofei Xu
Lan Xu
Mingze Xu
Songcen Xu
Weipeng Xu
Wenjia Xu
Wenju Xu
Xiangyu Xu
Xin Xu
Yinshuang Xu
Yixing Xu
Yuting Xu
Yanyu Xu
Zhenbo Xu
Zhiliang Xu
Zhiyuan Xu
Xiaohao Xu

Yanwu Xu
Yan Xu
Yiran Xu
Yifan Xu
Yufei Xu
Yong Xu
Zichuan Xu
Zenglin Xu
Zexiang Xu
Zhan Xu
Zheng Xu
Zhiwei Xu
Ziyue Xu
Shiyu Xuan
Hanyu Xuan
Fei Xue
Jianru Xue
Mingfu Xue
Qinghan Xue
Tianfan Xue
Chao Xue
Chuhui Xue
Nan Xue
Zhou Xue
Xiangyang Xue
Yuan Xue
Abhay Yadav
Ravindra Yadav
Kota Yamaguchi
Toshihiko Yamasaki
Kohei Yamashita
Chaochao Yan
Feng Yan
Kun Yan
Qingsen Yan
Qixin Yan
Rui Yan
Siming Yan
Xinchen Yan
Yaping Yan
Bin Yan
Qingan Yan
Shen Yan
Shipeng Yan
Xu Yan

Yan Yan
Yichao Yan
Zhaoyi Yan
Zike Yan
Zhiqiang Yan
Hongliang Yan
Zizheng Yan
Jiewen Yang
Anqi Joyce Yang
Shan Yang
Anqi Yang
Antoine Yang
Bo Yang
Baoyao Yang
Chenhongyi Yang
Dingkang Yang
De-Nian Yang
Dong Yang
David Yang
Fan Yang
Fengyu Yang
Fengting Yang
Fei Yang
Gengshan Yang
Heng Yang
Han Yang
Huan Yang
Yibo Yang
Jiancheng Yang
Jihan Yang
Jiawei Yang
Jiayu Yang
Jie Yang
Jinfa Yang
Jingkang Yang
Jinyu Yang
Cheng-Fu Yang
Ji Yang
Jianyu Yang
Kailun Yang
Tian Yang
Luyu Yang
Liang Yang
Li Yang
Michael Ying Yang

Yang Yang
Muli Yang
Le Yang
Qiushi Yang
Ren Yang
Ruihan Yang
Shuang Yang
Siyuan Yang
Su Yang
Shiqi Yang
Taojiannan Yang
Tianyu Yang
Lei Yang
Wanzhao Yang
Shuai Yang
William Yang
Wei Yang
Xiaofeng Yang
Xiaoshan Yang
Xin Yang
Xuan Yang
Xu Yang
Xingyi Yang
Xitong Yang
Jing Yang
Yanchao Yang
Wenming Yang
Yujiu Yang
Herb Yang
Jianfei Yang
Jinhui Yang
Chuanguang Yang
Guanglei Yang
Haitao Yang
Kewei Yang
Linlin Yang
Lijin Yang
Longrong Yang
Meng Yang
MingKun Yang
Sibei Yang
Shicai Yang
Tong Yang
Wen Yang
Xi Yang

Xiaolong Yang
Xue Yang
Yubin Yang
Ze Yang
Ziyi Yang
Yi Yang
Linjie Yang
Yuzhe Yang
Yiding Yang
Zhenpei Yang
Zhaohui Yang
Zhengyuan Yang
Zhibo Yang
Zongxin Yang
Hantao Yao
Mingde Yao
Rui Yao
Taiping Yao
Ting Yao
Cong Yao
Qingsong Yao
Quanming Yao
Xu Yao
Yuan Yao
Yao Yao
Yazhou Yao
Jiawen Yao
Shunyu Yao
Pew-Thian Yap
Sudhir Yarram
Rajeev Yasarla
Peng Ye
Botao Ye
Mao Ye
Fei Ye
Hanrong Ye
Jingwen Ye
Jinwei Ye
Jiarong Ye
Mang Ye
Meng Ye
Qi Ye
Qian Ye
Qixiang Ye
Junjie Ye

Sheng Ye
Nanyang Ye
Yufei Ye
Xiaoqing Ye
Ruolin Ye
Yousef Yeganeh
Chun-Hsiao Yeh
Raymond A. Yeh
Yu-Ying Yeh
Kai Yi
Chang Yi
Renjiao Yi
Xinping Yi
Peng Yi
Alper Yilmaz
Junho Yim
Hui Yin
Bangjie Yin
Jia-Li Yin
Miao Yin
Wenzhe Yin
Xuwang Yin
Ming Yin
Yu Yin
Aoxiong Yin
Kangxue Yin
Tianwei Yin
Wei Yin
Xianghua Ying
Rio Yokota
Tatsuya Yokota
Naoto Yokoya
Ryo Yonetani
Ki Yoon Yoo
Jinsu Yoo
Sunjae Yoon
Jae Shin Yoon
Jihun Yoon
Sung-Hoon Yoon
Ryota Yoshihashi
Yusuke Yoshiyasu
Chenyu You
Haoran You
Haoxuan You
Yang You

Quanzeng You
Tackgeun You
Kaichao You
Shan You
Xinge You
Yurong You
Baosheng Yu
Bei Yu
Haichao Yu
Hao Yu
Chaohui Yu
Fisher Yu
Jin-Gang Yu
Jiyang Yu
Jason J. Yu
Jiashuo Yu
Hong-Xing Yu
Lei Yu
Mulin Yu
Ning Yu
Peilin Yu
Qi Yu
Qian Yu
Rui Yu
Shuzhi Yu
Gang Yu
Tan Yu
Weijiang Yu
Xin Yu
Bingyao Yu
Ye Yu
Hanchao Yu
Yingchen Yu
Tao Yu
Xiaotian Yu
Qing Yu
Houjian Yu
Changqian Yu
Jing Yu
Jun Yu
Shujian Yu
Xiang Yu
Zhaofei Yu
Zhenbo Yu
Yinfeng Yu

Zhuoran Yu
Zitong Yu
Bo Yuan
Jiangbo Yuan
Liangzhe Yuan
Weihao Yuan
Jianbo Yuan
Xiaoyun Yuan
Ye Yuan
Li Yuan
Geng Yuan
Jialin Yuan
Maoxun Yuan
Peng Yuan
Xin Yuan
Yuan Yuan
Yuhui Yuan
Yixuan Yuan
Zheng Yuan
Mehmet Kerim Yücel
Kaiyu Yue
Haixiao Yue
Heeseung Yun
Sangdoo Yun
Tian Yun
Mahmut Yurt
Ekim Yurtsever
Ahmet Yüzügüler
Edouard Yvinec
Eloi Zablocki
Christopher Zach
Muhammad Zaigham
   Zaheer
Pierluigi Zama Ramirez
Yuhang Zang
Pietro Zanuttigh
Alexey Zaytsev
Bernhard Zeisl
Haitian Zeng
Pengpeng Zeng
Jiabei Zeng
Runhao Zeng
Wei Zeng
Yawen Zeng
Yi Zeng

Yiming Zeng
Tieyong Zeng
Huanqiang Zeng
Dan Zeng
Yu Zeng
Wei Zhai
Yuanhao Zhai
Fangneng Zhan
Kun Zhan
Xiong Zhang
Jingdong Zhang
Jiangning Zhang
Zhilu Zhang
Gengwei Zhang
Dongsu Zhang
Hui Zhang
Binjie Zhang
Bo Zhang
Tianhao Zhang
Cecilia Zhang
Jing Zhang
Chaoning Zhang
Chenxu Zhang
Chi Zhang
Chris Zhang
Yabin Zhang
Zhao Zhang
Rufeng Zhang
Chaoyi Zhang
Zheng Zhang
Da Zhang
Yi Zhang
Edward Zhang
Xin Zhang
Feifei Zhang
Feilong Zhang
Yuqi Zhang
GuiXuan Zhang
Hanlin Zhang
Hanwang Zhang
Hanzhen Zhang
Haotian Zhang
He Zhang
Haokui Zhang
Hongyuan Zhang

Hengrui Zhang
Hongming Zhang
Mingfang Zhang
Jianpeng Zhang
Jiaming Zhang
Jichao Zhang
Jie Zhang
Jingfeng Zhang
Jingyi Zhang
Jinnian Zhang
David Junhao Zhang
Junjie Zhang
Junzhe Zhang
Jiawan Zhang
Jingyang Zhang
Kai Zhang
Lei Zhang
Lihua Zhang
Lu Zhang
Miao Zhang
Minjia Zhang
Mingjin Zhang
Qi Zhang
Qian Zhang
Qilong Zhang
Qiming Zhang
Qiang Zhang
Richard Zhang
Ruimao Zhang
Ruisi Zhang
Ruixin Zhang
Runze Zhang
Qilin Zhang
Shan Zhang
Shanshan Zhang
Xi Sheryl Zhang
Song-Hai Zhang
Chongyang Zhang
Kaihao Zhang
Songyang Zhang
Shu Zhang
Siwei Zhang
Shujian Zhang
Tianyun Zhang
Tong Zhang

Tao Zhang
Wenwei Zhang
Wenqiang Zhang
Wen Zhang
Xiaolin Zhang
Xingchen Zhang
Xingxuan Zhang
Xiuming Zhang
Xiaoshuai Zhang
Xuanmeng Zhang
Xuanyang Zhang
Xucong Zhang
Xingxing Zhang
Xikun Zhang
Xiaohan Zhang
Yahui Zhang
Yunhua Zhang
Yan Zhang
Yanghao Zhang
Yifei Zhang
Yifan Zhang
Yi-Fan Zhang
Yihao Zhang
Yingliang Zhang
Youshan Zhang
Yulun Zhang
Yushu Zhang
Yixiao Zhang
Yide Zhang
Zhongwen Zhang
Bowen Zhang
Chen-Lin Zhang
Zehua Zhang
Zekun Zhang
Zeyu Zhang
Xiaowei Zhang
Yifeng Zhang
Cheng Zhang
Hongguang Zhang
Yuexi Zhang
Fa Zhang
Guofeng Zhang
Hao Zhang
Haofeng Zhang
Hongwen Zhang

Hua Zhang
Jiaxin Zhang
Zhenyu Zhang
Jian Zhang
Jianfeng Zhang
Jiao Zhang
Jiakai Zhang
Lefei Zhang
Le Zhang
Mi Zhang
Min Zhang
Ning Zhang
Pan Zhang
Pu Zhang
Qing Zhang
Renrui Zhang
Shifeng Zhang
Shuo Zhang
Shaoxiong Zhang
Weizhong Zhang
Xi Zhang
Xiaomei Zhang
Xinyu Zhang
Yin Zhang
Zicheng Zhang
Zihao Zhang
Ziqi Zhang
Zhaoxiang Zhang
Zhen Zhang
Zhipeng Zhang
Zhixing Zhang
Zhizheng Zhang
Jiawei Zhang
Zhong Zhang
Pingping Zhang
Yixin Zhang
Kui Zhang
Lingzhi Zhang
Huaiwen Zhang
Quanshi Zhang
Zhoutong Zhang
Yuhang Zhang
Yuting Zhang
Zhang Zhang
Ziming Zhang

Zhizhong Zhang
Qilong Zhangli
Bingyin Zhao
Bin Zhao
Chenglong Zhao
Lei Zhao
Feng Zhao
Gangming Zhao
Haiyan Zhao
Hao Zhao
Handong Zhao
Hengshuang Zhao
Yinan Zhao
Jiaojiao Zhao
Jiaqi Zhao
Jing Zhao
Kaili Zhao
Haojie Zhao
Yucheng Zhao
Longjiao Zhao
Long Zhao
Qingsong Zhao
Qingyu Zhao
Rui Zhao
Rui-Wei Zhao
Sicheng Zhao
Shuang Zhao
Siyan Zhao
Zelin Zhao
Shiyu Zhao
Wang Zhao
Tiesong Zhao
Qian Zhao
Wangbo Zhao
Xi-Le Zhao
Xu Zhao
Yajie Zhao
Yang Zhao
Ying Zhao
Yin Zhao
Yizhou Zhao
Yunhan Zhao
Yuyang Zhao
Yue Zhao
Yuzhi Zhao

Bowen Zhao
Pu Zhao
Bingchen Zhao
Borui Zhao
Fuqiang Zhao
Hanbin Zhao
Jian Zhao
Mingyang Zhao
Na Zhao
Rongchang Zhao
Ruiqi Zhao
Shuai Zhao
Wenda Zhao
Wenliang Zhao
Xiangyun Zhao
Yifan Zhao
Yaping Zhao
Zhou Zhao
He Zhao
Jie Zhao
Xibin Zhao
Xiaoqi Zhao
Zhengyu Zhao
Jin Zhe
Chuanxia Zheng
Huan Zheng
Hao Zheng
Jia Zheng
Jian-Qing Zheng
Shuai Zheng
Meng Zheng
Mingkai Zheng
Qian Zheng
Qi Zheng
Wu Zheng
Yinqiang Zheng
Yufeng Zheng
Yutong Zheng
Yalin Zheng
Yu Zheng
Feng Zheng
Zhaoheng Zheng
Haitian Zheng
Kang Zheng
Bolun Zheng

Haiyong Zheng
Mingwu Zheng
Sipeng Zheng
Tu Zheng
Wenzhao Zheng
Xiawu Zheng
Yinglin Zheng
Zhuo Zheng
Zilong Zheng
Kecheng Zheng
Zerong Zheng
Shuaifeng Zhi
Tiancheng Zhi
Jia-Xing Zhong
Yiwu Zhong
Fangwei Zhong
Zhihang Zhong
Yaoyao Zhong
Yiran Zhong
Zhun Zhong
Zichun Zhong
Bo Zhou
Boyao Zhou
Brady Zhou
Mo Zhou
Chunluan Zhou
Dingfu Zhou
Fan Zhou
Jingkai Zhou
Honglu Zhou
Jiaming Zhou
Jiahuan Zhou
Jun Zhou
Kaiyang Zhou
Keyang Zhou
Kuangqi Zhou
Lei Zhou
Lihua Zhou
Man Zhou
Mingyi Zhou
Mingyuan Zhou
Ning Zhou
Peng Zhou
Penghao Zhou
Qianyi Zhou

Shuigeng Zhou
Shangchen Zhou
Huayi Zhou
Zhize Zhou
Sanping Zhou
Qin Zhou
Tao Zhou
Wenbo Zhou
Xiangdong Zhou
Xiao-Yun Zhou
Xiao Zhou
Yang Zhou
Yipin Zhou
Zhenyu Zhou
Hao Zhou
Chu Zhou
Daquan Zhou
Da-Wei Zhou
Hang Zhou
Kang Zhou
Qianyu Zhou
Sheng Zhou
Wenhui Zhou
Xingyi Zhou
Yan-Jie Zhou
Yiyi Zhou
Yu Zhou
Yuan Zhou
Yuqian Zhou
Yuxuan Zhou
Zixiang Zhou
Wengang Zhou
Shuchang Zhou
Tianfei Zhou
Yichao Zhou
Alex Zhu
Chenchen Zhu
Deyao Zhu
Xiatian Zhu
Guibo Zhu
Haidong Zhu
Hao Zhu
Hongzi Zhu
Rui Zhu
Jing Zhu

Jianke Zhu
Junchen Zhu
Lei Zhu
Lingyu Zhu
Luyang Zhu
Menglong Zhu
Peihao Zhu
Hui Zhu
Xiaofeng Zhu
Tyler (Lixuan) Zhu
Wentao Zhu
Xiangyu Zhu
Xinqi Zhu
Xinxin Zhu
Xinliang Zhu
Yangguang Zhu
Yichen Zhu
Yixin Zhu
Yanjun Zhu
Yousong Zhu
Yuhao Zhu
Ye Zhu
Feng Zhu
Zhen Zhu
Fangrui Zhu
Jinjing Zhu
Linchao Zhu
Pengfei Zhu
Sijie Zhu
Xiaobin Zhu
Xiaoguang Zhu
Zezhou Zhu
Zhenyao Zhu
Kai Zhu
Pengkai Zhu
Bingbing Zhuang
Chengyuan Zhuang
Liansheng Zhuang
Peiye Zhuang
Yixin Zhuang
Yihong Zhuang
Junbao Zhuo
Andrea Ziani
Bartosz Zieliński
Primo Zingaretti

Nikolaos Zioulis
Andrew Zisserman
Yael Ziv
Liu Ziyin
Xingxing Zou
Danping Zou
Qi Zou

Shihao Zou
Xueyan Zou
Yang Zou
Yuliang Zou
Zihang Zou
Chuhang Zou
Dongqing Zou

Xu Zou
Zhiming Zou
Maria A. Zuluaga
Xinxin Zuo
Zhiwen Zuo
Reyer Zwiggelaar

Contents – Part XIII

AU-Aware 3D Face Reconstruction through Personalized AU-Specific Blendshape Learning

Chenyi Kuang[1]([⊠]), Zijun Cui[1], Jeffrey O. Kephart[2], and Qiang Ji[1]

[1] Rensselaer Polytechnic Institute, Troy, USA
{kuangc2,cuiz3,jiq}@rpi.edu
[2] IBM Thomas J. Watson Research Center, Ossining, USA
kephart@us.ibm.com

Abstract. 3D face reconstruction and facial action unit (AU) detection have emerged as interesting and challenging tasks in recent years, but are rarely performed in tandem. Image-based 3D face reconstruction, which can represent a dense space of facial motions, is typically accomplished by estimating identity, expression, texture, head pose, and illumination separately via pre-constructed 3D morphable models (3DMMs). Recent 3D reconstruction models can recover high-quality geometric facial details like wrinkles and pores, but are still limited in their ability to recover 3D subtle motions caused by the activation of AUs. We present a multi-stage learning framework that recovers AU-interpretable 3D facial details by learning personalized AU-specific blendshapes from images. Our model explicitly learns 3D expression basis by using AU labels and generic AU relationship prior and then constrains the basis coefficients such that they are semantically mapped to each AU. Our AU-aware 3D reconstruction model generates accurate 3D expressions composed by semantically meaningful AU motion components. Furthermore, the output of the model can be directly applied to generate 3D AU occurrence predictions, which have not been fully explored by prior 3D reconstruction models. We demonstrate the effectiveness of our approach via qualitative and quantitative evaluations.

Keywords: 3DMM · 3D face reconstruction · Facial action unit

1 Introduction

With the first 3D morphable model (3DMM) proposed by Blanz et al. [7], 3D face modeling and reconstruction have gained sustained attention as a research topic and are frequently used in popular applications like AR/VR, 3D avatar animation, video games and communication. Most existing 3D face reconstruction

Supplementary Information The online version contains supplementary material available at https://doi.org/10.1007/978-3-031-19778-9_1.

methods [18, 42, 44, 62] are based on a pre-constructed 3DMM, which divides the space of 3D facial shapes into identity and expression dimensions. The 3DMMs are constructed from a large database of 3D scans. Among various representations, orthogonal PCA basis are widely used such as BFM [22] and FLAME [30] and blendshapes, such as FaceWarehouse [9], FaceScape [53] and Feafa [52]. While the PCA basis usually represents global vertex deformations and does not have semantic meaning, each blendshape basis represents local deformations related to specific facial movements. Responding to increasing demand for generating high quality 3D faces, more recent works [4, 5, 21, 53] have recovered detailed facial geometry from monocular or multi-view images by dynamically learning a displacement map to add a refinement layer to the 3D geometry. However, these approaches to 3D face reconstruction have not fully considered the inherent 3D nature of facial movement, which is based upon the muscle activation under a local region of the skin.

The Facial Action Coding System (FACS) [20] encodes facial expressions in terms of activation levels of action units (AUs), each of which corresponds to a specific underlying group of facial muscle movements. Thus AU intensities can provide a useful basis for interpreting emotions or other reflections of human internal state such as pain. The definition of AU is widely used in image-based facial behaviour analysis tasks such as AU detection. Many computational methods [14, 26, 38, 54] have been developed for directly inferring AU activation from appearance features. Except for image-based AU detection, combining AU with 3D faces has been explored in terms of learning 3D AU classifiers from 3D scans in BP4D dataset [56] and synthesizing facial images from a specified set of AU activation through a generative model [34, 47].

Little work, however, has been devoted to constructing the FACS-based correspondence between 3DMM basis and AUs. Such line of work is important for two reasons. First, semantically mapping the 3DMM basis to each AU can help reconstruct 3D subtle motions caused by AU activation, which in turn reflects the underlying muscle activation. Second, spatial relationships among AUs derived from general anatomical knowledge [26, 33, 57, 58] can be incorporated into the 3D geometric basis generating process. Achieving this type of coherency between AU and 3D face models benefits both synergistically: incorporating AU information in 3D geometry helps capture more accurate facial motions, while incorporating geometric information helps detect challenging AUs.

Based on the considerations above, we propose a multi-stage training framework that generates a finer-grained blendshape basis that is specific to each input subject and each AU. We explicitly apply AU labels and a pre-learned Bayesian Network that captures generic inter-relationships among AUs to constrain the 3D model coefficients during training. Our main original contributions include:

- We propose a deep learning framework that explicitly learns personalized and AU-explainable 3D blendshapes for accurate 3D face reconstruction.
- We perform a multi-stage training process and utilize AU labels and a generic AU relationship prior to constrain the AU specific blendshape learning process, using a mixture of AU-labeled and unlabeled images.
- Our model simultaneously generates an AU basis and a realistic 3D face reconstruction with improved capture of subtle motions. We achieve state-of-

art 3D reconstruction results on BU3DFE [55] and the Now Challenge [42] dataset. Moreover, our model directly performs 3D AU detection because the 3D coefficients are readily mapped to AU activation probabilities.

2   Related Works

Personalized 3D Face Models. 3DMMS were first proposed [7] to model in three dimensions human variations in facial shape, expression, skin color, etc. Since then, 3DMMs have been extended and used widely for 3D face representation or reconstruction tasks. They are usually constructed from a large 3D database and have separate bases for identity, expression, texture, etc. The Basel Face Model (BFM) [40], FLAME [30] and LSFM [8] are popular 3DMMs for 3D reconstruction tasks. More recently, FaceScape [53] and ICT-Face [29] have been proposed as "high-resolution" 3D face models that provide meticulous geometric facial details. Some researchers have attempted to dynamically generate or update accurate 3DMMs directly from images or videos. Tewari et al. [48] learned a 3D facial shape and appearance basis from multi-view images of the same person. Later, Tewari et al. extended their work to learn a more complete 3DMM including shape, expression and albedo from video data [49]. Chaudhuri et al. [11] proposed an alternative that learns a personalized 3D face model by performing on-the-fly updating on the shape and expression blendshapes.

3DMM-Based Face Reconstruction. Other researchers have explored using a pre-constructed 3DMM to perform 3D face reconstruction from monocular images. 3DMM parameters representing camera, head pose, identity, expression, texture and illumination are estimated via regression. 3DMM-based face reconstruction models have achieved great performance improvements in head pose estimation [1,51,61], 3D face alignment [1,23,61] and facial detail recovery [4,5,21,62]. Moreover, Chang et al. [10] utilize 3DMM to reconstruct 3D facial expressions and apply the expression coefficients for expression recognition. Feng et al. [21] propose to learn an animatable detailed 3D face model that can generate expression-dependent geometric details such as wrinkles. However, using a 3D face reconstruction model to capture subtle local facial motions caused by activation of AUs has not been explored previously.

3D AU Modeling and Detection. 3DMMs are closely related to 3D expression/AU modeling and synthesis. Liu et al. [35] applied 3DMMs to train an adversarial network to synthesize AU images with given AU intensities. Song et al. [47] conducted an unsupervised training scheme to regress 3D AU parameters and generate game-like AU images through differentiable rendering. Li et al. [29] constructs a non-linear 3DMM with expression shapes closely related to FACS units and can be used to produce high-quality 3D expression animation.

Except for 3D AU synthesis, AU detection from 3D data have been actively studied by researchers and 3D scans, 3D point clouds, or 3DMMs can be used. Given a target 3D mesh or scan, classifiers can be trained based on the extracted mesh surface features for 3D AU detection [6,17,25,28,43,60]. Similarly, for 3D

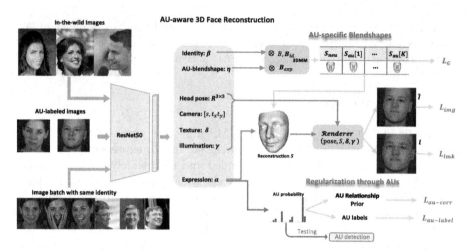

Fig. 1. Overview of our model structure and pipeline: (1) (grey) Basic module for regressing all 3D reconstruction parameters (2) (green) Pipeline for 3D face reconstruction, including subject neutral face generation, AU-specific blendshape construction and differentiable rendering process (3) (orange) Module for integrating AU prior knowledge and applying AU labels as constraints on $\boldsymbol{\alpha}$. During training the output AU probabilities are used to compute two AU regularization losses; during testing the output can be directly used for 3D AU detection. (Color figure online)

point cloud data, Reale et al. [41] trained a network to directly extract 3D point cloud features and support AU detection. Tulyakov et al. [50] learned a pose invariant face representation from the point cloud for more robust AU detection. Ariano et al. [3] propose a method of 3D AU detection by using 3DMM coefficients where they first remove the identity component from their SLC-3DMM and then train a classifier on 3D meshes for AU detection.

Our model differs from the above methods in that we construct person-specific and AU-specific 3D models for AU-interpretable face reconstruction without requiring any ground-truth 3D data for an input subject.

3 Proposed Method

In general 3D face reconstruction, the shape and expression spaces are spanned by pre-constructed bases. A target 3D face $\boldsymbol{S}$ can be represented by:

$$\boldsymbol{S} = \bar{B} + \boldsymbol{B}_{id}\beta + \boldsymbol{B}_{exp}\boldsymbol{\alpha} \tag{1}$$

where $\bar{B}$ is the 3DMM mean shape, $\boldsymbol{B}_{id}, \boldsymbol{B}_{exp}$ are shape bases and expression bases; $\beta, \boldsymbol{\alpha}$ are the vectors of shape and expression coefficients respectively.

The texture of S can also be represented by a linear model:

$$\boldsymbol{T} = \bar{T} + \boldsymbol{B}_{tex}\boldsymbol{\delta} \tag{2}$$

where $\boldsymbol{B}_{tex}$ is a texture basis (usually PCA) and $\boldsymbol{\delta}$ is a texture coefficient vector.

Our method, illustrated in Fig. 1, significantly extends the general 3DMM of Eq. 1. It contains three modules: (1) the basic module for regressing all 3D reconstruction parameters, including pose and camera parameters, identity coefficients

β, AU-blendshape coefficients η, expression coefficients α, texture coefficients δ and illumination parameters γ; (2) the module for constructing AU-specific blendshapes; (3) the module for incorporating AU regularization terms and AU detection. The remainder of this section discusses each of these in turn.

3.1 AU-specific 3D Model Learning

We describe the construction of an identity-consistent subject-neutral face and AU-specific blendshapes.

Identity-Consistent Parameters Learning. With the regressed identity coefficients β, the neutral blendshape for a subject is calculated by:

$$S_{neu} = \bar{B} + \boldsymbol{B}_{id}\beta \qquad (3)$$

Our model focuses on analysing 3D facial motions in sequence data like BP4D [56]. We want to reduce the identity bias during reconstruction for multiple frames of the same subject and therefore we can focus more on the non-rigid facial expressions. For the purpose of better estimating a subject-neutral face, we employ the identity-consistent constraint on the learning of identity parameter β. We sample a small batch of F images $I_1, \cdots , I_F$ for the same subject according to the identity labels and build F Siamese structures with shared network weights. For multi-frame input $[I_1, \cdots , I_F]$, from the output of Siamese structures, we extract identity coefficients $[\beta_1, \cdots , \beta_F]$ and enforce the similarity between every pair of identity coefficients by the following identity-consistency loss:

$$L_{id} = \frac{1}{2F(F-1)} \sum_{i,j=1}^{F} \|\beta_i - \beta_j\|_2 \qquad (4)$$

AU-Specific Blendshape Learning. A linear 3DMM usually contains an identity basis $\boldsymbol{B}_{id}$ and expression basis $\boldsymbol{B}_{exp}$, as expressed in Eq. 1. However, to adapt the 3D reconstruction model to an AU detection task, we want to construct an AU-specific blendshape for each of K blendshapes. For this purpose, we introduce an additional set of person-specific coefficients $\eta = [\eta_1, \cdots , \eta_K]$ to compose AU-specific blendshapes $\boldsymbol{B}_{au} = [[B_{au}[1], \cdots , B_{au}[K]]$.

$$B_{au}[k] = \sum_{m=1}^{M} \eta_{k,m} W_k \odot \boldsymbol{B}_{exp}[m], \forall k \in 1, ..., K \qquad (5)$$

where M is the number of expression bases and $B_{au}[k]$ is the subject blendshape for AU_k, and W_k is the pre-generated mask constraining local deformation in certain face regions for each AU. Each η_k has the dimension of the number of expression bases and $\eta_{k,m}$ is the m_{th} factor of η_k. For each input image, our model generates K subject-AU-specific blendshapes by predicting the AU coefficients η. By linearly combining the AU-specific blendshapes with the expression coefficients α, a 3D face can be expressed as:

$$S = S_{neu} + \boldsymbol{B}_{au}\alpha \qquad (6)$$

Combining Eq. 5 and 6, we find that α and η are coupled together to compose a 3D face shape and thus there may exist multiple solutions of α and η, making it impossible to properly match blendshapes with AUs. To jointly learn η and α, we constrain α by directly mapping it to AU occurrence probability.

3.2   AU-aware 3D Face Reconstruction

As depicted in Fig. 1, the expression coefficients α are the key factor to adapt the AU information to 3D geometry. In this section, we will demonstrate the process of applying two AU-related regularization terms as constraints of learning α.

AU Activation Probability. Before introducing AU-related regularization terms, we design mapping functions from 3D expression parameters α to AU occurrence probabilities. The intuition underlying the design of the mapping function is that α represents the deformation intensity in 3D space of each blendshape component, which is closer to the real-world AU activation defined in FACS [20] compared with 2D image features. Therefore, it is natural to apply a threshold on each dimension of $\alpha = [\alpha_1, \cdots, \alpha_K]^T$ to determine whether the corresponding AU is activated. We denote the activation status of AU_i as z_i with $z_i = \{0, 1\}$, and denote the probability of its occurrence as p_i with $p_i = p(z_i = 1)$. The mapping function $f : \alpha_i \to p_i$ then becomes:

$$p_i = p(z_i = 1) = \sigma(\frac{\alpha_i - \tau}{\epsilon}) \tag{7}$$

where $\sigma(x) = \frac{1}{1+e^{-x}}$ is the sigmoid function. τ is a threshold on expression intensity and ϵ is the temperature factor. Both τ and ϵ are pre-defined hyper-parameters. With the mapping in Eq. 7, AU-related regularization terms based on AU occurrence probability are then applied to optimize α by means described in detail below.

Regularization Through AUs. To learn semantically meaningful α, we derive constraints from both AU occurrence labels and generic prior knowledge on AU relationships, whereby the former applies to AU-annotated images and the latter applies to any dataset with various subjects. These constraints are incorporated into the proposed AU-specific blendshape learning as regularization terms.

A. Regularization with AU labels For images with available AU occurrence labels, we define a loss function based on the cross-entropy between the ground-truth label and predicted occurrence probability p_i:

$$L_{au-label} = -\frac{1}{|C|} \sum_{i \in C} (z_i^{gt} log(p_i) + (1 - z_i^{gt}) log(1 - p_i)) \tag{8}$$

where z_i^{gt} is the ground-truth label for AU_i and C is the set of annotated AUs.

Table 1. AU Correlation.

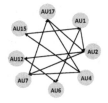

AU relations	AU pairs
	(1,2), (4,7), (4,9)
Positive correlated	(7,9),(6,12), (9,17)
	(15,17), (15,24), (17,24), (23,24)
Negative correlated	(2,6), (2,7), (12,15), (12,17)

Fig. 2. Pre-learned BN structure

B. Regularization with Generic AU Relationships. AU labels are not available for all training data. To further constrain the learning of B_{au} and α, we consider generic AU relationships defined by FACS [20]. AUs can be positively or negatively correlated, depending on the underlying muscle anatomy. We summarize the most commonly considered AU relationships in Table 1. These correlations are generic and are applicable across different subjects. AU correlations can be represented as probability inequality constraints [57]. For a positive correlated AU pair (i, j), given the occurrence of AU j, the probability of the occurrence of AU i is larger than the probability of its absence,

$$p(z_i = 1 | z_j = 1) > p(z_i = 0 | z_j = 1) \tag{9}$$

Similarly, we can derive probability constraints for negative correlations [57].

A Bayesian Network (BN) can then be learned from generic probability constraints by following [16]. The learned BN captures the joint probability of all possible configurations of 8 AUs. Its structure is visualized in Fig. 2.

Instead of employing the joint probability of all possible AUs [16], we focus on local probabilities of pairs of AUs. By employing local pairwise probabilities, we regularize α_i and α_j to be similar (or distinct) if AU_i and AU_j are positively (or negatively) correlated. Specifically, we obtain the pairwise probability of AU pair (i, j), i.e., $\boldsymbol{p}_{ij}^{prior}(z_i, z_j)$, from the learned Bayesian Network by marginalizing out the remaining nodes. The pre-generated pairwise probabilities for different AU pairs, i.e., $\boldsymbol{p}_{ij}^{prior}(z_i, z_j)$, encode generic AU relationship knowledge and apply to all subjects. Let C_2 represent the set of AU pairs (i, j) of interest[1]. The pre-generated pairwise probabilities $\{\boldsymbol{p}_{ij}^{prior}(z_i, z_j)\}_{(i,j) \in C_2}$ are then integrated into the learning of α through the proposed regularization term as follows:

$$L_{au-corr} = \frac{1}{|C_2|} \sum_{(i,j) \in C_2} (KL(p_i(z_i) \| \mathbb{E}_{p_j(z_j)} p^{prior}(z_i | z_j)) + KL(p_j(z_j) \| \mathbb{E}_{p_i(z_i)} p^{prior}(z_j | z_i))) \tag{10}$$

In Eq. 10, $p_i(z_i)$ and $p_j(z_j)$ are calculated with Eq. 7, $p^{prior}(z_j | z_j)$ are computed based on pairwise prior from the pre-learned BN: $p^{prior}(z_j | z_j) = \frac{p^{prior}(z_i, z_j)}{\sum_{z_i = 0,1} p^{prior}(z_i, z_j)}$. Both $p_i(z_i)$ and $\mathbb{E}_{p_j(z_j)} p^{prior}(z_i | z_j)$ are Bernoulli Distribution. $KL(\cdot \| \cdot)$ represents Kullback-Leibler divergence. By applying $L_{au-corr}$, AU prior relationships are leveraged to better learn AU-adaptive expression coefficients α.

---

[1] We select a set of eight AU pairs mentioned in Table 1 that are available in both the learned BN and the AU indices with $C_2 := \{(1, 2), (4, 7), (6, 12), (15, 17), (2, 6), (2, 7), (12, 15), (12, 17)\}$.

With the AU regularization terms above, our personalized AU basis are consistent with AUs. Reciprocally, AU-specific blendshapes support convenient 3D AU detection. One can apply Eq. 7 to the expression coefficients $\boldsymbol{\alpha}$ during testing to obtain the AU activation probabilities, and regard the AU_i as activated only if $p_i > 0.5$. The impact on AU detection performance is evaluated in Sect. 4.

3D Face Reconstruction The output of our model are 3D reconstruction parameters $\boldsymbol{\rho} = [s, \boldsymbol{R}, \boldsymbol{t}_{2d}, \boldsymbol{\beta}, \boldsymbol{\alpha}, \boldsymbol{\eta}, \boldsymbol{\delta}, \boldsymbol{\gamma}]$, where s is the scaling factor; $\boldsymbol{R}$ is the rotation matrix for head pose pitch, yaw and roll, $\boldsymbol{t}_{2d}$ is the 2d translation vector, $\boldsymbol{\alpha}$ are the predicted blendshape coefficients; $\boldsymbol{\delta}$ are the texture coefficients and $\boldsymbol{\gamma}$ is the illumination parameter. A weak perspective projection of the reconstructed 3D face can be expressed by

$$X = s * Pr * R * (\bar{B} + B_{id}\beta + B_{au}\alpha) + t \tag{11}$$

where $\boldsymbol{Pr} = \begin{bmatrix} 1 & 0 & 0 \\ 0 & 1 & 0 \end{bmatrix}$ is the weak perspective projection matrix. From projected vertices, we can select 68 facial landmarks $\boldsymbol{l} \in \mathbb{R}^{68 \times 2}$ and compute the projected landmark loss with ground-truth landmarks $\boldsymbol{l}^{gt}$ (detected by landmarks detectors) for 3D alignment.

For the illumination model, we follow the typical assumption that the face is a Lambertian surface and the illumination is modeled by Spherical Harmonics(SH) [37]. The color $\boldsymbol{c}$ of a vertex $\boldsymbol{x}_i$ with its surface normal $\boldsymbol{n}_i$ and texture $\boldsymbol{t}_i$ can be formulated as $\boldsymbol{c}(\boldsymbol{n}_i, \boldsymbol{t}_i | \gamma) = \boldsymbol{t}_i \sum_{k=1}^{K^2} \gamma_k \cdot \boldsymbol{H}_k(\boldsymbol{n}_i)$, where $\boldsymbol{H}_k : \mathbb{R}^3 \rightarrow \mathbb{R}$ is SH basis functions, γ_k are the corresponding SH coefficients and $K = 3, \boldsymbol{\gamma} \in \mathbb{R}^{K^2}$.

With a differentiable renderer module, we generate a synthetic image $\hat{I}$ using the projected 3D vertices $\boldsymbol{X}$ along with the texture and illumination parameters, i.e., $\hat{I} = \mathcal{R}(\boldsymbol{X}, \boldsymbol{\delta}, \boldsymbol{\gamma})$. By computing the pixel-level differences between the original image I and $\hat{I}$, the loss is back propagated to update $\boldsymbol{\rho}$.

3.3   Training Loss

We perform a three-stage training process, each stage progressively adding more terms to the loss function as described in Algorithm 1. For the first stage (training the 3D reconstruction), the model training is self-supervised with the identity-consistency constraint. The model takes image batches as input. At the second stage, we train our model only on AU-annotated data. For the last stage, we further fine-tune our model with AU priors introduced in Sect. 3.2.

The total training loss function for the final stage is:

$$\begin{aligned} L = &\lambda_{img}L_{img} + \lambda_{lmk}L_{lmk} + \lambda_{id}L_{id} + \lambda_G L_G + L_{sp} \\ &+ \lambda_{au-label}L_{au-label} + \lambda_{au-corr}L_{au-corr} \end{aligned} \tag{12}$$

The loss term L_{id} is defined in Eq. 4, the AU regularization terms $L_{au-label}$, $L_{au-corr}$ are defined in Eqs. 8 and 10. $L_{img}, L_{lmk}, L_{id}, L_G, L_{sp}$ are described below.

Algorithm 1 Multi-Stage Training Process

1: **Stage1: Identity-aware baseline model training**
2: Input: $B_{neu}^0, \boldsymbol{B}_{au}^0$,
$\{[I_1^{s_i}, \cdots, I_F^{s_i}], [\boldsymbol{l}_1^{s_i}, \cdots, \boldsymbol{l}_F^{s_i}]^{gt}[A_1^{s_i}, \cdots, A_F^{s_i}]\}_{i=1}^{N_2}$
3: Training Loss: $L_1 = \lambda_{img}L_{img} + \lambda_{lmk}L_{lmk} + \lambda_G L_G + \lambda_{id}L_{id} + \lambda_{sp}L_{sp}$
4: **Stage2: AU-adaptive training with AU labels**
5: Input: $\{I_i, \boldsymbol{l}_i^{gt}, A_i, \boldsymbol{z}_i^{gt}\}_{i=1}^{N_1}, B_{neu}^0, \boldsymbol{B}_{au}^0, \boldsymbol{p}_{ij}^{prior}$
6: Training Loss: $L_2 = \lambda_{img}L_{img} + \lambda_{lmk}L_{lmk} + \lambda_G L_G + \lambda_{au-label}L_{au-label} + \lambda_{sp}L_{sp}$
7: **Stage3: AU-adaptive training with AU prior**
8: Input: $\{I_i, \boldsymbol{l}_i^{gt}, A_i\}_{i=1}^{N_1}, B_{neu}^0, \boldsymbol{B}_{au}^0, \boldsymbol{p}_{ij}^{prior}$
9: Training Loss: $L_3 = \lambda_{img}L_{img} + \lambda_{lmk}L_{lmk} + \lambda_G L_G + \lambda_{sp}L_{sp} + \lambda_{au-corr}L_{au-corr}$

Photometric Loss. The main component of the training loss is the pixel-level loss between the synthetic image $\hat{I}$ and original image I, formulated as:

$$L_{img} = \frac{\sum_m A_m \|I - \hat{I}\|_2}{\sum_m A_m} \tag{13}$$

where A_m is pre-generated facial skin mask so that we only calculate the pixel difference in face region.

Projected Landmark Loss. We select 68 landmark vertices on the mesh model and define the landmark loss term as the distance between the projected 3D landmarks $\hat{l}$ and the pre-generated results l from landmark detectors.

$$L_{lmk} = \|\boldsymbol{l} - \boldsymbol{l}^{gt}\|_2 \tag{14}$$

Deformation Gradient Loss. Except for the soft constraints of AU labels and AU prior knowledge on expression coefficients $\boldsymbol{\alpha}$, we further apply a regularization term on the generated $\boldsymbol{B}_{au}$ to ensure they are locally deformed and semantically mapped to each AU. Inspired by the work of Chaudhur et al. [11] and Li et al. [27], we pre-define a template neutral face B_{neu}^0 the same number of AU-blendshape template $\boldsymbol{B}_{au}^0$ by performing Non-Rigis ICP [2] process from BFM template to ICT-Face [29] expression template and impose regularization term of deformation gradient similarity, formulated as below:

$$L_G = \sum_{k=1}^K \left\| \boldsymbol{G}_{(B_{au}[k] \to S_{neu})} - \boldsymbol{G}_{(B_{au}^0[k] \to B_{neu}^0)} \right\|_F \tag{15}$$

where $\boldsymbol{G}_{(B_{au}[k] \to S_{neu})}$, is the deformation gradient between the k_{th} AU-blendshape and neutral shape for a specific subject following the calculation defined in [12]. The loss L_G is utilized to enforce that the learned $\boldsymbol{B}_{au}$ are not exaggerated and have similar local deformations as the template ICT blendshapes so that $\boldsymbol{B}_{au}$ can semantically match with each AU. Without this loss, $\boldsymbol{B}_{au}$ will be deformed in a free-form manner and lose the interpretability as AU-blendshapes.

Coefficients Sparsity Loss. To avoid generating implausible faces we apply a regularization term to constrain small 3D coefficients, including β, α, δ, which is denoted as the sparsity loss L_{sp} and it's based on the L_2 norm of the coefficients.

$$L_{sp} = \lambda_{sp,1}\|\beta\|_2 + \lambda_{sp,2}\|\alpha\|_2 + \lambda_{sp,3}\|\delta\|_2 \tag{16}$$

The training process is described in Algorithm 1.

4   Experiments

Datasets. To fully assess the proposed model under different environments, we evaluate both face reconstruction performance and AU detection performance on the following benchmark datasets:

- **CelebA** [36] contains more than 200k celebrity images with annotations of 40 attributes. We utilize the full CelebA images and the corresponding landmark and identity annotation for training. The landmarks are used to crop and initially align the images; identity attributes are used to generate image triplets for the identity consistency training.
- **BP4D** [56] is a spontaneous database containing 328 sequences from 41 subjects performing different facial expressions. Each subject is involved in 8 expression tasks, and their spontaneous facial actions are encoded by binary AU labels and AU intensity labels. Around 140k frames with AU occurrence labels are employed for evaluation. Subject-exclusive three-fold cross-validation experiment protocol is employed for AU detection evaluation.
- **BU3DFE** [55] is a 3D facial expression database with 3D scans available for 2500 face shapes of neutral face and six expressions. We use BU3DFE for the evaluation of 3D reconstruction performance.
- **Now Challenge** [42] provides around 2k 2D multi-view images of 100 subjects categorized by neutral, expressional, occluded and selfie images. We employee Now dataset only for 3D reconstruction evaluation with provided ground-truth 3D scans.

Implementation Details. We use the BFM [22] 3DMM for face reconstruction. In Eq. 5, the deformation mask is generated by using expression shapes provided by the ICT-Face [29] model. We use NICP [2] tools to project each ICT-face vertex to the closest triangle of the BFM mesh. We first generate a binary weight map by thresholding the vertex deformation for each blendshape and then perform Gaussian smoothing on the boundary to generate W_k (visualizations are available in the supplementary material). We use CelebA and BP4D as our training data. At the first stage, we sampled small image batches from both databases with $F = 3$ in Eq. 4. In Eq. 7, we set the hyper-parameter $\tau = 0.15$ and $\epsilon = 0.05$ by grid-search. We assign $\epsilon = 0.01$, which is used to amplify the difference between α and τ.

For BP4D, we generate multiple triplet samples for each subject and each sequence. We train the **baseline** model for five epochs. At the second stage, we split BP4D into 3 folds and select two folds for AU-supervised training. The trained model is denoted as **baseline+AU label** model. For the last stage, we perform AU-adaptive training on both datasets by employing AU prior regularization term. The final model is denoted as **baseline+AU label+AU prior** model. We use CelebA and two folds of BP4D images for training. We train 170k iterations with batch size of 30.

4.1   Evaluation of 3D Reconstruction Error

To validate the reconstruction efficiency of AU-specific blendshapes, we perform quantitative and qualitative comparisons of the reconstruction results against state-of-the-art weakly-supervised 3D face reconstruction methods.

Table 2. 3D Reconstruction Error on BU3DFE [55]

Methods	Mean (mm)	SD
Chaudhuri et al. [11]	1.61	0.31
Shang et al. [44]	1.55	0.32
Bai et al. [4]	1.21	**0.25**
FML [48]	1.78	0.45
Ours-final	**1.11**	0.28

Table 3. 3D Reconstruction Error on **Now** [42] validation set

Methods	Mean (mm)	SD
Shang et al. [44]	1.87	2.63
Dib et al. [19]	1.57	1.31
RingNet [42]	1.53	1.31
Deep3dFaceRecon-pytorch [18]	1.41	1.21
DECA [21]	1.38	**1.18**
Ours-final	**1.33**	1.21

Table 4. Ablation Study on 3D Reconstruction

Stages with different losses (ResNet50)	BU3DFE [55]		Now [42]	
	Mean (mm)	SD	Mean (mm)	SD
backbone	1.62	0.68	1.90	1.45
backbone+L_{id}	1.58	0.50	1.84	1.56
backbone+L_G	1.37	0.35	1.52	1.36
backbone+$L_{id} + L_G$ (**baseline**)	1.32	0.32	1.47	1.38
backbone+$L_{id} + L_G + L_{au-label}$	1.18	0.30	1.39	**1.20**
Ours-final: *backbone*+$L_{id} + L_G + L_{au-label} + L_{au-corr}$	**1.11**	**0.28**	**1.33**	1.21

Quantitative Evaluation. We perform monocular face reconstruction evaluation on the BU3DFE and **Now** validation datasets. On the BU3DFE dataset, we follow the evaluation procedure of [48] and [5] to pre-generate a dense-correspondence map between each ground-truth scan and reconstructed 3D face, applying the Iterative-Closest-Point(ICP) algorithm using Open3d [59]. On the **Now** dataset, we compute the correspondence by following the RingNet evaluation procedure [42]. With the correspondence between each scan vertex and the BFM mesh surface, the reconstruction accuracy is evaluated in terms of vertex-to-plane mean square error (MSE) in units of mm and standard deviation (SD).

A. Comparison to State-of-the-Art Methods. We compare our model against four state-of-the-art methods: Chaudhuri et al. [11], Shang et al. [44], Bai et al. [4] and FML [48] on both the BU3DFE and **Now** datasets. Results are shown in Tables 2 and 3, respectively. On both benchmark datasets, our final model outperforms existing state-of-the-art methods. On BU3DFE, our model achieves an MSE of 1.11 MSE, which is 0.67 less than the MSE achieved by FML [48]. On the **Now** validation dataset, our final model's MSE is also better than the state-of-the-art methods [18, 19, 42, 44]. We provide visualizations examples of error maps on BU3DFE and **Now** in the supplementary materials.

B. Ablation Study. To further study the effectiveness of each component in Sect. 3.3, we report the performance of our model trained on the same training data but with different loss terms on both the BU3DFE and **Now** validation datasets. Results are shown in Table 4.

In the following, the "backbone" refers to the ResNet50 structure trained with basic loss terms including L_{img}, L_{lmk}, L_{sp}. We refer to the model trained with $L_{id} + L_G$ as identity-aware **baseline** model; model trained with $L_{id} + L_G + L_{au-label}$ is referred to as **baseline+AU label** model; our final model, i.e., the model trained with $L_{id} + L_G + L_{au-label} + L_{au-corr}$, is referred to as **baseline+AU label+AU prior** model.

The first four rows of Table 4 reveal that, prior to adding any AU regularization terms, adding L_G provides the most significant performance improvement. This demonstrates the effectiveness of constraining locally deformed blendshapes, even before they are made AU-specific. Advancing to the fifth and sixth rows of Table 4, where the regularization terms for AU labels and AU prior relationships are added, we observe that AU-based regularization provides another significant gain in 3D accuracy over the **baseline** model for both datasets. Furthermore, even at intermediate stages, our models can sometimes outperform state-of-the-art methods. For example, on BU3DFE, our **baseline+AU label** model achieves MSE = 1.18, which is better than MSE = 1.21 achieved by [4]. Since the available ground-truth scans in **Now** validation data do not have significant facial expressions, the degree to which AU regularization improves the final model is somewhat less than for BU3DFE. Even without AU regularization, our **baseline+AU label** model outperforms nearly all of the prior methods.

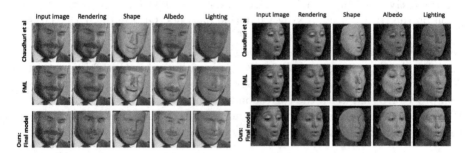

Fig. 3. Reconstruction result visualization on VoxCeleb2 [13] using **ours: baseline+AU label+AU prior**, Chaudhuri et al. [11] and FML [48]. Our model can produce accurate facial expressions.

Qualitative Evaluation. The PCA basis used in BFM [22] has no semantic meaning, and usually contains global deformations. In contrast, our learned AU-blendshapes have the advantage that they are capable of representing subtle local facial motions closely related to AUs, and moreover they are adapted to the known AU relationship priors described in Sect. 3.2. This advantage is illustrated qualitatively in Fig. 3, where we compare the 3D reconstruction result on VoxCeleb2 [13] images with the models of FML [48] and Chaudhur et al. [11]. It is evident from the examples given in Fig. 3 that our model can produce more reliable 3D facial motion details, especially in eye-brow motion and mouth motion. In Fig. 4, we perform a more comprehensive comparison of our model trained using different loss functions with state-of-art reconstruction methods. By self-comparison, our model (**C**) and (**D**) capture 3D expressions more accurately than our baseline model (**B**). In Fig. 5, we provide testing examples on **BU3DFE** and **Now**. For more qualitative results, please reference our supplementary materials.

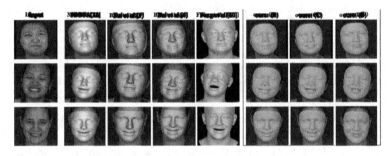

Fig. 4. Reconstruction result comparison of our model and state-of-art face reconstruction models: 3DDFA [23], Bai et al. [5], Bai et al. [4], Feng et al. [21] on BP4D [56] dataset. For our model, (**B**) is **baseline** model, (**C**) is **baseline+AU label** model and (**D**) is **baseline+AU label + AU prior** model.

(a) BU3DFE   (b) Now challenge

Fig. 5. Reconstruction visualization on BU3DFE samples and Now Challenge samples using our **baseline+AU label+AU prior** model.

Table 5. Comparison to state-of-the-art methods on BP4D (F1 score)

Method	AU1	AU2	AU4	AU6	AU7	AU10	AU12	AU14	AU15	AU17	AU23	AU24	Avg.
DRML [32]	36.4	[41.8]	43.0	55.0	67.0	66.3	65.8	54.1	33.2	48.0	31.7	30.0	48.3
ROI [31]	36.2	31.6	43.4	77.1	73.7	85.0	87.0	62.6	45.7	58.0	38.3	37.4	56.4
JAA-Net [45]	47.2	44.0	54.9	77.5	74.6	84.0	86.9	61.9	43.6	60.3	42.7	41.9	60.0
DSIN [15]	51.7	40.4	56.0	76.1	73.5	79.9	85.4	62.7	37.3	62.9	38.8	41.6	58.9
LP-Net [39]	43.4	38.0	54.2	77.1	76.7	**83.8**	**87.2**	63.3	45.3	60.5	48.1	54.2	61.0
ARL [46]	45.8	39.8	55.1	75.7	77.2	82.3	86.8	58.8	47.6	62.1	47.4	55.4	61.1
Jacob et al. [24]	51.7	49.3	**61.0**	**77.8**	**79.5**	82.9	86.3	**67.6**	**51.9**	**63.0**	43.7	**56.3**	**64.2**
Ours-final	**55.2**	**57.0**	53.7	66.7	77.8	76.4	79.7	59.8	44.1	60.1	**53.6**	46.0	60.8

4.2   Evaluation of 3D AU Detection Performance

Comparison to State-of-the-art Methods. To prove that the learned 3DMM is AU-interpretable with the proposed AU regularization terms, we perform AU detection directly using our 3D model and compare to state-of-the-art image-frame-based methods accordingly, including EAC-Net [32], ROI [31], JAA-Net [45], DSIN [15] and LP-Net [39], ARL [46], Jacob et al. [24]. We stress that our model performs AU detection as an outcome of 3D face reconstruction, which is a totally different mechanism from these SOTA methods, and yet our proposed method still achieves comparable AU detection performance for within-dataset evaluation on BP4D. During testing, given a set of predicted expression parameters α, we apply Eq. 7 to obtain activation probabilities and regard AU_i as active if $p_i > 0.5$. Results are shown in Table 5.

Table 6. Ablation Study on AU Detection

Models with different losses (`ReseNet50`)	Avg. (F1)
backbone	30.3
backbone+L_{id}	30.4
backbone+L_G	51.0
backbone+ $L_{id} + L_G$ (**baseline**)	56.0
backbone+$L_{id} + L_G + L_{au-label}$	60.0
Ours-final: *backbone*+$L_{id} + L_G + L_{au-label} + L_{au-corr}$	**60.8**

According to Table 5, the overall average F1-score of our 3D model achieves comparable performance compared to most of the frame-based methods. More importantly, our model performs significantly better performance on three challenging AUs: AU1, AU2 and AU23 and very close performance with [24] on AU7 and AU17. For AUs with distinguishable vertex deformations (like AU1 and AU2) that can be more easily identified from the overall geometry, our model can achieve good performance. For AUs with highly correlated blendshapes, i.e. the vertex deformations are overlapped and similar, our model is more susceptible to misclassification than image-based methods.

Ablation Study. To better understand whether the effect of each loss component on AU detection performance is consistent with 3D reconstruction, we employ the same model nomenclature as introduced in the previous section and report the average AU detection F1-score. During the training of the **baseline** model, no AU labels are used; only generic AU-blendshapes are used as weak constraints for AU modeling. Comparing the **baseline+AU label** F1-score to that of **baseline**, it is clear that AU label regularization helps significantly. Adding the AU relationship priors helps as well, albeit to a lesser extent (Table 6).

5   Conclusion

We have proposed a novel framework for learning subject-dependent AU blendshapes by directly applying AU-related regularization terms on a 3D face model.

With a learned AU-specific basis, our model is able to generate accurate 3D face reconstruction, especially for subtle motions in the eye and mouth regions, and can be directly utilized for AU detection. Experimental results demonstrate that our model achieves state-of-the-art 3D reconstruction accuracy and generates comparable AU detection results through integrating AU information during the model learning. Most importantly, quantitative evaluation of the two tasks shows that incorporating AU information in 3D geometry helps recover more realistic and explainable facial motions and 3D basis provide a new perspective of detecting challenging AUs, indicating a great potential for using our model in conjunction with image-based methods in a complementary fashion to create an AU detector that combines the best of both.

Acknowledgements. The work described in this paper is supported in part by the U.S. National Science Foundation award CNS 1629856.

References

1. Albiero, V., Chen, X., Yin, X., Pang, G., Hassner, T.: img2pose: face alignment and detection via 6dof, face pose estimation. In: Proceedings of the IEEE/CVF Conference on Computer Vision and Pattern Recognition, pp. 7617–7627 (2021)
2. Amberg, B., Romdhani, S., Vetter, T.: Optimal step nonrigid ICP algorithms for surface registration. In: 2007 IEEE Conference on Computer Vision and Pattern Recognition, pp. 1–8. IEEE (2007)
3. Ariano, L., Ferrari, C., Berretti, S., Del Bimbo, A.: Action unit detection by learning the deformation coefficients of a 3D morphable model. Sensors **21**(2), 589 (2021)
4. Bai, Z., Cui, Z., Liu, X., Tan, P.: Riggable 3D face reconstruction via in-network optimization. In: Proceedings of the IEEE/CVF Conference on Computer Vision and Pattern Recognition, pp. 6216–6225 (2021)
5. Bai, Z., Cui, Z., Rahim, J.A., Liu, X., Tan, P.: Deep facial non-rigid multi-view stereo. In: Proceedings of the IEEE/CVF Conference on Computer Vision and Pattern Recognition, pp. 5850–5860 (2020)
6. Bayramoglu, N., Zhao, G., Pietikäinen, M.: CS-3DLBP and geometry based person independent 3D facial action unit detection. In: 2013 International Conference on Biometrics (ICB), pp. 1–6. IEEE (2013)
7. Blanz, V., Vetter, T.: A morphable model for the synthesis of 3D faces. In: Proceedings of the 26th Annual Conference on Computer Graphics and Interactive Techniques, pp. 187–194 (1999)
8. Booth, J., Roussos, A., Zafeiriou, S., Ponniah, A., Dunaway, D.: A 3D morphable model learnt from 10,000 faces. In: Proceedings of the IEEE Conference on Computer Vision and Pattern Recognition, pp. 5543–5552 (2016)
9. Cao, C., Weng, Y., Zhou, S., Tong, Y., Zhou, K.: FaceWarehouse: a 3D facial expression database for visual computing. IEEE Trans. Visual Comput. Graphics **20**(3), 413–425 (2013)
10. Chang, F.J., Tran, A.T., Hassner, T., Masi, I., Nevatia, R., Medioni, G.: ExpNet: landmark-free, deep, 3D facial expressions. In: 2018 13th IEEE International Conference on Automatic Face & Gesture Recognition (FG 2018), pp. 122–129. IEEE (2018)

11. Chaudhuri, B., Vesdapunt, N., Shapiro, L., Wang, B.: Personalized face modeling for improved face reconstruction and motion retargeting. In: Vedaldi, A., Bischof, H., Brox, T., Frahm, J.-M. (eds.) ECCV 2020. LNCS, vol. 12350, pp. 142–160. Springer, Cham (2020). https://doi.org/10.1007/978-3-030-58558-7_9
12. Chu, W.S., la Torre, F.D., Cohn, J.F.: Selective transfer machine for personalized facial action unit detection. In: CVPR (2013)
13. Chung, J.S., Nagrani, A., Zisserman, A.: VoxCeleb2: deep speaker recognition. arXiv preprint arXiv:1806.05622 (2018)
14. Corneanu, C., Madadi, M., Escalera, S.: Deep structure inference network for facial action unit recognition. In: Ferrari, V., Hebert, M., Sminchisescu, C., Weiss, Y. (eds.) ECCV 2018. LNCS, vol. 11216, pp. 309–324. Springer, Cham (2018). https://doi.org/10.1007/978-3-030-01258-8_19
15. Corneanu, C., Madadi, M., Escalera, S.: Deep structure inference network for facial action unit recognition. In: Ferrari, V., Hebert, M., Sminchisescu, C., Weiss, Y. (eds.) ECCV 2018. LNCS, vol. 11216, pp. 309–324. Springer, Cham (2018). https://doi.org/10.1007/978-3-030-01258-8_19
16. Cui, Z., Song, T., Wang, Y., Ji, Q.: Knowledge augmented deep neural networks for joint facial expression and action unit recognition. In: Advances in Neural Information Processing Systems 33 (2020)
17. Danelakis, A., Theoharis, T., Pratikakis, I.: Action unit detection in 3D facial videos with application in facial expression retrieval and recognition. Multimedia Tools Appl. **77**(19), 24813–24841 (2018)
18. Deng, Y., Yang, J., Xu, S., Chen, D., Jia, Y., Tong, X.: Accurate 3D face reconstruction with weakly-supervised learning: From single image to image set. In: Computer Vision and Pattern Recognition Workshops, pp. 285–295 (2019)
19. Dib, A., Thebault, C., Ahn, J., Gosselin, P., Theobalt, C., Chevallier, L.: Towards high fidelity monocular face reconstruction with rich reflectance using self-supervised learning and ray tracing. In: Proceedings of the IEEE International Conference on Computer Vision (ICCV) (2021)
20. Ekman, P., Friesen, W.V., Hager, J.C.: Facial action coding system. A Human Face, Salt Lake City, UT (2002)
21. Feng, Y., Feng, H., Black, M.J., Bolkart, T.: Learning an animatable detailed 3D face model from in-the-wild images, vol. 40 (2021). https://doi.org/10.1145/3450626.3459936
22. Gerig, T., et al.: Morphable face models-an open framework. In: 2018 13th IEEE International Conference on Automatic Face & Gesture Recognition (FG 2018), pp. 75–82. IEEE (2018)
23. Guo, J., Zhu, X., Yang, Y., Yang, F., Lei, Z., Li, S.Z.: Towards fast, accurate and stable 3D dense face alignment. In: Vedaldi, A., Bischof, H., Brox, T., Frahm, J.-M. (eds.) ECCV 2020. LNCS, vol. 12364, pp. 152–168. Springer, Cham (2020). https://doi.org/10.1007/978-3-030-58529-7_10
24. Jacob, G.M., Stenger, B.: Facial action unit detection with transformers. In: Proceedings of the IEEE/CVF Conference on Computer Vision and Pattern Recognition, pp. 7680–7689 (2021)
25. Jiao, Y., Niu, Y., Tran, T.D., Shi, G.: 2D+ 3D facial expression recognition via discriminative dynamic range enhancement and multi-scale learning. arXiv preprint arXiv:2011.08333 (2020)
26. Li, G., Zhu, X., Zeng, Y., Wang, Q., Lin, L.: Semantic relationships guided representation learning for facial action unit recognition. In: AAAI (2019)
27. Li, H., Weise, T., Pauly, M.: Example-based facial rigging. ACM Trans. Graph. (TOG) **29**(4), 1–6 (2010)

28. Li, H., Sun, J., Xu, Z., Chen, L.: Multimodal 2D+ 3D facial expression recognition with deep fusion convolutional neural network. IEEE Trans. Multimedia **19**(12), 2816–2831 (2017)
29. Li, R., et al.: Learning formation of physically-based face attributes (2020)
30. Li, T., Bolkart, T., Black, M.J., Li, H., Romero, J.: Learning a model of facial shape and expression from 4D scans. ACM Trans. Graph. **36**(6), 1–194 (2017)
31. Li, W., Abtahi, F., Zhu, Z.: Action unit detection with region adaptation, multi-labeling learning and optimal temporal fusing. In: Proceedings of the IEEE Conference on Computer Vision and Pattern Recognition, pp. 1841–1850 (2017)
32. Li, W., Abtahi, F., Zhu, Z., Yin, L.: EAC-Net: deep nets with enhancing and cropping for facial action unit detection. IEEE Trans. Pattern Anal. Mach. Intell. **40**(11), 2583–2596 (2018)
33. Li, Y., Chen, J., Zhao, Y., Ji, Q.: Data-free prior model for facial action unit recognition. IEEE Trans. Affect. Comput. **4**(2), 127–141 (2013)
34. Liu, Z., Song, G., Cai, J., Cham, T.J., Zhang, J.: Conditional adversarial synthesis of 3D facial action units. Neurocomputing **355**, 200–208 (2019)
35. Liu, Z., Song, G., Cai, J., Cham, T.J., Zhang, J.: Conditional adversarial synthesis of 3D facial action units. Neurocomputing **355**, 200–208 (2019)
36. Liu, Z., Luo, P., Wang, X., Tang, X.: Deep learning face attributes in the wild. In: Proceedings of International Conference on Computer Vision (ICCV) (2015)
37. Müller, Claus: Spherical harmonics. LNM, vol. 17. Springer, Heidelberg (1966). https://doi.org/10.1007/BFb0094775
38. Niu, X., Han, H., Yang, S., Shan, S.: Local relationship learning with person-specific shape regularization for facial action unit detection. In: CVPR (2019)
39. Niu, X., Han, H., Yang, S., Huang, Y., Shan, S.: Local relationship learning with person-specific shape regularization for facial action unit detection. In: Proceedings of the IEEE Conference on Computer Vision and Pattern Recognition workshops (2019)
40. Paysan, P., Knothe, R., Amberg, B., Romdhani, S., Vetter, T.: A 3D face model for pose and illumination invariant face recognition. In: 2009 Sixth IEEE International Conference on Advanced Video and Signal Based Surveillance, pp. 296–301. IEEE (2009)
41. Reale, M.J., Klinghoffer, B., Church, M., Szmurlo, H., Yin, L.: Facial action unit analysis through 3d point cloud neural networks. In: 2019 14th IEEE International Conference on Automatic Face & Gesture Recognition (FG 2019), pp. 1–8. IEEE (2019)
42. Sanyal, S., Bolkart, T., Feng, H., Black, M.: Learning to regress 3D face shape and expression from an image without 3D supervision. In: Proceedings IEEE Conference on Computer Vision and Pattern Recognition (CVPR) (2019)
43. Savran, A., Sankur, B., Bilge, M.T.: Comparative evaluation of 3D vs. 2D modality for automatic detection of facial action units. Pattern Recogn. **45**(2), 767–782 (2012)
44. Shang, J., et al.: Self-supervised monocular 3D face reconstruction by occlusion-aware multi-view geometry consistency. In: Vedaldi, A., Bischof, H., Brox, T., Frahm, J.-M. (eds.) ECCV 2020. LNCS, vol. 12360, pp. 53–70. Springer, Cham (2020). https://doi.org/10.1007/978-3-030-58555-6_4
45. Shao, Z., Liu, Z., Cai, J., Ma, L.: Deep adaptive attention for joint facial action unit detection and face alignment. In: Ferrari, V., Hebert, M., Sminchisescu, C., Weiss, Y. (eds.) ECCV 2018. LNCS, vol. 11217, pp. 725–740. Springer, Cham (2018). https://doi.org/10.1007/978-3-030-01261-8_43

46. Shao, Z., Liu, Z., Cai, J., Wu, Y., Ma, L.: Facial action unit detection using attention and relation learning. IEEE Transactions on Affective Computing (2019)
47. Song, X., et al.: Unsupervised learning facial parameter regressor for action unit intensity estimation via differentiable renderer. In: Proceedings of the 28th ACM International Conference on Multimedia, pp. 2842–2851 (2020)
48. Tewari, et al.: FML: face model learning from videos. In: Proceedings of the IEEE/CVF Conference on Computer Vision and Pattern Recognition, pp. 10812–10822 (2019)
49. Tewari, A., et al.: Learning complete 3D morphable face models from images and videos. In: Proceedings of the IEEE/CVF Conference on Computer Vision and Pattern Recognition, pp. 3361–3371 (2021)
50. Tulyakov, S., Vieriu, R.L., Sangineto, E., Sebe, N.: Facecept3D: real time 3D face tracking and analysis. In: Proceedings of the IEEE International Conference on Computer Vision Workshops, pp. 28–33 (2015)
51. Wu, C.Y., Xu, Q., Neumann, U.: Synergy between 3Dmm and 3D landmarks for accurate 3D facial geometry. arXiv preprint arXiv:2110.09772 (2021)
52. Yan, Y., Lu, K., Xue, J., Gao, P., Lyu, J.: FEAFA: a well-annotated dataset for facial expression analysis and 3d facial animation. In: 2019 IEEE International Conference on Multimedia & Expo Workshops (ICMEW), pp. 96–101. IEEE (2019)
53. Yang, H., et al.: FaceScape: a large-scale high quality 3D face dataset and detailed riggable 3D face prediction. In: Proceedings of the IEEE/CVF Conference on Computer Vision and Pattern Recognition, pp. 601–610 (2020)
54. Yang, H., Wang, T., Yin, L.: Adaptive multimodal fusion for facial action units recognition. In: Proceedings of the 28th ACM International Conference on Multimedia, pp. 2982–2990 (2020)
55. Yin, L., Wei, X., Sun, Y., Wang, J., Rosato, M.J.: A 3D facial expression database for facial behavior research. In: 7th international conference on automatic face and gesture recognition (FGR06), pp. 211–216. IEEE (2006)
56. Zhang, X., et al.: BP4D-spontaneous: a high-resolution spontaneous 3D dynamic facial expression database. Image Vis. Comput. **32**(10), 692–706 (2014)
57. Zhang, Y., Dong, W., Hu, B., Ji, Q.: Classifier learning with prior probabilities for facial action unit recognition. In: CVPR (2018)
58. Zhang, Y., Dong, W., Hu, B., Ji, Q.: Weakly-supervised deep convolutional neural network learning for facial action unit intensity estimation. In: CVPR (2018)
59. Zhou, Q.Y., Park, J., Koltun, V.: Open3D: a modern library for 3D data processing. arXiv preprint arXiv:1801.09847 (2018)
60. Zhu, K., Du, Z., Li, W., Huang, D., Wang, Y., Chen, L.: Discriminative attention-based convolutional neural network for 3D facial expression recognition. In: 2019 14th IEEE International Conference on Automatic Face & Gesture Recognition (FG 2019), pp. 1–8. IEEE (2019)
61. Zhu, X., Liu, X., Lei, Z., Li, S.Z.: Face alignment in full pose range: a 3D total solution. In: IEEE Transactions on Pattern Analysis and Machine Intelligence (2017)
62. Zhu, X., et al.: Beyond 3DMM space: towards fine-grained 3D face reconstruction. In: Vedaldi, A., Bischof, H., Brox, T., Frahm, J.-M. (eds.) ECCV 2020. LNCS, vol. 12353, pp. 343–358. Springer, Cham (2020). https://doi.org/10.1007/978-3-030-58598-3_21

BézierPalm: A Free Lunch for Palmprint Recognition

Kai Zhao[1,2], Lei Shen[1], Yingyi Zhang[1], Chuhan Zhou[1], Tao Wang[1],
Ruixin Zhang[1], Shouhong Ding[1], Wei Jia[3], and Wei Shen[4(✉)]

[1] Tencent Youtu Lab, Shanghai, China
[2] University of California, Los Angeles, Los Angeles, USA
[3] School of Computer Science and Information Engineering,
Hefei University of Technology, Hefei, USA
[4] MoE Key Lab of Artificial Intelligence, AI Institute,
Shanghai Jiao Tong University, Shanghai, China
wei.shen@sjtu.edu.cn

Abstract. Palmprints are private and stable information for biometric recognition. In the deep learning era, the development of palmprint recognition is limited by the lack of sufficient training data. In this paper, by observing that palmar creases are the key information to deep-learning-based palmprint recognition, we propose to synthesize training data by manipulating palmar creases. Concretely, we introduce an intuitive geometric model which represents palmar creases with parameterized Bézier curves. By randomly sampling Bézier parameters, we can synthesize massive training samples of diverse identities, which enables us to pretrain large-scale palmprint recognition models. Experimental results demonstrate that such synthetically pretrained models have a very strong generalization ability: they can be efficiently transferred to real datasets, leading to significant performance improvements on palmprint recognition. For example, under the open-set protocol, our method improves the strong ArcFace baseline by more than 10% in terms of TAR@1e−6. And under the closed-set protocol, our method reduces the equal error rate (EER) by an order of magnitude. Code is available at http://kaizhao.net/palmprint.

Keywords: Deep learning · Palmprint recognition · Data synthesis · Bézier curve · Geometric models

1 Introduction

Palm information is privacy-by-design because the palm pattern is concealed inside your hand, and it is almost impossible to be tracked by public cameras without your consent. For its security and privacy, palmprint recognition is being

Supplementary Information The online version contains supplementary material available at https://doi.org/10.1007/978-3-031-19778-9_2.

adopted by AmazonOne for identification and payment [1]. In contrast, the widely used face recognition system can easily track people through public cameras without any consent. As a result, face recognition has received widespread criticism in the last few years due to the privacy concerns it creates [17,55].

It is precisely because of its privacy that palmprint recognition lacks a large-scale public dataset. To the best of our knowledge, the largest open dataset for palmprint recognition contains thousands of identities and tens of thousands of images [33]. In contrast, there are a number of million-scale face recognition datasets either based on webly collected faces [4,19,29] or surveillance cameras [41,58]. The lack of sufficient data has become the main bottleneck for palmprint recognition. In this paper, we propose to synthesize images to augment the training set for palmprint recognition.

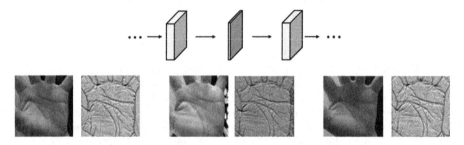

Fig. 1. Top: during training, we squeeze the intermediate features to 1-dimension for visualization. Middle and bottom: the input palm images and intermediate features. The intermediate features suggest that palmar creases are the key information to palmprint recognition.

By visualizing the intermediate features from a CNN-based palmprint recognition model, we observe that the palmar creases play a critical role. Specifically, we insert a 'squeeze-and-excite' operation into an existing CNN architecture. The 'squeeze-and-excite' first squeezes an intermediate feature map into 1-dimension and excites it back. Then we train this model on palmprint datasets. Finally, we visualize the 1-dimensional feature map on test images. As shown in Fig. 1, most of the texture and color information are ignored by the model, and the palmar creases are largely reserved. This reminds us that we may synthesize palmar creases to enrich the training data for palmprint recognition.

With the above observation, we propose to synthesize training data for palmprint recognition by manipulating palmar creases. An intuitive and simple geometric model is proposed to synthesize palm images by representing palmar creases with several parameterized Bézier curves. The identity of each synthesized data is controlled by the parameters of Bézier curves, *e.g.* number of curves, positions of endpoints, and control points. Our method is able to synthesize massive samples of diverse identities, which enables us to perform large-scale pretraining on such synthetic data. The synthetically pretrained models present promising generalization ability and can be efficiently transferred to real datasets.

Our method holds essential differences from other data generation methods such as generative adversarial networks (GANs) and data augmentation. First of all, both GANs and data augmentation rely on existing data: either train GANs with or add modifications to existing data. While our method creates new samples without any existing data. Second, neither GANs nor data augmentation can create samples of novel categories, while our method can control the category (identity) of synthesized samples. In addition, GANs require large amount of training data and thus cannot substantially improve the recognition performance. For example, [45] uses GAN-synthesized samples to train face recognition models. However, the synthetically trained models perform worse than models that are directly trained on dataset that is used to train GANs.

Extensive experiments under both open-set and closed-set evaluation protocols demonstrate that our method significantly improve the performance of strong baselines. Additionally, we evaluate on a private million-scale data to further confirm the scalability of our method.

The contributions of this paper are summarized as below:

– We visualize the intermediate features of CNN-based palmprint recognition models and observe that the palmar creases play an important role.
– We propose a simple yet effective model to synthesize training data by manipulating creases with parameterized curves. We pretrain deep palmprint recognition models with the synthetic data and then finetune them on real palmprint datasets.
– Extensive evaluation on 13 public datasets demonstrates that the synthetically pretrained models significantly outperform their 'train-from-scratch' counterparts and achieve state-of-the-art recognition accuracy.
– We test our method on a million-scale dataset, which is, to the best of our knowledge, the largest evaluation in palmprint recognition. The results verify the scalability of our method, showing its strong potential in the industry-level palmprint recognition.

2   Related Work

2.1   Palmprint Recognition

Traditional Palmprint Recognition. Traditional palmprint recognition methods in the literature can be roughly classified into two categories: holistic-based and local-based. In holistic-based methods, features are extracted from the whole image and then projected to a space of lower-dimensional to make it more compact and discriminative. PCA [38] and its 2D variant [46] are commonly used in this category. Besides, independent component analysis (ICA) is also used [7]. PCA seeks to find uncorrelated features while ICA attempts to find statistically independent features. Supervised projection methods including Linear Discriminant Analysis (LDA) and 2D-LDA [57] have also been explored. Another interesting method Locality Preserving Projection (LPP) [24] attempts to preserve the local structure of images. Hu *et al.* [26] extend LPP to 2D and

Feng *et al.* [13] introduce non-linear kernel to LPP. The holistic-based methods often suffer from degradation caused by distortion, illumination, and noise. To overcome these issues, the palm images are firstly transformed to another domain. Frequency [25,36], Cosine [34,35] and Radon [53] transforms are commonly used to overcome these degradations.

Local-based methods extract local features on the image and then fuse these features globally for recognition. Competitive coding (CompCode) [31] uses 2-D Gabor filters to extract orientation information from palm lines. FastCompCode [66] proposes a binary code for effective representation and matching. Other coding-based methods include SMCC [69], RLOC [27], ContourCode [30], double orientation code [11], *et al.* Wu *et al.* [59] extract local SIFT features and match palm images with RANSAC. Qian *et al.* [44] extract histogram of orientations.

Deep Learning Based Palmprint Recognition. Inspired by the success of deep learning in other recognition tasks such as person re-identification and face recognition [9,64], many researchers attempt to use deep learning technologies for palmprint recognition. Dian *et al.* [10] use the AlexNet as the feature extractor and match palm images with Hausdorff distance. Svoboda *et al.* [52] train CNNs with a novel loss function related to the d-prime index. Recently, margin-based loss functions have been proven to be effective for face recognition. The large margin loss [68] and additive angular margin loss [63] are introduced to palmprint recognition and impressive performance has been achieved. Graph neural networks are also used for palmprint recognition to model the geometric structure of palmprints [47]. Shao *et al.* [49] combine deep learning with hash coding to build efficient palmprint recognition models. Different from these studies that introduce new architectures or loss functions, our proposed method focuses on synthesizing training data for deep palmprint recognition.

2.2 Data Synthesis for Deep Models

Data synthesis aims at synthesizing training data to reduce the cost of data acquisition and labeling. Gaidon *et al.* [15] render the street views to pretrain deep models for object tracking. Tremblay *et al.* [54] render similar sceens for object detection. Yao *et al.* [60] use a graphic engine to simulate a large amount of training data for autonomous driving. Varol *et al.* [56] synthesize images from 3D sequences of human motion capture data for human pose estimation. Sharingan [43] Combines synthetic and real data for unsupervised geometry estimation. Baek *et al.* [3] synthesize depth maps with generative adversarial networks [18] for depth-based human pose estimation. To reduce the gap between synthetic and natural images, Shrivastava *et al.* [50] proposed the Simulated+Unsupervised learning paradigm and Chen *et al.* [6] propose a layer-wise learning rate selection method to improve the synthetic-to-real generalization performance. All these methods synthesize samples of *existing* and *known* categories, while our proposed method aims at generating samples for *novel* categories and augmenting the training identities for palmprint recognition.

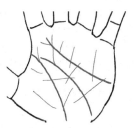

(a) A left palm with 3 principal lines (green) and several wrinkles (blue).

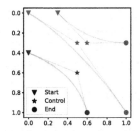

(b) Control points (Start (▼), control (⋆) and end (●)) of principal lines.

Fig. 2. An example hand (left) and control points of principal lines (right). (Color figure online)

3 Methodology

As illustrated in Fig. 2a, the palmprints are roughly composed of several (usually 3~5) principal lines and a number of thin wrinkles. To imitate the geometric appearance of palmprints, we use the Bèzier curves to parameterize the palmar creases. Specifically, we use several Bèzier curves to represent the principal lines and the wrinkles. For simplicity, we use second-order Bèzier curves with three parametric points in a 2D plane, a control point, a start point, and an end point. Figure 2b gives an example of the parametric points 3 principal lines of a left hand. Next, we will take the left hand as an example to detailedly illustrate how we determine the parameters of Bèzier curves, and the case for the right hand can be regarded as the mirror of the left hand.

3.1 Palmar Creases with Bèzier Curves

Let N and S be the number of total identities and number of samples for each identity, we will generate $N \times S$ samples in total. For each identity, we synthesize m principal lines and n wrinkles, where m and n are sampled from uniform

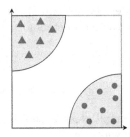

(a) Start and end points of principal lines are sampled from top-right and bottom-left corners.

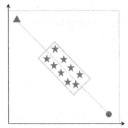

(b) The control point is sampled from a rectangle that is parallel to the line connecting starting and end points.

Fig. 3. Start (▼), end (●) and control (⋆) points.

distributions: $m \sim U(2,5)$ and $n \sim U(5,20)$. Take left hand as an example, the starting and end points of principal lines are randomly sampled from top-left and bottom-right corner of the plane, as shown in Fig. 3a. While the start and the end points of wrinkles are randomly sampled from the whole plane. Then, given the starting and end points, the control point is sampled from a rectangle that is parallel to the line connecting two points, as shown in Fig. 3b.

3.2   Parameters of Bèziers

We first determine the number of principal lines and wrinkles for each identity, and then randomly sample start, end, and control points for each crease.

Principal Lines. For each identity, we sample m principal lines starting from the top-left corner to the bottom-right corner. For left palms, the start/end points for each principal line are sampled from the top-left and bottom-right corner. Given the start/end points of a Bèzier, its control point is randomly sampled from a rectangle area in the middle of the line connecting start and end points.

Wrinkles. We generate $n = 5 \sim 15$ wrinkles for each identity. We do not restrict the directions of wrinkles and their start, end, and control points are randomly sampled from the whole plane:

$$Q = \text{random}\,(0, 1, \text{size} = (n, 3, 2)), \tag{1}$$

where Q is a randomly sampled tensor with shape $(n, 3, 2)$.

3.3   Within-Identity Diversity

We enhance the within-identity diversity of synthesized samples in two aspect: 1) we add small random noices to the parameters so that each sample is a little different from others; 2) we use a randomly selected natural image as the background of the synthesized sample.

Random Noice. Given parameters of a specific identity, we add small noises to P and Q to synthesize diverse samples. Formally, the parameters for the j-th sample of identity i are:

$$\begin{aligned} P_j^i &= P^i + N_p \\ Q_j^i &= Q^i + N_q, \end{aligned} \tag{2}$$

where $N_p \sim \mathcal{N}(\mu, 0.04)$ and $N_q \sim \mathcal{N}(\mu, 0.01)$ are small gaussian noises. Each crease is rendered with a random color c and stroke width w.

Random Background. For each sample we select a random image from the imagenet [8] dataset as the background of the synthesized sample.

Finally, sample S_j^i is synthesized with:

$$S_j^i = \text{synthesize}\,(P_j^i, Q_j^i, c, w, I), \tag{3}$$

where I is a randomly chosed image from the imagenet dataset. A overall algorithmic pipeline and some synthetical samples can be found in the supplementary material.

4   Experimental Settings

In this section, we introduce the detailed experimental settings including data preparation and evaluation protocols. Our experiments are mainly based on the ArcFace [9], a strong baseline for palm recognition [63]. During training, we use the ArcFace loss as supervision. During testing, we extract 512 dimensional features for each sample and the cosine similarity is used as the distance measurement.

4.1   Datasets and Data Preprocessing

Datasets. We use 13 public datasets in our experiments. The statistical information of these datasets is summarized in Table 1 and example ROIs of these datasets

Table 1. Statistics of the 13 public palmprint datasets.

Name	#IDs	#Images	Device	Name	#IDs	#Images	Device
MPD [63]	400	16,000	Phone	COEP [2]	167	1,344	Digital camera
XJTU_UP [48]	200	30,000	Phone	TCD [63]	600	12,000	Contactless
MOHI [22]	200	3,000	Phone	IITD [32]	460	2,601	Contactless
GPDS [14]	100	2,000	Web cam	CASIA [51]	620	5,502	Contactless
WEHI [22]	200	3,000	Web cam	PolyU-MS [61]	500	24,000	Contactless
PolyU(2d+3d) [28]	400	8,000	Web cam	CASIA-MS [21]	200	7,200	Contactless
XJTU_A [48]	114	1,130	CMOS camera				

The images in CASIA-MS [61] dataset are captured with multi-spectral devices and we only use visible spectra images. We remove the overlapped identities in MPD [63] and TCD [63] datasets. Finally, there are 3,268 identities and 59,162 images used in our experiments.

ROI Extraction. We follow the protocol of [62] for ROI extraction. Given a palm image, we first detect two landmarks and then crop the center area of the palm according to the landmarks. Figure 4 illustrates the landmarks (A and B) and ROI (blue box) of the left hand. As shown in Fig. 4, we use the intersection of the index finger and little finger as the first landmark (A), and the intersection of the ring finger and middle finger as the second landmark (B).

Table 2. Training/test splits of the open-set protocol.

Split	Mode	#IDs	#Images
train:test = 1:1	train	1,634	29,347
	test	1,632	29,815
train:test = 1:3	train	818	14,765
	test	2,448	44,397

Fig. 4. ROI extraction of a left hand. (Color figure online)

Then we set up a coordinate where $\boldsymbol{AB}$ is the x-axis and its perpendicular is the y-axis. Suppose $|\boldsymbol{AB}| = 1$ is the unit length, we crop a square with side length 7/6 as the ROI. The ROI of the right hand can be extracted similarly. Some example ROIs used in our experiments

4.2   Open-Set Protocol

Dataset Split. For the open-set protocol, we select part of identities from each dataset and combine them as a large training set, and the other identities are merged as a large test set. We test two different split settings. In the first setting, half of the identities are used for training, and half are used for testing. In the second setting, 1/4 of the identities are used for training and others for testing. The number of samples and identities in the two splits are summarized in Table 2.

Evaluation. The performance under the open-set protocol is evaluated in terms of TAR@FAR, where TAR and FAR stand for 'true accept rate' and 'false accept rate', respectively. Specifically, given several test images, we randomly sample several positive pairs where the two samples share the same identity, and negative pairs whose samples are from distinct identities. Let p^+, p^- be the positive/negative pairs and $sim(p)$ be the similarity between a pair of samples. We first fix the FAR and then calculate a proper threshold τ from negative pairs, finally we compute TAR using that threshold on the positive pairs.

Take FAR = 1e–3 as an example, we can search for a threshold τ on the negative pairs satisfying:

$$\text{FAR} = 10^{-3} = \frac{|\{p^- \mid sim(p^-) > \tau\}|}{|\{p^-\}|}. \tag{4}$$

With the threshold, we then calculate the TAR on the positive pairs:

$$\text{TAR} = \frac{|\{p^+ \mid sim(p^+) > \tau\}|}{|\{p^+\}|}. \tag{5}$$

Accordingly, we can calculate TAR under various FARs. In our experiments, we report the performance under FAR = 1e–3, 1e–4, 1e–5, 1e–6.

4.3   Closed-Set Protocol

The closed-set experiments are conducted on five datasets: CASIA, IITD, PolyU, TCD, and MPD. We perform 5-fold cross-validation on each dataset and report the average performance. The experiments are conducted individually on the five datasets. We use top-1 accuracy, EER to evaluate the performance of closed-set palmprint recognition. To compute the top-1 accuracy, we randomly select one sample from each identity as the *registry* and other samples are *queries*. Let $\mathcal{R} = \{r_i\}$ be the set of registries and $\mathcal{Q} = \{q_j\}$ the query set, and $sim(q_i, r_j)$ is the similarity between two samples. $y(\cdot)$ tells the identity label of a sample. The successfully matched queries are these queries that are of the same identity with their nearest registries:

$$\mathcal{Q}^+ = \left\{ q_i, \mid y\left(\text{argmax}_{r_j \in \mathcal{R}} \ \ sim(q_i, r_j) \right) = y(q_j) \right\} \tag{6}$$

Finally, the top-1 accuracy is the number of successfully matched queries divided by the total number of queries: $acc = |\mathcal{Q}^+|/|\mathcal{Q}|$. The EER is a point where FAR (False Acceptance Rate) and FRR (False Rejection Rate) intersect.

5   Experimental Results

In this section, we first compare our method with other traditional and deep learning based palmprint recognition methods. Then we conduct ablation studies to show the contribution of each component in our method.

5.1   Implementation Details

We implement our method with the PyTorch [42] framework. Two backbone networks, ResNet50 [23] and MobileFaceNet [5], are used in our experiments. The Bèzier curves are generated with an open-source package[1].

Data Synthesizing. By default, the synthetic dataset contains 4,000 identities, and each identity has 100 samples. The dimension of the synthetic image is 224×224. The stroke width w for principal lines and wrinkles are randomly selected from $1.5 \sim 3$ and $0.5 \sim 1.5$, respectively. We randomly blur the synthetic images using a gaussian kernel to improve generalization.

Model Training. For our proposed method, we first pretrain models on synthesized data for 20 epochs and then finetune on real palmprint datasets for 50 epochs. For the baseline, we directly train the models on real datasets for 50 epochs. We use the cosine annealing learning rate scheduler with a warmup start. The maximal learning rate for pretraining is 0.1 and 0.01 for finetune. All models are trained with mini-batch SGD algorithm. The momentum is 0.9 and

---

[1] https://bezier.readthedocs.io/.

weight decay is set to 1e–4. We use the *additive angular margin loss* (ArcFace [9]) with margin $m = 0.5$ and scale factor $s = 48$. Besides, we linearly warm up the margin from 0 in the first epoch to improve stability. We use 4 GPUs to run all training experiments and each GPU process 32 images in a batch, in total the effective batchsize is 128.

5.2   Open-Set Palmprint Recognition

We first test our method under the "open-set" protocol. Details about the "open-set" protocol can be found in Sect. 4.2. We test our method under two different training test ratios: 1:1 and 1:3, quantitative results are in Table 3. The TAR *v.s.* FAR curves of the 1:1 setting can be found in the supplementary material.

Table 3. Quantitative performance under the open-set protocol where the performance are evaluated in terms of TAR@FAR. 'MB' represents the MobileFaceNets [5] backbone and 'R50' is resnet50.

Method	Backbone	train : test = 1 : 1				train : test = 1 : 3			
		TAR@ 1e–3	TAR@ 1e–4	TAR@ 1e–5	TAR@ 1e–6	TAR@ 1e–3	TAR@ 1e–4	TAR@ 1e–5	TAR@ 1e–6
CompCode [31]	N/A	0.4800	0.4292	0.3625	0.2103	0.4501	0.3932	0.3494	0.2648
FastCompCode [66]	N/A	0.4243	0.3649	0.1678	0.2103	0.4188	0.3568	0.3100	0.2748
LLDP [39]	N/A	0.7382	0.6762	0.5222	0.1247	0.7372	0.6785	0.6171	0.2108
Ordinal Code [51]	N/A	0.4628	0.4074	0.3462	0.1993	0.4527	0.3975	0.3527	0.2422
BOCV [20]	N/A	0.4930	0.4515	0.3956	0.2103	0.4527	0.3975	0.3527	0.2422
RLOC [27]	N/A	0.6490	0.5884	0.4475	0.1443	0.6482	0.5840	0.5224	0.3366
DOC [11]	N/A	0.4975	0.4409	0.3712	0.1667	0.4886	0.4329	0.3889	0.2007
PalmNet [16]	N/A	0.7174	0.6661	0.5992	0.1069	0.7217	0.6699	0.6155	0.2877
C-LMCL [68]	MB	0.9290	0.8554	0.7732	0.6239	0.8509	0.7554	0.7435	0.5932
ArcFace [9]	MB	0.9292	0.8568	0.7812	0.7049	0.8516	0.7531	0.6608	0.5825
ArcFace [9]+Ours	MB	**0.9640**	**0.9438**	**0.9102**	**0.8437**	**0.9407**	**0.8861**	**0.7934**	**0.7012**
C-LMCL [68]	R50	0.9545	0.9027	0.8317	0.7534	0.8601	0.7701	0.6821	0.6254
ArcFace [9]	R50	0.9467	0.8925	0.8252	0.7462	0.8709	0.7884	0.7156	0.6580
ArcFace [9]+Ours	R50	**0.9671**	**0.9521**	**0.9274**	**0.8956**	**0.9424**	**0.8950**	**0.8217**	**0.7649**

As shown in Table 3, since traditional methods do not rely on training data, they behave similar performance under 1:1 and 1:3 settings, and deep learning based methods perform much better under the 1:1 setting than under the 1:3 setting. Among all traditional methods, LLDP [39] performs the best. Deep Learning based methods [9,16,68] significantly outperform traditional methods, and margin-based methods, *e.g.* C-LMCL [68] and ArcFace [9], present superior performance. Our proposed method remarkably improves the ArcFace baseline and achieves state-of-the-art performance under both 1:1 and 1:3 settings. Under the 1:3 setting, our performance even exceeds the performance of ArcFace under the 1:1 setting.

5.3   Closed-Set Palmprint Recognition

Here we report quantitative results of our method as well as other methods under the closed-set protocol. Our experiments are conducted on five datasets, and the performance is evaluated in terms of top-1 accuracy and EER. Detailed setting about the experiments was described in Sect. 4.3.

As shown in Table 4, though the results on the closed-set protocol are nearly saturated, our method still improves the baseline with a clear margin, advancing the top-1 accuracies to nearly 100%. Besides, our method significantly decreases the EER to an unprecedented level of 1e–3, surpassing all existing methods.

Table 4. Top-1 accuracy and EER under the 'closed-set' protocol. Our method significantly improves the top-1 accuracy and EER with a clear margin.

Method	CASIA	IITD	PolyU	TCD	MPD
CompCode [31]	79.27 / 1.08	77.79 / 1.39	99.21 / 0.68	– / –	– / –
Ordinal Code [51]	73.32 / 1.75	73.26 / 2.09	99.55 / 0.23	– / –	– / –
DoN [67]	99.30 / 0.53	99.15 / 0.68	100.0 / 0.22	– / –	– / –
PalmNet [16]	97.17 / 3.21	97.31 / 3.83	99.95 / 0.39	99.89 / 0.40	91.88 / 6.22
FERNet [40]	97.65 / 0.73	99.61 / 0.76	99.77 / 0.15	98.63 / –	– / –
DDBC [12]	96.41 / –	96.44 / –	–	98.73 / –	– / –
RFN [37]	– / –	99.20 / 0.60	– / –	– / –	– / –
C-LMCL [68]	– / –	– / –	100.0 / 0.13	99.93 / 0.26	– / –
JCLSR [65]	98.94 / –	98.17 / –	– / –	– / –	– / –
ArcFace [9] + MB	97.92 / 0.009	98.73 / 0.012	98.58 / 0.014	98.83 / 0.008	96.12 / 0.022
ArcFace [9] + MB + Ours	99.75 / 0.004	100.0 / 0.000	100.0 / 0.000	100.0 / 0.000	99.96 / 0.001

5.4   Cross-Dataset Validation

We perform cross-dataset validation to test the generalization of the proposed method. We train our method, as well as the baseline (ArcFace), on one dataset and test the performance on the other dataset. We test 5 different cross-dataset settings using the MobileFaceNet backbone, results are summarized in Table 5. The performance is evaluated in terms of both TAR@FAR, EER.

As shown in Table 5, our method consistently improves the performance of ArcFace on all the 5 settings, showing strong cross-dataset generalization ability.

5.5   Palmprint Recognition at Million Scale

To verify the scalability of our proposed method, we test our method on our internal dataset with million samples. The training set contains 19,286 identities and 2.87 million samples, while the test set has 1,000 identities and 0.18 million samples. The images of the dataset are collected parallelly in three places by 19 difference mobile phones (different brands and modes) and 2 IoT cameras. Images of each identity was collected in one seesion by 4 devices (2 IoT and 2 random mobile phones) and 4 different man-made light conditions. More detailed information and example images of this dataset can be found in

Table 5. Cross-dataset validation. 'M', 'P', 'T' and 'I' represent MPD, PolyU, TCD, and IITD datasets, respectively. M→P indicates the model is trained on M and evaluated on P.

Datasets	Method	TAR@FAR=			Top-1	EER
		1e–3	1e–4	1e–5		
M→P	AF	0.9759	0.9499	0.9210	99.93	0.007
	Ours	0.9935	0.9766	0.9622	100.0	0.002
T→P	AF	0.9347	0.8981	0.8509	98.22	0.018
	Ours	0.9918	0.9748	0.9591	100.0	0.003
I→P	AF	0.9364	0.9001	0.8020	97.67	0.019
	Ours	0.9688	0.9224	0.8728	99.04	0.009
T→I	AF	0.8533	0.7872	0.7306	97.47	0.033
	Ours	0.9896	0.9864	0.9745	98.85	0.007
M→I	AF	0.9927	0.9846	0.9717	99.76	0.004
	Ours	1.0000	1.0000	1.0000	100.0	0.000

Table 6. Palmprint recognition performance on million scale dataset.

Method	Backbone	TAR@				
		1e–5	1e–6	1e–7	1e–8	1e–9
AF [9]	MB	0.9911	0.9770	0.9550	0.9251	0.8833
Ours		0.9934	0.9803	0.9605	0.9301	0.9015
AF [9]	R50	0.9997	0.9986	0.9964	0.9931	0.9879
Ours		0.9999	0.9996	0.9975	0.9943	0.9911

We synthesize 20,000 identities and totally 2 million samples to pretrain the models in this experiment. The performance is evaluated under open-set protocol and results are summarized in Table 6, and the FAR *v.s.* TAR curves can be found in the supplementary material. The results show that our method consistently improves the performance of the baseline ArcFace method, showing great potential in large-scale palmprint recognition.

5.6   Palmprint Recognition with Limited Identities

The model performance under a limited number of training identities is critical to privacy-sensitive conditions where collecting training set with large-scale identities is infeasible. Here we test our method with various training identities. Specifically, under the open-set protocol (train:test = 1:1), we fix the test set and train models with 400, 800 and 1,600 identities.

As demonstrated in Table 7, our method maintains high performance while the ArcFace baseline degrades quickly as the drop of training identities. Even trained with 400 identities, our method still performs on par with the ArcFace counterpart that is trained with 1,600 identities, showing its superiority in identity-constrained scenarios.

Table 7. Performance under various training identities. The models are based on the MobileFaceNet backbone.

Method	#ID	TAR@FAR=			
		1e–3	1e–4	1e–5	1e–6
ArcFace	1,600	0.9292	0.8568	0.7812	0.7049
ArcFace+Ours		0.9640	0.9438	0.9102	0.8437
ArcFace	800	0.8934	0.7432	0.7104	0.6437
ArcFace+Ours		0.9534	0.9390	0.9025	0.8164
ArcFace	400	0.8102	0.7050	0.6668	0.3320
ArcFace+Ours		0.9189	0.8497	0.7542	0.6899

5.7   Ablation Study

In this section, we ablate the components and design choices of our method. All the experiments in this ablation study are conducted using the MobileFaceNet [5] and evaluated under the open-set protocol.

Components. The main components in our synthesized samples are the principal lines, the wrinkles, and the background images. Table 8 presents the results of models with and without these components. 'P', 'W' and 'B' represent the principal lines, wrinkles and image background in the synthesized samples, respectively. Synthesizing principal lines significantly improves the performance over the baseline at higher FARs, and the improvements at lower FARs are marginal. With wrinkles, the performance can be further improved especially at lower FARs. Finally, using natural images as the background helps achieve higher performance.

Table 8. Ablation studies on components.

P	W	B	TAR@FAR=			
			1e–3	1e–4	1e–5	1e–6
Baseline			0.9102	0.8259	0.7458	0.7217
✓			0.9514	0.9003	0.7613	0.7513
✓	✓		0.9597	0.9307	0.8949	0.8061
✓	✓	✓	**0.9640**	**0.9438**	**0.9102**	**0.8437**

Table 9. Comparison with an imagenet pretrained model.

Pretrain	TAR@FAR=			
	1e–3	1e–4	1e–5	1e–6
Imagenet	0.9608	0.9135	0.8294	0.7256
Ours	0.9640	0.9438	0.9102	0.8437

Compared to Imagenet Pretrain. Many down-stream vision tasks, *e.g.* detection, and segmentation, strongly rely on the imagenet [8] pretrained models. In this experiment, we compare the performance of our synthetically pretrained models to the imagenet pretrained models. We pretrain the MobileFaceNets with the imagenet dataset and our synthesized samples and compare their performance under the open-set protocol (train:test = 1:1). For imagenet pretraining, we follow the training configuration of [23]. It is worth noting that there are 1.2 million images in the imagenet training set and our synthesized dataset consists of only 0.4 million samples (4,000 identities with 100 samples per identity). As demonstrated in Table 8, even pretrained with one-third of samples, our proposed method still outperforms the imagenet pretrained model with a clear margin, especially under lower FARs. The experimental result tells that our synthesized dataset is specifically more suitable for palmprint recognition than general vision datasets, *e.g.* imagenet.

Number of Synthesized Samples and Identities. By default, we synthesize 4,000 identities and each of them has 100 images. In this ablation, we fix one number as the default and vary the other, and evaluate the finetuned performance in terms of FAR@1e–6. The results in Fig. 5 reveal that increasing both the number of samples and identities improves the performance. The number of identities has a greater impact on the fine-tuned performance and the number of samples has less impact.

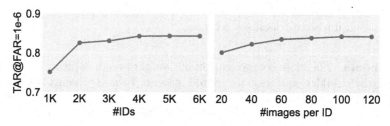

Fig. 5. TAR@FAR = 1e–6 of models pretrained with different synthetic samples and identities.

6   Conclusion

We proposed a simple yet effective geometric model to synthesize palmar creases by manipulating parameterized Bèzier curves. The synthetic samples are used to pretrain deep palmprint recognition models and improve model performance. Different from other data synthesizing methods, our method synthesizes samples of novel categories to augment both the identities and samples of the training set. Competitive results on several public benchmarks demonstrate the superiority and great potentials of our approach. Besides, experiments on a million-scale dataset verify the scalability of our method. We also believe our method could benefit some other tasks, *e.g.* fingerprint recognition.

Acknowledgment. We would like to acknowledge Haitao Wang and Huikai Shao for their assistance in processing experimental results. This work is partly supported by grants of the NSFC 62076086, 62176159 and Shanghai Municipal Science and Technology Major Project 2021SHZDZX0102.

References

1. Amazon one. https://one.amazon.com/
2. The ceop dataset. https://www.coep.org.in/resources/coeppalmprintdatabase
3. Baek, S., Kim, K.I., Kim, T.K.: Augmented skeleton space transfer for depth-based hand pose estimation. In: CVPR, pp. 8330–8339 (2018)
4. Cao, Q., Shen, L., Xie, W., Parkhi, O.M., Zisserman, A.: VGGFace2: a dataset for recognising faces across pose and age. In: FG 2018, pp. 67–74. IEEE (2018)
5. Chen, S., Liu, Y., Gao, X., Han, Z.: MobileFaceNets: efficient CNNs for accurate real-time face verification on mobile devices. In: Zhou, J., et al. (eds.) CCBR 2018. LNCS, vol. 10996, pp. 428–438. Springer, Cham (2018). https://doi.org/10.1007/978-3-319-97909-0_46
6. Chen, W., Yu, Z., Wang, Z., Anandkumar, A.: Automated synthetic-to-real generalization, pp. 1746–1756. In: PMLR (2020)
7. Connie, T., Jin, A.T.B., Ong, M.G.K., Ling, D.N.C.: An automated palmprint recognition system. Image Vis. Comput. **23**(5), 501–515 (2005)
8. Deng, J., Dong, W., Socher, R., Li, L.J., Li, K., Fei-Fei, L.: ImageNet: a large-scale hierarchical image database. In: CVPR, pp. 248–255. IEEE (2009)
9. Deng, J., Guo, J., Xue, N., Zafeiriou, S.: ArcFace: additive angular margin loss for deep face recognition. In: CVPR, pp. 4690–4699 (2019)
10. Dian, L., Dongmei, S.: Contactless palmprint recognition based on convolutional neural network. In: IEEE ICSP, pp. 1363–1367. IEEE (2016)
11. Fei, L., Xu, Y., Tang, W., Zhang, D.: Double-orientation code and nonlinear matching scheme for palmprint recognition. PR **49**, 89–101 (2016)
12. Fei, L., Zhang, B., Xu, Y., Guo, Z., Wen, J., Jia, W.: Learning discriminant direction binary palmprint descriptor. IEEE TIP **28**(8), 3808–3820 (2019)
13. Feng, G., Hu, D., Zhang, D., Zhou, Z.: An alternative formulation of kernel LPP with application to image recognition. Neurocomputing **69**(13–15), 1733–1738 (2006)
14. Ferrer, M.A., Vargas, F., Morales, A.: Bispectral contactless hand based biometric system. In: CONATEL 2011, pp. 1–6. IEEE (2011)
15. Gaidon, A., Wang, Q., Cabon, Y., Vig, E.: Virtual worlds as proxy for multi-object tracking analysis. In: CVPR, pp. 4340–4349 (2016)
16. Genovese, A., Piuri, V., Plataniotis, K.N., Scotti, F.: PalmNet: Gabor-PCA convolutional networks for touchless palmprint recognition. IEEE TIFS **14**(12), 3160–3174 (2019)
17. Gibney, E.: The battle for ethical AI at the world's biggest machine-learning conference. Nature **577**(7791), 609–610 (2020)
18. Goodfellow, I., et al.: Generative adversarial nets. In: Ghahramani, Z., Welling, M., Cortes, C., Lawrence, N., Weinberger, K.Q. (eds.) NeurIPS, vol. 27. Curran Associates, Inc. (2014). https://proceedings.neurips.cc/paper/2014/file/5ca3e9b122f61f8f06494c97b1afccf3-Paper.pdf
19. Guo, Y., Zhang, L., Hu, Y., He, X., Gao, J.: MS-Celeb-1M: a dataset and benchmark for large-scale face recognition. In: Leibe, B., Matas, J., Sebe, N., Welling, M. (eds.) ECCV 2016. LNCS, vol. 9907, pp. 87–102. Springer, Cham (2016). https://doi.org/10.1007/978-3-319-46487-9_6
20. Guo, Z., Zhang, D., Zhang, L., Zuo, W.: Palmprint verification using binary orientation co-occurrence vector. PRL **30**(13), 1219–1227 (2009)
21. Hao, Y., Sun, Z., Tan, T., Ren, C.: Multispectral palm image fusion for accurate contact-free palmprint recognition. In: ICIP, pp. 281–284. IEEE (2008)

22. Hassanat, A., Al-Awadi, M., Btoush, E., Al-Btoush, A., Alhasanat, E., Altarawneh, G.: New mobile phone and webcam hand images databases for personal authentication and identification. Procedia Manufact. **3**, 4060–4067 (2015). https://doi.org/10.1016/j.promfg.2015.07.977

23. He, K., Zhang, X., Ren, S., Sun, J.: Deep residual learning for image recognition. In: CVPR, pp. 770–778 (2016)

24. He, X., Niyogi, P.: Locality preserving projections. NeurIPS **16**, 153–160 (2003)

25. Hennings-Yeomans, P.H., Kumar, B.V., Savvides, M.: Palmprint classification using multiple advanced correlation filters and palm-specific segmentation. IEEE TIFS **2**(3), 613–622 (2007)

26. Hu, D., Feng, G., Zhou, Z.: Two-dimensional locality preserving projections (2dlpp) with its application to palmprint recognition. PR **40**(1), 339–342 (2007)

27. Jia, W., Huang, D.S., Zhang, D.: Palmprint verification based on robust line orientation code. PR **41**(5), 1504–1513 (2008)

28. Kanhangad, V., Kumar, A., Zhang, D.: Contactless and pose invariant biometric identification using hand surface. IEEE TIP **20**(5), 1415–1424 (2010). https://doi.org/10.1109/TIP.2010.2090888

29. Kemelmacher-Shlizerman, I., Seitz, S.M., Miller, D., Brossard, E.: The megaface benchmark: 1 million faces for recognition at scale. In: CVPR, pp. 4873–4882 (2016)

30. Khan, Z., Mian, A., Hu, Y.: Contour code: robust and efficient multispectral palmprint encoding for human recognition. In: ICCV, pp. 1935–1942. IEEE (2011)

31. Kong, A.K., Zhang, D.: Competitive coding scheme for palmprint verification. In: ICPR, vol. 1, pp. 520–523. IEEE (2004)

32. Kumar, A.: Incorporating cohort information for reliable palmprint authentication. In: Indian Conference on Computer Vision, Graphics and Image Processing, pp. 583–590. ICVGIP '08, IEEE, Bhubaneswar, India (2008). https://doi.org/10.1109/ICVGIP.2008.73

33. Kumar, A.: Toward more accurate matching of contactless palmprint images under less constrained environments. IEEE TIFS **14**(1), 34–47 (2018)

34. Laadjel, M., Al-Maadeed, S., Bouridane, A.: Combining fisher locality preserving projections and passband DCT for efficient palmprint recognition. Neurocomputing **152**, 179–189 (2015)

35. Leng, L., Li, M., Kim, C., Bi, X.: Dual-source discrimination power analysis for multi-instance contactless palmprint recognition. Multimedia Tools Appl. **76**(1), 333–354 (2017)

36. Li, H., Wang, L.: Palmprint recognition using dual-tree complex wavelet transform and compressed sensing. In: Proceedings of 2012 International Conference on Measurement, Information and Control, vol. 2, pp. 563–567. IEEE (2012)

37. Liu, Y., Kumar, A.: Contactless palmprint identification using deeply learned residual features. IEEE TBBIS **2**(2), 172–181 (2020)

38. Lu, G., Zhang, D., Wang, K.: Palmprint recognition using eigenpalms features. PRL **24**(9–10), 1463–1467 (2003)

39. Luo, Y.T., et al.: Local line directional pattern for palmprint recognition. PR **50**, 26–44 (2016)

40. Matkowski, W.M., Chai, T., Kong, A.W.K.: Palmprint recognition in uncontrolled and uncooperative environment. IEEE TIFS (2019). https://doi.org/10.1109/TIFS.2019.2945183

41. Maze, B., et al.: IARPA Janus benchmark - C: face dataset and protocol. In: ICB, pp. 158–165. IEEE (2018)

42. Paszke, A., et al.: PyTorch: an imperative style, high-performance deep learning library. NeurIPS **32**, 8026–8037 (2019)

43. PNVR, K., Zhou, H., Jacobs, D.: Sharingan: Combining synthetic and real data for unsupervised geometry estimation. In: CVPR, pp. 13974–13983 (2020)
44. Qian, J., Yang, J., Gao, G.: Discriminative histograms of local dominant orientation (D-HLDO) for biometric image feature extraction. PR **46**(10), 2724–2739 (2013)
45. Qiu, H., Yu, B., Gong, D., Li, Z., Liu, W., Tao, D.: SynFace: face recognition with synthetic data. In: CVPR, pp. 10880–10890 (2021)
46. Sang, H., Yuan, W., Zhang, Z.: Research of palmprint recognition based on 2DPCA. In: Yu, W., He, H., Zhang, N. (eds.) ISNN 2009. LNCS, vol. 5552, pp. 831–838. Springer, Heidelberg (2009). https://doi.org/10.1007/978-3-642-01510-6_93
47. Shao, H., Zhong, D.: Few-shot palmprint recognition via graph neural networks. Electron. Lett. **55**(16), 890–892 (2019)
48. Shao, H., Zhong, D., Du, X.: Effective deep ensemble hashing for open-set palmprint recognition. J. Electron. Imaging **29**(1), 013018 (2020)
49. Shao, H., Zhong, D., Du, X.: Deep distillation hashing for unconstrained palmprint recognition. IEEE TIM **70**, 1–13 (2021)
50. Shrivastava, A., Pfister, T., Tuzel, O., Susskind, J., Wang, W., Webb, R.: Learning from simulated and unsupervised images through adversarial training. In: CVPR, pp. 2107–2116 (2017)
51. Sun, Z., Tan, T., Wang, Y., Li, S.Z.: Ordinal palmprint represention for personal identification [representation read representation]. In: CVPR, vol. 1, pp. 279–284. IEEE (2005)
52. Svoboda, J., Masci, J., Bronstein, M.M.: Palmprint recognition via discriminative index learning. In: ICPR, pp. 4232–4237. IEEE (2016)
53. Tamrakar, D., Khanna, P.: Noise and rotation invariant RDF descriptor for palmprint identification. Multimedia Tools Appl. **75**(10), 5777–5794 (2016)
54. Tremblay, J., et al.: Training deep networks with synthetic data: bridging the reality gap by domain randomization. In: CVPRW, pp. 969–977 (2018)
55. Van Noorden, R.: The ethical questions that haunt facial-recognition research (2020)
56. Varol, G., Romero, J., Martin, X., Mahmood, N., Black, M.J., Laptev, I., Schmid, C.: Learning from synthetic humans. In: CVPR, pp. 109–117 (2017)
57. Wang, M., Ruan, Q.: Palmprint recognition based on two-dimensional methods. In: ICSP, vol. 4. IEEE (2006)
58. Whitelam, C., et al.: IARPA Janus benchmark-b face dataset. In: CVPRW, pp. 90–98 (2017)
59. Wu, X., Zhao, Q., Bu, W.: A sift-based contactless palmprint verification approach using iterative ransac and local palmprint descriptors. PR **47**(10), 3314–3326 (2014)
60. Yao, Y., Zheng, L., Yang, X., Naphade, M., Gedeon, T.: Simulating content consistent vehicle datasets with attribute descent. In: Vedaldi, A., Bischof, H., Brox, T., Frahm, J.-M. (eds.) ECCV 2020. LNCS, vol. 12351, pp. 775–791. Springer, Cham (2020). https://doi.org/10.1007/978-3-030-58539-6_46
61. Zhang, D., Guo, Z., Lu, G., Zhang, L., Zuo, W.: An online system of multispectral palmprint verification. IEEE TIM **59**(2), 480–490 (2009)
62. Zhang, Y., Zhang, L., Liu, X., Zhao, S., Shen, Y., Yang, Y.: Pay by showing your palm: a study of palmprint verification on mobile platforms. In: 2019 IEEE International Conference on Multimedia and Expo (ICME), pp. 862–867. IEEE (2019)
63. Zhang, Y., Zhang, L., Zhang, R., Li, S., Li, J., Huang, F.: Towards palmprint verification on smartphones. arXiv preprint arXiv:2003.13266 (2020)

64. Zhao, K., Xu, J., Cheng, M.M.: RegularFace: deep face recognition via exclusive regularization. In: CVPR, pp. 1136–1144 (2019)
65. Zhao, S., Zhang, B.: Joint constrained least-square regression with deep convolutional feature for palmprint recognition. IEEE TSMC (2020)
66. Zheng, Q., Kumar, A., Pan, G.: Suspecting less and doing better: new insights on palmprint identification for faster and more accurate matching. IEEE TIFS **11**(3), 633–641 (2015)
67. Zheng, Q., Kumar, A., Pan, G.: A 3D feature descriptor recovered from a single 2D palmprint image. IEEE TPAMI **38**(6), 1272–1279 (2016)
68. Zhong, D., Zhu, J.: Centralized large margin cosine loss for open-set deep palmprint recognition. IEEE TCSVT (2019). https://doi.org/10.1109/TCSVT.2019.2904283
69. Zuo, W., Lin, Z., Guo, Z., Zhang, D.: The multiscale competitive code via sparse representation for palmprint verification. In: CVPR, pp. 2265–2272. IEEE (2010)

Adaptive Transformers for Robust Few-shot Cross-domain Face Anti-spoofing

Hsin-Ping Huang[1]([✉]), Deqing Sun[2], Yaojie Liu[2], Wen-Sheng Chu[2],
Taihong Xiao[1], Jinwei Yuan[2], Hartwig Adam[2], and Ming-Hsuan Yang[1,2,3]

[1] University of California, Merced, USA
hhuang79@ucmerced.edu
[2] Google Research, Mountain View, USA
[3] Yonsei University, Seoul, South Korea

Abstract. While recent face anti-spoofing methods perform well under the intra-domain setups, an effective approach needs to account for much larger appearance variations of images acquired in complex scenes with different sensors for robust performance. In this paper, we present adaptive vision transformers (ViT) for robust cross-domain face anti-spoofing. Specifically, we adopt ViT as a backbone to exploit its strength to account for long-range dependencies among pixels. We further introduce the ensemble adapters module and feature-wise transformation layers in the ViT to adapt to different domains for robust performance with a few samples. Experiments on several benchmark datasets show that the proposed models achieve both robust and competitive performance against the state-of-the-art methods for cross-domain face anti-spoofing using a few samples.

1 Introduction

Face biometrics is widely applied to identity authentication applications due to its security, convenience, and no-contact nature, compared to conventional methods such as passcodes and fingerprints [24]. Other than face recognition, there is an additional step needed to keep the authentication systems secure from spoof presentation attacks, which is called face anti-spoofing. For example, printed photos, digital images, and 3D masks can deceive mobile platforms to authenticate the attacker as the genuine user, which would cause severe security breach. As a result, face anti-spoofing has been an important topic with studies for almost two decades.

In early systems, face authentication is mainly applied to controlled scenarios with fixed sensors such as building access and border control. With controlled environments and limited variations (*e.g.*, lighting and poses), all faces can be regarded as from one single domain. Numerous simple yet effective methods [4,14,26] can be

Supplementary Information The online version contains supplementary material available at https://doi.org/10.1007/978-3-031-19778-9_3.

applied to determine whether spoof attacks occur or not. Recently, mobile applications such as unlock and payment have increased the risk of spoofing attacks. Face images may be acquired from wider angles, complex scenes, and different devices, which can be regarded as a set of mixed data domains. In addition, an anti-spoof module may be deployed to new devices (*i.e.*, unseen domains). Accordingly, face anti-spoofing is required to not only handle large variations, but also well generalize or quickly adapt to unseen scenes and sensors.

Existing methods use intra-database testing and cross-database testing to evaluate the intra-domain and cross-domain face anti-spoofing performance. The former one trains and evaluates models on data splits from the same database, while the latter one does from different databases. Recent methods have already shown saturated performance on intra-database evaluations [1,3,4] in well-controlled scenarios. In recent years, numerous methods have been proposed to tackle cross-domain face anti-spoofing [20,34,43]. Although significant progress has been made, existing methods do not perform well on cross-dataset tests, *e.g.*, on CASIA, intra-testing *vs.* cross-testing can be 0% *vs.* 10% on half total error rate. Thus, it is of great interest to develop robust anti-spoofing methods for cross-domain scenarios.

There are a few challenges for cross-domain face anti-spoofing applications:

- **Domain gap.** The domain gap is highly correlated to the key factor of recognizing spoof: visual appearance. Spoofing cues, such as moire pattern and color distortion, can dramatically change or disappear with different camera devices, illuminations, and image resolutions. For example, images from Oulu-NPU [5] are in 1080P resolution, while images from Idiap Replay [9] are only in 480P resolution. The sensor noise and low image quality of Idiap Replay can lead to a biased prediction as spoof from a model trained on Oulu-NPU.
- **Limited data.** Compared to datasets for other vision tasks, *e.g.*, CelebA [36] and FFHQ [21], commonly used datasets for face anti-spoofing (such as CASIA [71], Idiap Replay [9], MSU-MFSD [57], and Oulu-NPU [5]) are considerably smaller in scale. Hence, models trained with limited data can easily over-fit the training data, and thereby generalize poorly to other domains. It is similar to training a model for downstream object recognition tasks with limited data but no ImageNet pre-trained modules.

In this work, we address these challenges and propose a robust cross-domain model that performs as well as for intra-domain tasks. The proposed model learns to exploit important visual information related to face spoofing from the training data and adapt well to new domains with a few samples. Specifically, we introduce the vision transformer [11] as the backbone module for cross-domain face anti-spoofing. To facilitate cross-domain adaption with a few samples, we propose adaptive transformers by integrating ensemble adapter modules and feature-wise transformation layers. Extensive experimental results show our proposed models outperform the state-of-the-art method on the widely-used benchmark datasets. We also provide insightful analysis on why the proposed adaptive transformer outperforms the evaluated methods. The main contributions of this work are:

- We propose adaptive transformers with ensemble adapters and feature-wise transforms for robust cross-domain face anti-spoofing with a few samples.

- We achieve state-of-the-art cross-domain face anti-spoofing results on widely-used benchmark datasets. Our approach closes the gap between intra-database evaluation and performance in real-world applications.
- We conduct in-depth analysis of adaptive transformers and show model explainability with insights for face anti-spoofing.

2 Related Work

Face Anti-spoofing. Early works exploit spontaneous human behaviors (*e.g.*, eye blinking, head motion) [23,41] or predefined movements (*e.g.*, head turning, expression changes) [8] to address face anti-spoofing. Due to the clear weaknesses in video replaying attacks and the inconvenience from user interaction, recent approaches evolve into modeling material properties (*i.e.*, texture). Several methods utilize hand-crafted features to describe spoof related patterns, *e.g.*, LBP [4,14], HoG [25,61] and SIFT [43] features, and train a live/spoof classifier using support vector machines or linear discriminant analysis. More recently, deep neural networks have been applied to anti-spoofing [20,34,35,47,66] and achieved state-of-the-art performance than conventional methods [12,26,42,60].

As limited spoof data is available for learning classifiers or deep neural networks, auxiliary supervisory signals have been introduced to infuse the models with prior knowledge, such as facial depth map [33], rPPG signal [32], reflection [63], and face albedo [38]. To improve model interpretability, feature disentanglement is proposed along with advances in generative adversarial networks [35,66]. Furthermore, customized deep network architectures are shown to be more effective for face anti-spoofing, *e.g.*, tree-like structure [34], network architecture search [64,65].

Most recently, a model based on a vision transformer is proposed to detect spoofing attack [15]. Although this transformer-based method is able to detect certain spoofs, it does not perform well on challenging print and replay attacks (*e.g.*, 5.84/15.20 [15] *vs.* 2.1/10.0 [34] EER on SiW-M dataset). These results suggest large headroom to improve models in detecting low-level texture cues. In this work, we propose an adaptive transformer model to robustly handle challenging print and replay spoof attacks across different datasets using a few-shot setting (*i.e.*, as few as 5 samples).

Domain Generalization. Domain generalization for face anti-spoofing aims to learn a model from multiple source datasets, and the model should generalize to the unseen target dataset. Several approaches [20,22,46,47] based on adversarial training and triplet loss have been developed to learn a shared feature space for multiple source domains that can generalize to the target domain. On the other hand, meta-learning formulations [7,48,55] are exploited to simulate the domain shift at training time to learn a representative feature space. Furthermore, disentangled representation for spoof and ID features [54] and sample re-weighting [31] improve generalization for face anti-spoofing. In contrast, we tackle a real-world anti-spoofing problem when only a few images are available from target datasets. In this work, we propose an effective cross-domain few-shot framework based on an adaptive transformer that achieves state-of-the-art performance.

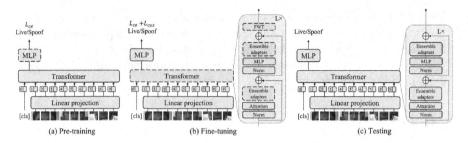

Fig. 1. Overview of our robust cross-domain face anti-spoofing framework.
The module or layer colored in wheat or green means that the weights are trainable
or fixed. The transformer receives image patches and an extra learnable classification
embedding [cls] as inputs, and a multi-layer perceptron (MLP) is used for live/spoof
face classification. At the pre-training stage (a), the backbone is fixed and only the
MLP head is trained using L_{ce}. At the fine-tuning stage (b), we insert two ensemble
adapter modules and a feature-wise transformation (FWT) layer to each transformer
block, and train all ensemble adapters and FWT layers using $L_{ce} + L_{cos}$ when other
layers are fixed. During testing (c), the FWT layers are removed from the model.

Few-shot Learning. Few-shot learning methods [2,13,18,45,49,50,53,56] aim
to adapt models to novel classes from a few samples from each class (assuming the classes used for training are disjoint with the novel classes seen at test
time). Cross-domain few-shot learning [17,52,69] further addresses the problem
when the novel classes are sampled from a different domain with different data
distribution. In contrast, few-shot supervised domain adaptation aims to adapt
models to new domains with the assistance of a few examples [39,40,51,58].
Anti-spoofing methods based on few-shot and zero-shot learning [34,44] are proposed to detect multiple spoof attacks. The SASA method [59] studies a similar
cross-domain problem by using a few target samples to better generalize, and the
features are learned within the adversarial learning framework. As shown in [59],
cross-domain model performance is unstable under different protocols. In contrast, we propose to learn features from balanced data from the source domains
and a few samples from the target domain. We also propose an adaptive transformer based on an adapter and a feature-wise transformation to improve the
model stability.

3   Method

In this work, we assume that there exist N source datasets $\mathbf{S} =
\{S_1, S_2, S_3, \ldots, S_N\}$ from different domains and one target dataset $\mathcal{T}$, where
each source dataset S_i consists of real and fake images $S_i = \{X_r^{S_i}, X_f^{S_i}\}$. The
goal of few-shot cross-domain anti-spoofing is to learn a classification model that
generalizes to the target domain $\mathcal{T}$ by accessing source datasets $\mathbf{S}$ as well as a
few samples (*e.g.*, 5 samples) from the target set $\mathcal{T}' = \{X_r^{\mathcal{T}'}, X_f^{\mathcal{T}'}\} \subseteq \mathcal{T}$.

To achieve this goal, we propose a robust framework based on the vision
transformer (ViT) [11] and the adaptive modules for few-shot cross-domain face

anti-spoofing. The proposed approach consists of three components: vision transformer, ensemble adapters and feature-wise transformation. Figure 1 shows the overall framework, and Fig. 2 presents the adaptive modules. We describe each component in the following sections.

3.1   Vision Transformer

We adopt the vision transformers (ViT) [11] as our backbone module to tackle the face anti-spoofing problem. Following the standard pipeline of ViT training, we split and reshape the input image into a sequence of flattened 2D patches. We use ViT to obtain the image representations and a multi-layer perceptron (MLP) head to get the classification prediction, $i.e.$, whether the input image is a live or a spoof face. At each training iteration, we form a balanced batch by sampling the same amount of live and spoof images from N source domain and a small subset of target domain $\{X_r^{S_i}, X_f^{S_i}, X_r^{T'}, X_f^{T'}\}$, where the sample size is B. The model prediction is $\{\hat{y}_r^{S_i}, \hat{y}_f^{S_i}, \hat{y}_r^{T'}, \hat{y}_f^{T'}\}$. We use the cross entropy loss L_{ce} to train our model, which is defined by

$$L_{ce} = \frac{1}{B(N+1)} \sum_{j=1}^{B} \left(\sum_{i=1}^{N} (\log(\hat{y}_{r_j}^{S_i}) + \log(1 - \hat{y}_{f_j}^{S_i})) + \log(\hat{y}_{r_j}^{T'}) + \log(1 - \hat{y}_{f_j}^{T'}) \right).$$

(1)

Unlike other object classification tasks where holistic information plays an essential role, we need to detect local spoof-related cues appearing possibly all over the image for the face anti-spoofing problem. Empirically, it has been shown that patch-based face anti-spoofing methods [3,62] improve the performance as the network extracts more discriminative local features by using patches as inputs. However, these methods use convolutional neural networks to extract patch features and predict spoof scores for each patch independently. Furthermore, they use global pooling to fuse the scores for final prediction, which fails to apply global reasoning by considering the correlation among patches. In contrast, ViT captures the long-range dependency among different patches via the global self-attention mechanism. As a result, the local spoof-related cues can be detected independently and accumulated globally for better spoof predictions. Therefore, ViT is suitable for face anti-spoofing.

3.2   Ensemble Adapters

One straightforward transfer learning strategy is to train a classifier on top of features extracted by a backbone network pre-trained on ImageNet [10] using anti-spoofing data. However, this strategy yields poor performance on the face anti-spoofing task for two reasons. First, the backbone pre-trained using a generic dataset cannot adapt well to the specific anti-spoofing facial data. Second, features extracted from the pre-trained backbone network are high-level, thus not suitable for the face anti-spoofing task where the subtle low-level information is crucial.

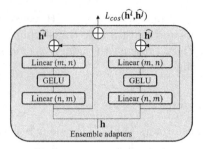

Fig. 2. Ensemble adapters. The ensemble adapters contain multiple adapters which take the same hidden representation as inputs, and the outputs of multiple adapters are aggregated. A cosine similarity loss is applied to pairs of outputs of adapters to enforce each adapter to learn diverse representations that complement with each other. Each adapter is a bottleneck layer with skipped connections. When the training starts, the adapter layers are close to identity layers, and they can be adapted for face anti-spoofing task or retained as the identity function.

Instead, one can fine-tune a classifier and the backbone on anti-spoofing data. Although good performance could be achieved on the source domain, the performance on the target domain becomes unstable even when the training loss approaches convergence as shown in Fig. 3 and Sect. 4.3. We attribute the instability to two factors. 1) When fine-tuning large models with few samples, the catastrophic forgetting problem usually causes training instability. 2) The domain gap between the target samples and the source domain is large such that the target samples are close to the decision boundary and have high uncertainty. An intuitive remedy is to freeze a majority of the backbone and partially fine-tune the network. However, the approach with fine-tuning only top layers of backbone networks does not address this issue. In the following, we propose to use ensemble adapter layers to achieve stable cross-domain performance.

Adaptive Module. In natural language processing, the adapterBERT [19] has been shown to successfully transfer the pre-trained BERT model to various downstream tasks without re-training the whole network. In this work, we introduce the adapter layer to alleviate the instability issue. The adapter has a bottleneck architecture containing few parameters relative to the feedforward layers. As shown in Fig. 2, it first linearly projects the n-dimensional features into a lower dimension m, applies a non-linear activation function GELU, and then projects back to n dimensions. As the adapter also contains a skip-connection, it is nearly an identity function if the parameters of the projection head are initialized to near-zero. As shown in Fig. 1(b), two adaptive modules are inserted into each transformer block. During the fine-tuning stage, we fix the original transformer backbone and update the weights of adaptive modules. As adapters contain only a few parameters ($\approx 3\%$ parameters of the original model), they can be learned without optimization difficulties. Thanks to the skip-connections, the adapters generate representations with less deviation from the pre-trained models and alleviate the catastrophic forgetting problem, thereby improving training stability.

Adapters also help adjust the feature distribution of the pre-trained transformer blocks to the face anti-spoofing data, maintaining the discriminative strength and good generalization ability of pre-trained transformer representations.

Ensemble Adapters and Cosine Similarity Loss. In this work, we introduce the ensemble adapters module to achieve higher accuracy and minimize training instability issues. Instead of having two naive adapters in each transformer block, we insert two ensemble adapter modules in each block. The ensemble adapters contain K adapters in parallel. Specifically, in each ensemble adapter module, the representation $\mathbf{h}$ is the input to K adapters and the outputs of adapters $\hat{\mathbf{h}}^k$ are aggregated and forwarded to the next layer. However, by simply ensembling the adapter outputs, multiple adapters learn repetitive information which does not improve the discriminability of the features and leads to limited performance improvements. In order to learn diverse features from multiple adapters, we use a cosine similarity loss which constrains multiple outputs of adapters to be complementary. Specifically, we minimize the cosine distance between each pair of outputs of the adapters $\hat{\mathbf{h}}^i$ and $\hat{\mathbf{h}}^j$. The cosine loss enforces the outputs of adapters to be dissimilar to each other and help learn diverse features. Assume the input image has N tokens and the feature dimension is D, we compute the cosine distance along the feature dimension and average over the number of tokens N. The cosine loss L_{cos} is defined by

$$\hat{\mathbf{h}} = \sum_{k=1}^{K} \hat{\mathbf{h}}^k = \sum_{k=1}^{K} Adapter_k(\mathbf{h}), \tag{2}$$

$$L_{cos} = \sum_{1 \le i,j \le K, i \ne j} \frac{1}{N} \sum_{n=1}^{N} \left(\frac{\hat{\mathbf{h}}_n^i \cdot \hat{\mathbf{h}}_n^j}{\left\| \hat{\mathbf{h}}_n^i \right\| \left\| \hat{\mathbf{h}}_n^j \right\|} \right)^2. \tag{3}$$

As the ensemble is conducted at the bottleneck network, our ensemble module is lightweight. Adding each additional adapter requires $\approx 3\%$ additional FLOPs and parameters, which are relatively low overheads. In practice, our model takes 15% additional inference time compared to naive ViT.

3.3 Feature-wise Transformation

Our goal is to learn a model that generalizes well to the target domain using source datasets and a small subset of the target dataset. Due to the distribution mismatch of the source and target domains, the model is prone to over-fitting since we only have access to limited target domain data during training. Thus, we include a feature-wise transformation (FWT) layer [52] into the transformer blocks. We first sample the scaling and bias terms of affine transformations from Gaussian distributions,

$$\alpha^d \sim N(0, \text{softplus}(W_\alpha^d)), \quad d = 1, \ldots, D, \tag{4}$$

$$\beta^d \sim N(0, \text{softplus}(W_\beta^d)), \quad d = 1, \ldots, D, \tag{5}$$

where W_α^d and W_β^d denote learnable sampling hyper-parameters, and D denotes the channel dimension of the activation map of each transformer block. We then compute the modulated features by applying the sampled affine transformations to intermediate features of layer $\mathbf{x}_l$ as follows:

$$\hat{\mathbf{x}}_l = \mathbf{x}_l + \boldsymbol{\alpha}_l \cdot \mathbf{x}_l + \boldsymbol{\beta}_l, \quad l = 1, \dots, L. \tag{6}$$

In practice, the same affine transformation is applied across all patch embeddings.

As shown in Fig. 1(b), we insert one FWT layer in each transformer block. The FWT layer is used only at training time as augmentation, and not used at test time. The FWT layer serves as feature-level data augmentation to increase the diversity of training samples, thus dramatically reducing over-fitting and improving stability and performance. The FWT layer is complementary to image-level augmentation and we apply both to help model training at the same time.

3.4   Adaptive Transformer

The proposed adaptive transformer consists of three stages: pre-training, fine-tuning and testing, as shown in Fig. 1. At the pre-training stage, we fix the ViT backbone initialized with pre-trained weights from ImageNet [10] and train the MLP head using the binary cross entropy loss L_{ce}. At the fine-tuning stage, we insert two ensemble adaptor modules and an FWT layer to each transformer block, and train all ensemble adaptors and FWT layers with all the other weights fixed until convergence using cross entropy loss and cosine loss $L_{ce} + L_{cos}$. During the testing stage, we remove the FWT layers and keep ensemble adaptors for cross-domain classification.

4   Experiments

4.1   Experimental Setups

Datasets and protocols. Two evaluation protocols are used in this work. In **Protocol 1**, we provide evaluations on four widely-used benchmark datasets: CASIA [71], Idiap Replay attack [9], MSU-MFSD [57], and Oulu-NPU [5]. Following the prior works, we regard each dataset as one domain and apply the leave-one-out testing protocol to evaluate the cross-domain generalization. In **Protocol 2**, we conduct similar cross-domain evaluations on the larger-scale datasets: CASIA-SURF [67,68], CASIA-CeFA [27,28], and WMCA [16]. Compared to datasets in **Protocol 1**, datasets in **Protocol 2** have much more subjects and richer environment variations, and thus the results can better reflect model performance. In both protocols, we include CelebA-Spoof [70] as the supplementary training data to increase the diversity of training samples to learn better spoof representations.

Implementation Details. The input images are cropped and resized to $224 \times 224 \times 3$ and split into a patch size of 16×16. We use an Adam optimizer with an initial learning rate of 1e-4 and weight decay of 1e-6. The batch size is 8 for each training domain. We use ViT-Base as our backbone whose output embedding dimension is 768, and the MLP head contains two fully-connected layers whose dimensions are 512 and 2. The adapter layers have dimension $n = 768$ and $m = 64$. We set the number of ensemble adapters $K = 2$ in the experiments. More experimental results of the ensemble adapters are in the supplementary materials. We first train the MLP head for 100 iterations in the pre-training stage and then the ensemble adapters and FWT layers for 4000 iterations in the fine-tuning stage. Our method is implemented using Pytorch.

Evaluation Metrics. We evaluate the model performance using three metrics: Half Total Error Rate (HTER), Area Under Curve (AUC), and True Positive Rate (TPR) at a fixed False Positive Rate (FPR). While HTER and AUC assess the theoretical performance, TPR at a certain FPR is adept at reflecting how well the model performs in practice. We use TPR@FPR=1% as the metric which is a high usability setting.

Evaluation Against State-of-the-Art Methods. We evaluate our model against the state-of-the-art cross-domain face anti-spoofing SSDG [20] method under several settings:

- 0-shot SSDG[†]: we do not add CelebA-Spoof, which is under the same setting as the SSDG paper [20].
- 0-shot SSDG: CelebA-Spoof is included as one of the source domains.
- 5-shot SSDG: CelebA-Spoof is included as one of the source domains, and the 5-shot samples are included at training time.

We include reported results of recent 0-shot methods in Table 1 for completeness. These methods do not outperform our SSDG baseline model. We are not able to evaluate these methods in the few-shot settings as the codes are not released.

Proposed Methods. We include these variants of our methods for evaluation:

- ViT: a ViT is used as the backbone, and the whole backbone along with the MLP layer are updated during training.
- ViTF: a ViT with FWT layers is used as the backbone, and the whole network along with the MLP layer are updated during training.
- ViTA: a ViT with naive single adapters is used as the backbone. Only the adapter layers are updated during training.
- ViTAF: a ViT with naive single adapters and FWT layers is used as the backbone. Only the adapter and FWT layers are updated during training.
- ViTAF*: a ViT with ensemble adapters and FWT layers is used as the backbone. The ensemble adapters and FWT layers are updated during training.

4.2 Cross-domain Performance

Tables 1 and 2 show the cross-domain performance for **Protocol 1** and **Protocol 2** respectively.

Table 1. Evaluation of cross-domain face anti-spoofing among CASIA (**C**), Replay (**I**), MSU-MFSD (**M**), and Oulu-NPU (**O**) databases. Methods are compared at their best performance based on the evaluation process in [20]. SSDG† denotes the cross-domain performance reported in [20] without using CelebA-Spoof as the supplementary source dataset.

	Method	OCI → M			OMI → C			OCM → I			ICM → O		
		HTER	AUC	TPR@ FPR=1%	HTER	AUC	TPR@ FPR=1%	HTER	AUC	TPR@ FPR=1%	HTER	AUC	TPR@ FPR=1%
0-shot	AS-FAS [65]	16.85	90.42	–	15.21	92.64	–	11.63	96.98	–	13.16	94.18	–
	DRDG [31]	12.43	95.81	–	19.05	88.79	–	15.56	91.79	–	15.63	91.75	–
	D^2AM [7]	12.70	95.66	–	20.98	85.58	–	15.43	91.22	–	15.27	90.87	–
	Self-DA [55]	15.40	91.80	–	24.50	84.40	–	15.60	90.10	–	23.10	84.30	–
	ANRL [30]	10.83	96.75	–	17.85	89.26	–	16.03	91.04	–	15.67	91.90	–
	FGHV [29]	9.17	96.92	–	12.47	93.47	–	16.29	90.11	–	13.58	93.55	–
0-shot	SSDG† [20]	7.38	97.17	–	10.44	95.94	–	11.71	96.59	–	15.61	91.54	–
	SSDG	6.58	97.21	48.33	12.91	93.92	56.43	**7.01**	**98.28**	63.85	12.47	94.87	51.55
	ViT	**1.58**	**99.68**	**96.67**	5.70	98.91	88.57	9.25	97.15	51.54	**7.47**	**98.42**	**69.30**
5-shot	SSDG	8.42	97.39	63.33	12.91	93.59	60.71	4.48	99.14	80.77	7.81	97.46	67.61
	ViT	3.42	98.60	95.00	1.98	99.75	94.00	2.31	99.75	87.69	7.34	97.77	66.90
	ViTA	4.75	98.84	76.67	5.00	99.13	82.14	5.37	98.57	76.15	7.16	97.97	73.24
	ViTAF	3.42	99.30	88.33	1.40	99.85	95.71	3.74	99.34	85.38	7.17	98.26	71.97
	ViTAF*	**2.92**	**99.62**	**91.66**	**1.40**	**99.92**	**98.57**	**1.64**	**99.64**	**91.53**	**5.39**	**98.67**	**76.05**

Table 2. Evaluation on cross-domain protocols among CASIA-SURF (**S**), CASIA-CeFA (**C**), and WMCA (**W**) databases. Methods are compared at their best performance based on the evaluation process in [20].

	Method	CS → W			SW → C			CW → S		
		HTER	AUC	TPR@ FPR=1%	HTER	AUC	TPR@ FPR=1%	HTER	AUC	TPR@ FPR=1%
0-shot	SSDG	12.64	94.35	55.72	12.25	94.78	51.67	27.08	80.05	12.06
	ViT	**7.98**	**97.97**	**73.61**	**11.13**	**95.46**	47.59	**13.35**	**94.13**	**49.97**
5-shot	SSDG	5.08	99.02	77.49	6.72	98.11	74.28	18.88	88.25	23.42
	ViT	4.30	99.16	83.55	7.69	97.66	68.33	12.26	94.40	42.59
	ViTA	3.77	99.42	85.78	6.02	98.47	78.29	15.67	91.86	51.21
	ViTAF	4.51	99.44	88.23	7.21	97.69	70.87	11.74	94.13	50.87
	ViTAF*	**2.91**	**99.71**	**92.65**	**6.00**	**98.55**	**78.56**	**11.60**	**95.03**	**60.12**

Effectiveness of CelebA-Spoof. As shown in Table 1, the 0-shot SSDG model outperforms 0-shot SSDG† on three out of four targets, which results in an average improvement of 0.76 AUC. The improvement can be attributed to two reasons. First, the CelebA-Spoof dataset can increase the diversity of source domain training data. Therefore, the distance between some source samples and the target samples is reduced, which benefits the cross-domain classification. Second, using more diverse training data could smooth the decision boundary and result in better model generalization ability.

0-Shot Performance. ViT outperforms SSDG on AUC scores for six out of total seven target domains: M (+2.5), C (+5.0), O (+3.6), W (+3.6), C (+0.7), S (+14.1), except for I (−1.1). The result shows that ViT is a strong backbone that generalizes better to the unseen target datasets. A ViT backbone fine-tuned on the source datasets with only a standard cross entropy loss can achieve competitive performance upon baseline approaches that employ special domain generalization techniques such as triplet loss and adversarial training. We also find that adding additional triplet loss or adversarial learning does not bring performance gain to the ViT backbone.

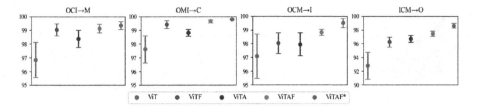

Fig. 3. Ablation study. We analyze different components of our model including ensemble adapter layers and feature-wise transformation (FWT) layers. We report the average AUC and standard deviation of the last eight checkpoints when the training is converged. The naive adapter and the FWT layer (ViTA, ViTF, ViTAF) both improve the performance. Our ensemble adapters (ViTAF*) further boost the average test performance and the stability.

From 0-Shot to 5-Shot. 5-shot SSDG improves upon 0-shot SSDG for six out of seven target domains with an average of 2.78 AUC. Similarly, 5-shot ViT improves upon 0-shot ViT for five out of seven target domains with an average of 0.77 AUC. These results demonstrate that using only 5-shot samples can effectively adapt the model to the target domain. Due to camera devices, illuminations, and image resolutions, a large domain gap exists between the source and target domains. In this case, a few target samples can effectively reveal some crucial characteristics and differences between live and spoof faces of the target domain, thereby facilitating the model adaptation to the target domain. It is worth noticing that 5-shot test samples are a relatively small subset in terms of dataset size, taking 4.7/1.6/1.2/0.3% of the target domain data in **Protocol 1** and approximately 0.1% of the target domain data in **Protocol 2**.

5-Shot Performance. ViTA outperforms 5-shot SSDG for six out of seven target domains: M (+1.45), C (+5.54), O (+0.51), W (+0.40), C (+0.35), S (+3.60), except for I (−0.57). Combining adapters and FWTs, the ViTAF model outperforms 5-shot SSDG for six out of seven target domains: M (+1.90), C (+6.26), O (+0.80), I (+0.20), W (+0.42), S (+5.88), except for C (−0.42).

Comparison of ViTA and ViTAF. Comparing ViTA with ViTAF, FWT layers achieves consistent improvement for **Protocol 1**: M (+0.46), C (+0.72), I (+0.77), O (+0.29). For **Protocol 2**, ViTAF achieves improvements only for the S domain (+2.28). This is likely due to the smaller size of datasets in **Protocol 1**, which highlights the importance of FWT layers to generate a more diverse distribution and increase the dataset size.

Comparison of ViTAF and ViTAF*. With the ensemble adapters, our full model ViTAF* achieves consistent improvement for all the targets over ViTAF: M (+0.32), C(+0.07), I(+0.30), O(+0.41), W(+0.27), C(+0.86), S(+0.90). The results show that the ensemble adapters and the cosine similarity loss facilitate learning diverse features from multiple adapters which are complementary with each other. Overall, our model achieves state-of-the-art results for all target domains, demonstrating the effectiveness of our method to adapt the model to the target domain with few samples. We further discuss the variants of our method in the following section.

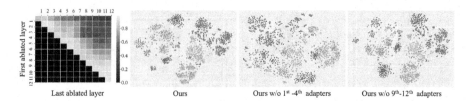

Fig. 4. Visualization of adapter. We visualize the TPR@FPR=1% score of ablated continuous adapter layers in the left-most sub-figure. For example, the value at the second row in the fifth column represents the model performance by removing the adapters from the second to fifth layers. We find that removing the adapters in the first four layers (the top left) causes a relatively severe performance drop than in the last four layers (the bottom right). We plot the feature distribution in the three figures to the right. A unique color represents the live or spoof sample from each domain. We observe that the data samples are less separable by removing the adapters in the first four layers than the last ones.

4.3   Ablation Study

We conduct ablation studies to analyze the contributions of each module using the 5-shot setting and **Protocol 1**. As discussed in Sect. 3.2, the performance of 5-shot ViT model may fluctuate among different checkpoints even the training loss converges. The best performance among all the checkpoints is reported in Tables 1 and 2, following [20]. In Fig. 3, we show the average AUC and standard deviation of the last eight checkpoints when the training process converges. Although the *best* performance of ViT is good in Table 1, the performance fluctuates and has lower *average* performance in Fig. 3. Comparing ViT with ViTF, ViTA and ViTAF, both FWT layers and adapter layers achieve better *average* performance with smaller standard deviation for all targets. Our full model ViTAF* achieves the best performance with the lowest standard deviation, which validates the robust performance achieved by the ensemble adapters.

4.4   Visualization

Adapter. Figure 4 shows the TPR@FPR=1% score of ablated continuous adapter layers. For example, the value at the second row in the fifth column represents the model performance by removing the adapter from the second to fifth layers. The diagonal numbers are generally good, indicating that ablating a single adapter layer does not affect model performance significantly. On the other hand, removing more adapter layers causes performance drops, which can be verified by the numbers in the upper triangular region. Moreover, the numbers at the top left are relatively smaller than those at the bottom right, which indicates that removing the adapters in the first few layers causes a more significant performance drop while removing the adapters in the last few layers does not.

We further plot the feature distribution using t-SNE [37]. We can observe that samples of all categories are well separated in our method. Moreover, we find that removing adapters in the first four layers leads to less separable distribution

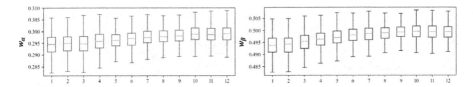

Fig. 5. Visualization of the feature-wise transformation layers. We present the quartile plot of learned sampling parameters W_α^d and W_β^d of all FWT layers. The box edges in each column mark the 25th and 75th percentiles of all $D = 768$ values. Note that W_α^d and W_β^d are initialized as 0.3 and 0.5, respectively. The values in shallow layers (1st-4th) deviate more from the initial values than those in deep layers (9th-12th), which suggests that the low-level features are adapted more and influence more to the target task.

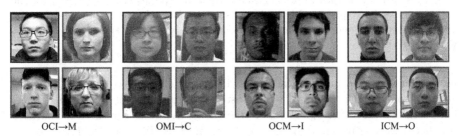

OCI→M   OMI→C   OCM→I   ICM→O

Fig. 6. Failure cases of our method. The live faces misclassified as spoof faces are shown in blue boxes and the spoof faces misclassified as live faces are shown in red boxes. The live faces classified as spoof faces (blue) are mostly in special light conditions or low-quality sensors, suggesting that our method still suffers from domain-specific environments. The spoof faces classified as live faces (red) show that our model has difficulties detecting spoof faces with better visual quality than live faces, detecting the unseen spoof types, and detecting paper attacks with local texture differences. (Color figure online)

than the last four layers. These results show that the low-level features of the transformer are more critical than high-level features for the anti-spoofing task.

Feature-Wise Transformation. Figure 5 shows the magnitude of the learned sampling parameters of FWT layers. We can observe that the values of both the scaling and the bias terms are closer to the initial values in deeper layers (9th-12th) and adjusted more in shallower layers (1st-4th), suggesting that the adaptation occurs mainly in the low-level features. This result also coincides with the findings in Fig. 4.

Failure Cases and Limitations. Figure 6 shows the common types of incorrect predictions by our methods. For the live faces classified as spoof faces (blue boxes), the results show that these faces are mostly in special light conditions or captured by low-quality sensors, e.g., strong yellow light (**OCI → M**), sensors with weird color temperatures (**OMI → C**), dark light (**OCM → I**). It suggests that our method still suffers from the domain-specific light condition. Due to the extreme light condition, a live face in one domain may look like a spoof face

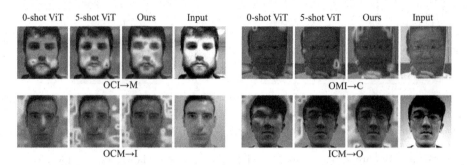

Fig. 7. Transformer attention on spoof images. We visualize the attention maps of transformers using Transformer Explainability [6]. Transformers focus on face regions with a bright reflection for MSU, hand and paper boundaries for CASIA, background paper textures for Replay, and background shadows for Oulu-NPU. Our model generates more accurate and conspicuous attention maps to capture spoof cues compared with naive ViTs.

in another domain. For spoof faces classified as live faces (red boxes), the replay attack displaying a fixed photo is the most challenging type for **OCM → I**. These images have even better visual quality than other live images in the same dataset, which causes confusion. Paper attacks are more challenging for **ICM → O**, which has the highest resolution among all datasets. While paper attacks show texture differences, there is no clear region of spoof cues, and thus the high-resolution spoof images in **O** may look closer to live images in other datasets. Paper attacks with real human eyes are challenging for **OMI → C**. It is difficult to detect this specific attack that only appears in **C** and does not show up in other datasets, including CelebA-Spoof. Researchers should note that for the responsible development of this technology, it is important to consider issues of potential unfair bias and consider testing for fairness.

Attention Maps. As shown in Fig. 7, we visualize the attention maps of different transformers on spoof images using Transformer Explainability [6]. We observe that different regions are highlighted by transformers to make predictions for different spoof face domains. For example, transformers make predictions mainly based on the bright reflection regions for the replay attack in **OCI → M**. For paper attacks, transformers focus on hands and paper boundaries in **OMI → C**, and the background paper texture in **OCM → I**. As for the replay attack in **ICM → O**, transformers pay more attention to the background shadows. Moreover, our model can better capture the spoof cues compared to the naive ViT, as the attention region are more conspicuous.

5   Conclusion

In this work, we study the task of cross-domain face anti-spoofing with a few samples. We introduce vision transformer with ensemble adapters and feature-wise transforms to adapt to new domains. The proposed ensemble adapters significantly facilitate both stable training process and consistent model performance. Experiments on widely-used benchmark datasets validate that our method achieves state-of-the-art performance for few-shot cross-domain face anti-spoofing.

References

1. Agarwal, A., Singh, R., Vatsa, M.: Face anti-spoofing using haralick features. In: International Conference on Biometrics Theory, Applications and Systems (BTAS) (2016)
2. Antoniou, A., Storkey, A., Edwards, H.: Data augmentation generative adversarial networks. In: International Conference on Learning Representations (ICLR) (2018)
3. Atoum, Y., Liu, Y., Jourabloo, A., Liu, X.: Face anti-spoofing using patch and depth-based CNNs. In: International Joint Conference on Biometrics (IJCB) (2017)
4. Boulkenafet, Z., Komulainen, J., Hadid, A.: Face anti-spoofing based on color texture analysis. In: International Conference on Image Processing (ICIP) (2015)
5. Boulkenafet, Z., Komulainen, J., Li, L., Feng, X., Hadid, A.: OULU-NPU: a mobile face presentation attack database with real-world variations. In: International Conference on Automatic Face & Gesture Recognition (FG) (2017)
6. Chefer, H., Gur, S., Wolf, L.: Transformer interpretability beyond attention visualization. In: IEEE Conference on Computer Vision and Pattern Recognition (CVPR) (2021)
7. Chen, Z., et al.: Generalizable representation learning for mixture domain face anti-spoofing. In: Association for the Advancement of Artificial Intelligence (AAAI) (2021)
8. Chetty, G.: Biometric liveness checking using multimodal fuzzy fusion. In: IEEE International Conference on Fuzzy Systems (FUZZ-IEEE) (2010)
9. Chingovska, I., Anjos, A., Marcel, S.: On the effectiveness of local binary patterns in face anti-spoofing. In: Proceedings of the International Conference of Biometrics Special Interest Group (BIOSIG) (2012)
10. Deng, J., Dong, W., Socher, R., Li, L.J., Li, K., Fei-Fei, L.: Imagenet: a large-scale hierarchical image database. In: IEEE Conference on Computer Vision and Pattern Recognition (CVPR) (2009)
11. Dosovitskiy, A., et al.: An image is worth 16×16 words: transformers for image recognition at scale. In: International Conference on Learning Representations (ICLR) (2021)
12. Feng, L., et al.: Integration of image quality and motion cues for face anti-spoofing: a neural network approach. J. Vis. Commun. Image Represent. **38**, 451–460 (2016)
13. Finn, C., Abbeel, P., Levine, S.: Model-agnostic meta-learning for fast adaptation of deep networks. In: International Conference on Machine Learning (ICML) (2017)
14. de Freitas Pereira, T., Anjos, A., De Martino, J.M., Marcel, S.: LBP-TOP based countermeasure against face spoofing attacks. In: Asian Conference on Computer Vision (ACCV) (2012)
15. George, A., Marcel, S.: On the effectiveness of vision transformers for zero-shot face anti-spoofing. In: International Joint Conference on Biometrics (IJCB) (2021)
16. George, A., Mostaani, Z., Geissenbuhler, D., Nikisins, O., Anjos, A., Marcel, S.: Biometric face presentation attack detection with multi-channel convolutional neural network. IEEE Trans. Inf. Forensics Secur. **15**, 42–55 (2020)

17. Guo, Y., et al.: A broader study of cross-domain few-shot learning. In: Vedaldi, A., Bischof, H., Brox, T., Frahm, J.-M. (eds.) ECCV 2020. LNCS, vol. 12372, pp. 124–141. Springer, Cham (2020). https://doi.org/10.1007/978-3-030-58583-9_8

18. Hariharan, B., Girshick, R.: Low-shot visual recognition by shrinking and hallucinating features. In: IEEE International Conference on Computer Vision (ICCV) (2017)

19. Houlsby, N., et al.: Parameter-efficient transfer learning for NLP. In: International Conference on Machine Learning (ICML) (2019)

20. Jia, Y., Zhang, J., Shan, S., Chen, X.: Single-side domain generalization for face anti-spoofing. In: IEEE Conference on Computer Vision and Pattern Recognition (CVPR) (2020)

21. Karras, T., Laine, S., Aila, T.: A style-based generator architecture for generative adversarial networks. In: IEEE Conference on Computer Vision and Pattern Recognition (CVPR) (2019)

22. Kim, T., Kim, Y.: Suppressing spoof-irrelevant factors for domain-agnostic face anti-spoofing. IEEE Access. **9**, 86966–86974 (2021)

23. Kollreider, K., Fronthaler, H., Faraj, M.I., Bigun, J.: Real-time face detection and motion analysis with application in "lliveness" assessment. Trans. Inf. Forens. Secur. (TIFS) **2**(3), 548–558 (2007)

24. Komando, K.: Smartphone security: what's better to use a pin, facial recognition, or your fingerprint? Fox News (2019)

25. Komulainen, J., Hadid, A., Pietikäinen, M.: Context based face anti-spoofing. In: International Conference on Biometrics: Theory, Applications and Systems (BTAS) (2013)

26. Li, L., Feng, X., Boulkenafet, Z., Xia, Z., Li, M., Hadid, A.: An original face anti-spoofing approach using partial convolutional neural network. In: International Conference on Image Processing Theory, Tools and Applications (IPTA) (2016)

27. Liu, A., Tan, Z., Wan, J., Escalera, S., Guo, G., Li, S.Z.: CASIA-SURF CEFA: a benchmark for multi-modal cross-ethnicity face anti-spoofing. In: Winter Conference on Applications of Computer Vision (WACV) (2021)

28. Liu, A., et al.: Cross-ethnicity face anti-spoofing recognition challenge: a review. IET Biomet. **10**, 24–43 (2020)

29. Liu, S., Lu, S., Xu, H., Yang, J., Ding, S., Ma, L.: Feature generation and hypothesis verification for reliable face anti-spoofing. In: Association for the Advancement of Artificial Intelligence (AAAI) (2022)

30. Liu, S., et al.: Adaptive normalized representation learning for generalizable face anti-spoofing. In: ACM International Conference on Multimedia (ACM MM) (2021)

31. Liu, S., et al.: Dual reweighting domain generalization for face presentation attack detection. In: International Joint Conference on Artificial Intelligence (IJCAI) (2021)

32. Liu, S., Yuen, P.C., Zhang, S., Zhao, G.: 3D mask face anti-spoofing with remote photoplethysmography. In: Leibe, B., Matas, J., Sebe, N., Welling, M. (eds.) ECCV 2016. LNCS, vol. 9911, pp. 85–100. Springer, Cham (2016). https://doi.org/10.1007/978-3-319-46478-7_6

33. Liu, Y., Jourabloo, A., Liu, X.: Learning deep models for face anti-spoofing: binary or auxiliary supervision. In: IEEE Conference on Computer Vision and Pattern Recognition (CVPR) (2018)

34. Liu, Y., Stehouwer, J., Jourabloo, A., Liu, X.: Deep tree learning for zero-shot face anti-spoofing. In: IEEE Conference on Computer Vision and Pattern Recognition (CVPR) (2019)

35. Liu, Y., Stehouwer, J., Liu, X.: On disentangling spoof trace for generic face anti-spoofing. In: Vedaldi, A., Bischof, H., Brox, T., Frahm, J.-M. (eds.) ECCV 2020. LNCS, vol. 12363, pp. 406–422. Springer, Cham (2020). https://doi.org/10.1007/978-3-030-58523-5_24
36. Liu, Z., Luo, P., Wang, X., Tang, X.: Deep learning face attributes in the wild. In: IEEE International Conference on Computer Vision (ICCV) (2015)
37. van der Maaten, L., Hinton, G.: Viualizing data using T-SNE. J. Mach. Learn. Res. (JMLR) **9**, 2579–2605 (2008)
38. Mishra, S.K., Sengupta, K., Horowitz-Gelb, M., Chu, W.S., Bouaziz, S., Jacobs, D.: Improved detection of face presentation attacks using image decomposition. arXiv preprint arXiv:2103.12201 (2021)
39. Motiian, S., Jones, Q., Iranmanesh, S., Doretto, G.: Few-shot adversarial domain adaptation. In: Neural Information Processing Systems (NeurIPS) (2017)
40. Motiian, S., Piccirilli, M., Adjeroh, D.A., Doretto, G.: Unified deep supervised domain adaptation and generalization. In: IEEE International Conference on Computer Vision (ICCV) (2017)
41. Pan, G., Sun, L., Wu, Z., Lao, S.: Eyeblink-based anti-spoofing in face recognition from a generic webcamera. In: IEEE International Conference on Computer Vision (ICCV) (2007)
42. Patel, K., Han, H., Jain, A.K.: Cross-database face antispoofing with robust feature representation. In: Chinese Conference on Biometric Recognition (CCBR) (2016)
43. Patel, K., Han, H., Jain, A.K.: Secure face unlock: spoof detection on smartphones. Trans. Inf. Forens. Secur. (TIFS) **11**(10), 2268–2283 (2016)
44. Qin, Y., et al.: Learning meta model for zero-and few-shot face antispoofing. In: Association for the Advancement of Artificial Intelligence (AAAI) (2020)
45. Ravi, S., Larochelle, H.: Optimization as a model for few-shot learning. In: International Conference on Learning Representations (ICLR) (2017)
46. Saha, S., et al..: Domain agnostic feature learning for image and video based face anti-spoofing. In: IEEE Conference on Computer Vision and Pattern Recognition Workshops (CVPRW) (2020)
47. Shao, R., Lan, X., Li, J., Yuen, P.C.: Multi-adversarial discriminative deep domain generalization for face presentation attack detection. In: IEEE Conference on Computer Vision and Pattern Recognition (CVPR) (2019)
48. Shao, R., Lan, X., Yuen, P.C.: Regularized fine-grained meta face anti-spoofing. In: Association for the Advancement of Artificial Intelligence (AAAI) (2020)
49. Snell, J., Swersky, K., Zemel, R.: Prototypical networks for few-shot learning. In: Neural Information Processing Systems (NeurIPS) (2017)
50. Sung, F., Yang, Y., Zhang, L., Xiang, T., Torr, P.H., Hospedales, T.M.: Learning to compare: Relation network for few-shot learning. In: IEEE Conference on Computer Vision and Pattern Recognition (CVPR) (2018)
51. Teshima, T., Sato, I., Sugiyama, M.: Few-shot domain adaptation by causal mechanism transfer. In: International Conference on Machine Learning (ICML) (2020)
52. Tseng, H.Y., Lee, H.Y., Huang, J.B., Yang, M.H.: Cross-domain few-shot classification via learned feature-wise transformation. In: International Conference on Learning Representations (ICLR) (2020)
53. Vinyals, O., Blundell, C., Lillicrap, T., kavukcuoglu, k., Wierstra, D.: Matching networks for one shot learning. In: Neural Information Processing Systems (NeurIPS) (2016)
54. Wang, G., Han, H., Shan, S., Chen, X.: Cross-domain face presentation attack detection via multi-domain disentangled representation learning. In: IEEE Conference on Computer Vision and Pattern Recognition (CVPR) (2020)

55. Wang, J., Zhang, J., Bian, Y., Cai, Y., Wang, C., Pu, S.: Self-domain adaptation for face anti-spoofing. In: Association for the Advancement of Artificial Intelligence (AAAI) (2021)
56. Wang, Y.X., Girshick, R., Hebert, M., Hariharan, B.: Low-shot learning from imaginary data. In: IEEE Conference on Computer Vision and Pattern Recognition (CVPR) (2018)
57. Wen, D., Han, H., Jain, A.K.: Face spoof detection with image distortion analysis. Trans. Inf. Forensics Secur. (TIFS) **10**(4), 746–761 (2015)
58. Xu, X., Zhou, X., Venkatesan, R., Swaminathan, G., Majumder, O.: D-SNE: domain adaptation using stochastic neighborhood embedding. In: IEEE Conference on Computer Vision and Pattern Recognition (CVPR) (2019)
59. Yang, B., Zhang, J., Yin, Z., Shao, J.: Few-shot domain expansion for face anti-spoofing. arXiv preprint arXiv:2106.14162 (2021)
60. Yang, J., Lei, Z., Li, S.Z.: Learn convolutional neural network for face anti-spoofing. arXiv preprint arXiv:1408.5601 (2014)
61. Yang, J., Lei, Z., Liao, S., Li, S.Z.: Face liveness detection with component dependent descriptor. In: International Conference on Biometrics (ICB) (2013)
62. Yang, X., et al.: Face anti-spoofing: model matters, so does data. In: IEEE Conference on Computer Vision and Pattern Recognition (CVPR) (2019)
63. Yu, Z., Li, X., Niu, X., Shi, J., Zhao, G.: Face anti-spoofing with human material perception. In: Vedaldi, A., Bischof, H., Brox, T., Frahm, J.-M. (eds.) ECCV 2020. LNCS, vol. 12352, pp. 557–575. Springer, Cham (2020). https://doi.org/10.1007/978-3-030-58571-6_33
64. Yu, Z., et al.: Auto-FAS: searching lightweight networks for face anti-spoofing. In: IEEE International Conference on Acoustics, Speech and SP (ICASSP) (2020)
65. Yu, Z., Wan, J., Qin, Y., Li, X., Li, S., Zhao, G.: NAS-FAS: static-dynamic central difference network search for face anti-spoofing. IEEE Trans. Pattern Recogn. Mach. Intell. (PAMI) **43**, 3005–3023 (2021)
66. Zhang, K.-Y., et al.: Face anti-spoofing via disentangled representation learning. In: Vedaldi, A., Bischof, H., Brox, T., Frahm, J.-M. (eds.) ECCV 2020. LNCS, vol. 12364, pp. 641–657. Springer, Cham (2020). https://doi.org/10.1007/978-3-030-58529-7_38
67. Zhang, S., et al.: CASIA-surf: a large-scale multi-modal benchmark for face anti-spoofing. In: IEEE Transactions on Biometrics, Behavior, and Identity Science (T-BIOM) (2020)
68. Zhang, S., et al.: A dataset and benchmark for large-scale multi-modal face anti-spoofing. In: IEEE Conference on Computer Vision and Pattern Recognition (CVPR) (2019)
69. Zhang, X., Meng, D., Gouk, H., Hospedales, T.M.: Shallow Bayesian meta learning for real-world few-shot recognition. In: IEEE International Conference on Computer Vision (ICCV) (2021)
70. Zhang, Y., et al.: CelebA-spoof: large-scale face anti-spoofing dataset with rich annotations. In: Vedaldi, A., Bischof, H., Brox, T., Frahm, J.-M. (eds.) ECCV 2020. LNCS, vol. 12357, pp. 70–85. Springer, Cham (2020). https://doi.org/10.1007/978-3-030-58610-2_5
71. Zhang, Z., Yan, J., Liu, S., Lei, Z., Yi, D., Li, S.Z.: A face antispoofing database with diverse attacks. In: International Conference on Biometrics (ICB) (2012)

Face2Face$^\rho$: Real-Time High-Resolution One-Shot Face Reenactment

Kewei Yang[1] , Kang Chen[1]($\boxtimes$) , Daoliang Guo[1] , Song-Hai Zhang[2] ,
Yuan-Chen Guo[2] , and Weidong Zhang[1]

[1] NetEase Games AI Lab, Hangzhou, People's Republic of China
{yangkewei,ckn6763,guodaoliang,zhangweidong02}@corp.netease.com
[2] Tsinghua University, Beijing, People's Republic of China

Abstract. Existing one-shot face reenactment methods either present obvious artifacts in large pose transformations, or cannot well-preserve the identity information in the source images, or fail to meet the requirements of real-time applications due to the intensive amount of computation involved. In this paper, we introduce Face2Face$^\rho$, the first **R**eal-time **H**igh-resolution and **O**ne-shot (RHO, ρ) face reenactment framework. To achieve this goal, we designed a new 3DMM-assisted warping-based face reenactment architecture which consists of two fast and efficient sub-networks, i.e., a u-shaped rendering network to reenact faces driven by head poses and facial motion fields, and a hierarchical coarse-to-fine motion network to predict facial motion fields guided by different scales of landmark images. Compared with existing state-of-the-art works, Face2Face$^\rho$ can produce results of equal or better visual quality, yet with significantly less time and memory overhead. We also demonstrate that Face2Face$^\rho$ can achieve real-time performance for face images of 1440×1440 resolution with a desktop GPU and 256×256 resolution with a mobile CPU.

Keywords: Face reenactment · One-shot · Real-time · High-resolution

1 Introduction

Face reenactment is the task of synthesizing realistic images of a source actor, with head poses and facial expressions synchronized with a specified driving actor. Such technology has great potential for media and entertainment applications. Traditional reenactment solutions [1] typically rely on costly CG techniques to create a high-fidelity digital avatar for the source actor, and to transfer the facial movements of the driving actor onto the digitized avatar via motion capture systems. To bypass the expensive graphics pipeline, image-based methods have been proposed, which synthesize reenacted faces using image retrieval

Supplementary Information The online version contains supplementary material available at https://doi.org/10.1007/978-3-031-19778-9_4.

Fig. 1. One-shot face reenactment results synthesized by Face2Face$^\rho$. Left: 1440×1440 resolution images generated at 25 fps on a desktop GPU (Nvidia GeForce RTX 2080Ti); the source images are from the internet. Right: 256×256 resolution images generated at 25 fps on a mobile CPU (Qualcomm Kryo 680). Notice that the time overhead of all required computations (e.g., facial landmark detection, shape and expression regression, etc.) for each frame is accounted in the fps calculation, not just the synthesis module.

and blending algorithms [8,35,38], generative adversarial networks [16,17,19,46] or neural textures [36,37]. Nevertheless, all these methods require a considerable amount of video footage (i.e., several minutes or hours) of the source actor, which is often infeasible in practical application scenarios.

Hence, few-shot/one-shot solutions have been developed, which can animate an unseen actor with only a small number of example face images. The key idea behind these methods is to decouple an actor's facial appearance and motion information with two separate encodings, allowing the network to learn the facial appearance and motion priors from a large collection of video data in a self-supervised fashion. Based on the way how motion information is encoded in the network, classic algorithms can be divided into two categories [24,49], i.e., warping-based and direct synthesis. Warping-based methods [2,32–34,45] learn to warp the source face based on an explicitly estimated motion field, while direct synthesis methods [5,27,50,52] encode both the appearance and motion information into some low-dimensional latent representation and then synthesize the reenacted image by decoding from the corresponding latent codes. Although both are capable of producing photo-realistic reenactment results, each approach has its advantages and disadvantages. Warping-based techniques work perfectly for a small range of motion, but may easily break when large pose transformations appear. On the contrary, direct synthesis solutions have better robustness against large pose changes, but the overall fidelity of the synthesized faces tends to be lower than those produced by warping-based methods, e.g., even the identity of the source actor may not be well-preserved [7].

In this context, the main focus of later researches in one-shot face reenactment is to achieve high-fidelity reenactment results for a wide range of poses. For instance, Meshry et al. [24] relieve the identity preserving problem in direct synthesis approaches by additionally employing an encoding concerning actors' facial layouts, Wang et al. [43] incorporate 3D motion fields in the warping-based methods to improve the performance on large poses, and Doukas et al. [7] propose a hybrid framework by injecting warped appearance features into a typical direct synthesize backbone so that the two types of methods can complement each other. Although these strategies improve the overall quality of generated images, they also significantly increase the networks' computational complexity. To our best knowledge, none of the current state-of-the-art one-shot approaches can be successfully adapted to meet the requirements of real-time applications, especially on mobile devices. The only algorithm that reports having barely achieved 25 fps inference speed is [49], but given the additional computational cost for facial landmark detection, GPU-CPU copy operations, etc., it still fails to support a real-time face reenactment system. In addition, [49] sacrifices too much quality for speed, as the quality produced results are clearly below state-of-the-art.

In this paper, we tackle a new challenging problem in one-shot face reenactment, i.e., building a real-time system that can produce results of state-of-the-art quality. To achieve this goal, we introduce Face2Face$^\rho$, the first real-time high-resolution and one-shot face reenactment framework. Specifically, Face2Face$^\rho$ can reenact faces at 25 fps for images of 1440 × 1440 resolution on a desktop GPU and 256 × 256 resolution on a mobile CPU (see Fig. 1). The key idea behind this framework is that warping-based backbones have better potentials in building a light-weighted reenactment framework, since the warped feature maps already depict most parts of the target face, leaving the generator a relatively easier task (i.e., refining and in-painting) to learn. In this spirit, we present a new way to combine the warping-based and direct synthesis approaches, i.e., injecting the 3D head pose encodings into a light-weighted u-shaped warping-based backbone. Further, we introduce a novel hierarchical motion prediction network that coarse-to-finely estimates the required motion fields based on different scales of landmark images. Such design achieves over 3 times speedup in both rendering and motion field prediction without damaging the visual quality or prediction precision. Our experiments also demonstrate that Face2Face$^\rho$ has the ability to perform state-of-the-art face reenactment with significantly less time and memory overhead than existing methods.

2   Related Work

We briefly review previous few-shot/one-shot methods in this section. As mentioned before, existing methods can be literately categorized into warping-based methods, direct synthesis methods, and hybrid methods.

Warping-Based Methods. These methods represent the pose and expression transformations using explicit motion fields, and then learn to warp and synthesize the target faces base on the estimated motion fields. Early methods [45] typically conduct warping directly on the source image, which often leads to unnatural head deformation. A more recent warping-based framework is introduced by Siarohin et al. [32] which performs warping on the latent feature maps and uses relative keypoint locations in the driving images to estimate motion fields. Followup works use a first-order approximation for keypoints [33] or keyregions [34] to improve the accuracy and robustness of motion field estimation, but still follow the relative motion transfer scheme. However, relative motion transfer would lead to obvious flaws if the initial driving face and the source face are different in head poses or expressions. Therefore, 3D morphable face models [3] which can explicitly estimate pose and expression information of 2D faces are incorporated to allow absolute motion transfer [9,47,48]. Nonetheless, previous warping-based methods share a common limitation, i.e., they only work well for a limited range of head poses. The latest work [43] overcomes this limitation to some extent by lifting the 2D motion fields to the 3D space. However, expensive operators like 3D convolution also make it unsuitable for real-time or mobile applications.

Direct Synthesis Methods. Zakharov et al. [50] introduce the first direct synthesis method, which projects both the appearance and motion into latent feature space and synthesizes target faces by decoding from corresponding latent codes. This framework also demonstrates that it is possible to directly synthesize reasonable reenactment results without an explicit warp field. However, [50] uses driving faces' landmarks for computing motion encodings. As facial landmarks are person-specific, motion encodings extracted from driving faces' landmarks would also contain some identity-related information, causing noticeable identity gaps in the synthesized face. Later works try to solve this problem by eliminating the driving actors' identity information from the motion codes. Various strategies have been proposed, e.g., FReeNet [52] trains a landmark converter to adapt the motion of an arbitrary person to the target person in the latent space, LPD [5] applies pose augmentation to improve cross-person reenactment performance, DAE-GAN [51] utilizes a deforming autoencoder [31] to learn pose-invariant embedded faces, etc. The latest method [24] additionally involves an encoding for the actors facial layouts, which can further relieve the identity preservation problem in some sense. Overall, direct synthesis methods can handle a much wider range of head pose changes, however, the fidelity of the generated images is typically lower than their warping-based counterparts under the same condition, because the high-frequency details may easily be lost when projecting the source face into a low-dimensional appearance embedding space. Besides, direct synthesis backbones also tend to be slower than warping-based ones, because the motion fields provide strong priors about the motion information, while direct synthesis methods learn everything from scratch.

Hybrid Methods. Inspired by FS-VID2VID [41], hybrid methods [7,49] that combine warping and synthesis have been proposed. Bi-layer [49] combines them in a parallel fashion, i.e., a direct synthesis branch to generate low-frequency components of the face image and a warping-based branch to add high-frequency details. Such combination makes the fastest one-shot reenactment network ever (i.e., 25 fps inference speed for 256×256 resolution images on mobile GPU), however, its quality of results are clearly below state-of-the-art. Moreover, it is still not fast enough to support real-time face reenactment applications, because other required operations like facial landmark detection and GPU-CPU copy operations also cost nonignorable computational time. HeadGAN [7] combines them in another way, injecting the warped appearance features into a direct synthesis backbone. Such design achieves the best visual performance among

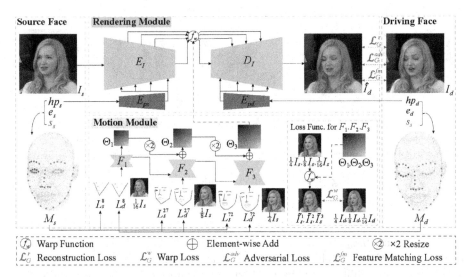

Fig. 2. Training pipeline of Face2Face$^\rho$. We first regress the 3DMM coefficients from the source image I_s and driving image I_d, and reconstruct three different scales of landmark images (i.e., L_s^n and L_d^n). The landmark images and the resized source images are fed to the motion module to coarse-to-finely predict facial motion fields, i.e., Θ_1, Θ_2 and Θ_3. Θ_3 and I_s are sent to the rendering module to generate the reenacted image $\hat{I}_d$. Head pose information is also injected into the encoder E_I and decoder D_I to improve the performances on large poses. The image sizes are adjusted for better illustration.

all existing algorithms but also makes HeadGAN [7] one of the most complex frameworks, unusable for time-critical applications. Face2Face$^\rho$ also follows the hybrid scheme, but we combine warping and synthesis in a new way. Specifically, we inject the pose encodings which are normally used in direct synthesis methods, into a warping-based generator backbone. We demonstrate that such architecture allows us to build a better one-shot face reenactment framework, which produces state-of-the-art results with significantly less time and memory overhead.

3   Method

The training pipeline of Face2Face$^\rho$ is illustrated in Fig. 2. For each pair of source and driving face images, we calculate their shape coefficients, expression coefficients, head poses, and landmark images with the help of 3DMM (Sect. 3.1), and then, the rendering module learns to synthesize the reenacted face image based on the source image, the estimated motion field, and the source/driving head pose pairs (Sect. 3.2), while the motion module learns to coarse-to-finely recover the motion fields from three different scales of landmark images (Sect. 3.3). Training and inference details are described in Sect. 3.4.

3.1   3DMM Fitting

Similar to previous methods [7,48], our method also relies on 3DMM [3] to disentangle face shape $s \in \mathbb{R}^{50}$, expression $e \in \mathbb{R}^{51}$ and head pose $hp \in \mathbb{R}^6$. We

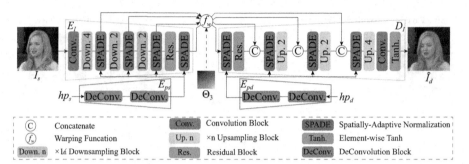

Fig. 3. Architecture of rendering module.

fit 3DMM to the source and driving image based on [44], yielding two vectors $[hp_s, e_s, s_s]$ and $[hp_d, e_d, s_d]$, where the subscripts s and d denote source and driving respectively. Each vector corresponds to a 3D face mesh in the 3DMM space. However, unlike previous methods, our framework does not require the entire face mesh to be constructed, thus, we only use the fitting 3DMM information to compute the locations of a set of pre-specified 3D keypoints (i.e., M_s and M_d) on the 3DMM face template. In our implementation, 72 keypoints were selected (as shown in Fig. 4) which are a subset of the 106-point facial landmark specification [20]. Using the standard 68-point specification [4] (i.e., two fewer points at the boundary of each eye) is also OK. It is also worth noting that, M_d is calculated using $[hp_d, e_d, s_s]$ rather than $[hp_d, e_d, s_d]$ to eliminate the interference of driving actor's identity.

3.2 Rendering Module

As mentioned before, the network structure of our rendering module is derived from a warping-based backbone. Previous warping-based methods [32–34,43] support at most 4 times downsampling. Further downsampling layers would quickly reduce the network's performance, resulting in intensive time and memory consumption when dealing with high-solution images. To address this problem, we present a much more effective rendering network architecture that supports 16 times downsampling without damaging the quality of results. The detailed structure of the rendering module is shown in Fig. 3, which is a u-shaped encoder-decoder architecture with a warp field applied to each connected feature map between the image encoder E_I and decoder D_I. Since each downsampling operation would discard some detail, we add skip connections to compensate for the information loss, as suggested in other high-speed rendering networks [23,54]. Such design allows the encoder to employ two additional downsampling blocks, making the network 3 times faster than previous warping-based backbones.

The major drawback of standard warping-based methods is that they can only handle a limited range of pose changes. Since using pose information to supervise the synthesis process proves to be an effective way to improve the robustness against large poses in recent direct synthesis approaches [5,50], we

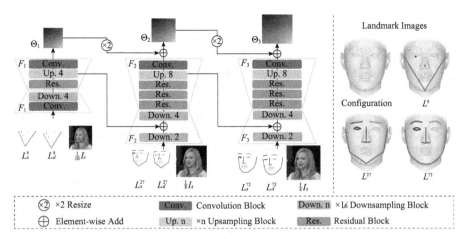

Fig. 4. Left: architecture of motion module, three scales of motion fields (i.e., $\frac{1}{16}$, $\frac{1}{8}$ and $\frac{1}{4}$ the size of the input image) are estimated from coarse to fine. Right: different scales of landmark images, top left shows the pre-configured 72 keypoints on the mesh template, and keypoints of the coarse-scale landmark images are subsets of these points.

inject pose encodings into the image encoder E_I and decoder D_I. The commonly used inputs to account for head poses are 2D facial landmarks [41,49,50], 3D facial landmarks [43] and rasterized 3DMM face meshes [7]. However, producing or processing such input information would cost non-negligible computational time. Alternatively, we directly provide the head rotations and translations estimated in the 3DMM fitting process, as pose encodings, to the rendering network. The 6-dimensional head pose vectors are reshaped into square matrices by deconvolution (i.e., E_{ps} and E_{pd}), and injected into the rendering backbone via SPADE [28]. Actually, AdaIn [11] can also be utilized for the same purpose, but the MLP layers therein tend to be more time-consuming. As no noticeable differences can be found between these two strategies in our experiments, we adopt SPADE [28] in our implementation.

3.3 Motion Module

The precision of the estimated motion field is of vital importance to a warping-based pipeline. As fitting 3DMM meshes have proven to be the best guidance information for such purpose [7,48], our motion module also follows a 3DMM-assisted fashion. However, different from previous 3DMM-assisted approaches which require the building and/or rendering of the entire face mesh, our method only needs to track the 3D positions of a small set of pre-configured 3D keypoints on the 3DMM template mesh, since a reasonable number of sparse keypoints are already sufficient to reveal the global motion field [32,33,43]. The tracked sparse 3D keypoints are then projected to the image space and transformed into a face sketch, which we refer to as a landmark image. The main advantage of such design is that it successfully avoids soft rasterizing (i.e., a very costly operation) the whole mesh, ensuring all inputs of the motion module to be quickly generated even on mobile CPUs.

The classic backbone for predicting the motion field is the single-scale hourglass network [32–34], effective but low-efficient. Inspired by recent optical flow estimation algorithms (e.g., [12]) which progressively produce high-resolution optical flow maps based on lower ones, we apply a similar coarse-to-fine strategy to motion field estimation, and successfully increase the inference speed of the motion branch by 3.5 times without sacrificing precision. As shown in Fig. 4, the motion module predicts three scales of motion fields Θ_1, Θ_2 and Θ_3, with three sub-networks F_1, F_2 and F_3 respectively. Each sub-network takes a different scale of the source and landmark images, and the feature maps after the upsampling block in each sub-network are accumulated to the subsequent sub-network to help convergence, as suggested in [42]. Notice that the number of keypoints n used when generating different scales of landmark images (i.e., L_s^n and L_d^n) also follows a coarse-to-fine scheme, where $n = 8, 27, 72$ (see right of Fig. 4).

3.4 Training and Inference

We train Face2Face$^\rho$ on the VoxCeleb dataset [26], which contains over 20k video sequences of different actors. For each video frame, we pre-compute its 3DMM coefficients as described in Sect. 3.1. Notice that the shape coefficients for the same video are forced to be identical in the 3DMM fitting process. Training pairs of source image I_s and driving image I_d are sampled from the same video. The rendering and motion module are jointly trained in an adversarial way for 380k iterations with a batch size of 6. We use an Adam [18] optimizer with $\beta_1 = 0.9$ and $\beta_2 = 0.999$, respectively. The learning rate is 0.0002 for the first 330k iterations and then linearly decays to 0. We adopt the commonly used training loss configuration in face reenactment [5,7,9,33,41,43], and the loss for the generator G (i.e., rendering and motion module) is calculated as:

$$\mathcal{L}_G = \lambda_G^r \mathcal{L}_G^r + \lambda_G^w \mathcal{L}_G^w + \lambda_G^{adv} \mathcal{L}_G^{adv} + \lambda_G^{fm} \mathcal{L}_G^{fm}, \tag{1}$$

where $\mathcal{L}_G^r$, $\mathcal{L}_G^w$, $\mathcal{L}_G^{adv}$ and $\mathcal{L}_G^{fm}$ denote the reconstruction loss, warp loss, adversarial loss, and feature matching loss respectively. The corresponding balancing weights λ's are set to 15, 500, 1 and 1, which are determined by grid searching.

The reconstruct loss $\mathcal{L}_G^r$ ensures the output image looks similar to the ground truth. Specifically, we adopt the perceptual loss of Wang et al. [43] to measure the distance between the driving image I_d and the synthesized image $\hat{I}_d$:

$$\mathcal{L}_G^r(I_d, \hat{I}_d) = \sum_{i=1}^{N} \left\| VGG_i(I_d) - VGG_i(\hat{I}_d) \right\|_1, \tag{2}$$

where $VGG_i(\cdot)$ is the ith feature layer extracted from a pre-trained VGG-19 network [15] and $N = 5$. We have tried adding an additional loss using a pre-trained VGGFace network [29], but no noticeable improvements in identity preservation can be observed. The reason is that the 3DMM already disentangles the identity (shape), expression and head pose, as discussed in [7,17,47].

Similar to [7,31,45], we also adopt a warping loss $\mathcal{L}_G^w$ to force the motion module to learn correct motion fields, which is defined as:

$$\mathcal{L}_G^w = \sum_{i=1}^{3} \left\| I_d - \widetilde{I}_s^i \right\|_1, \tag{3}$$

where $\widetilde{I}_s^i = f_w(I_s, \Theta_i)$ denotes the warped source image according to the ith motion field Θ_i. $f_w(\cdot, \cdot)$ is the warping function, which is implemented using a bilinear sampler. We downsample I_d to match the size of each warped image.

The generator is trained by minimizing an adversarial loss $\mathcal{L}_G^{adv}$ as well, which is calculated by using the PatchGAN discriminator D [13] and the least-square GAN objective [21]. According to [21], $\mathcal{L}_G^{adv}$ is defined as:

$$\mathcal{L}_G^{adv} = (D(\hat{I}_d, L_d^{72}) - 1)^2, \tag{4}$$

where L_d^{72} is the top-scale landmark image of the driving image. We also add a feature matching loss $\mathcal{L}_G^{fm}$ to help stabilize the training process [42]. The discriminator D is optimized by minimizing:

$$\mathcal{L}_{adv}^D = (D(I_d, L_d^{72}) - 1)^2 + D(\hat{I}_d, L_d^{72})^2. \tag{5}$$

During inference, the source actor's the 3DMM coefficients $[hp_s, e_s, s_s]$, landmark images L_s^n and encodings from E_I and E_{ps} in the rendering module can all be pre-computed and recorded in the offline phase, while the others are computed online (e.g., the driving actor's 3DMM coefficients $[hp_d, e_d, s_d]$, motion fields Θ_{1-3}, etc.). The inference speed is fast enough to support real-time applications on both PC and mobile devices. Demos are provided in the supplementary video.

4 Evaluation

In this section, we compare Face2Face$^\rho$ with the state-of-the-art works and perform an ablation study to evaluate some of our key design choices.

4.1 Comparisons

The state-of-the-art one-shot methods which we chose as the baselines are FS-VID2VID [41], Bi-layer [49], LPD [5], FOMM [33], MRAA [34] and HeadGAN [7]. For a fair comparison, all methods were implemented using PyTorch [30], and trained on the VoxCeleb dataset (i.e., randomly sampled 3M pairs for training and 3k pairs for testing). The authors' official implementations were used for Bi-layer, LPD, FOMM, MRAA and FS-VID2VID, while HeadGAN was implemented by ourselves since its source code was not publicly available. All models are trained using their recommended training configurations in the papers.

Table 1. Complexity comparisons. The inference time (Inf.) and GPU memory (Mem.) are measured on an Nvidia GeForce RTX 2080Ti GPU with FP32 and FP16 mode respectively. The "-" indicates unmeasurable, due to GPU memory limits or not supporting FP16 mode.

Method	256×256			512×512			1024×1024		
	MACs↓ ×10^9	Inf.(ms)↓ FP32/FP16	Mem.(GB)↓ FP32/FP16	MACs↓ ×10^9	Inf.(ms)↓ FP32/FP16	Mem.(GB)↓ FP32/FP16	MACs↓ ×10^9	Inf.(ms)↓ FP32/FP16	Mem.(GB)↓ FP32/FP16
FS-VID2VID	40.8	42.8/–	2.4/–	163.5	86.8/–	3.4/–	653.9	296.1/–	10.5/–
Bi-layer	3.8	5.6/5.4	0.9/0.9	15.3	12.6/10.0	1.1/1.0	61.2	36.2/25.8	1.9/1.6
LPD	30.3	11.8/10.1	1.3/1.0	121.2	27.9/18.5	1.7/1.3	484.9	95.6/53.9	3.2/2.6
FOMM	53.7	15.4/–	1.4/–	173.5	38.5/–	1.65/–	694.0	138.8/–	3.2/–
MRAA	53.7	15.6/–	1.4/–	173.5	39.1/–	1.65/–	694.0	145.9/–	3.2/–
HeadGAN	69.9	16.0/10.1	1.1/0.9	279.8	57.4/35.2	1.4/1.2	1119.4	224.3/147.2	3.1/2.3
Face2Face$^\rho$	**1.9**	**5.3/4.8**	**0.9/0.9**	**9.2**	**10.9/9.5**	**1.0/0.9**	**37.0**	**27.1/18.9**	**1.4/1.2**

Method	1440×1440			1536×1536			2048×2048		
	MACs↓ ×10^9	Inf.(ms)↓ FP32/FP16	Mem.(GB)↓ FP32/FP16	MACs↓ ×10^9	Inf.(ms)↓ FP32/FP16	Mem.(GB)↓ FP32/FP16	MACs↓ ×10^9	Inf.(ms)↓ FP32/FP16	Mem.(GB)↓ FP32/FP16
FS-VID2VID	–	–/–	–/–	–	–/–	–/–	–	–/–	–/–
Bi-layer	120.3	73.1/55.7	2.9/2.2	138.0	77.2/58.6	3.2/2.4	245.5	125.6/100.3	4.5/3.4
LPD	960.1	185.8/106.9	5.1/4.0	1091.2	198.9/114.3	5.6/4.3	1939.2	322.2/185.1	7.8/6.0
FOMM	1372.3	291.4/–	5.1/–	1561.4	310.4/–	5.7/–	2776.8	541.8/–	7.9/–
MRAA	1372.3	304.2/–	5.1/–	1561.4	327.6/–	5.8/–	2776.8	564.9/–	8.0/–
HeadGAN	2213.6	485.6/275.3	5.2/3.8	2518.6	518.4/295.6	5.8/4.2	4478.5	858.4/490.4	7.9/5.7
Face2Face$^\rho$	**71.8**	**52.1/32.5**	**1.8/1.6**	**82.8**	**56.7/34.8**	**2.0/1.8**	**146.2**	**95.8/60.2**	**2.7/2.4**

Notice that we omitted the side-by-side comparisons with some earlier works, e.g., X2Face [45] and FSTH [50], because their performances have been extensively compared and proved to be below our baselines [5,7,33,49]. Besides, a small-scale qualitative comparison with other state-of-the-art methods and also a many-shot method [36] are provided in the supplementary document.

Computational Complexity. We first evaluate the time and spatial complexity of each reenactment backbone in the inference phase. The time complexity is measured by the inference time and the number of multiply-accumulate operations (MACs), while the spatial complexity is measured by the run-time GPU memory overhead. The results shown in Table 1 demonstrate that Face2Face$^\rho$ is overwhelmingly superior in terms of computational complexity. Setting the speed requirement for real-time applications to 25 fps and considering the additional time (i.e., around 3–6 ms) required for some necessary auxiliary modules, only Bi-layer and LPD can handle 512×512 resolution images, and only Bi-layer still survives when the resolution increases to 1024×1024. In contrast, the resolution limit for Face2Face$^\rho$ is 1440×1440. We provide more high-resolution (i.e., 1440×1440) results synthesized by Face2Face$^\rho$ in the supplementary document.

Notice that there are currently no available high-resolution datasets that are suitable for the face reenactment task. So the high-resolution version of Face2Face$^\rho$ was trained using the upscaled images from VoxCeleb (i.e., 512×512), which inevitably limits the performance of Face2Face$^\rho$ on some true high-definition images. However, compared with the faked 1440×1440 results produced by simply upscaling the outputs of a 512×512 model, the results generated by a 1440×1440 model clearly have better visual quality (see supplementary document). Therefore, despite the absence of high-resolution datasets, supporting high-resolution images is still beneficial.

Source   Driving   FS-VID2VID Bi-layer   LPD   FOMM   MRAA   HeadGAN Face2Face$^\rho$

Fig. 5. Qualitative comparisons with the baselines, on the task of reenactment.

Reenactment. Next, we compare the quality of reenactment results. Since no ground truth is available for this task, we use FID [10] to measure image realism and use CSIM [6] to measure the identity gaps. We also adopt Average Rotation Distance (ARD) and Action Units Hamming distance (AU-H) used in [7] to evaluate the accuracy of the pose and expression transfer respectively. The statistics shown in Table 2 demonstrate that Face2Face$^\rho$ achieves state-of-the-art quality in each measurement. Figure 5 highlights some results where the source and the driving images have relatively large head pose differences, i.e., the head pose changes are from 30°–45° in either roll, pitch or yaw. Notice that the most recent works [7,43] that focus on pose editing typically only allow pose changes up to around 30°, so such range of pose variance can already be considered as *large* in one-shot face reenactment. From the results, we can see that methods HeadGAN and Face2Face$^\rho$ are clearly better than their counterparts. Methods with low CSIM scores (i.e., FS-VID2VID and Bi-layer) cannot correctly preserve the source actor's identity, while methods with high FID scores (i.e., Bi-layer and LPD) tend to generate blurry results. Besides, unnatural deformations can be observed in the results of two warping-based methods (i.e., MRAA and FOMM) when head pose deformations are large (e.g., last two rows of Fig. 5). Furthermore, since they both follow a relative motion transfer scheme, which cannot correctly transfer head pose when there are large pose gaps between the initial driving face and source face (e.g., first two rows of Fig. 5). Most importantly, the results demonstrate that Bi-layer sacrifices too much quality for fast inference speed, whereas Face2Face$^\rho$ achieves even faster inference speed without compromising quality. Notice that the CSIM/FID of FOMM and MRAA in Table 2 are inconsistent with their visual quality in Fig. 5, because Fig. 5 only highlights the cases of large head pose transformations while these scores are averaged over all 3k test pairs. The dynamic results shown in the supplementary video are better in line with these statistics. Besides, the video also demonstrates that our method

Source   Driving FS-VID2VID Bi-layer   LPD   FOMM   MRAA   HeadGAN Face2Face$^\rho$

Fig. 6. Qualitative comparisons with the baselines, on the task of reconstruction.

Table 2. Quantitative comparisons with the baselines.

Method	Reenactment				Reconstruction	
	FID↓	CSIM↑	ARD↓	AU-H↓	LPIPS↓	AKD↓
FS-VID2VID	57.3	0.571	3.43	0.29	0.167	3.20
Bi-layer	101.8	0.534	3.32	0.26	0.171	2.56
LPD	81.9	0.675	4.89	0.23	0.165	2.79
FOMM	46.8	0.736	7.61	0.27	0.160	2.44
MRAA	49.4	**0.741**	7.73	0.28	0.155	2.45
HeadGAN	48.1	0.690	3.06	0.23	0.137	1.49
Face2Face$^\rho$	**44.5**	0.729	**2.82**	**0.22**	**0.123**	**1.48**

Table 3. Quantitative comparisons with the ablation study cases.

Method	Reenactment				Reconstruction	
	FID↓	CSIM↑	ARD↓	AU-H↓	LPIPS↓	AKD↓
$r_1+p_0+m_0$	72.5	0.599	3.13	0.25	0.169	1.64
r_2+m_0	51.7	0.692	3.83	0.26	0.164	1.74
$r_0+p_1+m_0$	50.9	0.702	3.53	0.26	0.158	1.68
$r_0+p_2+m_0$	**43.4**	0.722	2.85	0.23	0.123	1.45
$r_0+p_3+m_0$	45.1	0.713	**2.81**	0.24	0.127	**1.44**
$r_0+p_0+m_1$	45.3	0.715	3.17	0.32	0.131	1.48
Face2Face$^\rho$	44.5	**0.729**	2.82	**0.22**	**0.123**	1.48

presents good temporal coherency though we do not explicitly enforce it in the training process (i.e., as did in [41]). This is achieved by a simple but effective strategy, i.e., applying bilateral filtering on the fitted 3DMM coefficients.

Reconstruction (Self-reenactment). Finally, we compare the results in the self-reenactment task (see Fig. 6), where the source and driving images are of the same actor. Since the driving image can also be viewed as the ground truth in this scenario, the reconstruction quality can be directly measured by comparing the similarity between the driving image and the synthesized image. In our experiments, the AlexNet-based LPIPS metric [53] and the average keypoint distance (AKD) [33] were adopted for such purpose. Statistics are also shown in Table 2, which demonstrate Face2Face$^\rho$ achieves the best scores in this task.

4.2   Ablation Study

In this section, we evaluate how some key choices would affect the performance of Face2Face$^\rho$. For clarity purposes, we denote the proposed rendering module,

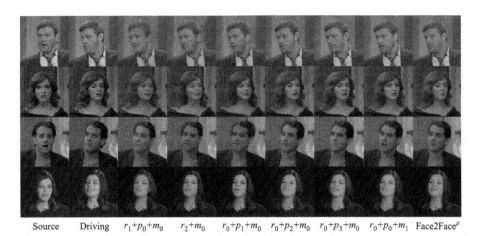

Source   Driving $r_1{+}p_0{+}m_0$ $r_2{+}m_0$ $r_0{+}p_1{+}m_0$ $r_0{+}p_2{+}m_0$ $r_0{+}p_3{+}m_0$ $r_0{+}p_0{+}m_1$ Face2Face$^\rho$

Fig. 7. Qualitative comparisons with the ablation study cases.

3DMM head pose encoding network and motion module as r_0, p_0 and m_0 respectively. Then, the alternatives to be studied can be defined as follows. 1) r_1: r_0 without skip connections, 2) r_2: r_0 without head pose injection, 3) p_1: 2D landmarks for pose encoding, 4) p_2: 3D landmarks for pose encoding, 5) p_3: depth map for pose encoding, 6) m_1: single-scale motion estimation network used in [32,33], with the number of channels reduced to match the complexity of m_0.

The results of different combinations are shown in Table 3, Fig. 7 and the supplementary video. We can see that r_1 and r_2 tend to have problems in large head pose changes, expressions generated by m_1 are often inconsistent with the driving actor (see the eyes and mouths in the 2nd and 3rd rows of Fig. 7)), and the performance of head pose encoding p_0 is almost equal to p_2 and p_3, despite p_2 and p_3 consume more computational time (i.e., 2–5 ms). Notice that using 2D landmarks for pose encoding p_1 actually does not help in handling large poses. Besides, we also conduct another ablation study to assess the significance of each loss term in the supplementary document.

4.3   Limitation

While our framework is generally robust, it shares some common limitations with other state-of-the-art one-shot methods. As illustrated in Fig. 8, some visible artifacts may appear in the background regions when the head transformations are large, and abnormal objects (e.g., hands or microphone) in the foreground may lead to blurry results.

5   Mobile Device Deployment

We use MNN [14] to deploy Face2Face$^\rho$ on mobile devices (see the supplementary video for a mobile demo). The 3DMM fitting and landmark image generation

Source   Driving   Face2Face$^\rho$ Source   Driving   Face2Face$^\rho$

Fig. 8. Example limitations. Left: large pose modification sometimes cause visible artifacts in the background. Right: abnormal objects (e.g., hands or microphone) in the foreground may lead to blurry results.

Table 4. Running time for different resolution images on Mobile CPU (Kryo 680, 4 threads) and GPU (Adreno 660, FP16).

Step	256×256 CPU/GPU (ms)	384×384 CPU/GPU (ms)	512×512 CPU/GPU (ms)
3DMM fitting	6.9	7.0	7.1
Landmark image generation	0.1	0.1	0.2
Motion field estimation	5.6/4.1	11.2/5.7	16.3/8.9
Feature warping	1.5/0.5	4.0/0.6	8.9/0.7
Decoding	25.1/12.7	59.9/27.5	110.7/49.4
GPU-CPU communication	–/3.8	–/16.7	–/29.1
Total	39.2/28.1	82.2/57.6	143.2/95.4

run on the CPU, while all other steps run on the CPU or the GPU. The running time for each step is listed in Table 4. As can be seen, Face2Face$^\rho$ only requires a Mobile CPU to achieve real-time performance for images of 256×256 resolution. Theoretically, Face2Face$^\rho$ supports higher resolution images when running on the GPU, but the expensive GPU-CPU communication operations limit its ability.

6 Conclusion

In this paper, we present Face2Face$^\rho$, the first real-time high-resolution one-shot face reenactment framework that consists of two fast and efficient networks: a u-shaped rendering network and a hierarchical coarse-to-fine motion network. Experimental results demonstrate that Face2Face$^\rho$ achieves state-of-the-art quality, while significantly reducing the computational complexity. Specifically, it can run in real-time for generating face images of 1440×1440 resolution with a desktop GPU and 256×256 resolution with a mobile CPU.

Besides, our method supports using a single photo to generate an inauthentic video, so it has the potential to be used for illegal activities. A prime example of this is the growing misuse of DeepFakes [25,39]. However, as more and more people can access such techniques, the threat has also become more well-aware. Accordingly, image forensic techniques [22,40] have been proposed. As there is no guarantee to detect all fake images by these methods, it is strictly prohibited to use our method to generate and publish unauthorized videos.

Acknowledgements. We thank Weitong Yao for his help in presenting our supplementary video.

References

1. Alexander, O., et al.: The digital emily project: achieving a photorealistic digital actor. IEEE Comput. Graphics Appl. **30**(4), 20–31 (2010)
2. Averbuch-Elor, H., Cohen-Or, D., Kopf, J., Cohen, M.F.: Bringing portraits to life. ACM TOG **36**(6), 1–13 (2017)
3. Blanz, V., Vetter, T.: A morphable model for the synthesis of 3D faces. In: SIGGRAPH, pp. 187–194 (1999)
4. Bulat, A., Tzimiropoulos, G.: How far are we from solving the 2D & 3D face alignment problem? (and a dataset of 230,000 3D facial landmarks). In: ICCV, pp. 1021–1030 (2017)
5. Burkov, E., Pasechnik, I., Grigorev, A., Lempitsky, V.: Neural head reenactment with latent pose descriptors. In: CVPR, pp. 13786–13795 (2020)
6. Deng, J., Guo, J., Xue, N., Zafeiriou, S.: ArcFace: additive angular margin loss for deep face recognition. In: CVPR, pp. 4690–4699 (2019)
7. Doukas, M.C., Zafeiriou, S., Sharmanska, V.: HeadGAN: one-shot neural head synthesis and editing. In: ICCV, pp. 14398–14407 (2021)
8. Garrido, P., et al.: VDub: modifying face video of actors for plausible visual alignment to a dubbed audio track. Comput. Graph. Forum **34**(2), 193–204 (2015)
9. Ha, S., Kersner, M., Kim, B., Seo, S., Kim, D.: MarioNETte: few-shot face reenactment preserving identity of unseen targets. In: AAAI, pp. 10893–10900 (2020)
10. Heusel, M., Ramsauer, H., Unterthiner, T., Nessler, B., Hochreiter, S.: GANs trained by a two time-scale update rule converge to a local nash equilibrium. In: NIPS, pp. 6626–6637 (2017)
11. Huang, X., Belongie, S.: Arbitrary style transfer in real-time with adaptive instance normalization. In: ICCV, pp. 1501–1510 (2017)
12. Huang, Z., Zhang, T., Heng, W., Shi, B., Zhou, S.: RIFE: real-time intermediate flow estimation for video frame interpolation. arXiv preprint arXiv:2011.06294 (2020)
13. Isola, P., Zhu, J.Y., Zhou, T., Efros, A.A.: Image-to-Image translation with conditional adversarial networks. In: CVPR, pp. 1125–1134 (2017)
14. Jiang, X., et al.: MNN: a universal and efficient inference engine. In: MLSys (2020)
15. Johnson, J., Alahi, A., Fei-Fei, L.: Perceptual losses for real-time style transfer and super-resolution. In: Leibe, B., Matas, J., Sebe, N., Welling, M. (eds.) ECCV 2016. LNCS, vol. 9906, pp. 694–711. Springer, Cham (2016). https://doi.org/10.1007/978-3-319-46475-6_43
16. Kim, H., et al.: Neural style-preserving visual dubbing. ACM TOG **38**(6), 1–13 (2019)
17. Kim, H., et al.: Deep video portraits. ACM TOG **37**(4), 1–14 (2018)
18. Kingma, D.P., Ba, J.: Adam: a method for stochastic optimization. In: ICLR (2015)
19. Koujan, M.R., Doukas, M.C., Roussos, A., Zafeiriou, S.: Head2Head: video-based neural head synthesis. In: FG, pp. 16–23 (2020)
20. Liu, Y., et al.: Grand challenge of 106-point facial landmark localization. In: ICMEW, pp. 613–616. IEEE (2019)
21. Mao, X., Li, Q., Xie, H., Lau, R.Y., Wang, Z., Paul Smolley, S.: Least squares generative adversarial networks. In: ICCV, pp. 2794–2802 (2017)

22. Marra, F., Gragnaniello, D., Cozzolino, D., Verdoliva, L.: Detection of GAN-generated fake images over social networks. In: MIPR, pp. 384–389. IEEE (2018)
23. Martin-Brualla, R., et al.: LookinGood: enhancing performance capture with real-time neural re-rendering. ACM TOG **37**(6), 1–14 (2018)
24. Meshry, M., Suri, S., Davis, L.S., Shrivastava, A.: Learned spatial representations for few-shot talking-head synthesis. In: ICCV, pp. 13829–13838 (2021)
25. Mirsky, Y., Lee, W.: The creation and detection of deepfakes: a survey. ACM Comput. Surv. **54**(1), 1–41 (2021)
26. Nagrani, A., Chung, J.S., Zisserman, A.: VoxCeleb: a large-scale speaker identification dataset. In: INTERSPEECH, pp. 2616–2620 (2017)
27. Nirkin, Y., Keller, Y., Hassner, T.: FSGAN: subject agnostic face swapping and reenactment. In: ICCV, pp. 7184–7193 (2019)
28. Park, T., Liu, M.Y., Wang, T.C., Zhu, J.Y.: Semantic image synthesis with spatially-adaptive normalization. In: CVPR, pp. 2337–2346 (2019)
29. Parkhi, O.M., Vedaldi, A., Zisserman, A.: Deep face recognition. In: BMVC (2015)
30. Paszke, A., et al.: PyTorch: an imperative style, high-performance deep learning library. In: NIPS, pp. 8024–8035 (2019)
31. Shu, Z., Sahasrabudhe, M., Alp Güler, R., Samaras, D., Paragios, N., Kokkinos, I.: Deforming autoencoders: unsupervised disentangling of shape and appearance. In: Ferrari, V., Hebert, M., Sminchisescu, C., Weiss, Y. (eds.) ECCV 2018. LNCS, vol. 11214, pp. 664–680. Springer, Cham (2018). https://doi.org/10.1007/978-3-030-01249-6_40
32. Siarohin, A., Lathuilière, S., Tulyakov, S., Ricci, E., Sebe, N.: Animating arbitrary objects via deep motion transfer. In: CVPR, pp. 2377–2386 (2019)
33. Siarohin, A., Lathuilière, S., Tulyakov, S., Ricci, E., Sebe, N.: First order motion model for image animation. In: Advances in Neural Information Processing Systems, pp. 7135–7145 (2019)
34. Siarohin, A., Woodford, O.J., Ren, J., Chai, M., Tulyakov, S.: Motion representations for articulated animation. In: CVPR, pp. 13653–13662 (2021)
35. Suwajanakorn, S., Seitz, S.M., Kemelmacher-Shlizerman, I.: Synthesizing Obama: learning lip sync from audio. ACM TOG **36**(4), 1–13 (2017)
36. Thies, J., Elgharib, M., Tewari, A., Theobalt, C., Nießner, M.: Neural voice puppetry: audio-driven facial reenactment. In: Vedaldi, A., Bischof, H., Brox, T., Frahm, J.-M. (eds.) ECCV 2020. LNCS, vol. 12361, pp. 716–731. Springer, Cham (2020). https://doi.org/10.1007/978-3-030-58517-4_42
37. Thies, J., Zollhöfer, M., Nießner, M.: Deferred neural rendering: image synthesis using neural textures. ACM TOG **38**(4), 1–12 (2019)
38. Thies, J., Zollhofer, M., Stamminger, M., Theobalt, C., Nießner, M.: Face2Face: real-time face capture and reenactment of RGB videos. In: CVPR, pp. 2387–2395 (2016)
39. Tolosana, R., Vera-Rodriguez, R., Fierrez, J., Morales, A., Ortega-Garcia, J.: Deepfakes and beyond: a survey of face manipulation and fake detection. Information Fusion **64**, 131–148 (2020)
40. Wang, S.Y., Wang, O., Zhang, R., Owens, A., Efros, A.A.: CNN-generated images are surprisingly easy to spot... for now. In: CVPR, pp. 8695–8704 (2020)
41. Wang, T., Liu, M., Tao, A., Liu, G., Catanzaro, B., Kautz, J.: Few-shot video-to-video synthesis. In: NIPS, pp. 5014–5025 (2019)
42. Wang, T.C., Liu, M.Y., Zhu, J.Y., Tao, A., Kautz, J., Catanzaro, B.: High-resolution image synthesis and semantic manipulation with conditional GANs. In: CVPR, pp. 8798–8807 (2018)

43. Wang, T.C., Mallya, A., Liu, M.Y.: One-shot free-view neural talking-head synthesis for video conferencing. In: CVPR, pp. 10039–10049 (2021)
44. Weng, Y., Cao, C., Hou, Q., Zhou, K.: Real-time facial animation on mobile devices. Graph. Models **76**(3), 172–179 (2014)
45. Wiles, O., Koepke, A.S., Zisserman, A.: X2Face: a network for controlling face generation using images, audio, and pose codes. In: Ferrari, V., Hebert, M., Sminchisescu, C., Weiss, Y. (eds.) ECCV 2018. LNCS, vol. 11217, pp. 690–706. Springer, Cham (2018). https://doi.org/10.1007/978-3-030-01261-8_41
46. Wu, W., Zhang, Y., Li, C., Qian, C., Loy, C.C.: ReenactGAN: learning to reenact faces via boundary transfer. In: Ferrari, V., Hebert, M., Sminchisescu, C., Weiss, Y. (eds.) ECCV 2018. LNCS, vol. 11205, pp. 622–638. Springer, Cham (2018). https://doi.org/10.1007/978-3-030-01246-5_37
47. Yao, G., et al.: One-shot face reenactment using appearance adaptive normalization. In: AAAI, pp. 3172–3180 (2021)
48. Yao, G., Yuan, Y., Shao, T., Zhou, K.: Mesh guided one-shot face reenactment using graph convolutional networks. In: ACM MM, pp. 1773–1781 (2020)
49. Zakharov, E., Ivakhnenko, A., Shysheya, A., Lempitsky, V.: Fast bi-layer neural synthesis of one-shot realistic head avatars. In: Vedaldi, A., Bischof, H., Brox, T., Frahm, J.-M. (eds.) ECCV 2020. LNCS, vol. 12357, pp. 524–540. Springer, Cham (2020). https://doi.org/10.1007/978-3-030-58610-2_31
50. Zakharov, E., Shysheya, A., Burkov, E., Lempitsky, V.: Few-shot adversarial learning of realistic neural talking head models. In: ICCV, pp. 9459–9468 (2019)
51. Zeng, X., Pan, Y., Wang, M., Zhang, J., Liu, Y.: Realistic face reenactment via self-supervised disentangling of identity and pose. In: AAAI, pp. 12757–12764 (2020)
52. Zhang, J., et al.: FReeNet: multi-identity face reenactment. In: CVPR, pp. 5326–5335 (2020)
53. Zhang, R., Isola, P., Efros, A.A., Shechtman, E., Wang, O.: The unreasonable effectiveness of deep features as a perceptual metric. In: CVPR, pp. 586–595 (2018)
54. Zhang, R., et al.: Real-time user-guided image colorization with learned deep priors. ACM TOG **36**(4), 1–11 (2017)

Towards Racially Unbiased Skin Tone Estimation via Scene Disambiguation

Haiwen Feng, Timo Bolkart, Joachim Tesch, Michael J. Black, and Victoria Abrevaya[⊠]

Max Planck Institute for Intelligent Systems, Tübingen, Germany
{hfeng,tbolkart,jtesch,black,vabrevaya}@tuebingen.mpg.de

Abstract. Virtual facial avatars will play an increasingly important role in immersive communication, games and the metaverse, and it is therefore critical that they be inclusive. This requires accurate recovery of the albedo, regardless of age, sex, or ethnicity. While significant progress has been made on estimating 3D facial geometry, appearance estimation has received less attention. The task is fundamentally ambiguous because the observed color is a function of albedo and lighting, both of which are unknown. We find that current methods are biased towards light skin tones due to (1) strongly biased priors that prefer lighter pigmentation and (2) algorithmic solutions that disregard the light/albedo ambiguity. To address this, we propose a new evaluation dataset (FAIR) and an algorithm (TRUST) to improve albedo estimation and, hence, fairness. Specifically, we create the first facial albedo evaluation benchmark where subjects are balanced in terms of skin color, and measure accuracy using the Individual Typology Angle (ITA) metric. We then address the light/albedo ambiguity by building on a key observation: the image of the full scene –as opposed to a cropped image of the face– contains important information about lighting that can be used for disambiguation. TRUST regresses facial albedo by conditioning on both the face region and a global illumination signal obtained from the scene image. Our experimental results show significant improvement compared to state-of-the-art methods on albedo estimation, both in terms of accuracy and fairness. The evaluation benchmark and code are available for research purposes at https://trust.is.tue.mpg.de.

1 Introduction

For critical systems such as face recognition, automated decision making or medical diagnosis, the development of machine-learning-based methods has been followed by questions about how to make their decisions fair to all sectors of the population [1,8,32,46]. For example, Buolamwini and Gebru [8] identify race and gender biases in face analysis methods, which disproportionately misclassify

---

Supplementary Information The online version contains supplementary material available at https://doi.org/10.1007/978-3-031-19778-9_5.

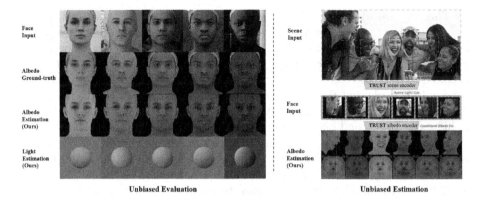

Fig. 1. FAIR (left) is a new dataset for unbiased albedo estimation that uses high-quality facial scans, varied lighting, and a new evaluation metric to benchmark current approaches in terms of accuracy and fairness. We also propose a new network, **TRUST** (right), for facial albedo estimation that reduces bias by addressing the light/albedo ambiguity using scene disambiguation cues.

dark-skinned females; Rajkomar et al. [50] note an influence of historical biases in machine learning methods for health care; and Kim et al. [30] point out how rendering algorithms in computer graphics are designed mostly for light-skinned people.

However, no such analysis exists for the task of 3D facial avatar creation. Here the problem involves estimating the 3D geometry and albedo from one or more images, where albedo is defined as a texture map corresponding to the diffuse reflection of the face (including skin tone, lips, eye, etc.). With growing interest in on-line virtual communication, gaming, and the metaverse, the role of facial avatars in our lives will likely increase. It is then critical that such technology is equally accessible to all and that every person can be represented faithfully, independent of gender, age, or skin color.

In this paper we address, for the first time, the problem of fairness in 3D avatar creation from images in-the-wild, and show that current methods are biased towards estimating albedo with a light skin color. While skin-tone bias has been extensively studied in the field of face recognition [18,62], here we examine a different problem. Specifically, we consider bias within methods that *regress* facial albedo (of which skin tone is only one aspect) and discuss the particular challenges that this involves. We analyze three main sources for this bias. First, existing statistical albedo models are trained from unbalanced datasets, producing strongly biased priors. Second, existing albedo regression methods are unable to factor lighting from albedo. When combined with a biased prior, they simply infer dim illumination to compensate for dark skin. Finally, there is, to date, no standard evaluation protocol that quantitatively reveals bias in albedo estimation. This has led to the field largely ignoring issues of fairness in albedo estimation.

This work makes several key contributions to advance fairness in facial albedo estimation. First, we create a new dataset of realistic synthetic images of faces in varying lighting conditions. We use this dataset, together with specifically designed metrics, as a benchmark for evaluating accuracy and fairness of facial albedo reconstruction (Fig. 1, left); we call the benchmark FAIR for Facial Albedo Independent of Race. With this we are able, for the first time, to quantify the bias of existing methods. We find that all existing methods are biased to light skin tones, and analyze the technical reasons behind this.

Finally, we introduce a new neural network model called TRUST (Towards Racially Unbiased Skin Tone estimation) that produces state-of-the-art results in terms of accuracy, as well as less biased albedo estimates (Fig. 1, right). The key to TRUST is the design of a novel architecture and losses that explicitly address the light/albedo ambiguity. Specifically, we propose a two-branch network to leverage scene cues for disambiguation. The first branch recovers the illumination signal in the form of Spherical Harmonics (SH) [51], both from the entire scene image and the individual facial crops. The second branch estimates diffuse albedo from the individual crops, conditioned on the intensity of the SH vector. This provides cues about the global illumination and helps the albedo network to better decide on the overall skin tone. The network is further coupled with a new statistical albedo model trained using a balanced sample of subjects. The proposed approach achieves 56% improvement over the best alternative method when evaluated on the new FAIR benchmark, highlighting the importance of tackling fairness both from the dataset and the algorithmic point of view.

In summary, our contributions are: (1) We identify, analyze and quantify the problem of biased facial albedo estimation. (2) We propose a new synthetic benchmark, as well as new metrics that measure performance in terms of skin tone and diversity. (3) We propose a solution for albedo estimation that significantly improves fairness by explicitly addressing the light/albedo ambiguity problem through scene disambiguation cues. (4) The benchmark, code, and model are publicly available for research purposes.

2   Related Work

3D Face and Appearance Estimation. Face albedo estimation is typically approached as an inverse rendering problem, in which face geometry, reflectance and illumination parameters are estimated from a single image. Methods can be roughly categorized into optimization-based [2,6,7,56,66] and learning-based [11,16,22,26,29,58,65]; see Egger et al. [20] for a review. The majority of these estimate appearance parameters of a 3D morphable model (3DMM) [7,27,48] trained from two-hundred white European subjects. This lack of diversity results in a strong bias towards light-skinned appearance when jointly estimating reflectance and lighting.

To obtain more varied appearance, Smith et al. [61] build an albedo model from light-stage data, and Gecer et al. [25] build a neural generative model from 10 K texture maps. Several other methods learn flexible appearance models directly from images, while jointly learning to reconstruct 3D shape and appearance [10,40,54,57,60,63,64,67,68,70]. Another line of work synthesizes high-frequency appearance details from images [37,55,72]. All of these methods treat the face in isolation by only analyzing a tightly cropped face region. In contrast, our approach exploits cues from the entire scene that help decouple albedo from lighting in unconstrained in-the-wild images.

A related line of work directly estimates *skin tone* from images – i.e. a single vector value (e.g. RGB) that summarizes the color of the face. This can be used as a proxy for color correction [5,12,43] and for cosmetology purposes [33,34]. Here we focus on estimating the full albedo map, but evaluate the accuracy of both albedo and skin tone, with the goal of identifying potential fairness issues.

Disambiguating Appearance and Lighting. Given the RGB values of a pixel, the proportion of color explained by light versus intrinsic appearance cannot be recovered without further knowledge [51]. While the use of a statistical appearance prior limits the variability of the intrinsic face color, it does not fully resolve the ambiguity. To address this, Aldrian et al. [2] regularize the light by imposing a "gray world" constraint that encourages the environment to be, on average, gray. Hu et al. [28] regularize the albedo by imposing symmetry, thus preventing illumination variation from strong point lights being explained by the appearance. Egger et al. [19] learn a statistical prior of in-the-wild SH coefficients and use this to constrain the light in an inverse rendering application. These methods impose priors or regularizers over the estimated light or appearance, using heuristics to complement the statistical face model. Instead of using the tightly cropped face in isolation, we estimate the environment light from the scene and use this in learning to disambiguate light and albedo.

Racial Face Bias. Several works identify demographic bias (sex, age, race) for algorithms in the context of biometrics (e.g., face verification, age estimation, race classification, emotion classification, etc.); see Drozdowski et al. [18] for a review. Dedicated benchmark datasets were proposed in [53,69] to support the study of racial biases in face recognition. Wang et al. [69] show bias in four commercial face recognition systems, and propose an algorithmic solution to mitigate this. Buolamwini and Gebru [8] report bias in gender classification systems correlated to skin tone and sex, where darker-skinned females are misclassified most frequently. Kim et al. [30] describe racial bias in existing quantitative metrics used to group skin colors and hair types, and propose an evaluation scheme based on complex numbers to alleviate this bias. No other previous work has quantitatively assessed bias in facial albedo estimation methods, nor is there any existing dataset for this task. Hence, FAIR provides an important new resource to the community.

3   Dataset and Metrics for Quantifying Skin Tone Bias

To develop unbiased algorithms it is important to first identify potential problems. Since it is difficult to acquire ground-truth appearance, there is to date no

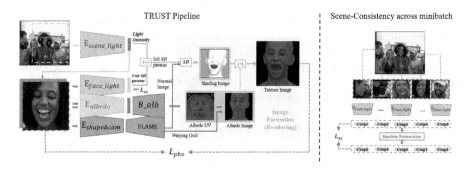

Fig. 2. We address biased albedo estimates by tackling the light/albedo ambiguity using scene disambiguation cues. Given an image of a scene with faces, we first obtain the 3-channel global light intensity factor using the E_{scene_light} encoder. We next extract facial crops, and condition the albedo encoder E_{albedo} by concatenating the intensity as an extra channel to the input. Finally, a crop-based light encoder E_{face_light} estimates normalized SH parameters, which are combined with the color intensity to obtain the final light estimate for the crop. The network is trained using a scene consistency loss, which requires the light from all faces in an image to be the same (i.e. permutation invariant).

albedo evaluation dataset available, much less one that covers a wide range of ethnicities and scenes. To address this, we describe a new dataset for evaluating single-image albedo reconstruction methods, constructed using high-quality facial scans. We additionally propose a set of metrics that measure fidelity of the estimated albedo, as well as accuracy and diversity of the overall skin tone.

Balancing skin type There are many types of bias but here we focus on skin color, which means we need an evaluation dataset that is balanced across this factor. There are several ways to quantify the skin color of a person. While self-reported ethnicity labels are commonly used in the literature (e.g. [38,69]), ethnicity is not well defined and there can be a large variety of skin types within ethnic groups. In dermatology, an extensively used system is the Fitzpatrick scale [23], employed also in computer vision research for balancing datasets [8,17,36, 71]. However, the scale is based on subjective assessments of skin sensitivity and tanning ability, and it has been shown to work sub-optimally for certain populations [49,73]. Instead, we employ the Individual Typology Angle (ITA) [9], also recently considered in [45]. The metric is based on the L* (lightness) and B* (yellow/blue) components of the CIE L*a*b* color space, and is computed as

$$\text{ITA}(L^*, b^*) = \frac{\arctan(\frac{L^*-50}{b^*}) \times 180}{\pi}. \tag{1}$$

We consider the ITA score of an albedo map to be the average of all pixel-wise ITA values within a pre-computed skin region area (defined on the UV map). ITA can be used to classify the skin according to six categories, ranging from very light (category I) to dark (category VI) [9, 15]. It has the advantage of being an objective metric, easily computable from images, and significantly correlated with skin pigmentation [14]. More details can be found in Sup. Mat.

Dataset Construction. The dataset is constructed using 206 high-quality 3D head scans purchased from Triplegangers[1]. The scans were selected such that they cover a relatively balanced range of sexes and skin colors (ITA skin group). Ages range from 18 to 78 years old. All of the scans were captured under neutral expression and uniform lighting. We obtain UV texture maps compatible with FLAME [39] by registering the FLAME model to the scans using the approach in [39] and we treat the texture maps as approximate ground-truth albedo.

To create a photo-realistic dataset we rendered the scans in complex scenes. Specifically, we used 50 HDR environment maps from Poly Haven[2] covering both natural and artificial lighting. In each scene we rendered three head scans under the same illumination. To ensure a balanced distribution of skin types, each image was constructed by first randomly selecting a skin type, and then randomly selecting a sample scan within the type. Our final testing dataset contains 721 images and 2163 facial crops under different illumination, with approximate ground-truth UV maps. Details and examples are provided in Sup. Mat.

Evaluation Metrics. To focus on both accuracy and fairness, we use the following metrics:

- ITA Error. We compute fidelity of skin tone by taking the average error in ITA (degrees, see Eq. 1) between predicted and ground-truth UV maps, over a skin mask region (see Sup. Mat.). We report average error per skin type (I to VI), as well as average ITA error across all groups.

- Bias Score. We quantify the *bias* of a method in terms of skin color by measuring the standard deviation across the *per-group* ITA errors (note that this is not the same as the standard deviation over the full dataset). A low value indicates roughly equal performance (i.e. unbiased) across all skin tones.

- Total Score. We summarize average ITA and bias score into a single score, which is the sum of the two.

- MAE. We also report results with a commonly employed image metric, namely mean average error. Here we calculate errors over the entire UV map, as opposed to only the skin region.

---

[1] https://triplegangers.com/.
[2] https://polyhaven.com/.

Fairness of Albedo Estimates of Current Methods. Using the above evaluation criteria, we benchmark several recent methods for facial albedo estimation from images in the wild. These are summarized in the top rows of Tab. 1. When observing the "ITA per skin type" column, we note that the accuracy of all methods varies with skin type, performing best on those values that are better represented by the statistical model[3]. In particular, extreme skin types such as I and VI tend to have noticeably larger errors. Low (bold) numbers for some types and high ones for others on each line indicates bias. An unbiased algorithm should have roughly equal errors across skin types.

4   Reasons Behind Racially Biased Albedo Estimations

Recovering the 3D shape and appearance of an object from a single RGB image is a highly ill-posed problem due to fundamental ambiguities arising from the interplay between geometry [4,21] and lighting [51] in the image formation process. For known objects such as the human face, a standard strategy is to use a strong prior in the form of a low-dimensional statistical model, e.g. the 3D Morphable Model (3DMM) [7,48] and its variants [13,39,61], to constrain the solution to the space of valid shapes and appearances. This idea has been widely adopted and has led to impressive advances in the field [20]. Yet, no careful consideration has been given to ensure that the models cover a balanced demographic distribution; indeed, the most widely used appearance model [48] was built using two-hundred white subjects. Several 3DMM variants have been made available (e.g. [38,61]) but none of them ensure a balanced distribution of skin tones. It is worth noting that a biased albedo model, employed within a neural network, can still be trained to produce outputs that are far away from the statistical mean. This is the case for example of MGCNet [58] (see Tab. 1), which uses low regularization weights to extrapolate results for type V skin tones. However, these are noisy estimates that do not faithfully represent the albedo, and the model still cannot extrapolate to type VI skin tones.

Even if one had an unbiased statistical model of face albedo, the problem remains ill-posed, leading to an *algorithmic* source of bias [44]. There is a fundamental ambiguity between scene lighting and albedo that cannot be resolved without strong assumptions [51]. Even with a good statistical model of face albedo, there are an infinite number of valid combinations of light and albedo that can explain the image. For example, an image of a darked-skin person can be explained by both dark skin and a bright light, or light skin and a dim light. This can be easily observed by looking at the shading equation commonly used for diffuse objects:

$$I_R = I_A \odot I_S, \tag{2}$$

where I_R is the final rendered image, I_S is the shading image, I_A is the albedo image, and $\odot$ denotes the Hadamard product. When both the albedo and light

---

[3] For GANFIT [25], the albedos contain a significant amount of baked-in lighting, and were captured with lower light conditions, hence the tendency to do well on dark skin tones.

Table 1. Comparison to state of the art on the FAIR benchmark. We show: average ITA error over all skin types; bias score (standard deviation); total score (avg. ITA+Bias); mean average error; and avg. ITA score per skin type in degrees (I: very light, VI: very dark). Our method achieves more balanced estimates, as can be seen in the bias score, as well as accurate skin color predictions.

Method	Avg. ITA ↓	Bias ↓	Score ↓	MAE ↓	ITA per skin type ↓					
					I	II	III	IV	V	VI
Deng et al. [16]	22.57	24.44	47.02	27.98	**8.92**	9.08	8.15	10.90	28.48	69.90
GANFIT [25]	62.29	31.81	94.11	63.31	94.80	87.83	76.25	65.05	38.24	**11.59**
MGCNet [58]	21.41	17.58	38.99	25.17	19.98	12.76	8.53	9.21	22.66	55.34
DECA [22]	28.74	29.24	57.98	38.17	9.34	11.66	11.58	16.69	39.10	84.06
INORig [3]	27.68	28.18	55.86	33.20	23.25	11.88	**4.86**	9.75	35.78	80.54
CEST [70]	35.18	12.14	47.32	29.92	50.98	38.77	29.22	23.62	21.92	46.57
Ours (BFM)	16.19	15.33	31.52	21.82	12.44	**6.48**	5.69	9.47	16.67	46.37
Ours (AlbedoMM)	17.72	15.28	33.00	19.48	15.50	10.48	8.42	**7.86**	**15.96**	48.11
Ours (BalancedAlb)	**13.87**	**2.79**	**16.67**	**18.41**	11.90	11.87	11.20	13.92	16.15	18.21

are unknown there is a scale ambiguity: for a fixed target image I_R, an increase in I_S by a factor of s results in a decrease in I_A by a factor of $1/s$. Given that skin tone dominates the albedo color in I_A, an overly bright estimate of the light will result in an overly dark estimate of the skin tone, and vice-versa. To address this we next propose a method that exploits scene lighting to reduce ambiguity in conjunction with an improved prior.

5   Unbiased Estimation via Scene Disambiguation Cues

Resolving the ambiguity above requires additional information. While most methods in the literature work with a cropped face image, our key insight is that the larger image contains important disambiguation cues.

5.1   Model

We begin by describing the image formation model employed throughout this work.

Geometry. We reconstruct geometry using the FLAME [39] statistical model, which parameterizes a face/head mesh using identity $\beta \in \mathbb{R}^{|\beta|}$, pose $\theta \in \mathbb{R}^{3k+3}$ (with $k = 4$ the number of joints), and expression $\psi \in \mathbb{R}^{|\psi|}$ latent vectors.

Albedo. We use a low-dimensional linear model to represent diffuse albedo. To avoid the biases present in current publicly available models, we purchased 54 uniformly lit 3D head scans from 3DScanStore[4], covering the full range of

---

[4] https://www.3dscanstore.com/.

skin types as measured by the ITA score. We converted these into the $d \times d$ FLAME UV texture space, and used Principal Component Analysis (PCA) to learn a model that, given albedo parameters $\alpha \in \mathbb{R}^{|\alpha|}$, outputs a UV albedo map $A(\alpha) \in \mathbb{R}^{d \times d \times 3}$. The albedo image is reconstructed as $I_A = W(A(\alpha))$, where W is a warping function that converts the UV map into camera space.

Illumination. We take the standard approach of approximating environment lighting using spherical harmonics (SH). Using this, the color of pixel (i,j) is computed as

$$
\begin{aligned}
I_R(i,j) &= I_A(i,j) \cdot I_S(i,j) \\
&= I_A(i,j) \cdot \sum_{k=1}^{B^2} \gamma_k \mathbf{H}_k(N(i,j)) \quad\quad (3) \\
&= I_A(i,j) \cdot \gamma \cdot \mathbf{h}(i,j)
\end{aligned}
$$

where $I_R(i,j)$ is the intensity at pixel (i,j) (computed once for each channel); $B = 3$ is the number of SH bands; $\gamma = (\gamma_1, \ldots, \gamma_{B^2})$ is the vector containing the SH parameters; $\mathbf{H}_k$, $k = 1 \ldots B^2$, are the orthogonal SH basis functions, $\mathbf{h}(i,j) \in \mathbb{R}^{B^2}$ is the vectorised version of $\mathbf{H}_k(N(i,j))$, and N is the normal image.

Since the overall intensity of the image can be described by either the albedo I_A or the shading I_S, we mitigate this fact by decomposing the SH coefficient vector of each color channel into a unit-scale vector and its norm:

$$
I_R(i,j) = ||\gamma|| \cdot I_A(i,j) \cdot \frac{\gamma}{||\gamma||} \cdot \mathbf{h}(i,j). \quad\quad (4)
$$

The scale factor $||\gamma||$ can now be regarded as the overall light intensity (one value per RGB channel), while the unit-scale SH parameters $\frac{\gamma}{||\gamma||}$ contain the light directional information. Given a fixed directional SH parameter, the scale is the key variable that modulates the skin tone. We estimate this value independent of the albedo and the normalized SH vector.

5.2   TRUST Network

An image of a face is typically only a small part of a larger image. Our key novelty here is to address the light/albedo ambiguity problem by leveraging *scene cues* to regularize the ill-posed problem. This is implemented by three design choices: (1) a novel *scene consistency* loss, (2) a two-branch architecture that exploits the SH decomposition from Eq. 4, and (3) a light-conditioned albedo estimation network.

Scene Consistency Loss. First, we observe that a scene containing multiple faces can provide hints about the illumination. Taking inspiration from human color constancy, we can assume a single model of illumination for the entire scene, such that when we observe a variety of skin colors we know that the difference is due to albedo and not lighting[5]. While other works have considered albedo consistency among different views as a cue for disambiguation [59, 63], *light consistency* within an image has been mostly unexplored. We formalize the idea by requiring the SH parameters of different faces in a same image to be close to each other. Specifically, given the set of all the estimated SH vectors $\{\gamma^i\}_{i=\{1..N\}}$, where N is the number of faces in the image, we penalize the difference between any two facial crops as $L_{sc} = ||P(\{\gamma^i\}) - \{\gamma^i\}||_1$, where $P(\cdot)$ is a random permutation function (illustrated in Fig. 2 right).

However, we note that this loss alone cannot ensure a correct albedo reconstruction: it can only work when there is a variety of skin tones present in the scene, otherwise the estimated albedos can still be consistently brighter or darker than the true albedo.

Two-Branch Architecture. As a complementary cue, we leverage the decomposition of SH into norm and direction described in Eq. 4, and exploit the fact that the global illuminant can provide additional information about the overall skin tone. To see why, consider the example of a dark-skinned person during daylight. The albedo can be correctly predicted as a dark skin under bright light, or incorrectly predicted as a light skin under dark light; the choice will depend largely on the bias of the prior. Yet, a coarse estimate of the global illuminant will reveal that the first case is the correct one. This provides a strong cue about where the output should lie in the skin color palette.

We implement this observation by proposing a two-branch architecture, shown in Fig. 2, left. First, the input image is passed through a *scene light encoder* E_{scene_light} that predicts the norm of the scene spherical harmonics $||\gamma||$ for each RGB channel, thus capturing the overall light intensity and color. We next obtain facial crops using an off-the-shelf face detector (or ground-truth values at training time). From these crops, an *albedo encoder* E_{albedo} predicts the albedo parameters of the model α, while a *crop-based light encoder* E_{face_light} predicts the normalized SH vector $\gamma' = \gamma/||\gamma||$. The outputs of E_{scene_light} and E_{face_light} are then combined to obtain the final SH prediction γ.

Light-Conditioned Albedo Estimation. We note that during test time, the albedo estimator E_{albedo} does not contain information about the scene, which can still introduce ambiguities. To address this, we propose to condition E_{albedo} on the estimated light intensity. For this, we broadcast the intensity factor from the scene light encoder into an image of the same size as the facial crop, and concatenate it with the input as an additional channel.

Semi-supervised Training. Given that unsupervised disentanglement cannot be solved without proper inductive biases [41] or without a limited amount of potentially imprecise supervision [42], here we use a semi-supervised learning

---

[5] There are exceptions to this, such as a scenes where some faces are in shadow or where the lighting is high-frequency.

strategy. Specifically, we generate a synthetic training set of 50k images using 1170 scans acquired from Renderpeople[6], combined with 273 panoramic HDR images from Poly Haven[7]. We train the networks using a combined synthetic/real dataset to ensure generalization.

Training. TRUST is trained using the following loss function:

$$\mathcal{L} = \lambda_{pho} L_{pho} + \lambda_{sc} L_{sc} + \mathbb{I}\lambda_{SH} L_{SH} + \mathbb{I}\lambda_{alb} L_{alb}. \tag{5}$$

Here, $L_{pho} = ||I - I_R||_1$ is the L1 photometric loss between the input image and rendered image, and L_{sc} is the scene consistency loss. $\mathbb{I}$ is an indicator function with value 1 for supervised training data and 0 for real. When training with synthetic data we also employ an L1 loss $L_{SH} = ||\gamma - \tilde{\gamma}||_1^1$ between ground-truth SH coefficients γ and the estimates $\tilde{\gamma}$, as well as an L1 loss between the rendered albedo and ground-truth. Note that we include the self-supervised loss on synthetic data since the ground-truth light and albedo are only approximations to the physical ground-truth. We set $\lambda_{pho} = 10, \lambda_{sc} = 10, \lambda_{SH} = 20, \lambda_{alb} = 20$ to weight the loss terms based on validation-set performance.

To compute the photometric loss we need an estimate of the geometry and camera. For this we use a pre-trained state-of-the-art geometry estimation network, DECA [22], which provides FLAME shape and expression coefficients, as well as weak perspective camera parameters. This module is fixed during training.

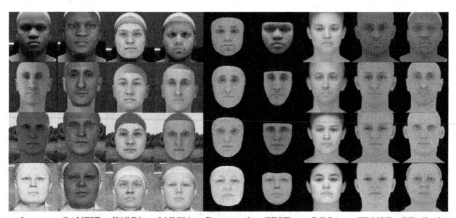

Input   GANFIT   INORig   MGCNet   Deng et al   CEST   DECA   TRUST   GT-albedo

Fig. 3. Comparison with recent face reconstruction methods on the proposed albedo benchmark. From left to right: input image, GANFIT [24], INORig [3], MGCNet [58], Deng et al. [16], CEST [70], DECA [22], TRUST (ours) and ground-truth albedo rendering.

---

[6] https://renderpeople.com/.

[7] Note that these scenes are completely different from those used in the evaluation benchmark.

5.3 Implementation Details

We implemented our approach in PyTorch [47], using the differentiable rasterizer from Pytorch3D [52] for rendering. We use Adam [31] as the optimizer with a learning rate of $1e-4$. All of the encoders use Resnet-50 architectures with input images of size 224×224 (in the case of full scene images, we first randomly crop a square and then resize). The UV space size is $d = 256$. To get shape, expression and camera parameters we use DECA [22] to regress the FLAME parameters $|\boldsymbol{\beta}| = 100$ and $|\boldsymbol{\psi}| = 50$. To train with real data, we use the subset of the OpenImages dataset [35] that contains faces.

We apply a two-stage training strategy. The first stage employs fully supervised training with a batch size of 32 using the synthetic dataset for one epoch. The second stage uses semi-supervised training with a batch size of 48 and all proposed losses for 4 epochs. More details can be found in Sup. Mat.

Table 2. Ablation study. We show comparisons to the following alternatives: (1) light estimation from crops ("faceSH") with self-supervised (self) and semi-supervised (semi) training sets; (2) SH intensity estimation from the scene, with SH directional estimation from crops ("fuseSH"); (3) fuseSH with scene consistency loss ("sc"); (4) fuseSH with conditioning ("cond"); (5) Ours: fuseSH with scene consistency and conditioning.

Method	Avg. ITA ↓	Bias ↓	Score ↓	MAE ↓
faceSH + self	24.17	11.46	35.62	25.81
faceSH + semi	14.70	6.60	21.31	17.64
fuseSH	15.22	11.08	26.31	**17.02**
fuseSH + sc	15.82	3.50	19.32	20.37
fuseSH + cond	**14.16**	6.56	20.72	17.05
Ours	14.18	**2.63**	**16.81**	19.08

6 Evaluation

We compare TRUST qualitatively and quantitatively with several SOTA methods. MGCNet [58], Deng et al. [16], INORig [3] and DECA [22] use the Basel Face Model (BFM) [48] for albedo estimation; GANFIT [25] uses its own GAN-based appearance model; and CEST [70] is a model-free approach.

6.1 Qualitative Results

We provide qualitative results on both real images (Fig. 4a) and synthetic images from the FAIR benchmark (Fig. 3), showing faces with a variety of skin colors and scene illuminations. We observe that (1) GANFIT [25], INORig [3], and DECA [22] produce albedo maps with low variety, hence achieving low ITA

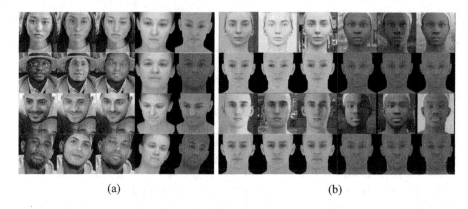

(a)   (b)

Fig. 4. (a) Qualitative comparisons on *real world images*. From left to right: 1) Input, 2) INORig [3], 3) MGCNet [58], 4) DECA [22], 5) TRUST (Ours). **(b)** Given images of the same subject (from the FAIR benchmark test set) under varying lighting (Rows 1 & 3), TRUST outputs similar albedos (Rows 2 and 4).

values on specific skin types, but high ITA values for other skin types; (2) the model-free approach CEST [70] bakes in a significant amount of light, since they cannot properly disentangle it from the albedo; (3) MGCNet [58] and, to a certain degree, Deng et al. [16] produce more diverse albedos, but since the BFM model does not include dark skin tones in the training dataset, these can only be encoded by extrapolating considerably, introducing noise. For more qualitative examples, see Sup. Mat.

To evaluate robustness we apply TRUST on images of a same subject under different lighting, and with varying backgrounds. Figure 4b shows that the estimated albedo, per subject, is consistent across lighting and background variations, and that skin tones are well captured.

6.2   Quantitative Comparisons

We quantitatively compare several albedo estimation methods on the FAIR benchmark as described in Sec. 3. Table 1 shows that the proposed approach (using the balanced albedo model) outperforms existing methods on all aggregated measures (i.e. Avg. ITA, Bias, Score, and MAE), and produces a more uniform (low) error across skin types. Note that while Deng et al. [16], INORig [3], and GANFIT [25] obtain the lowest scores for individual skin types, they have large errors for others, indicating their bias towards particular skin tones, which results in higher aggregated errors.

It is worth noting that, while shading information acts locally and provides gradients for geometry reconstruction, the skin tone is a global property of the albedo (low-frequency component). Hence, correct shape estimation does not necessarily imply good skin tone estimation (and vice-versa), which explains why methods such as DECA can achieve state-of-the-art results on shape estimation, even with strong regularization on the albedo coefficients that lead to incorrect skin tone estimates.

6.3   Ablation Studies

Effect of Albedo Model Space. We investigate how much a biased albedo space affects the final performance. To this end, we train two additional versions of our final network, but using instead the BFM albedo space [48] and AlbedoMM [61]. Both model variants show large improvements on most skin types compared to prior work (see Tab. 1). This demonstrates that addressing the light/albedo ambiguity is important for unbiased albedo estimation, and allows to push the albedo space to its representational limit. Both model variants perform similarly (see Tab. 1) in Avg. ITA error and Bias scores (std), but around 20% and 580% higher than our final model with a balanced albedo space. Most errors of these two variants come from type V and VI, which shows the importance of using a balanced albedo model to cover the full range of skin tones.

Light and Albedo Estimation from Facial Crops (faceSH): Here, both light and albedo encoders use facial crops as input, which is comparable to prior methods. We evaluate this setting using self-supervised training and semi-supervised training, to test the importance of the synthetic vs in-the-wild training set for reducing racial bias. Results are shown in the first two rows of Table 2, where we see that all metrics are significantly improved with access to synthetic data.

Scene Light Estimation (FuseSH): We next consider the case where the light intensity is estimated from the scene image, as in our approach, but with the following differences: (1) without conditioning and without scene consistency (fuseSH), (2) with scene consistency alone (fuseSH+sc), (3) with conditioning alone (fuseSH + cond). We observe in Table 2 that each of these components improves a different aspect: while conditioning results in better skin color predictions, the scene consistency encourages fairer estimates. Our final model, which uses both scene-consistency and conditioning, achieves the lowest total score.

7   Conclusions

This work presented initial steps towards unbiased estimation of facial albedo from images in the wild, using two main contributions. First, we built a new evaluation benchmark that is balanced in terms of skin type. We used this benchmark to highlight biases in current methods. We further proposed a new albedo estimation approach that addresses the light/albedo ambiguity problem, hence encouraging fairer estimates. Our solution is built on the idea that the scene image can be exploited as a cue to disambiguate light and albedo, resulting in more accurate predictions. The experimental results confirm that scene information helps to obtain fairer albedo reconstructions. We hope that this work will encourage the development of methods that are designed not just towards realism, but also towards fairness.

Acknowledgements. We thank S. Sanyal for the helpful suggestions, O. Ben-Dov, R. Danecek, Y. Wen for helping with the baselines, N. Athanasiou, Y. Feng, Y. Xiu for proof-reading, and B. Pellkofer for the technical support.

Disclosure: MJB has received research gift funds from Adobe, Intel, Nvidia, Meta/Facebook, and Amazon. MJB has financial interests in Amazon, Datagen Technologies, and Meshcapade GmbH. While MJB was a part-time employee of Amazon during a portion of this project, his research was performed solely at, and funded solely by, the Max Planck Society. While TB is a part-time employee of Amazon, his research was performed solely at, and funded solely by, MPI.

References

1. Adamson, A.S., Smith, A.: Machine learning and health care disparities in dermatology. JAMA Dermatol. **154**(11), 1247–1248 (2018)
2. Aldrian, O., Smith, W.A.: Inverse rendering of faces with a 3D morphable model. Trans. Pattern Anal. Mach. Intell. (PAMI) **35**(5), 1080–1093 (2012)
3. Bai, Z., Cui, Z., Liu, X., Tan, P.: Riggable 3D face reconstruction via in-network optimization. In: Conference on Computer Vision and Pattern Recognition (CVPR), pp. 6216–6225 (2021)
4. Bas, A., Smith, W.A.P.: What does 2D geometric information really tell us about 3D face shape? Int. J. Comput. Vis. (IJCV) **127**(10), 1455–1473 (2019)
5. Bianco, S., Schettini, R.: Adaptive color constancy using faces. Trans. Pattern Anal. Mach. Intell. (PAMI) **36**(8), 1505–1518 (2014)
6. Blanz, V., Romdhani, S., Vetter, T.: Face identification across different poses and illuminations with a 3D morphable model. In: International Conference on Automatic Face & Gesture Recognition (FG), pp. 202–207 (2002)
7. Blanz, V., Vetter, T.: A morphable model for the synthesis of 3d faces. In: SIGGRAPH, pp. 187–194 (1999)
8. Buolamwini, J., Gebru, T.: Gender shades: intersectional accuracy disparities in commercial gender classification. In: Conference on Fairness, Accountability and Transparency, pp. 77–91. PMLR (2018)
9. Chardon, A., Cretois, I., Hourseau, C.: Skin colour typology and suntanning pathways. Int. J. Cosmet. Sci. **13**(4), 191–208 (1991)
10. Chaudhuri, B., Vesdapunt, N., Shapiro, L., Wang, B.: Personalized face modeling for improved face reconstruction and motion retargeting. In: Vedaldi, A., Bischof, H., Brox, T., Frahm, J.-M. (eds.) ECCV 2020. LNCS, vol. 12350, pp. 142–160. Springer, Cham (2020). https://doi.org/10.1007/978-3-030-58558-7_9
11. Chen, A., Chen, Z., Zhang, G., Mitchell, K., Yu, J.: Photo-realistic facial details synthesis from single image. In: International Conference on Computer Vision (ICCV), pp. 9429–9439 (2019)
12. Choi, H., Choi, K., Suk, H.: Performance of the 14 skin-colored patches in accurately estimating human skin color. In: Computational Imaging XV, pp. 62–65 (2017)
13. Dai, H., Pears, N., Smith, W., Duncan, C.: Statistical modeling of craniofacial shape and texture. Int. J. Comput. Vis. (IJCV) **128**(2), 547–571 (2019)
14. Del Bino, S., Sok, J., Bessac, E., Bernerd, F.: Relationship between skin response to ultraviolet exposure and skin color type. Pigment Cell Res. **19**(6), 606–614 (2006)

15. Del Bino, S., Bernerd, F.: Variations in skin colour and the biological consequences of ultraviolet radiation exposure. Br. J. Dermatol. **169**, 33–40 (2013)
16. Deng, Y., Yang, J., Xu, S., Chen, D., Jia, Y., Tong, X.: Accurate 3D face reconstruction with weakly-supervised learning: from single image to image set. In: Conference on Computer Vision and Pattern Recognition Workshops (CVPR-W) (2019)
17. Dooley, S., et al.: Comparing human and machine bias in face recognition. arXiv preprint arXiv:2110.08396 (2021)
18. Drozdowski, P., Rathgeb, C., Dantcheva, A., Damer, N., Busch, C.: Demographic bias in biometrics: a survey on an emerging challenge. Trans. Technol. Soc. **1**(2), 89–103 (2020)
19. Egger, B., Schönborn, S., Schneider, A., Kortylewski, A., Morel-Forster, A., Blumer, C., Vetter, T.: Occlusion-aware 3D morphable models and an illumination prior for face image analysis. Int. J. Comput. Vis. (IJCV) **126**(12), 1269–1287 (2018)
20. Egger, B., et al.: 3D morphable face models - past, present, and future. Trans. Graph. (TOG) **39**(5), 1–38 (2020)
21. Egger, B., Sutherland, S., Medin, S.C., Tenenbaum, J.: Identity-expression ambiguity in 3D morphable face models. arXiv preprint arXiv:2109.14203 (2021)
22. Feng, Y., Feng, H., Black, M.J., Bolkart, T.: Learning an animatable detailed 3D face model from in-the-wild images. Trans. Graph. (Proc. SIGGRAPH) **40**(4), 1–13 (2021)
23. Fitzpatrick, T.B.: The validity and practicality of sun-reactive skin types I through VI. Arch. Dermatol. **124**(6), 869–871 (1988)
24. Gecer, B., Deng, J., Zafeiriou, S.: Ostec: one-shot texture completion. In: Conference on Computer Vision and Pattern Recognition (CVPR), pp. 7628–7638 (2021)
25. Gecer, B., Ploumpis, S., Kotsia, I., Zafeiriou, S.: Ganfit: Generative adversarial network fitting for high fidelity 3d face reconstruction. In: Conference on Computer Vision and Pattern Recognition (CVPR), pp. 1155–1164 (2019)
26. Genova, K., Cole, F., Maschinot, A., Sarna, A., Vlasic, D., Freeman, W.T.: Unsupervised training for 3D morphable model regression. In: Conference on Computer Vision and Pattern Recognition (CVPR), pp. 8377–8386 (2018)
27. Gerig, T., et al.: Morphable face models - an open framework. In: International Conference on Automatic Face & Gesture Recognition (FG), pp. 75–82 (2018)
28. Hu, G., Mortazavian, P., Kittler, J., Christmas, W.: A facial symmetry prior for improved illumination fitting of 3D morphable model. In: 2013 International Conference on Biometrics (ICB), pp. 1–6. IEEE (2013)
29. Kim, H., Zollhöfer, M., Tewari, A., Thies, J., Richardt, C., Theobalt, C.: Inverse-FaceNet: deep monocular inverse face rendering. In: Conference on Computer Vision and Pattern Recognition (CVPR), pp. 4625–4634 (2018)
30. Kim, T., et al.: Countering racial bias in computer graphics research. arXiv preprint arXiv:2103.15163 (2021)
31. Kingma, D.P., Ba, J.: Adam: a method for stochastic optimization. arXiv preprint arXiv:1412.6980 (2014)
32. Kinyanjui, N.M., et al.: Fairness of classifiers across skin tones in dermatology. In: Martel, A.L., et al. (eds.) MICCAI 2020. LNCS, vol. 12266, pp. 320–329. Springer, Cham (2020). https://doi.org/10.1007/978-3-030-59725-2_31
33. Kips, R., Gori, P., Perrot, M., Bloch, I.: CA-GAN: weakly supervised color aware GAN for controllable makeup transfer. In: Bartoli, A., Fusiello, A. (eds.) ECCV 2020. LNCS, vol. 12537, pp. 280–296. Springer, Cham (2020). https://doi.org/10.1007/978-3-030-67070-2_17

34. Kips, R., Tran, L., Malherbe, E., Perrot, M.: Beyond color correction: skin color estimation in the wild through deep learning. Electronic Imaging **2020**(5), 1–82 (2020)
35. Krasin, I., et al.: Openimages: a public dataset for large-scale multi-label and multi-class image classification, **2**(3), 18 (2017). Dataset available from https://github.com/openimages
36. Krishnapriya, K.S., Albiero, V., Vangara, K., King, M.C., Bowyer, K.W.: Issues related to face recognition accuracy varying based on race and skin tone. IEEE Trans. Technol. Soc. **1**(1), 8–20 (2020). https://doi.org/10.1109/TTS.2020.2974996
37. Lattas, A., et al.: AvatarMe: realistically renderable 3D facial reconstruction. In: Conference on Computer Vision and Pattern Recognition (CVPR), pp. 760–769 (2020)
38. Li, R., et al.: Learning formation of physically-based face attributes. In: Proceedings of the IEEE/CVF Conference on Computer Vision and Pattern Recognition, pp. 3410–3419 (2020)
39. Li, T., Bolkart, T., Black, M.J., Li, H., Romero, J.: Learning a model of facial shape and expression from 4D scans. ACM Transactions on Graphics, (Proc. SIGGRAPH Asia) **36**(6), 1–17 (2017). https://doi.org/10.1145/3130800.3130813
40. Lin, J., Yuan, Y., Shao, T., Zhou, K.: Towards high-fidelity 3D face reconstruction from in-the-wild images using graph convolutional networks. In: Conference on Computer Vision and Pattern Recognition (CVPR), pp. 5891–5900 (2020)
41. Locatello, F., et al.: Challenging common assumptions in the unsupervised learning of disentangled representations. arXiv preprint arXiv:1811.12359 (2018)
42. Locatello, F., et al.: Disentangling factors of variation using few labels. arXiv preprint arXiv:1905.01258 (2019)
43. Marguier, J., Bhatti, N., Baker, H., Harville, M., Süsstrunk, S.: Assessing human skin color from uncalibrated images. Int. J. Imaging Syst. Technol. **17**(3), 143–151 (2007)
44. Mehrabi, N., Morstatter, F., Saxena, N., Lerman, K., Galstyan, A.: A survey on bias and fairness in machine learning. ACM Comput. Surv. **54**(6) (2021). https://doi.org/10.1145/3457607
45. Merler, M., Ratha, N., Feris, R.S., Smith, J.R.: Diversity in faces. arXiv preprint arXiv:1901.10436 (2019)
46. Osoba, O.A., Welser IV, W.: An intelligence in our image: the risks of bias and errors in artificial intelligence. Rand Corporation (2017)
47. Paszke, A., et al.: PyTorch: an imperative style, high-performance deep learning library. In: Advances in Neural Information Processing Systems (NeurIPS) (2019)
48. Paysan, P., Knothe, R., Amberg, B., Romdhani, S., Vetter, T.: A 3D face model for pose and illumination invariant face recognition. In: 2009 Sixth IEEE International Conference on Advanced Video and Signal Based Surveillance. pp. 296–301. IEEE (2009)
49. Pichon, L.C., Landrine, H., Corral, I., Hao, Y., Mayer, J.A., Hoerster, K.D.: Measuring skin cancer risk in african americans: is the fitzpatrick skin type classification scale culturally sensitive. Ethn. Dis. **20**(2), 174–179 (2010)
50. Rajkomar, A., Hardt, M., Howell, M.D., Corrado, G., Chin, M.H.: Ensuring fairness in machine learning to advance health equity. Ann. Intern. Med. **169**(12), 866–872 (2018)
51. Ramamoorthi, R., Hanrahan, P.: A signal-processing framework for inverse rendering. In: Pocock, L. (ed.) SIGGRAPH, pp. 117–128 (2001)
52. Ravi, N., et al.: PyTorch3d. https://github.com/facebookresearch/pytorch3d (2020)

53. Robinson, J.P., Livitz, G., Henon, Y., Qin, C., Fu, Y., Timoner, S.: Face recognition: too bias, or not too bias? In: Proceedings of the IEEE/CVF Conference on Computer Vision and Pattern Recognition Workshops (2020)

54. Sahasrabudhe, M., Shu, Z., Bartrum, E., Güler, R.A., Samaras, D., Kokkinos, I.: Lifting autoencoders: unsupervised learning of a fully-disentangled 3D morphable model using deep non-rigid structure from motion. In: International Conference on Computer Vision Workshops (ICCV-W), pp. 4054–4064 (2019)

55. Saito, S., Wei, L., Hu, L., Nagano, K., Li, H.: Photorealistic facial texture inference using deep neural networks. In: Conference on Computer Vision and Pattern Recognition (CVPR), pp. 5144–5153 (2017)

56. Schönborn, S., Egger, B., Morel-Forster, A., Vetter, T.: Markov chain monte Carlo for automated face image analysis. Int. J. Comput. Vis. (IJCV) **123**(2), 160–183 (2017)

57. Sengupta, S., Kanazawa, A., Castillo, C.D., Jacobs, D.W.: SfSNet: learning shape, reflectance and illuminance of facesin the wild. In: Conference on Computer Vision and Pattern Recognition (CVPR), pp. 6296–6305 (2018)

58. Shang, J., et al.: Self-supervised monocular 3D face reconstruction by occlusion-aware multi-view geometry consistency. In: Vedaldi, A., Bischof, H., Brox, T., Frahm, J.-M. (eds.) ECCV 2020. LNCS, vol. 12360, pp. 53–70. Springer, Cham (2020). https://doi.org/10.1007/978-3-030-58555-6_4

59. Shi, F., Wu, H.T., Tong, X., Chai, J.: Automatic acquisition of high-fidelity facial performances using monocular videos. ACM Trans. Graph. (TOG) **33**(6), 1–13 (2014)

60. Shu, Z., Yumer, E., Hadap, S., Sunkavalli, K., Shechtman, E., Samaras, D.: Neural face editing with intrinsic image disentangling. In: Conference on Computer Vision and Pattern Recognition (CVPR), pp. 5541–5550 (2017)

61. Smith, W.A.P., Seck, A., Dee, H., Tiddeman, B., Tenenbaum, J., Egger, B.: A morphable face albedo model. In: Conference on Computer Vision and Pattern Recognition (CVPR), pp. 5010–5019 (2020)

62. Terhörst, P., Kolf, J.N., Huber, M., Kirchbuchner, F., Damer, N., Moreno, A.M., Fierrez, J., Kuijper, A.: A comprehensive study on face recognition biases beyond demographics. IEEE Trans. Technol. Soc. **3**(1), 16–30 (2021)

63. Tewari, A., et al.: FML: face model learning from videos. In: Proceedings of the IEEE Conference on Computer Vision and Pattern Recognition, pp. 10812–10822 (2019)

64. Tewari, A., et al.: Self-supervised multi-level face model learning for monocular reconstruction at over 250 Hz. In: Proceedings of the IEEE Conference on Computer Vision and Pattern Recognition, pp. 2549–2559 (2018)

65. Tewari, A., et al.: MoFA: model-based deep convolutional face autoencoder for unsupervised monocular reconstruction. In: International Conference on Computer Vision (ICCV) (2017)

66. Thies, J., Zollhöfer, M., Stamminger, M., Theobalt, C., Nießner, M.: Face2Face: real-time face capture and reenactment of RGB videos. In: Conference on Computer Vision and Pattern Recognition (CVPR), pp. 2387–2395 (2016)

67. Tran, L., Liu, F., Liu, X.: Towards high-fidelity nonlinear 3D face morphable model. In: Proceedings of the IEEE Conference on Computer Vision and Pattern Recognition, pp. 1126–1135 (2019)

68. Tran, L., Liu, X.: Nonlinear 3D face morphable model. In: Proceedings of the IEEE conference on computer vision and pattern recognition, pp. 7346–7355 (2018)

69. Wang, M., Deng, W., Hu, J., Tao, X., Huang, Y.: Racial faces in the wild: reducing racial bias by information maximization adaptation network. In: International Conference on Computer Vision (ICCV), pp. 692–702 (2019)

70. Wen, Y., Liu, W., Raj, B., Singh, R.: Self-supervised 3D face reconstruction via conditional estimation. In: International Conference on Computer Vision (ICCV), pp. 13289–13298 (2021)

71. Wilson, B., Hoffman, J., Morgenstern, J.: Predictive inequity in object detection. arXiv preprint arXiv:1902.11097 (2019)

72. Yamaguchi, S., et al.: High-fidelity facial reflectance and geometry inference from an unconstrained image. Trans. Graph. (TOG) **37**(4), 1–14 (2018)

73. Youn, J., et al.: Relationship between skin phototype and med in korean, brown skin. Photodermatol. Photoimmunol. Photomed. **13**(5–6), 208–211 (1997)

BoundaryFace: A Mining Framework with Noise Label Self-correction for Face Recognition

Shijie Wu[ID] and Xun Gong[(✉)][ID]

School of Computing and Artificial Intelligence, Southwest Jiaotong University,
Chengdu, Sichuan, China
xgong@swjtu.edu.cn

Abstract. Face recognition has made tremendous progress in recent years due to the advances in loss functions and the explosive growth in training sets size. A properly designed loss is seen as key to extract discriminative features for classification. Several margin-based losses have been proposed as alternatives of softmax loss in face recognition. However, two issues remain to consider: 1) They overlook the importance of hard sample mining for discriminative learning. 2) Label noise ubiquitously exists in large-scale datasets, which can seriously damage the model's performance. In this paper, starting from the perspective of decision boundary, we propose a novel mining framework that focuses on the relationship between a sample's ground truth class center and its nearest negative class center. Specifically, a closed-set noise label self-correction module is put forward, making this framework work well on datasets containing a lot of label noise. The proposed method consistently outperforms SOTA methods in various face recognition benchmarks. Training code has been released at https://gitee.com/swjtugx/classmate/tree/master/OurGroup/BoundaryFace.

Keywords: Face recognition · Noise label · Hard sample mining · Decision boundary

1 Introduction

Face recognition is one of the most widely studied topics in the computer vision community. Large-scale datasets, network architectures, and loss functions have fueled the success of Deep Convolutional Neural Networks (DCNNs) on face recognition. Particularly, with an aim to extract discriminative features, the latest works have proposed some intuitively reasonable loss functions.

For face recognition, the current existing losses can be divided into two approaches: one deems the face recognition task to be a general classification problem, and networks are therefore trained using softmax [1, 3, 5, 12, 16, 24–26, 31]; the other approaches the problem using metric learning and directly learns an embedding, such as [17, 20, 21]. Since metric learning loss usually suffers from sample batch combination explosion and semi-hard sample mining, the

© The Author(s), under exclusive license to Springer Nature Switzerland AG 2022
S. Avidan et al. (Eds.): ECCV 2022, LNCS 13673, pp. 91–106, 2022.
https://doi.org/10.1007/978-3-031-19778-9_6

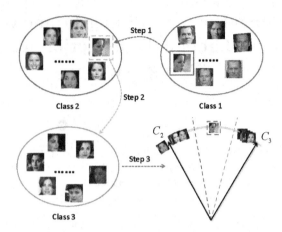

Fig. 1. The motivation of BoundaryFace. Step 1 denotes closed-set noise label self-correction. Step 2 denotes nearest negative class match. Step 3 denotes hard sample handle. For a noisy hard sample, we first correct its label, then match the nearest negative class based on the correct label, and finally emphasize it using the decision boundary consisting of this sample's ground truth class center and the nearest negative class center.

second problem needs to be addressed by more sophisticated sampling strategies. Loss functions have therefore attracted increased attention.

It has been pointed out that the classical classification loss function (*i.e.*, Softmax loss) cannot obtain discriminative features. Based on current testing protocols, the probe commonly has no overlap with the training images, so it is particularly crucial to extract features with high discriminative ability. To this end, Center loss [29] and NormFace [25] have been successively proposed to obtain discriminative features. Wen *et al.* [29] developed a center loss that learns each subject's center. To ensure the training process is consistent with testing, Wang *et al.* [25] made the features extracted by the network and the weight vectors of the last fully connected layer lay on the unit hypersphere. Recently, some margin-based softmax loss functions [3,12,13,24,26] have also been proposed to enhance intra-class compactness while enlarging inter-class discrepancy, resulting in more discriminative features.

The above approaches have achieved relatively satisfactory results. However, there are two very significant issues that must still be addressed: 1) Previous research has ignored the importance of hard sample mining for discriminative learning. As illustrated in [2,8], hard sample mining is a crucial step in improving performance. Therefore, some mining-based softmax losses have emerged. Very recently, MV-Arc-Softmax [28], and CurricularFace [9] were proposed. They were inspired by integrating both margin and mining into one framework. However, both consider the relationship between the sample ground truth class and all negative classes, which may complicate the optimization of the decision boundary. 2) Both margin-based softmax loss and mining-based softmax loss ignore the influence of label noise. Noise in face recognition datasets is composed of two types: *closed-set noise*, in which some samples are falsely given the labels of other identities within the same dataset, and *open-set noise*, in which a subset of samples that do not belong to any of the classes, are mistakenly assigned one of their labels, or contain some non-faces. Wang *et al.* [23] noted that noise, especially closed-set noise, can seriously impact model's performance. Unfortunately, removing noise is expensive and, in many cases, impracticable. Intuitively, the mining-based softmax loss functions can negatively impact the model if the training set is noisy. That is, mining-based softmax is likely to perform less well than baseline methods on datasets with severe noise problems. Designing a loss function that can perform hard sample mining and tolerate noise simultaneously is still an open problem.

In this paper, starting from the perspective of decision boundary, we propose a novel mining framework with tolerating closed-set noise. Figure 1 illustrates our motivation using a noisy hard sample processing. Specifically, based on the premise of closed-set noise label correction, the framework directly emphasizes hard sample features that are between the ground truth class center and the nearest negative class center. We find out that if a sample is a closed-set noise, there is a high probability that the sample is distributed within the nearest negative class's decision boundary, and the nearest negative class is likely to be the ground truth class of the noisy sample. Based on this finding, we propose a module that automatically discovers closed-set noise during training and dynamically corrects its labels. Based on this module, the mining framework can work well on large-scale datasets under the impact of severe noise. To sum up, the contributions of this work are:

- We propose a novel mining framework with noise label self-correction, named BoundaryFace, to explicitly perform hard sample mining as a guidance of the discriminative feature learning.
- The closed-set noise module can be used in any of the existing margin-based softmax losses with negligible computational overhead. To the best of our knowledge, this is the first solution for closed-set noise from the perspective of the decision boundary.
- We have conducted extensive experiments on popular benchmarks, which have verified the superiority of our BoundaryFace over the baseline softmax and the mining-based softmax losses.

2 Related Work

2.1 Margin-Based Softmax

Most recently, researchers have mainly focused on designing loss functions in the field of face recognition. Since basic softmax loss cannot guarantee facial features that are sufficiently discriminative, some margin-based softmax losses [3,12,13,24,26,33], aiming at enhancing intra-class compactness while enlarging inter-class discrepancy, have been proposed. Liu *et al.* [13] brought in multiplicative margin to face recognition in order to produce discriminative feature. Liu *et al.* [12] introduced an angular margin (A-Softmax) between ground truth class and other classes to encourage larger inter-class discrepancy. Since multiplicative margin could encounter optimization problems, Wang *et al.* [26] proposed an additive margin to stabilize optimization procedure. Deng *et al.* [3] changed the form of the additive margin, which generated a loss with clear geometric significance. Zhang *et al.* [33] studied on the effect of two crucial hyper-parameters of traditional margin-based softmax losses, and proposed the AdaCos, by analyzing how they modulated the predicted classification probability. Even these margin-based softmax losses have achieved relatively good performance, none of them takes into account the effects of hard sample mining and label noise.

2.2 Mining-Based Softmax

There are two well-known hard sample mining methods, *i.e.*, Focal loss [11], Online Hard Sample Mining (OHEM) [19]. Wang *et al.* [28] has shown that naive combining them to current popular face recognition methods has limited improvement. Some recent work, MV-Arc-Softmax [28], and CurricularFace [9] are inspired by integrating both margin and mining into one framework. MV-Arc-Softmax explicitly defines mis-classified samples as hard samples and adaptively strengthens them by increasing the weights of corresponding negative cosine similarities, eventually producing a larger feature margin between the ground truth class and the corresponding negative target class. CurricularFace applies curriculum learning to face recognition, focusing on easy samples in the early stage and hard samples in the later stage. However, on the one hand, both take the relationship between the sample ground truth class and all negative classes into consideration, which may complicate the optimization of the decision boundary; on the other hand, label noise poses some adverse effect on mining. It is well known that the success of face recognition nowadays benefits from large-scale training data. Noise is inevitably in these million-scale datasets. Unfortunately, Building a "clean enough" face dataset, however, is both costly and difficult. Both MV-Arc-Softmax and CurricularFace assume that the dataset is clean (*i.e.*, almost noiseless), but this assumption is not true in many cases. Intuitively, the more noise the dataset contains, the worse performance of the mining-based softmax loss will be. Unlike open-set noise, closed-set noise can be part of the clean data as soon as we correct their labels. Overall, our method differs from the currently popular mining-based softmax in that our method can conduct hard sample mining along with the closed-set noise well being handled, while the current methods cannot do so.

3 The Proposed Approach

3.1 Preliminary Knowledge

Margin-Based Softmax. The original softmax loss formula is as follows:

$$L = -\log \frac{e^{W_{y_i} x_i + b_{y_i}}}{\sum_{j=1}^{n} e^{W_j x_i + b_j}} \tag{1}$$

where x_i denotes the feature of the i-th sample belonging to y_i class in the min-batch, W_j denotes the j-th column of the weight matrix W of the last fully connected layer, and b_j and n denote the bias term and the number of identities, respectively.

To make the training process of the face recognition consistent with the testing, Wang et $al.$ [25] let the weight vector W_j and the sample features x_i lie on a hypersphere by l_2 normalization. And to make the networks converge better, the sample features are re-scaled to s. Thus, Eq. 1 can be modified as follows:

$$L = - \log \frac{e^{s(\cos \theta_{y_i})}}{\sum\limits_{j=1}^{n} e^{s(\cos \theta_j)}} \tag{2}$$

With the above modification, W_j has a clear geometric meaning which is the class center of j-th class and we can even consider it as a feature of the central sample of j-th class. θ_{y_i} can be seen as the angle between the sample and its class center, in particular, it is also the geodesic distance between the sample and its class center from the unit hypersphere perspective. However, as mentioned before, the original softmax does not yield discriminative features, and the aforementioned corrections ($i.e.$, Eq. 2) to softmax do not fundamentally fix this problem, which has been addressed by some variants of softmax based on margin. They can be formulated in a uniform way:

$$L = - \log \frac{e^{sf(\cos \theta_{y_i})}}{e^{sf(\cos \theta_{y_i})} + \sum\limits_{j=1, j \neq y_i}^{n} e^{s(\cos \theta_j)}} \tag{3}$$

E.g, in baseline softmax ($e.g.$, ArcFace), $f(\cos \theta_{y_i}) = \cos(\theta_{y_i} + m)$. As can be seen, the currently popular margin-based softmax losses all achieve intra-class compactness and inter-class discrepancy by squeezing the distance between a sample and its ground truth class center.

Mining-Based Softmax. Hard sample mining is to get the network to extra focus valuable, hard-to-learn samples. There are two main categories in the existing mining methods that are suitable for face recognition: 1) focusing on samples with large loss values from the perspective of loss. 2) focusing on samples misclassified by the network from the relationship between sample ground truth class and negative classes. They can be formed by a unified formula as below:

$$L = -I(p(x_i)) \log \frac{e^{sf(\cos \theta_{y_i})}}{e^{sf(\cos \theta_{y_i})} + \sum\limits_{j=1, j \neq y_i}^{n} e^{sg(t, \cos \theta_j)}} \tag{4}$$

where $p(x_i) = \dfrac{e^{sf(\cos \theta_{y_i})}}{e^{sf(\cos \theta_{y_i})} + \sum\limits_{j=1, j \neq y_i}^{n} e^{sg(t, \cos \theta_j)}}$ is the predicted ground truth probability and $I(p(x_i))$ is an indicator function. For type 1, such as Focal loss,

Fig. 2. Left: Each row represents one person. The red box includes a closed-set noise sample. **Right:** The distribution of the samples in the left figure is shown from the perspective of the decision boundary. The dashed arrows represent the optimized direction of the samples.

$I(p(x_i)) = (1 - p(x_i))^\lambda$, $f(\cos\theta_{y_i}) = \cos\theta_{y_i}$ and $g(t, \cos\theta_j) = \cos\theta_j$, λ is a modulating factor. For type 2, MV-Arc-Softmax and CurricularFace handle hard samples with varying $g(t, \cos\theta_j)$. Let $N = f(\cos\theta_{y_i}) - \cos\theta_j$, thus, MV-Arc-Softmax is described as:

$$g(t, \cos\theta_j) = \begin{cases} \cos\theta_j, & N \geq 0 \\ \cos\theta_j + t, & N < 0 \end{cases} \tag{5}$$

and CurricularFace formula is defined as follows:

$$g(t, \cos\theta_j) = \begin{cases} \cos\theta_j, & N \geq 0 \\ \cos\theta_j(t + \cos\theta_j), & N < 0 \end{cases} \tag{6}$$

From the above formula, we can see that if a sample is a easy sample, then its negative cosine similarity will not change. Otherwise, its negative cosine similarity will be amplified. Specially, in MV-Arc-Softmax, $\cos\theta_j + t > \cos\theta_j$ always holds true since t is a fixed hyper parameter and is always greater than 0. That is, the model always focuses on hard samples. In contrast, t is calculated based on the Exponential Moving Average (EMA) in CurricularFace, which is gradually changing along with iterations. Moreover, the $\cos\theta_j$ can reflect the difficulty of the samples, and these two changes allow the network to learn easy samples in the early stage and hard samples in the later stage.

3.2 Label Self-correction

In this section, we discuss the mining framework's noise tolerance module. Unlike open-set noise, a closed-set noise sample is transformed into a clean sample if its label can be corrected appropriately. The existing mining-based softmax losses, as their prerequisite, assume that the training set is a clean dataset. Suppose the labels of most closed-set noise in a real noisy dataset are corrected; in that case, poor results from hard sample mining methods on noisy datasets can be

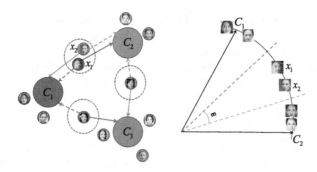

Fig. 3. Left: Blue, orange, and green represent three individuals. The samples in the ellipse are the hard samples. The solid arrows represent distance maximization, and the dashed arrows represent distance minimization. **Right:** The sample distribution of two persons in the left from the perspective of decision boundary. (Color figure online)

adequately mitigated. More specifically, we find that when trained moderately, networks have an essential ability for classification; and that closed-set noise is likely to be distributed within the nearest negative class's decision boundary. Additionally, the negative class has a high probability of being the ground truth class of this sample. As shown in Fig. 2, the red box includes a closed-set noise sample, which is labeled as class 1, but the ground truth label is class 2. The closed-set noise will be distributed within the decision boundary of class 2. At the same time, we dynamically change that sample's label so that the sample is optimized in the correct direction. That is, before the label of this closed-set noise is corrected, it is optimized in the direction of C_1 (*i.e.*, the "before" arrow); after correction, it is optimized in the direction of C_2 (*i.e.*, the "after" arrow). The label self-correction formula, named BoundaryF1, is defined as follows:

$$L = -\frac{1}{N} \sum_{i=1}^{N} \log \frac{e^{s\cos(\theta_{y_i}+m)}}{e^{s\cos(\theta_{y_i}+m)} + \sum_{j=1,j\neq y_i}^{n} e^{s\cos\theta_j}} \qquad (7)$$

where $if \max\{\cos(\theta_k + m) \ for \ all \ k \neq y_i\} - \cos\theta_{y_i} > 0 : y_i = k$. It means that, before each computing of Eq. 7, we decide whether to correct the label based on whether the sample is distributed within the decision boundary of the nearest negative class. Noted that, as a demonstration, apply this method to ArcFace. It can be applied to other margin-based losses could also be used.

3.3 BoundaryFace

Unlike the mining-based softmax's semantic for assigning hard samples, we only consider samples located in the margin region between the ground truth class and the nearest negative class. In other words, as each sample in the high-dimensional feature space has a nearest negative class center, if the sample feature is in the margin region between its ground truth class center and the nearest negative class center, then we label it as a hard sample. As shown in Fig. 3 (left), the nearest negative class for each class's sample may be different (*e.g.*, the nearest negative classes of two samples belonging to the C_1 class are C_2 and C_3, respectively). In Fig. 3, the right image presents the two classes of the left subfigure from the perspective of the decision boundary. Since samples x_1 and x_2 are in the margin region between their ground truth class and the nearest negative class, we treat them as hard samples. An additional regularization term f is added to allow the network to strengthen them directly. Additionally, to ensure its effectiveness on noisy datasets, we embed the closed-set noise label correction module into the mining framework. As shown in Fig. 4, after the network has obtained discriminative power, for each forward propagation; and based on the normalization of feature x_i and the weight matrix W, we obtain the cosine similarity $\cos \theta_j$ of sample feature x_i to each class center W_j. Next, we calculate the position of feature x_i at the decision boundary based on $\cos \theta_j$. Assuming that the nearest negative class of the sample is y_n. If it is distributed within the nearest negative class's decision boundary, we dynamically correct its label y_i to y_n; otherwise proceed to the next step. We then calculate $\cos(\theta_{y_i} + m)$. After that, we simultaneously calculate two lines: one is the traditional pipeline; and the other primarily determines whether the sample is hard or not. These two lines contribute to each of the final loss function's two parts. Since our idea is based on the perspective of the decision boundary, we named our approach BoundaryFace. The final loss function is defined as follows:

$$L = -\frac{1}{N} \sum_{i=1}^{N} (\log \frac{e^{sT(\cos\theta_{y_i})}}{e^{sT(\cos(\theta_{y_i}))} + \sum_{j=1,j\neq y_i}^{n} e^{s\cos\theta_j}} - \lambda f)$$

$$T(\cos\theta_{y_i}) = \cos(\theta_{y_i} + m),$$
$$f = \max\{0, \max\{\cos\theta_j|\, for\ all\ j \neq y_i\} - T(\cos\theta_{y_i})\} \tag{8}$$

where $if \max\{\cos(\theta_k + m)\, for\ all\ k \neq y_i\} - \cos\theta_{y_i} > 0 : y_i = k$. λ is a balance factor. As with BoundaryF1, before each computing of final loss, we decide whether to correct the label based on whether the sample is distributed within the decision boundary of the nearest negative class.

Optimization. In this part, we show that out BoundaryFace is trainable and can be easily optimized by the classical stochastic gradient descent (SGD). Assuming x_i denotes the deep feature of i-th sample which belongs to the y_i class, $L_1 = -\log(\frac{e^{f_{y_i}}}{\sum_k e^{f_k}})$, $L_2 = \lambda \max\{0, \max\{\cos\theta_k|\, for\ all\ k \neq y_i\} - \cos(\theta_{y_i} + m)\}$, the input of the L_1 is the logit f_k, where k denotes the k-th class.

In the forward propagation, when $k = y_i$, $f_k = s\cos(\theta_{y_i} + m)$, when $k \neq y_i$, $f_k = s\cos(\theta_k)$. Regardless of the relationship of k and y_i, there are two cases for L_2, if x_i is a easy sample, $L_2 = 0$. Otherwise, it will be constituted as $L_2 = \lambda(\max\{\cos\theta_k|\, for\ all\ k \neq y_i\} - \cos(\theta_{y_i} + m))$. In the backward propagation process, the gradients w.r.t. x_i and w_k can be computed as follows:

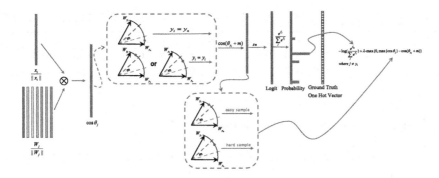

Fig. 4. Overview of BoundaryFace. The part included in the upper dashed box represents the closed-set noise processing. The part included in the lower dashed box represents the judgment of whether it is a hard sample or not.

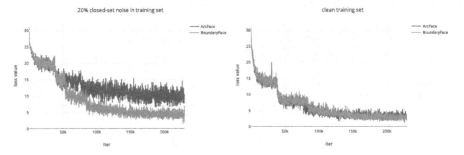

Fig. 5. Convergence process of BoundaryFace.

when $k = y_i$

$$\frac{\partial L}{\partial x_i} = \begin{cases} \frac{\partial L_1}{\partial f_{y_i}} \left(s \frac{\sin(\theta_{y_i} + m)}{\sin \theta_{y_i}} \right) \frac{w_{y_i}}{||w_{y_i}||} X, & easy \\ \left(\frac{\partial L_1}{\partial f_{y_i}} s + \frac{\partial L_2}{\partial \cos(\theta_{y_i} + m)} \right) \frac{\sin(\theta_{y_i} + m)}{\sin \theta_{y_i}} \frac{w_{y_i}}{||w_{y_i}||} X, & hard \end{cases} \tag{9}$$

$$\frac{\partial L}{\partial w_k} = \begin{cases} \frac{\partial L_1}{\partial f_{y_i}} \left(s \frac{\sin(\theta_{y_i} + m)}{\sin \theta_{y_i}} \right) \frac{x_i}{||x_i||} W, & easy \\ \left(\frac{\partial L_1}{\partial f_{y_i}} s + \frac{\partial L_2}{\partial \cos(\theta_{y_i} + m)} \right) \frac{\sin(\theta_{y_i} + m)}{\sin \theta_{y_i}} \frac{x_i}{||x_i||} W, & hard \end{cases} \tag{10}$$

when $k \neq y_i$

$$\frac{\partial L}{\partial x_i} = \begin{cases} \frac{\partial L_1}{\partial f_k} s \frac{w_k}{||w_k||} X, & easy \\ \left(\frac{\partial L_1}{\partial f_k} s + \frac{\partial L_2}{\partial \cos \theta_k} \right) \frac{w_k}{||w_k||} X, & hard \end{cases} \tag{11}$$

$$\frac{\partial L}{\partial w_k} = \begin{cases} \frac{\partial L_1}{\partial f_k} s \frac{x_i}{||x_i||} W, & easy \\ \left(\frac{\partial L_1}{\partial f_k} s + \frac{\partial L_2}{\partial \cos \theta_k} \right) \frac{x_i}{||x_i||} W, & hard \end{cases} \tag{12}$$

Algorithm 1: BoundaryFace

Input   : The feature of i-th sample x_i with its label y_i, last fully-connected
              layer parameters W, cosine similarity $\cos \theta_j$ of two vectors, embedding
              network parameters Θ, and margin m

iteration number $k \leftarrow 0$, parameter $m \leftarrow 0.5$, $\lambda \leftarrow \pi$;

while *not converged* **do**

    for all $j \neq y_i$,

    if $\max\{\cos(\theta_j + m)\} > \cos \theta_{y_i}$ **then**

    | $y_i = j$;

    else

    | $y_i = y_i$;

    end

    if $\cos(\theta_{y_i} + m) > \max\{\cos \theta_j\}$ **then**

    | $f = 0$;

    else

    | $f = \max\{\cos \theta_j\} - \cos(\theta_{y_i} + m)$;

    end

    Compute the loss L by Eq. 3.3;

    Compute the gradients of x_i and W_j by Eq. 9, 10, 11, 12;

    Update the parameters W and Θ;

    $k \leftarrow k + 1$;

end

Output: W, Θ

---

where, both X and W are symmetric matrices.

Further, in Fig. 5, we give the loss curves of baseline and BoundaryFace on the clean dataset and the dataset containing 20% closed-set noise, respectively. It can be seen that our method converges faster than baseline. The training procedure is summarized in Algorithm 1.

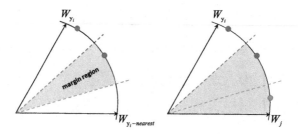

Fig. 6. The difference between BoundaryFace and SOTA methods in emphasizing the region where the hard samples are located.

3.4   Discussions with SOTA Loss Functions

Comparison with Baseline Softmax. The baseline softmax (*i.e.*, ArcFace, CosFace) introduces a margin from the perspective of positive cosine similarity, and they treat all samples equally. Our approach mining hard sample by introducing a regularization term to make the network pay extra attention to the hard samples.

Comparison with MV-Arc-Softmax and CurricularFace. MV-Arc-Softmax and CurricularFace assign the same semantics to hard samples, only differing in the following handling stage. As shown in Fig. 6 (right), both treat mis-classified samples as hard samples and focus on the relationship between the ground truth class of the sample and all negative classes. Instead, in Fig. 6 (left), our approach regards these samples located in the margin region as hard samples and focuses only on the relationship between the ground truth class of the sample and the nearest negative class. Moreover, the labels of both blue and orange samples are y_i, but the orange sample ground truth class is j-th class. Obviously, if there is closed-set noise in the dataset, SOTA methods not only emphasize hard samples but also reinforce closed-set noise.

4 Experiments

4.1 Implementation Details

Datasets. CASIA-WebFace [30] which contains about 0.5M of 10K individuals, is the training set that is widely used for face recognition, and since it has been cleaned very well, we take it as a clean dataset. In order to simulate the situation where the dataset contains much of noise, based on the CASIA-WebFace, we artificially synthesize noisy datasets which contain a different ratio of noise. In detail, for closed-set noise, we randomly flip the sample labels of CASIA-WebFace; for open-set noise, we choose MegaFace [10] as our open-set noise source and randomly replace the samples of CASIA-WebFace. Finally, we use the clean CASIA-WebFace and noisy synthetic datasets as our training set, respectively. We extensively test our method on several popular benchmarks, including LFW [7], AgeDB [14], CFP-FP [18], CALFW [35], CPLFW [34], SLLFW [4], RFW [27]. RFW consists of four subsets: Asian, Caucasian, Indian, and African. Note that in the tables that follow, CA denotes CALFW, CP denotes CPLFW, and Cau denotes Caucasian.

Training Setting. We follow [3] to crop the 112×112 faces with five landmarks [22,32]. For a fair comparison, all methods should be the same to test different loss functions. To achieve a good balance between computation and accuracy, we use the ResNet50 [6] as the backbone. The output of backbone gets a 512-dimension feature. Our framework is implemented in Pytorch [15]. We train modules on 1 NVIDIA TitanX GPU with batch size of 64. The models are trained with SGD algorithm, with momentum 0.9 and weight decay $5e-4$. The learning rate starts from 0.1 and is divided by 10 at 6, 12, 19 epochs. The training process is finished at 30 epochs. We set scale $s = 32$ and margin $m = 0.3$ or $m = 0.5$. Moreover, to make the network with sufficient discrimination ability, we first pre-train the network for 7 epochs using margin-based loss. The margin-based loss can also be seen as a degenerate version of our BoundaryFace.

Table 1. Verification performance (%) of our BoundaryFace with different hyper-parameter λ.

Method	SLLFW	CFP-FP
$\lambda = 2$	98.05	94.8
$\lambda = 2.5$	97.9	94.71
$\lambda = \pi$	**98.12**	**95.03**
$\lambda = 3.5$	97.8	94.9

Table 2. Verification performance (%) of ArcFace with different hyper-parameter m on datasets which contain different noise mixing ratios (%).

m	Closed-set ratio	Open-set ratio	LFW	AgeDB
0.3	10%	30%	**99.07**	**91.82**
0.5	10%	30%	98.22	89.02
0.3	30%	10%	98.42	88.5
0.5	30%	10%	**98.73**	**89.93**

4.2   Hyper-parameters

Parameter λ. Since the hyper-parameter λ plays an essential role in the proposed BoundaryFace, we mainly explore its possible best value in this section. In Table 1, we list the performance of our proposed BoundaryFace with λ varies in the range [2, 3.5]. We can see that our BoundaryFace is insensitive to the hyper-parameter λ. And, according to this study, we empirically set $\lambda = \pi$.

Parameter m. Margin m is essential in both margin-based softmax loss and mining-based softmax loss. For clean datasets, we follow [3] to set margin $m = 0.5$. In Tab. 2, we list the performance of different m for ArcFace on datasets with different noise ratios. It can be concluded that if most of the noise in the training set are open-set noise, we set $m = 0.3$; otherwise, we set $m = 0.5$.

4.3   Comparisons with SOTA Methods

Results on a Dataset that is Clean or Contains only Closed-Set Noise. In this section, we first train our BoundaryFace on the clean dataset as well as datasets containing only closed-set noise. We use BoundaryF1 (Eq. 7) as a reference to illustrate the effects of hard sample mining. Table 3 provides the quantitative results. It can be seen that our BoundaryFace outperforms the baseline and achieves comparable results when compared to the SOTA competitors on the clean dataset; our method demonstrates excellent superiority over baseline and SOTA methods on closed-set noise datasets. Furthermore, we can easily draw the following conclusions: 1) As the closed-set noise ratio increases, the performance of every compared baseline method drops quickly; this phenomenon did

Table 3. Verification performance (%) of different loss functions when the training set contains different ratios of closed-set noise. Ratio 0% means that the training set is the original CASIA-WebFace (*i.e.*, clean dataset).

Ratio	Method	LFW	AgeDB	CFP	CA	CP	SLLFW	Asian	Cau	Indian	African
0%	ArcFace	99.38	94.05	94.61	93.43	89.45	97.78	86.5	93.38	89.9	86.72
	MV-Arc-Softmax	99.4	94.17	94.96	93.38	89.48	97.88	86.23	93.27	90.12	87.03
	CurricularFace	99.42	94.37	94.94	**93.52**	89.7	98.08	86.43	**94.05**	**90.55**	**88.07**
	BoundaryF1	99.41	94.05	95.01	93.27	**89.8**	97.75	85.72	92.98	89.98	86.43
	BoundaryFace	**99.42**	**94.4**	**95.03**	93.28	89.4	**98.12**	**86.5**	93.75	90.5	87.3
10%	ArcFace	99.33	93.81	94.34	93.11	89.1	97.67	85.87	92.98	90.15	86.52
	MV-Arc-Softmax	**99.43**	93.9	94.27	93.15	**89.47**	97.82	85.7	93.17	90.45	87.28
	CurricularFace	99.33	93.92	93.97	93.12	88.78	97.52	85.43	92.98	89.53	86.53
	BoundaryF1	99.4	94.02	94.3	93.18	89.32	97.85	86.5	93.32	90.33	86.95
	BoundaryFace	99.35	**94.28**	**94.79**	**93.5**	89.43	**98.15**	**86.55**	**93.53**	90.33	**87.37**
20%	ArcFace	99.3	93	93.49	92.78	88.12	97.57	84.85	91.92	88.82	85.08
	MV-Arc-Softmax	99.12	93.12	93.26	93.12	88.3	97.37	85.15	92.18	89.08	85.32
	CurricularFace	99.13	91.88	92.56	92.28	87.17	96.62	84.13	91.13	87.7	83.6
	BoundaryF1	99.32	94.02	**94.5**	93.18	**89.03**	97.63	86	**93.28**	89.88	86.48
	BoundaryFace	**99.38**	**94.22**	93.89	**93.4**	88.45	**97.9**	**86.23**	93.22	90	**87.27**

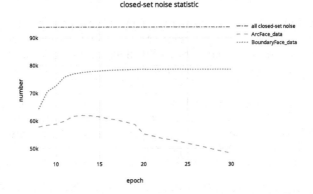

Fig. 7. Comparison of closed-set noise detected by BoundaryFace and ArcFace, respectively. The dash dot line indicates the total number of closed-set noise in the training set.

not occur when using our method. 2) Mining-based softmax has the opposite effect when encountering closed-set noisy data, and the better the method performs on the clean dataset, the worse the results tend to be. In addition, in Fig. 7, given 20% closed-set noise, we present the detection of closed-set noise by BoundaryFace during training and compare it with ArcFace. After closed-set noise is detected, our BoundaryFace dynamically corrects its labels. Correct labels result in a shift in the direction of the closed-set noise being optimized from wrong to right, and also lead to more accurate class centers. Furthermore, more accurate class centers in turn allow our method to detect more closed-set noise at each iteration, eventually reaching saturation.

Table 4. Verification performance (%) of different loss functions when the training set contains different mixing noise ratios. C denotes closed-set noise ratio (%). O denotes open-set noise ratio (%).

C	O	Method	LFW	AgeDB	CFP	CA	CP	SLLFW	Asian	Cau	Indian	African
20	20	ArcFace	98.87	89.55	89.56	90.43	84.4	94.87	80.97	88.37	85.83	79.72
		MV-Arc-Softmax	98.93	89.95	89.61	91.67	84.9	95.67	82.25	88.98	86.22	80.6
		CurricularFace	98.33	88.07	88.29	90.18	83.65	93.87	80.3	87.78	84.43	77.35
		BoundaryF1	99.12	92.5	89.66	92.27	84.43	96.75	84.42	91.4	88.33	**84.55**
		BoundaryFace	**99.2**	**92.68**	**93.28**	**92.32**	**87.2**	**96.97**	**84.78**	**91.88**	**88.8**	84.48
10	30	ArcFace	99.07	91.82	91.34	91.7	85.6	96.45	83.35	90	87.33	81.83
		MV-Arc-Softmax	98.92	91.23	91.27	91.9	85.63	96.17	83.98	90.15	87.57	82.33
		CurricularFace	98.88	91.58	91.71	91.83	85.97	96.17	82.98	89.97	86.97	82.13
		BoundaryF1	99	92.23	92.07	**92.05**	**86.62**	96.42	83.97	90.47	87.83	82.98
		BoundaryFace	**99.17**	**92.32**	**92.4**	91.95	86.22	**96.55**	**84.15**	**91.05**	**88.17**	**83.28**
30	10	ArcFace	98.73	89.93	89.21	91.02	82.93	95.15	81.25	88.33	85.87	80.03
		MV-Arc-Softmax	98.78	89.73	88.54	91.22	82.57	95.22	81.52	88.47	85.83	80.12
		CurricularFace	98.18	87.65	88.1	90.12	82.82	93.13	79.7	86.65	84.1	77.22
		BoundaryF1	99.1	92.3	**90.34**	92.28	**85.28**	96.7	83.52	90.9	87.53	83.12
		BoundaryFace	**99.1**	**93.38**	88.24	**92.5**	82.22	**96.88**	**83.77**	**91.18**	**88.18**	**83.67**

Results on Noisy Synthetic Datasets. The real training set contains not only closed-set noise but also open-set noise. As described in this section, we train our BoundaryFace on noisy datasets with different mixing ratios and compare it with the SOTA competitors. In particular, we set the margin $m = 0.5$ for the training set containing closed-set noise ratio of 30% and open-set noise ratio of 10%, and we set the margin $m = 0.3$ for the other two mixing ratios. As reported in Tab. 4, our method outperforms the SOTA methods on all synthetic datasets. Even on the dataset containing 30% open-set noise, our method still performs better than baseline and SOTA competitors.

5 Conclusions

In this paper, we propose a novel mining framework (*i.e.*, BoundaryFace) with tolerating closed-set noise for face recognition. BoundaryFace largely alleviates the poor performance of mining-based softmax on datasets with severe noise problem. BoundaryFace is easy to implement and converges robustly. Moreover, we investigate the effects of noise samples that might be optimized as hard samples. Extensive experiments on popular benchmarks have demonstrated the generalization and effectiveness of our method when compared to the SOTA.

Acknowledgement. This work was supported in part by the National Natural Science Foundation of China (61876158), Fundamental Research Funds for the Central Universities (2682021ZTPY030).

References

1. Cao, D., Zhu, X., Huang, X., Guo, J., Lei, Z.: Domain balancing: face recognition on long-tailed domains. In: Proceedings of the IEEE/CVF Conference on Computer Vision and Pattern Recognition, pp. 5671–5679 (2020)
2. Chen, B.: Angular visual hardness. In: International Conference on Machine Learning, pp. 1637–1648. PMLR (2020)
3. Deng, J., Guo, J., Xue, N., Zafeiriou, S.: ArcFace: additive angular margin loss for deep face recognition. In: Proceedings of the IEEE/CVF Conference on Computer Vision and Pattern Recognition, pp. 4690–4699 (2019)
4. Deng, W., Jiani, H., Zhang, N., Chen, B., Guo, J.: Fine-grained face verification: FGLFW database, baselines, and human-DCMN partnership. Pattern Recogn. **66**, 63–73 (2017)
5. Guo, J., Zhu, X., Zhao, C., Cao, D., Lei, Z., Li, S.Z.: Learning meta face recognition in unseen domains. In: Proceedings of the IEEE/CVF Conference on Computer Vision and Pattern Recognition, pp. 6163–6172 (2020)
6. He, K., Zhang, X., Ren, S., Sun, J.: Deep residual learning for image recognition. In: Proceedings of the IEEE Conference on Computer Vision and Pattern Recognition, pp. 770–778 (2016)
7. Huang, G.B., Mattar, M., Berg, T., Learned-Miller, E.: Labeled faces in the wild: a database for studying face recognition in unconstrained environments. In: Workshop on Faces in 'Real-Life' Images: Detection, Alignment, and Recognition (2008)
8. Huang, Y., et al.: Improving face recognition from hard samples via distribution distillation loss. In: Vedaldi, A., Bischof, H., Brox, T., Frahm, J.-M. (eds.) ECCV 2020. LNCS, vol. 12375, pp. 138–154. Springer, Cham (2020). https://doi.org/10.1007/978-3-030-58577-8_9
9. Huang, Y., et al.: CurricularFace: adaptive curriculum learning loss for deep face recognition. In: Proceedings of the IEEE/CVF Conference on Computer Vision and Pattern Recognition, pp. 5901–5910 (2020)
10. Kemelmacher-Shlizerman, I., Seitz, S.M., Miller, D., Brossard, E.: The MegaFace benchmark: 1 million faces for recognition at scale. In: Proceedings of the IEEE Conference on Computer Vision and Pattern Recognition, pp. 4873–4882 (2016)
11. Lin, T.-Y., Goyal, P., Girshick, R., He, K., Dollár, P.: Focal loss for dense object detection. In: Proceedings of the IEEE International Conference on Computer Vision, pp. 2980–2988 (2017)
12. Liu, W., Wen, Y., Yu, Z., Li, M., Raj, B., Song, L.: SphereFace: deep hypersphere embedding for face recognition. In: Proceedings of the IEEE Conference on Computer Vision and Pattern Recognition, pp. 212–220 (2017)
13. Liu, W., Wen, Y., Yu, Z., Yang, M.: Large-margin softmax loss for convolutional neural networks. In: ICML, vol. 2, p. 7 (2016)
14. Moschoglou, S., Papaioannou, A., Sagonas, C., Deng, J., Kotsia, I., Zafeiriou, S.: AgeDB: the first manually collected, in-the-wild age database. In: Proceedings of the IEEE Conference on Computer Vision and Pattern Recognition Workshops, pp. 51–59 (2017)
15. Paszke, A., et al.: Automatic differentiation in PyTorch (2017)
16. Ranjan, R., Castillo, C.D., Chellappa, R.: L2-constrained softmax loss for discriminative face verification. arXiv preprint arXiv:1703.09507 (2017)
17. Schroff, F., Kalenichenko, D., Philbin, J.: FaceNet: a unified embedding for face recognition and clustering. In: Proceedings of the IEEE Conference on Computer Vision and Pattern Recognition, pp. 815–823 (2015)

18. Sengupta, S., Chen, J.-C., Castillo, C., Patel, V.M., Chellappa, R., Jacobs, D.W.: Frontal to profile face verification in the wild. In: 2016 IEEE Winter Conference on Applications of Computer Vision (WACV), pp. 1–9. IEEE (2016)
19. Shrivastava, A., Gupta, A., Girshick, R.: Training region-based object detectors with online hard example mining. In: Proceedings of the IEEE Conference on Computer Vision and Pattern Recognition, pp. 761–769 (2016)
20. Sohn, K.: Improved deep metric learning with multi-class n-pair loss objective. In: Advances in Neural Information Processing Systems, pp. 1857–1865 (2016)
21. Sun, Y.: Deep learning face representation by joint identification-verification. The Chinese University of Hong Kong, Hong Kong (2015)
22. Tai, Y., et al.: Towards highly accurate and stable face alignment for high-resolution videos. In: Proceedings of the AAAI Conference on Artificial Intelligence, vol. 33, pp. 8893–8900 (2019)
23. Wang, F., et al.: The devil of face recognition is in the noise. In: Ferrari, V., Hebert, M., Sminchisescu, C., Weiss, Y. (eds.) ECCV 2018. LNCS, vol. 11213, pp. 780–795. Springer, Cham (2018). https://doi.org/10.1007/978-3-030-01240-3_47
24. Wang, F., Cheng, J., Liu, W., Liu, H.: Additive margin softmax for face verification. IEEE Signal Process. Lett. **25**(7), 926–930 (2018)
25. Wang, F., Xiang, X., Cheng, J., Yuille, A.L.: NormFace: L2 hypersphere embedding for face verification. In: Proceedings of the 25th ACM International Conference on Multimedia, pp. 1041–1049 (2017)
26. Wang, H., et al.: CosFace: large margin cosine loss for deep face recognition. In: Proceedings of the IEEE Conference on Computer Vision and Pattern Recognition, pp. 5265–5274 (2018)
27. Wang, M., Deng, W., Hu, J., Peng, J., Tao, X., Huang, Y.: Racial faces in-the-wild: reducing racial bias by deep unsupervised domain adaptation. arXiv preprint arXiv:1812.00194 (2018)
28. Wang, X., Zhang, S., Wang, S., Tianyu, F., Shi, H., Mei, T.: MIS-classified vector guided softmax loss for face recognition. In: Proceedings of the AAAI Conference on Artificial Intelligence, vol. 34, pp. 12241–12248 (2020)
29. Wen, Y., Zhang, K., Li, Z., Qiao, Yu.: A discriminative feature learning approach for deep face recognition. In: Leibe, B., Matas, J., Sebe, N., Welling, M. (eds.) ECCV 2016. LNCS, vol. 9911, pp. 499–515. Springer, Cham (2016). https://doi.org/10.1007/978-3-319-46478-7_31
30. Yi, D., Lei, Z., Liao, S., Li, S.Z.: Learning face representation from scratch. arXiv preprint arXiv:1411.7923 (2014)
31. Yuan, Y., Yang, K., Zhang, C.: Feature incay for representation regularization. arXiv preprint arXiv:1705.10284 (2017)
32. Zhang, K., Zhang, Z., Li, Z., Qiao, Yu.: Joint face detection and alignment using multitask cascaded convolutional networks. IEEE Signal Process. Lett. **23**(10), 1499–1503 (2016)
33. Zhang, X., Zhao, R., Qiao, Y., Wang, X., Li, H.: AdaCos: adaptively scaling cosine logits for effectively learning deep face representations. In: Proceedings of the IEEE/CVF Conference on Computer Vision and Pattern Recognition, pp. 10823–10832 (2019)
34. Zheng, T., Deng, W.: Cross-pose LFW: a database for studying cross-pose face recognition in unconstrained environments. Beijing University of Posts and Telecommunications, Technical report, 5:7 (2018)
35. Zheng, T., Deng, W., Hu, J.: Cross-age LFW: a database for studying cross-age face recognition in unconstrained environments. arXiv preprint arXiv:1708.08197 (2017)

Pre-training Strategies and Datasets for Facial Representation Learning

Adrian Bulat[1]([✉])(iD), Shiyang Cheng[1], Jing Yang[2](iD), Andrew Garbett[1],
Enrique Sanchez[1](iD), and Georgios Tzimiropoulos[1,3](iD)

[1] Samsung AI Cambridge, Cambridge, UK
adrian@adrianbulat.com, {shiyang.c,a.garbett}@samsung.com
[2] University of Nottingham, Nottingham, UK
jing.yang2@nottingham.ac.uk
[3] Queen Mary University London, London, UK
g.tzimiropoulos@qmul.ac.uk

Abstract. What is the best way to learn a universal face representation? Recent work on Deep Learning in the area of face analysis has focused on supervised learning for specific tasks of interest (e.g. face recognition, facial landmark localization etc.) but has overlooked the overarching question of how to find a facial representation that can be readily adapted to several facial analysis tasks and datasets. To this end, we make the following 4 contributions: (a) we introduce, for the first time, a comprehensive evaluation benchmark for facial representation learning consisting of 5 important face analysis tasks. (b) We systematically investigate two ways of large-scale representation learning applied to faces: supervised and unsupervised pre-training. Importantly, we focus our evaluations on the case of few-shot facial learning. (c) We investigate important properties of the training datasets including their size and quality (labelled, unlabelled or even uncurated). (d) To draw our conclusions, we conducted a very large number of experiments. Our main two findings are: (1) Unsupervised pre-training on completely in-the-wild, uncurated data provides consistent and, in some cases, significant accuracy improvements for all facial tasks considered. (2) Many existing facial video datasets seem to have a large amount of redundancy. We will release code, and pre-trained models to facilitate future research.

Keywords: Face recognition · Face alignment · Emotion recognition · 3D face reconstruction · Representation learning

1 Introduction

Supervised learning with Deep Neural Networks has been the standard approach to solving several Computer Vision problems over the recent past years [27,29,39,53,59]. Among others, this approach has been very successfully

---

Supplementary Information The online version contains supplementary material available at https://doi.org/10.1007/978-3-031-19778-9_7.

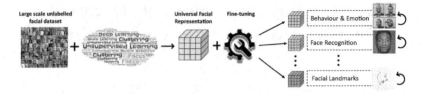

Fig. 1. We advocate for a new paradigm to solving face analysis based on the following pipeline: (1) collection of large-scale unlabelled facial dataset, (2) (task agnostic) network pre-training for universal facial representation learning, and (3) facial task-specific fine-tuning. **Our main result** is that even when training on a completely in-the-wild, uncurated dataset downloaded from Flickr, this generic pipeline provides consistent and, in some cases, significant accuracy improvements for all facial tasks considered.

applied to several face analysis tasks including face detection [6,17,36,80], recognition [16,57,67,68,77] and landmark localization [2,3,69,86]. For example, face recognition was one of the domains where even very early attempts in the area of deep learning demonstrated performance of super-human accuracy [49,61]. Beyond deep learning, this success can be largely attributed to the fact that for most face-related application domains, large scale datasets could be readily collected and annotated, see for example [3,7].

There are several concerns related to the above approach. Firstly, from a practical perspective, collecting and annotating new large scale face datasets is still necessary; examples of this are context-dependent domains like emotion recognition [23,62,63] and surveillance [5,21], or new considerations of existing problems like fair face recognition [54,60]. Secondly, from a methodological point of view, it is unsatisfactory for each application to require its own large-scale dataset, although there is only one object of interest - the human face.

To this end, we investigate, for the first time to our knowledge, the task of large-scale learning universal facial representation in a principled and systematic manner. In particular, we shed light to the following research questions:

– *"What is the best way to learn a universal facial representation that can be readily adapted to new tasks and datasets? Which facial representation is more amenable to few-shot facial learning?"*
– *"What is the importance of different training dataset properties (including size and quality) in learning this representation? Can we learn powerful facial feature representations from uncurated facial data as well?"*

To address this, **we make** the following **4 contributions**:

1. We introduce, for the first time, a comprehensive and principled evaluation benchmark for facial representation learning consisting of 5 important face analysis tasks, namely face recognition, AU recognition, emotion recognition, landmark localization and 3D reconstruction.
2. Within this benchmark, and for the first time, we systematically evaluate 2 ways of large-scale representation learning applied to faces: supervised and

unsupervised pre-training. Importantly, we focus our evaluations on the case of few-shot facial learning where only a limited amount of data is available for the downstream tasks.

3. We systematically evaluate the role of datasets in learning the facial feature presentations by constructing training datasets of varying size and quality. To this end, we considered ImageNet, several existing curated face datasets but also a new in-the-wild, uncurated face dataset downloaded from Flickr.

4. We conducted extensive experiments to answer the aforementioned research questions and from them we were able to draw several interesting observations and conclusions.

Our main findings are: (a) Even when training on a completely in-the-wild, uncurated dataset downloaded from Flickr, unsupervised pre-training pipeline provides consistent and, in some cases, significant accuracy improvements for all facial tasks considered. (b) We found that many existing facial video datasets seem to have a large amount of redundancy. Given that unsupervised pre-training is cheap and that the cost of annotating facial datasets is often significant, some of our findings could be particularly important for researchers when collecting new facial datasets is under consideration. Finally, we will release code and pre-trained models to facilitate future research.

2   Related Work

Facial Transfer Learning: Transfer learning in Computer Vision typically consists of ImageNet pre-training followed by fine-tuning on the downstream task [10, 15,53]. Because most recent face-related works are based on the collection of larger and larger facial datasets [3,24,44], the importance of transfer learning has been overlooked in face analysis and, especially, the face recognition literature. ImageNet pre-training has been applied to face analysis when training on small datasets is required, for example for emotion recognition [45], face anti-spoofing [48] and facial landmark localization [69]. Furthermore, the VGG-Face [47] or other large face datasets (e.g. [44]) have been identified as better alternatives by several works, see for example [19,30,31,33,37,48,51,52,76]. To our knowledge, we are the first to systematically evaluate supervised network pre-training using both ImageNet and VGG-Face datasets on several face analysis tasks.

Facial Datasets: The general trend is to collect larger and larger facial datasets for the face-related task in hand [3,24,44]. Also it is known that label noise can severely impact accuracy (e.g. see Table 6 of [16]). Beyond faces, the work of [40] presents a study which shows the benefit of *weakly supervised* pre-training on much larger datasets for general image classification and object detection. Similarly, we also investigate the impact of the size of facial datasets on *unsupervised pre-training* for facial representation learning. Furthermore, one of our main results is to show that a high-quality facial representation can be learned even when a completely uncurated face dataset is used.

Few-shot Face Analysis: Few-shot refers to both low data and label regime. There is very little work in this area. To our knowledge, there is no prior work on few-shot face recognition where the trend is to collect large-scale datasets with millions of samples (e.g. [24]). There is no systematic study for the task of emotion recognition, too. There is only one work on few-shot learning for facial landmark localization, namely that of [1] which, different to our approach, proposes an auto-encoder approach for network pre-training. To our knowledge, our evaluation framework provides the very first comprehensive attempt to evaluate the transferability of facial representations for few-shot learning for several face analysis tasks.

Semi-supervised Face Analysis: Semi-supervised learning has been applied to the domain of Action Unit recognition where data labelling is extremely laborious [82–84]. Although these methods work with few labels, they are domain specific (as opposed to our work), assuming also that extra annotations are available in terms of "peak" and "valley" frames which is also an expensive operation.

Unsupervised Learning: There is a very large number of recently proposed unsupervised/self-supervised learning methods, see for example [8,9,11,12,22, 25,43,73,79]. To our knowledge, only very few attempts from this line of research have been applied to faces so far. The authors of [71] learn face embeddings in a self-supervised manner by predicting the motion field between two facial images. The authors of [65] propose to combine several facial representations learned using an autoencoding framework. In this work, we explore learning facial representations in an unsupervised manner using the state-of-the-art method of [9] and show how to effectively fine-tune the learned representations to the various face analysis tasks of our benchmark.

3   Method

Supervised deep learning directly applied to large labelled datasets is the de facto approach to solving the most important face analysis tasks. In this section, we propose to take a different path to solving face analysis based on the following 2-stage pipeline: (task agnostic) network pre-training followed by task adaptation. Importantly, we argue that network pre-training should be actually considered as part of the method and not just a simple initialization step. We explore two important aspects of network pre-training: (1) the method used, and (2) the dataset used. Likewise, we highlight hyper-parameter optimization for task adaptation as an absolutely crucial component of the proposed pipeline. Finally, we emphasize the importance of evaluating face analysis on low data regimes, too. We describe important aspects of the pipeline in the following sections.

3.1   Network Pre-training

Supervised Pre-training of face networks on ImageNet or VGG datasets is not new. We use these networks as strong baselines. For the first time, we comprehensively evaluate their impact on the most important face analysis tasks.

Unsupervised Pre-training: Inspired by [9,22,26,43], we explore, for the first time in literature, large-scale unsupervised learning on facial images to learn a universal, task-agnostic facial representation. To this end, we adopt the recently proposed SwAV [9] which simultaneously clusters the data while enforcing consistency between the cluster assignments produced for different augmentations of the same image. The pretext task is defined as a "swapped" prediction problem where the code of one view is predicted from the representation of another: $\mathcal{L}(\mathbf{z}_0, \mathbf{z}_1) = \ell(\mathbf{z}_0, \mathbf{q}_1) + \ell(\mathbf{z}_1, \mathbf{q}_0)$, where $\mathbf{z}_0, \mathbf{z}_1$ are the features produced by the network for two different views of the same image and $\mathbf{q}_0, \mathbf{q}_1$ their corresponding codes computed by matching these feature using a set of prototypes. ℓ is a cross-entropy (with temperature) loss. See supplementary material for training details.

3.2 Pre-training Datasets

With pre-training being now an important part of the face analysis pipeline, it is important to investigate what datasets can be used to this end. We argue that supervised pre-training is sub-optimal due to two main reasons: (a) the resulting models may be overly specialized to the source domain and task (e.g. face recognition pre-training) or be too generic (e.g. ImageNet pre-training), and (b) the amount of labeled data may be limited and/or certain parts of the natural data distribution may not be covered. To alleviate this, for the first time, we propose to explore large scale unsupervised pre-training on 4 facial datasets of interest, under two settings: using curated and uncurated data. The later departs from the common paradigm that uses carefully collected data that already includes some forms of explicit annotations and post-processing. In contrast, in the later case, all acquired facial images are used.

Curated Datasets. For unsupervised pre-training we explore 3 curated datasets, collected for various facial analysis tasks: (a) Full VGG-Face ($\sim 3.4M$), (b) Small VGG-Face ($\sim 1M$) and (c) Large-Scale-Face ($> 5.0M$), consisting of VGG-Face2 [7], 300W-LP [85], IMDb-face [66], AffectNet [44] and Wider-Face [78]. During unsupervised pre-training we drop all labels using only the facial images. See supplementary material for more details.

Uncurated Datasets. For a more realistic and practical scenario, we go beyond sanitized datasets, by creating a completely uncurated, in-the-wild, dataset, coined Flickr-Face, of $\sim 1.5M$ facial images by simply downloading images from Flickr (using standard search keywords like "faces", "humans", etc.) and filtering them with a face detector [17] (the dataset will be made available). In total we collected 1.793.119 facial images. For more details, see supp. material.

3.3 Facial Task Adaptation

End Facial Tasks: To draw as safe conclusions as possible, we used a large variety of face tasks (5 in total) including face recognition (classification), facial Action Unit intensity estimation (regression), emotion recognition in terms of valence and arousal (regression), 2D facial landmark localization (pixel-wise regression), and 3D face reconstruction (GCN regression). For these tasks, we used, in total, 10 datasets for evaluation purposes.

Adaptation Methods: We are given a pre-trained model on task m, composed of a backbone $g(.)$ and a network head $h^m(.)$. The model follows the ResNet-50 [27] architecture. We considered two widely-used methods for task adaptation: (a) *Network fine-tuning* adapts the weights of $g(.)$ to the new task m_i. The previous head is replaced with a task-specific head $h^{m_i}(.)$ that is trained from scratch. (b) *Linear layer adaptation* keeps the weights of $g(.)$ fixed and trains only the new head $h^{m_i}(.)$. Depending on the task, the structure of the head varies. This will be defined for each task in the corresponding section. See also Sect. 5.

Hyper-parameter Optimization: We find that, without a proper hyper-parameters selection for each task and setting, the produced results are often misleading. In order to alleviate this and ensure a fair

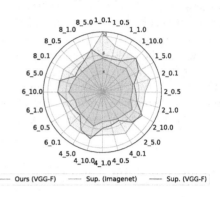

Fig. 2. Facial landmark localization accuracy in terms of NME (%) of 3 different pre-training methods for selected combinations of hyperparameters. The labels on the figure's perimeter show the scheduler length (first value) and backbone relative's learning rate (second value) separated by an underscore. Each circle on the radar plot denotes a constant error level. Points located closer to the center correspond to lower error levels. Accuracy greatly varies for different hyperparameters.

comparison, we search for the following optimal hyper-parameters: (a) learning rate, (b) scheduler duration and (c) backbone learning rate for the pre-trained ResNet-50. This search is repeated for *each data point* defined by the tuple (task, dataset, pre-training method and % of training data). In total, this yields in an extraordinary number of experiments for discovering the optimal hyperparameters.

Figure 2 shows the importance of hyperparameters on accuracy for the task of facial landmark localization. In particular, for 1 specific value of learning rate, about 40 different combinations of scheduler duration and backbone relative's learning rate are evaluated. 24 of those combinations are placed on the perimeter of the figure. The 3 closed curves represent the Normalized Mean Error (NME) for each hyperparameter combination for each pre-training method. We observe that accuracy greatly varies for different hyperparameters.

3.4 Few-Shot Learning-Based Evaluation

We explore, for the first time, evaluating the face models using a varying percentage of training data for each face analysis task. Specifically, beyond the standard evaluation using 100% of training data, we emphasize the importance of the low data regime, in particular 10% and 2%, which has a clear impact when new datasets are to be collected and annotated. The purpose of the proposed evaluation is not only to show which method works the best for this setting but also to draw interesting conclusions about the redundancy of existing facial datasets. See also Sect. 6.

Table 1. Comparison between the facial representations learned by MoCov2 and SwAV, by fine-tuning the models on 2% of 300W and DISFA.

Method	300W	DISFA
	NME (%)	ICC
Scratch	13.5	.237
MoCov2	11.9	.280
SwAV	**4.97**	**.560**
SwAV (256)	5.00	.549

3.5 Self-distillation for Semi-supervised Learning

The low data regime of the previous section refers to having both few data and few labels. We further propose to investigate the case of semi-supervised learning [12,35,74,75] where a full facial dataset has been collected but only few labels are provided. To this end, we propose a simple self-distillation technique which fully utilizes network pre-training: we use the fine-tuned network to generate in an online manner new labels for training an identically sized student model on unlabeled data. The student is initialized from a pre-trained model trained in a fully unsupervised manner. The self-distillation process is repeated iteratively for T steps, where, at each step, the previously trained model becomes the teacher. Formally, the knowledge transfer is defined as $\mathrm{argmin}_{\theta_t} \mathcal{L}((f(x, \theta_{t-1}), f(x, \theta_t)))$, where x is the input sample, θ_{t-1} and θ_t are the parameters of the teacher and the student, respectively, and $\mathcal{L}$ is the task loss (e.g. pixel-wise ℓ_2 loss for facial landmark localization).

4 Ablation Studies

In this section, we study and answer key questions related to our approach.

Fine-Tuning vs. Linear Adaptation: Our results, provided in Table 7, show that linear adaptation results in significant performance degradation. As our ultimate goal is high accuracy for the end facial task, linear adaptation is not considered for the rest of our experiments.

How Much Facial Data Is Required? Unlike supervised, unsupervised pre-training does not require labels and hence it can be applied easily to all types of combinations of facial datasets. Then, a natural question arising is how much data is needed to learn a high-quality representation. To this end, we used 3 datasets of varying size. The first one, comprising $\sim 3.3M$ images, is the original

VGG-Face dataset (VGG-Face). The second comprises $\sim 1M$ images randomly selected from VGGFace2 (VGG-Face-small). The last one, coined as Large-Scale-Face, comprises over 5M images, and is obtained by combining VGG-Face, 300W-LP [85], IMDb-face [66], AffectNet [44] and WiderFace [78]. For more details regarding the datasets see Sect. 3.2. We trained 3 models on these datasets and evaluated them for the tasks of facial landmark localization, AU intensity estimation and face recognition. As the results from Table 2 show, VGG-Face vs. VGG-Face-small yields small yet noticeable improvements especially for the case of 2% of labelled data. We did not observe further gains by training on Large-Scale-Face.

Curated vs. Uncurated Datasets: While the previous section investigated the quantity of data required, it did not explore the question of data quality. While we did not use any labels during the unsupervised pre-training phase, one may argue that all datasets considered are sanitized as they were collected by human annotators with a specific task in mind. In this section, we go beyond sanitized datasets, by experimenting with the newly completely uncurated, in-the-wild, dataset, coined Flickr-Face, introduced in Sect. 3.2.

We trained a model on it and evaluated it on the same tasks/datasets of the previous section. Table 2 shows some remarkable results: the resulting

Table 2. Impact of different datasets on the facial representations learned *in an unsupervised manner* for the tasks of facial landmark localization (300W), AU intensity estimation (DISFA) and face recognition (IJB-B).

Data amount	Unsup. data	300W	DISFA	IJBB
		NME	ICC	10^{-4}
100%	VGG-Face-small	3.91	.583	0.910
	VGG-Face	3.85	**.598**	**0.912**
	Large-Scale-Face	**3.83**	.593	**0.912**
	Flickr-Face	3.86	.590	0.911
10%	VGG-Face-small	4.37	.572	0.887
	VGG-Face	**4.25**	.592	0.889
	Large-Scale-Face	4.30	**.597**	**0.892**
	Flickr-Face	4.31	.581	0.887
2%	VGG-Face-small	5.46	.550	0.729
	VGG-Face	**4.97**	.560	**0.744**
	Large-Scale-Face	4.98	.551	0.743
	Flickr-Face	5.05	**.571**	0.740

model is on par with the one trained on the full VGG-Face dataset (Sect. 5 shows that it outperforms all other pre-training methods, too). We believe that this result can pave a whole new way to how practitioners, both in industry and academia, collect and label facial datasets for new tasks and applications.

Pre-training Task or Data? In order to fully understand whether the aforementioned gains are coming from the unsupervised task alone, the data, or both, we pre-trained a model on ImageNet dataset using *both* supervised and unsupervised pre-training. Our experiments showed that both models performed similarly (e.g. 4.97% vs 5.1% on 300W@2% of data) and significantly more poorly than models trained on face datasets. We conclude that *both unsupervised pretraining and data* are required for high accuracy.

Effect of Unsupervised Method: Herein, we compare the results obtained by changing the unsupervised pre-training method from SwAV to Moco-v2 [26]. Table 1 shows that SwAV largely outperforms Moco-v2, emphasizing the importance of utilizing the most powerful available unsupervised method. Note, that better representation learning as measured on imagenet, doesn't equate with better representation in general [13], hence way it's important to validate the performance of different methods for faces too. Furthermore, we evaluated SwAV models using different batch-sizes which is shown to be an important hyperparameter. We found both models to perform similarly. See SwAV (256) in Table 1 for the model trained with batch-size 256. With small batch-size training requires less resources, yet we found that it was prolonged by 2×.

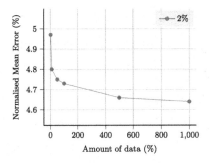 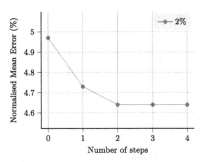

Fig. 3. Self-distillation accuracy for facial landmark vs. (left) amount of unlabeled data (100% corresponds to 300 W), and (right) number of distillation steps.

Self-distillation for Semi-supervised Learning: Herein, we evaluate the effectiveness of network pre-training on self-distillation (see Sect. 3.5) for the task of semi-supervised facial landmark localization (300W).

We compare unsupervised vs. supervised pre-training on VGG-Face as well as training from scratch. These networks are fine-tuned on 300W using 100% and, the most interesting, 10% and 2% of the data. Then, they are used as students for self-distillation. Figure 4 clearly shows the effectiveness of unsupervised student pre-training.

Furthermore, a large pool of unlabelled data was formed by 300W, AFLW [32], WFLW [72] and COFW [4,20]), and then used for self-distillation. Figure 3 (left) shows the impact on the accuracy of the final model by adding more and more unlabelled data to the self-distillation process. Clearly, self-distillation based on network pre-training is capable of effectively utilizing a large amount of unlabelled data. Finally, Fig. 3 (right) shows the impact of the number of self-distillation steps on accuracy.

Fig. 4. Effectiveness of network pre-training on self-distillation for the tasks of facial landmark localization.

Other Supervised Pre-training: Our best supervised pre-trained network is that based on training CosFace [68] on VGG-Face. Herein, for completeness, we compare this to supervised pre-training on another task/dataset, namely facial landmark localization. As Table 3 shows, the supervised pre-trained model on VGG-Face outperforms it by large margin. This is expected due to the massive size of VGG-Face.

Table 3. Supervised pre-training applied to different datasets. The models are evaluated for AU intensity estimation on DISFA.

Data amount	Pretrain. method		
	Sup. (ImageNet)	Sup. (VGG-F)	Sup. (300 W)
100%	.560	.575	.463
10%	.556	.560	.460
1%	.453	.542	.414

5   Main Results

In this section, we thoroughly test the generalizability of the universal facial representations by adapting the resulting models to the most important facial analysis tasks. The full training and implementation details for each of this tasks is detailed in the corresponding sub-section. Training code will be made available.

Data & Label Regime: For all datasets and tasks, we used fine-tuning for network adaptation using 3 data and label regimes: full (100%), low (10%) and very low (2% or less). For all low data scenarios, we randomly sub-sampled a set of annotated images without accounting for the labels (i.e. we don't attempt to balance the classes). Once formed, the same subset is used for all subsequent experiments to avoid noise induced by different sets of images. For face recognition, we deviated slightly from the above setting by enforcing that at least 1/4 of the identities are preserved for the very low data regime of 2%. This is a consequence of the training objective used for face recognition that is sensitive to both the number of identities and samples per identity.

Models Compared: For unsupervised network pre-training, we report the results of two models, one trained on the full VGG-Face and one on Flickr-Face. These models are denoted as Ours (VGG-F) and Ours (Flickr-F). These models are compared with supervised pre-training on ImageNet and VGG-Face (denoted as VGG-F), as well as the model trained from scratch.

Comparison with SOTA: Where possible, we also present the results reported by state-of-the-art methods for each task on the few-shot setting. Finally, for each task, and, to put our results into perspective, we report the accuracy of a state-of-the-art method for the given task. We note however, that the results are not directly comparable, due to different networks, losses, training procedure, and even training datasets.

Table 4. Face recognition results in terms of TAR on IJB-B and IJB-C.

Data amount	Pretrain. method	IJB-B					IJB-C				
		10^{-6}	10^{-5}	10^{-4}	10^{-3}	10^{-2}	10^{-6}	10^{-5}	10^{-4}	10^{-3}	10^{-2}
100%	Scratch	0.389	0.835	**0.912**	0.950	0.975	0.778	0.883	0.931	0.961	0.981
	Sup. (ImageNet)	0.390	**0.843**	**0.912**	0.950	0.975	0.831	**0.891**	0.931	0.961	0.981
	Ours (Flickr-F)	0.406	0.834	0.911	**0.951**	0.975	0.807	0.880	**0.932**	**0.962**	**0.982**
	Ours (VGG-F)	**0.432**	0.835	**0.912**	0.950	**0.976**	**0.882**	0.882	**0.932**	0.961	0.981
10%	Scratch	0.326	0.645	0.848	0.926	0.965	0.506	0.7671	0.8840	0.940	0.721
	Sup. (ImageNet)	0.320	0.653	0.858	0.926	0.966	0.503	0.779	0.891	0.941	0.973
	Ours (Flickr-F)	0.334	0.758	0.887	0.940	0.970	0.715	0.834	0.909	0.952	**0.978**
	Ours (VGG-F)	**0.392**	**0.784**	**0.889**	**0.941**	**0.972**	**0.733**	**0.847**	**0.911**	**0.953**	0.977
2%	Scratch	0.086	0.479	0.672	0.800	0.909	0.400	0.570	0.706	0.829	0.922
	Sup. (ImageNet)	0.264	0.553	0.694	0.820	0.915	**0.493**	0.599	0.723	0.841	0.928
	Ours (Flickr-F)	0.282	**0.558**	0.740	0.870	0.944	0.486	**0.649**	**0.786**	0.891	0.954
	Ours (VGG-F)	**0.333**	0.547	**0.744**	**0.873**	**0.948**	0.455	0.637	**0.786**	**0.893**	**0.956**
SOTA (from paper) [16]		0.401	0.821	0.907	0.950	0.978	0.0.767	0.879	0.929	0.964	0.984

5.1 Face Recognition

For face recognition, we fine-tuned the models on the VGGFace [7] and tested them on the IJB-B [70] and IJB-C [42] datasets. The task specific head $h(.)$ consists of a linear layer. The whole network was optimized using the CosFace loss [68]. Note that, for this experiment, since training was done on VGGFace [7], the results of supervised pre-training on VGG-Face are omitted (as meaningless). For training details, see supplementary material.

Results are shown in Table 4. Both *Ours (VGG-F)* and *Ours (Flickr-F)* perform similarly and both they outperform the other baselines by large margin for the low (10%) and very low (2%) data regimes. For the latter case, the accuracy drops significantly for all cases.

5.2 Facial Landmark Localization

We fine-tuned the pre-trained models for facial landmark localization on 300W [55], AFLW-19 [32], WFLW [72] and COFW-68 [4,20] reporting results in terms of $\mathrm{NME_{i\text{-}o}}$ [55] or $\mathrm{NME_{diag}}$ [32]. We followed the current best practices based on heatmap regression [3]. In order to accommodate for the pixel-wise nature of the task, the task specific head $h(.)$ is defined as a set of 3 1×1 conv. layers with 256 channels, each interleaved with bilinear upsampling operations for recovering part of the lost resolution. Additional high resolution information is brought up via skip connections and summation from the lower part of the network.

Table 5. Comparison against state-of-the-art in few-shot facial landmark localization.

300W	100%	10%	1.5%
RCN+ [28]	3.46	4.47	–
TS^3 [18]	3.49	5.03	–
3FabRec [1]	3.82	4.47	5.10
Ours (VGG-F)	**3.20**	**3.48**	**4.13**
AFLW	100%	10%	1%
RCN+ [28]	1.61	–	2.88
TS^3 [18]	–	2.14	–
3FabRec [1]	1.87	2.03	2.38
Ours (VGG-F)	**1.54**	**1.70**	**1.91**
WFLW	100%	10%	0.7%
SA [50]	4.39	7.20	–
3FabRec [1]	5.62	6.73	8.39
Ours (VGG-F)	**4.57**	**5.44**	**7.11**

Despite the simple and un-optimized architecture we found that the network

Table 6. Facial landmark localization results on 300W (test set), COFW, WFLW and AFLW in terms of NME$_{\text{inter-ocular}}$, except for AFLW where NME$_{\text{diag}}$ is used.

Data amount	Pretrain. method	300W	COFW	WFLW	AFLW
100%	Scratch	4.50	4.10	5.10	1.59
	Sup. (ImageNet)	4.16	3.63	4.80	1.59
	Sup. (VGG-F)	3.97	3.51	4.70	1.58
	Ours (Flickr-F)	3.86	3.45	4.65	1.57
	Ours (VGG-F)	**3.85**	**3.32**	**4.57**	**1.55**
10%	Scratch	6.61	5.63	6.82	1.84
	Sup. (ImageNet)	5.15	5.32	6.56	1.81
	Sup. (VGG-F)	4.55	4.46	5.87	1.77
	Ours (Flickr-F)	4.31	4.27	5.45	**1.73**
	Ours (VGG-F)	**4.25**	**3.95**	**5.44**	1.74
2%	Scratch	13.52	14.7	10.43	2.23
	Sup. (ImageNet)	8.04	8.05	8.99	2.09
	Sup. (VGG-F)	5.45	5.55	6.94	2.00
	Ours (Flickr-F)	5.05	5.18	6.53	**1.86**
	Ours (VGG-F)	**4.97**	**4.70**	**6.29**	1.88
SOTA (from paper) [69]		3.85	3.45	4.60	1.57
SOTA (from paper) [34]		–	–	4.37	1.39

performs very well, thanks to the strong facial representation learned. All models were trained using a pixel-wise MSE loss. For full training details, see supp. material.

Results are shown in Table 6: unsupervised pre-training (both models) outperform the other baselines for all data regimes, especially for the low and very low cases. For the latter case, *Ours (VGG-F)* outperforms *Ours (Flickr-F)* probably because *Ours (VGG-F)* contains a more balanced distribution of facial poses. The best supervised pre-training method is VGG-F showing the importance of pre-training on facial datasets.

Furthermore, Table 5 shows comparison with few very recent works on few-shot face alignment. Our method scores significantly higher across all data regimes and datasets tested setting a new state-of-the-art despite the straight-forward network architecture and the generic nature of our method.

5.3   Action Unit (AU) Intensity Estimation

We fine-tuned and evaluated the pre-trained models for AU intensity estimation on the corresponding partitions of BP4D [64,81] and DISFA [41] datasets. The network head $h(.)$ is implemented using a linear layer. The whole network is trained to regress the intensity value of each AU using an ℓ_2 loss. We report results in terms of intra-class correlation (ICC) [58]. For training details, see supplementary material.

Results are shown in Table 7: unsupervised pre-training (both models) outperform the other baselines for all data regimes. Notably, our models achieve very high accuracy even for the case when 2% of data was used. Supervised pre-training on VGG-F also works well.

Furthermore, Table 8 shows comparison with very recent works on semi-supervised AU intensity estimation. We note that these methods had access to all training data; only the amount of labels was varied. Our methods, although trained under both very low data and label regimes, outperformed them by a significant margin.

Table 7. AU intensity estimation results in terms of ICC on BP4D and DISFA.

Data amount	Pretrain. method	DISFA		BP4D	
		Finetune	Linear	Finetune	Linear
100%	Scratch	.318	–	.617	–
	Sup. (ImageNet)	.560	.316	.708	.587
	Sup. (VGG-F)	.575	.235	.700	.564
	Ours (Flickr-F)	.590	**.373**	.715	.599
	Ours (VGG-F)	**.598**	.342	**.719**	**.610**
10%	Scratch	.313	–	.622	–
	Sup. (ImageNet)	.556	.300	.698	.573
	Sup. (VGG-F)	.560	.232	.692	.564
	Ours (Flickr-F)	.581	**.352**	.699	.603
	Ours (VGG-F)	**.592**	.340	**.706**	**.604**
1%	Scratch	.237	–	.586	–
	Sup. (ImageNet)	.453	.301	.689	.564
	Sup. (VGG-F)	.542	.187	.690	.562
	Ours (Flickr-F)	**.571**	.321	**.695**	**.596**
	Ours (VGG-F)	.560	**.326**	.694	.592
SOTA (from paper) [46]		0.57	–	0.72	–

Table 8. Comparison against state-of-the-art on few-shot Facial AU intensity estimation on the BP4D dataset.

Method	Data amount	AU					Avg.
		6	10	12	14	17	
KBSS [82]	1%	.760	.725	.840	.445	.454	.645
KJRE [84]	6%	.710	.610	.870	.390	.420	.600
CLFL [83]	1%	.766	.703	.827	.411	**.600**	.680
SSCFL [56]	2%	.766	.749	.857	.475	.553	.680
Ours	1%	**.789**	**.756**	**.882**	**.529**	.578	**.707**

5.4   Emotion Recognition

We observe similar behaviour on the well-established AffectNet [44] for emotion recognition. For details and results, see supplementary material.

5.5   3D Face Reconstruction

We fine-tuned all models on the 300W-LP [85] dataset and tested them on AFLW2000-3D [85]. Our task specific head is implemented with a GCN based on spiral convolutions [38]. The network was trained to minimise the ℓ_1 distance between the predicted and the ground truth vertices.

Table 9. 3D face reconstruction reconstruction in terms of NME (68 points) on AFLW2000-3D.

Data	Pretrain. method				
	Scratch	Sup. (Imagenet)	Sup. (VGG-F)	Ours (Flickr-F)	Ours (VGG-F)
100%	3.70	3.58	3.51	3.53	**3.42**
10%	4.72	4.06	3.82	3.81	**3.72**
2%	7.11	6.15	4.42	4.50	**4.31**
SOTA (from paper) [14]: 3.39					

Training Details: Since 300W-LP has a small number of identities, during training we randomly augment the data using the following transformations: scaling($0.85 \times -1.15 \times$), in-plane rotation ($\pm 45°$), and random 10% translation w.r.t image width and height. Depending on the setting, we trained the model between 120 and 360 epochs using a learning rate of 0.05, a weight decay of 10^{-4} and SGD with momentum (set to 0.9). All models were trained using 2 GPUs.

Results are shown in Table 9: it can be seen that, *for all* data regimes, our unsupervised models outperform the supervised baselines. Supervised pre-training on VGG-F also works well. For more results, see supplementary material.

6   Discussion and Conclusions

Several conclusions can be drawn from our results: Unsupervised pre-training followed by task-specific fine-tuning provides very strong baselines for face analysis. For example, we showed that such generically built baselines outperformed recently proposed methods for few-shot/semi-supervised learning (e.g. for facial landmark localization and AU intensity estimation) some of which are based on quite sophisticated techniques. Moreover, we showed that unsupervised pre-training largely boosts self-distillation. Hence, it might be useful for newly-proposed task-specific methods to consider such a pipeline for both development and evaluation especially when newly-achieved accuracy improvements are to be reported.

Furthermore, these results can be achieved even by simply training on uncurated facial datasets that can be readily downloaded from image repositories. The excellent results obtained by pre-training on Flickr-Face are particularly encouraging. Note that we could have probably created a better and more balanced dataset in terms of facial pose by running a method for facial pose estimation.

When new datasets are to be collected, such powerful pre-trained networks can be potentially used for minimizing data collection and label annotation labour. Our results show that many existing datasets (e.g. AFLW, DISFA, BP4D, even AffectNet) seem to have a large amount of redundancy. This is more evident for video datasets (e.g. DISFA, BP4D).

Note that by no means our results imply or suggest that all face analysis can be solved with small labelled datasets. For example, for face recognition, it was absolutely necessary to fine-tune on the whole VGG-Face in order to get high accuracy.

References

1. Browatzki, B., Wallraven, C.: 3FabRec: fast few-shot face alignment by reconstruction. In: Proceedings of the IEEE/CVF Conference on Computer Vision and Pattern Recognition, pp. 6110–6120 (2020)
2. Bulat, A., Tzimiropoulos, G.: Two-stage convolutional part heatmap regression for the 1st 3D face alignment in the wild (3DFAW) challenge. In: Hua, G., Jégou, H. (eds.) ECCV 2016. LNCS, vol. 9914, pp. 616–624. Springer, Cham (2016). https://doi.org/10.1007/978-3-319-48881-3_43
3. Bulat, A., Tzimiropoulos, G.: How far are we from solving the 2D & 3D face alignment problem? (and a dataset of 230,000 3D facial landmarks). In: Proceedings of the IEEE International Conference on Computer Vision, pp. 1021–1030 (2017)
4. Burgos-Artizzu, X.P., Perona, P., Dollár, P.: Robust face landmark estimation under occlusion. In: Proceedings of the IEEE International Conference on Computer Vision, pp. 1513–1520 (2013)
5. Burton, A.M., Wilson, S., Cowan, M., Bruce, V.: Face recognition in poor-quality video: evidence from security surveillance. Psychol. Sci. **10**(3), 243–248 (1999)
6. Cai, Z., Fan, Q., Feris, R.S., Vasconcelos, N.: A unified multi-scale deep convolutional neural network for fast object detection. In: Leibe, B., Matas, J., Sebe, N., Welling, M. (eds.) ECCV 2016. LNCS, vol. 9908, pp. 354–370. Springer, Cham (2016). https://doi.org/10.1007/978-3-319-46493-0_22
7. Cao, Q., Shen, L., Xie, W., Parkhi, O.M., Zisserman, A.: VGGFace2: a dataset for recognising faces across pose and age. In: 2018 13th IEEE International Conference on Automatic Face & Gesture Recognition (FG 2018), pp. 67–74. IEEE (2018)
8. Caron, M., Bojanowski, P., Joulin, A., Douze, M.: Deep clustering for unsupervised learning of visual features. In: Ferrari, V., Hebert, M., Sminchisescu, C., Weiss, Y. (eds.) Computer Vision – ECCV 2018. LNCS, vol. 11218, pp. 139–156. Springer, Cham (2018). https://doi.org/10.1007/978-3-030-01264-9_9
9. Caron, M., Misra, I., Mairal, J., Goyal, P., Bojanowski, P., Joulin, A.: Unsupervised learning of visual features by contrasting cluster assignments. arXiv preprint arXiv:2006.09882 (2020)
10. Chen, L.C., Papandreou, G., Kokkinos, I., Murphy, K., Yuille, A.L.: Semantic image segmentation with deep convolutional nets and fully connected CRFs. arXiv preprint arXiv:1412.7062 (2014)
11. Chen, T., Kornblith, S., Norouzi, M., Hinton, G.: A simple framework for contrastive learning of visual representations. arXiv (2020)
12. Chen, T., Kornblith, S., Swersky, K., Norouzi, M., Hinton, G.: Big self-supervised models are strong semi-supervised learners. arXiv preprint arXiv:2006.10029 (2020)
13. Chen, X., He, K.: Exploring simple Siamese representation learning. arXiv preprint arXiv:2011.10566 (2020)
14. Cheng, S., Tzimiropoulos, G., Shen, J., Pantic, M.: Faster, better and more detailed: 3D face reconstruction with graph convolutional networks. In: Ishikawa, H., Liu, C.-L., Pajdla, T., Shi, J. (eds.) ACCV 2020. LNCS, vol. 12626, pp. 188–205. Springer, Cham (2021). https://doi.org/10.1007/978-3-030-69541-5_12
15. Dai, J., Li, Y., He, K., Sun, J.: R-FCN: object detection via region-based fully convolutional networks. In: NIPS (2016)
16. Deng, J., Guo, J., Xue, N., Zafeiriou, S.: ArcFace: additive angular margin loss for deep face recognition. In: Proceedings of the IEEE Conference on Computer Vision and Pattern Recognition, pp. 4690–4699 (2019)

17. Deng, J., Guo, J., Zhou, Y., Yu, J., Kotsia, I., Zafeiriou, S.: RetinaFace: single-stage dense face localisation in the wild. arXiv preprint arXiv:1905.00641 (2019)
18. Dong, X., Yang, Y.: Teacher supervises students how to learn from partially labeled images for facial landmark detection. In: Proceedings of the IEEE International Conference on Computer Vision, pp. 783–792 (2019)
19. Fan, Y., Lu, X., Li, D., Liu, Y.: Video-based emotion recognition using CNN-RNN and C3D hybrid networks. In: ACM International Conference on Multimodal Interaction (2016)
20. Ghiasi, G., Fowlkes, C.C.: Occlusion coherence: detecting and localizing occluded faces. arXiv preprint arXiv:1506.08347 (2015)
21. Grgic, M., Delac, K., Grgic, S.: SCface-surveillance cameras face database. Multimedia Tools Appl. **51**(3), 863–879 (2011)
22. Grill, J.B., et al.: Bootstrap your own latent: a new approach to self-supervised learning. arXiv preprint arXiv:2006.07733 (2020)
23. Gunes, H., Pantic, M.: Automatic, dimensional and continuous emotion recognition. Int. J. Synth. Emot. (IJSE) **1**(1), 68–99 (2010)
24. Guo, Y., Zhang, L., Hu, Y., He, X., Gao, J.: MS-Celeb-1M: a dataset and benchmark for large-scale face recognition. In: Leibe, B., Matas, J., Sebe, N., Welling, M. (eds.) ECCV 2016. LNCS, vol. 9907, pp. 87–102. Springer, Cham (2016). https://doi.org/10.1007/978-3-319-46487-9_6
25. He, K., Fan, H., Wu, Y., Xie, S., Girshick, R.: Momentum contrast for unsupervised visual representation learning. arXiv (2019)
26. He, K., Fan, H., Wu, Y., Xie, S., Girshick, R.: Momentum contrast for unsupervised visual representation learning. In: Proceedings of the IEEE/CVF Conference on Computer Vision and Pattern Recognition, pp. 9729–9738 (2020)
27. He, K., Zhang, X., Ren, S., Sun, J.: Deep residual learning for image recognition. In: CVPR, pp. 770–778 (2016)
28. Honari, S., Molchanov, P., Tyree, S., Vincent, P., Pal, C., Kautz, J.: Improving landmark localization with semi-supervised learning. In: Proceedings of the IEEE Conference on Computer Vision and Pattern Recognition, pp. 1546–1555 (2018)
29. Huang, G., Liu, Z., Van Der Maaten, L., Weinberger, K.Q.: Densely connected convolutional networks. In: Proceedings of the IEEE Conference on Computer Vision and Pattern Recognition, pp. 4700–4708 (2017)
30. Kaya, H., Gürpınar, F., Salah, A.A.: Video-based emotion recognition in the wild using deep transfer learning and score fusion. Image Vis. Comput. **65**, 66–75 (2017)
31. Knyazev, B., Shvetsov, R., Efremova, N., Kuharenko, A.: Convolutional neural networks pretrained on large face recognition datasets for emotion classification from video. arXiv preprint arXiv:1711.04598 (2017)
32. Koestinger, M., Wohlhart, P., Roth, P.M., Bischof, H.: Annotated facial landmarks in the wild: a large-scale, real-world database for facial landmark localization. In: 2011 IEEE International Conference on Computer Vision Workshops (ICCV Workshops), pp. 2144–2151. IEEE (2011)
33. Kossaifi, J., Toisoul, A., Bulat, A., Panagakis, Y., Hospedales, T.M., Pantic, M.: Factorized higher-order CNNs with an application to spatio-temporal emotion estimation. In: CVPR (2020)
34. Kumar, A., et al.: LUVLi face alignment: estimating landmarks' location, uncertainty, and visibility likelihood. In: Proceedings of the IEEE/CVF Conference on Computer Vision and Pattern Recognition, pp. 8236–8246 (2020)
35. Lee, D.H.: Pseudo-label: the simple and efficient semi-supervised learning method for deep neural networks. In: Workshop on Challenges in Representation Learning, ICML, vol. 3 (2013)

36. Li, J., et al.: DSFD: dual shot face detector. In: Proceedings of the IEEE Conference on Computer Vision and Pattern Recognition, pp. 5060–5069 (2019)
37. Li, S., Deng, W.: Deep facial expression recognition: a survey. IEEE Trans. Affect. Comput. **13**, 1195–1215 (2020)
38. Lim, I., Dielen, A., Campen, M., Kobbelt, L.: A simple approach to intrinsic correspondence learning on unstructured 3D meshes. In: Leal-Taixé, L., Roth, S. (eds.) ECCV 2018. LNCS, vol. 11131, pp. 349–362. Springer, Cham (2019). https://doi.org/10.1007/978-3-030-11015-4_26
39. Long, J., Shelhamer, E., Darrell, T.: Fully convolutional networks for semantic segmentation. In: Proceedings of the IEEE Conference on Computer Vision and Pattern Recognition, pp. 3431–3440 (2015)
40. Mahajan, D., et al.: Exploring the limits of weakly supervised pretraining. In: Ferrari, V., Hebert, M., Sminchisescu, C., Weiss, Y. (eds.) ECCV 2018. LNCS, vol. 11206, pp. 185–201. Springer, Cham (2018). https://doi.org/10.1007/978-3-030-01216-8_12
41. Mavadati, S.M., Mahoor, M.H., Bartlett, K., Trinh, P., Cohn, J.F.: DISFA: a spontaneous facial action intensity database. IEEE Trans. Affect. Comput. **4**(2), 151–160 (2013)
42. Maze, B., et al.: IARPA Janus benchmark-C: face dataset and protocol. In: IEEE International Conference on Biometrics (ICB) (2018)
43. Misra, I., van der Maaten, L.: Self-supervised learning of pretext-invariant representations. arXiv (2019)
44. Mollahosseini, A., Hasani, B., Mahoor, M.H.: AffectNet: a database for facial expression, valence, and arousal computing in the wild. IEEE Trans. Affect. Comput. **10**(1), 18–31 (2017)
45. Ng, H.W., Nguyen, V.D., Vonikakis, V., Winkler, S.: Deep learning for emotion recognition on small datasets using transfer learning. In: Proceedings of the 2015 ACM on International Conference on Multimodal Interaction, pp. 443–449 (2015)
46. Ntinou, I., Sanchez, E., Bulat, A., Valstar, M., Tzimiropoulos, G.: A transfer learning approach to heatmap regression for action unit intensity estimation. IEEE Trans. Affective Comput. (2021)
47. Parkhi, O.M., Vedaldi, A., Zisserman, A.: Deep face recognition (2015)
48. Parkin, A., Grinchuk, O.: Recognizing multi-modal face spoofing with face recognition networks. In: CVPR-W (2019)
49. Phillips, P.J., et al.: Face recognition accuracy of forensic examiners, superrecognizers, and face recognition algorithms. Proc. Natl. Acad. Sci. **115**(24), 6171–6176 (2018)
50. Qian, S., Sun, K., Wu, W., Qian, C., Jia, J.: Aggregation via separation: boosting facial landmark detector with semi-supervised style translation. In: Proceedings of the IEEE International Conference on Computer Vision, pp. 10153–10163 (2019)
51. Ranjan, R., Patel, V.M., Chellappa, R.: HyperFace: a deep multi-task learning framework for face detection, landmark localization, pose estimation, and gender recognition. IEEE TPAMI **41**(1), 121–135 (2017)
52. Ranjan, R., Sankaranarayanan, S., Castillo, C.D., Chellappa, R.: An all-in-one convolutional neural network for face analysis. In: IEEE FG 2017 (2017)
53. Ren, S., He, K., Girshick, R., Sun, J.: Faster R-CNN: towards real-time object detection with region proposal networks. In: Advances in Neural Information Processing Systems, pp. 91–99 (2015)
54. Robinson, J.P., Livitz, G., Henon, Y., Qin, C., Fu, Y., Timoner, S.: Face recognition: too bias, or not too bias? In: Proceedings of the IEEE/CVF Conference on Computer Vision and Pattern Recognition Workshops, pp. 0–1 (2020)

55. Sagonas, C., Antonakos, E., Tzimiropoulos, G., Zafeiriou, S., Pantic, M.: 300 faces in-the-wild challenge: database and results. Image Vis. Comput. **47**, 3–18 (2016)
56. Sanchez, E., Bulat, A., Zaganidis, A., Tzimiropoulos, G.: Semi-supervised au intensity estimation with contrastive learning. arXiv preprint arXiv:2011.01864 (2020)
57. Schroff, F., Kalenichenko, D., Philbin, J.: FaceNet: a unified embedding for face recognition and clustering. In: Proceedings of the IEEE Conference on Computer Vision and Pattern Recognition, pp. 815–823 (2015)
58. Shrout, P.E., Fleiss, J.L.: Intraclass correlations: uses in assessing rater reliability. Psychol. Bull. **86**(2), 420 (1979)
59. Simonyan, K., Zisserman, A.: Very deep convolutional networks for large-scale image recognition. arXiv preprint arXiv:1409.1556 (2014)
60. Sixta, T., Junior, J., Jacques, C., Buch-Cardona, P., Vazquez, E., Escalera, S.: FairFace challenge at ECCV 2020: analyzing bias in face recognition. arXiv preprint arXiv:2009.07838 (2020)
61. Taigman, Y., Yang, M., Ranzato, M., Wolf, L.: DeepFace: closing the gap to human-level performance in face verification. In: Proceedings of the IEEE Conference on Computer Vision and Pattern Recognition, pp. 1701–1708 (2014)
62. Tzirakis, P., Trigeorgis, G., Nicolaou, M.A., Schuller, B.W., Zafeiriou, S.: End-to-end multimodal emotion recognition using deep neural networks. IEEE J. Sel. Top. Sig. Process. **11**(8), 1301–1309 (2017)
63. Valstar, M., et al.: AVEC 2016: depression, mood, and emotion recognition workshop and challenge. In: Proceedings of the 6th International Workshop on Audio/Visual Emotion Challenge, pp. 3–10 (2016)
64. Valstar, M.F., et al.: FERA 2015-second facial expression recognition and analysis challenge. In: 2015 11th IEEE International Conference and Workshops on Automatic Face and Gesture Recognition (FG), vol. 6, pp. 1–8. IEEE (2015)
65. Vielzeuf, V., Lechervy, A., Pateux, S., Jurie, F.: Towards a general model of knowledge for facial analysis by multi-source transfer learning (2020)
66. Wang, F., et al.: The devil of face recognition is in the noise. In: Ferrari, V., Hebert, M., Sminchisescu, C., Weiss, Y. (eds.) ECCV 2018. LNCS, vol. 11213, pp. 780–795. Springer, Cham (2018). https://doi.org/10.1007/978-3-030-01240-3_47
67. Wang, F., Cheng, J., Liu, W., Liu, H.: Additive margin softmax for face verification. IEEE Signal Process. Lett. **25**(7), 926–930 (2018)
68. Wang, H., et al.: CosFace: large margin cosine loss for deep face recognition. In: Proceedings of the IEEE Conference on Computer Vision and Pattern Recognition, pp. 5265–5274 (2018)
69. Wang, J., et al.: Deep high-resolution representation learning for visual recognition. IEEE Trans. Pattern Anal. Mach. Intell. **43**, 3349–3364 (2020)
70. Whitelam, C., et al.: IARPA Janus benchmark-B face dataset. In: Proceedings of the IEEE Conference on Computer Vision and Pattern Recognition Workshops, pp. 90–98 (2017)
71. Wiles, O., Koepke, A., Zisserman, A.: Self-supervised learning of a facial attribute embedding from video. In: BMVC (2018)
72. Wu, W., Qian, C., Yang, S., Wang, Q., Cai, Y., Zhou, Q.: Look at boundary: A boundary-aware face alignment algorithm. In: Proceedings of the IEEE Conference on Computer Vision and Pattern Recognition, pp. 2129–2138 (2018)
73. Wu, Z., Xiong, Y., Yu, S.X., Lin, D.: Unsupervised feature learning via non-parametric instance discrimination. In: Proceedings of the IEEE Conference on Computer Vision and Pattern Recognition, pp. 3733–3742 (2018)

74. Xie, Q., Luong, M.T., Hovy, E., Le, Q.V.: Self-training with noisy student improves ImageNet classification. In: Proceedings of the IEEE/CVF Conference on Computer Vision and Pattern Recognition, pp. 10687–10698 (2020)
75. Yalniz, I.Z., Jégou, H., Chen, K., Paluri, M., Mahajan, D.: Billion-scale semi-supervised learning for image classification. arXiv preprint arXiv:1905.00546 (2019)
76. Yang, J., et al.: Neural aggregation network for video face recognition. In: CVPR (2017)
77. Yang, J., Bulat, A., Tzimiropoulos, G.: Fan-face: a simple orthogonal improvement to deep face recognition. In: AAAI, pp. 12621–12628 (2020)
78. Yang, S., Luo, P., Loy, C.C., Tang, X.: WIDER FACE: a face detection benchmark. In: IEEE Conference on Computer Vision and Pattern Recognition (CVPR) (2016)
79. Ye, M., Zhang, X., Yuen, P.C., Chang, S.F.: Unsupervised embedding learning via invariant and spreading instance feature. In: Proceedings of the IEEE Conference on Computer Vision and Pattern Recognition, pp. 6210–6219 (2019)
80. Zhang, S., Zhu, X., Lei, Z., Shi, H., Wang, X., Li, S.Z.: S3FD: single shot scale-invariant face detector. In: Proceedings of the IEEE International Conference on Computer Vision, pp. 192–201 (2017)
81. Zhang, X., et al.: BP4D-spontaneous: a high-resolution spontaneous 3D dynamic facial expression database. Image Vis. Comput. **32**(10), 692–706 (2014)
82. Zhang, Y., Dong, W., Hu, B.G., Ji, Q.: Weakly-supervised deep convolutional neural network learning for facial action unit intensity estimation. In: Proceedings of the IEEE Conference on Computer Vision and Pattern Recognition, pp. 2314–2323 (2018)
83. Zhang, Y., Jiang, H., Wu, B., Fan, Y., Ji, Q.: Context-aware feature and label fusion for facial action unit intensity estimation with partially labeled data. In: Proceedings of the IEEE International Conference on Computer Vision, pp. 733–742 (2019)
84. Zhang, Y., et al.: Joint representation and estimator learning for facial action unit intensity estimation. In: Proceedings of the IEEE Conference on Computer Vision and Pattern Recognition, pp. 3457–3466 (2019)
85. Zhu, X., Lei, Z., Liu, X., Shi, H., Li, S.Z.: Face alignment across large poses: a 3D solution. In: Proceedings of the IEEE Conference on Computer Vision and Pattern Recognition, pp. 146–155 (2016)
86. Zhu, X., Liu, X., Lei, Z., Li, S.Z.: Face alignment in full pose range: a 3D total solution. IEEE Trans. Pattern Anal. Mach. Intell. **41**(1), 78–92 (2017)

Look Both Ways: Self-supervising Driver Gaze Estimation and Road Scene Saliency

Isaac Kasahara[1]([✉]) [iD], Simon Stent[2] [iD], and Hyun Soo Park[1] [iD]

[1] University of Minnesota, Minneapolis, USA
{kasah011,hspark}@umn.edu
[2] Toyota Research Institute, Cambridge, MA, USA
simon.stent@tri.global

Abstract. We present a new on-road driving dataset, called "Look Both Ways", which contains synchronized video of both driver faces and the forward road scene, along with ground truth gaze data registered from eye tracking glasses worn by the drivers. Our dataset supports the study of methods for non-intrusively estimating a driver's focus of attention while driving - an important application area in road safety. A key challenge is that this task requires accurate gaze estimation, but supervised appearance-based gaze estimation methods often do not transfer well to real driving datasets, and in-domain ground truth to supervise them is difficult to gather. We therefore propose a method for self-supervision of driver gaze, by taking advantage of the geometric consistency between the driver's gaze direction and the saliency of the scene as observed by the driver. We formulate a 3D geometric learning framework to enforce this consistency, allowing the gaze model to supervise the scene saliency model, and vice versa. We implement a prototype of our method and test it with our dataset, to show that compared to a supervised approach it can yield better gaze estimation and scene saliency estimation with no additional labels.

Keywords: Driving · 3D gaze · Saliency · Self-supervised learning · ADAS

1 Introduction

For the past decade, computer vision has played an increasingly important role in self-driving cars, to help them understand what is happening *outside* the vehicle (see e.g. [6,13,40]). But the vast majority of vehicles on the road today remain human-controlled, and will stay that way for the foreseeable future, with partially automated systems (SAE Levels 2–3 [2]) set to become the norm [1]. Given this trend, it is important to pay close attention to what is happening *inside* the vehicle: to better understand the behaviors of human drivers. As driving becomes the activity of a cooperative human-AI team, building good representations of drivers will be critical to help ensure a safe and efficient system.

Supplementary Information The online version contains supplementary material available at https://doi.org/10.1007/978-3-031-19778-9_8.

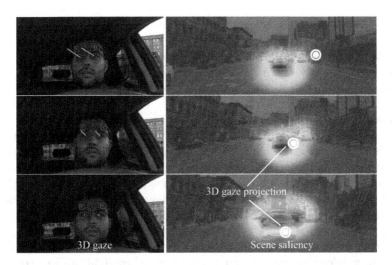

Fig. 1. Motivation. Estimating a driver's focus of attention is important to determine if they have sufficient situational awareness to drive safely. Here we show the test-time output of our method, with estimated gaze overlaid on the input face image, 3D gaze projected into the scene camera view, and saliency prediction from the scene image.

This work concerns one important aspect of driver behavior: their **visual focus of attention**. Attention is a major indicator of the intent and decision-making of drivers, and humans in general [20]. An ability to precisely estimate a driver's attention is a stepping stone towards vehicles being able to understand the situational awareness of a driver and adapt their behavior to provide better assistance to drivers in need through warnings or interventions. For example, in Fig. 1, a vehicle which can tell whether the driver has seen the braking vehicle up ahead may be able to warn them or apply braking earlier, to help prevent a collision. Knowledge of human visual attention can also be used to help machines attend to the driving task more efficiently [3]. Due to its importance, a number of companies exist which specialize in developing driver monitoring systems centered around estimating aspects of driver state such as eye gaze. However, commercial systems, which typically (though not exclusively) use near infra-red, glint- and model-based tracking to achieve high precision, are black-box systems and require specific camera and lighting setups. For these reasons, research into open models which relax these constraints, such as appearance-based gaze models powered by deep learning [18,49], has continued. One challenge with this work has been the lack of domain-specific data: while synthetic datasets have found some success [37,39,44], collecting ground truth gaze data across many subjects and conditions in the target domain of driving is expensive. As a consequence, existing appearance-based 3D gaze estimation models can be highly fragile when applied to new drivers in real driving scenes. There is a need for both a more label-efficient method to adapt gaze estimation models to drivers, and a dataset to support it.

To try to address these needs, we make the following contributions.

Firstly, we collect **a new on-road dataset for visual focus of attention estimation**. The *Look Both Ways* (LBW) dataset features seven hours of driving captured from 28 drivers with synchronized and calibrated facial RGB-D video (looking at the driver), driving scene stereo videos (looking at the road), and ground-truth gaze from eye-tracking glasses.

Secondly, we present a **self-supervised learning method to improve appearance-based driver gaze estimation** without annotations. Our main insight is that driver attention is highly correlated with 3D scene semantics (or visual saliency). For example, drivers tend to focus on vanishing points, tangent points on curving roads, pedestrians, relevant traffic signals, or approaching cars [20]. To take advantage of this, we set up our gaze learning framework to encourage geometric consistency between gaze direction and visual saliency through 3D reconstruction. Our system takes the driver face and stereo scene images as input, and outputs 3D gaze direction and an estimate of scene saliency.

Finally, we demonstrate that our self-supervised method can **improve performance** of a recent appearance-based gaze tracking method in this applied setting. As a byproduct, our method can also improve the performance of driving scene saliency. Our dataset and experimental code is available at https://github.com/Kasai2020/look_both_ways.

2   Related Work

Appearance-Based Gaze Estimation. Methods to non-intrusively estimate human gaze from facial images have been studied in computer vision for many decades [14]. Artificial neural networks were first used for appearance-based gaze estimation in the early 1990s [4], but modern deep learning techniques and the availability of larger training datasets have significantly improved their performance [18,49,50]. Researchers have explored techniques to further improve the data-efficiency, generalization and accuracy of these methods, for example by injecting more structure into the learned representations [9,31], leveraging synthetic data in novel ways [37,39,44], and personalizing gaze models to individuals with minimal supervision [21,30]. Despite this progress, supervised appearance-based models are still known to experience performance degradation at test-time, as they may struggle to transfer to new appearances (including occluders such as glasses), lighting conditions, or head poses outside of the training data. While exciting progress has been made recently in self-supervised gaze representation learning [41,48], these methods do not yet attempt to leverage supervisory signals that may be freely available from the environment, such as the scene which the subject is looking at. Our work presents a method, dataset and evidence for how self-supervision from the environment can be used to boost appearance-based gaze estimation in an applied setting.

Leveraging the Relationship Between Gaze and Saliency. Understanding where people look has long been a topic of interest in human perception and computer vision [47]. The computational modeling of visual saliency has advanced significantly, moving beyond the detection of low-level salient patterns towards higher-level reasoning [5,10,26,43]. Saliency models can now serve practical purposes, for example to predict (and therefore influence) website engagement [36,51]. The idea of relating the saliency of the environment to a person's attention—which we leverage in this paper—is not new. Early work by Sugano *et al.* [38] aggregated on-screen saliency maps corresponding to similar-looking eye appearances over time to help construct an appearance-based gaze estimator in the lab without ground truth. Recasens *et al.* showed how saliency can be used to help an appearance-based gaze estimator for images containing subjects looking elsewhere within the image [33], and in follow-up work with multi-view data showed how saliency, appearance-based gaze, and geometric relationships between camera views can be solved for simultaneously using only gaze as supervision [34]. Chang *et al.* [8] propose the use of saliency information to calibrate an existing gaze model. Most related to our work, Park *et al.* [29] demonstrated a method for end-to-end video-based eye-tracking which showed that the accuracy of appearance-based gaze models for subjects watching visual stimuli on screen could be improved with knowledge of saliency. Inspired by this prior work, we explore whether saliency and gaze can be used to supervise one another outside of the screen-in-the-lab setting, and in a real, 3D driving environment.

Gaze Estimation for Driving. Driving is a complex task which requires paying attention to many different static and dynamic areas of the vehicle and road scene, and therefore involves a range of eye movement strategies [20]. Vehicles which can accurately predict driver gaze can provide assistance which is more in tune with the needs of the driver. There are numerous datasets for the study of driver behaviors, including Brain4Cars [16], BDD-A [46], DrEYEve [28], Drive&Act [24], DMD [27], DADA2000 [11], and INAGT [45]. However, no dataset exists which combines driver-facing video, scene-facing video and ground truth gaze. In Sect. 3, we describe our dataset contribution and how it supports the exploration of gaze and saliency self-supervision for the important task of driver gaze estimation.

3   Look Both Ways (LBW) Dataset

To build the LBW dataset, we created a setup shown in Fig. 2(a) which captured two synchronized streams of data 15 Hz (downsampled 5 Hz for processing):

1. 3D gaze data consisting of: *(i)* face images, I_g, *(ii)* ground truth 3D gaze directions **g**, and *(iii)* 3D eye centers, $\{e_l, e_r\}$, with respect to the scene camera. A Kinect Azure RGB-D camera was used to capture the face image and the 3D location of eyes ("Gaze camera"). Drivers wore Tobii Pro Glasses to measure driver gaze in a glasses-centric co-ordinate system ("Gaze glasses"), which could later be transformed into ground truth gaze **g**.
2. Left and right pairs of stereo scene images, $\{I_s^l, I_s^r\}$, captured with an additional pair of Kinect Azure cameras ("Scene stereo") synchronized with the gaze camera.

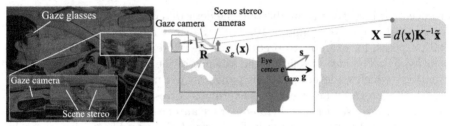

(a) LBW data capture setup and geometry

(b) Data samples showing a variety of driver appearances and driving conditions.

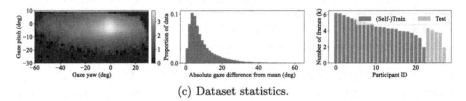

(c) Dataset statistics.

Fig. 2. The Look Both Ways (LBW) Dataset. *(a) Dataset collection setup.* We used synchronized and calibrated driver-facing monocular and scene-facing stereo cameras, and driver-mounted eye tracking glasses, in order to gather data of driver 3D gaze registered to real driving scenes. *(b) Samples from the dataset.* LBW is collected with 28 drivers who drive in various areas including urban, rural, residential, and campus, under sunny, rainy, cloudy, and snowy weather. The data includes driver face images, road-facing scene images, and 3D gaze direction from a head-mounted eye tracker. *(c) Dataset statistics.* (Left) Log-frequency histogram of ground truth gaze pitch and yaw, showing a concentration of gaze towards the road ahead. (Center) The distribution of fixations away from the mean is heavy tailed, corresponding to glances away from the forward road scene. (Right) Data was gathered from 28 subjects, of which 5 were held out from all supervised and self-supervised training as a test set.

3.1 Calibration and Pre-processing

The gaze and stereo cameras were rigidly attached to a mechanical frame as shown in Fig. 2(a), where their relative transformation $\mathbf{R}$ and intrinsic parameters $\mathbf{K}$ are constant. We calibrated these parameters using COLMAP, an off-the-shelf structure-from-motion algorithm [35]. Since the cameras face opposite

Fig. 3. Ground truth gaze registration. We map the gaze focal point $\mathbf{x}_g$ from the gaze glasses camera view (left) to the scene image $\mathbf{x}_s$ (center) using a homography $\mathbf{H}$ (right) estimated by matching local image features between the two images.

directions where matches cannot be found, we capture a calibration sequence by rotating the mechanical frame outside the vehicle in order to acquire feature correspondences across time.

Localizing the gaze glasses in the coordinate system defined by the scene cameras is non-trivial as the glasses are in constant motion. One possible approach is to estimate the 3D rotation and translation of the glasses in the driver-facing camera by tracking AprilTags [42] which we mounted rigidly to the frame. However, the result was highly sensitive to the small noisy in the recovered rotation. Instead, similar to [28], we opted to directly register the gaze focal point projected into the glasses' own scene-facing video stream, against our own scene-facing video:

$$\mathbf{g} = \mathbf{R}\frac{\mathbf{X}_g - \mathbf{e}}{\|\mathbf{X}_g - \mathbf{e}\|}, \quad \text{where} \quad \mathbf{X}_g = d(\mathbf{x}_s)\mathbf{K}^{-1}\widetilde{\mathbf{x}}_s, \quad \widetilde{\mathbf{x}}_s \propto \mathbf{H}\widetilde{\mathbf{x}}_g, \tag{1}$$

where $\mathbf{g} \in \mathbb{S}^2$ is the 3D gaze direction, $\mathbf{x}_g \in \mathbb{R}^2$ is the gaze focal point that is measured by the gaze glasses, $\mathbf{e} \in \mathbb{R}^3$ is the center of eyes in the scene camera coordinate, $\mathbf{x}_s \in \mathbb{R}^2$ is the transferred gaze focal point in the scene image, and $\mathbf{H}$ is the homography that directly maps the gaze glass image to the scene image as shown in Fig. 3. $d(\mathbf{x}_s)$ is the depth at the gaze focal point $\mathbf{x}_s$, $\widetilde{\mathbf{x}}$ is the homogeneous representation of $\mathbf{x}$, and $\mathbf{R} \in SO(3)$ is the rotation matrix that transforms from the scene image coordinate system to the face image coordinate system. We approximate this transformation as a homography (i.e., pure rotation) assuming that the distance from the scene to the camera is sufficiently far, i.e., weak perspective. We estimate this homography by leveraging local image feature matching [23] with RANSAC [12].

We use RAFT-Stereo [22] to reconstruct scene depth from our stereo image pair, and we measure the physical baseline distance between the stereo cameras to reconstruct to metric scale, validating by capturing an object of known size.

3.2 Final Collection

We collected the data by complying with an Institutional Research Board (IRB) protocol. Each driver signed a consent form reviewed by the IRB. All drivers were older than 18 years old and held a US driver's license. During driving, an

Table 1. Comparison of recent driver-facing datasets. Our dataset is unique in containing driver-facing imagery (Driver), scene-facing imagery (Scene) along with ground truth gaze fixations (Gaze). Among other things, LBW therefore supports the development of self-supervised methods to study and improve estimation of driver focus of attention (FoA) using scene saliency.

Dataset	Primary Task	Driver	Scene	Scenario	Gaze	# Subj	Size(h)
Brain4Cars [16]	Maneuver Pred	RGB	Mono	Real	No	10	*10
Drive&Act [24]	State/Act.Rec	RGB+D, NIR	–	Sim	No	15	12
DMD [27]	State/Act.Rec	RGB+D, NIR	–	Both	No	37	41
INAGT [45]	HMI Timing	RGB	Mono	Real	No	46	38
BDD-A [46]	Visual FoA	–	Mono	Sim	Yes	1,232	4
DrEYEve [28]	Visual FoA	–	Mono	Real	Yes	8	6
LBW (Ours)	Visual FoA/Gaze	RGB+D	Stereo	Real	Yes	28	7

instructor was on board in the passenger seat to provide safety instruction and directional guidance.

After calibration, we filter the videos to remove missed gaze registrations, missed driver detections via OpenPose [7], and dropped frames. The final fully-annotated dataset consists of 6.8 h of free driving on public roads. We captured 28 drivers (22 male, 6 female), totalling 123,297 synchronized driver face and stereo scene images with ground truth 3D gaze. This includes various road types (*e.g.* urban, residential and rural) and various weather conditions (sunny, cloudy, rainy, and snowy) with various lighting conditions (daytime and dusk).

Figures 2(b) and 2(c) illustrate the diversity of our dataset. Driver gaze is widely spread across yaw and pitch angles. For driving scenarios, the gaze distribution is slightly biased to the negative yaw angle because the driver seat is located on the left sides. Each participant collected more than 2,000 clean data samples. Table 1 compares LBW against recent driving datasets.

4   Self-supervised Gaze

Given a set of images that capture face appearance and the driving scene, we present a self-supervised learning framework to predict the 3D gaze direction. We represent a measure of visual saliency as a function of the 3D gaze direction, which allows us to encourage geometric consistency between the 3D gaze and visual saliency prediction.

4.1   Gaze-Driven Saliency

From an image of the driver's face, $\mathbf{I}_g \in [0,1]^{H_g \times W_g \times 3}$, where H_g and W_g are its height and width, we wish to predict the 3D gaze direction $\mathbf{g} \in \mathbb{S}^2$:

$$\mathbf{g} = f_g(\mathbf{I}_g; \boldsymbol{\theta}_g), \tag{2}$$

where f_g is a learnable function, parameterized by the weights $\boldsymbol{\theta}_g$. While f_g can be learned in a supervised fashion, using a number of pairs of 3D gaze direction

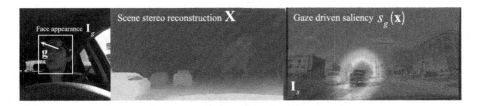

Fig. 4. Processed data sample. We represent a measure of visual saliency $s_g(\mathbf{x})$ as a function of the 3D gaze direction $\mathbf{g}$ that can be predicted by the face appearance image $\mathbf{I}_g$. Given the depth estimates from the stereo scene cameras in $\mathbf{X}$, we reconstruct 3D points and project them to the eye center $\mathbf{e}$ to form directions $\mathbf{s}$. The angular difference between $\mathbf{s}$ and the gaze direction $\mathbf{g}$ is used to model the projected scene saliency s_g.

and appearance, the learned model may not generalize well unless the training set is very large and diverse.

Our main insight is that the 3D gaze direction is highly correlated with the visual semantics (or visual saliency) observed by the scene image $\mathbf{I}_s \in [0,1]^{H_s \times W_s \times 3}$ with its height H_s and width W_s. We represent a measure of visual saliency s_g over the scene image as follows:

$$s_g(\mathbf{x}) = \frac{\exp\left(\kappa \mathbf{g}^\mathsf{T} \mathbf{s}(\mathbf{x})\right)}{\sum_{\mathbf{x} \in \mathcal{R}(\mathbf{I}_s)} \exp(\kappa \mathbf{g}^\mathsf{T} \mathbf{s}(\mathbf{x}))}, \tag{3}$$

where $s_g(\mathbf{x}) \in [0,1]$ is the visual saliency geometrically derived from the 3D gaze direction $\mathbf{g}$, the pixel $\mathbf{x} \in [0, W_s) \times [0, H_s)$ lies in the scene image, and κ is a concentration parameter that determines the variance of salience given the 3D gaze direction[1].

The directional unit vector $\mathbf{s}(\mathbf{x}) \in \mathbb{S}^2$ corresponds to scene image point $\mathbf{x}$:

$$\mathbf{s}(\mathbf{x}) = \mathbf{R}\frac{\mathbf{X} - \mathbf{e}}{\|\mathbf{X} - \mathbf{e}\|}, \quad \mathbf{X} = d(\mathbf{x})\mathbf{K}^{-1}\tilde{\mathbf{x}}, \tag{4}$$

where $\mathbf{X} \in \mathbb{R}^3$ is the 3D point that is reconstructed from the scene image $\mathbf{x}$ given the intrinsic parameter $\mathbf{K}$ and the depth $d(\mathbf{x}) \in \mathbb{R}_+$ as shown in Fig. 2(a). $\mathbf{R} \in SO(3)$ is the rotation matrix that transforms from the scene image coordinate system to the face image coordinate system. $\mathbf{e} \in \mathbb{R}^3$ is the 3D location of the eye center, i.e., $\mathbf{s}(\mathbf{x})$ is the direction of the 3D point $\mathbf{X}$ corresponding to $\mathbf{x}$ seen from the eye location.

Figures 2(a) and 4 illustrate the geometry of gaze-driven visual saliency $s_g(\mathbf{x})$. The saliency at a pixel location $\mathbf{x}$ can be measured by the angle between the gaze direction $\mathbf{g}$ and the corresponding direction $\mathbf{s}$ that can be obtained by 3D reconstruction of $\mathbf{x}$, i.e., scene stereo reconstruction with the depth $d(\mathbf{x})$. To obtain eye locations $\mathbf{e}$ in 3D, we run OpenPose [7] to detect the eyes in the RGB image and read off depth at those pixels.

---

[1] We use a von Mises-Fisher density function where κ is equivalent to the standard deviation of a Gaussian density function.

4.2   Losses and Network Design

In the previous section we described the computation of scene saliency from registered gaze. Visual saliency can also be predicted from the scene image directly using a saliency model:

$$s_s(\mathbf{x}) = f_s(\mathbf{x}, \mathbf{I}_s; \boldsymbol{\theta}_s), \tag{5}$$

where $s_s(\mathbf{x}) \in [0, 1]$ is the scene saliency at the pixel location $\mathbf{x}$, and f_s is a learnable function that predicts the saliency from a scene image, parametrized by the weights $\boldsymbol{\theta}_s$.

Ideally, the visual saliency derived by the gaze $s_g(\mathbf{x})$ agrees with the visual scene saliency predicted from the scene image $s_s(\mathbf{x})$. We leverage this relationship to allow self-supervision of gaze estimation, by encouraging consistency between $s_g(\mathbf{x})$ and $s_s(\mathbf{x})$ through a loss term:

$$\mathcal{L}_{\text{self}}(\boldsymbol{\theta}_g, \boldsymbol{\theta}_s) = \sum_{\{\mathbf{I}_g, \mathbf{I}_s\} \in \mathcal{D}} \left(\sum_{\mathbf{x} \in \mathcal{R}(\mathbf{I}_s)} (f_s(\mathbf{x}, \mathbf{I}_s; \boldsymbol{\theta}_s) - s_g(\mathbf{x}))^2 \right), \tag{6}$$

where $\mathcal{D}$ is the set of pairs of face and scene images, and $\mathcal{R}(\mathbf{I}_s) = [0, W_s] \times [0, H_s]$. No ground truth is needed to measure $\mathcal{L}_{\text{self}}$, so a large number of unlabeled data instances may be used.

Optimizing for this self-supervised loss alone may lead to a trivial solution, such as a constant gaze prediction outside the field of view of the scene image. We therefore constrain f_g and f_s with a small set of ground truth gaze data:

$$\mathcal{L}_g(\boldsymbol{\theta}_g) = \sum_{\{\widehat{\mathbf{g}}, \mathbf{I}_g\} \in \mathcal{D}_g} \left(1 - f_g(\mathbf{I}_g; \boldsymbol{\theta}_g)^\mathsf{T} \widehat{\mathbf{g}} \right)^2, \tag{7}$$

$$\mathcal{L}_s(\boldsymbol{\theta}_s) = \sum_{\{\widehat{s}, \mathbf{I}_s\} \in \mathcal{D}_s} \mathcal{L}_{\text{KL}} + \lambda_c \mathcal{L}_{\text{NCC}}, \tag{8}$$

where $\mathcal{D}_g$ is the set of the ground truth pairs of the eye appearance and the 3D gaze direction where $\widehat{\mathbf{g}}$ is the ground truth 3D gaze direction, and $\mathcal{D}_s$ is the set of the ground truth pairs of the scene image and visual saliency. $\mathcal{L}_{\text{KL}}$ and $\mathcal{L}_{\text{NCC}}$ measure the Kullback-Leibler (KL) divergence and normalized cross-correlation between the visual saliency prediction f_s and the ground truth saliency, as used in [10]:

$$\mathcal{L}_{\text{KL}} = \sum_{\mathbf{x}} \widehat{s}(\mathbf{x}) \log \left(\frac{\widehat{s}(\mathbf{x})}{f_s(\mathbf{x})} \right), \quad \mathcal{L}_{\text{NCC}} = -\frac{\sum_{\mathbf{x}} \widehat{s}(\mathbf{x}) f_s(\mathbf{x})}{\sqrt{\sum_{\mathbf{x}} f_s(\mathbf{x})^2} \sqrt{\sum_{\mathbf{x}} \widehat{s}(\mathbf{x})^2}}, \tag{9}$$

where $f_s(\mathbf{x}, \mathbf{I}_s; \boldsymbol{\theta}_s)$ is denoted $f_s(\mathbf{x})$ and $\sum_{\mathbf{x} \in \mathcal{R}(\mathbf{I}_s)}$ by $\sum_{\mathbf{x}}$. λ_c is the weight to balance between KL divergence and normalized correlation, set to 0.1.

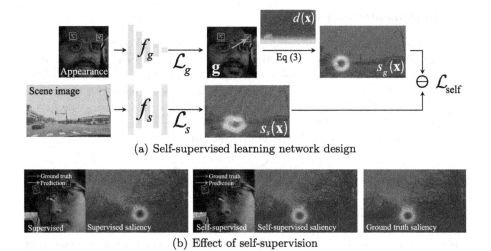

(a) Self-supervised learning network design

(b) Effect of self-supervision

Fig. 5. Model overview. (a) *Network design.* We jointly learn the gaze estimator f_g and saliency predictor f_s by enforcing the geometric consistency between them. The estimate gaze $\mathbf{g}$ is transformed to the visual saliency map $s_g(\mathbf{x})$ through Eq. (3). This visual saliency map is supervised by the scene saliency prediction $s(\mathbf{x})$, i.e., minimizing $\mathcal{L}_{\text{self}}$. For the labeled data, the supervised losses $\mathcal{L}_g$ and $\mathcal{L}_s$ are used. (b) *Effect of self-supervision.* We use the geometric relationship between the gaze and scene saliency to self-supervise the gaze direction. (Left) Supervised gaze direction where the predicted gaze is deviated from the ground truth. (Middle) The self-supervision enforces the geometric consistency between the gaze and scene saliency, which improves the gaze prediction and the saliency prediction. (Right) Ground truth scene saliency.

Our overall loss is then:

$$\mathcal{L}(\boldsymbol{\theta}_g, \boldsymbol{\theta}_s) = \mathcal{L}_{\text{self}}(\boldsymbol{\theta}_g, \boldsymbol{\theta}_s) + \lambda_g \mathcal{L}_g(\boldsymbol{\theta}_g) + \lambda_s \mathcal{L}_s(\boldsymbol{\theta}_s), \qquad (10)$$

where $\mathcal{L}_{\text{self}}$ is the self-supervised loss that ensures consistency between estimated gaze and estimated saliency without requiring ground truth data, and $\mathcal{L}_g$ and $\mathcal{L}_s$ are the supervised losses that prevent deviation from the ground truth. The hyperparameters λ_g and λ_s control the balance between supervised and self-supervised losses.

Our overall model is illustrated in Fig. 5(a). The gaze estimator f_g takes as input a face appearance image and outputs the gaze direction $\mathbf{g}$. With the reconstructed depth image $d(\mathbf{x})$, we transform the gaze direction to the scene image to form the visual saliency map $s_g(\mathbf{x})$. This saliency map is self-supervised by the saliency prediction of the scene image (and vice versa) via f_s by minimizing $\mathcal{L}_{\text{self}}$. When labeled data is available, we minimize the supervised losses $\mathcal{L}_g$ and $\mathcal{L}_s$ for the gaze and saliency, respectively. Figure 5(b) illustrates the positive effect of self-supervision on both gaze and saliency estimation.

4.3   Implementation Details

Any end-to-end trainable gaze estimator f_g or saliency predictor f_s can be used in our framework, but we opt for simple but strong models which have pre-trained weights available. For gaze estimation we use the ETH XGaze model [49] based on a ResNet-50 [15], and for saliency estimation we use Unisal [10] (MNetV2-RNN-Decoder). Our framework is implemented in PyTorch [32], using the Adam optimizer [19] with a fixed 0.5×10^{-9} learning rate and a batch size of 6. For λ_g and λ_s a value of 2.0 was used. We will release all code, models and data.

5   Experiments

We split our data into three: supervised training, self-supervised training, and held-out testing. The supervised split includes the ground truth labels of gaze directions and saliency maps. The self-supervised split does not: self-supervised learning uses geometric consistency as described in the previous section to learn from this data without annotations. Three data split configurations are tested: {supervised, self-supervised, test} = {5%, 75%, 20%}, {20%, 60%, 20%}, {40%, 40%, 20%}, {60%, 20%, 20%}, using the same test split each time. Splits are by subject, to be able to assess generalization to new subjects.

5.1   Evaluation Metrics

We measure the mean absolute error (MAE) with its standard deviation for the gaze and saliency predictions:

$$\text{MAE}_g = \frac{1}{N} \sum_i \cos^{-1}\left(\mathbf{g}_i^\top \widehat{\mathbf{g}}_i\right), \tag{11}$$

$$\text{MAE}_s = \frac{1}{N} \sum_i \left(\sum_{\mathbf{x} \in \mathcal{R}(\mathbf{I}_s)} |s_i(\mathbf{x}) - \widehat{s}_i(\mathbf{x})| \right), \tag{12}$$

where $\mathbf{g}_i$ and $s_i(\mathbf{x})$ are the ith predictions for gaze and saliency, and N is the number of test data samples.

5.2   Baselines

Gaze. We evaluate our self-supervised gaze estimation by comparing with strong recent appearance-based gaze estimation baselines. We note that our goal is not necessarily to target state-of-the-art accuracy, but rather to demonstrate the use of our dataset to explore saliency-based self-supervision to boost performance of a simple but strong baseline on real data.

(1) **Gaze360** [18]: we use the static model, pre-trained on a large-scale in-the-wild gaze dataset captured from 238 subjects in indoor and outdoor environments. This is an example of an off-the-shelf gaze estimator for "in-the-wild"

Table 2. Gaze performance. We compare appearance based gaze estimation in MAE_g (degrees, lower is better). Our method yields small but consistent improvement over baselines. "Self" and "Test" correspond to performance on the Self-Supervised and Testing splits. We test on four sets of splits with varying levels of supervised and self-supervised training: {Supervised %, Self-supervised %, Test %}.

Method	{5/75/20}		{20/60/20}		{40/40/20}		{60/20/20}	
	Self	Test	Self	Test	Self	Test	Self	Test
Gaze360 [18]	18.7	20.3	21.4	20.3	23.0	20.3	17.2	20.3
ETH XGaze [49]	11.6	15.6	11.9	15.6	12.6	15.6	15.4	15.6
Mean	9.5	9.2	9.5	9.2	9.0	9.2	8.7	9.2
Supervised-only	9.7	**7.8**	**6.9**	6.8	8.1	7.4	7.0	**6.7**
Ours	**8.2**	**7.8**	**6.9**	**6.5**	**7.4**	**7.2**	**6.2**	**6.7**

Table 3. Saliency performance. We compare saliency prediction in MAE_s (lower is better). Our method again yields small but consistent improvement over baselines. "Self" and "Test" correspond to performance on the Self-Supervised and Testing splits. We test on four sets of splits with varying levels of supervised and self-supervised training: {Supervised %, Self-supervised %, Test %}.

Method	{5/75/20}		{20/60/20}		{40/40/20}		{60/20/20}	
	Self	Test	Self	Test	Self	Test	Self	Test
Unisal [10]	1.57	1.60	1.57	1.60	1.56	1.60	1.58	1.60
Supervised-only	1.14	1.16	1.06	1.07	1.00	**1.03**	0.97	**1.03**
Ours	**1.12**	**1.14**	**1.05**	**1.06**	**0.99**	**1.03**	**0.96**	**1.03**

use. (2) **ETH XGaze** [49]: this is a ResNet-50 based model trained on the ETH XGaze dataset, a multi-view high-resolution gaze dataset captured in a controlled environment. We use the pre-trained model to evaluate on our dataset. (3) **Mean**: We compute the mean gaze over the entire LBW dataset and use it as a predictor. (4) **Supervised-only**: We re-train the ETH XGaze model (ResNet-50) on our LBW training dataset with the ground truth labels.

Saliency. (1) **Unisal** [10]: We use the saliency model pre-trained on multiple large-scale saliency datasets including DHF1K [43], Hollywood-2 and UCF-Sports [25] and SALICON [17] to evaluate on our dataset. (2) **Supervised-only**: We re-train Unisal on our LBW training dataset with ground truth labels.

5.3 Quantitative Evaluation

Tables 2 and 3 summarize the quantitative results of our experiments on gaze and saliency estimation, comparing our self-supervised learning method against the baselines described.

Gaze. The Gaze360 and ETH XGaze baselines produce relatively higher gaze estimation error for all splits because of the train-test domain gap. One significant source of difference is that all of our quantitative evaluation data features drivers wearing gaze tracking glasses, which can sometimes partially occlude the eye region and cause spurious estimations. The appearance of LBW face data is closer to the higher-resolution ETH XGaze dataset, which may explain the improvement over Gaze360. The mean gaze predictor is a competitive baseline because the attention of the driver is highly biased to the center (forward roadway and vanishing point). The supervised-only method improves performance as it allows domain adaptation using limited labeled data. Our method, which adds in geometric self-supervision, produces consistent performance improvements of up to 10% against the supervised-only method. Interestingly, its performance on the test splits is on par with the supervised-only method, indicating that it would still benefit from further adaptation. We argue that this is possible with our self-supervised learning method as no ground truth data is needed.

Saliency. A similar observation can be made for the saliency predictors as summarized in Table 3. Although Unisal is a competitive saliency predictor, the supervised-only method outperforms the baseline by adapting the model to the driving domain with limited labeled data. Our self-supervised learning method matches or improves on the supervised learning method consistently across splits.

5.4   Qualitative Evaluation

We show further qualitative output from our model in Fig. 6(a) over a range of drivers in the test split. It correctly predicts gaze direction in the presence of low lighting as the scene saliency provides an informative signal to refine the gaze. On the other hand, the scene saliency can sometimes mislead gaze estimation as it is biased towards the vanishing point in the scene, as shown in Fig. 6(b).

6   Discussion

We have presented a new dataset called Look Both Ways, which facilitates study into the problem of estimating a driver's focus of attention while on the road. We introduced a new approach for geometric self-supervision of 3D gaze from facial images and visual scene saliency, to take advantage of the natural relationship between the two. Using the LBW dataset, we showed that our end-to-end trained system can improve upon purely supervised methods for gaze estimation and saliency estimation, by virtue of being able to take advantage of unlabelled face and scene depth image pairs.

(a) Qualitative results for gaze and saliency using self-supervision

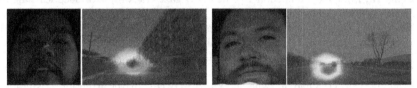

(b) Sample failure cases

Fig. 6. Qualitative Results. We visualize some further outputs of our model trained with self-supervised gaze and saliency. Successful results shown in (a) show the model working well in a variety of scenes and lighting conditions. Failure cases shown in (b) show how self-supervised learning can mislead the gaze estimation as the scene saliency prediction is highly biased to the vanishing point.

We believe that our dataset will be helpful for the community to further study driver attention in vehicles. Although we acknowledge that 3D gaze technology can potentially be used for surveillance applications, we hope to inspire an application that positively influences our thinking about the use of gaze estimation in vehicles, as a means to support improved assistance for drivers on the road.

Acknowledgement. This research is based on work supported by Toyota Research Institute and the NSF under IIS #1846031. The views and conclusions contained herein are those of the authors and should not be interpreted as representing the official policies, either expressed or implied, of the sponsors.

References

1. International Data Corporation: Worldwide Autonomous Vehicle Forecast, 2020–2024 (2020)
2. SAE Levels of Driving Automation Refined for Clarity and International Audience (2021). https://www.sae.org/blog/sae-j3016-update
3. Baee, S., Pakdamanian, E., Kim, I., Feng, L., Ordonez, V., Barnes, L.: MEDIRL: predicting the visual attention of drivers via maximum entropy deep inverse reinforcement learning. In: ICCV (2021)
4. Baluja, S., Pomerleau, D.: Non-intrusive gaze tracking using artificial neural networks (1993)
5. Bylinskii, Z., Recasens, A., Borji, A., Oliva, A., Torralba, A., Durand, F.: Where should saliency models look next? In: Leibe, B., Matas, J., Sebe, N., Welling, M. (eds.) ECCV 2016. LNCS, vol. 9909, pp. 809–824. Springer, Cham (2016). https://doi.org/10.1007/978-3-319-46454-1_49
6. Caesar, H., et al.: nuScenes: a multimodal dataset for autonomous driving. In: CVPR (2020)
7. Cao, Z., Hidalgo Martinez, G., Simon, T., Wei, S., Sheikh, Y.A.: OpenPose: real-time multi-person 2D pose estimation using part affinity fields. TPAMI 43, 172–186 (2019)
8. Chang, Z., Matias Di Martino, J., Qiu, Q., Espinosa, S., Sapiro, G.: SalGaze: personalizing gaze estimation using visual saliency. In: ICCV Workshops (2019)
9. Deng, H., Zhu, W.: Monocular free-head 3D gaze tracking with deep learning and geometry constraints. In: ICCV (2017)
10. Droste, R., Jiao, J., Noble, J.A.: Unified image and video saliency modeling. In: Vedaldi, A., Bischof, H., Brox, T., Frahm, J.-M. (eds.) ECCV 2020. LNCS, vol. 12350, pp. 419–435. Springer, Cham (2020). https://doi.org/10.1007/978-3-030-58558-7_25
11. Fang, J., Yan, D., Qiao, J., Xue, J., Yu, H.: DADA: driver attention prediction in driving accident scenarios. IEEE Trans. Intell. Transp. Syst. 23, 4959–4971 (2021)
12. Fischler, M.A., Bolles, R.C.: Random sample consensus: a paradigm for model fitting with applications to image analysis and automated cartography. ACM Commun. 24, 381–395 (1981)
13. Geiger, A., Lenz, P., Urtasun, R.: Are we ready for autonomous driving? The KITTI vision benchmark suite. In: CVPR (2012)
14. Hansen, D.W., Ji, Q.: In the eye of the beholder: a survey of models for eyes and gaze. TPAMI 32, 478–500 (2009)
15. He, K., Zhang, X., Ren, S., Sun, J.: Deep residual learning for image recognition. In: CVPR (2016)
16. Jain, A., Koppula, H.S., Raghavan, B., Soh, S., Saxena, A.: Car that knows before you do: anticipating maneuvers via learning temporal driving models. In: ICCV (2015)
17. Jiang, M., Huang, S., Duan, J., Zhao, Q.: SALICON: saliency in context. In: CVPR (2015)
18. Kellnhofer, P., Recasens, A., Stent, S., Matusik, W., Torralba, A.: Gaze360: physically unconstrained gaze estimation in the wild. In: ICCV (2019)
19. Kingma, D.P., Ba, J.L.: Adam: a method for stochastic optimization. arXiv (2014)
20. Land, M.F.: Eye movements and the control of actions in everyday life. Prog. Retinal Eye Res. 25, 296–324 (2006)

21. Lindén, E., Sjostrand, J., Proutiere, A.: Learning to personalize in appearance-based gaze tracking. In: ICCV Workshops (2019)
22. Lipson, L., Teed, Z., Deng, J.: RAFT-stereo: multilevel recurrent field transforms for stereo matching. In: 23DV (2021)
23. Lowe, D.G.: Object recognition from local scale-invariant features. IJCV (1999)
24. Martin, M., et al.: Drive&Act: a multi-modal dataset for fine-grained driver behavior recognition in autonomous vehicles. In: ICCV (2019)
25. Mathe, S., Sminchisescu, C.: Actions in the eye: dynamic gaze datasets and learnt saliency models for visual recognition. TPAMI **37**, 1408–1424 (2015)
26. Min, K., Corso, J.J.: TASED-Net: temporally-aggregating spatial encoder-decoder network for video saliency detection. In: ICCV (2019)
27. Ortega, J.D., et al.: DMD: a large-scale multi-modal driver monitoring dataset for attention and alertness analysis. In: Bartoli, A., Fusiello, A. (eds.) ECCV 2020. LNCS, vol. 12538, pp. 387–405. Springer, Cham (2020). https://doi.org/10.1007/978-3-030-66823-5_23
28. Palazzi, A., Abati, D., Solera, F., Cucchiara, R., et al.: Predicting the driver's focus of attention: the DR(eye)VE project. TPAMI **41**, 1720–1733 (2018)
29. Park, S., Aksan, E., Zhang, X., Hilliges, O.: Towards end-to-end video-based eye-tracking. In: Vedaldi, A., Bischof, H., Brox, T., Frahm, J.-M. (eds.) ECCV 2020. LNCS, vol. 12357, pp. 747–763. Springer, Cham (2020). https://doi.org/10.1007/978-3-030-58610-2_44
30. Park, S., Mello, S.D., Molchanov, P., Iqbal, U., Hilliges, O., Kautz, J.: Few-shot adaptive gaze estimation. In: ICCV (2019)
31. Park, S., Spurr, A., Hilliges, O.: Deep pictorial gaze estimation. In: Ferrari, V., Hebert, M., Sminchisescu, C., Weiss, Y. (eds.) ECCV 2018. LNCS, vol. 11217, pp. 741–757. Springer, Cham (2018). https://doi.org/10.1007/978-3-030-01261-8_44
32. Paszke, A., et al.: PyTorch: an imperative style, high-performance deep learning library. In: NeurIPS (2019)
33. Recasens, A., Khosla, A., Vondrick, C., Torralba, A.: Where are they looking? In: NeurIPS (2015)
34. Recasens, A., Vondrick, C., Khosla, A., Torralba, A.: Following gaze in video. In: ICCV (2017)
35. Schönberger, J.L., Frahm, J.M.: Structure-from-motion revisited. In: CVPR (2016)
36. Shen, C., Zhao, Q.: Webpage saliency. In: Fleet, D., Pajdla, T., Schiele, B., Tuytelaars, T. (eds.) ECCV 2014. LNCS, vol. 8695, pp. 33–46. Springer, Cham (2014). https://doi.org/10.1007/978-3-319-10584-0_3
37. Shrivastava, A., Pfister, T., Tuzel, O., Susskind, J., Wang, W., Webb, R.: Learning from simulated and unsupervised images through adversarial training. In: CVPR (2017)
38. Sugano, Y., Matsushita, Y., Sato, Y.: Appearance-based gaze estimation using visual saliency. TPAMI **35**, 329–341 (2013)
39. Sugano, Y., Matsushita, Y., Sato, Y.: Learning-by-synthesis for appearance-based 3D gaze estimation. In: CVPR (2014)
40. Sun, P., et al.: Scalability in perception for autonomous driving: Waymo open dataset. In: CVPR (2020)
41. Sun, Y., Zeng, J., Shan, S., Chen, X.: Cross-encoder for unsupervised gaze representation learning. In: ICCV (2021)
42. Wang, J., Olson, E.: AprilTag 2: efficient and robust fiducial detection. In: IROS (2016)
43. Wang, W., Shen, J., Xie, J., Cheng, M.M., Ling, H., Borji, A.: Revisiting video saliency prediction in the deep learning era. TPAMI **43**, 220–237 (2021)

44. Wood, E., Baltrusaitis, T., Zhang, X., Sugano, Y., Robinson, P., Bulling, A.: Rendering of eyes for eye-shape registration and gaze estimation. In: ICCV (2015)
45. Wu, T., Martelaro, N., Stent, S., Ortiz, J., Ju, W.: Learning when agents can talk to drivers using the INAGT dataset and multisensor fusion. ACM Interact. Mob. Wearable Ubiquit. Technol. **5**, 1–28 (2021)
46. Xia, Y., Zhang, D., Kim, J., Nakayama, K., Zipser, K., Whitney, D.: Predicting driver attention in critical situations. In: Jawahar, C.V., Li, H., Mori, G., Schindler, K. (eds.) ACCV 2018. LNCS, vol. 11365, pp. 658–674. Springer, Cham (2019). https://doi.org/10.1007/978-3-030-20873-8_42
47. Yarbus, A.L.: Eye Movements and Vision. Springer, New York (2013). https://doi.org/10.1007/978-1-4899-5379-7
48. Yu, Y., Odobez, J.M.: Unsupervised representation learning for gaze estimation. In: CVPR (2020)
49. Zhang, X., Park, S., Beeler, T., Bradley, D., Tang, S., Hilliges, O.: ETH-XGaze: a large scale dataset for gaze estimation under extreme head pose and gaze variation. In: Vedaldi, A., Bischof, H., Brox, T., Frahm, J.-M. (eds.) ECCV 2020. LNCS, vol. 12350, pp. 365–381. Springer, Cham (2020). https://doi.org/10.1007/978-3-030-58558-7_22
50. Zhang, X., Sugano, Y., Fritz, M., Bulling, A.: Appearance-based gaze estimation in the wild. In: CVPR (2015)
51. Zheng, Q., Jiao, J., Cao, Y., Lau, R.W.H.: Task-driven webpage saliency. In: Ferrari, V., Hebert, M., Sminchisescu, C., Weiss, Y. (eds.) Computer Vision – ECCV 2018. LNCS, vol. 11218, pp. 300–316. Springer, Cham (2018). https://doi.org/10.1007/978-3-030-01264-9_18

MFIM: Megapixel Facial Identity Manipulation

Sanghyeon Na[✉]

Kakao Brain, Seongnam, South Korea
orca.na@kakaobrain.com

Abstract. Face swapping is a task that changes a facial identity of a given image to that of another person. In this work, we propose a novel face-swapping framework called *Megapixel Facial Identity Manipulation (MFIM)*. The face-swapping model should achieve two goals. First, it should be able to generate a high-quality image. We argue that a model which is proficient in generating a megapixel image can achieve this goal. However, generating a megapixel image is generally difficult without careful model design. Therefore, our model exploits pretrained Style-GAN in the manner of GAN-inversion to effectively generate a megapixel image. Second, it should be able to effectively transform the identity of a given image. Specifically, it should be able to actively transform ID attributes (e.g., face shape and eyes) of a given image into those of another person, while preserving ID-irrelevant attributes (e.g., pose and expression). To achieve this goal, we exploit 3DMM that can capture various facial attributes. Specifically, we explicitly supervise our model to generate a face-swapped image with the desirable attributes using 3DMM. We show that our model achieves state-of-the-art performance through extensive experiments. Furthermore, we propose a new operation called ID mixing, which creates a new identity by semantically mixing the identities of several people. It allows the user to customize the new identity.

1 Introduction

Face swapping is a task that changes the facial identity of a given image to that of another person. It has now been applied in various applications and services in entertainment [23], privacy protection [29], and theatrical industry [31].

In technical terms, a face-swapping model should be able to generate a high-quality image. At the same time, it should be able to transfer the ID attributes (e.g., face shape and eyes) from the source image to the target image, while preserving the ID-irrelevant attributes (e.g., pose and expression) of the target image as shown in Fig. 1. In other words, the face-swapping model has two goals: i) generating high-quality images and ii) effective identity transformation. Our model, *Megapixel Facial Identity Manipulation (MFIM)*, is designed to achieve both of these goals.

Supplementary Information The online version contains supplementary material available at https://doi.org/10.1007/978-3-031-19778-9_9.

S. Avidan et al. (Eds.): ECCV 2022, LNCS 13673, pp. 143–159, 2022.
https://doi.org/10.1007/978-3-031-19778-9_9

Fig. 1. Megapixel facial identity manipulation. (*Top*) **Face swapping.** Our model faithfully synthesizes a high-quality megapixel image by blending ID (e.g., eyes and face shape) and ID-irrelevant attributes (e.g., pose and expression) of source and target images, respectively. (*Middle*) **Face swapping with large gaps** between the source and target images (e.g., gender and age). (*Bottom*) **ID mixing** using two source images: blending global (e.g., face shape) and local ID attributes (e.g., eyes) of global and local source images, respectively.

Firstly, to generate a high-quality image, we propose a face-swapping framework that exploits pretrained StyleGAN [22] in the manner of GAN-inversion. Specifically, we design an encoder called facial attribute encoder that effectively extracts ID and ID-irrelevant representations from the source and target images, respectively. These representations are forwarded to the pretrained StyleGAN generator. Then, the generator blends these representations and generates a high-quality megapixel face-swapped image.

Basically, our facial attribute encoder extracts style codes, which is similar to existing StyleGAN-based GAN-inversion encoders [3,33,37]. Specifically, our facial attribute encoder extracts ID and ID-irrelevant style codes from the source and target images, respectively. Here, one of the important things for faithful face swapping is that the details of the target image such as expression or background should be accurately reconstructed. However, the ID-irrelevant style codes, which do not have spatial dimensions, can fail to preserve the details of the target image. Therefore, our facial attribute encoder extracts not only the style codes, but also the style maps which have spatial dimensions from the target image. The style maps, which take advantages from its spatial dimensions, can complement the ID-irrelevant style codes by propagating additional information about the details of the target image. As a result, our facial attribute encoder, which extracts the style codes and style maps, can effectively capture the ID attributes from the source image and the ID-irrelevant attributes including details from the target image. MegaFS [45], the previous model that exploits pretrained StyleGAN, suffers from reconstructing the details of target image because it only utilizes the style codes. To solve this problem, they use a segmentation label to take the details from the target image. However, we resolve this drawback by extracting the style maps instead of using the segmentation label.

Secondly, we utilize 3DMM [16] which can capture various facial attributes for the effective identity transformation. We especially focus on the transformation of face shape which is one of the important factors in recognizing an identity. However, it is difficult to transform the face shape while preserving the ID-irrelevant attributes of the target image at the same time because these two goals are in conflict with each other [25]. Specifically, making the generated image have the same face shape with that of the source image enforces the generated image to *differ* a lot from the target image. In contrast, making it preserve the ID-irrelevant attributes of the target image enforces it to be *similar* to the target image. To achieve these two conflicting goals simultaneously, we utilize 3DMM which can accurately and distinctly capture the various facial attributes such as shape, pose, and expression from a given image. In particular, we explicitly supervise our model to generate a face-swapped image with the desirable attributes using 3DMM, i.e., the same face shape with the source image, but the same pose and expression with the target image. The previous models [1, 10, 17, 25, 27, 45] without such explicit supervision struggle with achieving two conflicting goals simultaneously. In contrast, our model can transform the face shape well, while preserving the ID-irrelevant attributes of the target image. HiFiFace [39], the previous model that exploits 3DMM, requires 3DMM not only at the training phase, but even at the inference phase. In contrast, our model does not use 3DMM at the inference phase.

Finally, we propose a new additional task, ID mixing, which means face swapping with a new identity created with multiple source images instead of a single source image. Here, we aim to design a method that allows the user to semantically control the identity creation process. For example, when using two source images, the user can extract the global ID attributes (e.g., face shape) from one source image and the local ID attributes (e.g., eyes) from the other source image, and create the new identity by blending them as shown in Fig. 1. The user can customize the new identity as desired with this operation. Furthermore, this operation does not require any additional training or segmentation label. To the best of our knowledge, we are the first to propose this operation.

Table 1. Comparison of our model (MFIM) with the previous face-swapping models (✓: positive, ✗ : negative, ✓ : partially positive). In terms of the 3DMM supervision, HifiFace also exploits the 3DMM supervision, but it requires 3DMM even at the inference phase, while MFIM does not.

	FaceShifter	HifiFace	InfoSwap	MegaFS	SmoothSwap	**MFIM**
Megapixel	✗	✗	✓	✓	✗	✓
W/o segmentation labels	✓	✗	✓	✗	✓	✓
3DMM supervision	✗	✓	✗	✗	✗	✓
ID mixing	✗	✗	✗	✗	✗	✓

In conclusion, the main contributions of this work include the following:

- We propose an improved framework for face swapping by adopting GAN-inversion method with pretrained StyleGAN that takes both style codes and style maps. It allows our model to generate high-quality megapixel images without additional labels in order to preserve the details of the target image.
- We introduce a 3DMM supervision method for the effective identity transformation, especially, the face shape. It allows our model to transform the face shape and preserve the ID-irrelevant attributes at the same time. Moreover, our model does not require 3DMM at the inference phase.
- We propose a new operation, ID mixing, which allows the user to customize the new identity using multiple source images. It does not require any additional training or segmentation label.

2   Related Work

Face Swapping. Faceshifter [27] proposes a two-stage framework in order to achieve occlusion aware method. Simswap [10] focuses on designing a framework to transfer an arbitrary identity to the target image. InfoSwap [17] proposes explicit supervision based on the IB principle for disentangling identity and identity-irrelevant information from source and target image. MegaFS [45] uses pre-trained StyleGAN [22] in order to generate megapixel samples by adopting GAN-inversion method. However, it does not introduce 3DMM supervision and relies on the segmentation labels. HifiFace [39] utilizes 3DMM for the effective identity transformation. However, HifiFace [39] requires 3DMM not only in the training phase, but also in the inference phase. On the contrary, our model only takes advantage of 3DMM at training phase and no longer needs it at the inference phase. Most recently, SmoothSwap [25] proposes a smooth identity embedder to improve learning stability and convergence speed. The key differences between our model and the previous models are given in Table 1.

Learning-Based GAN-Inversion. Generative Adversarial Networks (GAN) [18] framework has been actively employed in the various image manipulation applications [5, 11–13, 19, 26, 30, 32, 42, 44]. Recently, as remarkable GAN frameworks (e.g., BigGAN [7] and StyleGAN [22]) have emerged, GAN-inversion [41] is being actively studied. Especially, learning-based GAN-inversion aims to train an extra encoder to find a latent code that can reconstruct a given image using a pretrained generator as a decoder. Then, one can edit the given image by manipulating the latent code. pSp [33] and e4e [37] use the pretrained StyleGAN generator as a decoder. However, they have difficulty in accurate reconstruction of the given image. To solve this problem, ReStyle [3] and HFGI [38] propose iterative refinement and distortion map, respectively. However, these methods require multiple forward passes. StyleMapGAN [24] replaces the style codes of StyleGAN with the style maps. Our model also exploits the style maps, but as additional inputs to the style codes, not as replacements for the style codes to fully utilize the capability of the pretrained StyleGAN generator.

3DMM. A 3D morphable face model (3DMM) produces vector space representations that capture various facial attributes such as shape, expression and pose [4,6,8,15,16]. Although the previous 3DMM methods [4,6,8] have limitations in estimating face texture and lighting conditions accurately, recent methods [15,16] overcome these limitations. We utilize the state-of-the-art 3DMM [16] to effectively capture the various facial attributes and supervise our model.

3   MFIM: Megapixel Facial Identity Manipulation

Figure 2a shows an overall architecture of our model. Our goal is to capture the ID and ID-irrelevant attributes from the source image, $x_{src} \in \mathbb{R}^{3 \times 256 \times 256}$, and target image, $x_{tgt} \in \mathbb{R}^{3 \times 256 \times 256}$, respectively, and synthesize a megapixel image, $x_{swap} \in \mathbb{R}^{3 \times 1024 \times 1024}$, by blending these attributes. Note that x_{swap} should have the same ID attributes with those of x_{src}, while the same ID-irrelevant attributes with those of x_{tgt}. For example, in Fig. 2, x_{swap} has the same eyes and face shape with x_{src}, and the same pose and expression with x_{tgt}.

To achieve this goal, we firstly design a facial attribute encoder that encodes x_{src} and x_{tgt} into ID and ID-irrelevant representations, respectively. These representations are forwarded to the pretrained StyleGAN generator (Sect. 3.1). Secondly, for the effective identity transformation, especially the face shape, we additionally supervise our model with 3DMM. Note that 3DMM is only used at the training phase and no more used at the inference phase (Sect. 3.2). After training, our model can perform a new operation called *ID mixing* as well as face swapping. Whereas conventional face swapping uses only one source image, ID mixing uses multiple source images to create a new identity. (Section 3.3).

3.1   Facial Attribute Encoder

We introduce our facial attribute encoder. As shown in Fig. 2a, it first extracts hierarchical latent maps from a given image like pSp encoder [33]. Then, map-to-code (M2C) and map-to-map (M2M) blocks produce the style codes and style maps respectively, which are forwarded to the pretrained StyleGAN generator.

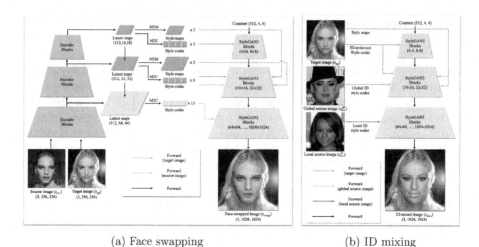

(a) Face swapping   (b) ID mixing

Fig. 2. The architecture of MFIM. Figure 2a shows the process of face swapping. The facial attribute encoder extracts style codes and style maps from source and target images. These are given to the pretrained StyleGAN generator as inputs. Figure 2b shows the process of ID mixing. The ID-style codes are extracted from two source images, instead of a single source image.

Style Code. Among the many latent spaces of the pretrained StyelGAN generator (e.g., $\mathcal{Z}$ [21], $\mathcal{W}$ [21], $\mathcal{W}^+$ [2], and $\mathcal{S}$ [40]), our facial attribute encoder maps a given image to $\mathcal{S}$, so it extracts twenty-six style codes from a given image. The extracted style codes transform the generator feature maps via weight demodulation operation [22]. As demonstrated in previous work [21], among the twenty-six style codes, we expect that the style codes corresponding to coarse spatial resolutions (e.g., from 4×4 to 16×16) synthesize the global aspects of an image (e.g., overall structure and pose). In contrast, the style codes corresponding to fine spatial resolutions (e.g., from 32×32 to 1024×1024), synthesize the relatively local aspects of an image (e.g., face shape, eyes, nose, and lips).

Based on this expectation, as shown in Fig. 2a, the style codes for the coarse resolutions are extracted from x_{tgt} and encouraged to transfer the global aspects of x_{tgt} such as overall structure and pose. In contrast, the style codes for the fine resolutions are extracted from x_{src} and encouraged to transfer the relatively local aspects of x_{src} such as face shape, eyes, nose, and lips. In this respect, we call the style codes extracted from x_{tgt} and x_{src} ID-irrelevant style codes and ID style codes, respectively. However, it is important to reconstruct the details of the target image (e.g., expression and background), but the ID-irrelevant style codes, which do not have spatial dimensions, lose those details.

Style Map. To preserve the details of x_{tgt}, our encoder extracts the style maps from x_{tgt} which have the spatial dimensions. Specifically, the M2M blocks in our encoder produce the style maps with the same size of the incoming latent maps.

Then, these style maps are given as noise inputs to the pretrained StyleGAN generator, which are known to generate fine details of the image.

Note that MegaFS [45] also adopts GAN-inversion method, but it struggles with reconstructing the details of x_{tgt}. To solve this problem, it relies on the segmentation label that detects background and mouth to copy those from x_{tgt}. In contrast, our model can reconstruct the details of x_{tgt} due to the style maps.

3.2   Training Objectives

ID Loss. To ensure x_{swap} has the same identity with x_{src}, we formulate ID loss which calculates cosine similarity between them as

$$\mathcal{L}_{id} = 1 - cos(R(x_{swap}), R(x_{src})), \tag{1}$$

where R is the pretrained face recognition model [14].

Reconstruction Loss. In addition, x_{swap} should be similar to x_{tgt} in most regions except for ID-related regions. To impose this constraint, we define reconstruction loss by adopting pixel-level L_1 loss and LPIPS loss [43] as

$$\mathcal{L}_{recon} = L_1(x_{swap}, x_{tgt}) + LPIPS(x_{swap}, x_{tgt}). \tag{2}$$

Adversarial Loss. To make x_{swap} realistic, we use the non-saturating adversarial loss [18], $\mathcal{L}_{adv}$, and R1 regularization [28], $\mathcal{L}_{R_1}$.

3DMM Supervision. We explicitly enforce x_{swap} to have the same face shape with that of x_{src}, and same pose and expression with those of x_{tgt}. For these constraints, we formulate the following losses using 3DMM [16]:

$$\mathcal{L}_{shape} = ||s_{swap} - s_{src}||_2, \tag{3}$$

$$\mathcal{L}_{pose} = ||p_{swap} - p_{tgt}||_2, \tag{4}$$

$$\mathcal{L}_{exp} = ||e_{swap} - e_{tgt}||_2, \tag{5}$$

where s, p, and e are the shape, pose, and expression parameters extracted from a given image by 3DMM [16] encoder, respectively, with a subscript that denotes the image from which the parameter is extracted (e.g., s_{swap} is the shape parameter extracted from x_{swap}). $\mathcal{L}_{shape}$ encourages x_{swap} to have the same face shape with that of x_{src}. On the other hand, $\mathcal{L}_{pose}$ and $\mathcal{L}_{exp}$ encourage x_{swap} to have the same pose and expression with those of x_{tgt}, respectively.

Note that HifiFace [39] also utilizes 3DMM, but it requires 3DMM even at the inference phase. This is because HiFiFace takes 3DMM parameters as inputs to generate a face-swapped image. In contrast, our model does not take 3DMM parameters as inputs to generate a face-swapped image, so 3DMM is no more used at the inference phase. Furthermore, in terms of loss function, HifiFace formulates the landmark-based loss, but we formulate the parameter-based losses. We compare these methods in the supplementary material.

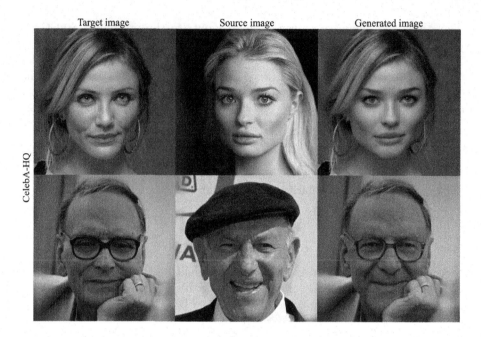

Fig. 3. Qualitative results on CelebA-HQ. The generated images have the same ID attributes (e.g., face shape and eyes) with the source images, but the same ID-irrelevant attributes (e.g., pose and expression) with the taget images.

Full Objective. Finally, we formulate the full loss as

$$\mathcal{L} = \lambda_{id}\mathcal{L}_{id} + \lambda_{recon}\mathcal{L}_{recon} + \lambda_{adv}\mathcal{L}_{adv} + \lambda_{R_1}\mathcal{L}_{R_1}$$
$$+\lambda_{shape}\mathcal{L}_{shape} + \lambda_{pose}\mathcal{L}_{pose} + \lambda_{exp}\mathcal{L}_{exp}. \tag{6}$$

3.3   ID Mixing

Our model can create a new identity by mixing multiple identities. We call this operation *ID mixing*. In order to allow the user to semantically control the identity creation process, we design a method to extract the ID style codes from multiple source images and then mix them like style mixing [21]. Here, we describe ID mixing using two source images, but it can be generalized to use multiple source images more than two. Specifically, when using two source images, the user can take *global* ID attributes (e.g., face shape) from one source image and *local* ID attributes (e.g., eyes) from the other source image and mix them to synthesize an ID-mixed image, x_{mix}.

Figure 2b describes this process. The ID-irrelevant style codes and style maps are extracted from x_{tgt} (red arrow in Fig. 2b). However, the ID style codes are extracted from two source images, global and local source images. We denote them as x_{src}^{gb} and x_{src}^{lc}, respectively, and the style codes extracted from them

Fig. 4. Qualitative comparison. See Sect. 4.2 for the discussion.

are called global (light blue arrow in Fig. 2b) and local ID style codes (dark blue arrow in Fig. 2b), respectively. These ID style codes transform the specific generator feature maps. In particular, the global ID style codes transform the ones with coarse spatial resolution (e.g., 32×32), while the local ID style codes are for the ones with fine spatial resolutions (e.g., from 64×64 to 1024×1024). In this manner, the global ID style codes transfer the global ID attributes (e.g., face shape) of x^{gb}_{src}, while the local ID style codes transfer the local ID attributes (e.g., eyes) of x^{lc}_{src} due to the property of style localization [21].

MegaFS [45] which exploits pretrained StyleGAN also has the potential to perform ID mixing. However, MegaFS struggles with transforming the face shape (Sect. 4.2), so it is difficult to effectively perform ID mixing.

4 Experiments

We present our experimental settings and results to demonstrate the effectiveness of our model. Implementation details are in the supplementary material.

Table 2. Quantitative comparison on FaceForensics++. See Sect. 4.1 for the description of each metric, and Sect. 4.2 for the discussion.

	Identity ↓	Shape ↓	Expression ↓	Pose ↓	Pose-HN ↓
Deepfakes	120.907	0.639	0.802	0.188	4.588
FaceShifter	110.875	0.658	0.653	0.177	**3.175**
SimSwap	99.736	0.662	0.664	0.178	3.749
HifiFace	106.655	0.616	0.702	0.177	3.370
InfoSwap	104.456	0.664	0.698	0.179	4.043
MegaFS	110.897	0.701	0.678	0.182	5.456
SmoothSwap	101.678	0.565	0.722	0.186	4.498
MFIM (ours)	**87.030**	**0.553**	**0.646**	**0.175**	3.694

Table 3. Quantitative comparison on CelebA-HQ. See Sect. 4.1 for the description of each metric, and Sect. 4.2 for the discussion.

	Identity ↓	Shape ↓	Expression ↓	Pose ↓	Pose-HN ↓	FID ↓
MegaFS	108.571	0.906	0.438	0.071	4.880	14.446
MFIM (ours)	**91.469**	**0.782**	**0.400**	**0.057**	**4.095**	**4.946**

4.1 Experimental Settings

Baselines. We compare our model with Deepfakes [1], FaceShifter [27], Sim-Swap [10], HifiFace [39], InfoSwap [17], MegaFs [45], and SmoothSwap [25].

Datasets. We use FFHQ [21] for training, and FaceForensics++ [34] and CelebA-HQ [20] for evaluation. We do not extend the training dataset by combining multiple datasets, while some of the previous models [17,27,39,45] do.

Evaluation Metrics. We evaluate our model and the baselines with respect to identity, shape, expression, and pose following SmoothSwap [25]. In the case of ID and shape, the closer x_{swap} and x_{src} are, the better, and for the expression and pose, the closer x_{swap} and x_{tgt} are, the better. To measure the identity, we use L_2 distance in the feature space of the face recognition model [9]. On the other hand, to measure the shape, expression, and pose, we use L_2 distance in the parameter space of 3DMM [36] for each attribute. For the pose, L_2 distance in the feature space of a pose estimation model [35] is additionally used, and this score is denoted as pose-HN. All of these metrics are the lower the better.

4.2 Comparison with the Baselines

The generated images of our model can be seen in Fig. 3. The qualitative and quantitative comparisons between our model and the baselines are presented in Fig. 4 and Tables 2 and 3, respectively. We first compare our model to the

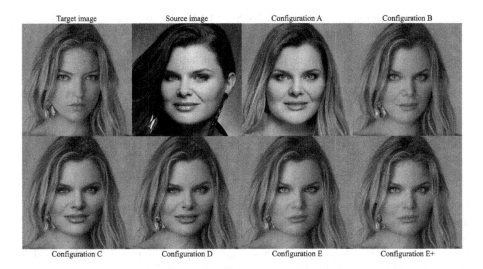

Fig. 5. Ablation study of MFIM. See Sect. 4.3 for the discussion.

baselines on FaceForensics++ [34], following the evaluation protocol of Smooth-Swap [25]. As shown in Table 2, our model is superior to the baselines in all metrics except for pose-HN. It is noteworthy that our model outperforms the baselines for the shape, expression, and pose at the same time, whereas the existing baselines do not perform well for all those three metrics at the same time. For example, among the baslines, SmoothSwap [25] and HifiFace [39] achieve good scores in the shape, but the expression scores of these baselines are not as good. On the other hand, FaceShifter [27] and SimSwap [10] achieve good scores in the expression and pose, but the shape scores of these baselines are not as good. However, our model accomplishes the state-of-the-art performance for the shape, expression, and pose metric at the same time.

In addition, we compare our model to the previous megapixel model, MegaFS [45], on CelebA-HQ. We generate 300,000 images following MegaFS [45]. Then, each model is evaluated with the same metrics used in the evaluation on FaceForenscis++. For FID, we use CelebA-HQ for the real distribution following MegaFS [45]. As shown in Table 3, our model outperforms MegaFS [45] in the all metrics.

4.3 Ablation Study of MFIM

We conduct an ablation study on CelebA-HQ to demonstrate the effectiveness of each component of our model following the evaluation protocol of the comparative experiment on CelebA-HQ (Sect. 4.2). The qualitative and quantitative results are presented in Fig. 5 and Table 4, respectively.

The configuration (A) is trained by using only the ID-irrelevant and ID style codes. The style maps and 3DMM supervision are not used in this configuration.

Table 4. Ablation study of MFIM. See Sect. 4.1 for the description of each metric, and Sect. 4.3 for the discussion.

Configuration	Identity ↓	Shape ↓	Expression ↓	Pose ↓	Pose-HN ↓
A. Baseline MFIM	70.160	0.383	1.116	0.145	7.899
B. + style maps	91.430	0.823	0.398	0.051	3.795
C. + $\mathcal{L}_{shape}$	86.476	0.635	0.864	0.085	5.091
D. + $\mathcal{L}_{pose}$	86.777	0.634	0.860	0.078	4.797
E. + $\mathcal{L}_{exp}$	91.469	0.782	0.400	0.057	4.095

In Fig. 5, the configuration (A) generates an image that has the overall structure and pose of x_{tgt}, but has the identity of x_{src} (e.g., eyes and face shape). This is because the ID-irrelevant style codes transform the generator feature maps with the coarser spatial resolutions (from 4×4 to 16×16) than the ID style codes (from 32×32 to 1024×1024), so the ID-irrelevant style codes synthesize more global aspects than the ID style codes do. However, the configuration (A) fails to reconstruct the details of x_{tgt} (e.g., expression, hair style, and background). This is because the ID-irrelevant style codes, which do not have the spatial dimensions, lose the details of x_{tgt}.

To solve this problem, we construct the configuration (B) by adding the style maps to the configuration (A). In Fig. 5, the configuration (B) reconstructs the details of x_{tgt} better than configuration (A). It is also supported by the improvement of the expression score in Table 4. These results show that the style maps, which have the spatial dimensions, can preserve the details of x_{tgt}. However, the generated image by configuration (B) does not have the same face shape with that of x_{src}, but with that of x_{tgt}.

Therefore, for the more effective identity transformation, we improve our model by adding the 3DMM supervision to the configuration (B). First, we construct the configuration (C) by adding $\mathcal{L}_{shape}$ to the configuration (B). As a result, the generated image by the configuration (C) has the same face shape with that of x_{src} rather than that of x_{tgt}. It leads to the improvement of the shape score in Table 4. However, the expression and pose scores are degraded. This result is consistent with Fig. 5 in that the generated image of configuration (C) has the same expression with x_{src}, not x_{tgt}, which is undesirable. We assume that this is because the expression and pose of x_{src} are leaked somewhat while the face shape of x_{src} is actively transferred by L_{shape}. It means that the ID and ID-irrelevant representations of MFIM are not perfectly disentangled. Improving our model to solve this problem can be future work.

In order to restore the pose and expression scores, we first construct the configuration (D) by adding $\mathcal{L}_{pose}$ to the configuration (C), and then construct the configuration (E) by adding $\mathcal{L}_{exp}$ to the configuration (D). As a result, as shown in Table 4, the pose and expression scores are restored to the similar scores to the configuration (B). Finally, the generated image by the configuration (E)

Fig. 6. ID mixing. Our model can create a new identity by blending the global (e.g., face shape) and local (e.g., eyes) ID attributes captured from the global and local source images, respectively.

in Fig. 5 has the same face shape with that of x_{src}, while the same pose and expression with that of x_{tgt}.

Although the configuration (E) can faithfully reconstruct the details of x_{tgt} such as background and hair style, we can further improve our model to reconstruct the high-frequency details by adding ROI only synthesis to the configuration (E) at the inference phase. This configuration is denoted as (E+). It allows our model to generate only the face region, but it does not require any segmentation label. More details on this are in the supplementary material. In Fig. 5, the configuration (E+) reconstructs the high-frequency details on hair. We use the configuration (E) for all the quantitative results, and the configuration (E+) for all the qualitative results.

4.4 ID Mixing

Figure 6 shows the qualitative results of ID mixing using our model. In Fig. 6, x_{mix} has the new identity with the global ID attributes (e.g., face shape) of x_{src}^{gb}, but the local ID attributes (e.g., eyes) of x_{src}^{lc}. This property of ID mixing allows the user to semantically control the ID creation process. We also compare our model with MegaFS [45] in terms of ID mixing in the supplementary material.

We quantitatively analyze the properties of ID mixing on CelebA-HQ. We prepare 30,000 triplets by randomly assigning one global source image and one local source image to each target image. Then, we define Relative Identity (R-ID) distance and Relative Shape (R-$Shape$) distance following SmoothSwap [25]. For example, R-$ID(gb)$ is defined as R-$ID(gb) = \dfrac{D_{ID}(x_{mix}, x_{src}^{gb})}{D_{ID}(x_{mix}, x_{src}^{gb}) + D_{ID}(x_{mix}, x_{src}^{lc})}$ where D_{ID} means L_2 distance on the feature

Table 5. Quantitative analysis of ID mixing. See Sect. 4.4 for the description of each metric and discussion.

	Overall identity		Face shape	
	R-ID (gb)	R-ID (lc)	R-Shape (gb)	R-Shape (lc)
Local	0.602	0.398	0.609	0.391
ID mixing	0.515	0.485	0.466	0.534
Global	0.399	0.601	0.378	0.622

space of the face recognition model [9]. This measures how similar the overall identity of x_{mix} is to that of x_{src}^{gb} compared to x_{src}^{lc}. $R\text{-}ID(lc)$ is defined similarly, so $R\text{-}ID(gb) + R\text{-}ID(lc) = 1$. In addition, $R\text{-}Shape(gb)$ and $R\text{-}Shape(lc)$ are defined in the same manner with $R\text{-}ID(gb)$ and $R\text{-}ID(lc)$, respectively, but they are based on the 3DMM [36] shape parameter distance to measure the similarity of face shape.

In Table 5, the two rows denoted by *local* and *global* show the results of conventional face swapping, not ID mixing, which uses a single source image. In particular, the row denoted by local is the result of conventional face swapping using only x_{src}^{lc} as the source image without using x_{src}^{gb}. For this reason, $R\text{-}ID(lc)$ and $R\text{-}Shape(lc)$ are smaller than $R\text{-}ID(gb)$ and $R\text{-}Shape(gb)$, respectively, which means that the generated image has the same overall identity and face shape as x_{src}^{lc}, not x_{src}^{gb}. Similarly, the row denoted by global shows that x_{mix} has the same overall identity and face shape as x_{src}^{gb}, not x_{src}^{lc}.

On the other hand, the row denoted by ID mixing shows the results of ID mixing, which uses both the x_{src}^{gb} and x_{src}^{lc} as described in Sect. 3.3. In contrast to when only one of x_{src}^{lc} or x_{src}^{gb} is used, $R\text{-}ID(gb)$ is similar to that of $R\text{-}ID(lc)$. It means that the overall identity of x_{mix} by ID mixing is like a new identity, a mixed identity of x_{src}^{lc} and x_{src}^{gb}. Furthermore, $R\text{-}Shape(gb)$ has a smaller value than $R\text{-}Shape(lc)$. It means that the face shape of the generated image is more similar to that of x_{src}^{gb} than that of x_{src}^{lc}, which is consistent with Fig. 6.

5   Conclusion

We present a state-of-the-art framework for face swapping, MFIM. Our model adopts the GAN-inversion method using pretrained StyleGAN to generate a megapixel image and exploits 3DMM to supervise our model. Finally, we design a new operation, ID mixing, that creates a new identity using multiple source images and performs face swapping with that new identity.

However, the face swapping model can cause **negative impacts** on society. For example, a video made with a malicious purpose (e.g., fake news) can cause fatal damage to the victim. Nevertheless, it has positive impacts on the entertainment and theatrical industry. In addition, generating elaborate face-swapped images can contribute to advances in deepfake detection.

References

1. Deepfakes. https://github.com/ondyari/FaceForensics/tree/master/dataset/ DeepFakes
2. Abdal, R., Qin, Y., Wonka, P.: Image2stylegan: how to embed images into the stylegan latent space? In: Proceedings of the IEEE/CVF International Conference on Computer Vision, pp. 4432–4441 (2019)
3. Alaluf, Y., Patashnik, O., Cohen-Or, D.: Restyle: a residual-based stylegan encoder via iterative refinement. In: Proceedings of the IEEE/CVF International Conference on Computer Vision, pp. 6711–6720 (2021)
4. Alexander, O., Rogers, M., Lambeth, W., Chiang, M., Debevec, P.: The digital emily project: photoreal facial modeling and animation. In: ACM SIGGRAPH 2009 courses, pp. 1–15 (2009)
5. Bahng, H., Chung, S., Yoo, S., Choo, J.: Exploring unlabeled faces for novel attribute discovery. In: Proceedings of the IEEE/CVF Conference on Computer Vision and Pattern Recognition, pp. 5821–5830 (2020)
6. Blanz, V., Vetter, T.: A morphable model for the synthesis of 3d faces. In: Proceedings of the 26th Annual Conference on Computer Graphics and Interactive Techniques, pp. 187–194 (1999)
7. Brock, A., Donahue, J., Simonyan, K.: Large scale GAN training for high fidelity natural image synthesis. arXiv preprint arXiv:1809.11096 (2018)
8. Cao, C., Weng, Y., Zhou, S., Tong, Y., Zhou, K.: FaceWarehouse: a 3d facial expression database for visual computing. IEEE Trans. Vis. Comput. Graph. **20**(3), 413–425 (2013)
9. Cao, Q., Shen, L., Xie, W., Parkhi, O.M., Zisserman, A.: Vggface2: a dataset for recognising faces across pose and age. In: 2018 13th IEEE International Conference on Automatic Face & Gesture Recognition (FG 2018), pp. 67–74. IEEE (2018)
10. Chen, R., Chen, X., Ni, B., Ge, Y.: SimSwap: an efficient framework for high fidelity face swapping. In: Proceedings of the 28th ACM International Conference on Multimedia, pp. 2003–2011 (2020)
11. Cho, W., Choi, S., Park, D.K., Shin, I., Choo, J.: Image-to-image translation via group-wise deep whitening-and-coloring transformation. In: Proceedings of the IEEE/CVF Conference on Computer Vision and Pattern Recognition, pp. 10639–10647 (2019)
12. Choi, Y., Choi, M., Kim, M., Ha, J.W., Kim, S., Choo, J.: StarGAN: Unified generative adversarial networks for multi-domain image-to-image translation. In: Proceedings of the IEEE Conference on Computer vision and Pattern Recognition, pp. 8789–8797 (2018)
13. Choi, Y., Uh, Y., Yoo, J., Ha, J.W.: StarGAN v2: diverse image synthesis for multiple domains. In: Proceedings of the IEEE/CVF Conference on Computer Vision and Pattern Recognition, pp. 8188–8197 (2020)
14. Deng, J., Guo, J., Xue, N., Zafeiriou, S.: ArcFace: additive angular margin loss for deep face recognition. In: Proceedings of the IEEE/CVF Conference on Computer Vision and Pattern Recognition, pp. 4690–4699 (2019)
15. Deng, Y., Yang, J., Xu, S., Chen, D., Jia, Y., Tong, X.: Accurate 3d face reconstruction with weakly-supervised learning: From single image to image set. In: Proceedings of the IEEE/CVF Conference on Computer Vision and Pattern Recognition Workshops (2019)
16. Feng, Y., Feng, H., Black, M.J., Bolkart, T.: Learning an animatable detailed 3D face model from in-the-wild images. vol. 40 (2021). https://doi.org/10.1145/3450626.3459936

17. Gao, G., Huang, H., Fu, C., Li, Z., He, R.: Information bottleneck disentanglement for identity swapping. In: Proceedings of the IEEE/CVF Conference on Computer Vision and Pattern Recognition, pp. 3404–3413 (2021)
18. Goodfellow, I., et al.: Generative adversarial nets. Adv. Neural Inf. Process. Syst. **27** (2014)
19. Isola, P., Zhu, J.Y., Zhou, T., Efros, A.A.: Image-to-image translation with conditional adversarial networks. In: Proceedings of the IEEE Conference on Computer Vision and Pattern Recognition, pp. 1125–1134 (2017)
20. Karras, T., Aila, T., Laine, S., Lehtinen, J.: Progressive growing of GANs for improved quality, stability, and variation. arXiv preprint arXiv:1710.10196 (2017)
21. Karras, T., Laine, S., Aila, T.: A style-based generator architecture for generative adversarial networks. In: Proceedings of the IEEE/CVF Conference on Computer Vision and Pattern Recognition, pp. 4401–4410 (2019)
22. Karras, T., Laine, S., Aittala, M., Hellsten, J., Lehtinen, J., Aila, T.: Analyzing and improving the image quality of StyleGAN. In: Proceedings of the IEEE/CVF Conference on Computer Vision and Pattern Recognition, pp. 8110–8119 (2020)
23. Kemelmacher-Shlizerman, I.: Transfiguring portraits. ACM Trans. Graph. (TOG) **35**(4), 1–8 (2016)
24. Kim, H., Choi, Y., Kim, J., Yoo, S., Uh, Y.: Exploiting spatial dimensions of latent in gan for real-time image editing. In: Proceedings of the IEEE/CVF Conference on Computer Vision and Pattern Recognition, pp. 852–861 (2021)
25. Kim, J., Lee, J., Zhang, B.T.: Smooth-swap: a simple enhancement for face-swapping with smoothness. arXiv preprint arXiv:2112.05907 (2021)
26. Lee, H.Y., Tseng, H.Y., Huang, J.B., Singh, M., Yang, M.H.: Diverse image-to-image translation via disentangled representations. In: Proceedings of the European Conference on Computer Vision (ECCV), pp. 35–51 (2018)
27. Li, L., Bao, J., Yang, H., Chen, D., Wen, F.: Faceshifter: towards high fidelity and occlusion aware face swapping. arXiv preprint arXiv:1912.13457 (2019)
28. Mescheder, L., Geiger, A., Nowozin, S.: Which training methods for GANs do actually converge? In: International Conference on Machine Learning, pp. 3481–3490. PMLR (2018)
29. Mosaddegh, S., Simon, L., Jurie, F.: Photorealistic face de-identification by aggregating donors' face components. In: Cremers, D., Reid, I., Saito, H., Yang, M.-H. (eds.) ACCV 2014. LNCS, vol. 9005, pp. 159–174. Springer, Cham (2015). https://doi.org/10.1007/978-3-319-16811-1_11
30. Na, S., Yoo, S., Choo, J.: Miso: mutual information loss with stochastic style representations for multimodal image-to-image translation. arXiv preprint arXiv:1902.03938 (2019)
31. Naruniec, J., Helminger, L., Schroers, C., Weber, R.M.: High-resolution neural face swapping for visual effects. In: Computer Graphics Forum, vol. 39, pp. 173–184. Wiley Online Library (2020)
32. Park, T., Liu, M.Y., Wang, T.C., Zhu, J.Y.: Semantic image synthesis with spatially-adaptive normalization. In: Proceedings of the IEEE/CVF Conference on Computer Vision and Pattern Recognition, pp. 2337–2346 (2019)
33. Richardson, et al.: Encoding in style: a Stylegan encoder for image-to-image translation. In: Proceedings of the IEEE/CVF Conference on Computer Vision and Pattern Recognition, pp. 2287–2296 (2021)
34. Rossler, A., Cozzolino, D., Verdoliva, L., Riess, C., Thies, J., Nießner, M.: Faceforensics++: learning to detect manipulated facial images. In: Proceedings of the IEEE/CVF International Conference on Computer Vision. pp. 1–11 (2019)

35. Ruiz, N., Chong, E., Rehg, J.M.: Fine-grained head pose estimation without keypoints. In: The IEEE Conference on Computer Vision and Pattern Recognition (CVPR) Workshops, June 2018
36. Sanyal, S., Bolkart, T., Feng, H., Black, M.J.: Learning to regress 3d face shape and expression from an image without 3d supervision. In: Proceedings of the IEEE/CVF Conference on Computer Vision and Pattern Recognition, pp. 7763–7772 (2019)
37. Tov, O., Alaluf, Y., Nitzan, Y., Patashnik, O., Cohen-Or, D.: Designing an encoder for Stylegan image manipulation. ACM Trans. Graph. (TOG) **40**(4), 1–14 (2021)
38. Wang, T., Zhang, Y., Fan, Y., Wang, J., Chen, Q.: High-fidelity gan inversion for image attribute editing. arXiv preprint arXiv:2109.06590 (2021)
39. Wang, Y., et al.: Hififace: 3d shape and semantic prior guided high fidelity face swapping. arXiv preprint arXiv:2106.09965 (2021)
40. Wu, Z., Lischinski, D., Shechtman, E.: StyleSpace analysis: Disentangled controls for stylegan image generation. In: Proceedings of the IEEE/CVF Conference on Computer Vision and Pattern Recognition, pp. 12863–12872 (2021)
41. Xia, W., Zhang, Y., Yang, Y., Xue, J.H., Zhou, B., Yang, M.H.: Gan inversion: a survey. IEEE Trans. Pattern Anal. Mach. Intell. 1–17 (2022)
42. Yoo, S., Bahng, H., Chung, S., Lee, J., Chang, J., Choo, J.: Coloring with limited data: Few-shot colorization via memory augmented networks. In: Proceedings of the IEEE/CVF Conference on Computer Vision and Pattern Recognition, pp. 11283–11292 (2019)
43. Zhang, R., Isola, P., Efros, A.A., Shechtman, E., Wang, O.: The unreasonable effectiveness of deep features as a perceptual metric. In: Proceedings of the IEEE Conference on Computer Vision and Pattern Recognition, pp. 586–595 (2018)
44. Zhu, J.Y., Park, T., Isola, P., Efros, A.A.: Unpaired image-to-image translation using cycle-consistent adversarial networks. In: Proceedings of the IEEE International Conference on Computer Vision, pp. 2223–2232 (2017)
45. Zhu, Y., Li, Q., Wang, J., Xu, C.Z., Sun, Z.: One shot face swapping on megapixels. In: Proceedings of the IEEE/CVF Conference on Computer Vision and Pattern Recognition. pp. 4834–4844 (2021)

3D Face Reconstruction with Dense Landmarks

Erroll Wood[1]($\boxtimes$), Tadas Baltrušaitis[1], Charlie Hewitt[1], Matthew Johnson[1], Jingjing Shen[1], Nikola Milosavljević[2], Daniel Wilde[1], Stephan Garbin[1], Toby Sharp[1], Ivan Stojiljković[2], Tom Cashman[1], and Julien Valentin[3]

[1] Microsoft, Cambridge, UK
errollw@gmail.com
[2] Microsoft, Belgrade, Serbia
[3] Microsoft, Zurich, Switzerland
valentin.julien@microsoft.com

Abstract. Landmarks often play a key role in face analysis, but many aspects of identity or expression cannot be represented by sparse landmarks alone. Thus, in order to reconstruct faces more accurately, landmarks are often combined with additional signals like depth images or techniques like differentiable rendering. Can we keep things simple by just using more landmarks? In answer, we present the first method that accurately predicts 10× as many landmarks as usual, covering the whole head, including the eyes and teeth. This is accomplished using synthetic training data, which guarantees perfect landmark annotations. By fitting a morphable model to these dense landmarks, we achieve state-of-the-art results for monocular 3D face reconstruction in the wild. We show that dense landmarks are an ideal signal for integrating face shape information across frames by demonstrating accurate and expressive facial performance capture in both monocular and multi-view scenarios. Finally, our method is highly efficient: we can predict dense landmarks and fit our 3D face model at over 150FPS on a single CPU thread. Please see our website: https://microsoft.github.io/DenseLandmarks/.

Keywords: Dense correspondences · 3D Morphable model · Face alignment · Landmarks · Synthetic data

1 Introduction

Landmarks are points in correspondence across all faces, like the tip of the nose or the corner of the eye. They often play a role in face-related computer vision, e.g., being used to extract facial regions of interest [33], or helping to constrain 3D model fitting [25,78]. Unfortunately, many aspects of facial identity or expression cannot be encoded by a typical sparse set of 68 landmarks alone. For example, without landmarks on the cheeks, we cannot tell whether or not someone has high cheek-bones. Likewise, without landmarks around the outer eye region, we cannot tell if someone is softly closing their eyes, or scrunching up their face.

Supplementary Information The online version contains supplementary material available at https://doi.org/10.1007/978-3-031-19778-9_10.

S. Avidan et al. (Eds.): ECCV 2022, LNCS 13673, pp. 160–177, 2022.
https://doi.org/10.1007/978-3-031-19778-9_10

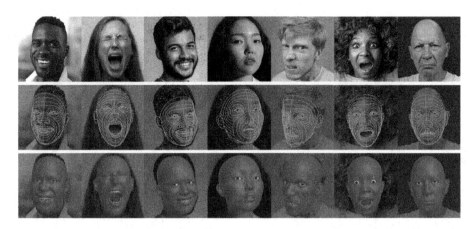

Fig. 1. Given a single image (top), we first robustly and accurately predict 703 landmarks (middle). To aid visualization, we draw lines between landmarks. We then fit our 3D morphable face model to these landmarks to reconstruct faces in 3D (bottom).

In order to reconstruct faces more accurately, previous work has therefore used additional signals beyond color images, such as depth images [63] or optical flow [13]. However, these signals may not be available or reliable to compute. Instead, given color images alone, others have approached the problem using analysis-by-synthesis: minimizing a photometric error [25] between a generative 3D face model and an observed image using differentiable rendering [18,26]. Unfortunately, these approaches are limited by the approximations that must be made in order for differentiable rendering to be computationally feasible. In reality, faces are not purely Lambertian [23], and many important illumination effects are not explained using spherical harmonics alone [18], e.g., ambient occlusion or shadows cast by the nose.

Faced with this complexity, wouldn't it be great if we could just use more landmarks? We present the first method that predicts over 700 landmarks both accurately and robustly. Instead of only the frontal "hockey-mask" portion of the face, our landmarks cover the entire head, including the ears, eyeballs, and teeth. As shown in Fig. 1, these landmarks provide a rich signal for both facial identity and expression. Even with as few as 68, it is hard for humans to precisely annotate landmarks that are not aligned with a salient image feature. That is why we use synthetic training data which guarantees consistent annotations. Furthermore, instead of representing each landmark as just a 2D coordinate, we predict each one as a random variable: a 2D circular Gaussian with position and uncertainty [37]. This allows our predictor to express uncertainty about certain landmarks, e.g., occluded landmarks on the back of the head.

Since our dense landmarks represent points of correspondence across all faces, we can perform 3D face reconstruction by fitting a morphable face model [6] to them. Although previous approaches have fit models to landmarks in a similar way [76], we are the first to show that landmarks are the only signal required to achieve state-of-the-art results for monocular face reconstruction in the wild.

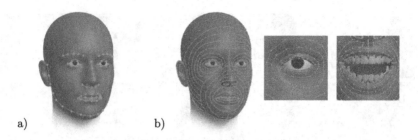

Fig. 2. Compared to a typical sparse set of 68 facial landmarks (a), our dense landmarks (b) cover the entire head in great detail, including ears, eyes, and teeth. These dense landmarks are better at encoding facial identity and subtle expressions.

The probabilistic nature of our predictions also makes them ideal for fitting a 3D model over a temporal sequence, or across multiple views. An optimizer can discount uncertain landmarks and rely on more certain ones. We demonstrate this with accurate and expressive results for both multi-view and monocular facial performance capture. Finally, we show that predicting dense landmarks and then fitting a model can be highly efficient by demonstrating real-time facial performance capture at over 150FPS on a single CPU thread.

In summary, our main contribution is to show that you can achieve more with less. You don't need parametric appearance models, illumination models, or differentiable rendering for accurate 3D face reconstruction. All you need is a sufficiently large quantity of accurate 2D landmarks and a 3D model to fit to them. In addition, we show that combining probabilistic landmarks and model fitting lets us intelligently aggregate face shape information across multiple images by demonstrating robust and expressive results for both multi-view and monocular facial performance capture.

2   Related Work

Reconstructing faces in 3D from images is a mature field at the intersection of vision and graphics. We focus our literature review on methods that are closer to our own, and refer the reader to Morales et al. [46] for an extensive survey.

Regression-Based 3D Face Reconstruction. DNN-based regression has been extensively used as a tool for 3D face reconstruction. Techniques fall into two broad categories: supervised, and self-supervised. Approaches either use 3D Morphable Models (3DMMs) [7,27,40], or eschew linear models and instead learn a non-linear one as part of the training process [65].

Fully supervised techniques either use parameter values from a 3DMM that is fit to the data via optimization as labels [14,67,72], or known face geometry is posed by sampling from a 3DMM and rendered to create synthetic datasets [21,26,50,56]. Self-supervised approaches commonly use landmark reprojection error and/or perceptual loss via differentiable rendering [17,23,26,30,31,44,51,

54,61,62,65,66]. Other techniques augment this with 3D or multiview constraints [20,43,57,60,73,74]. While this is similar to our technique, we only use a DNN to regress landmark positions which are then used to optimize 3DMM parameters, as in the large body of hybrid model-fitting methods [8,32].

Optimization-Based 3D Face Reconstruction. Traditionally, markerless reconstruction of face geometry is achieved with multi-view stereo [4,55], followed by optical flow based alignment, and then optimisation using geometric and temporal priors [5,9,49]. While such methods produce detailed results, each step takes hours to complete. They also suffer from drift and other issues due to their reliance on optical flow and multi-view stereo [15]. While our method cannot reconstruct faces in such fine detail, it accurately recovers the low-frequency shape of the face, and aligns it with a common topology. This enriches the raw data with semantics, making it useful for other tasks.

If only a single image is available, dense photometric [18,64], depth [63], or optical flow [13] constraints are commonly used to recover face shape and motion. However, these methods still rely on sparse landmarks for initializing the optimization close to the dense constraint's basin of convergence, and coping with fast head motion [78]. In contrast, we argue that dense landmarks alone are sufficient for accurately recovering the overall shape of the face.

Dense Landmark Prediction. While sparse landmark prediction is a main-stay of the field [12], few methods directly predict dense landmarks or corre-spondences. This is because annotating a face with dense landmarks is a highly ambiguous task, so either synthetic data [70], pseudo-labels made with model-fitting [16,24,77], or semi-automatic refinement of training data [35,36] are used. Another issue with predicting dense landmarks is that heatmaps, the *de facto* technique for predicting landmarks [11,12], rise in computational complexity with the number of landmarks. While a few previous methods have predicted dense frontal-face landmarks via cascade regression [35] or direct regression [16,28,36], we are the first to accurately and robustly predict over 700 land-marks covering the whole head, including eyes and teeth.

Some methods choose to predict dense correspondences as an image instead, where each pixel corresponds to a fixed point in a UV-unwrapping of the face [1,24] or body [29,59]. Such parameterization suffers from several drawbacks. How does one handle self-occluded portions of the face, e.g., the back of the head? Furthermore, what occurs at UV-island boundaries? If a pixel is half-nose and half-cheek, to which does it correspond? Instead, we choose to discretize the face into dense landmarks. This lets us predict parts of the face that are self-occluded, or lie outside image bounds. Having a fixed set of correspondences also benefits the model-fitter, making it more amenable to running in real-time.

3 Method

In recent years, methods for 3D face reconstruction have become more and more complicated, involving differentiable rendering and complex neural net-work training strategies. We show instead that success can be found by keeping

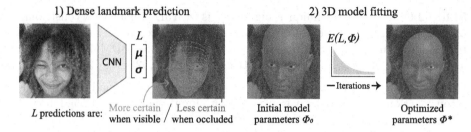

Fig. 3. Given an image, we first predict probabilistic dense landmarks L, each with position μ and certainty σ. Then, we fit our 3D face model to L, minimizing an energy E by optimizing model parameters Φ.

Fig. 4. Examples of our synthetic training data. Without the perfectly consistent annotations provided by synthetic data, dense landmark prediction would not be possible.

things simple. Our approach consists of two stages: First we predict probabilistic dense 2D landmarks L using a traditional convolutional neural network (CNN). Then, we fit a 3D face model, parameterized by Φ, to the 2D landmarks by minimizing an energy function $E(\Phi; L)$. Images themselves are not part of this optimization; the only data used are 2D landmarks.

The main difference between our work and previous approaches is the number and quality of landmarks. No one before has predicted so many 2D landmarks, so accurately. This lets us achieve accurate 3D face reconstruction results by fitting a 3D model to these landmarks alone.

3.1 Landmark Prediction

Synthetic Training Data. Our results are only possible because we use synthetic training data. While a human can consistently label face images with e.g., 68 landmarks, it would be almost impossible for them to annotate an image with dense landmarks. How would it be possible to consistently annotate occluded landmarks on the back of the head, or multiple landmarks over a largely featureless patch of skin e.g., the forehead? In previous work, pseudo-labelled real images with dense correspondences are obtained by fitting a 3DMM to images [1], but the resulting label consistency heavily depends on the quality of the 3D fitting. Using synthetic data has the advantage of guaranteeing perfectly consistent labels. We

Fig. 5. When parts of the face are occluded by e.g. hair or clothing, the corresponding landmarks are predicted with high uncertainty (red), compared to those visible (green). (Color figure online)

rendered a training dataset of 100 k images using the method of Wood et al. [70] with some minor modifications: we include expression-dependent wrinkle texture maps for more realistic skin appearance, and additional clothing, accessory, and hair assets. See Fig. 4 for some examples.

Probabilistic Landmark Regression. We predict each landmark as a random variable with the probability density function of a circular 2D Gaussian. So $L_i = \{\boldsymbol{\mu}_i, \sigma_i\}$, where $\boldsymbol{\mu}_i = [x_i, y_i]$ is the expected position of that landmark, and σ_i (the standard deviation) is a measure of uncertainty. Our training data includes labels for landmark positions $\boldsymbol{\mu}'_i = [x'_i, y'_i]$, but not for σ. The network learns to output σ in an unsupervised fashion to show that it is certain about some landmarks, e.g., visible landmarks on the front of the face, and uncertain about others, e.g., landmarks hidden behind hair (see Fig. 5). This is achieved by training the network with a Gaussian negative log likelihood (GNLL) loss [37]:

$$\text{Loss}(L) = \sum_{i=1}^{|L|} \lambda_i \left(\underbrace{\log\left(\sigma_i^2\right)}_{\text{Loss}_\sigma} + \underbrace{\frac{\|\boldsymbol{\mu}_i - \boldsymbol{\mu}'_i\|^2}{2\sigma_i^2}}_{\text{Loss}_\mu} \right) \tag{1}$$

Loss_σ penalizes the network for being too uncertain, and Loss_μ penalizes the network for being inaccurate. λ_i is a per-landmark weight that focuses the loss on certain parts of the face. This is the only loss used during training.

The probabilistic nature of our landmark predictions is important for accuracy. A network trained with the GNLL loss is more accurate than a network trained with L2 loss on positions only. Perhaps this is the result of the CNN being able to discount challenging landmarks (e.g., fully occluded ones), and spend more capacity on making precise predictions about visible landmarks.

Landmarks are commonly predicted via heatmaps [11]. However, generating heatmaps is computationally expensive [41]; it would not be feasible to output over 700 heatmaps in real-time. Heatmaps also prevent us predicting landmarks outside image bounds. Instead, we keep things simple, and directly regress position and uncertainty using a traditional CNN. We are able to take any off-the-shelf architecture, and alter the final fully-connected layer to output three values per-landmark: two for position and one for uncertainty. Since this final layer represents a small percentage of total CNN compute, our method scales well with landmark quantity.

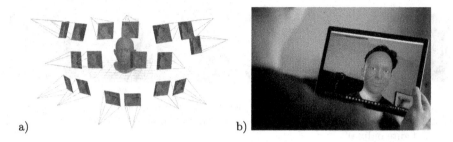

a)   b)

Fig. 6. We implemented two versions of our approach: one for processing multi-view recordings offline (a), and one for real-time facial performance capture (b).

Training Details. Landmark coordinates are normalized from $[0, S]$ to $[-1, 1]$, for a square image of size $S \times S$. Rather than directly outputting σ, we predict $\log \sigma$, and take its exponential to ensure σ is positive. Using PyTorch [47], we train ResNet [34] and MobileNet V2 [53] models from the timm [69] library using AdamW [45] with automatically determined learning rate [22]. We use data augmentation to help our synthetic data cross the domain gap [70].

3.2 3D Model Fitting

Given probabilistic dense 2D landmarks L, our goal is to find optimal model parameters $\mathbf{\Phi}^*$ that minimize the following energy:

$$E(\mathbf{\Phi}; L) = \underbrace{E_{\text{landmarks}}}_{\text{Data term}} + \underbrace{E_{\text{identity}} + E_{\text{expression}} + E_{\text{joints}} + E_{\text{temporal}} + E_{\text{intersect}}}_{\text{Regularizers}}$$

$E_{\text{landmarks}}$ is the only term that encourages the 3D model to explain the observed 2D landmarks. The other terms use prior knowledge to regularize the fit.

Part of the beauty of our approach is how naturally it scales to multiple images and cameras. In this section we present the general form of our method, suitable for F frames over C cameras, i.e., multi-view performance capture.

3D Face Model. We use the face model described in [70], comprising $N = 7{,}667$ vertices and $K = 4$ skeletal joints (the head, neck, and two eyes). Vertex positions are determined by the mesh-generating function $\mathcal{M}(\boldsymbol{\beta}, \boldsymbol{\psi}, \boldsymbol{\theta}): \mathbb{R}^{|\beta|+|\psi|+|\theta|} \to \mathbb{R}^{3N}$ which takes parameters $\boldsymbol{\beta} \in \mathbb{R}^{|\beta|}$ for identity, $\boldsymbol{\psi} \in \mathbb{R}^{|\psi|}$ for expression, and $\boldsymbol{\theta} \in \mathbb{R}^{3K+3}$ for skeletal pose (including root joint translation).

$$\mathcal{M}(\boldsymbol{\beta}, \boldsymbol{\psi}, \boldsymbol{\theta}) = \mathcal{L}(\mathcal{T}(\boldsymbol{\beta}, \boldsymbol{\psi}), \boldsymbol{\theta}, \mathcal{J}(\boldsymbol{\beta}); \mathbf{W})$$

where $\mathcal{L}(\mathbf{V}, \boldsymbol{\theta}, \mathbf{J}; \mathbf{W})$ is a standard linear blend skinning (LBS) function [39] that rotates vertex positions $\mathbf{V} \in \mathbb{R}^{3N}$ about joint locations $\mathbf{J} \in \mathbb{R}^{3K}$ by local joint rotations in $\boldsymbol{\theta}$, with per-vertex weights $\mathbf{W} \in \mathbb{R}^{K \times N}$. The face mesh and joint locations in the bind pose are determined by $\mathcal{T}(\boldsymbol{\beta}, \boldsymbol{\psi}): \mathbb{R}^{|\beta|+|\psi|} \to \mathbb{R}^{3N}$ and $\mathcal{J}(\boldsymbol{\beta}): \mathbb{R}^{|\beta|} \to \mathbb{R}^{3K}$ respectively. See Wood et al. [70] for more details.

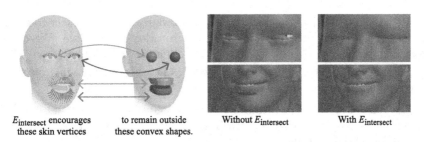

$E_{\text{intersect}}$ encourages   to remain outside   Without $E_{\text{intersect}}$ With $E_{\text{intersect}}$
these skin vertices   these convex shapes.

Fig. 7. We encourage the optimizer to avoid face mesh self-intersections by penalizing skin vertices that enter the convex hulls of the eyeballs or teeth parts.

Cameras are described by a world-to-camera rigid transform $\mathbf{X} \in \mathbb{R}^{3\times4} = [\mathbf{R}|\mathbf{T}]$ comprising rotation and translation, and a pinhole camera projection matrix $\mathbf{\Pi} \in \mathbb{R}^{3\times3}$. Thus, the image-space projection of the jth landmark in the ith camera is $\mathbf{x}_{i,j} = \mathbf{\Pi}_i \mathbf{X}_i \mathcal{M}_j$. In the monocular case, $\mathbf{X}$ can be ignored.

Parameters $\mathbf{\Phi}$ are optimized to minimize E. The main parameters of interest control the face, but we also optimize camera parameters if they are unknown.

$$\mathbf{\Phi} = \{\underbrace{\boldsymbol{\beta}, \mathbf{\Psi}_{F\times|\psi|}, \mathbf{\Theta}_{F\times|\theta|}}_{\text{Face}}; \underbrace{\mathbf{R}_{C\times3}, \mathbf{T}_{C\times3}, \mathbf{f}_C}_{\text{Camera(s)}}\}$$

Facial identity $\boldsymbol{\beta}$ is shared over a sequence of F frames, but expression $\mathbf{\Psi}$ and pose $\mathbf{\Theta}$ vary per frame. For each of our C cameras we have six degrees of freedom for rotation $\mathbf{R}$ and translation $\mathbf{T}$, and a single focal length parameter f. In the monocular case, we only optimize focal length.

$E_{\text{landmarks}}$ encourages the 3D model to explain the predicted 2D landmarks:

$$E_{\text{landmarks}} = \sum_{i,j,k}^{F,C,|L|} \frac{\|\mathbf{x}_{ijk} - \boldsymbol{\mu}_{ijk}\|^2}{2\sigma_{ijk}^2} \tag{2}$$

where, for the kth landmark seen by the jth camera in the ith frame, $[\boldsymbol{\mu}_{ijk}, \sigma_{ijk}]$ is the 2D location and uncertainty predicted by our dense landmark CNN, and $\mathbf{x}_{ijk} = \mathbf{\Pi}_j \mathbf{X}_j \mathcal{M}(\boldsymbol{\beta}, \boldsymbol{\psi}_i, \boldsymbol{\theta}_i)_k$ is the 2D projection of that landmark on our 3D model. The similarity of Eq. 2 to Loss_μ in Eq. 1 is no accident: treating landmarks as 2D random variables during both prediction and model-fitting allows our approach to elegantly handle uncertainty, taking advantage of landmarks the CNN is confident in, and discounting those it is uncertain about.

E_{identity} penalizes unlikely face shape by maximizing the relative log-likelihood of shape parameters $\boldsymbol{\beta}$ under a multivariate Gaussian Mixture Model (GMM) of G components fit to a library of 3D head scans [70]. $E_{\text{identity}} = -\log(p(\boldsymbol{\beta}))$ where $p(\boldsymbol{\beta}) = \sum_{i=1}^{G} \gamma_i \, \mathcal{N}(\boldsymbol{\beta}|\boldsymbol{\nu}_i, \mathbf{\Sigma}_i)$. $\boldsymbol{\nu}_i$ and $\mathbf{\Sigma}_i$ are the mean and covariance matrix of the ith component, and γ_i is the weight of that component.

$E_{\text{expression}} = \|\psi\|^2$ and $E_{\text{joints}} = \|\theta_{i:i\in[2,K]}\|^2$ encourage the optimizer to explain the data with as little expression and joint rotation as possible. We do not penalize global translation or rotation by ignoring the root joint θ_1.
$E_{\text{temporal}} = \sum_{i=2,j,k}^{F,C,|L|} \|\mathbf{x}_{i,j,k} - \mathbf{x}_{i-1,j,k}\|^2$ reduces jitter by encouraging face mesh vertices $\mathbf{x}$ to remain still between neighboring frames $i-1$ and i.

$E_{\text{intersect}}$ encourages the optimizer to find solutions without intersections between the skin and eyeballs or teeth (Fig. 7). Please refer to the supplementary material for further details.

3.3   Implementation

We implemented two versions of our system: one for processing multi-camera recordings offline, and one for real-time facial performance capture.

Our **offline** system produces the best quality results without constraints on compute. We predict 703 landmarks with a ResNet 101 [34]. To extract a facial Region-of-Interest (ROI) from an image we run a full-head probabilistic landmark CNN on multi-scale sliding windows, and select the window with the lowest uncertainty. When fitting our 3DMM, we use PyTorch [47] to minimize $E(\Phi)$ with L-BFGS [42], optimizing all parameters across all frames simultaneously.

For our **real-time** system, we trained a lightweight dense landmark model with MobileNet V2 architecture [53]. To compensate for a reduction in network capacity, we predict 320 landmarks rather than 703, and modify the ROI strategy: aligning the face so it appears upright with the eyes a fixed distance apart. This makes the CNN's job easier for frontal faces at the expense of profile ones.

Real-Time Model Fitting. We use the Levenberg-Marquardt algorithm to optimize our model-fitting energy. Camera and identity parameters are only fit occasionally. For the majority of frames we fit pose and expression parameters only. We rewrite the energy E in terms of the vector of residuals, $\mathbf{r}$, as $E(\Phi) = \|\mathbf{r}(\Phi)\|^2 = \sum_i r_i(\Phi)^2$. Then at each iteration k of our optimization, we can compute $\mathbf{r}(\Phi_k)$ and the Jacobian, $J(\Phi_k) = \frac{\partial \mathbf{r}(\Phi)}{\partial \Phi}|^{\Phi=\Phi_k}$, and use these to solve the symmetric, positive-semi-definite linear system, $(J^T J + \lambda \text{diag}(J^T J))\delta_k = -J^T \mathbf{r}$ via Cholesky decomposition. We then apply the update rule, $\Phi_{k+1} = \Phi_k + \delta_k$.

In practice we do not actually form the residual vector $\mathbf{r}$ nor the Jacobian matrix J. Instead, for performance reasons, we directly compute the quantities $J^T J$ and $J^T \mathbf{r}$ as we visit each term $r_i(\Phi_k)$ of the energy. Most of the computational cost is incurred in evaluating these products for the landmark data term, as expected. However, the Jacobian of landmark term residuals is not fully dense. Each individual landmark depends on its own subset of expression parameters, and is invariant to other expression parameters. We performed a static analysis of the sparsity of each landmark term with respect to parameters, $\partial r_i / \partial \Phi_j$, and we use this set of i, j indices to reduce the cost of our outer products from $O(|\Phi|^2)$ to $O(m_i^2)$, where m_i is the sparsified dimensionality of $\partial r_i / \partial \Phi$. We further enhance the sparsity by ignoring any components of the Jacobian with an absolute value below a certain empirically-determined threshold.

Method	Common NME	Challenging NME	Private FR$_{10\%}$
LAB [72]	● 2.98	5.19	0.83
AWING [69]	● **2.72**	● **4.52**	● 0.33
ODN [76]	3.56	6.67	-
3FabRec [10]	3.36	5.74	● **0.17**
Wood et al. [71]	3.09	4.86	● 0.50
LUVLi [39]	● 2.76	5.16	-
ours (L2)	3.30	● 5.12	● 0.33
ours (GNLL)	3.03	● 4.80	● **0.17**

Fig. 8. Left: results on 300W dataset, lower is better. Note competitive performance of our model (despite being evaluated across-dataset) and importance of GNLL loss. Right: sample predictions (top row) with label-translated results (bottom row).

By exploiting sparsity in this way, the landmark term residuals and their derivatives become very cheap to evaluate. This formulation avoids the correspondence problem usually seen with depth images [58], which requires a more expensive optimization. In addition, adding more landmarks does not significantly increase the cost of optimization. It therefore becomes possible to implement a very detailed and well-regularized fitter with a relatively small compute burden, simply by adding a sufficient number of landmarks. The cost of the Cholesky solve for the update δ_k is independent of the number of landmarks.

4   Evaluation

4.1   Landmark Accuracy

We measure the accuracy of a ResNet 101 dense landmark model on the **300W** [52] dataset. For benchmark purposes only, we employ label translation [70] to deal with systematic inconsistencies between our 703 predicted dense landmarks and the 68 sparse landmarks labelled as ground truth (see Table 8). While previous work [70] used label translation to evaluate a synthetically-trained sparse landmark predictor, we use it to evaluate a dense landmark predictor.

We use the standard normalized mean error (NME) and failure rate (FR$_{10\%}$) error metrics [52]. Our model's results in Table 8 are competitive with the state of the art, despite being trained with synthetic data alone. Note: these results provide a conservative estimate of our method's accuracy as the translation network may introduce error, especially for rarely seen expressions.

Ablation Study. We measured the importance of predicting each landmark as a random variable rather than as a 2D coordinate. We trained two landmark prediction models, one with our proposed GNLL loss (Eq. 1), and one with a simpler L2 loss on landmark coordinate only. Results in Table 8 confirm that including uncertainty in landmark regression results in better accuracy.

Qualitative Comparisons are shown in Fig. 9 between our real-time dense landmark model (MobileNet V2) and MediaPipe Attention Mesh [28], a publicly available dense landmark method designed for mobile devices. Our method

MediaPipe [29]   ours   MediaPipe [29]   ours

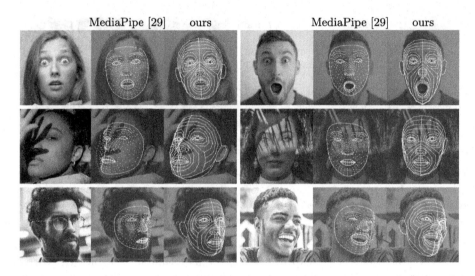

Fig. 9. We compare our real-time landmark CNN (MobileNet V2) with MediaPipe Attention Mesh [28], a publicly available method for dense landmark prediction. Our approach is more robust to challenging expressions and illumination.

is more robust, perhaps due to the consistency and diversity of our synthetic training data. See the supplementary material for additional qualitative results, including landmark predictions on the Challenging subset of 300W.

4.2   3D Face Reconstruction

Quantitatively, we compare our offline approach with recent methods on two benchmarks: the NoW Challenge [54] and the MICC dataset [2].

The Now Challenge [54] provides a standard evaluation protocol for measuring the accuracy and robustness of 3D face reconstruction in the wild. It consists of 2054 face images of 100 subjects along with a 3D head scan for each subject which serves as ground truth. We undertake the challenge in two ways: *single view*, where we fit our face model to each image separately, and *multi-view*, where we fit a per-subject face model to all image of a particular subject. As shown in Fig. 10, we achieve state of the art results.

The MICC Dataset [2] consists of 3D face scans and videos of 53 subjects. The videos were recorded in three environments: a "cooperative" laboratory environment, an indoor environment, and an outdoor environment. We follow Deng et al. [17], and evaluate our method in two ways: *single view*, where we estimate one face shape per frame in a video, and average the resulting face meshes, and *multi-view*, where we fit a single face model to all frames in a video jointly. As shown in Table 1, we achieve state of the art results.

Note that many previous methods are incapable of aggregating face shape information across multiple views. The fact ours can benefit from multiple views highlights the flexibility of our hybrid model-fitting approach.

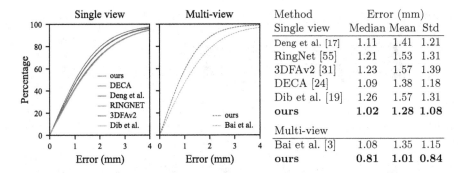

Fig. 10. Results for the now challenge [54]. We outperform the state of the art on both single- and multi-view 3D face reconstruction.

Table 1. Results on the MICC dataset [2], following the single and multi-frame evaluation protocol of Deng et al. [17]. We achieve state-of-the-art results.

Method	Error (mm), mean		
Single view	Coop.	Indoor	Outdoor
Tran et al. [67]	1.97	2.03	1.93
Genova et al. [26]	1.78	1.78	1.76
Deng et al. [17]	1.66	1.66	1.69
ours	**1.64**	**1.62**	**1.61**

Method	Error (mm), mean		
Multi-view	Coop.	Indoor	Outdoor
Piotraschke and Blanz [48]	1.68	1.67	1.72
Deng et al. [17]	1.60	1.61	1.63
ours	**1.43**	**1.42**	**1.42**

Ablation Studies. We conducted an experiment to measure the importance of landmark quantity for 3D face reconstruction. We trained three landmark CNNs, predicting 703, 320, and 68 landmarks respectively, and used these on the NoW Challenge (validation set). As shown in Fig. 11, fitting with more landmarks results in more accurate 3D face reconstruction.

In addition, we investigated the importance of using landmark uncertainty σ in model fitting. We fit our model to 703 landmark predictions on the NoW validation set, but using fixed rather than predicted σ. Figure 11 (bottom row of table) shows that fitting without σ leads to worse results.

Qualitative Comparisons between our work and several publicly available methods [17,23,30,54,57] can be found in Fig. 13.

4.3   Facial Performance Capture

Multi-view. Good synthetic training data requires a database of facial expression parameters from which to sample. We acquired such a database by conducting markerless facial performance capture for 108 subjects. We recorded each subject in our 17-camera studio, and processed each recording with our offline multi-view model fitter. For a 520 frame sequence it takes 3 min to predict dense landmarks for all images, and a further 9 min to optimize face model parameters. See Fig. 12 for some of the 125,000 frames of expression data captured with

Fit with:	68 ldmks.	320 ldmks.	703 ldmks.

Number of Landmarks	Error (mm)		
	Median	Mean	Std
68	1.10	1.38	1.16
320	1.00	1.24	1.02
703	**0.95**	**1.17**	**0.97**
703 (without σ)	1.02	1.26	1.03

Fig. 11. Ablation studies on the NoW [54] validation set confirm that denser is better: model fitting with more landmarks leads to more accurate results. In addition, we see that fitting without using σ leads to worse results.

Fig. 12. We demonstrate the robustness and reliability of our method by using it to collect a massive database of 125,000 facial expressions, fully automatically.

our system. As the system which is used to create the database is then subsequently re-trained with it, we produced several databases in this manner until no further improvement was seen. We do not reconstruct faces in fine detail like previous multi-view stereo approaches [5,9,49]. However, while previous work can track a detailed 3D mesh over a performance, our approach reconstructs the performance with richer semantics: identity and expression parameters for our generative model. In many cases it is sufficient to reconstruct the low-frequency shape of the face accurately, without fine details.

Real-Time Monocular. See the last two columns of Fig. 13 for a comparison between our offline and real-time systems for monocular 3D model-fitting. While our offline system produces the best possible results by using a large CNN and optimizing over all frames simultaneously, our real-time system can still produce accurate and expressive results fitting frame-to-frame. Please refer to the supplementary material for more results. Running on a single CPU thread (i5-11600K), our real-time system spends 6.5 ms processing a frame (150FPS), of which 4.1 ms is spent predicting dense landmarks and 2.3 ms is spent fitting our face model.

5   Limitations and Future Work

Our method depends entirely on accurate landmarks. As shown in Fig. 14, if landmarks are poorly predicted, the resulting model fit suffers. We plan to address

| RingNet [55] | Deng et al. [17] | 3DFAv2 [31] | MGCNet [58] | DECA [24] | ours (offline) | ours (real-time) |

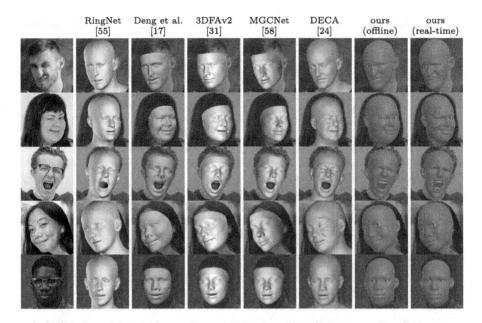

Fig. 13. Compared to previous recent monocular 3D face reconstruction methods, ours better captures gaze, expressions like winks and sneers, and subtleties of facial identity. In addition, our method can run in real time with only a minor loss of fidelity.

Fig. 14. Bad landmarks result in bad fits, and we are incapable of tracking the tongue.

this by improving our synthetic training data. Additionally, since our model does not include tongue articulation we cannot recover tongue movement.

Heatmaps have dominated landmark prediction for some time [11,12]. We were pleasantly surprised to find that directly regressing 2D landmark coordinates with unspecialized architectures works well and eliminates the need for computationally-costly heatmap generation. In addition, we were surprised that predicting σ helps accuracy. We look forward to further investigating direct probabilistic landmark regression as an alternative to heatmaps in future work.

In conclusion, we have demonstrated that dense landmarks are an ideal signal for 3D face reconstruction. Quantitative and qualitative evaluations have shown that our approach outperforms those previous by a significant margin, and excels at multi-view and monocular facial performance capture. Finally, our approach is highly efficient, and runs at over 150FPS on a single CPU thread.

Acknowledgments. Thanks to Chirag Raman and Jamie Shotton for their contributions, and Jiaolong Yang and Timo Bolkart for help with evaluation.

References

1. Alp Güler, R., Trigeorgis, G., Antonakos, E., Snape, P., Zafeiriou, S., Kokkinos, I.: DenseReg: fully convolutional dense shape regression in-the-wild. In: CVPR (2017)
2. Bagdanov, A.D., Del Bimbo, A., Masi, I.: The Florence 2D/3D hybrid face dataset. In: Workshop on Human Gesture and Behavior Understanding. ACM (2011)
3. Bai, Z., Cui, Z., Liu, X., Tan, P.: Riggable 3D face reconstruction via in-network optimization. In: CVPR (2021)
4. Beeler, T., Bickel, B., Beardsley, P., Sumner, B., Gross, M.: High-quality single-shot capture of facial geometry. In: ACM Transactions on Graphics (2010)
5. Beeler, T., et al.: High-quality passive facial performance capture using anchor frames. In: ACM Transactions on Graphics (2011)
6. Blanz, V., Vetter, T.: A morphable model for the synthesis of 3D faces. In: Computer Graphics and Interactive Techniques (1999)
7. Blanz, V., Vetter, T.: Face recognition based on fitting a 3d morphable model. TPAMI **25**(9), 1063–1074 (2003)
8. Bogo, F., Kanazawa, A., Lassner, C., Gehler, P., Romero, J., Black, M.J.: Keep It SMPL: automatic estimation of 3d human pose and shape from a single image. In: Leibe, B., Matas, J., Sebe, N., Welling, M. (eds.) ECCV 2016. LNCS, vol. 9909, pp. 561–578. Springer, Cham (2016). https://doi.org/10.1007/978-3-319-46454-1_34
9. Bradley, D., Heidrich, W., Popa, T., Sheffer, A.: High resolution passive facial performance capture. In: ACM Transactions on Graphics, vol. 29, no. 4 (2010)
10. Browatzki, B., Wallraven, C.: 3FabRec: Fast Few-shot Face alignment by Reconstruction. In: CVPR (2020)
11. Bulat, A., Sanchez, E., Tzimiropoulos, G.: Subpixel heatmap regression for facial landmark Localization. In: BMVC (2021)
12. Bulat, A., Tzimiropoulos, G.: How far are we from solving the 2d & 3d face alignment problem? (and a dataset of 230,000 3D facial landmarks). In: ICCV (2017)
13. Cao, C., Chai, M., Woodford, O., Luo, L.: Stabilized real-time face tracking via a learned dynamic rigidity prior. ACM Trans. Graph. **37**(6), 1–11 (2018)
14. Chandran, P., Bradley, D., Gross, M., Beeler, T.: Semantic deep face models. In: International Conference on 3D Vision (3DV) (2020)
15. Cong, M., Lan, L., Fedkiw, R.: Local geometric indexing of high resolution data for facial reconstruction from sparse markers. CoRR abs/1903.00119 (2019). www.arxiv.org/abs/1903.00119
16. Deng, J., Guo, J., Ververas, E., Kotsia, I., Zafeiriou, S.: RetinaFace: single-shot multi-level face localisation in the wild. In: CVPR (2020)
17. Deng, Y., Yang, J., Xu, S., Chen, D., Jia, Y., Tong, X.: Accurate 3d face reconstruction with weakly-supervised learning: from single image to image set. In: CVPR Workshops (2019)
18. Dib, A., et al.: Practical face reconstruction via differentiable ray tracing. Comput. Graph. Forum **40**(2), 153–164 (2021)
19. Dib, A., Thebault, C., Ahn, J., Gosselin, P.H., Theobalt, C., Chevallier, L.: Towards high fidelity monocular face reconstruction with rich reflectance using self-supervised learning and ray tracing. In: CVPR (2021)
20. Dou, P., Kakadiaris, I.A.: Multi-view 3D face reconstruction with deep recurrent neural networks. Image Vis. Comput. **80**, 80–91 (2018)

21. Dou, P., Shah, S.K., Kakadiaris, I.A.: End-to-end 3D face reconstruction with deep neural networks. In: CVPR (2017)
22. Falcon, W., et al.: Pytorch lightning **3**(6) (2019). GitHub. Note. https://github.com/PyTorchLightning/pytorch-lightning
23. Feng, Y., Feng, H., Black, M.J., Bolkart, T.: Learning an animatable detailed 3D face model from in-the-wild images. ACM Trans. Graph. (ToG) **40**(4), 1–13 (2021)
24. Feng, Y., Wu, F., Shao, X., Wang, Y., Zhou, X.: Joint 3d face reconstruction and dense alignment with position map regression network. In: ECCV (2018)
25. Garrido, P., et al.: Reconstruction of personalized 3d face rigs from monocular video. ACM Trans. Graph. **35**(3), 1–15 (2016)
26. Genova, K., Cole, F., Maschinot, A., Sarna, A., Vlasic, D., Freeman, W.T.: Unsupervised training for 3d morphable model regression. In: CVPR (2018)
27. Gerig, T., et al.: Morphable face models-an open framework. In: Automatic Face & Gesture Recognition (FG). IEEE (2018)
28. Grishchenko, I., Ablavatski, A., Kartynnik, Y., Raveendran, K., Grundmann, M.: Attention mesh: high-fidelity face mesh prediction in real-time. In: CVPR Workshops (2020)
29. Güler, R.A., Neverova, N., Kokkinos, I.: Densepose: dense human pose estimation in the wild. In: CVPR (2018)
30. Guo, J., Zhu, X., Yang, Y., Yang, F., Lei, Z., Li, S.Z.: Towards fast, accurate and stable 3d dense face alignment. In: Vedaldi, A., Bischof, H., Brox, T., Frahm, J.-M. (eds.) ECCV 2020. LNCS, vol. 12364, pp. 152–168. Springer, Cham (2020). https://doi.org/10.1007/978-3-030-58529-7_10
31. Guo, Y., Cai, J., Jiang, B., Zheng, J., et al.: Cnn-based real-time dense face reconstruction with inverse-rendered photo-realistic face images. TPAMI **41**(6), 1294–1307 (2018)
32. Han, S., et al.: Megatrack: monochrome egocentric articulated hand-tracking for virtual reality. ACM Trans. Graph. (TOG) **39**(4), 1–87 (2020)
33. Hassner, T., Harel, S., Paz, E., Enbar, R.: Effective face frontalization in unconstrained images. In: CVPR (2015)
34. He, K., Zhang, X., Ren, S., Sun, J.: Deep residual learning for image recognition. In: CVPR (2016)
35. Jeni, L.A., Cohn, J.F., Kanade, T.: Dense 3D face alignment from 2D videos in real-time. In: Automatic Face and Gesture Recognition (FG). IEEE (2015)
36. Kartynnik, Y., Ablavatski, A., Grishchenko, I., Grundmann, M.: Real-time facial surface geometry from monocular video on mobile GPUs. In: CVPR Workshops (2019)
37. Kendall, A., Gal, Y.: What uncertainties do we need in bayesian deep learning for computer vision? In: Advances in Neural Information Processing Systems, vol. 30 (2017)
38. Kumar, A., et al.: Luvli face alignment: estimating landmarks' location, uncertainty, and visibility likelihood. In: CVPR (2020)
39. Lewis, J.P., Cordner, M., Fong, N.: Pose space deformation: a unified approach to shape interpolation and skeleton-driven deformation. In: SIGGRAPH (2000)
40. Li, T., Bolkart, T., Black, M.J., Li, H., Romero, J.: Learning a model of facial shape and expression from 4D scans. In: ACM Transactions on Graphics, (Proceedings SIGGRAPH Asia) (2017)
41. Li, Y., Yang, S., Zhang, S., Wang, Z., Yang, W., Xia, S.T., Zhou, E.: Is 2d heatmap representation even necessary for human pose estimation? (2021)

42. Liu, D.C., Nocedal, J.: On the limited memory BFGS method for large scale optimization. Math. Program. **45**(1), 503–528 (1989). https://doi.org/10.1007/BF01589116
43. Liu, F., Zhu, R., Zeng, D., Zhao, Q., Liu, X.: Disentangling features in 3D face shapes for joint face reconstruction and recognition. In: CVPR (2018)
44. Liu, Y., Jourabloo, A., Ren, W., Liu, X.: Dense face alignment. In: ICCV Workshops (2017)
45. Loshchilov, I., Hutter, F.: Decoupled weight decay regularization. In: ICLR (2019)
46. Morales, A., Piella, G., Sukno, F.M.: Survey on 3d face reconstruction from uncalibrated images. Comput. Sci. Rev. **40**, 100400 (2021)
47. Paszke, A., et al.: Pytorch: an imperative style, high-performance deep learning library. In: NeurIPS (2019)
48. Piotraschke, M., Blanz, V.: Automated 3D face reconstruction from multiple images using quality measures. In: CVPR (2016)
49. Popa, T., South-Dickinson, I., Bradley, D., Sheffer, A., Heidrich, W.: Globally consistent space-time reconstruction. Comput. Graph. Forum **29**(5), 1633–1642 (2010)
50. Richardson, E., Sela, M., Kimmel, R.: 3D face reconstruction by learning from synthetic data. In: 3DV. IEEE (2016)
51. Richardson, E., Sela, M., Or-El, R., Kimmel, R.: Learning detailed face reconstruction from a single image. In: CVPR (2017)
52. Sagonas, C., Antonakos, E., Tzimiropoulos, G., Zafeiriou, S., Pantic, M.: 300 faces in-the-wild challenge: database and results. Image Vis. Computi. (IMAVIS) **47**, 3–18 (2016)
53. Sandler, M., Howard, A., Zhu, M., Zhmoginov, A., Chen, L.C.: Mobilenet V2: Inverted residuals and linear bottlenecks. In: CVPR (2018)
54. Sanyal, S., Bolkart, T., Feng, H., Black, M.: Learning to regress 3d face shape and expression from an image without 3d supervision. In: CVPR (2019)
55. Seitz, S.M., Curless, B., Diebel, J., Scharstein, D., Szeliski, R.: A comparison and evaluation of multi-view stereo reconstruction algorithms. In: CVPR (2006)
56. Sela, M., Richardson, E., Kimmel, R.: Unrestricted facial geometry reconstruction using image-to-image translation. In: ICCV (2017)
57. Shang, J.: Self-supervised monocular 3d face reconstruction by occlusion-aware multi-view geometry consistency. In: Vedaldi, A., Bischof, H., Brox, T., Frahm, J.-M. (eds.) ECCV 2020. LNCS, vol. 12360, pp. 53–70. Springer, Cham (2020). https://doi.org/10.1007/978-3-030-58555-6_4
58. Taylor, J., et al.: Efficient and precise interactive hand tracking through joint, continuous optimization of pose and correspondences. ACM Trans. Graph. (ToG) **35**(4), 1–12 (2016)
59. Taylor, J., Shotton, J., Sharp, T., Fitzgibbon, A.: The vitruvian manifold: inferring dense correspondences for one-shot human pose estimation. In: CVPR (2012)
60. Tewari, A., et al.: FML: face model learning from videos. In: CVPR (2019)
61. Tewari, A., et al: Self-supervised multi-level face model learning for monocular reconstruction at over 250 Hz. In: CVPR (2018)
62. Tewari, A., et al.: Mofa: model-based deep convolutional face autoencoder for unsupervised monocular reconstruction. In: ICCV Workshops (2017)
63. Thies, J., Zollhöfer, M., Nießner, M., Valgaerts, L., Stamminger, M., Theobalt, C.: Real-time expression transfer for facial reenactment. ACM Trans. Graph. **34**(6), 1–183 (2015)
64. Thies, J., Zollhöfer, M., Stamminger, M., Theobalt, C., Nießner, M.: Face2Face: real-time face capture and reenactment of RGB videos. In: CVPR (2016)

65. Tran, L., Liu, F., Liu, X.: Towards high-fidelity nonlinear 3D face morphable model. In: CVPR (2019)
66. Tran, L., Liu, X.: Nonlinear 3d face morphable model. In: CVPR (2018)
67. Tuan Tran, A., Hassner, T., Masi, I., Medioni, G.: Regressing robust and discriminative 3D morphable models with a very deep neural network. In: CVPR (2017)
68. Wang, X., Bo, L., Fuxin, L.: Adaptive wing loss for robust face alignment via heatmap regression. In: ICCV (2019)
69. Wightman, R.: Pytorch image models (2019). https://www.github.com/rwightman/pytorch-image-models, https://doi.org/10.5281/zenodo.4414861
70. Wood, E., et al.: Fake it till you make it: Face analysis in the wild using synthetic data alone (2021)
71. Wu, W., Qian, C., Yang, S., Wang, Q., Cai, Y., Zhou, Q.: Look at boundary: a boundary-aware face alignment algorithm. In: CVPR (2018)
72. Yi, H., et al.: MMFace: a multi-metric regression network for unconstrained face reconstruction. In: CVPR (2019)
73. Yoon, J.S., Shiratori, T., Yu, S.I., Park, H.S.: Self-supervised adaptation of high-fidelity face models for monocular performance tracking. In: CVPR (2019)
74. Zhou, Y., Deng, J., Kotsia, I., Zafeiriou, S.: Dense 3d face decoding over 2500fps: joint texture & shape convolutional mesh decoders. In: CVPR (2019)
75. Zhu, M., Shi, D., Zheng, M., Sadiq, M.: Robust facial landmark detection via occlusion-adaptive deep networks. In: CVPR (2019)
76. Zhu, X., Lei, Z., Liu, X., Shi, H., Li, S.Z.: Face alignment across large poses: a 3d solution. In: CVPR (2016)
77. Zhu, X., Lei, Z., Liu, X., Shi, H., Li, S.Z.: Face alignment across large poses: a 3d solution. In: Proceedings of the IEEE Conference on Computer Vision and Pattern Recognition, pp. 146–155 (2016)
78. Zollhöfer, M., et al.: State of the art on monocular 3d face reconstruction, tracking, and applications. Comput. Graph. Forum **37**(2), 523–550 (2018)

Emotion-aware Multi-view Contrastive Learning for Facial Emotion Recognition

Daeha Kim📵 and Byung Cheol Song$^{(\boxtimes)}$📵

Inha University, Incheon, Republic of Korea
bcsong@inha.ac.kr

Abstract. When a person recognizes another's emotion, he or she recognizes the (facial) features associated with emotional expression. So, for a machine to recognize facial emotion(s), the features related to emotional expression must be represented and described properly. However, prior arts based on label supervision not only failed to explicitly capture features related to emotional expression, but also were not interested in learning emotional representations. This paper proposes a novel approach to generate features related to emotional expression through feature transformation and to use them for emotional representation learning. Specifically, the contrast between the generated features and overall facial features is quantified through contrastive representation learning, and then facial emotions are recognized based on understanding of angle and intensity that describe the emotional representation in the polar coordinate, i.e., the Arousal-Valence space. Experimental results show that the proposed method improves the PCC/CCC performance by more than 10% compared to the runner-up method in the wild datasets and is also qualitatively better in terms of neural activation map. Code is available at https://github.com/kdhht2334/AVCE_FER.

Keywords: Facial emotion recognition · Dimensional model of emotion · Human-computer interaction

1 Introduction

Facial emotion (or expression) is the most distinct attention information among human non-verbal cues. Facial emotion recognition (FER) has made significant technological progress in recent years, and it has been gradually extended to various fields such as robot-assisted therapy [27] and robot navigation [2]. However, since most FER methods are based on discrete (emotion) labels, they could not take into account the intensity of emotion or capture the continuous emotional change.

Therefore, Arousal-Valence (AV)-based FER utilizing continuous labels has been studied to overcome the above-mentioned limitations of categorical FER.

Supplementary Information The online version contains supplementary material available at https://doi.org/10.1007/978-3-031-19778-9_11.

Here, continuous AV space is based on activation (arousal) and positiveness (valence) of emotions [18]. Psychological studies [45] showed that human visual attention is closely related to AV value(s), which suggests that AV-based FER can imitate human's emotion recognition. Comparing with categorical FER, AV-based FER handling continuous labels can theoretically understand complex facial expressions and micro-facial expressions, and even detect hidden emotions [37, 44].

However, the existing AV-based FER approaches have not yet technically dealt with the following concerns.

• *What is the Key for Feature Learning of Facial Emotions?* According to Panda et al. [36] and Wei et al. [52], visual features for standard vision tasks such as classification and detection cannot be scaled up for FER-related tasks because FER should consider the pixel-level visual properties (e.g., edge, hue, illumination) as well as semantic features (e.g., landmarks). Prior arts for representation learning [14, 19] learned facial emotions only through quantitative differences, so they did not provide an explicit solution for learning semantic features. Therefore, representation learning that can understand even semantic features is required.
• *How Can We Extract Facial Emotion-aware Features?* In general, a human has a so-called visual perception ability that attends core regions such as eyes and mouth for FER while suppressing relatively unnecessary parts such as hair and background [16]. This fact suggests that properly extracting the features of core and non-core regions is a pre-requisite in representation learning for FER. So, it is necessary to extract emotion-aware features from the (latent) feature space that can learn semantic information [3]. However, due to the difficulty of the problem setting, AV-based FER that considers representation learning and visual perception ability simultaneously has not yet been reported as in Fig. 1.

This paper addresses the two concerns mentioned above. First, we propose a novel contrastive representation learning (CRL) mechanism and analyze the (semantic) feature relationship, i.e., emotional contrast (cf. Sect. 3.3). The proposed CRL with the similarity function performs discriminative learning based on projected features in the AV space (see the blue dotted box of Fig. 2(b)) [4, 12]. This CRL mechanism is suitable for the FER task, since it is important to differentiate

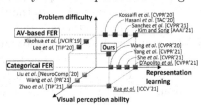

Fig. 1. Our emotion-aware representation learning is a novel method that has not been formally addressed and designed so far

the core regions in which emotions are expressed from the non-core regions in which emotions are not expressed [53]. Note that utilizing CRL as a regularization term can improve the generalization ability of convolutional neural networks (CNNs) and have the same effect on continuous label-based tasks [26]. Therefore, the proposed CRL mechanism for regularization can also enhance the generalization ability of emotional representations in the AV space.

Second, we propose feature transformations that generate multiple (semantic) "views" of a facial image, i.e., the facial emotion-aware features $\mathbf{z}_a$ and $\mathbf{z}_n$

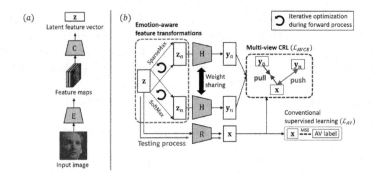

Fig. 2. (a) Input image encoding process. (b) The overall framework of the proposed method. Here, the green arrow indicates the testing process (Color figure online)

(see the red dotted box of Fig. 2(b)). Here, for transformation that has a significant impact on the performance of CRL, SparseMax [28] and SoftMax are adopted. z_a from SparseMax indicates facial features that are highly correlated with facial emotion. On the other hand, since SoftMax is based on weighted aggregation of features and is detrimental to the disentanglement representation [59], z_n obtained from SoftMax represents an average (facial) feature or a feature contrasting with z_a.

Therefore, the main contributions of this paper are summarized as follows:

- We succeeded in incorporating visual perception ability into representation learning for the first time in AV-based FER task. The proposed method overcame the limitations of problem setting in AV-based FER. Also, it showed better performance of more than 10% in the wild dataset than the state-of-the-art (SOTA) methods.
- The proposed feature transformations enable to focus on semantic regions that are important for emotional representation. We could observe the visual perception ability of transformed features focusing on semantic regions through activation map-based visualization.

2   Related Work

AV-Based FER Overview. With the advent of large-scale AV datasets [55], Hasani et al. [14] directly matched predictions using CNNs to continuous labels, i.e., ground-truths (GTs). Kossaifi et al. [23] proposed a factorized CNN architecture that achieved both computational efficiency and high performance based on low-rank tensor decomposition. However, the early methods mainly focused on quantitative differences between facial features. Only a few FER studies adopted adversarial learning capable of analyzing emotional diversity. For example, a personalized affective module based on adversarial learning of auto-encoding structure was proposed [1]. Kim and Song [19] divided image groups according to emotional intensity and analyzed complex emotional characteristics by using adversarial learning. Also, Sanchez et al. [42] tried to encode a contextual representation for understanding the temporal dependency of facial emotions.

Representative FER Approaches. Meanwhile, feature learning and various form of supervision information have been employed to overcome the limitations of discrete labels. Yang et al. [54] introduced polar coordinates on Mikel's Wheel [29] to analyze emotion polarity, type, intensity, and overcame the limitations of categorical FER through label distribution learning. However, since [54] uses simple MSE and KL divergence, it is difficult to analyze the diversity of visual emotions. Xue et al. [53] proposed a transformer [50] that learns relation-aware local representations and succeeded in learning diverse local patches of facial images for categorical FER. D'Apolito et al. [7] predicted and manipulated emotional categories through learnable emotion space instead of using hand-crafted labels. However, unlike the AV space, the discrete label-based emotion space cannot inherently handle micro-emotions. On the other hand, the proposed method that utilizes CRL based on the AV space and feature transformations can train CNNs similarly to human's FER mechanism.

Contrastive Representation Learning. Self-supervised learning (SSL) utilizes self-supervision which can represent hidden properties of images defined from pretext tasks. For example, Jigsaw puzzle [34] divided an image into patches and predicted shuffled patch positions. Gidaris et al. [11] predicted the angle of an image rotated by geometric transformation. CRL [4] that maximizes the agreement of self-supervisions generated by data augmentation has recently attracted attention, and CRL has been extended to multiview coding handling an arbitrary number of views [47]. Note that recent studies [40,41] have applied contrastive learning to the FER task. However, the categorical FER methods were verified only on a very limited dataset and cannot be extended to the AV space, so they are not dealt with in this paper.

3   Method

The goal of this paper is to enable CNNs to understand facial features through CRL with similarity function and feature transformations. Based on the insight and rationale derived from the latest CRL mechanism (Sect. 3.3), we propose similarity functions to describe emotional representation (Sect. 3.4), feature transformations (Sect. 3.5), and discriminative objective function (Sect. 3.6). The list below shows the nomenclature of this paper.

R, C, H	Regressor, Compressor and Projection head
$\mathbf{z}, \mathbf{z}_a, \mathbf{z}_n$	Latent feature and transformed features via Sparse(/Soft)Max
P_{XY}	Joint probability distribution of random variables X and Y
$P_X P_Y$	Product of marginal probability distributions
N, d	Sizes of mini-batch and latent feature

3.1 Overview

Figure 2 describes the overall framework of the proposed method. First, an encoder (E) [15, 25] and a compressor (C) encode an input (facial) image and convert into a latent feature (vector), respectively. Then, the latent feature $\mathbf{z}(\in \mathbb{R}^d)$ is converted to $\mathbf{x}(\in \mathbb{R}^2)$ by a regressor (R), and then conventional supervised learning $(\mathcal{L}_{AV})$ is applied for $\mathbf{x}$ and its AV label. At the same time, $\mathbf{z}_a$ and $\mathbf{z}_n(\in \mathbb{R}^d)$ (or multiple "views") are generated by an iterative optimization-based feature transformation [10, 28]. Based on a study [4] that mapping transformed features into objective function space is useful for representation learning, $\mathbf{z}_a$ and $\mathbf{z}_n$ are projected to $\mathbf{y}_a$ and $\mathbf{y}_n(\in \mathbb{R}^2)$ in the AV space through H, respectively. Then, CRL in the AV space $(\mathcal{L}_{AVCE})$ is performed through $\mathbf{x}$, $\mathbf{y}_a$, and $\mathbf{y}_n$ according to the 'push and pull' strategy. The model parameters are updated from $\mathcal{L}_{main}$ that is the summation of $\mathcal{L}_{AVCE}$ and $\mathcal{L}_{AV}$. In addition, discriminative learning $(\mathcal{L}_{dis})$ for boosting performance is applied through triplet tuple $(\mathbf{z}, \mathbf{z}_a, \mathbf{z}_n)$.

3.2 Preliminaries of CRL

Self-supervisions for CRL are designed to represent the hidden properties of an image (cf. Sect. 2), or to represent multiple views [49]. The latter aims at learning the contrast of multiple views, i.e., the gap of semantic-level information [47]. In other words, multi-view CRL injects the fact that different views $\mathbf{z}_a$ and $\mathbf{z}_n$ are contrastive each other into neural network parameters. As a result, H allows to focus on 'mouth and eyebrows', which are core regions in recognizing facial emotions (cf. Fig. 4), and helps the learning of R important for $\mathcal{L}_{AV}$ (see neural activation maps in Fig. 6). Multi-view CRL is designed through InfoNCE [35].

$$\mathcal{L}(X, Y) = \sup_{f \in \mathcal{F}} \mathbb{E}_{(\mathbf{x},\mathbf{y}_1) \sim P_{XY}, \{\mathbf{y}_j\}_{j=2}^{N} \sim P_Y} \log \left(\frac{e^{f(\mathbf{x},\mathbf{y}_1)}}{\frac{1}{N} \sum_{j=1}^{N} e^{f(\mathbf{x},\mathbf{y}_j)}} \right) \quad (1)$$

where $\mathbf{x}$ and $\mathbf{y}$ are the outcomes of random variables X and Y, respectively. Note that positive pairs $(\mathbf{x}, \mathbf{y}_1)$ and negative pairs $(\mathbf{x}, \mathbf{y}_{j>1})$ are sampled from P_{XY} and $P_X P_Y$, respectively. f is a similarity function belonging to a set of real-valued functions $\mathcal{F}$.

In general, maximizing the divergence between P_{XY} and $P_X P_Y$ in Eq. (1) encourages the learned representations X and Y to have high contrast. However, Eq. (1) cannot guarantee the stability of learning [32], and it is insufficient as a theoretical basis for designing f in the AV space.

3.3 Proposed Method: AVCE

We propose the so-called AVCE suitable for learning the Contrast of Emotions in AV space while following CRL mechanism of Eq. (1) (cf. Appendix for derivation). AVCE for learning emotional representations in AV space is defined by

$$\mathcal{L}_{AVCE}(X,Y) = \sup_{f \in \mathcal{F}} \mathbb{E}_{P_{XY}} f(\mathbf{x},\mathbf{y}) - \alpha \mathbb{E}_{P_X P_Y} f(\mathbf{x},\mathbf{y}) - \frac{\beta}{2} \mathbb{E}_{P_{XY}} f^2(\mathbf{x},\mathbf{y})$$

$$- \frac{\gamma}{2} \mathbb{E}_{P_X P_Y} f^2(\mathbf{x},\mathbf{y}) \quad \text{s.t.} \quad f(\mathbf{x},\mathbf{y}) = \left(1 - \frac{\theta(\mathbf{x},\mathbf{y})}{\pi}\right) \tag{2}$$

where as many as the number of mini-batches, positive and negative pairs(or views), i.e., $(\mathbf{x}, \mathbf{y}_a)$ and $(\mathbf{x}, \mathbf{y}_n)$ are sampled from P_{XY} and $P_X P_Y$, respectively. α, β, and γ are relative parameters that adjust the influence between pairs. Comparing with InfoNCE (Eq. (1)), Eq. (2) without exponential or logarithmic terms guarantees learning stability, so it can converge with small variance thanks to the relative parameters acting as regularizers. Also, Eq. (2) enables mini-batch-based empirical estimation through Monte-Carlo estimation, etc. [6].

Note that f of Eq. (2) is designed as the angular similarity based on θ that can describe an emotional representation in the AV space. Here, $\theta = \cos^{-1}\left(\frac{\mathbf{x} \cdot \mathbf{y}}{\|\mathbf{x}\|\|\mathbf{y}\|}\right)$ and $\|\cdot\|$ indicates L2 norm. To show that f is a function quantifying the emotional representation of pairs, we define emotional contrast (EC) and describe its property.

Definition 1. *Emotional contrast is a qualitative indicator that indicates the difference between emotions observed from two inputs (images)* [38].

If the two facial expressions look similar to each other, that is, if EC is small, then the two predicted emotions must be located close to each other in the AV space, and vice versa. The evidence that a qualitative indicator EC can be quantified through f is derived from the following Lemma.

Lemma 1. *The optimal solution of $\mathcal{L}_{AVCE}$ is $f^*(\mathbf{x},\mathbf{y}) = \frac{r(\mathbf{x},\mathbf{y})-\alpha}{\beta r(\mathbf{x},\mathbf{y})+\gamma}$ with density ratio $r(\mathbf{x},\mathbf{y}) = \frac{p(\mathbf{x},\mathbf{y})}{p(\mathbf{x})p(\mathbf{y})}$. Here, $f^*(\mathbf{x},\mathbf{y})$ is the optimal similarity that $\mathbf{x}$ and $\mathbf{y}$ can represent, and it can be obtained from the trained neural network.*

Proof. Please refer to Section A.1 in Appendix of [49].

In Lemma 1, $p(\mathbf{x},\mathbf{y})$ and $p(\mathbf{x})p(\mathbf{y})$ indicate the probability density functions of P_{XY} and $P_X P_Y$, respectively. Specifically, as the correlation of the two vectors becomes larger, the density ratio r gets larger [48]. In other words, EC and r are inversely proportional, i.e., EC $\propto \frac{1}{r}$. Also, in Lemma 1, if β is sufficiently larger than α and γ, f depends only on a constant. That is, $f \cong \frac{1}{\beta}$. So, in order to have an explicit (linear) relationship between r and the empirical estimate f, we set β to be smaller than α and γ. Then, we can approximate f as follows:

$$f(\mathbf{x},\mathbf{y}) \cong \frac{r(\mathbf{x},\mathbf{y})-\alpha}{\gamma} \propto \frac{1}{\text{EC}} \tag{3}$$

According to Eq. (3), the positive pair $(\mathbf{x}, \mathbf{y}_a)$ outputs larger f than the negative pair $(\mathbf{x}, \mathbf{y}_n)$ (same for r). Since EC $\propto \frac{1}{r}$, EC is also inversely proportional to f as shown in Eq. (3). Therefore, EC can be quantified with respect to θ of f.

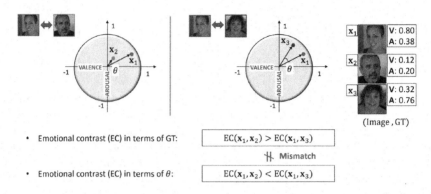

Fig. 3. A counterexample when quantifying EC using f of Eq. (2) on AffectNet dataset. Here, f only based on θ cannot properly reflect EC

Remarks. Prior arts such as [19, 40] constructed contrastive samples based only on quantitative emotion labels. However, even facial images annotated with the same emotion label can express different types of emotions. Therefore, $\mathcal{L}_{AVCE}$ reflecting the visual perception ability to the contrastive loss is effective to evaluate the unseen test DB.

3.4   Similarity Function Design

Basic Extension. On the other hand, EC cannot be quantified only depending on θ. Figure 3 illustrates a counterexample. If EC is defined in terms of GT (ideal case), EC increases as the two vectors are farther apart in AV space. That is, $EC(\mathbf{x}_1, \mathbf{x}_2)$ is greater than $EC(\mathbf{x}_1, \mathbf{x}_3)$. However, if EC is defined only in terms of θ (cf. Eq. (2)), the opposite result is obtained based on Eq. (3). The main reason for this counterexample is that the distance between the intensity components of $\mathbf{x}_1$ and $\mathbf{x}_2$ is not considered at all. Since intensity is a factor that generally quantifies the expression level of emotion [46], it is desirable to design f considering the difference in intensity as well as the directional difference between the two vectors, i.e., angular similarity. Therefore, we redefine f of Eq. (2) as follows:

$$f(\mathbf{x}, \mathbf{y}) = \left(1 - \frac{\theta(\mathbf{x}, \mathbf{y})}{\pi}\right) + \mu\left(1 - |\|\mathbf{x}\| - \|\mathbf{y}\||\right) \tag{4}$$

where μ is a balance factor and $|\cdot|$ outputs the absolute value of the input.

Different Ways to Represent Emotional Contrast. $f_1(\mathbf{x}, \mathbf{y}) = \|\mathbf{x}\|\|\mathbf{y}\| \cos\theta$ can be an alternative to Eq. (4). However, f in Eq. (4) can consider angle and intensity independently of each other, whereas the two components are entangled in f_1. Therefore, f is more advantageous than f_1 in dealing with multicultural cases [46] in which the influences of angle and intensity are expressed differently in the AV space. Meanwhile, facial emotions tend to be grouped mainly by the valence polarity [54]. So, emotion polarity can be added as follows:

$$f_2(\mathbf{x}, \mathbf{y}) = f(\mathbf{x}, \mathbf{y}) + \mathbf{1}_{pol}(\mathbf{x}, \mathbf{y}) \tag{5}$$

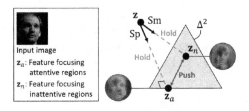

Fig. 4. Conceptual illustration for geometric interpretation of Sp and Sm. The circle-shaped pictures show the face region that each feature pays attention to. Red arrow and gray-dotted line indicate difference in semantic and content information, respectively (Color figure online)

where $\mathbf{1}_{pol}$ is a kind of penalty function that has 0 if the valence signs of the two inputs are the same, and -0.5 otherwise. As a result, Eq. (5), which independently describes angle, intensity, and polarity, can cover the universal meaning of emotions [17]. Default setting of the similarity function f is Eq. (4), and the comparison analysis of f_1 and f_2 is dealt with in Sect. 4.5.

3.5 Feature Transformations for Self-supervision

We adopt SparseMax (Sp) and SoftMax (Sm) [28] to generate attentive and inattentive regions from $\mathbf{z}$ on simplex Δ^{d-1}. Sp, which is in charge of a sparse neural attention mechanism, may be responsible for facial regions related to emotional expression. Since Sm is suitable for weighted aggregation of features [59] and is denser than Sp on Δ^{d-1} [33], it is used as a tool to obtain average attention information of the face. Unlike feature attention modules, Sp and Sm can explicitly get features that are relevant or less relevant to facial expressions. Sp and Sm are defined as follows.

$$\mathrm{Sp}(\mathbf{z}) := \underset{\mathbf{p}\in\Delta^{d-1}}{\arg\max}\langle\mathbf{z},\mathbf{p}\rangle - \frac{1}{2}\|\mathbf{p}\|^2 = \underset{\mathbf{p}\in\Delta^{d-1}}{\arg\min}\|\mathbf{p}-\mathbf{z}\|^2 \tag{6}$$

$$\mathrm{Sm}(\mathbf{z}) := \underset{\mathbf{p}\in\Delta^{d-1}}{\arg\max}\langle\mathbf{z},\mathbf{p}\rangle + \mathcal{H}(\mathbf{p}) = \frac{e^{\mathbf{z}}}{\sum_i e^{\mathbf{z}_i}} \tag{7}$$

where $\Delta^{d-1} = \{\mathbf{p}\in\mathbb{R}_+^d \mid \|\mathbf{p}\|_1 = 1\}$, $\mathcal{H}(\mathbf{p}) = -\sum_i p_i \ln p_i$, i.e., the negative Shannon entropy. Equations (6) and (7) that return $\mathbf{z}_a$ and $\mathbf{z}_n$ respectively are continuous and differentiable. Since the output of Sp corresponds to Euclidean projection onto the simplex, it is sparse. On the other hand, since $\exp(\cdot) > 0$, the output of Sm is dense. It is noteworthy that $\mathbf{z}_a$ and $\mathbf{z}_n$ are geometrically located on the edge and inside of Δ^2, respectively as in Fig. 4. Δ^2, where a vector in which emotions are strongly expressed is located outside, has a similar structural characteristics to the AV space. Even if dimension d increases ($d > 3$), the high-dimensional $\mathbf{z}_a$ and $\mathbf{z}_n$ on Δ^{d-1} can be projected while maintaining the relationship between Sp and Sm. So, Δ^{d-1} can be considered as the high-dimensional *emotional space*. Note that the projection head (H) for feature transformations plays a role of reducing the dimension from Δ^{d-1} to AV space while maintaining the emotional characteristics between $\mathbf{z}_a$ and $\mathbf{z}_n$.

Implementation. We generate $\mathbf{z}_a$ and $\mathbf{z}_n$ in each forward pass through an iterative optimization process based on the CVXPY library [10]. Specifically, ECOS (embedded conic solver) takes about 1.3 s per mini-batch on Xeon(R) E5-1650 CPU to generate $\mathbf{z}_a$ and $\mathbf{z}_n$ (cf. Appendix for forward/backward passes).

3.6   Discriminative Learning

In order to effectively realize the push and pull strategy of CRL, the emotion representation levels of two self-supervisions $\mathbf{z}_a$ and $\mathbf{z}_n$ should be differentiated from each other. At the same time, self-supervisions should preserve the content information of $\mathbf{z}$ to some extent. So, we construct the triplet tuple $Z = (\mathbf{z}, \mathbf{z}_a, \mathbf{z}_n)$, and define a discriminative objective function based on the triplet loss [43] as follows:

$$\mathcal{L}_{dis}(Z) = \sum_{(\mathbf{v},\mathbf{v}_a,\mathbf{v}_n)\in\mathcal{V}} \underbrace{\left[\delta_1 - \|\mathbf{v}_a - \mathbf{v}_n\|^2\right]_+}_{\text{Push term}} + \underbrace{(\|\bar{\mathbf{v}}_a\| - \delta_2) + (\|\bar{\mathbf{v}}_n\| - \delta_2)}_{\text{Hold terms}} \quad (8)$$

where δ_1 indicates the margin of $[\cdot]_+$, and δ_2 is a holding factor. Another projection head (H_1) projects $\mathbf{z}$ into $\mathbf{v}$ on metric space $\mathcal{V}$: $\mathbf{v} = \text{H}_1(\mathbf{z})$. $\bar{\mathbf{v}}_* = \frac{\mathbf{v}_*}{\|\mathbf{v}_*\|} - \frac{\mathbf{v}}{\|\mathbf{v}\|}$ indicates the (unit) vector difference. The first term of Eq. (8) is designed in such a way that $\mathbf{v}_a$ and $\mathbf{v}_n$ push each other within δ_1 so that $\mathcal{L}_{AVCE}$ can learn semantically discriminated views. The remaining terms properly hold the difference between $\mathbf{v}$ and $\mathbf{v}_a$ (or $\mathbf{v}_n$) so that the content information is preserved as shown in Fig. 4. Here, these terms were designed with inspiration from a previous study [51] where a powerful transformation (or augmentation) would be possible if content preserving semantic transformations were allowed.

Algorithm 1. Training Procedure of AVCE

Require: Input image IMG, learning rate ϵ_1, ϵ_2, ground-truth GT, parameters of E, C, R, H, H_1 $(\theta_e, \theta_c, \theta_r, \theta_h, \theta_{h1})$.
Ensure: Initialize $(\theta_e, \theta_c, \theta_r, \theta_h, \theta_{h1})$ to Normal distribution.
   while not converge $(\theta_e, \theta_c, \theta_r, \theta_h, \theta_{h1})$ **do**
      (Forward pass 1)
      $\mathbf{z} = (\text{C} \circ \text{E})(\text{IMG})$ ▷ Input image encoding
      $\mathbf{x} = \text{R}(\mathbf{z})$
      $\mathbf{z}_a, \mathbf{z}_n = \text{Sp}(\mathbf{z}), \text{Sm}(\mathbf{z})$ ▷ Feature transformations
      $\mathbf{y}_a, \mathbf{y}_n = \text{H}(\mathbf{z}_a), \text{H}(\mathbf{z}_n)$
      $\mathcal{L}_{main} \leftarrow \mathcal{L}_{AV}(\mathbf{x}, \text{GT}) + \mathcal{L}_{AVCE}(\mathbf{x}, \mathbf{y}_a, \mathbf{y}_n)$
      (Backward pass 1)
      $(\theta_e, \theta_c, \theta_r, \theta_h) \leftarrow (\theta_e, \theta_c, \theta_r, \theta_h) - \epsilon_1 \nabla_{(\theta_e, \theta_c, \theta_r, \theta_h)} \mathcal{L}_{main}$
      (Forward pass 2)
      $\mathcal{L}_{dis} \leftarrow \text{Triplet}(\text{H}_1(\mathbf{z}, \mathbf{z}_a, \mathbf{z}_n))$ ▷ Eq. (8)
      (Backward pass 2)
      $(\theta_e, \theta_c, \theta_{h1}) \leftarrow (\theta_e, \theta_c, \theta_{h1}) - \epsilon_2 \nabla_{(\theta_e, \theta_c, \theta_{h1})} \mathcal{L}_{dis}$
   end while

Training Procedure. The proposed method performs *two* forward/backward passes every iteration. Algorithm 1 describes the details of the objective functions calculated at each step and the neural networks to be trained. In the first pass, the encoding process of an input image and the feature transformation process are performed. Then, GT-based supervised learning ($\mathcal{L}_{AV}$) and contrastive learning ($\mathcal{L}_{AVCE}$) based on self-supervisions $\mathbf{y}_a$ and $\mathbf{y}_n$ are performed, respectively. These two loss functions are merged into $\mathcal{L}_{main}$ to update the trainable parameters $(\theta_e, \theta_c, \theta_r, \theta_h)$. In the second pass, discriminative learning ($\mathcal{L}_{dis}$) with triplet tuple Z as input is performed and parameters $(\theta_e, \theta_c, \theta_{h1})$ are updated.

4 Experiments

4.1 Datasets

We adopted open datasets only for research purposes, and informed consent was obtained if necessary. AFEW-VA [24] derived from the AFEW dataset [9] consists of about 600 short video clips annotated with AV labels frame by frame. Like [19], evaluation was performed through cross validation at a ratio of 5:1. Aff-wild [55] consists of about 300 video clips obtained from various subjects watching movies and TV shows. Since the test data of the Aff-wild was not disclosed, this paper adopted the sampled train set for evaluation purpose in the same way as previous works [14,19]. Aff-wild2 [22] is a dataset in which about 80 training videos and about 70 evaluation videos are added to Aff-wild to account for spontaneous facial expressions. AffectNet [31] consists of about 440K static images annotated with AV and discrete emotion labels, and landmarks.

4.2 Configurations

All networks were implemented in PyTorch, and the following experiments were performed on Intel Xeon CPU and RTX 3090 GPU. Each experiment was repeated five times. Encoder (E) was designed with parameter-reduced AlexNet [25] and ResNet18 [15] from scratch. Compressor (C) is composed of average pooling and FC layer. H(/H$_1$) and R are composed of FC layers and batch normalization (cf. Appendix for the network details). Adam optimizer [20] with a learning rate (LR) of 1e-4 was used to optimize E, C, and R. SGD [39] with LR 1e-2 was used to optimize H and H$_1$. AFEW-VA and AffectNet were trained for 50K iterations, and Aff-wild(/2) was trained for 100K iterations. Here, LR was reduced by 0.8 times at the initial 5K iterations, and decreased by 0.8 times every 20K iterations. The mini-batch sizes of AlexNet (AL) and ResNet18 (R18) were set to 256 and 128, respectively.

Hyperparameters. For face detection, the latest version of deep face detector [57] was used, and the detected facial regions were resized to 224×224 through random cropping (center cropping when testing). The dimensions of $\mathbf{z}$ and $\mathbf{v}$ were set to 32 and 8, respectively. In Eq. (2), α, β, and γ were set to 0.5, 0.005, and 0.5 according to Lemma 1. Angular similarity of Eq. (2) was clipped to lie in the range $(0, 1]$. In Eq. (4), the balance factor μ was set to 0.75. In Eq. (8), the margin δ_1 of the hinge function $[\cdot]_+$ and holding factor δ_2 were set to 1.0 and 0.8, respectively.

Evaluation Metrics. Root mean-squared error (RMSE) and sign agreement (SAGR) were used to measure the point-wise difference and overall emotional degree. In addition, Pearson correlation coefficient (PCC) and concordance correlation coefficient (CCC) were employed to measure the emotion tendency. For details on the above metrics, refer to the Appendix. Since the objective of emotional learning is to simultaneously achieve the minimization of RMSE and the maximization of PCC/CCC [19,23], $\mathcal{L}_{AV}$ is designed as follows: $\mathcal{L}_{AV} = \mathcal{L}_{RMSE} + \frac{(\mathcal{L}_{PCC}+\mathcal{L}_{CCC})}{2}$. Here, $\mathcal{L}_{C(/P)CC} = 1 - \frac{C(/P)CC_a+C(/P)CC_v}{2}$.

Table 1. Comparison results on the AFEW-VA dataset. *Red* and *blue* indicate the first and second-ranked values, respectively. For all comparison methods, the numerical values specified in the paper were used as they are

Case	Methods	RMSE (↓)		SAGR (↑)		PCC (↑)		CCC (↑)	
		(V)	(A)	(V)	(A)	(V)	(A)	(V)	(A)
Static	Kossaifi et al. [24]	0.27	0.23	–	–	0.41	0.45	–	–
	Mitenkova et al. [30]	0.40	0.41	–	–	0.33	0.42	0.33	0.40
	Kossaifi et al. [23]	0.24	0.24	0.64	0.77	0.55	0.57	0.55	0.52
	CAF (R18) [19]	0.17	0.18	0.68	0.87	0.67	0.60	0.59	0.54
	CAF (AL) [19]	0.20	0.20	0.66	0.83	0.67	0.63	0.58	0.57
	AVCE (R18) (Ours)	0.156	0.144	0.783	0.876	0.651	0.727	0.619	0.707
	AVCE (AL) (Ours)	0.162	0.170	0.790	0.834	0.730	0.686	0.629	0.622
Temporal	Kollias et al. [21]	–	–	–	–	0.51	0.58	0.52	0.56
	Kossaifi et al. [23]-scratch	0.28	0.19	0.53	0.75	0.12	0.23	0.11	0.15
	Kossaifi et al. [23]-trans	0.20	0.21	0.67	0.79	0.64	0.62	0.57	0.56

4.3 Quantitative Analysis

This section demonstrated the superiority of AVCE by comparing with the latest AV-based FER methods [14,19,23,42] which were verified in the wild datasets. Table 1 showed that AVCE outperforms other methods for AFEW-VA. This is because AVCE can discern even the subtle differences between positive and negative emotions. For example, AVCE (AL) showed about 0.13 higher SAGR (V) and about 0.05 higher CCC (V) than CAF (AL) [19], i.e., the runner-up method.

Next, AVCE showed a noticeable improvement in terms of PCC/CCC compared to CAF for Aff-wild. In Table 2, AVCE (AL) showed about 0.16 (16%) higher PCC (V) and about 0.14 (14%) higher CCC (V) than CAF (AL). Meanwhile, RMSE, which indicates the precision of prediction, was generally superior in R18, and PCC/CCC, which indicates the tendency of emotional change, showed superiority in AL. This tendency demonstrates that CNNs can improve precision in most over-parameterized settings, but CNNs are seldom generalized.

Table 2. Comparison results on the Aff-wild dataset. * was evaluated on Aff-wild's test set using ResNet50 backbone

Methods	RMSE (↓)		SAGR (↑)		PCC (↑)		CCC (↑)	
	(V)	(A)	(V)	(A)	(V)	(A)	(V)	(A)
Hasani et al. [13]	0.27	0.36	0.57	0.74	0.44	0.26	0.36	0.19
Hasani et al. [14]	0.26	0.31	0.77	0.75	0.42	0.40	0.37	0.31
Deng et al. [8]*	–	–	–	–	–	–	0.58	0.52
CAF (R18) [19]	0.22	0.20	0.70	0.76	0.57	0.57	0.55	0.56
CAF (AL) [19]	0.24	0.21	0.68	0.78	0.55	0.57	0.54	0.56
AVCE (R18) (Ours)	0.148	0.152	0.798	0.781	0.600	0.621	0.552	0.583
AVCE (AL) (Ours)	0.154	0.154	0.849	0.795	0.713	0.632	0.682	0.594

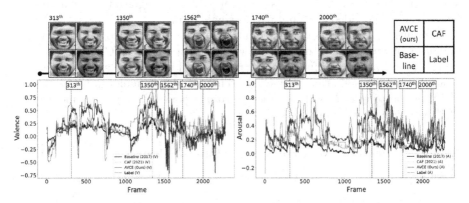

Fig. 5. Analysis of frame unit emotional fluctuations and corresponding mean neural activation maps on Aff-wild dataset. Baseline [31] and CAF [19] are reproduced for a fair experimental setup. Best viewed in color

Note that even in the Aff-wild2 dataset with various backgrounds and subjects added, AVCE (R18) showed 0.031 higher mean CCC than Sanchez et al. [42], that is the latest SOTA (see Table 3). Finally, AVCE shows superiority in both performance and network size on the AffectNet dataset. Please refer to the Appendix for the AffectNet results, additional backbone results, etc.

4.4   Qualitative Analysis

This section visualizes the performance of AVCE through neural activation map [58]. The activation map is computed from the feature maps and the weight matrices of the last layer of R(or H). Since it is important to consider both arousal and valence to capture emotional attention [18], we observed facial regions associated with emotional expression by averaging the two maps. Various examples of each of A and V are provided in the Appendix.

Fig. 6. Influence analysis of self-supervision through mean neural activation map on AffectNet. Best viewed in color

Figure 5 analyzes frame-by-frame emotional fluctuation by adopting CAF and baseline [31]. Overall, AVCE can successfully capture not only positive peaks but also negative changes. Seeing the 1562-th frame of the left (valence), the activation map of AVCE correctly captured the eye and lip regions and showed significant valence fluctuations. However, this variation showed the opposite direction to the GT. This indicates that it is sometimes difficult to grasp the global semantic context of the video clip only with a single frame.

In addition, we compared the activation maps of R and H to indirectly verify the effect of Sp, which is difficult to visualize. In Fig. 6, AVCE (H), which is trained to encourage the function of Sp, captured emotion-related regions well showing sparser results than AVCE (R). Through the examples in Fig. 6, we can find that the proposed method captures core regions (e.g. eyes and mouth) for FER better than other methods.

Table 3. Results on the validation set of Aff-wild2

Methods	CCC (V)	CCC (A)	Mean
ConvGRU [5]	0.398	0.503	0.450
Self-Attention [50]	0.419	0.505	0.462
Sanchez et al. [42]	0.438	0.498	0.468
AVCE (R18)	0.484	0.513	0.499
AVCE (AL)	0.496	0.500	0.498

Table 4. Ablation study on Aff-wild

CRL formula	f	f_1	f_2	CCC (↑) (V)	(A)
InfoNCE [35]	✓			0.637	0.546
		✓		0.651	0.550
Barlow-Twins [56]	✓			0.653	0.566
		✓		0.656	0.554
AVCE (AL) w/o $\mathcal{L}_{dis}$	✓			0.642	0.548
AVCE (AL)	✓			0.682	0.594
		✓		0.640	0.577
			✓	0.691	0.581

4.5   Ablation Study

Table 4 further analyzed the superiority of AVCE through representative CRL formulas and similarity functions of Sect. 3.4. InfoNCE (Eq. (1)) showed worse CCC (V) by 0.045 than AVCE (AL). This gap is lower than when $\mathcal{L}_{dis}$ was not used. Even a cutting-edge Barlow-Twins [56] showed 0.029 worse CCC (V) than AVCE. This proves the strength of AVCE, which reflects the structural property of the AV space well. On the other hand, f_1 based on dot product showed 0.042 lower CCC (V) than f. f_2, which gives a penalty on the valence axis, showed 0.009 high CCC (V) in AVCE, but decreased 0.013 in the arousal axis. In addition, the mining method [6] used as post-processing for negative pair sampling of AVCE shows an improvement of about 0.02 in terms of CCC (A). For details of the inference speed and the impact of AVCE, refer to the Appendix.

Voting Results of User Study. Finally, we conducted a user study to validate the emotion-aware ability of feature transformations. For this experiment, we prepared 32 pairs of examples generated by neural activation maps based on the same input image (cf. Figs. 3 and 4 in Appendix). For each example, 12 subjects were instructed to rank the images in the order of the best captures of emotional expression. As a result, AVCE, CAF, and baseline [31] showed top-1 accuracy of 67.96%, 25.78%, and 6.26%, respectively. Therefore, the superiority of the proposed method was proven through this user study once again.

5   Discussion of Limitations

Network Design. One may argue about the use of spatio-temporal network such as [42]. However, all methods showing excellent performance are based on static images (cf. Table 1). This shows that emotional expression-aware self-supervision, that is, attentive region of AVCE, is a more important clue for AV-based FER than quantitative differences in temporal features so far.

Data Imbalance. Since the datasets used in the experiments are biased towards positive emotions, training neural networks with only GT causes a bias towards positive emotions. In the future, study on weighted resampling or distribution shift that can explicitly deal with this data imbalance issue should be done.

Other Risk Factors. AV-based FER should be robust against both internal factors (e.g. skin color, face angle) and external factors (e.g. illumination and background) of a subject. This paper used datasets containing internal factors of various properties for learning, but did not directly focus on external factors. In the future, illumination and backgrounds-aware attention ability should be additionally considered in AVCE.

6   Conclusion

For the first time in the AV-based FER field, we presented a self-supervised method to learn emotion-aware facial features. Thanks to the features obtained from the novel iterative process, the proposed AVCE can understand the emotions from various perspectives. Experiments show that AVCE can detect core regions of wild facial emotions and regress continuous emotional changes without temporal learning.

Acknowledgments. This work was supported by IITP grants funded by the Korea government (MSIT) (No. 2021-0-02068, AI Innovation Hub and RS-2022-00155915, Artificial Intelligence Convergence Research Center(Inha University)), and was supported by the NRF grant funded by the Korea government (MSIT) (No. 2022R1A2C2010095 and No. 2022R1A4A1033549).

References

1. Barros, P., Parisi, G., Wermter, S.: A personalized affective memory model for improving emotion recognition. In: International Conference on Machine Learning, pp. 485–494 (2019)
2. Bera, A., Randhavane, T., Manocha, D.: Modelling multi-channel emotions using facial expression and trajectory cues for improving socially-aware robot navigation. In: Proceedings of the IEEE/CVF Conference on Computer Vision and Pattern Recognition Workshops (2019)
3. Cerf, M., Frady, E.P., Koch, C.: Faces and text attract gaze independent of the task: experimental data and computer model. J. Vis. 9(12), 10 (2009)
4. Chen, T., Kornblith, S., Norouzi, M., Hinton, G.: A simple framework for contrastive learning of visual representations. In: International Conference on Machine Learning, pp. 1597–1607 (2020)
5. Cho, K., et al.: Learning phrase representations using RNN encoder-decoder for statistical machine translation. In: Proceedings of the 2014 Conference on Empirical Methods in Natural Language Processing, 2014, Doha, Qatar, pp. 1724–1734. ACL (2014)
6. Chuang, C.Y., Robinson, J., Lin, Y.C., Torralba, A., Jegelka, S.: Debiased contrastive learning. In: Advances in Neural Information Processing Systems, vol. 33, pp. 8765–8775. Curran Associates, Inc. (2020)
7. d'Apolito, S., Paudel, D.P., Huang, Z., Romero, A., Van Gool, L.: Ganmut: learning interpretable conditional space for gamut of emotions. In: Proceedings of the IEEE/CVF Conference on Computer Vision and Pattern Recognition, pp. 568–577 (2021)
8. Deng, D., Chen, Z., Zhou, Y., Shi, B.: Mimamo net: integrating micro-and macro-motion for video emotion recognition. In: Proceedings of the AAAI Conference on Artificial Intelligence, vol. 34, pp. 2621–2628 (2020)
9. Dhall, A., Kaur, A., Goecke, R., Gedeon, T.: Emotiw 2018: audio-video, student engagement and group-level affect prediction. In: Proceedings of the 20th ACM International Conference on Multimodal Interaction, pp. 653–656 (2018)
10. Diamond, S., Boyd, S.: Cvxpy: A python-embedded modeling language for convex optimization. J. Mach. Learn. Res. 17(1), 2909–2913 (2016)
11. Gidaris, S., Singh, P., Komodakis, N.: Unsupervised representation learning by predicting image rotations. In: International Conference on Learning Representations (2018)
12. Grill, J.B., et al.: Bootstrap your own latent: a new approach to self-supervised learning. arXiv preprint. arXiv:2006.07733 (2020)
13. Hasani, B., Mahoor, M.H.: Facial affect estimation in the wild using deep residual and convolutional networks. In: Proceedings of the IEEE Conference on Computer Vision and Pattern Recognition Workshops, pp. 9–16 (2017)
14. Hasani, B., Negi, P.S., Mahoor, M.: Breg-next: facial affect computing using adaptive residual networks with bounded gradient. IEEE Trans. Affect. Comput. 13(2), 1023–1036 (2020)
15. He, K., Zhang, X., Ren, S., Sun, J.: Deep residual learning for image recognition. In: Proceedings of the IEEE Conference on Computer Vision and Pattern Recognition, pp. 770–778 (2016)
16. Itti, L., Koch, C.: Computational modelling of visual attention. Nat. Rev. Neurosci. 2(3), 194–203 (2001)

17. Jackson, J.C., et al.: Emotion semantics show both cultural variation and universal structure. Science **366**(6472), 1517–1522 (2019)
18. Jefferies, L.N., Smilek, D., Eich, E., Enns, J.T.: Emotional valence and arousal interact in attentional control. Psychol. Sci. **19**(3), 290–295 (2008)
19. Kim, D.H., Song, B.C.: Contrastive adversarial learning for person independent facial emotion recognition. In: Proceedings of the AAAI Conference on Artificial Intelligence, pp. 5948–5956 (2021)
20. Kingma, D.P., Ba, J.: Adam: a method for stochastic optimization. In: Bengio, Y., LeCun, Y. (eds.) 3rd International Conference on Learning Representations, ICLR 2015, San Diego, CA, USA, 7–9 May 2015, Conference Track Proceedings (2015). arxiv.org/abs/1412.6980
21. Kollias, D., et al.: Deep affect prediction in-the-wild: Aff-wild database and challenge, deep architectures, and beyond. Int. J. Comput. Vis. **127**(6), 907–929 (2019). https://doi.org/10.1007/s11263-019-01158-4
22. Kollias, D., Zafeiriou, S.: Expression, affect, action unit recognition: Aff-wild2, multi-task learning and arcface. In: 30th British Machine Vision Conference 2019, BMVC 2019, Cardiff, UK, 9–12 September 2019, p. 297 (2019). https://www.bmvc2019.org/wp-content/uploads/papers/0399-paper.pdf
23. Kossaifi, J., Toisoul, A., Bulat, A., Panagakis, Y., Hospedales, T.M., Pantic, M.: Factorized higher-order cnns with an application to spatio-temporal emotion estimation. In: Proceedings of the IEEE/CVF Conference on Computer Vision and Pattern Recognition. pp. 6060–6069 (2020)
24. Kossaifi, J., Tzimiropoulos, G., Todorovic, S., Pantic, M.: Afew-va database for valence and arousal estimation in-the-wild. Image Vis. Comput. **65**, 23–36 (2017)
25. Krizhevsky, A., Sutskever, I., Hinton, G.E.: Imagenet classification with deep convolutional neural networks. In: Advances in Neural Information Processing Systems, pp. 1097–1105 (2012)
26. Liu, X., Zhang, F., Hou, Z., Mian, L., Wang, Z., Zhang, J., Tang, J.: Self-supervised learning: Generative or contrastive. IEEE Trans. Knowl. Data Eng. (2021)
27. Marinoiu, E., Zanfir, M., Olaru, V., Sminchisescu, C.: 3d human sensing, action and emotion recognition in robot assisted therapy of children with autism. In: Proceedings of the IEEE Conference on Computer Vision and Pattern Recognition, pp. 2158–2167 (2018)
28. Martins, A., Astudillo, R.: From softmax to sparsemax: a sparse model of attention and multi-label classification. In: International Conference on Machine Learning, pp. 1614–1623 (2016)
29. Mikels, J.A., Fredrickson, B.L., Larkin, G.R., Lindberg, C.M., Maglio, S.J., Reuter-Lorenz, P.A.: Emotional category data on images from the international affective picture system. Behav. Res. Methods **37**(4), 626–630 (2005). https://doi.org/10.3758/BF03192732
30. Mitenkova, A., Kossaifi, J., Panagakis, Y., Pantic, M.: Valence and arousal estimation in-the-wild with tensor methods. In: 2019 14th IEEE International Conference on Automatic Face & Gesture Recognition (FG 2019), pp. 1–7 (2019)
31. Mollahosseini, A., Hasani, B., Mahoor, M.H.: Affectnet: a database for facial expression, valence, and arousal computing in the wild. IEEE Trans. Affect. Comput. **10**(1), 18–31 (2017)
32. Mroueh, Y., Melnyk, I., Dognin, P., Ross, J., Sercu, T.: Improved mutual information estimation. In: Proceedings of the AAAI Conference on Artificial Intelligence, pp. 9009–9017 (2021)

33. Niculae, V., Martins, A., Blondel, M., Cardie, C.: Sparsemap: differentiable sparse structured inference. In: International Conference on Machine Learning, pp. 3799–3808 (2018)
34. Noroozi, M., Favaro, P.: Unsupervised learning of visual representations by solving jigsaw puzzles. In: Leibe, B., Matas, J., Sebe, N., Welling, M. (eds.) ECCV 2016. LNCS, vol. 9910, pp. 69–84. Springer, Cham (2016). https://doi.org/10.1007/978-3-319-46466-4_5
35. Oord, A.v.d., Li, Y., Vinyals, O.: Representation learning with contrastive predictive coding. arXiv preprint. arXiv:1807.03748 (2018)
36. Panda, R., Zhang, J., Li, H., Lee, J.Y., Lu, X., Roy-Chowdhury, A.K.: Contemplating visual emotions: Understanding and overcoming dataset bias. In: Proceedings of the European Conference on Computer Vision (ECCV), pp. 579–595 (2018)
37. Posner, J., Russell, J.A., Peterson, B.S.: The circumplex model of affect: an integrative approach to affective neuroscience, cognitive development, and psychopathology. Dev. Psychopathol. **17**(3), 715–734 (2005)
38. Rafaeli, A., Sutton, R.I.: Emotional contrast strategies as means of social influence: Lessons from criminal interrogators and bill collectors. Acad. Manag. J. **34**(4), 749–775 (1991)
39. Robbins, H., Monro, S.: A stochastic approximation method. Ann. Math. Stat. **22**(3), 400–407 (1951)
40. Roy, S., Etemad, A.: Self-supervised contrastive learning of multi-view facial expressions. arXiv preprint. arXiv:2108.06723 (2021)
41. Roy, S., Etemad, A.: Spatiotemporal contrastive learning of facial expressions in videos. arXiv preprint. arXiv:2108.03064 (2021)
42. Sanchez, E., Tellamekala, M.K., Valstar, M., Tzimiropoulos, G.: Affective processes: stochastic modelling of temporal context for emotion and facial expression recognition. In: Proceedings of the IEEE/CVF Conference on Computer Vision and Pattern Recognition, pp. 9074–9084 (2021)
43. Schroff, F., Kalenichenko, D., Philbin, J.: Facenet: a unified embedding for face recognition and clustering. In: Proceedings of the IEEE Conference on Computer Vision and Pattern Recognition, pp. 815–823 (2015)
44. Song, B.C., Kim, D.H.: Hidden emotion detection using multi-modal signals. In: Extended Abstracts of the 2021 CHI Conference on Human Factors in Computing Systems, pp. 1–7 (2021)
45. Srivastava, P., Srinivasan, N.: Time course of visual attention with emotional faces. Attention Percept. Psychophysics **72**(2), 369–377 (2010). https://doi.org/10.3758/APP.72.2.369
46. Taverner, J., Vivancos, E., Botti, V.: A multidimensional culturally adapted representation of emotions for affective computational simulation and recognition. IEEE Trans. Affect. Comput. (2020)
47. Tian, Y., Krishnan, D., Isola, P.: Contrastive multiview coding. In: Vedaldi, A., Bischof, H., Brox, T., Frahm, J.-M. (eds.) ECCV 2020. LNCS, vol. 12356, pp. 776–794. Springer, Cham (2020). https://doi.org/10.1007/978-3-030-58621-8_45
48. Tsai, Y.H., Zhao, H., Yamada, M., Morency, L.P., Salakhutdinov, R.: Neural methods for point-wise dependency estimation. In: Proceedings of the Neural Information Processing Systems Conference (Neurips) (2020)
49. Tsai, Y.H.H., Ma, M.Q., Yang, M., Zhao, H., Morency, L.P., Salakhutdinov, R.: Self-supervised representation learning with relative predictive coding. In: International Conference on Learning Representations (2021)
50. Vaswani, A., et al.: Attention is all you need. In: Advances in Neural Information Processing Systems, vol. 30, pp. 5998–6008. Curran Associates, Inc. (2017)

51. Wang, Y., Pan, X., Song, S., Zhang, H., Huang, G., Wu, C.: Implicit semantic data augmentation for deep networks. Adv. Neural. Inf. Process. Syst. **32**, 12635–12644 (2019)

52. Wei, Z., Zhang, J., Lin, Z., Lee, J.Y., Balasubramanian, N., Hoai, M., Samaras, D.: Learning visual emotion representations from web data. In: Proceedings of the IEEE/CVF Conference on Computer Vision and Pattern Recognition, pp. 13106–13115 (2020)

53. Xue, F., Wang, Q., Guo, G.: Transfer: learning relation-aware facial expression representations with transformers. In: Proceedings of the IEEE/CVF International Conference on Computer Vision, pp. 3601–3610 (2021)

54. , Yang, J., Li, J., Li, L., Wang, X., Gao, X.: A circular-structured representation for visual emotion distribution learning. In: Proceedings of the IEEE/CVF Conference on Computer Vision and Pattern Recognition, pp. 4237–4246 (2021)

55. Zafeiriou, S., Kollias, D., Nicolaou, M.A., Papaioannou, A., Zhao, G., Kotsia, I.: Aff-wild: valence and arousal'in-the-wild'challenge. In: Proceedings of the IEEE Conference on Computer Vision and Pattern Recognition Workshops, pp. 34–41 (2017)

56. Zbontar, J., Jing, L., Misra, I., LeCun, Y., Deny, S.: Barlow twins: self-supervised learning via redundancy reduction. In: Proceedings of the 38th International Conference on Machine Learning, Virtual Event, vol. 139, pp. 12310–12320. PMLR (2021)

57. Zhang, K., Zhang, Z., Li, Z., Qiao, Y.: Joint face detection and alignment using multitask cascaded convolutional networks. IEEE Signal Process. Lett. **23**(10), 1499–1503 (2016)

58. Zhou, B., Khosla, A., Lapedriza, A., Oliva, A., Torralba, A.: Learning deep features for discriminative localization. In: Proceedings of the IEEE Conference on Computer Vision and Pattern Recognition, pp. 2921–2929 (2016)

59. Zhu, X., Xu, C., Tao, D.: Where and what? examining interpretable disentangled representations. In: Proceedings of the IEEE/CVF Conference on Computer Vision and Pattern Recognition, pp. 5861–5870 (2021)

Order Learning Using Partially Ordered Data via Chainization

Seon-Ho Lee🆔 and Chang-Su Kim$^{(\boxtimes)}$🆔

School of Electrical Engineering, Korea University, Korea, South Korea
seonholee@mcl.korea.ac.kr, changsukim@korea.ac.kr

Abstract. We propose the chainization algorithm for effective order learning when only partially ordered data are available. First, we develop a binary comparator to predict missing ordering relations between instances. Then, by extending the Kahn's algorithm, we form a chain representing a linear ordering of instances. We fine-tune the comparator over pseudo pairs, which are sampled from the chain, and then re-estimate the linear ordering alternately. As a result, we obtain a more reliable comparator and a more meaningful linear ordering. Experimental results show that the proposed algorithm yields excellent rank estimation performances under various weak supervision scenarios, including semi-supervised learning, domain adaptation, and bipartite cases. The source codes are available at https://github.com/seon92/Chainization.

Keywords: Order learning · Topological sorting · Rank estimation · Facial age estimation · Aesthetic assessment · Facial expression recognition

1 Introduction

In ordered data, objects are sorted according to their classes representing ranks or priorities. For instance, in facial age estimation, face photos are sorted according to the ages. Also, in a video streaming platform, videos can be sorted according to user preferences. For these ordered data, various attempts [5,9,11,12,17,24] have been made to estimate the ranks of objects. In particular, order learning algorithms [9,12,24] have shown promising rank estimation performances on diverse ordered data recently.

Order learning is based on the idea that relative assessment is easier than absolute assessment; telling the older one between two people is easier than estimating their exact ages. Hence, in order learning [9,12], a pairwise comparator to predict pairwise ordering relations is trained. Then, the rank of a test object is estimated by comparing it with the references with known ranks. To obtain a reliable comparator, they exploit the ordering relation for every pair of training objects. This complete ordering information, however, is not always available because it is hard to annotate the exact rank of every object [29].

Supplementary Information The online version contains supplementary material available at https://doi.org/10.1007/978-3-031-19778-9_12.

S. Avidan et al. (Eds.): ECCV 2022, LNCS 13673, pp. 196–211, 2022.
https://doi.org/10.1007/978-3-031-19778-9_12

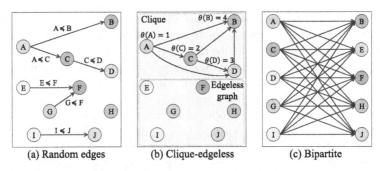

(a) Random edges   (b) Clique-edgeless   (c) Bipartite

Fig. 1. Three cases of partial orderings. In each graph, nodes and edges represent objects and known ordering relations, respectively. A directed edge from node x to node y means that $x \preccurlyeq y$. In (b), $\theta(x)$ denotes the rank of x.

A partial ordering means that ordering relations are known only for restricted pairs of objects. As illustrated in Fig. 1, we can consider three cases of partial orderings according to the types of underlying graphs.

- **Random edge case:** Ordering relations are given for randomly selected pairs of objects. For example, an extreme scenario that the relations are known for only 0.01% of all possible pairs is also considered in this paper. This case is represented by a simple directed graph as in Fig. 1(a).
- **Clique-edgeless case:** The ground-truth ranks are available for a subset of training objects. Thus, the ordering relation is known for every pair of objects in the subset, while no information is available for the other pairs. This case is represented by a sum of a clique and an edgeless graph as in Fig. 1(b). Note that typical semi-supervised learning [25,28] and unsupervised domain adaptation [13,30] scenarios belong to this case.
- **Bipartite case:** Objects are partitioned into two groups such that every object in one group has a higher rank than every object in the other group. Within each group, no ordering information is available. For example, face photos are simply dichotomized into either young ones or old ones. This case is represented by a complete bipartite graph in Fig. 1(c).

In these partial ordering cases, order learning yields poor results due to insufficient ordering information for training. To address the lack of supervision, many researches [13,25,28,30] have been conducted. Nevertheless, to the best of our knowledge, no algorithm has been proposed for these partially ordered data. Topological sorting algorithms [7,8,19,20] may be exploited to complement the incomplete ordering information. From a known partial ordering, these algorithms estimate a linear ordering, representing the ordering relation for every pair of objects. However, they do not consider the quality of the resultant linear ordering; for example, if it is known that $w \prec y$ and $x \prec z$, they may yield an arbitrary one of $w \prec x \prec y \prec z$ or $x \prec z \prec w \prec y$ or many other possibilities. Thus, the obtained linear ordering may be unreliable or even meaningless.

In this paper, under the three scenarios in Fig. 1, we aim to obtain a meaningful linear ordering from a given partial ordering and to enhance order learning performances. To this end, we propose a unified approach called *chainization*. First, to obtain a meaningful linear ordering, ordering criteria, such as age in face photos, should be recognized from known ordering relations, and unknown ordering relations should be estimated reliably. Hence, we train a pairwise comparator with given ordering relations. Then, using the comparator, we estimate unknown ordering relations and sort all instances to form a linear ordering. Second, we sample pseudo pairs from the obtained linear ordering and fine-tune the comparator using the pseudo pairs iteratively. The proposed algorithm yields a more accurate comparator than conventional order learning techniques [9, 12], since the pseudo pairs make up for insufficient training data. Last, we estimate the rank of an unseen test object by comparing it with references. Experimental results demonstrate that the proposed algorithm provides meaningful ordering results as well as excellent ranking performances under weakly supervised scenarios, including semi-supervised learning, unsupervised domain adaptation, and bipartite cases.

This work has the following major contributions:

- We improve order learning performances on various types of partially ordered data via the proposed chainization.
- The proposed chainization outperforms conventional techniques in both semi-supervised learning and unsupervised domain adaptation tests.
- We achieve competitive rank estimation performances even with a restricted set of training data. Notably, on the Adience dataset [10], we achieve state-of-the-art age estimation results using less than 0.1% of the training pairs.

2   Related Work

2.1   Order Learning

Lim *et al.* [12] first proposed the notion of order learning, which learns ordering relations between objects and determines the rank of an unseen object. It trains a pairwise comparator to categorize the relation between two objects into one of three cases: one object is bigger than, similar to, or smaller than the other. Then, it predicts the rank of a test object by comparing it with references with known ranks. It yields promising results since relative assessment is easier than absolute assessment in general. Based on similar motivations, some learning-to-rank methods [18, 26] also model a ranking function to estimate the priorities of objects via pairwise comparisons. Also, Shin *et al.* [24] modified the classification approach in [12] to develop a regression-based order learning algorithm.

However, not every pair of objects are easily comparable. Hence, Lee and Kim [9] proposed the order-identity decomposition network to decompose object information into an order-related feature and an identity feature. They showed that objects with similar identity features can be compared more reliably. These order learning techniques [9, 12, 24] assume that the rank of every training object is known. In contrast, we assume that only pairwise ordering relations between limited pairs of objects are known. Then, we attempt to discover the ordering relations across all objects from the given incomplete data. As a result, the proposed algorithm can reduce the amount of annotated pairs required for order learning significantly (*e.g.* by a factor of $\frac{1}{100}$).

2.2 Linear Extension of Partial Order

In order theory [6, 23], linear extension of a partial order means finding a linear order compatible with the partial order. In other words, an ordering relation between any elements should be determined without conflicting with the partial order. By generating a directed graph for the partial order, this problem can be converted to the topological sorting of the vertices in the graph [3]: linear extension and topological sorting are the same problem.

Various algorithms [7, 8, 19, 20, 27] have been proposed for linear extension. In [7], Kahn proposed a simple algorithm based on the breadth-first search (BFS). It first constructs a directed graph, in which vertices correspond to objects and directed edges represent ordering relations. It then repeatedly outputs a vertex with no incoming edge and deletes its outgoing edges from the graph. However, the Kahn's algorithm decides unknown ordering relations arbitrarily. Thus, one may want to obtain all possible linear orders and then evaluate each of them to find the best one. By exploiting the backtracking, Knuth [8] developed an algorithm to generate all possible linear extension results.

Depth-first search (DFS) algorithms also have been proposed. Tarjan [27] and Reingold *et al.* [20] use DFS to obtain a spanning forest of the directed graph, and then output the vertices before any of their descendants in the forest. In [19], DFS is performed both forward and backward to reduce the time complexity. These DFS methods [19, 20, 27] also determine unknown ordering relations randomly. In contrast, the proposed algorithm yields a meaningful linear ordering by estimating the missing ordering relations.

3 Proposed Algorithm

3.1 Preliminary

Mathematically, an *order* or *partial order* [23] is a binary relation, denoted by $\leq$, on a set $\Theta = \{\theta_1, \theta_2, \ldots, \theta_c\}$ that satisfies the three properties of

- Reflexivity: $\theta_i \leq \theta_i$ for all i;
- Antisymmetry: $\theta_i \leq \theta_j$ and $\theta_j \leq \theta_i$ imply $\theta_i = \theta_j$;
- Transitivity: $\theta_i \leq \theta_j$ and $\theta_j \leq \theta_k$ imply $\theta_i \leq \theta_k$.

Then, Θ is called a *partially ordered set*. Furthermore, if every pair of elements is comparable ($\theta_i \leq \theta_j$ or $\theta_j \leq \theta_i$ for all i, j), Θ is called a *chain* or *linearly ordered set*. In such a case, the partial order is called a *linear order*.

In practice, an order describes the ranks or priorities of classes in the set $\Theta = \{\theta_1, \ldots, \theta_c\}$, where each class represents one or more object instances. For example, in age estimation, θ_i may represent i-year-olds, and $\theta_{20} < \theta_{42}$ represents that 20-year-olds are younger than 42-year-olds. Let $\theta(\cdot)$ be the class function, and let x and y be instances. For example, $\theta(x) = \theta_{20}$ means that person x is 20-year-old. To represent the *ordering* between instances, we use '$\prec, \approx, \succ, \preccurlyeq, \succcurlyeq$' instead of '$<, =, >, \leq, \geq$' to avoid confusion. Specifically, $x \prec y$, $x \approx y$, and $x \preccurlyeq y$ mean that $\theta(x) < \theta(y)$, $\theta(x) = \theta(y)$, and $\theta(x) \leq \theta(y)$, respectively. Also, we use the expression *ordering* to describe instance relations, while using *order* exclusively for class relations.

3.2   Problem Definition

Suppose that there are n training instances in $\mathcal{X} = \{x_1, x_2, \ldots, x_n\}$. Let $\mathcal{L} = \{(x, y) : x \preccurlyeq y \text{ and } x, y \in \mathcal{X}\}$ be the set of increasingly ordered pairs of instances whose ordering relations are known. In order learning [9,12,24], it is assumed that $\mathcal{L}$ is a *linear ordering* of instances:

$$(x, y) \in \mathcal{L} \text{ or } (y, x) \in \mathcal{L} \text{ for all } x, y \in \mathcal{X}. \tag{1}$$

Note that both (x, y) and (y, x) belong to $\mathcal{L}$ if $x \approx y$, and thus $|\mathcal{L}| \geq \binom{n}{2}$. In other words, order learning assumes that the ground-truth class of every training instance is known, as well as the linear order on the set of classes. However, such information may be unavailable. In age estimation, annotating the exact age of a person is difficult, but telling the older one between two people is relatively easy [29]. Therefore, only the binary ordering information (*i.e.* who is older) between some selected pairs of people may be available. In such a case, we are given a *partial ordering* of instances,

$$\mathcal{P} = \{(x, y) : \text{It is known that } x \preccurlyeq y\} \subset \mathcal{L}. \tag{2}$$

We consider the case that the number of ordered pairs in $\mathcal{P}$ is considerably smaller than that in $\mathcal{L}$, $|\mathcal{P}| \ll |\mathcal{L}|$. Then, we formulate the problem as follows.

Problem. *Given a partial ordering $\mathcal{P}$ of instances, the objective is to obtain its superset $\mathcal{L}$ that is a linear ordering.*

In other words, we aim to linearly extend or 'chainize' $\mathcal{P}$ to $\mathcal{L}$. To this end, we propose the chainization algorithm. Note that if $\mathcal{L}$ is estimated reliably, order learning performance can be enhanced by using $\mathcal{L}$ as auxiliary information for training. The chainization algorithm also produces a pairwise comparator, using which we can estimate the rank of an unseen test instance. First, in Sect. 3.3, we present the chainization algorithm on the random edge case in Fig. 1(a). Then, we describe how to apply the chainization to the other cases in Sect. 3.4. Last, we explain the rank estimation scheme in Sect. 3.5.

3.3   Chainization – Basics

The chainization algorithm extends a partial ordering $\mathcal{P}$ on an instance set $\mathcal{X}$ to a linear ordering $\mathcal{L}$. First, we train a pairwise comparator using available information. Second, we use the comparator to estimate the ordering between every pair of instances in $\mathcal{X}$, yielding a linear ordering $\mathcal{L}$. These two steps are iterated to refine both the comparator and the linear ordering.

Graph Representation of Partial Ordering: We use a directed acyclic graph $G = (\mathcal{V}, \mathcal{E})$ to represent a partial ordering $\mathcal{P}$ of instances in $\mathcal{X}$. Initially, we construct the vertex set $\mathcal{V} = \{v_1, v_2, \ldots, v_n\}$ so that each vertex v_i corresponds to an instance $x_i \in \mathcal{X}$. We also construct the edge set $\mathcal{E} = \{(v_i, v_j) : (x_i, x_j) \in \mathcal{P}\}$ so that there is a directed edge from v_i to v_j if $x_i \preccurlyeq x_j$. In the initial graph,

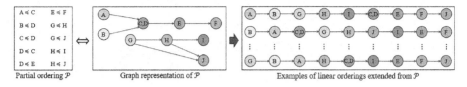

Fig. 2. Graph representation of a partial ordering $\mathcal{P}$ and its possible linear extension results.

cycles may occur because both (x_i, x_j) and (x_j, x_i) may belong to $\mathcal{P}$ if $x_i \approx x_j$. In such a case, we merge all vertices on each cycle into a single vertex and modify incident edges accordingly. Consequently, each vertex represents a set of one or more instances, which equal ($\approx$) one another.

Figure 2 shows an example of the graph representation: the partial ordering $\mathcal{P}$ is defined on a set $\mathcal{X}$ of 10 instances, but there are 9 vertices only because 'C' and 'D' are merged into one vertex.

After constructing the graph G, the linear extension of $\mathcal{P}$ to $\mathcal{L}$ can be regarded as finding a vertex sorting function

$$\sigma : \mathcal{V} \rightarrow \{1, 2, \ldots, |\mathcal{V}|\} \tag{3}$$

satisfying the constraint

$$\sigma(v_i) < \sigma(v_j) \text{ for all } (v_i, v_j) \in \mathcal{E}. \tag{4}$$

Note that $\sigma(\cdot)$ is a sorting index. For example, $\sigma(v_i) = 1$ means that v_i is the first in the sorted list of all vertices. If σ is obtained, a linear ordering $\mathcal{L}$ can be easily derived from the σ;

$$\mathcal{L} = \{(x_i, x_j) : \sigma(v_i) \leq \sigma(v_j) \text{ and } x_i, x_j \in \mathcal{X}\} \tag{5}$$

where v_i and v_j are the vertices containing x_i and x_j, respectively. It is guaranteed that $\mathcal{L} \supset \mathcal{P}$ due to the constraint in (4), but a linearly extended ordering $\mathcal{L}$ is not unique in general. As in Fig. 2, there are many possible linear orderings extended from the same partial ordering $\mathcal{P}$. Among them, we aim to determine a desirable linear ordering, which sorts all instances in $\mathcal{X}$ in a meaningful way.

Comparator: To obtain such an ordering, we develop a pairwise comparator in Fig. 3, which classifies the ordering between instances x and y into two cases: $x \preccurlyeq y$ or $x \succcurlyeq y$. The Siamese feature extractor [2] maps x and y to feature vectors, respectively, and then the classifier yields a softmax probability $p^{xy} = (p^{xy}_{\preccurlyeq}, p^{xy}_{\succcurlyeq})$. We first train the comparator using the known ordered pairs in $\mathcal{P}$. Specifically, we optimize it to minimize the loss

$$\ell = [x \not\approx y]\ell_{\mathrm{ce}}(p^{xy}, q^{xy}) + [x \approx y]D(p^{xy} \| q^{xy}) \tag{6}$$

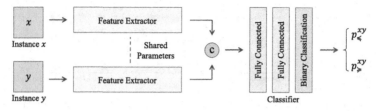

Fig. 3. An overview of the pairwise comparator, where ⓒ denotes concatenation.

Algorithm 1. Chainization

Input: Directed acyclic graph $G = (\mathcal{V}, \mathcal{E})$ for $\mathcal{P}$

 1: Train a comparator on $\mathcal{P}$ for warm-up epochs;
 2: **repeat**
 3:     $\mathcal{Q} \leftarrow \varnothing; \quad t \leftarrow 1;$
 4:     Add all vertices $v \in \mathcal{V}$ with $\delta(v) = 0$ to $\mathcal{Q}$;
 5:     **while** $\mathcal{Q} \neq \varnothing$ **do**
 6:         Remove the optimal v^* in (8) from $\mathcal{Q}$;
 7:         $\sigma(v^*) \leftarrow t; \quad t \leftarrow t + 1;$
 8:         **for all** adjacent vertex w of v^* in G **do**
 9:             Remove edge (v^*, w) from $\mathcal{E}$;
10:             **if** $\delta(w) = 0$ **then**
11:                 Add w to $\mathcal{Q}$;
12:             **end if**
13:         **end for**
14:     **end while**
15:     Obtain a chain from the sorting function σ;
16:     Shorten it to yield the linear ordering $\mathcal{L}$ in (9);
17:     Build a set $\mathcal{T}$ of pseudo pairs;
18:     Fine-tune the comparator on $\mathcal{P} \cup \mathcal{T}$;
19: **until** predefined number of epochs;

Output: Linear ordering $\mathcal{L}$, comparator

---

where $[\cdot]$ is the indicator function. If $x \prec y$ or $x \succ y$, we use the cross-entropy loss ℓ_{ce} with the ground-truth one-hot vector $q^{xy} = (q^{xy}_{\prec}, q^{xy}_{\succ})$. However, if $x \approx y$, we set $q^{xy}_{\prec} = q^{xy}_{\succ} = 0.5$ and use the KL-divergence D, instead of the cross-entropy. This is because the cross-entropy loss with $q^{xy} = (0.5, 0.5)$ produces near zero gradients for most p^{xy}, delaying the training unnecessarily.

Chainization: To determine the sorting function σ in (3), equivalently to find the linear ordering $\mathcal{L}$ in (5), we propose the chainization algorithm in Algorithm 1, which is based on the Kahn's topological sorting algorithm [7]. However, whereas the Kahn's algorithm obtains an arbitrary linear extension of $\mathcal{P}$, the proposed algorithm yields a meaningful linear ordering by estimating missing ordering information, not included in $\mathcal{P}$, using the pairwise comparator.

As in [7], we iteratively select a vertex v from the graph G and append it to the sorted list. In other words, at iteration t, we select v and set $\sigma(v) = t$. First,

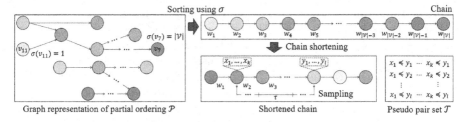

Fig. 4. An overview of the chainization.

we form a set $\mathcal{Q}$ to include all vertices v with indegree $\delta(v) = 0$. Note that at least one such vertex with no incoming edge exists, because the graph G for $\mathcal{P}$ is acyclic by construction. Also, such vertices precede the others in G. Second, we select an optimal vertex v^* from $\mathcal{Q}$, which is most likely to contain the smallest instances (*e.g.* the youngest people in age estimation). To this end, we define the probability that a vertex v precedes another vertex w as

$$p(v, w) = \tfrac{1}{kl} \sum_{i=1}^{k} \sum_{j=1}^{l} p_{\prec}^{x_i y_j} \qquad (7)$$

where $v = \{x_1, \ldots, x_k\}$ and $w = \{y_1, \ldots, y_l\}$. We also define the priority score π of each vertex $v \in \mathcal{Q}$ as $\pi(v) = \sum_{w \in \mathcal{Q}: w \neq v} p(v, w)$. We then choose the highest priority vertex

$$v^* = \arg\max_{v \in \mathcal{Q}} \pi(v) \qquad (8)$$

and set $\sigma(v^*) = t$. Then, we remove all outgoing edges of v^* from $\mathcal{E}$. We repeat this process until $\mathcal{Q} = \varnothing$ and thus $\sigma(v)$ is determined for all $v \in \mathcal{V}$.

Pseudo Pair Sampling: The sorting function σ lists all vertices in $\mathcal{V}$ increasingly, which can be represented by a chain as illustrated in Fig. 4. Let $(w_1, w_2, \ldots, w_{|\mathcal{V}|})$ denote this chain, where $w_i = v_j$ if $\sigma(v_j) = i$. The chain may represent linearly ordered classes. However, in general, $|\mathcal{V}|$ is much larger than the number of actual classes, since the graph representation is performed without full annotations of instance equalities ($\approx$).

We hence merge vertices in the chain, which likely come from the same underlying class. Specifically, we merge the adjacent vertices w_i and w_{i+1} with the lowest probability $p(w_i, w_{i+1})$ in (7) into one vertex. This is because a low $p(w_i, w_{i+1})$ implies that the instances in w_i are not clearly smaller ($\prec$) than those in w_{i+1}, and all those instances may belong to the same class. However, for any $x \in w_i$ and $y \in w_{i+1}$, if $x \prec y$ is known in the partial ordering $\mathcal{P}$, the merging is not allowed and the pair with the second lowest probability is merged. This is performed iteratively, until the number of vertices reaches a predefined threshold or no vertices can be merged, to yield a shortened chain.

The linear ordering $\mathcal{L}$ can be derived from the shortened chain by

$$\mathcal{L} = \{(x, y) : x \in w_i, y \in w_j \text{ and } i \leq j\}. \qquad (9)$$

Notice that $\mathcal{L}$ is obtained using the output of the comparator in (7), which is trained on the partial ordering $\mathcal{P}$. The additional information in $\mathcal{L}$, in turn, can be used to fine-tune the comparator. To this end, as shown in Fig. 4, we form a set $\mathcal{T}$ of pseudo training pairs. First, we sample an ordered pair (x, y), where $x \in w_i$, $y \in w_j$, and $j - i > \tau$, and add it to $\mathcal{T}$. It is called a *pseudo* pair, since the ordering $x \prec y$ is an estimated result using the comparator, instead of a ground-truth in the training set $\mathcal{P}$. In general, a larger threshold τ yields a more reliable $\mathcal{T}$. However, at a large τ, sampled pairs may be less informative, for their relations are relatively easy to predict. The impacts of τ will be analyzed in the supplemental document. Second, we also sample every possible pair (x, y) from each vertex w and add both (x, y) and (y, x) to $\mathcal{T}$ to indicate that $x \approx y$.

Next, we fine-tune the comparator using the augmented training set $\mathcal{P} \cup \mathcal{T}$. The comparator is, in turn, used to update the linear ordering $\mathcal{L}$ and the pseudo pair set $\mathcal{T}$. This is repeated as described in Algorithm 1.

3.4   Chainization – Applications

Clique-Edgeless Case: Let us consider the clique-edgeless case in which training instances in $\mathcal{X}$ are partitioned into two subsets $\mathcal{X}_c$ and $\mathcal{X}_e$, and the ground-truth ranks are available only for the instances in $\mathcal{X}_c$. Thus, the instances in $\mathcal{X}_c$ form a clique, whereas those in $\mathcal{X}_e$ form an edgeless subgraph in G, as shown in Fig. 1(b). Note that the clique-edgeless case can represent the semi-supervised learning scenario [25,28] if $|\mathcal{X}_c| \ll |\mathcal{X}_e|$. Also, it can represent the unsupervised domain adaptation scenario [13,30] when $\mathcal{X}_c$ and $\mathcal{X}_e$ are different source and target datasets, respectively.

The proposed chainization can be applied to this clique-edgeless case as well. We first train the comparator using the known ordering relations on $\mathcal{X}_c$. Then, we sort all instances via the chainization. However, at early iterations, the instances in $\mathcal{X}_e$ may not be ordered reliably, since no supervision is provided for them. Hence, we do not shorten the chain at early iterations. Also, to form a pseudo pair set $\mathcal{T}$, we use a gradually decreasing threshold τ, so that we can sample more reliable pairs at early iterations and more informative pairs at later iterations. The supplemental document describes the scheduling of τ in detail.

Bipartite Case: Training instances in $\mathcal{X}$ are partitioned into two subsets $\mathcal{X}_0$ and $\mathcal{X}_1$, and the only annotations are that every instance in $\mathcal{X}_0$ is no larger than ($\preccurlyeq$) every instance in $\mathcal{X}_1$. This special partial ordering $\mathcal{P}$ is represented by a complete bipartite graph G in Fig. 1(c). Even in this challenging case, the chainization algorithm can sort all instances in $\mathcal{X}$ meaningfully and yield a chain by adopting the same strategy used in the clique-edgeless case.

3.5   Rank Estimation

Based on order learning [12], we can estimate the rank of an unseen instance x by comparing it with multiple references with known ranks. For the rank estimation, Lee and Kim [9] developed the MAP estimator. However, their algorithm adopts a ternary classifier as the comparator and yields a probability vector of $p^{xy} = (p^{xy}_\prec, p^{xy}_\approx, p^{xy}_\succ)$ by comparing x with reference y. In contrast, we do not compute the probability $p_{\approx}^{xy}$ of the equal case explicitly, since it requires a threshold to define the equality between instances [12]. Thus, we modify the MAP estimation rule accordingly, which is detailed in the supplemental document.

4 Experiments

We conduct various experiments on facial age estimation [10,21], aesthetic assessment [22] and facial expression recognition [1] datasets to assess the proposed algorithm under the three different scenarios: random edge case, clique-edgeless case, and bipartite case. Due to the space limitation, implementation details and more results are available in the supplemental document.

4.1 Datasets

MORPH II [21]: It provides 55,134 facial images labeled with the exact ages in range [16, 77]. For evaluation, we select 5,492 images of the Caucasian race and divide them randomly into two subsets: 80% for training and 20% for test.

Adience [10]: It contains 26,580 images annotated with one of the eight age group labels: '0–2,' '4–6,' '8–13,' '15–20,' '25–32,' '38–43,' '48–53,' and '60–100.' For evaluation, we adopt the standard 5-fold cross validation [5,10,11].

Aesthetics [22]: It provides 15,687 image URLs on Flickr, where 13,929 images are available but the others are lost. Each image is annotated with a 5-scale aesthetic score. We use the 5-fold cross validation for evaluation.

FER+ [1]: It contains 32,298 grayscale images for facial expression recognition. Each image is categorized by 10 annotators into one of eight emotion classes, and the ground-truth class is determined by the majority rule.

4.2 Metrics

Linear Extension: To measure the quality of linear extension of $\mathcal{P}$ to $\mathcal{L}$, we use two metrics: Spearman's ρ [4] and pairwise error (PE). The Spearman's ρ computes the correlation coefficient between two instance rankings, which correspond to an estimated linear ordering $\hat{\mathcal{L}}$ and its ground-truth $\mathcal{L}$, respectively. PE is defined as $\text{PE} = 1 - 1/|\hat{\mathcal{L}}| \sum_{(x,y) \in \hat{\mathcal{L}}} [(x, y) \in \mathcal{L}]$, which measures the ratio of disordered pairs in $\hat{\mathcal{L}}$.

Rank Estimation: We assess rank estimation results by the mean absolute error (MAE) and the classification accuracy. MAE is the average absolute error between estimated and ground-truth ranks. For the classification accuracy, the closest rank to the MAP estimation result is regarded as the estimated rank. Note that rank estimation can be regarded as finding a meaningful linear ordering of unseen test instances.

Table 1. Linear extension results on MORPH II, Adience, and Aesthetics.

	MORPH II						Adience						Aesthetics					
	γ = 0.05%		γ = 0.1%		γ = 0.15%		γ = 0.01%		γ = 0.02%		γ = 0.03%		γ = 0.01%		γ = 0.02%		γ = 0.03%	
	PE (↓)	ρ (↑)	PE (↓)	ρ (↑)	PE (↓)	ρ (↑)	PE (↓)	ρ (↑)	PE (↓)	ρ (↑)	PE (↓)	ρ (↑)	PE (↓)	ρ (↑)	PE (↓)	ρ (↑)	PE (↓)	ρ (↑)
Lower bounds [7]	0.419	0.205	0.321	0.483	0.238	0.698	0.407	0.057	0.353	0.225	0.281	0.439	0.270	0.057	0.274	0.106	0.290	0.119
DRA [26]	0.126	0.892	0.108	0.924	0.099	0.927	0.115	0.814	0.113	0.823	0.095	0.851	0.080	0.679	0.071	0.802	0.066	0.836
OL [12]	0.128	0.897	0.108	0.923	0.096	0.930	0.120	0.809	0.113	0.821	0.100	0.847	0.083	0.665	0.069	0.805	0.067	0.822
Proposed	0.114	0.918	0.100	0.936	0.089	0.949	0.061	0.908	0.033	0.948	0.027	0.959	0.063	0.838	0.052	0.853	0.034	0.872

4.3   Random Edge Case

First, we evaluate the linear extension and rank estimation performances in the random edge case. Let $\gamma = 100 \times \frac{|\mathcal{P}|}{|\mathcal{L}|}$ denote the percentage of available known pairs in a partial ordering $\mathcal{P}$ over all pairs in the linear ordering $\mathcal{L}$. Hence, at a lower γ, the linear extension of $\mathcal{P}$ to $\mathcal{L}$ is more difficult.

Linear Extension: Table 1 summarizes the linear extension results on three datasets: MORPH II, Adience, and Aesthetics. Note that there is no conventional technique to extend a partial ordering to a meaningful linear ordering. Hence, for comparison, we provide the results of the Kahn's topological sorting algorithm [7] and conventional comparison-based relative rank estimators, DRA [26] and OL [12], which also can be trained on a partial ordering $\mathcal{P}$. The Kahn's algorithm yields one of the possible linear orderings arbitrarily, so it performs poorly in terms of both PE and Spearman's ρ. Nevertheless, its results can be regarded as the performance lower bounds. Both DRA and OL do not provide a method to extend $\mathcal{P}$ to $\mathcal{L}$. Hence, instances are sorted by their estimated ranks.

First, even at $\gamma = 0.05\%$ on MORPH II, the proposed algorithm achieves a high ρ of 0.918 using only 0.05% of ordered pairs in $\mathcal{L}$ as supervision. This indicates that the proposed algorithm predicts the other missing 99.95% pairs in $\mathcal{L}$ reliably. Second, Adience has eight age group classes, whereas MORPH II has more than 60 age classes. Hence, the linear ordering $\mathcal{L}$ of the Adience data can be more easily estimated: even when γ is as low as 0.01%, the proposed algorithm obtains a high ρ of 0.908 and a low PE of 0.061. Third, due to subjectivity and ambiguity of aesthetic criteria, Aesthetics is more challenging than Adience is. So, it yields relatively low scores at the same γ.

Rank Estimation: Figure 5 compares the rank estimation (age group classification) accuracies of the proposed algorithm and the conventional order learning algorithm OL [12] on the Adience test set. To estimate the rank of an instance, OL requires reference instances with known ranks because it performs comparison-based rank estimation. Thus, for each rank, an instance is randomly selected from the training set as a reference. The proposed algorithm also uses the same references for the rank estimation. At all γ's, the proposed algorithm outperforms OL. Especially, at a low $\gamma = 0.005\%$, OL fails to obtain a reliable comparator due to the lack of training pairs, resulting in a poor accuracy of 31.8%. In contrast, the proposed algorithm achieves a much higher accuracy of 56.7% by optimizing the comparator over pseudo pairs.

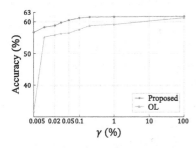

Fig. 5. Comparison of the proposed chainization with OL [12] on Adience. The x-axis is in a logarithmic scale.

Table 2. Comparison of rank estimation results on Adience.

Algorithm	Accuracy (%)	MAE
OR-CNN [16]	56.7 ± 6.0	0.54 ± 0.08
CNNPOR [14]	57.4 ± 5.8	0.55 ± 0.08
GP-DNNOR [15]	57.4 ± 5.5	0.54 ± 0.07
SORD [5]	59.6 ± 3.6	0.49 ± 0.05
POE [11]	60.5 ± 4.4	0.47 ± 0.06
Proposed ($\gamma = 100\%$)	**61.7 ± 4.3**	**0.46 ± 0.05**
Proposed ($\gamma = 0.08\%$)	60.5 ± 4.2	0.48 ± 0.05
Proposed ($\gamma = 0.03\%$)	59.7 ± 4.0	0.49 ± 0.05
Proposed ($\gamma = 0.02\%$)	58.8 ± 4.2	0.51 ± 0.06
Proposed ($\gamma = 0.01\%$)	58.3 ± 4.5	0.53 ± 0.06

Table 2 compares the proposed algorithm with conventional ordinal regressors [5,11,14–16] on the Adience test set. We provide the results of the proposed algorithm at $\gamma = 100\%$ as the performance upper bounds, which achieve the best scores among all methods. Here, the comparator is trained using the ground-truth linear ordering $\mathcal{L}$ of the training set. With weaker supervision, the performances are lowered but still competitive. For example, using only 0.03% of the ordering relations in $\mathcal{L}$, the proposed algorithm performs better than the others, except for POE [11]. Moreover, at $\gamma = 0.08\%$, the proposed algorithm reaches the performances of POE. This confirms that the comparator is effectively fine-tuned with the partial data augmented by pseudo pairs.

4.4   Clique-Edgeless Case

To assess the proposed algorithm in the clique-edgeless case, we employ typical semi-supervised learning and unsupervised domain adaptation protocols.

First, in the semi-supervised learning test, we compare the proposed algorithm with the state-of-the-art ordinal regressors, POE [11] and SORD [5], at various supervision levels s, which means that the ground-truth ranks are known for $s\%$ of the training instances. However, the ordinal regressors assume that the ground-truth rank of every training instance is given. Hence, we utilize recent semi-supervised learning algorithms, FlexMatch [28] and FixMatch [25], together with the ordinal regressors so that they can use unlabeled instances for training. Figure 6 compares the results. The performances of SORD are severely degraded at low levels of s. Its performances do not improve even when it is combined with FlexMatch and FixMatch. Compared to SORD, POE and its combined versions with FlexMatch and FixMatch provide better results. However, the proposed algorithm achieves the best accuracies at all levels of s with large margins. Notably, the proposed algorithm at $s = 30\%$ shows competitive results to the fully supervised POE. This indicates that the chainization can effectively reduce the amount of supervision required for obtaining a good rank estimator.

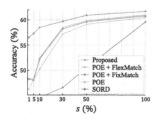

Fig. 6. Semi-supervised learning performances on Adience.

Table 3. Domain adaptation results from Adience to MORPH II.

Algorithm	ρ	MAE	Accuracy (%)
POE [11]	0.614	0.66	43.4
SORD [5]	0.560	0.85	37.5
OL [12]	0.630	0.68	43.8
Proposed	**0.798**	**0.54**	**51.5**

Next, we compare the proposed algorithm under the domain adaptation protocol. We use Adience and MORPH II as the source and target domains, respectively. Table 3 compares the sorting and rank estimation results. To compute ρ of POE and SORD, instances are sorted by their estimated ranks. Although the source and target datasets contain images of different characteristics, the proposed algorithm performs reliably and provides better results than the conventional algorithms in [5, 11, 12]. Notably, compared to OL, the proposed algorithm improves the performances meaningfully via the chainization.

4.5 Bipartite Case

In the bipartite case, all instances in $\mathcal{X}$ are partitioned into two subsets $\mathcal{X}_0$ and $\mathcal{X}_1$ so that every instance in $\mathcal{X}_0$ is smaller than every instance in $\mathcal{X}_1$. In other words, every ordering relation across the two subsets is known. Hence, to evaluate the quality of linear extension, we measure the ρ and PE scores for $\mathcal{X}_0$ and $\mathcal{X}_1$ separately and report the average scores over the subsets.

Table 4 lists the performances on MORPH II and Adience. The Kahn's algorithm [7] yields almost zero ρ's, since no ordering information within $\mathcal{X}_0$ or $\mathcal{X}_1$ is available in $\mathcal{P}$. In contrast, the proposed algorithm sorts the instances in $\mathcal{X}$ meaningfully, outperforming DRA and OL by large margins. The ρ coefficient for Adience is relatively low since its subset $\mathcal{X}_1$ has a severe class imbalance. Also, we compare the rank estimation results of OL and the proposed algorithm in terms of MAE. In this test, we use randomly selected references for each rank. Due to the extremely limited information for training, OL yields poor results. In contrast, the proposed algorithm provides decent MAE results, 5.9 for the 62 ranks in MORPH II and 0.8 for the 8 ranks in Adience.

Figure 7 shows the linear extension results on MORPH II in more detail. After sorting the instances in $\mathcal{X}$ based on $\hat{\mathcal{L}}$, we compute the moving average age of 100 consecutive instances from the youngest to the oldest. Although no ordering information within $\mathcal{X}_0$ or $\mathcal{X}_1$ is available, the proposed algorithm estimates such information quite reliably and yields generally increasing curves.

Last, we assess the performances on the FER+ dataset [1]. There is no explicit order between the emotion classes in FER+, so we consider the two classes of 'sadness' and 'happiness' and assume that 'sadness' precedes ($<$) 'happiness.' In other words, 'sadness' is assumed to be the opposite feeling of 'happiness' on

Table 4. Linear extension results in the bipartite case.

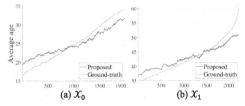

(a) $\mathcal{X}_0$ (b) $\mathcal{X}_1$

Fig. 7. Sorting $\mathcal{X}_0$ and $\mathcal{X}_1$ of MORPH II.

	MORPH II			Adience		
	MAE($\downarrow$)	PE ($\downarrow$)	ρ ($\uparrow$)	MAE ($\downarrow$)	PE ($\downarrow$)	ρ ($\uparrow$)
Lower Bounds [7]	–	0.484	0.003	–	0.341	0.007
DRA [26]	–	0.334	0.405	–	0.270	0.228
OL [12]	8.696	0.450	0.068	1.682	0.307	0.128
Proposed	**5.903**	**0.246**	**0.638**	**0.807**	**0.192**	**0.452**

Fig. 8. Sorting of the instances in 'sadness' and 'happiness' classes in the FER+ dataset. More examples are shown in the supplemental document.

the same axis. Then, the instances belonging to 'sadness' and 'happiness' are assigned to $\mathcal{X}_0$ and $\mathcal{X}_1$, respectively. Even in this challenging case, the chainization can sort all the instances in a meaningful order. Figure 8 shows examples of the sorted instances. The instances in the 'sadness' class are sorted meaningfully from 'weeping' to 'wailing,' and those in the 'happiness' class are from 'smiling tightly' to 'laughing.' The proposed algorithm discovers these subclasses without any intra-class supervision; it discovers them based on the inter-class order assumption only. The proposed algorithm determines that the wailing instance is happier than the weeping one. One possible explanation for this counter-intuitive ordering is that wailing entails emitting a cry by opening ones mouth wide, similar to when one laughs.

5 Conclusions

We proposed the chainization algorithm to improve order learning performances on partially ordered data. First, we estimate unknown ordering relations of instances using a comparator trained on the partial ordering. Then, based on the estimated relations, we obtain a linear ordering and then sample pseudo pairs. We then fine-tune the comparator using the pseudo pairs iteratively. As a result, we obtain a more accurate comparator than conventional order learning. Extensive experiments on various datasets showed that the proposed algorithm provides meaningful sorting results and excellent rank estimation performances under diverse weak supervision scenarios.

Acknowledgments. This work was supported by the NRF grants funded by the Korea government (MSIT) (No. NRF-2021R1A4A1031864 and No. NRF-2022R1A2B5B03002310) and also by IITP grant funded by the Korea government (MSIT) (No. 2021-0-02068, Artificial Intelligence Innovation Hub).

References

1. Barsoum, E., Zhang, C., Ferrer, C.C., Zhang, Z.: Training deep networks for facial expression recognition with crowd-sourced label distribution. In: ICMI (2016)
2. Bromley, J., Guyon, I., LeCun, Y., Säckinger, E., Shah, R.: Signature verification using a "Siamese" time delay neural network. In: NIPS (1993)
3. Cormen, T.H., Leiserson, C.E., Rivest, R.L., Stein, C.: Introduction to Algorithms. MIT press (2009)
4. Diaconis, P., Graham, R.L.: Spearman's footrule as a measure of disarray. J. Roy. Stat. Soc.: Ser. B (Methodol.) **39**(2), 262–268 (1977)
5. Diaz, R., Marathe, A.: Soft labels for ordinal regression. In: CVPR (2019)
6. Jech, T.J.: The Axiom of Choice. Courier Corporation (2008)
7. Kahn, A.B.: Topological sorting of large networks. Commun. ACM **5**(11), 558–562 (1962)
8. Knuth, D.E., Szwarcfiter, J.L.: A structured program to generate all topological sorting arrangements. Inf. Process. Lett. **2**(6), 153–157 (1974)
9. Lee, S.H., Kim, C.S.: Deep repulsive clustering of ordered data based on order-identitiy decomposition. In: ICLR (2021)
10. Levi, G., Hassner, T.: Age and gender classification using convolutional neural networks. In: CVPR Workshops (2015)
11. Li, W., Huang, X., Lu, J., Feng, J., Zhou, J.: Learning probabilistic ordinal embeddings for uncertainty-aware regression. In: CVPR (2021)
12. Lim, K., Shin, N.H., Lee, Y.Y., Kim, C.S.: Order learning and its application to age estimation. In: ICLR (2020)
13. Liu, X., Li, S., Ge, Y., Ye, P., You, J., Lu, J.: Recursively conditional gaussian for ordinal unsupervised domain adaptation. In: ICCV (2021)
14. Liu, Y., Kong, A.W.K., Goh, C.K.: A constrained deep neural network for ordinal regression. In: CVPR (2018)
15. Liu, Y., Wang, F., Kong, A.W.K.: Probabilistic deep ordinal regression based on Gaussian processes. In: CVPR (2019)
16. Niu, Z., Zhou, M., Wang, L., Gao, X., Hua, G.: Ordinal regression with multiple output CNN for age estimation. In: CVPR (2016)
17. Pan, H., Han, H., Shan, S., Chen, X.: Mean-variance loss for deep age estimation from a face. In: CVPR (2018)
18. Parikh, D., Grauman, K.: Relative attributes. In: ICCV (2011)
19. Pearce, D.J., Kelly, P.H.: A dynamic topological sort algorithm for directed acyclic graphs. J. Exp. Algorithmics **11**, 1–7 (2007)
20. Reingold, E.M., Nievergelt, J., Deo, N.: Combinatorial Algorithms: Theory and Practice. Prentice Hall (1977)
21. Ricanek, K., Tesafaye, T.: MORPH: A longitudinal image database of normal adult age-progression. In: FGR (2006)
22. Schifanella, R., Redi, M., Aiello, L.M.: An image is worth more than a thousand favorites: Surfacing the hidden beauty of Flickr pictures. In: ICWSM (2015)
23. Schröder, B.S.W.: Ordered Sets: An Introduction. Springer (2003)
24. Shin, N.H., Lee, S.H., Kim, C.S.: Moving window regression: a novel approach to ordinal regression. In: CVPR (2022)
25. Sohn, K., et al.: FixMatch: simplifying semi-supervised learning with consistency and confidence. In: NIPS (2020)
26. Souri, Y., Noury, E., Adeli, E.: Deep relative attributes. In: ACCV (2016)

27. Tarjan, R.: Finding dominators in directed graphs. SIAM J. Comput. **3**(1), 62–89 (1974)

28. Zhang, B., et al.: FlexMatch: boosting semi-supervised learning with curriculum pseudo labeling. In: NIPS (2021)

29. Zhang, Y., Liu, L., Li, C., Loy, C.C.: Quantifying facial age by posterior of age comparisons. In: BMVC (2017)

30. Zou, Y., Yang, X., Yu, Z., Kumar, B.V.K.V., Kautz, J.: Joint disentangling and adaptation for cross-domain person re-identification. In: Vedaldi, A., Bischof, H., Brox, T., Frahm, J.-M. (eds.) ECCV 2020. LNCS, vol. 12347, pp. 87–104. Springer, Cham (2020). https://doi.org/10.1007/978-3-030-58536-5_6

Unsupervised High-Fidelity Facial Texture Generation and Reconstruction

Ron Slossberg[1](✉), Ibrahim Jubran[2], and Ron Kimmel[1]

[1] Technion Institute, Haifa, Israel
ronslos@gmail.com , ron@cs.technion.ac.il
[2] University of Haifa, Haifa, Israel

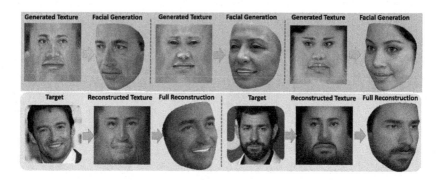

Abstract. Many methods have been proposed over the years to tackle the task of facial 3D geometry and texture recovery from a single image. Such methods often fail to provide high-fidelity texture without relying on 3D facial scans during training. In contrast, the complementary task of 3D facial generation has not received as much attention. As opposed to the 2D texture domain, where GANs have proven to produce highly realistic facial images, the more challenging 3D domain has not yet caught up to the same levels of realism and diversity. In this paper, we propose a novel unified pipeline for both tasks, generation of texture with coupled geometry, and reconstruction of high-fidelity texture. Our texture model is learned, in an unsupervised fashion, from natural images as opposed to scanned textures. To our knowledge, this is the first such unified framework independent of scanned textures. Our novel training pipeline incorporates a pre-trained 2D facial generator coupled with a deep feature manipulation methodology. By applying our two-step geometry fitting process, we seamlessly integrate our modeled textures into synthetically generated background images forming a realistic composition of our textured model with background, hair, teeth, and body. This enables us to apply transfer learning from the 2D image domain, thus leveraging the high-quality

R. Slossberg and I. Jubran—These authors contributed equally to this work.

Supplementary Information The online version contains supplementary material available at https://doi.org/10.1007/978-3-031-19778-9_13.

results obtained in this domain. We provide a comprehensive study on several recent methods comparing our model in generation and reconstruction tasks. As the extensive qualitative, as well as quantitative analysis, demonstrate, we achieve state-of-the-art results for both tasks.

1   Introduction

Generation of 3D facial geometry and full texture, as well as their reconstruction from a single 2D image, are highly challenging and important tasks at the intersection of computer vision, graphics, and machine learning. These tasks arise within endless applications ranging from virtual reality to facial editing.

Our main motivation is that while 2D generation methods have been successful, it is difficult to carefully control attributes such as expression, pose and lighting within such image generators. At the other end, achieving similar results in the 3D domain is difficult due to lack of data and the requirement for generating corresponding geometries for each texture map. Our goal is to enable such control while maintaining the convenience of training on 2D images. In addition, we propose to construct a joint pipeline for both tasks for the sake of resource conservation as well as model standardization for applications where both generated and reconstructed faces are used.

At the heart of such generation and reconstruction methods lies a hidden common assumption that natural facial geometries and textures reside on a low-dimensional manifold. Following this assumption, the above tasks can be carried out within this simpler representation space, instead of the original high-dimensional space. The recovery of this manifold is termed *facial modeling* and the mathematical bridge between the high and low dimensional representations is termed a *facial model*. Many different types of facial models have been proposed over the years, including linear, non-linear, deep learning-based, hybrid, implicit, and dense landmark regression models, to name a few. While most models are geared towards reconstruction tasks, only a few models are successful at synthetically generating realistic samples due to the added complication of sampling the facial manifold. In addition, regardless of the models used, the facial generation process must account for the inter-dependency between geometry and texture, thus, producing compatible geometry-texture pairs in order to achieve realistic 3D facial generations. Ideally, when performed correctly, the newly generated faces will reside on the combined geometry-texture manifold.

In previous efforts, training a generative model for facial geometry and texture depended either on (i) 3D facial scans, via supervised learning, that yielded high-quality results, or (ii) on 2D facial images only, via unsupervised or semi-supervised learning, which produced lower-quality results; see overview in Sect. 2. Here we combine the best of both worlds, and provide an unsupervised training pipeline, independent of a dataset of 3D facial scans, producing state-of-the-art facial generation results. In addition to performing 3D facial texture generation, which is our main contribution, the proposed model can also be utilized for the task of full-texture recovery from a single 2D image for which we also demonstrate results on par with fully supervised methods. The proposed high-resolution model is achieved by incorporating a linear as well as a direct regression facial model, a pre-trained 2D generative model, a deep feature manipulation component, and a differentiable rendering layer, all integrated as building blocks for a novel unsupervised training pipeline.

2   Background and Related Efforts

Next, we review related efforts. Techniques incorporated in the proposed pipeline are described in detail. Table 1 summarizes the fundamental differences between our work and relevant prior works.

The 3D Morhpable Model (3DMM) [1] is arguably the most commonly used model both when generating or reconstructing facial geometries and textures; see [9]. The 3DMM model is obtained by semantically aligning facial scans to a template model comprised of n vertices and performing PCA [16] on the geometry, texture and expression vectors. The obtained k principal components for shape and expression $\mathbf{U}_s, \mathbf{U}_e \in \mathbb{R}^{3n \times k}$ and mean shape $\mathbf{M} \in \mathbb{R}^{3n}$ comprise the 3DMM geometry model. Given a set of shape and expression parameters $(\mathbf{p}_s, \mathbf{p}_e \in \mathbb{R}^k)$, the facial geometry is constructed as $\mathbf{S} = \mathbf{M} + \mathbf{U}_s \cdot \mathbf{p}_s + \mathbf{U}_e \cdot \mathbf{p}_e$. Texture modeling and formation are produced per-vertex in a similar manner. Many improvements were suggested, for example, [2,3,22], who improve the data acquisition and registration processes. However, due to their linear nature, such models usually produce unrealistic samples [35].

3DMM Fitting. Given a 2D face image and the 3DMM geometry and expression basis, the goal of *3DMM fitting* is to recover the 3DMM geometry and expression coefficients as well as a 3D rigid transformation. Numerous approaches have been suggested for tackling this problem, ranging from optimization-based methods [1,12], to one-shot deep learning pipelines originated in [31,45], and followed up in [7,14,15,39] to name a few. In this work, we utilize the model introduced in [7], due to its high precision in estimating model parameters, as well as the available code and pre-trained model; see Sect. 3.

Non-linear and Hybrid Model Fitting. Recent efforts have built upon classical 3DMMs, proposing both hybrid [4,12,32–36,38] and non-linear models [42,44]. These deep network-based methods may also incorporate linear components. Some models are presented only in the context of monocular geometry and texture recovery while others are also utilized for synthesis.

Dense Landmark Regression. In [20], a regression network is trained to predict a dense collection of landmarks directly on a given facial 2D image. These landmarks represent the projected vertex locations of a 3D canonical facial model. This method achieves better alignment relative to the target image and is not constrained to the limitations of the linear model. However, the landmark based facial representation presents low-detail geometry due to the limited number of recovered landmarks. We therefore propose a two-step fitting scheme combining both landmark regression as well as 3DMM geometry reconstruction in order to gain the benefits of both regimes; see details in Sect. 3.3.

Realistic 2D Face Generation. In a long line of efforts culminating in [17], various models have been proposed for the task of 2D face image generation.

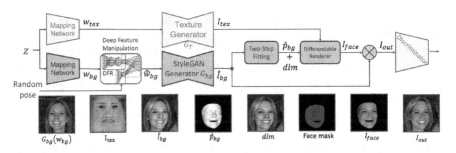

Fig. 1. Our training pipeline. A vector $\mathbf{z} \in \mathbb{R}^{512}$ of Gaussian random noise is plugged into two identical mapping networks [19], producing two latent vectors $\mathbf{w}_{tex}, \mathbf{w}_{bg} \in \mathbb{R}^{18 \times 512}$, respectively. The facial image obtained by feeding $\mathbf{w}_{bg}$ into *Style-GAN* is illustrated on the lower left. The vector $\mathbf{w}_{bg}$ is plugged into a deep feature manipulation network [37] called *StyleRig* to obtain the (manipulated) latent vector $\hat{\mathbf{w}}_{bg} \in \mathbb{R}^{18 \times 512}$ which encodes the same facial information as $\mathbf{w}_{bg}$ (*e.g.* facial expression, identity, lighting, etc.) but with a modified facial orientation. We then feed $\mathbf{w}_{tex}$ and $\hat{\mathbf{w}}_{bg}$ into our texture and pre-trained *StyleGAN* generators G_T and G_{bg}, outputting a texture image I_{tex} and a 2D facial image $\hat{I}_{bg}$ respectively. Then, we apply a two-step fitting approach to recover 3DMM parameters ($\hat{\mathbf{p}}_{bg}$) [7] as well as a dense landmarks mask (dlm) [20] that best fit $\hat{I}_{bg}$; see Sect. 3.3. We then use $\hat{\mathbf{p}}_{bg}$ to render the texture I_{tex} into a 2D facial image I_{face}, and perform a masking operation according to the face mask extracted from the dlm. The masked facial (foreground) image I_{face} and the (background) image $\hat{I}_{bg}$ are then composed together to form I_{out}. Finally, I_{out} is fed into a pre-trained discriminator which is further trained. Trainable and frozen models are depicted in green and red respectively

Such models are capable of generating highly realistic 2D facial images as well as project real 2D facial images onto the model's latent manifold. As we aim to mitigate the need for 3D scans of facial textures, we heavily rely on well-established 2D facial generative models as the basis for the proposed pipeline. Throughout the proposed pipeline, we utilize the framework and pre-trained model weights provided by the seminal papers of Karras *et al.* [17,18], which are regarded the golden standard for this task; see Sect. 3.

Manipulating Facial Properties via Deep Feature Mapping. Most synthesis methods described above, specifically [18], learn to map an input random noise vector, through some latent representation, into a realistic 2D facial image. Following this popular approach, a variety of papers have emerged which learn to manipulate this latent vector to change some desired facial properties in the output 2D image. Such manipulation can be either statistics-based [5] or, more often, learning based [37]; see [40] with references therein.

As discussed in detail in Sect. 3, our pipeline makes use of a 2D facial image generator to compensate for the lack of 3D facial scans. However, it is infeasible to compensate for 3D geometry and full facial texture using only *uncontrolled randomly generated* 2D facial images. We thus utilize a method providing control over the pose of generated images and show that the *controlled* 2D images indeed suffice for full-texture learning. To this end, we utilize the method of [37] for deep feature manipulation; see Sect. 3.

Generation. While most prior efforts have focused on 3D reconstruction from a 2D image, few methods have been proposed for the generation of random but realistic facial models. In [25], a GAN-based approach was also proposed for improving facial recognition models via synthetic augmentation; however, their pipeline focuses more on controlling model parameters intending to supplement the training data. This, as opposed to the realistic generation of completely random faces, leads to a less desirable outcome in terms of realism and resolution. Hence, the results are not visually pleasing; see Fig. 4. In [12, 34, 35], 3DMMs combined with generative models were used for either generation or reconstruction of realistic textures. However, these methods rely on proprietary high-quality facial scans during training, obtained by specialized facial scanners. This makes these results difficult to reproduce. Moreover, such scanned data is far less diverse than abundant facial 2D images in common datasets.

Reconstruction. Many methods have been previously suggested for 3D face reconstruction from a given 2D image. In [8, 31–33], a mapping from 2D images to a 3D geometric representation is learned based on synthetic data. In [12, 13], real facial textures were utilized, to obtain, in a supervised manner, a realistic reconstruction. However, acquiring such textures requires laborious and expensive 3D scanning, hence, impractical to scale to large numbers. In this paper, we provide an unsupervised alternative that requires only the freely available geometric models, and does not directly require 3D scans, and achieves either comparable or higher quality reconstructions. A pipeline for completion of a facial texture containing large holes was suggested in [6], however, they also rely on scanned textures as training data. A one-shot learning approach was proposed in [11] which applies an iterative and slow optimization process to complete a facial texture.

Two additional methods that do not rely on 3D scanned data were proposed by Lin *et al.* and Kim *et al.* [21,23]. In Kim *et al.* [21] an unsupervised model for partial texture completion is trained by combining a global and a local patch discriminator to the full rendering as well as the uv mapped texture. The uv maps in this work are of dimension 512×512, a quarter of the resolution presented by our maps. Lin *et al.* [23] takes a different approach to the completion task by utilizing Graph Convolutional Networks. However, by not basing their pipelines on a 2D image generator which can produce controlled 2D images (*e.g. StyleGAN* combined with a model as [37]), their method is not intended for the task of generation of expressive 3D models and does not account for the coupling of geometry and texture. See detailed comparison with [21,23] in Sect. 4.

2.1 Our Contribution

The main contributions of our method are the following:

(i) We provide the first unsupervised high-fidelity generation pipeline capable of producing realistic textures coupled with corresponding geometries; See Table 1 and Sect. 3. This is achieved by a novel training pipeline which successfully decouples intrinsic texture features related to the person's identity, from extrinsic properties such as pose and Lambertian illumination.

Table 1. Comparison to prior art.

Method	Unsupervised training	High-fidelity output	Supports generation	Supports reconstruction
Deng et al. [7]	✓			✓
Lin et al. [23]	✓	✓		✓
Kim et al. [21]	✓	✓		✓
Deng et al. [6]		✓		✓
Gecer et al. [12]		✓		✓
Shamai et al. [34,35]		✓	✓	
Marriott et al. [25]	✓		✓	
Ours	✓	✓	✓	✓

(ii) In addition to texture generation, we utilize the very same model for the task of texture recovery from a single image, successfully reconstructing frontal as well as peripheral facial details; see Sect. 3.2.

(iii) We present state-of-the-art results in both model generation as well as full texture recovery. We support this claim via both qualitative as well as quantitative results and comparisons; see Sect. 4. We prepared an additional demonstration video with further results; see supplementary material.

(iv) Our results are fully reproducible as only freely available datasets and models are required during training and inference. In addition, we provide all our trained model weights for both generation and reconstruction tasks [26].

3   Unsupervised Learning of Facial Textures and Geometries

In this section, we detail our unsupervised pipeline for generation and reconstruction of full facial textures and coupled geometries. While the proposed pipeline generates and recovers both texture as well as corresponding geometry, we rely on existing methods and models for geometric recovery and generation, and focus our attention mainly on high-quality texture modeling. We are guided by the notion that the main effect on the perception of model realism stems from high-resolution texture rather than highly detailed geometry. This idea was also noted *e.g.* by [35]. Nevertheless, recovery of highly detailed geometry is still an important research topic with many successful efforts such as [4,32,33,41].

An overview of the suggested training and inference pipelines is depicted in Figs. 1 and 2 respectively. The proposed approach to unsupervised learning of facial textures utilizes an adversarial loss to train a texture generator, G_T, while harnessing a pre-trained 2D facial image generator, G_{bg}, in the following fashion. We start by generating, via G_{bg}, a 2D facial image which we term a *background image*. We then fit a corresponding geometry to the background image using a two-step geometry recovery process utilizing [7,20]; see Sect. 3.3. We proceed to generate a facial texture I_{tex} via our trainable texture generator G_T. The generated synthetic texture is stored as a 2D image coupled with a canonical UV parametrization relating between image locations to the vertices of the 3D facial model. We base our UV unwraping on Floater [10]. The model fitted to

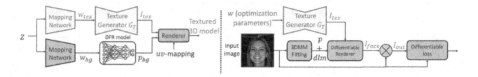

Fig. 2. Our inference pipelines. During inference, we drop some components related to the training pipeline (see Fig. 1). **(Left) Generation:** As before, a single latent vector **z** is used to generate $\mathbf{w}_{tex}$ and $\mathbf{w}_{bg}$ via two mapping networks. The latent vector $\mathbf{w}_{bg}$ is used to generate 3DMM geometry parameters $\mathbf{p}_{bg}$ via the trained DFR model while $\mathbf{w}_{tex}$ is introduced to the trained texture generator yielding the corresponding texture image I_{tex}. The parameters $\mathbf{p}_{bg}$ are used, along with our canonical UV parametrization, to generate the 3DMM geometry which we render using I_{tex} as the mesh texture. **(Right) Reconstruction:** A given input image I is first plugged into our two-step fitting model producing its 3DMM parameters **p** and a dense landmark mask dlm. A latent vector **w** containing our optimization parameters is then inserted into our trained texture generator producing a texture image I_{tex}. Using a differentiable renderer, **p** and I_{tex} are rendered into a 2D face image I_{face}, which is blended with I according to the dlm to produce our output I_{out}. Finally, a VGG loss similar to [17] is evaluated between I and I_{out}

the background image enables the seamless mapping of the synthetic texture image I_{tex} into the background image as depicted in Fig. 1.

The texture generator is trained within a GAN framework for which a discriminator model is trained to differentiate between blended and real images and thus continuously improves the generator quality. In order to generate high-resolution facial textures from all viewing angles, it is crucial to control various properties within the images generated by G_{bg}. For example, we require that each generated identity appears under a range of poses. We therefore utilize a deep feature manipulation component, as in [37], that encodes the desired properties within the input of G_{bg}. In addition, in order to disentangle between the albedo and shading components of the texture, we estimate the Lambertian lighting conditions in G_{bg} and apply them to our texture within the rendering process. Section 3.2 further elaborates on these components.

Learning from 3D Facial Scans. Prior efforts approached the task of training facial texture models by relying on difficult-to-obtain 3D scans. For example, in [12,35], high-resolution scans obtained by a 3DMD scanner are geometrically aligned and mapped to a canonical 2D domain. The mapped textures are used as training data for a GAN which is tasked to generate new and realistic ones. This methodology suffers from two main drawbacks: (i) The 3D scans are not easily obtained or freely distributed, thus posing a significant barrier in reproducing such models. (ii) High-quality 3D scanners are expensive and cumbersome, limiting the ability to collect data. Hence, even when available, such datasets are comprised of at most a few thousand subjects, which can not encompass the huge variety of human faces. We mitigate the above issues by eliminating the dependency on scans and replacing them with widely available 2D facial images and freely distributed geometric models, thus, providing a more accessible method and producing a more diverse texture model.

Replacing 3D Facial Scans with 2D Facial Images. Replacing 3D facial scans with prevalent 2D facial images is commonly achieved by utilizing a differentiable rendering layer. The rendering of 3D textured models into 2D images enables the incorporation of 2D image-related architectures and losses. This process also requires a 3D mesh, usually represented by a pair (V, Tri) of vertex coordinates $V \in \mathbb{R}^{N_v \times 3}$ and triangulation $Tri \in \mathbb{R}^{N_f \times 3}$, as well as a uv parametrization $\phi : \{1, \cdots, N_v\} \to [0,1] \times [0,1]$ that maps every vertex to coordinates on the canonical plane. To obtain the desired facial rendering I_{face}, the vertex coordinates are first projected onto the 2D camera plane and the final pixel colors are determined by a rasterization process mapping the facial texture onto the projected mesh according to the predetermined UV parametrization.

Using this methodology, we can transform our training losses from the 3D to the 2D domain. We can thus utilize the vast corpus of prior art regarding 2D images, including pre-trained models as well as large, high resolution, and freely available datasets; see Sect. 3.1.

Having established the above, the question remains how to obtain synthetic facial renderings which are indistinguishable from real facial images, considering that the rendered images lack hair, ears, inside of the mouth, background, etc. Possible solutions include segmenting-out the background in the real image, or adding a synthetic background to the rendered (synthetic) facial image. The former can be achieved via image segmentation or 3D model fitting, both of which produce sub-optimal results that are easily distinguishable from the synthetic image, due to artifacts at the face boundary. We therefore choose the latter option and propose to generate an additional 2D facial image I_{bg}, *e.g.* using *StyleGAN*, and utilize I_{bg} as the background to our (foreground) rendered image I_{face}. This is achieved by first fitting a geometric model to I_{bg} (see Sect. 3.3), which serves as the 3D mesh required for rendering I_{tex} into a 2D image I_{face}, as previously detailed. This process embeds our synthetic facial texture image I_{tex} into I_{bg}, enforcing the facial texture to be generated in a way that realistically blends with the surrounding parts in I_{bg}, like hair and ears; see Fig. 1.

3.1 Transfer Learning

The process described above results in a 2D facial image, enabling the use of standard 2D image losses. As common in generative models, we use an adversarial loss to discriminate between real and fake images. Fortunately, many such pre-trained GANs are available for the task of 2D facial image generation [17]. We base our mapping network, texture generator, and discriminator, on the architecture proposed in *StyleGAN2* [19]. As facial textures are closely related to 2D facial images, we initialize the above models with the pre-trained *Style-GAN2* weights. This transfer learning approach has dramatically reduced our pipeline training time and improves texture quality, as was also reported by [17].

3.2 Pose and Illumination Invariant Textures

As detailed above, the proposed unsupervised approach relies on rendering 2D images from the generated textures. However, this approach alone, has two inherent problem: (i) Since every input vector z corresponds to a facial image in a specific known pose, the generator can leverage this correlation and generate high-resolution details only in the visible regions with no penalty on occluded regions within the rendered 2D image. We propose to mitigate this issue by introducing random facial rotations during training via *deep feature manipulation*, as detailed below. (ii) Without properly addressing scene illumination, the generator will incorporate the lighting effects into the generated textures; see Fig. 5. We thus aim to decouple the albedo from the illumination effects, enabling post-relighting of the texture. To this end, we relight the models during training using the lighting parameters recovered by [7], forcing the generator to produce textures without baked-in lighting effects. Here, we assume a simplified Lambertian lighting model and do not consider reflective effects.

Deep Feature Pose Manipulation. In order to overcome the orientation-decoupling problem, we manipulate the latent vector w_{bg}, related to the background image I_{bg} enforcing the generation of faces in a variety of orientations. This successfully decouples the pose from the input vector z, thus encouraging our texture generator to produce full high resolution texture from all viewing angles. We adopt the deep feature manipulation methodology proposed in [37].

The manipulation model, termed *StyleRig*, is comprised of two parts. A Differentiable Face Reconstruction Network, or DFR model, which takes as input the latent vector $\mathbf{w}$ and produces estimated 3DMM parameters $\mathbf{p} = DFR(\mathbf{w})$ which include $(\mathbf{p_s}, \mathbf{p_e}, \mathbf{p_t}, \gamma, \mathbf{R}, \mathbf{t})$, shape, expression, texture and lighting, rotation and translation parameters respectively. We train our model utilizing the highly versatile 3DMM model generated by [3].

A second network termed *StyleRig* takes as input a latent vector $\mathbf{w}$ and a set of parameters $\mathbf{p}$ and outputs a modified latent parameter vector $\hat{\mathbf{w}}$, where ideally the image $I = G_{bg}(\hat{\mathbf{w}})$ portrays the face $G_{StyleGan}(\mathbf{w})$ produced by $\mathbf{w}$ but modified to fit the parameters $\mathbf{p}$. In order to produce a rotated version of I_{bg} we first modify the rotation parameters of $\mathbf{p}_{bg} := DFR(\mathbf{w}_{bg})$ to derive $\hat{\mathbf{p}}_{bg}$ and then apply $\hat{\mathbf{w}}_{bg} = StyleRig(\hat{\mathbf{p}}_{bg}, \mathbf{w}_{bg})$. The image $\hat{I}_{bg} = G_{bg}(\hat{\mathbf{w}}_{bg})$ contains a rotated version of the same person as in I_{bg}. We then generate a texture image using the latent vector $\mathbf{w}_{tex}$, regardless of the rotation angles which were modified in $\mathbf{w}_{bg}$. This yields the desired pose-invariance within the texture generator; see Fig. 1

The same DFR model used above will later also be utilized during inference in order to recover corresponding geometries for our generated textures; see Sect. 3.3 and Fig. 2. This allows us to efficiently generate corresponding geometries directly from latent vectors without requiring the trained *StyleGAN* generator during inference.

Training for Re-illumination. To generate textures without Lambertian illumination effects, we first estimate the background scene lighting and relight the texture during training. Assuming a simplified Lambertian reflectance model, we estimate the parameters $\gamma \in \mathbb{R}^{3 \times 9}$ from I_{bg}, as coefficients of 9 Spherical

Harmonics (SH) basis functions [28,29] for R,G and B illumination bands, and relight the rendered image I_{face} under the recovered illumination. The coefficients γ with the computed vertex normals $\{\mathbf{n}_i\}$ and SH functions Φ produce the per-vertex lighting value $\mathbf{C}(\mathbf{n}_i|\gamma)_l = \sum_{b=1}^{9} \gamma_{l,b}\Phi_b(\mathbf{n}_i)$. We perform two rendering passes, one for the illumination component and another for the albedo. The final illuminated rendering is obtained by pixelwise multiplication of the two rendering results.

$$I_{face} = \mathcal{R}(\mathbf{S}(p_s, p_e), G_T(w_{tex})) \cdot \mathcal{R}(\mathbf{S}(p_s, p_e), \mathbf{C}(\mathbf{n}_i|\gamma)),$$

where $\mathcal{R}(G, T)$ signifies the rendering operator applied to a geometry G and a texture T, $\mathbf{p}_s, \mathbf{p}_e$ are respectively shape and expression parameters recovered from I_{bg}, and $\mathbf{w}_{tex}$ is the input latent vector for the texture generator.

This process results in the texture generator producing textures with no baked-in Lambertian lighting effects, so that the re-illuminated texture via γ would match the lighting present in I_{bg} and seem realistic to the discriminator.

3.3 Recovering Corresponding Geometry via Two-Step Fitting

In order to facilitate the realistic incorporation of foreground rendering and background image we propose a two step geometry fitting approach. We observed that, in general, geometry reconstruction methods tend to exhibit a trade-off between geometry realism and precise image alignment. For example, while 3DMM based fitting methods produce high-resolution facial meshes, the mesh alignment relative to the target image is imperfect. In contrast, landmark regression based methodologies are precisely aligned to the target facial image but produce a very sparse geometry reconstruction based on the landmark arrangement. To achieve a realistic blending between the foreground rendering I_{face} and synthetic background image I_{bg}, both accuracy as well as high-resolution geometry are crucial.

To this end, we propose a two step fitting scheme comprising of the 3DMM recovery proposed by [7] followed by a dense landmark regression model [20], gaining the benefits of both. This is achieved by extracting the geometry parameters $\hat{\mathbf{p}}_{bg}$ from the former while utilizing the boundary mask dlm from the latter. While [7] provides a good high-resolution fitting which can be realistically rendered, we use the dense landmark mask (dlm) from [20] in order to perform foreground blending with high precision. By adopting the two-step approach we harness the strengths from both fitting techniques enabling us to perform accurate and realistic blending. In Sect. 4.3 we provide an ablation study comparing the naive one-step 3DMM-only approach to our proposed two-step fitting approach. Indeed we observe that the two-step approach helps mitigate unwanted misalignment artifacts, especially in the mouth region.

3.4 Unsupervised Training

The proposed pipeline above generates full facial textures along with corresponding geometries, and, using a differentiable renderer, synthesizes a 2D facial image.

Adhearing to the GAN framework, the composed facial image along with a real 2D facial image are fed into a discriminator network tasked to differentiate between the real and the fake samples. Such 2D real images are widespread and can be taken from any dataset of facial images, for example, [18].

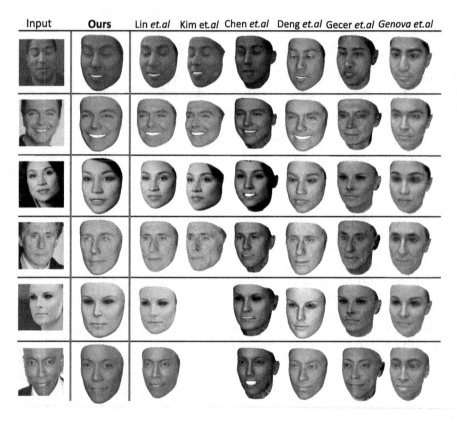

Fig. 3. Qualitative Reconstruction Comparison Results: We present texture reconstruction results on the MOFA test-set [39] compared to previous methods by [4, 7, 12, 14, 21, 23], respectively. This figure is best viewed when zoomed in.

4   Experimental Results

We compare the proposed approach to several state-of-the-art 3D generation and texture reconstruction methods. We provide quantitative and qualitative evidence that our model performance is on par with and often outperforms previous methods, both supervised and unsupervised by scanned textures (see Table 1), in terms of texture reconstruction quality, realism, and details. Our supplementary material contains additional reconstruction results for extreme

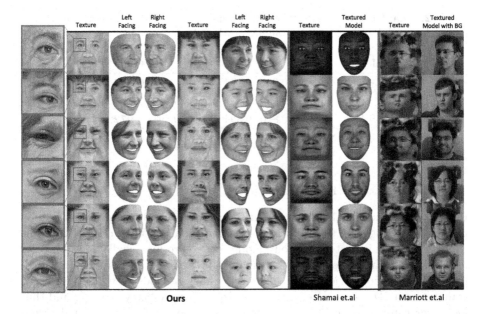

Fig. 4. Facial Synthesis: We visually compare our output textures and rendered textured geometries to: Shamai *et al.* [34] and Mariott *et al.* [25]. Our high resolution textures provide highly realistic faces spanning a wide variety of ages, ethnicity and appearance. The leftmost column provides a zoomed-in crop, highlighting the high resolution details. The proposed method presents finer details and realism as compared to both previous methods, even though [34] is supervised by scanned textures

side views, as well as a demonstration video presenting more viewing angles for our output results. Our code and pre-trained models are available[1].

Implementation Details. We implemented our pipeline in Python using Pytorch [27] and Pytorch3D [30], and trained it on 4 RTX 3090 GPUs on the FFHQ dataset [18] consisting of $70k$ facial images. We initialized our models from the pre-trained weights of *StyleGAN* [19], using default parameters and losses, we train for 3 epochs; see Sect. 3.1. The 2D images as well as the generated textures are of size 1024×1024.

4.1   Face Generation

We randomly generated textures and corresponding geometries via the proposed inference pipeline; see Sect. 3 and Fig. 2. We present the texture images with zoomed-in areas to highlight the high level of detail and realism. We compare our results to the supervised model of [34] and the unsupervised model from [25]; see Fig. 4. See supplementary material for additional results.

---

[1] Link for our open-source code on Github: https://github.com/ronslos/Unsupervised-High-Fidelity-Facial-Texture-Generation-and-Reconstruction.

Table 2. Quantitative Evaluation: We evaluate reprojected reconstruction similarity on the CelebA [24] test-set, containing nearly 20k images

Metric	[7]	[23]	[6]	Ours
L_1 distance ↓	0.052	0.034	/	**0.0244**
PSNR ↑	26.58	29.69	22.9~26.5	**32.889**
SSIM ↑	0.826	0.894	0.887~0.898	**0.972**
LightCNN [43] ↑	0.724	0.900	/	**0.96**

4.2 Facial Texture Reconstruction

Figure 3 presents a qualitative comparison between our texture reconstruction pipeline from Fig. 2 to several state-of-the-art prior works [4,7,12,14,23]. The comparison demonstrates that our model can reproduce challenging textures *e.g.* difficult lighting conditions, makeup, and extreme expressions and compares favorably to previous approaches, including methods based on supervised training from 3D scans. Note, that we utilize [7] for geometry recovery and thus focus our comparison on texture recovery only; see Sect. 3. Additional reconstruction results produced from high-resolution images are depicted in Fig. 1 and the supplementary material, which also presents reconstructions from side views. The results demonstrate that our model is capable of high-resolution texture recovery when presented with high-quality input images. We note that our proposed texture recovery method consists of a weight regularization term balancing between texture fidelity and realism. This is set manually to a constant desirable value throughout all our experiments. See supplementary for details alongside additional results obtained for varying regularization values.

4.3 Ablation Study

In Fig. 5 we present an ablation study, where the full proposed model is shown to produce more realistic results compared to its variants with missing components. Additional ablation results are placed in the supplementary material. This suggests that each of our pipeline components is crucial for producing satisfactory output results. We show that: (i) model rotations during training are crucial for generating high details on the peripheral areas of the texture; see Sect. 3.2, (ii) the two-step fitting eliminates the unwanted teeth artifacts; see Sect. 3.3, and (iii) model illumination during training successfully disentangles albedo from Lambertian shading effects, producing models that can be realistically integrated into scenes with varying lighting conditions; see Sect. 3.2.

Training Stability. The ablation study depicts three different training pipelines with parts of the original pipeline missing. However, the model still converges very similarly, maintains identities and only differs by the manner expected by the removal of each block. This demonstrated that our training is robust to modification of the pipeline.

4.4   Quantitative Results

Table 2 presents a quantitative study for the task of texture reconstruction, using the CelebA [24] test-set. Our method achieves better scores in all tested metrics compared to previous state-of-the-art methods [6,7,23]. In contrast to [23], we do not omit problematic areas by semantically masking difficult regions.

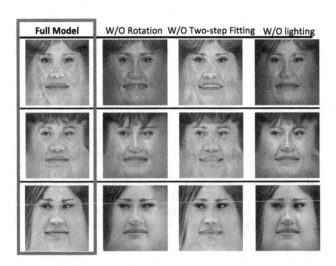

Fig. 5. Ablation Study. Left to right: (i) full model, (ii) without applying our deep feature manipulation component (see Sect. 3.2), (ii) without the two-step fitting, *i.e.* using only the 3DMM during the geometry fitting process, without the facial masking step (see Sect. 3.3), and (iii) without relighting the model (see Sect. 3.2). This leads to poor details in the texture periphery, unwanted teeth artifact, and baked-in Lambertian lighting effects, respectively; see Sect. 4.3

5   Discussion, Limitations, and Future Work

We introduced a novel unsupervised pipeline for generation as well as reconstruction of high resolution realistic facial textures. Our pipeline matches the geometry and texture via a single unified random input vector $\mathbf{z}$, and combines common pre-existing building blocks, in a non-trivial manner, with new novel ideas, to achieve SOTA result. Those ideas include the incorporation of a background image during training, the decoupling of pose from texture by feature vector manipulation, the ability to generate coupled geometry and texture at inference directly from random features, and our two-step fitting approach.

Our experiments demonstrate that we surpass prior art in realism and quality, in both tasks, including models supervised by scanned facial textures.

Due to the presence of subjects wearing glasses within the FFHQ dataset used for training, in some cases, our output texture might contain glasses; See supplementary material. This can be mitigated in future work by using latent feature manipulation. In addition, while Lambertian lighting is disentangled within our pipeline, we do not tackle the challenging problem of specular disentanglement. Moreover, we noticed that during reconstruction, on occasion, the eye color is not consistent with the input image. In future work it is possible to explore regional weighting of the reconstruction loss in order to better control reconstruction trade-offs. Lastly, we did not utilize non-linear geometric representations as we note that high-resolution texture is the most crucial component in the quest for realistic facial generation.

References

1. Blanz, V., Vetter, T.: A morphable model for the synthesis of 3d faces. In: Proceedings of the 26th Annual Conference on Computer Graphics and Interactive Techniques, pp. 187–194 (1999)
2. Booth, J., Roussos, A., Ponniah, A., Dunaway, D., Zafeiriou, S.: Large scale 3d morphable models. Int. J. Comput. Vision **126**(2), 233–254 (2018)
3. Booth, J., Roussos, A., Zafeiriou, S., Ponniah, A., Dunaway, D.: A 3d morphable model learnt from 10,000 faces. In: Proceedings of the IEEE Conference on Computer Vision and Pattern Recognition, pp. 5543–5552 (2016)
4. Chen, A., Chen, Z., Zhang, G., Mitchell, K., Yu, J.: Photo-realistic facial details synthesis from single image. In: Proceedings of the IEEE/CVF International Conference on Computer Vision, pp. 9429–9439 (2019)
5. Chen, Y.C., et al.: Facelet-bank for fast portrait manipulation. In: Proceedings of the IEEE Conference on Computer Vision and Pattern Recognition, pp. 3541–3549 (2018)
6. Deng, J., Cheng, S., Xue, N., Zhou, Y., Zafeiriou, S.: Uv-gan: adversarial facial uv map completion for pose-invariant face recognition. In: Proceedings of the IEEE Conference on Computer Vision and Pattern Recognition, pp. 7093–7102 (2018)
7. Deng, Y., Yang, J., Xu, S., Chen, D., Jia, Y., Tong, X.: Accurate 3d face reconstruction with weakly-supervised learning: from single image to image set. In: Proceedings of the IEEE/CVF Conference on Computer Vision and Pattern Recognition Workshops, pp. 0 (2019)
8. Dou, P., Shah, S.K., Kakadiaris, I.A.: End-to-end 3d face reconstruction with deep neural networks. In: proceedings of the IEEE Conference on Computer Vision and Pattern Recognition, pp. 5908–5917 (2017)
9. Egger, B., Smith, W.A., Tewari, A., Wuhrer, S., Zollhoefer, M., Beeler, T., Bernard, F., Bolkart, T., Kortylewski, A., Romdhani, S., Theobalt, C., Blanz, V., Vetter, T.: 3d morphable face models-past, present, and future. ACM Trans. Graph. (TOG) **39**(5), 1–38 (2020)
10. Floater, M.S.: Parametrization and smooth approximation of surface triangulations. Comput. Aided Geometric Design **14**(3), 231–250 (1997)
11. Gecer, B., Deng, J., Zafeiriou, S.: Ostec: one-shot texture completion. In: Proceedings of the IEEE/CVF Conference on Computer Vision and Pattern Recognition, pp. 7628–7638 (2021)

12. Gecer, B., Ploumpis, S., Kotsia, I., Zafeiriou, S.: Ganfit: generative adversarial network fitting for high fidelity 3d face reconstruction. In: Proceedings of the IEEE/CVF Conference on Computer Vision and Pattern Recognition, pp. 1155–1164 (2019)

13. Gecer, B., Ploumpis, S., Kotsia, I., Zafeiriou, S.: Fast-ganfit: generative adversarial network for high fidelity 3d face reconstruction. arXiv preprint arXiv:2105.07474 (2021)

14. Genova, K., Cole, F., Maschinot, A., Sarna, A., Vlasic, D., Freeman, W.T.: Unsupervised training for 3d morphable model regression. In: Proceedings of the IEEE Conference on Computer Vision and Pattern Recognition, pp. 8377–8386 (2018)

15. Guo, J., Zhu, X., Yang, Y., Yang, F., Lei, Z., Li, S.Z.: Towards fast, accurate and stable 3D dense face alignment. In: Vedaldi, A., Bischof, H., Brox, T., Frahm, J.-M. (eds.) ECCV 2020. LNCS, vol. 12364, pp. 152–168. Springer, Cham (2020). https://doi.org/10.1007/978-3-030-58529-7_10

16. Jolliffe, I.T.: Principal components in regression analysis. In: Principal component analysis, pp. 129–155. Springer, New York (1986). https://doi.org/10.1007/978-1-4757-1904-8_8

17. Karras, T., Aittala, M., Hellsten, J., Laine, S., Lehtinen, J., Aila, T.: Training generative adversarial networks with limited data. In: Proceedings of the NeurIPS (2020)

18. Karras, T., Laine, S., Aila, T.: A style-based generator architecture for generative adversarial networks. In: Proceedings of the IEEE/CVF Conference on Computer Vision and Pattern Recognition, pp. 4401–4410 (2019)

19. Karras, T., Laine, S., Aittala, M., Hellsten, J., Lehtinen, J., Aila, T.: Analyzing and improving the image quality of stylegan. In: Proceedings of the IEEE/CVF Conference on Computer Vision and Pattern Recognition, pp. 8110–8119 (2020)

20. Kartynnik, Y., Ablavatski, A., Grishchenko, I., Grundmann, M.: Real-time facial surface geometry from monocular video on mobile gpus. In: Proceedings of CVPR Workshops (2019)

21. Kim, J., Yang, J., Tong, X.: Learning high-fidelity face texture completion without complete face texture (2021)

22. Li, T., Bolkart, T., Black, M.J., Li, H., Romero, J.: Learning a model of facial shape and expression from 4D scans. ACM Trans. Graph. (Proc. SIGGRAPH Asia) 36(6), 194:1–194:17 (2017). https://doi.org/10.1145/3130800.3130813

23. Lin, J., Yuan, Y., Shao, T., Zhou, K.: Towards high-fidelity 3d face reconstruction from in-the-wild images using graph convolutional networks. In: Proceedings of the IEEE/CVF Conference on Computer Vision and Pattern Recognition, pp. 5891–5900 (2020)

24. Liu, Z., Luo, P., Wang, X., Tang, X.: Deep learning face attributes in the wild. In: Proceedings of International Conference on Computer Vision (ICCV), December 2015

25. Marriott, R.T., Romdhani, S., Chen, L.: A 3d gan for improved large-pose facial recognition. In: Proceedings of the IEEE/CVF Conference on Computer Vision and Pattern Recognition, pp. 13445–13455 (2021)

26. Models, P.: The weights for all our pretrained models. (2021), the authors commit to publish upon acceptance of this paper or reviewer request

27. Paszke, A., Gross, S., Massa, F., Lerer, A., Bradbury, J., Chanan, G., Killeen, T., Lin, Z., Gimelshein, N., Antiga, L., et al.: Pytorch: an imperative style, high-performance deep learning library. Adv. Neural. Inf. Process. Syst. 32, 8026–8037 (2019)

28. Ramamoorthi, R., Hanrahan, P.: An efficient representation for irradiance environment maps. In: Proceedings of the 28th Annual Conference on Computer Graphics and Interactive Techniques, pp. 497–500 (2001)
29. Ramamoorthi, R., Hanrahan, P.: A signal-processing framework for inverse rendering. In: Proceedings of the 28th Annual Conference on Computer Graphics and Interactive Techniques, pp. 117–128 (2001)
30. Ravi, N., Reizenstein, J., Novotny, D., Gordon, T., Lo, W.Y., Johnson, J., Gkioxari, G.: Accelerating 3d deep learning with pytorch3d. arXiv preprint arXiv:2007.08501 (2020)
31. Richardson, E., Sela, M., Kimmel, R.: 3d face reconstruction by learning from synthetic data. In: 2016 Fourth International Conference on 3D Vision (3DV), pp. 460–469. IEEE (2016)
32. Richardson, E., Sela, M., Or-El, R., Kimmel, R.: Learning detailed face reconstruction from a single image. In: Proceedings of the IEEE conference on computer vision and pattern recognition. pp. 1259–1268 (2017)
33. Sela, M., Richardson, E., Kimmel, R.: Unrestricted facial geometry reconstruction using image-to-image translation. In: Proceedings of the IEEE International Conference on Computer Vision, pp. 1576–1585 (2017)
34. Shamai, G., Slossberg, R., Kimmel, R.: Synthesizing facial photometries and corresponding geometries using generative adversarial networks. ACM Trans. Multimed. Comput. Commun. Appl. (TOMM) 15(3s), 1–24 (2019)
35. Slossberg, R., Shamai, G., Kimmel, R.: High quality facial surface and texture synthesis via generative adversarial networks. In: Leal-Taixé, L., Roth, S. (eds.) ECCV 2018. LNCS, vol. 11131, pp. 498–513. Springer, Cham (2019). https://doi.org/10.1007/978-3-030-11015-4_36
36. Tewari, A., et al.: Fml: face model learning from videos. In: Proceedings of the IEEE Conference on Computer Vision and Pattern Recognition, pp. 10812–10822 (2019)
37. Tewari, A., et al.: Stylerig: rigging stylegan for 3d control over portrait images. In: Proceedings of the IEEE/CVF Conference on Computer Vision and Pattern Recognition, pp. 6142–6151 (2020)
38. Tewari, A., et al.: Self-supervised multi-level face model learning for monocular reconstruction at over 250 hz. In: The IEEE Conference on Computer Vision and Pattern Recognition (CVPR) (2018)
39. Tewari, A., Zollhofer, M., Kim, H., Garrido, P., Bernard, F., Perez, P., Theobalt, C.: Mofa: model-based deep convolutional face autoencoder for unsupervised monocular reconstruction. In: Proceedings of the IEEE International Conference on Computer Vision Workshops, pp. 1274–1283 (2017)
40. Tolosana, R., Vera-Rodriguez, R., Fierrez, J., Morales, A., Ortega-Garcia, J.: Deepfakes and beyond: A survey of face manipulation and fake detection. Information Fusion 64, 131–148 (2020)
41. Tran, A.T., Hassner, T., Masi, I., Paz, E., Nirkin, Y., Medioni, G.: Extreme 3d face reconstruction: Seeing through occlusions. In: Proceedings of the IEEE Conference on Computer Vision and Pattern Recognition, pp. 3935–3944 (2018)
42. Tran, L., Liu, X.: Nonlinear 3d face morphable model. In: In: Proceeding of IEEE Computer Vision and Pattern Recognition. Salt Lake City, UT, June 2018
43. Wu, X., He, R., Sun, Z., Tan, T.: A light cnn for deep face representation with noisy labels. IEEE Trans. Inf. Forensics Secur. 13(11), 2884–2896 (2018)

44. Yenamandra, T., Tewari, A., Bernard, F., Seidel, H.P., Elgharib, M., Cremers, D., Theobalt, C.: i3dmm: Deep implicit 3d morphable model of human heads. In: Proceedings of the IEEE/CVF Conference on Computer Vision and Pattern Recognition. pp. 12803–12813 (2021)
45. Zhu, X., Lei, Z., Liu, X., Shi, H., Li, S.Z.: Face alignment across large poses: a 3d solution. In: Proceedings of the IEEE Conference on Computer Vision and Pattern Recognition, pp. 146–155 (2016)

Multi-domain Learning for Updating Face Anti-spoofing Models

Xiao Guo[✉][iD], Yaojie Liu[iD], Anil Jain[iD], and Xiaoming Liu[iD]

Michigan State University, Michigan, USA
{guoxia11,liuyaoj1,jain,liuxm}@cse.msu.edu

Abstract. In this work, we study multi-domain learning for face anti-spoofing (MD-FAS), where a pre-trained FAS model needs to be updated to perform equally well on both source and target domains while only using target domain data for updating. We present a new model for MD-FAS, which addresses the forgetting issue when learning new domain data, while possessing a high level of adaptability. First, we devise a simple yet effective module, called spoof region estimator (SRE), to identify spoof traces in the spoof image. Such spoof traces reflect the source pre-trained model's responses that help upgraded models combat catastrophic forgetting during updating. Unlike prior works that estimate spoof traces which generate multiple outputs or a low-resolution binary mask, SRE produces one single, detailed pixel-wise estimate in an unsupervised manner. Secondly, we propose a novel framework, named FAS-wrapper, which transfers knowledge from the pre-trained models and seamlessly integrates with different FAS models. Lastly, to help the community further advance MD-FAS, we construct a new benchmark based on SIW, SIW-Mv2 and Oulu-NPU, and introduce four distinct protocols for evaluation, where source and target domains are different in terms of spoof type, age, ethnicity, and illumination. Our proposed method achieves superior performance on the MD-FAS benchmark than previous methods. Our code is available at https://github.com/CHELSEA234/Multi-domain-learning-FAS.

1 Introduction

Face anti-spoofing (FAS) comprises techniques that distinguish genuine human faces and faces on spoof mediums [6], such as printed photographs, screen replay, and 3D masks. FAS is a critical component of the face recognition pipeline that ensures only genuine faces are being matched. As face recognition systems are widely deployed in real world applications, a laboratory-trained FAS model is often required to deploy in a new target domain with face images from novel camera sensors, ethnicities, ages, types of spoof attacks, *etc.*, which differ from the source domain training data in the laboratory.

Supplementary Information The online version contains supplementary material available at https://doi.org/10.1007/978-3-031-19778-9_14.

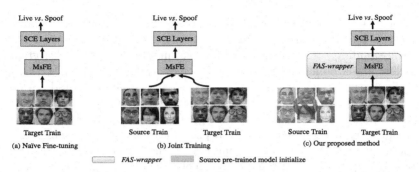

Fig. 1. We study multi-domain learning face anti-spoofing (MD-FAS), in which the model is trained only using target domain data. We first derive the general formulation of FAS models, which contains Spoof Cue Estimate Layers (SCE layers) and multi-scale feature extractor (MsFE). Based on these two components, we propose *FAS-wrapper* that can be adopted for any FAS models, as depicted in (c). (a) and (b) represent the naive fine-tuning and joint training.

In the presence of a large domain-shift [23,50,58] between the source and target domain, it is necessary to employ new target domain data for updating the pre-trained FAS model, in order to perform well in the new test environment. Meanwhile, the source domain data might be inaccessible during updating, due to data privacy issues, which happens more and more frequently for Personally Identifiable Information (PII). Secondly, the FAS model needs to be evaluated jointly on source and target domains, as spoof attacks should be detected regardless of which domain they originate from. Motivated by these challenges, the goal of this paper is to answer the following question:

How can we update a FAS model using only target domain data, so that the upgraded model can perform well in both the source and target domains?

We define this problem as multi-domain learning face anti-spoofing (MD-FAS), as depicted in Fig. 1. Notably, Domain Adaptation (DA) works [14,27, 31,38,51] mainly evaluate on the target domain, whereas MD-FAS requires a joint evaluation. Also, MD-FAS is related to Multiple Domain Learning (MDL) [17,44,45], which aims to learn a universal representation for images in many generic image domains, based on one unchanged model. In contrast, MD-FAS algorithm needs to be model-agnostic for the deployment, which means the MD-FAS algorithm can be tasked to update FAS models with various architectures or loss functions. Lastly, the source domain data is unavailable during the training in MD-FAS, which is different from previous domain generalization methods in FAS [20,36,42,53] or related manipulation detection problems [5].

There are two main challenges in MD-FAS. First, the source domain data is unavailable during the updating. As a result, MD-FAS easily suffers from the long-standing *catastrophic forgetting* [25] in learning new tasks, gradually degrading source domain performance. The most common solution [12,22,29] to such a forgetting issue is to use logits and class activation map (grad-CAM) [52] restoring prior model responses when processing the new data. However, due to the increasingly sophisticated spoof image, using logits and grad-CAM empirically fail to precisely pinpoint spatial pixel locations where spoofness occurs, unable to uncover the decision making behind the FAS model. To this end, we propose a simple yet effective module, namely *spoof region estimator (SRE)*, to identify the spoof regions given an input spoof image. Such spoof traces serve as responses of the pre-trained model, or better replacement to logits and activation maps in the MD-FAS scenario. Notably, unlike using multiple traces to pinpoint spoofness or manipulation in image [31,69], or low-resolution binary mask as manipulation indicator [10,33,64], our *SRE* offers a single and high-resolution detailed binary mask representing pixel-wise spatial locations of spoofness. Also, many anti-forgetting algorithms [8,13,40,46,49,54] usually require extra memory for restoring exemplar samples or expanding the model size, which makes them inefficient in real-world situations.

Secondly, to develop an algorithm with a high level of adaptability, it is desirable to keep original FAS models intact for the seamless deployment while changing the network parameters. Unlike methods proposed in [44,45] that specialize on the certain architecture (*e.g.*, ResNet), we first derive the general formulation after studying FAS models [30,34,37,53,63,65], then based on such a formulation we propose a novel architecture, named *FAS-wrapper* (depicted in Fig. 2), which can be deployed for FAS models with minimum changes on the architecture.

In summary, this paper makes the following contributions:

⋄ Driven by the deployment in real-world applications, we define a new problem of MD-FAS, which requires to update a pre-trained FAS model only using target domain data, yet evaluate on both source and target domains. To facilitate the MD-FAS study, we construct the FASMD benchmark, based on existing FAS datasets [7,34,36], with four evaluation protocols.

⋄ We propose a *spoof region estimator (SRE)* module to identify spoof traces in the input image. Such spoof traces serve as the prior model's responses to help tackle the *catastrophic forgetting* during the FAS model updating.

⋄ We propose a novel method, *FAS-wrapper*, which can be adopted by any FAS models for adapting to target domains while preserving the source domain performance.

⋄ Our method demonstrates superior performance over prior works, on both source and target domains in the FASMD benchmark. Moreover, our method also generalizes well in the cross-dataset scenario.

Table 1. We study the multi-domain learning face anti-spoofing, which is different to prior works.

Paradigm	Method	Source free	Learning new domain	Joint evaluation	Model agnostic	Anti-forgetting mechanism
Face anti-spoofing domain learning	SSDG [20]	✗	✓	✓	✓	N/A
	MADDoG [53]	✗	✓	✓	✓	N/A
	FSDE-FAS [61]	✗	✓	✓	✓	N/A
Anti-forgetting learning	EWC [25]	✓	✗	✓	✓	Prior-driven
	iCaRL [46]	✓	✗	✓	✓	Replay
	MAS [4]	✓	✗	✓	✓	Prior-driven
	LwF [29]	✓	✗	✓	✓	Data-driven (class prob.)
	LwM [12]	✓	✗	✓	✓	Data-driven (feat. map)
Multi-domain learning	DAN [14]	✗	✓	✗	✓	N/A
	OSBP [51]	✗	✓	✗	✓	N/A
	STA [31]	✗	✓	✗	✓	N/A
	CIDA [27]	✓	✓	✗	✗	N/A
	Seri. Adapter [44]	✓	✓	✓	✗	N/A
	Para. Adapter [45]	✓	✓	✓	✗	N/A
Multi-domain learning face anti-spoofing	FAS-wrapper (Ours)	✓	✓	✓	✓	Data-driven (spoof region)

2   Related Works

Face Anti-spoofing Domain Adaptation. In Domain Adaption (DA) [14, 27,31,38,51], many prior works assume the source data is accessible, but in our setup, source domain data is unavailable. The DA performance evaluation is biased towards the target domain data, as source domain performance may deteriorate, whereas FAS models need to excel on both source and target domain data. There are some FAS works that study the cross-domain scenario [20,36, 43,53,56,59,61]. [61] is proposed for the scenario where source and a few labeled new domain data are available, with the idea to augment target data by style transfer [62]. [53] learns a shared, indiscriminative feature space without the target domain data. Besides, [20] constructs a generalized feature space that has a compact real faces feature distribution in different domains. [36] also works on unseen domain generalization. But the same as the other works, the new domain is not based on bio-metric patterns (*i.e.*, age). Being orthogonal to prior works, the source domain data in our study is unavailable, which is a more challenging setting, as shown in Table 1.

Anti-forgetting Learning. The main challenge in MD-FAS is the long-studied *catastrophic forgetting* [25]. According to [11], there exist four solutions: replay [8,46,54], parameter isolation [13,40,49], prior-driven [4,25,28] and data-driven [12,22,29]. The replay method requires to restore a fraction of training data which breaks our source-free constraint, *e.g.*, [47] needs to store the exemplar training data. Parameter isolation methods [13,40,49] dynamically expand the network, which is also discouraged due to the memory expense. The prior-driven methods [4,25,28] are proposed based on the assumption that model parameters obey the Gaussian distribution, which is not always the case. The data-driven method [3,15,16,19] is always more favored in the community, due to its effectiveness and low computation cost. However, the development of data-driven methods is dampened in the FAS, since the commonly-used pre-trained model responses (*e.g.*, class probabilities [29] and grad-CAM [12]) fail to capture spoof regions. In this context, our SRE is a simple yet effect way of estimating the spoof trace in the image, which serves as the responses of the pre-train model.

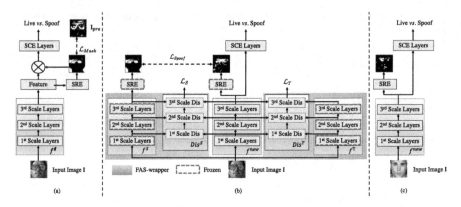

Fig. 2. (a) Given the source pre-trained model that contains feature extractor f^S, we fine-tune it with the proposed *spoof region estimator* (SRE) on the target domain data, in which we use preliminary mask ($\mathbf{I}_{pre}$) to assist the learning (see Sect. 3.2). Then, we obtain a well-trained *SRE* and a new feature extractor f^T which specializes in the target domain. (b) In *FAS-wrapper*, SRE helps f^S and updated model (f^{new}) generate binary masks indicating spoof cues, which serve as model responses given an input image ($\mathbf{I}$). $\mathcal{L}_{Spoof}$ prevents the divergence between estimated spoof traces, to combat *catastrophic forgetting*. Meanwhile, using two multi-scale discriminators (Dis^S and Dis^T), *FAS-wrapper* transfers the knowledge from two teacher models (f^S and f^T) to f^{new} via the adversarial training. (c) The update model f^{new} and SRE can be used for the inference.

Multi-domain Learning. Mostly recently, many large-scale FAS datasets with rich annotations have been collected [30,67,68] in the community, among which [30] studies cross-ethnicity and cross-gender FAS. However they work on multi-modal datasets, whereas our input is a single RGB image. In the literature, our work is similar to the multi-domain learning (MDL) [41,44,45], where a re-trained model is required to perform well on both source and target domain data. The common approaches are proposed from [44,45] based on ResNet [18], which, compared to [26,55], has advantages in increasing the abstraction by convoluation operations. In contrast, an ideal MD-FAS algorithm, such as *FAS-wrapper*, should work in a model-agnostic fashion.

3   Proposed Method

This section is organized as follows. Section 3.1 summarizes the general formulation of recent FAS models. Sectons 3.2 and 3.3 introduce the *spoof region estimator* and overall *FAS-wrapper* architecture. Training and inference procedures are reported in Sect. 3.4.

3.1   FAS Models Study

We investigate the recently proposed FAS methods (see Table 2) and observe that these FAS models have two shared characteristics. **Spoof Cue Estimate.**

Beyond treating FAS as a binary classification problem, many SOTA works emphasize on estimating spoof clues from a given image. Such spoof clues are detected in two ways: (a) optimizing the model to predict auxiliary signals such as depth map or rPPG signals [34,63,65]; (b) interpreting the spoofness from different perspectives: the method in [21] aims to disentangle the spoof noise, including color distortions and different types of artifacts, and spoof traces are interpreted in [35,37] as multi-scale and physical-based traces.

Multi-scale Feature Extractor. Majority of previous FAS methods adopt the multi-scale feature. We believe such a multi-scale structure assists in learning information at different frequency levels. This is also demonstrated in [37] that low-frequency traces (*e.g.*, makeup strokes and specular highlights) and high-frequency content (*e.g.*, Moiré patterns) are equally important for the FAS models' success.

Table 2. Summary of recent FAS models.

Method	Year	Number of scale	Spoof cue estimate
Auxiliary [34]	2018	3	Depth and rPPG signal
Despoofing [21]	2018	3	Color distortions, and display artifacts
MADD [53]	2019	3	Depth
CDCN [65]	2020	3	Depth
STDN [37]	2020	3	Color range bias, content and texture pattern, and depth
BCN [63]	2020	3	Patch, reflection and depth
PSMM-Net [30]	2021	4	Depth, RGB and infrared image
PhySTD [35]	2022	4	Additive and inpainting trace, and depth

As a result, we formalize the generic FAS model using two components: feature extractor f and spoof cue estimate (SCE) layers (or decoders) g. When f takes an input face image, denoted as $\mathbf{I}$, the output feature map at t-th layer of the feature extractor f is $f_t(\mathbf{I})$. The size of $f_t(\mathbf{I})$ is $C_t \times H_t \times W_t$, where C_t is the channel number, and H_t and W_t are respectively the height and width of feature maps.

3.2 Spoof Region Estimator

Motivation. Apart from the importance of identifying spoof cues for FAS performance, we observe that spoof trace also serves as a key reflection of how different models make the binary decision, namely, different models' activations on the input image. In other words, although different models might unanimously classify the same image as spoof, they in fact could make decisions based on distinct spatial regions, as depicted in Fig. 6. Thus, we attempt to prevent the divergence between spoof regions estimated from the new model (*i.e.*, f^{new}) and source domain pre-trained model (*i.e.*, f^S), such that we can enable f^{new} to perceive spoof cues from the perspective of f^S, thereby combating the *catastrophic forgetting* issue. To this end, we propose a *spoof region estimator* (*SRE*) to localize spatial pixel positions with spoof artifacts or covered by spoof materials.

Formulation. Let us formulate the spoof region estimate task. We denote the pixel collection in an image as $D_{\mathbf{I}} = \{(x_1, y_1), (x_2, y_2), ..., (x_n, y_n)\}$, the proposed method aims to predict the region where the area of presentation attack can be represented as a binary mask, denoted as $D_{pred} = \{(x_1, y_1'), (x_2, y_2'), ..., (x_n, y_n')\}$, where x_i, y_i and y_i' respectively represent the pixel, ground truth pixel label, and predicted label at i th pixel. Also, the spoof region estimate task can be regarded

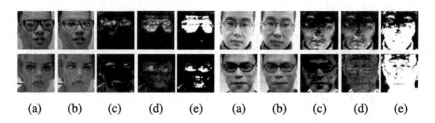

Fig. 3. The preliminary mask generation process: (a) the spoof image, (b) the live reconstruction, (c) and (d) are difference image in RGB and gray format, and (e) is the preliminary spoof mask.

as a pixel-level binary classification problem, namely pixel being live or spoof, thus we have $y_i \in \{o^{Live}, o^{Spoof}\}$. Note that $i \in \{1, 2, 3..., n\}$ and n is the total number of pixels in the image.

Method. As depicted in Fig. 2, we insert a *SRE* module in the source pre-trained model, between the feature extractor f^S and spoof cue estimate layers g^S. The region estimator converts $f^s(\mathbf{I})$ to a binary mask $\mathbf{M}$ with the size $H_{t'} \times W_{t'}$. In the beginning of the training, we create the preliminary mask to supervise *SRE* for generating the spoof region. The preliminary mask generation is based on the reconstruction method proposed in [37], as illustrated in Fig. 3. In particular, we denote input spoof image as $\mathbf{I}_{spoof}$ and use the method in [37] to reconstruct its live counterpart $\hat{I}_{live}$. By subtracting $\mathbf{I}_{spoof}$ from $\hat{I}_{live}$, and taking the absolute value of the resulting image, we obtain the different image $\mathbf{I}_d$, whose size is $C_0 \times H_0 \times W_0$ where C_0 is 3. We convert $\mathbf{I}_d$ to a gray image $\hat{\mathbf{I}}_d$, by summing along with its channel dimension. Apparently, $\hat{\mathbf{I}}_d$ has the size as $C_1 \times H_0 \times W_0$ where C_1 is 1. We assign each pixel value in the preliminary mask by applying a predefined threshold T,

$$p'_{ij} = \begin{cases} 0 & p_{ij} < T \\ 1 & p_{ij} \geq T, \end{cases} \tag{1}$$

where pixels in $\hat{\mathbf{I}}_d$ and $\mathbf{I}_{pre}$ are p_{ij} and p'_{ij} respectively.

Evidently, the supervisory signal $\mathbf{I}_{pre}$ is not the ground truth. Inspired by [10] that a model can generate the manipulation mask by itself during training procedure, we only use $\mathbf{I}_{pre}$ as the supervision at the first a few training epochs, then steer the model itself to find the optimal spoof region by optimizing towards a higher classification accuracy. More details are in Sect. 3.4.

Discussion. Firstly, we discuss the difference to prior spoof region estimate works. The previous methods [35,37] use various traces to help live or spoof image reconstruction, while our goal is to pinpoint the region with spoof artifacts, which serves as pre-trained model's responses to help the new model behave similar to the pre-trained one(s), alleviating the forgetting issue. [10] offers low-resolution binary masks as the supervisory signal, but our self-generated $\mathbf{I}_{pre}$ can only bootstrap the system. Also, [69] proposes an architecture for producing multiple masks, which is not practical in our scenario. Thus our mask generation method is different from theirs. Finally, SRE can be a plug-in module for any given FAS model, and details are in Sect. 5.4.

3.3 *FAS-Wrapper* Architecture

Motivation. We aim to deliver an update algorithm that can be effortlessly deployed to different FAS models. Thus, it is important to design a model agnostic algorithm that allows the FAS model to remain intact, thereby maintaining the original FAS model performance. Our *FAS-wrapper* operates in a model-agnostic way where only external expansions are made, largely maintaining the original FAS model's ability.

As depicted in Fig. 2, we denote the source pre-trained feature extractor f^S as *source teacher*, and the feature extractor after the fine-tuning procedure as *target teacher* (f^T). Instead of using one single teacher model like [20], we use f^S and f^T to regularize the training, offering the more informative and instructive supervision for the newly upgraded model, denoted as f^{new}. Lastly, unlike prior FAS works [20,53,61] which apply the indiscriminative loss on the final output embedding or logits from f^S, we construct multi-scale discriminators that operate at the feature-map level for aligning intermediate feature distributions of f^{new} to those of teacher models (*i.e.*, f^T and f^S). Motivations of the multi-scale discriminators are: (a) the multi-scale features, as a common FAS model attribute (Sect. 3.1), should be considered; (b) the adversarial learning can be used at the feature-map level which contains the richer information than final output logits.

Method. We construct two multi-scale discriminators, Dis^S and Dis^T, for transferring semantic knowledge from f^S and f^T to f^{new} respectively, via an adversarial learning loss. Specifically, at l-th scale, Dis_l^S and Dis_l^T take the previous discriminator output and the l-th scale feature generated from feature extractors. We use $\mathbf{d}_l^S$ and $\mathbf{d}_l^T$ to represent two discriminators' outputs at l-th level while taking teacher generated features (*i.e.*, $f_l^S(\mathbf{I})$ and $f_l^T(\mathbf{I})$), and $\mathbf{d}_l'^S$ and $\mathbf{d}_l'^T$ while taking upgraded model generated feature, $f_l^{new}(\mathbf{I})$. Therefore, the first-level discriminator output are:

$$\mathbf{d}_1^S = Dis_1^S(f_1^S(\mathbf{I})), \quad \mathbf{d}_1^T = Dis_1^T(f_1^T(\mathbf{I})), \tag{2}$$

$$\mathbf{d}_1'^S = Dis_1^S(f_1^{new}(\mathbf{I})), \quad \mathbf{d}_1'^T = Dis_1^T(f_1^{new}(\mathbf{I})), \tag{3}$$

and discriminators at following levels take the l-th ($l > 1$) backbone layer output feature and the previous level discriminator output, so we have:

$$\mathbf{d}_l^S = Dis_l^S(f_l^S(\mathbf{I})) \oplus \mathbf{d}_{l-1}^S, \quad \mathbf{d}_l^T = Dis_l^T(f_l^T(\mathbf{I})) \oplus \mathbf{d}_{l-1}^T, \tag{4}$$

$$\mathbf{d}_l'^S = Dis_l^S(f_l^{new}(\mathbf{I})) \oplus \mathbf{d}_{l-1}'^S, \quad \mathbf{d}_l'^T = Dis_l^T(f_l^{new}(\mathbf{I})) \oplus \mathbf{d}_{l-1}'^T. \tag{5}$$

After obtaining the output from the last-level discriminator, we define $\mathcal{L}_{D_S}$ and $\mathcal{L}_{D_T}$ to train Dis_s and Dis_t, and $\mathcal{L}_S$ and $\mathcal{L}_T$ to supervise f^{new}.

$$\mathcal{L}_S = -\mathbb{E}_{x_p \sim P_s}[log(\mathbf{d}_l^S)] - \mathbb{E}_{x_f \sim P_{new}}[log(1 - \mathbf{d}_l'^S)], \tag{6}$$

$$\mathcal{L}_T = -\mathbb{E}_{x_p \sim P_t}[log(\mathbf{d}_l^T)] - \mathbb{E}_{x_f \sim P_{new}}[log(1 - \mathbf{d'}_l^T)], \qquad (7)$$

$$\mathcal{L}_{D_s} = -\mathbb{E}_{x_p \sim P_s}[log(1 - \mathbf{d}_l^S)] - \mathbb{E}_{x_f \sim P_{new}}[log(\mathbf{d'}_l^S)], \qquad (8)$$

$$\mathcal{L}_{D_t} = -\mathbb{E}_{x_p \sim P_t}[log(1 - \mathbf{d}_l^T)] - \mathbb{E}_{x_f \sim P_{new}}[log(\mathbf{d'}_l^T)]. \qquad (9)$$

Discussion. The idea of adopting adversarial training on the feature map for knowledge transfer is similar to [9]. However, the method in [9] is for the online task and transferring knowledge from two models specialized in the same domain. Conversely, our case is to learn from heterogeneous models which specialize in different domains. Additionally, using two regularization terms with symmetry based on the two pre-trained models, is similar to work in [66] on the knowledge distillation topic that is different to FAS. However, the same is the effect of alleviating the imbalance between classification loss and regularization terms, as reported in [24,66].

3.4 Training and Inference

Our training procedure contains two stages, as depicted in Fig. 2. Firstly, we fine-tune given any source pre-trained FAS model with the proposed SRE, on the target dataset. We optimize the model by minimizing the ℓ_1 distance (denoted as $\mathcal{L}_{Mask}$) between the predicted binary mask $\mathbf{M}$ and $\mathbf{I}_{pre}$, and the original loss $\mathcal{L}_{Orig}$ that is used in the training procedure of original FAS models. After the fine-tuning process, we obtain well-trained SRE and a feature extractor (f^T) that is able to work reasonably well on target domain data. Secondly, we integrate the well-trained SRE with the updated model (f^{new}) and the source pre-trained model (f^S), such that we can obtain estimated spoof cues from perspectives of two models. We use $\mathcal{L}_{Spoof}$ to prevent the divergence between spoof regions estimated from f^{new} and f^S. Lastly, we use $\mathcal{L}_S$ and $\mathcal{L}_T$ as introduced in Sect. 3.3 for transferring knowledge from the f^S and f^T to f^{new}, respectively. Therefore, the overall objective function in the training is denoted as $\mathcal{L}_{total}$:

$$\mathcal{L}_{total} = \lambda_1 \mathcal{L}_{Orig} + \lambda_2 \mathcal{L}_{Spoof} + \lambda_3 \mathcal{L}_S + \lambda_4 \mathcal{L}_T, \qquad (10)$$

where λ_1-λ_4 are the weights to balance the multiple terms. In inference, we only keep new feature extract f^{new} and SRE, as depcited in Fig. 2 (c).

4 FASMD Dataset

We construct a new benchmark for MD-FAS, termed FASMD, based on SiW [34], SiW-Mv2 [36][1] and Oulu-NPU [7]. MD-FAS consists of five sub-datasets: dataset A is the source domain dataset, and B, C, D and E are four target domain datasets, which introduce unseen spoof type, new ethnicity distribution, age distribution and novel illumination, respectively. The statistics of the FASMD benchmark are reported in Table 3.

---

[1] We release SiW-Mv2 on CVLab website.

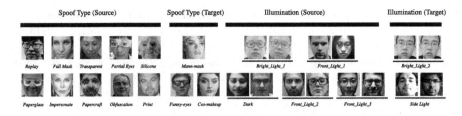

Fig. 4. Representative examples in source and target domain for spoof and illumination protocols.

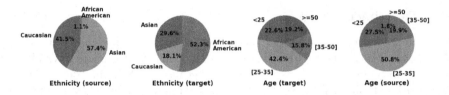

Fig. 5. The distribution of ethnicity and age in source and target domain subsets.

New Spoof Type. As illustrated in Fig. 4, target domain dataset B has novel spoof types that are excluded from the source domain dataset (A). The motivation for this design is, compared with the *print* and *replay* that are prevalent nowadays, other new spoof types are more likely to emerge and cause threats. As a result, given the fact that, five macro spoof types are introduced

Table 3. The FASMD benchmark. [Keys: eth.= ethnicity, illu.= illumination.]

Video Num/Subject Num		
Dataset ID	Train	Test
A (Source)	4, 983/603	2, 149/180
B (New spoof type)	1, 392/301	383/71
C (New eth. distribution)	1, 024/360	360/27
D (New age distribution)	892/157	411/43
E (New illu. distribution)	1, 696/260	476/40

in SIW-Mv2 (*print, replay, 3D mask, makeup* and *partial manipulation attack*), we select one micro spoof type from other three macro spoof types besides *print* and *replay* to constitute the dataset B, which are *Mannequin mask, Cosmetic makeup* and *Funny eyes*.

New Ethnicity Distribution. In reality, pre-trained FAS models can be deployed to organizations with certain ethnicity distribution (*e.g.*, African American sports club). Therefore, we manually annotate the ethnicity information of each subject in three datasets, then devise the ethnicity protocol where dataset A has only 1.1% African American samples, but this proportion increases to 52.3% in dataset C, as depicted in Fig. 5.

New Age Distribution, Likewise, a FAS model that is trained on source domain data full of college students needs to be deployed to the group with a different age distribution, such as a senior care or kindergartens. We estimate the age information by the off-the-shelf tool [48], and construct dataset D to have a large portion of subjects over 50 years old, as seen in Fig. 5.

New Illumination. Oulu-NPU dataset has three different illumination sessions, and we use methods proposed in [71] to estimate the lighting condition for each sample in SIW and SIW-Mv2 datasets. Then we apply K-means [39] to cluster them into K groups. For the best clustering performance, we use "eblow method" [57] to decide the value of K. We annotate different illumination sessions as *Dark*, three *Front Light*, *Side Light*, and two *Bright Light* (Fig. 4), then dataset E introduces the new illumination distribution.

5   Experimental Evaluations

5.1   Experiment Setup

We evaluate our proposed method on the FASMD dataset. In Sect. 5.3, we report *FAS-wrapper* performance with different FAS models, and we choose PhySTD [35] as the FAS model for analysis in Sect. 5.2, because PhySTD has demonstrated competitive empirical FAS results. Firstly, we compare to anti-forgetting methods (*e.g.*, LwF [29], MAS [4] and LwM [12]). Specifically, based on the architecture of PhySTD, we concatenate feature maps generated by last convolution layers in different branches, then employ Global Average Pooling and fully connected (FC) layers to convert concatenated features into a 2-dimensional vector. We fix the source pre-trained model weights and only train added FC layers in the original FAS task, as a binary classifier. In this way, we can apply methods in [4,12,29] to this binary classifier. For multi-domain learning methods (*e.g.*, Serial and Parallel Res-Adapter [44,45]), we choose the 1×1 kernel size convolution filter as the adapter and incorporate into the PhySTD as described in original works (see details in the supplementary material). We use standard FAS metrics to measure the performance, which are Attack Presentation Classification Error Rate (APCER), Bona Fide Presentation Classification Error Rate (BPCER), and Average Classification Error Rate ACER [1], Receiver Operating Characteristic (ROC) curve.

Implementation Details. We use Tensorflow [2] in implementation, and we run experiments on a single NVIDIA TITAN X GPU. In the source pre-train stage, we use a learning rate 3e–4 with a decay rate 0.99 for every epoch and the total epoch number is 180. We set the mini-batch size as 8, where each mini-batch contains 4 live images and 4 spoof images (*e.g.*, 2 SIW-Mv2 images, 1 image in SIW and OULU-NPU, respectively). Secondly, we keep the same hyper-parameter setting as the pre-train stage, fine-tune the source domain pre-trained model with *SRE* at a learning rate 1e–6. The overall FAS-wrapper is trained with a learning rate 1e–7.

5.2   Main Results

Table 4 reports the detailed performance from different models on all four protocols. Overall, our method surpasses the previous best method on source and target domain evaluation in *all categories*, with the only exception of the target domain performance in the illumination protocol (0.3% worse than [12]).

Table 4. The main performance reported in TPR@FPR=0.5%. Scores before and after "/" are performance on the source and target domains respectively. [Key: Best, Second Best, except for two teacher models and upper bound performance in the first three rows (■)].

Method	Training data	Spoof	Age	Ethnicity	Illumination	Average
Upper Bound	Source + Target	89.5/52.5	86.7/82.3	87.7/62.8	89.0/74.4	88.2/68.0
Source Teacher	Source	84.2/39.8	84.2/72.8	84.2/59.2	84.2/64.4	84.2/59.1
Target Teacher	Target	73.5/51.5	67.9/80.8	77.2/61.9	65.0/71.8	70.9/66.3
LwF [29]	Target	74.8/50.8	71.7/77.9	71.0/59.8	65.3/69.2	70.7/64.4
LwM [12]	Target	76.5/51.0	71.5/80.0	76.0/62.0	71.0/71.8	73.8/**65.9**
MAS [4]	Target	73.4/48.8	68.3/78.6	73.5/60.9	66.0/65.9	71.4/63.5
Seri. RA [44]	Target	74.3/**51.4**	72.6/79.8	72.0/61.7	67.0/70.4	71.5/65.8
Para. RA [45]	Target	75.5/51.2	73.0/79.7	72.0/61.5	68.0/69.3	72.1/65.4
Ours - $(\mathcal{L}_T + \mathcal{L}_S)$	Target	80.3/50.5	77.1/79.0	75.1/61.3	77.2/69.4	77.4/65.1
Ours - $\mathcal{L}_T$	Target	**80.5**/50.8	**79.0**/79.4	**76.1**/61.5	**78.3**/70.2	**78.5**/77.4
Ours - $\mathcal{L}_{Spoof}$	Target	75.5/51.0	70.4/79.3	74.9/**62.1**	70.1/70.0	72.7/65.6
Ours	Target	81.8/51.5	79.5/80.6	76.8/62.3	79.6/**71.5**	79.4/66.4

More importantly, regarding performance on source domain data, it is impressive that our method surpasses the best previous method in all protocols by a large margin (*e.g.*, 5.3%, 6.5%, 0.8% and 8.6%, and 5.6% on average). We believe that, the proposed SRE can largely alleviate the *catastrophic forgetting* as mentioned above, thereby yielding the superior source domain performance than prior works. However, the improvement diminishes on the new ethnicity protocol. One possible reason is that the *print* and *replay* attacks account for a large portion of data in new ethnicity distribution, and different methods, performance on these two common presentation attacks are similar.

Additionally, Table 5 reports the average performance on four protocols in terms of ACPER, BCPER and ACER. Our method still remains the best, besides BPCER on the target domain performance. It is worth mentioning that we have 4.2% APCER on source domain data and 8.9% ACER on target domain data, which are better than best results from prior works, namely 5.6% APCER in [12] and 11.0% ACER in [45]. Furthermore, in Sect. 5.4, we examine the adaptability of our proposed method, by incorporating it with different FAS methods.

Table 5. The average performance of the different methods in four protocols. The scores before and after "/" are performance on source and target domains. [Key: Best, Second Best, except for two teacher models and upper bound performance in first three rows (■)].

Method	APCER (%)	BCPER (%)	ACER (%)
Upper Bound	3.7/4.5	5.8/13.3	5.2/13.3
Source Teacher	4.1/4.8	7.4/23.0	6.1/23.0
Target Teacher	6.6/4.6	6.4/14.2	5.5/10.0
LwF [29]	6.4/5.6	8.1/15.9	6.8/11.2
LwM [12]	5.6/**4.3**	8.0/14.0	**6.3**/11.1
MAS [4]	6.7/5.3	8.4/13.9	6.8/11.2
Seri. RA [44]	6.3/5.0	8.4/15.0	6.7/11.3
Para. RA [45]	6.2/7.6	8.4/13.4	6.7/11.0
Ours - $(\mathcal{L}_S + \mathcal{L}_T)$	4.8/6.5	9.1/15.6	6.9/11.1
Ours - $\mathcal{L}_T$	**4.5**/5.2	8.3/14.9	6.4/**10.1**
Ours - $\mathcal{L}_{Spoof}$	6.0/8.8	**8.0**/14.2	7.0/11.5
Ours	4.2/4.2	7.8/**13.5**	6.0/8.9

Table 6. (a) The *FAS-wrapper* performance with different FAS models; (b) Performance of adopting different architecture design choices.

TPR@FPR=0.5% (Source/Target)	PhySTD [35]	CDCN [65]	Auxi.-CNN [34]
Naive Fine.	70.9/66.3	69.2/63.2	63.3/61.3
Full (Ours)	**79.4/66.4**	**74.8/62.7**	**70.3**/61.3
Full - $\mathcal{L}_{Spoof}$	72.7/65.6	74.1/62.5	69.0/**61.4**
Full - $\mathcal{L}_{D_i}$	78.5/64.4	73.1/62.3	69.1/61.3
Full - $(\mathcal{L}_T + \mathcal{L}_S)$	77.3/65.1	71.6/62.1	65.6/61.3

	TPR@FPR=0.5%
$\mathcal{L}_{Spoof}$ + Multi-disc. (Ours)	**79.4/66.4**
$\mathcal{L}_{Spoof}$ + Multi-disc. (same weights)	75.0/65.8
$\mathcal{L}_{Spoof}$ + Single disc. (concat.)	74.4/66.0
$\mathcal{L}_{Spoof}$ + [60]	65.2/63.2

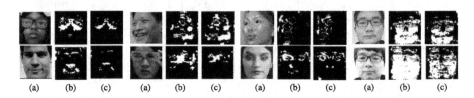

(a)   (b)   (c)   (a)   (b)   (c)   (a)   (b)   (c)   (a)   (b)   (c)

Fig. 6. Spoof region estimated from different models. Given input image (a), (b) and (c) are model responses from [35] and [34], respectively. Detailed analyses in Sect. 5.4.

Ablation Study Using $\mathcal{L}_{Spoof}$. *SRE* plays a key role in *FAS-wrapper* for learning the new spoof type, as ablating the $\mathcal{L}_{Spoof}$ largely decreases the source domain performance, namely from 79.4% to 72.7% on TPR@FPR = 0.5% (Table 4) and 1.8% on APCER (Table 5). Such a performance degradation supports our statement that, $\mathcal{L}_{Spoof}$ prevents divergence between spoof traces estimated from the source teacher and the upgraded model, which helps to combat the *catastrophic forgetting* issue, and maintain the source domain performance.

Ablation Study Using $\mathcal{L}_S$ and $\mathcal{L}_T$. Without the adversarial learning loss ($\mathcal{L}_S + \mathcal{L}_T$), the model performance constantly decreases, according to Table 4, although such impacts are less than removal of $\mathcal{L}_{Spoof}$, which still causes 2.0% and 1.3% average performance drop on source and target domains. Finally, we have a regularization term $\mathcal{L}_T$ which also contributes to performance. That is, removing $\mathcal{L}_T$ hinders the FAS performance (*e.g.*, 1.0% ACER on target domain performance), as reported in Table 5.

5.3   Adaptability Analysis

We apply *FAS-wrapper* on three different FAS methods: Auxi.-CNN [34], CDCN [65] and PhySTD [35]. CDCN uses a special convolution (*i.e.*, Central Difference Convolution) and Auxi.-CNN is the flagship work that learns FAS via auxiliary supervisions. As shown in Table 6 (a), *FAS-wrapper* can consistently improve the performance of naive fine-tuning. When ablating the $\mathcal{L}_{Spoof}$, PhySTD [35] experiences the large performance drop (6.7%) on the source domain, indicating the importance of SRE in the learning the new domain. Likewise, the removal of adversarial learning loss (*e.g.*, $\mathcal{L}_T + \mathcal{L}_S$) leads to difficulty in preserving the source domain performance, which can be shown from, on the source domain, CDCN [65] decreases 3.2% and Auxi-CNN [34] decreases 4.7%.

This means dual teacher models, in the *FAS-wrapper*, trained with adversarial learning benefit the overall FAS performance. Also, we visualize the spoof region generated from *SRE* with [34,35] in Fig. 6. We can see the spoof cues are different, which supports our hypothesis that, although FAS models make the same final binary prediction, they internally identify spoofness in different areas.

5.4   Algorithm Analysis

Spoof Region Visualization. We feed output features from different models (*i.e.*, f^S, f^T and f^{new}) to a well-trained *SRE* to generate the spoof region, as depicted in Fig. 7. In general, the f^S produces more accurate activated spoof regions on the source domain images. For example, two source images in new spoof category have detected makeup spoofness on eyebrows and mouth (first row) and more intensive activation on the funny eye region (second row). f^T has the better spoof cues estimated on the target domain image. For example, two target images in the new spoof category, where spoofness estimated from f^T is stronger and more comprehensive; in the novel ethnicity category, the spoofness covers the larger region. With $\mathcal{L}_{Spoof}$, the updated model (f^{new}) identifies the spoof traces in a more accurate way.

Explanability. We compare *SRE* with the work which generate binary masks indicating the spoofness [10], and works which explain how a model makes a binary classification decision [52,70]. In Fig. 8, we can observe that our generated spoof traces can better capture the manipulation area, regardless of spoof types. For example, in the first *print* attack image, the entire face is captured as spoof in our method but other three methods fail to achieve so. Also, our binary mask is more detailed and of higher resolution than that of [10], and more accurate and robust than [52,70]. Notably, we do not include works in [35,37,69] which use many outputs to identify spoof cues.

Architecture Design. We compare to some other architecture design choices, such as all multi-scale discriminators with the same weights, concatenation of

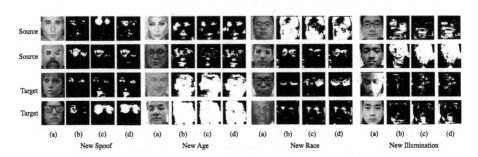

Fig. 7. Given the input spoof image (a), spoof regions generated by *SRE* with two teacher models (*i.e.*, f^S and f^T) in (b) and (c), and the new upgraded model (f^{new}) in (d), for different protocols. Detailed analyses are in Sect. 5.4.

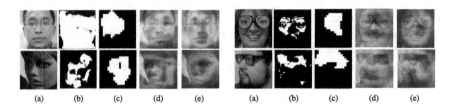

Fig. 8. Different spoof estimate methods. Given input image (a), (b) and (c) are the spoof regions estimated from ours and [10]. (d) and (e) are the activated map from methods in [52,70].

different scale features and one single discriminator. Moreover, we use correlation similarity table in [60] instead of multi-scale discriminators for transfering knowledge from f^S and f^T to f^{new}. Table 6(b) demonstrates the superiority of our architectural design.

5.5   Cross-Dataset Study

We evaluate our methods in the cross-dataset scenario and compare to SSDG [20] and MADDG [53]. Specifically, we denote OULU-NPU [7] as O, SIW [34] as S, SIW-Mv2 [36] as M, and HKBU-MARs [32] as H. We use three datasets as source domains for training and one remaining dataset for testing. We train three individual source domain teacher models on three source datasets respectively. Then, as depicted in Fig. 9, inside *FAS-wrapper*, three multi-scale discriminators are employed to transfer knowledge from three teacher models to the updated model f^{new} which is then evaluated on the target domain. Notably, we remove proposed *SRE* in this cross-dataset scenario, as there is no need to restore the prior model responses.

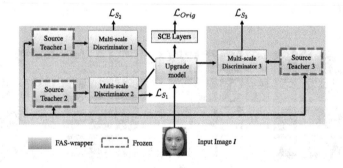

Fig. 9. We adapt *FAS-wrapper* for the cross-dataset scenario.

Table 7. The cross-dataset comparison.

	O&M&H to S		O&W&H to M		M&S&H to O		M&S&O to H	
	HTER(%)	AUC(%)	HTER(%)	AUC(%)	HTER(%)	AUC(%)	HTER(%)	AUC(%)
MADDG [53]	16.7	90.5	50.3	60.7	17.6	73.0	33.2	73.5
SSDG-M [20]	**11.1**	93.4	29.6	67.1	**12.1**	**89.0**	**25.0**	82.5
SSDG-R [20]	13.3	93.4	29.3	**69.5**	13.3	83.4	28.9	81.0
Ours	15.4	**93.6**	**28.1**	68.4	14.8	85.6	27.1	**83.8**

The results are reported in Table 7, indicating that our *FAS-wrapper* also exhibits a comparable performance on the cross-dataset scenario as prior works.

6 Conclusion

We study the multi-domain learning face anti-spoofing (MD-FAS), which requires the model perform well on both source and novel target domains, after updating the source domain pre-trained FAS model only with target domain data. We first summarize the general form of FAS models, then based on which we develop a new architecture, *FAS-wrapper*. *FAS-wrapper* contains spoof region estimator which identifies the spoof traces that help combat *catastrophic forgetting* while learning new domain knowledge, and the *FAS-wrapper* exhibits a high level of flexibility, as it can be adopted by different FAS models. The performance is evaluated on our newly-constructed FASMD benchmark, which is also the first MD-FAS dataset in the community.

Acknowledgement. This research is based upon work supported by the Office of the Director of National Intelligence (ODNI), Intelligence Advanced Research Projects Activity (IARPA), via IARPA R&D Contract No. 2017-17020200004. The views and conclusions contained herein are those of the authors and should not be interpreted as necessarily representing the official policies or endorsements, either expressed or implied, of the ODNI, IARPA, or the U.S. Government. The U.S. Government is authorized to reproduce and distribute reprints for Governmental purposes notwithstanding any copyright annotation thereon.

References

1. international organization for standardization. Iso/iec jtc 1/sc 37 biometrics: Information technology biometric presentation attack detection part 1: Framework. https://www.iso.org/obp/ui/iso. Accessed 3 Mar 2022
2. Abadi, M., et al.: TensorFlow: a system for large-scale machine learning. In: OSDI (2016)
3. AbdAlmageed, W., et al.: Assessment of facial morphologic features in patients with congenital adrenal hyperplasia using deep learning. JAMA Netw. Open **3** (2020)

4. Aljundi, R., Babiloni, F., Elhoseiny, M., Rohrbach, M., Tuytelaars, T.: Memory aware synapses: learning what (not) to forget. In: Ferrari, V., Hebert, M., Sminchisescu, C., Weiss, Y. (eds.) ECCV 2018. LNCS, vol. 11207, pp. 144–161. Springer, Cham (2018). https://doi.org/10.1007/978-3-030-01219-9_9

5. Asnani, V., Yin, X., Hassner, T., Liu, S., Liu, X.: Proactive image manipulation detection. In: CVPR (2022)

6. Atoum, Y., Liu, Y., Jourabloo, A., Liu, X.: Face anti-spoofing using patch and depth-based CNNS. In: IJCB (2017)

7. Boulkenafet, Z., Komulainen, J., Li, L., Feng, X., Hadid, A.: OULU-NPU: a mobile face presentation attack database with real-world variations. In: IEEE International Conference on Automatic Face and Gesture Recognition (2017)

8. Chaudhry, A., Ranzato, M., Rohrbach, M., Elhoseiny, M.: Efficient lifelong learning with a-gem. ICLR (2019)

9. Chung, I., Park, S., Kim, J., Kwak, N.: Feature-map-level online adversarial knowledge distillation. In: ICML (2020)

10. Dang*, H., Liu*, F., Stehouwer*, J., Liu, X., Jain, A.: On the detection of digital face manipulation. In: CVPR (2020)

11. Delange, M., et al.: A continual learning survey: Defying forgetting in classification tasks. In: TPAMI (2021)

12. Dhar, P., Singh, R.V., Peng, K.C., Wu, Z., Chellappa, R.: Learning without memorizing. In: CVPR (2019)

13. Fernando, C., et al.: PathNet: evolution channels gradient descent in super neural networks. arXiv preprint arXiv:1701.08734 (2017)

14. Ganin, Y., et al.: Domain-adversarial training of neural networks. J. Mach. Learn. Res. **17**, 2096–2030 (2016)

15. Guo, X., Choi, J.: Human motion prediction via learning local structure representations and temporal dependencies. In: AAAI (2019)

16. Guo, X., Mirzaalian, H., Sabir, E., Jaiswal, A., Abd-Almageed, W.: Cord19sts: Covid-19 semantic textual similarity dataset. arXiv preprint arXiv:2007.02461 (2020)

17. Guo, Y., Li, Y., Wang, L., Rosing, T.: Depthwise convolution is all you need for learning multiple visual domains. In: AAAI (2019)

18. He, K., Zhang, X., Ren, S., Sun, J.: Deep residual learning for image recognition. In: CVPR (2016)

19. Hsu, I., et al.: Discourse-level relation extraction via graph pooling. arXiv preprint arXiv:2101.00124 (2021)

20. Jia, Y., Zhang, J., Shan, S., Chen, X.: Single-side domain generalization for face anti-spoofing. In: CVPR (2020)

21. Jourabloo, A., Liu, Y., Liu, X.: Face de-spoofing: Anti-spoofing via noise modeling. In: ECCV (2018)

22. Jung, H., Ju, J., Jung, M., Kim, J.: Less-forgetting learning in deep neural networks. arXiv preprint arXiv:1607.00122 (2016)

23. Khosla, A., Zhou, T., Malisiewicz, T., Efros, A.A., Torralba, A.: Undoing the damage of dataset bias. In: Fitzgibbon, A., Lazebnik, S., Perona, P., Sato, Y., Schmid, C. (eds.) ECCV 2012. LNCS, vol. 7572, pp. 158–171. Springer, Heidelberg (2012). https://doi.org/10.1007/978-3-642-33718-5_12

24. Kim, J.Y., Choi, D.W.: Split-and-bridge: Adaptable class incremental learning within a single neural network. In: AAAI (2021)

25. Kirkpatrick, J., et al.: Overcoming catastrophic forgetting in neural networks. In: Proceedings of the National Academy of Sciences (2017)

26. Krizhevsky, A., Sutskever, I., Hinton, G.E.: ImageNet classification with deep convolutional neural networks. In: NeuriPS (2012)
27. Kundu, J.N., Venkatesh, R.M., Venkat, N., Revanur, A., Babu, R.V.: Class-incremental domain adaptation. In: ECCV (2020)
28. Lee, S.W., Kim, J.H., Jun, J., Ha, J.W., Zhang, B.T.: Overcoming catastrophic forgetting by incremental moment matching. In: NeurIps (2017)
29. Li, Z., Hoiem, D.: Learning without forgetting. In: TPAMI (2017)
30. Liu, A., Tan, Z., Wan, J., Escalera, S., Guo, G., Li, S.Z.: URF CeFA: a benchmark for multi-modal cross-ethnicity face anti-spoofing. In: WACV (2021)
31. Liu, H., Cao, Z., Long, M., Wang, J., Yang, Q.: Separate to adapt: open set domain adaptation via progressive separation. In: CVPR (2019)
32. Liu, S., Yang, B., Yuen, P.C., Zhao, G.: A 3d mask face anti-spoofing database with real world variations. In: CVPR Workshop (2016)
33. Liu, X., Liu, Y., Chen, J., Liu, X.: PSSC-Net: progressive spatio-channel correlation network for image manipulation detection and localization. In: T-CSVT (2022)
34. Liu, Y., Jourabloo, A., Liu, X.: Learning deep models for face anti-spoofing: Binary or auxiliary supervision. In: CVPR (2018)
35. Liu, Y., Liu, X.: Physics-guided spoof trace disentanglement for generic face anti-spoofing. In: TPAMI (2022)
36. Liu, Y., Stehouwer, J., Jourabloo, A., Liu, X.: Deep tree learning for zero-shot face anti-spoofing. In: CVPR (2019)
37. Liu, Y., Stehouwer, J., Liu, X.: On disentangling spoof trace for generic face anti-spoofing. In: Vedaldi, A., Bischof, H., Brox, T., Frahm, J.-M. (eds.) ECCV 2020. LNCS, vol. 12363, pp. 406–422. Springer, Cham (2020). https://doi.org/10.1007/978-3-030-58523-5_24
38. Long, M., Cao, Y., Wang, J., Jordan, M.: Learning transferable features with deep adaptation networks. In: ICML (2015)
39. MacQueen, J., et al.: Some methods for classification and analysis of multivariate observations. In: Proceedings of the Fifth Berkeley Symposium on Mathematical Statistics and Probability (1967)
40. Mallya, A., Lazebnik, S.: Packnet: Adding multiple tasks to a single network by iterative pruning. In: CVPR (2018)
41. Mancini, M., Ricci, E., Caputo, B., Bulò, S.R.: Adding new tasks to a single network with weight transformations using binary masks. In: Leal-Taixé, L., Roth, S. (eds.) ECCV 2018. LNCS, vol. 11130, pp. 180–189. Springer, Cham (2019). https://doi.org/10.1007/978-3-030-11012-3_14
42. Qin, Y., et al.: Learning meta model for zero-and few-shot face anti-spoofing. In: AAAI (2020)
43. Quan, R., Wu, Y., Yu, X., Yang, Y.: Progressive transfer learning for face anti-spoofing. In: TIP (2021)
44. Rebuffi, S.A., Bilen, H., Vedaldi, A.: Learning multiple visual domains with residual adapters. In: NeurIPS (2017)
45. Rebuffi, S.A., Bilen, H., Vedaldi, A.: Efficient parametrization of multi-domain deep neural networks. In: CVPR (2018)
46. Rebuffi, S.A., Kolesnikov, A., Sperl, G., Lampert, C.H.: ICARL: incremental classifier and representation learning. In: CVPR (2017)
47. Rostami, M., Spinoulas, L., Hussein, M., Mathai, J., Abd-Almageed, W.: Detection and continual learning of novel face presentation attacks. In: ICCV (2021)
48. Rothe, R., Timofte, R., Van Gool, L.: DEX: deep expectation of apparent age from a single image. In: ICCV Workshops (2015)D

49. Rusu, A.A., et al.: Progressive neural networks. arXiv preprint arXiv:1606.04671 (2016)
50. Saenko, K., Kulis, B., Fritz, M., Darrell, T.: Adapting Visual category models to new domains. In: Daniilidis, K., Maragos, P., Paragios, N. (eds.) ECCV 2010. LNCS, vol. 6314, pp. 213–226. Springer, Heidelberg (2010). https://doi.org/10. 1007/978-3-642-15561-1_16
51. Saito, K., Yamamoto, S., Ushiku, Y., Harada, T.: Open set domain adaptation by backpropagation. In: ECCV (2018)
52. Selvaraju, R.R., Cogswell, M., Das, A., Vedantam, R., Parikh, D., Batra, D.: Grad-CAM: visual explanations from deep networks via gradient-based localization. International Journal of Computer Vision **128**(2), 336–359 (2019). https:// doi.org/10.1007/s11263-019-01228-7
53. Shao, R., Lan, X., Li, J., Yuen, P.C.: Multi-adversarial discriminative deep domain generalization for face presentation attack detection. In: CVPR (2019)
54. Shin, H., Lee, J.K., Kim, J., Kim, J.: Continual learning with deep generative replay. NeurIPS (2017)
55. Simonyan, K., Zisserman, A.: Very deep convolutional networks for large-scale image recognition. arXiv preprint arXiv:1409.1556 (2014)
56. Stehouwer, J., Jourabloo, A., Liu, Y., Liu, X.: Noise modeling, synthesis and classification for generic object anti-spoofing. In: CVPR (2020)
57. Thorndike, R.L.: Who belongs in the family? Psychometrika **18**, 267–276 (1953)
58. Torralba, A., Efros, A.A.: Unbiased look at dataset bias. In: CVPR (2011)
59. Tu, X., Ma, Z., Zhao, J., Du, G., Xie, M., Feng, J.: Learning generalizable and identity-discriminative representations for face anti-spoofing. In: TIST (2020)
60. Tung, F., Mori, G.: Similarity-preserving knowledge distillation. In: ICCV (2019)
61. Yang, B., Zhang, J., Yin, Z., Shao, J.: Few-shot domain expansion for face anti-spoofing. arXiv preprint arXiv:2106.14162 (2021)
62. Yoo, J., Uh, Y., Chun, S., Kang, B., Ha, J.W.: Photorealistic style transfer via wavelet transforms. In: ICCV (2019)
63. Yu, Z., Li, X., Niu, X., Shi, J., Zhao, G.: Face anti-spoofing with human material perception. In: Vedaldi, A., Bischof, H., Brox, T., Frahm, J.-M. (eds.) ECCV 2020. LNCS, vol. 12352, pp. 557–575. Springer, Cham (2020). https://doi.org/10.1007/ 978-3-030-58571-6_33
64. Yu, Z., Li, X., Shi, J., Xia, Z., Zhao, G.: Revisiting pixel-wise supervision for face anti-spoofing. Behavior, and Identity Science, IEEE Trans. Biomet. 3, 285–295 (2021)
65. Yu, Z., et al.: Searching central difference convolutional networks for face anti-spoofing. In: CVPR (2020)
66. Zhang, J., et al.: Class-incremental learning via deep model consolidation. In: WACV (2020)
67. Zhang, S., et al.: CASIA-SURF: a large-scale multi-modal benchmark for face anti-spoofing. Behavior, and Identity Science, IEEE Trans. Biomet. **2**, 182–193 (2020)
68. Zhang, Y., et al.: CelebA-Spoof: large-scale face anti-spoofing dataset with rich annotations. In: Vedaldi, A., Bischof, H., Brox, T., Frahm, J.-M. (eds.) ECCV 2020. LNCS, vol. 12357, pp. 70–85. Springer, Cham (2020). https://doi.org/10. 1007/978-3-030-58610-2_5

69. Zhao, H., Zhou, W., Chen, D., Wei, T., Zhang, W., Yu, N.: Multi-attentional deepfake detection. In: CVFPR (2021)
70. Zhou, B., Khosla, A., Lapedriza, A., Oliva, A., Torralba, A.: Learning deep features for discriminative localization. In: CVPR (2016)
71. Zhou, H., Hadap, S., Sunkavalli, K., Jacobs, D.W.: Deep single-image portrait relighting. In: ICCV (2019)

Towards Metrical Reconstruction
of Human Faces

Wojciech Zielonka$^{(\boxtimes)}$, Timo Bolkart, and Justus Thies

Max Planck Institute for Intelligent Systems, Tübingen, Germany
`wojciech.zielonka@tuebingen.mpg.de`

Abstract. Face reconstruction and tracking is a building block of numerous applications in AR/VR, human-machine interaction, as well as medical applications. Most of these applications rely on a metrically correct prediction of the shape, especially, when the reconstructed subject is put into a metrical context (i.e., when there is a reference object of known size). A metrical reconstruction is also needed for any application that measures distances and dimensions of the subject (e.g., to virtually fit a glasses frame). State-of-the-art methods for face reconstruction from a single image are trained on large 2D image datasets in a self-supervised fashion. However, due to the nature of a perspective projection they are not able to reconstruct the actual face dimensions, and even predicting the average human face outperforms some of these methods in a metrical sense. To learn the actual shape of a face, we argue for a supervised training scheme. Since there exists no large-scale 3D dataset for this task, we annotated and unified small- and medium-scale databases. The resulting unified dataset is still a medium-scale dataset with more than 2k identities and training purely on it would lead to overfitting. To this end, we take advantage of a face recognition network pretrained on a large-scale 2D image dataset, which provides distinct features for different faces and is robust to expression, illumination, and camera changes. Using these features, we train our face shape estimator in a supervised fashion, inheriting the robustness and generalization of the face recognition network. Our method, which we call MICA (MetrIC fAce), outperforms the state-of-the-art reconstruction methods by a large margin, both on current non-metric benchmarks as well as on our metric benchmarks (15% and 24% lower average error on NoW, respectively). **Project website:** https://zielon.github.io/mica/

1 Introduction

Learning to reconstruct 3D content from 2D imagery is an ill-posed inverse problem [4]. State-of-the-art RGB-based monocular facial reconstruction and tracking methods [18,23] are based on self-supervised training, exploiting an underlying metrical face model which is constructed using a large-scale dataset

Supplementary Information The online version contains supplementary material available at https://doi.org/10.1007/978-3-031-19778-9_15.

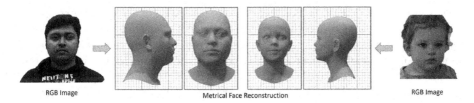

RGB Image   Metrical Face Reconstruction   RGB Image

Fig. 1. An RGB image of a subject serves as input to MICA, which predicts a metrical reconstruction of the human face. Images from NoW [59], StyleGan2 [38].

of registered 3D scans (e.g., 33000 scans for the FLAME [47] model). However, when assuming a perspective camera, the scale of the face is ambiguous since a large face can be modeled by a small face that is close to the camera or a gigantic face that is far away. Formally, a point $x \in \mathbb{R}^3$ of the face is projected to a point $p \in \mathbb{R}^2$ on the image plane with the projective function $\pi(\cdot)$ and a rigid transformation composed of a rotation $R \in \mathbb{R}^{3\times3}$ and a translation $t \in \mathbb{R}^3$:

$$p = \pi(R \cdot x + t) = \pi(s \cdot (R \cdot x + t)) = \pi(R \cdot (s \cdot x) + (s \cdot t))).$$

The perspective projection is invariant to the scaling factor $s \in \mathbb{R}$, and thus, if x is scaled by s, the rigid transformation can be adapted such that the point still projects onto the same pixel position p by scaling the translation t by s. In consequence, face reconstruction methods might result in a good 2D alignment but can fail to reconstruct the metrical 3D surface and the meaningful metrical location in space. However, a metric 3D reconstruction is needed in any scenario where the face is put into a metric context. E.g., when the reconstructed human is inserted into a virtual reality (VR) application or when the reconstructed geometry is used for augmented reality (AR) applications (teleconferencing in AR/VR, virtual try-on, etc.). In these scenarios, the methods mentioned above fail since they do not reproduce the correct scale and shape of the human face. In the current literature [25,59,83], we also observe that methods use evaluation measurements not done in a metrical space. Specifically, to compare a reconstructed face to a reference scan, the estimation is aligned to the scan via Procrustes analysis, including an optimal scaling factor. This scaling factor favors the estimation methods that are not metrical, and the reported numbers in the publications are misleading for real-world applications (relative vs. absolute/metrical error). In contrast, we aim for a metrically correct reconstruction and evaluation that directly compares the predicted geometry to the reference data without any scaling applied in a post-processing step which is fundamentally different. As discussed above, the self-supervised methods in the literature do not aim and cannot reconstruct a metrically correct geometry. However, training these methods in a supervised fashion is not possible because of the lack of data (no large-scale 3D dataset is available). Training on a small- or medium-scale 3D dataset will lead to overfitting of the networks (see study in the supplemental document). To this end, we propose a hybrid method that can be trained on a medium-scale 3D dataset, reusing powerful descriptors from a pretrained face recognition network (trained on a large-scale 2D dataset). Specifically, we propose the usage of existing 3D datasets like LYHM [16],

FaceWarehouse [10], Stirling [26], etc., that contain RGB imagery and corresponding 3D reconstructions to learn a metrical reconstruction of the human head. To use these 3D datasets, significant work has been invested to unify the 3D data (i.e., to annotate and non-rigidly fit the FLAME model to the different datasets). This unification provides us with meshes that all share the FLAME topology. Our method predicts the head geometry in a neutral expression, only given a single RGB image of a human subject in any pose or expression. To generalize to unseen in the wild images, we use a state-of-the-art face recognition network [17] that provides a feature descriptor for our geometry-estimating network. This recognition network is robust to head poses, different facial expressions, occlusions, illumination changes, and different focal lengths, thus, being ideal for our task (see Fig. 3). Based on this feature, we predict the geometry of the face with neutral expression within the face space spanned by FLAME [47], effectively disentangling shape and expression. As an application, we demonstrate that our metrical face reconstruction estimator can be integrated in a new analysis-by-synthesis face tracking framework which removes the requirement of an identity initialization phase [70]. Given the metrical face shape estimation, the face tracker is able to predict the face motion in a metrical space.

In summary, we have the following contributions:

- a dataset of 3D face reference data for about 2300 subjects, built by unifying existing small- and medium-scale datasets under common FLAME topology.
- a metrical face shape predictor—MICA—which is invariant to expression, pose and illumination, by exploiting generalized identity features from a face recognition network and supervised learning.
- a hybrid face tracker that is based on our (learned) metrical reconstruction of the face shape and an optimization-based facial expression tracking.
- a metrical evaluation protocol and benchmark, including a discussion on the current evaluation practise.

2   Related Work

Reconstructing human faces and heads from monocular RGB, RGB-D, or multi-view data is a well-explored field at the intersection of computer vision and computer graphics. Zollhöfer et al. [85] provide an extensive review of reconstruction methods, focusing on optimization-based techniques that follow the principle of analysis-by-synthesis. Primarily, the approaches that are based on monocular inputs are based on a prior of face shape and appearance [6,7,27,28,40,66–71,77,78]. The seminal work of Blanz et al. [8] introduced such a 3D morphable model (3DMM), which represents the shape and appearance of a human in a compressed, low-dimensional, PCA-based space (which can be interpreted as a decoder with a single linear layer). There is a large corpus of different morphable models [21], but the majority of reconstruction methods use either the Basel Face Model [8,52] or the Flame head model [47]. Besides using these models for an analysis-by-synthesis approach, there is a series of learned regression-based methods. An overview of these methods is given by Morales et al. [50]. In the following, we will discuss the most relevant related work for monocular RGB-based reconstruction methods.

Optimization-Based Reconstruction of Human Faces. Along with the introduction of a 3D morphable model for faces, Blanz et al. [8] proposed an optimization-based reconstruction method that is based on the principle of analysis-by-synthesis. While they used a sparse sampling scheme to optimize the color reproduction, Thies et al. [69,70] introduced a dense color term considering the entire face region that is represented by a morphable model using differentiable rendering. This method has been adapted for avatar digitization from a single image [36] including hair, is used to reconstruct high-fidelity facial reflectance and geometry from a single images [79], for reconstruction and animation of entire upper bodies [71], or avatars with dynamic textures [51]. Recently, these optimization-based methods are combined with learnable components such as surface offsets or view-dependent surface radiance fields [32]. In addition to a photometric reconstruction objective, additional terms based on dense correspondence [35] or normal [1,32] estimations of neural network can be employed. Optimization-based methods are also used as a building block for neural rendering methods such as deep video portraits [40], deferred neural rendering [68], or neural voice puppetry [67]. Note that differentiable rendering is not only used in neural rendering frameworks but is also a key component for self-supervised learning of regression-based reconstruction methods covered in the following.

Regression-Based Reconstruction of Human Faces. Learning-based face reconstruction methods can be categorized into supervised and self-supervised approaches. A series of methods are based on synthetic renderings of human faces to perform a supervised training of a regressor that predicts the parameters of a 3D morphable model [20,41,56,57]. Genova et al. [31] propose a 3DMM parameter regression technique that is based on synthetic renderings (where ground truth parameters are available) and real images (where multi-view identity losses are applied). It uses FaceNet [60] to extract features for the 3DMM regression task. Tran et al. [72] and Chang et al. [11] (ExpNet) directly regress 3DMM parameters using a CNN trained on fitted 3DMM data. Tu et al. [75] propose a dual training pass for images with and without 3DMM fittings. Jackson et al. [37] propose a model-free approach that reconstructs a voxel-based representation of the human face and is trained on paired 2D image and 3D scan data. PRN [24] is trained on 'in-the-wild' images with fitted 3DMM reconstructions [84]. It is not restricted to a 3DMM model space and predicts a position map in the UV-space of a template mesh. Instead of working in UV-space, Wei et al. [76] propose to use graph convolutions to regress the coordinates of the vertices. MoFA [65] is a network trained to regress the 3DMM parameters in a self-supervised fashion. As a supervision signal, it uses the dense photometric losses of Face2Face [70]. Within this framework, Tewari et al. proposed to refine the identity shape and appearance [64] as well as the expression basis [63] of a linear 3DMM. In a similar setup, one can also train a non-linear 3DMM [74] or personalized models [12]. RingNet [59] regresses 3DMM parameters and is trained on 2D images using losses on the reproduction of 2D landmarks and shape consistency (different images of the same subject) and shape inconsistency (images of different subjects) losses. DECA [23] extends RingNet with expression dependent offset predictions in UV space. It uses dense photometric losses to train the 3DMM parameter regression and the offset prediction network. This separation of a coarse 3DMM model and a detailed bump map has been introduced by Tran et al. [73]. Chen et al. [13] use a hybrid training composed of self-supervised and supervised training based on renderings to predict texture and displacement maps. Deng et al. [18] train a 3DMM parameter regressor based on multi-image consistency losses and 'hybrid-level' losses (photometric reconstruction loss with skin attention masks, and a perception-level loss based on FaceNet [60]). On the NoW challenge [59], DECA [23] and the method of Deng et al. [18] show on-par state-of-the-art results. Similar to DECA's offset prediction, there are GAN-based methods that predict detailed color maps [29,30] or skin properties [44,45,58,79] (e.g., albedo, reflectance, normals) in UV-space of a 3DMM-based face reconstruction. In contrast to these methods, we are interested in reconstructing a metrical 3D representation of a human face and not fine-scale details. Self-supervised methods suffer from the depth-scale ambiguity (the face scale, translation away from the camera, and the perspective projection are ambiguous) and, thus, predict a wrongly scaled face, even though 3DMM models are by construction in a metrical space. We rely on a strong supervision signal to learn the metrical reconstruction of a face using high-quality 3D scan datasets which we unified. In combination with an identity encoder [17] trained on in-the-wild 2D data, including occlusions, different illumination, poses, and expressions, we achieve robust geometry estimations that significantly outperform state-of-the-art methods.

3   Metrical Face Shape Prediction

Based on a single input RGB image I, MICA aims to predict a metrical shape of a human face in a neutral expression. To this end, we leverage both 'in-the-wild' 2D data as well as metric 3D data to train a deep neural network, as shown in Fig. 2. We employ a state-of-the-art face recognition network [17] which is trained on 'in-the-wild' data to achieve a robust prediction of an identity code, which is interpreted by a geometry decoder.

Identity Encoder. As an identity encoder, we leverage the ArcFace [17] architecture which is pretrained on Glint360K [2]. This ResNet100-based network is trained on 2D image data using an additive angular margin loss to obtain highly discriminative features for face recognition. It is invariant to illumination, expression, rotation, occlusion, and camera parameters which is ideal for a robust shape prediction. We extend the ArcFace architecture by a small mapping network $\mathcal{M}$ that maps the ArcFace features to our latent space, which can then be interpreted by our geometry decoder:

$$z = \mathcal{M}(ArcFace(I)),$$

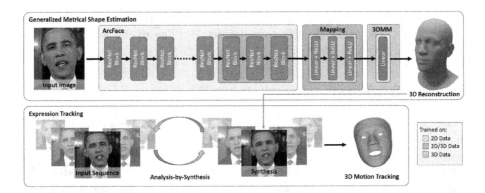

Fig. 2. We propose a method for metrical human face shape estimation from a single image which exploits a supervised training scheme based on a mixture of different 2D,2D/3D and 3D datasets. This estimation can be used for facial expression tracking using analysis-by-synthesis which optimizes for the camera intrinsics, as well as the per-frame illumination, facial expression and pose.

where $z \in \mathbb{R}^{300}$. Our mapping network $\mathcal{M}$ consists of three fully-connected linear hidden layers with ReLU activation and the final linear output layer.

Geometry Decoder. There are essentially two types of geometry decoders used in the literature, model-free and model-based. Throughout the project of this paper, we conducted experiments on both types and found that both perform similarly on the evaluation benchmarks. Since a 3DMM model efficiently represents the face space, we focus on a model-based decoder. Specifically, we use FLAME [47] as a geometry decoder, which consists of a single linear layer:

$$\mathcal{G}_{3DMM}(z) = B \cdot z + A,$$

where $A \in \mathbb{R}^{3N}$ is the geometry of the average human face and $B \in \mathbb{R}^{3N \times 300}$ contains the principal components of the 3DMM and $N = 5023$.

Supervised Learning. The networks described above are trained using paired 2D/3D data from existing, unified datasets $\mathcal{D}$ (see Sect. 5). We fix large portions of the pre-trained ArcFace network during the training and refine the last 3 ResNet blocks. Note that ArcFace is trained on a much larger amount of identities, therefore, refining more hidden layers results in worse predictions due to overfitting. We found that using the last 3 ResNet blocks gives the best generalization (see supplemental document). The training loss is:

$$\mathcal{L} = \sum_{(I,\mathcal{G}) \in \mathcal{D}} |\kappa_{mask}(\mathcal{G}_{3DMM}(\mathcal{M}(ArcFace(I))) - \mathcal{G})|, \tag{1}$$

where $\mathcal{G}$ is the ground truth mesh and κ_{mask} is a region dependent weight (the face region has weight 150.0, the back of the head 1.0, and eyes with ears 0.01). We use AdamW [49] for optimization with fixed learning rate $\eta = 1e-5$ and weight decay $\lambda = 2e{-}4$. We select the best performing model based on the validation set loss using the Florence dataset [3]. The model was trained for $160k$ steps on Nvidia Tesla V100.

4   Face Tracking

Based on our shape estimate, we demonstrate optimization-based face tracking on monocular RGB input sequences. To model the non-rigid deformations of the face, we use the linear expression basis vectors and the linear blendskinning of the FLAME [47] model, and use a linear albedo model [22] to reproduce the appearance of a subject in conjunction with a Lambertian material assumption and a light model based on spherical harmonics. We adapt the analysis-by-synthesis scheme of Thies et al. [70]. Instead of using a multi-frame model-based bundling technique to estimate the identity of a subject, we use our one-shot shape identity predictor. We initialize the albedo and spherical harmonics based on the same first frame using the energy:

$$E(\phi) = w_{dense}E_{dense}(\phi) + w_{lmk}E_{lmk}(\phi) + w_{reg}E_{reg}(\phi), \qquad (2)$$

where ϕ is the vector of unknown parameters we are optimizing for. The energy terms $E_{dense}(\phi)$ and $E_{reg}(\phi)$ measure the dense color reproduction of the face (ℓ_1-norm) and the deviation from the neutral pose respectively. The sparse landmark term $E_{lmk}(\phi)$ measures the reproduction of 2D landmark positions (based on Google's mediapipe [33,39] and Face Alignment [9]). The weights w_{dense}, w_{lmk} and w_{reg} balance the influence of each sub-objectives on the final loss. In the first frame vector ϕ contains the 3DMM parameters for albedo, expression, and rigid pose, as well as the spherical harmonic coefficients (3 bands) that are used to represent the environmental illumination [54]. After initialization, the albedo parameters are fixed and unchanged throughout the sequence tracking.

Optimization. We optimize the objective function Eq. (2) using Adam [42] in PyTorch. While recent soft-rasterizers [48,55] are popular, we rely on a sampling based scheme as introduced by Thies et al. [70] to implement the differentiable rendering for the photo-metric reproduction error $E_{dense}(\phi)$. Specifically, we use a classical rasterizer to render the surface of the current estimation. The rasterized surface points that survive the depth test are considered as the set of visible surface points $\mathcal{V}$ for which we compute the energy term $E_{dense}(\phi) = \sum_{i \in \mathcal{V}} |I(\pi(\mathbf{R} \cdot p_i(\phi) + t)) - c_i(\phi)|$ where p_i and c_i being the i-th vertex and color of the reconstructed model, and I the RGB input image.

5   Dataset Unification

In the past, methods and their training scheme were limited by the availability of 3D scan datasets of human faces. While several small and medium-scale datasets are available, they are in different formats and do not share the same topology. To this end, we unified the available datasets such that they can be used as

Table 1. Overview of our unified datasets. The used datasets vary in the capture modality and the capture protocol. Here, we list the number of subject, the minimum number of images per subjects, and whether the dataset includes facial expressions. In total our dataset contains 2315 subjects with FLAME topology.

Dataset		#Subj.	#Min. Img.	Expr.
Stirling [26]	☑	133	8	✓
D3DFACS [15]	☑	10	videos	✓
Florence 2D/3D [3]	☑	53	videos	✓
BU-3DFE [81]	☑	100	83	✓
LYHM [16]	☑	1211	2	✗
FaceWarehouse [10]	☑	150	119	✓
FRGC [53]	☑	531	7	✓
BP4D+ [82]	☑	127	videos	✓

a supervision signal for face reconstruction from 2D images. Specifically, we register the FLAME [47] head model to the provided scan data. In an initial step, we fit the model to landmarks and optimize for the FLAME parameters based on an iterative closest point (ICP) scheme [5]. We further jointly optimize FLAME's model parameters, and refine the fitting with a non-rigid deformation regularized by FLAME, similar to Li and Bolkart et al. [47]. In Table 1, we list the datasets that we unified for this project. We note that the datasets vary in the capturing modality and capturing script (with and without facial expressions, with and without hair caps, indoor and outdoor imagery, still images, and videos), which is suitable for generalization. The datasets are recorded in different regions of the world and are often biased towards ethnicity. Thus, combining other datasets results in a more diverse data pool. In the supplemental document, we show an ablation on the different datasets. *Upon agreement of the different dataset owners, we will share our unified dataset, i.e., for each subject one registered mesh with neutral expression in FLAME topology.* Note that in addition to the datasets listed in Table 1, we analyzed the FaceScape dataset [80]. While it provides a large set of 3D reconstructions (∼17k), which would be ideal for our training, the reconstructions are not done in a metrical space. Specifically, the data has been captured in an uncalibrated setup and faces are normalized by the eye distance, which has not been detailed in their paper (instead, they mention sub-millimeter reconstruction accuracy which is not valid). This is a fundamental flaw of this dataset, and also questions their reconstruction benchmark [83].

6   Results

Our experiments mainly focus on the metrical reconstruction of a human face from in the wild images. In the supplemental document, we show results for the sequential tracking of facial motions using our metrical reconstruction as initialization. The following experiments are conducted with the original models of

Table 2. Quantitative evaluation of the face shape estimation on the *NoW Challenge* [59]. Note that we list two different evaluations: the non-metrical evaluation from the original NoW challenge and our new metrical evaluation (including a cumulative error plot on the left). The original NoW challenge cannot be considered metrical since Procrustes analysis is used to align the reconstructions to the corresponding reference meshes, including scaling. We list all methods from the original benchmark and additionally show the performance of the average human face of FLAME [47] as a reference (first row).

NoW-Metric Challenge	Method	Non-Metrical [59]			Metrical (mm)		
		Median	Mean	Std	Median	Mean	Std
	Average Face (FLAME [47])	1.21	1.53	1.31	1.49	1.92	1.68
	3DMM-CNN [72]	1.84	2.33	2.05	3.91	4.84	4.02
	PRNet [24]	1.50	1.98	1.88	–	–	–
	Deng et al [18] (TensorFlow)	1.23	1.54	1.29	2.26	2.90	2.51
	• Deng et al [18] (PyTorch)	1.11	1.41	1.21	1.62	2.21	2.08
	• RingNet [59]	1.21	1.53	1.31	1.50	1.98	1.77
	• 3DDFA-V2 [34]	1.23	1.57	1.39	1.53	2.06	1.95
	• MGCNet [62]	1.31	1.87	2.63	1.70	2.47	3.02
	UMDFA [43]	1.52	1.89	1.57	2.31	2.97	2.57
	• Dib et al. [19]	1.26	1.57	1.31	1.59	2.12	1.93
	• DECA [23]	1.09	1.38	1.18	1.35	1.80	1.64
	• FOCUS [46]	1.04	1.30	1.10	1.41	1.85	1.70
	• **Ours**	**0.90**	**1.11**	**0.92**	**1.08**	**1.37**	**1.17**

the respective publications including their reconstructions submitted to the given benchmarks. Note that these models are trained on their large-scale datasets, training them on our medium-scale 3D dataset would lead to overfitting.

6.1 Face Shape Estimation

In recent publications, face shape estimation is evaluated on datasets where reference scans of the subjects are available. The NoW Challenge [59] and the benchmark of Feng et al. [25] which is based on Stirling meshes [26] are used in the state-of-the-art methods [18,23,59]. We conduct several studies on these benchmarks and propose different evaluation protocols.

Non-metrical Benchmark. The established evaluation methods on these datasets are based on an optimal scaling step, i.e., to align the estimation to the reference scan, they optimize for a rigid alignment and an additional scaling factor which results in a non-metric/relative error. This scaling compensates for shape mispredictions, e.g., the mean error evaluated on the NoW Challenge for the average FLAME mesh (Table 2) drops from 1.92 mm to 1.53 mm because of the applied scale optimization. This is an improvement of around 20% which has nothing to do with the reconstruction quality and, thus, creates a misleading benchmark score where methods appear better than they are. Nevertheless, we

Table 3. Quantitative evaluation of the face shape estimation on the *Stirling Reconstruction Benchmark* [25] using the NoW protocol [59]. We list two different evaluations: the non-metric evaluation from the original benchmark and the metric evaluation. *Note that for this experiment, we exclude the Stirling dataset from our training set.*

Stirling (NoW Protocol)	Non-Metrical						Metrical (mm)					
	Median		Mean		Std		Median		Mean		Std	
	LQ	HQ	LQ	HQ	LQ	HQ	LQ	HQ	LQ	HQ	LQ	HQ
Average Face (FLAME [47])	1.23	1.22	1.56	1.55	1.38	1.35	1.44	1.40	1.84	1.79	1.64	1.57
RingNet [59]	1.17	1.15	1.49	1.46	1.31	1.27	1.37	1.33	1.77	1.72	1.60	1.54
3DDFA-V2 [34]	1.26	1.20	1.63	1.55	1.52	1.45	1.49	1.38	1.93	1.80	1.78	1.68
Deng et al. [18] (TensorFlow)	1.22	1.13	1.57	1.43	1.40	1.25	1.85	1.81	2.41	2.29	2.16	1.97
Deng et al. [18] (PyTorch)	1.12	0.99	1.44	1.27	1.31	1.15	1.47	1.31	1.93	1.71	1.77	1.57
DECA [23]	1.09	1.03	1.39	1.32	1.26	1.18	1.32	1.22	1.71	1.58	1.54	1.42
Ours w/o. Stirling	**0.96**	**0.92**	**1.22**	**1.16**	**1.11**	**1.04**	**1.15**	**1.06**	**1.46**	**1.35**	**1.30**	**1.20**

Table 4. Quantitative evaluation of the face shape estimation on the *Stirling Reconstruction Benchmark* [25]. We list two different evaluations: the non-metric evaluation from the original benchmark and the metric evaluation. This benchmark is based on an alignment protocol that only relies on reference landmarks and, thus, is very noisy and dependent on the landmark reference selection (in our evaluation, we use the landmark correspondences provided by the FLAME [47] model). We use the image file list from [59] to compute the scores (i.e., excluding images where a face is not detectable). *Note that for this experiment, we exclude the Stirling dataset from our training set.*

Stirling/ESRC Benchmark	Non-metrical [25]						Metrical (mm)					
	Median		Mean		Std		Median		Mean		Std	
	LQ	HQ	LQ	HQ	LQ	HQ	LQ	HQ	LQ	HQ	LQ	HQ
Average Face (FLAME [47])	1.58	1.62	2.06	2.08	1.82	1.83	1.70	1.62	2.19	2.09	1.96	1.85
RingNet [59]	1.56	1.60	2.01	2.05	1.75	1.76	1.67	1.64	2.16	2.09	1.90	1.81
3DDFA-V2 [34]	1.58	1.49	2.03	1.90	1.74	1.63	1.70	1.56	2.16	1.98	1.88	1.70
Deng et al. [18] (TensorFlow)	1.56	1.41	2.02	1.84	1.77	1.63	2.13	2.14	2.71	2.65	2.33	2.12
Deng et al. [18] (PyTorch)	1.51	1.29	1.95	1.64	1.71	1.39	1.78	1.54	2.28	1.97	1.97	1.68
DECA [23]	1.40	1.32	1.81	1.72	1.59	1.50	1.56	1.45	2.03	1.87	1.81	1.64
Ours w/o. Stirling	**1.26**	**1.22**	**1.62**	**1.55**	**1.41**	**1.34**	**1.36**	**1.26**	**1.73**	**1.60**	**1.48**	**1.37**

evaluate our method on these benchmarks and significantly outperform all state-of-the-art methods as can be seen in Tables 2 and 4 ('Non-Metrical' column).

Metrical Benchmark. Since for a variety of applications, actual metrical reconstructions are required, we argue for a new evaluation scheme that uses a purely rigid alignment, i.e., without scale optimization (see Fig. 5). The error is calculated using an Euclidean distance between each scan vertex and the closest point on the mesh surface. This new evaluation scheme enables a comparison of methods based on metrical quantities (see Tables 2 and 4) and, thus, is *fundamentally* different from the previous evaluation schemes. In addition, the benchmark of Feng et al. [25] is based on the alignment using sparse facial (hand-selected) landmarks. Our experiments showed that this scheme is highly dependent on the

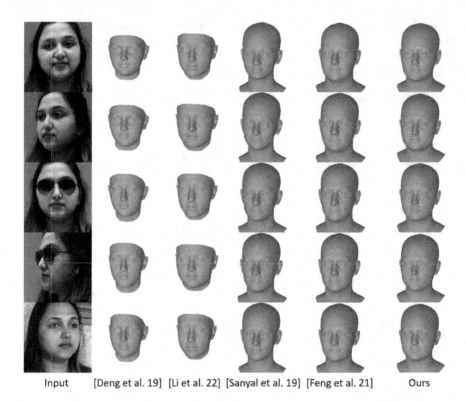

Input   [Deng et al. 19] [Li et al. 22] [Sanyal et al. 19] [Feng et al. 21]   Ours

Fig. 3. Qualitative results on NoW Challenge [59] to show the invariance of our method to changes in illumination, expression, occlusion, rotation, and perspective distortion in comparison to other methods.

selection of these markers and results in inconsistent evaluation results. In our listed results, we use the marker correspondences that come with the FLAME model [47]. To get a more reliable evaluation scheme, we evaluate the benchmark of Feng et al. using the dense iterative closest point (ICP) technique from the NoW challenge, see Table 3. On all metrics, our proposed method significantly improves the reconstruction accuracy. Note that some methods are even performing worse than the mean face [47].

Qualitative Results. In Fig. 3, we show qualitative results to analyze the stability of the face shape prediction of a subject across different expressions, head rotation, occlusions, or perspective distortion. As can be seen, our method is more persistent compared to others, especially, in comparison to Deng et al. [18] where shape predictions vary the most. Figure 4 depicts the challenging scenario of reconstructing toddlers from single images. Instead of predicting a small face for a child, the state of the art methods are predicting faces of adults. In contrast, MICA predicts the shape of a child with a correct scale.

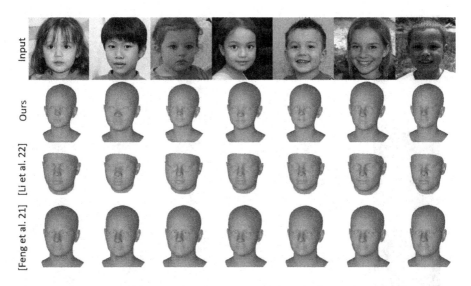

Fig. 4. Current methods are not predicting metrical faces, which becomes visible when displaying them in a metrical space and not in their image spaces. To illustrate we render the prediction of the faces of toddlers in a common metrical space using the same projection. State-of-the-art approaches trained in a self-supervised fashion like DECA [23] or weakly-supervised like FOCUS [46] scale the face of an adult to fit the observation in the image space, thus, the prediction in 3D is non-metrical. In contrast, our reconstruction method is able to recover the physiognomy of the toddlers. Input images are generated by StyleGan2 [38].

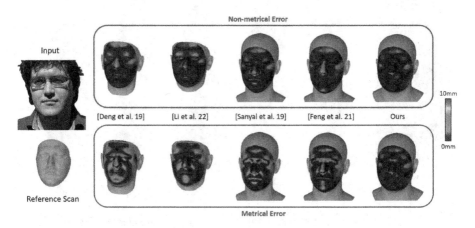

Fig. 5. Established evaluation benchmarks like [25,59] are based on a non-metrical error metric (top-row). We propose a new evaluation protocol which measures reconstruction errors in a metrical space (bottom row) (c.f. Table 2). Image from the NoW [59] validation set.

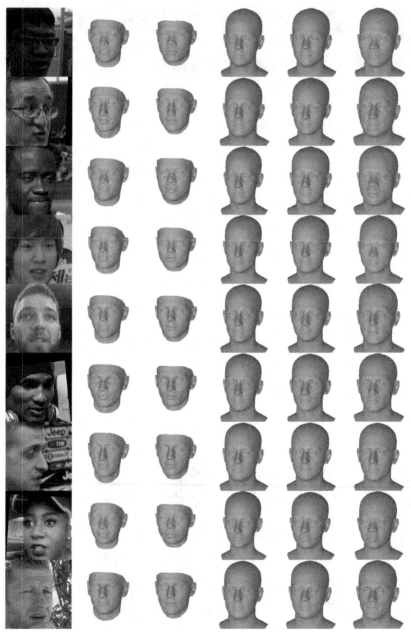

Input   [Deng et al. 19] [Li et al. 22] [Sanyal et al. 19] [Feng et al. 21]   Ours

Fig. 6. Qualitative comparison on randomly sampled images from the VoxCeleb2 [14] dataset. Our method is able to capture face shape with intricate details like nose and chin, while being metrical plausible (c.f., Tables 2 and 4).

In Fig. 6 reconstructions for randomly sampled identities from the VoxCeleb2 [14] dataset are shown. Some of the baselines, especially, RingNet [59], exhibits strong bias towards the mean human face. In contrast, our method is able to not only predict better overall shape but also to reconstruct challenging regions like nose or chin, even though the training dataset contains a much smaller identity and ethnicity pool. Note that while the reconstructions of the baseline methods look good under the projection, they are not metric as shown in Tables 2 and 4.

6.2 Limitations

Our method is not designed to predict shape and expressions in one forward pass, instead, we reconstruct the expression separately using an optimization-based tracking method. However, this optimization-based tracking leads to temporally coherent results, as can be seen in the suppl. video. In contrast to DECA [23] or Deng et al. [18], the focus of our method is the reconstruction of a metrical 3D model, reconstructing high-frequent detail on top of our prediction is an interesting future direction. Our method fails, when the used face detector [61] does not recognize a face in the input.

7   Discussion and Conclusion

A metrical reconstruction is key for any application that requires the measurement of distances and dimensions. It is essential for the composition of reconstructed humans and scenes where objects of known size are in, thus, it is especially important for virtual reality and augmented reality applications. However, we show that recent methods and evaluation schemes are not designed for this task. While the established benchmarks report numbers in millimeters, they are computed with an optimal scale to align the prediction and the reference. We strongly argue against this practice, since it is misleading and the errors are not absolute metrical measurements. To this end, we propose a simple, yet fundamental adjustment of the benchmarks to enable metrical evaluations. Specifically, we remove the optimal scaling, and only allow rigid alignment of the prediction with the reference shape. As a stepping stone towards metrical reconstructions, we unified existing small- and medium-scale datasets of paired 2D/3D data. This allows us to establish 3D supervised losses in our novel shape prediction framework. While our data collection is still comparably small (around 2k identities), we designed MICA that uses features from a face recognition network pretrained on a large-scale 2D image dataset to generalize to in-the-wild image data. We validated our approach in several experiments and show state-of-the-art results on our newly introduced metrical benchmarks as well as on the established scale-invariant benchmarks. We hope that this work inspires researchers to concentrate on metrical face reconstruction.

Acknowledgement. We thank Haiwen Feng for support with NoW and Stirling evaluations, and Chunlu Li for providing FOCUS results. The authors thank the International Max Planck Research School for Intelligent Systems (IMPRS-IS) for supporting Wojciech Zielonka.

Disclosure. While TB is part-time employee of Amazon, his research was performed solely at, and funded solely by MPI. JT is supported by Microsoft Research gift funds.

References

1. Abrevaya, V.F., Boukhayma, A., Torr, P.H., Boyer, E.: Cross-modal deep face normals with deactivable skip connections. In: Conference on Computer Vision and Pattern Recognition (CVPR), pp. 4978–4988 (2020)
2. An, X., et al.: Partial fc: Training 10 million identities on a single machine. In: Arxiv 2010.05222 (2020)
3. Bagdanov, A.D., Del Bimbo, A., Masi, I.: The florence 2D/3D hybrid face dataset. In: Proceedings of the 2011 Joint ACM Workshop on Human Gesture and Behavior Understanding, J-HGBU 2011, pp. 79–80. Association for Computing Machinery, New York, NY, USA (2011). https://doi.org/10.1145/2072572.2072597, https://doi.org/10.1145/2072572.2072597
4. Bas, A., Smith, W.A.P.: What does 2D geometric information really tell us about 3D face shape? Int. J. Comput. Visi. **127**(10), 1455–1473 (2019)
5. Besl, P.J., McKay, N.D.: Method for registration of 3-D shapes. In: Sensor Fusion IV: Control Paradigms and Data Structures, vol. 1611, pp. 586–606. International Society for Optics and Photonics, Bellingham (1992)
6. Blanz, V., Basso, C., Poggio, T., Vetter, T.: Reanimating faces in images and video. In: EUROGRAPHICS (EG), vol. 22, pp. 641–650 (2003)
7. Blanz, V., Scherbaum, K., Vetter, T., Seidel, H.P.: Exchanging faces in images. Comput. Graph. Forum **23**(3), 669–676 (2004)
8. Blanz, V., Vetter, T.: A morphable model for the synthesis of 3D faces. In: SIGGRAPH, pp. 187–194 (1999)
9. Bulat, A., Tzimiropoulos, G.: How far are we from solving the 2D & 3D face alignment problem? (and a dataset of 230,000 3d facial landmarks). In: International Conference on Computer Vision (2017)
10. Cao, C., Weng, Y., Zhou, S., Tong, Y., Zhou, K.: FaceWarehouse: a 3D facial expression database for visual computing. Trans. Visual. Comput. Graph. **20**, 413–425 (2013)
11. Chang, F.J., Tran, A.T., Hassner, T., Masi, I., Nevatia, R., Medioni, G.: ExpNet: landmark-free, deep, 3d facial expressions. In: International Conference on Automatic Face & Gesture Recognition (FG), pp. 122–129 (2018)
12. Chaudhuri, B., Vesdapunt, N., Shapiro, L., Wang, B.: Personalized face modeling for improved face reconstruction and motion retargeting. In: Vedaldi, A., Bischof, H., Brox, T., Frahm, J.-M. (eds.) ECCV 2020. LNCS, vol. 12350, pp. 142–160. Springer, Cham (2020). https://doi.org/10.1007/978-3-030-58558-7_9
13. Chen, A., Chen, Z., Zhang, G., Mitchell, K., Yu, J.: Photo-realistic facial details synthesis from single image. In: Proceedings of the IEEE International Conference on Computer Vision, pp. 9429–9439 (2019)
14. Chung, J.S., Nagrani, A., Zisserman, A.: VoxCeleb2: deep speaker recognition. In: "INTERSPEECH" (2018)

15. Cosker, D., Krumhuber, E., Hilton, A.: A FACS valid 3d dynamic action unit database with applications to 3d dynamic morphable facial modeling. In: 2011 International Conference on Computer Vision, pp. 2296–2303 (2011). https://doi. org/10.1109/ICCV.2011.6126510

16. Dai, H., Pears, N., Smith, W., Duncan, C.: Statistical modeling of craniofacial shape and texture. Int. J. Comput. Vision **128**(2), 547–571 (2019). https://doi. org/10.1007/s11263-019-01260-7

17. Deng, J., Guo, J., Liu, T., Gong, M., Zafeiriou, S.: Sub-center ArcFace: boosting face recognition by large-scale noisy web faces. In: Vedaldi, A., Bischof, H., Brox, T., Frahm, J.-M. (eds.) ECCV 2020. LNCS, vol. 12356, pp. 741–757. Springer, Cham (2020). https://doi.org/10.1007/978-3-030-58621-8_43

18. Deng, Y., Yang, J., Xu, S., Chen, D., Jia, Y., Tong, X.: Accurate 3D face reconstruction with weakly-supervised learning: From single image to image set. In: Conference on Computer Vision and Pattern Recognition Workshops (CVPR-W) (2019)

19. Dib, A., Thebault, C., Ahn, J., Gosselin, P., Theobalt, C., Chevallier, L.: Towards high fidelity monocular face reconstruction with rich reflectance using self-supervised learning and ray tracing. In: International Conference on Computer Vision (ICCV), pp. 12819–12829 (2021)

20. Dou, P., Shah, S.K., Kakadiaris, I.A.: End-to-end 3D face reconstruction with deep neural networks Arch. Computat. Methods Eng **29**, 3475–3507 (2017)

21. Egger, B., et al.: 3D morphable face models - past, present and future. Transa. Graph. **39**(5) (2020). https://doi.org/10.1145/3395208

22. Feng, H., Bolkart, T.: Photometric FLAME fitting (2020). https://github.com/ HavenFeng/photometric_optimization

23. Feng, Y., Feng, H., Black, M.J., Bolkart, T.: Learning an animatable detailed 3D face model from in-the-wild images. Trans. Graph. (Proc. SIGGRAPH) **40**(8) (2021)

24. Feng, Y., Wu, F., Shao, X., Wang, Y., Zhou, X.: Joint 3D face reconstruction and dense alignment with position map regression network. In: Ferrari, V., Hebert, M., Sminchisescu, C., Weiss, Y. (eds.) Computer Vision – ECCV 2018. LNCS, vol. 11218, pp. 557–574. Springer, Cham (2018). https://doi.org/10.1007/978-3-030-01264-9_33

25. Feng, Z., et al.: Evaluation of dense 3D reconstruction from 2D face images in the wild. In: International Conference on Automatic Face & Gesture Recognition (FG), pp. 780–786 (2018). https://doi.org/10.1109/FG.2018.00123

26. Feng, Z., et al.: Evaluation of dense 3d reconstruction from 2D face images in the wild. CoRR abs/1803.05536 (2018), https://arxiv.org/abs/1803.05536

27. Garrido, P., Valgaerts, L., Rehmsen, O., Thormaehlen, T., Perez, P., Theobalt, C.: Automatic face reenactment. In: Conference on Computer Vision and Pattern Recognition (CVPR), pp. 4217–4224 (2014)

28. Garrido, P., et al.: VDub - modifying face video of actors for plausible visual alignment to a dubbed audio track. In: EUROGRAPHICS (EG), pp. 193–204 (2015)

29. Gecer, B., Ploumpis, S., Kotsia, I., Zafeiriou, S.: GANFIT: generative adversarial network fitting for high fidelity 3D face reconstruction. In: The IEEE Conference on Computer Vision and Pattern Recognition (CVPR), June 2019

30. Gecer, B., Ploumpis, S., Kotsia, I., Zafeiriou, S.P.: Fast-GANFIT: generative adversarial network for high fidelity 3d face reconstruction. IEEE Trans. Pattern Anal. Mach. Intell.. (2021)

31. Genova, K., Cole, F., Maschinot, A., Sarna, A., Vlasic, D., Freeman, W.T.: Unsupervised training for 3d morphable model regression (2018)

32. Grassal, P.W., Prinzler, M., Leistner, T., Rother, C., Nießner, M., Thies, J.: Neural Head Avatars from Monocular RGB Videos (2021). https://doi.org/10.48550/ARXIV.2112.01554, https://arxiv.org/abs/2112.01554
33. Grishchenko, I., Ablavatski, A., Kartynnik, Y., Raveendran, K., Grundmann, M.: Attention Mesh: High-fidelity Face Mesh Prediction in Real-time (2020). https://doi.org/10.48550/ARXIV.2006.10962, https://arxiv.org/abs/2006.10962
34. Guo, J., Zhu, X., Yang, Y., Yang, F., Lei, Z., Li, S.Z.: Towards Fast, Accurate and Stable 3D Dense Face Alignment (2020). https://doi.org/10.48550/ARXIV.2009.09960, https://arxiv.org/abs/2009.09960
35. Güler, R.A., Trigeorgis, G., Antonakos, E., Snape, P., Zafeiriou, S., Kokkinos, I.: DenseReg: Fully Convolutional Dense Shape Regression In-the-Wild (2016). https://doi.org/10.48550/ARXIV.1612.01202, https://arxiv.org/abs/1612.01202
36. Hu, L., et al.: Avatar digitization from a single image for real-time rendering. ACM Trans. Graph. 36(6), 14 (2017). https://doi.org/10.1145/3130800.31310887
37. Jackson, A.S., Bulat, A., Argyriou, V., Tzimiropoulos, G.: Large Pose 3D Face Reconstruction from a Single Image via Direct Volumetric CNN Regression (2017). https://doi.org/10.48550/ARXIV.1703.07834, https://arxiv.org/abs/1703.07834
38. Karras, T., Laine, S., Aittala, M., Hellsten, J., Lehtinen, J., Aila, T.: Analyzing and improving the image quality of StyleGAN. In: Proceedings of CVPR (2020)
39. Kartynnik, Y., Ablavatski, A., Grishchenko, I., Grundmann, M.: Real-time facial surface geometry from monocular video on mobile GPUs (2019)
40. Kim, H., et al.: Deep video portraits. Trans. Graph. 37(4), 1–14 (2018)
41. Kim, H., Zollhöfer, M., Tewari, A., Thies, J., Richardt, C., Theobalt, C.: InverseFaceNet: deep monocular inverse face rendering. In: Conference on Computer Vision and Pattern Recognition (CVPR), June 2018
42. Kingma, D.P., Ba, J.: Adam: a method for stochastic optimization. CoRR abs/1412.6980 (2015)
43. Koizumi, T., Smith, W.A.P.: Look Ma, No Landmarks – unsupervised, model-based dense face alignment. In: Vedaldi, A., Bischof, H., Brox, T., Frahm, J.-M. (eds.) ECCV 2020. "look ma, no landmarks!" - unsupervised, model-based dense face alignment, vol. 12347, pp. 690–706. Springer, Cham (2020). https://doi.org/10.1007/978-3-030-58536-5_41
44. Lattas, A., et al.: AvatarMe: realistically renderable 3D facial reconstruction in-the-wild". In: Conference on Computer Vision and Pattern Recognition (CVPR), pp. 760–769 (2020)
45. Lattas, A., Moschoglou, S., Ploumpis, S., Gecer, B., Ghosh, A., Zafeiriou, S.P.: AvatarMe++: facial shape and BRDF inference with photorealistic rendering-aware GANs. Trans. Pattern Anal. Mach. Intell. (PAMI) (2021)
46. Li, C., Morel-Forster, A., Vetter, T., Egger, B., Kortylewski, A.: To fit or not to fit: model-based face reconstruction and occlusion segmentation from weak supervision. CoRR abs/2106.09614 (2021), https://arxiv.org/abs/2106.09614
47. Li, T., Bolkart, T., Black, M.J., Li, H., Romero, J.: Learning a model of facial shape and expression from 4D scans. Trans. Grap. (Proc. SIGGRAPH Asia) 36(6), 194:1–194:17 (2017., https://doi.org/10.1145/3130800.3130813
48. Liu, S., Li, T., Chen, W., Li, H.: Soft rasterizer: a differentiable renderer for image-based 3D reasoning. In: International Conference on Computer Vision (ICCV), October 2019
49. Loshchilov, I., Hutter, F.: Fixing weight decay regularization in Adam. CoRR abs/1711.05101 (2017), https://arxiv.org/abs/1711.05101
50. Morales, A., Piella, G., Sukno, F.M.: Survey on 3D face reconstruction from uncalibrated images (2021)

51. Nagano, K., et al.:paGAN: real-time avatars using dynamic textures. ACM Trans. Graph. **37**(6) (2018). https://doi.org/10.1145/3272127.3275075

52. Paysan, P., Knothe, R., Amberg, B., Romdhani, S., Vetter, T.: A 3D face model for pose and illumination invariant face recognition. In: International Conference on Advanced Video and Signal Based Surveillance, pp. 296–301 (2009)

53. Phillips, P., et al.: Overview of the face recognition grand challenge. In: 2005 IEEE Computer Society Conference on Computer Vision and Pattern Recognition (CVPR'05), vol. 1, pp. 947–954 (2005). https://doi.org/10.1109/CVPR.2005.268

54. Ramamoorthi, R., Hanrahan, P.: An efficient representation for irradiance environment maps. In: Proceedings of the 28th Annual Conference on Computer Graphics and Interactive Techniques, SIGGRAPH 2001, pp. 497–500. Association for Computing Machinery, New York, NY, USA (2001). https://doi.org/10.1145/383259.383317

55. Ravi, N., et al.: Accelerating 3D deep learning with pytorch3d. arXiv:2007.08501 (2020)

56. Richardson, E., Sela, M., Kimmel, R.: 3D Face Reconstruction by Learning from Synthetic Data (2016). https://doi.org/10.48550/ARXIV.1609.04387, https://arxiv.org/abs/1609.04387

57. Richardson, E., Sela, M., Or-El, R., Kimmel, R.: Learning detailed face reconstruction from a single image. In: 2017 IEEE Conference on Computer Vision and Pattern Recognition (CVPR)(2017)

58. Saito, S., Wei, L., Hu, L., Nagano, K., Li, H.: Photorealistic facial texture inference using deep neural networks (2016)

59. Sanyal, S., Bolkart, T., Feng, H., Black, M.: Learning to regress 3D face shape and expression from an image without 3d supervision. In: Conference on Computer Vision and Pattern Recognition (CVPR) (2019)

60. Schroff, F., Kalenichenko, D., Philbin, J.: FaceNet: a unified embedding for face recognition and clustering. In: 2015 IEEE Conference on Computer Vision and Pattern Recognition (CVPR), June 2015. https://doi.org/10.1109/cvpr.2015.7298682

61. Serengil, S.I., Ozpinar, A.: Hyperextended lightface: a facial attribute analysis framework. In: 2021 International Conference on Engineering and Emerging Technologies (ICEET), pp. 1–4. IEEE (2021). https://doi.org/10.1109/ICEET53442.2021.9659697

62. Shang, J., et al.: Self-supervised monocular 3D face reconstruction by occlusion-aware multi-view geometry consistency. In: Vedaldi, A., Bischof, H., Brox, T., Frahm, J.-M. (eds.) ECCV 2020. LNCS, vol. 12360, pp. 53–70. Springer, Cham (2020). https://doi.org/10.1007/978-3-030-58555-6_4

63. Tewari, A., et al.: FML: face model learning from videos. In: Proceedings of the IEEE Conference on Computer Vision and Pattern Recognition, pp. 10812–10822 (2019)

64. Tewari, A., et al.: Self-supervised multi-level face model learning for monocular reconstruction at over 250 hz. In: The IEEE Conference on Computer Vision and Pattern Recognition (CVPR) (2018)

65. Tewari, A., et al.: MoFA: model-based deep convolutional face autoencoder for unsupervised monocular reconstruction. In: The IEEE International Conference on Computer Vision (ICCV) (2017)

66. Thies, J., Zollhöfer, M., Stamminger, M., Theobalt, C., Nießner, M.: Facevr: Real-time gaze-aware facial reenactment in virtual reality. ACM Trans. Graph. **37** (2018)

67. Thies, J., Elgharib, M., Tewari, A., Theobalt, C., Nießner, M.: Neural voice puppetry: audio-driven facial reenactment. In: Vedaldi, A., Bischof, H., Brox, T., Frahm, J.-M. (eds.) ECCV 2020. LNCS, vol. 12361, pp. 716–731. Springer, Cham (2020). https://doi.org/10.1007/978-3-030-58517-4_42

68. Thies, J., Zollhöfer, M., Nießner, M.: Deferred neural rendering: image synthesis using neural textures. Trans. Graph. **38**(4), 1–12 (2019)

69. Thies, J., Zollhöfer, M., Nießner, M., Valgaerts, L., Stamminger, M., Theobalt, C.: Real-time expression transfer for facial reenactment. Trans. Graph. **34**(6) (2015)

70. Thies, J., Zollhöfer, M., Stamminger, M., Theobalt, C., Nießner, M.: Face2Face: real-time face capture and reenactment of RGB videos. In: Conference on Computer Vision and Pattern Recognition (CVPR), pp. 2387–2395 (2016)

71. Thies, J., Zollhöfer, M., Theobalt, C., Stamminger, M., Niessner, M.: Headon: real-time reenactment of human portrait videos. ACM Transa. Graph. **37**(4), 1–13 (2018) 10.1145/3197517.3201350, https://dx.doi.org/10.1145/3197517.3201350

72. Tran, A.T., Hassner, T., Masi, I., Medioni, G.: Regressing robust and discriminative 3D morphable models with a very deep neural network. In: Proceedings of the IEEE Conference on Computer Vision and Pattern Recognition (CVPR), pp. 1599–1608 (2017)

73. Tran, A.T., Hassner, T., Masi, I., Paz, E., Nirkin, Y., Medioni, G.: Extreme 3D face reconstruction: seeing through occlusions. In: Conference on Computer Vision and Pattern Recognition (CVPR) (2018)

74. Tran, L., Liu, F., Liu, X.: Towards high-fidelity nonlinear 3D face morphable model. In: In Proceeding of IEEE Computer Vision and Pattern Recognition. Long Beach, CA, June 2019

75. Tu, X., et al.: Joint 3D face reconstruction and dense face alignment from a single image with 2D-assisted self-supervised learning. arXiv preprint arXiv:1903.09359 (2019)

76. Wei, H., Liang, S., Wei, Y.: 3D dense face alignment via graph convolution networks (2019)

77. Weise, T., Bouaziz, S., Li, H., Pauly, M.: Realtime performance-based facial animation. In: Trans. Graph. **30** (2011)

78. Weise, T., Li, H., Gool, L.J.V., Pauly, M.: Face/Off: live facial puppetry. In: SIGGRAPH/Eurographics Symposium on Computer Animation (SCA), pp. 7–16 (2009)

79. Yamaguchi, S., et al.: High-fidelity facial reflectance and geometry inference from an unconstrained image. ACM Trans. Graph. **37**(4) (2018). https://doi.org/10.1145/3197517.3201364, https://doi.org/10.1145/3197517.3201364

80. Yang, H., Zhu, H., Wang, Y., Huang, M., Shen, Q., Yang, R., Cao, X.: FaceScape: a large-scale high quality 3d face dataset and detailed riggable 3D face prediction. In: IEEE/CVF Conference on Computer Vision and Pattern Recognition (CVPR), June 2020

81. Yin, L., Wei, X., Sun, Y., Wang, J., Rosato, M.: A 3d facial expression database for facial behavior research. In: 7th International Conference on Automatic Face and Gesture Recognition (FGR06), pp. 211–216 (2006). https://doi.org/10.1109/FGR.2006.6

82. Zhang, Z., et al.: Multimodal spontaneous emotion corpus for human behavior analysis. In: 2016 IEEE Conference on Computer Vision and Pattern Recognition (CVPR), pp. 3438–3446 (2016). https://doi.org/10.1109/CVPR.2016.374

83. Zhu, H., et al.: FacesCape: 3D facial dataset and benchmark for single-view 3D face reconstruction. arXiv preprint arXiv:2111.01082 (2021)

84. Zhu, X., Lei, Z., Liu, X., Shi, H., Li, S.Z.: Face alignment across large poses: a 3D solution. In: Conference on Computer Vision and Pattern Recognition (CVPR). pp. 146–155. IEEE Computer Society, Los Alamitos, CA, USA, June 2016. https://doi.org/10.1109/CVPR.2016.23, https://doi.ieeecomputersociety.org/10.1109/CVPR.2016.23

85. Zollhöfer, M., et al.: State of the art on monocular 3D face reconstruction, tracking, and applications. Comput. Graph. Forum (Eurographics State of the Art Reports) **37**(2) (2018)

Discover and Mitigate Unknown Biases with Debiasing Alternate Networks

Zhiheng Li[1], Anthony Hoogs[2], and Chenliang Xu[1(✉)]

[1] University of Rochester, Rochester, USA
{zhiheng.li,chenliang.xu}@rochester.edu
[2] Kitware, Inc., Clifton Park, USA
anthony.hoogs@kitware.com

Abstract. Deep image classifiers have been found to learn biases from datasets. To mitigate the biases, most previous methods require labels of protected attributes (e.g., age, skin tone) as full-supervision, which has two limitations: 1) it is infeasible when the labels are unavailable; 2) they are incapable of mitigating unknown biases—biases that humans do not preconceive. To resolve those problems, we propose Debiasing Alternate Networks (DebiAN), which comprises two networks—a Discoverer and a Classifier. By training in an alternate manner, the discoverer tries to find multiple unknown biases of the classifier without any annotations of biases, and the classifier aims at unlearning the biases identified by the discoverer. While previous works evaluate debiasing results in terms of a single bias, we create Multi-Color MNIST dataset to better benchmark mitigation of multiple biases in a multi-bias setting, which not only reveals the problems in previous methods but also demonstrates the advantage of DebiAN in identifying and mitigating multiple biases simultaneously. We further conduct extensive experiments on real-world datasets, showing that the discoverer in DebiAN can identify unknown biases that may be hard to be found by humans. Regarding debiasing, DebiAN achieves strong bias mitigation performance.

Keywords: Bias identification · Bias mitigation · Fairness · Unsupervised debiasing

1 Introduction

Many studies have verified that AI algorithms learn undesirable biases from the dataset. Some biases provide shortcuts [18] for the network to learn superficial features instead of the intended decision rule causing robustness issues, *e.g.*, static cues for action recognition [7,11,40]. Other biases make AI algorithms discriminate against different protected demographic groups such as

---

Supplementary Information The online version contains supplementary material available at https://doi.org/10.1007/978-3-031-19778-9_16.

genders[1] [3,25–27,58,61,66] and skin tones [9,23], leading to serious fairness problems. Therefore, it is imperative to mitigate the biases in AI algorithms. However, most previous bias mitigation methods [4,54,60,64,66] are supervised methods—requiring annotations of the biases, which has several limitations: First, bias mitigation cannot be performed when labels are not available due to privacy concerns. Second, they cannot mitigate *unknown* biases—biases that humans did not preconceive, making the biases impossible to be labeled and mitigated.

Since supervised debiasing methods present many disadvantages, in this work, we focus on a more challenging task—unsupervised debiasing, which mitigates the *unknown* biases in a learned classifier without any annotations. Without loss of generality, we focus on mitigating biases in image classifiers. Solving this problem contains two steps [2,14,36,45,52]: bias identification and bias mitigation.

Due to the absence of bias annotations, the first step is to assign the training samples into different bias groups as the pseudo bias labels, which is challenging since the biases are even unknown. The crux of the problem is to define the unknown bias. Some previous works make strong assumptions about the unknown biases based on empirical observations, such as biases are easier to be learned [45], samples from the same bias group are clustered in feature space [52], which can be tenuous for different datasets or networks. Other works quantify the unknown biases by inversely using the debiasing objective functions [2,14], which can face numerical or convergence problems (more details in Sect. 2). Unlike previous works, we follow an axiomatic principle to define the unknown biases—classifier's predictions that violate a fairness criterion [13,17,21,22,35,46,55]. Based on this definition, we propose a novel *Equal Opportunity Violation* (EOV) loss to train a *discoverer* network to identify the classifier's biases. In specific, it shepherds the *discoverer* network to predict bias group assignments such that the *classifier* violates the Equal Opportunity [22,46] fairness criterion (Figs. 1, 2).

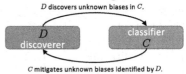

D discovers unknown biases in *C*.

C mitigates unknown biases identified by *D*.

Fig. 1. DEBIASING ALTERNATE NETWORKS (DebiAN). We alternately train two networks—a *discover* and a *classifier*. *Discoverer* actively identifies *classifier*'s unknown biases. At the same time, the *classifier* mitigates the biases identified by the *discoverer*.

Regarding debiasing as the second step, most previous approaches [2,14,52] preprocess the identified biases into pseudo bias labels and resort to other supervised bias mitigation methods [6,47] for debiasing. In contrast, we propose a novel *Reweighted Cross-Entropy* (RCE) loss that leverages soft bias group assignments predicted by the *discoverer* network to mitigate the biases in the *classifier* (Fig. 1). In this way, the *classifier* is guided to meet the Equal Opportunity.

In addition, many previous works [2,14,52] treat bias identification and bias mitigation as two isolated steps. In [2,14], the biases are identified from an undertrained classifier, which is suboptimal since the classifier may learn different

---

[1] In this work, "gender" denotes visually perceived gender, not real gender identity.

biases at different training stages. Consequently, these two-stage methods fail to mitigate other biases learned by the classifier at later training stages. In contrast, we employ an alternate training scheme to carry out bias identification and bias mitigation simultaneously. We jointly update the *discoverer* and *classifier* in an interleaving fashion (Figs. 1 and 2). In this way, the *discoverer* can repetitively inspect multiple biases that the *classifier* learns at the entire training stage.

We integrate our novel losses and training scheme into a unified framework— DEBIASING ALTERNATE NETWORKS (DebiAN), which contains two networks—a *discoverer* D and a *classifier* C (see Fig. 1). We jointly train the two networks in an alternate manner. Supervised by our novel EOV loss, D tries to discover C's multiple unknown biases that violate the Equal Opportunity fairness criterion. Trained with our RCE loss, C aims at mitigating multiple biases identified by the *discoverer* D to satisfy Equal Opportunity. After the alternate training, the unknown biases in *classifier* C are mitigated, leading to a fairer and more robust classification model. Besides, when employed with other network explanation methods [49,50,67], the *discoverer* is helpful to interpret the discovered unknown biases, facilitating dataset curators to locate dataset biases [53].

While previous works [7,31,41,45,47] only evaluate debiasing results in terms of a single bias, we create Multi-Color MNIST dataset with two biases in the dataset, which benchmarks debiasing algorithms in the multi-bias setting. Our new dataset surfaces the problems in previous methods (*e.g.*, LfF [45]) and demonstrates the advantage of DebiAN in discovering and mitigating multiple biases. We further conduct extensive experiments to verify the efficacy of DebiAN in real-world image datasets. In the face image domain, DebiAN achieves better gender bias mitigation results on CelebA [43] and bFFHQ [32] datasets. On the gender classification task, DebiAN achieves better debiasing results on CelebA w.r.t.multiple bias attributes. We further show an interesting unknown bias discovered by DebiAN in gender classification—`visible hair area`. Lastly, we show that DebiAN applies to other image domains for broader tasks, such as action recognition and scene classification. Our method not only achieves better debiasing results, but also identifies interesting unknown biases in scene classifiers.

Our contributions are summarized as follows: (1) We propose a novel objective function, *Equal Opportunity Violation* (EOV) loss, for identifying unknown biases of a classifier based on Equal Opportunity. (2) We propose a *Reweighted Cross-Entropy* (RCE) loss to mitigate the discovered unknown biases by leveraging the soft bias group assignments. (3) We create Multi-Color MNIST dataset to benchmark debiasing algorithms in a multi-bias setting. (4) Our DEBIASING ALTERNATE NETWORKS (DebiAN) outperforms previous unsupervised debiasing methods on both synthetic and real-world datasets.

2   Related Work

Bias Identification. Most previous works identify *known* biases based on bias labels. In [9], face images are labeled with gender and skin tone to identify the performance gaps across intersectional groups. Balakrishnan *et al.* [8] further synthesize intersectional groups of images and analyze the biases with additional labels.

Beyond face images, recent works [44,56] compute the statistics of labels based on the rule mining algorithm [1] or external tools. [34] uses clustering on image embeddings to discover unknown biases. [37,42] discovers *unknown* biases without labels. However, these works rely on GAN [20,29] to synthesize images, which suffers from image quality issues. In contrast, DebiAN directly classifies real images into different bias attribute groups to discover the unknown biases.

Supervised Debiasing. Supervised debiasing methods use bias labels for debiasing. [28] proposes a supervised reweighing method. Wang *et al.* [62] benchmark recent supervised debiasing methods [4,54,64,66]. [15] lets the model be flexibly fair to different attributes during testing. [48] uses disentanglement for debiasing. Singh *et al.* [51] propose a feature splitting approach to mitigate contextual bias. [16,19] use adversarial training to mitigate biases in face recognition.

Known Bias Mitigation with Prior knowledge. Without using labels, some works use prior knowledge to mitigate certain known biases. ReBias [7] uses model capacity as the inductive bias to mitigate texture bias and static bias in image and video classification. HEX [57] introduces a texture extractor to mitigate the texture bias. Beyond image classification, RUBi [10] and LearnedMixin [12] mitigate unimodal bias for visual question answering [5] with prior knowledge.

Unsupervised Debiasing. In the field of mitigating unknown biases, Sohoni *et al.* [52] apply clustering on samples in each class and use the clustering assignment as the predicted bias labels, which could be inaccurate due to its unsupervised nature. Li *et al.* [39,40] fix the parameters of feature extractors and focus on mitigating the representation bias. LfF [45] identifies biases by finding easier samples in the training data through training a bias-amplified network supervised by GCE loss [65], which up-weights the samples with smaller loss values and down-weights the samples with larger loss values. In other words, GCE loss does not consider the information of the classifier, *e.g.*, the classifier's output. Therefore, LfF's bias-amplified network blindly finds the biases in the data samples instead of the classifier. Unlike LfF, the EOV loss in DebiAN actively identifies biases in the classifier based on the classifier's predictions, leading to better debiasing performance. Following LfF, BiaSwap [32] uses LfF to discover biases and generate more underrepesented images via style-transfer for training. Other works [2,14,36,59] inversely use the debiasing objective function to maximize an unbounded loss (*e.g.*, gradient norm penalty in IRMv1 [6]) for bias identification, which may encounter numerical or convergence problems. As a comparison, our EOV loss (Eq. (2)) minimizes negative log-likelihood, which is numerically stable and easier to converge.

3   Method

Overview. The overview of our proposed DEBIASING ALTERNATE NETWORKS (DebiAN) is shown in Fig. 2. It contains two networks—a *discoverer* D and a *classifier* C. As shown in Fig. 2 (a), the *discoverer* D tries to discover the unknown biases in the *classifier* C by optimizing our proposed EOV loss ($\mathcal{L}_{\text{EOV}}$)

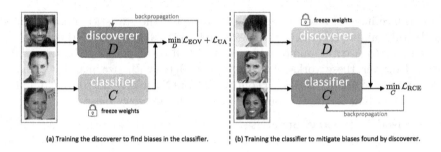

(a) Training the discoverer to find biases in the classifier.   (b) Training the classifier to mitigate biases found by discoverer.

Fig. 2. Overview of DEBIASING ALTERNATE NETWORKS (DebiAN). DebiAN consists of two networks—a *discoverer* D and a *classifier* C. D is trained with $\mathcal{L}_{EOV}$ and $\mathcal{L}_{UA}$ (Sect. 3.1) to find the unknown biases in C. C is optimized with $\mathcal{L}_{RCE}$ (Sect. 3.2) to mitigate the biases identified by D

and UA penalty ($\mathcal{L}_{UA}$) (Sect. 3.1). As shown in Fig. 2 (b), the *classifier* C's goal is to mitigate the biases identified by D via a novel *Reweighted Cross-Entropy* loss ($\mathcal{L}_{RCE}$) (Sect. 3.2). Lastly, we train the two networks in an alternate manner as the full model for discovering and mitigating the unknown biases (Sect. 3.3).

Background. To better explain our motivation for discovering the *unknown* biases (without manual annotations of biases), let us first revisit the traditional approach for identifying *known* biases when labels of biases (*e.g.*, protected attributes) are available, which is illustrated in Fig. 3 (a). The following are given for identifying *known* biases—a well-trained *classifier* C for predicting a target attribute, n testing images $\{\mathbf{I}_i\}_{i=1}^n$, target attribute labels of each image $\{y_i\}_{i=1}^n$, and bias attribute labels $\{b_i\}_{i=1}^n$. We denote the i-th image target attribute as $y_i \in \{1, 2, ...K\}$ and K is the number of classes. We consider the bias attribute that is binary or continuously valued (*i.e.*, $b_i \in \{0, 1\}$ or $b_i \in [0, 1]$), such as biological gender (*e.g.*, female and male) and skin tones (*e.g.*, from dark skin tones to light skin tones in Fitzpatrick skin type scale). We leave bias attributes with multi-class values for future works. Then, the given *classifier* C is tested for predicting the target attribute $\hat{y}_i$ for each testing image $\mathbf{I}_i$. Finally, we check whether the predictions meet a fairness criterion, such as Equal Opportunity [22]:

$$\Pr\{\hat{y} = k \mid b = 0, y = k\} = \Pr\{\hat{y} = k \mid b = 1, y = k\}, \tag{1}$$

where the LHS and RHS are true positive rates (TPR) in negative ($b = 0$) and positive ($b = 1$) bias attribute groups, respectively. $k \in \{1...K\}$ is a target attribute class. Equal Opportunity requires the same TPR across two different bias attribute groups. That is, if the TPR is significantly different in two groups of the bias attribute, we conclude that *classifier* C contains the bias of attribute b because C violates the Equal Opportunity fairness criterion. For example, as shown in Fig. 3 (a), although all images are female, a gender classifier may have a larger TPR for the group of long-hair female images than the group of short-hair female images. Thus the gender classifier is biased against different hair lengths.

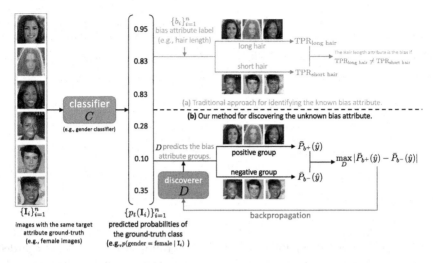

Fig. 3. (a): The traditional approach for identifying the *known* bias attribute (*e.g.*, hair length) by comparing true positive rates (TPR) of the target attribute (*e.g.*, gender) in two groups of bias attributes (*e.g.*, long hair and short hair), where the group assignment of bias attribute is based on the labels of the bias attribute. **(b)**: Our method trains a *discoverer* (D) to predict the groups of the unknown bias attribute such that the difference of averaged predicted probabilities on the target attribute (*e.g.*, gender) in two groups are maximized (see Eq. 2)

3.1 Unknown Bias Discovery

As for identifying unknown biases, we do not have the labels to assign images into two groups for comparing TPR since 1) we do not assume images come with bias attribute labels, and 2) the type of bias is even unknown. However, we can compare the difference in TPR for any group assignments based on speculated biases—a significant difference in TPR hints that the Equal Opportunity fairness criterion is most violated (our method mainly focuses on the Equal Opportunity fairness criterion, and we leave other fairness criteria for future work). Motivated by this finding, instead of using labels of bias attribute $\{b_i\}_{i=1}^{n}$ for group assignment, we train a *discoverer* D to predict the group assignment for each image, *i.e.*, $p(\hat{b} \mid \mathbf{I}_i) := D(\mathbf{I}_i)$. By optimizing loss functions below, we find the most salient bias of the *classifier* C that violates the Equal Opportunity fairness criterion, which is illustrated in Fig. 3 (b).

Equal Opportunity Violation (EOV) Loss. To shepherd the *discoverer* D to find the group assignment where *classifier* C violates the Equal Opportunity fairness criterion, we propose the *Equal Opportunity Violation* (EOV) loss, denoted by $\mathcal{L}_{\text{EOV}}$, as the objective function to train D. For computing $\mathcal{L}_{\text{EOV}}$, we sample a set of n images $\{\mathbf{I}_i\}_{i=1}^{n}$ with the *same* target attribute labels (*i.e.*, $\forall_i y_i = k$), *e.g.*, all images in Fig. 3 (b) are female. The *classifier* C has been trained for predicting the target attribute y of the images (*i.e.*, $p(\hat{y} \mid \mathbf{I}_i) := C(\mathbf{I}_i)$). For simplicity, we denote p_t as C's prediction on images of the ground-truth class (*i.e.*, $p_t(\mathbf{I}_i) = p(\hat{y} = y_i \mid \mathbf{I}_i)$). Meanwhile, the same set of images $\{\mathbf{I}_i\}$ are fed to the *discoverer* D for predicting the binary bias attribute group assignment: $p(\hat{b} \mid \mathbf{I}_i) := D(\mathbf{I}_i)$. Finally, we define the EOV loss as:

$$\mathcal{L}_{\text{EOV}} = -\log\left(\left|\bar{P}_{b+}(\hat{y}) - \bar{P}_{b-}(\hat{y})\right|\right), \tag{2}$$

where $\bar{P}_{b+}(\hat{y})$ and $\bar{P}_{b-}(\hat{y})$ are defined by:

$$
\begin{aligned}
\bar{P}_{b+}(\hat{y}) &= \frac{\sum_{i=1}^{n} p(\hat{b}=1 \mid \mathbf{I}_i) p_t(\mathbf{I}_i)}{\sum_{i=1}^{n} p(\hat{b}=1 \mid \mathbf{I}_i)}, \\
\bar{P}_{b-}(\hat{y}) &= \frac{\sum_{i=1}^{n} p(\hat{b}=0 \mid \mathbf{I}_i) p_t(\mathbf{I}_i)}{\sum_{i=1}^{n} p(\hat{b}=0 \mid \mathbf{I}_i)}.
\end{aligned} \tag{3}
$$

Intuitively, $\bar{P}_{b+}(\hat{y})$ and $\bar{P}_{b-}(\hat{y})$ are the weighted average predicted probabilities of the target attribute in two bias attribute groups, which can be regarded as a relaxation to Equal Opportunity's true positive rate (Eq. 1) where the predicted probabilities are binarized into predictions with a threshold (*e.g.*, 0.5). Minimizing $\mathcal{L}_{\text{EOV}}$ leads D to maximize the discrepancy of averaged predicted probabilities of target attributes in two bias attribute groups (*i.e.*, see $\max_D |\bar{P}_{b+}(\hat{y}) - \bar{P}_{b-}(\hat{y})|$ in Fig. 3), thus finding the bias attribute group assignments where C violates the Equal Opportunity fairness criterion. For example, in Fig. 3 (b), if the gender classifier C is biased against different hair lengths, then by optimizing $\mathcal{L}_{\text{EOV}}$, D can assign the female images into two bias attribute groups (*i.e.*, short hair and long hair) with the predicted bias attribute group assignment probability $p(\hat{b} \mid \mathbf{I}_i)$, such that the difference of averaged predicted probabilities on gender in these two groups is maximized.

Unbalanced Assignment (UA) Penalty. However, we find that optimizing $\mathcal{L}_{\text{EOV}}$ alone may let the *discoverer* D find a trivial solution—assigning all images into one bias attribute group. For example, suppose D assigns all images to the positive bias attribute group (*i.e.*, $\forall_i,\ p(\hat{b}=1 \mid \mathbf{I}_i) = 1$). In that case, $\bar{P}_{b-}(\hat{y})$ becomes zero since the negative group contains no images. $\bar{P}_{b+}(\hat{y})$ becomes a large positive number by simply averaging $p_t(\mathbf{I}_i)$ for all of the n images, which can trivially increase $|\bar{P}_{b+}(\hat{y}) - \bar{P}_{b-}(\hat{y})|$, leading to a small $\mathcal{L}_{\text{EOV}}$. To prevent this trivial solution, we propose the *Unbalanced Assignment* (UA) loss denoted by:

$$\mathcal{L}_{\text{UA}} = -\log\left(1 - \frac{1}{n}\left|\sum_{i=1}^{n} p(\hat{b}=1 \mid \mathbf{I}_i) - p(\hat{b}=0 \mid \mathbf{I}_i)\right|\right). \tag{4}$$

Intuitively, minimizing $\mathcal{L}_{\text{UA}}$ penalizes the unbalanced assignment that leads to large difference between $\sum_{i=1}^{n} p(\hat{b}=1 \mid \mathbf{I}_i)$ and $\sum_{i=1}^{n} p(\hat{b}=0 \mid \mathbf{I}_i)$, which can be regarded as the numbers of images assigned into positive and negative bias attribute groups, respectively. Therefore, $\mathcal{L}_{\text{EOV}}$ is jointly optimized with $\mathcal{L}_{\text{UA}}$ to prevent the trivial solution. We acknowledge a limitation of the UA penalty. Although it resolves the trivial solution, it introduces a trade-off since the bias attribute groups are usually spuriously correlated with the target attribute (*e.g.*, more long-hair females than the short-hair females in the dataset). Hence encouraging balanced assignments may make the *discoverer* harder to find the correct assignment. However, our ablation study shows that the benefits of using $\mathcal{L}_{UA}$ outweigh its limitations. The results are shown in Sect. 4.1 and Table 1.

3.2 Unknown Bias Mitigation by Reweighing

We further mitigate C's unknown biases identified by D. To this end, we propose a novel *Reweighted Cross-Entropy* loss that adjusts the weight of each image's classification loss. Based on the bias attribute group assignment $p(\hat{b} \mid \mathbf{I}_i)$ predicted by D, we define the weight $\mathcal{W}(\mathbf{I}_i)$ of classification loss for each image $\mathbf{I}_i$ as:

$$
\begin{aligned}
\mathcal{W}(\mathbf{I}_i) = & \mathbb{1}\left[\bar{P}_{b+}(\hat{y}) \geq \bar{P}_{b-}(\hat{y})\right] p(\hat{b} = 0 \mid \mathbf{I}_i) \\
& + \mathbb{1}\left[\bar{P}_{b+}(\hat{y}) < \bar{P}_{b-}(\hat{y})\right] p(\hat{b} = 1 \mid \mathbf{I}_i),
\end{aligned}
\tag{5}
$$

where $\mathbb{1}$ is an indicator function. Then, the *Reweighted Cross-Entropy* loss ($\mathcal{L}_{RCE}$) is defined by:

$$
\mathcal{L}_{RCE} = -\frac{1}{n}\sum_{i=1}^{n}(1 + \mathcal{W}(\mathbf{I}_i))\log p_t(\mathbf{I}_i).
\tag{6}
$$

For example, when C performs better on images from the positive bias attribute group (*i.e.*, $\bar{P}_{b+}(\hat{y}) \geq \bar{P}_{b-}(\hat{y})$), we use $p(\hat{b} = 0 \mid \mathbf{I}_i)$ as the weight, which up-weights the images from the negative bias attribute group, where classifier C is worse-performed. At the same time, it down-weights the images from the positive bias attribute group where C is already better-performed. Adding one to the weight in Eq. (6) lets the loss function degenerate to standard cross-entropy loss when $\mathcal{W}(\mathbf{I}_i) = 0$. By minimizing the *Reweighted Cross-Entropy* loss, C is guided to meet Equal Opportunity.

3.3 Full Model

We summarize the proposed losses in Sect. 3.1 and Sect. 3.2 for the full model of DEBIASING ALTERNATE NETWORKS (DebiAN), which is shown in Fig. 2. When the task is to only discover (*i.e.*, not mitigate) the unknown biases of a given classifier, the classifier's parameters are fixed and we only train the *discoverer* D by minimizing $\mathcal{L}_{EOV}$ (Eq. 2) and $\mathcal{L}_{UA}$ (Eq. 4) on the classifier's training data. When the task is to mitigate the unknown biases, we jointly train two networks in an alternate fashion:

$$
\min_{D} \mathcal{L}_{EOV} + \mathcal{L}_{UA},
\tag{7}
$$

$$
\min_{C} \mathcal{L}_{RCE}.
\tag{8}
$$

In Eq. 7, C's parameters are fixed, and D is optimized to identify C's unknown biases where C violates the Equal Opportunity. Through Eq. 8, C is optimized for mitigating the unknown biases discovered by D to satisfy the Equal Opportunity while D's parameters are frozen. After the alternate training, C's unknown biases identified by D are mitigated, leading to a fairer and more robust *classifier*. The pseudocode of the complete algorithm is in Appendix A.

4 Experiment

We conduct extensive experiments to verify the efficacy of DebiAN. First, we evaluate the results on our newly created Multi-Color MNIST dataset (Sect. 4.1) in a multi-bias setting. We further conduct experiments on real-world datasets in multiple image domains–face (Sect. 4.2) and other image domains (*e.g.*, scene, action recognition) (Sect. 4.3). More details (*e.g.*, evaluation metrics) are introduced in each subsection. The code and our newly created Multi-Color MNIST dataset are released at https://github.com/zhihengli-UR/DebiAN.

Comparison Methods. We mainly compare with three unsupervised debiasing methods: 1) LfF [45] uses Generalized Cross-entropy (GCE) loss [65] to train a "biased model" for reweighing the classifier; 2) EIIL [14] identifies the bias groups by optimizing bias group assignment to maximize the IRMv1 [6] objective function. The identified bias groups will serve as pseudo bias labels for other supervised debiasing methods to mitigate the biases. Following [14], IRM [6] is used as the debiasing algorithm for EIIL. 3) PGI [2] follows EIIL to identify the biases by training a small multi-layer perceptron for bias label predictions. Concerning debiasing, PGI minimizes the KL-divergence of the classifier's predictions across different bias groups. We use the officially released code of LfF, EIIL, and PGI in our experiment. Besides, we also compare with vanilla models, which do not have any debiasing techniques (*i.e.*, only using standard cross-entropy loss for training). On bFFHQ [32] and BAR [45] datasets, we also compare with BiaSwap [32], which follows LfF to identify unknown biases, and then uses style-transfer to generate more underrepresented images for training. Since its code has not been released, we cannot compare DebiAN with BiaSwap on other datasets. All results shown below are the mean results over three random seeds of runs, and we also report the standard deviation as the error bar.

4.1 Experiment on Multi-Color MNIST

Many previous works use synthetic datasets to benchmark bias mitigation performance. For example, Colored MNIST [7,31,41] adds color bias to the original MNIST [38] dataset, where each digit class is spuriously correlated with color (see Fig. 4 (a)). We compare DebiAN with other methods on the Colored MNIST dataset in Appendix E. However, we believe that the single-bias setting is an oversimplification of the real-world scenario where multiple biases may exist. For instance, Lang *et al.* [37] find that gender classifiers are biased with multiple independent bias attributes, including wearing lipsticks, eyebrow thickness, nose width, *etc.*. The benchmarking results on such a single-bias synthetic dataset may not help us to design better debiasing algorithms for real-world usage.

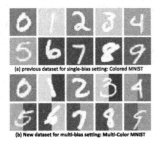

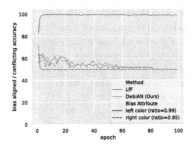

Fig. 4. Comparison between (a) previous Colored MNIST [7,31,41] with a single color bias and **(b)** our new Multi-Color MNIST dataset that contains *two* bias attributes—`left color` and `right color`

Fig. 5. Evaluating bias discovery w.r.t.`left color`, `right color` biases throughout the training epochs on Multi-Color MNIST. LfF only finds the more salient `left color` bias (ratio=0.99), whereas DebiAN's *discoverer* finds both biases at the early training stage. Then accuracies gradually converge to 50% as debiasing is performed in the *classifier*, making the *discoverer* harder to find biases

To this end, we propose **Multi-Color MNIST** dataset to benchmark debiasing methods under the multi-bias setting. In the training set, each digit class is spuriously correlated with *two* bias attributes—`left color` and `right color` (Fig. 4 (b)). Following the terms used in LfF [45], we call samples that can be correctly predicted with the bias attribute as bias-aligned samples. Samples that cannot be correctly predicted with the bias attribute are called bias-conflicting samples. For example, if most digit "0" images are in red `left color` in the training set, we call them bias-aligned samples w.r.t.`left color` attribute, and we regard digit "0" images in a different `left color` (*e.g.*, yellow) as bias-conflicting samples. Since the dataset contains two bias attributes, there exist images that are bias-aligned w.r.t.to `left color` and bias-conflicting w.r.t.`right color` simultaneously, or vice versa. Following [45], we use the *ratio* of the bias-aligned samples for each bias attribute to indicate how strong the spurious correlation is in the training set. The two ratios for two bias attributes can be different, which is more common in the real-world scenario. The images in the testing set also contain two background colors, but the testing set has a balanced distribution of bias-aligned and bias-conflicting samples w.r.t.each bias attribute.

Evaluation Metrics and Settings. Following [45], we report the accuracy results in bias-aligned and bias-conflicting samples on the testing set. Since Multi-Color MNIST contains two bias attributes, we report the four accuracy results in the combination of (bias-aligned, bias-conflicting) × (`left color`, `right color`), *e.g.*, middle four rows in Table 1 for each method. We also report the unbiased accuracy, which averages the four results above. Here, we choose

Table 1. Debiasing results on multi-color MNIST dataset. The accuracy results in the four combinations of two bias attributes, (*i.e.*, left color and right color) and (bias-aligned and bias-conflicting) are reported. Unbiased accuracy averages the results over all four combinations. We bold top-2 results and underline lowest results

left color Ratio = 0.99	right color Ratio = 0.95	Vanilla	LfF	EIIL	PGI	w/o $\mathcal{L}_{\mathrm{UA}}$ (Ours)	DebiAN (Ours)
Bias-aligned	Bias-aligned	**100.0 ± 0.0**	99.6 ± 0.5	**100.0 ± 0.0**	98.6 ± 2.3	**100.0 ± 0.0**	**100.0 ± 0.0**
Bias-aligned	Bias-conflicting	97.1 ± 0.5	4.7 ± 0.5	**97.2 ± 1.5**	82.6 ± 19.6	**97.2 ± 0.5**	95.6 ± 0.8
Bias-conflicting	Bias-aligned	27.5 ± 3.6	**98.6 ± 0.4**	70.8 ± 4.9	26.6 ± 5.5	71.6 ± 0.7	**76.5 ± 0.7**
Bias-conflicting	Bias-conflicting	5.2 ± 0.4	5.1 ± 0.4	10.9 ± 0.8	9.5 ± 3.2	**13.8 ± 1.1**	**16.0 ± 1.8**
Unbiased accuracy		57.4 ± 0.7	52.0 ± 0.1	69.7 ± 1.0	54.3 ± 4.0	**70.6 ± 0.3**	**72.0 ± 0.8**

0.99 as the ratio of bias-aligned samples w.r.t. left color and 0.95 as the ratio of bias-aligned samples w.r.t. right color. In this way, the left color is a *more salient* bias than the right color. We report the results of other ratio combinations in Appendix C.3. We strictly use the same set of hyperparameters used in (single) Colored MNIST in LfF. More details are in Appendix B.

Debiasing Results on Multi-Color MNIST. The debiasing results are shown in Table 1. Except for LfF, all other methods achieve higher accuracy results on left color bias-aligned samples (1st and 2nd rows) than right color bias-aligned samples (1st and 3rd rows), indicating that most methods are more biased w.r.t. the more salient bias, *i.e.*, left color (ratio=0.99) in the multi-bias setting. Unlike all other methods, LfF gives abnormal results— high accuracy results (*e.g.*, 99.6, 98.6) for the right color bias-aligned samples and low accuracy results (*e.g.*, 4.7, 5.1) for the right color bias-conflicting samples. Consequently, LfF achieves the worst unbiased accuracy (52.0). The results indicate that LfF only mitigates the more salient left color bias, rendering the classifier to learn the less salient right color bias (ratio=0.95). Compared with all other methods, DebiAN achieves better unbiased accuracy results (72.0). More importantly, DebiAN achieves much better debiasing result (16.0) in bias-conflicting samples w.r.t. both left color and right color attributes, where neither color can provide the shortcut for the correct digit class prediction, demonstrating better debiasing results of DebiAN for mitigating multiple biases simultaneously in the multi-bias setting, which is closer to the real-world scenarios.

Bias Discovery: LfF vs. DebiAN. We further evaluate the bias discovery results throughout the entire training epochs, which helps us better understand LfF's abnormal results and DebiAN's advantages. We use LfF's "biased model" and DebiAN's *discoverer* to predict if a given image is bias-aligned or bias-conflicting w.r.t. a bias attribute (*i.e.*, binary classification, more details in Appendix D.1). We show the accuracy results of bias discovery w.r.t. each bias attribute at the end of each epoch in Fig. 5, which shows that LfF only discovers the more salient left color bias attribute (100% accuracy), but completely ignores the less salient right color bias (50% accuracy) throughout the entire

Table 2. Results of mitigating the gender bias of `Blond Hair` classifier on CelebA [43]

	Vanilla	LfF	EIIL	PGI	DebiAN (Ours)
Avg. Group Acc.	79.8 ± 0.3	80.9 ± 1.4	82.0 ± 1.1	81.6 ± 0.3	**84.0 ± 1.4**
Worst Group Acc.	37.9 ± 1.1	43.3 ± 3.0	46.1 ± 4.9	40.9 ± 6.4	**52.9 ± 4.7**

Table 3. Accuracy results on bias-conflicting samples on bFFHQ [32]

Vanilla	LfF	PGI	EIIL	BiaSwap	DebiAN
51.03	55.61	55.2 ± 5.3	59.2 ± 1.9	58.87	**62.8 ± 0.6**

training stage. It reveals the problem of LfF's definition of the unknown bias—an attribute in the dataset that is easier, which only holds in the single-bias setting but does not generalize to the multi-bias setting. In contrast, DebiAN uses the principled definition to define the bias—classifier's predictions that violate equal opportunity, enabling *discoverer* to find both biases accurately at the beginning (it achieves about 60% to 70% accuracy because debiasing is simultaneously performed before the end of the first epoch). At the same time, DebiAN's alternate training scheme lets the classifier mitigate both biases, making the *discoverer* harder to predict the biases, *e.g.*, accuracies of both bias attributes gradually converge to 50%. More discussions are in Appendix D.4.

Ablation Study on UA Penalty. We conduct an ablation study to show the effectiveness of Unbalanced Assignment (UA) penalty (Sect. 3.1). Table 1 shows that $\mathcal{L}_{UA}$ improves the debiasing results (see w/o $\mathcal{L}_{UA}$). Besides, we also conduct ablation studies on different batch sizes, which are included in Appendix C.2.

4.2 Experiments on Face Image Dataset

Gender Bias Mitigation. In the face image domain, we conduct experiments to evaluate gender bias mitigation results on CelebA [43] dataset, which contains 200K celebrity faces annotated with 40 binary attributes. The dataset has spurious correlations between gender and `Blond Hair`, leading to gender biases when performing hair color classification. We follow most of the settings used in LfF, such as using ResNet-18 [24] as the backbone, using Adam [33] optimizer, *etc.*. The only difference is that LfF reports the results on the validation set of CelebA, whereas we use the validation set to select the epoch with the best validation set accuracy (bias labels in the validation set are not used) to report the results on the testing set. All methods (including LfF) are benchmarked under the same setting. We report results in two evaluation metrics: 1) Average Group Accuracy (Avg. Group Acc.), which calculates the unweighted average of accuracies in four groups between target attribute and bias attribute, *i.e.*, (male, female) × (blond, not blond); 2) Worst Group Accuracy (Worst Group Acc.) [47], which takes the lowest accuracy in the four groups. As shown in Table 2, DebiAN achieves better Average and Worst Group accuracy results, which shows that DebiAN can better mitigate gender bias without labels. We also conduct experiments on bFFHQ [32] where the training data contains the spurious correlation between age and gender. We compare DebiAN with other methods of gender bias mitigation. We strictly follow the setting in [32]. We

Table 4. Results of mitigating multiple biases (*i.e.*, `Wearing Lipstick` and `Heavy Makeup`) in gender classifier on CelebA dataset

Bias attribute	Metric	Vanilla	LfF	PGI	EIIL	DebiAN (Ours)
`Wearing Lipstick`	Avg. Group Acc.	86.6 ± 0.4	87.0 ± 0.9	86.9 ± 3.1	86.3 ± 1.0	**88.5 ± 1.1**
	Worst Group Acc.	53.9 ± 1.2	55.3 ± 3.6	56.0 ± 11.7	52.4 ± 3.2	**61.7 ± 4.2**
`Heavy Makeup`	Avg. Group Acc	85.1 ± 0.0	85.5 ± 0.6	85.4 ± 3.4	84.0 ± 1.2	**87.8 ± 1.3**
	Worst Group Acc.	45.4 ± 0.0	46.9 ± 2.6	46.9 ± 13.1	40.9 ± 4.5	**56.0 ± 5.2**

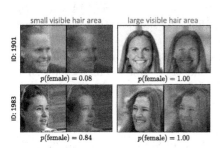

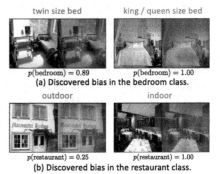

(a) Discovered bias in the bedroom class.

(b) Discovered bias in the restaurant class.

Fig. 6. Discovered bias of gender classifier: `visible hair area` based on *discoverer*'s saliency map. p(female) is vanilla classifier's predicted probability of the face is female. In the two groups predicted by D, the visible hair areas are different, where the classifier has different confidences on gender for the same identity

Fig. 7. Discovered biases in Places [68] dataset. We apply CAM on *discoverer* to generate saliency map. The value p(bedroom) (p(restaurant)) is vanilla classifier's predicted probability of the scene image is bedroom (restaurant)

report the age accuracy results on the bias-conflicting samples in the testing set in Table 3. The results of vanilla, LfF, and BiaSwap are from [32] and [32] does not provide the error bars. DebiAN achieves the best unsupervised results for mitigating gender bias.

Mitigating Multiple Biases in Gender Classifier. The results on Multi-Color MNIST dataset suggest that DebiAN better mitigates multiple biases in the classifier. In the face image domain, a recent study [37] shows that gender classifier is biased by multiple attributes, such as `Heavy Makeup` and `Wearing Lipstick`. Hence, we train gender classifiers on CelebA dataset and evaluate Average Group Accuracy and Worst Group Accuracy w.r.t.these two bias attributes. As shown in Table 4, DebiAN achieves better debiasing results w.r.t.both bias attributes, proving that the *discoverer* can find multiple biases in the classifier C during the alternate training, enabling *classifier* to mitigate multiple biases simultaneously.

Table 5. Results on biased action recognition (BAR) [45] dataset

Vanilla	LfF	PGI	EIIL	BiaSwap	DebiAN
51.85 ± 5.92	62.98 ± 2.76	65.19 ± 1.32	65.44 ± 1.17	52.44	**69.88 ± 2.92**

Table 6. Scene classification accuracy results on the *unseen* LSUN [63] dataset

vanilla	LfF	PGI	EIIL	DebiAN (Ours)
79.3 ± 0.3	71.1 ± 1.0	74.1 ± 1.9	79.4 ± 0.2	**80.0 ± 0.4**

Identified Unknown Bias in Gender Classifier. Gender classifier can have more biases beyond `Wearing Lipstick` and `Heavy Makeup`. For example, Balakrishnan *et al.* [8] leverages StyleGAN2 [30] to generate high-quality synthesized images and identify the `hair length` bias of the gender classifier, *e.g.*, longer hair length makes the classifier predict the face as female. Related to their finding, the *discoverer* D in DebiAN identifies an interesting unknown bias: `visible hair area`. We use D to predict the bias attribute group assignment on images in CelebA. To better interpret the bias attribute, we further use the identity labels in CelebA to cluster images with the same identity. Figure 6 shows that D assigns images of the same identity into two distinct groups based on the visible hair area, which is verified by D's CAM [67] saliency maps. Strictly speaking, all females in Fig. 6 have long hair. However, due to the hairstyle, pose, or occlusion, visible hair areas differ between the two groups. As a result, the gender classifier has lower predicted probabilities on the female images with smaller visible hair areas. More visualizations are shown in Appendix G.1.

4.3 Experiments on Other Image Domains

Our method is not limited to synthetic and face image domains. Here we conduct experiments on action recognition and scene classification tasks.

Mitigating Place Bias in Action Recognition. We conduct experiments on Biased Action Recognition (BAR) dataset [45], an image dataset with the spurious correlation between action and place in the training set. The testing set only contains bias-conflicting samples. Hence, higher accuracy results on the testing set indicate better debiasing results. The accuracy results in Table 5 show that DebiAN achieves better debiasing results than other methods.

Improving Cross-dataset Generalization on Scene Classification. We conduct experiments on the more challenging scene classification task, where datasets are more complex and may contain multiple unknown biases. The biases in this task are underexplored by previous works partly due to the lack of attribute labels. Due to the absence of attribute labels, we use cross-dataset generalization [53] to evaluate the debiasing results. Concretely, models are trained on Places [68] with ten classes overlapped with LSUN [63] (*e.g.*, bedroom, classroom, *etc.*), and evaluated on the *unseen* LSUN dataset. The results are shown in Table 6. DebiAN achieves the best result on the unseen LSUN dataset, showing that DebiAN unlearns the dataset biases [53] in Places to improve the robustness against distributional shifts between different datasets.

Identified Unknown Biases in Scene Classifier. DebiAN discovers Places dataset's unknown biases that humans may not preconceive. In Fig. 7, the *discoverer* separates bedroom and restaurant images based on `size` of beds and `indoor/outdoor`. The vanilla classifier performs worse on bedroom images with twin-size beds and outdoor restaurant images (see more in Appendix G.2).

5   Conclusion

We propose DEBIASING ALTERNATE NETWORKS to discover and mitigate the unknown biases. DebiAN identifies unknown biases that humans may not preconceive and achieves better unsupervised debiasing results. Our Multi-Color MNIST dataset surfaces previous methods' problems and demonstrates DebiAN's advantages in the multi-bias setting. Admittedly, our work has some limitations, *e.g.*, DebiAN focuses on binary or continuously valued bias attributes, not multi-class ones. We hope our work can facilitate research on bias discovery and mitigation.

Acknowledgement. This work has been partially supported by the National Science Foundation (NSF) under Grant 1764415, 1909912, and 1934962 and by the Center of Excellence in Data Science, an Empire State Development-designated Center of Excellence. The article solely reflects the opinions and conclusions of its authors but not the funding agents.

References

1. Agrawal, R., Srikant, R.: Fast algorithms for mining association rules in large databases. In: International Conference on Very Large Data Bases (1994)
2. Ahmed, F., Bengio, Y., van Seijen, H., Courville, A.: Systematic generalisation with group invariant predictions. In: International Conference on Learning Representations (2021)
3. Albiero, V., KS, K., Vangara, K., Zhang, K., King, M.C., Bowyer, K.W.: Analysis of gender inequality in face recognition accuracy. In: The IEEE Winter Conference on Applications of Computer Vision Workshops (WACVW) (2020)
4. Alvi, M., Zisserman, A., Nellaaker, C.: Turning a blind eye: explicit removal of biases and variation from deep neural network embeddings. In: The European Conference on Computer Vision Workshop (ECCVW) (2018)
5. Antol, S., et al.: VQA: visual question answering. In: The IEEE International Conference on Computer Vision (ICCV) (2015)
6. Arjovsky, M., Bottou, L., Gulrajani, I., Lopez-Paz, D.: invariant risk minimization. arXiv:1907.02893 [cs, stat] (2020)
7. Bahng, H., Chun, S., Yun, S., Choo, J., Oh, S.J.: Learning de-biased representations with biased representations. In: International Conference on Machine Learning (2020)
8. Balakrishnan, G., Xiong, Y., Xia, W., Perona, P.: Towards causal benchmarking of bias in face analysis algorithms. In: The European Conference on Computer Vision (ECCV) (2020)

9. Buolamwini, J., Gebru, T.: Gender shades: intersectional accuracy disparities in commercial gender classification. In: ACM Conference on Fairness, Accountability, and Transparency (2018)
10. Cadene, R., Dancette, C., Ben younes, H., Cord, M., Parikh, D.: RUBi: reducing unimodal biases for visual question answering. In: Advances in Neural Information Processing Systems (2019)
11. Choi, J., Gao, C., Messou, J.C.E., Huang, J.B.: Why can't i dance in the mall? Learning to mitigate scene bias in action recognition. In: Advances in Neural Information Processing Systems (2019)
12. Clark, C., Yatskar, M., Zettlemoyer, L.: don't take the easy way out: ensemble based methods for avoiding known dataset biases. In: Empirical Methods in Natural Language Processing (2019)
13. Corbett-Davies, S., Pierson, E., Feller, A., Goel, S., Huq, A.: Algorithmic decision making and the cost of fairness. In: Proceedings of the 23rd ACM SIGKDD International Conference on Knowledge Discovery and Data Mining (2017)
14. Creager, E., Jacobsen, J.H., Zemel, R.: Environment inference for invariant learning. In: International Conference on Machine Learning (2021)
15. Creager, E., et al.: Flexibly fair representation learning by disentanglement. In: International Conference on Machine Learning (2019)
16. Dhar, P., Gleason, J., Roy, A., Castillo, C.D., Chellappa, R.: PASS: protected attribute suppression system for mitigating bias in face recognition. In: The IEEE International Conference on Computer Vision (ICCV) (2021)
17. Dwork, C., Hardt, M., Pitassi, T., Reingold, O., Zemel, R.: Fairness through awareness. In: Proceedings of the 3rd Innovations in Theoretical Computer Science Conference (2012)
18. Geirhos, R., et al.: Shortcut learning in deep neural networks. Nat. Mach. Intell. **2**(11), 665–673 (2020)
19. Gong, S., Liu, X., Jain, A.K.: Jointly de-biasing face recognition and demographic attribute estimation. In: The European Conference on Computer Vision (ECCV) (2020)
20. Goodfellow, I., et al.: Generative adversarial nets. In: Advances in Neural Information Processing Systems (2014)
21. Grgic-Hlaca, N., Zafar, M.B., Gummadi, K.P., Weller, A.: The case for process fairness in learning: Feature selection for fair decision making. In: NIPS Symposium on Machine Learning and the Law (2016)
22. Hardt, M., Price, E., Srebro, N.: Equality of opportunity in supervised learning. In: Advances in Neural Information Processing Systems (2016)
23. Hazirbas, C., Bitton, J., Dolhansky, B., Pan, J., Gordo, A., Ferrer, C.C.: Towards measuring fairness in AI: the casual conversations dataset. arXiv:2104.02821 [cs] (2021)
24. He, K., Zhang, X., Ren, S., Sun, J.: Deep residual learning for image recognition. In: The IEEE Conference on Computer Vision and Pattern Recognition (CVPR) (2016)
25. Hendricks, L.A., Burns, K., Saenko, K., Darrell, T., Rohrbach, A.: Women also snowboard: overcoming bias in captioning models. In: The European Conference on Computer Vision (ECCV) (2018)
26. Jia, S., Meng, T., Zhao, J., Chang, K.W.: Mitigating gender bias amplification in distribution by posterior regularization. In: Annual Meeting of the Association for Computational Linguistics (2020)

27. Joo, J., Kärkkäinen, K.: Gender slopes: counterfactual fairness for computer vision models by attribute manipulation. In: International Workshop on Fairness, Accountability, Transparency and Ethics in Multimedia (2020)
28. Kamiran, F., Calders, T.: Data preprocessing techniques for classification without discrimination. Knowl. Inf. Syst. **33**, 1–33 (2012). https://doi.org/10.1007/s10115-011-0463-8
29. Karras, T., Laine, S., Aila, T.: A style-based generator architecture for generative adversarial networks. In: The IEEE Conference on Computer Vision and Pattern Recognition (CVPR) (2019)
30. Karras, T., Laine, S., Aittala, M., Hellsten, J., Lehtinen, J., Aila, T.: Analyzing and improving the image quality of StyleGAN. In: The IEEE Conference on Computer Vision and Pattern Recognition (CVPR) (2020)
31. Kim, B., Kim, H., Kim, K., Kim, S., Kim, J.: Learning not to learn: training deep neural networks with biased data. In: The IEEE Conference on Computer Vision and Pattern Recognition (CVPR) (2019)
32. Kim, E., Lee, J., Choo, J.: BiaSwap: removing dataset bias with bias-tailored swapping augmentation. In: The IEEE International Conference on Computer Vision (ICCV) (2021)
33. Kingma, D.P., Ba, J.: Adam: a method for stochastic optimization. In: International Conference on Learning Representations (2015)
34. Krishnakumar, A., Prabhu, V., Sudhakar, S., Hoffman, J.: UDIS: unsupervised discovery of bias in deep visual recognition models. In: British Machine Vision Conference, BMVC (2021)
35. Kusner, M.J., Loftus, J., Russell, C., Silva, R.: Counterfactual fairness. In: Advances in Neural Information Processing Systems (2017)
36. Lahoti, P., et al.: Fairness without demographics through adversarially reweighted learning. In: Advances in Neural Information Processing Systems (2020)
37. Lang, O., et al.: Explaining in style: training a GAN to explain a classifier in StyleSpace. In: The IEEE International Conference on Computer Vision (ICCV) (2021)
38. Lecun, Y., Bottou, L., Bengio, Y., Haffner, P.: Gradient-based learning applied to document recognition. In: Proceedings of the IEEE (1998)
39. Li, W., et al.: Object-driven text-to-image synthesis via adversarial training. In: The IEEE Conference on Computer Vision and Pattern Recognition (CVPR) (2019)
40. Li, Y., Li, Y., Vasconcelos, N.: RESOUND: towards action recognition without Representation Bias. In: The European Conference on Computer Vision (ECCV) (2018)
41. Li, Y., Vasconcelos, N.: REPAIR: removing representation bias by dataset resampling. In: The IEEE Conference on Computer Vision and Pattern Recognition (CVPR) (2019)
42. Li, Z., Xu, C.: Discover the unknown biased attribute of an image classifier. In: The IEEE International Conference on Computer Vision (ICCV) (2021)
43. Liu, Z., Luo, P., Wang, X., Tang, X.: Deep learning face attributes in the wild. In: The IEEE International Conference on Computer Vision (ICCV) (2015)
44. Manjunatha, V., Saini, N., Davis, L.S.: Explicit bias discovery in visual question answering models. In: The IEEE Conference on Computer Vision and Pattern Recognition (CVPR) (2019)
45. Nam, J., Cha, H., Ahn, S., Lee, J., Shin, J.: Learning from failure: training debiased classifier from biased classifier. In: Advances in Neural Information Processing Systems (2020)

46. Pleiss, G., Raghavan, M., Wu, F., Kleinberg, J., Weinberger, K.Q.: On fairness and calibration. In: Advances in Neural Information Processing Systems (2017)
47. Sagawa*, S., Koh*, P.W., Hashimoto, T.B., Liang, P.: Distributionally robust neural networks for group shifts: on the importance of regularization for worst-case generalization. In: International Conference on Learning Representations (2020)
48. Sarhan, M.H., Navab, N., Albarqouni, S.: Fairness by learning orthogonal disentangled representations. In: The European Conference on Computer Vision (ECCV) (2020)
49. Selvaraju, R.R., Cogswell, M., Das, A., Vedantam, R., Parikh, D., Batra, D.: Gradcam: visual explanations from deep networks via gradient-based localization. In: The IEEE International Conference on Computer Vision (ICCV) (2017)
50. Selvaraju, R.R., Cogswell, M., Das, A., Vedantam, R., Parikh, D., Batra, D.: Grad-CAM: visual explanations from deep networks via gradient-based localization. Int. J. Comput. Vis. **128**(2), 336–359 (2020). https://doi.org/10.1007/s11263-019-01228-7
51. Singh, K.K., Mahajan, D., Grauman, K., Lee, Y.J., Feiszli, M., Ghadiyaram, D.: Don't judge an object by its context: learning to overcome contextual bias. In: The IEEE Conference on Computer Vision and Pattern Recognition (CVPR) (2020)
52. Sohoni, N.S., Dunnmon, J.A., Angus, G., Gu, A., Ré, C.: No subclass left behind: fine-grained robustness in coarse-grained classification problems. In: Advances in Neural Information Processing Systems (2020)
53. Torralba, A., Efros, A.A.: Unbiased look at dataset bias. In: The IEEE Conference on Computer Vision and Pattern Recognition (CVPR) (2011)
54. Tzeng, E., Hoffman, J., Darrell, T., Saenko, K.: Simultaneous deep transfer across domains and tasks. In: The IEEE International Conference on Computer Vision (ICCV) (2015)
55. Verma, S., Rubin, J.: Fairness definitions explained. In: 2018 IEEE/ACM International Workshop on Software Fairness (FairWare) (2018)
56. Wang, A., Narayanan, A., Russakovsky, O.: REVISE: a tool for measuring and mitigating bias in image datasets. In: The European Conference on Computer Vision (ECCV) (2020a)
57. Wang, H., He, Z., Lipton, Z.C., Xing, E.P.: Learning robust representations by projecting superficial statistics out. In: International Conference on Learning Representations (2019a)
58. Wang, J., Liu, Y., Wang, X.E.: Are gender-neutral queries really gender-neutral? mitigating gender bias in image search. In: Empirical Methods in Natural Language Processing (2021a)
59. Wang, T., Yue, Z., Huang, J., Sun, Q., Zhang, H.: Self-supervised learning disentangled group representation as feature. In: Advances in Neural Information Processing Systems (2021b)
60. Wang, X., Ang, M.H., Lee, G.H.: Cascaded refinement network for point cloud completion. In: The IEEE Conference on Computer Vision and Pattern Recognition (CVPR) (2020b)
61. Wang, Z., et al.: CAMP: cross-modal adaptive message passing for text-image retrieval. In: The IEEE International Conference on Computer Vision (ICCV) (2019b)
62. Wang, Z., Qinami, K., Karakozis, I.C., Genova, K., Nair, P., Hata, K., Russakovsky, O.: Towards fairness in visual recognition: effective strategies for bias mitigation. In: The IEEE Conference on Computer Vision and Pattern Recognition (CVPR) (2020c)

63. Yu, F., Seff, A., Zhang, Y., Song, S., Funkhouser, T., Xiao, J.: LSUN: construction of a large-scale image dataset using deep learning with humans in the loop. arXiv:1506.03365 [cs] (2016)
64. Zhang, B.H., Lemoine, B., Mitchell, M.: Mitigating unwanted biases with adversarial learning. In: AAAI/ACM Conference on AI, Ethics, and Society (2018)
65. Zhang, Z., Sabuncu, M.: Generalized cross entropy loss for training deep neural networks with noisy labels. In: Advances in Neural Information Processing Systems (2018)
66. Zhao, J., Wang, T., Yatskar, M., Ordonez, V., Chang, K.W.: Men also like shopping: reducing gender bias amplification using corpus-level constraints. In: Empirical Methods in Natural Language Processing (2017)
67. Zhou, B., Khosla, A., Lapedriza, A., Oliva, A., Torralba, A.: Learning deep features for discriminative localization. In: The IEEE Conference on Computer Vision and Pattern Recognition (CVPR) (2016)
68. Zhou, B., Lapedriza, A., Khosla, A., Oliva, A., Torralba, A.: Places: a 10 million image database for scene recognition. IEEE Trans. Pattern Anal. Mach. Intell. **40**(6), 1452–1464 (2018)

Unsupervised and Semi-supervised Bias Benchmarking in Face Recognition

Alexandra Chouldechova, Siqi Deng$^{(\boxtimes)}$, Yongxin Wang, Wei Xia, and Pietro Perona

AWS AI Labs, Seattle, USA
siqideng@amazon.com

Abstract. We introduce Semi-supervised Performance Evaluation for Face Recognition (SPE-FR). SPE-FR is a statistical method for evaluating the performance and algorithmic bias of face verification systems when identity labels are unavailable or incomplete. The method is based on parametric Bayesian modeling of the face embedding similarity scores. SPE-FR produces point estimates, performance curves, and confidence bands that reflect uncertainty in the estimation procedure. Focusing on the unsupervised setting wherein no identity labels are available, we validate our method through experiments on a wide range of face embedding models and two publicly available evaluation datasets. Experiments show that SPE-FR can accurately assess performance on data with no identity labels, and confidently reveal demographic biases in system performance.

Keywords: Algorithmic bias · Semi-supervised evaluation · Face verification · Bayesian inference

1 Introduction

Measuring a system's accuracy and its algorithmic bias prior to deployment is a cornerstone of responsible AI [8,22,31,43,54]. This is especially important in the context of computer vision applications, such as face analysis and recognition [5, 8,23,45,53]. Assessing system performance and bias is not a one-off affair. There is no guarantee that a model that is found to perform equally across ethnic groups and genders, say, on a given benchmarking dataset will continue to do so in a different use case. This is because system operating characteristics depend on the statistics of data, which generally differ across use cases. Ideally, each organization that plans to adopt AI technology would conduct a performance and bias evaluation of the proposed system in each use case prior to deployment.

In practice, however, benchmarking vision algorithms is a tall order for most organizations. A key problem is acquiring appropriately annotated test data that

---

A. Chouldechova and W. Xia—Work done when at Amazon.
A. Chouldechova and S. Deng—Equal contribution.

Supplementary Information The online version contains supplementary material available at https://doi.org/10.1007/978-3-031-19778-9_17.

S. Avidan et al. (Eds.): ECCV 2022, LNCS 13673, pp. 289–306, 2022.
https://doi.org/10.1007/978-3-031-19778-9_17

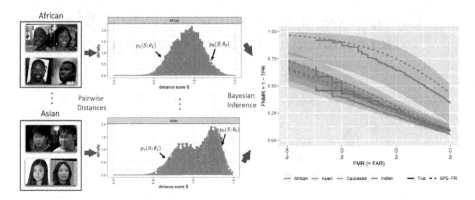

Fig. 1. SPE-FR methodology and sample results. SPE-FR models the similarity scores S_{ij} in each group as coming from a mixture of two parametric distributions, $p_1(S; \theta_1)$ for matching identities and $p_0(S; \theta_0)$ for impostors. Bayesian inference estimates parameters θ_0, θ_1 and proportion of true matches, π (middle). The right panel shows corresponding unsupervised error estimates, where SPE-FR was applied to the Racial Faces in the Wild (RFW) [57] dataset. SPE-FR estimates using no id labels are shown as dashed lines with credible confidence bands overlaid. Ground truth performance from fully labeled data is shown in solid lines ("True"). The face recognition model ("AA") being tested was trained on BUPT-BalancedFace [58] while leaving out the "African" group in order to artificially introduce bias (Sect. 4.1). SPE-FR correctly and confidently reveals racial bias, i.e. accuracy on the "African" group is worse than the other groups.

mirror the statistics of the use case. In particular, annotating accurate test data is expensive and time-consuming. *This pain is particularly acute in face recognition*, which relies on identity annotations. Reliable identity ground truth for faces is extremely difficult to obtain. Typically it is obtained by government organizations through access to identity documents [23], or through the subjective judgment of human annotators [37]. The first approach is not available to most organizations, and the second is fraught and highly unreliable because people are not accurate and often biased in recognizing the faces of strangers [2,40,42,52].

This raises the question: *What's the best an organization can do with limited resources?* We believe that the most practical scenario for face recognition is the following: data (images of faces) is plentiful, but collecting a large number of high-quality identity annotations may not be feasible. Instead, it is feasible to collect annotations as to membership in demographic or morphological groups, e.g. perceived ethnicity, gender, body shape, etc. Indeed, prior studies have found that human annotators provide reasonably reliable and consistent annotations of these types of characteristics [5,34]. Thus, we pose the following challenge: Given a large data set of face images, where each image is annotated for group membership *but not identity*, estimate the overall performance and algorithmic bias of a face recognition system on the data. We focus here on the question of whether this is feasible at all, and how to do it.

To summarize our contributions, we introduce in this paper a method we call SPE-FR (Semi-supervised Performance Evaluation for Face Recognition), which enables one to accomplish precisely this task in the setting of face verification. We believe SPE-FR is the first semi- and un-supervised method for evaluating bias in face recognition algorithms. SPE-FR produces point estimates and uncertainty bands (specifically, Bayesian posterior credible bands) for common performance metrics used in face recognition settings, and enables the metrics to be compared across different subgroups of the population as part of an algorithmic bias assessment. Figure 1 previews the kinds of results we are able to obtain with no access to identity information. Our experiments demonstrate the surprising result that it is possible to reliably estimate the performance and bias of face verification systems *even when no test data identity annotations are available* (what we term the *unsupervised* setting). While the methodology is presented in the more general semi-supervised setting where partial identity annotations may be available, the experimental results presented in the main paper focus on what we believe to be the more interesting and realistic unsupervised setting.

2   Related Work

Algorithmic Bias in Face Recognition. Prior work has studied demographic bias in the performance of face recognition systems, exploring whether systems have disparate error rates across different demographic groups [1,36,45,48,51, 53]. Of particular note is NIST's Face Recognition Vendor Test (FRVT), which is conducted on US government data [23]. Findings of bias have also inspired a body of work on bias mitigation strategies [28,32,33,35,38,59]. To meet the many calls for more thorough bias benchmarking of face recognition systems, a number of public data sets have become available that contain demographic information alongside identity information [39,47,57]. Meanwhile, it has become clear that accuracy and bias measurements on a given dataset may not generalize to new domains and use cases [5,6,17,61]. Therefore, we believe that, ultimately, accuracy and bias measurements may need to be carried out per use case.

Semi- and Un-supervised Performance Evaluation on New Domains. The absence of high-quality annotated target domain test data poses a persistent obstacle to the thorough performance and bias evaluation of AI systems prior to new deployments. In classification, methods have been introduced to estimate model performance on unlabelled or partly labelled test data. [60] developed the *Semi-supervised Performance Evaluation* (SPE) method for estimating the performance of classification systems, [18] proposed training a model to predict system error across different target data sets, and [24] proposed a method based on differences in model scores. [21] learns a confidence threshold such that the proportion of unlabelled examples exceeding the threshold is a reasonable estimate of model accuracy. [32] introduced the *Bayesian Calibration* (BC) method that learns a calibration function using a small sample of labelled data and then applies it to unlabelled examples to estimate model performance and bias.

Our proposed method, SPE-FR, differs in several ways from existing work. (i) None of these methods were developed for face recognition settings or consider tasks such as 1:1 verification, which is not inherently a classification task; and only [32] directly considers bias assessment. (ii) Except for [32], the methods do not output uncertainty assessments (e.g., confidence intervals or posterior credible regions) alongside point estimates of performance. (iii) None of the methods have been assessed in high-performance regimes of the kind that are relevant in face verification. That is, the methods are developed primarily for estimating overall accuracy and are not tested in challenging settings such as estimating false non-match rates at false match rates well below 0.01. In our experimental evaluation of BC [32], we found that BC performs well at estimating overall accuracy, and yet it is not suitable for estimating metrics relevant to benchmarking face recognition systems.

SPE-FR takes inspiration from the SPE [60] method. In particular, we adopt a similar approach to modeling model scores (in our case similarity or distance scores) as following user-specified parametric distributions. Our work improves upon SPE [60] in several important ways. SPE does not consider the unsupervised setting with no labels, face recognition systems, or bias evaluation. Whereas they focused on estimating Precision-Recall curves across the full range of recall (TPR), we focus on low False Match Rate (FMR < 0.01) and low False Non-Match Rate (FNMR < 0.01) regimes that are not considered in this or other work. We discuss further innovations and adaptations that went into SPE-FR in our methodology section below.

3   Semi-supervised Bias Evaluation Methodology

In a typical modern face recognition system, a face embedding model ϕ is applied to extract identity information from a pre-processed (e.g., cropped and aligned) face image $x_i, i \in \{1, \ldots, I\}$ to produce a feature embedding vector $\mathbf{z}_i = \phi(x_i) \in \mathbb{R}^d$, for a choice of feature dimension, d. A common use case for face recognition models is 1:1 *face verification*. Face verification (FV) aims to determine whether two face images, x_i and x_j, belong to the same person. This is often done by applying a similarity or distance function to the embedding vectors $\mathbf{z}_i, \mathbf{z}_j$, and calling the pair a "match" if the similarity exceeds a pre-specified threshold (equivalently, if the distance falls below some threshold). Common functions include the *cosine similarity* $S_{cos}(\mathbf{z}_i, \mathbf{z}_j) = \mathbf{z}_i \cdot \mathbf{z}_j / \|\mathbf{z}_i\|_2 \|\mathbf{z}_j\|_2$, and the *Euclidean distance* $D_2(\mathbf{z}_i, \mathbf{z}_j) = \|\mathbf{z}_i - \mathbf{z}_j\|_2$.

The most common metrics used in evaluating the performance of a face verification system are the False Non-Match Rate (FNMR) and False Match Rate (FMR) [23]. Let $S_{ij} = S(\mathbf{z}_i, \mathbf{z}_j)$ denote the similarity score of images i and j and $Y_{ij} \in \{0, 1\}$ denote the ground truth indicator that i and j correspond to the same person. The FNMR and FMR at threshold τ are then defined as:

$$\text{FNMR}(\tau) = \mathbb{P}(S_{ij} < \tau \mid Y_{ij} = 1), \qquad \text{FMR}(\tau) = \mathbb{P}(S_{ij} \geq \tau \mid Y_{ij} = 0). \quad (1)$$

The FNMR-FMR curve of FNMR plotted as a function of FMR is a common summary of the accuracy of the FV system and its bias across different demographics. A common one-number summary is the FNMR at a particular FMR level (e.g., FNMR@FMR=10^{-3}). If ground truth identity labels are available (i.e., Y_{ij} is known for all pairs) then these quantities can be estimated through empirical proportions. E.g., $\widehat{\text{FNMR}}(\tau) = \frac{1}{N_1} \sum_{i<j} \mathbb{1}(S_{ij} < \tau) Y_{ij}$, where $N_1 = \sum_{i<j} Y_{ij}$ is the number of true matches among all image pairs and $\mathbb{1}(x)$ is the indicator function. Our proposed method (Sect. 3.1) enables the estimation of such metrics even when Y_{ij} is unknown for most, or even *all*, pairs.

3.1 Semi-supervised Performance Evaluation for Face Verification

We now proceed to present the formalism of the SPE-FR method. The intuition behind SPE-FR is twofold. First, any performance metric that involves the scores S and matches indicator Y can be computed from the joint distribution of (S, Y), as we will detail in Sect. 3.4. Second, empirical evidence suggests that the match-conditional distributions of $S \mid Y$ are well-behaved across a range of face embedding model architectures and test datasets, and may be estimated through mixture modeling *even when Y is unknown*.

More formally, in SPE-FR we model the similarity scores S within match class $Y = y$ as following some user-specified distribution $p_y(s \mid \theta)$, parameterized by $\theta \in \mathbb{R}^p$. In Sect. 3.3 we describe a specific parametric family that, we find, works well for face recognition systems. Let n denote the number of images and let N denote the total number of *image pairs*. Let $\mathcal{L} = \{(i, j) : i < j, Y_{ij} \text{ is known}\}$ denote the subset of image pairs for which identity match is known, and let $Y_{\mathcal{L}}$ denote the set of known Y's. In the unsupervised setting that we focus on in our experiments, where we assume no identity annotations are available, $\mathcal{L} = \emptyset$. Let $\mathcal{U}$ denote all image pairs for which identity match is *unknown*—in the unsupervised setting, $\mathcal{U}$ is *all* image pairs. Lastly, let $\pi = \mathbb{P}(Y_{ij} = 1)$ denote the proportion of true matches among all image pairs. In this notation, we can write down the likelihood of the observed data given unknown parameters π and θ as,

$$p(S, Y_{\mathcal{L}} \mid \pi, \theta) = \prod_{(i,j) \in \mathcal{L}} \pi^{y_{ij}} (1-\pi)^{1-y_{ij}} p_{y_{ij}}(s_{ij} \mid \theta_{y_{ij}}) \times \prod_{(i,j) \in \mathcal{U}} ((1-\pi) p_0(s_{ij} \mid \theta_0) + \pi p_1(s_{ij} \mid \theta_1)), \quad (2)$$

where we think of $\theta = (\theta_0, \theta_1)$ as parameterizing the two distinct class-conditional densities. There are many approaches one can take to estimating the parameters (π, θ). For instance, one can attempt maximum likelihood estimation on Eq. (2) through methods such as the EM algorithm [41]. In this work, we take a Bayesian inference approach. More precisely, given a prior distribution $p(\pi, \theta)$, we base our inference on the posterior distribution,

$$p(\pi, \theta \mid S, Y_{\mathcal{L}}) \propto p(S, Y_t \mid \pi, \theta) \, p(\pi, \theta). \quad (3)$$

The posterior distribution on (π, θ) then implies a posterior for any performance metrics that can be calculated from the joint distribution of (S, Y).

This approach is based on the same philosophy as the Semi-supervised Performance Evaluation (SPE) method introduced in [60] for evaluating binary classification models. SPE-FR includes a number of innovations, which we outline in the next few subsections. To begin with SPE [60] does not consider the *unsupervised* setting, does not consider *Face Recognition (FR) systems*, nor *groups* (i.e., no bias evaluation). We introduce and study the unsupervised case, i.e. that **performance and bias evaluation** are possible with **no Y labels** (this is a surprising result), and focus on FR. Moreover, as we now briefly discuss, the FR regime required more sophisticated statistical methods to address acute challenges. (i) Estimating accuracy at the low FNMR and FMR regime differs from the accuracy estimation when errors are relatively frequent. FR accuracy is often much higher than in typical classification problems, so correct approximation of the tails of the class-conditionals is crucial. Existing methods operate in much higher error settings. E.g., [60] showed results for Precision-Recall curves (not ROC or FNMR-FMR) across the whole $[0, 1]$ recall range, which can hide poor performance at the edges. (ii) Distribution tail behavior. In our extensive empirical analysis (Supplemental C) we found that the parametric families considered in [60] fail to model distance/similarity scores output by FR systems. We use instead the "two-piece" (TP) family of scale-location-shape distributions from the statistics literature on heavy-tailed distributions, which we demonstrate do a good job of approximating FR system scores across different models and different data sets (MORPH and RFW). We also provide a tailored prior specification. Our two-piece distributions approximate well the ground truth across different datasets (Supplemental C). (iii) We consider highly imbalanced data: [60], [32], and other methods do not handle extreme class imbalance. In real world FR studies, non-matches ($Y = 0$) far outnumber true matches ($Y = 1$). To adapt SPE to this highly imbalanced setting we found that an informative prior on π, the proportion of true matches, is often necessary. We show how techniques from false discovery rate control in statistical genetics can be used to estimate π and inform the prior (Supplemental D).

3.2   Bias Evaluation in Face Recognition Systems

We are interested in evaluating not only overall performance but bias as well. The most common way to assess a face verification system for *bias* is to compare performance metrics across different groups. For the purpose of this paper we assume that for each image i we have a *known* or *inferred* group membership variable $A_i \in \{1, ..., K\}$ (e.g., gender, race, combinations thereof, etc.). In cases where A_i is inferred, such as through the use of a classifier, we will think of our method as estimating performance for the *inferred* rather than the true groups.[1]

There are two principal ways of extending SPE to perform bias evaluation. In the "stratified" approach, one can perform SPE-FR separately within each group, and then assess differences in the resulting group-level performance estimates. Alternatively, one can apply Bayesian hierarchical modeling to pool information across data from different groups in estimating parameters. Specifically, one can introduce parameters ν_Y to form the hierarchical specification:

---

[1] Some have developed methods for estimating group fairness metrics in the presence of noisy or inferred group membership labels [4,9,10,44]. Understanding how SPE-FR performs with respect to the true unknown groups using inferred group information is an interesting and important question, but beyond the scope of the present work.

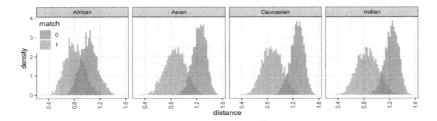

Fig. 2. Normal model. (Top) Empirical distribution of the class-conditional distances computed by the AA model (see Table 1) on the RFW dataset (each face pair is from the same ethnicity, "match" indicates a genuine identity match).

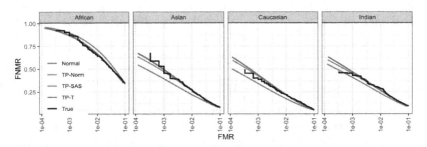

Fig. 3. Parametric estimates of algorithmic error compared with ground truth (Black). Comparison of Normal, Two-piece Normal (TP-Norm), Two-piece sinh-arcsinh (TP-SAS), and Two-piece Student-t (TP-T) parametric approximations of the AA model on the RFW (Sect. 3.2). The TP distributions capture skewness and kurtosis (i.e., heavy-tailedness) in the class-conditional score distributions, producing better approximations of the true performance curves. TP-Norm and TP-T curves are visually indistinguishable from this data.

$$\pi_A \mid A \sim \text{Beta}(\alpha, \beta) \qquad Y \mid A \sim \text{Bernoulli}(\pi_A) \qquad (4a)$$

$$\nu_Y \mid Y \sim p(\nu_Y) \qquad \theta_{Y,A} \mid Y, A, \nu_Y \sim p(\theta_{Y,A} \mid \nu_Y) \qquad (4b)$$

$$S \mid Y, A, \theta \sim p_{Y,A}(s \mid \theta_{Y,A}) \qquad (4c)$$

We provide details and experiments on the model specification in Sect. 3.3 and Bayesian inference strategy in Sect. 3.4 for the stratified approach.

3.3 Parametric Conditional Distributions and Priors

Distribution and Prior Selection for Fitting. To have SPE-FR perform effectively, we need to have good parametric models for the match-conditional distributions $S \mid Y, \pi, \theta$. In Fig. 2 we show class-conditional score densities for the 4 most prevalent race/ethnicity groups in the RFW data. The densities are unimodal and most are close to symmetric. However, a closer analysis of the data using Normal-QQ plots (Supplemental C) reveals that only the scores for the African group approximately follow a Normal distribution. The rest are significantly skewed. It is therefore important that our choice of parametric family $p_Y(s \mid \theta_Y)$ be able to capture at least skewness.

While there are classical skewed parametric families of distributions such as the Gamma, log-Normal and Weibull, and SPE-FR can be used with any parametric families, we found through extensive experimentation that these models were often a poor fit to the observed data. Our experiments revealed that so-called *two-piece* distributions [49] provided a much better approximation, a finding that appears robust to the choice of model architecture and data set. These distributions, which have not previously been considered in the computer vision literature, allow flexible control of skewness and tail behavior in a single simple parametric family [19,20]. Given a symmetric unimodal density, f, centered at 0, the parametric family of *two-piece distributions generated by* f is given by:

$$g(x; \mu, \sigma_1, \sigma_2, \delta) = \begin{cases} \frac{2}{\sigma_1 + \sigma_2} f\left(\frac{x-\mu}{\sigma_1}; \delta\right) & x < \mu \\ \frac{2}{\sigma_1 + \sigma_2} f\left(\frac{x-\mu}{\sigma_2}; \delta\right) & x \geq \mu \end{cases}. \tag{5}$$

Here μ denotes the mode of the distribution, the σ_k control skewness, and δ is a shape parameter that controls kurtosis ("heavy-tailedness"). For instance, when f is chosen to be the Student-t distribution, δ denotes the degrees of freedom. Figure 3 shows that two-piece distributions provide a much closer approximation than the standard Normal to the true FNMR-FMR curves on the RFW data. The corresponding plot for Morph (Supplemental C) shows even greater improvements in approximation accuracy.

Prior Specification. We now outline the model specification used in our experiments in the stratified setting for a given group (and hence omit the group membership A to simplify notation). Let $\tau_{jk} = 1/\sigma_{jk}^2$ denote the precision parameter in match class $Y = j \in \{0,1\}$ of the $k \in \{1,2\}$ component of the two-piece distribution. Here $k = 1$ denotes the parameters for the left half of the two-piece distribution and $k = 2$ denotes the right. Our model specification is:

$$\pi \sim \text{Unif}(\text{L}, \text{U}) \qquad Y \sim \text{Bernoulli}(\pi) \tag{6a}$$

$$\mu_j \sim N(\eta_j, 0.25^2) \qquad \tau_{jk} \sim \text{Gamma}(10, \beta_{jk}^\tau) \tag{6b}$$

$$\delta_j \sim \text{Gamma}(\alpha_j^\delta, \beta_j^\delta) \qquad S \mid Y, \theta \sim TP(\mu_Y, \tau_{1Y}, \tau_{2Y}, \delta_Y), \tag{6c}$$

where TP denotes a two-piece distribution, and the Gamma distribution is shape-rate parameterized, so that $\mathbb{E}[\text{Gamma}(\alpha, \beta)] = \alpha/\beta$. For the experiments in the main paper, we show results using a two-piece Student-t (TP-T) for RFW and a Two-piece sinh-arcsinh (TP-SAS) for MORPH. The TP-SAS has previously been used specifically to model skewed heavy-tailed data [50], which is precisely the kind of distribution we expect to see for non-match scores.

Table 1. Training sets derived from BUPT-BalancedFace. Starting from the full training (FT) set, we obtained a number of training sets by removing selectively some identities. These "ablated" sets are used to produce corresponding face recognition models. We hypothesize that these bias-controlled models contain different types and degrees of biases, thus suitable for inspection purposes (as verified in Fig. 4). *: IDs counted from majority voting of image predictions.

Name	FT	RT	M	EA	CC	AA
Left-out set	None	Random 90%	Male	East Asian	Caucasian	African
# Identities	28000	2800	7541*	21000	21000	21000

3.4 Bayesian Inference Strategy

Markov Chain Monte Carlo (MCMC) Inference. Because the posterior distribution of the parameters $(\pi, \theta) = (\pi, \mu_j, \tau_{jk}, \delta_j)$ in model specification (6) is analytically intractable, we rely on MCMC methods to obtain a sample from the posterior distribution. For our experiments we used the BayesianTools [27] implementation of the Differential Evolution MCMC sampler (DEzs) originally proposed in [7]. Given a posterior sample $\{(\pi_i, \theta_i)\}_{i=1}^T$, we can calculate values of FNMR and FMR at a given threshold τ by evaluating the tail probabilities:

$$\text{FMR}_i(\tau; \theta) = \int_\tau^\infty p_0(s; \theta_{i0})ds \qquad \text{FNMR}_i(\tau; \theta) = \int_{-\infty}^\tau p_1(s; \theta_{i1})ds$$

For a given metric $M(\tau; \pi, \theta)$, e.g. FNMR at a threshold τ, we obtain point estimates of M using the posterior mean $\frac{1}{T}\sum_1^T M(\tau; \pi_i, \theta_i)$. To obtain $(1-\alpha)\%$ posterior credible intervals, we take the $\alpha/2$ and $1-\alpha/2$ quantiles of $\{M(\tau; \pi_i, \theta_i)\}$.

Hierarchical Clustering Procedure for Constructing Confidence Bands for Performance Curves. We can also obtain posterior credible confidence bands for entire FNMR-FMR curves. The procedure we present here is specifically tailored to produce non-trivial confidence bands at low FMR values. Standard approaches will generally produce FNMR confidence intervals of the form $[0, u]$: i.e., the lower endpoint of the FNMR band will be 0. Let $\text{FNMR}(\zeta; \theta_i)$ denote the FNMR curve as a function of $\zeta = \text{FMR}$ at parameter values θ_i. To construct the confidence band, we first apply agglomerative hierarchical single-linkage clustering with Canberra distance to the (logged) $\text{FNMR}(\zeta; \theta_i)$ curves at a grid of ζ values evenly spaced on the logarithmic scale. We then cut the cluster tree at a level such that at least $(1 - \alpha)\%$ of the curves are contained in the largest component. The envelope generated by the curves in that component provides a $(1 - \alpha)\%$ confidence band: if the parametric assumptions of the model are met, it provides uniform coverage for the entire FNMR-FMR curve, not simply pointwise coverage.

4 Experiments

We mimic the setting in which an organization has a large collection of face images x_i, many of which are of the same people. We assume that we *do not*

Table 2. Models trained under various settings. We trained face embedding models on various popular training datasets, model architectures and loss functions and verified the effectiveness of SPE-FR (Sect. 4.2).

Training data	IMDB [55]	DeepGlint [11]	BUPT-BalancedFace [58]		
Loss function	Sub-Center Arc	Sub-Center Arc	Sub-Center Arc	CosFace [56]	ℓ_2-Softmax [46]
Architecture	R101	R101	R18	R101	R101 [29]
AA ablation	✗	✗	✓	✓	✓

have access to identity indicators Y_{ij}, and that we have access to true or inferred group label identities A_i for the purpose of assessing bias. For privacy reasons, organizations wishing to assess the performance of a third-party system on their data may be unwilling or prohibited from sharing image data with system developers, who are in many cases, commercial vendors. Since SPE-FR relies only on the scores S_{ij}, it is sufficient for owners of the test data to provide just the scores from running the 1:1 verification system on their data. Sharing of the raw face images x_i is not required; the resulting S_{ij} and A_i are sufficient to run SPE-FR. *The goal of our experiments is to evaluate whether the SPE-FR algorithm can assess group-level performance well enough to reflect existing trends and to reveal demographic bias in system performance.* We compare the results of SPE-FR to ground truth assessed using fully identity-annotated data. SPE-FR is applied in the *unsupervised* setting where $N_{\mathcal{L}} = 0$, i.e. *no identity labels are available.* "Ground truth" values are calculated from known Y_{ij} for all image pairs, to which SPE-FR does not have access.

Our experiments are performed on the RFW [57] and MORPH [47] datasets. Details about the test sets and protocols, specifics on the Bayesian inference MCMC configurations and hyperparameters estimation process (Sect. 3.4), as well as ablation study on $N_{\mathcal{L}}$ comparing the unsupervised setting ($N_{\mathcal{L}} = 0$) with the semi-supervised ones ($N_{\mathcal{L}} > 0$), may be found in the Supplemental B.

4.1   Face Embedding Model Training for Bias Analysis

We apply our method to two sets of face recognition (FR) models: (i) demographically "biased" models trained using a common architecture to assess whether SPE-FR can reveal bias in the performance of 1:1 verification systems; and (ii) models trained with various datasets, network architectures, and loss functions that allow us to examine whether SPE-FR performs well across different settings.

Model Training with Controlled Biases. We employ BUPT-BalancedFace dataset [58] as our training set. This dataset provides images across 4 race/ethnicity groups (African, Asian, Caucasian, and Indian), each with 7,000 identities. We adopt the popular state-of-the-art Sub-center ArcFace [12] method in our face recognition model and employ a variant of ResNet [30] as our feature extractor.

In order to explore bias, we train a set of models by using all but one particular race or gender group from the BUPT-BalancedFace dataset. In this way, we can obtain several different training sets with different types or degrees of bias. Configurations of the training sets is detailed in Table 1[2]. We evaluate each model's performance and bias on the test sets and use ground truth labels to compute the *true* performance (in the form of FNMR-FMR curves) for comparing with SPE-FR estimates.

Model Training for Generalization Validation. To validate if SPE-FR is applicable to face embedding models trained across different settings, we test on the second set of FR models trained to represent state-of-the-art for popular training datasets, model architectures, and loss functions. See Table 2 for details. We share more details on model training in Supplemental F.

4.2   Result and Analysis

Results on Models Trained with Controlled Biases. To validate the effectiveness of SPE-FR, we evaluate the models trained with controlled biases (Table 1) on several test datasets where face verification performance is compared across cohorts of face pairs representing different genders and races. Figure 1 shows the results of applying unsupervised SPE-FR to estimate the RFW data performance of the system trained excluding African faces from the training data. SPE-FR produces estimates (dashed lines) and 89% posterior credible regions (shaded bands) for the full FNMR vs FMR curves for each of the 4 racial/ethnic groups coded in the data. While the confidence bands are wide, in part due to the relatively small dataset, SPE-FR has good coverage of the true (solid) curves and correctly reveals that the system under-performs on African faces. Figure 5 shows the unsupervised SPE-FR results for MORPH disaggregated by race/ethnicity and gender. Even though the confidence bands fail to capture the true (solid) curves, they are in the right ballpark, and SPE-FR still confidently and correctly identifies significant gender bias across all race/ethnicity groups. As we show in the Supplemental C), poor confidence band prediction on MORPH is not due to the TP-SAS parametric model being an overall poor fit to the score distributions within each group and match class. In particular, if all labels Y_{ij} are made available, the TP-SAS distribution results in good approximations of the FNMR-FMR curve on the MORPH data. Confidence band prediction of SPE-FR on MORPH can in principle be improved by using SPE-FR in the semi-supervised setting and obtaining Y_{ij} for pairs with borderline similarity scores. However, this requires obtaining true identity annotations for pairs that are somewhat difficult for the system to distinguish, and which therefore may be difficult for humans to correctly annotate. Figure 4a **and Fig.** 4b show estimated FNMR at an overall target FMR for five different models (Table 1) on the RFW and MORPH datasets. The overall target FMR is set to be 0.001 on MORPH and 0.005 on RFW. The SPE-FR estimates are highly accurate for RFW but slightly overestimate the error on MORPH across the board. The results are nevertheless useful: They reflect trends in the ground truth, such as the poor performance of the RT model compared to others.

---

[2] BUPT-BalancedFace does not provide gender annotations, we generated pseudo labels from open-source face analysis repository Insightface [3,13–16,25,26].

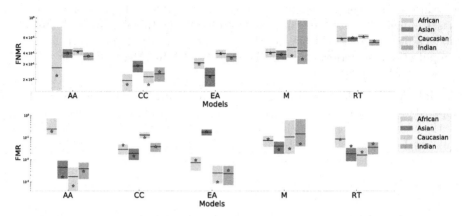

(a) **Ground truth bias vs Unsupervised SPE-FR estimates on RFW.**

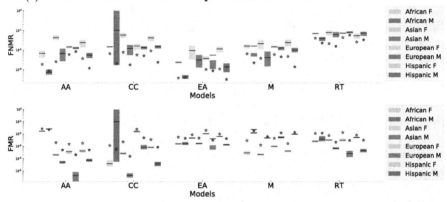

(b) **Ground truth model vs Unsupervised SPE-FR estimates on MORPH.**

Fig. 4. Unsupervised SPE-FR model bias estimates vs ground truth. We show the error rates of models that were trained using five different training settings (Table 1) derived from BUPT [58]. SPE-FR was used to assess the error rates of each model on RFW (a) and MORPH (b). We show False Match Rate (FMR) and False Non-Match Rate (FNMR). We set the number of labeled instances $N_{\mathcal{L}} = 0$, for unsupervised estimates. Here we apply one decision threshold per model, across all demographic groups. The threshold is selected so that FMR = 0.05 for RFW and FMR = 0.001 for MOPRH over the entire dataset containing all demographic groups. Then FMR and FNMR at each model's selected threshold are produced on each group-specific benchmark. The ⋆ indicates the ground truth performance (FMR or FNMR) measured with fully labeled data. The horizontal lines and colored bars are the corresponding performance point estimates and 89% confidence bands. On RFW, unsupervised estimates of SPE-FR are on target (stars within the confidence intervals) for both FNMR and FMR, and the error rate differences across groups are predicted correctly. On the MORPH dataset, SPE-FR overestimates the ground truth FNMR and underestimates the ground truth FMR. Since the overestimate and underestimate are consistent across settings, the error rate differences across groups are predicted correctly (as confirmed in Fig. 5).

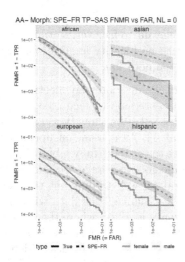

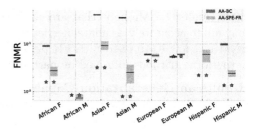

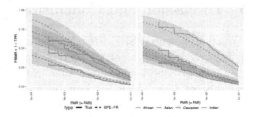

Fig. 6. Comparison with BC adapted to face verification systems. Evaluation of AA model on MORPH. Results show Bayesian Calibration [32] (left) and SPE-FR (right) estimates for each group, with corresponding Bayesian confidence intervals. True performance from full label is marked with stars. Both BC and SPE-FR over-estimate FNMR, but our estimates are significantly more close to the ground truth.

Fig. 5. Unsupervised SPE-FR estimates of the FNMR vs FMR curve. AA model applied to MORPH, SPE-FRE estimates shown as dashed lines with credible confidence bands overlaid (see Sect. 3.4 for details), ground truth ("True") performance from fully labeled data shown in solid lines. The jagged shape in the true performance curve is caused by insufficient sample size at the operating ranges. SPE-FR correctly reveals gender bias within each ethnic group, where females are recognized less accurately.

Fig. 7. Unsupervised SPE-FR estimates of the FNMR vs FMR curve. Two models are evaluated on RFW: (left) FR model trained on IMDB with Sub-Center Arcface loss and Res101 backbone; (right) FR model trained on BUPT with CosFace loss and Res101 backbone.

Comparison to Bayesian Calibration [32]. We compare SPE-FR to the Bayesian Calibration (BC) [32] method by analogously recasting verification in a manner such that BC can be applied despite originally developed for binary classification (implementation details in Supplemental H). We apply the BC method under setting $N_{\mathcal{L}} = 256$ to the "AA" model. On MORPH, BC's estimate of the *overall system accuracy* is close to the ground truth (Supplemental H). However, at the same threshold introduced in Fig. 4, we can see from Fig. 6 that BC's estimates of FNMR underperform SPE-FR by a large margin, especially considering that the BC is applied with partial annotation ($N_{\mathcal{L}} = 256$), whereas SPE-FR with none ($N_{\mathcal{L}} = 0$). There are two important takeaways from these results: (i) Methods that are effective at estimating overall performance may fail to accurately estimate metrics that are relevant to face verification (e.g., FNMR at low FMR); (ii) SPE-FR performed with no identity annotations can outperform methods informed by partial identity annotation.

Results on Generalization Capability Test. We evaluate the effectiveness of SPE-FR for performance estimation and bias detection of face recognition models trained under a wide range of settings (Table 2). We show two examples in Fig. 7 (the rest may be found in Supplemental A). As is seen, unsupervised SPE-FR ($N_{\mathcal{L}} = 0$) produces estimated curves close to the true (fully labeled) performance curves, and the confidence bands provide good coverage of the ground truth values. This indicates that SPE-FR generalizes well to different training pipelines. On the three models trained on BUPT-BalancedFace data with the leave-one-out setting, we again observe similar trends as Fig. 1 where the performance and bias estimates are dead-on. As is seen, SPE-FR performs well across different optimization functions model architectures. This also provides evidence that the two-piece family of distributions we propose in SPE-FR is a good choice across a range of training pipelines and test datasets.

5   Discussion and Conclusions

We have presented SPE-FR, the first unsupervised method for measuring bias in face recognition algorithms. It is based on parametric modeling of the distribution of confidence values that are assigned by the algorithm to proposed matches of faces. SPE-FR can be applied to assess the performance of face recognition systems both in the unsupervised setting where no identity annotations are available and in the semi-supervised setting where some annotations are available. SPE-FR produces Bayesian posterior intervals for any performance metric that can be evaluated from the joint distribution of the match indicator Y and the algorithmic score S. In particular, it can be used to estimate entire performance curves (such as the FNMR vs FMR curve) and produces confidence bands to communicate the uncertainty in the estimation. We validated SPE-FR with experiments on a carefully constructed set of FR models and datasets. The main observations are fourfold: First, it is effective in revealing demographic biases in model performance. Second, our method can estimate performance even when the test set is rather small, and when the ratio of true matches to non-matches is low, as is the case for certain subgroups in the MORPH data. Third, even when the confidence bands do not contain the ground truth, the degree of misestimation is found to be fairly consistent across groups, and thus SPE-FR can still provide a strong indication of demographic bias in system performance. Lastly, our experiments show that SPE-FR can be applied off-the-shelf to a wide range of face embedding models with state-of-the-art designs and trained on different datasets. Therefore, SPE-FR can be especially useful to companies and agencies prior to system adoption who may otherwise be unable to estimate system performance or detect potential biases as they cannot collect reliable identity annotations for their data.

References

1. Albiero, V., KS, K., Vangara, K., Zhang, K., King, M.C., Bowyer, K.W.: Analysis of gender inequality in face recognition accuracy. In: Proceedings of the IEEE/CVF Winter Conference on Applications of Computer Vision Workshops, pp. 81–89 (2020)
2. Albright, T.D.: Why eyewitnesses fail. Proc. Natl. Acad. Sci. **114**(30), 7758–7764 (2017)
3. An, X., et al: Partial fc: training 10 million identities on a single machine. In: Arxiv 2010.05222 (2020)
4. Awasthi, P., Beutel, A., Kleindessner, M., Morgenstern, J., Wang, X.: Evaluating fairness of machine learning models under uncertain and incomplete information. In: Proceedings of the 2021 ACM Conference on Fairness, Accountability, and Transparency, pp. 206–214 (2021)
5. Balakrishnan, G., Xiong, Y., Xia, W., Perona, P.: Towards causal benchmarking of bias in face analysis algorithms. In: Vedaldi, A., Bischof, H., Brox, T., Frahm, J.-M. (eds.) ECCV 2020. LNCS, vol. 12363, pp. 547–563. Springer, Cham (2020). https://doi.org/10.1007/978-3-030-58523-5_32
6. Beery, S., Van Horn, G., Perona, P.: Recognition in terra incognita. In: Ferrari, V., Hebert, M., Sminchisescu, C., Weiss, Y. (eds.) ECCV 2018. LNCS, vol. 11220, pp. 472–489. Springer, Cham (2018). https://doi.org/10.1007/978-3-030-01270-0_28
7. ter Braak, C.J., Vrugt, J.A.: Differential evolution Markov chain with snooker updater and fewer chains. Stat. Comput. **18**(4), 435–446 (2008)
8. Buolamwini, J., Gebru, T.: Gender shades: intersectional accuracy disparities in commercial gender classification. In: Conference on Fairness, Accountability and Transparency, pp. 77–91. PMLR (2018)
9. Chen, J., Kallus, N., Mao, X., Svacha, G., Udell, M.: Fairness under unawareness: assessing disparity when protected class is unobserved. In: Proceedings of the Conference on Fairness, Accountability, and Transparency, pp. 339–348 (2019)
10. Coston, A., et al.: Fair transfer learning with missing protected attributes. In: Proceedings of the 2019 AAAI/ACM Conference on AI, Ethics, and Society, pp. 91–98 (2019)
11. Deepglint: https://trillionpairs.deepglint.com/overview. https://trillionpairs. deepglint.com/overview
12. Deng, J., Guo, J., Liu, T., Gong, M., Zafeiriou, S.: Sub-center arcface: Boosting face recognition by large-scale noisy web faces. In: European Conference on Computer Vision, pp. 741–757. Springer (2020)
13. Deng, J., Guo, J., Liu, T., Gong, M., Zafeiriou, S.: Sub-center ArcFace: boosting face recognition by large-scale noisy web faces. In: Vedaldi, A., Bischof, H., Brox, T., Frahm, J.-M. (eds.) ECCV 2020. LNCS, vol. 12356, pp. 741–757. Springer, Cham (2020). https://doi.org/10.1007/978-3-030-58621-8_43
14. Deng, J., Guo, J., Niannan, X., Zafeiriou, S.: Arcface: Additive angular margin loss for deep face recognition. In: CVPR (2019)
15. Deng, J., Guo, J., Ververas, E., Kotsia, I., Zafeiriou, S.: Retinaface: single-shot multi-level face localisation in the wild. In: CVPR (2020)
16. Deng, J., et al.: The menpo benchmark for multi-pose 2d and 3d facial landmark localisation and tracking. IJCV (2018)
17. Deng, S., Xiong, Y., Wang, M., Xia, W., Soatto, S.: Harnessing unrecognizable faces for improving face recognition. arXiv preprint arXiv:2106.04112 (2021)

18. Deng, W., Zheng, L.: Are labels always necessary for classifier accuracy evaluation? In: Proceedings of the IEEE/CVF Conference on Computer Vision and Pattern Recognition, pp. 15069–15078 (2021)
19. Fechner, G.T.: Kollektivmasslehre. Engelmann (1897)
20. Fernández, C., Steel, M.F.: On bayesian modeling of fat tails and skewness. J. Am. Stat. Assoc. **93**(441), 359–371 (1998)
21. Garg, S., Balakrishnan, S., Lipton, Z.C., Neyshabur, B., Sedghi, H.: Leveraging unlabeled data to predict out-of-distribution performance. arXiv preprint arXiv:2201.04234 (2022)
22. GoogleAI: Responsible ai practices. https://ai.google/responsibilities/responsible-ai-practices/
23. Grother, P.J., Ngan, M.L., Hanaoka, K.K., et al.: Face recognition vendor test part 3: demographic effects (2019)
24. Guillory, D., Shankar, V., Ebrahimi, S., Darrell, T., Schmidt, L.: Predicting with confidence on unseen distributions. In: Proceedings of the IEEE/CVF International Conference on Computer Vision, pp. 1134–1144 (2021)
25. Guo, J., Deng, J., Lattas, A., Zafeiriou, S.: Sample and computation redistribution for efficient face detection. arXiv preprint arXiv:2105.04714 (2021)
26. Guo, J., Deng, J., Xue, N., Zafeiriou, S.: Stacked dense u-nets with dual transformers for robust face alignment. In: BMVC (2018)
27. Hartig, F., Minunno, F., Paul, S.: BayesianTools: general-purpose MCMC and SMC samplers and tools for bayesian statistics (2019). https://CRAN.R-project. org/package=BayesianTools, r package version 0.1.7
28. Hashimoto, T., Srivastava, M., Namkoong, H., Liang, P.: Fairness without demographics in repeated loss minimization. In: International Conference on Machine Learning,pp. 1929–1938. PMLR (2018)
29. He, K., Zhang, X., Ren, S., Sun, J.: Deep residual learning for image recognition. In: Proceedings of the IEEE Coference on Computer Vision and Pattern Recognition,pp. 770–778 (2016)
30. He, K., Zhang, X., Ren, S., Sun, J.: Identity mappings in deep residual networks. In: Leibe, B., Matas, J., Sebe, N., Welling, M. (eds.) ECCV 2016. LNCS, vol. 9908, pp. 630–645. Springer, Cham (2016). https://doi.org/10.1007/978-3-319-46493-0_38
31. IBM: Trustworthy ai.https://www.ibm.com/watson/trustworthy-ai
32. Ji, D., Smyth, P., Steyvers, M.: Can i trust my fairness metric? assessing fairness with unlabeled data and bayesian inference. arXiv preprint arXiv:2010.09851 (2020)
33. Kearns, M., Roth, A.: The ethical algorithm: The science of socially aware algorithm design. Oxford University Press (2019)
34. Keles, U., Lin, C., Adolphs, R.: A cautionary note on predicting social judgments from faces with deep neural networks. Affective Sci. **2**(4), 438–454 (2021)
35. Kortylewski, A., Egger, B., Schneider, A., Gerig, T., Morel-Forster, A., Vetter, T.: Analyzing and reducing the damage of dataset bias to face recognition with synthetic data. In: Proceedings of the IEEE/CVF Conference on Computer Vision and Pattern Recognition Workshops,pp. 0 (2019)
36. Krishnapriya, K., Albiero, V., Vangara, K., King, M.C., Bowyer, K.W.: Issues related to face recognition accuracy varying based on race and skin tone. IEEE Trans. Technol. Soc. **1**(1), 8–20 (2020)
37. Krivosheev, E., Bykau, S., Casati, F., Prabhakar, S.: Detecting and preventing confused labels in crowdsourced data. Proc. VLDB Endowment **13**(12), 2522–2535 (2020)

38. Lahoti, P., et al.: Fairness without demographics through adversarially reweighted learning. arXiv preprint arXiv:2006.13114 (2020)
39. Maze, B., et al.: Iarpa janus benchmark-c: Face dataset and protocol. In: 2018 International Conference on Biometrics (ICB), pp. 158–165. IEEE (2018)
40. McKone, E., Dawel, A., Robbins, R.A., Shou, Y., Chen, N., Crookes, K.: Why the other-race effect matters: poor recognition of other-race faces impacts everyday social interactions. British J. Psychol. (2021)
41. Muthén, B., Shedden, K.: Finite mixture modeling with mixture outcomes using the em algorithm. Biometrics **55**(2), 463–469 (1999)
42. Phillips, P.J., Yates, A.N., Hu, Y., Hahn, C.A., Noyes, E., Jackson, K., Cavazos, J.G., Jeckeln, G., Ranjan, R., Sankaranarayanan, S., et al.: Face recognition accuracy of forensic examiners, superrecognizers, and face recognition algorithms. Proc. Natl. Acad. Sci. **115**(24), 6171–6176 (2018)
43. PricewaterhouseCoopers: Responsible ai toolkit. https://www.pwc.com/gx/en/issues/data-and-analytics/artificial-intelligence/what-is-responsible-ai.html
44. Prost, F., et al.: Measuring model fairness under noisy covariates: a theoretical perspective. In: Proceedings of the 2021 AAAI/ACM Conference on AI, Ethics, and Society, pp. 873–883 (2021)
45. Raji, I.D., Gebru, T., Mitchell, M., Buolamwini, J., Lee, J., Denton, E.: Saving face: Investigating the ethical concerns of facial recognition auditing. In: Proceedings of the AAAI/ACM Conference on AI, Ethics, and Society, pp. 145–151 (2020)
46. Ranjan, R., Castillo, C.D., Chellappa, R.: L2-constrained softmax loss for discriminative face verification. arXiv preprint arXiv:1703.09507 (2017)
47. Ricanek, K., Tesafaye, T.: Morph: A longitudinal image database of normal adult age-progression. In: 7th International Conference on Automatic Face and Gesture Recognition (FGR06), pp. 341–345. IEEE (2006)
48. Robinson, J.P., Livitz, G., Henon, Y., Qin, C., Fu, Y., Timoner, S.: Face recognition: too bias, or not too bias? In: Proceedings of the ieee/cvf Conference on Computer Vision and Pattern Recognition Workshops, p. 1 (2020)
49. Rubio, F., Steel, M.: The family of two-piece distributions. Significance **17**, 12–13 (2020). https://doi.org/10.1111/j.1740-9713.2020.01352.x
50. Rubio, F.J., Ogundimu, E.O., Hutton, J.L.: On modelling asymmetric data using two-piece sinh-arcsinh distributions. Brazilian J. Probability Stat., 485–501 (2016)
51. Srinivas, N., Ricanek, K., Michalski, D., Bolme, D.S., King, M.: Face recognition algorithm bias: performance differences on images of children and adults. In: Proceedings of the IEEE/CVF Conference on Computer Vision and Pattern Recognition Workshops (2019)
52. Tanaka, J.W., Kiefer, M., Bukach, C.M.: A holistic account of the own-race effect in face recognition: Evidence from a cross-cultural study. Cognition **93**(1), B1–B9 (2004)
53. Vangara, K., King, M.C., Albiero, V., Bowyer, K., et al.: Characterizing the variability in face recognition accuracy relative to race. In: Proceedings of the IEEE/CVF Conference on Computer Vision and Pattern Recognition Workshops, pp. 0 (2019)
54. Vorvoreanu, M., Walker, K.: Advancing ai trustworthiness: Updates on responsible ai research, February 2022. https://www.microsoft.com/en-us/research/blog/advancing-ai-trustworthiness-updates-on-responsible-ai-research/
55. Wang, F., et al.: The devil of face recognition is in the noise. In: Ferrari, V., Hebert, M., Sminchisescu, C., Weiss, Y. (eds.) ECCV 2018. LNCS, vol. 11213, pp. 780–795. Springer, Cham (2018). https://doi.org/10.1007/978-3-030-01240-3_47

56. Wang, H., et al.: Cosface: large margin cosine loss for deep face recognition. In: Proceedings of the IEEE Conference on Computer Vision and Pattern Recognition, pp. 5265–5274 (2018)

57. Wang, M., Deng, W., Hu, J., Tao, X., Huang, Y.: Racial faces in the wild: Reducing racial bias by information maximization adaptation network. In: Proceedings of the IEEE/CVF International Conference on Computer Vision, pp. 692–702 (2019)

58. Wang, M., Zhang, Y., Deng, W.: Meta balanced network for fair face recognition. IEEE Trans. Pattern Anal. Mach. Intell. (2021)

59. Wang, Z., et al.: Towards fairness in visual recognition: effective strategies for bias mitigation. In: Proceedings of the IEEE/CVF Conference on Computer Vision and Pattern Recognition, pp. 8919–8928 (2020)

60. Welinder, P., Welling, M., Perona, P.: A lazy man's approach to benchmarking: Semisupervised classifier evaluation and recalibration. In: Proceedings of the IEEE Conference on Computer Vision and Pattern Recognition, pp. 3262–3269 (2013)

61. Zhou, K., Liu, Z., Qiao, Y., Xiang, T., Loy, C.C.: Domain generalization in vision: a survey. arXiv preprint arXiv:2103.02503 (2021)

Towards Efficient Adversarial Training on Vision Transformers

Boxi Wu[1], Jindong Gu[2], Zhifeng Li[3], Deng Cai[1(✉)], Xiaofei He[1],
and Wei Liu[3(✉)]

[1] State Key Lab of CAD&CG, Zhejiang University, Zhejiang, China
boxiwu@zju.edu.cn, {dengcai,xiaofeihe}@cad.zju.edu.cn
[2] University of Munich, Munich, Germany
[3] Tencent Data Platform, Shenzhen, China
michaelzfli@tencent.com, wl2223@columbia.edu

Abstract. Vision Transformer (ViT), as a powerful alternative to Convolutional Neural Network (CNN), has received much attention. Recent work showed that ViTs are also vulnerable to adversarial examples like CNNs. To build robust ViTs, an intuitive way is to apply adversarial training since it has been shown as one of the most effective ways to accomplish robust CNNs. However, one major limitation of adversarial training is its heavy computational cost. The self-attention mechanism adopted by ViTs is a computationally intense operation whose expense increases quadratically with the number of input patches, making adversarial training on ViTs even more time-consuming. In this work, we first comprehensively study fast adversarial training on a variety of vision transformers and illustrate the relationship between the efficiency and robustness. Then, to expedite adversarial training on ViTs, we propose an efficient Attention Guided Adversarial Training mechanism. Specifically, relying on the specialty of self-attention, we actively remove certain patch embeddings of each layer with an attention-guided dropping strategy during adversarial training. The slimmed self-attention modules accelerate the adversarial training on ViTs significantly. With only 65% of the fast adversarial training time, we match the state-of-the-art results on the challenging ImageNet benchmark.

Keywords: Robustness · Adversarial training · Vision transformer

1 Introduction

Vision Transformers with the self-attention mechanism have been broadly studied and become de facto state-of-the-art models for many benchmarks. Recent works broadly investigated the traits of this new genre of architectures on computer vision tasks. Meanwhile, the adversarial robustness of Vision Transformers has also been intensively studied [1,1,7,9,22,29,32,44–46,48,52,60,64,84]. To

---

B. Wu and J. Gu—Equal contribution.

S. Avidan et al. (Eds.): ECCV 2022, LNCS 13673, pp. 307–325, 2022.
https://doi.org/10.1007/978-3-031-19778-9_18

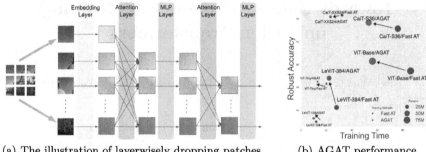

(a) The illustration of layerwisely dropping patches   (b) AGAT performance

Fig. 1. (a) AGAT chooses to drop a certain proportion of image embeddings based on the attention information at each self-attention layer. (b) We plot the robust accuracy against the training time (hours) for various ViTs. AGAT substantially accelerates adversarial training, while maintaining or improving the robustness at the same time.

build robust Vision Transformers, an intuitive way is to apply adversarial training [25,63] since it has been shown to be one of the most effective ways to achieve robust CNNs [5,23,43]. However, one major limitation of adversarial training is its expensive computational cost. Adversarial training is known for requiring no extra cost during testing but greatly increasing the training cost. Huge efforts have been devoted to overcome this deficit [3,30,31,51,62,66,76,81]. However, the philosophy of designing stronger ViTs has largely lifted up the computation intensity and weakened the performance of previously-proposed techniques. The specialty of the newly-proposed self-attention design [13,19] in ViTs also introduces new challenges for accelerating adversarial training.

In this paper, we study the problem of how to efficiently carry out adversarial training on Vision Transformers. We first apply the state-of-the-art Fast Adversarial Training (Fast AT) algorithm [62,81] on a variety of vision transformers and analyze how factors like attention mechanism, computational complexity, and parameter size influence the training quality. To the best of our knowledge, we are the first to accomplish a broad investigation on this topic. Our survey shows that, although ViTs outperform CNNs by a great margin on robustness, they have hugely increased the computational complexity. The self-attention mechanism adopted by ViTs is a computationally intense operation whose cost increases quadratically with the number of input patches. This newly-emerged module hampers the utilization of several techniques for accelerating adversarial training. Meanwhile, we find that large ViTs models also suffer from obvious catastrophic over-fitting problems [56]. This eventually leads to the degradation of robustness on ViTs with increasingly large capacity.

To make adversarial training efficient on the heavy-weight vision transformers, we investigate in accelerating adversarial training for vision transformers. Particularly, we leverage the specialty that the self-attention mechanism of transformers is capable of processing variable-length inputs. This specialty of ViTs has been utilized in a wide range of applications, including processing variable-length word sequences for translations [19], mining graphs with unlimited edges [75], etc. Recently, on vision tasks, several works [16,55,70] explored the possibility of dropping input image patches during training or testing for acceleration purposes. However, randomly dropping a certain number of input patches will inevitably hurt the training quality. Thus, many works have proposed adaptive designs [50,83] in the scenarios of a variety of targeted tasks.

Enlightened by the above works, we propose an Attention-Guided Adversarial Training (AGAT) mechanism, where we drop the patches based on the attention information. As illustrated by Fig. 1(a), our method intends to drop image embeddings after each layer of self-attention. Note that the self-attention layer is non-parametric and thus is not limited to a static number of inputs. We drop the embeddings with lower attention and keep the higher ones. Such a design will better preserve the feed-forward process and therefore guard the backward gradient computation of generating the adversarial examples. As shown in Fig. 1(b), AGAT gets to keep the training quality mostly unchanged or be improved by taking only 65% training time. Our work matches the state-of-the-art results of adversarial robustness on the challenging benchmark of ImageNet.

2   Relate Works

Adversarial Training. Adversarial attacks [23,38,39,43,67,80] intend to endanger the performance of deep networks via repeatedly optimizing the input images with respect to the output of the model. To counter this unwanted deficit, various defensive approaches were proposed [20,27,40,41,47,61,65,82]. Among these defenses, the methodology of adversarial training withstands most kinds of examinations and has become one of a few defenses that can consistently improve the robustness of deep networks when facing most attacks [5]. However, adversarial training is known to suffer from complexity issues [54,62,81]. Particularly, Fast AT [81] enhances the single-step adversarial training with random initialization. Fast AT shows promising results on benchmark datasets. Later works [3,4,33,51,66,76] also proposed improved variants of Fast AT.

Vision Transformer. The Transformer architecture and its self-attention mechanism were first proposed in the field of natural language processing (NLP) [13, 19,74] and then adopted in the scenario of computer vision [17,79,85]. After the huge efforts of a surge of explorations [21,71,77], the Vision Transformer (ViT) has shown the potential to surpass the traditional convolutional neural networks. Then, researchers keep pushing this new philosophy of model design into a wide range of fields like high-resolution vision tasks [42,78]. Meanwhile, to reduce the huge computational expense that is brought by the densely modeled self-attention mechanism, various techniques have been proposed [17,77].

Adversarial Robustness of ViT. The adversarial robustness of ViT has also achieved great attention due to its impressive performance [8,10,12,26,49,53, 63,64]. Some works [10,12,63] first reported positive results where they showed that standard ViTs perform more robust than standard CNNs under adversarial attacks. The later works [8,26] revealed that ViTs are not more robust than CNNs if both are trained in the same training framework. By adopting Transformers' training recipes, CNNs can become as robust as Transformers on defending against adversarial attacks. In both sides, we can observe that the clean accuracy of standard models can be easily reduced to near zero under standard attack protocols. In addition, Fu et al. [22] studied attacking ViTs in a patch-wise approach, which reveals the unique vulnerability of ViTs. To boost the adversarial robustness of ViTs, recent works [6,68] explored multiple-step adversarial training to ViTs. Shao et al. [63], tested the vanilla adversarial training on CIFAR10. However, multi-step adversarial training is computationally expensive. And in this work, we take the step of exploring fast single-step adversarial training on ViT models.

3   Fast Adversarial Training on Vision Transformers

We first comprehensively study the Fast AT [81] algorithm on vision transformers. Fast AT is designed to be efficient so that it can be applied to large models (e.g., ResNet-101 [28]) on large-scale datasets (e.g., ImageNet [58]). Specifically, Fast AT refines the standard single-step FGSM [23] algorithm by adopting a large random perturbation as the starting point for searching adversarial examples. By doing so, Fast AT is supposed to effectively resist the catastrophic overfitting [81] of training with the plain FGSM. Thus, Fast AT preserves the effectiveness while significantly improves the efficiency over the multi-step PGD [43] algorithm. To better understand the robustness of the newly-developed ViT models, in this section, we apply Fast AT to a wide range of ViTs.

We select nineteen models of different sizes from five vision transformer families, including ViT [21], CaiT [73], LeViT [24], SwinTransformer [42], and CrossFormer [78]. The selected models cover a wide range of model designs, including hybrid models [24], slim models [24,78], constrained attention [42,78], and multi-scale attention [24,78]. Following the settings of Fast AT [81], we set the perturbation radius to $2/255$ for ImageNet and test the adversarially trained models with the 100-step PGD attack. Our training schedule aligns with Swin-Transformer [42] and DeiT [72]. We keep all hyper-parameters, e.g., image size, training epoch, and data augmentation, identical for all models. We also present the results of Fast AT on the CNN models of ResNet-50 and ResNet-101 for comparison. As shown by Fig. 2(a), ViTs are consistently more robust than CNNs. This aligns with concurrent researches on model robustness [69]. We conclude draw novel observations as follows:

1. **Within the same transformer family, larger transformers do not always result in better robustness.** In Fig. 2(a), the transformer families of LeViT, CaiT, and ViT exhibit a pattern of over-fitting. Namely, as the models get larger, the network robustness learned by Fast AT degrades conversely. For instance, Cait-S36 performs worse than CaiT-XXS24. Figure 2(b)

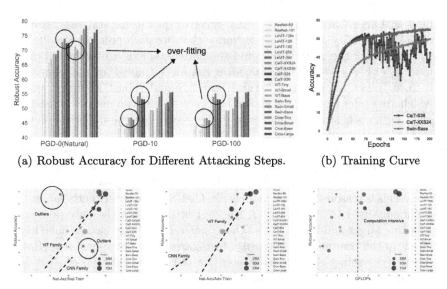

(a) Robust Accuracy for Different Attacking Steps.   (b) Training Curve

(c) Performance Outliers   (d) Performance Alignment   (e) Computation Intensity

Fig. 2. (a) Robust accuracy for various ViTs. (b) Large ViTs like CaiT-S36 may suffer from obvious unstable training and over-fitting, while designs like window attention [42] can alleviate the issue. (c) The performance of ViTs on Fast AT may not align with their natural accuracy of natural training. (d) In contrast, the natural and robust accuracies of ViTs align with each other when both are under Fast AT. (e) Large ViTs greatly increase the computational complexity.

provides more details of the above over-fitting issue. The optimization of the CaiT-S36 model gradually degrades after a certain point. In contrast, the CaiT-XXS24 model possesses a monotonically increasing training curve. This aligns with previous findings that ViTs may suffer from more severe over-fitting on natural tasks and need the assistance of aggressive data augmentation schedules [72]. Moreover, transformers with a constrained attention mechanism can alleviate the over-fitting problem. In Fig. 2(b), unlike CaiT-S36, the large model of Swin-Base shows a steady training curve.

2. **Among different transformer families, the attention mechanism designed for better natural performance not necessarily results in better robustness.** In Fig. 2(c), for each transformer architecture, we plot its natural performance under natural training against its robust performance under Fast AT. Among different transformer architectures, the two metrics of natural accuracy and robust accuracy approximately form a line, indicating the close relation between natural and robust performances. Compared with the line formed by CNNs, vision transformers consistently achieve better robustness on models with similar natural performance. However, we can observe a few outliers of models from the LeViT and CaiT families. Specifically, the hybrid design of LeViT can achieve high robustness with very small

models. Large CaiTs, despite being effective on the natural task, result in obvious inferiority on robustness. Notice that, for each point in Fig. 2(c), the two metrics of the vertical axis and the horizontal axis are evaluated on two models, either adversarially-trained or naturally-trained, of the same architecture. When we plot the natural accuracy and robust accuracy, both of which are under Fast AT, as shown by Fig. 2(d), the two metrics consistently align with each other without any outlier, revealing the difference between Fast AT and standard training.

3. **SOTA ViTs suffer from a severe efficiency issue and require much more training time than SOTA CNNs.** The above over-fitting problem mainly shows on large ViTs like Cait-S36 or LeViT-384, but not on the small ones. This is reasonable since models like Cait-S36 are consistently larger than commonly-used CNNs. However, the over-fitting is not the only problem of adopting larger and larger ViTs. These increasingly large models have hugely lifted up the computation intensity. In Fig. 2(e), we plot robustness (Robust Accuracy) against computation intensity (GFLOPs). State-of-the-art ViTs can be a few times larger than CNNs. This makes utilizing Fast AT even harder since the self-attention module is more intricate to accelerate.

4   Efficient Adversarial Training on Vision Transformers

As discussed in the last section, one major problem that hinders the deployment of adversarial training on vision transformers is the efficiency issue. Adversarial training is known to be computationally intensive. This greatly hampers its usage on large-scale models or datasets. Various techniques have been proposed to mitigate this problem. However, with the revolution brought by vision transformers, many existing techniques such as variable-resolution training [81] have been unusable. More importantly, there is a rising trend of adopting increasingly large ViTs for better performance. The complexity of these enormous ViTs is too large to afford, even for efficient algorithms like Fast AT.

In this section, we first analyze the computational complexity of popular ViTs. Our analysis shows that ViT requires a much longer time to finish adversarial training, which is caused by the large computational cost of ViT brought by a large number of input patches. Then, we explore the input patches to reduce the brought computational cost. Given the fact that the flexibility of self-attention allows ViTs to process an arbitrary length of image patches, we explore a random patch dropping strategy to reduce the computation. The dropping operation with the reduced number of patches can accelerate adversarial training, as expected. However, the naive dropping strategy will also hurt robustness. To address the above issues, we propose our Attention-Guided Adversarial Training algorithm, which selectively drops patches based on attention magnitude.

4.1   Computation Intensity of ViTs

We first formally formulate our task. For each matrix, we present its shape in the lower right corner and its index in the upper right corner. Denote the input feature as $\mathbf{X}_{p\times d}$, which consists of a sequence of p embeddings with the dimension being $d : \mathbf{X} = [X_d^1, X_d^2, ..., X_d^p]$. Each embedding relates to a specific non-overlapped patch of the input image. Vision transformer consists of a list of blocks, each of which consists of two kinds of computation, i.e., the Multi-head Self-Attention layer (MSA) and the Multi-Layer Perceptron layer (MLP). In the MSA module, $\mathbf{X}$ is first normalized via Layer Normalization and then transformed to the *query, key, and value* matrices ($\mathbf{K}$, $\mathbf{Q}$, $\mathbf{V}$).

$$[\mathbf{K}_{p\times d}, \ \mathbf{Q}_{p\times d}, \ \mathbf{V}_{p\times d}] = \text{LayerNorm}(\mathbf{X}_{p\times d})\mathbf{W}_{d\times 3d}^1. \tag{1}$$

For the multi-head design, we partition the $\mathbf{K}$, $\mathbf{Q}$, $\mathbf{V}$ matrices of shape $p \times d$ into h heads, with each part having a shape of $p \times \frac{d}{h}$. Then, taking the first head as an example, $\mathbf{V}^1$ will be re-weighted by $\mathbf{A}^1$ with the following form:

$$\text{Attn}(\mathbf{K}_{p\times\frac{d}{h}}^1, \mathbf{Q}_{p\times\frac{d}{h}}^1, \mathbf{V}_{p\times\frac{d}{h}}^1) = \text{SoftMax}(\mathbf{Q}^1\mathbf{K}^{1\top}/\sqrt{d} + \mathbf{B})\mathbf{V}^1 = \mathbf{A}_{p\times p}^1\mathbf{V}^1. \tag{2}$$

$\mathbf{B}$ is a learnable bias. Note that all the column vectors of $\mathbf{A}^1$ are normalized by Softmax and thus have a summation of 1 in each. Then, $\mathbf{AV}$ value of each head will be concatenated and transformed to the output of MSA.

$$\mathbf{X}_{p\times d}' = \text{Concat}(\mathbf{A}^1\mathbf{V}^1, \mathbf{A}^2\mathbf{V}^2, ..., \mathbf{A}^h\mathbf{V}^h)_{p\times d}\mathbf{W}_{d\times d}^2. \tag{3}$$

A following MLP module will take in the output of MSA, $\mathbf{X}'$, and transform each embedding with Layer Normalization and GELU activation.

$$\mathbf{X}_{p\times c}'' = \text{GELU}\Big[\text{LayerNorm}(\mathbf{X}_{p\times d}')\mathbf{W}_{d\times 4d}^3\Big]\mathbf{W}_{4d\times d}^4. \tag{4}$$

The computational complexity of the above process is:

$$\Omega(\text{MSA}) = 4pd^2 + 2p^2d + pd; \quad \Omega(\text{MLP}) = 8pd^2 + pd. \tag{5}$$

A typical vision transformer will consecutively conduct the above process to generate the final image representation for prediction. Take the ViT-Base model as an example. Each layer has $d = 768$. Therefore, we have $\Omega(\text{MSA}) + \Omega(\text{MLP}) = 7 \times 10^6 p + 1.5 \times 10^3 p^2$. Since $7 \times 10^6 \gg 1.5 \times 10^3$ and p is mostly around 2×10^2, the computational complexity of the entire ViT is approximately linear to p.

4.2 Dropping Patch: The Flexibility of Self-attention

Different from the convolutional operation where the hyperparameters (e.g., kernel size, padding size) are supposed to be fixed, the self-attention operation does not require the inputs with fixed length. For instance, this flexibility of self-attention is leveraged to process an arbitrary length of words in NLP tasks. Similarly, the flexibility makes its adaption to graph data feasible, in which different nodes can have a different number of connected edges [75]. When transformers with self-attention mechanisms have been introduced into computer vision tasks, researchers also investigate dynamically dropping the patches or

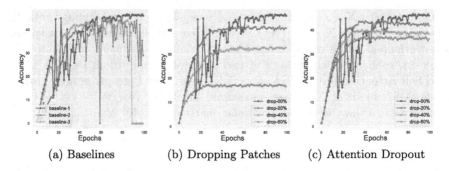

(a) Baselines   (b) Dropping Patches   (c) Attention Dropout

Fig. 3. (a) We repeat the baseline without any dropping for three times. We can observe the training is very unstable. (b) Training curve when we drop various rates of input patches. (c)Training curve when we adopt various rates of attention dropout.

the embeddings in the forward pass of a ViT model [16,55,70]. It is found that, when a constrained quantity of patches are dropped, the forward inference can be significantly accelerated. Meanwhile, the performance of the model will be only slightly degraded [50,83]. Several works utilize this feature to design new mechanisms for their own unique purposes.

In this work, we also explore a patch dropping strategy to accelerate adversarial training given the excellent trade-off it achieves. We first test the scheme of randomly dropping a certain number of input patches to see how it influences the training quality of Fast AT. We report the results in Fig 3(b), where we plot the robustness against the training epoch for different ratios of dropping. Note that no patches will be dropped during inference in the testing stage. When the number of input patches is reduced, the forward inference of ViT can be accelerated. Surprisingly, from the figure, we also observe that the dropping operation also stabilizes the adversarial training and alleviates the phenomenon of catastrophic over-fitting [34,59,81]. As shown by Fig 3(a), we repeat Fast AT without any dropping for three times. The training procedure can be very unstable and occasionally drop to zero accuracy. We conjecture that it is the regularization effect brought by the patch dropping operation that stabilizes Fast AT. To further verify this conjecture, we test ViTs equipped with the dropout operation as in DeiT [72]. The dropout module is applied right after the self-attention module. As shown in Fig 3(c), like dropping patches, the attention dropout module also stabilizes Fast AT. Unlike dropping patches, the dropout module cannot save computation. However, the final robust accuracy can be reduced in both cases when dropping is applied. The random patch dropping strategy poses a dilemma. Namely, it brings both acceleration and performance degradation. In the following section, we will present our attention-guided patch dropping strategy, where we achieve a better trade-off between efficiency and effectiveness.

4.3 Attention-Guided Adversarial Training

It is known that adversarial training utilizes adversarial attacks to generate examples so that the network can learn to fit the generated adversarial examples.

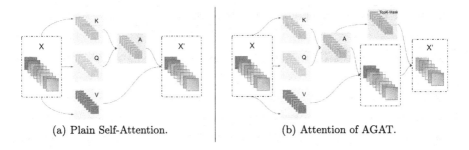

(a) Plain Self-Attention.   (b) Attention of AGAT.

Fig. 4. The illustration of the plain self-attention layer and the attention layer of AGAT. The embedding mask is directly generated from **A** and is non-parametric. Thus, for the same model, one can adopt our AGAT during training and the plain self-attention during testing, respectively.

This is a typical hard example mining framework. The more powerful the adversarial examples are, the more robust the learned network will be. The quality of the adversarial examples relies on the adversarial attacking algorithm. And the attack algorithm depends on accurately estimating the gradient of the input pixels with respect to the loss function. Thus, a major insight of achieving our goal is to drop the patches that will barely hamper the gradient estimation. A similar philosophy has been utilized for sparse attacks or black-box attacks.

Recent works studied the learned attention and found that the magnitude of the attention can reveal how salient an embedding is [15]. This enlightens us that we can utilize this ready-made information to filter salient embeddings. Thus, we sum $\frac{1}{h}\sum_{i=1}^{h} \mathbf{A}^i$ by row and generate an index vector **a**. Note that the column of $\frac{1}{h}\sum_{i=1}^{h} \mathbf{A}^i$ is the weighted-average parameter and thus always equal to 1. It indicates how much a generated embedding receives the information of each input embedding. In contrast, the row of $\frac{1}{h}\sum_{i=1}^{h} \mathbf{A}^i$ reveals how much each input embedding influences the output embeddings. This value differs from embedding to embedding. Thus, we choose to select the top-k embeddings based on their magnitude in **a**. Then, the formulation of (3) becomes:

$$\mathbf{X}'_{k \times d} = \text{MaskBy}\Big[\text{Concat}(\mathbf{A}^1 \mathbf{V}^1, ..., \mathbf{A}^h \mathbf{V}^h), \text{Topk}(\mathbf{a})\Big]_{k \times d} \mathbf{W}^2_{d \times d}. \qquad (6)$$

We drop the embeddings after the weighted average calculation of **AV** so that the magnitude of embeddings will be kept stable. The number of embeddings will reduce from p to k. To fully utilize the attention information in each layer, we propose a layer-wise exponential dropping scheme. Namely, in each layer, we drop a constant proportion of patches. Thus, this scheme will drop more embeddings on deeper layers, where the embeddings are consistently more redundant [55]. We set the dropping rate to 0.9. On a 12-layer ViT-Base model, the final layer will process only 31% number of embeddings and save more than 40% FLOPs of the entire model. A detailed implementation of our Attention-Guided Adversarial Training is shown in Algorithm 1. Our AGAT only modifies the training process. During testing, we use the original model for prediction. The class token will not be dropped when it involves the feed-forward procedure.

Algorithm 1. AGAT attention code (PyTorch-like)

```
def init(num_heads, dim, drop_rate):
    head_dim = dim // num_heads # num_heads: the number of heads, dim: embedding dimension
    scale = head_dim ** -0.5

    qkv = nn.Linear(dim, dim * 3)
    proj = nn.Linear(dim, dim)

def forward(self, x): # x: input tensor with the shape of (b, p, d);
    b, p, d = x.shape # b: batch size; p: patch number
    q, k, v = qkv(x).reshape(b, p, 3, num_heads, head_dim).permute(2, 0, 3, 1, 4).unbind(0)

    attn = (q @ k.transpose(-2, -1)) * scale
    attn = attn.softmax(dim=-1) # b num_heads p p

    own_attn = torch.sum(torch.sum(attn, dim=1), dim=-2) # b p
    kept_num = int(p * drop_rate) - 1 # compute the number of kept embeddings
    _, rank_indices = torch.topk(own_attn[:,1:], k=kept_num, dim=-1) # b k
    rank_indices = rank_indices.unsqueeze(-1).repeat(1,1,dim) # for the API of torch.gather

    x = (attn @ v).transpose(1, 2).reshape(B, N, C)
    x = torch.gather(x, dim=1, index=rank_indices) # drop embeddings

    return proj(x)
```

---

5 Experiments

5.1 Experimental Setup

Dataset. We evaluate our method on the challenging ImageNet [57] dataset. Due to the huge computational expense of adversarial training, most adversarial training approaches are only verified on relatively small datasets such as CIFAR10 [36] or MNIST [37]. Our efforts on improving the efficiency of adversarial training allow us to apply adversarial training to large-scale datasets. The input image size is 224 on all models for a fair comparison.

Training Schedule. Following previous works [72,78], we use the AdamW [35] optimizer for training for 300 epochs with a cosine decay learning rate schedule. The initial learning rate is set to 0.001. The first 20 epochs adopt the linear warm-up strategy. The batch size is 1024 split on 8 NVIDIA A100 GPUs.

Evaluation Metrics. We report our major results on two metrics, robust accuracy and GFLOPs. We mainly focus on improving the speed of training and keeping the learned robustness unchanged at the mean time. For a direct impression of training speed, we also record the training time for each method. Note that the training time is not only determined by the efficiency of the training algorithm, but also the IO speed and many other nonnegligible factors.

Adversarial Attack. We choose the powerful multi-step PGD attack [43] with the perturbation radius being 2/255 or 4/255 and the optimization step being 20 or 100 [82]. We also test different kinds of attacks, including black-box attacks, to rule out the possibility of obfuscated gradient [5].

Vision Transformers. Our AGAT can be directly used on the self-attention model and most of its variants. We apply our AGAT to three commonly-used models ViT [21], CaiT [73], and LeViT [24]. All the three models are built on the original self-attention module and can fully reveal the effectiveness of our AGAT. In future work, we will explore combining our AGAT with more sophisticated attention mechanism like window attention [42] or multi-scale attention [78].

Table 1. Adversarial Training on The ImageNet Dataset. In most cases, our Attention-Guided Adversarial Training on ViTs achieves comparable clean performance and robust accuracy to Fast-AT with much less time. The conclusion still holds when different perturbation ranges are applied.

Model	Params	Block number	Training method	Dropping rate	FLOPs	Training time	$\epsilon = 2/255$			$\epsilon = 4/255$		
							Nat-Acc.	PGD-20	PGD-100	Nat-Acc.	PGD-20	PGD-100
ResNet-50 [28]	25.6M	16	Free AT [62]	–	3.8G	46H	62.28	**43.77**	**43.44**	58.31	30.89	30.71
			Fast AT [81]	–	3.8G	**14H**	58.20	43.62	43.31	52.62	30.17	30.13
			Grad Align [4]	–	3.8G	**14H**	57.44	42.61	42.46	53.66	**31.18**	**31.01**
ResNet-101 [28]	44.5M	33	Free AT [62]	–	7.6G	51H	64.37	43.27	43.14	60.41	31.17	31.14
			Fast AT [81]	–	7.6G	**17H**	60.90	**44.57**	**44.11**	55.62	**33.02**	**33.26**
			Grad Align [4]	–	7.6G	**17H**	60.12	43.28	43.04	53.94	30.27	30.21
CaiT-XXS24 [73]	12.0M	24	Fast AT [81]	0.0	2.5G	32H	72.84	54.31	54.26	68.77	32.14	32.09
			Random	0.4	**1.5G**	22H	65.62	39.81	39.52	60.87	31.54	31.46
			AGAT	0.05	**1.5G**	23H	71.15	54.17	54.08	68.32	31.46	31.39
CaiT-XXS36 [73]	17.3M	36	Fast AT [81]	0.0	3.8G	38H	74.01	55.58	55.41	73.54	34.61	34.28
			Random	0.4	2.7G	**25H**	69.25	50.13	49.89	65.12	28.00	27.91
			AGAT	0.03	2.7G	**25H**	73.83	**55.81**	**55.72**	73.91	**35.22**	**35.19**
CaiT-S36 [73]	68.2M	36	Fast AT [81]	0.0	13.9G	76H	72.51	53.12	52.76	71.20	33.02	32.84
			Random	0.4	7.8G	**51H**	70.46	51.27	51.03	66.62	28.95	28.75
			AGAT	0.03	**7.7G**	53H	72.69	**53.66**	**53.48**	71.06	**33.46**	**33.17**
LeViT-128 [24]	7.8M	9	Fast AT [81]	0.0	0.4G	12H	67.30	45.00	44.87	64.66	**32.11**	**32.09**
			Random	0.4	0.2G	10H	58.14	30.62	30.52	54.94	28.05	28.01
			AGAT	0.15	0.2G	10H	67.19	**45.30**	**45.21**	64.98	32.02	31.88
LeViT-256 [24]	11.0M	12	Fast AT [81]	0.0	0.6G	15H	68.69	46.94	46.89	66.24	**33.81**	**33.62**
			Random	0.4	**0.4G**	12H	60.71	31.45	31.18	57.64	29.89	29.66
			AGAT	0.1	**0.4G**	13H	68.90	**47.37**	**47.06**	65.98	33.12	33.05
LeViT-384 [24]	39.0M	12	Fast AT [81]	0.0	2.35G	28H	70.01	46.24	46.13	65.38	31.22	31.04
			Random	0.4	**1.3G**	**20H**	63.70	33.74	33.26	60.11	28.51	28.02
			AGAT	0.1	**1.3G**	22H	69.73	**48.80**	**48.59**	67.02	**33.48**	**33.35**
ViT-Tiny [21]	5.1M	12	Fast AT [81]	0.0	1.1G	20H	69.09	48.32	48.28	64.03	**31.68**	**31.20**
			Random	0.4	0.6G	**13H**	61.11	31.58	31.16	58.10	27.43	27.25
			AGAT	0.1	0.6G	**13H**	69.64	**48.50**	**48.46**	63.02	31.17	31.04
ViT-Small [21]	22M	12	Fast AT [81]	0.0	4.6G	47H	71.37	**49.49**	**49.41**	66.92	**34.07**	**33.82**
			Random	0.4	2.7G	33H	63.62	33.58	33.29	60.18	29.10	28.91
			AGAT	0.1	**2.6G**	**32H**	70.62	49.00	48.85	66.10	33.62	33.40
ViT-Base [21]	86M	12	Fast AT [81]	0.0	17.5G	86H	70.31	50.55	50.06	63.59	33.59	33.39
			Random	0.4	10.5G	**55H**	65.80	37.04	36.81	61.16	30.07	30.01
			AGAT	0.1	**10.1G**	56H	70.41	**51.23**	**51.11**	67.93	**34.94**	**34.78**

Training Algorithm. For vision transformers, we compare our AGAT with FastAT and the random dropping strategy (Random). we also provide results of Free AT [62] and Grad Align [4] algorithms on the ResNet [28] models.

5.2 Improved Efficiency of Adversarial Training on ImageNet

We present the performance of AGAT in Table 1. Because AGAT drops a static rate of embeddings for each self-attention layer, the depth of the ViTs will decide

Table 2. Evaluation of Adversarially Trained Models under Various Attacks. Robust accuracy of adversarially trained models is reported in this table. The robust accuracy achieved by our AGAT is comparable to that by Fast-AT under various attack evaluations and different perturbation ranges.

Method	Model	$\epsilon = 2/255$					$\epsilon = 4/255$				
		PGD	C&W	APGD-CE	APGD-DLR	Square	PGD	C&W	APGD-CE	APGD-DLR	Square
ViT-Tiny [21]	Fast AT	48.28	48.02	48.20	48.05	58.21	31.20	31.09	31.11	31.00	37.97
	AGAT	48.46	48.17	48.37	48.24	58.33	31.04	31.03	31.01	30.85	37.84
ViT-Base [21]	Fast AT	50.06	49.87	50.01	49.52	59.28	33.39	33.36	33.28	33.10	40.81
	AGAT	51.11	50.84	51.23	50.45	61.12	34.78	34.42	34.54	34.20	42.24
CaiT-XXS24 [73]	Fast AT	54.26	54.19	54.20	54.13	63.22	32.09	32.01	32.08	31.90	38.02
	AGAT	54.08	53.88	54.00	53.98	62.35	31.39	31.22	31.20	31.11	37.48
CaiT-S36 [73]	Fast AT	52.76	52.51	52.70	52.53	61.75	32.84	32.73	32.79	32.61	39.71
	AGAT	53.48	53.13	53.37	53.02	62.86	33.17	33.08	33.10	33.00	40.12
LeViT-128 [24]	Fast AT	44.87	44.81	44.73	44.60	56.89	32.09	32.03	32.02	31.95	38.90
	AGAT	45.21	45.19	45.19	45.06	57.12	31.88	31.77	31.87	31.76	38.61
LeViT-384 [24]	Fast AT	46.13	45.98	46.02	45.93	56.39	31.25	31.00	31.22	30.82	37.99
	AGAT	48.59	48.26	48.58	48.49	58.90	33.35	33.24	33.29	33.17	40.22

the total number of dropped features. Thus, we adjust the dropping rate for ViTs with different numbers of blocks so that the complexity of the feed-forward process will be approximately reduced by 40% of the baseline. For instance, we set the dropping rate to 0.1 for models with 12 blocks but 0.03 for models with 36 blocks. For the baseline of randomly dropping input patches, we can always set the dropping rate to 0.4 since the total amount of saved computation will not be affected by the number of blocks.

As shown by Table 1, for each vision transformer, the Fast AT baseline achieves high robustness but is time-consuming, while the Random dropping strategy saves training time but achieves inferior robustness. In contrast, AGAT achieves comparable robustness with Fast AT using much less training time. Particularly, on the ViT-Base model, AGAT achieves similar robustness to Fast AT but only takes 65% of training time. Meanwhile, since slim models such as ViT-Tiny and LeViT-128 do not possess the same level of model redundancy as their large-sized counterparts, the robustness of these slim models degrades more dramatically than larger ones when we randomly drop patches. When trained with AGAT, the robustness of slim models matches the plain Fast AT.

5.3   Ablation Study

Results Under Various Attacks. Adversarial robustness is known to be hard to examine. Several defensive algorithms were found to be vulnerable to tailored attacks. One of the most important and typical representatives of such phenomena is the obfuscated gradient problem. Our AGAT does not fall into this category, considering the algorithm neither utilizes any stochastic process nor hampers the gradient computation. In fact, our AGAT only takes effect on the training stage and does not modify any procedure during evaluation. To further show the robustness of the learned ViTs, we present the robust accuracy of our learned models under various different attacks in Table 2. We select the attacking criteria of C&W [14], Square [2], APGD-CE [18], and APGD-DLR [18]. The AGAT models achieve the same level of robustness as Fast AT.

Table 3. Ablation Study on Dropping Strategy. We compare our attention-guided dropping strategy with random dropping. Ours outperforms random dropping constantly in different dropping rates.

Model	Method	Attack	$\epsilon = 2/255$				$\epsilon = 4/255$			
			0%	20%	40%	60%	0%	20%	40%	60%
ViT-Tiny [21]	Random	PGD	48.28	39.02	31.16	21.01	31.20	29.64	27.25	24.11
	AGAT	PGD	48.28	**48.15**	**48.46**	**46.60**	31.20	**31.15**	**31.04**	**28.13**
ViT-Small [21]	Random	PGD	49.41	40.62	33.29	28.81	33.82	30.13	28.91	25.25
	AGAT	PGD	49.41	**49.43**	**48.85**	**47.90**	33.82	**33.29**	**33.40**	**32.10**
ViT-Base [21]	Random	PGD	49.26	45.02	36.81	33.17	33.39	32.61	30.01	28.86
	AGAT	PGD	49.26	**49.80**	**50.02**	**48.20**	33.39	**34.15**	**34.78**	**32.90**

Robustness and Dropping Rate. We cross-validate the rate of dropping of our AGAT in Table 3. To provide a clear comparison with the random dropping strategy, we compare their learned robust accuracy when both dropping strategies reduce approximately the same amount of computation. Due to the difference between the two algorithms (layer-wise vs input-wise), the actual learning rates are different across the two methods. It can be told that AGAT can maintain the learned robustness in a wide range of dropping rates. In contrast, the random dropping strategy significantly degrades the performance, especially for the slim model of ViT-Tiny. Dropping more than 40% computation will bring obvious degradation on robustness, even for AGAT. Thus, we consider this dropping rate as a good trade-off between effectiveness and efficiency.

Visualization. To better get an insight of how AGAT takes effect, we visualize the internal results of the ViT-Base model. For each of the 12 blocks in ViT-Base, we show the position of the dropped embeddings by masking out the corresponding image patches. In Fig. 5, the position of the dropped embedding mainly concentrates on the relatively unimportant positions like background, while the patches of the main object are mostly kept. This indicates that our AGAT successfully guards the feed-forward procedure and thus secures the generation of adversarial examples. We also visualize the corresponding value of attention for each patch. The darkness of each patch position indicates how much the corresponding embedding of this patch influences the other embeddings. For each block, we normalize all the values of attention by dividing the maximum value of attention. This visualization also demonstrates that the dropping rate of AGAT gets to cover the embeddings on the position of the main object. Therefore, dropping rates larger than the chosen value may lose crucial information for inference and thus hamper the generation of adversarial examples for training.

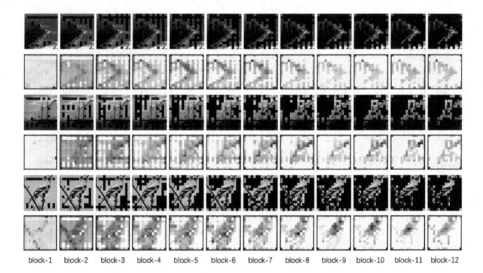

Fig. 5. Visualizations of dropped image patches and the distribution of attention. AGAT mainly cuts off the computation of non-object embeddings and thus maintains the performance and gradient computation.

6   Conclusions

Adversarial training is one of the most effective defense methods to boost the adversarial robustness of models. However, it is computationally expensive, even after many efforts have been made to address it. The emergence of ViTs, whose computational cost increases quadratically with the number of input patches, makes adversarial training more challenging. In this work, we first thoroughly examined the most popular fast adversarial training on various ViTs. Our investigation shows that ViT achieves higher robust accuracy than ResNet, while it does suffer from a large computation burden, as expected. Our further exploration showed that random input patch dropping can accelerate and stabilize the adversarial training, which, however, sacrifices the final robust accuracy. To overcome the dilemma, we proposed an Attention-Guided Adversarial Training (AGAT) mechanism based on the specialty of the self-attention mechanism. Our AGAT leverages the attention to guide the patch dropping process, which accelerates the adversarial training significantly and maintains the high robust accuracy of ViTs. We hope that this work can serve the community as a baseline for research on efficient adversarial training on vision transformers.

Acknowledgement. This work was supported in part by The National Key Research and Development Program of China (Grant Nos: 2018AAA0101400), in part by The National Nature Science Foundation of China (Grant Nos: 62036009, U1909203, 61936006, 62133013), in part by Innovation Capability Support Program of Shaanxi (Program No. 2021TD-05).

References

1. Aldahdooh, A., Hamidouche, W., Deforges, O.: Reveal of vision transformers robustness against adversarial attacks. arXiv:2106.03734 (2021)
2. Andriushchenko, M., Croce, F., Flammarion, N., Hein, M.: Square attack: a query-efficient black-box adversarial attack via random search. In: Vedaldi, A., Bischof, H., Brox, T., Frahm, J.-M. (eds.) ECCV 2020. LNCS, vol. 12368, pp. 484–501. Springer, Cham (2020). https://doi.org/10.1007/978-3-030-58592-1_29
3. Andriushchenko, M., Flammarion, N.: Understanding and improving fast adversarial training. In: NeurIPS (2020)
4. Andriushchenko, M., Flammarion, N.: Understanding and improving fast adversarial training. In: Larochelle, H., Ranzato, M., Hadsell, R., Balcan, M., Lin, H. (eds.) Advances in Neural Information Processing Systems 33: Annual Conference on Neural Information Processing Systems 2020, NeurIPS 2020, pp. 6–12 (2020). https://proceedings.neurips.cc/paper/2020/hash/b8ce47761ed7b3b6f48b583350b7f9e4-Abstract.html
5. Athalye, A., Carlini, N., Wagner, D.A.: Obfuscated gradients give a false sense of security: circumventing defenses to adversarial examples. In: ICML. Proceedings of Machine Learning Research, vol. 80, pp. 274–283. PMLR (2018)
6. Bai, J., Yuan, L., Xia, S., Yan, S., Li, Z., Liu, W.: Improving vision transformers by revisiting high-frequency components. CoRR abs/2204.00993 (2022). https://doi.org/10.48550/arXiv.2204.00993
7. Bai, Y., Mei, J., Yuille, A., Xie, C.: Are transformers more robust than CNNs? arXiv:2111.05464 (2021)
8. Bai, Y., Mei, J., Yuille, A., Xie, C.: Are transformers more robust than CNNs? In: Beygelzimer, A., Dauphin, Y., Liang, P., Vaughan, J.W. (eds.) Advances in Neural Information Processing Systems (2021). https://openreview.net/forum?id=hbHkvGBZB9
9. Benz, P., Ham, S., Zhang, C., Karjauv, A., Kweon, I.S.: Adversarial robustness comparison of vision transformer and MLP-mixer to CNNs. CoRR abs/2110.02797 (2021). https://arxiv.org/abs/2110.02797
10. Benz, P., Ham, S., Zhang, C., Karjauv, A., Kweon, I.S.: Adversarial robustness comparison of vision transformer and MLP-mixer to CNNs. arXiv preprint arXiv:2110.02797 (2021)
11. Bhojanapalli, S., Chakrabarti, A., Glasner, D., Li, D., Unterthiner, T., Veit, A.: Understanding robustness of transformers for image classification. CoRR abs/2103.14586 (2021). https://arxiv.org/abs/2103.14586
12. Bhojanapalli, S., Chakrabarti, A., Glasner, D., Li, D., Unterthiner, T., Veit, A.: Understanding robustness of transformers for image classification. arXiv:2103.14586 (2021)
13. Brown, T.B., et.al.: Language models are few-shot learners. In: Neural Information Processing Systems, NeurIPS (2020)
14. Carlini, N., Wagner, D.A.: Towards evaluating the robustness of neural networks. In: SP, pp. 39–57. IEEE Computer Society (2017)
15. Caron, M., et al.: Emerging properties in self-supervised vision transformers. In: 2021 IEEE/CVF International Conference on Computer Vision, ICCV 2021, Montreal, QC, Canada, 10–17 October 2021, pp. 9630–9640. IEEE (2021). https://doi.org/10.1109/ICCV48922.2021.00951

16. Chen, T., Cheng, Y., Gan, Z., Yuan, L., Zhang, L., Wang, Z.: Chasing sparsity in vision transformers: an end-to-end exploration. CoRR abs/2106.04533 (2021). https://arxiv.org/abs/2106.04533
17. Chu, X., et al.: Twins: revisiting spatial attention design in vision transformers. CoRR abs/2104.13840 (2021)
18. Croce, F., Hein, M.: Reliable evaluation of adversarial robustness with an ensemble of diverse parameter-free attacks. In: ICML (2020)
19. Devlin, J., Chang, M., Lee, K., Toutanova, K.: BERT: pre-training of deep bidirectional transformers for language understanding. In: Conference of the North American Chapter of the Association for Computational Linguistics, NAACL, pp. 4171–4186 (2019)
20. Dhillon, G.S., et.al.: Stochastic activation pruning for robust adversarial defense. In: ICLR (2018)
21. Dosovitskiy, A., et.al.: An image is worth 16×16 words: transformers for image recognition at scale. In: International Conference on Learning Representations, ICLR (2021)
22. Fu, Y., Zhang, S., Wu, S., Wan, C., Lin, Y.: Patch-fool: are vision transformers always robust against adversarial perturbations? In: International Conference on Learning Representations (2022)
23. Goodfellow, I.J., Shlens, J., Szegedy, C.: Explaining and harnessing adversarial examples. In: Bengio, Y., LeCun, Y. (eds.) ICLR (2015). https://arxiv.org/abs/1412.6572
24. Graham, B., El-Nouby, A., Touvron, H., Stock, P., Joulin, A., Jégou, H., Douze, M.: LeViT: a vision transformer in convnet's clothing for faster inference. CoRR abs/2104.01136 (2021). https://arxiv.org/abs/2104.01136
25. Gu, J., Tresp, V., Qin, Y.: Are vision transformers robust to patch perturbations? CoRR abs/2111.10659 (2021). https://arxiv.org/abs/2111.10659
26. Gu, J., Tresp, V., Qin, Y.: Are vision transformers robust to patch perturbations? In: arXiv preprint arXiv:2111.10659 (2021)
27. Guo, C., Rana, M., Cisse, M., Van Der Maaten, L.: Countering adversarial images using input transformations. In: ICLR (2018)
28. He, K., Zhang, X., Ren, S., Sun, J.: Deep residual learning for image recognition. In: CVPR, pp. 770–778 (2016). https://doi.org/10.1109/CVPR.2016.90, https://doi.org/10.1109/CVPR.2016.90
29. Hu, H., Lu, X., Zhang, X., Zhang, T., Sun, G.: Inheritance attention matrix-based universal adversarial perturbations on vision transformers. IEEE Signal Process. Lett. **28**, 1923–1927 (2021)
30. Jia, X., Zhang, Y., Wu, B., Ma, K., Wang, J., Cao, X.: LAS-AT: adversarial training with learnable attack strategy. In: Proceedings of the IEEE/CVF Conference on Computer Vision and Pattern Recognition (CVPR), pp. 13398–13408, June 2022
31. Jia, X., Zhang, Y., Wu, B., Wang, J., Cao, X.: Boosting fast adversarial training with learnable adversarial initialization. IEEE Trans. Image Process. **31**, 4417–4430 (2022)
32. Joshi, A., Jagatap, G., Hegde, C.: Adversarial token attacks on vision transformers. arXiv:2110.04337 (2021)
33. Kim, H., Lee, W., Lee, J.: Understanding catastrophic overfitting in single-step adversarial training. In: Thirty-Fifth AAAI Conference on Artificial Intelligence, AAAI 2021, Thirty-Third Conference on Innovative Applications of Artificial Intelligence, IAAI 2021, The Eleventh Symposium on Educational Advances in Artificial Intelligence, EAAI 2021, Virtual Event, 2–9 February 2021, pp. 8119–8127. AAAI Press (2021). https://ojs.aaai.org/index.php/AAAI/article/view/16989

34. Kim, H., Lee, W., Lee, J.: Understanding catastrophic overfitting in single-step adversarial training. In: Thirty-Fifth AAAI Conference on Artificial Intelligence, AAAI 2021, Thirty-Third Conference on Innovative Applications of Artificial Intelligence, IAAI 2021, The Eleventh Symposium on Educational Advances in Artificial Intelligence, EAAI 2021, Virtual Event, 2–9 February 2021, pp. 8119–8127. AAAI Press (2021). https://ojs.aaai.org/index.php/AAAI/article/view/16989

35. Kingma, D.P., Ba, J.: Adam: a method for stochastic optimization. In: Bengio, Y., LeCun, Y. (eds.) 3rd International Conference on Learning Representations, ICLR 2015, San Diego, CA, USA, May, pp. 7–9 (2015) Conference Track Proceedings (2015). https://arxiv.org/abs/1412.6980

36. Krizhevsky, A., Hinton, G., et al.: Learning multiple layers of features from tiny images (2009)

37. LeCun, Y., Cortes, C.: MNIST handwritten digit database (2010). https://yann.lecun.com/exdb/mnist/

38. Liang, S., Wei, X., Yao, S., Cao, X.: Efficient adversarial attacks for visual object tracking. In: Vedaldi, A., Bischof, H., Brox, T., Frahm, J.-M. (eds.) ECCV 2020. LNCS, vol. 12371, pp. 34–50. Springer, Cham (2020). https://doi.org/10.1007/978-3-030-58574-7_3

39. Liang, S., Wu, B., Fan, Y., Wei, X., Cao, X.: Parallel rectangle flip attack: a query-based black-box attack against object detection. In: Proceedings of the IEEE/CVF International Conference on Computer Vision, pp. 7697–7707 (2021)

40. Liao, F., Liang, M., Dong, Y., Pang, T., Hu, X., Zhu, J.: Defense against adversarial attacks using high-level representation guided denoiser. In: CVPR, pp. 1778–1787 (2018)

41. Liu, W., Jiang, Y., Luo, J., Chang, S.: Noise resistant graph ranking for improved web image search. In: The 24th IEEE Conference on Computer Vision and Pattern Recognition, CVPR 2011, Colorado Springs, CO, USA, 20–25 June 2011, pp. 849–856. IEEE Computer Society (2011). https://doi.org/10.1109/CVPR.2011.5995315, https://doi.org/10.1109/CVPR.2011.5995315

42. Liu, Z., et.al.: Swin transformer: hierarchical vision transformer using shifted windows. CoRR abs/2103.14030 (2021)

43. Madry, A., Makelov, A., Schmidt, L., Tsipras, D., Vladu, A.: Towards deep learning models resistant to adversarial attacks. In: ICLR. OpenReview.net (2018). https://openreview.net/forum?id=rJzIBfZAb

44. Mahmood, K., Mahmood, R., Van Dijk, M.: On the robustness of vision transformers to adversarial examples. In: Proceedings of the IEEE/CVF International Conference on Computer Vision, pp. 7838–7847 (2021)

45. Mao, X., et al.: Towards robust vision transformer. arXiv:2105.07926 (2021)

46. Mao, X., et al.: Rethinking the design principles of robust vision transformer. arXiv:2105.07926 (2021)

47. Meng, D., Chen, H.: MagNet: a two-pronged defense against adversarial examples. In: Proceedings of the 2017 ACM SIGSAC Conference on Computer and Communications Security, pp. 135–147 (2017)

48. Mu, N., Wagner, D.: Defending against adversarial patches with robust self-attention. In: ICML 2021 Workshop on Uncertainty and Robustness in Deep Learning (2021)

49. Naseer, M.M., Ranasinghe, K., Khan, S.H., Hayat, M., Shahbaz Khan, F., Yang, M.H.: Intriguing properties of vision transformers. In: Advances in Neural Information Processing Systems, vol. 34 (2021)

50. Pan, B., Jiang, Y., Panda, R., Wang, Z., Feris, R., Oliva, A.: IA-RED^2: interpretability-aware redundancy reduction for vision transformers. CoRR abs/2106.12620 (2021). https://arxiv.org/abs/2106.12620

51. Park, G.Y., Lee, S.W.: Reliably fast adversarial training via latent adversarial perturbation. In: ICCV (2021)

52. Paul, S., Chen, P.: Vision transformers are robust learners. CoRR abs/2105.07581 (2021). https://arxiv.org/abs/2105.07581

53. Paul, S., Chen, P.Y.: Vision transformers are robust learners. arXiv:2105.07581 (2021)

54. Qin, C., et.al.: Adversarial robustness through local linearization. In: NeurIPS (2019)

55. Rao, Y., Zhao, W., Liu, B., Lu, J., Zhou, J., Hsieh, C.: DynamicViT: efficient vision transformers with dynamic token sparsification. CoRR abs/2106.02034 (2021). https://arxiv.org/abs/2106.02034

56. Rice, L., Wong, E., Kolter, J.Z.: Overfitting in adversarially robust deep learning. CoRR abs/2002.11569 (2020). https://arxiv.org/abs/2002.11569

57. Russakovsky, O., et.al.: ImageNet large scale visual recognition challenge (2015)

58. Russakovsky, O., et al.: ImageNet large scale visual recognition challenge. Int. J. Comput. Vision. IJCV **115**, 211–252 (2015)

59. S., V.B., Babu, R.V.: Single-step adversarial training with dropout scheduling. In: 2020 IEEE/CVF Conference on Computer Vision and Pattern Recognition, CVPR 2020, Seattle, WA, USA, June 13–19, 2020, pp. 947–956. Computer Vision Foundation/IEEE (2020). https://doi.org/10.1109/CVPR42600.2020.00103. https://openaccess.thecvf.com/content_CVPR_2020/html/B.S._Single-Step_Adversarial_Training_With_Dropout_Scheduling_CVPR_2020_paper.html

60. Salman, H., Jain, S., Wong, E., Madry, A.: Certified patch robustness via smoothed vision transformers. arXiv:2110.07719 (2021)

61. Samangouei, P., Kabkab, M., Chellappa, R.: Defense-GAN: protecting classifiers against adversarial attacks using generative models. In: ICLR (2018)

62. Shafahi, A., et al.: Adversarial training for free! In: NeurIPS (2019)

63. Shao, R., Shi, Z., Yi, J., Chen, P.Y., Hsieh, C.J.: On the adversarial robustness of visual transformers. arXiv:2103.15670 (2021)

64. Shi, Y., Han, Y.: Decision-based black-box attack against vision transformers via patch-wise adversarial removal. arXiv preprint arXiv:2112.03492 (2021)

65. Song, Y., Kim, T., Nowozin, S., Ermon, S., Kushman, N.: PixelDefend: leveraging generative models to understand and defend against adversarial examples. In: ICLR (2018)

66. Sriramanan, G., et al.: Towards efficient and effective adversarial training. In: NeurIPS (2021)

67. Szegedy, C., et al.: Intriguing properties of neural networks. In: Bengio, Y., LeCun, Y. (eds.) ICLR (2014). https://arxiv.org/abs/1312.6199

68. Tang, S., et al.: RobustART: benchmarking robustness on architecture design and training techniques. arXiv preprint arXiv:2109.05211 (2021)

69. Tang, S., et al.: RobustART: benchmarking robustness on architecture design and training techniques. arXiv preprint arXiv:2109.05211 (2021)

70. Tang, Y., et.al.: Patch slimming for efficient vision transformers. CoRR abs/2106.02852 (2021). https://arxiv.org/abs/2106.02852

71. Touvron, H., Cord, M., Douze, M., Massa, F., Sablayrolles, A., Jégou, H.: Training data-efficient image transformers & distillation through attention. In: International Conference on Machine Learning, ICML, vol. 139, pp. 10347–10357 (2021)

72. Touvron, H., Cord, M., Douze, M., Massa, F., Sablayrolles, A., Jégou, H.: Training data-efficient image transformers & distillation through attention. In: Meila, M., Zhang, T. (eds.) Proceedings of the 38th International Conference on Machine Learning, ICML 2021, 18–24 July 2021, Virtual Event. Proceedings of Machine Learning Research, vol. 139, pp. 10347–10357. PMLR (2021). https://proceedings.mlr.press/v139/touvron21a.html

73. Touvron, H., Cord, M., Sablayrolles, A., Synnaeve, G., Jégou, H.: Going deeper with image transformers. CoRR abs/2103.17239 (2021). https://arxiv.org/abs/2103.17239

74. Vaswani, A., et al.: Attention is all you need. In: Neural Information Processing Systems, NeurIPS, pp. 5998–6008 (2017)

75. Velickovic, P., Cucurull, G., Casanova, A., Romero, A., Liò, P., Bengio, Y.: Graph attention networks. In: 6th International Conference on Learning Representations, ICLR 2018, Vancouver, BC, Canada, April 30–3 May 2018, Conference Track Proceedings. OpenReview.net (2018). https://openreview.net/forum?id=rJXMpikCZ

76. Vivek, B., Babu, R.V.: Single-step adversarial training with dropout scheduling. In: CVPR (2020)

77. Wang, W., et.al.: Pyramid vision transformer: a versatile backbone for dense prediction without convolutions. CoRR abs/2102.12122 (2021)

78. Wang, W., et.al.: Crossformer: a versatile vision transformer hinging on cross-scale attention. In: International Conference on Learning Representations (2022). https://openreview.net/forum?id=_PHymLIxuI

79. Wang, Z., Jiang, W., Zhu, Y., Yuan, L., Song, Y., Liu, W.: DynaMixer: a vision MLP architecture with dynamic mixing. In: Chaudhuri, K., Jegelka, S., Song, L., Szepesvári, C., Niu, G., Sabato, S. (eds.) International Conference on Machine Learning, ICML 2022, 17–23 July 2022, Baltimore, Maryland, USA. Proceedings of Machine Learning Research, vol. 162, pp. 22691–22701. PMLR (2022). https://proceedings.mlr.press/v162/wang22i.html

80. Wei, X., Liang, S., Chen, N., Cao, X.: Transferable adversarial attacks for image and video object detection. In: Proceedings of the 28th International Joint Conference on Artificial Intelligence, pp. 954–960 (2019)

81. Wong, E., Rice, L., Kolter, J.Z.: Fast is better than free: revisiting adversarial training. CoRR abs/2001.03994 (2020). https://arxiv.org/abs/2001.03994

82. Xie, C., Wang, J., Zhang, Z., Ren, Z., Yuille, A.: Mitigating adversarial effects through randomization. In: ICLR (2018)

83. Xu, Y., et.al.: Evo-ViT: slow-fast token evolution for dynamic vision transformer. CoRR abs/2108.01390 (2021). https://arxiv.org/abs/2108.01390

84. Yu, Z., Fu, Y., Li, S., Li, C., Lin, Y.: MIA-former: efficient and robust vision transformers via multi-grained input-adaptation. arXiv preprint arXiv:2112.11542 (2021)

85. Zhang, Q., Yang, Y.: ResT: an efficient transformer for visual recognition. CoRR abs/2105.13677 (2021)

MIME: Minority Inclusion for Majority Group Enhancement of AI Performance

Pradyumna Chari[1], Yunhao Ba[1], Shreeram Athreya[1], and Achuta Kadambi[1,2]

[1] Department of Electrical and Computer Engineering, UCLA, Los Angeles, USA
{pradyumnac,yhba,shreeram}@ucla.edu, achuta@ee.ucla.edu
[2] Department of Computer Science, UCLA, Los Angeles, USA

Abstract. Several papers have rightly included minority groups in artificial intelligence (AI) training data to improve test inference for minority groups and/or society-at-large. A society-at-large consists of both minority and majority stakeholders. A common misconception is that minority inclusion does not increase performance for majority groups alone. In this paper, we make the surprising finding that including minority samples can improve test error for the majority group. In other words, minority group inclusion leads to majority group enhancements (MIME) in performance. A theoretical existence proof of the MIME effect is presented and found to be consistent with experimental results on six different datasets. Project webpage: https://visual.ee.ucla.edu/mime.htm/.

Keywords: Fairness · Bias · Data diversity

1 Introduction

Inclusion of minorities in a dataset impacts the performance of artificial intelligence (AI). Recent research has presented the value of inclusive datasets to improve AI performance on minorities and also for society-at-large [11,21,23, 29,30,34,35,37,44]. A society-at-large consists of both majority and minority stakeholders. However, an objection (often silently posed) to minority inclusion efforts, is that the inclusion of minorities can diminish performance for the majority. This is based on a "rule of thumb" that AI performance is maximized when one trains and tests on the same distribution. A devil's advocate position against minority inclusion might be presented as: "In a fictitious society where we are absolutely certain that only blue-skinned humans will exist in the test set, why include out of distribution orange-skinned humans in the training set?".

In this paper, we make the surprising finding that inclusion of minority samples improves AI performance not just for minorities, not just for society-at-large, but *even for majorities*. We refer to this effect as Minority Inclusion, Majority Enhancement (MIME), illustrated in Fig. 2. Specifically, we note that

Supplementary Information The online version contains supplementary material available at https://doi.org/10.1007/978-3-031-19778-9_19.

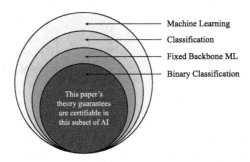

Machine Learning
Classification
Fixed Backbone ML
Binary Classification

This paper's theory guarantees are certifiable in this subset of AI

Fig. 1. This paper proves* that including minorities improves majority performance. *When do the provable guarantees hold? The guarantees are certifiable for fixed backbone binary classification (e.g. one uses a head network with pretrained weights and fine-tunes a downstream layer for classification). The fixed backbone ML is far from a toy scenario (it is considered SoTA by some authors [31]) and also enables provable certification - ordinarily it is hard to prove things for neural network settings.

including some minority samples in the train set improves majority group test performance. However, continued addition of minority samples leads to performance drop. The effect holds under statistical conditions that are represented in traditional computer vision datasets including FairFace [32], UTKFace [56], pets [22], medical imaging datasets [40] and even non-vision data [9]. Although deep learning is used for these problems, the flattening layer of a network can be empirically approximated to elementary distributions like Gaussian Mixture Models (GMMs). A GMM facilitates closed-form analysis to prove the existence of the MIME effect. Additionally, we show existence of MIME on general distributions. Classification experiments on neural networks validate using Gaussian mixtures: complex neural networks exhibit feature embeddings in flat layers, distributed with approximately Gaussian density, across six datasets, in and beyond computer vision, and across many realizations and configurations.

Fairness in machine learning is an exceedingly popular area, and our results benefit from several key papers published in recent years. Sample reweighting approaches recognize the need to preferentially weight difficult examples [14,18,43]. Active and online learning benefit from insights into sample "informativeness" (i.e. given a budget on the number of training samples, which would be the best sample to include [13,16]). Domain randomization literature indicates that surprising perturbations to the training set can improve generalization performance [27,47,54]. We extend some of these theoretical insights to the sphere of analyzing benefits of minority inclusion on majority performance.

1.1 Contributions

While some works [24,34] have observed related phenomena for isolated tasks, to the best of our knowledge, characterizing benefits to majority groups by including minority data is largely unexplored theoretically. Our contributions are as follows:

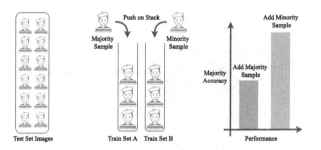

Fig. 2. Inclusion of minorities can improve performance for majorities.
We theoretically describe an effect called Minority Inclusion, Majority Enhancement
(MIME). The figure depicts test classification of blue mimes, and an initial training
stack, also of blue mimes. If allowed to add one more training sample, it can be better
to push an orange mime onto the training stack rather than a blue mime. Test accuracy
can increase by pushing orange, even though the test set consists of blue mimes alone.

- We introduce the Minority Inclusion Majority Enhancement (MIME) effect
  in a theoretical and empirical setting.
- Theoretically: we derive in closed form, the existence of the MIME effect both
  with and without domain gap (Key Results 1 and 2) and for general sample
  distributions (Key Result 3).
- Empirically: we test the MIME effect on six datasets, as varied as animals to
  medical images, and observe the existence of MIME consistent with theory.

1.2   Outline of Theoretical Scope

Figure 1 describes the theoretical scope. Through three key results (Theorem 1,
Theorem 2 and Theorem 3), this paper offers an existence proof of the MIME
effect. An existence proof can leverage a tractable setting. As in Fig. 2, training
data is a stack of $K - 1$ majority samples. Test data is all majority samples. We
can push one additional training sample to increase the stack size to K. We are
allowed the choice of having the K-th sample drawn from the minority or majority
group. Theorem 1 proves that, under the assumptions in Sect. 3, pushing a minority sample is superior for majority group performance improvements. Theorem 2
generalizes this result to a more realistic scenario, with domain gap. Theorem 3
extends the existence proof to general sample distributions. Empirical results on
real-world AI tasks offer validation for theoretical assumptions.

2   Related Work

Debiasing and Fairness: It has been widely reported that biases in training
data lead to biased algorithmic performance [10,11,26]. Work has been carried
out in identifying and quantifying biases [2,4,49] and a range of methods exist to
address them [23,37]. Early approaches suggest oversampling strategies [8,19].
Other methods propose resampling based on individual performance [35]. Some

works utilize information bottlenecks to disentangle biased attributes [46]. Still other methods propose bias mitigation solutions based on adversarial learning [55] or include considerations like protected class-specific classifiers [50]. Generative models have also found use in creating synthetic datasets with debiased attributes [41]. Xu *et al.* [52] identify inherent bias amplification as a result of adversarial training and propose a framework to mitigate these biases. Our goals are different – while these aim to reduce test time performance bias across groups, we analyze influence of minority samples on majority group performance.

Learning from Multiple Domains: Domain adaptation literature explores learning from multiple sources [42]. It could therefore be one potential way to analyze our problem of training on combinations of majority and minority data. In our setting, data arising from distinct domains is seen as being drawn from different distributions with a domain gap [6]. Between these domains, [5] establishes error bounds for learning from combinations of domains. However, these error estimates and bounds do not take into account the notion of majority and minority groups; therefore, describing the MIME effect is outside their scope.

Dataset Diversity: An important push towards fairness is through analysis of dataset composition. Several works indicate the importance of diverse datasets [21,29]. Ryu *et al.* [44] note that class imbalance in the training set leads to performance reduction. Wang *et al.* [49] highlight that perfectly balanced datasets may still not lead to balanced performance. For designing medical devices, [30] emphasizes the importance of diverse datasets. Through experiments on X-ray datasets, [34] observe that imbalanced training sets adversely affect performance on the disadvantaged group. They also observe that an unbiased training set shows the best overall accuracy. However, their inferences are related empirical observations on a few medical tasks and datasets. From an application perspective, the task of remote photoplethysmography enables analysis of the bias problem. Prior work notes that camera-based heart rate estimation exhibits skin tone bias [39], and [1,51] propose synthetic augmentations to mitigate this. Additionally, [12,48] establish that camera based heart rate estimation is fundamentally biased against dark skin tone subjects, establishing a notion of task complexity. While all these works recognize that data composition affects bias, none to our knowledge describe the effect of varying minority group proportions on majority group accuracy.

3   Statistical Origins of the MIME Effect

For more concise exposition, we make assumptions in the main paper derivation and defer extended generality to the supplement. Assumptions include:

– Assumption 1: one-dimensional data samples and binary labels, $x \in \mathbb{R}$, $y \in \{1, 2\}$. This is relevant to modern classification problems since the final classification decision is based on a one dimensional projection of the feature representation of the sample with respect to the learnt hyperplane (discussed in Fig. 1, Sect. 4). Additionally, existence proof of MIME holds for more general vectorized notation, as discussed in the supplement.

– Assumption 2: the binary classifier used is a perceptron: this assumption relates to real neural networks since the last layer is perceptron-like [38].

We now introduce some key definitions that follow from these assumptions.

Definition 1: (Task complexity): *For binary classification we define task complexity for a group of data θ as a continuous variable in $[0,1]$, such that,*

$$\theta = \arg\min_{h \in H} \epsilon(h), \tag{1}$$

where $\epsilon(h)$ is the classification error for hypothesis h (the classifier), H is the space of feasible hypotheses. It is noted later that this is empirically equivalent to distributional overlap. This definition is not new. Hard-sample mining [18] establishes the of use performance measures as an indicator of difficulty.

Definition 2: (Majority Group): *Group class (i.e. group label $g = major$) on which the task performs better. Quantified by training a network only with majority group data and evaluating test performance:* $\theta^{major} = \arg\min_{h \in H} \epsilon^{major}(h)$.

Definition 3: (Minority Group): *Group class (i.e. group label $g = minor$) on which the task performs worse. Quantified by training a network only with minority class data and evaluating test performance:* $\theta^{minor} = \arg\min_{h \in H} \epsilon^{minor}(h)$.

Definition 4: (Minority Training Ratio (β)): *Ratio of minority to majority samples in the data under consideration (training set, in the context of this paper).*

Definition 5: (MIME Domain Gap): Measure of how classification differs for minorities and majorities. Quantified as a difference between ideal hyperplanes. Note that this definition for domain gap could be different from other definitions. In this work, domain gap should be taken to mean MIME domain gap.

Empirical observations on cutting-edge machine learning tasks demonstrate the real-world applicability of the assumptions above. We now discuss three key results. For ease of understanding, we make two simplifying assumptions for Key Results 1 and 2: (i) simplified distributions that follow a symmetric Gaussian Mixture Model, and (ii) equally likely class labels, i.e. $Pr(y = 1) = Pr(y = 2)$. These assumptions are relaxed in Key Result 3.

Key Result 1: A minority sample can be more valuable for majority classifiers than another majority sample

Our first key result shows that it can benefit performance on the majority group more if one adds minority data (instead of majority data). Consider a binary classification setting with data samples $x \in \mathbb{R}$ and labels $y \in \{1, 2\}$. Samples from the two classes are drawn from distributions with distinct means:

$$\begin{aligned} x|y = 1 &\sim p_1(x|\mu_1, \sigma_1) \\ x|y = 2 &\sim p_2(x|\mu_2, \sigma_2). \end{aligned} \tag{2}$$

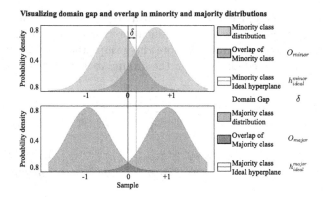

Fig. 3. Visualizating of gaussian mixture model parameters. We plot GMMs with different task complexities. The domain gap δ is visualized as the difference in the ideal threshold locations. The overlap/task complexity metric can be visually seen.

Maximum likelihood (ML) can be used to estimate the label as

$$\widehat{y} = \arg\max_{y} \mathcal{L}(x|y). \tag{3}$$

An ideal hyperplane for ML $\mathcal{H}_{\text{ideal}}$ is a set of data samples such that:

$$\mathcal{H}_{\text{ideal}} = \left\{ x \mid \mathcal{L}(x|y=1) = \mathcal{L}(x|y=2) \right\}. \tag{4}$$

We consider the hyperplane's geometry to be linear in this one dimensional setting. Therefore the hyperplane can be represented as a normal vector: $\mathbf{h}_{\text{ideal}}$. The normalized hyperplane is represented by a two dimensional vector, $\mathbf{h} = [1 \ b]^T$. Here, b is the offset/bias. In general, a hyperplane $\mathbf{h}$ may not be ideal. The accuracy of a hyperplane is based on a performance measure $\mathcal{P}\{\mathbf{h}\}$, where the operator $\mathcal{P}$ takes as input the hyperplane and outputs the closeness to the ideal hyperplane $\mathbf{h}_{\text{ideal}}$. A goal of a learning based classifier is to obtain:

$$\widehat{\mathbf{h}} = \arg\min_{\mathbf{h}} \mathcal{P}\{\mathbf{h}\} = \arg\min_{\mathbf{h}} \|\mathbf{h} - \mathbf{h}_{\text{ideal}}\|, \tag{5}$$

where $\widehat{\mathbf{h}}$ is the best learnt estimate of the ideal hyperplane. The ideal hyperplane is the global minimizer of this objective. Now, assume we are provided a finite training set of labelled data $\mathcal{D}_{K-1} = \{(x_i, y_i)\}_{i=1}^{K-1}$. Let the estimated hyperplane be $\mathbf{h}_{K-1}$, denoting that $K-1$ samples have been used to learn the hyperplane. If one additional data sample is made available, then the learnt hyperplane would be $\mathbf{h}_K$. From Eq. 2, the k-th sample is drawn from one of two distributions:

$$\begin{aligned} x_k|y=1 &\sim p_1(x|\mu_1, \sigma_1) \\ x_k|y=2 &\sim p_2(x|\mu_2, \sigma_2). \end{aligned} \tag{6}$$

We now introduce the notion of majority and minority sampling.

Introducing Majority/Minority Distributions: Suppose that the k-th data sample could be drawn for the same classification task from a minority or majority group. Let $g \in \{\text{major}, \text{minor}\}$ denote the group label (for the group class). Equation 2 can now be conditioned on the group label, such that there are four possible distributions from which the k-th sample can be drawn:

$$
\left.\begin{aligned}
x_k|g = \text{major}, y = 1 &\sim p_1^{\text{major}}(x|\mu_1^{\text{major}}, \sigma_1^{\text{major}}) \\
x_k|g = \text{major}, y = 2 &\sim p_2^{\text{major}}(x|\mu_2^{\text{major}}, \sigma_2^{\text{major}})
\end{aligned}\right\} \begin{array}{l} \textit{Majority} \\ \textit{group} \end{array}
$$

$$
\left.\begin{aligned}
x_k|g = \text{minor}, y = 1 &\sim p_1^{\text{minor}}(x|\mu_1^{\text{minor}}, \sigma_1^{\text{minor}}) \\
x_k|g = \text{minor}, y = 2 &\sim p_2^{\text{minor}}(x|\mu_2^{\text{minor}}, \sigma_2^{\text{minor}})
\end{aligned}\right\} \begin{array}{l} \textit{Minority} \\ \textit{group} \end{array}
\tag{7}
$$

Overlap: Let the ideal decision hyperplane be located at $x = d_{\text{ideal}}$. Then, given equal likelihood of the two labels for y, the overlap for the majority group is defined as the probability of erroneous sample classification:

$$
O_{\text{major}} = 0.5 \int_{x=-\infty}^{d_{\text{ideal}}} p_2^{\text{major}}(x)dx + 0.5 \int_{x=d_{\text{ideal}}}^{\infty} p_1^{\text{major}}(x)dx. \tag{8}
$$

The same definition holds true for the minority class as well. Therefore, by definition, $O_{\text{major}} < O_{\text{minor}}$. The task complexities θ^{major} and θ^{minor} are empirical estimates of the respective overlaps. Hereafter, we assume that all four marginal distributions are Gaussian and symmetric (this is relaxed later for Key Result 3). Figure 3 visually highlights relevant parameters. $O_{\text{minor}} > O_{\text{major}}$ occurs through the interplay of component means and variances.

The expectation over the class label yields majority and minority sampling:

$$
\begin{aligned}
x_k^{\text{major}} &\triangleq x_k|g = \text{major} \sim \mathbb{E}_y\big[x_k|g = \text{major}, y\big] \\
x_k^{\text{minor}} &\triangleq x_k|g = \text{minor} \sim \mathbb{E}_y\big[x_k|g = \text{minor}, y\big],
\end{aligned}
\tag{9}
$$

where we have defined x_k^{major} or x_k^{minor} as having the k-th sample come from the majority or minority distributions.

Armed with an expression for the k-th sample, we can consider a scope similar to active/online learning [3,7,16,17,20,28,33,45]. Suppose a dataset of $K - 1$ samples has been collected on majority samples, such that there exists a dataset stack $\mathcal{D}_{K-1}^{\text{major}} = \left\{(x_i^{\text{major}}, y_i^{\text{major}})\right\}_{i=1}^{K-1}$. A hyperplane $\mathbf{h}_{K-1}$ is learnt on this dataset and can be improved by expanding the dataset size. Consider pushing sample index K, denoted as x_K onto the stack. Now we have a choice of pushing x_K^{major} or x_K^{minor}, to create one of two datasets:

$$
\begin{aligned}
\mathcal{D}_K^+ &= \{\mathcal{D}_{K-1}^{\text{major}}, x_K^{\text{major}}\} \\
\mathcal{D}_K^- &= \{\mathcal{D}_{K-1}^{\text{major}}, x_K^{\text{minor}}\},
\end{aligned}
\tag{10}
$$

where $\mathcal{D}_K^-$ represents the interesting case where we choose to push a minority sample onto a dataset with all majority samples (e.g. adding a dark skinned sample to a light skinned dataset). Denote $\mathbf{h}_K^+$ and $\mathbf{h}_K^-$ as hyperplanes learnt on $\mathcal{D}_K^+$ and $\mathcal{D}_K^-$. We now arrive at the following result.

Theorem 1: *Let* $\mathcal{P}^{major}\{\cdot\}$ *be the performance of a hyperplane on the majority group. Let* $\Delta = \mathcal{P}^{major}\{\mathbf{h}_{K-1}\}$. *Assume that the minority group distribution has an overlap* O_{minor} *while the majority group has an overlap* $O_{major} < O_{minor}$. *Both have the same ideal hyperplane* $\mathbf{h}_{ideal}$. *Under the definitions of* $\mathbf{h}_K^-$ *and* $\mathbf{h}_K^+$ *as above, assuming* Δ *is sufficiently small and the group class distribution variances are not very large,*

$$\mathbb{E}_{x_K^{minor}} \mathcal{P}^{major}\{\mathbf{h}_K^-\} < \mathbb{E}_{x_K^{major}} \mathcal{P}^{major}\{\mathbf{h}_K^+\}, \tag{11}$$

stating that, perhaps surprisingly, expected performance for majorities improves more by pushing a minority sample on the stack, rather than a majority sample.

Proof (Sketch): *A sketch is provided, please see the supplement for the full proof. The general idea is to show that samples closer to* $\mathbf{h}_{ideal}$ *are more beneficial, and minority distributions may sample these with higher likelihood. Without loss of generality, we assume that* $\mathbf{h}_{K-1}$ *is located, non-ideally, closer to the task class* $y = 2$ *(arbitrarily called the positive class) than* $\mathbf{h}_{ideal}$. *For our perceptron update rule, the improvement in the estimated hyperplane due to* x_K *is proportional to the difference between the false negative rate (FNR) and the false positive rate (FPR) for* $\mathbf{h}_{K-1}$, *with respect to the distribution of* x_K. *For sufficiently small* Δ, $FNR - FPR$ *can be approximated in terms of the likelihood l that* x_K *is on the ideal hyperplane. The likelihood l is directly proportional to* $FPR - FNR$. *Under the assumptions of the theorem, a direct relation is established between the overlap and l for each of the group classes. Then, it is shown that an additional minority sample, with overlap* $O_{minor} > O_{major}$ *leads to greater expected gains as compared to an additional majority sample, concluding the proof.* ∎

Key Result 2: MIME holds under domain gap

In the previous key result we described the MIME effect in a restrictive setting where a minority and majority group have the same target hyperplane. However, it is rarely the case that minorities and majorities have the same decision boundary. We now consider the case with non-zero domain gap, to show that MIME holds on a more realistic setting. Domain gap can be quantified in terms of ideal decision hyperplanes. If $\mathbf{h}_{ideal}^{major}$ and $\mathbf{h}_{ideal}^{minor}$ denote ideal hyperplanes for the majority and minority groups respectively, then domain gap $\delta = \|\mathbf{h}_{ideal}^{major} - \mathbf{h}_{ideal}^{minor}\|$.

A visual illustration of domain gap is provided in Fig. 3. Next, we define relative hyperplane locations in terms of halfspaces (since all hyperplanes in the one dimensional setting are parallel). We say two hyperplanes $\mathbf{h}_1$ and $\mathbf{h}_2$ lie in the same halfspace of a reference hyperplane $\mathbf{h}_0$ if their respective offsets/biases satisfy the condition $(b_1 - b_0)(b_2 - b_0) > 0$. For occupancy in different halfspaces, the condition is $(b_1 - b_0)(b_2 - b_0) < 0$. We now enter into the second key result.

Theorem 2: *Let* $\delta \neq 0$ *be the domain gap between the majority and minority groups. Assume that the minority group distribution has an ideal hyperplane* $\mathbf{h}_{ideal}^{minor}$; *while the majority group has an ideal hyperplane* $\mathbf{h}_{ideal}^{major}$. *Then, if* $\delta < \Delta$,

$\delta + \Delta$ is small enough, and the group class distribution variances are not very large, it can be shown that if either of the following two cases:

1. $\mathbf{h}_{K-1}$ and $\mathbf{h}_{ideal}^{minor}$ lie in different halfspaces of $\mathbf{h}_{ideal}^{major}$,
2. $\mathbf{h}_{K-1}$ and $\mathbf{h}_{ideal}^{minor}$ lie in the same halfspace of $\mathbf{h}_{ideal}^{major}$, and if

$$\frac{O_{major}}{O_{minor}} < (1 - \frac{\delta}{\Delta})f, \tag{12}$$

are true, then:

$$\mathbb{E}_{x_K^{minor}} \mathcal{P}^{major}\{\mathbf{h}_K^-\} < \mathbb{E}_{x_K^{major}} \mathcal{P}^{major}\{\mathbf{h}_K^+\}, \tag{13}$$

where f is a non-negative constant that depends on the majority and minority means and standard deviations for all the individual GMM components.

Proof (Sketch): A sketch is provided, please see the supplement for the full proof. We prove independently for both cases.

1. When $\mathbf{h}_{K-1}$ and $\mathbf{h}_{ideal}^{minor}$ lie in different halfspaces of $\mathbf{h}_{ideal}^{major}$, it can be shown that the expected improvement in the hyperplane is higher for the minority group as compared to the majority group, using a similar argument as in Theorem 1. This proves the theorem for Case 1.
2. When $\mathbf{h}_{K-1}$ and $\mathbf{h}_{ideal}^{minor}$ lie in the same halfspace of $\mathbf{h}_{ideal}^{major}$, and assuming that $\mathbf{h}_{K-1}$ is located closer to the positive class, we approximate the $FNR - FPR$ value as function of δ, Δ and the likelihood l as defined for Theorem 1. Then, through algebraic manipulation, constraints can be established in terms of the two likelihoods l_{minor} and l_{major}. Under the assumptions of the theorem, a relation can be established between the ratios $\frac{l_{minor}}{l_{major}}$ and $\frac{O_{minor}}{O_{major}}$. This proves the theorem for Case 2, and concludes the proof. ∎

Key Result 3: MIME holds for general distributions

We now relax the symmetric Gaussian and equally likely labels requirements to arrive at a general condition for MIME existence. Let p_1^{major} and p_2^{major} be general distributions describing the majority group $y = 1$ and $y = 2$ classes. Additionally, $Pr(y = 1) \neq Pr(y = 2)$. Minority group distributions are described similarly. We define the signed tail weight for the majority group as follows:

$$T^{major}(x_d) = \pi^{major} \int_{x=-\infty}^{x_d} p_2^{major}(x)dx - (1 - \pi^{major}) \int_{x=x_d}^{\infty} p_1^{major}(x)dx, \tag{14}$$

where $\pi^{major} = Pr(x = 2)$ for the majority group. $T^{minor}(\cdot)$ is similarly defined. This leads us to our third key result.

Theorem 3: Consider majority and minority groups, with general sample distributions and unequal prior label distributions. If,

$$min\{T^{minor}(d_{ideal} + \Delta), -T^{minor}(d_{ideal} - \Delta)\}$$
$$> max\{T^{major}(d_{ideal} + \Delta), -T^{major}(d_{ideal} - \Delta)\}, \tag{15}$$

then $\mathbb{E}_{x_K^{minor}} \mathcal{P}^{major}\{\mathbf{h}_K^-\} < \mathbb{E}_{x_K^{major}} \mathcal{P}^{major}\{\mathbf{h}_K^+\}$.

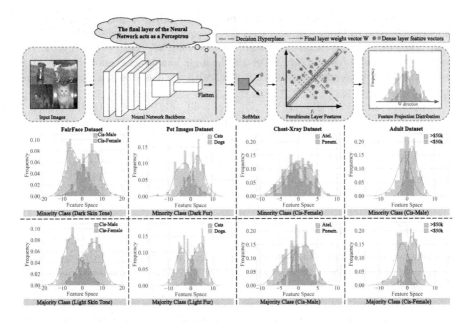

Fig. 4. The use of Gaussian mixtures to represent minority and majority distributions is consistent with behaviors in modern neural networks, on real-world datasets. (top row) The last layer of common neural architectures is a linear classifier on features. Histograms of the penultimate layer projections are generated for models with $\beta = 0.5$. (middle row) Minority histograms: note the greater difficulty due to less separation of data. (bottom row) Majority histograms: note smaller overlap and easier classification. Figure can be parsed on a per-dataset basis. Within each column, the reader can compare the domain gap and overlap in the two histograms.

Proof (Sketch): *A sketch is provided, please see the supplement for the full proof. The perceptron algorithm update rule is proportional to $FNR - FPR$ (if $\mathbf{h}_{K-1}$ is located closer to the positive class) or the $FPR - FNR$ (if $\mathbf{h}_{K-1}$ is located closer to the negative class). The MIME effect exists in the scenario where the worst case update for the minority group is better than the best case update for the majority group (described in Eq. 15). This proves the theorem.* ∎

Generalizations of Theorem 3 to include domain gap are discussed in the supplement, for brevity. Theorems 1 and 2 are special cases of the general Theorem 3, describing MIME existence for specific group distributions.

4   Verifying MIME Theory on Real Tasks

In the previous section, we provide existence conditions for the MIME phenomenon for general sample distributions. However, experimental validation of the phenomenon requires quantification in terms of measurable quantities such as overlap. Theorem 2 provides us these resources. Here, we verify that the assumptions in Theorem 2 are validated by experiments on real tasks.

Table 1. Experimental measures of overlap and domain gap are consistent with the theory in Sect. 3. Note that the majority group consistently has lower overlap. Domain gaps are found to be small. DS-1 is FairFace, DS-2 is Pet Images, DS-4 is Chest-Xray14 and DS-5 is Adult. DS-6 is the high domain gap gender classification experiment. DS-3 is excluded here since it deals with a 9 class classification problem.

Dataset (Task)	DS-1 [32] (Gender)	DS-2 [22] (Species)	DS-4 [40] (Diagnosis)	DS-5 [9] (Income)	DS-6 [53,56] (Gender)
Major. overlap	0.186	0.163	0.294	0.132	0.09
Minor. overlap	0.224	0.198	0.369	0.208	0.19
Domain gap	0.276	0.518	0.494	0.170	1.62

4.1   Verifying Assumptions

Verifying Gaussianity: Theorem 2 assumes that data x is drawn from a Gaussian Mixture Model. At first glance, this quantification may appear to be unrelated to complex neural networks. However, as illustrated at the top of Fig. 4, a ConvNet is essentially a feature extractor that feeds a flattened layer into a simple perceptron or linear classifier. The flattened layer can be orthogonally projected onto the decision boundary to generate, in analogy, an x used for linear classification (Fig. 1, fixed-backbone configuration). We use this as a first approximation to the end-to-end configuration used in our experiments.

Plotting empirical histograms of these flattened layers (Fig. 4) shows Gaussian-like distribution. This is consistent with the Law of Large Numbers – linear combination of several random variables follows an approximate Gaussian distribution. Hence, Theorem 2 is approximately related in this setting. Details about implementation and comparison to Gaussians are deferred to the supplement.

Verifying Minority/Majority Definitions: The MIME proof linked minority and majority definitions to distributional overlap and domain gap. Given the histogram embeddings from above, it is seen that minority groups on all four vision tasks have greater overlap. There also exists a domain gap between majority and minority but this is small compared to distribution spread (except for the high domain gap experiment). This establishes applicability of small domain gap requirements. Quantification is provided in Table 1. Code is in the supplement.

4.2   MIME Effect Across Six, Real Datasets

Implementation: Six multi-attribute datasets are used to assess the MIME effect (five are in computer vision). For a particular *experiment*, we identify a task category to evaluate accuracy over (e.g. gender), and a group category (e.g. race). The best test accuracy on the majority group across all epochs is recorded as our accuracy measure. Each experiment is run for a fixed number of *minority training ratios* (β). For each minority training ratio, the total number of training samples remains constant. That is, the minority samples replace the majority

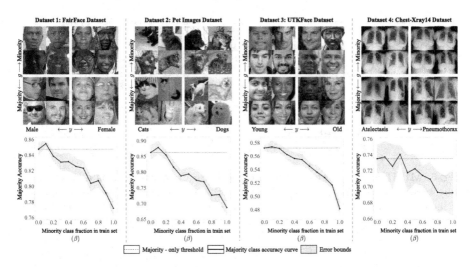

Fig. 5. When domain gap is small, the MIME effect holds. On four vision datasets, majority performance is maximized with some inclusion of minorities. All experiments are run for several trials and realizations (described in Sect. 4.2).

samples, instead of being appended to the training set. Each experiment is also run for a finite number of *trials*. Different trials have different random train and test sets (except for the FairFace dataset [32] where we use the provided test split). Averaging is done across trials. Note that minority samples to be added are randomly chosen – the MIME effect is not specific to particular samples. For the vision datasets, we use a ResNet-34 architecture [25], with the output layer appropriately modified. For the non-visual dataset, a fully connected network is used. Average accuracy and trend error, across trials are used to evaluate performance. Specific implementation details are in the supplement.

MIME Effect on Gender Classification: The FairFace dataset [32] is used to perform gender classification ($y = 1$ is male, $y = 2$ is female). The majority and minority groups $g = \{\text{major}, \text{minor}\}$ are light and dark skin, respectively. Results are averaged over five trials. Figure 5 describes qualitative accuracy. The accuracy trends indicate that adding 10% of minority samples to the training set leads to approximately a 1.5% gain in majority group (light skin) test accuracy.

MIME Effect on Animal Species Identification: We manually annotate light and dark cats and dogs from the Pets dataset [22]. We classify between cats ($y = 1$) and dogs ($y = 2$). The majority and minority groups are light and dark fur color respectively. Figure 5 shows qualitative results. Over five trials, we see a majority group accuracy gain of about 2%, with a peak at $\beta = 10\%$.

MIME Effect on Age Classification: We use a second human faces dataset, the UTKFace dataset [56], for the age classification task (9 classes of age-intervals). We pre-process the UTKFace age labels into class bins to match the

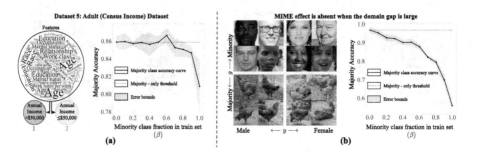

Fig. 6. MIME effect is observed in non-vision datasets, and is absent in the case of large domain gap. (a) The Adult Dataset [9] uses Census data to predict an income label. (b) On dataset six, gender classification is rescoped to occur in a high domain gap setting. Majority group is chickens [53] and minority group is humans [56].

FairFace dataset format. The majority and minority groups are male and female respectively. The proportion of task class labels is kept the same across group classes. Results are averaged over five trials. Figure 5 shows trends. We observe a smaller average improvement for the 10% minority training ratio. However, since these are average trends, this indicates consistent gain. Results on this dataset also empirically highlight the existence of the MIME effect beyond two class settings.

MIME Effect on X-ray Diagnosis Classification: We use the NIH Chest-Xray14 dataset [40] to analyze trends on a medical imaging task. We perform binary classification of scans belonging to 'Atelectasis' ($y = 1$) and 'Pneumothorax' ($y = 2$) categories. The male and female genders are the majority and minority groups respectively. Results are averaged over seven trials (due to noisier trends). From Fig. 5, we observe noisy trends - specifically we see a performance drop for $\beta = 0.2$, prior to an overall gain for $\beta = 0.3$. The error bounds also have considerably more noise. However, confidence in the peak and the MIME effect, as seen from the average trends and the error bounds, remains high.

MIME Effect on Income Classification: For validation in a non-vision setting, we use the Adult (Census Income) dataset [9]. The data consists of census information with annual income labels (income less than or equal to $50,000 is $y = 1$, income greater than $50,000 is $y = 2$). The majority and minority groups are female and male genders respectively. Results are averaged over five trials. Figure 6(a) highlights a prominent accuracy gain for $\beta = 0.6$.

MIME Effect and Domain Gap: Theorem 2 (Sect. 3) suggests that large domain gap settings will not show the MIME effect. We set up an experiment to verify this (Fig. 6(b)). Gender classification among chickens (majority group) and humans (minority group) has a high domain gap due to minimal common context (validated by the domain gap estimates, Table 1). With increasing β, the majority accuracy decreases. This (and Fig. 4, Table 1 that show low domain gap for other datasets) validates Theorem 2. Note that while this result may not be unexpected, it further validates our proposed theory.

Table 2. Additional evaluation metrics provide further evidence of MIME existence across all datasets. The table highlights: (i) number of trials with MIME performance gain (i.e. majority accuracy at some $\beta > 0$ is greater than majority accuracy at $\beta = 0$), and (ii) the mean MIME performance gain across trials (in % points).

Dataset	DS-1 [32]	DS-2 [22]	DS-3 [56]	DS-4 [40]	DS-5 [9]
#MIME trials/Total trials	4/5	4/5	5/5	6/7	4/5
Avg. MIME perf. gain	0.72%	1.84%	0.70%	1.89%	0.98%

5 Discussion

Secondary Validation and Analysis: Table 2 supplies additional metrics to analyze MIME. Across datasets, almost all trials show existence, with every dataset showing average MIME performance gain. Some readers may view the error bars in Figs. 5 and 6 as large, however they are comparable to other empirical ML works [15,36]; they may appear larger due to scaling. Reasons for error bars include variations in train-test data and train set size (Table B and C, supplement). Further analysis, including interplay with debiasing methods (e.g. hard-sample mining [18]) and reconciliation with work on equal representation datasets [11,21,23,29,30,34,35,37,44] is deferred to the supplement.

Optimality of Inclusion Ratios: Our experiments show that there can exist an optimal amount of minority inclusion to benefit the majority group the most. This appears true across all experiments in Figs. 5, 6. However, beyond a certain amount, accuracy decreases consistently, with lowest accuracy on majority samples observed when no majorities are used in training. This optimal β depends on individual task complexities, among other factors. Since identifying it is outside our scope (Sect. 1.1, 1.2), our experiments use 10% sampling resolution for β. Peaks at $\beta = 10\%$ for some datasets are due to this lower resolution; optimal peak need not lie there for all datasets (e.g. X-ray [40] & Adult [9]). Future work can identify optimal ratios through finer analysis over β.

Limitations: The theoretical scope is certifiable within fixed-backbone binary classification, which is narrower than all of machine learning (Fig. 1). Should this theory be accepted by the community, follow-up work can generalize theoretical claims. Another limitation is the definition-compatibility of majority and minority groups. Our theory is applicable to task-advantage definitions; some scholars in the community instead define majorities and minorities by proportion. Our theory is applicable to these authors as well, albeit with a slight redefinition of terminology. Additional considerations are included in the supplement.

Conclusion: In conclusion, majority performance benefits from a non-zero fraction of inclusion of minority data given a sufficiently small domain gap.

Acknowledgements. We thank members of the Visual Machines Group for their feedback and support. A.K. was partially supported by an NSF CAREER award IIS-2046737 and Army Young Investigator Award. P.C. was partially supported by a Cisco PhD Fellowship.

References

1. Ba, Y., Wang, Z., Karinca, K.D., Bozkurt, O.D., Kadambi, A.: Overcoming difficulty in obtaining dark-skinned subjects for remote-PPG by synthetic augmentation. arXiv preprint arXiv:2106.06007 (2021)
2. Balakrishnan, G., Xiong, Y., Xia, W., Perona, P.: Towards causal benchmarking of bias in face analysis algorithms. In: Vedaldi, A., Bischof, H., Brox, T., Frahm, J.-M. (eds.) ECCV 2020. LNCS, vol. 12363, pp. 547–563. Springer, Cham (2020). https://doi.org/10.1007/978-3-030-58523-5_32
3. Balcan, M.-F., Broder, A., Zhang, T.: Margin based active learning. In: Bshouty, N.H., Gentile, C. (eds.) COLT 2007. LNCS (LNAI), vol. 4539, pp. 35–50. Springer, Heidelberg (2007). https://doi.org/10.1007/978-3-540-72927-3_5
4. Bellamy, R.K., et al.: Ai fairness 360: an extensible toolkit for detecting and mitigating algorithmic bias. IBM J. Res. Dev. **63**(4/5), 1–4 (2019)
5. Ben-David, S., Blitzer, J., Crammer, K., Kulesza, A., Pereira, F., Vaughan, J.W.: A theory of learning from different domains. Mach. Learn. **79**(1), 151–175 (2010)
6. Ben-David, S., Blitzer, J., Crammer, K., Pereira, F., et al.: Analysis of representations for domain adaptation. In: Advances in Neural Information Processing Systems, vol. 19, p. 137 (2007)
7. Beygelzimer, A., Hsu, D.J., Langford, J., Zhang, T.: Agnostic active learning without constraints. In: Advances in Neural Information Processing Systems, vol. 23, pp. 199–207 (2010)
8. Bickel, S., Brückner, M., Scheffer, T.: Discriminative learning under covariate shift. J. Mach. Learn. Res. **10**(9), 2137–2155 (2009)
9. Blake, C.L., Merz, C.J.: UCI repository of machine learning databases, 1998 (1998)
10. Bolukbasi, T., Chang, K.W., Zou, J.Y., Saligrama, V., Kalai, A.T.: Man is to computer programmer as woman is to homemaker? Debiasing word embeddings. In: Advances in Neural Information Processing Systems, vol. 29, pp. 4349–4357 (2016)
11. Buolamwini, J., Gebru, T.: Gender shades: intersectional accuracy disparities in commercial gender classification. In: Conference on Fairness, Accountability and Transparency, pp. 77–91. PMLR (2018)
12. Chari, P., et al.: Diverse R-PPG: camera-based heart rate estimation for diverse subject skin-tones and scenes. arXiv preprint arXiv:2010.12769 (2020)
13. Choi, J., Elezi, I., Lee, H.J., Farabet, C., Alvarez, J.M.: Active learning for deep object detection via probabilistic modeling. arXiv preprint arXiv:2103.16130 (2021)
14. Cui, Y., Jia, M., Lin, T.Y., Song, Y., Belongie, S.: Class-balanced loss based on effective number of samples. In: Proceedings of the IEEE/CVF Conference on Computer Vision and Pattern Recognition, pp. 9268–9277 (2019)
15. d'Ascoli, S., Gabrié, M., Sagun, L., Biroli, G.: On the interplay between data structure and loss function in classification problems. In: Advances in Neural Information Processing Systems, vol. 34, pp. 8506–8517 (2021)
16. Dasgupta, S.: Two faces of active learning. Theoret. Comput. Sci. **412**(19), 1767–1781 (2011)

17. Dasgupta, S., Hsu, D.J., Monteleoni, C.: A general agnostic active learning algorithm. Citeseer (2007)
18. Dong, Q., Gong, S., Zhu, X.: Class rectification hard mining for imbalanced deep learning. In: Proceedings of the IEEE/CVF International Conference on Computer Vision, pp. 1851–1860 (2017)
19. Elkan, C.: The foundations of cost-sensitive learning. In: International Joint Conference on Artificial Intelligence, vol. 17, pp. 973–978. Lawrence Erlbaum Associates Ltd (2001)
20. Ertekin, S., Huang, J., Bottou, L., Giles, L.: Learning on the border: active learning in imbalanced data classification. In: Proceedings of the Sixteenth ACM Conference on Conference on Information and Knowledge Management, pp. 127–136 (2007)
21. Gebru, T., et al.: Datasheets for datasets. arXiv preprint arXiv:1803.09010 (2018)
22. Golle, P.: Machine learning attacks against the Asirra captcha. In: Proceedings of the 15th ACM Conference on Computer and Communications Security, pp. 535–542 (2008)
23. Gong, Z., Zhong, P., Hu, W.: Diversity in machine learning. IEEE Access 7, 64323–64350 (2019)
24. Gwilliam, M., Hegde, S., Tinubu, L., Hanson, A.: Rethinking common assumptions to mitigate racial bias in face recognition datasets. In: Proceedings of the IEEE/CVF International Conference on Computer Vision, pp. 4123–4132 (2021)
25. He, K., Zhang, X., Ren, S., Sun, J.: Deep residual learning for image recognition. In: Proceedings of the IEEE/CVF Conference on Computer Vision and Pattern Recognition, pp. 770–778 (2016)
26. Hendricks, L.A., Burns, K., Saenko, K., Darrell, T., Rohrbach, A.: Women also snowboard: overcoming bias in captioning models. In: Ferrari, V., Hebert, M., Sminchisescu, C., Weiss, Y. (eds.) ECCV 2018. LNCS, vol. 11207, pp. 793–811. Springer, Cham (2018). https://doi.org/10.1007/978-3-030-01219-9_47
27. Huang, J., Guan, D., Xiao, A., Lu, S.: FSDR: frequency space domain randomization for domain generalization. In: Proceedings of the IEEE/CVF Conference on Computer Vision and Pattern Recognition, pp. 6891–6902 (2021)
28. Huang, S.J., Jin, R., Zhou, Z.H.: Active learning by querying informative and representative examples. In: Advances in Neural Information Processing Systems, vol. 23, pp. 892–900 (2010)
29. Jo, E.S., Gebru, T.: Lessons from archives: Strategies for collecting sociocultural data in machine learning. In: Proceedings of the 2020 Conference on Fairness, Accountability, and Transparency, pp. 306–316 (2020)
30. Kadambi, A.: Achieving fairness in medical devices. Science 372(6537), 30–31 (2021)
31. Kang, B., et al.: Decoupling representation and classifier for long-tailed recognition. arXiv preprint arXiv:1910.09217 (2019)
32. Karkkainen, K., Joo, J.: FairFace: face attribute dataset for balanced race, gender, and age for bias measurement and mitigation. In: Proceedings of the IEEE/CVF Winter Conference on Applications of Computer Vision, pp. 1548–1558 (2021)
33. Kremer, J., Steenstrup Pedersen, K., Igel, C.: Active learning with support vector machines. Wiley Interdisc. Rev. Data Min. Knowl. Discovery 4(4), 313–326 (2014)
34. Larrazabal, A.J., Nieto, N., Peterson, V., Milone, D.H., Ferrante, E.: Gender imbalance in medical imaging datasets produces biased classifiers for computer-aided diagnosis. Proc. Natl. Acad. Sci. 117(23), 12592–12594 (2020)
35. Li, Y., Vasconcelos, N.: Repair: removing representation bias by dataset resampling. In: Proceedings of the IEEE/CVF Conference on Computer Vision and Pattern Recognition, pp. 9572–9581 (2019)

36. Liu, T., Vietri, G., Wu, S.Z.: Iterative methods for private synthetic data: unifying framework and new methods. In: Advances in Neural Information Processing Systems, vol. 34, pp. 690–702 (2021)

37. Mehrabi, N., Morstatter, F., Saxena, N., Lerman, K., Galstyan, A.: A survey on bias and fairness in machine learning. ACM Comput. Surv. (CSUR) **54**(6), 1–35 (2021)

38. Mohri, M., Rostamizadeh, A.: Perceptron mistake bounds. arXiv preprint arXiv:1305.0208 (2013)

39. Nowara, E.M., McDuff, D., Veeraraghavan, A.: A meta-analysis of the impact of skin tone and gender on non-contact photoplethysmography measurements. In: Proceedings of the IEEE/CVF Conference on Computer Vision and Pattern Recognition Workshops, pp. 284–285 (2020)

40. Rajpurkar, P., et al.: ChexNet: radiologist-level pneumonia detection on chest x-rays with deep learning. arXiv preprint arXiv:1711.05225 (2017)

41. Ramaswamy, V.V., Kim, S.S., Russakovsky, O.: Fair attribute classification through latent space de-biasing. In: Proceedings of the IEEE/CVF Conference on Computer Vision and Pattern Recognition, pp. 9301–9310 (2021)

42. Redko, I., Morvant, E., Habrard, A., Sebban, M., Bennani, Y.: A survey on domain adaptation theory: learning bounds and theoretical guarantees. arXiv preprint arXiv:2004.11829 (2020)

43. Ren, M., Zeng, W., Yang, B., Urtasun, R.: Learning to reweight examples for robust deep learning. In: International Conference on Machine Learning, pp. 4334–4343. PMLR (2018)

44. Ryu, H.J., Adam, H., Mitchell, M.: InclusiveFaceNet: improving face attribute detection with race and gender diversity. arXiv preprint arXiv:1712.00193 (2017)

45. Settles, B.: Active learning literature survey (2009)

46. Tartaglione, E., Barbano, C.A., Grangetto, M.: EnD: entangling and disentangling deep representations for bias correction. In: Proceedings of the IEEE/CVF Conference on Computer Vision and Pattern Recognition, pp. 13508–13517 (2021)

47. Tremblay, J., et al.: Training deep networks with synthetic data: bridging the reality gap by domain randomization. In: Proceedings of the IEEE/CVF Conference on Computer Vision and Pattern Recognition Workshops, pp. 969–977 (2018)

48. Vilesov, A., et al.: Blending camera and 77 GHz radar sensing for equitable, robust plethysmography. ACM Trans. Graph. (SIGGRAPH) **41**(4), 1–14 (2022)

49. Wang, T., Zhao, J., Yatskar, M., Chang, K.W., Ordonez, V.: Balanced datasets are not enough: estimating and mitigating gender bias in deep image representations. In: Proceedings of the IEEE/CVF International Conference on Computer Vision, pp. 5310–5319 (2019)

50. Wang, Z., et al.: Towards fairness in visual recognition: effective strategies for bias mitigation. In: Proceedings of the IEEE/CVF Conference on Computer Vision and Pattern Recognition, pp. 8919–8928 (2020)

51. Wang, Z., et al.: Synthetic generation of face videos with plethysmograph physiology. In: Proceedings of the IEEE/CVF Conference on Computer Vision and Pattern Recognition (CVPR), pp. 20587–20596 (2022)

52. Xu, H., Liu, X., Li, Y., Jain, A., Tang, J.: To be robust or to be fair: towards fairness in adversarial training. In: International Conference on Machine Learning, pp. 11492–11501. PMLR (2021)

53. Yao, Y., Yu, H., Mu, J., Li, J., Pu, H.: Estimation of the gender ratio of chickens based on computer vision: dataset and exploration. Entropy **22**(7), 719 (2020)

54. Yue, X., Zhang, Y., Zhao, S., Sangiovanni-Vincentelli, A., Keutzer, K., Gong, B.: Domain randomization and pyramid consistency: Simulation-to-real generalization without accessing target domain data. In: Proceedings of the IEEE/CVF International Conference on Computer Vision, pp. 2100–2110 (2019)

55. Zhang, B.H., Lemoine, B., Mitchell, M.: Mitigating unwanted biases with adversarial learning. In: Proceedings of the 2018 AAAI/ACM Conference on AI, Ethics, and Society, pp. 335–340 (2018)

56. Zhang, Z., Song, Y., Qi, H.: Age progression/regression by conditional adversarial autoencoder. In: Proceedings of the IEEE/CVF Conference on Computer Vision and Pattern Recognition, pp. 5810–5818 (2017)

Studying Bias in GANs Through the Lens of Race

Vongani H. Maluleke[(✉)], Neerja Thakkar, Tim Brooks, Ethan Weber,
Trevor Darrell, Alexei A. Efros, Angjoo Kanazawa, and Devin Guillory

UC Berkeley, Berkeley, CA, USA
vongani_maluleke@berkeley.edu

Abstract. In this work, we study how the performance and evaluation
of generative image models are impacted by the racial composition
of their training datasets. By examining and controlling the racial distributions in various training datasets, we are able to observe the impacts
of different training distributions on generated image quality and the
racial distributions of the generated images. Our results show that the
racial compositions of generated images successfully preserve that of the
training data. However, we observe that truncation, a technique used
to generate higher quality images during inference, exacerbates racial
imbalances in the data. Lastly, when examining the relationship between
image quality and race, we find that the highest perceived visual quality
images of a given race come from a distribution where that race is well-
represented, and that annotators consistently prefer generated images of
white people over those of Black people.

Keywords: GANs · Racial bias · Truncation · Data imbalance

1 Introduction

The computer vision community has wrestled with problems of bias for decades
[45,50]. As vision algorithms are starting to become practically useful in the
real world, this issue of bias has manifested as a serious problem in society
[6,11,43,47]. In particular, GANs [17] have significantly increased in quality and
popularity over the past few years [8,31], and these models have been shown
to contain racial biases [14,27,28]. As GANs are increasingly used for synthetic
data generation and creative applications, there is the potential for racial bias
to propagate to downstream applications, and the need for an understanding
of the cause of biased outputs. In generative image models, the question of
whether the source of biased outputs comes from the data with which models

---

V. H. Maluleke and N. Thakkar—Equal contribution in alphabetical order.

Supplementary Information The online version contains supplementary material
available at https://doi.org/10.1007/978-3-031-19778-9_20.

S. Avidan et al. (Eds.): ECCV 2022, LNCS 13673, pp. 344–360, 2022.
https://doi.org/10.1007/978-3-031-19778-9_20

are trained (data distribution bias) or the algorithms themselves (algorithmic bias) is unanswered.

In this work, we aim to understand the source of bias in GANs in the context of perceived race[1], i.e., can dataset imbalance alone sufficiently describe issues of racial representation in generative image models? Or do algorithmic choices also contribute [25]? We consider the following types of bias in generative image models as they pertain to class distributions and image quality: 1) *Data distribution bias*: imbalances in training data that are replicated in the generated data, 2) *Symmetric algorithmic bias*: imbalances in training data that are exacerbated in the generated data, irrespective of which race labels are over or under-represented in the data, and 3) *Asymmetric algorithmic bias*: unequal effects on different classes, dependent on or independent of class representation in the training data.

We conduct a systematic study, exploring the following research questions:

1. Will a racially imbalanced training dataset lead to an even more imbalanced generated dataset?
2. Will improving sample quality using the commonly employed "truncation trick" exacerbate an underlying racial imbalance?
3. If a generator is trained on an imbalanced dataset, will perceived visual quality of the generated images change depending on class representation?

We explore these research questions in the context of StyleGAN2-ADA [33] trained to generate human faces. To measure the impact of dataset imbalance, we first label a subset of FFHQ [31], to understand the racial composition of this popular and representative dataset for training generative models of face images. We also train StyleGAN2-ADA on three datasets with varying controlled ratios of images of persons perceived as Black or white. We then measure the perceived racial distribution of training and generated data, with and without truncation, and study the relationship between quality and race class label distribution. To obtain the perceived racial distribution, we use Amazon Mechanical Turk Annotation (AMT) annotations, as well as a classifier that is calibrated against human performance. The AMT annotations are also used to measure the perceived visual quality of real and generated images.

Our findings show that 1) GANs appear to preserve the racial composition of training data, even for imbalanced datasets, exhibiting data distribution bias 2) however, truncation exacerbates discrepancies in the racial distribution equally amongst race class labels, exhibiting symmetric algorithmic bias, and 3) when ranking images by quality, we find that generated images of a given perceived race are of higher perceived quality when they come from a generator that is over-represented for images labeled as white, while images labeled as Black retain constant quality regardless of the training data's racial composition. We also find that both real and generated white labeled facial images are consistently annotated as higher quality than real and generated images of

---

[1] We do not objectively evaluate the underlying actual race, but rather measure the perceived race of the image. This is because race is a complex social construct and it is not sufficient to evaluate race with only visual features. See Sect. 3.1.

Black people. It is unclear whether this observed asymmetric algorithmic bias is caused by StyleGAN2-ADA, our human-centric system of evaluation, underlying qualitative discrepancies in training data, or a combination thereof.

2   Related Work

Racial Bias in Computer Vision. Machine learning models and their applications have a well-documented history of racial bias, spanning vision [11,35], language [9,10,46], and predictive algorithms that have a heavy impact on real peoples' lives [29,42,43]. Numerous research efforts have aimed to evaluate, understand, and mitigate bias, particularly in computer vision. Buolamwini *et al.* [11] analyzed three automated facial analysis algorithms, and found that all classifiers performed worse on images of individuals with a darker skin type compared to counterparts with a lighter skin type [11]. A similar conclusion was made in earlier research by Klare *et al.* [35], who found that face recognition algorithms consistently performed poorly on young Black females. Phillip *et al.* [44] showed that machine learning algorithms suffer from the "other race effect" (humans recognize faces of people from their race more accurately compared to faces of other races) [44].

Racial Bias in Generative Models. Image generation models have been shown to contain racial biases [14,27,28]. AI Gahaku [14], an AI art generator that turns user-submitted photos into Renaissance-style paintings, often turns photos of people of color into paintings that depict white people. The Face Depixelizer, a tool based on PULSEGAN [40], which super-resolves a low-resolution face image, also tends to generate an image of a white person, regardless of input race. Jain *et al.* [28] demonstrated that popular GAN models exacerbate biases along the axes of gender and skin tone when given a skewed distribution of faces; for example, Snapchats beautification face filter lightens skin tones of people of color and morphs their faces to have euro-centric features. GANs can inherit, reinforce and even exacerbate biases when generating synthetic data [27].

Racial Bias Mitigation. Several works have proposed ways to mitigate racial bias in facial recognition systems by modifying models directly or with data sampling strategies [19,51,52]. To reduce racial bias via model modification, Wang *et al.* [51] proposed a deep information maximization adaptation network (IMAN), with white faces as the source domain and other races as target domains. William *et al.* [19] performed facial recognition experiments by manipulating the race data distribution to understand and mitigate racial bias. Their work demonstrated that skewing the training distribution with a majority of African labeled images tends to mitigate racial bias better than balanced training data set.

Generative Adversarial Networks. GANs [16], a class of implicit generative models, learn to generate data samples by optimizing a minimax objective between discriminator and generator networks. The discriminator is tasked with differentiating training images from generated images, and the generator aims to fool the discriminator. Modern GANs [8,31,33] are capable of producing high quality images and are increasingly leveraged for image manipulation tasks [1,26].

GAN Truncation. The "truncation trick" introduced by Brock *et al.* [8] is a sampling technique that allows deliberate control of the trade-off between variety and fidelity in GAN models. At the loss of some diversity, the fidelity of generated images can be improved by sampling from a shrunk or truncated distribution [2,8,39]. StyleGAN implements truncation by interpolating towards the mean intermediate latent vector in W space [31]. In this work we evaluate the impact of truncation on racial diversity in images generated with StyleGAN2-ADA [30].

GAN Mode Collapse. GANs are known to exhibit mode collapse or mode dropping, where certain features present in the training dataset distribution are missing from the distribution of generated images [15]. Many works propose solutions to address mode collapse, such as Wasserstein GANs [3,18], Prescribed GANs [13], and Mode Seeking GANs [38]. In spite of these works, mode dropping is not fully understood. Arora *et al.* [4] show that the generated distribution of a GAN has a relatively low support size (diversity of images) compared to the training distribution. In the work "Seeing What a GAN Cannot Generate," Bau *et al.* [5] visualized regions of images that GANs are unable to reproduce. They found that higher-quality GANs better match the dataset in terms of the distribution of pixel area belonging to each segmentation class, and that certain classes, such as people, were particularly challenging for the GANs. These works indicate that GANs may exacerbate bias in the training data distribution by dropping certain features or classes in generated images—in this work, we also analyze whether these effects occur regarding racial bias.

3   Methodology

3.1   Racial Categorizations

Race is a dynamic and complex social construct. People can be of multiple races and perception of race is heavily dependent on culture and geography with different meanings and interpretations. As such, all discussion in this work pertains to perceived race by annotators. Despite the complexities and subjectivity involved in analyzing racial perceptions, we choose to study the bias in GANs through the lens of race as this is a topic of societal consequence [14,27,28].

The decision to use perceived racial classifications over skin color *(tone/shade)* estimates and categorizations (such as Individual Typology Angle (ITA) and Fitzpatrick skin phototype [53]) was driven by the notion that perceived racial categorization is an informative lens through which to study racial bias [20], and the availability of the FairFace dataset, a large-scale face dataset with seven race categorizations. Furthermore, Karkkainen *et al.* [36] found that solely relying on skin color/ITA in the FairFace dataset is not sufficient to distinguish race categories. We condense the seven race categories into three: Black, white, and Non-Black or Non-white, to further reduce perceptual ambiguity (see Sect. 4.1). This study does not aim to minimize the importance of understanding these questions in Non-Black or Non-white races, but as a first study we simplify the categorization.

80B-20W Training	50B-50W Training	20B-80W Training

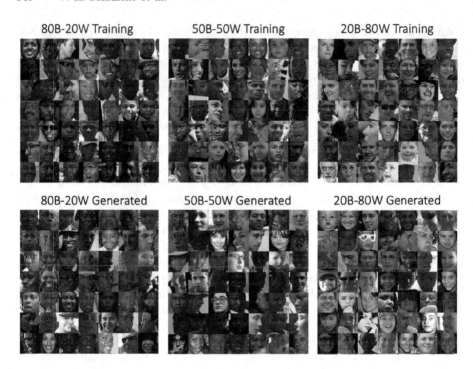

80B-20W Generated	50B-50W Generated	20B-80W Generated

Fig. 1. Training Data and Generated Data. The top row shows real data from the FairFace dataset used for training generative models, sampled in ratios used for training. The bottom row shows generated data from models trained on the 80B-20W, 50B-50W, and 20B-80W datasets (left to right).

3.2 Datasets

This section describes the FFHQ and FairFace datasets. It also explains how we use the datasets: we quantify the racial distribution of FFHQ, train generative models on both datasets to answer our three research questions, and also use FairFace to train a classifier on perceived race.

Flickr Faces HQ (FFHQ) is one of the most commonly-used datasets for the development of high fidelity GANs that generate faces, such as StyleGAN [31] and StyleGANV2 [33]. It contains 70,000 high-quality 1024×1024 resolution images scraped from Flickr, which were automatically aligned and cropped [32]. We quantify the racial distribution of face images on a subset of FFHQ, as well as that of a StyleGANV2 model trained on FFHQ with and without truncation.

FairFace consists of 108,501 images annotated by age, gender and race, which are cropped, aligned and 224×224 [36]. The representative faces in this dataset come from public images without public figures, minimizing selection bias. As described in Sect. 3.1, we use the FairFace race categorization choices as a starting point.

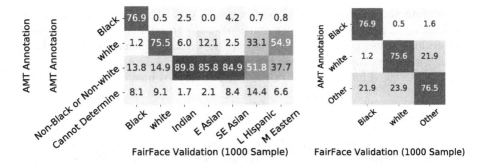

FairFace Validation (1000 Sample)   FairFace Validation (1000 Sample)

Fig. 2. Consistency of AMT annotation labels vs. Full FairFace labels. (Left) A confusion matrix of AMT annotations and the 7 FairFace labels on 1000 random samples of the FairFace validation set. (Right) A condensed version of the confusion matrix. All numbers are shown in percentages. Overall, there is 76% agreement between the FairFace labels and our collected annotations.

We use this dataset to train a perceived race classifier and multiple StyleGAN2-ADA models. From the FairFace dataset, we create three overlapping subsets of 12K images, each with images randomly sampled in the following ratios: 80% Black/20% white (80B-20W), 50% Black/50% white (50B-50W), and 20% Black/80% white (20B-80W). Six different 128 × 128 resolution StyleGAN2-ADA models [30] were trained using an "other races" dataset, an all Black dataset, an all white dataset, and each of the three FairFace datasets described above (i.e., 80B-20W, 50B-50W, and 20B-80W). All StyleGAN2-ADA models were trained with 2 GPUs, batch size 64, and an R1-gamma parameter value 0.0128, ensuring high fidelity images for 25000 kimg. Example generated images trained with the FairFace datasets can be seen in the bottom row of Fig. 1.

3.3 Amazon Mechanical Turk Annotation

Amazon Mechanical Turk (AMT) workers labeled tasks associated with the following three questions:

1. **Race Classification:** What is the race of the person in the image? [Choices: Black, white, Cannot Determine, Non-Black or Non-white.]
2. **Real/Fake Classification:** Is this image real or fake?
3. **Image Quality Ranking:** Which image is more likely to be a fake image?

In our tasks, 1000 randomly sampled real images from FairFace and FFHQ, respectively, and 1000 images from each dataset of generated images were labeled. More details are in the supplementary material.

4 Experiments and Results

In this section, we first establish the reliability of our AMT annotation process and how we condense and use race labels, and then use the AMT annotations to compute the racial composition of a subset of FFHQ. We then assess the relationship between the racial distributions of the training and generated data, and evaluate the impact of truncation on the racially imbalance in the data. Finally, we assess the relationship between the training data racial distribution and the perceived image quality of the GAN-generated images.

4.1 The Racial Distribution of Training and GAN-Generated Data

Annotation Consistency Analysis. We use annotations to measure the racial distribution of the training and generated images. We first assess the performance and reliability of our procedure by collecting annotations from a random sample of 1000 images from the FairFace validation set. The confusion matrix in Fig. 2 shows the difference in labels on the FairFace validation set and the annotations collected using our AMT protocol, demonstrating the inherent limitations in attempting to establish racial categorizations on visual perception alone. However, we find that the ambiguity in visual discernment is lowest between images perceived as Black and white, making these two classes suitable for analysis of racial bias. Limiting the observed racial categories leads to more consistent labeling, allowing for a thorough examination of the impacts between two race class labels from the data.

The Racial Distribution of FFHQ. We analyze the racial distribution of FFHQ by selecting a random subset of 1000 images and collecting images on AMT using our procedure for task one described in Sect. 3.3. We find that FFHQ is composed of 69% white, 4% Black, and 27% non-Black or non-white facial images. Compared to the global Black population, FFHQ is under-representative.

Relationship Between Training and GAN-Generated Data Distributions. On our first research question, regarding if an imbalanced dataset further exacerbates the generated dataset distribution, our experiments indicate that StyleGAN2-ADA's generated data distribution preserves the training data distribution. We compute the perceived racial distributions of FFHQ and FairFace (20B-80W, 50B-50W, and 80B-20W) training data and generated data, based on our AMT annotations. To explicitly showcase the ratio of Black and white race class labels in the training and generated data, we excluded the "Non-Black or Non-white" and "Cannot Determine" class labels. It can be seen in Fig. 3 that the training and generated data distributions are statistically close - the red bars represent the 95% Wald's confidence interval (CI) of each generated data distribution. The training data distributions all fall within the 95% confidence interval of the observed sample means, and as such we conclude that the generators successfully preserve the training distributions and exhibits data distribution bias. See the supplementary material for more information on CI calculations.

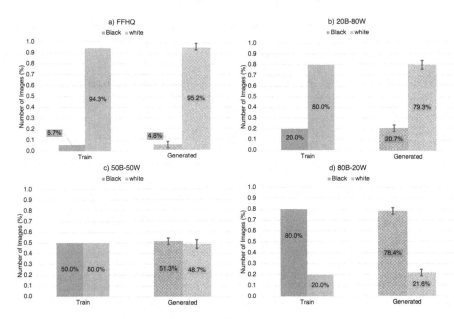

Fig. 3. Racial distribution of training and GAN-generated data. Distributions for (a) FFHQ, (b) 20B-80W, (c) 50B-50W and (d) 80B-20W. The red bars represent the 95% confidence interval for the expected distribution of the generated data. All class labels aside from Black and white are excluded. All of the generative models preserve the distribution of the training data.

Impact of Truncation on FFHQ Generated Data Distribution. This section studies our second research question on the effect of truncation on racial imbalance. We follow the same protocol as above on truncation levels 1 (no truncation), 0.75, and 0.5, and find that applying truncation when generating data exacerbates the racial imbalance in StyleGAN2-ADA. Figure 4(a) shows the AMT annotation distribution of the FFHQ training data, and Fig. 4(b) shows the distribution of StyleGAN-2 ADA trained on FFHQ without truncation. As greater truncation levels are applied, the generated data becomes increasingly racially imbalanced. The percentage of images of Black people in the generated data distribution in Fig. 4 drops from 4% to 0% at a truncation level of 0.5. We observe an inverse effect for images of white people, where more truncation increases the percentage of the white class labeled images in the generated data distribution.

Automatic Race Classifier. In order to conduct a more fine-grained study on the effect of truncation level, we scale the AMT annotation process by using an automatic race classifier to classify perceived race. A ResNet-18 model [21] was used to carry out three-way classification on face images. The model was trained on the FairFace training split augmented with equal quantities of generated images from StyleGAN2-ADA models trained on all-Black, all-white, and

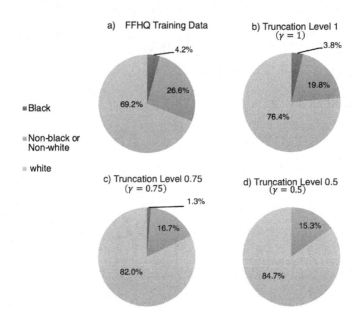

Fig. 4. The racial distribution of FFHQ with truncation. The top row shows the FFHQ training data distribution (left) and the generated data distribution without truncation (right). The bottom row shows the generated data distribution with a truncation level of 0.75 (left) and an increased truncation level of 0.5 (right). While the model without truncation closely preserves the original training data distribution, as the level of truncation increases, the ratio of white to Non-white class labels increases.

all-"other"-races datasets. Confusion matrices showing the performance of the classifier on the FairFace validation set and our collected annotations are shown in Fig. 5. While the automatic classifier performance is not perfect, at 84% accuracy, it suffices as a reasonable proxy for AMT annotations, given that the confusion between the classifier labels and our collected annotations on images labeled as Black and white is similar to the confusion between our collected annotations and the FairFace labels seen in Fig. 2.

Evaluation of Truncation. We evaluate levels of truncation and observe the following trend across all models: as the level of truncation increases, racial diversity decreases, converging to the average face of the dataset. Images were generated from StyleGAN2 trained on FFHQ and the 80B-20W, 50B-50W, and 80B-20W FairFace-trained generators at truncation levels ranging from $\gamma = 0$ to 1 at intervals of 0.1. The perceived race labels were automatically classified for 10K generated images at each truncation level, for a total of 110K images, with results in Fig. 6. We observe that truncation in a dataset with predominantly images of white people, such as FFHQ, increases the frequency of generating images classified as white. Similarly, when the majority of images in a dataset

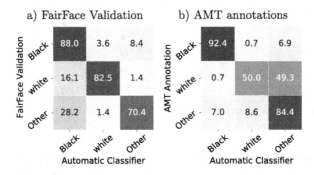

Fig. 5. Automatic Classifier Performance. Confusion matrices for the automatic classifier on the entire FairFace validation set (left) and the automatic classifier on 1000 images with collected annotations (right). On our AMT annotations, the classifier confuses images labeled as Black and white at a level comparable to that of our annotations and the FairFace labels (Fig. 2).

are of Black people, as in the 80B-20W dataset, the truncated generated data distribution has predominantly images classified as Black. Examples of generated face images at different levels of truncation can be seen in the supplementary material.

4.2 GAN Quality

From the AMT Image Quality Ranking task, we perform pairwise comparisons of the generators' respective data distributions against each other. We determine that when trained with FairFace splits, images from the generator trained on more images of white people are always preferred at a greater proportion, and on FFHQ with truncation, images with more truncation are seen as higher quality.

This finding comes from counting the number of times images from one generator are preferred over images from another generator Results of this comparison can be seen in Table 1 for FairFace and Table 2 for FFHQ. Error bars are computed using the Wald's method for a 95% confidence interval. For FairFace, we find that the generator trained on a higher percentage of images of white people tends to be preferred in more comparisons by a narrow margin that often surpasses error bounds. For FFHQ with truncation, an increased truncation level always leads to a generator being more preferred, indicating that truncation increases perceptual sample quality.

Correlation with FID. Fréchet inception distance (FID) [22] is a common GAN metric that measures image quality by comparing distributions of features extracted with the Inception network [49] between training and generated images. Higher quality models receive a lower FID score. The FIDs of our FairFace-trained generators are 5.60, 5.63, and 5.68 for the 20B-80W, 50B-50W, and 80B-20W models respectively, not revealing a clear difference in perceived visual quality based on this automatic metric.

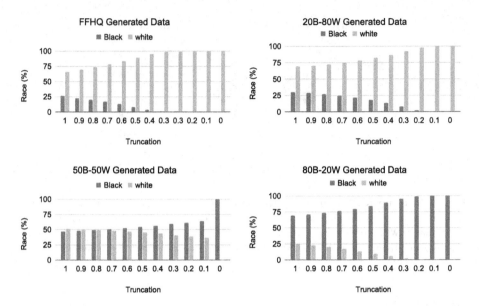

Fig. 6. Automatic evaluation of truncation. Automatically evaluated results of StyleGAN models trained on various datasets, with 110,000 images total generated at levels of truncation from $\gamma = 1.0$ (no truncation) to $\gamma = 0.0$ (full truncation). The y-axis represents the racial breakdown of the dataset, which becomes more polarized as truncation increases.

4.3   Perceived Visual Image Quality and Race

To address the third research question, i.e., to determine if there is a relationship between perceived race and generated image quality, we examine the results of our binary real/fake classification task and our pairwise image quality ranking task. Our findings on the real or fake classification task do not yield a clear relationship between the training data distribution and generated image quality; please see the supplementary material for details. However, pairwise image quality comparisons provide a more fine-grained analysis. From a perceptual quality ranking obtained from pairwise comparisons, we find that the average perceived visual quality of generated images of a particular race increases as the proportion of training images of that race increases. We also find that generated images of white people tend to be perceived as higher quality than images of Black people, regardless of the training distribution.

Using 3000 FairFace 80B-20W, 50B-50W, 20B-80W dataset images, 54000 pairwise comparisons were evaluated within and across the datasets. From these pairwise comparisons, we use the choix package's [37] implementation of the Bradley-Terry model [12] to rank the 3000 images in descending order of image quality. From this global ranking, we obtain a ranked ordering of all images labeled as Black and white. Table 3 investigates the breakdown of the top K images. In order to obtain weighted percentage scores, the raw counts for the top K images (which can be seen in the supplementary material) of a particular race

Table 1. Pairwise image quality comparison of FairFace generators. 9000 comparisons were conducted between each pair of generators, resulting in a total of 27000 comparisons. We report the percentage of images that are preferred from the left generator over the right, with the accompanying 95% Wald's CI. Generators trained on datasets with a greater number of images of white people tend to be perceived as having better image quality.

Generator A	Generator B	Percentage Gen. A Preferred
20B-80W	80B-20W	53.9 ± 1.02
20B-80W	50B-50W	52.0 ± 1.03
50B-50W	80B-20W	51.0 ± 1.03

Table 2. Pairwise image quality comparison of FFHQ at different truncation levels. The percentage of images that are preferred when generated with the left truncation over the right, with a Wald's 95% CI. A truncation level of $\gamma = 1$ corresponds to no truncation, and $\gamma = 0.5$ corresponds to the most truncation. Images generated with more truncation are perceived as being of higher quality.

Truncation A	Truncation B	Percentage Trunc. A Preferred
0.50	1.00	58.7 ± 1.02
0.75	1.00	55.4 ± 1.02
0.50	0.75	52.5 ± 1.03

are normalized by the expected frequency of the images from the corresponding race found in each data split. Then, the weighted numbers are divided by the sum of all scores for that race and value of K. The results indicate that the highest quality images of a particular race are more likely to come from a data split where the race class is over-represented or represented in parity. From the global ranking, a precision-recall curve for each race from each data split over the top K images, and the area under the PR curves, are shown in Fig. 7. Images labeled as white are overall ranked as higher quality than images labeled as Black. Furthermore, for white labels, being in the majority (i.e., from the 20B-80W split) yields better quality than in the minority (i.e., from the 80B-20W split).

These results raise the question of whether a predisposition towards white generated faces is a by-product of our learned generative models, or is a result of other parts of our data collection and evaluation process. In order to gain insight on this question, we conducted 1700 pairwise comparisons between real face images from the FairFace data labeled as Black and white, using the same AMT protocol as for generated data. By removing generative models from this evaluation, we can determine whether external factors such as original real image quality or annotator bias may play a role in our observed results. An evaluation procedure invariant to the perceived races of images should produce results where real images perceived as white are preferred over real images perceived

Table 3. Top K image composition per-race. Given a ranking of images labeled as Black and white across all data splits, we break down the data split that each image came from. The highest quality images ($K = 10, 25, 50$) are more likely to come from a data split where they are over-represented or represented in parity

	White				Black		
K	80B-20W	50B-50W	20B-80W	K	80B-20W	50B-50W	20B-80W
10	0.00	0.29	**0.71**	10	**0.49**	0.23	0.28
25	0.00	0.38	**0.62**	25	**0.57**	0.19	0.24
50	0.22	0.36	**0.42**	50	**0.45**	0.37	0.17
100	0.26	**0.41**	0.33	100	**0.37**	0.32	0.31
500	0.33	**0.36**	0.31	500	**0.35**	0.33	0.32

as Black 50% of the time. Instead, they were preferred 55.2% of the time with a 95% Wald's confidence interval of 55.2% ± 2.3%. This indicates that even though our system of evaluation is based on pairwise comparisons, a standard and well-regarded GAN quality metric [7], it has a detectable bias towards selecting images labeled as white over those labeled as Black.

The source of this propensity towards selecting images perceived as white is unclear. Captured images of Black people in the dataset could be of lower quality than that of images of white people, potentially because of camera or sensor bias. Due to prevalence, collecting high quality images of white-appearing faces might be easier. Another possibility is the "other race effect" [44], where annotators are biased toward their own race, however, the demographics of the annotators in our study are unknown. A future in-depth study of these factors causing asymmetric algorithmic bias should be a subject of future investigations.

5 Discussion

Through a systematic investigation into the role of racial composition in generative models, we find that state-of-the-art GANs such as StyleGAN2-ADA closely mirror the racial composition of their training data, exhibiting data distribution bias. Our study reveals that in FFHQ, the most prominent dataset of generative models of facial images, Black people are substantially underrepresented at 4%, as compared to the global population. Practitioners should be aware of this bias when using this dataset. We recommend that generative modeling practitioners have more awareness of the racial composition of their training dataset, particularly when the downstream application requires a well-balanced model. When the training data has known biases or imbalances, we recommend transparency through mechanisms such as model cards [41].

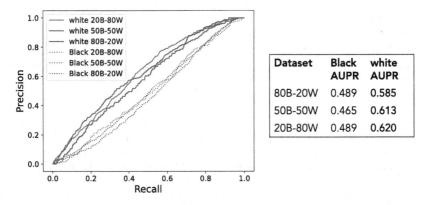

Fig. 7. PR curves (left). PR curves for each race within each generated dataset. For a given K between 0 and 3000, precision, shown on the y-axis, is defined as the count of images of a particular perceived race and dataset in the top K images, normalized by the total number of images of each race and dataset. Recall, shown on the x-axis, is defined as the number of images seen out of the total images (K/N, where $N = 3000$). **Area under the PR curves (right).** A larger number indicates high image quality; images labeled as white are consistently perceived as higher quality than those labeled as Black, regardless of the generated dataset they come from.

Downstream applications, even generative model demos, often employ the truncation trick to improve the visual fidelity of generated images. Our work shows that this qualitative improvement comes at the expense of exacerbating existing bias. Our studies show that using a well balanced dataset can mitigate this issue of symmetric algorithmic bias. We suggest researchers be transparent on their usage and level of truncation, and encourage research for alternative algorithms to truncation. Interesting future directions include correlating FID to other quality metrics, performing this study on different GAN architectures and other generative models such as VAEs [34,48] and diffusion models [23]. In particular, with diffusion models, it would be interesting to see if classifier-free guidance [24] exhibits the same symmetric algorithmic bias as the truncation trick. Another interesting direction is to perform an intersectional study probing similar questions, by considering other attributes such as gender in addition to race.

Acknowledgement. We thank Hany Farid, Judy Hoffman, Aaron Hertzmann, Bryan Russell, and Deborah Raji for useful discussions and feedback. This work was supported by the BAIR/BDD sponsors, ONR MURI N00014-21-1-2801, and NSF Graduate Fellowships. The study of annotator bias was performed under IRB Protocol ID 2022-04-15236.

References

1. Abdal, R., Qin, Y., Wonka, P.: Image2StyleGAN++: how to edit the embedded images? In: Proceedings of the IEEE/CVF Conference on Computer Vision and Pattern Recognition, pp. 8296–8305 (2020)
2. Ackley, D.H., Hinton, G.E., Sejnowski, T.J.: A learning algorithm for Boltzmann machines. Cogn. Sci. **9**(1), 147–169 (1985)
3. Arjovsky, M., Chintala, S., Bottou, L.: Wasserstein generative adversarial networks. In: Precup, D., Teh, Y.W. (eds.) Proceedings of the 34th International Conference on Machine Learning. Proceedings of Machine Learning Research, vol. 70, pp. 214–223. PMLR, 06–11 August 2017. https://proceedings.mlr.press/v70/arjovsky17a.html
4. Arora, S., Zhang, Y.: Do GANs actually learn the distribution? An empirical study (2017)
5. Bau, D., et al.: Seeing what a GAN cannot generate (2019)
6. Benjamin, R.: Race after technology: abolitionist tools for the new Jim code. Social forces (2019)
7. Borji, A.: Pros and cons of GAN evaluation measures. Comput. Vis. Image Underst. **179**, 41–65 (2019)
8. Brock, A., Donahue, J., Simonyan, K.: Large scale GAN training for high fidelity natural image synthesis. arXiv preprint arXiv:1809.11096 (2018)
9. Brown, T., Askell, A., et al.: Language models are few-shot learners. Adv. Neural. Inf. Process. Syst. **33**, 1877–1901 (2020)
10. Brunet, M.E., Alkalay-Houlihan, C., Anderson, A., Zemel, R.: Understanding the origins of bias in word embeddings. In: International Conference on Machine Learning, pp. 803–811. PMLR (2019)
11. Buolamwini, J., Gebru, T.: Gender shades: intersectional accuracy disparities in commercial gender classification. In: Conference on Fairness, Accountability and Transparency, pp. 77–91. PMLR (2018)
12. Caron, F., Doucet, A.: Efficient Bayesian inference for generalized Bradley-terry models. J. Comput. Graph. Stat. **21**(1), 174–196 (2012)
13. Dieng, A.B., Ruiz, F.J.R., Blei, D.M., Titsias, M.K.: Prescribed generative adversarial networks (2019)
14. Gahaku, A.: Ai gahaku (2019)
15. Goodfellow, I.: NIPS 2016 tutorial: generative adversarial networks (2017)
16. Goodfellow, I., et al.: Generative adversarial nets. In: Advances in Neural Information Processing Systems, pp. 2672–2680 (2014)
17. Goodfellow, I.J., et al.: Generative adversarial networks (2014)
18. Gulrajani, I., Ahmed, F., Arjovsky, M., Dumoulin, V., Courville, A.: Improved training of Wasserstein GANs (2017)
19. Gwilliam, M., Hegde, S., Tinubu, L., Hanson, A.: Rethinking common assumptions to mitigate racial bias in face recognition datasets. In: Proceedings of the IEEE/CVF International Conference on Computer Vision (ICCV) Workshops, pp. 4123–4132, October 2021
20. Hanna, A., Denton, E., Smart, A., Smith-Loud, J.: Towards a critical race methodology in algorithmic fairness. CoRR abs/1912.03593 (2019). https://arxiv.org/abs/1912.03593
21. He, K., Zhang, X., Ren, S., Sun, J.: Deep residual learning for image recognition. In: Proceedings of the IEEE Conference on Computer Vision and Pattern Recognition, pp. 770–778 (2016)

22. Heusel, M., Ramsauer, H., Unterthiner, T., Nessler, B., Hochreiter, S.: GANs trained by a two time-scale update rule converge to a local nash equilibrium. In: Proceedings of the 31st International Conference on Neural Information Processing Systems, NIPS 2017, pp. 6629–6640 (2017)
23. Ho, J., Jain, A., Abbeel, P.: Denoising diffusion probabilistic models. Adv. Neural. Inf. Process. Syst. **33**, 6840–6851 (2020)
24. Ho, J., Salimans, T.: Classifier-free diffusion guidance. arXiv preprint arXiv:2207.12598 (2022)
25. Hooker, S.: Moving beyond "algorithmic bias is a data problem." Patterns **2**(4), 100241 (2021) https://doi.org/10.1016/j.patter.2021.100241. https://www.sciencedirect.com/science/article/pii/S2666389921000611
26. Härkönen, E., Hertzmann, A., Lehtinen, J., Paris, S.: GANSpace: discovering interpretable GAN controls. In: Proceedings of the NeurIPS (2020)
27. Jain, N., Manikonda, L., Hernandez, A.O., Sengupta, S., Kambhampati, S.: Imagining an engineer: on GAN-based data augmentation perpetuating biases. arXiv preprint arXiv:1811.03751 (2018)
28. Jain, N., Olmo, A., Sengupta, S., Manikonda, L., Kambhampati, S.: Imperfect imaganation: Implications of GANs exacerbating biases on facial data augmentation and snapchat selfie lenses. arXiv preprint arXiv:2001.09528 (2020)
29. Jeff, L., Surya, M., Lauren, K., Julia, A.: How we analyzed the COMPAS recidivism algorithm. Propublica (2016)
30. Karras, T., Aittala, M., Hellsten, J., Laine, S., Lehtinen, J., Aila, T.: Training generative adversarial networks with limited data. arXiv preprint arXiv:2006.06676 (2020)
31. Karras, T., Laine, S., Aila, T.: A style-based generator architecture for generative adversarial networks. In: Proceedings of the IEEE/CVF Conference on Computer Vision and Pattern Recognition, pp. 4401–4410 (2019)
32. Karras, T., Laine, S., Aila, T.: A style-based generator architecture for generative adversarial networks (2019)
33. Karras, T., Laine, S., Aittala, M., Hellsten, J., Lehtinen, J., Aila, T.: Analyzing and improving the image quality of StyleGAN. In: Proceedings of the IEEE/CVF Conference on Computer Vision and Pattern Recognition, pp. 8110–8119 (2020)
34. Kingma, D.P., Welling, M.: Auto-encoding variational bayes. arXiv preprint arXiv:1312.6114 (2013)
35. Klare, B.F., Burge, M.J., Klontz, J.C., Vorder Bruegge, R.W., Jain, A.K.: Face recognition performance: role of demographic information. IEEE Trans. Inf. Forensics Secur. **7**(6), 1789–1801 (2012). https://doi.org/10.1109/TIFS.2012.2214212
36. Kärkkäinen, K., Joo, J.: Fairface: face attribute dataset for balanced race, gender, and age for bias measurement and mitigation. In: 2021 IEEE Winter Conference on Applications of Computer Vision (WACV), pp. 1547–1557 (2021). https://doi.org/10.1109/WACV48630.2021.00159
37. Lucas, M., Brendan, H.: Github (2022). https://github.com/lucasmaystre/choix.git
38. Mao, Q., Lee, H.Y., Tseng, H.Y., Ma, S., Yang, M.H.: Mode seeking generative adversarial networks for diverse image synthesis. In: Proceedings of the IEEE/CVF Conference on Computer Vision and Pattern Recognition (CVPR), June 2019
39. Marchesi, M.: Megapixel size image creation using generative adversarial networks (2017)
40. Menon, S., Damian, A., Hu, S., Ravi, N., Rudin, C.: PULSE: self-supervised photo upsampling via latent space exploration of generative models. CoRR abs/2003.03808 (2020). https://arxiv.org/abs/2003.03808

41. Mitchell, M., et al.: Model cards for model reporting. CoRR abs/1810.03993 (2018). https://arxiv.org/abs/1810.03993
42. Noble, S.U.: Algorithms of Oppression: How Search Engines Reinforce Racism. New York University Press, New York (2018)
43. O'Neil, C.: Weapons of Math Destruction How Big Data Increases Inequality and Threatens Democracy. Penguin Books, London (2018)
44. Phillips, P.J., Jiang, F., Narvekar, A., Ayyad, J., O'Toole, A.J.: An other-race effect for face recognition algorithms. ACM Trans. Appl. Percept. **8**(2) (2011). https://doi.org/10.1145/1870076.1870082
45. Ponce, J., et al.: Dataset issues in object recognition. In: Ponce, J., Hebert, M., Schmid, C., Zisserman, A. (eds.) Toward Category-Level Object Recognition. LNCS, vol. 4170, pp. 29–48. Springer, Heidelberg (2006). https://doi.org/10.1007/11957959_2
46. Radford, A., et al.: Learning transferable visual models from natural language supervision. In: International Conference on Machine Learning, pp. 8748–8763. PMLR (2021)
47. Raji, I.D., Buolamwini, J.: Actionable auditing: investigating the impact of publicly naming biased performance results of commercial AI products. In: Proceedings of the 2019 AAAI/ACM Conference on AI, Ethics, and Society, pp. 429–435 (2019)
48. Razavi, A., Van den Oord, A., Vinyals, O.: Generating diverse high-fidelity images with VQ-VAE-2. In: Advances in Neural Information Processing Systems 32 (2019)
49. Szegedy, C., et al.: Going deeper with convolutions. In: Proceedings of the IEEE Conference on Computer Vision and Pattern Recognition, pp. 1–9 (2015)
50. Torralba, A., Efros, A.A.: Unbiased look at dataset bias. In: CVPR 2011, pp. 1521–1528. IEEE (2011)
51. Wang, M., Deng, W., Hu, J., Tao, X., Huang, Y.: Racial faces in the wild: reducing racial bias by information maximization adaptation network. In: 2019 IEEE/CVF International Conference on Computer Vision (ICCV), pp. 692–702 (2019)
52. Wang, Z., et al.: Towards fairness in visual recognition: effective strategies for bias mitigation. CoRR abs/1911.11834 (2019). https://arxiv.org/abs/1911.11834
53. Wilkes, M., Wright, C.Y., du Plessis, J.L., Reeder, A.: Fitzpatrick skin type, individual typology angle, and melanin index in an African population: steps toward universally applicable skin photosensitivity assessments. JAMA Dermatol. **151**(8), 902–903 (2015)

Trust, but Verify: Using Self-supervised Probing to Improve Trustworthiness

Ailin Deng[(✉)], Shen Li, Miao Xiong, Zhirui Chen, and Bryan Hooi

National University of Singapore, Singapore, Singapore
{ailin,shen.li,miao.xiong,zhiruichen}@u.nus.edu
bhooi@comp.nus.edu.sg

Abstract. Trustworthy machine learning is of primary importance to the practical deployment of deep learning models. While state-of-the-art models achieve astonishingly good performance in terms of accuracy, recent literature reveals that their predictive confidence scores unfortunately cannot be trusted: e.g., they are often overconfident when wrong predictions are made, or so even for obvious outliers. In this paper, we introduce a new approach of *self-supervised probing*, which enables us to check and mitigate the overconfidence issue for a trained model, thereby improving its trustworthiness. We provide a simple yet effective framework, which can be flexibly applied to existing trustworthiness-related methods in a plug-and-play manner. Extensive experiments on three trustworthiness-related tasks (misclassification detection, calibration and out-of-distribution detection) across various benchmarks verify the effectiveness of our proposed probing framework.

1 Introduction

Deep neural networks have recently exhibited remarkable performance across a broad spectrum of applications, including image classification and object detection. However, the ever-growing range of applications of neural networks has also led to increasing concern about the reliability and trustworthiness of their decisions [17,32], especially in safety-critical domains such as autonomous driving and medical diagnosis. This concern has been exacerbated with observations about their overconfidence, where a classifier tends to give a wrong prediction with high confidence [18,27]. Such disturbing phenomena are also observed on out-of-distribution data [16]. The overconfidence issue thus poses great challenges to the application of models in the tasks of misclassification detection, calibration and out-of-distribution detection [14,16,18], which we collectively refer to as *trustworthiness*.

Researchers have since endeavored to mitigate this overconfidence issue by deploying new model architectures under the Bayesian framework so as to yield well-grounded uncertainty estimates [3,12,22]. However, these proposed frameworks usually incur accuracy drops and heavier computational overheads. Deep

---

Supplementary Information The online version contains supplementary material available at https://doi.org/10.1007/978-3-031-19778-9_21.

S. Avidan et al. (Eds.): ECCV 2022, LNCS 13673, pp. 361–377, 2022.
https://doi.org/10.1007/978-3-031-19778-9_21

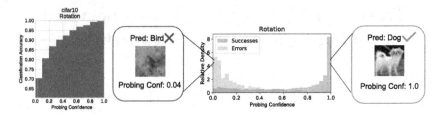

Fig. 1. *Left*: Positive correlation between probing confidence and classification accuracy. *Right*: Images with lower probing confidence can be visually hard to detect and cause errors, while the images with higher probing confidences are sharp and clear, and lead to successful predictions. The visualized probing confidence is calculated from the self-supervised rotation task on CIFAR-10.

ensemble models [6,24] obtain uncertainty estimates from multiple classifiers, but also suffer from heavy computational cost. Some recent works [8,21] favor improving misclassification detection performance given a trained classifier. In particular, Trust Score [21] relies on the training data to estimate the test sample's misclassification probability, while True Class Probability [8] uses an auxiliary deep model to predict the true class probability in the original softmax distribution. Like these methods, our approach is plug-and-play and does not compromise the performance of the classifier, or require retraining it. Our method is complementary to existing trustworthiness methods, as we introduce the use of *probing* as a new source of information that can be flexibly combined with trustworthiness methods.

Probing [2,20] was proposed as a general tool for understanding deep models without influencing the original model. Specifically, probing is an analytic framework that uses the representations extracted from an original model to train another classifier (termed 'probing classifier') for a certain designed probing task to predict some properties of interest. The performance (*e.g.*, accuracy) of the learned probing classifier can be used to evaluate or understand the original model. For example, one probing framework proposed in [20] evaluates the quality of sentence embeddings using the performance on the probing task of sentence-length or word-order prediction, while [2] uses probing to understand the dynamics of intermediate layers in a deep network.

Though probing has been utilized in natural language processing for linguistics understanding, the potential of probing in mitigating the overconfidence issue in deep visual classifiers remains unexplored. Intuitively, our proposed framework uses probing to 'assess' a classifier, so as to distinguish inputs where it can be trusted from those where it cannot, based on the results on the probing task. To achieve this goal, we need both 1) well-designed probing tasks, which should be different but highly related to the original classification task, and 2) a framework for how to use the probing results.

So the first question is: *what probing tasks are related to the original visual classification problem yet naturally available and informative?* We relate this question with the recent advancement of self-supervised learning. Existing literature suggests that a model that can tell the rotation, colorization or some other properties of objects is expected to have learned semantic information that is useful for downstream object classification [11,13,28,36]. Reversing this, we may expect that a pretrained supervised model with good classification performance can tell the properties of an object, *e.g.*, rotation degrees. In addition, recently [10] observes a strong correlation between rotation prediction accuracy and classification accuracy at the dataset level, under a multi-task learning scheme. This observation suggests that self-supervised tasks, *e.g.*, rotation or translation prediction, can help in assessing a model's trustworthiness.

In our work, we first present a novel empirical finding that the 'probing confidence', or the confidence of the probing classifier, highly correlates with the classification accuracy, as shown in Figs. 1 and 3. Motivated by this finding, we propose our *self-supervised probing* framework, which exploits the probing confidence for trustworthiness tasks, in a flexible and plug-and-play manner. Finally, we verify the effectiveness of our framework by conducting experiments on the three trustworthiness-related tasks.

Overall, the contributions and benefits of our approach are as follows[1]:

- (Empirical Findings) We show that the probing confidence highly correlates with classification accuracy, showing the value of probing confidence as an auxiliary information source for trustworthiness tasks.
- (Generality) We provide a simple yet effective framework to incorporate the probing confidence into existing trustworthiness methods without changing the classifier architecture.
- (Effectiveness) We verify that our self-supervised probing framework achieves generally better performance in three trustworthiness related problems: misclassification detection, calibration and OOD detection.

2 Related Work

2.1 Trustworthiness in Deep Learning

The overconfidence issue [16,18] raises major concerns about deep models' trustworthiness, and has been studied in several related problems: calibration, misclassification detection, and out-of-distribution (OOD) detection [14,16,18].

Calibration algorithms aim to align a model's predictive confidence scores with their ground truth accuracy. Among these methods, a prominent approach is to calibrate the confidence without changing the original prediction, such as Temperature Scaling [14] and Histogram Binning [4].

For misclassification and OOD detection, a common approach is to incorporate uncertainty estimation to get a well-grounded confidence score. For example, [5,25] attempt to capture the uncertainty of every sample using a Dirichlet distribution. Ensemble-based methods such as Monte-Carlo Dropout [12] and Deep Ensembles [24] calculate uncertainty from multiple trials either with the

---

[1] Our code is available at https://github.com/d-ailin/SSProbing.

Bayesian formalism or otherwise. However, these uncertainty estimation algorithms have a common drawback that they involve modifying the classification architecture, thus often incurring accuracy drops. Besides, ensembling multiple overconfident classifiers can still produce overconfident predictions.

The practical demand for uncertainty estimation on pretrained models has led to a line of research developing *post-hoc* methods. Trust Score [21] utilizes neighborhood information as a metric of trustworthiness, assuming that samples in a neighborhood are most likely to have the same class label. True Class Probability [8] aims to train a regressor to capture the softmax output score associated with the true class.

Compared to these works, we introduce *probing confidence* as a valuable additional source of information for trustworthiness tasks. Rather than replacing existing trustworthiness methods, our approach is complementary to them, flexibly incorporating them into our self-supervised probing framework.

2.2 Self-supervised Learning

Self-supervised learning leverages supervisory signals from the data to capture the underlying structure of unlabeled data. Among them, a prominent paradigm [11,11,28,36] is to define a prediction problem for a certain property of interest (known as pretext tasks) and train a model to predict the property with the associated supervisory signals for representation learning. For example, some works train models to predict any given image's rotation degree [13], or the relative position of image patches [28], or use multi-task learning combining supervised training with pretext tasks [19]. The core intuition behind these methods is that the proposed pretext tasks are highly related to the semantic properties in images. As such, well-trained models on these tasks are expected to have captured the semantic properties in images. Motivated by this intuition but from an opposite perspective, we expect that the supervised models that perform well in object classification, should have grasped the ability to predict relevant geometric properties of the data, such as rotation angle and translation offset.

2.3 Probing in Neural Networks

Early probing papers [23,30] trained 'probing classifiers' on static word embeddings to predict various semantic properties. This analytic framework was then extended to higher-level embeddings, such as sentence embedding [1] and contextual embedding [31], by developing new probing tasks such as predicting the properties of the sentence structure (*e.g.*, sentence length) or other semantic properties. Apart from natural language processing, probing has also been used in computer vision to investigate the dynamics of each intermediate layer in the neural network [2]. However, most probing frameworks are proposed as an explanatory tool for analyzing certain characteristics of learned representations or models. Instead, our framework uses the probing framework to mitigate the overconfidence issue, by using the probing results to distinguish samples on which the model is trustworthy, from samples on which it is not.

3 Methodology

3.1 Problem Formulation

Let us consider a dataset $\mathcal{D}$ which consists of N i.i.d training samples, i.e., $\mathcal{D} = (\mathbf{x}^{(i)}, y^{(i)})_{i=1}^{N}$ where $\mathbf{x}^{(i)} \in \mathcal{R}^d$ is the i-th input sample and $y^{(i)} \in \mathcal{Y} = \{1, \ldots, K\}$ is the corresponding true class.

A classification neural network consists of two parts: the backbone parameterized by $\boldsymbol{\theta}_b$ and the linear classification layer parameterized by $\boldsymbol{\theta}_c$. Given an input $\mathbf{x}$, the neural network obtains a latent feature vector $\mathbf{z} = f_{\boldsymbol{\theta}_b}(\mathbf{x})$ followed by the softmax probability output and the predictive label:

$$\hat{P}(Y \mid \mathbf{x}, \boldsymbol{\theta}_b, \boldsymbol{\theta}_c) = \mathsf{softmax}(f_{\boldsymbol{\theta}_c}(\mathbf{z})) \tag{1}$$

$$\hat{y} = \underset{k \in \mathcal{Y}}{\operatorname{argmax}} \, \hat{P}(Y = k \mid \mathbf{x}, \boldsymbol{\theta}_b, \boldsymbol{\theta}_c). \tag{2}$$

The obtained maximum softmax probability (MSP) $\hat{p} := \hat{P}(Y = \hat{y} \mid \mathbf{x}, \boldsymbol{\theta}_b, \boldsymbol{\theta}_c)$ is broadly applied in the three trustworthiness tasks: misclassification detection, out-of-distribution detection and calibration [14,18].

Misclassification Detection is also known as error or failure prediction [8,18], and aims to predict whether a trained classifier makes an erroneous prediction for a test example. In general, it requires a confidence estimate for any given sample's prediction, where a lower confidence indicates that the prediction is more likely to be wrong.

For a standard network, the baseline method is to use the maximum softmax output as the confidence estimate for misclassification detection [14,18]:

$$\hat{P}(\hat{y} \neq y) := 1 - \hat{p}. \tag{3}$$

Out-of-Distribution Detection aims to detect whether a test sample is from a distribution that is different or semantically shifted from the training data distribution [34]. [18] proposed to use the maximum softmax scores for OOD detection. By considering the out-of-distribution data to come from a class that is not in $\mathcal{Y}$ (e.g. class $K + 1$), we can write this as:

$$\hat{P}(y \in \mathcal{Y}) := \hat{p}, \tag{4}$$

where y is the true label for sample $\mathbf{x}$. The minimum value of this score is $1/K$, so an ideal classifier when given out-of-distribution data is expected to assign a flat softmax output probability of $1/K$ for each class [25].

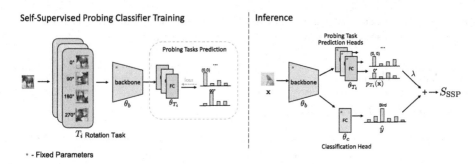

Fig. 2. Our self-supervised probing framework, which first trains a probing classifier (left); then at test time, combines the probing confidence with the confidence obtained from the classifier.

Calibration aims to align the predicted confidence $\hat{P}$ with the ground truth prediction accuracy. For example, with a well-calibrated model, samples predicted with confidence of 0.9 should be correctly predicted 90% of the time. Formally, we define perfect calibration as

$$\mathbb{P}(\hat{Y} = Y \mid \hat{P} = p) = p, \ \forall \ p \in [0, 1],$$

where $\hat{P}$ is estimated as the maximum softmax probability in the standard supervised multi-class classification setup. However, these scores have commonly been observed to be miscalibrated, leading to a line of research into calibration techniques for neural networks, such as [14,26].

On the whole, the baseline confidence scores (MSP) $\hat{p}$ have been observed to be often overconfident, even on misclassified as well as out-of-distribution samples [14,16,18]. This degrades the performance of the baseline approach on all three tasks: misclassification detection, OOD detection and calibration. Our work aims to show that self-supervised probing provides a valuable source of auxiliary information, which helps to mitigate the overconfidence issue and improve performance on these three tasks in a post-hoc setting.

3.2   Self-supervised Probing Framework

Overview. Our self-supervised probing framework computes the *probing confidence*, and uses it as an auxiliary source of information for the three trustworthiness tasks, given a trained classifier. Our framework involves two steps:

1. Training the self-supervised probing classifier to obtain the probing confidence for each sample;
2. Incorporating probing confidence into the three trustworthiness tasks. Specifically, for misclassification and OOD detection, we incorporate probing confidence by combining it with the original confidence scores. For calibration, we propose a simple and novel scheme which uses the probing confidence as prior information for input-dependent temperature scaling.

This framework is illustrated in Fig. 2.

Self-supervised Probing Tasks. Recall that our goal is to use probing tasks to assess the trustworthiness of the classifier. This requires probing tasks that are semantically relevant to the downstream classification task (but without using the actual class labels). The observations made in [13,28,36] suggest that simple tasks which apply a discrete set of transformations (e.g. a set of rotations or translations), and then require the model to predict which transformation was applied, should be suitable as probing tasks.

Formally, we denote the set of probing tasks as $\mathcal{T} = \{T_1, T_2, \ldots, T_M\}$, where each task T_i consists of k_i transformations $T_i = \{t_i^{(0)}, t_i^{(1)}, \ldots, t_i^{(k_i-1)}\}$, where $t_i^{(0)}$ is the identity transformation. For example, one can create a rotation probing task defined by four rotation transformations associated with rotation degrees of $\{0°, 90°, 180°, 270°\}$, respectively.

Training Probing Classifier. As our goal is to provide auxiliary uncertainty support for a given model, we avoid modifying or fine-tuning the original model and fix the model's backbone throughout training. Thus, for a given probing task $T_i \in \mathcal{T}$, we fix the supervised model's backbone f_{θ_b} and train the *probing classifier* as a fully-connected (FC) layer with parameters θ_{T_i}. Optimization proceeds by minimizing the cross entropy loss $\mathcal{L}_{CE}$ over θ_{T_i} only:

$$\hat{P}(Y_{T_i} \mid t(\mathbf{x}), \theta_b, \theta_{T_i}) := \mathsf{softmax}(f_{\theta_{T_i}}(f_{\theta_b}(t(\mathbf{x})))) \tag{5}$$

$$\min_{\theta_{T_i}} \mathcal{L}_{T_i} := \mathbb{E}_{(\mathbf{x},y)\sim\mathcal{D}} \sum_{t\in T_i} \mathcal{L}_{CE}(\mathbf{y}_{T_i}, \hat{P}(Y_{T_i} \mid t(\mathbf{x}), \theta_b, \theta_{T_i})), \tag{6}$$

where $\mathbf{y}_{T_i}$ is the one hot label for the probing task and $\mathcal{L}_{CE}$ denotes the cross entropy loss.

As the backbone is fixed for all probing tasks and there are no other shared parameters among probing tasks, the training for all probing tasks are performed in parallel. After training, we obtain M probing classifiers for the probing tasks $\mathcal{T}$ ($|\mathcal{T}| = M$).

Computing Probing Confidence. During inference, for each test image $\mathbf{x}$ and probing task T_i, we will now compute the *probing confidence* to help assess the model's trustworthiness on $\mathbf{x}$. Intuitively, if the model is trustworthy on $\mathbf{x}$, the probing classifier should correctly recognize that $\mathbf{x}$ corresponds to an identity transformation (since it is the original untransformed test image). Thus, we probe the model by first passing the test image through the backbone, followed by applying the probing classifier corresponding to task T_i. Then, we compute the probing confidence $p_{T_i}(\mathbf{x}) \in \mathbb{R}$ as the probing classifier's predictive confidence for the identity transformation label (i.e. for label 0) in the softmax probability distribution:

$$p_{T_i}(\mathbf{x}) := \hat{P}(\mathbf{y}_{T_i}^{(0)} \mid \mathbf{x}, \theta_b, \theta_{T_i}) \tag{7}$$

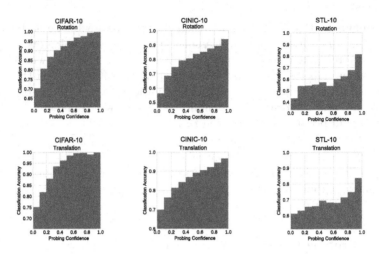

Fig. 3. Clear positive correlation between classification accuracy and probing confidence under the rotation and translation probing tasks on CIFAR-10, CINIC-10 and STL-10.

Empirical Evidence. From Fig. 3, we observe that for both rotation and translation probing tasks, and on three datasets, the probing confidence has a clear positive correlation with the classification accuracy. This empirical evidence indicates that the samples with higher probing confidence tend to be predicted correctly in the classification task. This validates our use of probing confidence for assessing predictive confidence given a sample.

Incorporating Probing Confidence. For the misclassification detection task, we compute our *self-supervised probing* score by combining the probing confidence from the different probing tasks with any existing misclassification score $S(\mathbf{x})$, which can be the classifier's maximum softmax probability, entropy, or any other existing indicator scores [8,21]:

$$S_{\mathrm{SSP}}(\mathbf{x}) := S(\mathbf{x}) + \sum_{i=1}^{M} \lambda_i p_{T_i}(\mathbf{x}), \tag{8}$$

where λ_i's are hyperparameters and are determined corresponding to the best AUPR-ERR performance on the validation set. The proposed $S_{\mathrm{SSP}}(\mathbf{x})$ is the combined result from the original indicator and the probing confidence scores.

Similarly, we do the same for OOD detection, where $S(\mathbf{x})$ can be any existing OOD score, e.g. maximum softmax probability or entropy.

Input-Dependent Temperature Scaling. For the calibration task, we design our input-dependent temperature scaling scheme to calibrate the original predictive confidence as an extension of temperature scaling [14]. Classical temperature scaling uses a single scalar temperature parameter a_0 to rescale the softmax distribution. Using our probing confidence $p_{T_i}(\mathbf{x})$ for each sample $\mathbf{x}$ as prior information, we propose to obtain a scalar temperature $\tau(\mathbf{x})$ as a learned function of the probing confidence:

$$\tau(\mathbf{x}) := a_0 + \sum_{i=1}^{M} a_i p_{T_i}(\mathbf{x}) \tag{9}$$

$$\tilde{P}(Y \mid \mathbf{x}) := \mathsf{softmax}\left(\frac{f_{\theta_c}\left(f_{\theta_b}(\mathbf{x})\right)}{\tau(\mathbf{x})} \right) \tag{10}$$

Here, $\tilde{P}(Y \mid \mathbf{x})$ contains our output calibrated probabilities. a_0 and a_i are learnable parameters; they are optimized via negative likelihood loss on the validation set, similarly to in classical temperature scaling [14]. For each sample $\mathbf{x}$, we obtain $\tau(\mathbf{x})$ as its input-dependent temperature. With $\tau(\mathbf{x}) = 1$, we recover the original predicted probabilities $\hat{p}$ for the sample. As all logit outputs of a sample are divided by the same scalar, the predictive label is unchanged. In this way, we calibrate the softmax distribution based on the probing confidence, without compromising the model's accuracy.

4 Experiments

In this section, we conduct experiments on the three trustworthiness-related tasks: misclassification, OOD detection and calibration. The main results including ablation study and case study focus on the misclassification detection task, while the experiments on calibration and OOD performance aim to verify the general effectiveness of probing confidence for trustworthiness-related tasks.

4.1 Experimental Setup

Datasets. We conduct experiments on the benchmark image datasets: CIFAR-10 [33], CINIC-10 [9] and STL-10 [7]. We use the default validation split from CINIC-10 and split 20% data from the labeled training data as validation set for CIFAR-10 and STL-10. All the models and baselines share the same setting. Further details about these datasets, architectures, training and evaluation metrics can be found in the supplementary material.

Network Architectures. Our classification network architectures adopt the popular and effective models including VGG16 [29] and ResNet-18 [15]. For fairness, all methods share the same classification network. We train each probing task with a FC layer. The hyperparameters λ_i's are selected according to the best AUPR-ERR performance on the corresponding validation set.

Evaluation Metrics. The evaluation metrics for misclassification, OOD detection and calibration follow the standard metrics used in the literature [8,14,18]. We relegate the details to the supplementary material.

Table 1. Comparison of misclassification detection methods. All methods share the same trained classification network. All values are percentages. +SSP indicates incorporating our self-supervised probing. **Bold** numbers are the superior results.

Dataset	Model	FPR@95% ↓	AUPR-ERR ↑	AUPR-SUCC ↑	AUROC ↑
		Base/+SSP			
CIFAR-10 VGG16	MSP	50.50/**48.87**	46.21/**46.98**	99.13/**99.16**	91.41/**91.53**
	MCDropout	50.25/**49.37**	46.64/**47.23**	99.15/**99.17**	91.46/**91.58**
	TCP	45.74/**45.61**	47.70/**47.93**	99.16/**99.19**	91.85/**91.88**
	TrustScore	47.87/**45.61**	46.50/**47.65**	98.99/**99.16**	90.47/**91.68**
CIFAR-10 ResNet-18	MSP	47.01/**45.30**	44.39/**45.48**	99.02/**99.32**	90.63/**92.10**
	MCDropout	43.47/**38.18**	42.04/**52.60**	**99.53**/99.51	93.09/**94.05**
	TCP	**40.88**/40.88	**50.37** /50.36	99.48/**99.48**	**93.74**/93.73
	TrustScore	31.62/**30.77**	59.57/**60.12**	99.46/**99.47**	94.29/**94.38**
CINIC-10 VGG16	MSP	67.23/**66.49**	53.21/**54.40**	**96.67**/96.11	**86.33**/85.53
	MCDropout	64.74/**64.62**	54.02/**54.76**	94.41/**96.19**	84.85/**86.45**
	TCP	67.80/**65.95**	53.19/**54.27**	96.57/**96.58**	86.51/**86.62**
	TrustScore	68.36/**65.65**	51.83/**53.66**	96.19/**96.46**	85.25/**86.01**
CINIC-10 ResNet-18	MSP	62.57/**62.48**	53.18/**53.29**	**97.73**/97.57	**88.39**/88.04
	MCDropout	59.32/**58.21**	52.55/**57.20**	**98.23**/98.23	89.50/**90.16**
	TCP	59.66/**58.95**	55.08/**55.27**	97.87/**97.89**	89.07/**89.17**
	TrustScore	62.26/**60.08**	53.06/**54.53**	97.64/**97.73**	88.07/**88.50**
STL-10 ResNet-18	MSP	77.12/**76.67**	58.81/**59.19**	89.59/**89.81**	78.99/**79.35**
	MCDropout	74.09/**73.86**	60.49/**61.01**	**92.20**/91.33	81.55/**81.59**
	TCP	79.19/**79.07**	54.72/**54.94**	85.18/**85.59**	74.79/**75.17**
	TrustScore	72.48/**71.99**	61.36/**62.10**	90.60/**90.81**	80.57/**80.95**

4.2   Results on Misclassification Detection

Performance. To demonstrate the effectiveness of our framework, we implemented the baseline methods including Maximum Softmax Probabilty [18], Monte-Carlo Dropout (MCDropout) [12], Trust Score [21] and True Class Probability (TCP) [8]. Our implementation is based on the publicly released code (implementation details can be found in supplementary materials). To show the effectiveness of probing confidence for these existing trustworthiness scores, we compare the performance of models with and without our self-supervised probing approach (refer to Eq. (8), where we use the existing baseline methods as $S(\mathbf{x})$).

The results are summarized in Table 1. From the table, we observe that our method outperforms baseline scores in most cases. This confirms that probing confidence is a helpful indicator for failure or success prediction, and improves the existing state-of-the-art methods in a simple but effective way.

Q1: When Does Self-supervised Probing Adjust the Original Decision to Be More (or Less) Confident? As our goal is to provide auxiliary evidence support for predictive confidence based on self-supervised probing tasks, we investigate what kinds of images are made more or less confident by the addition of the probing tasks.

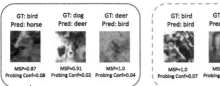 

Fig. 4. Analysis of the examples in CIFAR-10 for the rotation probing task. The red box contains the samples that are wrongly predicted on both probing and classification tasks. The green dashed box contains the samples predicted wrongly on the probing task but predicted correctly for classification. The green solid box contains the samples predicted correctly on both probing tasks and classification. The objects that are visually harder to detect tend to fail in the probing task.

Figure 4 illustrates three cases, demonstrating what kind of images tend to fail or succeed in the probing tasks. From the figure, we observe that samples with objects that are intrinsically hard to detect (e.g., hidden, blurred or blending in with their surroundings) tend to fail in the probing task, whereas samples with clear and sharp objects exhibit better performance in the probing task. The former type of samples are likely to be less trustworthy, which validates the intuition for our approach.

Q2: How Do Different Combinations of Probing Tasks Affect Performance? To further investigate the effect of the probing tasks, we design different combinations of probing tasks and observe how these combinations affect the performance in misclassification tasks.

We first demonstrate the performance with or without rotation and translation probing tasks to see how each task can affect the performance. The result is based on the ResNet-18 model trained on CIFAR-10 and reported in Table 2. The result shows that the rotation probing task contributes more than the translation task to the overall improvement. The combination of rotation and translation probing tasks outperforms each one individually, implying that multiple probing tasks better identifies the misclassified samples, by combining different perspectives.

To further investigate the influence of the number of transformations for each probing task, we conduct experiments by varying the numbers of transformations in the probing task. The details of the experimental setting are provided in the supplementary material and the result is shown in Fig. 5.

We observe that the larger dataset (CINIC-10) shows stable performance under the probing tasks with varying number of transformations, but the smaller dataset (STL-10) shows a drop in performance when using the probing tasks with more transformations. As the number of transformations in a probing task can

Table 2. The performance of different combinations of probing tasks for CIFAR-10. Combining both probing tasks outperforms the individual task setting, suggesting that multiple tasks effectively assesses trustworthiness from multiple perspectives.

Rotation	Translation	CIFAR-10			
		FPR@95% ↓	AUPR-ERR ↑	AUPR-SUCC ↑	AUROC ↑
✓	✓	**45.30**	**45.48**	**99.32**	**92.10**
✓		45.58	45.36	99.28	91.78
	✓	46.15	44.61	99.24	91.42

be regarded as the complexity of the probing task, this suggests that on smaller datasets, the probing tasks should be designed with fewer transformations to allow the probing classifier to effectively learn the probing task.

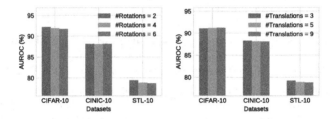

Fig. 5. The performance (AUROC) when using different numbers of transformations (#Rotations / #Translations) in the rotation and translation probing tasks. The probing tasks with more transformations decrease the performance in most case, especially for the small dataset (STL-10).

Q3: Feasibility of Other Self-supervised Tasks Than Rotation and Translation Prediction. Other than rotation and translation, there are self-supervised tasks such as jigsaw puzzles [28], *i.e.*, predicting the jigsaw puzzle permutations. Since our self-supervised probing framework can extract the probing confidence for any proposed self-supervised probing tasks flexibly, we also experiment with jigsaw puzzle prediction as a probing task. However, we found that the training accuracy for jigsaw puzzle prediction is low, resulting in less informative probing confidence scores. This is probably because shuffling patches of an image breaks down the image semantics, making it challenging for the supervised backbone to yield meaningful representations for the self-supervised probing task.

In general, probing tasks should be simple yet closely related to visual semantic properties, so that the probing confidence correlates with classification accuracy. The rotation and translation tasks assess a model's ability to identify the correct orientation and position profile of the object of interest, which are closely related to the classification task; but more complex tasks (e.g., jigsaw) can lead to greater divergence between probing and classification. We leave the question of using other potential probing tasks in the further study.

Table 3. AUROC (%) of OOD detection trained on in-distribution data (a) CIFAR-10 and (b) CINIC-10. The baseline methods are Maximum Softmax Probability and Entropy. +SSP indicates incorporating our self-supervised probing.

Backbone	Method	CIFAR-10 →				
		SVHN	LSUN	ImageNet	LSUN(FIX)	ImageNet(FIX)
VGG16	MSP	91.05	88.98	88.08	85.64	86.01
	MSP+SSP	**92.57**	**90.39**	**90.08**	**86.93**	**87.41**
	Entropy	91.79	89.55	88.60	86.04	86.46
	Entropy+SSP	**92.57**	**90.70**	**90.09**	**86.76**	**87.34**
ResNet-18	MSP	88.80	91.17	88.86	85.26	85.75
	MSP+SSP	**91.71**	**92.62**	**91.27**	**89.71**	**89.65**
	Entropy	89.27	91.94	89.44	85.54	86.06
	Entropy+SSP	**92.13**	**93.55**	**92.02**	**90.04**	**90.03**
		CINIC-10 →				
Backbone	Method	SVHN	LSUN	ImageNet	LSUN(FIX)	ImageNet(FIX)
VGG16	MSP	81.48	81.17	80.36	76.45	76.76
	MSP+SSP	**85.25**	**84.73**	**83.53**	**80.92**	**80.36**
	Entropy	83.24	82.96	81.92	77.83	77.93
	Entropy+SSP	**85.07**	**84.57**	**83.32**	**79.90**	**79.68**
ResNet-18	MSP	88.81	86.11	83.03	83.25	81.59
	MSP+SSP	**90.33**	**87.87**	**86.20**	**83.69**	**83.43**
	Entropy	87.65	83.34	80.96	83.59	81.34
	Entropy+SSP	**89.75**	**85.46**	**83.26**	**85.09**	**83.31**

4.3 Results on Out-of-Distribution Detection

Besides misclassification detection, we also conduct experiments on out-of-distribution detection with S_{SSP}. All hyperparameters λ_i share the same setting as in misclassification detection. Since our goal is to verify that our self-supervised probing approach can be combined with common existing methods to enhance their performance, we build upon the most commonly used methods for OOD detection: Maximum Softmax Probability (MSP) and the entropy of the softmax probability distribution (refer to Eq. (8)).

The results are reported with the AUROC metric in Table 3, indicating that our self-supervised probing consistently improves the OOD detection performance on both MSP and entropy methods.

4.4 Results on Calibration

In this section, we verify our proposed input-dependent temperature scaling as described in Sect. 3.2. Specifically, we compare the common calibration baselines,

Table 4. The reported performance in calibration. Our approach (Scaling+SSP) compare with uncalibrated softmax probability (MSP) [18], Histogram Binning binning (Hist. Binning) [35] and Temperature Scaling (Temp. Scaling) [14].

		ECE (%) ↓	MCE (%) ↓	NLL ↓	Brier Score (×10⁻³) ↓
CIFAR-10 VGG16	MSP (uncalibrated)	5.0	31.43	0.39	13.17
	Hist. Binning	1.65	20.68	0.35	12.88
	Temp. Scaling	1.03	**7.53**	**0.26**	**12.03**
	Scaling+SSP	**0.93**	9.15	**0.26**	**12.03**
CIFAR-10 ResNet-18	MSP (uncalibrated)	4.31	28.16	0.28	11.55
	Hist. Binning	1.17	27.95	0.31	10.73
	Temp. Scaling	1.40	18.91	0.23	10.72
	Scaling+SSP	**0.75**	**7.92**	**0.22**	**10.48**
CINIC-10 VGG16	MSP (uncalibrated)	9.68	24.29	0.71	27.82
	Hist. Binning	2.95	28.40	0.67	26.44
	Temp. Scaling	0.62	**2.46**	**0.55**	25.34
	Scaling+SSP	**0.53**	3.42	**0.55**	**25.28**
CINIC-10 ResNet-18	MSP (uncalibrated)	7.94	23.08	0.55	23.43
	Hist. Binning	2.26	21.09	0.56	22.20
	Temp. Scaling	1.41	13.30	0.45	21.56
	Scaling+SSP	**0.77**	**10.22**	**0.44**	**21.51**
STL-10 ResNet-18	MSP (uncalibrated)	16.22	26.76	1.18	46.73
	Hist. Binning	7.80	17.73	1.92	46.30
	Temp. Scaling	1.56	9.08	**0.89**	42.22
	Scaling+SSP	**1.17**	**7.61**	**0.89**	**42.15**

including Temperature Scaling [14] and Histogram Binning [35]. Temperature Scaling is the key baseline for verifying the effectiveness of our use of probing confidence as prior information to obtain a temperature for each sample.

The result is shown in Table 4. We observe that our proposed calibration method generally outperforms the baseline methods under different evaluation metrics.

5   Conclusions

In this paper, we proposed a novel self-supervised probing framework for enhancing existing methods' performance on trustworthiness related problems. We first showed that the 'probing confidence' from the probing classifier highly correlates with classification accuracy. Motivated by this, our framework enables incorporating probing confidence into three trustworthiness related tasks: misclassification, OOD detection and calibration. We experimentally verify the benefits of our framework on these tasks. Our work suggests that self-supervised probing serves as a valuable auxiliary information source for trustworthiness tasks across a wide range of settings, and can lead to the design of further new methods incorporating self-supervised probing (and more generally, probing) into these and other tasks, such as continual learning and open-world settings.

Acknowledgments. This work was supported in part by NUS ODPRT Grant R252-000-A81-133.

References

1. Adi, Y., Kermany, E., Belinkov, Y., Lavi, O., Goldberg, Y.: Fine-grained analysis of sentence embeddings using auxiliary prediction tasks. arXiv preprint arXiv:1608.04207 (2016)
2. Alain, G., Bengio, Y.: Understanding intermediate layers using linear classifier probes. arXiv preprint arXiv:1610.01644 (2016)
3. Blundell, C., Cornebise, J., Kavukcuoglu, K., Wierstra, D.: Weight uncertainty in neural networks. arXiv abs/1505.05424 (2015)
4. Brier, G.W., et al.: Verification of forecasts expressed in terms of probability. Mon. Weather Rev. **78**(1), 1–3 (1950)
5. Charpentier, B., Zügner, D., Günnemann, S.: Posterior network: uncertainty estimation without OOD samples via density-based pseudo-counts. Adv. Neural. Inf. Process. Syst. **33**, 1356–1367 (2020)
6. Chen, J., Liu, F., Avci, B., Wu, X., Liang, Y., Jha, S.: Detecting errors and estimating accuracy on unlabeled data with self-training ensembles. In: Advances in Neural Information Processing Systems 34 (2021)
7. Coates, A., Ng, A., Lee, H.: An analysis of single-layer networks in unsupervised feature learning. In: Proceedings of the Fourteenth International Conference on Artificial Intelligence and Statistics, pp. 215–223. JMLR Workshop and Conference Proceedings (2011)
8. Corbière, C., Thome, N., Bar-Hen, A., Cord, M., Pérez, P.: Addressing failure prediction by learning model confidence. arXiv preprint arXiv:1910.04851 (2019)
9. Darlow, L.N., Crowley, E.J., Antoniou, A., Storkey, A.J.: CINIC-10 is not imagenet or CIFAR-10. arXiv preprint arXiv:1810.03505 (2018)
10. Deng, W., Gould, S., Zheng, L.: What does rotation prediction tell us about classifier accuracy under varying testing environments? In: International Conference on Machine Learning, pp. 2579–2589. PMLR (2021)
11. Doersch, C., Gupta, A., Efros, A.A.: Unsupervised visual representation learning by context prediction. In: Proceedings of the IEEE International Conference on Computer Vision, pp. 1422–1430 (2015)
12. Gal, Y., Ghahramani, Z.: Dropout as a Bayesian approximation: representing model uncertainty in deep learning. In: International Conference on Machine Learning, pp. 1050–1059. PMLR (2016)
13. Gidaris, S., Singh, P., Komodakis, N.: Unsupervised representation learning by predicting image rotations. arXiv preprint arXiv:1803.07728 (2018)
14. Guo, C., Pleiss, G., Sun, Y., Weinberger, K.Q.: On calibration of modern neural networks. In: International Conference on Machine Learning, pp. 1321–1330. PMLR (2017)
15. He, K., Zhang, X., Ren, S., Sun, J.: Deep residual learning for image recognition. In: Proceedings of the IEEE Conference on Computer Vision and Pattern Recognition, pp. 770–778 (2016)

16. Hein, M., Andriushchenko, M., Bitterwolf, J.: Why ReLu networks yield high-confidence predictions far away from the training data and how to mitigate the problem. In: Proceedings of the IEEE/CVF Conference on Computer Vision and Pattern Recognition, pp. 41–50 (2019)
17. Hendrycks, D., Carlini, N., Schulman, J., Steinhardt, J.: Unsolved problems in ML safety. arXiv preprint arXiv:2109.13916 (2021)
18. Hendrycks, D., Gimpel, K.: A baseline for detecting misclassified and out-of-distribution examples in neural networks. In: Proceedings of International Conference on Learning Representations (2017)
19. Hendrycks, D., Mazeika, M., Kadavath, S., Song, D.: Using self-supervised learning can improve model robustness and uncertainty. In: Advances in Neural Information Processing Systems 32 (2019)
20. Hewitt, J., Liang, P.: Designing and interpreting probes with control tasks. arXiv preprint arXiv:1909.03368 (2019)
21. Jiang, H., Kim, B., Guan, M.Y., Gupta, M.: To trust or not to trust a classifier. In: Proceedings of the 32nd International Conference on Neural Information Processing Systems, pp. 5546–5557 (2018)
22. Kendall, A., Gal, Y.: What uncertainties do we need in Bayesian deep learning for computer vision? In: Advances in Neural Information Processing Systems 30 (2017)
23. Köhn, A.: What's in an embedding? analyzing word embeddings through multilingual evaluation (2015)
24. Lakshminarayanan, B., Pritzel, A., Blundell, C.: Simple and scalable predictive uncertainty estimation using deep ensembles. Advances in Neural Information Processing Systems 30 (2017)
25. Malinin, A., Gales, M.: Predictive uncertainty estimation via prior networks. In: Advances in Neural Information Processing Systems 31 (2018)
26. Mukhoti, J., Kulharia, V., Sanyal, A., Golodetz, S., Torr, P.H.S., Dokania, P.: Calibrating deep neural networks using focal loss. arXiv abs/2002.09437 (2020)
27. Nguyen, A., Yosinski, J., Clune, J.: Deep neural networks are easily fooled: high confidence predictions for unrecognizable images. In: Proceedings of the IEEE Conference on Computer Vision and Pattern Recognition, pp. 427–436 (2015)
28. Noroozi, M., Favaro, P.: Unsupervised learning of visual representations by solving jigsaw puzzles. In: Leibe, B., Matas, J., Sebe, N., Welling, M. (eds.) ECCV 2016. LNCS, vol. 9910, pp. 69–84. Springer, Cham (2016). https://doi.org/10.1007/978-3-319-46466-4_5
29. Simonyan, K., Zisserman, A.: Very deep convolutional networks for large-scale image recognition. arXiv preprint arXiv:1409.1556 (2014)
30. Sohn, K., Lee, H., Yan, X.: Learning structured output representation using deep conditional generative models. Adv. Neural. Inf. Process. Syst. **28**, 3483–3491 (2015)
31. Tenney, I., et al.: What do you learn from context? probing for sentence structure in contextualized word representations. arXiv preprint arXiv:1905.06316 (2019)
32. Toreini, E., Aitken, M., Coopamootoo, K., Elliott, K., Zelaya, C.G., Van Moorsel, A.: The relationship between trust in AI and trustworthy machine learning technologies. In: Proceedings of the 2020 conference on fairness, accountability, and transparency, pp. 272–283 (2020)
33. Torralba, A., Fergus, R., Freeman, W.T.: 80 million tiny images: a large data set for nonparametric object and scene recognition. IEEE Trans. Pattern Anal. Mach. Intell. **30**(11), 1958–1970 (2008)

34. Yang, J., Zhou, K., Li, Y., Liu, Z.: Generalized out-of-distribution detection: a survey. arXiv preprint arXiv:2110.11334 (2021)

35. Zadrozny, B., Elkan, C.: Obtaining calibrated probability estimates from decision trees and Naive Bayesian classifiers. In: ICML, vol. 1, pp. 609–616. CiteSeer (2001)

36. Zhang, R., Isola, P., Efros, A.A.: Colorful image colorization. In: Leibe, B., Matas, J., Sebe, N., Welling, M. (eds.) ECCV 2016. LNCS, vol. 9907, pp. 649–666. Springer, Cham (2016). https://doi.org/10.1007/978-3-319-46487-9_40

Learning to Censor by Noisy Sampling

Ayush Chopra[1]([✉]), Abhinav Java[2], Abhishek Singh[1], Vivek Sharma[1],
and Ramesh Raskar[1]

[1] Massachusetts Institute of Technology, Cambridge, MA, USA
ayushc@mit.edu
[2] Delhi Technological University, New Delhi, India

Abstract. Point clouds are an increasingly ubiquitous input modality and the raw signal can be efficiently processed with recent progress in deep learning. This signal may, often inadvertently, capture sensitive information that can leak semantic and geometric properties of the scene which the data owner does not want to share. The goal of this work is to protect sensitive information when learning from point clouds; by censoring the sensitive information before the point cloud is released for downstream tasks. Specifically, we focus on preserving utility for perception tasks while mitigating attribute leakage attacks. The key motivating insight is to leverage the localized saliency of perception tasks on point clouds to provide good privacy-utility trade-offs. We realise this through a mechanism called *Censoring by Noisy Sampling* (*CBNS*), which is composed of two modules: i) Invariant Sampling: a differentiable point-cloud sampler which learns to remove points invariant to utility and ii) Noise Distorter: which learns to distort sampled points to decouple the sensitive information from utility, and mitigate privacy leakage. We validate the effectiveness of CBNS through extensive comparisons with state-of-the-art baselines and sensitivity analyses of key design choices. Results show that CBNS achieves superior privacy-utility trade-offs on multiple datasets. The code for our work can be found https://github.com/java-abhinav07/CBNS-ECCV2022.

1 Introduction

Proliferation of 3D acquisition systems such as LiDARs, ToF cameras, structured-light scanners has made it possible to sense and capture the real-world with high fidelity. Point clouds are emerging as the preferred mode to store the outputs of these 3D sensors given that they are lightweight in memory and simple in form. Recent advances in deep learning have allowed to directly process the raw sensor output; which has enabled use of point clouds for diverse perception tasks across classification [1–6], semantic segmentation [7–10], object detection [11–14], and registration [15,16]. This is facilitating algorithms for critical applications across autonomous navigation, precision surgery and secure authentication.

The deployment of downstream algorithms in these critical domains implies that the sensor often captures sensitive information, which the user would like to keep private. This is then inadvertently encoded in representations learned from

© The Author(s), under exclusive license to Springer Nature Switzerland AG 2022
S. Avidan et al. (Eds.): ECCV 2022, LNCS 13673, pp. 378–395, 2022.
https://doi.org/10.1007/978-3-031-19778-9_22

the signal [17], leaking several semantic and geometric properties of the scene. Consider for instance, the robotic vacuum cleaners which use LiDAR sensors to efficiently navigate inside the house. The captured signal is also sufficient to localize and map the entire house (via SLAM) as well as track and surveil individuals (via object detection). Similarly, this is also valid for the popular *face-id* experience in recent smartphones which use structured light to capture point clouds of the owner(s) face and use it for authentication, locally on-device. It is well understood that a lot of semantic information (age, gender, expression etc.) can be perceived from the point cloud - which the user may not be willing to share. With the emergence of strict regulations on data capture and sharing such as HIPAA [18], CCPA[1], capturing such sensitive information can create legal liabilities. The goal of this paper is to alleviate such privacy concerns, while preserving utility, by transforming the point cloud to censor sensitive information *before* it is released for downstream utility tasks.

In practice, the design of such transformation functions depends upon the definition of the utility task and privacy attack. Most prior work has focused on preserving the utility of geometric tasks (image-based localization, SLAM, SfM, etc.) while protecting against input reconstruction attacks [19]. For these setups, the dominant idea is to transform the point cloud into 3D line cloud [20] which obfuscates the semantic structure of the scene while preserving utility for camera localization [21], SLAM [22], SfM [23] etc. In contrast, we focus on providing utility for perception tasks (classification, detection, segmentation etc.) while mitigating sensitive attribute leakage [24]. We posit that projecting to line clouds is an infeasible transformation for perception tasks because: i) line clouds disintegrates the semantic structure of the scene required for perception which worsens the utility. This is visualized in [20] and validated by our analysis in Sect. 6; and ii) line clouds are now also vulnerable to inversion attacks, as recently shown in [25], which worsens the privacy. We propose *Censoring by Noisy Sampling (CBNS)* as an alternate transformation for censoring point clouds, which provides improved privacy-utility trade-offs.

The motivating insight for *CBNS* is that performance on perception tasks (utility) only depends upon only a small subset of points (critical points) such that removing (or *sampling*) other non-critical points does not change prediction. Leveraging this for censoring point clouds presents two challenges: *First,* conventional point cloud sampling methods are designed to improve compute efficiency while retaining maximal information about a specific task. Hence, we need to design methods that can jointly sample critical points for the utility task and remove information *invariant* to utility. *Second,* this invariant sampling is necessary but not sufficient, as critical points for task and sensitive attributes can overlap; as we observe through quantitative analysis in Sect. 3.1. We develop *CBNS* to overcome these challenges - i) by introducing an invariant sampler that balances privacy-utility trade-off in its sampling via an adversarial contrastive objective (ℓ_{aco}); ii) by designing a noisy distortion network that adds sample-

---

[1] https://leginfo.legislature.ca.gov/faces/billTextClient.xhtml?bill_id=201720180AB3 75.

specific noise to minimize the overlap between task and sensitive information in a utility conducive manner.

Contributions: Our CBNS is an end-to-end learning framework for protecting sensitive information in perception tasks by dynamically censoring point clouds. CBNS is composed of: i) an invariant sampler that learns to sample non-sensitive points in a task-oriented manner by balancing privacy-utility, ii) a noisy distorter that learns to randomize sampled points for utility conducive removal of sensitive information. We demonstrate the effectiveness of our framework through extensive comparisons against strong baselines and analyses of key design choices. Results show that CBNS significantly improves privacy-utility trade-offs on multiple datasets.

2   Problem Formulation

This section formalises the notation for our task, the threat and attack models, and our privacy definition.

Notation: Consider a data owner O with a point cloud dataset $D_O = (P, Y)$ of N datapoints and (p, y) denotes a paired sample, for $p \in P$ and $y \in Y$. Specifically, $p \in R^{m \times d}$ is a *point cloud* defined as an unordered set of m elements with d features; and y is a *label set* of k attributes describing p. For instance, p can be a 3D point cloud representing a human face ($p \in R^{m \times 3}$) with the *set y* containing categorical attributes that indicate the {*age, gender, expression*} ($k = 3$) of the individual. For every pair $(p, y) \in D_O$, certain attributes in the label set y represent sensitive information which the data owner (O) wants to keep private (y_s) but is comfortable sharing the non-sensitive (or task) information (y_t), such that ($y = y_s \cup y_t$). The risk of leaking this sensitive information prevents the data owner from sharing D_O with untrusted parties; especially with recent progress in deep learning where attackers can efficiently learn functions (F) that can directly map the raw point cloud p to any attribute $a \in y$, where $a = F(p)$ [6,14]. Trivially omitting y_s from y to share the dataset of paired samples $\{(p, y_t)\}$ is not enough since the sensitive information is encoded in p and can be inferred by attackers (*e.g.* using pre-trained models or auxilliary datasets). Hence, to facilitate data sharing with untrusted parties, it is essential to *censor* the sensitive information in p (that leaks y_s) *before* the dataset can be released. Our goal is to learn such a transformation function ($T(\theta_T; \cdot)$) that censors each sample in D_O by generating $\hat{p} = T(p)$. This allows to release ($\hat{p}, y_t$) instead of (p, y_t). Henceforth, we denote this *censored dataset* as ($\hat{P}, \hat{Y}$). The key challenge for T is to preserve utility of the task information (y_t) while protecting privacy of sensitive information (y_s). In practice, the design of T depends upon definition of the utility task and privacy attack. We focus on providing utility for perception tasks while mitigating attribute leakage attacks [24].

Threat Model: We assume that the attacker gains access to a subset of censored point clouds ($\hat{P}, Y$) intending to infer sensitive attributes (y_s). This is practical since data owners typically share data with external entities for storage and also

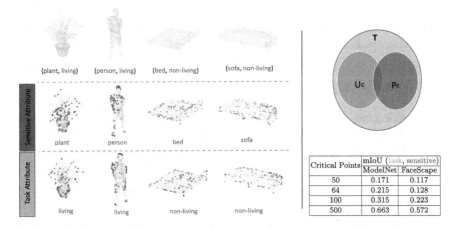

Fig. 1. Premise validation. (*Left*) - perception on point clouds depends upon few critical points. (*Right - bottom*) table shows overlap of critical points for sensitive (P_c) and task (U_c) attributes; (*Right - top*) goal of a censoring mechanism is to remove $T - U_c$ and reduce $P_c \cap U_c$. We bridge these ideas in Sect. 3.1 and introduce CBNS in Sect. 3.2 to accomplish both goals.

for monetary incentives. Further, the threat is also valid if the attacker gains access to the learned censoring function T which can be used to simulate a dataset that mimics the censored point cloud distribution. This is practical if the attacker is one of the data owners that has access to T. We note that unlike differential privacy [26] that protects identifiability, our threat model protects sensitive attribute leakage [24].

Attack Model: We model an attacker that uses the released dataset to train state-of-the-art DNN models that can directly predict the sensitive attribute from the point cloud. This attacker may use arbitrary models which are not accessible during training, and hence we mimic a proxy attacker for learning the censoring transformation. We represent the proxy attacker by a state-of-the-art DNN parameterized as $f_A(\theta_A; \cdot)$ and trained on censored point clouds $\hat{P}$.

Privacy: Following the setup described by Hamm *et al.* [27], we define privacy as the expected loss over the estimation of sensitive information by the attacker. This privacy loss L_{priv}, given ℓ_p norm, for an attacker can be stated as:

$$L_{priv}(\theta_T, \theta_A) \triangleq E[\ell_p(f_A(T(p; \theta_T); \theta_A), y_s)]$$

Under this definition, releasing sensitive information while preserving privacy manifests as a *min-max* optimization between the data owner and the attacker. However, for training the model parameters, we use a proxy adversary from which gradients can be propagated. We refer to the attack performed by this proxy attacker as an *online attack* and note that this allows mimicking worst-case setups where the attacker can also dynamically adapt using protected data and sensitive label information [28]. We note that our definition of privacy significantly differs from differential privacy [26] since we aim to protect sensitive attributes instead of the identity of the data owner.

3   Methodology

In this section, we introduce *Censoring by Noisy Sampling (CBNS)* - a mechanism to censor point clouds for enabling utility of perception tasks while protecting leakage attack on sensitive attributes. We begin by discussing our key motivating insight and then delineate the proposed *CBNS* mechanism.

3.1   Premise Validation

State-of-the-art DNN models such as PointNet [1], PointNet++ [2], DGCNN [3] have successfully handled the irregularity of the raw point cloud and achieved remarkable progress on perception tasks such as classification, segmentation etc. Extensive empirical analysis of these networks shows that classification performance depends upon only a small subset of points (*critical points*) such that removing other non-critical points does not change prediction. Figure 1 visualizes the critical points for perceiving the category (*plant, person, bed, sofa*) and super-type (*living, non-living*) of a few ModelNet dataset samples [29] by training PointNet. The observed *localized* (i.e. depends on critical points) and *task-oriented* (different across category and super-type) saliency is a key motivating insight for censoring point clouds for privacy-utility release.

Assume a privacy-utility scenario where the super-type is task (utility) and the category is the sensitive attribute (privacy). In principle, we achieve good utility (predicting super-type) by only keeping the necessary critical points. Since critical points are visualized via post-training analysis, in practice, this presents two challenges for data release: *First,* conventional point cloud sampling methods are designed to improve compute efficiency while retaining maximal information for a specific task. Hence, we need to design methods that can jointly sample critical points for the utility task and remove information *invariant* to utility. *Second,* this invariant sampling is necessary but not sufficient, as critical points for task and sensitive attributes can overlap. For instance, the top-100 critical points for super-type and category in ModelNet have mIoU of *31%* (table in Fig. 1). Hence we also need to distort the sampled points to decouple the sensitive and task attributes. The venn-diagram in Fig. 1 helps visualize this constraint. Intuitively, we want to learn a censoring transformation that can concurrently remove $T - U_c$ and reduce $P_c \cap U_c$. With this motivation, next we describe our proposed mechanism to censor point clouds.

3.2   Censoring by Noisy Sampling

The task of censoring to mitigate information leakage involves three key entities: i) Data Owner (O), ii) User (U) and iii) Attacker (A). O censors each sample in

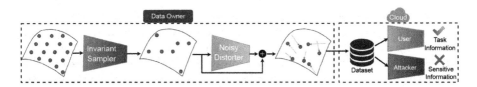

Fig. 2. Censoring by noisy sampling through a three-player game: i) Data Owner (O), ii) User (U) and iii) Attacker (A). O censors every sample in the dataset and shares it with U to train a model on the task information. A intercepts the released dataset and attempts to leak the sensitive information. We design *CBNS*, composed of two modules: a) *Invariant Sampler* and b) *Noise Distorter*, to help O enable U's task and avert A's attack. The design of the mechanism is delineated in Sect. 3.2.

the dataset to protect sensitive information and releases it for U, an untrusted but honest entity, to learn a model on the non-sensitive information. A intercepts the released dataset and queries it to leak the sensitive information. We design *Censoring by Noisy Sampling* (**CBNS**) to help O facilitate the task of U and prohibit the task of A. This three-player game [30] is summarized in Fig. 2 and described below:

a) Owner. owns the point cloud dataset (P, Y) which is to be released. This entity censors the sensitive information in each sample (p, y) for $p \in P$ and $y \in Y$. CBNS is composed of two parametric modules, applied sequentially: i) *Invariant Sampler* $(f_S(\theta_S; \cdot))$, ii) *Noisy Distorter* $(f_D(\theta_D; \cdot))$.

First, $p \in R^{m \times d}$ is passed through $f_S(\theta_S; \cdot)$, differentiable DNN sampler built upon [31], which selects a subset of r points relevant for encoding task information to generate an intermediate point cloud $p_s \in R^{r \times d}$, where $r << m$. In contrast to conventional sampling methods which are aimed at improving compute efficiency while preserving all information, f_S is a lossy sampler designed to remove points *invariant* to utility. The extent and quality of censoring depends upon design of f_S, which we analyse in Sect. 6. Releasing this p_s may still leak sensitive attribute through points which overlap with utility (mIoU table in Fig. 1). *Next,* p_s is passed through $f_D(\theta_D; \cdot)$ which generates task-oriented noise to distort p_s. This is done to decouple overlapping sensitive (privacy) and task (utility) information and executed in the following steps: i) $\mu, \sigma = f_D(p_s; \theta_D)$, ii) $z_s \sim \mathcal{N}(\mu, \sigma^2)$, iii) $\hat{p} = p_s + z_s$ where the sampled noise $z_s \in R^{r \times d}$. All the censored point cloud samples $(\hat{p}, \hat{y})$ are aggregated into the dataset $(\hat{P}, \hat{Y})$ and then released for use by untrusted parties.

b) User is an untrusted but honest entity that receives the released dataset $(\hat{P}, \hat{Y})$ and uses it to infer the non-sensitive task attributes. The *User* trains a state-of-the-art DNN model that can learn to directly map the raw point cloud signal to the task attribute (y_t). For training *CBNS*, we mimic the real user using a proxy user which is parameterized with $f_U(\theta_U; \cdot)$ that consumes $\hat{p} \in \hat{P}$ to predict $y_t \in \hat{Y}$.

c) **Attacker** is an untrusted semi-honest entity that acquires access to $(\hat{P}, Y)$ with the intention to leak sensitive information about the data owner. The attacker is parameterized with $(f_A(\theta_A; \cdot))$ which is not accessible during design of *CBNS*. Hence, for training, we use a proxy attacker that consumes $\hat{p} \in \hat{P}$ to predict the sensitive attribute (y_s). We note that f_A is a proxy attacker used for training *CBNS*, while a *distinct offline attacker* (f), not used for training, is employed for evaluation tasks.

Training: The utility loss is approximated based on the performance of the proxy user which depends upon parameters θ_T $(\theta_T = \theta_S \cup \theta_D)$ and θ_U that are learned during training. The objective function is given by:

$$L_{util}(\theta_S, \theta_D, \theta_U) \triangleq E[\ell_u(f_U(f_D(f_S(p; \theta_S)\theta_D); \theta_U), y_t)] \qquad (1)$$

where, θ_S, θ_D are parameters of CBNS and θ_U are parameters of the proxy user network; and ℓ_u is the cross entropy loss (ℓ_{cce}).

The privacy loss is approximated based on the performance of the proxy attacker which depends upon parameters θ_T, θ_A learned during training. The objective function is given by:

$$L_{priv}(\theta_S, \theta_D, \theta_A) \triangleq E[\ell_a(f_A(f_D(f_S(p; \theta_S)\theta_D); \theta_A), y_s)] \qquad (2)$$

where, θ_S, θ_D are parameters of CBNS and θ_A are parameters of the proxy attacker; and ℓ_a denotes the attacker loss. For training CBNS, we define ℓ_a with the following objective function:

$$\ell_a = \alpha * (\ell_{cce}(f_A(f_D(p_s)), y_s)) + (1 - \alpha) * \ell_{aco}(f_D(p_s), y_s, y_t) \qquad (3)$$

where ℓ_{cce} is categorical cross-entropy and ℓ_{aco} is an adversarial contrastive loss, inspired from [32]; and α is a scalar hyperparameter.

Adversarial Contrastive Loss (ℓ_{aco}): Our analysis in Sect. 6 shows that using ℓ_{aco} significantly improves privacy-utility trade-offs. Consider, for instance, age (y_s) to be the sensitive attribute. In the conventional contrastive loss, we encourage to pull positive samples (same age) closer within the local neighborhood and negative samples (different age) apart. In contrast, ℓ_{aco} pulls negative samples closer (different age) and positive samples (same age) apart. The goal here is to map all different ages within a very small neighborhood of each other, to deter the attacker from learning discriminative representations of age. Intuitively, this guides *CBNS* to transform the released point cloud to introduce ambiguity in representations used by an attacker to correctly discriminate between ages, resulting in better privacy. In other words, the ℓ_{aco} forces to map the different ages to a single point in the embedding space.

The proxy attacker and proxy user have access to supervised data and attempt to minimize their losses L_{util} and L_{priv} respectively. CBNS is trained to minimize L_{util} and maximize L_{priv}, simulating an implicit min-max optimization for these two components. Furthermore, CBNS also minimizes a soft-projection loss [31] (L_{sample}) to improve stability of f_S and ensure that the sampler is constrained to *select* points from the input set (instead of interpolating). This overall objective can be summarized as:

$$\min_{\theta_S, \theta_D} \left[\max_{\theta_A} L_{priv}(\theta_S, \theta_D, \theta_A) + \lambda \min_{\theta_S, \theta_D, \theta_U} L_{util}(\theta_S, \theta_D, \theta_U) + \min_{\theta_S} L_{sample}(\theta_S) \right]$$

(4)

Here, λ is a chosen hyperparameter to help regulate the trade-off between privacy and utility.

Inference: A data owner with access to a point cloud dataset (P, Y) can use CBNS to generate the censored dataset $(\hat{P}, \hat{Y})$ and release it for use by untrusted parties. This released dataset can be used for either: i) training new models or ii) running inference using pre-trained models. This is possible only because the output space of the censoring mechanism is same as the input space. In other words, censoring a point cloud using CBNS also generates a point cloud. In contrast: i) most work for censoring images requires releasing neural activations which cannot be processed by arbitrary designed networks [28,32,33] and ii) prior work for censoring point clouds releases line clouds [20,21] which, while useful for geometric tasks, are incompatible for off-the-shelf perception networks.

4   Experiments

In this section, we specify the datasets and baselines used, define the evaluation protocols and summarize implementation details for the results presented in this work. Details about the code are included in the appendix.

Datasets: a) FaceScape [34] consists of 16,940 textured 3D faces, captured from 938 subjects each with multiple categorical labels for age (100), gender (2) and expression (20). For our experiments, we sample 1024 3D points from the surface of each face mesh using Pytorch 3D [35]. To simulate privacy-utility analysis, we use the expression as the task attribute (utility) and gender as the sensitive attribute (privacy). We choose this configuration because the default critical points for the two attributes overlap (need for noisy distorter) and are also distributed across the point cloud (need for invariant sampling), but human performance motivates that they are can be inferred independently. This provides a good benchmark for testing the efficacy of CBNS. **b) ModelNet** [29] consists of 12,311 CAD-generated meshes across 40 categories (object types) of which 9,843 training and 2,468 testing data points. For our experiments, we uniformly sample 2048 3D points from the mesh surface and then project them onto a unit sphere. Since each input sample only has one attribute (object type), we adapt the strategy used by [30] to simulate our privacy-utility analysis. Specifically, to identify an additional attribute, we divide the 40 classes into two super-types: living and non-living. We anticipate living objects to have visually discriminative features instead of geometric shapes of non-living objects. For example, the task of classifying an object as living (*person, plant*) or non-living (*sofa, bed*) should not reveal any information about its underlying identity (*person, plant, sofa, bed*). We use super-types as task attribute and object type as sensitive attribute.

Baselines: Prior work in censoring point clouds has largely focused on geometric tasks (image-based localization, SLAM, SfM, etc.) via line clouds [20–23]. However, our analysis (Sect. 6) shows that line clouds are a weak baseline for perception tasks (classification, detection, etc.). To ensure rigorous analysis, we define multiple baselines inspired by work in 2D vision that has focused on censoring images (and their activations) for perception tasks while mitigating attribute leakage. The baselines differ in the design of sampling and noisy distorter modules - which may be task-oriented (learned using data) or task-agnostic (deterministic). Our mechanism *CBNS* is equivalent to the *Oriented Sampling - Oriented Noise (OS-ON)* configuration. The baselines are summarized below, with more details in the appendix:

- **Agnostic Sampling - Agnostic Noise (AS-AN):** Uses farthest point sampling (FPS) with fixed gaussian distribution for noise. This is inspired from [36] which formalises differential privacy for images through Gaussian noise, without any learning. While [36] adds noise to images, we add it to a sampled point cloud obtained via FPS.
- **Agnostic Sampling - Oriented Noise (AS-ON):** Uses FPS and learns parameters of the gaussian distribution for noise (as in CBNS) using *maximum likelihood* attacker training. This is inspired from [33] which learn a noise distribution to obfuscate image activations. While [33] adds noise to image activations, we add it to a sampled point cloud obtained via FPS.
- **Oriented Sampling - Agnostic Noise (OS-AN):** Uses differentiable point cloud sampling (as in CBNS) with fixed gaussian distribution for noise. This is inspired from [28] which does channel pruning of image activations to remove sensitive information. While [28] trains a DNN to prune neural activations, we train a DNN to sample point clouds [31].

Evaluation Protocol: We evaluate different techniques by comparing the *privacy-utility trade-off*. For each technique, utility is a measure of *User*'s performance by training on the *censored* dataset and privacy is of the *Attacker*'s performance (as described in Sect. 2). Specifically, we quantify information leakage from the dataset by comparing the performance of an attacker to correctly infer sensitive information from the censored dataset. For this analysis, we simulate a *worst case* attacker that dynamically adapts to the privatization scheme. Inspired by [30], we quantify privacy-utility trade-offs curves by different techniques using area under the pareto-optimal curve denoted as the normalized hypervolume (**NHV**) [37]. *Higher NHV value indicates a better privacy-utility trade-off.*

Implementation Details: Unless stated otherwise, we use 3D-point clouds ($d = 3$) with the Invariant Sampler producing 64 points ($m = 64$) and with PointNet [1] as the backbone architecture for both f_U and f_A. For FaceScape, $n = 1024$ and the dataset split is 80% training and 20% testing examples. For ModelNet, $n = 2048$ and we restrict experimentation to a smaller set of 4 classes: 2 living and 2 non-living to ensure ease of analysis and avoid data imbalance issues (ModelNet has 2 living and 38 non-living objects).

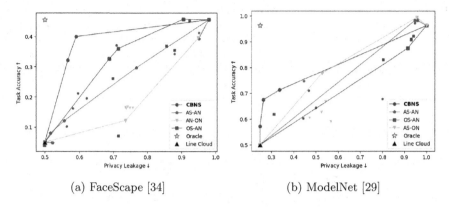

(a) FaceScape [34]   (b) ModelNet [29]

Fig. 3. Privacy-utility trade-off comparison for different techniques by interpolating their best performing points. The oracle point refers to the best possible censoring mechanism. We note that the line cloud [20,22] techniques do not yield any trade-off due to its incompatibility with perception tasks.

5   Results

We report performance comparison with baselines on ModelNet and FaceScape, in Table 1. For completeness, apart from the baselines defined in Sect. 4, we also benchmark with two extreme scenarios: i) **No-privacy**: default case where the data is released without any censoring and, ii) **Oracle**: best possible case with some ideal censoring mechanism which *does not exist*. Results show that **CBNS** significantly outperforms all baselines, on both datasets; as evident from higher NHV. *First,* **CBNS** consistently provides the best privacy leakage - often very close to random chance. Specifically, privacy leakage with CBNS is 0.5890 for 2-way classification in FaceScape and 0.2657 for 4-way classification in ModelNet. *Second,* the peak privacy-utility trade-off for **CBNS** is closest to the oracle, on both datasets. Specifically, when CBNS is used for data release on FaceScape, the *User* achieves a utility of *0.4013* (88% of the oracle) while the *Attacker* performance is close to random chance (0.5890). This corresponds to *13% less privacy leakage while also providing 4% more utility* than the closest baseline (OS-AN). However, a higher fall in utility is observed on ModelNet, which can be attributed to the fact that the task and sensitive attributes are more strongly coupled, than in FaceScape. *Finally,* these observations are corroborated visually by the privacy-utility trade-off curves in Fig. 3 where CBNS has the highest area-under-curve (correlated with the hyper-volume).

6   Discussion

We analyse the impact of key design choices for censoring by noisy sampling. Specifically, we study the characterization of both *CBNS* modules: i) Invariant Sampler and ii) Noisy Distorter; and impact of the perception network. For

Table 1. Comparison for sensitive attribute leakage. We compare our approach on sensitive attribute leakage with the existing works and baseline. CBNS outperforms Line Cloud [20,22], AS-AN [36], AS-ON [33], OS-AN [28] and achieves the best privacy-utility trade-off on FaceScape and ModelNet datasets. For the FaceScape, sensitive attribute is gender and task attribute is expression; and for the ModelNet, sensitive attribute is underlying object type and task attribute is super-types (living or non-living).

Method	FaceScape			ModelNet		
	Privacy ($\downarrow$)	Utility ($\uparrow$)	NHV ($\uparrow$)	Privacy ($\downarrow$)	Utility ($\uparrow$)	NHV ($\uparrow$)
No-privacy	0.9515	0.4549	–	0.95	0.9625	–
Line Cloud [20,22]	0.5000	0.0500	–	0.2500	0.5000	–
AS-AN [36]	0.9511	0.4122	0.1524	0.9469	0.9612	0.6113
AS-ON [33]	0.9391	0.3875	0.1250	0.5281	0.7781	0.6088
OS-AN [28]	0.7143	0.3602	0.1439	0.3125	0.6187	0.6356
CBNS (Ours)	**0.5890**	**0.4013**	**0.1885**	**0.2657**	**0.6750**	**0.6492**
Oracle	0.5000	0.4549	–	0.2500	0.9625	–

Table 2. Design of Invariant Sampler. Privacy-utility trade-off is influenced by whether transformation is learned, and how it is learned. For FaceScape, sensitive attribute is gender and task attribute is expression. l_{cce}, l_{me} and l_a denotes cross entropy loss, max-entropy loss and CBNS loss respectively.

Technique	Privacy ($\downarrow$)	Utility ($\uparrow$)	NHV ($\uparrow$)
AS-ON [33] (ℓ_{cce})	0.9297	0.3954	0.1322
OS-AN [28] (ℓ_{cce})	0.6942	0.3602	0.1439
CBNS (ℓ_{me})	0.6839	0.413	0.1596
CBNS (ℓ_{cce})	0.5787	0.3638	0.1615
CBNS (ℓ_a)	**0.5707**	**0.3997**	**0.1885**

completeness, we also analyse the viability of line clouds for perception tasks. For ease of exposition, we restrict the scope of this analysis to FaceScape dataset.

- Design of Invariant Sampler: We study the role of two design choices: i) learning a task-oriented sampler and ii) the attacker loss that is used to optimize the parameters of the learned sampler. Results are presented in Table 2. Please note that we follow the baselines from Sect. 4 and explicitly mention (L_{priv}) the attacker objective in parenthesis. Specifically, l_{cce} is the cross-entropy loss, l_a is our proposed loss (Eq. 3) and l_{me} is a max-entropy loss used in [30]. We observe the following: *First,* using a learned task-oriented sampler reduces privacy-leakage by 35% without any loss to utility (row 1 vs 4 and 5) in contrast to a task-agnostic sampler. *Second,* using the proposed adversarial contrastive loss in L_{priv} improves privacy-utility trade-off by increasing utility by 3% without any additional privacy leakage (row 4 vs 5). *Third,* using l_{me} improves utility

Table 3. Design of Noisy Distorter. Privacy-utility trade-off is influenced by the learned noise and the granularity of the noise parameters (*shared v.s pointwise*). For FaceScape, sensitive attribute is gender and task attribute is expression. l_{cce} and l_a denotes cross entropy loss and CBNS loss respectively.

Technique	Privacy ($\downarrow$)	Utility ($\uparrow$)	NHV ($\uparrow$)
OS (ℓ_{cce})	0.5787	0.3638	0.1615
OS-AN [28] (ℓ_{cce})	0.6942	0.3602	0.1439
CBNS (*shared, ℓ_{cce}*)	0.9051	0.4532	0.1586
CBNS (*shared, ℓ_a*)	0.8600	0.4217	0.1625
CBNS (*pointwise, ℓ_{cce}*)	0.5689	0.4013	0.1530
CBNS (*pointwise, ℓ_a*)	**0.5707**	**0.3997**	**0.1885**

but with a significant increase in privacy-leakage; as evident from lower NHV. l_{me} is successful for images [30] but fails to generalize to point clouds, which can be attributed to the irregularity in the data structure.

- Design of Noisy Distorter: We study the role of three design choices: i) learning task-oriented noise, ii) the attacker loss used to optimize parameters of the learned noise (l_a or l_{cce}) and iii) the granularity of the noise parameters (*shared v.s pointwise*). *Shared* implies that each point is distorted using noise from the same learned distribution (i.e. $z_s \in R^1$) and *Pointwise* implies that each point is distorted from a unique independently learned distributions (i.e. $z_s \in R^r$). Results are presented in Table 3. We follow the baselines from Sect. 4 and define *OS* (row 1) as additional baseline which only uses sampling (*without* noisy deformation). We observe the following: *First,* using noise task-agnostic (row 1 vs 2), or ii) shared task-oriented (row 1 vs 3, 4) does not provide benefit; and are infact worse than no noise baseline (*SO*). *Second, pointwise* noise distributions *significantly* improves performance. (row 3 vs 5; 4 vs 6). This increase in NHV as well as peak privacy-utility trade-offs can be attributed to improved flexibility for adapting to characteristics of sensitive, task attributes and their relationship.. *Third,* the objective function used for learning noise is also important where using l_{aco} in l_a improves privacy-utility trade-off (row 3 vs 4; row 5 vs 6).

- Impact of Perception Network: In our threat model, the *Owner* releases dataset for post-hoc access by the *User* and *Attacker*. Hence, the censoring mechanism should be independent of the type of perception networks used by these entities for downstream tasks. We analyse this sensitivity by comparing two different proxy attacker and user networks. Specifically, we use DGCNN [3] which is a recent state-of-the-art network with higher capacity and distinct saliency properties than PointNet [38]. Results are presented in Table 4. We observe the following: *First,* increasing capacity of proxy networks further improves learning of CBNS as evident from better privacy-utility trade-offs (row 1 vs 2; row 3 vs 4). For instance, when CBNS is trained with DGCNN (as against PointNet), the censored dataset provides a better utility of 0.4100 (vs 0.3997) while also

Table 4. Impact of Perception Network and Incompatibility of Line Clouds.
For FaceScape, sensitive attribute is gender and task attribute is expression. CBNS is
invariant to the type of attacker network. Using stronger perception network (DGCNN)
further improves performance over PointNet and helps achieve near optimal trade-
off with our proposed CBNS. Resampling line clouds provides poor (random chance)
privacy-utility trade-off.

Technique	Backbone	Privacy ($\downarrow$)	Utility ($\uparrow$)	NHV ($\uparrow$)
OS-AN [28]	PointNet	0.6942	0.3602	0.1439
	DGCNN	0.7056	0.4718	0.2136
CBNS (Ours)	PointNet	0.5707	0.3997	0.1885
	DGCNN	**0.4848**	**0.4100**	**0.2361**
Line Cloud [20, 22]	PointNet	0.5000	0.0500	-
	DGCNN	0.5000	0.0500	-

significantly reducing privacy leakage to 0.4848 (vs 0.5707). *Second,* importantly,
we see that noisy sampling is independent of the downstream network and can
generalize to multiple perception networks. Specifically, this is very encouraging
since CBNS can concurrently mitigate stronger *attackers* from leaking information by improving the utility of *users* with the stronger perception backbones.

- **Incompatibility of Line Clouds:** We posit that line clouds are an incompatible baseline for perception tasks because i) they destroy semantic structure
of the input point cloud which is essential for perception (see visualizations
in [20]), and ii) any off-the-shelf perception network: used by both *User* and
Attacker cannot train on line clouds. To benchmark the performance of line
clouds, we generate point clouds by re-sampling line clouds and evaluate performance on our perception queries. Results in Table 4 show that: i) re-sampling
line clouds provides extremely poor utility (random chance), and ii) the privacy-
utility trade-off cannot be tuned (hence no NHV). Specifically, we observe that
resampled line cloud obtain privacy leakage of 0.5000 (for 2-way classification)
and utility of 0.05 (on a 20-way classification). Finally, we acknowledge recent
work has attacked line clouds to reconstruct point clouds [25] but note that this
is equivalent to our No-Privacy baseline which can improve utility but requires
mechanisms like noisy sampling to provide privacy.

7   Related Work

Private Imaging. A majority of the existing works in privately sharing data
focus on identifiability and anonymization [26,39,40]. In contrast to this line of
work, we focus on protecting sensitive attributes. Among the techniques that
focus on protecting sensitive attributes [28,32,33,41,42], their tasks are typically limited to image datasets. More recently, privacy for 3D point clouds has
emerged with a focus on geometric queries protecting privacy by releasing line

clouds [20,23]. However, To the best of our knowledge, this is the first work in protecting sensitive information leakage for perception tasks in point clouds. Adjacent to research in privately sharing data, privately sharing ML model [43–47] has received interest recently. However, unlike protecting sensitive attributes, model sharing protects the identifiability of training data.

Learning on Point Clouds. Recent advances in deep learning (DL) have allowed to learn directly on raw point clouds; enabling use in diverse perception tasks such as classification, semantic segmentation, object detection, registration etc. Various DL architectures have been proposed starting with PointNet [1], PointNet++ [2] and follow-up works in [4,5,8,48–53] that improve the performance over a given task by capturing task-oriented representations. Zheng *et al.* [38] observe that saliency of the point cloud networks is localized and network rely on a small subset of the signal for the task. This observation has led to extensive work in privacy and security [54–57] utilizing the localized saliency used to design adversarial attack (and defence) mechanisms on the trained models. We note that our setting significantly differs from adversarial defence work since we *protect the dataset* that can be used to train arbitrary models while adversarial methods focus on protecting the model predictions.

Sampling of Point Clouds. Processing point clouds can be computationally intensive making sampling a popular pre-processing step to alleviate this challenge. Classical methods such as random sampling and FPS [2,4] are task-agnostic and deterministic algorithms for sampling point sets. However, not utilizing task knowledge when sampling hinders performance. Recent techniques [31,58] introduce task-oriented mechanisms for sampling through differentiable approximations. The focus is to improve compute efficiency while preserving the entire signal in the sampled subset. In contrast, our goal is to censor sensitive information during the sampling process. We build upon prior work to introduce a task-oriented point-cloud sampler that censors sensitive information.

Noisy Sampling for Censoring. While not motivated for point clouds, similar intuition has been used for tabular datasets for private coresets [59,60] combines subset (coreset) selection and differentially-private noise to achieve good privacy utility trade-off. Our work is different because: i) our queries involve neural networks so computing sensitivity for DP-noise is infeasible, ii) we only want to protect sensitive attribute. We empirically validate privacy-utility trade-off using benchmark metrics, as described in Sect. 4 and present results in Sect. 5.

8   Conclusion

This focus of this paper is to censor point clouds to provide utility for perception tasks while mitigating attribute leakage attacks. The key motivating insight is to leverage the localized saliency of perception tasks on point clouds to provide good privacy-utility trade-offs. We achieve this through our mechanism called censoring by noisy sampling (*CBNS*), which is composed of two modules: i) Invariant Sampling - a differentiable point-cloud sampler which learns to remove points invariant to utility and ii) Noise Distorter - which learns to distort sampled points to decouple the sensitive information from utility, and mitigate privacy leakage. We validate the effectiveness of CBNS through extensive comparisons with state-of-the-art baselines and sensitivity analyses of key design choices. Results show that CBNS achieves superior privacy-utility trade-offs.

References

1. Qi, C.R., Su, H., Mo, K., Guibas, L.J.: PointNet: deep learning on point sets for 3d classification and segmentation (2017)
2. Qi, C.R., Yi, L., Su, H., Guibas, L.J.: PointNet++: deep hierarchical feature learning on point sets in a metric space. In: 30th Proceedings of the Conference on Advances in Neural Information Processing Systems (2017)
3. Wang, Y., et al.: Dynamic graph CNN for learning on point clouds. ACM Trans. Graph. **38**(5), 1–12 (2019)
4. Li, Y., Bu, R., Sun, M., Wu, W., Di, X., Chen, B.: PointCNN: convolution on x-transformed points. In: 31st Proceedings of the Conference on Advances in Neural Information Processing Systems (2018)
5. Wu, W., Qi, Z., Fuxin, L.: PointConv : deep convolutional networks on 3D point clouds. In: Proceedings of the IEEE/CVF Conference on Computer Vision and Pattern Recognition., pp. 9621–9630 (2019)
6. Zhao, H., Jiang, L., Jia, J., Torr, P.H., Koltun, V.: Point transformer. In: Proceedings of the IEEE/CVF International Conference on Computer Vision, pp. 16259–16268 (2021)
7. Xu, C., et al.: SqueezeSegV3: spatially-adaptive convolution for efficient point-cloud segmentation. In: Vedaldi, A., Bischof, H., Brox, T., Frahm, J.-M. (eds.) ECCV 2020. LNCS, vol. 12373, pp. 1–19. Springer, Cham (2020). https://doi.org/10.1007/978-3-030-58604-1_1
8. Hu, Q., et al.: Randla-Net: efficient semantic segmentation of large-scale point clouds. In: Proceedings of the IEEE/CVF Conference on Computer Vision and Pattern Recognition, pp. 11108–11117 (2020)
9. Zhang, Y., Zhou, Z., David, P., Yue, X., Xi, Z., Gong, B., Foroosh, H.: PolarNet: an improved grid representation for online lidar point clouds semantic segmentation. In: Proceedings of the IEEE/CVF Conference on Computer Vision and Pattern Recognition, pp. 9601–9610 (2020)
10. Chen, C., Qian, S., Fang, Q., Xu, C.: HAPGN: hierarchical attentive pooling graph network for point cloud segmentation. IEEE Trans. Multim. **23**, 2335–2346 (2020)
11. Qi, C.R., Liu, W., Wu, C., Su, H., Guibas, L.J.: Frustum pointnets for 3D object detection from RGB-D data. In: Proceedings of the IEEE conference on Computer Vision and Pattern Recognition, pp. 918–927 (2018)
12. Qi, C.R., Litany, O., He, K., Guibas, L.J.: Deep Hough voting for 3d object detection in point clouds. In: Proceedings of the IEEE/CVF International Conference on Computer Vision, pp. 9277–9286 (2019)
13. Martin, S., et al.: Complex-yolo: real-time 3D objectdetection on point clouds. In: Computer Vision and Pattern Recognition. (2018)
14. Shi, S., Wang, X., Li, H.: PointrCnn: 3D object proposal generation and detection from point cloud. In: Proceedings of the IEEE/CVF Conference on Computer Vision and Pattern Recognition, pp. 770–779 (2019)

15. Sarode, V., Li, X., Goforth, H., Aoki, Y., Srivatsan, R.A., Lucey, S., Choset, H.: PcrNet: point cloud registration network using pointnet encoding. arXiv preprint arXiv:1908.07906 (2019)
16. Aoki, Y., Goforth, H., Srivatsan, R.A., Lucey, S.: PointNetLK: robust & efficient point cloud registration using pointNet. In: Proceedings of the IEEE/CVF Conference on Computer Vision and Pattern Recognition, pp. 7163–7172 (2019)
17. Song, C., Shmatikov, V.: Overlearning reveals sensitive attributes. arXiv preprint arXiv:1905.11742 (2019)
18. Atchinson, B.K., Fox, D.M.: From the field: the politics of the health insurance portability and accountability act. Health Aff. **16**(3), 146–150 (1997)
19. Arora, S., Liang, Y., Ma, T.: Why are deep nets reversible: a simple theory, with implications for training. CoRR abs/1511.05653 (2015)
20. Speciale, P., Kang, S.B., Pollefeys, M., Schönberger, J., Sinha, S.: Privacy preserving image-based localization. In: 2019 Conference on Computer Vision and Pattern Recognition (CVPR), IEEE, June 2019
21. Speciale, P., Schonberger, J.L., Sinha, S.N., Pollefeys, M.: Privacy preserving image queries for camera localization. In: Proceedings of the IEEE/CVF International Conference on Computer Vision, pp. 1486–1496 (2019)
22. Shibuya, M., Sumikura, S., Sakurada, K.: Privacy preserving visual SLAM. In: Vedaldi, A., Bischof, H., Brox, T., Frahm, J.-M. (eds.) ECCV 2020. LNCS, vol. 12367, pp. 102–118. Springer, Cham (2020). https://doi.org/10.1007/978-3-030-58542-6_7
23. Geppert, M., Larsson, V., Speciale, P., Schönberger, J.L., Pollefeys, M.: Privacy preserving structure-from-motion. In: Vedaldi, A., Bischof, H., Brox, T., Frahm, J.-M. (eds.) ECCV 2020. LNCS, vol. 12346, pp. 333–350. Springer, Cham (2020). https://doi.org/10.1007/978-3-030-58452-8_20
24. Jia, J., Gong, N.Z.: {AttriGuard}: a practical defense against attribute inference attacks via adversarial machine learning. In: 27th USENIX Security Symposium (USENIX Security 18), pp. 513–529 (2018)
25. Chelani, K., Kahl, F., Sattler, T.: How privacy-preserving are line clouds? recovering scene details from 3D lines (2021)
26. Dwork, C., McSherry, F., Nissim, K., Smith, A.: Calibrating noise to sensitivity in private data analysis. In: Halevi, S., Rabin, T. (eds.) TCC 2006. LNCS, vol. 3876, pp. 265–284. Springer, Heidelberg (2006). https://doi.org/10.1007/11681878_14
27. Hamm, J.: Minimax filter: learning to preserve privacy from inference attacks. J. Mach. Learn. Res. **18**(129), 1–31 (2017)
28. Singh, A., et al.: DISCO: dynamic and invariant sensitive channel obfuscation for deep neural networks. In: 2021 IEEE/CVF Conference on Computer Vision and Pattern Recognition (CVPR) (2021)
29. Wu, Z., Song, S., Khosla, A., Yu, F., Zhang, L., Tang, X., Xiao, J.: 3D shapeNets: a deep representation for volumetric shapes. In: Proceedings of the IEEE Conference on Computer Vision and Pattern Recognition, pp. 1912–1920 (2015)
30. Roy, P.C., Boddeti, V.N.: Mitigating information leakage in image representations: a maximum entropy approach. In: Proceedings of the IEEE/CVF Conference on Computer Vision and Pattern Recognition, pp. 2586–2594
31. Lang, I., Manor, A., Avidan, S.: SampleNet: differentiable point cloud sampling. In: 2020 IEEE/CVF Conference on Computer Vision and Pattern Recognition (CVPR) (2020)
32. Osia, S.A., et al.: A hybrid deep learning architecture for privacy-preserving mobile analytics. IEEE Internet Things J. **7**(5), 4505–4518 (2020)

33. Mireshghallah, F., Taram, M., Ramrakhyani, P., Jalali, A., Tullsen, D., Esmaeilzadeh, H.: Shredder: Learning noise distributions to protect inference privacy. In: Proceedings of the Twenty-Fifth International Conference on Architectural Support for Programming Languages and Operating Systems, pp. 3–18 (2020)

34. Yang, H., et al.: FaceScape: a large-scale high quality 3d face dataset and detailed riggable 3D face prediction. In: IEEE/CVF Conference on Computer Vision and Pattern Recognition (CVPR). June 2020

35. Ravi, N., et al.: Accelerating 3d deep learning with pytorch3d. arXiv:2007.08501 (2020)

36. Fan, L.: Image pixelization with differential privacy. In: Kerschbaum, F., Paraboschi, S. (eds.) DBSec 2018. LNCS, vol. 10980, pp. 148–162. Springer, Cham (2018). https://doi.org/10.1007/978-3-319-95729-6_10

37. Ishibuchi, H., Imada, R., Setoguchi, Y., Nojima, Y.: How to specify a reference point in hypervolume calculation for fair performance comparison. Evol. Comput. **26**(3), 411–440 (2018)

38. Zheng, T., Chen, C., Yuan, J., Li, B., Ren, K.: PointCloud saliency maps. In: Proceedings of the IEEE/CVF International Conference on Computer Vision, pp. 1598–1606 (2019)

39. Samarati, P., Sweeney, L.: Protecting privacy when disclosing information: k-anonymity and its enforcement through generalization and suppression. J. Am. Med. Inform. Assoc. **15**(5), 627–637 (1998)

40. Wang, T., Zhang, X., Feng, J., Yang, X.: A comprehensive survey on local differential privacy toward data statistics and analysis. Sensors **20**(24), 7030 (2020)

41. Xiao, T., Tsai, Y.H., Sohn, K., Chandraker, M., Yang, M.H.: Adversarial learning of privacy-preserving and task-oriented representations. In: Proceedings of the AAAI Conference on Artificial Intelligence., vol.34, pp. 12434–12441 (2020)

42. Liu, Z., Wu, Z., Gan, C., Zhu, L., Han, S.: DataMix: efficient privacy-preserving edge-cloud inference. In: Vedaldi, A., Bischof, H., Brox, T., Frahm, J.-M. (eds.) ECCV 2020. LNCS, vol. 12356, pp. 578–595. Springer, Cham (2020). https://doi.org/10.1007/978-3-030-58621-8_34

43. McMahan, H.B., Moore, E., Ramage, D., y Arcas, B.A.: Federated learning of deep networks using model averaging. arXiv preprint arXiv:1602.05629 (2016)

44. Gupta, O., Raskar, R.: Distributed learning of deep neural network over multiple agents. J. Netw. Comput. Appl. **116**, 1–8 (2018)

45. Du, J., Li, S., Feng, M., Chen, S.: Dynamic differential-privacy preserving sgd. arXiv preprint arXiv:2111.00173 (2021)

46. Ho, S., Qu, Y., Gu, B., Gao, L., Li, J., Xiang, Y.: DP-GAN: differentially private consecutive data publishing using generative adversarial nets. J. Netw. Comput. Appl. **185**, 103066 (2021)

47. Jordon, J., Yoon, J., Van Der Schaar, M.: Pate-GAN: generating synthetic data with differential privacy guarantees. In: International Conference on Learning Representations. (2018)

48. Liu, Z., Hu, H., Cao, Y., Zhang, Z., Tong, X.: A Closer Look at Local Aggregation Operators in Point Cloud Analysis. In: Vedaldi, A., Bischof, H., Brox, T., Frahm, J.-M. (eds.) ECCV 2020. LNCS, vol. 12368, pp. 326–342. Springer, Cham (2020). https://doi.org/10.1007/978-3-030-58592-1_20

49. Yan, X., Zheng, C., Li, Z., Wang, S., Cui, S.: PointASNL: robust point clouds processing using nonlocal neural networks with adaptive sampling. In: Proceedings of the IEEE/CVF Conference on Computer Vision and Pattern Recognition, pp. 5589–5598 (2020)

50. Bytyqi, Q., Wolpert, N., Schömer, E.: Local-area-learning network: Meaningful local areas for efficient point cloud analysis. arXiv preprint arXiv:2006.07226 (2020)

51. Xu, Q., Sun, X., Wu, C.Y., Wang, P., Neumann, U.: GRID-GCN for fast and scalable point cloud learning. In: Proceedings of the IEEE/CVF Conference on Computer Vision and Pattern Recognition, pp. 5661–5670 (2020)

52. Xiang, T., Zhang, C., Song, Y., Yu, J., Cai, W.: Walk in the cloud: learning curves for point clouds shape analysis. In: Proceedings of the IEEE/CVF International Conference on Computer Vision, pp. 915–924

53. Lin, C., Li, C., Liu, Y., Chen, N., Choi, Y.K., Wang, W.: Point2skeleton: Learning skeletal representations from point clouds. In: Proceedings of the IEEE/CVF Conference on Computer Vision and Pattern Recognition, pp. 4277–4286 (2021)

54. Lang, I., Kotlicki, U., Avidan, S.: Geometric adversarial attacks and defenses on 3D point cloud. In: 2021 International Conference on 3D Vision (3DV) (2021)

55. Yang, J., Zhang, Q., Fang, R., Ni, B., Liu, J., Tian, Q.: Adversarial attack and defense on point sets (2021)

56. Liu, D., Yu, R., Su, H.: Extending adversarial attacks and defenses to deep 3D point cloud classifiers (2019)

57. Lee, K., Chen, Z., Yan, X., Urtasun, R., Yumer, E.: ShapeAdv: generating shape-aware adversarial 3d point clouds. arXiv preprint arXiv:2005.11626 (2020)

58. Dovrat, O., Lang, I., Avidan, S.: Learning to sample. In:: 2019 IEEE/CVF Conference on Computer Vision and Pattern Recognition (CVPR), pp. 2755–2764 (2019)

59. Gupta, A., Ligett, K., McSherry, F., Roth, A., Talwar, K.: Differentially private combinatorial optimization. In: Proceedings of the Twenty-first Annual ACM-SIAM Symposium on Discrete Algorithms, SIAM, pp. 1106–1125 (2010)

60. Feldman, D., Fiat, A., Kaplan, H., Nissim, K.: Private coresets. In: Proceedings of the Forty-First Annual ACM Symposium on Theory of computing, pp. 361–370 (2009)

An Invisible Black-Box Backdoor Attack Through Frequency Domain

Tong Wang[1], Yuan Yao[1(✉)], Feng Xu[1], Shengwei An[2], Hanghang Tong[3],
and Ting Wang[4]

[1] State Key Laboratory for Novel Software Technology,
Nanjing University, Jiangsu, China
mg20330065@smail.nju.edu.cn, {y.yao,xf}@nju.edu.cn
[2] Purdue University, West Lafayette, USA
an93@purdue.edu
[3] University of Illinois Urbana-Champaign, Champaign, USA
htong@illinois.edu
[4] Pennsylvania State University, State College, USA
ting@psu.edu

Abstract. Backdoor attacks have been shown to be a serious threat against deep learning systems such as biometric authentication and autonomous driving. An effective backdoor attack could enforce the model misbehave under certain predefined conditions, i.e., *triggers*, but behave normally otherwise. The triggers of existing attacks are mainly injected in the pixel space, which tend to be visually identifiable at both training and inference stages and detectable by existing defenses. In this paper, we propose a simple but effective and invisible black-box backdoor attack FTROJAN through trojaning the frequency domain. The key intuition is that triggering perturbations in the frequency domain correspond to small pixel-wise perturbations dispersed across the entire image, breaking the underlying assumptions of existing defenses and making the poisoning images visually indistinguishable from clean ones. Extensive experimental evaluations show that FTROJAN is highly effective and the poisoning images retain high perceptual quality. Moreover, we show that FTROJAN can robustly elude or significantly degenerate the performance of existing defenses.

Keywords: Backdoor attack · Black-box attack · Frequency domain · Invisibility

1 Introduction

CNNs are vulnerable to backdoor/trojan attacks [20,34]. Specifically, a typical backdoor attack poisons a small subset of training data with a *trigger*, and

Supplementary Information The online version contains supplementary material available at https://doi.org/10.1007/978-3-031-19778-9_23.

S. Avidan et al. (Eds.): ECCV 2022, LNCS 13673, pp. 396–413, 2022.
https://doi.org/10.1007/978-3-031-19778-9_23

enforces the backdoored model misbehave (e.g., misclassify the test input to a target label) when the trigger is present but behave normally otherwise at inference time. Such attacks can cause serious damages such as deceiving biometric authentication that is based on face recognition or misleading autonomous cars that rely on camera inputs.

An ideal backdoor attack should satisfy the three desiderata of *efficacy*, *specificity*, and *fidelity* from the adversary's perspective [39]. Here, efficacy means that the target CNN model can be successfully misled by the triggers, specificity means that the trained model should perform normally on the benign inputs, and fidelity means the poisoning images should retain the perceptual similarity to the original clean images. The latter two aspects are related to the *stealthiness* of a backdoor attack. That is, if either the trigger is clearly visible or the backdoored model performs relatively poor on the benign inputs, users may easily detect such an anomaly.

(a)   (b)

Fig. 1. The poisoning images of existing backdoor attacks. (a) Poisoning images from BADNET [20], Blend [11], TrojanNN [34], Clean Label [49], Dynamic Backdoor [41], IAB [37], Latent Backdoor [58], and Composite Backdoor [31]. (b) Poisoning images from SIG [7] and REFOOL [35].

Motivation. While various existing backdoor attacks perform relatively well on the efficacy and specificity aspects, they tend to fall short in terms of satisfying the fidelity requirement, i.e., the triggers are visually identifiable (see Fig. 1). The fundamental reason is that existing attacks directly inject or search for triggers in the spatial domain (i.e., pixel space) of an image. In this domain, it is a dilemma to find triggers that are simultaneously recognizable by CNNs and invisible to humans. Figure 1(a) shows the poisoning images from existing backdoor attacks whose triggers are concentrated in a small area, and thus the triggers are visually identifiable to a large extent. In view of this, several work proposes to disperse the trigger to a larger area to make it less visible. Figure 1(b) shows two black-box backdoor attacks on this thread. However, they are still generally detectable by humans (e.g., the wave pattern in the background or the abnormal reflective phenomenon). Recently, several work has successfully created invisible and effective white-box backdoor attacks [17,30,38]. However, they all require the control over the training process with knowledge of the learning model in use, which limits their usages in practice.

Insight and Contribution. In this paper, we propose a simple but effective and invisible black-box backdoor attack FTROJAN through trojaning the frequency domain of images. It opens the door for various future backdoor attacks and defenses. Our key insights are two-fold. First, adding small perturbations in the mid- and high-frequency components can result in poisoning images with high fidelity [45,56]. Second, recent research has provided evidence that frequency-domain triggers, although dispersed throughout the entire image, are still recognizable and learnable by CNNs [52,54,55,59]. Armed with the above insights, we first transform the images from RGB channels to YUV channels as UV channels correspond to chrominance components that are less sensitive to the human visual system (HVS). Next, we divide an image into a set of disjoint blocks and inject the trigger at both mid- or high-frequency components of the UV channels in each block. Through the above design, we can not only maintain the high fidelity of poisoning images, but also disperse the trigger throughout the entire image breaking the underlying assumptions of many existing defenses.

We evaluate our attack in several datasets and tasks including traffic sign recognition, objection classification, and face recognition. The results show that the proposed attack FTROJAN achieves 98.78% attack success rate on average without significantly degrading the classification accuracy on benign inputs (0.56% accuracy decrease on average). Moreover, we compare the fidelity aspect with several existing backdoor attacks and show that the poisoning images by FTROJAN are visually indistinguishable and retain higher perceptual quality. We also evaluate the proposed attack against state-of-the-art backdoor defensing systems including NEURAL CLEANSE [51], ABS [33], STRIP [18], FEBRUUS [16], and NAD [29], as well as adaptive defenses based on anomaly detection and signal smoothing in the frequency domain. The results show that FTROJAN can robustly bypass or significantly degenerate the performance of these defenses.

2   Attack Design

Overview. In the black-box setting of backdoor attacks, the adversary does not have the access or control to the CNN model, and he/she can only access part of the training data [20,41]. Consequently, the key issue of such an attack is to design the triggers. To make the trigger invisible and effective, our FTROJAN consists of the following steps. First, given an input RGB image, we first convert it to YUV channels. The reason is that YUV channels contain the bandwidth for chrominance components (i.e., UV channels) that are less sensitive to the HVS. Second, we transform the UV channels of the image from the spatial domain to the frequency domain via discrete cosine transform (DCT). Here, a small perturbation on the frequency domain may correspond to a large area in the spatial domain. In practice, we divide the images into a set of disjoint *blocks* and perform DCT on each block. Blocks that are too large would make the

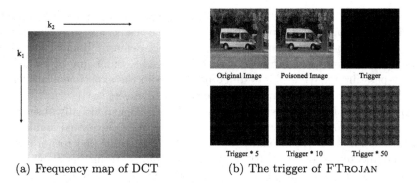

(a) Frequency map of DCT (b) The trigger of FTROJAN

Fig. 2. (a) Frequency map of DCT. Each frequency band is indicated by the 2-D frequency index (k_1, k_2). (b) An illustration of the trigger of FTROJAN. The trigger is scattered over the entire image and invisible to the HVS. To better visualize the trigger, we multiply each pixel value with a given factor in the second row.

computation time-consuming, and too small could cause serious distortion to the image. We set block size to 32×32 in this work, and the frequency map of a block is shown in Fig. 2(a), where we use $index\ (k_1, k_2)$ to indicate each frequency band (the frequency goes from high to low from the upper left to the bottom right).[1] Third, FTROJAN chooses a *frequency band* with a fixed magnitude in the frequency domain to serve as the trigger. We will later discuss different trigger generation strategies related to what frequency is the trigger placed on and what is the magnitude of the trigger. Finally, after the frequency trigger is generated, we apply inverse DCT to obtain the trigger in the spatial domain denoted by YUV channels, and transform the YUV channels back to the RGB channels since CNN models are mainly trained on the RGB color space.

Note that, once the trigger is defined in the frequency domain, it corresponds to fixed pixels (with fixed values) in the spatial domain. Therefore, we can use these pixels as the trigger to superimpose the original pixels to poison an image, without the need of repeatedly computing the above transforms.

Trigger Generation. Trigger generation involves the following two orthogonal dimensions, i.e., *trigger frequency* and *trigger magnitude.*

We first need to decide the specific frequency band that we aim to place the trigger on. On the one hand, placing the trigger at higher frequency would make the poisoning image even less sensitive to human perception, but such triggers could be erased by low-pass filters. On the other hand, triggers at lower frequency are robust against low-pass filters but could cause visual abnormalities if its magnitude is too large. In this work, we choose a more robust *mix mode*, i.e., placing one trigger at mid frequency and one at high frequency.

---

[1] Other design choices such as choosing to poison smaller blocks or fewer blocks are also studied, and the results, included in the supplementary material, show little difference in a wide range.

For trigger magnitude, larger magnitude may be easier for CNNs to learn and also robust against low-pass filters; however, it also comes at a risk of being detected by human perception or existing backdoor defenses. Smaller magnitude may bypass human perception and existing defenses, but being attenuated by the low-pass filters. We evaluate different choices in the experiment and choose a moderate magnitude depending on the specific datasets.

An example of our trigger is shown in Fig. 2(b). We can visually observe that the poisoning images by our method retain very high perceptual similarity to their original images. Additionally, we can observe from the first row of Fig. 2(b) that, the injected trigger is nearly invisible to humans. To further show how the trigger looks like, we multiply each pixel value of the trigger by a factor and show the results in the second row of the figure. We can observe that the trigger is scattered over the entire image. More examples of poisoning images are shown in the supplementary material.

Table 1. Summary of the datasets and the classifiers used in our experiments.

Task	Dataset	# of Training/Test images	# of Labels	Image size	Model architecture
Handwritten digit recognition	MNIST	60,000/10,000	10	$32 \times 32 \times 1$	2 Conv + 2 Dense
Traffic sign recognition	GTSRB	39,209/12630	43	$32 \times 32 \times 3$	6 Conv + 1 Dense
Object classification	CIFAR10	50,000/10,000	10	$32 \times 32 \times 3$	6 Conv + 1 Dense
Object classification	ImageNet	20,567/1,315	16	$224 \times 224 \times 3$	ResNet50
Face recognition	PubFig	5,274/800	60	$224 \times 224 \times 3$	ResNet50

3   Evaluation

3.1   Experimental Setup

Tasks, Datasets, and Models. As summarized in Table 1, we conduct experiments on several benchmark tasks/datasets, including handwritten digit recognition on the MNIST data [27], traffic sign recognition on the GTSRB data [46], object classification on the CIFAR10 data [26] and the ImageNet data [15], and face recognition on the PubFig data [26]. We resize the images, and train different models for these tasks depending on the image size and complexity. For the GTSRB data, we follow standard processing such as histogram equalization in the HSV color space. For the ImageNet data, we randomly sampled 16 labels. For the PubFig data, we use the sampled subset of 60 persons from [35].

Evaluation Metrics. For efficacy and specificity, we measure the *attack success rate (ASR)* and the *accuracy on benign data (BA)*, respectively. For fidelity, it is still an open problem to measure it. In this work, we mainly consider if human eyes are sensitive to the poisoning images and use metrics *peak signal-to-noise ratio (PSNR)* [24], *structural similarity index (SSIM)* [53], and *inception score (IS)* [8,42].

Implementations. For the proposed FTROJAN attack, we implement it with two versions in both PyTorch and Tensorflow 2.0.[2] Our default settings are as follows. For trigger frequency, we place the trigger at frequency bands $(15, 15)$ and $(31, 31)$ where $(15, 15)$ belongs to the mid-frequency component and $(31, 31)$ belongs to the high-frequency component. Based on the size of images, we set the trigger magnitude to 30 for MNIST, CIFAR10, GTSRB, and 50 for ImageNet, PubFig. The injection rate is fixed to 5% for simplicity. We use the Adam optimizer with learning rate 0.0005 for MNIST and GTSRB, and the RMSprop optimizer with learning rate 0.001 for the rest datasets. The batch size is set to 64. In the following, we use FTROJAN to denote the default setting unless otherwise stated. The target label is set to 8 for all the datasets. All the experiments were carried out on a server equipped with 256 GB RAM, one 20-core Intel i9-10900KF CPU at 3.70GHz and one NVIDIA GeForce RTX 3090 GPU.

Table 2. Efficacy and specificity results of FTROJAN variants. All the results are percentiles. For the default FTROJAN (i.e., 'UV+mix' variant), it can achieve 98.78% ASR, while the BA decreases by 0.56% on average.

FTROJAN Variant	MNIST		GTSRB		CIFAR10		ImageNet		PubFig	
	BA	ASR	BA	ASR	BA	ASR	BA	ASR	BA	ASR
No attack	99.40	–	97.20	–	87.12	–	79.60	–	89.50	–
UV+mix	99.36	99.94	96.63	99.25	86.05	99.97	78.63	99.38	88.62	99.83
UV+mid	99.40	99.22	96.91	98.59	86.90	99.90	78.50	99.75	89.13	97.86
UV+high	99.39	99.81	96.63	99.12	86.90	99.90	78.75	99.14	88.25	99.93
YUV+mix	–	–	96.82	98.35	86.76	99.96	79.13	99.38	88.08	99.93
RGB+mix	–	–	97.16	92.05	86.33	95.99	78.70	95.46	89.37	99.25

3.2 Attack Performance

(A) Overall Performance. We first evaluate different trigger generation strategies of the proposed FTROJAN attack. The BA and ASR results are shown in Table 2, and the corresponding fidelity results are included in the supplementary material due to the space limit. For the variants in the table, 'UV', 'YUV', and 'RGB' indicate injected channels of the trigger,[3] and 'mid', 'high', and 'mix' mean the trigger frequencies. Here, 'mix' is our default setting as mentioned above, and frequency bands $(15, 15)$ and $(31, 31)$ are used for 'mid' and 'high', respectively.

We can first observe that all the FTROJAN variants are effective, namely, decreasing little on BA and having a high ASR. For example, on average, the default FTROJAN (i.e., 'UV+mix') can achieve 98.78% ASR, while the BA

---

[2] The code is available at https://github.com/SoftWiser-group/FTrojan.

[3] The MNIST images are gray-scale and have only one channel. We directly inject the trigger into this channel for Table 2.

decreases by only 0.56%. Additionally, comparing different trigger frequencies, we can observe that all the three choices are closely effective and trojaning at high frequency tends to have higher fidelity results in general (based on the fidelity results in the supplementary material).

(B) Performance versus Injection Rate, Trigger Frequency, and Trigger Magnitude. We next evaluate the effectiveness of FTROJAN when the injection rate of poisoning images in training data varies. We increase the injection rate from 0.01% to 10% and show the results in Fig. 3(a) and 3(b). In the following, we mainly report results on GTSRB and CIFAR10 as training on these two datasets is more efficient. We can observe from the figure that BA does not change significantly when the injection rate is in a wide range. Additionally, when the injection rate is no less than 1%, FTROJAN can achieve a high ASR for both datasets. This experiment also shows that different datasets have different sensitivity to the injection rate. For example, injecting 0.1% poisoning images could already achieve a high ASR on CIFAR10.

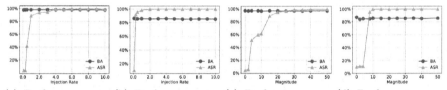

(a) Performance vs. injection rate on GTSRB

(b) Performance vs. injection rate on CIFAR10

(c) Performance vs. trigger magnitude on GTSRB

(d) Performance vs. trigger magnitude on CIFAR10

Fig. 3. Performance vs. injection rate and trigger magnitude. FTROJAN can achieve a high ASR when the injection rate is around 0.1%–1%, and when the frequency magnitude is larger than a certain threshold. We fix the magnitude to 30 for GTSRB and CIFAR10, and fix injection rate to 5% in this work to ensure high ASR.

For trigger frequency, we study different frequency indices while keeping the other settings as default. It is observed that the backdoor attack is effective when the triggers are placed on mid- and high-frequency components. In this work, we choose a mix mode by default, i.e., triggering one mid-frequency index and one high-frequency index. The results are included in the supplementary material.

We next explore the effectiveness of FTROJAN w.r.t. the trigger magnitude. We vary the trigger magnitude from 1 to 50, and show the results on GTSRB and CIFAR10 in Fig. 3(c) and 3(d). We can observe that as long as the frequency magnitude is larger than a certain threshold, our backdoor attack will succeed with a high ASR. Based on our experiments, the poisoning images will not cause identifiable visual abnormalities when the trigger magnitude is no more than 100 in mid- and high-frequency components (e.g., see the images in the supplementary material). To ensure high ASR and robustness against filtering methods such as Gaussian filters, we set trigger magnitude to 30–50 for different datasets based on the size of the images.

(C) Comparisons with Existing Attacks. Here, we compare FTROJAN with existing backdoor attacks including BADNET [20], SIG [7], REFOOL [35], and IAB [37]. For BADNET, we implement it ourselves and add a 4 × 4 white block in the lower right corner as the trigger. For REFOOL, we use the implementation provided by the authors [6]. For SIG, we use the public implementation in the NAD repository [4]. For IAB, we also use its implementation from the authors [3]. Since REFOOL does not provide its implementations on MNIST and IAB does not provide its implementations on ImageNet and PubFig, we still report the results on GTSRB and CIFAR10 as shown in Table 3.

We can first observe from the table that our FTROJAN attack achieves higher ASR scores than the competitors on both datasets. The BA scores of FTROJAN are also very close to those of the clean model. Second, FTROJAN outperforms the competitors for all the three fidelity metrics. Together with the visual results in Fig. 1, we can conclude that the proposed FTROJAN attack is better than the competitors in the fidelity aspect.

Table 3. Comparison results with existing attacks. All the BA and ASR results are percentiles. Larger PSNR and SSIM, and smaller IS are better. FTROJAN achieves higher ASR than the competitors on both datasets, and it outperforms the competitors for all the three fidelity metrics. Best results are in bold.

Attack method	GTSRB					CIFAR10				
	BA	ASR	PSNR	SSIM	IS	BA	ASR	PSNR	SSIM	IS
No attack	97.20	–	INF	1.000	0.000	87.12	–	INF	1.000	0.000
BADNET	96.51	84.98	24.9	0.974	0.090	86.01	94.80	23.8	0.941	0.149
SIG	96.49	92.56	25.3	0.973	1.353	85.70	95.76	25.2	0.871	1.905
REFOOL	96.41	56.52	19.1	0.923	1.035	85.87	73.20	17.3	0.769	0.910
IAB	92.12	64.84	23.8	0.956	0.226	85.10	79.70	13.2	0.829	2.240
FTROJAN	**96.63**	**99.25**	**40.9**	**0.995**	**0.017**	**86.05**	**99.97**	**40.9**	**0.995**	**0.135**

Table 4. Defense results of NEURAL CLEANSE. FTROJAN can bypass NEURAL CLEANSE (i.e., the abnormal index is smaller than 2).

Dataset	Abnormal index	
	Clean	Backdoored
GTSRB	1.33	1.62
CIFAR10	1.25	1.85

In summary, the above results show that: 1) in the efficacy and specificity aspects, the proposed FTROJAN achieves a high attack success rate without significantly degrading the classification accuracy on benign inputs; and 2) in the fidelity aspects, FTROJAN produces images with higher fidelity and perceptual quality under three evaluation metrics compared to the existing backdoor attacks.

3.3 Evaluations Against Defenses

NEURAL CLEANSE. NEURAL CLEANSE [51] detects triggers via searching for a small region with a fixed trigger pattern. The basic idea is that, no matter what the input is, the existence of the trigger pattern will lead the model to predict a fixed label. Then, it compares the norms of each identified pattern to determine the abnormal index of the classifier. Abnormal index larger than 2 is considered to be a backdoored model. We use the NEURAL CLEANSE implementation provided by the authors [5], and the detection results are shown in Table 4. We can first observe that FTROJAN can bypass NEURAL CLEANSE on GTSRB and CIFAR10. The reason is that, based on the design nature, NEURAL CLEANSE is effective when the trigger is relatively small and fixed. However, the injected trigger of FTROJAN is dispersed over the entire image, and thus makes NEURAL CLEANSE less effective in such cases.

Table 5. Defense results of ABS. Small REASR values mean that FTROJAN successfully bypass the detection of ABS.

Dataset	REASR (Feature Space)		REASR (Pixel space)	
	Clean	Backdoored	Clean	Backdoored
CIFAR10	0	0	0	0

Table 6. Defense results of STRIP. Most of the poisoned images by FTROJAN can bypass the detection of STRIP.

Dataset	False rejection rate	False acceptance rate
GTSRB	4.10%	98.00%
CIFAR10	10.95%	77.40%

ABS. ABS [33] is a defense technique that scans through each neuron to see if its stimulation substantially and unconditionally increases the prediction probability of a particular label. It then reverses the trigger based on the identified neurons, and uses the trigger to attack benign inputs. If the ASR of the reversed trigger (i.e., REASR) is high, ABS reports the model as being backdoored. We use the implementation of ABS provided by the authors [1], which provides a binary executable file to run on CIFAR10. Thus, we only report the results on CIFAR10 in Table 5. We can observe that ABS cannot detect the backdoored model by our FTROJAN attack. The probable reason is as follows. ABS is effective in terms of identifying one neuron or a few neurons that are responsible for a target label. However, the injected trigger by FTROJAN scatters over the entire image in the spatial domain, which may affect a large number of neurons.

STRIP. STRIP [18] is an online inspection method working at inference stage. Its basic idea is that, if a given test image contains a trigger, superimposing the test image with clean images would result in a relatively lower classification entropy. Then, STRIP uses the entropy of the superimposed image to decide whether the test image contains a trigger. We apply STRIP on the test inputs and the results are shown in Table 6. We implement STRIP ourselves. The key parameter of STRIP is the entropy boundary, and we search it within our best efforts. The boundary is set to 0.133 for GTSRB and 0.30 for CIFAR10. In the table, we report the false rejection rate (the probability that a benign input is regarded as a poisoning input) and false acceptance rate (the probability that a poisoning image is regarded as a benign input) as suggested by STRIP. We can observe that STRIP yields a high false acceptance rate on both datasets, meaning that most of the poisoning images by FTROJAN can bypass the detection of STRIP. For example, on CIFAR10 data, over three quarters of the poisoning images can bypass STRIP detection, and over 10% clean images are misclassified as poisoning images. The reason for the ineffectiveness of STRIP is that, when multiple images are superimposed in the spatial domain, the frequency domain of the superimposed image would change dramatically compared to the original test input. Consequently, the trigger would be ineffective after superimposition and thus cannot be detected by STRIP.

Table 7. Defense results of FEBRUUS. All the results are percentiles. FTROJAN significantly degenerates FEBRUUS's effectiveness. After applying FEBRUUS, although the ASR decreases by 15–25%, the BA decreases up to 75%.

Dataset	Before FEBRUUS		After FEBRUUS	
	BA	ASR	BA	ASR
GTSRB	97.56	88.62	22.15	72.82
CIFAR10	86.42	99.55	10.60	76.73

Table 8. Defense results of NAD. All the results are percentiles. NAD is ineffective in terms of defending against FTROJAN. The ASR is still high after applying NAD.

Dataset	Before NAD		After NAD	
	BA	ASR	BA	ASR
GTSRB	96.47	98.46	96.33	98.15
CIFAR10	81.12	99.80	78.16	99.41

FEBRUUS. With the assumption that triggers are usually not in the center part of an image, FEBRUUS [16] first identifies and removes the suspicious area in the image that contributes most to the label prediction using GradCAM [43], and then uses GAN to restore the removed area. We use the implementation of FEBRUUS provided by the authors [2], and keep the default parameter settings. The results are shown in Table 7. It can be observed that after the images are sent to FEBRUUS for sanitization, although the ASR decreases by 15–25%, the BA drops significantly by up to 75%. The reason that FEBRUUS's performance significantly degenerates against our FTROJAN attack is as follows. The trigger of FTROJAN is placed on the entire image in the spatial domain, making it difficult to spot the suspicious area (see Fig. 4 for examples). Additionally, when a relatively large area is removed (which is often the case of our attack), the restored image would introduce serious distortions, and thus make the training on such images less effective on the benign inputs.

NAD. NAD [29] utilizes a teacher network trained on a small set of clean data to guide the fine-tuning of the backdoored student network, so as to erase the effect of triggers. The teacher network shares the same architecture with the student network. During knowledge transfer from the teacher network to the student network, NAD requires the alignment of the intermediate-layer's attention. We use the implementation provided by the authors [4] and keep the default parameters. The results are shown in Table 8.[4] It can be observed from the table that after applying NAD, the ASR is still very high meaning that NAD is ineffective in terms of erasing the impact of our attack. The possible reason is that the parameters of the backdoored model do not deviate significantly from those in the clean model, as our triggers are very small (in terms of pixel values) and dispersed across the entire image. Therefore, knowledge transferring from clean model may not help in such cases.

clean   poisoning   clean   poisoning

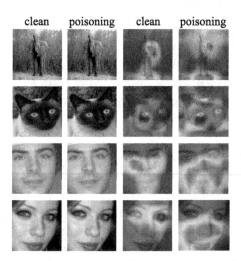

Fig. 4. The responsible region for prediction by GradCAM [43]. Our attack does not introduce unusual regions as existing spatial triggers.

Visual Capture by GradCAM. We next illustrate the reason of the ineffectiveness of existing defenses. Specifically, we use GradCAM [43] to capture

---

[4] Here, for better reproducibility of the results, we use the same model in the NAD repository instead of our CNN models. Therefore, the BA scores in the table is slightly lower than the previous results.

the influential area in an image that is responsible for the prediction, and some examples are shown in Fig. 4. Warmer colors indicate more influence. The first two and last two images are selected from ImageNet and PubFig, respectively. We can observe that the warm areas of the poisoning images do not contain unusual regions as existing spatial triggers (see the supplementary material for some examples). Additionally, the warm areas of poisoning images are similar to that of clean images, but generally covering a relatively larger area. This breaks the underlying assumptions of existing defenses that rely on identifying a small, unusual region that significantly determines the prediction results.

Adaptive Defenses. Finally, we evaluate the effectiveness of FTROJAN against adaptive defenses that directly operate on the frequency domain. In particular, we consider two adaptive defenses, i.e., *anomaly detection* and *signal smoothing* in the frequency domain. For the former, we evaluate whether the attack can be identified by applying existing anomaly detection methods on the images, and the results show that such defenses are ineffective (see the supplementary material for detailed results). For the latter, we consider three filters, i.e., Gaussian filter, Wiener filter, and BM3D [14], which are widely used in image denoising and restoration. We apply these filters to the training data before feeding them to the model. We evaluate these filters in a wide range of parameters and observe similar results. The results are shown in Table 9. It is observed that although these filters are effective in terms of lowering the ASR, they also significantly degenerate the BA performance (e.g., from 4.33% to 33.91% absolute decrease). For Gaussian filter and Wiener filter, the minimum window size is 3×3, and larger w leads to stronger smoothing. We observe that even with the minimum window size, the BA already significantly decreases (e.g., 17.40% and 16.88% absolute decreases for Gaussian filter and Wiener filter on CIFAR10). For BM3D, we vary the noise standard deviation parameter σ, with larger σ indicating stronger smoothing. It is observed that even with $\sigma = 0.5$, the BA still significantly decreases. Overall, these results imply a fundamental accuracy-robustness trade-off for the above defenders.

Table 9. Defense results of Gaussian filter, Wiener filter, and BM3D. Although these filters lower the ASR of FTROJAN, they also significantly degenerate the BA performance.

Filters and parameters	GTSRB			CIFAR10		
	BA	ASR	BA decrease	BA	ASR	BA decrease
Original	97.20	–	–	87.12	–	–
Gaussian filter ($w = (3, 3)$)	90.81	8.45	–6.39	69.72	26.38	–17.40
Gaussian filter ($w = (5, 5)$)	89.20	6.40	–8.00	53.21	19.48	–33.91
Wiener filter ($w = (3, 3)$)	92.87	3.54	–4.33	70.24	9.16	–16.88
Wiener filter ($w = (5, 5)$)	89.79	3.08	–7.41	61.04	5.84	–26.08
BM3D ($\sigma = 0.5$)	92.31	4.42	–4.89	82.34	15.84	–4.78
BM3D ($\sigma = 1.0$)	91.53	10.82	–5.67	81.40	19.33	–5.72

In summary, the above results show that our FTROJAN *attack can bypass or significantly degenerate the performance of the state-of-the-art defenses, as well as anomaly detection and signal smoothing techniques in the frequency domain. These results indicate that new defending techniques are still in demand to protect against our* FTROJAN *attacks.*

4   Related Work

Backdoor Attacks. Backdoor attacks are introduced by [11,20], where pre-defined triggers are injected into training data so that the trained model would mis-predict the backdoored instances/images as a target label. Later, researchers pay more attention to robust backdoor attacks that could reduce the effectiveness of existing backdoor defenses [22,31,37,40,41,44,58]. For example, Yao et al. [58] generate triggers whose information is stored in the early internal layers. Salem et al. [41] and Eguyen et al. [37] propose dynamic backdoor attacks to generate dynamic triggers conditioned on the input images. For the above backdoor attacks, although their evaluations show that they can bypass some defenses such as NEURAL CLEANSE [51] and STRIP [18], the generated triggers are still visually identifiable to a large extent.

Later, several researchers propose to make the triggers less visible by dispersing the trigger to a much larger area of the image. For example, SIG [7] transfers the images with superimpose signals (e.g., a ramp signal or a sinusoidal signal), and triggers are contained in the varying background. REFOOL [35] defines triggers resembling to the natural reflection phenomenon, and shows that it is resistant to several defenses including Fine-pruning [32] and NEURAL CLEANSE [51]. Although these attacks follow the black-box setting, the triggers are still visually detectable. Recent work [17,28,30,38] has successfully created invisible and effective backdoor attacks. For example, Doan et al. [17] jointly learn the stealthy trigger and the optimal classifier under a constrained optimization framework. Li et al. [30] borrow the idea from image steganography [61] by hiding an attacker-specified string into images. However, they all require the control over the training process with knowledge of the learning model in use. Different from the above work, we propose the first black-box backdoor attack that is both effective and invisible through trojaning in the frequency domain of images.

There also exist backdoor attacks that directly inject triggers into the trained networks without accessing the training data [13,34,39,47]. In these attacks, the triggers can be inverted from the trained networks and then injected into the test images. For example, TrojanNN [34] identifies triggers that could maximize the activations of certain specific neurons, and retrains the model with generated images (both with and without triggers). Pang et al. [39] further study the connections between adversarial attacks and model poisoning attacks, leading to optimized version of TrojanNN against existing defenses. However, the generated triggers of these attacks are still visually identifiable.

Defenses Against Backdoor Attacks. Existing backdoor defenses can be roughly divided into three categories, i.e., *model inspection, trigger detection or* *erasion*, and *model tuning*. Defenses in the first category focus on inspecting whether a given DNN has been backdoored [9, 10, 21, 23, 25, 33, 51]. For example, Neural Cleanse [51] propose to identify the shortcuts (small perturbations) across different labels to decide whether a model is backdoored or not. If the model is backdoored, it further reverts the trigger from the identified perturbations, and propose mitigate the attacks based on the reverted trigger. DeepInspect [10] is similar to Neural Cleanse except that it does not require the access to training data and the model parameters. Instead, DeepInspect infers the training data via model inversion [57]. ABS [33] first identifies the neurons that substantially maximize the activation of a particular label, and then examines whether these neurons lead to a trigger.

Assuming that the given DNN has been backdoored, defenses in the second category mainly aim to detect whether an instance has been corrupted or how to erase the triggers in the input images [12, 16, 18, 36, 48, 50]. For example, Tran et al. [48] find that corrupted instances usually have a signature in the spectrum of the covariance of their features, and train a classify to detect such instances. STRIP [18] propose to add perturbations on the test image to check if it has a trigger, based on the intuition that trojaned images usually make the consistent prediction (i.e., the target label) even when various perturbations are added. Februus [16] first deletes the influential region in an image identified by GradCAM [43], and then restores the image via GAN.

In the third category, the defenses still assume that the model has been backdoored and propose to directly mitigate the effect of the backdoor attacks by tuning the models [29, 32, 60]. For example, Fine-pruning [32] prunes and fine-tunes the neurons that are potentially responsible for the backdoor attacks; however, it was observed that Fine-pruning could bring down the overall accuracy of the given model. Zhao et al. [60] introduce mode connectivity [19] into backdoor mitigation, and found that the middle range of a path (in the loss landscapes) connecting two backdoored models provides robustness. NAD [29] uses a teacher network trained on clean data to erase the triggers' effect in the backdoored student network via knowledge distillation.

5   Conclusion and Discussion

In this paper, we propose a black-box, frequency-domain backdoor attack FTRO-JAN. We explore the design space and show that trojaning at UV channels, and injecting mid- and high-frequency triggers in each block with medium magnitude can achieve high attack success rate without degrading the prediction accuracy on benign inputs. The poisoning images of FTROJAN are also of higher perceptual quality compared with several existing backdoor attacks. In terms of defending against our backdoor attacks, we show that the proposed FTROJAN can bypass or significantly degenerate the performance of existing defenses and adaptive defenses.

Currently, we evaluate our attack against CNNs only. How can it be extended to other models and how does it perform on other learning tasks such as natural language processing tasks are unclear. We plan to explore such directions in future work. To defend against the proposed attacks, we also plan to design more robust defenses that go beyond the current assumption of backdoor attacks in the spatial domain. For example, one possible direction is to explore the subtle behavior difference between poisoning samples and benign samples.

Acknowledgement. We would like to thank Yingqi Liu for help reproducing the evaluation of ABS defense and providing comments. This work is supported by the National Natural Science Foundation of China (No. 62025202), and the Collaborative Innovation Center of Novel Software Technology and Industrialization. Hanghang Tong is partially supported by NSF (1947135, 2134079, and 1939725). Ting Wang is partially supported by the National Science Foundation under Grant No. 1953893, 1951729, and 2119331.

References

1. Abs implementation. https://github.com/naiyeleo/ABS
2. Februus implementation. https://github.com/AdelaideAuto-IDLab/Februus
3. Inputaware backdoor implementation. https://github.com/VinAIResearch/input-aware-backdoor-attack-release
4. Nad implementation. https://github.com/bboylyg/NAD
5. Neural cleanse implementation. https://github.com/bolunwang/backdoor
6. Refool implementation. https://github.com/DreamtaleCore/Refool
7. Barni, M., Kallas, K., Tondi, B.: A new backdoor attack in CNNs by training set corruption without label poisoning. In: 2019 IEEE International Conference on Image Processing (ICIP), pp. 101–105. IEEE (2019)
8. Barratt, S., Sharma, R.: A note on the inception score. arXiv preprint arXiv:1801.01973 (2018)
9. Chen, B., et al.: Detecting backdoor attacks on deep neural networks by activation clustering. In: Workshop on Artificial Intelligence Safety, Co-Located with the Thirty-Third AAAI Conference on Artificial Intelligence (2019)
10. Chen, H., Fu, C., Zhao, J., Koushanfar, F.: DeepInspect: a black-box trojan detection and mitigation framework for deep neural networks. In: Proceedings of the Twenty-Eighth International Joint Conference on Artificial Intelligence (IJCAI) (2019)
11. Chen, X., Liu, C., Li, B., Lu, K., Song, D.: Targeted backdoor attacks on deep learning systems using data poisoning. arXiv preprint arXiv:1712.05526 (2017)
12. Cohen, J., Rosenfeld, E., Kolter, Z.: Certified adversarial robustness via randomized smoothing. In: International Conference on Machine Learning (ICML), pp. 1310–1320. PMLR (2019)
13. Costales, R., Mao, C., Norwitz, R., Kim, B., Yang, J.: Live trojan attacks on deep neural networks. In: Proceedings of the IEEE/CVF Conference on Computer Vision and Pattern Recognition Workshops, pp. 796–797 (2020)
14. Dabov, K., Foi, A., Katkovnik, V., Egiazarian, K.: Image denoising by sparse 3-d transform-domain collaborative filtering. IEEE Trans. Image Process. **16**(8), 2080–2095 (2007)
15. Deng, J., Dong, W., Socher, R., Li, L.J., Li, K., Fei-Fei, L.: ImageNet: a large-scale hierarchical image database. In: 2009 IEEE Conference on Computer Vision and Pattern Recognition (CVPR), pp. 248–255. IEEE (2009)

16. Doan, B.G., Abbasnejad, E., Ranasinghe, D.C.: Februus: input purification defense against trojan attacks on deep neural network systems. In: Proceedings of the Annual Computer Security Applications Conference (ACSAC), pp. 897–912 (2020)
17. Doan, K., Lao, Y., Zhao, W., Li, P.: Lira: learnable, imperceptible and robust backdoor attacks. In: Proceedings of the IEEE/CVF International Conference on Computer Vision (ICCV), pp. 11966–11976 (2021)
18. Gao, Y., Xu, C., Wang, D., Chen, S., Ranasinghe, D.C., Nepal, S.: Strip: a defence against trojan attacks on deep neural networks. In: Proceedings of the 35th Annual Computer Security Applications Conference (ACSAC), pp. 113–125 (2019)
19. Garipov, T., Izmailov, P., Podoprikhin, D., Vetrov, D., Wilson, A.G.: Loss surfaces, mode connectivity, and fast ensembling of DNNs. In: Proceedings of the 32nd International Conference on Neural Information Processing Systems (NeurIPS), pp. 8803–8812 (2018)
20. Gu, T., Dolan-Gavitt, B., Garg, S.: BadNets: identifying vulnerabilities in the machine learning model supply chain. arXiv preprint arXiv:1708.06733 (2017)
21. Guo, W., Wang, L., Xing, X., Du, M., Song, D.: Tabor: a highly accurate approach to inspecting and restoring trojan backdoors in AI systems. arXiv preprint arXiv:1908.01763 (2019)
22. He, Y., Shen, Z., Xia, C., Hua, J., Tong, W., Zhong, S.: Raba: a robust avatar backdoor attack on deep neural network. arXiv preprint arXiv:2104.01026 (2021)
23. Huang, S., Peng, W., Jia, Z., Tu, Z.: One-pixel signature: characterizing CNN models for backdoor detection. In: Vedaldi, A., Bischof, H., Brox, T., Frahm, J.-M. (eds.) ECCV 2020. LNCS, vol. 12372, pp. 326–341. Springer, Cham (2020). https://doi.org/10.1007/978-3-030-58583-9_20
24. Huynh-Thu, Q., Ghanbari, M.: Scope of validity of PSNR in image/video quality assessment. Electron. Lett. **44**(13), 800–801 (2008)
25. Kolouri, S., Saha, A., Pirsiavash, H., Hoffmann, H.: Universal litmus patterns: revealing backdoor attacks in CNNs. In: Proceedings of the IEEE/CVF Conference on Computer Vision and Pattern Recognition (CVPR), pp. 301–310 (2020)
26. Krizhevsky, A., Hinton, G., et al.: Learning multiple layers of features from tiny images (2009)
27. LeCun, Y., Bottou, L., Bengio, Y., Haffner, P.: Gradient-based learning applied to document recognition. Proc. IEEE **86**(11), 2278–2324 (1998)
28. Li, S., Xue, M., Zhao, B., Zhu, H., Zhang, X.: Invisible backdoor attacks on deep neural networks via steganography and regularization. IEEE Trans. Dependable Secure Comput. **18**(5), 2088–2105 (2020)
29. Li, Y., Koren, N., Lyu, L., Lyu, X., Li, B., Ma, X.: Neural attention distillation: Erasing backdoor triggers from deep neural networks. In: Proceedings of the International Conference on Learning Representations (ICLR) (2021)
30. Li, Y., Li, Y., Wu, B., Li, L., He, R., Lyu, S.: Invisible backdoor attack with sample-specific triggers. In: Proceedings of the IEEE/CVF International Conference on Computer Vision (ICCV), pp. 16463–16472 (2021)
31. Lin, J., Xu, L., Liu, Y., Zhang, X.: Composite backdoor attack for deep neural network by mixing existing benign features. In: Proceedings of the ACM SIGSAC Conference on Computer and Communications Security (CCS), pp. 113–131 (2020)
32. Liu, K., Dolan-Gavitt, B., Garg, S.: Fine-pruning: defending against backdooring attacks on deep neural networks. In: Bailey, M., Holz, T., Stamatogiannakis, M., Ioannidis, S. (eds.) RAID 2018. LNCS, vol. 11050, pp. 273–294. Springer, Cham (2018). https://doi.org/10.1007/978-3-030-00470-5_13

33. Liu, Y., Lee, W.C., Tao, G., Ma, S., Aafer, Y., Zhang, X.: Abs: scanning neural networks for back-doors by artificial brain stimulation. In: Proceedings of the 2019 ACM SIGSAC Conference on Computer and Communications Security (CCS), pp. 1265–1282 (2019)

34. Liu, Y., et al.: Trojaning attack on neural networks. In: Annual Network and Distributed System Security Symposium (NDSS) (2018)

35. Liu, Y., Ma, X., Bailey, J., Lu, F.: Reflection backdoor: a natural backdoor attack on deep neural networks. In: Vedaldi, A., Bischof, H., Brox, T., Frahm, J.-M. (eds.) ECCV 2020. LNCS, vol. 12355, pp. 182–199. Springer, Cham (2020). https://doi.org/10.1007/978-3-030-58607-2_11

36. Ma, S., Liu, Y.: NIC: detecting adversarial samples with neural network invariant checking. In: Proceedings of the 26th Network and Distributed System Security Symposium (NDSS 2019) (2019)

37. Nguyen, T.A., Tran, A.: Input-aware dynamic backdoor attack. In: Proceedings of the Annual Conference on Neural Information Processing Systems (NeurIPS) (2020)

38. Nguyen, T.A., Tran, A.T.: Wanet-imperceptible warping-based backdoor attack. In: International Conference on Learning Representations (ICLR) (2021)

39. Pang, R., et al.: A tale of evil twins: adversarial inputs versus poisoned models. In: Proceedings of the 2020 ACM SIGSAC Conference on Computer and Communications Security (CCS). pp. 85–99 (2020)

40. Saha, A., Subramanya, A., Pirsiavash, H.: Hidden trigger backdoor attacks. In: Proceedings of the AAAI Conference on Artificial Intelligence (AAAI), pp. 11957–11965 (2020)

41. Salem, A., Wen, R., Backes, M., Ma, S., Zhang, Y.: Dynamic backdoor attacks against machine learning models. arXiv preprint arXiv:2003.03675 (2020)

42. Salimans, T., Goodfellow, I., Zaremba, W., Cheung, V., Radford, A., Chen, X.: Improved techniques for training GANs. In: Proceedings of the 30th International Conference on Neural Information Processing Systems (NeurIPS), pp. 2234–2242 (2016)

43. Selvaraju, R.R., Cogswell, M., Das, A., Vedantam, R., Parikh, D., Batra, D.: Gradcam: Visual explanations from deep networks via gradient-based localization. In: Proceedings of the IEEE international conference on computer vision (ICCV). pp. 618–626 (2017)

44. Shokri, R., et al.: Bypassing backdoor detection algorithms in deep learning. In: 2020 IEEE European Symposium on Security and Privacy (EuroS&P), pp. 175–183. IEEE (2020)

45. Sonka, M., Hlavac, V., Boyle, R.: Image processing, analysis, and machine vision. Cengage Learning (2014)

46. Stallkamp, J., Schlipsing, M., Salmen, J., Igel, C.: The German traffic sign recognition benchmark: a multi-class classification competition. In: The 2011 International Joint Conference on Neural Networks (IJCNN), pp. 1453–1460. IEEE (2011)

47. Tang, R., Du, M., Liu, N., Yang, F., Hu, X.: An embarrassingly simple approach for trojan attack in deep neural networks. In: Proceedings of the 26th ACM SIGKDD International Conference on Knowledge Discovery & Data Mining (KDD), pp. 218–228 (2020)

48. Tran, B., Li, J., Madry, A.: Spectral signatures in backdoor attacks. In: Proceedings of the 32nd International Conference on Neural Information Processing Systems (NeurIPS), pp. 8011–8021 (2018)

49. Turner, A., Tsipras, D., Madry, A.: Clean-label backdoor attacks (2018)

50. Udeshi, S., Peng, S., Woo, G., Loh, L., Rawshan, L., Chattopadhyay, S.: Model agnostic defence against backdoor attacks in machine learning. arXiv preprint arXiv:1908.02203 (2019)

51. Wang, B., et al.: Neural cleanse: Identifying and mitigating backdoor attacks in neural networks. In: 2019 IEEE Symposium on Security and Privacy (SP), pp. 707–723. IEEE (2019)

52. Wang, H., Wu, X., Huang, Z., Xing, E.P.: High-frequency component helps explain the generalization of convolutional neural networks. In: Proceedings of the IEEE/CVF Conference on Computer Vision and Pattern Recognition (CVPR), pp. 8684–8694 (2020)

53. Wang, Z., Bovik, A.C., Sheikh, H.R., Simoncelli, E.P.: Image quality assessment: from error visibility to structural similarity. IEEE Trans. Image Process. **13**(4), 600–612 (2004)

54. Xu, Z.Q.J., Zhang, Y., Luo, T., Xiao, Y., Ma, Z.: Frequency principle: fourier analysis sheds light on deep neural networks. arXiv preprint arXiv:1901.06523 (2019)

55. Xu, Z.-Q.J., Zhang, Y., Xiao, Y.: Training behavior of deep neural network in frequency domain. In: Gedeon, T., Wong, K.W., Lee, M. (eds.) ICONIP 2019. LNCS, vol. 11953, pp. 264–274. Springer, Cham (2019). https://doi.org/10.1007/978-3-030-36708-4_22

56. Yamaguchi, S., et al.: High-fidelity facial reflectance and geometry inference from an unconstrained image. ACM Trans. Graph. (TOG) **37**(4), 1–14 (2018)

57. Yang, Z., Zhang, J., Chang, E.C., Liang, Z.: Neural network inversion in adversarial setting via background knowledge alignment. In: Proceedings of the 2019 ACM SIGSAC Conference on Computer and Communications Security (CCS), pp. 225–240 (2019)

58. Yao, Y., Li, H., Zheng, H., Zhao, B.Y.: Latent backdoor attacks on deep neural networks. In: Proceedings of the 2019 ACM SIGSAC Conference on Computer and Communications Security (CCS), pp. 2041–2055 (2019)

59. Yin, D., Lopes, R.G., Shlens, J., Cubuk, E.D., Gilmer, J.: A fourier perspective on model robustness in computer vision. In: Annual Conference on Neural Information Processing Systems (NeurIPS), pp. 13255–13265 (2019)

60. Zhao, P., Chen, P.Y., Das, P., Ramamurthy, K.N., Lin, X.: Bridging mode connectivity in loss landscapes and adversarial robustness. In: Proceedings of the International Conference on Learning Representations (ICLR) (2020)

61. Zhu, J., Kaplan, R., Johnson, J., Fei-Fei, L.: Hidden: hiding data with deep networks. In: Proceedings of the European conference on computer vision (ECCV), pp. 657–672 (2018)

FairGRAPE: Fairness-Aware GRAdient Pruning mEthod for Face Attribute Classification

Xiaofeng Lin⬤, Seungbae Kim⬤, and Jungseock Joo$^{(\boxtimes)}$⬤

University of California, Los Angeles, Los Angeles, CA 90024, USA
bernardo1998@g.ucla.edu, sbkim@cs.ucla.edu, jjoo@comm.ucla.edu

Abstract. Existing pruning techniques preserve deep neural networks' overall ability to make correct predictions but could also amplify hidden biases during the compression process. We propose a novel pruning method, Fairness-aware GRAdient Pruning mEthod (FairGRAPE), that minimizes the disproportionate impacts of pruning on different subgroups. Our method calculates the per-group importance of each model weight and selects a subset of weights that maintain the relative between-group total importance in pruning. The proposed method then prunes network edges with small importance values and repeats the procedure by updating importance values. We demonstrate the effectiveness of our method on four different datasets, FairFace, UTKFace, CelebA, and ImageNet, for the tasks of face attribute classification where our method reduces the disparity in performance degradation by up to 90% compared to the state-of-the-art pruning algorithms. Our method is substantially more effective in a setting with a high pruning rate (99%). The code and dataset used in the experiments are available at https://github.com/Bernardo1998/FairGRAPE

1 Introduction

Deep neural networks (DNNs) are widely used in applications running on mobile or wearable devices where computational resources are limited [62]. A common strategy to improve the inference efficiency of deep models in such environments is model compression by pruning and removing insignificant nodes or connections between nodes, resulting in sparser networks than the original ones [4,13,14, 19,34,50]. These methods have been known to reduce the computational cost significantly with almost negligible loss in prediction accuracy [7].

Despite the prevalence of model compression, recent studies have also reported that compressed models may suffer from hidden biases, *i.e.* accuracy disparity, more severely than the original models [3,25,26]. The pruned models

---

Supplementary Information The online version contains supplementary material available at https://doi.org/10.1007/978-3-031-19778-9_24.

S. Avidan et al. (Eds.): ECCV 2022, LNCS 13673, pp. 414–432, 2022.
https://doi.org/10.1007/978-3-031-19778-9_24

may be accurate overall or on some sub-groups (*e.g.* White males), while resulting more severe performance decrease from the original model on specific sub-groups. This bias is particularly problematic for model pruning methods, which attempt to identify and remove insignificant parameters. The parameter-wise significance considered in such methods is estimated from in-the-wild datasets, which are typically unbalanced and biased [30,51]. The societal impact of this bias is also huge because the compressed models are commonly used in consumer devices for daily use such as mobile phones and personal assistant devices.

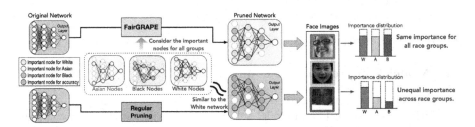

Fig. 1. Illustration of our proposed model compression method for face attribute classification. Since the compressed model pruned by a regular pruning method shows disparity results over different groups, our proposed pruning method aims to fairly treat all groups by preserving important nodes for sensitive attributes (*e.g.* race, gender) in networks.

To address this critical issue, we propose a novel model pruning method, Fairness-aware GRAdient Pruning mEthod – **FairGRAPE**. Our method aims at preserving per-group accuracy as well as overall accuracy in classification tasks. Figure 1 illustrates the fundamental idea of our proposed method. Existing pruning methods disregard demographic groupings and prune the nodes with the smallest weights to preserve the model's overall accuracy. However, some nodes may be critical only for a sub-population underrepresented in the dataset and consequently pruned, leading to a biased compressed model. In contrast, our method considers each node's importance to each sub-group separately so that it can retain important features for all groups.

Specifically, our method computes the group-wise importance of each parameter to get the distribution of the total importance of each group in a model. It then iteratively selects network edges that most closely maintain both the magnitude and share of importance for each group. By selecting such edges, our method equalizes the importance loss across groups, reducing performance disparity.

To evaluate the effectiveness of our method, we conduct extensive experiments on the face attribute classification tasks where demographic labels are readily available. We use four popular face datasets, FairFace [30], UTKFace [63], CelebA [38], and the person subtree in the ImageNet [56]. The experimental results show that FairGRAPE not only preserves the overall classification accuracy but also minimizes the performance gap between sub-groups after pruning, compared to other state-of-the-art pruning methods. We summarize our contributions as follows.

- We show that existing pruning methods disproportionately prune important features for different demographic groups, leading to a more considerable accuracy disparity in the compressed model than in the original model.
- We propose a novel, simple, and generally applicable pruning method that maintains the layer-wise distribution of group importance.
- We evaluate our method on four large-scale face datasets compared to four widely used pruning methods.

2   Related Work

2.1   Model Compression via Pruning

Compression of deep models involves various methods to reduce computation cost without significant loss in model performance. Major categories of compression techniques include Parameter pruning [13,20]; Parameter quantification [19]; Lower-rank factorization [47]; knowledge distillation [24]. In this paper, we focus on examining the first one: parameter pruning, which reduces the number of weights associated with nodes or edges in a network.

Prior research in pruning has focused on the following aspects: how to maintain certain structural elements of the original model [23,35,53], how to rank the importance of individual features [11,34,37,40,41,50,60], whether pruning should be done at once or across several steps [13,59], and how many pruning and retraining iterations are required [4,20].

2.2   Fairness in Computer Vision

Fairness has received much attention in the recent literature on computer vision and deep learning [5,6,16,21,29,36,39,48,49,51,52,55,57]. The most common goal in these works is to enhance fairness by reducing the *accuracy disparity* of a model between images from different demographic sub-groups. For example, a face attribute classifier may yield a disproportionately higher error rate on images of non-White or females [5,30]. Another line of work has investigated biased or spurious associations in public image datasets and models between different dimensions of sensitive groups and non-protected attributes such as semantic descriptions, facial expressions, and age [1,6,28,64,65]. Our paper focuses on the former: the mitigation of accuracy disparity.

The cause of demographic bias can be demographically imbalanced datasets and the design choice of learning algorithms or network architectures [10,32]. Prior works have found that a face dataset dominated by the White race produces a poor performance for other races, while a face dataset with balanced group distribution, from either real or synthesized data, can enhance fairness [15,17, 18,30,52,58]. Algorithmic bias can be mitigated through either explicit fairness constraints [31,61], matching learned representations to a target distribution or group-wise characteristics [8,44,45], or adversarial mitigation and decoupling to disconnect representation and sensitive groups that attempts to decorrelate sensitive attributes and model outputs [1,2,12,33,43,54]. Our method estimates the importance of each connection weight toward each sub-group and maintains between-group ratios in pruning.

2.3 Fairness in Model Compression

Only a few studies have been concerned with fairness in the compression of deep models. [25] reported that pruned models tend to forget specific subsets of data. It is examined in [26,46] that pruning can impact demographic subgroups disproportionately in face attribute classification and expression recognition. Another recent work [3] showed that knowledge distillation could reduce bias in pruned models. All these studies focus on measuring pruning-induced biases between output categories. To the best of our knowledge, our paper is the first to separate the pruning impact on output classes and sensitive groups and propose a pruning algorithm to mitigate biases in both dimensions.

3   Fairness-Aware GRAdient Pruning mEthod

3.1   Problem Statement and Objective

Consider a neural network f parameterized by $\theta \in \mathbb{R}^m$ and a dataset $D = \{(x_i, y_i, k_i)\}_{i=1}^n$, where $x_i \in \mathcal{X}$ is an input vector, $y_i \in \mathcal{Y}$ is a target output, and $k_i \in K$ is a sensitive attribute. The goal of network pruning is to find the following parameter set:

$$\theta' = \operatorname*{argmin}_{\theta} L(D, \theta) = \operatorname*{argmin}_{\theta} \frac{1}{n} \sum_{i=1}^n \ell(f(\theta, x_i), y_i), \text{ subject to } ||\theta||_0 \leq c \cdot m$$

(1)

Here $\ell(\cdot)$ denotes a loss function, and $c \in (0, 1)$ is the desired sparsity level.

We further examine the network's performance on different subsets of D. Let $D_k = \{(x_i, y_i, k_i) | k_i = k\}$ denote the subset of instances from a sensitive group $k \in K$. Given a performance metric $A(D_k; \theta)$, the difference in performance on D_k between the full model f and a compressed model f' is:

$$\Delta A(D_k; \theta') = A(D_k; \theta') - A(D_k; \theta)$$

(2)

The mean of all group-wise performance differences is:

$$\Delta \bar{A}(D; \theta') = \frac{1}{|K|} \sum_{k \in K} \Delta A(D_k; \theta')$$

(3)

Our goal is to minimize the variance of performance differences in a pruned model. This task can be formulated as finding the following θ^*:

$$\theta^* = \operatorname*{argmin}_{\theta'}[Var(\Delta A(D_k; \theta'))] = \operatorname*{argmin}_{\theta'}[\frac{1}{|K|}\sum_{k \in K}(\Delta A(D_k; \theta') - \Delta\bar{A}(D; \theta'))^2]$$

(4)

Note that the actual task of the model determines the choices of the performance metric $A(\theta; D_k)$. This paper focuses on classification tasks and thus uses accuracy, false positive rate (FPR), and false negative rate (FNR) as performance metrics. The output space $\mathcal{Y}$ and sensitive groups K can be either overlapping or disjoint, and this paper examines both cases.

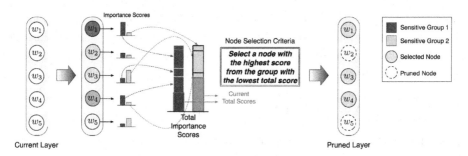

Fig. 2. Illustration of the proposed node selection method. FairGRAPE first computes the importance score of each individual weight for all groups layer-wise. Based on the total scores from the current layer, FairGRAPE selects a node with the highest score from the group with the greatest loss in importance score to minimize the variance of performance changes.

3.2   FairGRAPE: Fairness-Aware Gradient Pruning Method

The common idea behind model pruning methods is estimating the importance of edges and pruning less important ones. While the existing methods focus on measuring the importance to the whole dataset, our method aims to preserve important weights for each sensitive group to mitigate biases.

To this end, we propose to compute the group-wise importance score of each weight with respect to each sensitive group, and then use a greedy algorithm to select weights based on the scores. At each step, the method compares the current ratio of importance scores with the target ratio (*i.e.*, the ratio in the model before the current pruning step). Then the group that has the largest difference will be selected, and the method adds one weight with the highest importance for the selected group to the selected network. Once the desired number of weights is selected, the remaining weights are pruned. FairGRAPE compresses all layers of the model with this node selection process, which is illustrated in Fig. 2.

Group-Wise Importance. Let $w \in \theta'$ denote a parameter in f' and $L(D_k, \theta')$ denote the loss on sensitive group k. The gradient of $L(D_k, \theta')$ with respect to w is $g_w = \frac{\partial L(D_k, \theta')}{\partial w}$. Then the importance of w with respect to group k and the total model importance score for a group k are:

$$I_{k,w} = (L(D_k, \theta') - L(D_k, \theta'|w=0))^2 \qquad I_k = \sum_{w \in \theta'} I_{k,w} \qquad (5)$$

Computing the importance defined in Eq. 5 requires evaluating a different network for every parameter, which is often impractical. Alternatively, $I_{w,k}$ could be approximated by its first-order Taylor expansion, as explained in [41]:

$$I_{k,w} = (g_w w)^2 \qquad (6)$$

Maintaining Share of Importance. Based on the group importance scores, we compute the share of the importance of group k as follows:

$$P_k = \frac{I_k}{\sum_K I_k} \qquad (7)$$

The share of importance in the original model f is used as a target. In the pruned model f' with parameter set θ', the percentage change in the importance score compared to full model f is:

$$\Delta P_{k,f'} = \frac{P_{k,\theta'} - P_{k,\theta}}{P_{k,\theta}} \qquad (8)$$

As weights are pruned, the importance scores for each group would inevitably decrease. However, the disparate loss of importance across groups leads to an imbalanced loss in classification performance. Thus, we apply a layer-wise greedy algorithm to select the parameters that minimize the difference of $\Delta P_{k,f'}$ between the sensitive groups, as explained in Algorithm 1.

FairGRAPE iteratively prunes and fine-tunes a network: given a desired sparsity c and a step size r, the percentage of remaining weights to be pruned at each iteration, the total number of iterations is $Iters = \lceil (log_r(c)) \rceil$. In each iteration, the network is pruned layer by layer for all layers with weight attributes (*e.g.* convolutional and linear layers). Before pruning a layer, $P_{k,\theta}$ for each group k is calculated with all unpruned parameters θ. At the very beginning of the algorithm, θ' has not included any weights yet, and all group importance values are 0. So $P_{k,\theta'}$ are initialized to $1/|K|$. Then weights in θ are added to θ' one at a time. Before each selection, the sensitive group k with the minimum $\Delta P_{k,\theta'}$ is identified, as shown in line 9 of Algorithm 1. Then the weight that has the highest importance score for group k is added to the set of selected weights to minimize $P_{k,\theta'}$ (line 10). $P_{k,\theta'}$ and $\Delta P_{k,\theta'}$ are updated for all groups $k \in K$ (line 12). The selection for weights continues until $(1-r)\%$ of weights are selected. The weights not selected are removed by setting them to zero and thus no longer considered in further iterations. Then FairGRAPE proceeds to

---

Algorithm 1 FairGRAPE

1: $c \leftarrow$ desired sparsity
2: $r \leftarrow$ % of parameters to prune per iteration
3: $Iters \leftarrow \lceil log_r(c) \rceil$; $i \leftarrow 0$
4: $f \leftarrow$ pre-pruning network with parameter set $\boldsymbol{\theta}$
5: **while** $i < Iters$ **do**
6:     **for** θ_{layer} **in** $\boldsymbol{\theta}$ **do**
7:         $\theta'_{layer} \leftarrow \emptyset$
8:         **while** $|\theta'_{layer}| < ||\theta_{layer}||_0 \times (1 - r)$ **do**
9:             $\tilde{k} \leftarrow \min_k(\Delta P_{k,\theta'_{layer}})$ ▷ Find the greatest importance loss
10:             $\tilde{w} \leftarrow \text{argmax}_{w \in \theta'_{layer}}(I_{\tilde{k},w})$ ▷ Find the highest importance for $\tilde{k}$
11:             $\theta'_{layer} \leftarrow \theta'_{layer} \bigcup \{\tilde{w}\}$
12:             $\Delta P_{k,\theta'_{layer}} \leftarrow \frac{P_{k,\theta'_{layer}} - P_{k,\theta_{layer}}}{P_{k,\theta_{layer}}}, \forall k \in K$ ▷ Update importance losses
13:         **end while**
14:         $\theta_{prune} \leftarrow \{w | w \in \theta_{layer} \wedge w \notin \theta'_{layer}\}$
15:         $\theta_{prune} \leftarrow 0$ ▷ Prune weights that are not selected
16:     **end for**
17:     $f \leftarrow$ Train $(\boldsymbol{\theta}; D)$; $i \leftarrow i + 1$
18: **end while**

---

the next layer. Once all layers are pruned, the network is retrained for a fixed number of e epochs to adjust the weights to its current structure. Then the next iteration begins.

4 Experiments

4.1 Datasets

To evaluate our proposed FairGRAPE, we conducted extensive experiments with four face image datasets, including FairFace [30], UTKFace [63], CelebA [38], and the person subtree of ImageNet [56]. Table 1 shows the distributions of races and genders in all datasets. Images are fairly distributed across the seven race groups in the FairFace, while the white race is dominant in the UTKFace. This allows us to validate that the effect of our method remains consistent with the presence of data bias. In UTKFace, only one "*Asian*" contains both Asian and Southeast Asian faces. We excluded the "*Other*" category in UTKFace due to its ambiguity. Race/ethnicity information is not provided in CelebA and ImageNet. FairFace, UTKFace, and CelebA provide annotations for binary genders. While the ImageNet person subtree contains three gender classes: Male, Female, and Unsure (non-binary), we only use ImageNet samples with binary genders to stay consistent with other datasets. Following the practice in [56], Imagenet samples that are from "unsafe" categories or have imageability scores ≤ 4 are also excluded.

Table 1. Demographic composition of datasets.

Dataset	Images	White	Black	Hispanic	East Asian	Southeast Asian	Indian	Middle Eastern	Male	Female	Categories
FairFace [30]	97,698	18,612	13,789	14,990	13,837	12,210	13,835	10,425	51,778	45,920	–
UTKFace [63]	22,013	10,078	4,526	–	3,434	–	3,975	–	11,631	10,382	–
CelebA [38]	202,599	–	–	–	–	–	–	–	84,434	118,165	39
ImageNet (Person) [56]	10,215	–	–	–	–	–	–	–	6,590	3,625	103

4.2 Experiment Settings

Network Architectures: To ensure our method applies to different architectures, we use two popular deep networks: ResNet-34 [22] and MobileNet-V2 [27]. ResNet is widely applied for classification tasks, and the MobileNet is a compact network commonly used by mobile devices. All models are pre-trained on ImageNet [9].

Hyperparameters: We use a cross-entropy loss function with the ADAM optimizer for all training. All accuracy scores, overall and group-wise, are averaged across three trials to control for randomness in training. For iterative pruning methods, we retrain five epochs after each pruning iteration. Step size $r = 0.9$ on FairFace, CelebA and Imagenet and $r = 0.975$ on UTKFace. The training/validation/testing percentage is 80%/10%/10% in each dataset.

4.3 Baseline Methods

We deploy the following four baseline methods: **Single-Shot Network Pruning (SNIP)** [34]: calculates the connection sensitivity of edges by back-propagating on one mini-batch and prunes the edges with low sensitivity. **Weight Selection (WS)** [19]: prunes the weights with magnitudes below a threshold in a trained model. It is the most commonly used in mobile applications [42]. **Lottery Ticket Identification (Lottery)** [13]: records the initial state of the network; resets the model to its initial state after each pruning iteration. **Gradient Signal Preservation (GraSP)** [50]: removes the parameters with low Hessian-gradient scores to maximize gradient signal in the pruned model.

5 Results

To evaluate the effectiveness of our method, we conduct extensive experiments on three different settings, including (Sect. 5.1) gender and race classification tasks, (Sect. 5.2) non-sensitive attribute classification tasks, and (Sect. 5.3) model pruning based on unsupervised clustering. We also perform more in-depth analysis, including (Sect. 5.4) ablation studies, (Sect. 5.6) different sparsity levels, (Sect. 5.5) pruning on minority faces, and (Sect. 5.7) difference in importance score and structure, to understand the importance of components in Fair-GRAPE.

Table 2. The group-wise accuracy and biases in gender or race classification tasks. Hisp, E-A, SE-A and ME stand for Hispanic, East Asian, Southeast Asian and Middle Eastern. FairFace experiments are conducted on ResNet-34 pruned at 99% sparsity, UTKFace experiment on MobileNet-V2 pruned at 90% sparsity. $\rho(A)$ and $\rho(\Delta)$ are the standard deviation of accuracy and accuracy loss across sensitive groups, respectively.

Task	Method	Accuracy			Bias		Accuracy								Bias	
		All	Male	Female	$\rho(A)$	$\rho(\Delta)$	All	White	Black	Hisp	E-A	SE-A	Indian	ME	$\rho(A)$	$\rho(\Delta)$
FairFace, Gender	No-pruning	94.6	94.7	94.5	0.14	–	94.6	94.6	90.5	95.9	94.7	94.4	96.3	95.6	1.93	–
	Lottery	85.8	86.4	85.2	0.80	0.65	85.8	85.1	80.8	88.4	84.0	85.5	88.1	89.6	3.01	1.55
	SNIP	90.4	91.0	89.9	0.78	0.63	90.4	91.0	85.2	92.6	90.0	90.5	91.3	92.6	2.53	0.93
	WS	83.8	84.3	83.4	0.62	0.47	83.9	82.9	78.9	87.2	82.2	82.2	86.2	88.3	3.32	2.00
	GraSP	87.9	88.4	87.4	0.75	0.60	87.9	87.5	83.1	89.6	87.5	88.0	89.4	90.9	2.49	0.93
	FairGRAPE	**91.1**	91.3	91.0	**0.20**	**0.05**	**90.5**	90.4	85.4	92.3	90.1	90.5	91.9	92.8	**2.47**	**0.77**
FairFace, Race	No-pruning	72.0	71.2	72.9	1.23	–	72.0	73.9	83.2	59.6	77.6	66.9	75.4	66.2	8.02	–
	Lottery	57.1	55.3	59.1	2.64	1.42	57.1	69.7	78.8	33.0	74.1	43.5	61.7	30.4	20.0	12.9
	SNIP	62.3	60.4	64.3	2.78	1.55	62.3	74.1	80.8	44.5	73.7	53.7	66.0	34.8	17.1	10.7
	WS	47.9	47.3	48.5	**0.86**	**0.36**	47.9	64.7	77.9	8.61	78.3	31.1	37.8	30.0	26.9	19.9
	GraSP	57.9	56.0	60.1	2.88	1.55	57.9	69.6	77.3	38.6	72.0	47.0	62.1	30.7	18.0	11.3
	FairGRAPE	**66.8**	65.3	68.6	2.35	1.12	**65.1**	72.2	80.3	47.5	75.8	56.3	70.2	48.6	**13.4**	**6.13**
UTKFace, Gender	No-pruning	93.5	92.4	94.8	1.68	–	93.5	94.1	–	95.1	–	89.6	–	93.7	2.45	–
	Lottery	83.5	83.7	83.3	0.34	2.01	83.5	84.7	–	85.8	–	75.0	–	85.2	5.15	2.79
	SNIP	91.0	91.3	90.6	0.45	2.19	91.0	91.9	–	93.0	–	86.0	–	90.9	3.08	0.67
	WS	81.9	81.4	82.6	0.89	1.79	81.9	82.1	–	84.9	–	77.2	–	82.4	3.20	0.92
	GraSP	86.8	88.5	84.9	2.51	4.20	86.8	86.7	–	89.8	–	81.4	–	88.3	3.66	1.43
	FairGRAPE	**92.2**	92.0	92.5	**0.31**	**1.36**	**91.9**	92.7	–	94.0	–	87.9	–	91.3	**2.61**	**0.56**
UTKFace, Race	No-pruning	90.8	90.6	90.9	0.24	–	90.8	92.2	–	92.5	–	93.3	–	83.3	4.69	–
	Lottery	71.7	69.4	74.2	3.41	3.17	71.7	83.8	–	80.3	–	61.0	–	42.7	19.0	15.6
	SNIP	86.8	85.7	88.0	1.64	1.40	86.8	91.6	–	92.5	–	85.8	–	70.1	10.4	6.28
	WS	70.7	68.3	73.5	3.68	3.41	70.7	82.7	–	80.8	–	59.2	–	41.4	19.6	16.2
	GraSP	77.7	76.4	79.1	1.94	1.70	77.7	86.1	–	83.3	–	72.2	–	56.4	13.5	9.81
	FairGRAPE	**88.7**	88.2	89.3	**0.78**	**0.54**	**88.5**	90.6	–	92.2	–	88.9	–	79.0	**5.93**	**2.04**

5.1   Gender and Race Classification

We first perform experiments to verify bias mitigation in classifying sensitive attributes. Table 2 shows classification accuracy and biases on FairFace and UTKFace datasets where we compress the ResNet-34 and MobileNet-V2, respectively. The column 'Task' indicates the dataset and classification task. We report overall classification accuracy, accuracy by sensitive groups, and variances in accuracy degradation. FairGRAPE consistently produces a substantially higher accuracy, lower differences in accuracy, and lower variance in performance degradation than the baseline methods. For example, SNIP sometimes produces accuracy scores close to our method, but it has a remarkably larger accuracy variance than FairGRAPE, which implies the potential biases caused by model pruning. In the only cases of FairFace, WS produced a model with a smaller race classification accuracy gap between male and female images, but at the cost of drastically worsened accuracy for both groups. These results suggest that our proposed method successfully equalizes the impact of pruning on the sensitive groups regardless of the classification task, thus achieving a better trade-off between fairness and overall accuracy.

Furthermore, FairGRAPE shows solid performances in all settings with different architectures and datasets (balanced or imbalanced), proving the proposed

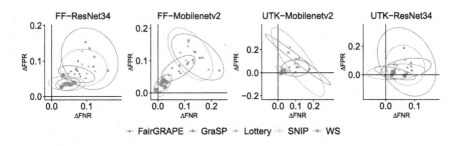

Fig. 3. Normalized FNR/FPR changes in race classification. Sparsity levels are 99% for ResNet-34 and 90% for MobileNet-V2. Each data point represents the mean value of a race. The ellipses are created by estimating 95% confidence ellipses, assuming multivariate t-distribution of points produced by each method.

method's robustness. See supplementary material for results when we jointly control race and gender groups.

We next visualize the proportion changes of False Negative Rates (FNRs)/False Positive Rate (FPRs) from the full model after pruning by Fair-GRAPE and other baseline methods in Fig. 3. Each point in the plot represents normalized FNR and FPR change of a specific race group in the model produced by one of the pruning methods, and the ellipses are created by estimating a 95% confidence region of data points. The results reveal that the proposed FairGRAPE produces data points closer to the origin than the other data points generated by the baseline methods. More importantly, FairGRAPE creates the smallest ellipse, which demonstrates that performance changes for each group are close to each other. Thus the distribution of induced bias across sensitive groups is fair.

5.2 Non-sensitive Attribute Classification

To evaluate the performance of FairGRAPE in more practical cases where output classes and sensitive groups are disjoint, we experiment with classification on CelebA and ImageNet datasets. CelebA contains the 39 non-sensitive categories of facial attributes such as eyeglasses, makeup, and lipsticks. We code each of these categories as a binary classification task. For the ImageNet experiment, we use the modified person subtree, which contains 10,215 images in 103 distinct classes (*e.g.*, basketball player, rapper) with gender labels [56]. We train the models to classify the class to which a given image belongs. Note that we use the ResNet-34 network at 50% sparsity for the ImageNet experiments and the MobileNet-V2 network at 90% sparsity for the CelebA experiments.

Table 3 shows the overall accuracy, accuracy of each gender, and the standard deviation of accuracy change. FairGRAPE achieves the highest accuracy on ImageNet. Although GraSP has a smaller accuracy gender gap than our method, its overall accuracy and variance of performance degradation are drastically worse. In the CelebA experiment, FairGRAPE has a significantly lower variance in accuracy change than other methods while achieving the highest accuracy. The results demonstrate that FairGRAPE performs well on sensitive attribute classification tasks and non-sensitive attributes, thus widely applicable in various applications.

Table 3. The average accuracy and biases in person category classification and facial attributes classification on ResNet-34 at 50% sparsity and MobileNet-V2 network at 90% sparsity, respectively. $\rho(\Delta)$ is the standard deviation of accuracy loss across genders.

Dataset	Task	Group	Methods	Accuracy			Bias	
				All	Male	Female	Diff	$\rho(\Delta)$
ImageNet	Person Subtree (103 classes)	Gender	No-Pruning	50.25	53.03	45.60	7.43	–
			Lottery	50.85	54.03	45.98	8.05	2.55
			SNIP	47.85	50.89	42.76	8.13	0.49
			WS	51.11	54.06	46.16	7.90	0.33
			GraSP	15.36	17.03	12.57	4.47	2.10
			FairGRAPE	**51.12**	54.01	46.16	**7.85**	**0.30**
CelebA	Non-sensitive Facial Attributes (39 classes)	Gender	No-Pruning	91.81	91.76	91.86	0.11	–
			Lottery	89.31	88.99	89.54	0.55	0.32
			SNIP	90.29	90.05	90.46	0.41	0.21
			WS	88.57	88.15	88.87	0.72	0.43
			GraSP	89.40	89.08	89.63	0.55	0.32
			FairGRAPE	**90.90**	90.74	91.01	**0.27**	**0.11**

5.3 Unsupervised Learning for Group Aware in Model Pruning

In practice, labels for sensitive attributes may not always be available. Therefore, we further examine the performance of our method on a dataset without demographic group labels through unsupervised group discovery.

Table 4 shows the accuracy and bias of experiments on the FairFace dataset. In this test, FairGRAPE conducts pruning by calculating the importance score of parameters for clusters learned from unsupervised learning as sensitive groups. Then we evaluate accuracy and bias with actual race labels. We labeled the seven clusters using K-means clustering on image embedding generated by the ResNet-34 network pre-trained on Imagenet. While all baseline methods have low accuracy and large variance of accuracy as they do not consider the sensitive groups, the FairGRAPE method consistently results in the lowest performance variance, suggesting that our proposed method has the potential to compress the model while reducing biases even in the absence of sensitive attribute information. The K-means algorithm's simplicity further reinforced our method's generalizability when the precise group partitioning is complex or noisy.

Table 4. The average accuracy and biases in race classification, where FairGRAPE pruning is performed based on groups clustered by unsupervised learning. Hisp, E-A, SE-A and ME stand for Hispanic, East Asian, Southeast Asian and Middle Eastern. $\rho(A)$ and $\rho(\Delta)$ are the standard deviation of accuracy and accuracy loss across sensitive races.

Task	Methods	Accuracy								Bias	
		All	White	Black	Hisp	E-A	SE-A	Indian	ME	$\rho(A)$	$\rho(\Delta)$
FairFace, Race	No-Pruning	72.0	73.9	83.2	59.6	77.6	66.9	75.5	66.2	8.03	–
	Lottery	57.1	69.7	78.8	33.0	74.1	43.5	61.7	30.4	20.0	12.9
	SNIP	62.3	74.1	80.8	44.5	73.7	53.7	66.0	34.8	17.1	10.7
	WS	47.9	64.7	78.0	8.6	78.3	31.1	37.8	30.0	26.9	19.9
	GraSP	57.9	69.6	77.3	38.6	72.0	47.0	62.1	30.7	18.0	11.3
	FairGRAPE	**63.5**	69.7	80.4	49.2	74.7	53.7	68.1	42.8	**14.1**	**7.40**

Table 5. The accuracy and biases under different pruning settings. The MobileNet-V2 networks are trained on CelebA attributes classification tasks and pruned at 90% sparsity. # iter is the number of pruning iterations, determined by the pruning step r which is the proportion of remain edges removed during each iteration. % training images represents the percentage of training images included in calculation of group importance scores. $\rho(\Delta)$ is the standard deviation of accuracy loss across genders.

Group importance	Iterative retraining (# iterations/r)	% Training images	Accuracy			Bias	
			All	Female	Male	Diff	$\rho(\Delta)$
✓	✓ (22/0.1)	20%	90.90	91.01	90.74	0.27	0.11
✓	✓ (22/0.1)	100%	90.66	90.81	90.45	0.36	0.18
✓	✓ (22/0.1)	50%	90.72	90.84	90.54	0.30	0.13
✓	✓ (22/0.1)	10%	90.84	90.97	90.67	0.30	0.13
✓	✓ (16/0.2)	20%	90.49	90.62	90.32	0.30	0.20
✓	✓ (3/0.5)	20%	90.34	90.52	90.10	0.42	0.22
✓	✗ (1/0.9)	20%	89.26	89.51	88.92	0.41	0.34
✗	✓ (22/0.1)	–	89.31	89.54	88.99	0.45	0.31
✗	✗ (1/0.9)	–	88.57	88.86	88.17	0.69	0.42

5.4   Ablation Studies: Group Importance and Iterative Pruning

Table 5 shows the performance of FairGRAPE with different group importance and iterative retraining settings. We first find that group importance is the essential component in our proposed method. The baseline method, which does not use both group importance and iterative retraining, has remarkably lower accuracy, gender gap, and variance of accuracy changes than our method, which utilizes both components. As the pruning step r at each iteration increased, the accuracy decreased, and the bias increased gradually.

More specifically, the model suffers from an obvious performance drop and bias increase when r increased from 0.1 to 0.2. This result agrees with previous findings [13] that iterative pruning improves performance.

Finally, we examine the percentage of training images used in importance calculation. FairGRAPE calculates group-wise importance score $I_{w,k} = (g_w w)^2$

Table 6. UTKFace gender classification accuracy on minority subsets. $\rho(A)$ and $\rho(\Delta)$ are the standard deviation of accuracy and accuracy loss across racs, respectively.

Methods	Accuracy					Bias	
	All	White	Black	Asian	Indian	$\rho(A)$	$\rho(\Delta)$
No-pruning	93.84	95.08	95.27	89.85	92.70	2.54	–
FairGRAPE	91.72	92.86	94.18	86.88	90.40	3.21	0.78
GraSP (Minority)	89.15	88.73	92.24	83.71	91.19	3.80	2.31
GraSP (All data)	88.33	88.80	91.05	82.47	89.13	3.73	1.77
SNIP (Minority)	90.55	91.60	92.79	83.91	91.19	4.03	1.90
SNIP (All data)	90.95	91.33	94.18	85.44	91.11	3.66	1.62

for each weight w, where g_w is calculated with respect to average loss across selected mini-batches of the training set. It has been found that the proportion of training images used in the calculation process affects pruning speed and accuracy [41]. We compared the performance using 100%, 50%, 20%, and 10% of training sets. The result indicates that 20% is the ideal ratio that produces the best performance.

5.5   Pruning on Images from Minority Races

This section examines whether rebalancing the dataset could mitigate pruning-induced bias. Using the UTKFace dataset, where white faces are dominant, we tested SNIP and GraSP with their gradient calculation and parameter selection conducted on non-white examples only (i.e., Black, Asian, Indian) Table 6 shows the result. Interestingly, using a subset of data did not significantly change overall accuracy. However, the overall biases increased compared to the case of using all data. This change shows that the problem of biases in pruned methods cannot be solved by simple data rebalancing and our method effectively addresses this challenging problem.

5.6   Analysis on Model Sparsity Levels

We next evaluate the performance of FairGRAPE across different sparsity levels to understand its effectiveness. Figure 4 shows changes in accuracy and biases over different sparsity levels. FairGRAPE outperforms the baseline methods by producing the highest accuracy and lowest disparity of performance degradation across sensitive groups at various pruning rates. As sparsity changes from 90% to 99%, most baseline methods exhibit a sharp decrease in accuracy and increase in bias, while performance change in FairGRAPE is substantially smaller. This confirms that our method can be widely deployed to real-world systems with various sparsity levels.

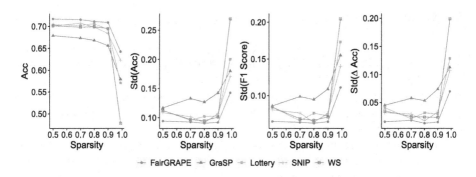

Fig. 4. Accuracy and biases of race classification across races at different sparsity levels. Experiments were conducted using ResNet-34 on FairFace dataset.

5.7 Layer-Wise Importance Scores and Bias

This subsection performs an in-depth structural analysis on pruned networks. Figure 5 visualizes the ratio of importance scores at each layer for each gender group. Each bar represents a convolutional or linear layer. And the width of a colored segment indicates the ratio of importance score for the corresponding gender group. FairGRAPE preserves the balanced importance distribution of the full network, with similar scores for both genders, leading to substantially smaller gaps in accuracy and accuracy change. The group-agnostic pruning methods, including SNIP and Weight Selection, select weights with higher importance for the female group, which is already showing higher accuracy in the original model. Consequently, the accuracy of the male group suffered from a substantially greater loss and the gap is much larger than the model pruned by FairGRAPE.

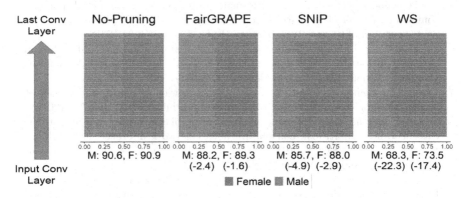

Fig. 5. The ratio of importance scores on MobileNet-V2. Networks are pruned to 90% sparsity and trained on UTKFace dataset. M and F indicate race classification accuracy on male and female images. Accuracy changes between the pruned models and the full model are shown in parenthesis.

6   Conclusion

In this paper, we proposed FairGRAPE, a novel pruning method that prunes weights based on their importance with respect to each demographic sub-group in the dataset. Empirical results show that our method can minimize performance degradation across sub-groups in different network architectures and datasets at various pruning rates. We also demonstrated that the association between distributions of gradient importance and performance biases has an important implication for understanding information loss during model compression. Our work will therefore contribute to developing fair light-weight models that can be deployed on many mobile devices by mitigating hidden biases.

Acknowledgement. This work was supported by NSF SBE-SMA #1831848.

References

1. Alvi, M., Zisserman, A., Nellåker, C.: Turning a blind eye: explicit removal of biases and variation from deep neural network embeddings. In: Leal-Taixé, L., Roth, S. (eds.) ECCV 2018. LNCS, vol. 11129, pp. 556–572. Springer, Cham (2019). https://doi.org/10.1007/978-3-030-11009-3_34

2. Bahng, H., Chun, S., Yun, S., Choo, J., Oh, S.J.: Learning de-biased representations with biased representations. In: III, H.D., Singh, A. (eds.) Proceedings of the 37th International Conference on Machine Learning (ICML). Proceedings of Machine Learning Research, vol. 119, pp. 528–539 (2020)

3. Blakeney, C., Huish, N., Yan, Y., Zong, Z.: Simon says: evaluating and mitigating bias in pruned neural networks with knowledge distillation. arXiv preprint arXiv:2106.07849 (2021)

4. Blalock, D., Gonzalez Ortiz, J.J., Frankle, J., Guttag, J.: What is the state of neural network pruning? Proc. Mach. Learn. Syst. **2**, 129–146 (2020)

5. Buolamwini, J., Gebru, T.: Gender shades: intersectional accuracy disparities in commercial gender classification. In: Proceedings of the 2020 Conference on Fairness, Accountability, and Transparency (FACCT), pp. 77–91 (2018)

6. Chen, Y., Joo, J.: Understanding and mitigating annotation bias in facial expression recognition. In: Proceedings of the IEEE/CVF International Conference on Computer Vision (ICCV), pp. 14980–14991 (2021)

7. Cheng, Y., Wang, D., Zhou, P., Zhang, T.: A survey of model compression and acceleration for deep neural networks. arXiv preprint arXiv:1710.09282 (2017)

8. Das, A., Dantcheva, A., Bremond, F.: Mitigating bias in gender, age and ethnicity classification: a multi-task convolution neural network approach. In: Leal-Taixé, L., Roth, S. (eds.) ECCV 2018. LNCS, vol. 11129, pp. 573–585. Springer, Cham (2019). https://doi.org/10.1007/978-3-030-11009-3_35

9. Deng, J., Dong, W., Socher, R., Li, L.J., Li, K., Fei-Fei, L.: ImageNet: a large-scale hierarchical image database. In: 2009 IEEE Conference on Computer Vision and Pattern Recognition (CVPR), pp. 248–255. IEEE (2009)

10. Du, M., Yang, F., Zou, N., Hu, X.: Fairness in deep learning: a computational perspective. IEEE Intell. Syst. **36**, 25–34 (2020)

11. Dubey, A., Chatterjee, M., Ahuja, N.: Coreset-based neural network compression. In: Ferrari, V., Hebert, M., Sminchisescu, C., Weiss, Y. (eds.) ECCV 2018. LNCS, vol. 11211, pp. 469–486. Springer, Cham (2018). https://doi.org/10.1007/978-3-030-01234-2_28

12. Dwork, C., Immorlica, N., Kalai, A.T., Leiserson, M.: Decoupled classifiers for group-fair and efficient machine learning. In: Conference on Fairness, Accountability and Transparency (FAACT), pp. 119–133. PMLR (2018)

13. Frankle, J., Carbin, M.: The lottery ticket hypothesis: finding sparse, trainable neural networks. In: Proceedings of the International Conference on Learning Representations (ICLR) (2019)

14. Frankle, J., Dziugaite, G.K., Roy, D.M., Carbin, M.: Stabilizing the lottery ticket hypothesis. arXiv preprint arXiv:1903.01611 (2019)

15. Frid-Adar, M., Klang, E., Amitai, M., Goldberger, J., Greenspan, H.: Synthetic data augmentation using GAN for improved liver lesion classification. In: 2018 IEEE 15th International Symposium on Biomedical Imaging (ISBI), pp. 289–293 (2018)

16. Garcia, R.V., Wandzik, L., Grabner, L., Krueger, J.: The harms of demographic bias in deep face recognition research. In: 2019 International Conference on Biometrics (ICB), pp. 1–6 (2019)

17. Georgopoulos, M., Panagakis, Y., Pantic, M.: Investigating bias in deep face analysis: the KANFace dataset and empirical study. Image Vis. Comput. **102**, 103954 (2020)

18. Gwilliam, M., Hegde, S., Tinubu, L., Hanson, A.: Rethinking common assumptions to mitigate racial bias in face recognition datasets. In: Proceedings of the IEEE/CVF International Conference on Computer Vision (ICCV) Workshops, pp. 4123–4132 (2021)

19. Han, S., Mao, H., Dally, W.J.: Deep compression: compressing deep neural networks with pruning, trained quantization and Huffman coding. In: Proceedings of the International Conference on Learning Representations (ICLR) (2016)

20. Han, S., Pool, J., Tran, J., Dally, W.: Learning both weights and connections for efficient neural network. In: Advances in Neural Information Processing Systems, vol. 28 (2015)

21. Hazirbas, C., Bitton, J., Dolhansky, B., Pan, J., Gordo, A., Ferrer, C.C.: Towards measuring fairness in AI: the casual conversations dataset. arXiv preprint arXiv:2104.02821 (2021)

22. He, K., Zhang, X., Ren, S., Sun, J.: Deep residual learning for image recognition. In: Proceedings of the IEEE Conference on Computer Vision and Pattern Recognition, pp. 770–778 (2016)

23. He, Y., Zhang, X., Sun, J.: Channel pruning for accelerating very deep neural networks. In: Proceedings of the IEEE International Conference on Computer Vision, pp. 1389–1397 (2017)

24. Hinton, G., Vinyals, O., Dean, J.: Distilling the knowledge in a neural network. In: NIPS Deep Learning and Representation Learning Workshop (2015)

25. Hooker, S., Courville, A., Clark, G., Dauphin, Y., Frome, A.: What do compressed deep neural networks forget? arXiv preprint arXiv:1911.05248 (2019)

26. Hooker, S., Moorosi, N., Clark, G., Bengio, S., Denton, E.: Characterising bias in compressed models (2020), arXiv preprint arXiv:2010.03058

27. Howard, A.G., et al.: MobileNets: efficient convolutional neural networks for mobile vision applications. arXiv preprint arXiv:1704.04861 (2017)

28. Joo, J., Kärkkäinen, K.: Gender slopes: counterfactual fairness for computer vision models by attribute manipulation. In: Proceedings of the 2nd International Workshop on Fairness, Accountability, Transparency and Ethics in Multimedia, pp. 1–5 (2020)
29. Jung, S., Chun, S., Moon, T.: Learning fair classifiers with partially annotated group labels. In: Proceedings of the IEEE/CVF Conference on Computer Vision and Pattern Recognition, pp. 10348–10357 (2022)
30. Karkkainen, K., Joo, J.: FairFace: face attribute dataset for balanced race, gender, and age for bias measurement and mitigation. In: Proceedings of the IEEE/CVF Winter Conference on Applications of Computer Vision (WACV), pp. 1548–1558 (2021)
31. Kleindessner, M., Samadi, S., Awasthi, P., Morgenstern, J.: Guarantees for spectral clustering with fairness constraints. In: Chaudhuri, K., Salakhutdinov, R. (eds.) Proceedings of the 36th International Conference on Machine Learning (ICML), vol. 97, pp. 3458–3467 (2019)
32. Krishnan, A., Almadan, A., Rattani, A.: Understanding fairness of gender classification algorithms across gender-race groups. In: 2020 19th IEEE International Conference on Machine Learning and Applications (ICMLA), pp. 1028–1035. IEEE (2020)
33. Lee, J., Kim, E., Lee, J., Lee, J., Choo, J.: Learning debiased representation via disentangled feature augmentation. In: Advances in Neural Information Processing Systems (NIPS) 34 (2021)
34. Lee, N., Ajanthan, T., Torr, P.: SNIP: single-shot network pruning based on connection sensitivity. In: Proceedings of the International Conference on Learning Representations (ICLR) (2019)
35. Li, H., Kadav, A., Durdanovic, I., Samet, H., Graf, H.P.: Pruning filters for efficient convnets. In: International Conference on Learning Representations (ICLR) (2017)
36. Li, Y., Vasconcelos, N.: REPAIR: removing representation bias by dataset resampling. In: Proceedings of the IEEE/CVF Conference on Computer Vision and Pattern Recognition (CVPR) (2019)
37. Liu, Z., Li, J., Shen, Z., Huang, G., Yan, S., Zhang, C.: Learning efficient convolutional networks through network slimming. In: Proceedings of the IEEE International Conference on Computer Vision, pp. 2736–2744 (2017)
38. Liu, Z., Luo, P., Wang, X., Tang, X.: Deep learning face attributes in the wild. In: Proceedings of the IEEE International Conference on Computer Vision, pp. 3730–3738 (2015)
39. Misra, I., Zitnick, C.L., Mitchell, M., Girshick, R.: Seeing through the human reporting bias: Visual classifiers from noisy human-centric labels. In: Proceedings of the IEEE Conference on Computer Vision and Pattern Recognition (CVPR) (2016)
40. Molchanov, P., Tyree, S., Karras, T., Aila, T., Kautz, J.: Pruning convolutional neural networks for resource efficient inference. In: International Conference on Learning Representations (ICLR) (2017)
41. Molchanov, P., Mallya, A., Tyree, S., Frosio, I., Kautz, J.: Importance estimation for neural network pruning. In: Proceedings of the IEEE/CVF Conference on Computer Vision and Pattern Recognition (CVPR), pp. 11264–11272 (2019)
42. Nan, K., Liu, S., Du, J., Liu, H.: Deep model compression for mobile platforms: a survey. Tsinghua Sci. Technol. **24**(6), 677–693 (2019)
43. Ramaswamy, V.V., Kim, S.S.Y., Russakovsky, O.: Fair attribute classification through latent space de-biasing. In: Proceedings of the IEEE/CVF Conference on Computer Vision and Pattern Recognition (CVPR), pp. 9301–9310 (2021)

44. Ryu, H.J., Adam, H., Mitchell, M.: InclusiveFaceNet: improving face attribute detection with race and gender diversity. arXiv preprint arXiv:1712.00193 (2017)

45. Schumann, C., Wang, X., Beutel, A., Chen, J., Qian, H., Chi, E.H.: Transfer of machine learning fairness across domains. Clinical Orthopaedics and Related Research (CoRR) (2019)

46. Stoychev, S., Gunes, H.: The effect of model compression on fairness in facial expression recognition. arXiv preprint arXiv:2201.01709 (2022)

47. Tai, C., Xiao, T., Zhang, Y., Wang, X., Weinan, E.: Convolutional neural networks with low-rank regularization. In: International Conference on Learning Representations (ICLR) (2016)

48. Terhöst, P., Kolf, J.N., Damer, N., Kirchbuchner, F., Kuijper, A.: Face quality estimation and its correlation to demographic and non-demographic bias in face recognition. In: 2020 IEEE International Joint Conference on Biometrics (IJCB), pp. 1–11 (2020)

49. Wang, A., Barocas, S., Laird, K., Wallach, H.: Measuring representational harms in image captioning. In: 2022 ACM Conference on Fairness, Accountability, and Transparency, pp. 324–335 (2022)

50. Wang, C., Zhang, G., Grosse, R.: Picking winning tickets before training by preserving gradient flow. In: International Conference on Learning Representations (ICLR) (2020)

51. Wang, M., Deng, W., Hu, J., Tao, X., Huang, Y.: Racial faces in the wild: Reducing racial bias by information maximization adaptation network. In: Proceedings of the IEEE Conference on Computer Vision and Pattern Recognition (CVPR) (2019)

52. Wang, T., Zhao, J., Yatskar, M., Chang, K.W., Ordonez, V.: Balanced datasets are not enough: estimating and mitigating gender bias in deep image representations. In: Proceedings of the IEEE/CVF International Conference on Computer Vision (ICCV) (2019)

53. Wang, W., Fu, C., Guo, J., Cai, D., He, X.: COP: customized deep model compression via regularized correlation-based filter-level pruning. In: Proceedings of the 28th International Joint Conference on Artificial Intelligence, pp. 3785–3791 (2019)

54. Wang, Z., et al.: Towards fairness in visual recognition: effective strategies for bias mitigation. In: Proceedings of the IEEE/CVF Conference on Computer Vision and Pattern Recognition (CVPR) (2020)

55. Xu, X., et al.: Consistent instance false positive improves fairness in face recognition. In: Proceedings of the IEEE/CVF Conference on Computer Vision and Pattern Recognition (CVPR), pp. 578–586 (2021)

56. Yang, K., Qinami, K., Fei-Fei, L., Deng, J., Russakovsky, O.: Towards fairer datasets: filtering and balancing the distribution of the people subtree in the ImageNet hierarchy. In: Proceedings of the 2020 Conference on Fairness, Accountability, and Transparency (FACCT), pp. 547–558 (2020)

57. Yang, Y., et al.: Explaining deep convolutional neural networks via latent visual-semantic filter attention. In: 5th AAAI/ACM Conference on AI, Ethics, and Society (2022)

58. Yang, Y., Kim, S., Joo, J.: Explaining deep convolutional neural networks via latent visual-semantic filter attention. In: Proceedings of the IEEE/CVF Conference on Computer Vision and Pattern Recognition, pp. 8333–8343 (2022)

59. You, H., et al.: Drawing early-bird tickets: toward more efficient training of deep networks. In: International Conference on Learning Representations (ICLR) (2020)

60. Yu, R., et al.: NISP: pruning networks using neuron importance score propagation. In: Proceedings of the IEEE Conference on Computer Vision and Pattern Recognition (CVPR), pp. 9194–9203 (2018)
61. Zafar, M.B., Valera, I., Rogriguez, M.G., Gummadi, K.P.: Fairness constraints: mechanisms for fair classification. In: Artificial Intelligence and Statistics, pp. 962–970. PMLR (2017)
62. Zhang, C., Patras, P., Haddadi, H.: Deep learning in mobile and wireless networking: a survey. IEEE Commun. Surv. Tutor. **21**(3), 2224–2287 (2019)
63. Zhang, Z., Song, Y., Qi, H.: Age progression/regression by conditional adversarial autoencoder. In: IEEE Conference on Computer Vision and Pattern Recognition (CVPR). IEEE (2017)
64. Zhao, D., Wang, A., Russakovsky, O.: Understanding and evaluating racial biases in image captioning. In: Proceedings of the IEEE/CVF International Conference on Computer Vision (ICCV), pp. 14830–14840 (2021)
65. Zhao, J., Wang, T., Yatskar, M., Ordonez, V., Chang, K.W.: Men also like shopping: reducing gender bias amplification using corpus-level constraints. In: Proceedings of the 2017 Conference on Empirical Methods in Natural Language Processing, pp. 2979–2989 (2017)

Attaining Class-Level Forgetting in Pretrained Model Using Few Samples

Pravendra Singh[1], Pratik Mazumder[2(✉)], and Mohammed Asad Karim[3]

[1] IIT Roorkee, Roorkee, India
pravendra.singh@cs.iitr.ac.in
[2] IIT Kanpur, Kanpur, India
pratikm@cse.iitk.ac.in
[3] Carnegie Mellon University, Pittsburgh, USA
mkarim2@cs.cmu.edu

Abstract. In order to address real-world problems, deep learning models are jointly trained on many classes. However, in the future, some classes may become restricted due to privacy/ethical concerns, and the restricted class knowledge has to be removed from the models that have been trained on them. The available data may also be limited due to privacy/ethical concerns, and re-training the model will not be possible. We propose a novel approach to address this problem without affecting the model's prediction power for the remaining classes. Our approach identifies the model parameters that are highly relevant to the restricted classes and removes the knowledge regarding the restricted classes from them using the limited available training data. Our approach is significantly faster and performs similar to the model re-trained on the complete data of the remaining classes.

1 Introduction

There are several real-world problems in which deep learning models have exceeded human-level performance. This has led to a wide deployment of deep learning models. Deep learning models generally train jointly on a number of categories/classes of data. However, the use of some of these classes may get restricted in the future (restricted classes), and a model with the capability to identify these classes may violate legal/privacy concerns. Individuals and organizations are becoming increasingly aware of these issues leading to an increasing number of legal cases on privacy issues in recent years. In such situations, the model has to be stripped of its capability to identify these categories (Class-level Forgetting). Due to legal/privacy concerns, the available training data may also be limited. In such situations, the problem becomes even more difficult to solve

---

All the authors have contributed equally.

Supplementary Information The online version contains supplementary material available at https://doi.org/10.1007/978-3-031-19778-9_25.

in the absence of the full training data. Real world problems such as incremental and federated learning also suffer from this problem as discussed in Sect. 3. We present a "Restricted Category Removal from Model Representations with Limited Data" (RCRMR-LD) problem setting that simulates the above problem. In this paper, we propose to solve this problem in a fast and efficient manner.

The objective of the RCRMR-LD problem is to remove the information regarding the restricted classes from the network representations of all layers using the limited training data available without affecting the ability of the model to identify the remaining classes. If we have access to the full training data, then we can simply exclude the restricted class examples from the training data and perform a full training of the model from scratch using the abundant data (FDR - full data retraining). However, the RCRMR-LD problem setting is based on the scenario that the directive to exclude the restricted classes is received in the future after the model has already been trained on the full data and now only a limited amount of training data is available to carry out this process. Since only limited training data is available in our RCRMR-LD problem setting, the FDR model violates our problem setting and is therefore, not a solution to our RCRMR-LD problem setting. Simply training the network from scratch on only the limited training data of the remaining classes will result in severe overfitting and significantly affect the model performance (Baseline 2, as shown in Table 1).

Another possible solution to this problem is to remove the weights of the fully-connected classification layer of the network corresponding to the excluded classes such that it can no longer classify the excluded classes. However, this approach suffers from a serious problem. Since, in this approach, we only remove some of the weights of the classification layer and the rest of the model remains unchanged, the model still contains the information required for recognizing the excluded classes. This information can be easily accessed through the features that the model extracts from the images and, therefore, we can use these features for performing classification. In this paper, we use a nearest prototype-based classifier to demonstrate that the model features still contain information regarding the restricted classes. Specifically, we use the model features of the examples from the limited training data to compute the average class prototype for each class and create a nearest class prototype-based classifier using them. Next, for any given test image, we extract its features using the model and then find the class prototype closest to the given test image. This nearest class prototype-based classifier performs close to the original fully-connected classifier on the excluded classes as shown in Table 1 (Baseline 1). Therefore, even after using this approach, the resulting model still contains information regarding the restricted classes. Another possible approach can be to apply the standard fine-tuning approach to the model using the limited available training data of the remaining classes (Baseline 8). However, fine-tuning on such limited training data is not able to sufficiently remove the restricted class information from the model representations (see Table 1), and aggressive fine-tuning on the limited training data may result in overfitting.

Considering the problems faced by the naive approaches mentioned above, we propose a novel "Efficient Removal with Preservation" (ERwP) approach to address the RCRMR-LD problem. First, we propose a novel technique to identify the model parameters that are highly relevant to the restricted classes, and to the best of our knowledge, there are no existing prior works for finding such class-specific relevant parameters. Next, we propose a novel technique that optimizes the model on the limited available training data in such a way that the restricted class information is discarded from the restricted class relevant parameters, and these parameters are reused for the remaining classes.

To the best of our knowledge, this is the first work that addresses the RCRMR-LD problem. We also propose several baseline approaches for this problem (see Sect. 6). Our proposed approach significantly outperforms all the proposed baseline approaches. Our proposed approach requires very few epochs to address the RCRMR-LD problem and is, therefore, very fast ($\sim$200$\times$ on ImageNet) and efficient. The model obtained after applying our approach forgets the excluded classes to such an extent that it behaves as though it was never trained on examples from the excluded classes. The performance of our model is very similar to the full data retraining (FDR) model (see Sect. 8.1 in the manuscript and Fig. 2 in the supplementary material). We also propose the performance metrics needed to evaluate the performance of any approach for the RCRMR-LD problem.

2 Problem Setting

In this work, we present the *restricted category removal from model representations with limited data (RCRMR-LD)* problem setting, in which a deep learning model M_o trained on a specific dataset has to be modified to exclude information regarding a set of restricted/excluded classes from all layers of the deep learning model without affecting its identification power for the remaining classes (see Fig. 1). The classes that need to be excluded are referred to as the restricted/excluded classes. Let $\{C_1^e, C_2^e, ..., C_{N_e}^e\}$ be the restricted/excluded classes, where N_e refers to the number of excluded classes. The remaining classes of the dataset are the remaining/non-excluded classes. Let $\{C_1^{ne}, C_2^{ne}, ..., C_{N_{ne}}^{ne}\}$ be the non-excluded classes, where N_{ne} refers to the number of remaining/non-excluded classes. Additionally, we only have access to a limited amount of training data for the restricted classes and the remaining classes, for carrying out this process. Therefore, any approach for addressing this problem can only utilize this limited training data.

3 RCRMR-LD Problem in Real World Scenarios

A real-world scenario where our proposed RCRMR-LD problem can arise is the incremental learning setting [16,21], where the model receives training data in the form of sequentially arriving tasks. Each task contains a new set of classes. During a training session t, the model receives the task t for training and cannot access the full data of the previous tasks. Instead, the model has access to very few exemplars of the classes in the previous tasks. Suppose before training a model on training session t, it is noticed that some classes from a previous task ($<t$) have to be removed from the model since those classes have become restricted due to privacy

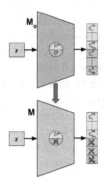

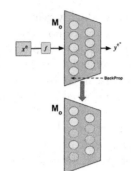

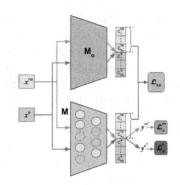

Fig. 1. The RCRMR-LD problem setting aims to remove the information regarding the restricted/excluded classes ($\{C_1^e, .., C_{N_e}^e\}$) from all layers of a trained model M_o while preserving its predictive power for the remaining classes ($\{C_1^{ne}, .., C_{N_{ne}}^{ne}\}$) using limited training data. The category removal (denoted by a red cross) has to take place at the classifier level (denoted as squares for each output logit) and at the feature/representation level (denoted as a circle) (Color figure online)

Fig. 2. ERwP identifies those parameters in the model that are highly relevant to the restricted classes. To obtain these parameters, ERwP modifies training images from a restricted class using a data augmentation f and performs back-propagation using the classification loss on these training images. ERwP then studies the gradient update that each parameter receives in this process in order to identify the highly relevant parameters for the restricted classes (denoted by dotted circles)

Fig. 3. ERwP only optimizes the restricted class relevant parameters in the model (denoted by dotted circles). ERwP uses $\mathcal{L}_c^e$, $\mathcal{L}_c^{ne}$ and $\mathcal{L}_{kd}$ losses to remove the restricted class information from the model while preserving its performance on the remaining classes. $\mathcal{L}_c^e$ and $\mathcal{L}_c^{ne}$ denote the classification loss on the restricted class training examples and the remaining class training example, respectively. $\mathcal{L}_{kd}$ denotes the knowledge distillation-based regularization loss that preserves the logits corresponding to only the remaining classes for all the training examples

or ethical concerns. In this case, only a limited number of exemplars are available for all these previous classes (restricted and remaining). This demonstrates that the RCRMR-LD problem is present in the incremental learning setting. We experimentally demonstrate in Sect. 8.3, how our approach can address the RCRMR-LD problem in the incremental learning setting.

Let us consider another example. The EU GDPR laws require a data provider to remove information about an individual from a dataset upon that individual's request. In face recognition, this may lead to cases where the model has to be retrained from scratch, leaving out the training data for the restricted classes. In many such cases, it may be highly impractical and inefficient for the model creators to retrain the entire model from scratch. The RCRMR problem simulates this problem setting. Other examples of this problem include ethical AI concerns where protected classes (pregnant women, prisoners, children, etc.) need to be removed. There can also be other real-world scenarios, such as federated learning, where our RCRMR-LD problem can arise. Please refer to Sect. 1 in the supplementary material for more details.

4 Proposed Method

4.1 Method Description

Let, B refer to a mini-batch (of size S) from the available limited training data, and B contains training datapoints from the restricted/excluded classes ($\{(x_i^e, y_i^e)|(x_1^e, y_1^e), ..., (x_{S_e}^e, y_{S_e}^e)\}$) and from the remaining/non-excluded classes ($\{(x_j^{ne}, y_j^{ne})|(x_1^{ne}, y_1^{ne}), ..., (x_{S_{ne}}^{ne}, y_{S_{ne}}^{ne})\}$). Here, (x_i^e, y_i^e) refers to a training datapoint from the excluded classes where x_i^e is an image, y_i^e is the corresponding label and $y_i^e \in \{C_1^e, C_2^e, ..., C_{N_e}^e\}$. (x_j^{ne}, y_j^{ne}) refers to a training datapoint from the non-excluded classes where x_j^{ne} is an image, y_j^{ne} is the corresponding label and $y_j^{ne} \in \{C_1^{ne}, C_2^{ne}, ..., C_{N_{ne}}^{ne}\}$. Here, S_e and S_{ne} refer to the number of training examples in the mini-batch from the excluded and non-excluded classes, respectively, such that $S = S_e + S_{ne}$. N_e and N_{ne} refer to the number of excluded and non-excluded classes, respectively. Let M refer to the deep learning model being trained using our approach and M_o is the original trained deep learning model.

In a trained model, some of the parameters may be highly relevant to the restricted classes, and the performance of the model on the restricted classes is mainly dependent on such highly relevant parameters. Therefore, in our approach, we focus on removing the excluded class information from these restricted class relevant parameters. Since the model is trained on all the classes jointly, the parameters are shared across the different classes. Therefore identifying these class-specific relevant parameters is very difficult. Let us consider a model that is trained on color images of a class. If we now train it on grayscale images of the class, then the model has to learn to identify these new images. In order to do so, the parameters relevant to that class will receive large gradient updates as compared to the other parameters (see Sect. 5.1 in the supplementary material). We propose a novel approach for identifying the relevant parameters for the restricted classes using this idea. For each restricted class, we choose the training images belonging to that class from the limited available training data. Next, we apply a grayscale data augmentation technique/transformation f to these images so that these images become different from the images that the original model was earlier trained on (assuming that the original model has not been trained on grayscale images). We can also use other data augmentation techniques that are not seen during the training process of the original model and that do not change the class of the image (refer to Sect. 5.6 in the supplementary material). Next, we combine the predictions for each training image into a single average prediction and perform backpropagation. During the backpropagation, we study the gradients for all the parameters in each layer of the model. Accordingly, we select the parameters with the highest absolute gradient as the relevant parameters for the corresponding restricted class. Specifically, for a given restricted class, we choose all the parameters from each network layer such that pruning (zeroing out) these parameters will result in the maximum degradation of model performance on that restricted class. We provide a detailed description of the process for identifying the restricted class relevant parameters in Sect. 2 of the supplementary material. The combined set of the relevant parameters for all the excluded classes is referred to as the restricted/excluded class relevant parameters Θ_{exrel} (see Fig. 2). Please note that we use this process only to identify Θ_{exrel}, and we do not update the model parameters during this step.

Pruning the relevant parameters for a restricted class can severely impact the performance of the model for that class (see Sect. 5.1 in the supplementary material). However, this may also degrade the performance of the model on the non-excluded classes because the parameters are shared across multiple classes. Therefore, we cannot address the RCRMR-LD problem by pruning the relevant parameters of the excluded classes. Finetuning these parameters on the limited remaining class data will also not be able to sufficiently remove the restricted class information from the model. Based on this, we propose to address the RCRMR-LD problem by optimizing the relevant parameters of the restricted classes to remove the restricted class information from them and to reuse them for the remaining classes.

After identifying the restricted class relevant parameters, our ERwP approach uses a classification loss based on the cross-entropy loss function to optimize the restricted class relevant parameters of the model on each mini-batch (see Fig. 3). We know that the gradient ascent optimization algorithm can be used to maximize a loss function and encourage the model to perform badly on the given input. Therefore, we use the gradient ascent optimization on the classification loss for the limited restricted class training examples to remove the information regarding the restricted classes from Θ_{exrel}. We achieve this by multiplying the classification loss for the training examples from the excluded classes by a constant negative factor of -1. We also optimize Θ_{exrel} using the gradient descent optimization on the classification loss for the limited remaining class training example, in order to reuse these parameters for the remaining classes. We validate using this approach through various ablation experiments as shown in Sect. 5.2 in the supplementary material. The classification loss for the examples from the excluded and non-excluded classes and the overall classification loss for each mini-batch are defined as follows.

$$\mathcal{L}_c^e = \sum_{i=1}^{S_e} -1 * \ell(y_i^e, y_i^{e*}) \tag{1}$$

$$\mathcal{L}_c^{ne} = \sum_{j=1}^{S_{ne}} \ell(y_j^{ne}, y_j^{ne*}) \tag{2}$$

$$\mathcal{L}_c = \frac{1}{S}(\mathcal{L}_c^e + \mathcal{L}_c^{ne}) \tag{3}$$

where, y_j^{e*} and y_j^{ne*} refer to the predicted class labels for x_i^e and x_j^{ne}, respectively. $\ell(.,.)$ refers to the cross-entropy loss function. $\mathcal{L}_c^e$ and $\mathcal{L}_c^{ne}$ refer to the classification loss for the examples from the excluded and non-excluded classes in the mini-batch, respectively. $\mathcal{L}_c$ refers to the overall classification loss for each mini-batch.

Since all the network parameters were jointly trained on all the classes (restricted and remaining), the restricted class relevant parameters also contain information relevant to the remaining classes. Applying the above process alone will still harm the model's predictive power for the non-excluded classes (as shown in Sect. 5.2, Table 2 in the supplementary material). This is because the gradient ascent optimization strategy will also erase some of the relevant information regarding the remaining classes. Further, applying $\mathcal{L}_c^{ne}$ on the limited training examples of the remaining classes will lead to overfitting and will not be effective enough to fully preserve the model performance on the remaining classes. In order to ensure that the model's predictive power for the non-excluded classes does not change, we use a knowledge distillation-based regularization loss. Knowledge distillation [14] ensures that the predictive power of the teacher network is replicated in the student network. In this problem setting, we want the final model to replicate the same predictive power of the original model for the remaining classes. Therefore, given any training example, we use the knowledge distillation-based regularization loss to ensure that the output logits produced by the model corresponding to only the non-excluded classes remain the same as that produced by the original model. We apply the knowledge distillation loss to the limited training examples from both the excluded and remaining classes, to preserve the non-excluded class logits of the model for any input image. We validate this knowledge distillation-based regularization loss through ablation experiments as shown in Table 2 in the supplementary material. We use the original model M_o (before applying ERwP) as the teacher network and the current model M being processed by ERwP as the student network, for the knowledge distillation process. Please note that the optimization for this loss is also carried out only for the restricted class relevant parameters of the model. Let KD refer to the knowledge distillation loss function. It computes the Kullback-Liebler (KL) divergence between the soft predictions of the teacher and the student networks and can be defined as follows:

$$KD(p_s, p_t) = KL(\sigma(p_s), \sigma(p_t)) \tag{4}$$

where, $\sigma(.)$ refers to the softmax activation function that converts logit a_i for each class i into a probability by comparing a_i with logits of other classes a_j, i.e., $\sigma(a_i) = \frac{exp^{a_i/\kappa}}{\sum_j exp^{a_j/\kappa}}$. κ refers to the temperature [14], KL refers to the KL-Divergence function. p_s, p_t refer to the logits produced by the student network and the teacher network, respectively.

The knowledge distillation-based regularization losses in our approach are defined as follows.

$$\mathcal{L}_{kd}^{e} = \sum_{i=1}^{S_e} KD(M(x_i^e)[C^{ne}], M_o(x_i^e)[C^{ne}]) \tag{5}$$

$$\mathcal{L}_{kd}^{ne} = \sum_{j=1}^{S_{ne}} KD(M(x_j^{ne})[C^{ne}], M_o(x_j^{ne})[C^{ne}]) \tag{6}$$

$$\mathcal{L}_{kd} = \frac{1}{S}(\mathcal{L}_{kd}^{e} + \mathcal{L}_{kd}^{ne}) \tag{7}$$

where, $M(\#)[C^{ne}]$ and $M_o(\#)[C^{ne}]$ refer to the output logits corresponding to the remaining classes produced by M and M_o, respectively. $\#$ can be either x_i^e or x_j^{ne}. $\mathcal{L}_{kd}^{e}$ and $\mathcal{L}_{kd}^{ne}$ refer to knowledge distillation-based regularization loss for the examples from the excluded and non-excluded classes, respectively. $\mathcal{L}_{kd}$ refers to the overall knowledge distillation-based regularization loss for each mini-batch. The $\mathcal{L}_{kd}^{ne}$ loss helps in preserving the model performance for the non-excluded classes. If some of the restricted classes are similar to some of the remaining/non-excluded classes, the $\mathcal{L}_{kd}^{e}$ loss ensures that the model performance on the remaining classes is not degraded due to this similarity. This is because the $\mathcal{L}_{kd}^{e}$ loss preserves the logits corresponding to the non-excluded classes for the restricted class training examples.

The total loss $\mathcal{L}_{erwp}$ of our approach for each mini-batch is defined as follows.

$$\mathcal{L}_{erwp} = \mathcal{L}_c + \beta\mathcal{L}_{kd} \tag{8}$$

where, β is a hyper-parameter that controls the contribution of the knowledge distillation-based regularization loss. We use this loss for fine-tuning the model for very few epochs.

5   Related Work

Pruning [1,11,12,25] involves removing redundant and unimportant weights [2, 7,9] or filters [10,13,17] from a deep learning model without affecting the model performance. Pruning approaches generally identify the important parameters in the network and remove the unimportant parameters. In the RCRMR-LD problem setting, the restricted class relevant parameters are also important parameters. However, we empirically observe that pruning the restricted class relevant parameters severely affects the model performance for the remaining classes since the parameters are shared among all the classes. Therefore, pruning approaches cannot be applied in the RCRMR-LD problem setting.

In the incremental learning setting [3,15,18,24], the objective is to preserve the predictive power of the model for previously seen classes while learning a new set of classes. The work in [22] uses a topology-preserving loss to prevent catastrophic forgetting by maintaining the topology in feature space. In contrast to the incremental learning setting, our proposed RCRMR-LD problem setting involves removing the information regarding specific classes from the pre-trained model while preserving the predictive power of the model for the remaining classes.

There has been some research involving deleting individual data points from trained machine learning models such as [5,6]. The work in [5] deals with data deletion in the context of a machine learning algorithm and model. It shows how to remove the influence of a data point from a k-means clustering model. Our work focuses on restricted category removal from deep learning models with limited data. Therefore, the approaches proposed in [5] cannot be applied to RCRMR-LD. Further, the objective of data deletion is to remove a data point without affecting the model performance on any classes, including the class of the deleted data point. This is in stark contrast to our RCRMR-LD problem, where the objective is to remove the knowledge of a set of classes or categories from the model. Further, data deletion methods will require access to the entire training data of a class in order to remove the entire knowledge of a class (refer to the appendix A.1. of [6]). This is because deep learning models have a high generalization power even on unseen examples of a class on which they have been trained, and simply deleting a few data points of a class from the knowledge base of the model will not be enough to forget that class. However, in our proposed problem setting, only a limited number of training examples are present for any class. Therefore, data-deletion approaches are not solutions to our proposed RCRMR-LD problem setting. This is why we have not applied these approaches in our problem setting.

Privacy-preserving deep learning [4,8,19] involves learning representations that incorporate features from the data relevant to the given task and ignore sensitive information (such as the identity of a person). The authors in [20] propose a simple variational approach for privacy-preserving representation learning. In contrast to existing privacy preservation works, the objective of the RCRMR-LD problem setting is to achieve class-level forgetting, i.e., if a class is declared as private/restricted, then all information about this class should be removed from the model trained on it, without affecting its ability to identify the remaining classes. To the best of our knowledge, this is the first work to address the class-level forgetting problem in the limited data regime, i.e., RCRMR-LD problem setting.

6   Baselines

We propose 9 baseline models for the RCRMR-LD problem and compare our proposed approach with them. The baseline 1 involves deleting the weights of the fully-connected classification layer corresponding to the excluded classes. Baselines 2, 3, 4, 5 involve training the model on the limited training data of the remaining classes. Baselines 2 and 4 both involve training a new model from scratch using the limited training examples of only the non-excluded classes, but baseline 4 initializes the model with the weights of the original model. Baselines 3 and 5 are similar to baselines 2 and 4, respectively, but also use a knowledge distillation loss to preserve the non-excluded class logits. Baselines 6, 7, 8, 9 involve fine-tuning the model on the available limited training data. Baselines 6 and 7 fine-tune the original model on the available limited data of all the classes after mapping the restricted classes to a single excluded class, but baseline 7 also uses a knowledge distillation loss. Baselines 8 and 9 fine-tune the original model on the available limited data of only the remaining classes, but baseline 9 also uses a knowledge distillation loss. Please refer to Sect. 3 in the supplementary material for details about the baselines.

7   Performance Metrics

In the RCRMR-LD problem setting, we propose three performance metrics to validate the performance of any method: forgetting accuracy (FA_e), forgetting prototype accuracy (FPA_e), and constraint accuracy (CA_{ne}). The forgetting accuracy refers to the fully-connected classification layer accuracy of the model for the excluded classes. The forgetting prototype accuracy refers to the nearest class prototype-based classifier accuracy of the model for the excluded classes. CA_{ne} refers to the fully-connected classification layer accuracy of the model for the non-excluded classes.

In order to judge any approach on the basis of these metrics, we follow the following sequence. First, we analyze the constraint accuracy (CA_{ne}) of the model produced by the given approach to verify if the approach has preserved the prediction power of the model for the non-excluded classes. CA_{ne} of the model should be close to that of the original model. If this condition is not satisfied, then the approach is not suitable for this problem, and we need not analyze the other metrics. This is because if the constraint accuracy is not maintained, then the overall usability of the model is hurt significantly. Next, we analyze the forgetting accuracy (FA_e) of the model to verify if the excluded class information has been removed from the model at the classifier level. FA_e of the model should be as close to 0% as possible. Finally, we analyze the forgetting prototype accuracy (FPA_e) of the model to verify if the excluded class information has been removed from the model at the feature level. FPA_e of the model should be significantly less than that of the original model. However, the FPA_e will not become zero since any trained model will learn to extract meaningful features, which will help the nearest class prototype-based classifier to achieve some non-negligible accuracy even on the excluded classes. Therefore, for a better analysis of the level of forgetting of the excluded classes at the feature level, we compare the FPA_e of the model with the FPA_e of the FDR model. The FDR model is a good candidate for this analysis since it has not been trained on the excluded classes (only trained on the complete dataset of the remaining classes), and it still achieves a non-negligible performance of the excluded classes (see Sec 8.1). However, it should be noted that this comparison is only for analysis and the comparison is not fair since the FDR model needs to train on the entire dataset (except the excluded classes).

A naive approach for measuring the capability of any approach for removing the excluded class information in this problem setting is to only consider how low the forgetting accuracy (FA_e) of the model for the excluded classes drops to after the excluded category removal process. However, using FA_e alone may be misleading since zero or random forgetting accuracy (FA_e) for a excluded class does not mean that the excluded class information has been removed from all layers of the model. In order to understand this point, let us consider the weight deletion (WD) baseline (baseline 1) that simply deletes the classification layer weights corresponding to the excluded classes and achieves a forgetting accuracy (FA_e) of 0% for the excluded classes. However, this does not mean that the excluded class information has been removed from all the layers of the network since the rest of the network remains intact. Therefore, using only (FA_e) metric is not enough. Now, if we consider the forgetting prototype accuracy (FPA_e) of the WD model, we will observe that the FPA_e of WD model is the same as that of the original model for the excluded classes. This clearly indicates that the excluded class information is still present in the layers of the network. Further, we also need to check whether the model performance for the remaining classes is maintained. We use our proposed constraint accuracy (CA_{ne}) of the non-excluded classes for this purpose. Therefore, the above discussion clearly demonstrates that a single metric is not effective in this problem setting.

8   Experiments

We have reported the experimental results for the CIFAR-100 and ImageNet-1k datasets in this section. We have also provided the results on the CUB-200 dataset in the supplementary material. Please refer to the supplementary material for the details regarding the datasets and implementation. We have provided the experimental results for the ablation experiments to validate the different components of our works in the supplementary material.

8.1   CIFAR-100 Results

We report the performance of different baselines and our proposed ERwP method on the RCRMR-LD problem using the CIFAR-100 dataset with different architectures in Table 1. We observe that the baseline 1 (weight deletion) achieves high constraint accuracy CA_{ne} and 0% forgetting accuracy FA_e. But its forgetting prototype accuracy FPA_e remains the same as the original model for all the three architectures, i.e., ResNet-20/56/164. Therefore, baseline 1 fails to remove the excluded class information from the model at the feature level. Baseline 2 is not able to preserve the constraint accuracy CA_{ne} even though it performs full training on the limited excluded class data. Baseline 3 achieves higher CA_{ne} than baseline 2, but the constraint accuracy is still too low. Baselines 4 and 5 demonstrate significantly better constraint accuracy than baseline 2 and 3, but their constraint accuracy is still significantly lower than the original model (except baseline 5 for ResNet-20). The baseline 5 with ResNet-20 maintains the constraint accuracy and achieves 0% forgetting accuracy FA_e but its FPA_e is still significantly high and, therefore, is unable to remove the excluded class information from the model at the feature level. The fine-tuning based baselines 6 and 7 are able to significantly reduce the forgetting accuracy FA_e but their constraint accuracy CA_{ne} drops significantly. The fine-tuning based baselines 8 and 9 only finetune the model on the limited remaining class data and as a result they are not able to sufficiently reduce either the FA_e or the FPA_e.

Table 1. Experimental results on the CIFAR-100 dataset for RCRMR-LD

Methods	ResNet-20			ResNet-56			ResNet-164		
	FA_e	FPA_e	CA_{ne}	FA_e	FPA_e	CA_{ne}	FA_e	FPA_e	CA_{ne}
Original	70.15%	65.25%	67.06%	70.80%	68.65%	69.88%	79.00%	76.40%	76.30%
No training									
Baseline 1 - WD	0.00%	65.25%	69.88%	0.00%	68.65%	72.44%	0.00%	76.40%	78.23%
Full train schedule									
Baseline 2 - TSLNRC	0.00%	22.20%	31.55%	0.00%	20.20%	30.21%	0.00%	33.05%	40.65%
Baseline 3 - TSLNRC-KD	0.00%	27.55%	40.81%	0.00%	22.50%	32.26%	0.00%	38.55%	45.74%
Baseline 4 - TOLNRC	0.00%	50.85%	58.01%	0.00%	48.60%	57.81%	0.00%	51.55%	63.78%
Baseline 5 - TOLNRC-KD	0.00%	60.25%	67.85%	0.00%	51.25%	61.14%	0.00%	52.80%	63.75%
Only fine-tuning									
Baseline 6 - FOLMRCSC	24.25%	59.55%	64.03%	13.35%	60.25%	65.23%	15.40%	59.20%	71.06%
Baseline 7 - FOLMRCSC-KD	13.50%	58.80%	63.79%	12.75%	64.95%	63.41%	16.75%	65.30%	68.61%
Baseline 8 - FOLNRC	59.05%	64.30%	68.34%	66.90%	68.45%	70.11%	77.35%	75.85%	75.95%
Baseline 9 - FOLNRC-KD	57.99%	64.40%	68.40%	65.95%	68.40%	70.01%	73.30%	73.55%	75.99%
ERwP (ours)	0.00%	48.06%	66.84%	0.00%	47.84%	69.32%	0.74%	56.23%	75.65%

Our proposed ERwP approach achieves a constraint accuracy CA_{ne} that is very close to the original model for all three architectures. It achieves close to 0% FA_e. Further, it achieves a significantly lower FPA_e than the original model. Specifically, the FPA_e of our approach is significantly lower than that of the original model by absolute margins of 17.19%, 20.81%, and 20.17% for the ResNet-20, ResNet-56, and ResNet-164 architectures, respectively. The FPA_e for the FDR model is 44.20%, 45.40% and 51.85% for the ResNet-20, ResNet-56 and ResNet-164 architectures, respectively. Therefore, the FPA_e of our approach is close to that of the FDR model by absolute margins of 3.86%, 2.44% and 4.38% for the ResNet-20, ResNet-56 and ResNet-164 architectures, respectively. Therefore, our ERwP approach makes the model behave similar to the FDR model even though it was trained on only limited data from the excluded and remaining classes. Further, our ERwP requires only 10 epochs to remove the excluded class information from the model. Since the available limited training data is only 10% of the entire CIFAR-100 dataset, therefore, our ERwP approach is approximately $30 * 10 = 300\times$ faster than the FDR method that is trained on the full training data for 300 epochs.

The FPA_e accuracy obtained using ERwP is significantly lower than the original model, e.g., for the ResNet-56 architecture FPA_e of ERwP is 47.84% compared to 68.65% of the original model for the CIFAR-100 dataset using the ResNet-56 model. However, this does not indicate the presence of much restricted category information. This is because the process for obtaining the FPA_e accuracy involves creating prototypes from the limited training data of the restricted classes and the remaining classes and finding the nearest neighbor class. Therefore, this process is dependent on the features generated by the deep learning model. Deep learning models generally produce highly discriminative features that can be used to create good prototype classifiers even for classes that the models were

Table 2. Experimental results on ImageNet-1k

Model	Methods	Top-1		Top-5	
		FA_e	CA_{ne}	FA_e	CA_{ne}
Res-18	Original	69.76%	69.76%	89.58%	89.02%
	ERwP	0.28%	69.13%	1.01%	88.93%
Res-50	Original	76.30%	76.11%	93.04%	92.84%
	ERwP	0.25%	75.45%	2.55%	92.39%
Mob-V2	Original	72.38%	70.83%	91.28%	90.18%
	ERwP	0.17%	70.81%	0.81%	89.95%

not trained on. For example, in the few-shot learning setting, the model is generally trained only on the base classes and then evaluated on novel class episodes using a prototype-based classifier. The prototype-based classifier of the few-shot learning setting is very effective in classifying the novel classes even though the deep model, which was used to obtain the features for the prototypes, was never trained on the novel classes. The discriminative nature of the features produced by deep learning models is the main reason why ImageNet pre-trained model features are used to train classifiers for other datasets and settings, such as in zero-shot learning. In order to better appreciate the effectiveness of our approach, we also consider the FDR model, which has not seen any training data of the restricted classes and still achieves a FPA_e accuracy close to that of our approach, e.g. FDR achieves a FPA_e accuracy of 45.40% for the CIFAR-100 dataset using the ResNet-56 model while our approach achieves an FPA_e accuracy of 47.84%. We provide this result as a reference to demonstrate that the non-zero accuracy of ERwP is due to the generalization power of deep CNNs and not due to the restricted classes information in the model. However, comparing FDR with our approach is not fair since FDR requires the full training data of the remaining classes, which violates the RCRMR-LD problem setting. Therefore, we have not provided the FDR results in the tables to maintain fairness.

8.2 ImageNet Results

Table 2 reports the experimental results for different approaches to RCRMR-LD problem over the ImageNet-1k dataset using the ResNet-18, ResNet-50 and MobileNet V2 architectures. Our proposed ERwP approach achieves a top-1 constraint accuracy CA_{ne} that is very close to that of the original model by absolute margins of 0.63%, 0.66% and 0.02% for the ResNet-18, ResNet-50 and MobileNet V2 architectures, respectively. It achieves close to 0% top-1 forgetting accuracy FA_e for all the three architectures. Therefore, our approach performs well even on the large-scale ImageNet-1k dataset. Further, our ERwP requires only 10 epochs to remove the excluded class information from the model. Since the available limited training data is only 5% of the entire ImageNet-1k dataset,

Table 3. Performance of ERwP in incremental learning setting using ResNet-18

Model	FA_e	CA_{ne}
Original model obtained after Session 4 [M4]	56.39%	58.32%
M4 modified with ERwP (ours)	0.20%	59.93%

therefore, our ERwP approach is approximately $20 * 10 = 200 \times$ faster than the FDR method that is trained on the full data for 100 epochs.

8.3   RCRMR-LD Problem in Incremental Learning

In this section, we experimentally demonstrate how the RCRMR-LD problem in the incremental learning setting is addressed using our proposed approach. We consider an incremental learning setting on the CIFAR-100 dataset in which each task contains 20 classes. We use the BIC [23] method for incremental learning on this dataset. The exemplar memory size is fixed at 2000 as per the setting in [23]. In this setting, there are 5 tasks. Let us assume that the model (M4) has already been trained on 4 tasks (80 classes), and we are in the fifth training session. Suppose, at this stage, it is noticed that all the classes in the first task (20 classes) have become restricted and need to be removed before the model is trained on task 5. However, we only have a limited number of exemplars of the 80 classes seen till now, i.e., $2000/80 = 25$ per class. We apply our proposed approach to the model obtained after training session 4, and the results are reported in Table 3. The results indicate that our approach modified the model obtained after session 4, such that the forgetting accuracy of the restricted classes approaches 0% and the constraint accuracy of the remaining classes is not affected. In fact, the modified model behaves as if, it was never trained on the classes from task 1. We can now perform the incremental training of the modified model on task 5.

9   Conclusion

In this paper, we present a "Restricted Category Removal from Model Representations with Limited Data" problem in which the objective is to remove the information regarding a set of excluded/restricted classes from a trained deep learning model without hurting its predictive power for the remaining classes. We propose several baseline approaches and also the performance metrics for this setting. We propose a novel approach to identify the model parameters that are highly relevant to the restricted classes. We also propose a novel efficient approach that optimizes these model parameters in order to remove the restricted class information and re-use these parameters for the remaining classes.

References

1. Carreira-Perpinán, M.A., Idelbayev, Y.: "learning-compression" algorithms for neural net pruning. In: Proceedings of the IEEE Conference on Computer Vision and Pattern Recognition, pp. 8532–8541 (2018)
2. Dong, X., Chen, S., Pan, S.J.: Learning to prune deep neural networks via layer-wise optimal brain surgeon. In: Proceedings of the 31st International Conference on Neural Information Processing Systems. NIPS 2017, pp. 4860–4874. Curran Associates Inc., Red Hook (2017)
3. Douillard, A., Cord, M., Ollion, C., Robert, T., Valle, E.: PODNet: pooled outputs distillation for small-tasks incremental learning. In: Vedaldi, A., Bischof, H., Brox, T., Frahm, J.-M. (eds.) ECCV 2020. LNCS, vol. 12365, pp. 86–102. Springer, Cham (2020). https://doi.org/10.1007/978-3-030-58565-5_6
4. Edwards, H., Storkey, A.: Censoring representations with an adversary. arXiv preprint arXiv:1511.05897 (2015)
5. Ginart, A., Guan, M.Y., Valiant, G., Zou, J.: Making AI forget you: data deletion in machine learning. arXiv preprint arXiv:1907.05012 (2019)
6. Golatkar, A., Achille, A., Ravichandran, A., Polito, M., Soatto, S.: Mixed-privacy forgetting in deep networks. In: Proceedings of the IEEE/CVF Conference on Computer Vision and Pattern Recognition, pp. 792–801 (2021)
7. Guo, Y., Yao, A., Chen, Y.: Dynamic network surgery for efficient DNNs. Adv. Neural. Inf. Process. Syst. **29**, 1379–1387 (2016)
8. Hamm, J.: Minimax filter: learning to preserve privacy from inference attacks. J. Mach. Learn. Res. **18**(1), 4704–4734 (2017)
9. Han, S., Mao, H., Dally, W.J.: Deep compression: compressing deep neural networks with pruning, trained quantization and Huffman coding. arXiv preprint arXiv:1510.00149 (2015)
10. He, Y., Kang, G., Dong, X., Fu, Y., Yang, Y.: Soft filter pruning for accelerating deep convolutional neural networks. In: IJCAI International Joint Conference on Artificial Intelligence (2018)
11. He, Y., Dong, X., Kang, G., Fu, Y., Yan, C., Yang, Y.: Asymptotic soft filter pruning for deep convolutional neural networks. IEEE Trans. Cybern. **50**(8), 3594–3604 (2019)
12. He, Y., Liu, P., Wang, Z., Hu, Z., Yang, Y.: Filter pruning via geometric median for deep convolutional neural networks acceleration. In: Proceedings of the IEEE/CVF Conference on Computer Vision and Pattern Recognition, pp. 4340–4349 (2019)
13. He, Y., Liu, P., Zhu, L., Yang, Y.: Meta filter pruning to accelerate deep convolutional neural networks. arXiv preprint arXiv:1904.03961 (2019)
14. Hinton, G., Vinyals, O., Dean, J.: Distilling the knowledge in a neural network. In: NIPS Deep Learning and Representation Learning Workshop (2014). https://fb56552f-a-62cb3a1a-s-sites.googlegroups.com/site/deeplearningworkshopnips2014/65.pdf
15. Hou, S., Pan, X., Loy, C.C., Wang, Z., Lin, D.: Learning a unified classifier incrementally via rebalancing. In: CVPR, pp. 831–839 (2019)
16. Kemker, R., Kanan, C.: FearNet: brain-inspired model for incremental learning. In: International Conference on Learning Representations (2018). https://openreview.net/forum?id=SJ1Xmf-Rb
17. Li, H., Kadav, A., Durdanovic, I., Samet, H., Graf, H.P.: Pruning filters for efficient convnets. arXiv preprint arXiv:1608.08710 (2016)

18. Liu, Y., Schiele, B., Sun, Q.: Adaptive aggregation networks for class-incremental learning. In: The IEEE/CVF Conference on Computer Vision and Pattern Recognition (CVPR) (2021)
19. Louizos, C., Swersky, K., Li, Y., Welling, M., Zemel, R.: The variational fair autoencoder. arXiv preprint arXiv:1511.00830 (2015)
20. Nan, L., Tao, D.: Variational approach for privacy funnel optimization on continuous data. J. Parallel Distrib. Comput. **137**, 17–25 (2020)
21. Rebuffi, S.A., Kolesnikov, A., Sperl, G., Lampert, C.H.: ICARL: incremental classifier and representation learning. In: Proceedings of the IEEE Conference on Computer Vision and Pattern Recognition, pp. 2001–2010 (2017)
22. Tao, X., Chang, X., Hong, X., Wei, X., Gong, Y.: Topology-preserving class-incremental learning. In: Vedaldi, A., Bischof, H., Brox, T., Frahm, J.-M. (eds.) ECCV 2020. LNCS, vol. 12364, pp. 254–270. Springer, Cham (2020). https://doi.org/10.1007/978-3-030-58529-7_16
23. Wu, Y., et al.: Large scale incremental learning. In: Proceedings of the IEEE/CVF Conference on Computer Vision and Pattern Recognition, pp. 374–382 (2019)
24. Yu, L., et al.: Semantic drift compensation for class-incremental learning. In: CVPR, pp. 6982–6991 (2020)
25. Zhang, T., et al.: A systematic DNN weight pruning framework using alternating direction method of multipliers. In: Ferrari, V., Hebert, M., Sminchisescu, C., Weiss, Y. (eds.) ECCV 2018. LNCS, vol. 11212, pp. 191–207. Springer, Cham (2018). https://doi.org/10.1007/978-3-030-01237-3_12

Anti-Neuron Watermarking: Protecting Personal Data Against Unauthorized Neural Networks

Zihang Zou[1]([✉]), Boqing Gong[2], and Liqiang Wang[1]

[1] University of Central Florida, Orlando, USA
{Zihang.Zou,Liqiang.Wang}@ucf.edu
[2] Google Research, Seattle, USA
bgong@google.com

Abstract. We study protecting a user's data (images in this work) against a learner's unauthorized use in training neural networks. It is especially challenging when the user's data is only a tiny percentage of the learner's complete training set. We revisit the traditional watermarking under modern deep learning settings to tackle the challenge. We show that when a user watermarks images using a specialized linear color transformation, a neural network classifier will be imprinted with the signature so that a third-party arbitrator can verify the potentially unauthorized usage of the user data by inferring the watermark signature from the neural network. We also discuss what watermarking properties and signature spaces make the arbitrator's verification convincing. To our best knowledge, this work is the first to protect an *individual* user's data ownership from unauthorized use in training neural networks.

1 Introduction

Recent advances in machine learning techniques have put personal data at significant risk. For example, in the scandal of "Cambridge Analytica" [38], millions of users' data are collected without consent to train machine learning models for political advertising. To protect personal data and privacy, there have been some legislations in place, such as Europe General Data Protection Regulation [11] (effective in May 2018), California Privacy Act [2] (effective in January 2021), and China Data Security Law [33] (effective in July 2021). They often require that personal data should be "processed lawfully, fairly and in a transparent manner" and can only be used "adequately, relevantly and limited to what is necessary in relation to the purposes ('data minimisation')" [11]. However, there is a lack of methods for detecting personal data breaches from machine learning models, which have increasingly become the primary motivation for a violator

Supplementary Information The online version contains supplementary material available at https://doi.org/10.1007/978-3-031-19778-9_26.

to break a user's data ownership because the models' efficacy heavily depends on data.

This paper studies personal image protection (PIP) from unauthorized usage in training deep neural networks (DNNs). The need for PIP arises when users expose their images to digital products and cloud services. In the era of big data and deep learning, a critical concern is that DNN learners may violate users' intents by using their data to train DNNs without authorization. It becomes worse when the DNN models consequently leak private user information [1,10, 27,31]. However, how can ordinary users know whether their images, which could be a tiny portion of the DNN learner's complete training set, have been used to train a DNN model?

Traditionally, PIP aims to prevent a user's images from duplicating, remixing, or exploiting (e.g., for a financial incentive) without the user's consent and relies on digital watermarking [5,19,25,35,42,46]. The digital watermarking enables a user to imprint images with unique patterns, such as signatures, logos, or stamps, to track and identify unauthorized *copies* of their pictures.

However, the rise of data-dependent deep learning poses another need for PIP, namely, protecting a user's images from unauthorized use in training DNNs. Could watermarking still fulfill this need?

One inspiring observation is that some DNNs do "memorize" certain training examples [1,9,10] in various ways, offering a user an opportunity to watermark their images to make them memorizable by the DNNs. We say this watermarking scheme is "anti-neuron" because its objective is to facilitate a third-party arbitrator to verify a DNN's use of a user's images in training and then hold the DNN learner accountable. However, we have to resolve two questions to make this anti-neuron watermarking work in practice. What watermarks make a user's images memorizable by DNNs? How can the third-party arbitrator verify that the user's images were indeed part of a DNN model's training set?

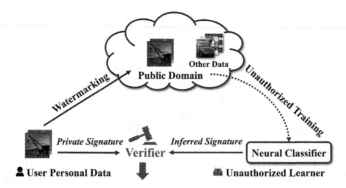

Does the inferred signature match the user private signature?

Fig. 1. Illustration of the anti-neuron watermarking for personal image protection (PIP) against unauthorized neural learners.

To answer the above questions, we first use Fig. 1 to formalize the anti-neuron watermarking for PIP against unauthorized DNN learners. First, a user watermarks images using a private signature before sharing them with the public (e.g., social media). An unauthorized learner then collects the user's watermarked images, along with images from other sources, to construct a training set to train a DNN image classifier. Finally, the user turns to a third-party arbitrator to check whether their images were used to train the DNN model. The arbitrator tries to recover the user's private signature for watermarking from the DNN model and the user's original images with no watermark—crucially, the arbitrator does not use the user's private signature to recover it. The arbitrator concludes that the user's images were part of the DNN's training set if the user's private signature can be recovered without knowing it in advance.

This paper proposes an empirically effective approach to the anti-neuron watermarking, and we leave more rigorous analyses to future work. In particular, a linear color transformation (LCT) in the hue space can be effectively used as a watermarking method. The resultant images remain as appealing as the original ones visually, so the unauthorized learner would not detect this type of watermark. Moreover, the LCT method is resilient to standard image augmentation techniques used in training neural models. Finally, we show that a DNN classifier indeed tends to memorize the LCT watermarking using extensive experiments. The arbitrator's verification method is simply iterating over the signature space, watermarking the user's original images using each signature, and returning the signature that reaches the lowest DNN classification loss.

In summary, our main contribution is to formalize the problem of user-focused anti-neuron watermarking for personal image protection from unauthorized usage in training DNNs. Moreover, we propose the LCT watermarking for ordinary users and a straightforward verification method for the third-party arbitrator, demonstrating a successful anti-neuron watermarking scenario for PIP. Additionally, we raise some critical questions for furthering the study of PIP against DNN learners: 1) What types of watermarking can imprint DNNs the best, especially when a user's watermarked images are only a tiny part of the training set? 2) What makes the imprinting of DNNs possible? Is it the DNN's memorization of training examples? 3) How can a trustworthy arbitrator recover a user's private watermark from DNN and the user's unwatermarked images? 4) How can anti-neuron watermarking work for multiple users? To the best of our knowledge, this work is the first to protect an individual user's data ownership from unauthorized use in training neural networks.

2   Related Work

Watermarking is a long-standing technique to declare ownership of objects. It can be traced back to paper marking [24] at 1282 in Italy, where a watermark was created via changing the thickness of the paper. Digital watermark is later introduced by [35] to code an undetectable digital watermark on gray scale images. Yu et al. [42] train a neural network for watermarking to embed hidden information in images. El et al. [8] add digital watermarks to video frames with neural networks. Zhong et al. [46] propose an automated and robust image watermarking based on deep neural networks. Recently, watermarking is used to protect the intellectual property of machine learning models [13,26,28,44]. These techniques follow similar ideas as trojan attacks [21] or backdoor attack [12], where models are trained with constructed samples to learn objective behaviors.

The most relevant works to this paper are *dataset tracing* and *membership inference*. **Dataset tracing** [20,23,29] protects the intellectual property of a dataset by appending traceable watermarks on data samples. Sablayrolles et al. [29] use pretrained model on a dataset itself to generate "radioactive data" to carry the class-specific watermarking vectors in high dimensional feature space. If a learner uses the "radioactive dataset" for training, the model's classifier would become more aligned with the watermarking vectors and thus can be used as an evidence of unauthorized usage. This kind of watermarking requires a pretrained model trained with the whole dataset. However, as such prior knowledge about the entire training data is unavailable for a common user, this kind of technique would be less applicable in real PIP scenarios.

Membership inference determines if a certain sample is inside a target dataset. Inference attack was first proposed for the attack and defense on medical datasets where users' medical records are extremely sensitive. By comparing genomic data with the statistical information of the training dataset, the presence of certain users can be inferred by attackers [15]. Shokri et al. [31] later introduce membership inference attack (MIA) into machine learning models. MIA trains a binary classifier to predict membership, on top of several shadow models being trained with the same data distribution as training. Alternatively, Yeom et al. [40] use the average of training error as the threshold to perform MIAs. Sablayrolles et al. [30] improve this threshold with Bayes optimal classifier to search for the best threshold using samples from both training and testing.

As MIAs determine whether given data samples belong to a training set or not, it is tempting to perform MIAs for personal data protection. However, similar to dataset tracing, as the training data distribution is unknown for common users, neither shadow models [31] nor threshold [30,40] can be obtained and existing MIA methods fail to work in protecting personal data.

3   Problem Statement

Consider image classification as a case study without loss of generality. Denote by $\mathcal{D}_u$ the set of personal images owned by a common user u. Assume $\mathcal{D}_u$ is unique and distinguished among identifiable users, as defined in GDPR [11]. Suppose the user u plans to expose $\mathcal{D}_u$ online, *e.g.*, by sharing them on social media. For the purpose of avoiding potential breach of personal data proprietary, the user watermarks images with a secret signature k^* before sharing them on social media. Denote by $\mathcal{D}_u^*$ the set of watermarked images carrying the signature k^*.

An unauthorized learner may use the user's data $\mathcal{D}_u^*$, along with many others', to construct a training set $\mathcal{D}$ to train a DNN classifier f without acquiring the user's permission. It is reasonable to assume that the user's data $\mathcal{D}_u^*$ is only a small portion of the whole training set $\mathcal{D}$ and the user u does not have any prior knowledge about the other users' data.

Let $g \in \mathcal{G}$ denote a watermarking method and $\mathcal{V}$ be a neutral third-party verification method that infers the user's private signature for watermarking without knowing it before. The arbitrator determines whether the user's personal images have been used in the training of neural classifier f as follows,

$$\mathcal{V}(f, \mathcal{D}_u, \mathcal{G}) = k^* \textbf{ iff } \mathcal{D}_u^* \subseteq \mathcal{D} \tag{1}$$

where the user's watermarked images $\mathcal{D}_u^* = g(D_u, k^*), g \in \mathcal{G}$. Namely, if the arbitrator can recover the user's private signature, she/he concludes that the user's images were part of the training set for learning the classifier f.

4 Approach

4.1 The Anti-Neuron Watermarking Method

Recent studies show that DNNs can "memorize" some training examples in various ways [1,9,10], and one can recover certain meaningful low-resolution images from DNNs [10]. Hence, it is tempting to conduct verification by recovering the user u's images from the neural classifier f. However, there are many challenges with this approach. First of all, the model f may memorize some training images but not this user u's. Moreover, even if the model happens to memorize some of this user's images, the recovery success rate is likely low. Existing methods (e.g., [10]) can recover semantically meaningful images from some DNNs, but they do not resemble any exact training images, to the best of our knowledge. Finally but not the least, the method in [10] incurs high computation cost, often by many iterations of gradient descent, and assumes that the DNN classifier f is a white box, disclosing its architecture and parameters.

An alternative approach to leveraging DNNs' memorization capability is to check a DNN's loss over a set of training images. Arguably, if the DNN model has memorized a majority of this set of images, the loss should be low. Following the above reasoning, we let a user u watermark her/his images $\mathcal{D}_u$ using a private signature k^* so the user has full control and knowledge of her/his watermarked images $\mathcal{D}_u^*$. This watermarking method eases the third-party arbitrator's job; instead of trying to recover the exact training images, the arbitrator can now search for the watermarking signature that leads to the lowest DNN loss, if the DNN model has memorized many images in $\mathcal{D}_u^*$ watermarked by user u.

Properties for Effective Watermarking. Formally, a user u chooses an anti-neuron watermarking function $g \in \mathcal{G}$ and generates the watermarked images as

$$\mathcal{D}_u^* = \{g(I, k^*), \forall I \in \mathcal{D}_u\} \tag{2}$$

We discuss the necessary properties needed to make a good anti-neuron watermarking function. The key is to make the watermarked images, and hence the signature, memorized by DNNs. First, the watermarking function g should *preserve an image's original content*. For example, for a user portrait or selfie, g should not change its identity. Besides, the watermarking function g should be *resilient to common image augmentations* used to train DNNs. The private signature should survive after the learner applies common image augmentations. Furthermore, the space K of watermarking signatures should be *large* and preferably *bounded*, such that the probability of an innocent classifier coincidentally matching the user signature is low, while the signature can be inferred efficiently during verification.

Linear Color Transformation. Based on the discussion above, we propose Linear Color Transformation (LCT) as our anti-neuron watermarking. Color provides a large signature space for images. Our watermarking function exploits hue transformation and uses the hue adjustment of images as a signature. Thanks to the sufficiently big hue space, the user's randomly chosen signature is likely different from other users' signatures. Moreover, the randomly chosen signature lifts the user images to a low-density region, making the resultant images be easily memorized by DNNs—according to Feldman's studies on memorization [9] and our experiments in Sect. 5.6, DNNs tend to memorize images of low-density regions.

Concretely, we first convert the RGB color space into the YIQ color space [37] by the following matrix:

$$T_{\mathrm{YIQ}} = \begin{bmatrix} 0.299 & 0.587 & 0.114 \\ 0.596 & -0.275 & -0.321 \\ 0.212 & -0.523 & 0.311 \end{bmatrix} \tag{3}$$

In the YIQ color space, hue is represented by two dimensional coordinates, forming a chromaticity diagram. As a result, watermarking images with signature k will be conducted by rotating the hue at an angle θ_k with the following matrix,

$$T_k = \begin{bmatrix} 1 & 0 & 0 \\ 0 & cos(\theta_k) & -sin(\theta_k) \\ 0 & sin(\theta_k) & cos(\theta_k) \end{bmatrix} \tag{4}$$

where $\theta_k = \frac{k\pi}{180}$. Hence, for every pixel $v = [v_r, v_g, v_b]^\mathsf{T}$ in image I, we can watermark v with signature k by:

$$v' = g_k v \tag{5}$$

where $g_k = T_{\mathrm{YIQ}} \cdot T_k \cdot T_{\mathrm{YIQ}}^{-1}$.

Making LCT More Versatile. An immediate extension to LCT is to make the color transformation matrix T_{YIQ} specifiable by users. A user chosen color transformation T_u can further enrich the watermarking signature space. We leave this extension to future work.

4.2   The Verification Method

We let a third-party arbitrator independent of the user and DNN learner determine whether the user's images were part of the DNN training set. The arbitrator has to infer a signature from a suspicious DNN classifier f and the user's original, unwatermarked images $\mathcal{D}_u$ without using the private watermark signature k^*. If the inferred signature matches the user's private one, we say that the DNN classifier is highly likely trained using the user's images $\mathcal{D}_u^*$.

Assume that the watermarking function $g(I, k^*)$ does not change the image's class label. Let y denote the class label of image $I \in \mathcal{D}_u$. We design a simple yet effective approach to recovering the watermarking signature:

$$\hat{k} \leftarrow \arg\min_{k \in \mathcal{K}} \sum_{(I,y) \in \mathcal{D}_u} \mathcal{L}(f(g(I, k)), y) \tag{6}$$

where $\mathcal{L}$ is a loss (e.g., cross-entropy) for learning the DNN classifier f, and $\mathcal{K}$ is the collection of all possible signatures.

If the inferred signature matches the user's private one, $\hat{k} \approx k^*$, the arbitrator concludes that the DNN learner has used the user's images $D_u^* = \{g(I, k^*), \forall I \in \mathcal{D}_u\}$ as part of the training set for DNN f. Otherwise, the DNN learner is likely innocent.

The Signature Space $\mathcal{K}$. It is important to discuss the success rate of the above verification method. Apparently, the signature space $\mathcal{K}$ should be sufficiently large to reduce the probability of an innocent classifier coincidentally matching a user's watermarked images. For the analysis purpose, we discretize the bounded signature space $\mathcal{K}$ into N equal-sized, non-overlapped slots, each with an interval 2τ. We say the recovered signature $\hat{k}$ matches the private one k^* when $|\hat{k} - k^*| < \tau$. Reserving one slot for no watermarking, the number of valid watermarking signatures is $N - 1$. Clearly, the larger N is, the more convincing the verification.

Some readers might wonder what if there is a large number of users. For example, given 1 million users but a small number N of signatures, would this setting fail the proposed anti-neuron watermarking? The answer is a pleasant no because, importantly, two users could choose the same private watermarking signature as long as their personal images are different, though the chance of using the same signature is low because each user independently chooses a signature. What happens when a user chooses not to watermark her/his images? A well-trained neural classifier should generalize well under the training distribution. Hence, if most training images are not watermarked, given the user's original unwatermarked data, the recovered signature from the well-trained classifier would approach no watermarking.

It is not necessary to have enormous N to avoid users having duplicated private signatures based on the above discussion. However, a sufficiently large N is still preferred for another reason, DNNs' memorization. Only when N is big, the chance becomes high for a user to watermark her/his images into a low-density region and hence can be memorized by DNNs.

A large signature space also benefits the memorization of user signatures. According to the study [9] on memorization, deep neural classifier must memorize atypical examples to perform well on the less frequent examples during inference. Since watermarking shift data distribution via signature from a large space, watermarking is highly likely to lift user images into lower density region and thus being better memorized by neural models.

Optimization Method and Computational Cost for Signature Inference. To solve Eq. (6) efficiently, we propose two optimization methods. **(i) Grid search:** the arbitrator can enumerate all signatures for watermarking and perform grid search over the bounded signature space with a linear computational cost as $O(N)$. If the signature is well memorized by a DNN, the DNN loss will reach minimum when the signature being evaluated equals or closely approximates the private signature used by the user. **(ii) Gradient search:** when the model is accessible, the arbitrator can watermark clean images with a random initial watermark signature and then infer the user's signature by descending along the gradient of training loss with respect to the signature. This technique infers the watermark signature more precisely than grid search and the computational cost might be less for a large N.

5   Experiments

5.1   Setup

We evaluate the proposed watermarking in image classification on the Cifar-10/Cifar-100 [3], CUB birds [36] and Tiny ImageNet [17] datasets.

A User Watermarks Their Personal Data. A portion of randomly chosen images from a training set (by default, 1% for Cifar and 0.1% for Tiny ImageNet) is defined as a user' personal data. The user data could contain samples from any class. Each user image is watermarked using Eq. (5) by a given signature in the space of $[30, 60, ..., 330]$, followed by clipping pixel values to the valid range of $[0,1]$. By default, we use 60 (*i.e.*, rotating hue by 60°) as the signature.

A Learner Trains Neural Classifiers Using Unauthorized User Data. An unauthorized learner trains neural classifiers using the above watermarked user data along with other training data. Images are randomly cropped, horizontal flipped, and normalized following the common data augmentation practice [14,18]. We use ResNet50 [14] as the default neural classifier and train every model from scratch for 90 epochs. The initial learning rate is 0.1 and decays by 0.1 for every 30 epochs.

A Verifier Infers The Watermark Signature. Given suspicious neural network models, a third-party verifier infers the user's signature following two approaches discussed above. For *grid search*, we iterate over all candidate signatures generated by dividing the whole signature space into $N = 12$ intervals whose length is $2\tau = 2 \times 15$. For *gradient search*, we exploit gradient descent to learn the signature. To avoid local optimum, multiple initial values are used and the best signature that leads to the lowest loss is returned.

5.2 Analyzing Effectiveness of Watermarking

We first show empirically how signatures are memorized by the neural classifiers. Here, we consider a single user watermarking their data for simplicity. (See Appendix for other experiments and the gradient search results.)

1. *Different Numbers of Watermarked Samples.* We study how many images are desired for making anti-neuron watermarking successful. The grid search result is shown in Fig. 2 (a, b, c) using Eq. (6). It is visually clear that most of the models achieve the minimum loss near the watermark signature, within the range of matching $|\hat{k} - k^*| < \tau$. However, with less watermarked data (*e.g.*, less than 5 samples), the inferred signature with minimum loss does not match the user's private signature.

2. *Different Watermark Signatures.* We verify whether different watermark signatures work equivalently. We experiment with different signatures on one user's data and show the grid search results in Fig. 2 (d, e, f) for different datasets. From these figures, we observe that all inferred signatures (marked in square) match the user's signatures for watermarking, indicating that different hue adjustments can all be used for anti-neuron watermarking.

3. *Different Neural Classifier Architectures.* We also evaluate the proposed watermarking for different neural classifier architectures, including Alexnet [18], VGG [32], ResNet [14], Wide ResNet [43] and DenseNet [16] trained with default settings. As shown in Fig. 2g, all inferred signatures match the user's, implying that our watermarking approach works well against a large variety of deep neural networks.

4. *Different Learning Capacities of Models.* We further investigate whether a model memorizes watermark signatures better when the model has more learning capacity (e.g., more parameters, deeper or wider) by exploring the ResNet family. As shown in Fig. 2h, as the networks go larger and deeper, the loss decreases faster and reaches the minimum around the watermark signature more sharply.

5. *High Resolution Images.* In Fig. 2i, we present our result on CUB-200-Birds, a fine-grained dataset with high-resolution images of 448×448. We use pre-trained ResNet50 from ImageNet and conduct a transfer learning on CUB-200-Birds. The dataset has fewer than 6000 images for training, and we assume the user has 60 images (1%) for watermarking. Strong data augmentations [41] are used to boost performance, including color jitter, random crop, random resize, random scale and random horizontal flip. Even under the strong data augmentations and the transfer learning setting, the result shows that ResNet50 memorizes the user's signature well.

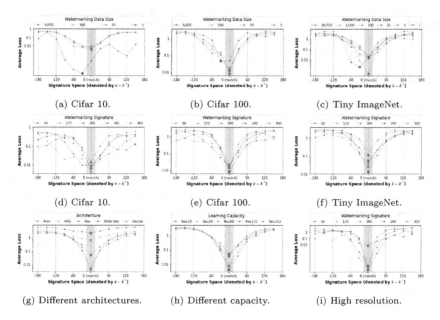

(a) Cifar 10.   (b) Cifar 100.   (c) Tiny ImageNet.

(d) Cifar 10.   (e) Cifar 100.   (f) Tiny ImageNet.

(g) Different architectures.   (h) Different capacity.   (i) High resolution.

Fig. 2. The first row shows variant of loss for models trained with **different quantity** of watermarked samples on Cifar and Tiny ImageNet. The second row shows variant of loss for models with **different signatures** on Cifar and Tiny ImageNet. The third row shows results for **different architectures**, **different capacity** on Tiny ImageNet and **high resolution** on CUB-200-Birds. The x-axis represents signature space (denoted by distance to the user private signature, *i.e.*, $k-k^*$), and the y-axis represents the average loss of user data with respect to signature k. The green region represents the range for a match ($< 2\tau$). If the inferred signature $\hat{k}$ (marked as **Square marker** indicating the point with minimum loss) lies in the green region ($|\hat{k} - k^*| < \tau$), it would be a match. Otherwise, it would be a miss. (Color figure online)

5.3   Analyzing Properties of Watermarking

We then evaluate how the properties discussed in Sect. 4.1 would help anti-neuron watermarking.

Resilience to Data Augmentation. We evaluate if our anti-neuron watermarking is resilient against various common data augmentations, especially those involving random hue transformations. We apply random crop and random horizontal flip in all our experiments following [14,18]. Besides, several widely adopted data augmentations including random cutout [6], label smoothing [34], Gaussian noise [4], adversarial training [22] and differential privacy [7] are evaluated. Finally, we test color jittering [18], which includes brightness, saturation, contrast and *the same* hue transformation we used for watermarking. As shown in Fig. 3, the watermark signatures can be inferred correctly for the aforementioned data augmentations. This shows empirically that LCT is an effective anti-neuron watermarking approach because it is resilient to common data augmentations in neural networks' training. We also evaluate privacy preserving techniques such as differential privacy [7]. Since we infer the signature using all user images, noise added to the output would be reduced by taking an average. Beside, we also consider two common *defense techniques* against watermarking: pruning and fine-tuning. We follow common settings [45] and find in Fig. 3g and Fig. 3h that LCT is also resilient to these defense methods.

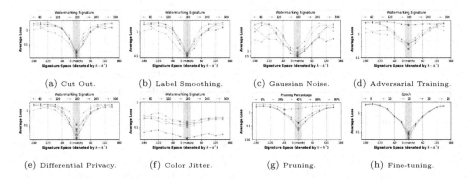

(a) Cut Out.   (b) Label Smoothing.   (c) Gaussian Noise.   (d) Adversarial Training.

(e) Differential Privacy.   (f) Color Jitter.   (g) Pruning.   (h) Fine-tuning.

Fig. 3. The variation of model loss for **different data augmentations**. Only the color jitter can significantly narrow down the loss difference between signatures.

Less Noticeable Watermarking. In Sect. 4.1, we discuss the watermarking should not change the major content of an image, and one of the desired features is to make watermarking unnoticeable to human. Rather than changing the hue of images globally, we study an alternative technique from traditional watermarking proposed in [42]. It adjusts the blue channel's intensity on pre-selected pixels. In this work, we adjust the intensity as a watermark signature on 512 randomly selected pixels. As shown in Fig. 4, the general appearance of watermarked images are less noticeable than changing the hue globally (adjusting hue for 4096 pixels by 60). For $\tau = 0.1$ and watermark signatures (the blue channel's intensity), 0.1, 0.3, 0.5, 0.12, 0.28, 0.44 are used in inference on selected pixels, matching the user's watermark signature. However, this kind of watermarking has its limitation. It introduces noise to images, and the images could look noisy when the color themes are dominated by red or green. To solve this problem, we may find some transformations that are invisible to humans but easy to learn by neural classifiers. We leave this challenge to future work.

5.4   Analyzing Signature Space for Verification

In Sect. 4.2, we discuss how the signature space could affect watermarking from the perspective of a third-party verifier. Here, we show experimentally how to have a trustful signature space for a convincing verification.

When User Data Was Not Used to Train Neural Classifiers. From previous experiments, we show that the inferred signature matches a user's private

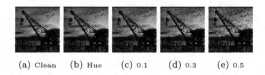

(a) Clean   (b) Hue   (c) 0.1   (d) 0.3   (e) 0.5

Fig. 4. Illustration of clean, hue-transformed and less noticeable watermarked samples. 0.1, 0.3 and 0.5 are the intensity of blue channel for selected pixels. (Color figure online)

watermark signature if the user's watermarked data have been used in training. Here we show the inferred signature approaches no watermarking when the user data was not used for training. To this end, we construct held-out users using auxiliary unseen data from validation. Pretrained models from Fig. 2h are used to infer signature from the held-out users. Not surprisingly, the inferred signatures approach 0 (no watermarking) for the held-out users, with $|\hat{k} - 0| = 4.3 \pm 1.4$.

Multiple Users with User-specific Watermarking Signatures. We examine multiple users for several scenarios. The training set of Tiny ImageNet is equally divided into 1,000 users. Then we evaluate the effectiveness of watermarking for different ratio of users exploiting the same LCT (Eq. (3)) or different LCTs. For the later, we sample 3×3 matrices from a uniform distribution $T_u \sim \mathcal{U}(-1, 1)$ per user. Each user chooses a random signature from $[30, 60, ..., 330]$, and τ is set to 15.

From the result shown in Fig. 5a, we can observe that when 20% of users watermark their images using LCT, their watermark signatures can be inferred correctly for almost all the users. As this ratio increases, the matching accuracy drops significantly if the users use the same LCT. However, if they use different LCTs, the matching accuracy remains above 80% even when all users data are watermarked independently. We also evaluate a special case when an adversary infers signatures using an arbitrary LCT. The arbitrary LCTs ($T_{u'} \sim \mathcal{U}(-1, 1)$) only achieve 10% matching accuracy, which is 70% less when LCTs are given. Such results indicate users can use unique and user-specific watermarking for a better protection rate when other users may also exploit watermarking.

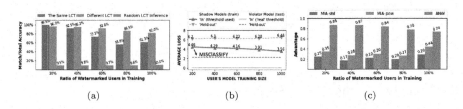

(a)   (b)   (c)

Fig. 5. (a) Watermarking performance for **multiple users**. (b) MIAs fail to work with user-specific shadow models because insufficient training data leads to much higher threshold. (c) Our ANW *vs.* MIAs using the adv^{P} metric.

5.5   Comparisons with Related Methods

Comparing to Membership Inference Attacks. We compare our anti-neuron watermarking (ANW) with two *threshold-based* membership inference attacks (MIAs): In MIA-std [40], few samples are known in violator's training set and their average training loss would be used as threshold ϵ to infer membership (if $\mathcal{L}_t < \epsilon$, target sample t is in training, *vice versa.*); In MIA-pow [30], few samples in training and held-out together determine a better threshold.

There are 3 scenarios making MIAs not applicable for PIP. **(i)** as a user has no knowledge about the violator's training distribution, MIAs cannot be applied as neither shadow models nor threshold can be obtained. **(ii)** Users could train shadow model using their own data and perform MIAs via shadow models [31], but MIAs would not work well because shadow models trained with user data would produce a much larger loss than the learner' models. Consequently, if a threshold is chosen from shadow models trained with user data, held-out sample would be misclassified as "in training" because the learner's model would produce smaller loss for both "training" and "held-out" samples. Here we compare MIAs by creating 10 users with individual data. 10 shadow models are trained respectively and MIA-std is performed with the threshold of average training loss. For ANW, 10 users data are watermarked with different signatures. Under different settings for user data size, we find out that ANW achieves 100% matching accuracy while MIA-std achieves 50% (misclassify all held-out samples). Figure 5b shows how the threshold from shadow models fails to classify sample membership for the learner. Similarly, MIA-pow along with other MIAs [23,31] relied on shadow models would also fail in this settings. **(iii)** At last, even if a user acquires all necessary information, the MIA results would still be less convincing. As MIAs only provide binary output (True/False), it is difficult to convince the verifier when random guess can still achieve about 50% success rate. To quantifiably and fairly compare with MIAs, we extend the classic *membership advantage* [39] into *protection advantage* (adv^P) considering both accuracy and fidelity:

$$\text{adv}^P = \int_x (\mathbb{P}_e(y = True|x) - \mathbb{P}_r(y = True|x))dx \qquad (7)$$

The adv^P metric quantifies quality of protection through the expectation gap between the empirical successful inference ($\mathbb{P}_e$) and successful random guess ($\mathbb{P}_r$). Note that the *membership advantage* [39] is a special case of adv^P metric when the second term is 0.5. For a Bernoulli experiment, the above formula could be calculated as $\frac{M-Np}{N}$, where M is the total matches in N experiments and p is the probability of a correct random guess. With above metric, we conduct comparison between our watermarking and two threshold-based MIAs [30,40] (See appendix for experiment settings.). As shown in Fig. 5c, our ANW significantly outperforms the MIA approaches under the adv^P metric with both accurate and convincing inference, showing that watermarking is a feasible method in the PIP problem.

Comparing to Dataset Tracing [29]. Dataset tracing [29] exploits pretrained classifier to generate traceable data. If neural classifier learns such dataset, the decision boundary of classifier would become more aligned with watermarking vectors (*i.e.*, cosine similarity becomes higher). In Table 1, we compare this approach [29] with ours when only 0.1% data being watermarked. For dataset tracing, it is computed by the classifier's weight vector and the watermarking vector. And for our method, it is computed by inferred and user watermarking signatures. The experimental results show that it is easier to memorize low dimensional signatures as our watermarking method lifts the cosine similarity significantly after training with tiny portion of watermarked data.

Table 1. Cosine similarity. With only 0.1% data watermarked, the dataset tracing shows almost no effects while our watermarking method improves the similarity to almost 1 after training.

	Before training	After training
Dataset tracing [29]	-0.005 ± 0.030	-0.005 ± 0.015
Our watermarking	0.045 ± 0.52	0.999 ± 0.001

5.6   Improving Memorization by Watermarking

Finally, we explore empirically why watermarking is effective against neural classifier by revisiting "Memorization Value Estimate" (MAE) [9]. MAE measures the generalization gap (difference of prediction between models trained with/without certain data) to quantify the memorization ability of neural networks toward such data. A higher MAE after watermarking indicates the model tends to memorize watermarked data than original data. For user data, we observe the MAE increases from 26.8% to 34.8% after applying watermarking, indicating that our approach increases memorization of user data and thus the signature would be easier memorized along with user data.

6   Conclusion

In this paper, we introduce a new personal data protection problem against unauthorized neural model training. To protect user personal data, we propose an anti-neuron watermarking approach based on linear color transformation. By watermarking user's images with private signature using LCT, unauthorized usage of user personal data can be verified by a third-party neutral arbitrator. Through extensive experiments, we show empirically that LCT-based watermarking is effective in protecting user data from unauthorized usage in a various realistic settings.

Acknowledgements. this work was supported in part by NSF-1704309 and NSF-1952792.

References

1. Carlini, N., Liu, C., Erlingsson, Ú., Kos, J., Song, D.: The secret sharer: evaluating and testing unintended memorization in neural networks. In: 28th USENIX Security Symposium (USENIX Security 2019), pp. 267–284 (2019)
2. CCPA: California privacy act, Januay 2021. https://oag.ca.gov/privacy/ccpa
3. Cifar (2009). https://www.cs.toronto.edu/~kriz/cifar.html cIFAR Dataset
4. Cohen, J., Rosenfeld, E., Kolter, Z.: Certified adversarial robustness via randomized smoothing. In: International Conference on Machine Learning, pp. 1310–1320. PMLR (2019)
5. Cox, I.J., Miller, M.L., Bloom, J.A., Honsinger, C.: Digital Watermarking. LNCS, vol. 53. Springer, Heidelberg (2002). https://doi.org/10.1007/3-540-36617-2
6. DeVries, T., Taylor, G.W.: Improved regularization of convolutional neural networks with cutout. arXiv preprint arXiv:1708.04552 (2017)
7. Dwork, C.: Differential privacy: a survey of results. In: Agrawal, M., Du, D., Duan, Z., Li, A. (eds.) TAMC 2008. LNCS, vol. 4978, pp. 1–19. Springer, Heidelberg (2008). https://doi.org/10.1007/978-3-540-79228-4_1
8. El'arbi, M., Amar, C.B., Nicolas, H.: Video watermarking based on neural networks. In: 2006 IEEE International Conference on Multimedia and Expo, pp. 1577–1580. IEEE (2006)
9. Feldman, V., Zhang, C.: What neural networks memorize and why: discovering the long tail via influence estimation. arXiv preprint arXiv:2008.03703 (2020)
10. Fredrikson, M., Jha, S., Ristenpart, T.: Model inversion attacks that exploit confidence information and basic countermeasures. In: Proceedings of the 22nd ACM SIGSAC Conference on Computer and Communications Security, pp. 1322–1333 (2015)
11. GDPR: Regulation (EU) 2016/679 (general data protection regulation) that is applicable as of may 25th, 2018 in all member states, is to the protection of natural persons with regard to the processing of personal data and rules relating to the free movement of personal data (2016). https://gdpr-info.eu/
12. Gu, T., Liu, K., Dolan-Gavitt, B., Garg, S.: BadNets: evaluating backdooring attacks on deep neural networks. IEEE Access **7**, 47230–47244 (2019)
13. Guo, J., Potkonjak, M.: Watermarking deep neural networks for embedded systems. In: 2018 IEEE/ACM International Conference on Computer-Aided Design (ICCAD), pp. 1–8. IEEE (2018)
14. He, K., Zhang, X., Ren, S., Sun, J.: Deep residual learning for image recognition. In: Proceedings of the IEEE Conference on Computer Vision and Pattern Recognition, pp. 770–778 (2016)
15. Homer, N., et al.: Resolving individuals contributing trace amounts of DNA to highly complex mixtures using high-density SNP genotyping microarrays. PLoS Genet. **4**(8), e1000167 (2008)
16. Huang, G., Liu, Z., Van Der Maaten, L., Weinberger, K.Q.: Densely connected convolutional networks. In: Proceedings of the IEEE Conference on Computer Vision and Pattern Recognition, pp. 4700–4708 (2017)
17. kaggle (2017). https://www.kaggle.com/c/tiny-imagenet, tiny Imagenet
18. Krizhevsky, A., Sutskever, I., Hinton, G.E.: ImageNet classification with deep convolutional neural networks. In: Pereira, F., Burges, C.J.C., Bottou, L., Weinberger, K.Q. (eds.) Advances in Neural Information Processing Systems, vol. 25, pp. 1097–1105. Curran Associates, Inc. (2012)

19. Kundur, D., Hatzinakos, D.: Digital watermarking using multiresolution wavelet decomposition. In: Proceedings of the 1998 IEEE International Conference on Acoustics, Speech and Signal Processing, ICASSP 1998 (Cat. No. 98CH36181), vol. 5, pp. 2969–2972. IEEE (1998)

20. Li, Y., Zhang, Z., Bai, J., Wu, B., Jiang, Y., Xia, S.T.: Open-sourced dataset protection via backdoor watermarking. arXiv preprint arXiv:2010.05821 (2020)

21. Liu, Y., et al.: Trojaning attack on neural networks. In: NDSS Symposium (2017)

22. Madry, A., Makelov, A., Schmidt, L., Tsipras, D., Vladu, A.: Towards deep learning models resistant to adversarial attacks. In: International Conference on Learning Representations (2018). https://openreview.net/forum?id=rJzIBfZAb

23. Maini, P., Yaghini, M., Papernot, N.: Dataset inference: ownership resolution in machine learning. arXiv preprint arXiv:2104.10706 (2021)

24. Meggs, P.B.: A History of Graphic Design. Wiley, Hoboken (1998)

25. Meng, Z., Morizumi, T., Miyata, S., Kinoshita, H.: Design scheme of copyright management system based on digital watermarking and blockchain. In: 2018 IEEE 42nd Annual Computer Software and Applications Conference (COMPSAC), vol. 2, pp. 359–364. IEEE (2018)

26. Nagai, Y., Uchida, Y., Sakazawa, S., Satoh, S.: Digital watermarking for deep neural networks. Int. J. Multimed. Inf. Retrieval $7(1)$, 3–16 (2018). https://doi.org/10.1007/s13735-018-0147-1

27. Nasr, M., Shokri, R., Houmansadr, A.: Comprehensive privacy analysis of deep learning: passive and active white-box inference attacks against centralized and federated learning. In: 2019 IEEE Symposium on Security and Privacy (SP), pp. 739–753. IEEE (2019)

28. Rouhani, B.D., Chen, H., Koushanfar, F.: DeepSigns: an end-to-end watermarking framework for protecting the ownership of deep neural networks. In: ACM International Conference on Architectural Support for Programming Languages and Operating Systems (2019)

29. Sablayrolles, A., Douze, M., Schmid, C., Jégou, H.: Radioactive data: tracing through training. In: International Conference on Machine Learning, pp. 8326–8335. PMLR (2020)

30. Sablayrolles, A., Douze, M., Schmid, C., Ollivier, Y., Jégou, H.: White-box vs black-box: Bayes optimal strategies for membership inference. In: International Conference on Machine Learning, pp. 5558–5567. PMLR (2019)

31. Shokri, R., Stronati, M., Song, C., Shmatikov, V.: Membership inference attacks against machine learning models. In: 2017 IEEE Symposium on Security and Privacy (SP), pp. 3–18. IEEE (2017)

32. Simonyan, K., Zisserman, A.: Very deep convolutional networks for large-scale image recognition. arXiv preprint arXiv:1409.1556 (2014)

33. Standing Committee of the National People's Congress: China data security law, July 2021. https://www.xinhuanet.com/2021-06/11/c_1127552204.htm

34. Szegedy, C., Vanhoucke, V., Ioffe, S., Shlens, J., Wojna, Z.: Rethinking the inception architecture for computer vision. In: Proceedings of the IEEE Conference on Computer Vision and Pattern Recognition, pp. 2818–2826 (2016)

35. Tirkel, A.Z., Rankin, G., Van Schyndel, R., Ho, W., Mee, N., Osborne, C.F.: Electronic watermark. In: Digital Image Computing, Technology and Applications (DICTA 1993), pp. 666–673 (1993)

36. Welinder, P., et al.: Caltech-UCSD Birds 200. Technical report CNS-TR-2010-001, California Institute of Technology (2010)

37. Wikipedia: Yiq (2015). https://en.wikipedia.org/wiki/YIQ

38. Wikipedia: Cambridge analytica (2018). https://en.wikipedia.org/wiki/Cambridge_Analytica
39. Yeom, S., Fredrikson, M., Jha, S.: The unintended consequences of overfitting: training data inference attacks. arXiv preprint arXiv:1709.01604, December 2017
40. Yeom, S., Giacomelli, I., Fredrikson, M., Jha, S.: Privacy risk in machine learning: analyzing the connection to overfitting. In: 2018 IEEE 31st Computer Security Foundations Symposium (CSF), pp. 268–282. IEEE (2018)
41. Yu, F., Wang, D., Shelhamer, E., Darrell, T.: Deep layer aggregation. In: Proceedings of the IEEE Conference on Computer Vision and Pattern Recognition, pp. 2403–2412 (2018)
42. Yu, P.T., Tsai, H.H., Lin, J.S.: Digital watermarking based on neural networks for color images. Sig. Process. **81**(3), 663–671 (2001)
43. Zagoruyko, S., Komodakis, N.: Wide residual networks. arXiv preprint arXiv:1605.07146 (2016)
44. Zhang, J., et al.: Model watermarking for image processing networks. In: Proceedings of the AAAI Conference on Artificial Intelligence, vol. 34, pp. 12805–12812 (2020)
45. Zhang, J., et al.: Passport-aware normalization for deep model protection. Adv. Neural. Inf. Process. Syst. **33**, 22619–22628 (2020)
46. Zhong, X., Huang, P.C., Mastorakis, S., Shih, F.Y.: An automated and robust image watermarking scheme based on deep neural networks. IEEE Trans. Multimed. **23**, 1951–1961 (2020)

An Impartial Take to the CNN vs Transformer Robustness Contest

Francesco Pinto[1,2]([✉]), Philip H. S. Torr[1], and Puneet K. Dokania[1,2]

[1] University of Oxford, Oxford, UK
francesco.pinto@eng.ox.ac.uk
[2] Five AI Ltd., Cambridge, UK

Abstract. Following the surge of popularity of Transformers in Computer Vision, several studies have attempted to determine whether they could be more robust to distribution shifts and provide better uncertainty estimates than Convolutional Neural Networks (CNNs). The almost unanimous conclusion is that they are, and it is often conjectured more or less explicitly that the reason of this supposed superiority is to be attributed to the self-attention mechanism. In this paper we perform extensive empirical analyses showing that recent state-of-the-art CNNs (particularly, ConvNeXt [20]) can be as robust and reliable or even sometimes more than the current state-of-the-art Transformers. However, there is no clear winner. Therefore, although it is tempting to state the definitive superiority of one family of architectures over another, they seem to enjoy similar extraordinary performances on a variety of tasks while also suffering from similar vulnerabilities such as texture, background, and simplicity biases.

Keywords: Transformers · CNNs · Robustness · Calibration

1 Introduction

Transformers are a family of neural network architectures that became extremely popular in natural language processing, and are primarily characterised by the extensive use of the attention mechanisms as defined in [37]. Before Vision Transformers (ViT) [8] were introduced, Transformers were considered difficult to use for computer vision applications due to the prohibitive computational complexity and memory requirements of the self-attention mechanism. Since then, several transformer variants that are efficient to train with performance more competitive with the state-of-the-art CNNs like BiT [17] (e.g. [19,36,41]) have been proposed.

The effectiveness of transformers compared to CNNs in computer vision applications has led to recent interest in comparing them in obtaining reliable predictive uncertainty and robustness to distribution shifts. The almost unanimous conclusion in the literature is that transformers exhibit: (1) better calibration [22], (2) better robustness to covariate shift [3,23,28,42], and (3) better

Supplementary Information The online version contains supplementary material available at https://doi.org/10.1007/978-3-031-19778-9_27.

S. Avidan et al. (Eds.): ECCV 2022, LNCS 13673, pp. 466–480, 2022.
https://doi.org/10.1007/978-3-031-19778-9_27

uncertainty estimation for tasks like out-of-distribution detection (OoD) [3,9]. Currently, these conclusions are mostly misleading as (1) the recent convolutional architectures (ConNeXt) were not available for proper comparisons; (2) the comparisons are often performed with questionable assumptions (e.g. comparing model capacity solely based on their parameter count) or training procedures (e.g. trying to make the training as similar as possible for both the families at the cost of damaging the performance of either); and (3) the choice of the evaluation metrics is often not carefully justified and the most subtle aspects of the interpretation of the results were not identified. Additionally, when it comes to explaining the outcome of the analysis, which mostly leads to concluding that Transformers are superior, the credit is often given (more or less explicitly) to the most prominent feature that distinguishes Transformers from CNNs: the self-attention mechanism. Yet, a fair comparison and an understanding of whether and how self-attention modules would allow learning superior features compared to convolutional models is needed before providing a definitive answer regarding the superiority of one over another.

Taking a step in this direction, we thoroughly evaluate the robustness and reliability of most recent state-of-the-art Transformers (ViT [8] and SwinT [19]) and CNN architectures (BiT [17] and ConvNeXt [20]) on ImageNet-1K [6]. We would like to highlight that we do not modify the training recipes of CNNs and Transformers to ensure that they are at their current best during comparisons. The main takeaways of our work are:

1. **Simplicity bias experiment** [34]. Transformers, just like CNNs, also suffer from the so-called simplicity bias. They are somewhat similar to CNNs in finding shortcuts (undesirable) to solve the desired task. Therefore, as opposed to the common notion, despite the capability of the self-attention modules to communicate globally, Transformers as well tend to focus on easy-to-discriminate parts of the input and conveniently ignore other complex-yet-discriminative ones. Hence, similar to CNNs, they might just be learning to combine sets of simple and potentially spurious features, rather than more complex and invariant ones. Based on this experiment, we discourage the common trend in the literature to give unnecessary praise to the self-attention module of Transformers anytime these perform better against CNNs. More theoretical developments, analyses, and well-thought experiments are needed to support such claims.

2. We show that for out-of-distribution detection task, CNNs and Transformers **perform equally well**. We also highlight why, unless domain-specific assumptions are made, preferring AURP over AUROC in situations of data imbalance (which generally is the case) might give the false impression of one model being significantly superior to others.

3. In-distribution calibration of the best performing CNN model (in terms of accuracy) is better than the best performing Transformer. However, there is **no clear winner** that performs the best in all the experiments including covariate shift.

4. Again, there is **no clear winner** in detecting misclassified inputs.

These takeaways also suggest that the inductive biases induced in CNNs by using the design components popularised by Transformers (e.g. GeLU [13] activations, LN normalization [2] etc.), but without using the self-attention mechanism, might be highly effective in bridging the gap between the two in terms of robustness. However, this speculation requires further analysis as there are too many variables involved in designing a model (from architectural design choices to optimization algorithms) and the interplay between them is not well understood yet.

2   Experimental Design and Choices

2.1   Setup

Models. We consider state-of-the-art convolutional and non-convolutional models for our analysis.

1. **BiT** [17]: It is a very commonly used family of fully convolutional architectures. Its members are ResNet variants that have been shown to achieve state-of-the-art accuracy on ImageNet classification and that, with an appropriate fine-tuning procedure, transfer well to many other datasets. In this paper we consider BiT-R50x1, BiT-R50x3, BiT-R101x1, BiT-R101x3, BiT-R152x2, BiT-R152x4 (where R50/101/152 indicates the ResNet variant, and the multiplicative factor scales the number of channels).
2. **ConvNeXt** [20]: A recent family of fully convolutional architecture that is very close to the non-convolutional Transformer models in terms of training recipes and design choices. Its members have been shown to produce either comparable or superior performance to Transformers on several large-scale datasets. ConvNeXt exemplifies how advancing state-of-the-art in one family of networks can yield architecture design choices that, if adapted properly, can benefit other families of networks too. Our conclusions heavily rely on the careful architecture design process of ConvNeXt. We consider ConvNeXt-B, ConvNeXt-L, ConvNeXt-XL variants. Here and also for other models, B, L and XL indicate the capacity (B = Base, L = Large, XL = Extra Large).
3. **ViT** [8]: First successful use of Transformers on vision tasks. Its members still exhibit state-of-the-art performances. We consider ViT-B/16 and ViT-L/16[1], where 16 indicates the input token patch size.
4. **SwinTransformer** [19]: A family of transformers implementing a hierarchical architecture employing a shifting window mechanism. We consider the Swin-B and Swin-L variants. We use patch size of 4 pixels and shifted windows of size 7 as they provide highly competitive performance.

Training. Unless stated otherwise, all the considered architectures have been pre-trained on ImageNet-21k [32] and fine-tuned on ImageNet-1k [6]. We use the

---

[1] We omit ViT-B/32 ViT-L/32 as we find them to always underperform with respect to ViT-B/16 and ViT-L/16 (a similar observation was made in [28]). Similarly, we also omit DeiT [36] as it underperforms compared to SwinTransformers.

trained checkpoints available in the `timm library` [39] except only for the simplicity bias experiments where we fine-tune the models on our own. Additional results showing the impact of pre-training are shown in Appendix A.

Datasets. Since the in-distribution dataset is ImageNet-1K, we use ImageNet-A [14], ImageNet-R [12], ImageNetv2 [31], ImageNet-Sketch [38] for the *domain-shift* experiments. For *out-of-distribution* detection experiments, we use ImageNet-O [14]. For our preliminary analyses to understand *existing biases* in Transformers and CNNs, we use ImageNet9 [40], the Cue-Conflict Stimuli dataset [38], and also *synthesize* a dataset by combining MNIST and CIFAR-10 datasets. For Imagenet experiments, we apply the standard preprocessing pipeline. Additional results showing the impact of input preprocessing are shown in Appendix A.

2.2   Yet Another Analysis?

Before we begin discussing our analyses, we would like to mention how we differ from the existing ones.

Closest to ours is a recent analysis presented by [3] which involves rather simpler architectures for both Transformers (DeiT) and CNNs (ResNet-50), and also drops transformer-specific training techniques (for instance, reducing training epochs to 100 from 300, removing augmentations and regularisation techniques etc.). This indeed brings DeiT down to CNNs in terms of training procedure, however, makes DeiT underperform significantly. Although they derive interesting insights, the applicability of these insights for a practitioner with an intent to identify the most robust and best performing model is somehow limited. Therefore, we not only consider a wider variety of CNNs and Tranformers in our analysis, we also do not modify their standard training recipes so that their best performance is being compared. In [29], authors do provide a partial and preliminary analysis questioning the existing literature, however, solid evidence is still lacking. Another work [35] showed superiority of CNNs over Transformers on natural covariate-shift datasets. Differently from them, our analysis not only considers these metrics, but also the performance in terms of calibration, misclassification detection, and out-of-distribution detection. Other recent work [23,42] performs partially overlapping analyses reaching the same conclusion about the superiority of Transformers. However, [23] do not consider recent CNN models, and also compare Transformers pre-trained on ImageNet-21K with CNNs that are trained from scratch on ImageNet-1K. Instead, [42] only compares with the extremely simple CNN variants.

We would also like to highlight that comparing different models based on their capacity (determined solely based on their number of parameters) might lead to wrong conclusions. How well a model would preform in practice is heavily dependent on the nature and the composition (hierarchy, depth etc.) of the underlying functions, not just on the number of parameters. To provide a widely known example, an MLP with one hidden layer and enough hidden units (large number of parameters) can theoretically fit most functions of interest, and it is known to be a universal function approximator [5,15]. However, in practice, they underperform compared to a deep network (with same or even less number of parameters). The interaction of inductive biases and training procedures plays an important role towards finding solutions that generalise well.

Therefore, although the number of parameters can be a proxy for comparing model capacity, in practice, it can be misleading. Indeed, when compute and memory constraints are imposed, a practitioner will always find the best performing model satisfying such constraints rather than choosing a model based on the parameter count[2]. We provide discussions and empirical findings (using standard complexity measures) to support our arguments above in Appendix B.

3   Empirical Evaluation and Analysis

3.1   Are Transformer Features More Robust Than CNN Ones?

There is no clear answer to this question in the literature. It is known that for a model to generalise to previously unseen domains, its predictions should not depend on spurious features that are specific to the distribution from which the training and test in-domain sets are sampled from, but on robust features that generalise across other domains under covariate-shift [30]. Typical examples of spurious features described in literature are the background's colour, textures and generally any simple pattern that correlates strongly with the labels in the training set but not in the test set [1].

It is usually conjectured in the literature that Transformers might be learning more robust features than CNNs because of the ability of their self-attention modules to communicate globally within a given input [28]. Which, in fact, is equivalent to implicitly criticizing the convolutional inductive biases of CNNs for their relatively poor robustness. Before we begin comparing these two families in terms of robustness, here we first present a few experiments to analyse their vulnerabilities. These experiments show that *the sole presence of the self-attention mechanism is not sufficient for Transformers to neglect spurious features*, and they result to be as biased as CNNs towards them.

Simplicity Bias Experiment. The intent of this experiment is to understand what Transformers and CNNs prefer to learn in situations where it is possible to focus only on the simple discriminative features of the input and ignore the complex discriminative ones in order to perform well on the task. This experiment was proposed and analysed on CNNs by [34]. Following their work, we first create a binary classification task where the input $X = [\mathbf{x}, \bar{\mathbf{x}}]$ is composed of the concatenation of $\mathbf{x}$ and $\bar{\mathbf{x}}$, both discriminative, and learning features for *either or both* will lead to an accurate classifier. We design this task such that, say, $\bar{\mathbf{x}}$ is

---

[2] Consider that ViT-L/32 has about 307M parameters, ViT-L/16 has 305M, yet ViT-L/32 requires about 15GFLOPS, while ViT-L/16 requires about 61GFLOPS, and ViT-L/32 exhibits lower accuracy and robustness than ViT-B/32 [28].

Table 1. Simplicity bias (SB), Background bias (BB) and Texture bias (TB) experiments. For **SB**, in-domain indicates the accuracy when MNIST and CIFAR images are associated as in the training set. *A model suffers from SB if R-MNIST accuracy is close to random whereas R-CIFAR accuracy is close to the in-domain.* For **BB**, we report the absolute accuracy on the original (O), mixed-same (MS), and mixed-random (MR) datasets, respectively. **BG-Gap** defined as the difference in accuracy between MS and MR, quantifies the impact of background in producing correct classifications. For **TB** we report the CCS accuracy. All quantities in the table are percentages (%).

	# params (M)	SB			BB				TB
		In-domain	R-MNIST	R-CIFAR	O (↑)	MS (↑)	MR (↑)	BG-Gap (↓)	CCS(↑)
BiT-R50×1	25	100	48.39	100	94.57	83.21	76.2	7.00	31.09
BiT-R50×3	217	100	48.14	100	95.14	85.14	80.22	4.92	33.12
BiT-R101×1	44	100	48.50	99.94	94.17	81.28	75.19	6.09	32.81
BiT-R101×3	387	100	48.19	99.89	94.32	81.19	76.67	4.52	32.58
BiT-R152×2	232	100	48.39	99.94	94.64	80.05	75.09	4.95	35.47
BiT-R152×4	936	100	48.19	100	95.01	81.16	75.33	5.83	37.19
ConvNeXt-B	88	100	48.29	99.94	97.95	93.95	90.42	3.53	30.63
ConvNeXt-L	196	100	48.20	99.89	98.2	95.19	91.63	3.56	35.16
ConvNeXt-XL	348	100	48.75	99.69	98.49	95.23	92.3	2.93	36.95
ViT-B/16	86	100	48.59	99.79	97.36	92.35	88	4.34	30.78
ViT-L/16	304	100	52.79	95.66	98.02	94.05	90.05	4	47.19
Swin-B	87	100	48.75	99.64	97.75	90.94	86.47	4.47	26.95
Swin-L	195	100	48.69	99.74	98.02	92.99	88.47	4.52	30.08

more complex[3] than **x**. Then, under this setting, a trained classifier suffers from simplicity bias if (1) fixing **x** and randomly modifying **x̄** in the input does not change its prediction, and (2) fixing **x̄** and randomly modifying **x** in the input drops the test accuracy to the random prediction baseline.

To create the dataset for the above experiment, **x** is taken from the MNIST dataset [7] (randomly sampled image of a certain digit) while **x̄** from the relatively more complex CIFAR-10 (randomly sampled image of a certain label). For instance, say digit **0** is associated to **car** and the whole concatenated image is assigned label +1, and digit **1** is associated to **truck** and the concatenated image is labelled −1. Refer to the top left of Fig. 1. During training, this relationship holds true for all the examples (in-domain). We fine-tune our classifiers on this dataset for 3 epochs (it is easy to converge on this dataset). At test time, we either randomise the MNIST part of the image (R-MNIST) or the CIFAR part of the image (R-CIFAR) for the analysis. Results are reported in Table 1.

As it can be seen, the accuracy is almost the same for all the models (except in ViT-L/16) even if the CIFAR (more complex) part of the input is completely randomized (R-CIFAR). However, the accuracy drops to nearly random (50%) when the MNIST part of the input is randomized (R-MNIST). This shows that

---

[3] We understand that defining complexity is subjective. Here we assume that something that is visually more complex (having more colors, shapes, textures etc.) across the training set would require learning more complex features.

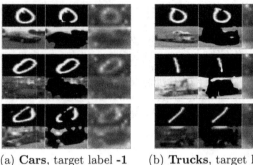
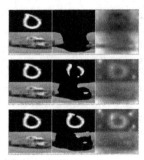

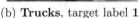

(a) **Cars**, target label **-1**   (b) **Trucks**, target label **1**   (c) Top to bottom: attention at layer 1, 4 and 12.

Fig. 1. Simplicity Bias Experiment for Transformers: For each triplet of images, from left to right: input image, test image without pixels on which the attention value is below the 70% quantile and the attention map visualization. The attention maps show that the Transformer (ViT-B/16) gives high attention values to simple features and neglect the complex ones.

both families, Transformers and CNNs, rely on MNIST for classification and are agnostic to the CIFAR component. Hence, both are prone to simplicity bias. To understand which are the most prominent features leveraged by the Transformer, we visualize the pixels that fall above the 70% quantile of the intensity values in the attention map, and blacken the ones that fall below it in Fig. 1. This figure confirms that Transformer's self-attention mechanism neglects complex features in favour of simple features. Figure 1 (c) also shows how the self-attention changes through the layers of the transformer. At the first layer there is no specific focus on the MNIST digit, but as the layers progress (i.e. as the features specialise to be useful for the classification), the attention values increase around the digit.

Reliance on Backgrounds and Texture. Here we measure the performance of several architectures on a benchmark that measures the reliance of features on backgrounds and textures: ImageNet9 [40] and the Cue-Conflict Stimuli [38].

The **ImageNet9** dataset selects a subset of labels and images from the original ImageNet dataset. In our experiments we measure the accuracy on the full images of the dataset (*original split*), images in which the background has been swapped with another image of same class (*mixed-same*), images in which the background has been swapped with another image of different class chosen at random (*mixed-random*). Sample images are provided in Appendix C. The authors of this dataset suggest taking the gap between the accuracy on mixed-same and mixed-random as a quantifier of the reliance on background information to produce accurate predictions. As it can be seen from Table 1, some of the highest capacity BiT models do not rely more on the background than ViT-B/16, SWIN-B and SWIN-L. ConvNeXt models rely on backgrounds even less than Transformers, suggesting that the self-attention mechanism might not be the only factor responsible for the difference observed between low-capacity ResNets and Transformers.

The **Cue-Conflict Stimuli** dataset alters the texture information of an image using style transfer: given an image of a certain class, it uses as style-image a sample from another class (sample images in Appendix C). The purpose is to deceive classifiers that overly rely on textures to make predictions. As it can be seen in Table 1, although the top performing model is ViT-L/16 (with a significant margin), Swin Transformers exhibit an even heavier reliance on texture than ConvNeXt models, and ViT-B/16 performs comparably to ConvNeXt-B. This suggests that the sole presence of the self-attention in an architecture is not sufficient for the model to not be biased towards texture information.

> **Conclusion 1**
>
> ○ Transformers can leverage spurious features just like CNNs. They can be comparably prone to various biases such as simplicity bias, background bias, and texture bias. The sole presence of self-attention might not be sufficient to avoid such biases.

3.2 Out-of-Distribution Detection

Current notion in the literature is that Transformers are better than CNNs at detecting OoD samples [28].

We compare various CNN and Transformer models at the task of detecting ImageNet-O samples from ImageNet-1K. ImageNet-O contains 2K samples in 200 classes, while the subset of ImageNet-1K used as the corresponding in-distribution set contains 10K samples [14] (therefore, there is a stark imbalance in the number of samples belonging to the two sets). Both ImageNet-O and ImageNet-1K (test) samples are fed to the classifier, for each point an uncertainty score is computed and a binary threshold-based classifier is used to distinguish between them. Since the choice of the threshold depends on the risk exposure desired for a certain application, a standard evaluation procedure considers all the risk thresholds and computes the AUROC (Area Under the Receiver Operating Characteristic curve) and the AUPR (Area Under the Precision-Recall curve).

AUPR vs AUROC? We start by observing that the apparent complexity in distinguishing ImageNet-O samples from ImageNet-1K observed in the literature (e.g. [14,28]) mostly depends on the interaction between specific evaluation choices. The AUPR, in the case of an imbalanced number of samples belonging to the positive and negative classes, is known to prefer one class over another. However, for out-of-distribution evaluation, unless additional domain-specific assumptions are made, there is no preferred mistake: confusing an in-distribution sample with an out-of-distribution sample or viceversa are both equally important mistakes. To exemplify why the AUPR can yield misleading conclusions, in Table 2 we consider different possible assignments of the positive class and apply a rebalancing technique as well. Recent work [14,28] concluding

Table 2. ImageNet-O: **OoD** performance analysis when in-distribution samples are assigned label 1 and OoD label 0, and vice-versa (with and without rebalancing). AUROC (%) is invariant whereas AUPR (%) is extremely sensitive to these design choices. The best performing method based on AUROC is in bold and the second best is underlined. The gap between the two is marginal.

| | IND = 1, OoD = 0 | | | | IND = 0, OoD = 1 | | | |
| | Imbalanced | | Balanced | | Imbalanced | | Balanced | |
	AUROC (↑)	AUPR (↑)	AUROC (↑)	AUPR (↑)	AUROC (↑)	AUPR (↑)	AUROC (↑)	AUPR (↑)
BiT-R50x1	65.17	90.15	65.17	65.81	65.17	23.30	65.17	60.13
BiT-R50x3	74.56	92.30	74.56	71.28	74.56	36.26	74.56	72.49
BiT-R101x1	70.34	91.35	70.34	68.75	70.34	28.53	70.34	66.11
BiT-R101x3	77.32	93.40	77.32	74.84	77.32	38.74	77.32	74.66
BiT-R152x2	77.46	93.51	77.46	75.23	77.46	38.24	77.46	74.43
BiT-R152x4	80.07	94.39	80.07	78.10	80.07	44.25	80.07	78.17
ConvNeXt-B	85.72	95.53	85.72	81.74	85.72	59.15	85.72	85.53
ConvNeXt-L	89.07	96.90	89.07	86.96	89.07	65.33	89.07	88.55
ConvNeXt-XL	<u>90.04</u>	97.19	<u>90.04</u>	88.11	<u>90.04</u>	68.50	<u>90.04</u>	89.75
ViT-B/16	79.89	95.26	79.89	82.30	79.89	36.77	79.89	73.77
ViT-L/16	**90.60**	97.85	**90.60**	91.27	**90.60**	64.58	**90.60**	88.90
Swin-B	83.74	95.29	83.74	81.01	83.74	52.93	83.74	82.80
Swin-L	87.76	96.55	87.76	85.67	87.76	62.51	87.76	87.27

that there exist a dramatic gap between CNNs and Transformers on OoD detection performance report values when OoD samples are considered as positives (third column from the right). In this setting, for instance, the performance of BiT-R50x1 is less than half of the performance of ViT-L/16, and extremely low (with respect to the attainable maximum of 100). However, only rebalancing the number of samples[4] the performance of BiT-R50x1 rises to more than two thirds of the performance of ViT-L/16 (last column on the right). Alternatively, if the choice of the positive and negative class is flipped, in an imbalance condition, one can obtain an absolute gap between the performance of BiT-R50x1 and ViT-L/16 of less than 8% (third column from the left). If one drew conclusions solely based on this column, one would think there is only a marginal difference between the performance of the two models. This gap widens when rebalancing the number of samples (fourth column from the left). This exemplifies how widely the AUPR can vary based on evaluation choices that, in the lack of domain-specific assumptions, are arbitrary. On the other hand, the AUROC does not vary across all the considered evaluation setups, because it gives the same importance to both types of errors that can occur. These results allow us to conclude that, for the considered models, ImageNet-O is evidently not as hard to distinguish from ImageNet as it is believed to be.

For completeness, in Appendix D we provide a proof to show that AUROC is invariant to the choice of positive and negative classes.

---

[4] We oversample OoD samples (4×) so that both in-distribution and OoD datasets have 10000 samples each. We could rebalance them also by randomly sampling 2000 out of the 10000 in-distribution samples, but this could induce some variance in the metrics; we also observed that the average of this strategy coincides with the balancing strategy.

Comparing Transformers and CNNs. From the AUROC values in Table 2 it is clear that the top-performing CNN (ConvNeXt-XL) is competitive to the top-performing Transformer (ViT-L/16). ConvNeXt-L outperforms Swin-L, and ConvNeXt-B outperforms Swin-B. The best performing BiT (BiT-R152×4) outperforms ViT-B.

Conclusion 2

○ CNNs can perform as well as Transformers for OoD detection.
○ With no domain-specific assumptions regarding the importance of one category over another (in-distribution vs OoD), AUROC should be preferred over AUPR as it is stable across evaluation choices.

3.3 Calibration on In-Distribution and Domain-Shift

A model is said to be calibrated if its confidence (i.e. the maximum probability score of the softmax output) and its accuracy match. The idea is to attribute to the confidence the frequentist probabilistic meaning of counting the amount of times the model is correct. Several measures have been proposed targeted specifically towards quantifying the said mismatch between a classifier's confidence and its accuracy. These measures are primarily the variants of the well-known Expected Calibration Error (ECE) [25] such as the recently proposed Adaptive Calibration Error (AdaECE) [24].

Comparing Transformers and CNNs. On in-domain data (Table 3), ViTs produce the lowest calibration error and Swin transformers are outperformed by

Table 3. **In-distribution** accuracy (%) and **calibration** (%) for ImageNet-1K.

	ImageNet-1K (test)		
	Acc. (↑)	ECE (↓)	AdaECE (↓)
BiT-R50x1	74.03	3.49	3.45
BiT-R50x3	77.92	6.56	6.51
BiT-R101x1	75.85	5.10	5.10
BiT-R101x3	78.20	7.63	7.63
BiT-R152x2	78.00	6.37	6.37
BiT-R152x4	78.16	9.38	9.38
ConvNeXt-B	85.53	2.87	2.82
ConvNeXt-L	86.29	2.27	2.34
ConvNeXt-XL	**86.58**	2.38	2.29
ViT-B/16	78.01	**1.40**	**1.41**
ViT-L/16	84.38	1.81	1.83
SWIN-B	84.71	8.40	8.40
SWIN-L	85.83	5.50	5.50

ConvNeXts. On covariate-shifted inputs (Table 4), ViTs produce higher calibration error than ConvNeXts and Swin transformers, and the model producing the lowest calibration error is the Swin-L. Consistently with [22], within a family of models, the ECE typically decreases as the number of parameters (and also the accuracy) increases.

Table 4. **Domain-shift** accuracy (%) and **calibration** (%) for ImageNet-1K.

| | Domain-shift | | | | | | | | | | | |
| | ImageNet-R | | | ImageNet-A | | | ImageNet-V2 | | | ImageNet-SK | | |
	Acc (↑)	ECE (↓)	AdaECE (↓)	Acc (↑)	ECE (↓)	AdaECE (↓)	Acc (↑)	ECE (↓)	AdaECE (↓)	Acc (↑)	ECE (↓)	AdaECE (↓)
BiT-R50x1	39.87	15.50	15.50	10.97	42.94	42.94	62.70	8.49	8.45	27.34	24.87	24.87
BiT-R50x3	46.39	14.65	14.65	24.08	34.48	34.48	66.36	13.13	13.13	33.47	28.55	28.55
BiT-R101x1	41.72	12.24	12.24	16.29	36.68	36.68	64.61	10.21	10.21	28.69	24.37	24.37
BiT-R101x3	47.00	15.80	15.80	27.11	32.92	32.92	66.44	14.44	14.39	34.15	30.67	30.67
BiT-R152x2	48.02	15.38	15.38	27.15	32.25	32.25	66.76	12.14	12.13	35.70	28.41	28.41
BiT-R152x4	47.57	15.32	15.32	30.84	29.93	29.93	67.12	15.75	15.67	35.08	31.45	31.45
ConvNeXt-B	62.46	2.57	2.51	52.63	8.28	8.31	75.43	**2.91**	**2.78**	48.64	8.85	8.84
ConvNeXt-L	64.57	3.00	3.08	58.23	7.57	7.26	76.77	3.72	3.85	50.08	10.31	10.31
ConvNeXt-XL	**66.01**	2.92	2.90	**61.11**	7.54	7.21	**77.20**	4.00	4.24	**52.67**	11.16	11.15
ViT-B16	43.15	5.21	5.21	24.17	22.89	22.89	66.25	4.71	4.68	18.18	13.02	13.02
ViT-L16	61.54	3.07	3.07	47.08	11.99	11.99	74.28	5.34	5.22	45.96	10.67	10.67
Swin-B	59.63	2.18	2.17	49.72	8.77	8.76	74.74	4.92	4.81	45.07	**7.75**	**7.75**
Swin-L	64.24	**2.14**	**2.11**	59.52	**6.19**	**6.33**	76.65	3.03	3.14	48.87	8.72	8.71

Conclusion 3

○ There is no one model that performs the best in all the covariate shift experiments in terms of calibration. Transformers or CNNs either can be better or worse depending on the experiment.

○ The best performing model in terms of accuracy is not the most calibrated one.

Is Low Calibration Error Enough for a Classifier to be Reliable? A perfectly calibrated classifier can still be highly inaccurate and unreliable. For example, consider the binary case where there are 70 negative test samples and 30 positives. A classifier that has learned to classify every sample to a negative class with a confidence of 0.7 will be perfectly calibrated, however, only 70% accurate. Since neural networks trained on cross-entropy loss are known to be overconfident [11], even if we somehow manage to calibrate them well, they still might be assigning higher confidence to the wrongly predicted samples than the correctly predicted ones. If the minority class samples (positives in the above example) are as important as the majority ones, this behaviour raises concerns relating to their reliability. Analysing and quantifying such behaviour is necessary to complement our understanding in terms of the reliability of neural networks. In the next section, we discuss this aspect as well.

3.4   Misclassified Input Detection

One of the tasks a reliable classifier should be good at is to reject samples on which they are likely to be wrong. This particular task did not receive much

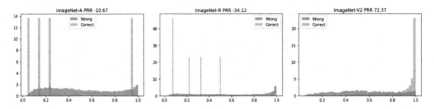

Fig. 2. From left to right: the distribution of the confidence values for wrong and right samples for ViT-L/16 on ImageNet-A, ImageNet-R and ImageNet-V2. As it can be seen, in several cases wrong samples are given higher confidence than correct samples (PRR < 0). In cases when PRR > 0, some wrong samples are still given higher confidences (similar to correct samples), but to a lesser extent.

attention in the Transformers vs CNNs comparisons performed by the existing literature. Several ways to evaluate a model at this task are available (e.g. metrics based on ROC [18] or Rejection-Accuracy curves [10,14]), however, it has already been observed that these metrics favour models that have higher test accuracy [4,21]. A recently proposed metric that allows comparison of different models in this aspect, agnostic to their individual accuracy, is Prediction Rejection Ratio (PRR) [21]. The sign of this metric is an indication of whether a model tend to provide lower confidence to correctly classified samples and higher to wrongly classified ones or not. The PRR ranges from −1 to 1. It is 0 if the rejection choice is performed at random, negative if the network is more confident on misclassified samples than on correctly classified ones, and positive viceversa. The optimal value of 1 is achieved when the classifier rejects only the misclassified samples while rejecting the most uncertain ones.

For instance, consider Fig. 2 where we show the distribution of the confidence values for samples that a ViT-L/16 wrongly and correctly classified on a few datasets. As observed, in many cases the network is more confident on wrongly classified samples than on the correctly classified ones. This is captured by the sign of PRR (reported in %). However, the corresponding miscalibration error values as shown in Table 4 are particularly low (especially on ImageNet-R). Therefore, as discussed in Sect. 3.3, low miscalibration solely can be misleading in providing a deep understanding of the reliability of different models.

Comparing Transformers and CNNs. As it can be seen form Table 5, in in-distribution ViT-L/16 is the best model, immediately followed by ConvNeXt-XL. ViT-B/16 slightly outperforms ConvNeXt-B and L, which in turn outperform Swin-B and L. On ImageNet-A, the best model is BiT-R152x4, with a significant margin with respect to any other model. The second best model is Swin-L, and the third best is BiT-R50x1. On ImageNet-R, the only model with positive PRR is Swin-L, and the models with highest negative PRR are ConvNeXt-XL and L, followed by BiT-R50x1 and 101x1. On ImageNet-Sketches ViT-L/16 and ConvNeXt-XL perform comparably, immediately followed by ConvNeXt-L and B. On ImageNetV2, ViT-L/16 is the best model, immediately followed by ViT-B/16 and all the ConvNeXts.

Table 5. Misclassification detection results using the PRR (%) metric.

	In-distribution	Domain-shift			
	ImageNet-1K (test)	ImageNet-A	ImageNet-R	ImageNet-SK	ImageNet-V2
	PRR (↑)				
BiT-R50x1	68.38	54.90	−25.60	58.70	63.13
BiT-R50x3	67.61	28.58	−42.72	60.25	64.09
BiT-R101x1	69.82	−0.42	−25.94	60.08	64.60
BiT-R101x3	68.93	29.50	−34.52	60.13	65.00
BiT-R152x2	68.03	31.56	−35.12	59.26	63.26
BiT-R152x4	67.00	**92.04**	−46.05	59.34	61.48
ConvNeXt-B	73.43	16.03	−39.91	67.44	69.84
ConvNeXt-L	73.48	40.56	−23.60	69.03	69.50
ConvNeXt-XL	<u>74.37</u>	35.96	<u>−19.32</u>	<u>69.29</u>	70.07
ViT-B16	74.17	11.54	−46.01	63.94	<u>70.51</u>
ViT-L16	**76.03**	−10.67	−34.12	**69.79**	**72.37**
Swin-B	72.04	32.65	−32.95	64.23	67.35
Swin-L	72.89	<u>56.54</u>	**36.53**	63.52	68.49

Conclusion 4

○ No single model is the winner in detecting misclassified samples.

○ The fact that several models are severely overconfident and wrong on ImageNet-R (PRR) while showing low calibration errors indicate that the calibration analysis should be complemented with experiments such as misclassification detection to understand their reliability.

---

4   Concluding Remarks

We performed an extensive analysis comparing current state-of-the-art Transformers and CNNs. With simple experiments, we have shown that Transformers, just like CNNs, are vulnerable to picking spurious or simple discriminative features in the training set instead of focusing on robust features that generalise under covariate shift conditions. Therefore, the presence of the self-attention mechanism might not be facilitating learning more complex and robust features. To show it is not even necessary, we observed that ConvNeXt models exhibit even superior robustness with respect to current Transformers without leveraging the self-attention mechanism in a few cases. We also conducted an in-depth analysis about the out-of-distribution, calibration, and misclassification detection properties of these models. We hope that our work will encourage development of modules within Transformers and CNNs that can avoid various biases. Additionally, our analysis in Appendix B regarding the lack of reliable metrics to quantify a model's capacity to open new avenues for future work.

Acknowledgements. This work is supported by the UKRI grant: Turing AI Fellowship EP/W002981/1 and EPSRC/MURI grant: EP/N019474/1. We would like to thank the Royal Academy of Engineering and FiveAI. Francesco Pinto's PhD is funded by the European Space Agency (ESA). PD would like to thank Anuj Sharma and Kemal Oksuz for their comments on the draft.

References

1. Arjovsky, M., Bottou, L., Gulrajani, I., Lopez-Paz, D.: Invariant risk minimization. arXiv e-Prints arXiv:1907.02893, July 2019
2. Ba, J.L., Kiros, J.R., Hinton, G.E.: Layer normalization. arXiv preprint arXiv:1607.06450 (2016)
3. Bai, Y., Mei, J., Yuille, A., Xie, C.: Are transformers more robust than CNNs? In: NeurIPS (2021)
4. Condessa, F., Kovacevic, J., Bioucas-Dias, J.: Performance measures for classification systems with rejection. Pattern Recogn. (2015)
5. Cybenko, G.: Approximation by superpositions of a sigmoidal function. Math. Control Sig. Syst. **2**, 303–314 (1989)
6. Deng, J., Dong, W., Socher, R., Li, L.J., Li, K., Fei-Fei, L.: ImageNet: a large-scale hierarchical image database. In: 2009 CVPR, pp. 248–255 (2009)
7. Deng, L.: The MNIST database of handwritten digit images for machine learning research. IEEE Sig. Process. Mag. **29**(6), 141–142 (2012)
8. Dosovitskiy, A., et al.: An image is worth 16x16 words: transformers for image recognition at scale. In: ICLR (2021)
9. Fort, S., Ren, J., Lakshminarayanan, B.: Exploring the limits of Out-of-Distribution detection. In: NeurIPS (2021)
10. Fumera, G., Roli, F.: Support vector machines with embedded reject option. In: Lee, S.-W., Verri, A. (eds.) SVM 2002. LNCS, vol. 2388, pp. 68–82. Springer, Heidelberg (2002). https://doi.org/10.1007/3-540-45665-1_6
11. Guo, C., Pleiss, G., Sun, Y., Weinberger, K.Q.: On calibration of modern neural networks. In: ICML 2017, pp. 1321–1330. JMLR.org (2017)
12. Hendrycks, D., et al.: The many faces of robustness: a critical analysis of out-of-distribution generalization. IN: ICCV (2021)
13. Hendrycks, D., Gimpel, K.: Bridging nonlinearities and stochastic regularizers with gaussian error linear units. CoRR abs/1606.08415 (2016). https://arxiv.org/abs/1606.08415
14. Hendrycks, D., Zhao, K., Basart, S., Steinhardt, J., Song, D.: Natural adversarial examples. In: CVPR (2021)
15. Hornik, K., Stinchcombe, M., White, H.: Multilayer feedforward networks are universal approximators. Neural Netw. **2**(5), 359–366 (1989)
16. Jiang, Y., Neyshabur, B., Mobahi, H., Krishnan, D., Bengio, S.: Fantastic generalization measures and where to find them. In: ICLR (2020)
17. Kolesnikov, A., et al.: Big transfer (BiT): general visual representation learning. In: Vedaldi, A., Bischof, H., Brox, T., Frahm, J.-M. (eds.) ECCV 2020. LNCS, vol. 12350, pp. 491–507. Springer, Cham (2020). https://doi.org/10.1007/978-3-030-58558-7_29
18. Landgrebe, T.C.W., Tax, D.M.J., Paclík, P., Duin, R.P.W.: The interaction between classification and reject performance for distance-based reject-option classifiers. Pattern Recogn. Lett. **27**(8), 908–917 (2006)
19. Liu, Z., et al.: Swin transformer: hierarchical vision transformer using shifted windows. In: ICCV (2021)

20. Liu, Z., Mao, H., Wu, C.Y., Feichtenhofer, C., Darrell, T., Xie, S.: A ConvNet for the 2020s. In: CVPR (2022)
21. Malinin, A., Mlodozeniec, B., Gales, M.: Ensemble distribution distillation. In: ICLR (2020)
22. Minderer, M., et al.: Revisiting the calibration of modern neural networks. In: NeurIPS (2021)
23. Morrison, K., Gilby, B., Lipchak, C., Mattioli, A., Kovashka, A.: Exploring corruption robustness: inductive biases in vision transformers and mlp-mixers, vol. abs/2106.13122 (2021). http://arxiv.org/abs/2106.13122
24. Mukhoti, J., Kulharia, V., Sanyal, A., Golodetz, S., Torr, P.H., Dokania, P.K.: Calibrating deep neural networks using focal loss. In: NeurIPS (2020)
25. Naeini, M.P., Cooper, G.F., Hauskrecht, M.: Obtaining well calibrated probabilities using Bayesian binning. In: Proceedigs of Conference on AAAI Artificial Intelligence 2015, pp. 2901–2907, January 2015
26. Neyshabur, B., Bhojanapalli, S., Mcallester, D., Srebro, N.: Exploring generalization in deep learning. In: Guyon, I., et al. (eds.) NeurIPS, vol. 30. Curran Associates, Inc. (2017)
27. Neyshabur, B., Bhojanapalli, S., Srebro, N.: A PAC-Bayesian approach to spectrally-normalized margin bounds for neural networks. In: ICLR (2018)
28. Paul, S., Chen, P.Y.: Vision transformers are robust learners. In: AAAI (2022)
29. Pinto, F., Torr, P., Dokania, P.: Are vision transformers always more robust than convolutional neural networks? In: NeurIPS Workshop on Distribution Shifts: Connecting Methods and Applications (2021)
30. Quionero-Candela, J., Sugiyama, M., Schwaighofer, A., Lawrence, N.D.: Dataset Shift in Machine Learning. The MIT Press, Cambridge (2009)
31. Recht, B., Roelofs, R., Schmidt, L., Shankar, V.: Do imagenet classifiers generalize to imagenet? In: ICML (2019)
32. Ridnik, T., Ben-Baruch, E., Noy, A., Zelnik-Manor, L.: Imagenet-21k pretraining for the masses (2021)
33. Sanyal, A., Torr, P.H.S., Dokania, P.K.: Stable rank normalization for improved generalization in neural networks and GANs. In: ICLR (2020)
34. Shah, H., Tamuly, K., Raghunathan, A., Jain, P., Netrapalli, P.: The pitfalls of simplicity bias in neural networks. In: NeurIPS (2020)
35. Tang, S., et al.: RobuStart: benchmarking robustness on architecture design and training techniques. arXiv (2021)
36. Touvron, H., Cord, M., Douze, M., Massa, F., Sablayrolles, A., Jégou, H.: Training data-efficient image transformers & distillation through attention. In: ICML (2021)
37. Vaswani, A., et al.: Attention is all you need. In: NeurIPS, vol. 30 (2017)
38. Wang, H., Ge, S., Lipton, Z., Xing, E.P.: Learning robust global representations by penalizing local predictive power. In: NeurIPS, pp. 10506–10518 (2019)
39. Wightman, R.: PyTorch image models (2019). https://github.com/rwightman/pytorch-image-models
40. Xiao, K., Engstrom, L., Ilyas, A., Madry, A.: Noise or signal: the role of image backgrounds in object recognition. In: ICLR (2021)
41. Yuan, L., et al.: Tokens-to-Token ViT: training vision transformers from scratch on ImageNet. In: ICCV (2021)
42. Zhang, C., et al.: Delving deep into the generalization of vision transformers under distribution shifts. In: CVPR (2022)

Recover Fair Deep Classification Models via Altering Pre-trained Structure

Yanfu Zhang⬤, Shangqian Gao⬤, and Heng Huang$^{(\boxtimes)}$⬤

Department of Electrical and Computer Engineering, University of Pittsburgh,
Pittsburgh, USA
{yaz91,shg84,heng.huang}@pitt.edu

Abstract. There have been growing interest in algorithmic fairness for
biased data. Although various pre-, in-, and post-processing methods are
designed to address this problem, new learning paradigms designed for
fair deep models are still necessary. Modern computer vision tasks usually
involve large generic models and fine-tuning concerning a specific task.
Training modern deep models from scratch is expensive considering the
enormous training data and the complicated structures. The recently
emerged intra-processing methods are designed to debias pre-trained
large models. However, existing techniques stress fine-tuning more, but
the deep network structure is less leveraged. This paper proposes a novel
intra-processing method to improve model fairness by altering the deep
network structure. We find that the unfairness of deep models are usually caused by a small portion of sub-modules, which can be uncovered
using the proposed differential framework. We can further employ several strategies to modify the corrupted sub-modules inside the unfair
pre-trained structure to build a fair counterpart. We experimentally verify our findings and demonstrate that the reconstructed fair models can
make fair classification and achieve superior results to the state-of-the-
art baselines. We conduct extensive experiments to evaluate the different
strategies. The results also show that our method has good scalability
when applied to a variety of fairness measures and different data types.

Keywords: Fairness · Model pruning

1 Introduction

Recently, machine learning models have been increasing in usage in different
applications. However, evidence shows that ML models can be biased just
as human decision-makers, resulting in serious problems in some high-stakes
decision-making, such as awarding loans, deciding probationers' risks, or detecting fraud. The bias in machine decision has two main sources, the intrinsic
algorithm design, and the flawed training data collection. For example, people
found some gender bias in Amazon's resume screening tool [11] and the credit
limits of Apple Card [39]. Algorithmic fairness is gaining growing interest to

© The Author(s), under exclusive license to Springer Nature Switzerland AG 2022
S. Avidan et al. (Eds.): ECCV 2022, LNCS 13673, pp. 481–498, 2022.
https://doi.org/10.1007/978-3-031-19778-9_28

alleviate this issue. Usually, some features used for the decision-making data indicate the underprivileged groups in the population. The classifiers learned with algorithmic fair-awareness are insensitive to these features, *a.k.a.* protected attributes. For example, a machine learning model is usually trained w.r.t. award loans based on user profiles, where gender and ethnicity are protected attributes. Algorithmic fairness prevents decision-making from being associated with gender or ethnicity. To fit into different application scenario, researchers proposed various definitions for algorithmic fairness, including individual fairness [13], demographic parity [8], equal odds and equal opportunities [21], disparate treatment, impact, and mistreatment [49]. Among the works attempting to achieve fairness commitments for classification models, some try to address a substantial source of the bias, i.e., the dataset itself. Alternatively, many methods try to rectify bias that manifests in models during training, which can be categorized into pre-, in-, or post-processing frameworks. Although these methods achieve great success in many tasks, some scenarios prevent their application. Due to the rapid growth of the size of modern machine learning problems, it is common to adopt some pre-trained backbone models and fine-tune them for some specific tasks. In real-world applications, the models are usually trained with the accumulation of data, and the potential data distribution may vary with time. In these cases, pre-processing and in-processing methods are expensive since they require retraining from scratch each time, and state-of-the-art models may require thousands of GPU hours. Post-processing methods sometimes cannot fully use the models since they are viewed as black boxes.

Recently, intra-processing algorithms have emerged to address these problems. An intra-processing approach has access to a pre-trained model and a dataset (typically differing from the biased training dataset). It outputs a debiased model by updating or augmenting the weights.

However, existing intra-processing methods are usually designed for general machine learning models, thus cannot fully use the deep network structure. This paper proposes a novel intra-processing framework to address this limitation—we alter the structure of an unfair model to recover a fair counterpart. Our contributions are summarized as follows,

- We propose a conjecture that the unfairness of a deep network is caused by only a small portion of its sub-modules. We design a differentiable scheme to identify those model weights corrupted by unfairness. We verify our findings empirically and show that the percentage of corrupted weights is quite low.
- We propose several strategies to reconstruct the fair classification model by modifying the corrupted networks. First, we can obtain a slim network by removing the unfair weights and applying off-the-shelf intra-process methods. Second, we can graft informative filters into the corrupted weights. And third, we can refine the slim network via network augmentation.
- We experimentally verified our findings and demonstrated that our algorithm outperforms state-of-the-art intra-processing baselines, and our approach generalizes well to various settings, e.g., tabular and vision datasets. We also conducted extensive experiments to study the corrupted weights and different model altering strategies.

2   Related Works

2.1   Fairness in Machine Learning

At a high level, algorithmic fairness can be mathematically defined by the group or individual, and various formal definitions of fairness have been proposed. Individually fair models [13] are based on the intuition that similar users deserve similar treatments. They map input metric spaces to output metric spaces, where individual fairness is defined as Lipschitz continuity of the models. Individual fairness has a preferable property that the Lipschitz continuity naturally implies statistical parity between subgroups of the population. On the other hand, group fairness (sometimes referred to as statistical parity) considers the invariance of the machine learning models on the protected non-overlapping subsets. Group fairness sometimes makes the computation simpler than individual fairness since it is compliant with statistical analysis. The core research problem for fairness is to identify the sources of unfairness and design the corresponding solutions. Imbalanced data concerning the protected attributes usually lead to an unfair model, i.e. the unfairness from the data. To address this problem, some works, including BUPT-Balancedface/RFW [40] and Fairface [27], try to build balanced data. Alternatively, some recent research finds that sometimes data imbalance doesn't necessarily lead to unfairness [17], which makes the problem more intriguing. Meanwhile, some methods aims at learning a fair classifier on top of the biased data [6,28,34,48,53]. Many debiasing algorithms can be split into three categories based on the processing of data and model. Pre-processing methods directly change the data. In-processing approaches train machine learning models tailored to making fairer prediction. Post-processing techniques refine the potentially biased predictions outputted by a fixed model. Our method is an intra-processing method [37] identifying the critical parts of the models causing the unfairness, while previous related methods promote the fairness via finetuning using partial knowledge of the models.

2.2   Fine-Tuning Over-Parameterized Network

Modern deep neural networks typically achieve higher performance from larger model scales. The model scales mainly come from two sources: the layer width and the network topology. Recent research shows that both the network weights and the network topology have redundancy concerning the model utility. For example, [22] benefits from huge convolution filter numbers. Some works show that carefully dropping part of network weights makes only a slight performance decrease [18], even when a substantial amount of the weights are removed. Many pruning methods are proposed to identify what weights are redundant. Magnitude pruning [20] removes weights with small norm values. Lottery ticket hypothesis (LTH) [15] shows that a sparse sub-network exists at the initialization time that can reach the performance of the full model. Moreover, the weight drop can be conducted at a different level, e.g., channel-wise [16,31,52] and weight-wise [20]. On the other hand, people found that long-distance connections can improve the model performance [24]. However, there is some inefficiency because the deeper layers consider the early features as "obsolete" ones and ignore them while learning new representations. CondenseNet [45] and ShuffleNet [51] alleviate this inefficiency through strategically pruning redundant connections and exponentially discarding cross-layer connections, respectively. One explanation for this phenomenon is that a deep neural network can be viewed as a large ensembled model, and only some sub-structures play a vital role in prediction performance. This argument is empirically supported by some network refinement methods [19,38]. Part of our framework is motivated by this body of research. Instead of refining special sub-structures, one can also train potential sub-networks with different sizes and use larger networks to help the training of smaller ones. A typical case is slimmable neural networks [47], which train sub-networks with different widths at the same time. On top of slimmable networks, universally slimmable networks [46] proposed enhanced training techniques that distill knowledge from larger sub-networks (including the full model) to smaller sub-networks. Recently, network augmentation [7] put small models into large models to improve the training of the small model.

Of note, our work is not directly related to the fair differentiable neural architecture search. FairDARTS [10] and FairNas [9] define Expectation Fairness (EF) and Strict Fairness (SF) to alleviate supernet bias and avoid the unfair advantage of skip connections for residual modules. They use the terminology "fairness" totally different from our paper (our work considers the classification fairness).

3 Methodology

In this section we first briefly recap the problem formulation of the algorithmic fairness for the intra-processing scenario to make our paper self-contained. Next, we describe our method to discover the candidate sub-modules for the model structure alteration. At last, we discuss several strategies to reconstruct a fair model with awareness of the corrupted sub-modules.

3.1 Problem Formulation

Intra-processing Debiasing: Our task is to adjust an unfair model using a validation dataset. Formally, $\mathcal{D} = \{(X_i, Y_i)\}$ denotes a dataset, where X_i is a data point containing one binary protected attribute A, and Y_i is the label. $f_\theta : \mathbb{R}^d \to [0, 1]$ is an unfair neural network with weights θ (we will drop θ when it is clear from context). $\hat{\mathcal{Y}} = \{f(X_i)|(X_i, Y_i)\}$ is the prediction. $\rho(\mathcal{Y}, \hat{\mathcal{Y}})$ denotes the performance of f, and we use balanced accuracy in this paper. Specifically, we assume f is l layers feed-forward neural network, and its ith layer is $f^{(i)}$. We denote $f = f^{(l)} \circ f'$, so that the first $l - 1$ layers $f' = f^{(l-1)} \circ \cdots \circ f^{(1)}$ can be viewed as an encoder to compute data representations. $\mu(\mathcal{D}, \hat{\mathcal{Y}}, A) \in [0, 1]$ is a bias measure. One typically chooses an appropriate definition of the fairness measure depending on the applications, which we will discuss later.

Since there is usually some trade-off between the performance ρ and the bias μ, we want to decrease the bias μ without significantly sacrifices the performance ρ. A common practice is to maximize the model performance subject to some predetermined tolerance ϵ to the bias, and we have the objective function,

$$\Phi_{\mu,\rho,\epsilon}(\mathcal{D}, \hat{\mathcal{Y}}, A) = \begin{cases} \rho & \text{if } \mu < \epsilon \\ 0 & \text{otherwise} \end{cases}. \tag{1}$$

An intra-processing algorithm takes in the validation dataset $\mathcal{D}_{val}$ and a trained model f_θ and outputs a fine-tuned $f_{\theta'}$ with weights θ' via optimizing the objective $\phi_{\mu,\rho,\epsilon}$. Note that the difference between intra-processing algorithms and pre-, in-, and post- methods makes these methods useful for different problem settings because these paradigms have different access to the data and model, i.e., pre- methods mainly consider the data, in- mainly consider the model training, and the post- sometimes cannot access the model details.

Fairness Measures: Now we describe the fairness measures used in this work. We first define the true positive and false positive rates as,

$$TPR_{A=a}(\mathcal{D}, \hat{\mathcal{Y}}) = \frac{|\{i|\hat{Y}_i = Y_i = 1, a_i = a\}|}{|\{i|\hat{Y}_i = Y_i = 1\}|} = P_{(X_i,Y_i)\in\mathcal{D}}(\hat{Y}_i = 1|a_i = a, Y_i = 1),$$
$$\tag{2}$$

$$FPR_{A=a}(\mathcal{D}, \hat{\mathcal{Y}}) = \frac{|\{i|\hat{Y}_i = 1, Y_i = 0, a_i = a\}|}{|\{i|\hat{Y}_i = 1, Y_i = 0\}|} = P_{(X_i,Y_i)\in\mathcal{D}}(\hat{Y}_i = 1|a_i = a, Y_i = 0).$$
$$\tag{3}$$

Next, we describe the fairness measures used in this paper.
Statistical Parity Difference (SPD),

$$SPD(\mathcal{D}, \hat{\mathcal{Y}}, A) = P_{(X_i,Y_i)\in\mathcal{D}}(\hat{Y}_i = 1|a_i = 0) - P_{(X_i,Y_i)\in\mathcal{D}}(\hat{Y}_i = 1|a_i = 1). \tag{4}$$

Equal opportunity difference (EOD),

$$EOD(\mathcal{D}, \hat{\mathcal{Y}}, A) = TPR_{A=0}(\mathcal{D}, \hat{\mathcal{Y}}) - TPR_{A=1}(\mathcal{D}, \hat{\mathcal{Y}}). \tag{5}$$

Average Odds Difference (AOD),

$$AOD(\mathcal{D}, \hat{\mathcal{Y}}, A) = \frac{1}{2} \left(\left(FPR_{A=0}(\mathcal{D}, \hat{\mathcal{Y}}) - FPR_{A=1}(\mathcal{D}, \hat{\mathcal{Y}}) \right) \right.$$
$$\left. \left(TPR_{A=0}(\mathcal{D}, \hat{\mathcal{Y}}) - TPR_{A=1}(\mathcal{D}, \hat{\mathcal{Y}}) \right) \right). \tag{6}$$

3.2   Finding Corrupted Sub-modules

As an intra-processing method, we will use the validation data and the model structure simultaneously. Here validation data refers to a few data points for fine-tuning without breaking the test integrity. Note that we only use the validation data of limited size instead of the complete training data, and the reasons are two-folded. First, fine-tuning the unfair model is sometimes prohibitive considering the size of the full training data, particularly when the model is also large. Second, the complete training data are usually biased in the protected attribute distribution. It is more viable to collect a small and unbiased validation set. For the second point, one implicitly assumes that primarily training on an imbalanced dataset is inherently disadvantageous. However, whether the assumption is valid in some application scenarios is still an open question. For example, in face recognition, training on only African faces induced less bias than training on a balanced distribution of faces and distributions biased to include more African faces produced more equitable models, and adding more images of existing identities to a dataset in place of adding new identities can lead to accuracy boosts across racial categories [17]. We believe that this assumption deserves further investigation concerning the specific tasks. In this paper, we deal with this issue in a conservative manner and focus on a balanced validation set. Specifically, this section assumes that we have the unfair model f and the balanced validation data $\mathcal{D}_{val}$. In the following, we describe our method to discover the sub-modules making substantial contribution to unfairness.

Modern deep neural networks are over-parameterized. Many works have shown that there are some redundant sub-structures inside a model regarding their contribution to the model performance, e.g., carefully removing a large number of channels or layer shortcuts [25,44] usually will not affect the model performance significantly. Moreover, deep neural networks are known for that they can memorize samples with random labels [3], and show some properties of ensembled models, e.g., dropout, as a frequently used technique, functions similar as bagging [42]. Motivated by these findings, we make a conjecture that different modules in a deep network make different contributions to the model prediction and fairness. With the help of the validation dataset, we can discover the influential weights leading to unfairness. Specifically, we freeze the unfair network and assign a mask network to the weights. Then we learn the mask networks to identify those corrupted weights. We will empirically verify this conjecture in the experiments. The model alteration will focus on these corrupted weights, which will be detailed in the next section.

Formally, let M be a binary mask, which has the same size of θ. We first initialize all entries in M with 1 and construct a masked network $f(X; \theta \odot M)$, which is identical to f in the prediction ability. We then identify the sub-networks causing unfairness with θ frozen via solving the following problem,

$$\min_{M \in \{0,1\}^N} \mathcal{L}_{ft}(f(X; \theta \odot M), y), \quad s.t. \ \|M\|_0/N \leq \tau. \tag{7}$$

here $\mathcal{L}_{ft}$ is the fine-tune loss, τ is a threshold, and $1 - \tau$ of the weights are identified as makes little contribution to algorithmic fairness. By solving the

---

Algorithm 1: Discover Model Weights Corrupted by Unfairness

Input: validation data $\mathcal{D}_{val}$, original classifier f, epochs E, parameters τ, β
Output: pruned mode f_{ft}

1 freeze θ in f, initialize m;
2 **for** $e := 1$ *to* E **do**
3   shuffle($\mathcal{D}_{val}$)
4   **for** *a mini-batch* (x, y) *in* $\mathcal{D}_{val}$ **do**
5   obtain masked f_M using m and $\epsilon_m \sim \mathcal{N}(0, \min(1, \max(0.05, 0.5m)))$;
6   compute gradients for m w.r.t. (9) and update it with ADAM;
7   **end**
8 **end**

---

problem in Eq. (7), we can have the optimal mask M^* and the corresponding weights $\theta_M = M^* \odot \theta$, which is a fair sub-structure inside the unfair model.

Solving the problem in Eq. 7 directly is difficult because of the constraint of L_0 norm. To overcome this difficulty, we reparameterize masks with continuous values, which becomes,

$$M = \begin{cases} 1 \text{ if sigmoid}(\hat{m}) \geq 0.5 \\ 0 \text{ if sigmoid}(\hat{m}) < 0.5 \end{cases} \tag{8}$$

here $\hat{m} = m + \epsilon_m$, which use the reparameterization trick. m is the learnable relaxed mask, ϵ_m is randomly drawn Gaussian noise whose variance is adaptive w.r.t. m. We use ϵ_m to avoid the discovery stuck in bad local minimum. Equation (8) is still not differentiable, to enable gradient calculation, we can use straight through estimator (STE) [5], and the gradients of m can be calculated by: $\frac{\partial M}{\partial m} = \frac{\partial M}{\partial \text{sigmoid}(m)} \frac{\partial \text{sigmoid}(m)}{\partial m}$.

Although binary masks are differentiable, the problem in Eq. 7 is in constraint form. To make the optimization easier, we can change the problem to the following form:

$$\min_m \mathcal{L}_{ft}(f(x; \mathcal{W} \odot M), y) + \beta \mathcal{R}(\|M\|_0/N, k), \tag{9}$$

where β is a coefficient parameter, $\mathcal{R}$ is a regularization term to push $\|M\|_0/N$ to a pre-defined threshold τ. Applying this regularization term will count the sparsity of all weights together. The optimization of binary masks is then more flexible than using the same sparsity rate for all layers. We choose $\mathcal{R}(\|M\|_0/N, \tau) = \log(\max(\|M\|_0/N, \tau)/\tau)$, instead of commonly used regression losses, like MAE or MSE, because both of them can not reach desired sparsity when τ is small (for example, $\tau = 0.01$).

After we obtain the mask θ_M, we can obtain the corresponding f_{θ_M}. In the next part, we will discuss several strategies to refine the fair classification model on top of f_{θ_M}. The full algorithm is described in Algorithm 1.

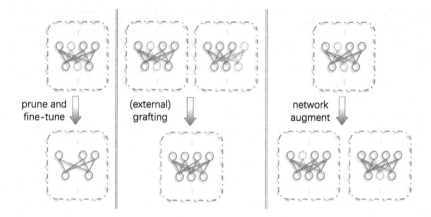

Fig. 1. Illustration of three strategies. The corrupted sub-modules are denoted by dashed circles and lines. The prune and fine-tune strategy builds a pruned model via removing all corrupted weights. The grafting strategy build a model via grafting the unfair weights using two independently discoveries (denoted by different color). The network augmentation strategy maintains the unfair model and refine the augmented fair subnetwork. (Color figure online)

3.3   Strategies to Recover the Fair Classification Model

A straightforward method to reconstruct the fair model is to remove all corrupted weights and only use the left structures. In this case, we no longer need the mask network. Rather, f_{θ_M} can be viewed as a fair subnetwork inside the unfair model, which is related to model compression to some degree. However, the fair subnetwork may lose some generalization ability to the classification problem. This phenomenon is also confirmed in the model pruning literature—the prediction accuracy decrease is usually non-negligible and grows with the pruning rate. Besides, training the pruned network from scratch instead of fine-tuning may lead to worse performance. In this section, we describe several strategies to reconstruct a fair model on top of the fair subnetwork. Figure 1 illustrates the three strategies.

Adversarial Fine-Tuning Pruned Model: A straightforward process to refine the fair subnetwork is to adjust the pruned f_{θ_M} using off-the-shelf in-processing methods. More specifically, we remove all zero weights in f_{θ_M} and run the adversarial fine-tuning [37]. Since the unfair full model can be processed similarly, we can compare the fine-tuning results between the fair subnetwork and the unfair full model to demonstrate the necessity of pruning for a better performance—in other words, verify our conjecture on the existence of the fair subnetwork. We will show the results in the experiments.

Network Grafting: Network grafting is a learning paradigm related to pruning. Model pruning attempts to improve the model efficiency via removing unimportant filters. Alternatively, network grafting aims to improve the representation capability of deep neural networks via grafting the external information into unimportant filters. We adopt the terminologies in filter grafting [33,38] and interpret the corrupted weights as the rootstocks. We re-activate these corrupted weights via grafting, i.e., replacing the corrupted weight values using some scions. There are three types of scions: noise, internal filters, and external filters. One can follow the filter grafting [33] for grafting the corrupted weights using noise and internal filters as scions. Here the noise scions are Gaussian noise having a larger ell_1 norm than the corrupted weights. The internal filters are the weights in the fair subnetwork with the largest ell_1 norms. For the external filters, we propose a variant. We independently discover two fair subnetworks from the unfair model. This step is feasible because the fair subnetwork pruning is to solve an integer problem using approximate methods, which usually results in different seeds. We then execute layer-level grafting. Since the location of the corrupted weights for the two subnetworks are generally different, they can learn mutual information from each other.

Network Augmentation: Training large neural networks usually uses regularization techniques (e.g., data augmentation, dropout) to overcome over-fitting. Some recent work [7] observes that these techniques might hurt the performance of tiny neural networks. Instead of augmenting the data, one should augment the model to avoid the under-fitting. This strategy maintains a large network, in which the tiny network is a subnetwork. Augmented nets are sampled from the large network and fine-tuned against the augmented loss function $\mathcal{L}_{aug} = \mathcal{L}(\theta_M) + \sum_i \alpha_i \mathcal{L}([\theta_M, \theta_i])$, where $[\theta_M, \theta_1]$ represents an augmented model that contains the tiny neural network and α_i is the scaling hyper-parameters. For our problem, the construction of the large augmented network is of particular convenience—we can directly use the unfair full model for that purpose. As such, we can sample the augmented net i containing the fair subnetwork from the full unfair model and update the unfair model i progressively using gradient-based optimization methods.

4   Results

We conduct the experiments on representative image and tabular datasets. The results demonstrate that our method achieves comparable or superior fairness compared to related fair algorithms.

4.1   Image Data Classification

We consider two image datasets, CIFAR-10 Skewed and CelebA. CIFAR-10 Skewed is a synthesized dataset serving as a benchmark for comparing intra-processing methods and the related schemes. We also include the necessary ablation study using this benchmark. CelebA is a real-world dataset to further verify

Table 1. Computational results on CIFAR-10S benchmark. Since the bias tolerance is 0.05, some approaches are not considered fair. Our method has the best accuracy under the fairness constraint.

	Accuracy	Bias
Baseline	0.892 ± 0.004	0.080
Uni.Conf. [2]	0.842 ± 0.011	0.097
Adv.Debias [50]	0.841 ± 0.011	0.099
Dom.Disc. [54]	0.904 ± 0.049	0.043
Dom.Ind. [41]	0.920 ± 0.009	0.005
RndPert [37]	0.913 ± 0.021	0.048
LayerwiseOpt [37]	0.898 ± 0.016	0.043
Adv.Ft [37]	0.917 ± 0.018	0.051
Prune + AdvFt	0.920 ± 0.014	0.033
NoiseGraft	0.909 ± 0.011	0.045
InterGraft	0.918 ± 0.013	0.013
ExtGraft	0.927 ± 0.009	0.028
NetAug	0.931 ± 0.016	0.014

Table 2. The performance of the baseline model and our approach for CIFAR-10S benchmark under different bias level.

Bias level	Baseline	Strategy		
		Adv.Ft	ExtGraft	NetAug
80%	0.935	0.941	0.944	0.946
90%	0.917	0.937	0.945	0.943
99%	0.894	0.916	0.912	0.915

Table 3. Computational results on CelebA dataset. The results are based on five runs and the mean bias column indicates the unfair models.

	Accuracy	Bias
Baseline	0.53 ± 0.00	> 0.05
ROC [26]	0.53 ± 0.01	<0.05
EqOdds [21]	0.98 ± 0.00	>0.05
CalibEqOdds [36]	0.51 ± 0.01	<0.05
RndPert	0.56 ± 0.03	>0.05
LayerwiseOpt	0.52 ± 0.02	<0.05
Adv.Ft	0.91 ± 0.00	<0.05
Prune + AdvFt	0.93 ± 0.00	<0.05
ExtGraft	0.94 ± 0.00	<0.05
NetAug	0.94 ± 0.01	<0.05

the advantage of our approach compared to other state-of-the-art methods. We detail the construction of the two datasets and the experimental evaluation in the following (Table 3).

Data Description: We use the *CIFAR-10 Skewed* (CIFAR-10S) benchmark [41] to show the effectiveness of the intra-processing scheme compared to the rest processing schemes. CIFAR-10S is based on CIFAR-10 [30], a dataset with 50,000 32×32 images evenly distributed between 10 object classes. In CIFAR-10S, each of the ten original classes is subdivided into two new domain subclasses, corresponding to color and grayscale domains within that class. Per class, the 5,000 training images are split 95% to 5% between the two domains; five classes are 95% color, and five classes are 95% grayscale. The total number of images allocated to each domain is thus balanced. We create two copies of the standard CIFAR-10 test set for testing: one in color and one in grayscale. These two datasets are considered separately, and only the 10-way classification decision boundary is relevant. The *CelebA* dataset [32] consists of over 200,000 images of celebrity headshots, along with binary attributes, but some binary categorization of attributes such as gender, hair color, and age does not reflect true human diversity and is problematic [12,41]. In this experiments we choose two models. One predicts whether or not the person is young, and the other predicts whether the person is smiling. We set the protected attribute to Fitzpatrick skin tones [14] in the range $4-6$ following [43], and label the attributes and use the same pre-training setting following [37].

Table 4. Computational results on Adult dataset. We use AOD and SPD as the fairness measure and race and sex as the protected attribute. − indicates that the bias is out of bound so that the accuracy cannot be accepted.

	AOD-sex		SPD-race	
	Accuracy	Bias	Accuracy	Bias
Baseline	~~0.86~~	0.175 ± 0.016	~~0.86~~	0.178 ± 0.013
ROC [26]	~~0.79~~	0.052 ± 0.009	0.71	0.050 ± 0.006
EqOdds [21]	~~0.66~~	0.081 ± 0.018	0.51	0.000 ± 0.001
CalibEqOdds [36]	~~0.84~~	0.299 ± 0.020	~~0.75~~	0.178 ± 0.019
Adv.Debias [50]	0.81	0.008 ± 0.011	0.65	0.042 ± 0.008
RndPert	0.73	0.044 ± 0.009	0.64	0.051 ± 0.001
LayerwiseOpt	0.62	0.024 ± 0.010	0.63	0.041 ± 0.010
Adv.Ft	0.61	0.032 ± 0.009	0.61	0.033 ± 0.011
Prune + AdvFt	0.77	0.049 ± 0.011	0.64	0.042 ± 0.008
ExtGraft	0.65	0.036 ± 0.013	0.61	0.028 ± 0.012
NetAug	0.65	0.036 ± 0.013	0.61	0.028 ± 0.012

Comparative Methods: For Cifar-10S, we consider the best-performing in the benchmarking [41] including uniform confusion loss [2], Adversarial Debiasing [50], prior shift inference [54], and domain-independent training [41]. We also include three intra-processing methods in [37], Random Perturbation, Layer-wise Optimization, and Adversarial Fine-tuning. For all methods, we use the standard 10-way classifier, following [41]. For CelebA, we focus on the comparison of the proposed method with the biased baseline model and several related methods, including the reject option classification post-processing algorithm [26], which is designed to minimize statistical parity difference; the equalized odds post-processing algorithm [21] for minimizing equal opportunity differences; the Calibrated equalized odds post-processing algorithm [36] for equal opportunity differences. We also consider Adversarial Debiasing [50] which is an in-processing method using the adversarial critic to predict the protected attribute and highly related to the intra-processing methods.

Our Setting: Prune + Adv.Ft is adversarial fine-tuning strategy. We fine-tune the model 90 epochs with 5 warmpup steps and cosine annealing learning rate scheduler, using ADAM optimizer with starting learning rate 0.01. Noise-, Inter-, and ExtGraft are grafting using noise, internal scions, and external scions, respectively. For ExtGraft, we consider two independent discovery and always use the first run as the final model the since the two perform close to each other. The model is trained for 100 epochs. NetAug is network augmentation. We use one augmentation per epoch, and train the network 100 epochs, and the scaling parameter is 1. We choose a small diversity factor of 0.05, since the prune rate is low. For both dataset we use a ResNet-18 [22] pretrained on ImageNet from the PyTorch library [35] as the initial model. We set $E = 80$, $\beta = 5$, and $\tau = 0.1$.

Table 5. Results on COMPAS dataset.

	Accuracy	Bias
Baseline	~~0.85~~	0.152 ± 0.147
ROC [26]	0.50	0.013 ± 0.028
EqOdds [21]	0.51	0.011 ± 0.009
CalibEqOdds [36]	0.36	0.023 ± 0.029
Adv.Debias [50]	~~0.62~~	0.081 ± 0.109
RndPert	~~0.68~~	0.084 ± 0.016
LayerwiseOpt	0.52	0.039 ± 0.043
Adv.Ft	0.59	0.036 ± 0.017
Prune + AdvFt	0.61	0.035 ± 0.014
ExtGraft	0.61	0.044 ± 0.011
NetAug	0.60	0.041 ± 0.012

4.2 Additional Results on Tabular Data Classification

Besides image datasets, we also consider two widely-used tabular binary classification datasets from AIF360 [4] to show that our approach can generalize to different application scenarios. Each dataset contains at least one protected feature. For all datasets, we follow [37] and use a feed-forward neural network with ten fully-connected layers of size 32. A BatchNorm layer follows each fully-connected layer. We use a dropout fraction of 0.2. For more details, please refer to [37]. The rest of the settings are similar to the image tasks. The results are obtained by averaging the fairness metrics on the test sets based on ten random initialization.

Income Prediction: The Adult dataset [29] is from the Census Bureau, and the task is to predict whether a given adult makes more than $50,000 a year based on attributes such as education, hours of work per week, etc., for approximately 45,000 individuals. In this experiment, *gender* (male or female) is used as the binary protected attribute. The computational results are presented in Table 4.

Recidivism Prediction: Correctional Offender Management Profiling for Alternative Sanctions (COMPAS) is a commercial tool to assess a criminal defendant's likelihood to re-offend. The task is to predict the recidivism risk based on the features for defendants, including the criminal history, jail and prison time, and demographics. In this experiment, *gender* (male or female) are used as binary protected attributes and EOD is the fairness measure.. The computational results are presented in Table 5.

4.3 Discussions

In this experiment, we have several observations. Table 1 shows that our method works are superior to all the baselines significantly. Table 2 further highlights the performance evolution w.r.t. bias, and we can find that for extremely high bias (i.e., 99%), our method still performs well. Our approach can achieve nearly perfect fairness when the bias is moderately high (i.e., 80%). We also notice that the model accuracy is relatively stable w.r.t. initialization. However, the model bias usually has a larger perturbation. The algorithmic design for specific fairness criteria cannot generalize to different scenarios. These results are consistent with the observation that many group fairness constraints are intrinsically incompatible so that trade-offs between them shall be considered [1]. Our approach usually has better-balanced accuracy and comparable (i.e., no statistical significance) bias than the state-of-the-art intra-processing baselines. This result indicates that our approach dominates the baselines Pareto-optimally.

We notice that the three recovering strategies show some performance difference particularly for vision dataset. The Prune+AdvFt strategy consistently outperforms the related baselines using the full model, which verifies the existence of the fair subnetwork. The best-performing grafting strategy is via external graft-ing. NetAug usually performs similar to the grafting strategy. For tabular data, there is no statistical difference between the naive strategy (i.e., Prune+Adv.Ft) and the complex strategies (i.e., grafting and NetAug). It should be mentioned that although grafting and NetAug sometimes yield better fair models, the train-ing time is significantly longer than the Prune+Adv.Ft strategy. In most cases, the Grafting strategy and the NetAug strategy have comparable performance. We recommend the Grafting strategy for general purpose model debiasing con-sidering the model and training complexity. For large-scale fairness problems, we expect NetAug is of some use since the network augmentation technique is designed to avoid under-fitting for tiny models. However, there still lacks such a benchmark to our best knowledge.

Table 6. Pruned results guided by different reconstructed fair models. For all entries, the value denotes accuracy/bias/final pruning rate (if applicable).

Ratio	Base	Teacherl		
		Adv.Ft	ExtGraft	NetAug
80%	0.912/0.054	0.907/0.040/15%	0.905/0.048/14%	0.900/0.036/17%
90%	0.901/0.072	0.898/0.041/15%	0.899/0.056/16%	0.893/0.044/12%
99%	0.879/0.115	0.874/0.066/13%	0.891/0.082/15%	0.878/0.063/14%

4.4 Further Study: Fair Subnetworks in Unfair Models

The empirical results provide some evidence on the existence of fair subnetwork in a unfair model. A further question is whether a completely unfair model can be adjust to become fair? To answer it, we consider the following problem,

$$\min_{m} H(f_t^u(x, \mathcal{W} \odot M), f^r(x)) + \gamma H(f_{t-1}^u(x), f_t^u(x)), \qquad (10)$$

where f^u is an unfair model, and f^r is a reconstructed fair model. t is the epoch. $H(\cdot)$ is the entropy function. The first term can be regarded as the knowledge distillation loss [23] with temperature 1.0. The second term is consistency reg-ularization between epochs. We let the unfair model mimic the outputs of the reconstructed fair model instead of the fair sub-networks, since the fair sub-network is sub-optimal before we apply the intra-process. During pruning, we fix model weights and only update the binary mask and ignore the pruning rate constraint in this problem to expand the possible search space of robust sub-networks. Table 6 summarizes the results on CIFAR-10S. We alter the ratio of color and grayscale images, and compute the pruned models concerning the reconstructed fair models using different strategies. The results show that simply removing the corrupted weights is adequate to obtain a fair model with accept-able accuracy. We also notice that the pruning rate is merely around 12% ∼ 17%, even for a high imbalance ratio. This result indicate that most weights in a non-robust deep neural network are robust or at least insensitive to unfairness.

5   Conclusion

In this paper, we propose a novel intra-processing fairness framework. Our framework includes two steps. First, we discover the fair sub-structure using model pruning techniques. Second, we propose several strategies to reconstruct the fair deep classification model. We benchmark the performance of the intra-processing method and show the effectiveness of our design. Extensive experiments demonstrate that our approach is suitable for various application scenarios and has a comparable performance $w.r.t.$ state-of-the-art methods.

Acknowledgement. This work was partially supported by NSF IIS 1845666, 1852606, 1838627, 1837956, 1956002, 2217003.

References

1. Inherent trade-offs in the fair determination of risk scores. arXiv preprint arXiv:1609.05807 (2016)
2. Alvi, M., et al.: Turning a blind eye: explicit removal of biases and variation from deep neural network embeddings. In: Proceedings of the European Conference on Computer Vision (ECCV) Workshops (2018)
3. Arpit, D., et al.: A closer look at memorization in deep networks. In: Proceedings of the 34th International Conference on Machine Learning, vol. 70, pp. 233–242. JMLR. org (2017)
4. Bellamy, R.K., et al.: Ai fairness 360: an extensible toolkit for detecting, understanding, and mitigating unwanted algorithmic bias. arXiv preprint arXiv:1810.01943 (2018)
5. Bengio, Y., Léonard, N., Courville, A.: Estimating or propagating gradients through stochastic neurons for conditional computation. arXiv preprint arXiv:1308.3432 (2013)
6. Bower, A., Niss, L., Sun, Y., Vargo, A.: Debiasing representations by removing unwanted variation due to protected attributes. arXiv preprint arXiv:1807.00461 (2018)
7. Cai, H., Gan, C., Lin, J., Han, S.: Network augmentation for tiny deep learning. arXiv preprint arXiv:2110.08890 (2021)
8. Calders, T., Kamiran, F., Pechenizkiy, M.: Building classifiers with independency constraints. In: 2009 IEEE International Conference on Data Mining Workshops, pp. 13–18. IEEE (2009)
9. Chu, X., Zhang, B., Xu, R.: Fairnas: rethinking evaluation fairness of weight sharing neural architecture search. In: Proceedings of the IEEE/CVF International Conference on Computer Vision, pp. 12239–12248 (2021)
10. Chu, X., Zhou, T., Zhang, B., Li, J.: Fair DARTS: eliminating unfair advantages in differentiable architecture search. In: Vedaldi, A., Bischof, H., Brox, T., Frahm, J.-M. (eds.) ECCV 2020. LNCS, vol. 12360, pp. 465–480. Springer, Cham (2020). https://doi.org/10.1007/978-3-030-58555-6_28

11. Dastin, J.: Amazon scraps secret ai recruiting tool that showed bias against women. Reuters (2018)
12. Denton, E., Hutchinson, B., Mitchell, M., Gebru, T.: Detecting bias with generative counterfactual face attribute augmentation (2019)
13. Dwork, C., et al.: Fairness through awareness. In: Proceedings of the 3rd Innovations in Theoretical Computer Science Conference, pp. 214–226 (2012)
14. Fitzpatrick, T.B.: The validity and practicality of sun-reactive skin types i through vi. Arch. Dermatol. **124**(6), 869–871 (1988)
15. Frankle, J., Carbin, M.: The lottery ticket hypothesis: finding sparse, trainable neural networks. In: International Conference on Learning Representations (2019). https://openreview.net/forum?id=rJl-b3RcF7
16. Ganjdanesh, A., Gao, S., Huang, H.: Interpretations steered network pruning via amortized inferred saliency maps. In: Proceedings of the European Conference on Computer Vision (ECCV) (2022)
17. Gwilliam, M., et al.: Rethinking common assumptions to mitigate racial bias in face recognition datasets. In: Proceedings of the IEEE/CVF International Conference on Computer Vision, pp. 4123–4132 (2021)
18. Han, S., Mao, H., Dally, W.J.: Deep compression: compressing deep neural networks with pruning, trained quantization and huffman coding. arXiv preprint arXiv:1510.00149 (2015)
19. Han, S., et al.: Dsd: regularizing deep neural networks with dense-sparse-dense training flow (2016)
20. Han, S., Pool, J., Tran, J., Dally, W.: Learning both weights and connections for efficient neural network. Adv. Neural Inf. Process. Syst. **28** (2015)
21. Hardt, M., Others: equality of opportunity in supervised learning. Adv. Neural Inf. Process. Syst. (2016)
22. He, K., Zheng, X.: Deep residual learning for image recognition. In: Proceedings of the IEEE Conference on Computer Vision and Pattern Recognition, pp. 770–778 (2016)
23. Hinton, G., Vinyals, O., Dean, J.: Distilling the knowledge in a neural network. arXiv preprint arXiv:1503.02531 (2015)
24. Huang, G., et al.: Densely connected convolutional networks. In: Proceedings of the IEEE Conference on Computer Vision and Pattern Recognition, pp. 4700–4708 (2017)
25. Huang, G., et al.: Condensenet: an efficient densenet using learned group convolutions. In: Proceedings of the IEEE Conference on Computer Vision and Pattern Recognition, pp. 2752–2761 (2018)
26. Kamiran, F., Karim, A., Zhang, X.: Decision theory for discrimination-aware classification. In: 2012 IEEE 12th International Conference on Data Mining, pp. 924–929. IEEE (2012)
27. Kärkkäinen, K., Joo, J.: Fairface: face attribute dataset for balanced race, gender, and age. arXiv preprint arXiv:1908.04913 (2019)
28. Kim, M., et al.: Fairness through computationally-bounded awareness. Adv. Neural Inf. Process. Syst., 4842–4852 (2018)
29. Kohavi, R.: Scaling up the accuracy of naive-bayes classifiers: A decision-tree hybrid. In: Kdd, vol. 96, pp. 202–207 (1996)
30. Krizhevsky, A., Hinton, G., et al.: Learning multiple layers of features from tiny images (2009)
31. Li, H., Kadav, A., Durdanovic, I., Samet, H., Graf, H.P.: Pruning filters for efficient convnets. In: International Conference on Learning Representations (ICLR) (2017)

32. Liu, Z., et al.: Deep learning face attributes in the wild. In: Proceedings of International Conference on Computer Vision (ICCV) (2015)
33. Meng, F., et al.: Filter grafting for deep neural networks. In: Proceedings of the IEEE/CVF Conference on Computer Vision and Pattern Recognition, pp. 6599–6607 (2020)
34. Mukherjee, D., et al.: Two simple ways to learn individual fairness metrics from data. arXiv preprint arXiv:2006.11439 (2020)
35. Paszke, A., et al.: Automatic differentiation in pytorch (2017)
36. Pleiss, G., et al.: On fairness and calibration. Adv. Neural Inf. Process. Syst. **30** (2017)
37. Savani, Y., White, C., Govindarajulu, N.S.: Intra-processing methods for debiasing neural networks. Adv. Neural Inf. Process. Syst. **33**, 2798–2810 (2020)
38. Shen, C., Wang, X., Yin, Y., Song, J., Luo, S., Song, M.: Progressive network grafting for few-shot knowledge distillation. arXiv preprint arXiv:2012.04915 (2020)
39. Vigdor, N.: Apple card investigated after gender discrimination complaints. The New York Times (2019)
40. Wang, M., et al.: Racial faces in the wild: reducing racial bias by information maximization adaptation network. In: Proceedings of the IEEE/CVF International Conference on Computer Vision, pp. 692–702 (2019)
41. Wang, Z., et al.: Towards fairness in visual recognition: Effective strategies for bias mitigation. In: Proceedings of the IEEE/CVF Conference on Computer Vision and Pattern Recognition, pp. 8919–8928 (2020)
42. Warde-Farley, D., Goodfellow, I.J., Courville, A., Bengio, Y.: An empirical analysis of dropout in piecewise linear networks. arXiv preprint arXiv:1312.6197 (2013)
43. Wilson, B., Hoffman, J., Morgenstern, J.: Predictive inequity in object detection. arXiv preprint arXiv:1902.11097 (2019)
44. Yang, F., Cisse, M., Koyejo, O.O.: Fairness with overlapping groups; a probabilistic perspective. Adv. Neural Inf. Process. Syst. **33** (2020)
45. Yang, L., et al.: Condensenet v2: sparse feature reactivation for deep networks. In: Proceedings of the IEEE/CVF Conference on Computer Vision and Pattern Recognition, pp. 3569–3578 (2021)
46. Yu, J., Huang, T.S.: Universally slimmable networks and improved training techniques. In: Proceedings of the IEEE/CVF International Conference on Computer Vision, pp. 1803–1811 (2019)
47. Yu, J., Yang, L., Xu, N., Yang, J., Huang, T.: Slimmable neural networks. In: International Conference on Learning Representations (2019). https://openreview.net/forum?id=H1gMCsAqY7
48. Yurochkin, M., et al.: Training individually fair ml models with sensitive subspace robustness. In: International Conference on Learning Representations (2019)
49. Zafar, M.B., et al.: Fairness beyond disparate treatment & disparate impact: learning classification without disparate mistreatment. In: Proceedings of the 26th International Conference on World Wide Web, pp. 1171–1180 (2017)
50. Zhang, B.H., Lemoine, B., Mitchell, M.: Mitigating unwanted biases with adversarial learning. In: Proceedings of the 2018 AAAI/ACM Conference on AI, Ethics, and Society, pp. 335–340 (2018)
51. Zhang, X.: Shufflenet: an extremely efficient convolutional neural network for mobile devices. In: Proceedings of the IEEE Conference on Computer Vision and Pattern Recognition, pp. 6848–6856 (2018)
52. Zhang, Y., Gao, S., Huang, H.: Exploration and estimation for model compression. In: Proceedings of the IEEE/CVF International Conference on Computer Vision, pp. 487–496 (2021)

53. Zhang, Y., Luo, L., Huang, H.: Unified fairness from data to learning algorithm. In: 2021 IEEE International Conference on Data Mining (ICDM), pp. 1499–1504. IEEE (2021)
54. Zhao, J., et al.: Men also like shopping: reducing gender bias amplification using corpus-level constraints. arXiv preprint arXiv:1707.09457 (2017)

Decouple-and-Sample: Protecting Sensitive Information in Task Agnostic Data Release

Abhishek Singh$^{(\boxtimes)}$, Ethan Garza, Ayush Chopra, Praneeth Vepakomma, Vivek Sharma, and Ramesh Raskar

Massachusetts Institute of Technology, Cambridge, USA
abhi24@mit.edu

Abstract. We propose *sanitizer*, a framework for secure and task-agnostic data release. While releasing datasets continues to make a big impact in various applications of computer vision, its impact is mostly realized when data sharing is not inhibited by privacy concerns. We alleviate these concerns by sanitizing datasets in a two-stage process. First, we introduce a *global decoupling* stage for decomposing raw data into sensitive and non-sensitive latent representations. Secondly, we design a *local sampling* stage to synthetically generate sensitive information with differential privacy and merge it with non-sensitive latent features to create a useful representation while preserving the privacy. This newly formed latent information is a task-agnostic representation of the original dataset with anonymized sensitive information. While most algorithms sanitize data in a task-dependent manner, a few task-agnostic sanitization techniques sanitize data by censoring sensitive information. In this work, we show that a better privacy-utility trade-off is achieved if sensitive information can be synthesized privately. We validate sanitizer's effectiveness by outperforming state-of-the-art baselines on the existing tasks and demonstrating tasks that are not possible using existing techniques. Our code and benchmark is available at https://github.com/splitlearning/sanitizer.

1 Introduction

Releasing datasets has resulted in methodological advancements in computer vision [14,62] and machine learning (ML). However, the advancement is still limited by datasets that comply with modern privacy standards. The goal of this work is to alleviate privacy concerns in dataset release when it contains sensitive information. Since datasets are released independently of downstream tasks, we focus on the problem of protecting sensitive information in a task-agnostic manner. We refer to this problem as **sanitization**. Releasing sanitized datasets could galvanize the research community to make progress in the areas where raw data access is not feasible.

Supplementary Information The online version contains supplementary material available at https://doi.org/10.1007/978-3-031-19778-9_29.

S. Avidan et al. (Eds.): ECCV 2022, LNCS 13673, pp. 499–517, 2022.
https://doi.org/10.1007/978-3-031-19778-9_29

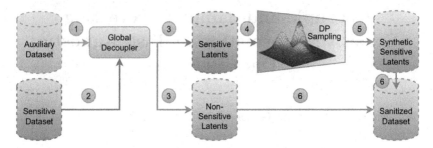

Fig. 1. Sanitizer pipeline First, we learn a latent model (global decoupler) of the data distribution using non-sensitive auxiliary dataset (in green). Next, we use the latent model to decouple sensitive (in red) and non-sensitive (in blue) information from the sensitive dataset to learn the distribution of sensitive latents. We synthetically generate sensitive latents by sampling from the distribution. Finally, we get the sanitized dataset by combining non-sensitive and synthetically generated sensitive latents. (Color figure online)

As a motivating example, consider a hospital with a dataset of face images where "ethnicity" and "age" of every face is a sensitive detail. The hospital is enabled to share the dataset with untrusted parties for several applications if we can *sanitize* all images in the dataset. To understand the benefit of sharing the dataset, we list the following use-cases that also motivate our experiments in Sect. 4.

UC1: A crowd-sourcing company can build a facial recognition model for medical diagnostics [10, 36, 61] from the sanitized dataset. This model will be deployed on cloud, therefore the prediction will be performed over sanitized images.

UC2: A group of researchers can develop a model of capturing keypoints from face images. Unlike UC1, they want the model to predict over unsanitized images. Hence sanitized images should be photo-realistic to prevent a domain mismatch.

UC3: The hospital wants to share a sanitized dataset with a company to build an ML model to predict "age". Similar to UC2, the hospital would perform prediction on unsanitized images hence the sanitized dataset should be photo-realistic. However, unlike UC2, prediction attribute "age" is also a sensitive attribute requiring privacy.

Since there can be many such use-cases, it is impractical to assume that the hospital knows all use-cases in advance before releasing the dataset. Therefore, the goal of *Sanitizer* is to transform the dataset by anonymizing sensitive information without the knowledge of the downstream use-cases. In addition to learning ML models, being task agnostic allows *sanitizer* to do inference queries on sensitive datasets such as counting the number of faces with "smiling" attribute, or counting X-ray images with "lung cancer". Trivially cropping the sensitive parts from the image is not feasible because the pixels that reveal the sensitive information are present everywhere in a face image. Furthermore, unlike face images, identifying sensitive information visually may not be possible. For instance, several recent works [4,5,29,30,73] show ways in which sensitive demographics can be leaked leak from biomedical images using ML models.

Many works in sanitizing data have a different scope from the one considered here. Typically identity [17] of individuals is treated as sensitive information. While this notion protects privacy, we *only* focus on a specific set of sensitive attributes. For example - in UC1, it is acceptable to share face images as long as "ethnicity" and "age" can be protected. In works that do consider specific sensitive attributes, their notion of utility is typically task-dependent as in [33,44,46]. Although *sanitizer* can be used for such problems due to its task-agnostic approach, not exploiting the knowledge about downstream tasks comes at the expense of a relatively lower utility. Existing works specifically in sanitization [23,31] protect sensitive information by *censoring* it. Unlike censoring based approaches, our main idea is to share synthetically generated sensitive information. While the data receiver can not infer the original sensitive information, our approach allows them to learn from anonymized sensitive information.

To design *sanitizer*, we posit that sensitive data can be anonymized by replacing sensitive information with a synthetic one. However, for images, this synthetic replacement is not trivial to perform since the sensitive information is not localized in a region and sensitive attributes and non-sensitive attributes can share the same parts of data (ex. - race and gender). Therefore, we introduce a *latent model* that exclusively isolates sensitive information into a smaller subspace. We learn the latent model using publicly available datasets and then use the model to isolate the sensitive information from the sensitive dataset. Next, we learn a generative model of the isolated sensitive information and synthesize sensitive latents by sampling from the model. We merge these samples with the non-sensitive latent representation to obtain sanitized data. We visualize the whole pipeline in Fig. 1.

Contributions: *First,* we introduce a joint optimization framework for isolating sensitive information from data. *Second,* we design a mechanism for anonymizing sensitive image datasets. *Third,* we empirically demonstrate various applications of sanitization to show the benefit of *sanitizer* over existing approaches, *Fourth,* we release a benchmark and dataset of sanitized representations obtained from baselines for rigorous attacks and defense evaluation in the future.

2   Problem Formulation

Terminology: Consider a data holder A with access to a dataset $\mathbf{D}^A = \{\mathbf{X}, \mathbf{Y}\}$ with N data points. Let $\mathbf{x} \in \mathbf{X}$ and $\mathbf{y} \in \mathbf{Y}$ represents a pair of sample and *set* of labels $(\mathbf{x}, \mathbf{y})$ describing distinct attributes of $\mathbf{x}$. For instance, if $\mathbf{x}$ is a face image of an individual, the *set* $\mathbf{y}$ may include the age, gender, and ethnicity of the individual. For A, certain attributes in the label set $\mathbf{y}$ represent sensitive information (called $\mathbf{y}_S$) while others are non-sensitive ($\mathbf{y}_{NS}$) such that $\mathbf{y} = \{\mathbf{y}_S \cup \mathbf{y}_{NS}\}$. These sensitive attributes are A's secrets that prevent A from sharing $\mathbf{D}^A$. While A can release $(\mathbf{x}, \mathbf{y}_{NS})$, an attacker can guess $\mathbf{y}_S$ using $\mathbf{x}$ by exploiting correlation between $\mathbf{x}$ and $\mathbf{y}_S$. Hence, to release $\mathbf{D}^A$ for arbitrary downstream tasks, sanitization techniques transform every sample in $\mathbf{D}^A$ from $(\mathbf{x}, \mathbf{y})$ to $(\tilde{\mathbf{x}}, \tilde{\mathbf{y}})$ resulting in sanitized dataset $\tilde{\mathbf{D}}^A$ that can be shared with untrusted parties. The key challenge is anonymizing sensitive information while maximally retaining the utility. We assume that an auxiliary dataset $\mathbf{D}^{aux}$ from the same distribution as $\mathbf{D}^A$ is publicly accessible to all parties.

Sanitizer Overview: We perform sanitization in a two stage process: i) *Global decoupling* and ii) *Local sampling*. *Global decoupling* stage learns a latent model (parameterized by θ, ϕ) of data using $\mathbf{D}^{aux}$ for decoupling raw data ($\mathbf{x}$) into sensitive ($\mathbf{z}_S$) and non-sensitive ($\mathbf{z}_{NS}$) latents. We assume that the auxiliary dataset and the sensitive dataset come from the same distribution $p(\mathbf{x}, \mathbf{y})$. This stage does not require access to A's dataset ($\mathbf{D}^A$) and hence can be performed independently making this stage *global* since the same model can be utilized by different sensitive-data owners. We discuss the design of the *global decoupler* in Sect. 3.1. *Local sampling* stage learns a generative model ($f(\psi, \cdot)$) of sensitive latents in $\mathbf{D}^A$. We obtain the sensitive latents in $\mathbf{D}^A$ using the *global decoupler* from the first stage. Finally, we obtain the sanitized dataset by merging every non-sensitive latent with independently sampled sensitive-latent. We discuss the *local sampling* stage in Sect. 3.2.

Threat Model: We assume that the *untrusted* data-receiver can act as an attacker by utilizing auxiliary dataset $\mathbf{D}^{aux}$, parameters of *global decoupler* (θ, ϕ) and *local sampler* ($f(\psi, \cdot)$) as a side information. The side information allows the attacker to generate a mapping between $\mathbf{D}^{aux}$ and its sanitized version $\tilde{\mathbf{D}}^{aux}$. The attacker's goal is to recover A's sensitive attribute $\mathbf{y}_S$ from the sanitized dataset $\tilde{\mathbf{D}}^A$. Since $\mathbf{D}^{aux}$ and $\mathbf{D}^A$ come from the same distribution, the attacker can model the problem of inferring the sensitive attributes as an ML problem. By learning a mapping between sanitized samples ($\tilde{\mathbf{x}} \in \tilde{\mathbf{X}}^{aux}, \tilde{\mathbf{y}} \in \tilde{\mathbf{Y}}^{aux}$) and sensitive attributes ($\mathbf{y}_S \in \mathbf{Y}_S^{aux}$) using $\mathbf{D}^{aux}$, the attacker can attempt inferring sensitive attributes from $\tilde{\mathbf{D}}^A$. This threat model is different from differential privacy [17] which seeks to protect identifiability.

Defining Information Leakage: Information leakage for sanitization has been typically defined statistically [15,37,57]; however, estimating these statistics requires estimation of probability distributions making it intractable for non-linear queries over higher-dimensional datasets (images). Alternatively, leakage can be quantified by simulating an attacker's performance by making some assumptions. The goal of sanitization is to minimize the distinguishability of the original sensitive attributes $\mathbf{y}_S$ from other possible values (domain($\mathbf{y}_S$)) sensitive attributes can take. For example, if "ethnicity" is a sensitive attribute then, informally, leakage is the likelihood of the attacker's correct *estimate* about the race of the sanitized face image. Formally, this can be modeled by a change in belief over the sensitive attribute before (prior $p(\mathbf{y}_S)$) and after (posterior $p(\mathbf{y}_S|\tilde{\mathbf{x}})$) observing the sanitized sample ($\tilde{\mathbf{x}}, \tilde{\mathbf{y}}$). A similar notion is formalized in the pufferfish framework [26] where the quantity $\frac{p(y_{s_j}|\tilde{\mathbf{x}},\theta)}{p(y_{s_i}|\tilde{\mathbf{x}},\theta)} / \frac{p(y_{s_j})}{p(y_{s_i})}$ for all possible sets of secrets (y_{s_i}, y_{s_j}) and for all possible priors on data θ is bounded by e^ϵ where ϵ is a privacy parameter. Note that satisfying this definition requires modeling various possible data evolution and attacker scenarios. We focus only on a single type of attacker described in the threat model and therefore use a data-driven approach to quantify leakage. This data-driven adversary learns the joint distribution $p(\tilde{\mathbf{X}}, \mathbf{Y}_S)$ using the side information. Finally, the leakage of the sanitized datasets is evaluated as the difference between the accuracy of the adversary to correctly estimate the sensitive information $p(\mathbf{y}_S|\tilde{\mathbf{x}}, \theta)$ and the estimation of an uninformed adversary $p(\mathbf{y}_S|\theta)$. We note that existing works in sanitization [23,31] use the same criterion to evaluate information leakage.

Desiderata: In both stages of *sanitizer*, we have two desirable properties corresponding to privacy and utility; in total, we get four desirable properties that we elaborate on now. The first stage is *global decoupling* where we learn to separate a sample $\mathbf{x}$ into sensitive and non-sensitive latent $\mathbf{z}_S$ and $\mathbf{z}_{NS}$ respectively. Therefore, the desirable property **P1** requires $(\mathbf{z}_S, \mathbf{z}_{NS})$ to be independent. In other words, **P1** requires non-sensitive latent $\mathbf{z}_{NS}$ does not leak information about $\mathbf{z}_S$. This property can be achieved trivially by sharing all zeroes therefore to enforce utility, we desire property **P2** that requires $p(\mathbf{x}|\mathbf{z}_S, \mathbf{z}_{NS})$ to be maximum. Property **P2** requires $(\mathbf{z}_S, \mathbf{z}_{NS})$ to be useful enough for describing the original sample $\mathbf{x}$. This completes the privacy-utility desiderata for the *global decoupling* stage. The *local sampling* stage focuses only on transforming the sensitive latent, therefore, both privacy and utility desideratum only focus on $\mathbf{z}_{NS}$. For the privacy desiderata **P3** in this stage, we require that sanitized sensitive latents $\tilde{\mathbf{z}}_S$ and $\tilde{\mathbf{z}}'_S$ obtained from $\mathbf{x}, \mathbf{x}' \in \mathbf{X}$ respectively are indistinguishable from each other. **P3** enforces that identifying original data sample based only on the sensitive information should not be possible, i.e. $p(\tilde{\mathbf{z}}_S \sim f_\psi(\mathbf{z}_S)) = p(\tilde{\mathbf{z}}_S \sim f_\psi(\mathbf{z}'_S))$. For the example of a face image with sensitive "ethnicity", **P3** requires synthetically generated $\tilde{\mathbf{z}}_S$ should be independent of the original "ethnicity" of the sample. We can trivially solve **P3** by sharing only zeroes, therefore to ensure utility, we introduce property **P4** that requires the *distribution* of original sensitive and synthetic sensitive latents to be the same. Specifically, the property implies $p(\mathbf{z}_S) = p(\tilde{\mathbf{z}}_S)$. Next, we model these desiderata to design our technique.

3   Method

We sanitize a sensitive dataset in a two-stage process. The first stage is *global decoupling* where we learn a latent model of the data distribution using auxiliary dataset $\mathbf{D}^{aux}$. Our goal is to learn a latent model of data that maximally *decorrelates* $\mathbf{z}_S$ and $\mathbf{z}_{NS}$ for every sample $\mathbf{x}$ (P1) and *preserves* all details of the sample in $\mathbf{z}$ (P2). We achieve this goal by designing *global-decoupler* in Sect. 3.1. The second stage is *local sampling* where we learn the distribution of the sensitive portion

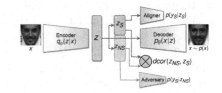

Fig. 2. Architecture for the proposed global-decoupler. The encoder samples $\mathbf{z} \sim q_\phi(\mathbf{z}|\mathbf{x})$) partitioned into $(\mathbf{z}_S, \mathbf{z}_{NS})$. Aligner encourages $\mathbf{z}_S$ to carry information relevant to $\mathbf{y}_S$. We use adversary to reduce information between $\mathbf{z}_{NS}$ and $\mathbf{y}_S$. Finally, we minimize distance correlation between $\mathbf{z}_S$ and $\mathbf{z}_{NS}$.

$\mathbf{Z}_S$ of our sensitive dataset $\mathbf{D}^A$. Our goal is to sample from the distribution $\tilde{\mathbf{Z}}_S$ such that estimating original sensitive attribute $\mathbf{Y}_S$ is not feasible (P3) and the distribution of $p(\mathbf{Z}_S)$ and $p(\tilde{\mathbf{Z}}_S)$ is similar (P4). We achieve this goal by designing *DP-sampling* mechanism in Sect. 3.2. We summarize the overall pipeline in Fig. 1.

3.1 Global Decoupling for Isolating Sensitive Information

Our goal is to design a latent model of the data distribution $p(\mathbf{x}, \mathbf{y})$ such that $\mathbf{x}$ can be decoupled into latents $\mathbf{z}_S$ and $\mathbf{z}_{NS}$. We call this latent model as *global decoupler*. We design it by integrating four components - i) generative model, ii) aligner, iii) decorrelator and iv) adversarial training. We describe the architecture of *global-decoupler* in Fig. 2. Generative models ([18,28,52]) are being increasingly used to perform such latent modeling . Specifically, we build upon VAE [28] since they provide the flexibility of modeling data with constraints on the probability density of the latent space $p(\mathbf{z})$. Given a dataset $\mathbf{X}$, VAEs [28,53] model the distribution of samples $p(\mathbf{x}), \forall \mathbf{x} \in \mathbf{X}$ by learning parameters ϕ of approximate posterior $q_\phi(\mathbf{z}|\mathbf{x})$ and θ for the likelihood $p_\theta(\mathbf{x}|\mathbf{z})$. β-VAE [21] improves the disentanglement between the components of $\mathbf{z}$ sampled from $q_\phi(\mathbf{z}|\mathbf{x})$ by regularizing the KL divergence between the prior $p(\mathbf{z})$ and approximate posterior $q_\phi(\mathbf{z}|\mathbf{x})$. To improve disentanglement between every $\mathbf{z}_i$, existing works such as Factor-VAE [27] and TCVAE [9] regularize the total correlation of $q(\mathbf{z})$ measured by $\mathsf{KL}(q(\mathbf{z})|| \prod_{i=1}^{m} q(\mathbf{z}_i))$ where KL refers to the KL divergence and m is the total number of components of $\mathbf{z}$. However, high degree of disentanglement between *every component* can hinder the reconstruction quality [21]. Therefore, instead of disentangling every pair of $(\mathbf{z}_i, \mathbf{z}_j)$, we propose a new regularized *global-decoupler* to focus on the disentanglement of $(\mathbf{z}_S, \mathbf{z}_{NS})$ instead.

A key characteristic of VAE is that the decoupled latent representations are unordered. Hence, there is no explicit control on which dimensions encode what semantic attributes. This is a challenge for our work that ideally requires that representations encoding the sensitive attributes be contiguous for decoupling. Intuitively, we decouple the vector $\mathbf{z} \sim q_\phi(\mathbf{z}|\mathbf{x})$ into $\mathbf{z}_S$ and $\mathbf{z}_{NS}$ with additional regularization constraints that encourage independence between $\mathbf{z}_S$ and $\mathbf{z}_{NS}$. Formally, we reformulate the original VAE objective with an *aligner* $g_u(\cdot)$ parameterized by u to estimate $\mathbf{y}_S$ from $\mathbf{z}_S$, the intuition is that the *aligner*'s gradient flow will encourage $q_\phi(\cdot)$ to maximize relevant information between $\mathbf{y}_S$ and $\mathbf{z}_S$. Since all latents are known to be correlated with each other to a certain extent, we need to prevent leakage of $\mathbf{y}_S$ in $\mathbf{z}_{NS} \sim q(\mathbf{z}_{NS}|\mathbf{x})$. Unlike FactorVAE [27] or TCVAE [9] that regularize the total correlation disentangling each dimension, we propose to regularize correlation between sensitive($q(\mathbf{z}_S)$) and non-sesntive($q(\mathbf{z}_{NS})$) latents. We re-formulate the objective for $q_\phi(\cdot)$ to minimize distance correlation [63] between $q(\mathbf{z}_S)$ and $q(\mathbf{z}_{NS})$. To motivate the use of distance correlation, we note that directly estimating probability density is intractable for high dimensional representations, various measures such as HSIC [19], MMD [6] and distance correlation [67] are used. Distance correlation between n samples of two vectors $\mathbf{x}$ and $\mathbf{y}$ can be obtained as following:

$$dcorr(\mathbf{x}, \mathbf{y}) = \frac{dcov(\mathbf{x}, \mathbf{y})}{\sqrt{dcov(\mathbf{x}, \mathbf{x}) * dcov(\mathbf{y}, \mathbf{y})}}$$

where $dcov()$ is the sample distance covariance analogue of covariance defined as $dcov(\mathbf{x}, \mathbf{y}) = \frac{1}{n^2} \sum_{j=1}^{n} \sum_{k=1}^{n} \hat{\mathbf{x}}_{j,k} \hat{\mathbf{y}}_{j,k}$. Here $\hat{\mathbf{x}}$ and $\hat{\mathbf{y}}$ are obtained by computing double centered euclidean distance matrices of $\mathbf{x}$ and $\mathbf{y}$. In particular, we use distance correlation ($dcorr$) because it can measure nonlinear correlations between samples from random variables of arbitrary dimensions ($\mathbf{z}_S$ and $\mathbf{z}_{NS}$ can have different dimensionality), allows for efficient gradient computation and does not require any kernel selection or parameter tuning, unlike HSIC and MMD. We do note that $dcorr$ is measured as a sample statistic and hence larger sample size is desirable for the unbiased sample statistic to represent the population notion of the distance correlation. To prevent information leakage of $\mathbf{y}_S$ from $\mathbf{z}_S$, we use a proxy attacker network $h_v(\cdot)$ that is trained adversarially to learn parameters v which constrains $\mathbf{z}_{NS}$ to not carry information relevant to $\mathbf{y}_S$. The final objective can be summarized as:

$$L_1(\theta, \phi, \beta) = \mathbb{E}_{q_\phi(\mathbf{z}|\mathbf{x})}[log p_\theta(\mathbf{x}|\mathbf{z})] - \beta D_{KL}(q_\phi(\mathbf{z}|\mathbf{x}) || p(\mathbf{z})) \tag{1}$$

$$L_2(\phi, u) = \ell_1(g_u(\mathbf{z}_i \sim q_\phi(\mathbf{x})|_{i \le k}), \mathbf{y}_S) \tag{2}$$

$$L_3(\phi) = dcorr(\mathbf{z}_i \sim q_\phi(\mathbf{x})|_{i \le k}, \mathbf{z}_i \sim q_\phi(\mathbf{x})|_{k < i \le m}) \tag{3}$$

$$L_4(\phi, v) = \ell_2(h_v(\mathbf{z}_i \sim q_\phi(\mathbf{x})|_{k < i \le m}), \mathbf{y}_S) \tag{4}$$

Here k and m are the dimensionalities of vectors $\mathbf{z}_S$ and $\mathbf{z}$, respectively. L_1 is the β-VAE [21] formulation of VAE's evidence lower bound where the parameter β encourages disentanglement between every component of $\mathbf{z}$. Increasing β favors the property P1 (by encouraging independence) but hurts the property P2 (by reducing reconstruction). L_2 is the objective for training the parameters of the aligner model. However, L_1 does not prevent $\mathbf{z}_{NS}$ from leaking information about $\mathbf{y}_S$. Hence, we optimize L_4 adversarially to prevent information leakage. Finally, we minimize distance correlation between $\mathbf{z}_S$ and $\mathbf{z}_{NS}$ to prevent $\mathbf{y}_{NS}$ from encoding information about $\mathbf{z}_S$ and encourage decoupling $\mathbf{z}_S$ and $\mathbf{z}_{NS}$. Jointly optimizing L_1, L_2, L_3 and L_4 helps achieve properties P1 and P2. We validate each component's benefit via ablation studies in Sect. 5.

ℓ_1, ℓ_2 can be cross-entropy or ℓ_p-norm (often $p = 2$) depending upon $\mathbf{y}_S$. The parameters ϕ, θ, u, v are trained jointly with following objective:

$$\min_{\theta, \phi, u} \alpha_1 L_1(\theta, \phi, \beta) + \alpha_2 L_2(\phi, u) + \alpha_3 L_3(\phi) - \alpha_4 \min_v L_4(\phi, v) \tag{5}$$

where $\beta, \alpha_1, \alpha_2, \alpha_3, \alpha_4$ are scalar hyper-parameters that yield a trade-off between the privacy (property P1) and utility (property P2). We reiterate that this stage only accesses auxiliary dataset $\mathbf{D}^{aux}$ for the training and evaluation. Hence the parameters of the global-decoupler do not leak any sensitive information.

3.2   Local Sampling for Synthesizing Sensitive Latents

In this stage, we design the *DP-sampling* mechanism to sanitize every sample in the sensitive dataset. A sanitized sample $(\tilde{\mathbf{x}}, \tilde{\mathbf{y}})$ is obtained from $(x, y) \in \mathbf{D}^A$

by extracting the sensitive and non-sensitive latents $(\mathbf{z}_S, \mathbf{z}_{NS})$ from the global-decoupler and replacing the sensitive latent with a synthetic one $(\tilde{\mathbf{z}}_S)$. To satisfy the privacy desiderata of our second stage P3, $\tilde{\mathbf{z}}_S$ is sampled independently of $\mathbf{z}_S$. In contrast to prior works [22, 32, 34] that focus on censoring sensitive attributes, a key benefit of our mechanism is in anonymizing the sensitive information for individual data points while enabling downstream tasks that may benefit from joint distribution $p(\mathbf{z}_S, \mathbf{y}_S)$. Motivated by the use-case UC3, we demonstrate in Sect. 4 under experiment E5 on how to train an ML model on a sanitized dataset that predicts the sensitive attributes of unsanitized images. To motivate our DP-sampling mechanism, we first discuss a trivial suppression-based mechanism and a naive DP mechanism.

a) Suppression: The key is to explicitly remove sensitive information by replacing $\mathbf{z}_S$ with a zero vector (i.e. $\tilde{\mathbf{z}}_S$ is a zero vector). While this approach censors the sensitive latent, it is not possible to learn the distribution $p(\mathbf{x}, \mathbf{y}_S)$ under this mechanism resulting in a violation of our desired property P4. Therefore, we sanitize the sensitive information $\mathbf{z}_S$ using DP mechanisms.

b) DP-Obfuscation: The key idea is to add privacy calibrated noise to $\mathbf{z}_S$. This calibration can be formalized using DP where a mechanism $\mathcal{M}$ is ϵ-differentially private [17] if for every neighboring datasets X, X' and every output set $S \subset Range(\mathcal{M})$, the following inequality holds: $\mathbb{P}(\mathcal{M}(X) \in S) \leq e^{\epsilon}\mathbb{P}(\mathcal{M}(X') \in S)$. Here, we use the laplace mechanism [15] that adds noise sampled from a laplace distribution with variance as the ℓ_1-sensitivity of the query q. In the context of our work, the ℓ_1 sensitivity is defined as an identity function. Hence, to bound the sensitivity, we fix a pre-defined range $[a, b] \in \mathbb{R}$ in which $\mathbf{z}_S$ can lie, giving us sensitivity as $||a - b||_1$. Any data sam-

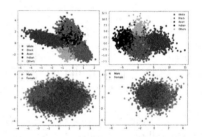

Fig. 3. Latent space visualization of $\mathbf{Z}_S$ by plotting its two components with the color of their sensitive attribute. We keep sensitive attributes as "race" and "gender" for the plots in the first and second row respectively using UTKFace [76].

ple $\mathbf{x}$ that results in $\mathbf{z}_S \notin [a, b]$ is truncated to the closest vector in the range. To summarize, the mechanism can be described as $f(\mathbf{z}_S) = \mathbf{z}_S + \Delta$ where Δ is sampled from a laplace distribution, i.e. $\Delta \sim Lap(0, \frac{||a-b||_1}{\epsilon})$. While this approach allows us to have a trade-off between the privacy property P3 and utility property P4 by controlling ϵ, we get a sub-optimal trade-off due to two reasons: i) truncation step discards the values outside the range $[a, b]$ ii) the noise is added independently to every component of $\mathbf{z}_S$ therefore throwing away the structure present in the distribution of $\mathbf{z}_S$ as shown in Fig. 3. This motivates developing a more utility conducive mechanism that can utilize structure in the latent space of $\mathbf{z}_S$.

c) DP-Sampling: Our goal is to utilize the structure present in the distribution of sensitive latents $p(\mathbf{z}_S)$ as shown in Fig. 3. We can observe the points to be clustered around their respective sensitive attribute. Therefore, *instead of adding uniform and independent noise, we propose to learn the distribution of* $\mathbf{z}_S$ *and sample from it.* Since the data is low dimensional, learning a Gaussian mixture model [39] suffices to model the distribution. However, sampling from the mixture model could leak sensitive information since our threat model considers the parameters of the sampling model are accessible to the attacker. Therefore, we learn the covariance matrix of $\mathbf{Z}_S$ and perturb it in a differentially private manner before sampling from it. If the learned model of the data satisfies DP then due to the post-processing invariance property [17] of DP, the samples obtained from this model would also satisfy DP. We learn the GMM model (parameterized by ψ) using the sensitive dataset $(\mathbf{Z}_S, \mathbf{Y}_S)$. Such a sampling scheme also provides the benefit of sampling labeled pairs $(\tilde{\mathbf{Z}}_S, \tilde{\mathbf{Y}}_S)$ which is required for performing supervised learning. We utilize RONGauss mechanism [8] to learn a differentially private covariance matrix of the sensitive latent dataset $\mathbf{Z}_S$. For each $\mathbf{z}_S \in \mathbf{Z}_S$, the mechanism performs random orthonormal projection to a lower-dimensional. We learn the mean and covariance for each category in a differentially private manner. Low dimensional projection improves utility by reducing the perturbation required for the same amount of privacy. Finally, we obtain synthetic sample $\tilde{\mathbf{z}}_S$ by sampling from the Gaussian model and reprojecting it back to the original dimensionality of $\mathbf{z}_S$. Formally, this can be written as $\tilde{\mathbf{z}}_S, \tilde{\mathbf{y}}_S \sim f_\psi(\tilde{\mathbf{z}}_S, \tilde{\mathbf{y}}_S)$, here ψ is learned using original sensitive dataset $\mathbf{Z}_S$. We note that, unlike standard GMM, here we use only a single mode from the GMM for every unique class. This is a more accurate description of the data since every sample $\mathbf{z}_S$ is uniquely associated with a single sensitive attribute $\mathbf{y}_S$. While the RONGauss mechanism learns and samples the whole data space for providing a uniform privacy guarantee, we only sample sensitive latents $\mathbf{z}_S$ instead of $\mathbf{z}$ since the goal is to protect sensitive attributes and not uniform privacy. We note that this DP-sampling does not give a uniform privacy guarantee on $\tilde{\mathbf{Z}}_S$ since information about sensitive attributes can leak from $\mathbf{Z}_{NS}$ too. We developed global-decoupler to address this specific issue. Our proposed sampling scheme can be extended to synthetic data release [64] by treating every component in $\mathbf{z}$ as sensitive (i.e. $k = m$) and presents interesting future work.

Remark: In this section, we presented our two-stage sanitization process. The main advantage of separating *sanitizer* as a two-stage process is that developing *global decoupling* is a one-time procedure and can be performed by a third party that distributes the trained model to different data owners A's which can apply sanitizing mechanisms individually. This modular process is an efficient way to release sensitive datasets if there are multiple A's involved. Furthermore, we believe that future works can improve either of the two stages independently.

4   Experiments

In this Section, we compare *sanitizer* with different baselines under multiple experimental setups. Each experimental setup is focused on simulating a unique use case. For all experiments, we use CelebA [35], UTKFace [76] and Fairface [25].

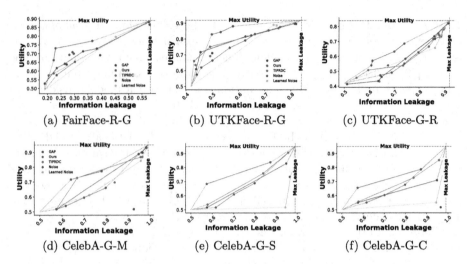

Fig. 4. E1: privacy-utility trade-off evaluation on different datasets: We plot sensitive information leakage as a proxy for privacy and one of the task attributes as a measure of utility for the sanitized dataset. Each point in this plot corresponds to training a *sanitizer* model and then evaluating its performance by training the adversary model and utility model on the sanitized dataset. *Sanitizer* performs better than all existing methods on all three datasets. Solid line represents the pareto-optimal curve for different methods. The dotted lines are extrapolation towards lowest and highest utility and leakage that is achievable trivially.

We split the dataset into $\mathbf{D}^{aux}$ for the first stage and $\mathbf{D}^A$ for the second stage. First, we train all techniques using $\mathbf{D}^{aux}$ and obtain sanitized dataset. Then we perform leakage assessment by training an adversary to learn a mapping between sanitized dataset and sensitive information. We discuss the rationale for such an adversary in Sect. 2. Finally, we evaluate the utility of the sanitized data based upon the experimental setup. Since our goal is task-agnostic data release, the *utility attribute is only used* after the sanitized dataset is released.

4.1   Baselines and Evaluation

Baselines: We compare against state-of-the-art visual sanitization techniques GAP [22] and TIPRDC [32], and introduce new baselines for exhaustive comparison. *GAP* [22]: is trained adversarially to maximize loss for a proxy adversary trying to infer sensitive attributes on the sanitized images. We replace the architecture proposed in the original paper with CNN architecture used in *sanitizer* to improve their results for higher dimensional image datasets. ii) *Learned Noise:* is built upon the TCNND architecture described in GAP [22] where a small dimensional noise is fed to a decoder that sanitizes the image by adding the noise vector. iii) *TIPRDC* [32]: is used as a baseline without any modification. iv) *Noise:* baseline sanitizes data by adding Gaussian noise in the pixel space; which is equivalent to the DP baseline used in TIPRDC [31].

Table 1. E1: Privacy-utility comparison: We report area under the curve (higher is better) to compare the privacy-utility trade-offs between *sanitizer* and baselines. UTKFace-R and UTKFace-G refer to the setup where *race* and *gender* is the sensitive attribute. Our method outperforms all baselines in all experiments.

Method	Fairface-R ↑	CelebA ↑	UTKFace-R ↑	UTKFace-G ↑
TIPRDC [32]	0.441	0.465	0.453	0.443
GAP [22]	0.447	0.442	0.450	0.434
Noise	0.438	0.422	0.435	0.431
Adversarial noise [22]*	0.432	0.422	0.420	0.439
Ours	**0.476**	**0.483**	**0.476**	**0.487**

Evaluation Metrics: We evaluate different techniques by comparing the *privacy-utility trade-off*. Here the utility is measured by the data receiver's test accuracy on the downstream task using sanitized dataset. For measuring privacy loss, we use the technique described in Sect. 2. Specifically, we quantify information leakage from the dataset by comparing the performance of an adversary inferring sensitive information from the sanitized dataset. We simulate a strong adversary that dynamically adapts to a sanitization scheme. This adaptation is modeled by a pretrained adversary model that is finetuned on the *sanitized* dataset and then evaluated on the sanitized test set. This privacy loss acts as a lower bound on the worst-case privacy loss. Since inferring sensitive attribute is similar to learn an optimal classifier, the difficulty in giving upper bound on the privacy loss is similar to upper bounding generalization error in ML models. Hence, our evaluation uses a similar approach of using test set accuracy. Inspired by [54] we quantify privacy-utility trade-offs curves by different techniques using area under the pareto-optimal curve (AuC). Higher AuC value denotes a better privacy-utility trade-off. Fore more experimental details and results, we refer the reader to supplementary material.

4.2   Experimental Setup and Results

Experiment E1. *Multi-category sensitive and Binary utility*: We test the use-case **UC1** by evaluating the privacy-utility trade-off on a task where sensitive information is multi-category "race" (fine-grained) and downstream utility task is "gender" (coarse). Intuitively, we should get a good trade-off from all techniques that can share coarse-grained data while obfuscating fine-grained sensitive detail.

Experiment E2. *Binary sensitive and Multi-category utility*: We use the setup as E1 but use "race" (coarse) as sensitive attribute and "gender" (fine-grained) as utility attribute. Intuitively, we expect degradation in an overall trade-off in comparison to E1. We perform the experiments on UTKFace [76] dataset and call this configuration *UTKFace-G*.

Experiment E3. *Single sensitive and Multiple utility*: We use the same setup as E1 but evaluate multiple utility tasks. We use CelebA [35] with sensitive attribute as "gender" and utility as "mouth open", "smiling" and "high cheekbone".

Table 2. E4, Classification Accuracy Score (CAS) evaluation: We train a classifier on privatized data samples and evaluate them on non-privatized samples.

	UTKFace		CelebA	
	Utility	Leakage	Utility	Leakage
Uniform noise	0.667	0.501	0.576	0.712
GAP [22]	0.615	0.499	0.723	0.686
Adversarial noise [22]	0.801	0.695	0.746	**0.663**
Ours	**0.86**	**0.474**	**0.9022**	0.6955

Table 3. E5, CAS for learning a model of sensitive attribute. We experiment with different mechanisms in the *local sampling* stage.

	UTKFace		CelebA	
	Utility	Leakage	Utility	Leakage
Suppression	0.208	0.498	0.7042	0.7177
Obfuscation	0.208	0.491	0.62	0.7129
DP-Sampling	**0.521**	**0.474**	**0.817**	**0.6955**

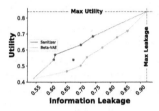

Fig. 5. Comparing β-VAE and global-decoupler by plotting the privacy-utility trade-off.

Table 4. Ablation on global-decoupler by cutting its different components. ✓ and ✗ denotes the presence and absence of the respective components.

Aligner	Dcorr	Adv.	Leakage ↓	Utility ↑
✗	✗	✓	0.6259	0.5474
✗	✓	✓	0.6238	0.5394
✓	✗	✗	0.6816	0.5137
✓	✗	✓	0.6318	0.5335
✓	✓	✗	0.6752	0.5386
✓	✓	✓	**0.6132**	**0.5698**

Experiment E4. *Learning transferable models*: We evaluate the use-case **UC2** by training a ML model on sanitized images and evaluate it on real images (non-sanitized). This setup is similar to Classification Accuracy Score(CAS) in the generative modeling community [49]. Note that it is not possible to include TIPRDC baseline since their output is constrained to embedding space.

Experiment E5. *Learn sensitive attribute distribution*: We test the use-case **UC3** of learning a ML model over the distribution $p(\mathbf{X}, \mathbf{Y}_S)$ while protecting individual sensitive information. We train the data-receiver's ML model on $(\tilde{\mathbf{X}}, \tilde{\mathbf{Y}}_S)$ and the attacker on $(\tilde{\mathbf{X}}, \mathbf{Y}_S)$. We evaluate data-receiver on $(\mathbf{X}, \mathbf{Y}_S)$ and the attacker on $(\tilde{\mathbf{X}}, \mathbf{Y}_S)$. This setup is not possible for our baselines since they censor sensitive information.

Results: For E1 and E2, we plot the privacy-utility trade-off for all techniques in Fig. 4 and Table 1. *Sanitizer* obtains a better privacy-utility trade-off consistently. For E3, we compare trade-off by evaluating on multiple downstream tasks and observe sanitizer's consistent better performance. We posit that the consistent improvement is due to explicit modeling of different privacy-utility constraints in *global-decoupler*. We compare the results for E4 in Table 2. Unlike previous experiments, here *sanitizer* achieves substantial gap in comparison to other techniques. We believe that synthetically replacing sensitive information allows *sanitizer* to produce realistic sanitized samples. While the leakage is slightly larger on CelebA dataset, the relative improvement in utility is much larger. For E5, we compare three mechanisms proposed in Sect. 3.2 in Table 3.

Under the same privacy budget, the proposed DP-Sampling technique achieves much better performance in both utility and leakage. Finally, we emphasize that E5 is not possible for baselines and is achieved only by the design of *sanitizer* and results for E4 and E5 validate that using *sanitizer* significantly improves performance for use-cases UC2 and UC3 (Sect. 1).

5   Discussion

Here, we analyze the design of global-decoupler by performing ablation study and discuss architectural limitations associated with it.

i) Ablation Study for Global-Decoupler: We perform ablation on each of the components described in the architecture in Fig. 2. We measure the sensitive information leakage and utility by comparing performance with and without each component in the objective given in Sect. 3. We can interpret this ablation study as keeping $\alpha_i = 0$ for the i'th component during the *global decoupling* stage. We enumerate the results in Table 4. We note that the presence of all components provides the best trade-off between the leakage and utility.

The global-decoupler is built upon β-VAE; therefore, we compare the trade-off between the two. We utilize latent space interpolation to randomize the sensitive attribute. First, we train a β-VAE model and obtain the mean representation of the sensitive latent by $z_{S_i} = \frac{1}{n_i} \sum_{j \in S_i} z_j \sim q_\phi(z|x_j)$ where S_i refers to a unique sensitive attribute category with n_i number of samples in the dataset. Finally, to randomize sensitive information in a given sample x, we transform the original latent $z = q_\phi(x)$ to obtain a sanitized latent $\tilde{z} = z - z_{S_i} + z_{S_j}$. For performing sensitive attribute randomization, i is the sensitive category of z, and j is chosen uniformly from the set of all categories including i. Finally, we obtain $\tilde{x} = p_\theta(\tilde{z})$ as a sanitized transformation of x. We evaluate this technique on UTKFace dataset [76] with same experimental setup as E2. We model the attacker same way as explained in Sect. 4 and show trade-off curves in Fig. 5.

ii) Architectural Limitations: The key goal of this work is to introduce a systematic framework and mechanisms for sanitization that could be useful for as many downstream tasks as possible under the privacy-utility trade-off. Here, we note two key limitations of the presented results, emerging from the generative modeling framework: i) *input sample size* - This limitation stems from the need for sufficient data points to learn a latent model of the data that generalizes between $\mathbf{D}^{aux}$ and $\mathbf{D}^A$. Designing latent models that can capture the distribution with a minimum number of samples is an active area of research in few-shot learning which will improve the impact of our results but is orthogonal to the scope of our work. ii) *output sample quality* - This limitation can be improved using hierarchical latent variable models [51,66] and we consider this as part of the future work. We believe that improvement in representation capacity can improve trade-offs even further for *sanitizer*.

6   Related Work

First, we discuss prior work in privacy-preserving data release for task-dependent and task-independent setups. *Next*, we draw parallels to techniques in fairness and conditional generation of images.

Task-dependent data release techniques transform data that is conducive to a particular task. Several techniques use central DP [17] as a formal privacy definition to answer aggregate queries. The queries can be summary statistics such as mean, median [16,17] or learning a ML model [1], sharing gradients in federated learning [70]. Recent work in adversarial learning has resulted in techniques for task-specific latent representation [20,33,34,40,45,46,55,56,60, 71]. While we share the same goal of protecting sensitive information, our work differs in its task-independent formulation.

Task-independent techniques share data in a non-interactive manner. Similar to central DP, several works consider identification as sensitive information, however without a trusted curator. This modified central DP setup is referred to as local-DP [48]. While variants of local-DP for attribute privacy exist, their focus is primarily on protecting dataset statistics [75], different rows of a dataset [2] or task-dependent [12,43]. Local-DP based generative models [8,24,65,72,77] learn data distribution privately to release samples. While we focus on specific sensitive information, we build upon the sampling strategy used in RonGauss [8] to sample sensitive data. TIPRDC [31] and GAP [23] are task-agnostic techniques that protect sensitive information by censoring it. While we solve a similar problem, our sampling-based approach allows performing certain tasks (eg. **E5** in Sect. 4) that are not possible with the censoring-based approach.

Fairness techniques aim to make predictive models unbiased with respect to *protected groups*. Among different approaches [7] used for fairness, works in censoring information [3,69,74,75] related to *protected groups* is the closest approach to our work. However, we differ significantly from the censoring approach because we release anonymized sensitive information instead of censoring it. Furthermore, the goal of the sanitization problem is to maximally retain original data insofar that all biases would exist after sanitization. While the objective and evaluation for the fairness community are different, we note that Sarhan et al. [58] use a similar objective as *sanitizer* by utilizing variational inference with orthogonality constraint for preventing leakage. However, they do not provide anonymization since two correlated vectors can be orthogonal.

Conditional generation which has a similar problem setup to sanitization [11,59]. While this has led to some relevant work in privacy, the techniques typically handcraft the objective to be task-specific for identity [13,41,42,47,50]. In contrast, *sanitizer* is agnostic of target utility and only depends upon sensitive attributes. Some recent works utilize uncertainty-based metrics [38,68] to fuse all sensitive attributes in latent space using adversarial training but hence, unlike *sanitizer*, generate highly unrealistic images (hence not being task agnostic) due to high uncertainty.

7   Conclusion

In this work, we presented sanitizer: a framework for minimizing sensitive information leakage to facilitate task-agnostic data release. We achieve this goal through a two-stage process - i) *global decoupling* for learning a latent model of data and ii) *local sampling* for securely synthesizing sensitive information. While our approach improves the privacy-utility trade-off, future work includes technique that allow privacy guarantees for the non-sensitive latent.

Acknowledgements. This work was supported by NSF award number 1729931.

References

1. Abadi, M., Chu, A., Goodfellow, I., McMahan, H.B., Mironov, I., Talwar, K., Zhang, L.: Deep learning with differential privacy. Proceedings of the 2016 ACM SIGSAC Conference on Computer and Communications Security, October 2016. https://dx.doi.org/10.1145/2976749.2978318
2. Acharya, J., Bonawitz, K., Kairouz, P., Ramage, D., Sun, Z.: Context aware local differential privacy. In: International Conference on Machine Learning, pp. 52–62. PMLR (2020)
3. Adeli, E., et al.: Bias-resilient neural network (2019)
4. Banerjee, I., et al.: Reading race: AI recognizes patient's racial identity in medical images. arXiv preprint arXiv:2107.10356 (2021)
5. Betzler, B.K., et al.: Gender prediction for a multiethnic population via deep learning across different retinal fundus photograph fields: retrospective cross-sectional study. JMIR Med. Inf. **9**(8), e25165 (2021)
6. Borgwardt, K.M., Gretton, A., Rasch, M.J., Kriegel, H.P., Schölkopf, B., Smola, A.J.: Integrating structured biological data by kernel maximum mean discrepancy. Bioinformatics **22**(14), e49–e57 (2006)
7. Caton, S., Haas, C.: Fairness in machine learning: a survey. arXiv preprint arXiv:2010.04053 (2020)
8. Chanyaswad, T., Liu, C., Mittal, P.: Ron-gauss: Enhancing utility in non-interactive private data release. Proc. Priv. Enhancing Technol. **2019**(1), 26–46 (2019)
9. Chen, R.T., Li, X., Grosse, R., Duvenaud, D.: Isolating sources of disentanglement in variational autoencoders. arXiv:1802.04942 (2018)
10. Chen, S., et al.: Development of a computer-aided tool for the pattern recognition of facial features in diagnosing turner syndrome: comparison of diagnostic accuracy with clinical workers. Sci. Rep. **8**(1), 1–9 (2018)
11. Chen, Y.C., Shen, X., Lin, Z., Lu, X., Pao, I., Jia, J., et al.: Semantic component decomposition for face attribute manipulation. In: CVPR (2019)
12. Cheng, J., Tang, A., Chinchali, S.: Task-aware privacy preservation for multidimensional data. arXiv preprint arXiv:2110.02329 (2021)
13. Chhabra, S., Singh, R., Vatsa, M., Gupta, G.: Anonymizing k-facial attributes via adversarial perturbations. arXiv preprint arXiv:1805.09380 (2018)
14. Deng, J., Dong, W., Socher, R., Li, L.J., Li, K., Fei-Fei, L.: ImageNet: a large-scale hierarchical image database. In: 2009 IEEE Conference on Computer Vision and Pattern Recognition, pp. 248–255. IEEE (2009)

15. Dwork, C., McSherry, F., Nissim, K., Smith, A.: Calibrating noise to sensitivity in private data analysis. In: Halevi, S., Rabin, T. (eds.) TCC 2006. LNCS, vol. 3876, pp. 265–284. Springer, Heidelberg (2006). https://doi.org/10.1007/11681878_14
16. Dwork, C., McSherry, F., Nissim, K., Smith, A.: Calibrating noise to sensitivity in private data analysis. In: Theory of Cryptography Conference (2006)
17. Dwork, C., Roth, A., et al.: The algorithmic foundations of differential privacy. Foundations Trends Theor. Comput. Sci. 9(3–4), 211–407 (2014)
18. Goodfellow, I.J., et al.: Generative adversarial networks. arXiv:1406.2661 (2014)
19. Gretton, A., Bousquet, O., Smola, A., Schölkopf, B.: Measuring statistical dependence with Hilbert-Schmidt norms. In: Jain, S., Simon, H.U., Tomita, E. (eds.) ALT 2005. LNCS (LNAI), vol. 3734, pp. 63–77. Springer, Heidelberg (2005). https://doi.org/10.1007/11564089_7
20. Hamm, J.: Minimax filter: learning to preserve privacy from inference attacks. J. Mach. Learn. Res. 18(129), 1–31 (2017). https://jmlr.org/papers/v18/16-501.html
21. Higgins, I., et al.: beta-VAE: Learning basic visual concepts with a constrained variational framework (2016)
22. Huang, C., Kairouz, P., Chen, X., Sankar, L., Rajagopal, R.: Context-aware generative adversarial privacy. Entropy 19(12), 656 (2017). arXiv: 1710.09549, https://doi.org/10.3390/e19120656
23. Huang, C., Kairouz, P., Chen, X., Sankar, L., Rajagopal, R.: Generative adversarial privacy. CoRR (2018)
24. Jordon, J., Yoon, J., Schaar, M.V.D.: PATE-GAN: generating synthetic data with differential privacy guarantees, September 2018. https://openreview.net/forum?id=S1zk9iRqF7
25. Kärkkäinen, K., Joo, J.: FairFace: face attribute dataset for balanced race, gender, and age. arXiv:1908.04913 (2019)
26. Kifer, D., Machanavajjhala, A.: Pufferfish: a framework for mathematical privacy definitions. ACM TODS 39(1), 1–36 (2014)
27. Kim, H., Mnih, A.: Disentangling by factorising. In: ICML (2018)
28. Kingma, D.P., Welling, M.: Auto-encoding variational bayes. arXiv:1312.6114 (2013)
29. Korot, E., et al.: Predicting sex from retinal fundus photographs using automated deep learning. Sci. Rep. 11(1), 1–8 (2021)
30. Kumar, D., Verma, C., Dahiya, S., Singh, P.K., Raboaca, M.S.: Cardiac diagnostic feature and demographic identification models: a futuristic approach for smart healthcare using machine learning (2021)
31. Li, A., Duan, Y., Yang, H., Chen, Y., Yang, J.: TIPRDC: task-independent privacy-respecting data crowdsourcing framework for deep learning with anonymized intermediate representations. In: ACM SIGKDD (2020)
32. Li, A., Duan, Y., Yang, H., Chen, Y., Yang, J.: TIPRDC: task-independent privacy-respecting data crowdsourcing framework for deep learning with anonymized intermediate representations. In: Proceedings of the 26th ACM SIGKDD International Conference on Knowledge Discovery & Data Mining, pp. 824–832 (2020)
33. Li, A., Guo, J., Yang, H., Chen, Y.: DeepObfuscator: adversarial training framework for privacy-preserving image classification (2019)
34. Liu, C., Chakraborty, S., Mittal, P.: DEEProtect: Enabling inference-based access control on mobile sensing applications. CoRR (2017)
35. Liu, Z., Luo, P., Wang, X., Tang, X.: Large-scale CelebFaces attributes (CelebA) dataset. Retrieved August 15, 11 (2018)

36. Loos, H.S., Wieczorek, D., Würtz, R.P., Malsburg, C.V.D., Horsthemke, B.: Computer-based recognition of dysmorphic faces. Eur. J. Hum. Genet. **11**(8), 555–560 (2003)

37. Makhdoumi, A., Fawaz, N.: Privacy-utility tradeoff under statistical uncertainty. In: Annual Allerton Conference on Communication, Control, and Computing (Allerton) (2013)

38. Martinsson, J., Zec, E.L., Gillblad, D., Mogren, O.: Adversarial representation learning for synthetic replacement of private attributes. arXiv preprint arXiv:2006.08039 (2020)

39. McLachlan, G.J., Lee, S.X., Rathnayake, S.I.: Finite mixture models. Ann. Rev. Stat. Appl. **6**, 355–378 (2019)

40. Mireshghallah, F., Taram, M., Ramrakhyani, P., Tullsen, D.M., Esmaeilzadeh, H.: Shredder: learning noise to protect privacy with partial DNN inference on the edge. CoRR abs/1905.11814 (2019). arxiv.org/abs/1905.11814

41. Mirjalili, V., Raschka, S., Ross, A.: FlowSAN: privacy-enhancing semi-adversarial networks to confound arbitrary face-based gender classifiers. IEEE Access **7**, 99735–99745 (2019)

42. Mirjalili, V., Raschka, S., Ross, A.: PrivacyNet: semi-adversarial networks for multi-attribute face privacy. IEEE Trans. Image Process. **29**, 9400–9412 (2020)

43. Murakami, T., Kawamoto, Y.: {Utility-Optimized} local differential privacy mechanisms for distribution estimation. In: 28th USENIX Security Symposium (USENIX Security 19), pp. 1877–1894 (2019)

44. Osia, S.A., et al.: A hybrid deep learning architecture for privacy-preserving mobile analytics. IEEE Internet Things J. **7**(5), 4505–4518 (2020)

45. Osia, S.A., et al.: A hybrid deep learning architecture for privacy-preserving mobile analytics. IEEE Internet Things J. **7**(5), 4505–4518 (2020). arXiv: 1703.02952, https://doi.org/10.1109/JIOT.2020.2967734

46. Osia, S.A., Taheri, A., Shamsabadi, A.S., Katevas, K., Haddadi, H., Rabiee, H.R.: Deep private-feature extraction (2018)

47. Othman, A., Ross, A.: Privacy of facial soft biometrics: suppressing gender but retaining identity. In: Agapito, L., Bronstein, M.M., Rother, C. (eds.) ECCV 2014. LNCS, vol. 8926, pp. 682–696. Springer, Cham (2015). https://doi.org/10.1007/978-3-319-16181-5_52

48. Raskhodnikova, S., Smith, A., Lee, H.K., Nissim, K., Kasiviswanathan, S.P.: What can we learn privately. In: FOCS (2008)

49. Ravuri, S., Vinyals, O.: Classification accuracy score for conditional generative models. arXiv:1905.10887 (2019)

50. Raynal, M., Achanta, R., Humbert, M.: Image obfuscation for privacy-preserving machine learning. arXiv preprint arXiv:2010.10139 (2020)

51. Razavi, A., Van den Oord, A., Vinyals, O.: Generating diverse high-fidelity images with VQ-VAE-2. Adv. Neural Inf. Process. Syst. **32** (2019)

52. Rezende, D., Mohamed, S.: Variational inference with normalizing flows. In: International Conference on Machine Learning, pp. 1530–1538. PMLR (2015)

53. Rezende, D.J., Mohamed, S., Wierstra, D.: Stochastic backpropagation and approximate inference in deep generative models. In: ICML (2014)

54. Roy, P.C., Boddeti, V.N.: Mitigating information leakage in image representations: a maximum entropy approach. In: CVPR (2019)

55. Roy, P.C., Boddeti, V.N.: Mitigating information leakage in image representations: a maximum entropy approach. In: Proceedings of the IEEE/CVF Conference on Computer Vision and Pattern Recognition (CVPR), June 2019

56. Samragh, M., Hosseini, H., Triastcyn, A., Azarian, K., Soriaga, J., Koushanfar, F.: Unsupervised information obfuscation for split inference of neural networks. arXiv preprint arXiv:2104.11413 (2021)
57. Sankar, L., Rajagopalan, S.R., Poor, H.V.: An information-theoretic approach to privacy. In: Allerton Conference on Communication, Control, and Computing (Allerton) (2010)
58. Sarhan, M.H., Navab, N., Eslami, A., Albarqouni, S.: Fairness by learning orthogonal disentangled representations. In: Vedaldi, A., Bischof, H., Brox, T., Frahm, J.-M. (eds.) ECCV 2020. LNCS, vol. 12374, pp. 746–761. Springer, Cham (2020). https://doi.org/10.1007/978-3-030-58526-6_44
59. Shen, W., Liu, R.: Learning residual images for face attribute manipulation. In: CVPR (2017)
60. Singh, A., et al.: Disco: dynamic and invariant sensitive channel obfuscation for deep neural networks. arXiv:2012.11025 (2020)
61. Stephen, I.D., Hiew, V., Coetzee, V., Tiddeman, B.P., Perrett, D.I.: Facial shape analysis identifies valid cues to aspects of physiological health in Caucasian, Asian, and African populations. Front. Psychol. 8, 1883 (2017)
62. Su, N.M., Crandall, D.J.: The affective growth of computer vision. In: Proceedings of the IEEE/CVF Conference on Computer Vision and Pattern Recognition, pp. 9291–9300 (2021)
63. Székely, G.J., Rizzo, M.L., Bakirov, N.K., et al.: Measuring and testing dependence by correlation of distances. Ann. Stat. 35(6), 2769–2794 (2007)
64. Tao, Y., McKenna, R., Hay, M., Machanavajjhala, A., Miklau, G.: Benchmarking differentially private synthetic data generation algorithms. arXiv preprint arXiv:2112.09238 (2021)
65. Torkzadehmahani, R., Kairouz, P., Paten, B.: DP-CGAN: differentially private synthetic data and label generation. In: Proceedings of the IEEE/CVF Conference on Computer Vision and Pattern Recognition Workshops (2019)
66. Vahdat, A., Kautz, J.: NVAE: A deep hierarchical variational autoencoder. Adv. Neural Inf. Process. Syst. 33, 19667–19679 (2020)
67. Vepakomma, P., Singh, A., Zhang, E., Gupta, O., Raskar, R.: NoPeek-Infer: preventing face reconstruction attacks in distributed inference after on-premise training. In: 2021 16th IEEE International Conference on Automatic Face and Gesture Recognition (FG 2021), pp. 1–8. IEEE (2021)
68. Wang, H.P., Orekondy, T., Fritz, M.: InfoScrub: towards attribute privacy by targeted obfuscation. In: Proceedings of the IEEE/CVF Conference on Computer Vision and Pattern Recognition, pp. 3281–3289 (2021)
69. Wang, T., Zhao, J., Yatskar, M., Chang, K.W., Ordonez, V.: Balanced datasets are not enough: Estimating and mitigating gender bias in deep image representations. In: Proceedings of the IEEE/CVF International Conference on Computer Vision, pp. 5310–5319 (2019)
70. Wei, K., et al.: Federated learning with differential privacy: algorithms and performance analysis. IEEE Trans. Inf. Forensics Secur. 15, 3454–3469 (2020)
71. Wu, Z., Wang, Z., Wang, Z., Jin, H.: Towards privacy-preserving visual recognition via adversarial training: a pilot study. In: Proceedings of the European Conference on Computer Vision (ECCV), pp. 606–624 (2018)
72. Xie, L., Lin, K., Wang, S., Wang, F., Zhou, J.: Differentially private generative adversarial network. arXiv preprint arXiv:1802.06739 (2018)
73. Yi, P.H., et al.: Radiology 'forensics': determination of age and sex from chest radiographs using deep learning. Emerg. Radiol. 28(5), 949–954 (2021)

74. Zemel, R., Wu, Y., Swersky, K., Pitassi, T., Dwork, C.: Learning fair representations. In: International Conference on Machine Learning, pp. 325–333. PMLR (2013)

75. Zhang, B.H., Lemoine, B., Mitchell, M.: Mitigating unwanted biases with adversarial learning. In: Proceedings of the 2018 AAAI/ACM Conference on AI, Ethics, and Society, pp. 335–340 (2018)

76. Zhang, Z., Song, Y., Qi, H.: Age progression/regression by conditional adversarial autoencoder. In: Proceedings of the IEEE Conference on Computer Vision and Pattern Recognition, pp. 5810–5818 (2017)

77. Zhang, Z., et al.: PrivSyn: differentially private data synthesis (2021)

Privacy-Preserving Action Recognition via Motion Difference Quantization

Sudhakar Kumawat$^{(\boxtimes)}$ ⓘ and Hajime Nagahara ⓘ

Osaka University, Suita, Japan
{sudhakar,nagahara}@ids.osaka-u.ac.jp

Abstract. The widespread use of smart computer vision systems in our personal spaces has led to an increased consciousness about the privacy and security risks that these systems pose. On the one hand, we want these systems to assist in our daily lives by understanding our surroundings, but on the other hand, we want them to do so without capturing any sensitive information. Towards this direction, this paper proposes a simple, yet robust privacy-preserving encoder called BDQ for the task of privacy-preserving human action recognition that is composed of three modules: *Blur*, *Difference*, and *Quantization*. First, the input scene is passed to the *Blur* module to smoothen the edges. This is followed by the *Difference* module to apply a pixel-wise intensity subtraction between consecutive frames to highlight motion features and suppress high-level privacy attributes. Finally, the *Quantization* module is applied to the motion difference frames to remove the low-level privacy attributes. The BDQ parameters are optimized in an end-to-end fashion via adversarial training such that it learns to allow action recognition attributes while inhibiting privacy attributes. Our experiments on three benchmark datasets show that the proposed encoder design can achieve state-of-the-art trade-off when compared with previous works. Furthermore, we show that the trade-off achieved is at par with the DVS sensor-based event cameras. Code available at: https://github.com/suakaw/BDQ_PrivacyAR

Keywords: Action recognition · Privacy · Motion difference · Quantization · Adversarial training

1 Introduction

For many decades, people have been fascinated with the idea of creating computer vision (CV) systems that can see and interpret the world around them. In today's world, as this dream turns into reality and such systems begin to be deployed in our personal spaces, there is an increased consciousness about "what"

Supplementary Information The online version contains supplementary material available at https://doi.org/10.1007/978-3-031-19778-9_30.

these systems see and "how" they interpret it. Nowadays, we want CV systems that can protect our visual privacy without compromising the user experience. Therefore, there is a growing interest in developing such CV systems that can prevent the camera system from obtaining detailed visual data that may contain any sensitive information, but allow it to capture useful information to successfully perform the CV task [14,26,30,33,37]. For a satisfactory user experience and strong privacy protection, a CV system must satisfy the following properties:

- **Good target task accuracy.** This is necessary for maintaining a good user experience. For example, a privacy-preserving face detection model must detect faces with high precision without revealing facial identity [33], a privacy-preserving pose estimation model must detect body key-points without revealing the person identity [14], and an action recognition model must recognize human actions without revealing their identity information [30,37].
- **Strong privacy protection.** Any privacy-preserving model, irrespective of the target task must preserve common visual privacy attributes such as identity, gender, race, color, gait, etc. [22]. Note that the definition of privacy attributes for a privacy-preserving model may vary depending on its application. Furthermore, strong privacy protection is guaranteed when the model is applied at the point of capture and it is impossible for any adversary to learn or reconstruct the privacy attributes.
- **Cost-effective and low space-time complexity.** The right to privacy is considered as one of the fundamental rights in the most countries. However, with the increasing availability of low-budget consumer cameras and smartphones, it cannot be fully guaranteed unless the privacy-preserving models are affordable to everyone. This calls for a focus on implementing such models, whether in software or hardware, in a cost-effective manner. Additionally, since the privacy-preserving model needs to be applied at the point of capture in consumer cameras and smartphones with low memory, computation, and power budgets, it must be of low space-time complexity.

In this paper, we are interested in developing a privacy-preserving encoder for the task of human action recognition while keeping the above properties in mind. In particular, we develop a simple and robust privacy-preserving encoder called BDQ that is composed of three modules: *Blur*, *Difference*, and *Quantization*. The modules are applied in a sequential manner such that *Blur* module smoothen the edges in the input frames. The *Difference* module computes pixel-wise intensity subtraction between consecutive frames to highlight motion features and suppress high-level privacy attributes. The *Quantization* module removes the low-level privacy attributes from the motion difference frames. The parameters of BDQ are optimized in an end-to-end manner via adversarial training such that it learns to facilitate action recognition while inhibiting privacy attributes. Note that, any successful action recognition model relies on the presence of both spatial and temporal cues in its input for good performance. However, in most cases, applying a privacy-preserving encoder often destroys the spatial resolution which is sometimes detrimental for action recognition as shown in Fig. 1. The design of our BDQ encoder is motivated to alleviate such issues such that

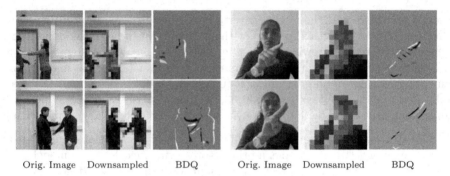

Orig. Image   Downsampled   BDQ   Orig. Image   Downsampled   BDQ

Fig. 1. Left- An example where downsampling is effective for privacy-preserving action recognition. Right- An example where down-sampling is detrimental for action recognition since the information about the number of fingers is lost. Unlike downsampling, the BDQ preserves both spatial and temporal resolutions.

it preserves both spatial and temporal cues that are essential for action recognition while discarding attributes that may reveal the privacy information. In summary, the contributions of this work are as follows.

- We propose a simple yet robust privacy-preserving encoder called BDQ for the task of human action recognition. The BDQ encoder allows important spatio-temporal cues for action recognition while preserving privacy attributes at a very low space-time complexity.
- We show that the BDQ encoder achieves state-of-the-art trade-off between action recognition and privacy preservation on three benchmark datasets SBU, KTH, and IPN, when compared with other privacy-preserving models. Moreover, we show that the trade-off achieved is at par with the DVS sensor-based event cameras.
- We provide an extensive analysis of the BDQ encoder. The analysis includes an ablation study on the components of BDQ, learning and reconstructing privacy attributes by different adversaries, and a subjective evaluation.
- Finally, we also discuss the feasibility of implementing the BDQ modules using existing hardware (please refer supplementary).

2   Related Work

In recent years, there is a growing interest in developing privacy-preserving vision systems for various computer vision tasks such as action recognition [30,37], face detection [33], pose estimation [14,32], fall detection [3], and posture classification [12]. Here, we provide a brief overview of privacy-preserving frameworks for various computer vision tasks, especially human action recognition.

Privacy-Preserving Computer Vision. Early privacy-preserving models used hand-crafted features such as blurring, down-sampling, pixelation, and face/object replacement for protecting sensitive information [2,7,23]. Unfortunately, such approaches require extensive domain knowledge about the problem setting which may not be feasible in practice. Modern privacy-preserving frameworks take a data-driven approach to hide sensitive information. Such frameworks learn to preserve privacy via adversarial training [28] using Deep Neural Networks (DNNs) that train the parameters of an encoder to actively inhibit the sensitive attributes in an visual data against an adversarial DNN whose task is to learn privacy attributes while allowing attributes that are essential for the computer vision task [5,16,21,24,33,37]. Note that the encoder can be a hardware module [14,33] or a software module [28,37]. Besides these works, there are other imaging systems that use optical operations to hide sensitive attributes. For example, in [25], the authors design camera systems that perform blurring and k-same face de-identification in hardware. Furthermore, in [6,35], authors explore coded aperture masks to enhance privacy.

Privacy-Preserving Action Recognition. Early works in this area proposed to learn human actions from low-resolution videos [9,29,30]. Ryoo *et al.* [29,30] proposed to learn image transformations to down-sample frames into low-resolution for action recognition. Wang *et al.* [35] proposed a lens-free coded aperture camera system for action recognition that is privacy-preserving. Note that the above frameworks are limited to providing visual privacy and it is not clear, to what extent they provide protection against adversaries like DNNs that may try to learn or reconstruct the privacy attributes. To solve this issue, Ren *et al.* [27] proposed to learn a video face anonymizer using adversarial training. The training uses a video anonymizer that modifies the original video to remove sensitive information while trying to maximize the action recognition performance and a discriminator that tries to extract sensitive information from the anonymized videos. Later, Wu *et al.* [36,37] proposed and compared multiple adversarial training frameworks for optimizing the parameters of the encoder function. They used a UNet-like encoder from [18] which can be seen as a 2D conv-based frame-level filter. The encoder is trained to allow important spatio-temporal attributes for action recognition, measured by a DNN, and to inhibit the privacy attributes in frames against an ensemble of DNN adversaries whose task is to learn the sensitive information. An important drawback of this framework is that the training requires an ensemble of adversaries in order to provide strong privacy protection. Concurrent to our work, Dave *et al.* [10] proposed a self-supervised framework for training a UNet-based privacy-preserving encoder.

3 Proposed Framework

In this section, we present the design of our BDQ encoder which is composed of a series of modules. We also discuss an adversarial training scheme to optimally train the parameters of these modules for the two seemingly contradictory tasks: protecting privacy and enabling action recognition.

3.1 BDQ: Blur Difference Quantization

The BDQ encoder, as the name suggests is composed of three modules: *Blur*, *Difference*, and *Quantization*. Given a scene, the three modules are applied to it in a sequential manner as shown in Fig. 2. Here, for each module, we provide a detailed description of its implementation and role in preserving privacy and enabling action recognition.

Blur. The goal of the *Blur* module is to blur the spatial edges while preserving important spatial features for action recognition. More importantly, its task is to suppress the obvious privacy features that may leak at the spatial edges in motion difference frames that will be produced by the *Difference* module. Given a frame v_i, we define a video as $V = \{v_i | i = 1, 2, .., t\}$ where t is the number of frames. The blurred frame B_{v_i} is convolution of video frame v_i and a 2D Gaussian kernel G_σ of σ standard deviation and defined as $B_{v_i} = G_\sigma v_i$, where $G_\sigma = \frac{1}{2\pi\sigma^2} exp(-\frac{x^2+y^2}{2\sigma^2})$. Window-size of the kernel is kept as 5×5 and σ is learned during the adversarial training. A small window-size is chosen since it stabilizes training and avoids losing important spatial features.

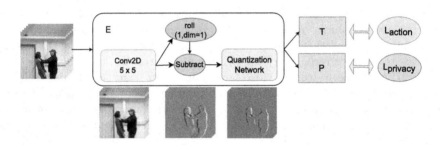

Fig. 2. The BDQ encoder architecture and adversarial training framework for privacy-preserving action recognition. $roll(1, dim = 1)$ operation shifts frames by one along the temporal dimension.

Difference. Given two consecutive frames from an action video after passing through the *Blur* module, this module performs pixel-wise numerical subtraction between their intensity values and outputs a single frame as $D(B_{v_i}, B_{v_j}) = B_{v_i} - B_{v_j}$. It serves two important purposes: First, it highlights the motion features between the two frames by bringing out the direction of motion which improves action recognition accuracy. This is evident from the fact that many current state-of-the-art action recognition methods such as [17,19,20,34] use such temporal-difference modules in the feature space to develop action recognition models. Second, it suppresses obvious high-level spatial privacy cues which helps in preserving privacy. Note that this module does not contain any learnable parameters. Furthermore, when implemented for online applications where frames are continuously being captured, it needs to store a copy of the previous frame for pixel-wise numerical subtraction.

Quantization. Although, the *Blur* and the *Difference* modules contribute to suppressing high-level spatial privacy cues, they cannot fully protect against adversaries (see Sect. 5.1). This is because they still allow low-level spatial privacy cues that are good enough for learning and reconstructing the privacy attributes (see Sect. 5.4). To alleviate this issue, the task of the *Quantization* module is to remove such information by applying a pixel-wise quantization function on the motion difference frames that are output by the *Difference module*. Conventionally, a quantization function is defined by $y = \sum_{n=1}^{N-1} \mathcal{U}(x - b_i)$, where y is the discrete output, x is a continuous input, $b_i = \{0.5, 1.5, 2.5, \ldots, N-1.5\}$, $N = 2^k$, k is the number of bits, and $\mathcal{U}$ is the Heaviside function. Unfortunately, such a formulation is not differentiable and therefore not suitable for back-propagation. Thus, following [33,38], we approximate the above quantization function with a differentiable version by replacing the Heaviside function with the sigmoid $\sigma()$ function, which results in the following formulation: $\sum_{n=1}^{N-1} \sigma(H(x - b_i))$, where H is a scalar hardness term. Here, the parameters learned are the b_i values. In this work, we fix the number of b_i values to be 15 and initialize them to the values $0.5, 1.5, \ldots, 14.5$. Furthermore, the input to the *Quantization* module is normalized to have values between 0 to 15. Note that, here we allow quantization output to be non-integer since no hardware constrain is imposed on BDQ.

3.2 Training BDQ Encoder

The BDQ encoder contains several parameters such as the standard deviation of the *Blur* module and the intervals of the *Quantization* module. Our goal is to set these parameters such that: (1) the privacy attributes cannot be learned from the BDQ output by any adversary, (2) recognizing action attributes must be feasible with high precision. Although, we can achieve this goal by setting these parameters heuristically, however, it has been shown that a better performance can be achieved if they are learned in a data-driven fashion [14,33,37].

Our training framework consists of three components: (1) the BDQ encoder denoted as E, (2) a 3D CNN for predicting target action attribute denoted as T, (3) and a 2D CNN for predicting privacy attribute denoted as P. The three components are connected as illustrated in Fig. 2 such that the output of E is simultaneously passed to the networks T and P. Following [28], the parameter optimization of E, T, and P is formulated as a three-player non-zero sum game where the goal of E is to maximize the likelihood of the target action attributes, measured by E, while maximizing the uncertainty in the privacy attributes, measured by P. Such a training procedure consists of two steps that are iterated until the privacy attributes are sufficiently preserved without a significant compromise in action recognition. In the first step, P is fixed and E and T are trained together using the following loss function.

$$\mathcal{L}(V, \theta_E, \theta_T) = \mathcal{XE}(T(E(V)), L_{action}) - \alpha \mathcal{E}(P(E(V))) \qquad (1)$$

Here, $\mathcal{XE}$ and $\mathcal{E}$ refer to the cross-entropy loss and entropy function, respectively. θ_E and θ_T denote parameters of E and T, respectively. L_{action} is the ground-truth action label and α is the adversarial weight that allows a trade-off between action and privacy recognition. In the second step, E and T are fixed, and P is trained using the following loss function. Here, θ_P denote the parameters of P and $L_{privacy}$ are the ground-truth privacy labels.

$$\mathcal{L}(V, \theta_P) = \mathcal{XE}(P(E(V)), L_{privacy}) \qquad (2)$$

4 Experiments

4.1 Datasets

SBU. The SBU Kinect Interaction Dataset [39] is a two-person interaction dataset for video-based action recognition, recorded at 15 fps. It consists of seven actors interacting in pairs in the following eight ways: approaching, departing, pushing, kicking, punching, exchanging objects, hugging, and shaking hands. Originally, the dataset comes divided into 21 sets such that each set corresponds to a pair of actors performing all the eight interactions. Furthermore, the 21 sets are created such that the same two actors may appear in two different sets. In such a case, in the first set, one actor acts and the other reacts and vice versa in the second set. For example, in set s01s02, actor 1 is acting and actor 2 is reacting; similarly, in set s02s01, actor 2 is acting and actor 1 is reacting. Since, such sets contain the same pair of actors, they can be combined into one class. Following this procedure, we reduce the number of 21 original sets to 13 different distinct actor-pair sets. For our setting, given a video, the target task is to classify it into one of the eight interaction/action classes while the privacy label prediction task is to recognize the actor-pair among the 13 actor-pairs. Note the above method is identical to the one followed in [36,37] for developing their privacy-preserving action recognition framework.

KTH. The KTH dataset [31] is a video-based action recognition dataset, recorded at 25 fps. It consists of 25 actors, each performing the following six actions: walk, jog, run, box, hand-wave, and hand clap. The different actions are recorded in different settings and variations including outdoor, outdoor with scale variation, outdoor with different clothes, and indoor. In our experiments, we use the six action classes for the action recognition task and the 25 actor identities for the privacy label prediction task.

IPN. The IPN hand gesture dataset [4] is a video-based hand gesture dataset, recorded at 30 fps. It consists of 50 actors, each performing the following 13 hand gestures that are common in interacting with a touch-less screen: pointing with one finger, pointing with two fingers, click with one finger, click with two fingers, throw up, throw down, throw left, throw right, open twice, double click with one finger, double click with two fingers, zoom in, and zoom out. In our experiments, we use the 13 hand gesture classes for the action recognition task and the gender (male/female, 2 classes) of the actors for the privacy label prediction task.

4.2 Implementation

Adversarial Training. Our adversarial training framework consists of three components: (1) the BDQ encoder, (2) an action recognition model which is set to a 3D ResNet-50 network, (3) and a privacy attribute prediction model which is set to a 2D ResNet-50 network. Furthermore, the 3D ResNet-50 and the 2D ResNet-50 networks are initialized with Kinetics-400 and ImageNet pre-trained weights, respectively. For training, we densely sample t consecutive frames ($t = 16$ for SBU, $t = 32$ for KTH and IPN) from the input video to form an input sequence. For spatial data augmentation, we randomly choose for each input sequence, a spatial position and a scale to perform a multi-scale cropping where the scale is picked from the set $\{1, \frac{1}{2^{1/4}}, \frac{1}{2^{3/4}}, \frac{1}{2}\}$. The final output is an input sequence with size 224×224. As shown in Fig. 2, the input sequence is then passed through the BDQ encoder whose output is then passed to the 3D ResNet-50 model for action recognition and 2D ResNet-50 model for predicting privacy labels. The optimization of parameters of the three networks is done according to the adversarial training framework discussed in Sect. 3.2 with $\alpha = 2, 1$, and 8, for SBU, KTH, and IPN, respectively. Scaler hardness H is set to 5 for all datasets. The adversarial training is performed for 50 epochs with SGD optimizer, $lr = 0.001$, cosine annealing scheduler, and batch size of 16.

Validation. We freeze the trained BDQ encoder and newly instantiate a 3D ResNet-50 model for action recognition and a 2D ResNet-50 model for privacy label prediction. Note that the 3D ResNet-50 and the 2D ResNet-50 models are initialized with Kinetics-400 and ImageNet pre-trained weights, respectively. We use the BDQ encoder output on the train set videos to train the 3D ResNet-50 model for action recognition and the 2D ResNet-50 model for predicting privacy labels. Both the networks are trained for 50 epochs with SGD optimizer, $lr = 0.001$, cosine annealing scheduler, and batch size 16. For validation, we sample consecutive t frames ($t = 16$ for SBU, $t = 32$ for KTH and IPN) from each input video without any random shift, producing an input sequence. We then center crop (without scaling) each frame in the sequence with a square region of size 224×224. For action recognition, we use the generated sequence on the 3D ResNet model to report the clip-1 crop-1 accuracy. For privacy prediction, we average the softmax outputs by the 2D ResNet-50 model over t frames and report the average accuracy.

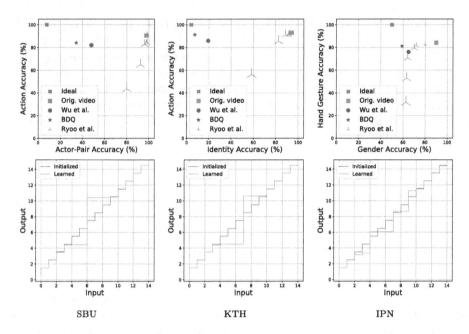

Fig. 3. Performance trade-off (row 1) and learned quantization steps (row 2) on the three datasets: SBU, KTH, and IPN.

4.3 Results

Figure 3 presents our results on the three datasets. We use the visualization proposed in [37] to illustrate the trade-off between the action/gesture recognition accuracy and the privacy label prediction accuracy. We compare our method with two different methods for preserving privacy in action videos: Ryoo *et al.* [30] and Wu *et al.* [36].

In Ryoo *et al.* [30], the degradation encoder is a down-sampling module. Here, a high-resolution action video is down-sampled into multiple videos of a fixed low resolution by applying different image transformations that are optimized for the action recognition task. These transformations include sub-pixel translation, scaling, rotation, and other affine transformations emulating possible camera motion. The low-resolution videos can then be used for training action recognition models. In our experiments, we consider the following low spatial resolutions: 112 × 112, 56 × 56, 28 × 28, 14 × 14, 7 × 7, and 4 × 4. For each resolution, we generate corresponding low-resolution videos by applying the learned transformations and train a 3D ResNet-50 model for action recognition and a 2D ResNet-50 model for predicting privacy labels. Figure 3 row 1 reports the results of this experiment where a bigger marker depicts a larger down-sampling rate. We observe that, as the down-sampling rate increases, the privacy label prediction accuracy drops for all the datasets. Unfortunately, the action recognition accuracy drops at a faster rate which is contradictory to the desired behavior.

In Wu *et al.* [36], the degradation encoder is a UNet-like network that is implemented using the model from [18]. It can be seen as a 2D convolution-based frame-level filter and converts each frame into a feature map of the same shape as the original frame. For training the encoder, we use the same adversarial training method as

Table 1. Comparison of space-time complexity of BDQ and Wu *et al.*

Method	Params.	Size	FLOPs
Wu *et al.*	1.3M	3.8Mb	166.4G
BDQ	16	3.4Kb	120.4M

described in Sect. 3.2 which is same as the original work. However, the privacy model is reset after certain iterations to improve performance as done in the original work. For a fair comparison, the adversarial training is performed using a 3D ResNet-50 model for action recognition and a 2D ResNet-50 model for predicting privacy labels. Furthermore, the validation method followed is identical to the one mentioned in Sect. 4.2. Figure 3 row 1 reports our evaluation results of these experiments. We observe that, in comparison to Ryoo *et al.* [30], Wu *et al.* [36] performs significantly better across all the datasets in terms of preserving privacy and enabling action recognition.

Our proposed BDQ encoder surpasses both Ryoo *et al.* [30] and Wu *et al.* [36] by a significant margin across all the datasets in preserving privacy and enabling action recognition. As seen in Fig. 3 row 1, it is closer to the ideal trade-off than any other method. Finally, Table 1 compares the space-time complexity of the BDQ and Wu *et al.* encoders. We observe that BDQ uses significantly less parameters and computation in comparison to the Wu *et al.* encoder.

5   Analysis

5.1   Ablation Study

As described in Sect. 3, the BDQ encoder consists of three modules: *Blur* (B), *Difference* (D), and *Quantization* (Q). Here, we study the role of each of these modules in preserving privacy and enabling action recognition. For this, we take the pre-trained BDQ encoder that was learned on the SBU dataset in Sect. 4

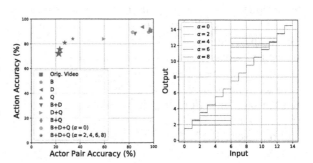

Fig. 4. Left- Results of the ablation study. Here, a bigger ★ corresponds to a higher value of α. Right- Effect of the adversarial parameter α on the quantization steps.

and select various combinations of its modules to study their contribution to action recognition and actor-pair recognition. For each combination, we freeze the parameters of its module(s) and use its output to train a 3D ResNet-50 (pre-trained on Kinetics-400) for action recognition and a 2D ResNet-50 (pre-trained on ImageNet) for actor-pair recognition. Note that, for both the networks, the training, and the validation procedures are identical to the one used in Sect. 4. Figure 4 provides results of this study on the SBU dataset. We observe that the combinations 'B', 'D', 'Q', 'B+D', and 'B+Q', have very little effect in preserving privacy information and achieve results close to the case when original video is used. Interestingly, the combination 'D' achieves a higher action recognition accuracy among all the combinations, signifying its ability to produce better temporal features. Furthermore, a good drop in privacy accuracy is observed when 'D' and 'Q' are used together. Moreover, this accuracy further drops drastically when all 'B', 'D', and 'Q' are used together. Finally, we also study the effect of the adversarial parameter α on these modules as shown in Fig. 4. We observe that when no adversarial training is performed, i.e. $\alpha = 0$, there is a very little drop in privacy accuracy. However, with the increase in the value of α, both action recognition and actor-pair accuracy begin to fall, with the action recognition accuracy falling more sharply. Figure 4 presents the learned quantization values corresponding to each value of α. We observe that with the increase in α the amount of quantization increases which leads to drop in action and actor-pair accuracies. Please refer to supplementary for more studies.

5.2   Strong Privacy Protection

A significant challenge for any privacy-preserving model is to provide protection against any possible, seen and unseen adversary, that may try to learn the privacy information. In order to show that our proposed framework provides such strong privacy protection, we prepare a list of ten state-of-the-art image classification networks (adversaries) as shown in Fig. 5. We take the pre-trained BDQ encoder from Sect. 4 and use its output (degraded video) to train the above networks for predicting the actor-pair labels on the SBU dataset. Furthermore, we also train these networks on the original videos to prepare corresponding baselines for comparison. Note that all the networks are initialized with ImageNet pre-trained weights, and the training and inference procedures are identical to the one used for the adversary in Sect. 4. From Fig. 5, we observe that the BDQ encoder consistently protects privacy information against all the networks with ResNet-50 [13] performing the best at 34.18% and MobileNet-v3 [15] performing the worst at 25.46%. Note that, among all the adversaries, the BDQ encoder had only seen ResNet-50 during its training.

5.3   Generalized Spatio-Temporal Features

In addition to strong privacy protection, a privacy-preserving model must allow task-specific features to be learned by any network that is designed for that task. In order to show that our proposed framework allows useful spatio-temporal cues for action recognition, we take the pre-trained BDQ encoder from Sect. 4 and use its output to separately train five 3D CNNs for predicting action classes on the SBU dataset, as shown in Fig. 6. Furthermore, similar to Sect. 5.2, we

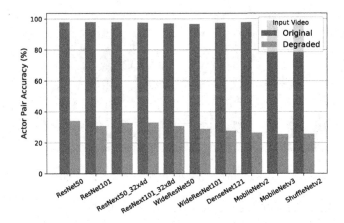

Fig. 5. Actor-pair accuracy on various image classification networks.

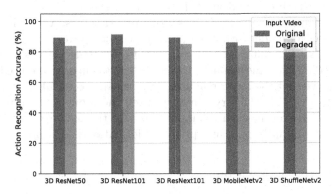

Fig. 6. Action recognition accuracy on various action recognition networks.

also train these networks on the original videos to prepare corresponding base-lines for comparison. Note that all the networks are initialized with Kinetics-400 pre-trained weights. From Fig. 6, we observe that the BDQ encoder consistently allows spatio-temporal information to be learned with 3D ResNext-101 perform-ing the best at 85.1% and 3D ShuffleNet-v2 performing the worst at 81.91%. Furthermore, all the networks achieve action recognition accuracy marginally lower than their corresponding baselines.

5.4   Robustness to Reconstruction Attack

In this section, we explore a scenario where an attacker has access to the BDQ encoder such that he/she can produce a large training set containing degraded videos along with their corresponding original videos. In such a case, the attacker can train an encoder-decoder network and try to reverse the effect of BDQ, recov-ering the privacy information. In order to show that our proposed framework is resistant to such an attack, we train a 3D UNet [8] model for 200 epochs on the

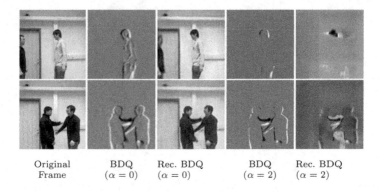

| Original
Frame | BDQ
($\alpha = 0$) | Rec. BDQ
($\alpha = 0$) | BDQ
($\alpha = 2$) | Rec. BDQ
($\alpha = 2$) |

Fig. 7. Visualization of reconstruction results for $\alpha = 0$ and 2.

SBU dataset with input as degraded videos from the pre-trained BDQ encoder of Sect. 4 and output original videos as ground-truth labels. Additionally, we also train the 3D UNet model with input as degraded videos from an untrained BDQ encoder. Figure 7 visualizes some examples of reconstruction when videos from untrained (column 4) and trained (column 5) BDQ encoder are used for training. We observe that the reconstruction network can successfully reconstruct the original video with satisfactory accuracy when the input is from an untrained BDQ encoder. However, when the input is from a trained BDQ encoder, reconstruction is significantly poor and privacy information is still preserved.

5.5   Subjective Evaluation

In Sect. 5.2 and 5.4, we show that our proposed framework is robust against adversaries that may try to learn or reconstruct the privacy attributes. However, such protection is of no use unless it provides visual privacy against the human visual system. In order to show that the BDQ encoder produces encodings that provide visual privacy, we conduct a user study on the videos from the SBU dataset. The user study is composed of 60 questions where each question consists of a video sampled from the SBU validation set and applied with the BDQ encoder learned in Sect. 4. Furthermore, each question has seven options showing cropped faces of actors from the SBU dataset. Given a BDQ output video where two persons are interacting, the task of the user is to select the identities of both the actors from the seven options. A total of 26 participants took part in the study. Note that the random chance of selecting two actors and both of them being correct is 4.76%. Similarly, the random chance of selecting two actors and at least one of them being correct is 52.38%. In the first case, the results of our user study reveal that the participants were able to recognize both the actors correctly with an accuracy of 8.65%. Similarly, the users' accuracy for the second case was 65.64% (more details in supplementary).

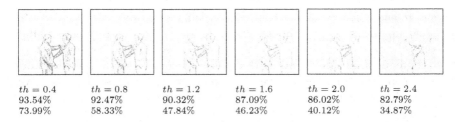

$th = 0.4$	$th = 0.8$	$th = 1.2$	$th = 1.6$	$th = 2.0$	$th = 2.4$
93.54%	92.47%	90.32%	87.09%	86.02%	82.79%
73.99%	58.33%	47.84%	46.23%	40.12%	34.87%

Fig. 8. Example event frames (Row 1), event threshold (Row 2), action recognition accuracy (Row 3) and actor-pair recognition accuracy (Row 4) on SBU.

5.6   Comparison with Event Camera

In recent years, Dynamic Vision Sensor (DVS) based cameras are being proposed as an in-home monitoring solution for privacy-preserving action detection and recognition [1]. Unlike traditional cameras that capture high-resolution videos and images, a DVS sensor detects the temporal changes in the pixel intensity at a pixel location. If the pixel intensity rises beyond a fixed threshold at a pixel, it is registered as a positive event. However, if it drops below a fixed threshold, it is registered as a negative event. Here, positive and negative events describe the direction of motion which can be encoded as outlines. At an abstract level, our BDQ encoder can be seen as a digital approximation of the DVS sensor that can be implemented in any traditional camera. In order to compare our framework with the DVS sensor, we first convert the videos from the SBU dataset into events using [11] which proposes a method for converting any video into synthetic events such that they can be simulated as events from a DVS sensor. Such a method is useful since training DNNs require huge amount of data and collecting such amount is not feasible using event cameras. Furthermore, the above method enables us to vary the pixel level threshold which decides if the intensity change (event) will be registered or not. Note that a high threshold leads to less events while a low threshold leads to more events being registered. Figure 8 displays the effect of threshold on an event frame. The events from the converted SBU dataset are first converted into event frames using [11] which are then used for training a 3D ResNet-50 model for action recognition and a 2D ResNet-50 model for actor-pair recognition. The initialization and training settings is identical to Sect. 4. Figure 8 reports the trade-off for each threshold. We observe that with the increase in threshold, both action recognition and actor-pair accuracy drops. Furthermore, the trade-off at threshold value 2.4 is close to the trade-off achieved by the BDQ encoder with $\alpha = 2$ (refer Sect. 4.3).

6   Conclusions

This paper proposes a novel encoder called BDQ for the task of privacy-preserving human action recognition. The BDQ encoder is composed of three modules: *Blur, Difference,* and *Quantization* whose parameters are learned in an end-to-end fashion via an adversarial training framework such that it learns to allow important spatio-temporal attributes for action recognition and inhibit spatial privacy attributes. We show that the proposed encoder achieves state-of-the-art trade-off on three benchmark datasets in comparison to previous works. Furthermore, the trade-off achieved is at par with the DVS sensor-based event cameras. Finally, we also provide an extensive analysis of the BDQ encoder including an ablation study on its components, robustness to various adversaries, and a subjective evaluation.

Limitation: Due to its design, our proposed framework for privacy preservation cannot work in cases when the subject or the camera does not move.

Acknowledgement. This work was supported by JSPS KAKENHI Grant Number JP20K20628.

References

1. www.samsung.com/au/smart-home/smartthings-vision-u999/GP-U999GTEEAAC/
2. Agrawal, P., Narayanan, P.: Person de-identification in videos. IEEE Trans. Circ. Syst. Video Technol. **21**(3), 299–310 (2011)
3. Asif, U., et al.: Privacy preserving human fall detection using video data. In: Machine Learning for Health Workshop, pp. 39–51. PMLR (2020)
4. Benitez-Garcia, G., Olivares-Mercado, J., Sanchez-Perez, G., Yanai, K.: Ipn hand: a video dataset and benchmark for real-time continuous hand gesture recognition. In: 2020 25th International Conference on Pattern Recognition (ICPR), pp. 4340–4347. IEEE (2021)
5. Brkic, K., Sikiric, I., Hrkac, T., Kalafatic, Z.: I know that person: generative full body and face de-identification of people in images. In: 2017 IEEE Conference on Computer Vision and Pattern Recognition Workshops (CVPRW), pp. 1319–1328. IEEE (2017)
6. Canh, T.N., Nagahara, H.: Deep compressive sensing for visual privacy protection in flatcam imaging. In: 2019 IEEE/CVF International Conference on Computer Vision Workshop (ICCVW), pp. 3978–3986. IEEE (2019)
7. Chen, D., Chang, Y., Yan, R., Yang, J.: Tools for protecting the privacy of specific individuals in video. EURASIP J. Adv. Signal Process. **2007**, 1–9 (2007)
8. Çiçek, Ö., Abdulkadir, A., Lienkamp, S.S., Brox, T., Ronneberger, O.: 3D U-Net: learning dense volumetric segmentation from sparse annotation. In: Ourselin, S., Joskowicz, L., Sabuncu, M.R., Unal, G., Wells, W. (eds.) MICCAI 2016. LNCS, vol. 9901, pp. 424–432. Springer, Cham (2016). https://doi.org/10.1007/978-3-319-46723-8_49
9. Dai, J., Wu, J., Saghafi, B., Konrad, J., Ishwar, P.: Towards privacy-preserving activity recognition using extremely low temporal and spatial resolution cameras. In: Proceedings of the IEEE Conference on Computer Vision and Pattern Recognition Workshops, pp. 68–76 (2015)

10. Dave, I.R., Chen, C., Shah, M.: Spact: self-supervised privacy preservation for action recognition. In: Proceedings of the IEEE/CVF Conference on Computer Vision and Pattern Recognition, pp. 20164–20173 (2022)
11. Gehrig, D., Gehrig, M., Hidalgo-Carrió, J., Scaramuzza, D.: Video to events: recycling video datasets for event cameras. In: Proceedings of the IEEE/CVF Conference on Computer Vision and Pattern Recognition, pp. 3586–3595 (2020)
12. Gochoo, M., Tan, T.H., Alnajjar, F., Hsieh, J.W., Chen, P.Y.: Lownet: privacy preserved ultra-low resolution posture image classification. In: 2020 IEEE International Conference on Image Processing (ICIP), pp. 663–667. IEEE (2020)
13. He, K., Zhang, X., Ren, S., Sun, J.: Deep residual learning for image recognition. In: Proceedings of the IEEE Conference on Computer Vision and Pattern Recognition, pp. 770–778 (2016)
14. Hinojosa, C., Niebles, J.C., Arguello, H.: Learning privacy-preserving optics for human pose estimation. In: Proceedings of the IEEE/CVF International Conference on Computer Vision, pp. 2573–2582 (2021)
15. Howard, A., et al.: Searching for mobilenetv3. In: Proceedings of the IEEE/CVF International Conference on Computer Vision, pp. 1314–1324 (2019)
16. Huang, C., Kairouz, P., Sankar, L.: Generative adversarial privacy: a data-driven approach to information-theoretic privacy. In: 2018 52nd Asilomar Conference on Signals, Systems, and Computers, pp. 2162–2166. IEEE (2018)
17. Jiang, B., Wang, M., Gan, W., Wu, W., Yan, J.: Stm: spatiotemporal and motion encoding for action recognition. In: Proceedings of the IEEE/CVF International Conference on Computer Vision, pp. 2000–2009 (2019)
18. Johnson, J., Alahi, A., Fei-Fei, L.: Perceptual losses for real-time style transfer and super-resolution. In: Leibe, B., Matas, J., Sebe, N., Welling, M. (eds.) ECCV 2016. LNCS, vol. 9906, pp. 694–711. Springer, Cham (2016). https://doi.org/10.1007/978-3-319-46475-6_43
19. Li, Y., Ji, B., Shi, X., Zhang, J., Kang, B., Wang, L.: Tea: temporal excitation and aggregation for action recognition. In: Proceedings of the IEEE/CVF Conference on Computer Vision and Pattern Recognition, pp. 909–918 (2020)
20. Liu, Z., et al.: Teinet: towards an efficient architecture for video recognition. In: Proceedings of the AAAI Conference on Artificial Intelligence, vol. 34, pp. 11669–11676 (2020)
21. Mirjalili, V., Raschka, S., Ross, A.: Flowsan: privacy-enhancing semi-adversarial networks to confound arbitrary face-based gender classifiers. IEEE Access 7, 99735–99745 (2019)
22. Orekondy, T., Schiele, B., Fritz, M.: Towards a visual privacy advisor: understanding and predicting privacy risks in images. In: Proceedings of the IEEE International Conference on Computer Vision, pp. 3686–3695 (2017)
23. Padilla-López, J.R., Chaaraoui, A.A., Flórez-Revuelta, F.: Visual privacy protection methods: a survey. Expert Syst. Appl. 42(9), 4177–4195 (2015)
24. Pittaluga, F., Koppal, S., Chakrabarti, A.: Learning privacy preserving encodings through adversarial training. In: 2019 IEEE Winter Conference on Applications of Computer Vision (WACV), pp. 791–799. IEEE (2019)
25. Pittaluga, F., Koppal, S.J.: Pre-capture privacy for small vision sensors. IEEE Trans. Pattern Anal. Mach. Intell. 39(11), 2215–2226 (2016)
26. Raval, N., Machanavajjhala, A., Cox, L.P.: Protecting visual secrets using adversarial nets. In: 2017 IEEE Conference on Computer Vision and Pattern Recognition Workshops (CVPRW), pp. 1329–1332. IEEE (2017)

27. Ren, Z., Lee, Y.J., Ryoo, M.S.: Learning to anonymize faces for privacy preserving action detection. In: Proceedings of the European Conference on Computer Vision (ECCV), pp. 620–636 (2018)

28. Roy, P.C., Boddeti, V.N.: Mitigating information leakage in image representations: a maximum entropy approach. In: Proceedings of the IEEE/CVF Conference on Computer Vision and Pattern Recognition, pp. 2586–2594 (2019)

29. Ryoo, M., Kim, K., Yang, H.: Extreme low resolution activity recognition with multi-siamese embedding learning. In: Proceedings of the AAAI Conference on Artificial Intelligence, vol. 32 (2018)

30. Ryoo, M.S., Rothrock, B., Fleming, C., Yang, H.J.: Privacy-preserving human activity recognition from extreme low resolution. In: Thirty-First AAAI Conference on Artificial Intelligence (2017)

31. Schuldt, C., Laptev, I., Caputo, B.: Recognizing human actions: a local svm approach. In: Proceedings of the 17th International Conference on Pattern Recognition, 2004. ICPR 2004, vol. 3, pp. 32–36. IEEE (2004)

32. Srivastav, V., Gangi, A., Padoy, N.: Human pose estimation on privacy-preserving low-resolution depth images. In: Shen, D., et al. (eds.) MICCAI 2019. LNCS, vol. 11768, pp. 583–591. Springer, Cham (2019). https://doi.org/10.1007/978-3-030-32254-0_65

33. Tan, J., et al.: Canopic: pre-digital privacy-enhancing encodings for computer vision. In: 2020 IEEE International Conference on Multimedia and Expo (ICME), pp. 1–6. IEEE (2020)

34. Wang, L., Tong, Z., Ji, B., Wu, G.: Tdn: temporal difference networks for efficient action recognition. In: Proceedings of the IEEE/CVF Conference on Computer Vision and Pattern Recognition, pp. 1895–1904 (2021)

35. Wang, Z.W., et al.: Privacy-preserving action recognition using coded aperture videos. In: Proceedings of the IEEE/CVF Conference on Computer Vision and Pattern Recognition Workshops (2019)

36. Wu, Z., Wang, H., Wang, Z., Jin, H., Wang, Z.: Privacy-preserving deep action recognition: an adversarial learning framework and a new dataset. IEEE Trans. Pattern Anal. Mach. Intell. (2020)

37. Wu, Z., Wang, Z., Wang, Z., Jin, H.: Towards privacy-preserving visual recognition via adversarial training: a pilot study. In: Proceedings of the European Conference on Computer Vision (ECCV), pp. 606–624 (2018)

38. Yang, J., et al.: Quantization networks. In: Proceedings of the IEEE/CVF Conference on Computer Vision and Pattern Recognition, pp. 7308–7316 (2019)

39. Yun, K., Honorio, J., Chattopadhyay, D., Berg, T.L., Samaras, D.: Two-person interaction detection using body-pose features and multiple instance learning. In: 2012 IEEE Computer Society Conference on Computer Vision and Pattern Recognition Workshops, pp. 28–35. IEEE (2012)

Latent Space Smoothing for Individually Fair Representations

Momchil Peychev[1]([✉]) [iD], Anian Ruoss[2] [iD], Mislav Balunović[1] [iD],
Maximilian Baader[1] [iD], and Martin Vechev[1] [iD]

[1] Department of Computer Science, ETH Zurich, Zürich, Switzerland
{momchil.peychev,mislav.balunovic,mbaader,martin.vechev}@inf.ethz.ch
[2] DeepMind, London, UK
anianr@deepmind.com

Abstract. Fair representation learning transforms user data into a representation that ensures fairness and utility regardless of the downstream application. However, learning individually fair representations, i.e., guaranteeing that similar individuals are treated similarly, remains challenging in high-dimensional settings such as computer vision. In this work, we introduce LASSI, the first representation learning method for certifying individual fairness of high-dimensional data. Our key insight is to leverage recent advances in generative modeling to capture the set of similar individuals in the generative latent space. This enables us to learn individually fair representations that map similar individuals close together by using adversarial training to minimize the distance between their representations. Finally, we employ randomized smoothing to provably map similar individuals close together, in turn ensuring that local robustness verification of the downstream application results in end-to-end fairness certification. Our experimental evaluation on challenging real-world image data demonstrates that our method increases certified individual fairness by up to 90% without significantly affecting task utility.

Keywords: Fair representation learning · Individual fairness · Smoothing

1 Introduction

Deep learning models are increasingly deployed in critical domains, such as face detection [74], credit scoring [38], or crime risk assessment [6], where decisions of the model can have wide-ranging impacts on society. Unfortunately, the models and datasets employed in these settings are biased [7,43], which raises concerns

---

A. Ruoss—Work partially done while the author was at ETH Zurich.

Supplementary Information The online version contains supplementary material available at https://doi.org/10.1007/978-3-031-19778-9_31.

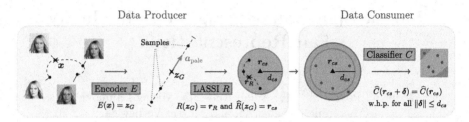

Fig. 1. Overview of our framework LASSI. The left part shows the data producer who captures the set of individuals similar to x by interpolating along the attribute vector a_{pale}. The data producer then uses adversarial training and center smoothing to compute a representation that provably maps all similar points into the ℓ_2-ball of radius d_{cs} around r_{cs}. The right part shows the data consumer who can certify individual fairness, i.e., prove that all similar individuals receive the same classification outcome, of the end-to-end model by checking whether the certified radius obtained via randomized smoothing exceeds d_{cs}.

against their usage for such tasks and causes regulators to hold organizations accountable for the discriminatory effects of their models [18,19,22,23,77].

In this regard, fair representation learning [88] is a promising bias mitigation approach that transforms data to prevent discrimination regardless of the concrete downstream application while simultaneously maintaining high task utility. The approach is highly modular [60]: the *data regulator* defines the fairness notion, the *data producer* learns a fair representation that encodes the data, and the *data consumers* employ the transformed data in downstream tasks. Recent work successfully augmented fair representation learning with guarantees [24,68], but its application to high-dimensional data, such as images, remains challenging.

Key Challenge: Scaling to High-Dimensional Data and Real-World Models. The two central challenges of *individually* fair representation learning, which requires similar individuals to be treated similarly, are: (i) designing a suitable input similarity metric [86,88] and (ii) enforcing that similar individuals are *provably* treated similarly according to that metric. For low-dimensional tabular data, prior work has typically measured input similarity in terms of the input features (age, income, etc.), using, e.g., logical constraints [68] or weighted ℓ_p-metrics [85]. However, characterizing the similarity of high-dimensional data, such as images, at the input-level, e.g., by comparing pixels, is infeasible. Moreover, proving that all points in the infinite set of similar individuals obtain the same classification requires propagating this set through the model. Unfortunately, for high-dimensional applications this is unattainable for prior work using (mixed-integer) linear programming solvers [16,76], which only scale to small networks.

This Work. In this work, we introduce latent space smoothing for individually fair representations (LASSI), a method that addresses both of the above challenges. Our approach leverages two recent advances: the emergence of powerful generative models [41], which enable the definition of image similarity for individual fairness, and the scalable certification of deep models [10], which allows proving individual fairness. A high-level overview of our approach is shown in Fig. 1. Concretely, we use generative modeling [41] to enable data regulators to define input similarity by varying a continuous attribute of the image, such as pale skin in Fig. 1. To enforce that similar individuals are provably treated similarly, we further base our approach on smoothing: (i) the data producer uses center smoothing [44] to learn a representation that provably maps similar individuals close together, and (ii) the data consumer certifies local ℓ_2-robustness using randomized smoothing [10], thereby proving individual fairness of the end-to-end model. Therefore, our approach enables data regulators to impose fairness notions of the form: *"For a given person, all people differing only in skin tone should receive the same classification"* and allows data producers and consumers to independently learn a representation and classification models that provably enforce this notion.

To measure input similarity, the data producer leverages the ability of a bijective generative model to interpolate along the direction of an attribute vector in the latent space, which is impractical in the pixel space. As a result, the set of similar individuals can be defined by a line segment in the latent space (center part of the data producer in Fig. 1), corresponding to an elaborate curve in the input space (left part of the data producer in Fig. 1), which cannot be concisely captured by, e.g., an ℓ_p-ball. Thus, the data producer learns a representation R that maps all points of the latent line segment close together in the representation space by using adversarial training to minimize the distance between similar individuals. However, as adversarial training cannot provide guarantees on this maximum distance, the data producer uses center smoothing [44] to adjust the representation such that its *smoothed* version $\widehat{R}$ provably maps all similar points into an ℓ_2-ball of radius d_{cs} around a center r_{cs} with high probability (right part of the data producer in Fig. 1). Finally, the data consumer only needs to prove that the certified radius (violet in the data consumer part of Fig. 1) of its *smoothed* classifier $\widehat{C}$ around r_{cs} is larger than d_{cs} to obtain an individual fairness certificate for the end-to-end model $M := \widehat{C} \circ \widehat{R} \circ E$.

Our experimental evaluation on several image classification tasks shows that training with LASSI significantly increases the number of individuals for which we can certify individual fairness, with respect to multiple different sensitive attributes, as well as their combinations. Overall, we certify up to 90% more than the baselines. Furthermore, we demonstrate that the representations obtained by LASSI can be used to solve classification tasks that were unseen during training.

Main Contributions. We make the following contributions:

- A novel input similarity metric for high-dimensional data defined via interpolation in the latent space of generative models.

- A scalable representation learning method with individual fairness certification for models using high-dimensional data via randomized smoothing.
- A large-scale evaluation of our method on various image classification tasks.

2 Related Work

In this work, we consider individual fairness, which requires that similar individuals be treated similarly [14]. In contrast, group fairness enforces specific classification statistics to be equal across different groups of the population [14,28]. While both fairness notions are desirable, they also both suffer from certain shortcomings. For instance, models satisfying group fairness may still discriminate against individuals [14] or subgroups [36]. In contrast, the central challenge limiting practical adoption of individual fairness is the lack of a widely accepted similarity metric [86]. While recent work has made progress in developing similarity metrics for tabular data [31,57,62,79,87], defining similarity concisely for high-dimensional data remains challenging and is a key contribution of our work.

Fair Representation Learning. A wide range of methods has been proposed to learn fair representations of user data. Most of these works consider group fairness and employ techniques such as adversarial learning [15,37,50,55], disentanglement [11,53,69], duality [73], low-rank matrix factorization [63], and distribution alignment [3,54,89]. Fair representation learning for individual fairness has recently gained attention, with similarity metrics based on logical formulas [68], Wasserstein distance [20,45], fairness graphs [46], and weighted ℓ_p-norms [88]. Unfortunately, none of these approaches can capture the similarity between individuals for the high-dimensional data we consider in our work.

Bias in High-Dimensional Data. A long line of work has investigated the biases of models operating on high-dimensional data, such as images [81,83] and text [5,49,64,75], showing, e.g., that black women obtain lower accuracy in commercial face classification [7,43,66]. Importantly, these models not only learn but also amplify the biases of the training data [29,90], even for balanced datasets [80]. A key challenge for bias mitigation in high-dimensional settings is that, unlike tabular data, sensitive attributes such as age or skin tone are not directly encoded as features. Thus, prior work has often relied on generative models [2,12,13,33,39,40,47,48,67,70] or computer simulations [59] to manipulate these sensitive attributes and check whether the perturbed instances are classified the same. However, unlike our work, these methods only tested for bias empirically and do not provide fairness guarantees. Recent work also explored using generative models to define [27,84] or certify [61] robustness, but without focusing on fairness.

Fairness Certification. Regulatory agencies are increasingly holding organizations accountable for the discriminatory effects of their machine learning models [18,19,22,23,77]. Accordingly, designing algorithms with fairness guarantees has become an active area of research [1,3,4,9,24,71]. However, unlike our work, most approaches for individual fairness certification consider pretrained models and thus cannot be employed in fair representation learning [32,78,85]. In contrast, [68] learn individually fair representations with provable guarantees for low-dimensional tabular data, providing a basis for our approach. However, neither the similarity notions nor the certification methods employed by [68] scale to high-dimensional data, which is the primary focus of our work.

3 Background

This section provides the necessary background on individual fairness, fair representation learning, generative modeling, and randomized smoothing.

Individual Fairness. The seminal work of [14] defined individual fairness as "treating similar individuals similarly". In this work, we consider the concrete instantiation of this notion from [68]: an individual x' is similar to x with respect to a binary input similarity metric $\phi \colon \mathbb{R}^n \times \mathbb{R}^n \to \{0,1\}$ if and only if $\phi(x, x') = 1$. A model $M \colon \mathbb{R}^n \to \mathcal{Y}$ is individually fair at $x \in \mathbb{R}^n$ if it classifies all individuals similar to x (as measured by ϕ) the same, i.e.,

$$\forall x' \in \mathbb{R}^n \colon \phi\left(x, x'\right) \implies M\left(x\right) = M\left(x'\right). \tag{1}$$

For example, a credit rating algorithm is individually fair for a given person if all similar applicants (e.g., similar income and repayment history) receive the same credit rating. Our goal is to learn a model M that maximizes the number of points x from the distribution for which we can *guarantee* that Eq. 1 is satisfied. Defining a suitable input similarity metric ϕ is one of the key challenges limiting practical applications of individual fairness, and in Sect. 4.1 we will show how to employ generative modeling to overcome this obstacle for high-dimensional data.

Fair Representation Learning. Fair representation learning [88] partitions the model $M \colon \mathbb{R}^n \to \mathcal{Y}$ into a data producer $P \colon \mathbb{R}^n \to \mathbb{R}^k$, which maps input points $x \in \mathbb{R}^n$ into a representation space $\mathbb{R}^k$ that satisfies a given fairness notion while maintaining downstream utility, and a data consumer $C \colon \mathbb{R}^k \to \mathcal{Y}$ that solves a downstream task taking only the transformed data points $r := P\left(x\right) \in \mathbb{R}^k$ as inputs. Importantly, the consumers (potentially indifferent to fairness) can employ standard training methods to obtain fair classifiers that are useful across a variety of different tasks. We base our approach on the LCIFR framework [68], which learns representations with individual fairness guarantees for low-dimensional tabular data. LCIFR defines a family of similarity notions and leverages (mixed-integer) linear programming methods for fairness certification. However, high-dimensional applications are out of reach for LCIFR because both the similarity notions and linear programming methods are tailored to low-dimensional tabular data. In particular, similarity is defined via logical formulas operating on the features of x, which is infeasible for, e.g., images, which cannot be compared solely at the pixel level. Moreover, while linear programming methods work well for small networks, they do not scale to real-world computer vision models. In this work, we show how to resolve these two key concerns to generalize the high-level idea of LCIFR to real-world, high-dimensional applications.

Generative Modeling. Normalizing flows, such as Glow [41], recently emerged as a promising generative modeling approach due to their exact log-likelihood evaluation, efficient inference and synthesis, and useful latent space for downstream tasks. Unlike GANs [25] or VAEs [42], normalizing flows are bijective models consisting of an encoder $E\colon \mathbb{R}^n \to \mathbb{R}^q$ and a decoder $D\colon \mathbb{R}^q \to \mathbb{R}^n$ for which $\boldsymbol{x} = D\left(E\left(\boldsymbol{x}\right)\right)$. Glow's input space $\mathbb{R}^n$ and latent space $\mathbb{R}^q$ have the same dimensionalities $n = q$. Its latent space captures important data attributes, thus enabling latent space interpolation such as changing the age of a person in an image. While attribute manipulation via latent space interpolation has also been investigated in the fairness context for GANs and VAEs [2,13,33,39,48,67], Glow's key advantages are the existence of an encoder (unlike GANs, which cannot represent an input point in the latent space efficiently) and the bijectivity of the end-to-end model (VAEs cannot reconstruct the input point exactly). Our key idea is to leverage Glow to define image similarity by interpolating along the directions defined by certain sensitive attributes in the latent space.

Smoothing. Unlike (mixed-integer) linear programming [16,76], smoothing approaches [10] can compute local robustness guarantees for any type of classifier $C\colon \mathbb{R}^k \to \mathcal{Y}$, regardless of its complexity and scale. To that end, [10] construct a smoothed classifier $\widehat{C}\colon \mathbb{R}^k \to \mathcal{Y}$, which returns the most probable classification of C for an input $\boldsymbol{r} \in \mathbb{R}^k$ when perturbed by random noise from $\mathcal{N}(0, \sigma_{rs}^2 I)$. Using a sampling-based approach, [10] establish a local robustness guarantee of the form: $\forall \boldsymbol{\delta} \in \mathbb{R}^k$ such that $\|\boldsymbol{\delta}\|_2 < d_{rs}$ we have $\widehat{C}\left(\boldsymbol{r} + \boldsymbol{\delta}\right) = \widehat{C}\left(\boldsymbol{r}\right)$ with probability $1 - \alpha_{rs}$, where α_{rs} can be made arbitrarily small. Thus, $\widehat{C}$ will classify all points in the ℓ_2-ball of radius d_{rs} around $\boldsymbol{r}$ the same with high probability. Recently, [44] introduced center smoothing, which extends this approach from classification to multidimensional regression. Concretely, for a function $R\colon \mathbb{R}^q \to \mathbb{R}^k$, center smoothing uses sampling and approximation to compute a smooth version $\widehat{R}\colon \mathbb{R}^q \to \mathbb{R}^k$, which maps $\boldsymbol{z} \in \mathbb{R}^q$ to the center point $\boldsymbol{r}_{cs} := \widehat{R}\left(\boldsymbol{z}\right)$ of a minimum enclosing ball containing at least half of the points $\boldsymbol{r}_i \sim R(\boldsymbol{z} + \mathcal{N}(0, \sigma_{cs}^2 I))$ for $i \in \{1, \ldots, m\}$. Then, for $\epsilon > 0$ and $\forall \boldsymbol{z}' \in \mathbb{R}^q$ such that $\|\boldsymbol{z} - \boldsymbol{z}'\|_2 \leq \epsilon$, we have $\|\widehat{R}\left(\boldsymbol{z}\right) - \widehat{R}\left(\boldsymbol{z}'\right)\|_2 \leq d_{cs}$ with probability at least $1 - \alpha_{cs}$. That is, center smoothing computes a sound upper bound d_{cs} on the ℓ_2-ball of the function outputs of $\widehat{R}$ for all points in the ℓ_2-ball of radius ϵ around $\boldsymbol{z}$.

4   High-Dimensional Individually Fair Representations

In this section, we describe how our method defines a set of similar individuals (Sect. 4.1), learns individually fair representations for these points (Sect. 4.2), and finally, certifies individual fairness for them (Sect. 4.4). Our approach is general, but we focus on images for presentational purposes.

4.1   Similarity via a Generative Model

We consider two individuals $\boldsymbol{x}$ and $\boldsymbol{x}'$ to be similar if they differ only in their continuous sensitive attributes. However, semantic attributes, such as skin color, cannot be captured conveniently via the input features of $\boldsymbol{x}$. Thus, our key idea is to define similarity in the latent space of a generative model G. We compute a vector $\boldsymbol{a} \in \mathbb{R}^q$ associated with the sensitive attribute, such that interpolating along the direction of $\boldsymbol{a}$ in the latent space and reconstructing back to the input space results in a meaningful semantic transformation of that attribute. There is active research investigating different ways of computing $\boldsymbol{a}$ [13,30,41,48,67], and we will empirically show that our method is compatible with any such method.

Computing $\boldsymbol{a}$. We define individual similarity in the latent space of Glow [41]. Our method is independent of the actual computation of $\boldsymbol{a}$, which we demonstrate by instantiating four different attribute vector types. Let $\boldsymbol{z}_G = E(\boldsymbol{x})$ be the latent code of $\boldsymbol{x}$ in the generative latent space. First, following [41], we compute $\boldsymbol{a}$ by calculating the average latent vectors $\boldsymbol{z}_{G,pos}$ for samples with the attribute and $\boldsymbol{z}_{G,neg}$ for samples without it and set $\boldsymbol{a}$ to their difference, $\boldsymbol{a} = \boldsymbol{z}_{G,pos} - \boldsymbol{z}_{G,neg}$. Second, following [13], we train a linear classifier $\text{sign}(\boldsymbol{a}^\top \boldsymbol{z}_G + b)$ to predict the presence of the attribute from $\boldsymbol{z}_G$ and take $\boldsymbol{a}$ to be the vector orthonormal to the decision boundary of the linear classifier. Finally, we employ [48] and [67] who build on these methods, accounting for the possible correlations between the sensitive and target attributes. In all cases, moving in one direction of $\boldsymbol{a}$ in the latent space increases the presence of the attribute and interpolating in the opposite direction decreases it. LASSI is independent of the sensitive attribute vector computation and will immediately benefit from all advancements in this area. We evaluate with vectors computed by [41] and [13] in the main paper (Sect. 5) and present further results with vectors from [48,67] in App. E.

Individual Similarity in Latent Space. Using the generative model G and the attribute vector $\boldsymbol{a}$, we define the set of individuals similar to $\boldsymbol{x}$ in the latent space of G as $S(\boldsymbol{x}) := \{\boldsymbol{z}_G + t \cdot \boldsymbol{a} \mid |t| \le \epsilon\} \subseteq \mathbb{R}^q$ (bottom of Fig. 2). Here, ϵ denotes the maximum perturbation level applied to the attribute. We consider G, $\boldsymbol{a}$, and ϵ to be a part of the similarity specification set by the data regulator. Crucially, $S(\boldsymbol{x})$ contains an infinite number of points but is compactly represented in the latent space of G as a line segment. In contrast, the same set represented directly in the input space, $S^{\text{in}}(\boldsymbol{x}) := D(S(\boldsymbol{x})) \subseteq \mathbb{R}^n$, obtained by decoding the latent representations in $S(\boldsymbol{x})$ with D, cannot be abstracted conveniently (top of Fig. 2). Moreover, this approach for constructing $S(\boldsymbol{x})$ can be extended to multiple sensitive attributes by interpolating along their attribute vectors simultaneously. Referring back to the notation in Sect. 3, we formally define the input similarity metric ϕ to satisfy $\phi(\boldsymbol{x}, \boldsymbol{x}') \iff \boldsymbol{x}' \in S^{\text{in}}(\boldsymbol{x})$.

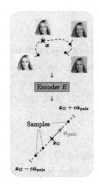

Fig. 2. Similarity in latent space.

4.2   Learning Individually Fair Representations

Assuming that the generative model $G = (E, D)$ is pretrained and given (e.g., by the data regulator), in this section we describe the learning of the representation $R\colon \mathbb{R}^q \to \mathbb{R}^k$, which maps from the generative latent space $\mathbb{R}^q$ directly to the representation space $\mathbb{R}^k$. The representation R is trained separately from the data consumer, the classifier C, whose training is explained in the next section.

Adversarial Loss. We encourage similar treatment for all points in $S^{\text{in}}(x)$ by training R to map them close to each other in $\mathbb{R}^k$, minimizing the loss

$$\mathcal{L}_{adv}(x) = \max_{z' \in S(x)} \|R(z_G) - R(z')\|_2. \tag{2}$$

Minimizing $\mathcal{L}_{adv}(x)$ is a min-max optimization problem, and adversarial training [56] is known to work well in such settings. Because the underlying domain of the inner maximization problem is simply the line segment $S(x)$, we perform a random adversarial attack in which we sample s points $z_i \sim \mathcal{U}(S(x))$ uniformly at random from $S(x)$ and approximate $\mathcal{L}_{adv}(x) \approx \max_{i=1}^{s} \|R(z_G) - R(z_i)\|_2$. This efficient attack is typically more effective [17] than the first-order methods such as FGSM [26] and PGD [56] when the search space is low-dimensional.

Classification Loss. To ensure that the learned representations remain useful for downstream tasks, we introduce an auxiliary classifier C_{aux} to predict a ground truth target label y by adding an additional classification loss term:

$$\mathcal{L}_{cls}(x, y) = \text{cross\_entropy}\left(C_{aux} \circ R(z_G), y\right). \tag{3}$$

Reconstruction Loss. The downstream task may not always be known to the data producer a priori, and thus our representations should ideally transfer to a variety of such tasks. To that end, we optionally utilize a reconstruction loss, which is designed to preserve the signal from the original data [55,68]:

$$\mathcal{L}_{recon}(x) = \|z_G - Q(R(z_G))\|_2, \tag{4}$$

where $Q\colon \mathbb{R}^k \to \mathbb{R}^q$ denotes a reconstruction network.

The representation R, the auxiliary classifier C_{aux}, and the reconstruction network Q are trained jointly using stochastic gradient descent to minimize the combined objective

$$\lambda_1 \mathcal{L}_{cls}(x, y) + \lambda_2 \mathcal{L}_{adv}(x) + \lambda_3 \mathcal{L}_{recon}(x). \tag{5}$$

Trading off fairness, accuracy, and transferability is a multi-objective optimization problem, an active area of research. Here, we follow [55,68] and use a linear scalarization scheme, with the hyperparameters λ_1, λ_2 and λ_3 balancing the three losses, but our method is also compatible with other schemes [51,58,82].

4.3 Training Classifier C

Once we have learned the representation R, we can use it to train any classifier C (often different from the auxiliary one C_{aux}). As we will apply smoothing to C, we train it by adding isotropic Gaussian noise to its inputs during the training process, as in [10]. We use the outputs of $R \circ E$ (and not the smoothed version $\widehat{R} \circ E$) as inputs to train C, since repeatedly smoothing the pipeline at this step is computationally expensive and because the distance between the smoothed and the unsmoothed outputs is generally small [44].

4.4 Certifying Individual Fairness via Latent Space Smoothing

With R and C trained as described above, we now construct the end-to-end model $M \colon \mathbb{R}^n \to \mathcal{Y}$ for which, given an input x, we can certify individual fairness of the form

$$\forall x' \in S^{\mathrm{in}}(x) : M(x) = M(x'), \tag{6}$$

with arbitrarily high probability.

Algorithm 1. Certifying the individual fairness of $\widehat{C} \circ \widehat{R} \circ E$ for the input x.

---

function CERTIFY(E, R, C, x)

Let $z_G = E(x)$. Then, $r_{cs} = \widehat{R}(z_G)$ and d_{cs} from center smoothing [44].

if center smoothing abstained **then return** ABSTAIN

Smooth C [10]: obtain the certified radius d_{rs} around r_{cs} (i.e., same classification)

if $d_{cs} < d_{rs}$ **then return** CERTIFIED

else return NOT CERTIFIED

Given a point z in the latent space of G, we define the function $g_z(t) := R(z + t \cdot a)$ for $t \in \mathbb{R}$. We apply the center smoothing procedure presented by [44] to obtain $\widehat{g}_z$, the smoothed version of g_z, and define $\widehat{R}(z) := \widehat{g}_z(0)$ such that for all $z' \in S(x)$, $\|\widehat{R}(z) - \widehat{R}(z')\|_2 \le d_{cs}$ (see Fig. 3). Next, we smooth the classifier C to obtain its ℓ_2-robustness radius d_{rs}. If $d_{cs} < d_{rs}$, then the end-to-end model $M = \widehat{C} \circ \widehat{R} \circ E$ certifiably satisfies individual fairness at x (as defined in Eq. 6) with high probability. Concretely, if we instantiate center smoothing with confidence α_{cs} and randomized smoothing with confidence α_{rs}, then the individual fairness certificate holds with probability at least $1 - \alpha_{cs} - \alpha_{rs}$ (union bound). The compositional certification procedure is summarized in Algorithm 1. Its correctness is formalized in Theorem 1 with a detailed proof in App. A.

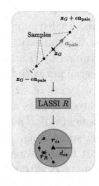

Fig. 3. Center smoothing the similarity set.

Theorem 1. *Assume that we have a bijective generative model* $G = (E, D)$ *used to define the similarity set* $S^{\mathrm{in}}(x)$ *for a given input* x. *Let Algorithm 1 perform*

*center smoothing [44] with confidence $1 - \alpha_{cs}$ and randomized smoothing [10]
with confidence $1 - \alpha_{rs}$. If Algorithm 1 returns* CERTIFIED *for the input $\boldsymbol{x}$, then
the end-to-end model $M = \widehat{C} \circ \widehat{R} \circ E$ is individually fair for $\boldsymbol{x}$ with respect to
$S^{\text{in}}(\boldsymbol{x})$ with probability at least $1 - \alpha_{cs} - \alpha_{rs}$.*

5   Experiments

We now evaluate LASSI and present the key findings: (i) LASSI enforces individual fairness and keeps accuracy high, (ii) LASSI handles various sensitive
attributes and attribute vectors, and (iii) LASSI representations transfer to
unseen tasks.

Datasets. We evaluate LASSI on two datasets. CelebA [52] contains 202,599
aligned and cropped face images of real-world celebrities. The images are annotated with the presence or absence of 40 face attributes with various correlations
between them [13]. As CelebA is highly imbalanced, we also experiment with Fair-
Face [34]. It is balanced on race and contains 97,698 released images (padding
0.25) of individuals from 7 race and 9 age groups. We split the training set randomly (80:20 ratio) and evaluate on the validation set because the test set is not
publicly shared. Further information about the datasets (including experimental
"unfairness" of different attributes computed on CelebA) is in App. B.

Experimental Setup. The following setup is used for all experiments, unless
stated otherwise. We use images of size 64×64, and for each dataset pretrain
a Glow model G with 4 blocks of 32 flows, using an open-source PyTorch [65]
implementation [72]. We use $\boldsymbol{a} = \boldsymbol{z}_{G,pos} - \boldsymbol{z}_{G,neg}$ and set $\epsilon = 1$ such that $S^{\text{in}}(\boldsymbol{x})$
contains realistic high-quality reconstructions (confirmed by manual inspection).
Thus, the similarity specification (Sect. 4.1) for enforcing individual fairness is
determined by G and the radius ϵ. We implement the representation R as a fully-
connected network that propagates Glow's latent code of an input $\boldsymbol{x}$ through two
hidden layers of sizes 2048 and 1024, mapping to a 512-dimensional space. The
final layer applies zero mean and unit variance normalization ensuring that all
components of R's output are in the same range when Gaussian noise is added
during smoothing. A linear classifier C is used for predicting the target label.
    Our fairness-unaware baseline (denoted as Naive) is standard representation
learning of R without adversarial and reconstruction losses ($\lambda_2 = \lambda_3 = 0$). When
training LASSI, we set the classification loss weight $\lambda_1 = 1$, except for the
transfer learning experiments. A recent work [67] proposed generating synthetic
images with a ProGAN [35] to balance the dataset. Their method is not concerned with individual fairness and their transformation of latent representations may change other, non-sensitive attributes. Nevertheless, we employ [67]'s
high-level idea of augmenting the training set with synthetic samples from a
generative model (Glow in our case). For each training sample $\boldsymbol{x}$, we synthesize
and randomly sample s additional images from $S^{\text{in}}(\boldsymbol{x})$ in every epoch. Then, we

proceed with representation learning of R on the augmented dataset. We denote this baseline, addapted to the individual fairness setting, as DataAug. We do not compare with LCIFR [68] as our individual similarity specifications cannot be directly encoded as logical formulas over the input features of x and because its certification is based on expensive solvers that do not scale to Glow and large models.

We list all selected hyperparameters for all experiments, based on an an extensive hyperparameter search on the validation sets, in App. C (details provided for the CelebA dataset). The hyperparameter study shows that LASSI works for a wide range of hyperparameter values and demonstrates that λ_2 controls the trade-off between accuracy and fairness. We report the accuracy and the certified individual fairness of the models measured on 312 samples from CelebA's test set (every 64-th) and 343 samples from FairFace's test set (every 32-nd). The certified fairness refers to the percentage of test samples for which Algorithm 1 returns CERTIFIED, i.e., for which we can prove that Eq. 6 holds, guaranteeing that all similar individuals (according to our similarity definition) are classified the same. This metric is denoted as "Fair" in the tables. The evaluation of a single data point takes up to 6 s due to the sampling required by the smoothing procedures, which is why we do not report results on the whole test sets. We ran the experiments on GeForce RTX 2080 Ti GPUs and release all the code and models to reproduce our results at https://github.com/eth-sri/lassi.

Single Sensitive Attribute. We experiment with 4 different continuous sensitive attributes from CelebA: Pale_Skin, Young, Blond_Hair and Heavy_Makeup on two tasks: predicting Smiling and Earrings. We chose attributes with different balance ratios that have been used in prior work [13], while avoiding attributes that perpetuate harmful stereotypes [13] (e.g., avoiding Male). Glow

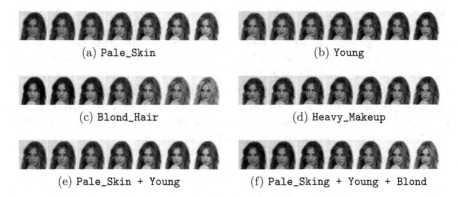

(a) Pale_Skin   (b) Young

(c) Blond_Hair   (d) Heavy_Makeup

(e) Pale_Skin + Young   (f) Pale_Sking + Young + Blond

Fig. 4. Similar points from $S^{\mathrm{in}}(x)$, as reconstructed by Glow, for multiple sensitive attribute combinations. Central images correspond to the original input. We vary t uniformly (left to right) in the $[-\frac{\epsilon}{\sqrt{n}}, \frac{\epsilon}{\sqrt{n}}]$ range, n = number of sensitive attributes, $\epsilon = 1$. For $n > 1$, all attribute vectors are multiplied by the same t.

can also be used to generate discrete attributes, but then fairness certification can be done via enumeration because partial eyeglasses or hats, for example, are not plausible. Figure 4 provides example images from $S^{\text{in}}(x)$ for a single x. The Earrings task is considerably more imbalanced than Smiling, with 78.21% majority class accuracy on our test subset. Because of the high correlation between Earrings and Makeup, we run LASSI with increased λ_2 for this pair of attributes.

We show the results in Table 1 averaged over 5 runs with different random seeds. The results indicate that data augmentation helps, but is not enough. LASSI significantly improves the certified fairness, compared to the baselines, with a minor loss of accuracy on Smiling and even acts as a helpful regularizer on the imbalanced Earrings task. In App. D we report the standard deviations demonstrating that LASSI consistently enforces individual fairness with low variance and further evaluate empirical (i.e., non-certifiable) fairness metrics.

Multiple Sensitive Attributes. In the next experiment, we combine the sensitive attributes Pale_Skin, Young and Blond_Hair and predict Smiling. The similarity sets w.r.t. which we certify individual fairness are defined as $S(x) = \{E(x) + \sum_i t_i \cdot a_i \mid \|t\|_2 \leq \epsilon\}$. The results in Table 1 (rows 5 – 6) show that the certified fairness drops as the similarity sets become more complex, as expected, but LASSI still successfully enforces individual fairness in these cases.

Larger Images and Different Attribute Vectors. Next, we explore if LASSI can also work with larger images. We increase the dimensionality of the CelebA images to 128×128, pretrain Glow with 5 blocks and keep the rest of the hyperparameters the same. The results are consistent with those already presented in Table 1: LASSI increases the certified individual fairness by up to 77% on the Smiling task (see App. D for detailed results). We also instantiate LASSI with the alternative attribute vector type [13] introduced in Sect. 4.1 (with $\epsilon = 10$). Although interpolating along the vector which is perpendicular to the linear decision boundary of the sensitive attribute possibly reduces the correlations leaked into the similarity sets, Table 2 shows that LASSI still improves the certified fairness by up to 16% compared to the baselines. This improvement is 9.7% and 6.1% for the attribute vectors proposed by [67] and [48] respectively, further demonstrating that LASSI can be useful for various attribute vector types. More details about these experiments are provided in App. E.

Table 1. Evaluation of LASSI on the CelebA dataset, showing that LASSI significantly increases certified individual fairness compared to the baselines without affecting the classification accuracy, even increasing it for imbalanced tasks. Reported means averaged over 5 runs, see App. D for standard deviations.

Task	Sensitive attribute(s)	Naive Acc.	Naive Fair	DataAug Acc.	DataAug Fair	LASSI (ours) Acc.	LASSI (ours) Fair
Smiling	Pale_Skin	**86.3**	0.6	85.7	12.2	85.9	**98.0**
	Young	**86.3**	38.2	85.9	43.0	**86.3**	**98.8**
	Blond_Hair	86.3	3.4	**86.6**	9.4	86.4	**94.7**
	Heavy_Makeup	**86.3**	0.4	85.3	13.7	85.6	**91.3**
	Pale+Young	**86.0**	0.4	85.8	9.9	85.8	**97.3**
	Pale+Young+Blond	86.2	0.0	**86.4**	3.6	85.5	**86.5**
Earrings	Pale_Skin	81.3	24.3	81.0	40.4	**85.0**	**98.5**
	Young	81.4	59.2	79.9	72.0	**84.5**	**98.0**
	Blond_Hair	81.4	9.2	82.2	30.5	**84.8**	**96.2**
	Heavy_Makeup	81.6	20.5	80.3	49.2	**82.3**	**98.7**

Table 2. Evaluation with a perpendicular to the linear decision boundary of the sensitive attribute [13] (Sect. 4.1) on the Smiling task, showing that LASSI is not limited to a specific attribute vector type.

Sensitive attribute(s)	Naive Acc.	Naive Fair	DataAug Acc.	DataAug Fair	LASSI (ours) Acc.	LASSI (ours) Fair
Pale_Skin	86.4	34.0	85.9	90.3	**86.5**	**98.8**
Young	86.3	73.1	86.2	90.3	**86.8**	**97.9**
Blond_Hair	86.2	71.4	86.1	88.8	**86.7**	**98.8**
Heavy_Makeup	86.2	11.5	86.3	87.4	**86.8**	**98.8**
Pale+Young	86.2	28.6	85.8	84.7	**86.5**	**98.6**
Pale+Young+Blond	86.2	23.7	85.9	82.2	**86.4**	**98.7**

Transfer Learning. To demonstrate the modularity of our approach, we show that LASSI can learn fair and transferable representations which are useful for unseen downstream tasks. To that end, we turn off the classification loss, consistent with prior work [55] ($\lambda_1 = 0$, i.e., the representation R is trained unsupervised), and enable the reconstruction loss ($\lambda_3 = 0.1$). The reconstruction network Q has an architecture symmetric to that of R. In Table 3 we report the accuracies and the certified fairness on 7 different, relatively well-balanced, downstream tasks. The models perform slightly worse compared to the case where the downstream task is known in advance, but the obtained certified individual fairness is still consistently high – more than 80% for the most complex similarity

Table 3. Transfer learning results, demonstrating that LASSI can still achieve high certified individual fairness even when the downstream tasks are not known.

Sens. attrib.:	Pale (P)		Young (Y)		Blond (B)		P + Y		P + Y + B	
Transfer task	Acc.	Fair	Acc.	Fair	Acc.	Fair	Acc.	Fair	Acc.	Fair
Smiling	86.2	93.1	86.0	95.4	85.1	93.8	85.9	92.2	85.1	87.0
High_Cheeks	81.7	92.6	82.3	96.0	81.3	92.2	80.8	93.0	80.6	84.5
Mouth_Open	81.5	91.2	82.4	94.3	82.4	87.5	81.6	90.1	82.5	80.8
Lipstick	88.3	94.0	85.8	95.8	86.8	91.2	85.1	90.6	86.2	81.0
Heavy_Makeup	86.5	93.0	83.5	95.3	85.6	89.3	83.7	90.0	83.3	80.4
Wavy_Hair	79.2	93.3	77.5	95.8	78.0	91.3	77.6	91.5	78.8	85.3
Eyebrows	78.3	92.1	78.3	94.7	78.9	89.6	77.8	92.2	78.7	85.6

specification (P+Y+B) and above 90% for the simpler ones. Standard deviations and baseline accuracies on these tasks are reported in App. D.

Training on FairFace Dataset. To verify that LASSI works well in different settings, we also evaluate on the FairFace [34] dataset. We select Race=Black as a sensitive attribute and predict Age. This is a very challenging multi-class task with around 60% state of the art accuracy. Therefore, we create two easier tasks: Age-2, predicting if an individual is younger or older than 30, and Age-3 with three target ranges: $[0 - 19]$, $[20 - 39]$, and 40+. Table 4 reports the results for $\epsilon = 0.5$. We verify that transfer learning also works in this setup by training on Age-2 and then transferring the representations to all three tasks. As the tasks are related, increasing the classification loss weight λ_1 on the base task from 0 to 0.01, increases both the transfer downstream accuracy and the certified fairness. The highest certified fairness is generally obtained when the downstream task is known and the model is trained on it (LASSI, $\lambda_1 = 1$).

Table 4. Results on FairFace, showing that LASSI can significantly improve the certified individual fairness even on balanced datasets. The adversarial loss weight is $\lambda_2 = 0.1$ for all models except Naive, the transfer models are trained on Age-2 with reconstruction loss weight $\lambda_3 = 0.1$. LASSI is trained on the corresponding tasks with adversarial but without reconstruction loss ($\lambda_1 = 1$, $\lambda_3 = 0$).

Task	Naive		DataAug		Transfer$_{\lambda_1=0}$		Transfer$_{\lambda_1=0.01}$		LASSI	
	Acc.	Fair	Acc.	Fair	Acc.	Fair	Acc.	Fair	Acc.	Fair
Age-2	69.0	5.7	68.9	4.8	66.4	91.7	**74.9**	91.7	72.0	**95.0**
Age-3	67.0	0.0	67.1	0.6	63.0	85.6	**67.7**	88.0	65.1	**90.8**
Age (all)	**42.2**	0.0	39.9	0.0	34.3	72.0	37.1	**77.5**	41.5	65.9

6 Limitations and Future Work

We now discuss some of the limitations of LASSI. First, our method trains individually fair models, but it does not guarantee that models satisfy other fairness notions, e.g., group fairness. While individual fairness is a well-studied research area, recent work argues that it does not qualify as a valid fairness notion as it can be insufficient to guarantee fairness in certain instances and risks encoding implicit human biases [21]. Moreover, the validity of our fairness certificates depends heavily on the generative model used by LASSI. In particular, the similarity sets $S(x)$ considered in our work may not be exhaustive enough as there can be latent points outside $S(x)$ that correspond to input points that would be perceived as similar to x by a human observer. This can also happen if the generative model is not powerful enough to generate all possible instances and combinations of similar individuals. For the above reasons, it is hard to obtain formal guarantees about G and the computed certificates may not always transfer from G to the real world. We explore this issue further in App. F where we experiment with 3D Shapes [8], a procedurally generated dataset with known ground truth similarity sets. Future work can consider addressing these challanges by performing extensive manual human inspection of reconstructions produced by G (similar to App. G). Moreover, all future advancements in the active research area of normalizing flows will immediately improve the quality of our certificates.

7 Conclusion

We proposed LASSI, which defines image similarity with respect to a generative model via attribute manipulation, allowing us to capture complex image transformations such as changing the age or skin color, which are otherwise difficult to characterize. Further, we were able to scale certified representation learning for individual fairness to real-world high-dimensional datasets by using randomized smoothing-based techniques. Our extensive evaluation yields promising results on several datasets and illustrates the practicality of our approach.

Acknowledgments. We thank Seyedmorteza Sadat for his help with preliminary investigations and the anonymous reviewers for their insightful feedback.

References

1. Albarghouthi, A., D'Antoni, L., Drews, S., Nori, A.V.: Fairsquare: probabilistic verification of program fairness. In: Proceedings of ACM Programming Language (2017)
2. Balakrishnan, G., Xiong, Y., Xia, W., Perona, P.: Towards causal benchmarking of biasin face analysis algorithms. In: Ratha, N.K., Patel, V.M., Chellappa, R. (eds.) Deep Learning-Based Face Analytics. ACVPR, pp. 327–359. Springer, Cham (2021). https://doi.org/10.1007/978-3-030-74697-1_15

3. Balunovic, M., Ruoss, A., Vechev, M.: Fair normalizing flows. In: International Conference on Learning Representations (2022). https://openreview.net/forum?id=BrFIKuxrZE

4. Bastani, O., Zhang, X., Solar-Lezama, A.: Probabilistic verification of fairness properties via concentration. In: Proceedings of ACM Programming Language (2019)

5. Bolukbasi, T., Chang, K., Zou, J.Y., Saligrama, V., Kalai, A.T.: Man is to computer programmer as woman is to homemaker? debiasing word embeddings. Adv. Neural Inf. Process. Syst. **29** (2016)

6. Brennan, T., Dieterich, W., Ehret, B.: Evaluating the predictive validity of the compas risk and needs assessment system. Crim. Just. Behav. **36**, 21–40 (2009)

7. Buolamwini, J., Gebru, T.: Gender shades: intersectional accuracy disparities in commercial gender classification. In: Conference on Fairness, Accountability and Transparency (2018)

8. Burgess, C., Kim, H.: 3d shapes dataset (2018). https://github.com/deepmind/3dshapes-dataset/

9. Choi, Y., Dang, M., den Broeck, G.V.: Group fairness by probabilistic modeling with latent fair decisions. In: Thirty-Fifth AAAI Conference on Artificial Intelligence (2021)

10. Cohen, J.M., Rosenfeld, E., Kolter, J.Z.: Certified adversarial robustness via randomized smoothing. In: Proceedings of the 36th International Conference on Machine Learning (2019)

11. Creager, E., Met al.: Flexibly fair representation learning by disentanglement. In: Proceedings of the 36th International Conference on Machine Learning (2019)

12. Dash, S., Sharma, A.: Evaluating and mitigating bias in image classifiers: a causal perspective using counterfactuals. In: Proceedings of the IEEE/CVF Winter Conference on Applications of Computer Vision (WACV), pp. 915–924 (2022)

13. Denton, E., Hutchinson, B., Mitchell, M., Gebru, T.: Detecting bias with generative counterfactual face attribute augmentation. CoRR (2019)

14. Dwork, C., Hardt, M., Pitassi, T., Reingold, O., Zemel, R.S.: Fairness through awareness. In: Innovations in Theoretical Computer Science (2012)

15. Edwards, H., Storkey, A.J.: Censoring representations with an adversary. In: 4th International Conference on Learning Representations (2016)

16. Ehlers, R.: Formal verification of piece-wise linear feed-forward neural networks. In: Automated Technology for Verification and Analysis - 15th International Symposium (2017)

17. Engstrom, L., Tran, B., Tsipras, D., Schmidt, L., Madry, A.: Exploring the landscape of spatial robustness. In: Proceedings of the 36th International Conference on Machine Learning (2019)

18. EU: Ethics guidelines for trustworthy AI (2019)

19. EU: Proposal for a regulation of the European parliament and of the council laying down harmonised rules on artificial intelligence (artificial intelligence act) and amending certain union legislative acts (2021)

20. Feng, R., Yang, Y., Lyu, Y., Tan, C., Sun, Y., Wang, C.: Learning fair representations via an adversarial framework. CoRR (2019)

21. Fleisher, W.: What's fair about individual fairness? In: AAAI/ACM Conference on AI, Ethics, and Society, Virtual Event (2021)

22. FTC: Using artificial intelligence and algorithms (2020)

23. FTC: Aiming for truth, fairness, and equity in your company's use of AI (2021)

24. Gitiaux, X., Rangwala, H.: Learning smooth and fair representations. In: The 24th International Conference on Artificial Intelligence and Statistics (2021)

25. Goodfellow, I.J., et al.: Generative adversarial nets. Adv. Neural Inf. Process. Syst. **27** (2014)
26. Goodfellow, I.J., Shlens, J., Szegedy, C.: Explaining and harnessing adversarial examples. In: 3rd International Conference on Learning Representations (2015)
27. Gowal, S., et al.: Achieving robustness in the wild via adversarial mixing with disentangled representations. In: IEEE/CVF Conference on Computer Vision and Pattern Recognition (2020)
28. Hardt, M., Price, E., Srebro, N.: Equality of opportunity in supervised learning. Adv. Neural Inf. Process. Syst. **29** (2016)
29. Hendricks, L.A., Burns, K., Saenko, K., Darrell, T., Rohrbach, A.: Women also snowboard: overcoming bias in captioning models. In: Ferrari, V., Hebert, M., Sminchisescu, C., Weiss, Y. (eds.) ECCV 2018. LNCS, vol. 11207, pp. 793–811. Springer, Cham (2018). https://doi.org/10.1007/978-3-030-01219-9_47
30. Higgins, I., et al.: beta-vae: learning basic visual concepts with a constrained variational framework. In: 5th International Conference on Learning Representations (2017)
31. Ilvento, C.: Metric learning for individual fairness. In: 1st Symposium on Foundations of Responsible Computing (2020)
32. John, P.G., Vijaykeerthy, D., Saha, D.: Verifying individual fairness in machine learning models. In: Proceedings of the Thirty-Sixth Conference on Uncertainty in Artificial Intelligence (2020)
33. Joo, J., Kärkkäinen, K.: Gender slopes: counterfactual fairness for computer vision models by attribute manipulation. In: Proceedings of the 2nd International Workshop on Fairness, Accountability, Transparency and Ethics in Multimedia, FATE/MM '20, pp. 1–5. Association for Computing Machinery, New York (2020). https://doi.org/10.1145/3422841.3423533
34. Kärkkäinen, K., Joo, J.: Fairface: face attribute dataset for balanced race, gender, and age for bias measurement and mitigation. In: IEEE Winter Conference on Applications of Computer Vision (2021)
35. Karras, T., Aila, T., Laine, S., Lehtinen, J.: Progressive growing of gans for improved quality, stability, and variation. In: 6th International Conference on Learning Representations, ICLR 2018, Vancouver, BC, Canada, 30 April–3 May 2018, Conference Track Proceedings. OpenReview.net (2018). https://openreview.net/forum?id=Hk99zCeAb
36. Kearns, M.J., Neel, S., Roth, A., Wu, Z.S.: Preventing fairness gerrymandering: auditing and learning for subgroup fairness. In: Proceedings of the 35th International Conference on Machine Learning (2018)
37. Kehrenberg, T., Bartlett, M., Thomas, O., Quadrianto, N.: Null-sampling for interpretable and fair representations. In: Vedaldi, A., Bischof, H., Brox, T., Frahm, J.-M. (eds.) ECCV 2020. LNCS, vol. 12371, pp. 565–580. Springer, Cham (2020). https://doi.org/10.1007/978-3-030-58574-7_34
38. Khandani, A.E., Kim, A.J., Lo, A.W.: Consumer credit-risk models via machine-learning algorithms. J. Bank. Finan. **34**, 2767–2787 (2010)
39. Kim, B., et al.: Interpretability beyond feature attribution: quantitative testing with concept activation vectors (TCAV). In: Proceedings of the 35th International Conference on Machine Learning (2018)
40. Kim, H., et al.: Counterfactual fairness with disentangled causal effect variational autoencoder. In: Thirty-Fifth AAAI Conference on Artificial Intelligence (2021)
41. Kingma, D.P., Dhariwal, P.: Glow: generative flow with invertible 1×1 convolutions. Adv. Neural Inf. Process. Syst. **31** (2018)

42. Kingma, D.P., Welling, M.: Auto-encoding variational bayes. In: 2nd International Conference on Learning Representations (2014)
43. Klare, B., Burge, M.J., Klontz, J.C., Bruegge, R.W.V., Jain, A.K.: Face recognition performance: role of demographic information. IEEE Trans. Inf. Forensics Secur. (2012)
44. Kumar, A., Goldstein, T.: Center smoothing: certified robustness for networks with structured outputs. Adv. Neural Inf. Process. Syst. **34** (2021)
45. Lahoti, P., Gummadi, K.P., Weikum, G.: ifair: learning individually fair data representations for algorithmic decision making. In: 35th IEEE International Conference on Data Engineering (2019)
46. Lahoti, P., Gummadi, K.P., Weikum, G.: Operationalizing individual fairness with pairwise fair representations. In: Proceedings of VLDB Endowment (2019)
47. Lang, O., et al.: Explaining in style: training a gan to explain a classifier in stylespace. In: Proceedings of the IEEE/CVF International Conference on Computer Vision (ICCV), pp. 693–702 (2021)
48. Li, Z., Xu, C.: Discover the unknown biased attribute of an image classifier. In: Proceedings of the IEEE/CVF International Conference on Computer Vision (ICCV), pp. 14970–14979 (2021)
49. Liang, P.P., Wu, C., Morency, L., Salakhutdinov, R.: Towards understanding and mitigating social biases in language models. In: Proceedings of the 38th International Conference on Machine Learning (2021)
50. Liao, J., Huang, C., Kairouz, P., Sankar, L.: Learning generative adversarial representations (GAP) under fairness and censoring constraints. CoRR (2019)
51. Lin, X., Zhen, H., Li, Z., Zhang, Q., Kwong, S.: Pareto multi-task learning. Adv. Neural Inf. Process. Syst. **32** (2019)
52. Liu, Z., Luo, P., Wang, X., Tang, X.: Deep learning face attributes in the wild. In: IEEE International Conference on Computer Vision (2015)
53. Locatello, F., Abbati, G., Rainforth, T., Bauer, S., Schölkopf, B., Bachem, O.: On the fairness of disentangled representations. Adv. Neural Inf. Process. Syst. **32** (2019)
54. Louizos, C., Swersky, K., Li, Y., Welling, M., Zemel, R.S.: The variational fair autoencoder. In: 4th International Conference on Learning Representations (2016)
55. Madras, D., Creager, E., Pitassi, T., Zemel, R.S.: Learning adversarially fair and transferable representations. In: Proceedings of the 35th International Conference on Machine Learning (2018)
56. Madry, A., Makelov, A., Schmidt, L., Tsipras, D., Vladu, A.: Towards deep learning models resistant to adversarial attacks. In: 6th International Conference on Learning Representations (2018)
57. Maity, S., Xue, S., Yurochkin, M., Sun, Y.: Statistical inference for individual fairness. In: 9th International Conference on Learning Representations (2021)
58. Martínez, N., Bertrán, M., Sapiro, G.: Minimax pareto fairness: a multi objective perspective. In: Proceedings of the 37th International Conference on Machine Learning (2020)
59. McDuff, D.J., Cheng, R., Kapoor, A.: Identifying bias in AI using simulation. CoRR (2018)
60. McNamara, D., Ong, C.S., Williamson, R.C.: Costs and benefits of fair representation learning. In: Proceedings of the 2019 AAAI/ACM Conference on AI, Ethics, and Society (2019)
61. Mirman, M., Hägele, A., Bielik, P., Gehr, T., Vechev, M.T.: Robustness certification with generative models. In: 42nd ACM SIGPLAN International Conference on Programming Language Design and Implementation (2021)

62. Mukherjee, D., Yurochkin, M., Banerjee, M., Sun, Y.: Two simple ways to learn individual fairness metrics from data. In: Proceedings of the 37th International Conference on Machine Learning (2020)

63. Oneto, L., Donini, M., Pontil, M., Maurer, A.: Learning fair and transferable representations with theoretical guarantees. In: 7th IEEE International Conference on Data Science and Advanced Analytics (2020)

64. Park, J.H., Shin, J., Fung, P.: Reducing gender bias in abusive language detection. In: Proceedings of the 2018 Conference on Empirical Methods in Natural Language Processing (2018)

65. Paszke, A., et al.: Pytorch: an imperative style, high-performance deep learning library. In: Wallach, H.M., Larochelle, H., Beygelzimer, A., d'Alché-Buc, F., Fox, E.B., Garnett, R. (eds.) Advances in Neural Information Processing Systems, vol. 32 (2019)

66. Raji, I.D., Buolamwini, J.: Actionable auditing: investigating the impact of publicly naming biased performance results of commercial AI products. In: Proceedings of the 2019 AAAI/ACM Conference on AI, Ethics, and Society (2019)

67. Ramaswamy, V.V., Kim, S.S.Y., Russakovsky, O.: Fair attribute classification through latent space de-biasing. In: IEEE Conference on Computer Vision and Pattern Recognition (2021)

68. Ruoss, A., Balunovic, M., Fischer, M., Vechev, M.T.: Learning certified individually fair representations. Adv. Neural Inf. Process. Syst. **33** (2020)

69. Sarhan, M.H., Navab, N., Eslami, A., Albarqouni, S.: Fairness by learning orthogonal disentangled representations. In: Vedaldi, A., Bischof, H., Brox, T., Frahm, J.-M. (eds.) ECCV 2020. LNCS, vol. 12374, pp. 746–761. Springer, Cham (2020). https://doi.org/10.1007/978-3-030-58526-6_44

70. Sattigeri, P., Hoffman, S.C., Chenthamarakshan, V., Varshney, K.R.: Fairness GAN: generating datasets with fairness properties using a generative adversarial network. IBM J. Res. Dev. (2019)

71. Segal, S., Adi, Y., Pinkas, B., Baum, C., Ganesh, C., Keshet, J.: Fairness in the eyes of the data: certifying machine-learning models. In: AAAI/ACM Conference on AI, Ethics, and Society (2021)

72. Seonghyeon, K.: Glow pytorch (commit: 97081ff1) (2020). https://github.com/rosinality/glow-pytorch

73. Song, J., Kalluri, P., Grover, A., Zhao, S., Ermon, S.: Learning controllable fair representations. In: The 22nd International Conference on Artificial Intelligence and Statistics (2019)

74. Sun, X., Wu, P., Hoi, S.C.H.: Face detection using deep learning: an improved faster RCNN approach. Neurocomputing **299**, 42–50 (2018)

75. Tatman, R.: Gender and dialect bias in youtube's automatic captions. In: Proceedings of the First ACL Workshop on Ethics in Natural Language Processing (2017)

76. Tjeng, V., Xiao, K.Y., Tedrake, R.: Evaluating robustness of neural networks with mixed integer programming. In: 7th International Conference on Learning Representations (2019)

77. UN: The right to privacy in the digital age (2021)

78. Urban, C., Christakis, M., Wüstholz, V., Zhang, F.: Perfectly parallel fairness certification of neural networks. In: Proceedings of ACM Programming Language (2020)

79. Wang, H., Grgic-Hlaca, N., Lahoti, P., Gummadi, K.P., Weller, A.: An empirical study on learning fairness metrics for COMPAS data with human supervision. CoRR (2019)

80. Wang, T., Zhao, J., Yatskar, M., Chang, K., Ordonez, V.: Balanced datasets are not enough: estimating and mitigating gender bias in deep image representations. In: IEEE/CVF International Conference on Computer Vision (2019)
81. Wang, Z., et al.: Towards fairness in visual recognition: effective strategies for bias mitigation. In: IEEE/CVF Conference on Computer Vision and Pattern Recognition (2020)
82. Wei, S., Niethammer, M.: The fairness-accuracy pareto front. Stat. Anal. Data Min. **15**(3), 287–302 (2022). https://doi.org/10.1002/sam.11560
83. Wilson, B., Hoffman, J., Morgenstern, J.: Predictive inequity in object detection. CoRR (2019)
84. Wong, E., Kolter, J.Z.: Learning perturbation sets for robust machine learning. In: 9th International Conference on Learning Representations (2021)
85. Yeom, S., Fredrikson, M.: Individual fairness revisited: transferring techniques from adversarial robustness. In: Proceedings of the Twenty-Ninth International Joint Conference on Artificial Intelligence (2020)
86. Yurochkin, M., Bower, A., Sun, Y.: Training individually fair ML models with sensitive subspace robustness. In: 8th International Conference on Learning Representations (2020)
87. Yurochkin, M., Sun, Y.: Sensei: sensitive set invariance for enforcing individual fairness. In: 9th International Conference on Learning Representations (2021)
88. Zemel, R.S., Wu, Y., Swersky, K., Pitassi, T., Dwork, C.: Learning fair representations. In: Proceedings of the 30th International Conference on Machine Learning (2013)
89. Zhao, H., Coston, A., Adel, T., Gordon, G.J.: Conditional learning of fair representations. In: 8th International Conference on Learning Representations (2020)
90. Zhao, J., Wang, T., Yatskar, M., Ordonez, V., Chang, K.: Men also like shopping: reducing gender bias amplification using corpus-level constraints. In: Proceedings of the 2017 Conference on Empirical Methods in Natural Language Processing (2017)

Parameterized Temperature Scaling for Boosting the Expressive Power in Post-Hoc Uncertainty Calibration

Christian Tomani[1]([⊠]), Daniel Cremers[1], and Florian Buettner[2,3]

[1] Technical University of Munich, Munich, Germany
christian.tomani@tum.de, cremers@tum.de
[2] German Cancer Research Center (DKFZ), Heidelberg, Germany
florian.buettner@dkfz.de
[3] Goethe University Frankfurt, Frankfurt, Germany

Abstract. We address the problem of uncertainty calibration and introduce a novel calibration method, Parametrized Temperature Scaling (PTS). Standard deep neural networks typically yield uncalibrated predictions, which can be transformed into calibrated confidence scores using post-hoc calibration methods. In this contribution, we demonstrate that the performance of accuracy-preserving state-of-the-art post-hoc calibrators is limited by their intrinsic expressive power. We generalize temperature scaling by computing prediction-specific temperatures, parameterized by a neural network. We show with extensive experiments that our novel accuracy-preserving approach consistently outperforms existing algorithms across a large number of model architectures, datasets and metrics (Source code available at: https://github.com/tochris/pts-uncertainty).

1 Introduction

Due to their high predictive power, neural network based systems are increasingly used for decision making in real-world applications. Models deployed in such real-world settings, require not only high accuracy, but also reliability and uncertainty-awareness. Especially in safety critical applications such as autonomous driving or in automated factories where average case performance is insufficient, a reliable estimate of the predictive uncertainty of models is crucial. This can be achieved via well-calibrated confidence scores that are representative of the true likelihood of a prediction.

Since modern neural networks tend to yield systematically overconfident predictions [4,13], a number of algorithms for post-hoc calibration have been proposed. These algorithms include parametric approaches that transform the outputs of neural networks based on simple linear models in form of Platt-scaling or Temperature scaling. Alternative non-parametric approaches include histogram- or regression-based models such as histogram-binning or isotonic regression. Recent research efforts have shown that combining and extending these base

S. Avidan et al. (Eds.): ECCV 2022, LNCS 13673, pp. 555–569, 2022.
https://doi.org/10.1007/978-3-031-19778-9_32

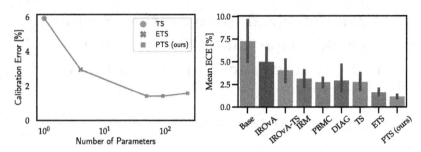

(a) Increased expressive power of post-hoc methods yields lower calibration error.

(b) Our approach improves substantially over baselines across 3 datasets and 9 architectures.

Fig. 1. (a) With increased expressive power, temperature scaling-based models yield lower expected calibration errors (ECE). All post-hoc calibration models were optimized to calibrate a MobileNetV2 trained on ImageNet. (b) Bars show the average ECE of all baseline methods. Average is taken over all architectures and baselines and lines indicate standard deviation. PTS improves substantially over all baselines with relative reduction of calibration error of 30% over ETS and even higher reductions for other baselines.

techniques [8,9,11,26] results in a plethora of approaches where no single approach performs best across datasets and model architectures. Temperature-scaling based approaches are a particularly appealing family of post-hoc calibrators since they do not affect the accuracy of the transformed model and have a high data efficiency, so that they can be applied also in low-data settings with only small validation sets available. However, they are collectively limited by a low expressive power (or model capacity): Temperature scaling [4] fits a single scalar parameter, extended temperature scaling [26] is based on a weighted ensemble of 3 fixed temperatures. While non-parametric models are more expressive, they usually do not preserve model accuracy and the accuracy of trained models may decrease substantially after calibration [4,26]. Importantly, all temperature-scaling based approaches are based on a fixed calibration map, that transforms all uncalibrated predictions of a neural network into calibrated predictions in the same manner without leveraging information from individual predictions.

We hypothesize that the performance of temperature-scaling based post-hoc calibration models is intrinsically limited by their expressive power, which stems from a lack of modeling a prediction-specific transformation. We show that our prediction-specific temperatures are indeed different for each model; in fact, they vary over a wide range of values, which is in stark contrast to only 1 or 3 temperatures for temperature scaling or ensemble temperature scaling and indicates that temperatures calculated based on each prediction separately yield more accurate uncertainty aware post-hoc calibration results.

1.1 Contributions

In this work we make the following contributions:

- We show that the limiting factor of TS-based post-hoc calibrators is the expressive power of the underlying calibration model.
- We generalize temperature scaling based on a highly expressive neural network that computes *prediction-specific* temperatures; we refer to our accuracy-preserving post-hoc calibration approach as Parameterized Temperature Scaling (PTS).
- We show that our approach has a similar data-efficiency as state-of-the-art prediction-agnostic post-hoc calibrators.
- We demonstrate in exhaustive experiments that PTS outperforms existing methods across a wide range of datasets and models as "one-size-fits-all" calibrator, without the need to optimize any hyperparameter.

2 Related Work

In this section, we review existing approaches for post-hoc calibration of trained neural networks. For this type of post-processing method a validation set, drawn from the generative distribution of the training data, is used to rescale the outputs returned by a trained neural network such that in-domain predictions are well calibrated. Related work can be categorized along two distinct axes, namely parametric vs non-parametric methods and accuracy-preserving methods vs. those where accuracy can change after calibration. While non-parametric approaches tend to have a higher expressive power than parametric models, most non-parametric methods suffer from the drawback that they do not preserve the accuracy of trained neural networks.

2.1 Non-parametric Methods

A popular non-parametric post-processing approach is histogram binning [24]. In brief, all uncalibrated confidence scores $\hat{P}_l$ are partitioned into M bins. Next, a calibrated score Q_m is assigned to each bin by optimizing a bin-wise squared loss. Extensions to histogram binning include isotonic regression [25] and Bayesian Binning into Quantiles (BBQ) [15]. For isotonic regression, uncalibrated confidence scores are divided into M intervals and a piecewise constant function f is fitted on the validation set. This isotonic function is then used to transform uncalibrated outputs into calibrated scores. BBQ is a Bayesian generalization of histogram binning using the concept of Bayesian model averaging. Recently proposed alternatives to histogram-based methods are Gaussian Process based calibration [23] and calibration via splines [5]. While these non-parametric methods do not preserve the accuracy of trained neural networks, Zhang et al. [26] have recently introduced an accuracy-preserving extension of isotonic regression by imposing strict isotonicity on the isotonic function.

2.2   Parametric Methods

In addition to these non-parametric approaches, also parametric alternatives for post-processing confidence scores exist. For example, the idea of Platt scaling [17] is based on transforming the non-probabilistic outputs (logits) $z_i \in \mathbb{R}$ of a binary classifier to calibrated confidence scores. While initially proposed in the context of support vector machines, Platt scaling has also been used for calibrating other classifiers, including neural networks. More specifically, the logits are transformed to calibrated confidence scores $\hat{Q}_i$ using logistic regression $\hat{Q}_i = \sigma(az_i + b)$, where σ is the sigmoid function. The two parameters a and b are fitted by optimising the negative log-likelihood of the validation set.

Guo et al. [4] generalized Platt scaling to the multi-class case: Temperature Scaling (TS) is a simple but popular post-processing approach where a scalar parameter T is used to re-scale the logits of a trained neural network. In the case of C-class classification, the logits are a C-dimensional vector $\mathbf{z}_i \in \mathbb{R}^C$, which are typically transformed into confidence scores $\hat{P}_i$ using the softmax function σ_{SM}. For temperature scaling, logits are rescaled with temperature T and transformed into calibrated confidence scores $\hat{Q}_i$ using σ_{SM} as

$$\hat{Q}_i = \max_c \sigma_{SM}(\mathbf{z}_i/T)^{(c)} \tag{1}$$

T is learned by minimizing the negative log-likelihood of the validation set. Zhang et al. [26] have recently introduced an extended temperature scaling, where calibrated predictions are obtained by a weighted sum of predictions re-scaled via three individual temperature terms: an adjustable temperature (as in vanilla temperature scaling), a fixed temperature of 1 and a fixed temperature of ∞. Other generalization of Platt scaling to the multi-class case are vector scaling and matrix scaling [4]. Matrix scaling applies a linear transformation $\mathbf{W}\mathbf{z}_i + \mathbf{b}$ to the logits, where $\mathbf{W}$ and $\mathbf{b}$ do not depend on individual predictions. For vector scaling, $\mathbf{W}$ is chosen to be diagonal, so that it can be interpreted as a generalization of Ensemble Temperature Scaling, where each dimension is transformed with its own temperature. In contrast to the non-parametric methods introduced above or other parametric multi-class calibrators such as vector scaling/matrix scaling or Dirichlet based scaling [12], Temperature Scaling-based methods have the advantage that they do not change the accuracy of the trained neural network. Since re-scaling does not affect the ranking of the logits, also the maximum of the softmax function remains unchanged. In this work, we build on temperature scaling in order to leverage its accuracy-preserving nature and introduce a generalized formulation that overcomes its limited expressive power.

More recently, a family of intra order-preserving function was proposed as post-hoc calibration functions that can preserve the top-k predictions of neural networks [18]. Confnet [22] is another calibration method that obtains better confidence scores by feeding logits into a neural network; however, it is an end-to-end framework optimizing also the weights of the classifier itself.

Algorithm 1 Parameterized Temperature Scaling (PTS)

Input: Trained classification model $(\hat{Y}, \hat{Z}) = h(X)$, validation set (X, Y), initialized calibration network $T = g_\theta(Z)$, number of training steps S, batch size β.

1: **for** ς in 1:S **do**
2:      Read minibatch $MB = (\{X_1, \ldots, X_\beta\}, \{Y_1, \ldots, Y_\beta\})$ from validation set
3:      **for** X_b in MB **do**
4:          Compute calibrated predictions $\sigma_{SM}(\mathbf{z}_b / g_\theta(\mathbf{z}_b^s))^{(c)}$ with $\mathbf{z}_b = h(X_b)$ (eq. 7)
5:      **end for**
6:      Compute L_θ based on MB and do one training step optimizing $\boldsymbol{\theta}$ based on MB
7: **end for**

---

3   Definitions and Problem Set-up

Let $X \in \mathbb{R}^D$ and $Y \in \{1, \ldots, C\}$ be random variables that denote the D-dimensional input and labels in a classification task with C classes with a ground truth joint distribution $\pi(X, Y) = \pi(Y|X)\pi(X)$. The dataset $\mathcal{D}$ consists of N i.i.d. samples $\mathcal{D} = \{(X_n, Y_n)\}_{n=1}^N$ drawn from $\pi(X, Y)$. Let $h(X) = (\hat{Y}, \hat{Z})$ be the output of a trained neural network classifier h predicting a class $\hat{Y}$ and an associated unnormalized logit tupel $\hat{Z}$ based on X. $\hat{Z}$ is then transformed into a confidence score $\hat{P}$ associated to $\hat{Y}$ via the softmax function σ_{SM} as $\hat{P} = \max_c \sigma_{SM}(\hat{Z})^{(c)}$. In this work, we develop a new approach to improve the quality of the predictive uncertainty of h by improving the calibration of its confidence scores $\hat{P}$.

Uncertainty (miss-)calibration. We define perfect calibration such that accuracy and confidence match for all confidence levels [4]:

$$\mathbb{P}(\hat{Y} = Y | \hat{P} = p) = p, \quad \forall p \in [0, 1] \tag{2}$$

Based on Eq. 2 it is straight-forward to define miss-calibration as the difference in expectation between confidence and accuracy:

$$\mathbb{E}_{\hat{P}} \left[\left| \mathbb{P}(\hat{Y} = Y | \hat{P} = p) - p \right| \right] \tag{3}$$

Measuring Calibration. The expected calibration error (ECE) [15] is a scalar summary measure estimating miss-calibration by approximating Eq. 3 based on predictions, confidence scores and ground truth labels $\{(Y_l, \hat{Y}_l, \hat{P}_l)\}_{l=1}^L$ of a finite number of L samples. ECE is computed by first partitioning all L confidence scores $\hat{P}_l$ into M equally sized bins of size $1/M$ and computing accuracy and average confidence of each bin. Let B_m be the set of indices of samples whose confidence falls into its associated interval $I_m = \left(\frac{m-1}{M}, \frac{m}{M} \right]$. $\text{conf}(B_m) = 1/|B_m| \sum_{i \in B_m} \hat{P}_i$ and $\text{acc}(B_m) = 1/|B_m| \sum_{i \in B_m} \mathbf{1}(\hat{Y}_i = Y_i)$ are the average confidence and accuracy associated with B_m, respectively. The ECE is then computed as

$$\text{ECE}^d = \sum_{m=1}^{M} \frac{|B_m|}{n} \|\text{acc}(B_m) - \text{conf}(B_m)\|_d \tag{4}$$

with d usually set to 1 for the l1-norm. While the ECE is the most commonly used measure of miss-calibration, it has some drawbacks. In particular, the choice of bins can result in biased estimates and/or volatility [1,9,26]. Therefore, alternative formulations to mitigate these issues have been suggested. For example, Zhang et al. [26] have proposed to replace histograms with non-parametric density estimators and present an ECE based on kernel density estimation (KDE). In addition to top-label ECE (Eq. 4), class-wise ECE has been proposed as a metric. However, they have been observed to be often contradictory [16]. Consequently, calibration gain, a dimensionality-independent solution to compare calibration maps was recently introduced [26]. This metric builds on the well-known calibration refinement decomposition [14] for the strictly proper scoring loss [3]. Orthogonal ways of evaluating calibration include testing a hypothesis of perfect calibration [21].

4   Highly Expressive Post-hoc Calibration via Parameterized Temperature Scaling

To overcome limitations in the expressive power of TS-based methods, we propose to parameterize the temperature in a flexible and expressive manner. Rather then learning a single temperature (or weighted sum of fixed temperatures), we introduce a dependency of the temperature on the un-normalized logits. In other words, while temperature scaling works by re-scaling any logit tupel of a trained model by the same temperature, PTS introduces a dependency of the temperature on the logit tuple itself. That is, our approach leverages the information present in a logit tupel to compute a prediction-specific temperature.

More formally, we propose the following post-hoc calibrator to map unnormalized logits $\mathbf{z}$ to calibrated confidence scores. We start by parameterizing the temperature T with a flexible neural network as follows:

$$T(\mathbf{z}; \boldsymbol{\theta}) = g_\theta(\mathbf{z}^s) \tag{5}$$

with $\boldsymbol{\theta}$ being the weights of a neural network g parameterizing the scalar temperature $T(\mathbf{z}; \boldsymbol{\theta})$ and $\mathbf{z}^s$ being an unnormalised logit tuple sorted by decreasing value.

The parameterized temperature is then used to obtain calibrated confidence scores $\hat{Q}_i$ for sample i based on unnormalized logits $\mathbf{z}_i$:

$$\hat{Q}_i(\mathbf{z}_i, \boldsymbol{\theta}) = \max_c \sigma_{SM}(\mathbf{z}_i/T(\mathbf{z}_i; \boldsymbol{\theta}))^{(c)} \tag{6}$$

$$= \max_c \sigma_{SM}(\mathbf{z}_i/g_\theta(\mathbf{z}_i^s))^{(c)} \tag{7}$$

We fit a post-hoc calibrator for a trained neural network $h(X)$ by optimizing a squared error loss L_θ with respect to $\boldsymbol{\theta}$.

$$L_\theta = \frac{1}{N} \sum_{n=1}^{N} \sum_{c=1}^{C} (I_{nc} - \sigma_{SM}(\mathbf{z}_i/g_\theta(\mathbf{z}_i^s))^{(c)})^2 \tag{8}$$

with I_{nc} being 1 if sample n has true class c, and 0 otherwise. PTS is summarized in Algorithm 1.

Like standard temperature scaling, PTS with a parameterized temperature $T(\mathbf{z}; \boldsymbol{\theta})$ does not change the accuracy of the trained model since the ranking of the logits remains unchanged.

We first explore the relation between calibration performance and expressive power of a post-hoc calibrator and demonstrate that performance of current state-of-the-art temperature-scaling based calibrators is limited by expressive power.

Next, we show that PTS is a one-size-fits-all approach for post-hoc calibration: in contrast to the common state-of the-art where performance varies widely between datasets and network architectures, our approach consistently outperforms state-of-the-art methods on a wide range of datasets and model architectures. We then demonstrate that in spite of the larger number of parameters, PTS has a similar data efficiency compared to low-parametric baselines such as temperature-scaling. Finally, we investigate the dependency structure between logits and their prediction-specific temperature and show that allowing for non-linearities in this relationship improves calibration performance.

4.1 Baseline Methods and Datasets

With data efficiency and the ability to preserve the trained model's accuracy being key desiderata of post-hoc calibration methods [26], we mainly focus on accuracy preserving baselines and/or temperature-scaling based methods. We compare our approach to the following baseline methods:

- Base: Uncalibrated baseline model
- Temperature scaling (TS): Post-hoc calibration by temperature scaling [4]
- Ensemble Temperature scaling (ETS): Ensemble version of TS with 4 parameters [26]
- Isotonic regression (IR) [25]
- Accuracy preserving version of Isotonic regression (IRM) [26]
- Composite model combining Temperature Scaling and Isotonic Regression (TS-IR) [26]
- The scaling-binning calibrator, combining temperature scaling with histogram binning (PBMC) [9]
- Accuracy and intra-order preserving calibration (DIAG) [18]

DIAG can be run with or without hyperparameter optimization; for a fair comparison, since all other baselines including ours have fixed hyperparameters, we report results without hyperparameter optimization.

We evaluate the performance of all models on three datasets, namely Imagenet, CIFAR-10 and CIFAR-100. For all datasets, we calibrate various neural network architectures and analyze a mix of complex and less complex settings. To complement the complex architectures needed to perform well on Imagenet and other complex datasets, we explore how our approach (and others) perform in simpler tasks that require less complex models. For Imagenet we used 5 pre-trained models provided as part of tensorflow, namely ResNet50, ResNet152 [6], DenseNet169 [7], Xception [2] and MobileNetv2 [19]. For CIFAR-10 and CIFAR-100, we trained VGG19 [20] and LeNet5 [10].

We used a standard setup for evaluating model calibration [4] and trained PTS as well as all baselines on the standard validation sets of all datasets. We then evaluated all models by computing the ECE on the standard test sets. For CIFAR-10 and CIFAR-100, we used a validation dataset consisting of 5000 samples and an independent test set of 10000 samples. For ImageNet, we randomly split the hold-out set into a validation set of 12500 samples and a test set of 37500 samples.

We quantify the quality of calibration for all experiments using the standard Expected Calibration Error ECE[1] based on 10 bins as well as and Expected Calibration Error based on kernel density estimates, ECE_{KDE}. In addition, we also report results from the dimensionality-independent calibration gain, which takes all classes into account [26].

PTS was trained as a neural network with 2 fully connected hidden layers with 5 nodes each. Hyperparameters were the same for all experiments, namely a learning rate of 0.00005, batch size of 1000 and stepsize of 100,000. We further limited $\mathbf{z}^s$ to the top 10 most confident predictions in all settings since we found that they convey sufficient information. That means, PTS can be used in a large variety of settings without the need to optimize hyperparameters.

5   Experiments and Results

5.1   Higher Expressive Power Leads to Better Calibration Performance

To assess the link between expressive power and calibration for temperature-scaling based models, we train our PTS calibrators with an increasing number of nodes in the hidden layers on the Imagenet validation set. We compare calibration performance of our neural-network-based parameterization of the temperature to post-hoc calibrators with fixed temperature on the Imagenet test set. Figure 1 illustrates that increasing the expressive power of temperature scaling (based on a single parameter) via a weighted ensembles of 3 temperatures (4 parameters) results in an improved ECE (50% for MobileNetV2 trained on ImageNet), as previously demonstrated. When further increasing the expressive power of temperature-scaling based calibrators via a neural network, we find that

Table 1. Expected calibration error ECE[1]. For all architectures our approach largely outperforms baseline post-hoc calibrators.

	Base	IROvA	IROvA-TS	IRM	PBMC	DIAG	TS	ETS	PTS (ours)
CIFAR LeNet5	1.91	1.99	1.92	1.57	2.14	1.94	1.91	1.67	**1.47**
CIFAR VGG19	7.92	1.10	**0.77**	1.03	1.66	1.51	1.37	1.34	0.84
CIFAR100 LeNet5	7.54	1.71	2.52	3.52	2.69	3.78	1.71	1.28	**0.70**
CIFAR100 VGG19	12.96	5.73	2.88	5.28	3.05	9.30	3.64	2.11	**0.82**
ImgNet ResNet50	6.26	6.60	5.66	2.86	3.47	1.53	1.85	1.35	**1.34**
ImgNet ResNet152	6.39	6.55	5.46	2.88	3.49	1.99	2.17	1.02	**0.97**
ImgNet DenNet169	6.13	6.61	5.64	2.74	3.39	1.89	1.97	1.08	**1.05**
ImgNet Xception	13.25	8.31	5.43	5.34	3.26	–	4.40	1.83	**1.59**
ImgNet MobNetV2	2.98	6.19	6.12	3.05	1.52	**1.41**	5.91	2.94	1.43

Table 2. Expected calibration error ECE$_{\text{KDE}}$. Overall rankings are largely consistent with ECE[1]. DIAG did not converge to a meaningful optimum for Xception.

	Base	IROvA	IROvA-TS	IRM	PBMC	DIAG	TS	ETS	PTS (ours)
CIFAR LeNet5	1.93	1.82	1.83	1.50	2.33	2.11	1.97	1.82	**1.49**
CIFAR VGG19	7.34	1.24	1.11	**1.07**	1.95	1.92	1.85	1.72	1.38
CIFAR100 LeNet5	7.54	1.76	2.66	3.52	2.70	4.08	1.73	1.07	**0.95**
CIFAR100 VGG19	12.32	5.29	2.50	5.23	3.73	9.24	3.43	2.31	**1.05**
ImgNet ResNet50	5.61	5.93	5.00	2.54	4.82	**1.17**	1.44	1.57	1.32
ImgNet ResNet152	5.69	5.73	4.82	2.48	4.88	1.76	1.85	1.39	**0.89**
ImgNet DenNet169	5.49	5.95	4.97	2.39	4.81	1.56	1.53	1.29	**1.03**
ImgNet Xception	12.59	7.72	4.79	4.77	3.62	–	4.01	1.98	**1.26**
ImgNet MobNetV2	3.10	5.75	5.63	2.93	2.09	1.55	5.91	3.02	**1.26**

the calibration error further decreases with a larger number of parameters until a plateau is reached (additional improvement in ECE of 52% for MobileNetV2 trained on ImageNet). We next evaluated the set of temperatures learnt by PTS for predictions from three different models on the Imagenet test set (Fig. 2). These temperatures span a wide range of values, which is in stark contrast to only 3 temperatures used in ETS, indicating that for ETS the ensemble of only 3 temperatures limits its calibration performance.

Taken together, this illustrates that the performance of conventional temperature-scaling based methods is limited by their inherent expressive power.

5.2   PTS Is a One-size-fits-all Post-hoc Calibrator

We next evaluate the performance of our approach on a total of 9 deep neural networks trained on CIFAR-10, CIFAR-100 and Imagenet.

Table 1 shows the standard ECE, Table 2 the KDE-based ECE and Table 3 calibration gain for all experiments. Rankings for all metrics are largely consistent and our approach outperforms baselines in all settings in terms of ECE[1].

Table 3. Calibration Gain (higher is better): Our approach (PTS) largely outperforms baseline post-hoc calibrators also for a dimensionality-independent calibration metric.

	IROvA	IROvA-TS	IRM	PBMC	DIAG	TS	ETS	PTS (ours)
CIFAR LeNet5	0.01	0.01	**0.03**	−0.05	0.00	0.01	0.02	**0.03**
CIFAR VGG19	0.91	**0.92**	0.91	0.88	0.87	0.87	0.91	0.91
CIFAR100 LeNet5	0.69	0.65	0.48	0.59	0.55	0.67	0.70	**0.72**
CIFAR100 VGG19	1.67	1.99	1.70	1.94	0.66	1.92	2.03	**2.09**
ImgNet ResNet50	−0.02	0.14	0.39	0.26	**0.47**	0.45	**0.47**	0.47
ImgNet ResNet152	0.01	0.17	0.39	0.24	0.43	0.42	0.46	**0.48**
ImgNet DenNet169	−0.03	0.10	0.36	0.22	0.40	0.39	0.42	**0.43**
ImgNet Xception	0.28	0.20	0.46	0.41	–	0.33	0.44	**0.49**
ImgNet MobNetV2	0.20	0.08	0.36	0.34	**0.38**	0.28	0.36	**0.38**

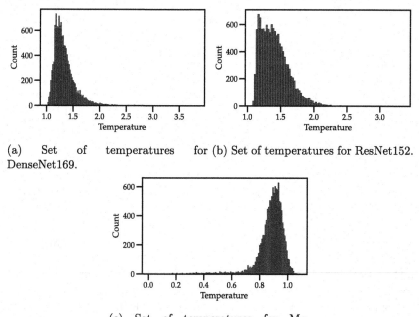

(a) Set of temperatures for DenseNet169.

(b) Set of temperatures for ResNet152.

(c) Set of temperatures for MobileNetV2.

Fig. 2. Prediction-specific temperatures inferred by PTS for all samples in the Imagenet test set. For all models, temperatures varied over a wide range of values, which is in stark contrast to only 3 temperatures used in ETS.

ECE_{KDE} suggests that in settings with low complexity - i.e. a simple dataset with low number of classes such as CIFAR-10 and/or a simple architecture such as LeNet - performance of PTS is comparable to ETS only. The more complex a setting, the larger the gain of PTS. This range of complex architectures and

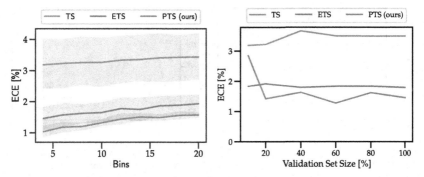

(a) Robustness in terms of number of bins.

(b) ECE for MobileNetV2 trained on ImageNet for different validation set sizes

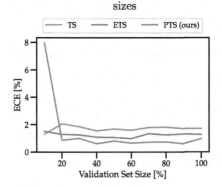

(c) ECE for LeNet5 trained on CIFAR-100 for different validation set sizes

Fig. 3. Robustness of TS-based methods. (a) Mean ECE across 5 architectures trained on ImageNet, with a confidence band illustrating one standard deviation. PTS has the lowest calibration error across all architectures, irrespective of the chosen number of bins. Robustness in terms of dataset size (b and c): ECE for post-hoc calibrators trained on increasingly smaller subsets of the validation sets of ImageNet (b) and CIFAR-100 (c), generated by subsampling decreasing fractions of the full validation set (10% to 100%). PTS maintains the high data efficiency inherent in TS methods with low ECE even for small validation sets.

datasets is particularly relevant in practice since Guo et al. [4] have shown that it is particularly modern architectures that are prone to mis-calibration. Additionally, Table 3 shows the calibration gain [26], which indicates that PTS yields an improved performance even for metrics, which are dimensionality-independent.

To make sure the choice of bin size when computing the ECE does not affect our findings, we computed ECE^1 for bin sizes M ranging from 5 to 20 in steps of 2. Figure 3 (a) illustrates the mean ECE across the 5 architectures trained on ImageNet and calibrated using TS, ETS and PTS. While small bin sizes result in a systematically smaller ECE - a known bias [9] - PTS outperforms the other TS-based methods for all bin sizes with rankings being unchanged.

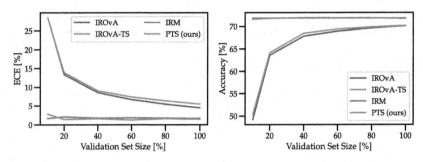

(a) ECE for MobileNetV2 trained on ImageNet

(b) Accuracy for MobileNetV2 trained on ImageNet

Fig. 4. ECE and accuracy for non-parametric post-hoc calibrators on validation sets of decreasing size. Non-parametric calibration methods suffer from a low data-efficiency and decrease in accuracy compared to PTS.

Table 4. Normalized ECE relative to PTS for 5 Imagenet models across different validation set sizes.

Validation Set Size [%]	IROvA	IROvA-TS	IRM	TS	ETS
10	6.84	6.81	0.83	0.71	0.40
20	11.92	11.42	2.62	2.12	1.11
40	7.85	7.14	2.50	2.14	1.13
60	6.17	5.59	2.16	1.92	1.00
80	5.96	5.09	2.47	2.13	1.00
100	5.67	4.81	2.63	2.28	1.16

5.3   PTS Is Data-efficient

A major advantage of TS-based models over other approaches is their high data-efficiency paired with accuracy-preserving properties. We therefore designed experiments to quantify the data-efficiency of PTS. To this end, we fitted our model on increasingly smaller subsets of the validation set to calibrate a MobileNetV2 architecture trained on ImageNet and a LeNet5 architecture trained on CIFAR-100. In both cases we varied the size of the subsets from 10% to 100% of the respective standard validation set size. When evaluating ECE on the test set, we found that like vanilla TS and ETS, our model yielded excellent performance even when trained on small fractions of the validation set, maintaining one of the key advantages of TS-based models (Fig. 3 (b) and (c)). We confirmed the robustness of these findings, by performing the dataset-size vs ECE experiment for all other models trained on imagenet. We summarized the results by normalizing ECE relative to PTS for each dataset size and model. We then took the average across all models. Table 4 shows that across all models, only for very small dataset sizes of 10%, PTS is outperformed by other approaches.

Table 5. ECE for linear and non-linear models on Imagenet. Indicates that generating temperatures using simply a linear model is not sufficient.

	Linear Model	PTS (ours)
ImgNet ResNet50	1.47	**1.34**
ImgNet ResNet152	1.02	**0.97**
ImgNet DenNet169	1.22	**1.05**
ImgNet Xception	1.62	**1.59**
ImgNet MobNetV2	1.49	**1.43**

These findings are in contrast to non-parametric models, which also tend to have a higher expressive power than standard TS approaches. When repeating the data-efficiency experiment for this family of models, we found that calibration error increased substantially with decreasing validation set size. In addition, IROVA and IROVA-TS also yielded a substantial decrease in accuracy (Fig. 4).

5.4 The Relationship Between Logits and Temperature Is Non-linear

We finally assessed whether the information present in the logits can be captured via a linear model or whether non-linearities need to be accounted for. To this end, we trained a linear version of our neural network without non-linear activation function (with the same number of parameters as PTS to ensure a fair comparison) as calibration map. Using this linear model to calibrate trained networks with all assessed architectures on Imagenet results on average in a substantially higher ECE of 1.36 compared to 1.28 using a nonlinear model (Table 5). This indicated that it is not sufficient to generate prediction-specific temperatures using a linear model, but that the relationship between logits and temperature is non-linear.

6 Conclusion

In this work, we have introduced a novel approach for accuracy-preserving post-hoc calibration by modeling prediction-specific temperatures. To boost the expressive power of TS-based models we introduce a dependency of the temperature on the predicted logits and propose a parameterization of the temperature itself using a neural network. These prediction-specific temperatures make up a highly expressive, accuracy-preserving and data-efficient generalization of temperature scaling. In extensive experiments, we show that this approach results in substantially lower calibration errors than existing post-hoc calibration approaches, with an average improvement over the current state-of-the-art (ETS) of 30%.

Acknowledgements. This work was supported by the Munich Center for Machine Learning and has been funded by the German Federal Ministry of Education and Research (BMBF) under Grant No. 01IS18036B.

References

1. Ashukha, A., Lyzhov, A., Molchanov, D., Vetrov, D.: Pitfalls of in-domain uncertainty estimation and ensembling in deep learning. arXiv preprint arXiv:2002.06470 (2020)
2. Chollet, F.: Xception: deep learning with depthwise separable convolutions. In: Proceedings of the IEEE Conference on Computer Vision and Pattern Recognition, pp. 1251–1258 (2017)
3. Gneiting, T., Raftery, A.E.: Strictly proper scoring rules, prediction, and estimation. J. Am. Stat. Assoc. **102**(477), 359–378 (2007)
4. Guo, C., Pleiss, G., Sun, Y., Weinberger, K.Q.: On calibration of modern neural networks. In: Proceedings of the 34th International Conference on Machine Learning, vol. 70, pp. 1321–1330. JMLR. org (2017)
5. Gupta, K., Rahimi, A., Ajanthan, T., Mensink, T., Sminchisescu, C., Hartley, R.: Calibration of neural networks using splines. arXiv preprint arXiv:2006.12800 (2020)
6. He, K., Zhang, X., Ren, S., Sun, J.: Deep residual learning for image recognition. In: Proceedings of the IEEE Conference on Computer Vision and Pattern Recognition, pp. 770–778 (2016)
7. Huang, G., Liu, Z., Van Der Maaten, L., Weinberger, K.Q.: Densely connected convolutional networks. In: Proceedings of the IEEE Conference on Computer Vision and Pattern Recognition, pp. 4700–4708 (2017)
8. Jang, S., Lee, I., Weimer, J.: Improving classifier confidence using lossy label-invariant transformations. In: International Conference on Artificial Intelligence and Statistics, pp. 4051–4059. PMLR (2021)
9. Kumar, A., Liang, P.S., Ma, T.: Verified uncertainty calibration. In: Advances in Neural Information Processing Systems, vol. 32, pp. 3792–3803 (2019)
10. LeCun, Y., Bottou, L., Bengio, Y., Haffner, P.: Gradient-based learning applied to document recognition. Proc. IEEE **86**(11), 2278–2324 (1998)
11. Ma, X., Blaschko, M.B.: Meta-Cal: well-controlled post-hoc calibration by ranking. In: International Conference on Machine Learning, pp. 7235–7245. PMLR (2021)
12. Milios, D., Camoriano, R., Michiardi, P., Rosasco, L., Filippone, M.: Dirichlet-based gaussian processes for large-scale calibrated classification. arXiv preprint arXiv:1805.10915 (2018)
13. Minderer, M.: Revisiting the calibration of modern neural networks. Adv. Neural. Inf. Process. Syst. **34**, 15682–15694 (2021)
14. Murphy, A.H.: A new vector partition of the probability score. J. Appl. Meteorol. Climatol. **12**(4), 595–600 (1973)
15. Naeini, M.P., Cooper, G., Hauskrecht, M.: Obtaining well calibrated probabilities using bayesian binning. In: Twenty-Ninth AAAI Conference on Artificial Intelligence (2015)
16. Nixon, J., Dusenberry, M.W., Zhang, L., Jerfel, G., Tran, D.: Measuring calibration in deep learning. In: CVPR Workshops. vol. 2 (2019)
17. Platt, J.C.: Probabilistic outputs for support vector machines and comparisons to regularized likelihood methods. Adv. Large Margin Classifiers. **10**, 61–74 (1999)

18. Rahimi, A., Shaban, A., Cheng, C.A., Hartley, R., Boots, B.: Intra order-preserving functions for calibration of multi-class neural networks. In: Advances in Neural Information Processing System, vol. 33, pp. 13456–13467 (2020)
19. Sandler, M., Howard, A., Zhu, M., Zhmoginov, A., Chen, L.C.: MobileNetV 2: inverted residuals and linear bottlenecks. In: Proceedings of the IEEE Conference on Computer Vision and Pattern Recognition, pp. 4510–4520 (2018)
20. Simonyan, K., Zisserman, A.: Very deep convolutional networks for large-scale image recognition. arXiv preprint arXiv:1409.1556 (2014)
21. Vaicenavicius, J., Widmann, D., Andersson, C., Lindsten, F., Roll, J., Schön, T.: Evaluating model calibration in classification. In: The 22nd International Conference on Artificial Intelligence and Statistics, pp. 3459–3467. PMLR (2019)
22. Wan, S., Wu, T.Y., Wong, W.H., Lee, C.Y.: ConfNet: predict with confidence. In: 2018 IEEE International Conference on Acoustics, Speech and Signal Processing (ICASSP), pp. 2921–2925 (2018)
23. Wenger, J., Kjellström, H., Triebel, R.: Non-parametric calibration for classification. In: International Conference on Artificial Intelligence and Statistics, pp. 178–190. PMLR (2020)
24. Zadrozny, B., Elkan, C.: Obtaining calibrated probability estimates from decision trees and Naive Bayesian classifiers. In: ICML, vol. 1, pp. 609–616. Citeseer (2001)
25. Zadrozny, B., Elkan, C.: Transforming classifier scores into accurate multiclass probability estimates. In: Proceedings of the Eighth ACM SIGKDD International Conference on Knowledge Discovery and Data Mining, pp. 694–699 (2002)
26. Zhang, J., Kailkhura, B., Han, T.: Mix-n-Match: ensemble and compositional methods for uncertainty calibration in deep learning. arXiv preprint arXiv:2003.07329 (2020)

FairStyle: Debiasing StyleGAN2 with Style Channel Manipulations

Cemre Efe Karakas⬤, Alara Dirik$^{(\boxtimes)}$⬤, Eylül Yalçınkaya⬤, and Pinar Yanardag⬤

Department of Computer Engineering, Boğaziçi University, Istanbul, Turkey
alara.dirik@gmail.com

Abstract. Recent advances in generative adversarial networks have shown that it is possible to generate high-resolution and hyperrealistic images. However, the images produced by GANs are only as fair and representative as the datasets on which they are trained. In this paper, we propose a method for directly modifying a pre-trained StyleGAN2 model that can be used to generate a balanced set of images with respect to one (e.g., *eyeglasses*) or more attributes (e.g., *gender and eyeglasses*). Our method takes advantage of the style space of the StyleGAN2 model to perform disentangled control of the target attributes to be debiased. Our method does not require training additional models and directly debiases the GAN model, paving the way for its use in various downstream applications. Our experiments show that our method successfully debiases the GAN model within a few minutes without compromising the quality of the generated images. To promote fair generative models, we share the code and debiased models at http://catlab-team.github.io/fairstyle.

Keywords: GANs · Fairness · Bias correction · StyleGAN

1 Introduction

Generative Adversarial Networks (GANs) [9] are popular image generation models capable of synthesizing high-quality images, and they have been used for a variety of visual applications [19, 29, 34, 35, 42, 43]. Like most of the deep learning models, GANs are essentially statistical models trained to learn a data distribution and generate realistic data that is indistinguishable to the discriminator from that in the training set. To achieve this, GANs exploit and favor the samples that provide the most information, and may neglect minority ones. Therefore, a well-trained GAN favors learning the majority attributes, and the samples they generate suffer from the same biases in the datasets on which they are trained.

C. E. Karakas and A. Dirik—Equal contributions.

Supplementary Information The online version contains supplementary material available at https://doi.org/10.1007/978-3-031-19778-9_33.

(a) Black and Female   (b) Black and Male

(c) Male with Eyeglasses   (d) Non-Black and Male

Fig. 1. Sample outputs from the StyleGAN2 model debiased using our method with respect to **Black+Gender** attributes.

For example, a GAN trained on a face dataset with few images of non-Caucasian individuals, will generate images of mostly Caucasians [22,30]. Our preliminary analysis of the pre-trained StyleGAN2-FFHQ [16] model confirms the significance of the generation bias: out of 10K randomly generated images, the *male* attribute is present in 42%, the *young* attribute is present in 70%, and the *eyeglasses* attribute is present in 20%. Our analysis shows that these biases also exist in the FFHQ training data with 42%, 72%, and 22% for the *male, young* and *eyeglasses* attributes, respectively (see Appendix B for more details). These examples show that GANs not only inherit biases from the training data, but also carry over to the applications built on top of them. This is a particularly important issue because pre-trained large-scale GANs such as StyleGAN2 are often used as the backbone of various computer vision applications in a variety of domains such as image processing, image generation and manipulation, anomaly detection, dataset generation and augmentation. Therefore, any model or application that depends on large pre-trained models such as StyleGAN2 would inherit or even amplify their biases and is therefore bound to be unfair.

In this paper, we address the problem of fairness in GANs by debiasing a pre-trained StyleGAN2 model with respect to single or multiple attributes. After debiasing, the edited StyleGAN2 models allow the user to generate unbiased images in which the target attributes are fairly represented. Unlike previous work that requires extensive preprocessing or training an additional model for each target attribute, our approach directly debiases the GAN model to produce more balanced outputs, and it can also be used for various downstream applications. Moreover, our approach does not require any sub-sampling of the input or output data, and is able to debias the GAN model within minutes without compromising the image quality. Our main contributions are as follows:

- We first propose a simple method that debiases the GAN model with respect to a single attribute, such as *gender* or *eyeglasses*.
- We then extend our method for jointly debiasing multiple attributes such as *gender and eyeglasses*.
- To handle more complex attributes such as *race*, we propose a third method based on CLIP [25], where we debias StyleGAN2 with text-based prompts such as *'a black person'* or *'an asian person'*.
- We perform extensive comparisons between our proposed method and other approaches to enforce fairness for a variety of attributes. We empirically show that our method is very effective in de-biasing the GAN model to produce balanced datasets without compromising the quality of the generated images.

2   Related Work

In this section, we first review related work in fairness and bias. We then discuss studies that specifically address fairness and bias in generative models. Finally, we discuss related work in the area of latent space manipulation.

2.1   Fairness and Bias in AI

Fairness and bias detection in deep neural networks have attracted much attention in recent years [6,23]. Most existing work on fairness focuses on studying the fairness of classifiers, as the predictions of these models can be directly used for discriminatory purposes or associate unjustified stereotypes with a particular class. Approaches to eliminating model bias can be divided into three main categories: Preprocessing methods that aim to collect balanced training data [20,21,41], methods to introduce constraints or regularizers into the training process [2,37,40], and post-processing methods that modify the posteriors of the trained models to debias them [7,12]. In our work, we focus on debiasing and fairness methods developed specifically for GANs, which we discuss below.

2.2   Detecting and Eliminating Biases in GANs

The fairness of generative models is much less studied compared to the fairness of discriminative models. Most research on the bias and fairness of GANs aims to either eliminate the negative effects of using imbalanced data on generation results or to identify and explain the biases. Research on bias and fairness of GANs can be divided into three main categories: improving the training and generation performance of GANs using biased datasets, identifying and explaining biases, and debiasing pre-trained GANs.

The first research category, training GANs on biased datasets, aims to solve the problem of low quality image generation when the model is trained on imbalanced datasets with disjoint manifolds and fails to learn the true data distribution. [32] proposes a heuristic motivated by rejection sampling to inject *disconnectedness* into GAN training to improve learning on disconnected manifolds. [31] proposes Discriminator Optimal Transport (DOT), a gradient ascent method driven by a Wasserstein discriminator to improve samples. [3] uses a rejection sampling method to approximately correct errors in the distribution of the GAN generator. [10] proposes a weakly supervised method to detect bias in existing datasets and assigns importance weights to samples during training. The second category of research aims to detect or explain bias in generative models. [18] proposes to use attribute-specific classifiers and train a generative model to specifically explain which style channels of StyleGAN2 contribute to the underlying classifier decisions. The third line of research aims to debias and improve the sample quality of pre-trained GANs. [11] proposes to train a probabilistic classifier to distinguish samples from two distributions and use this likelihood-free importance weighting method to correct for bias in generative models. However, this method requires training a classifier for each attribute targeted for debiasing and cannot handle biases in multiple attributes (e.g., *gender and eyeglasses*). [30] proposes a conditional latent space sampling method to generate attribute-balanced images. More specifically, latent codes from StyleGAN2 are sampled and classified. Then, a Gaussian Mixture Model (GMM) is trained for each attribute to create a set of balanced latent codes. Another recent work, [26], proposes to use the latent codes from the W-space of StyleGAN2 to train a linear SVM model for each attribute and then use the normal vector to the separation hyperplane to steer the latent code away from or towards acquiring the target attribute for debiasing. Unlike [26,30], our method does not require model training and aims to directly debias the GAN model which can be used to generate attribute-balanced image sets.

2.3   Latent Space Manipulation

Several methods have been proposed to exploit the latent space of GANs for image manipulation, which can be divided into two broad categories: supervised and unsupervised methods. Supervised approaches typically benefit from pre-trained attribute classifiers that guide the optimization process to discover meaningful directions in the latent space, or use labeled data to train new classifiers that directly aim to learn directions of interest [8,27]. Other work shows that it is possible to find meaningful directions in latent space in an unsupervised manner [14,33]. GANSpace [13] proposes to apply principal component analysis [36] to randomly select the latent vectors of the intermediate layers of the BigGAN [5] and StyleGAN models. A similar approach is used in SeFA

[28], where they directly optimize the intermediate weight matrix of the GAN model in closed form. LatentCLR [39] proposes a contrastive learning approach to find unsupervised directions that are transferable to different classes. In addition, both StyleCLIP [24] and StyleMC [17] use CLIP to find text-based directions within StyleGAN2 and perform both coarse and fine-grained manipulations of different attributes. Another recent work, StyleFlow [1], proposes a method for attribute-conditioned sampling and attribute-controlled editing with Style-GAN2. With respect to GAN editing, [4] proposes a method to permanently change the parameters of a GAN to produce images in which the desired attribute (e.g., clouds, thick eyebrows) is always present. However, they did not aim to debias GANs for fairness and their methodology differs from ours.

3   Methodology

In this section, we propose three methods to debias a pre-trained StyleGAN2 model. We begin with a brief description of the StyleGAN2 architecture and then describe our methods for debiasing a single attribute, joint debiasing of multiple attributes, and debiasing with text-based directions. Figure 2 illustrates a general view of our framework.

3.1   Background on StyleGAN2

The generator of StyleGAN2 contains several latent spaces: $\mathcal{Z}$, $\mathcal{W}$, $\mathcal{W}+$ and $\mathcal{S}$, also referred to as the style space. $\mathbf{z} \in \mathcal{Z}$ is a latent vector drawn from a prior distribution $p(\mathbf{z})$, typically chosen as a Gaussian. The generator $\mathcal{G}$ acts as a mapping function $\mathcal{G} : \mathcal{Z} \rightarrow \mathcal{X}$, where $\mathcal{X}$ is the target image domain. Therefore, $\mathcal{G}$ transforms the vectors from $\mathbf{z}$ into an intermediate latent space $\mathcal{W}$ by forward propagating them through 8 fully connected layers. The resulting latent vectors $\mathbf{w} \in \mathcal{W}$ are then transformed into channel-wise style parameters, forming the *style space*, denoted $\mathcal{S}$. In our work, we use the style space $\mathcal{S}$ to perform manipulations, as it is shown [38] to be the most disentangled, complete and informative space of StyleGAN2.

The synthesis network of the generator in StyleGAN2 consists of several blocks, each block having two convolutional layers for synthesizing feature maps. Each main block has an additional 1×1 convolutional layer that maps the output feature tensor to RGB colors, referred to as $tRGB$. The three different style code vectors are referred to as $\mathbf{s}_{B1}$, $\mathbf{s}_{B2}$, and $\mathbf{s}_{B+tRGB}$, where B indicates the block number. Given a block B, the style vectors $\mathbf{s}_{B1}$ and $\mathbf{s}_{B2}$ of each block consist of style channels that control disentangled visual attributes. The style vectors of each layer are obtained from the intermediate latent vectors $\mathbf{w} \in \mathcal{W}$ of the same layer by three affine transformations, $\mathbf{w}_{B1} \rightarrow \mathbf{s}_{B1}, \mathbf{w}_{B2} \rightarrow \mathbf{s}_{B2}, \mathbf{w}_{B2} \rightarrow \mathbf{s}_{B+tRGB}$.

3.2   Measuring Generation Bias

To assess whether our method produces a balanced distribution of attributes, we begin by formulating and quantifying the bias in the generated images. Given an

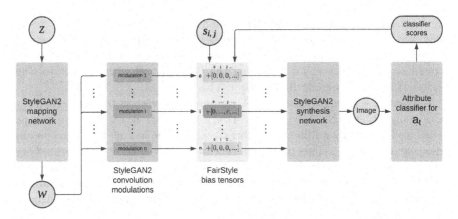

Fig. 2. An overview of the FairStyle architecture, $\mathbf{z}$ denotes a random vector drawn from a Gaussian distribution, $\mathbf{w}$ denotes the latent vector generated by the mapping network of StyleGAN2. Given a target attribute a_t, $s_{i,j}$ represents the style channel with layer index i and channel index j controlling the target attribute. We introduce *fairstyle* bias tensors into the GAN model, in which we edit the corresponding style channel $s_{i,j}$ for debiasing. The edited vectors are then fed into the generator to get a new batch of images from which we obtain updated classifier results for a_t. The fairstyle bias tensors are iteratively edited until the GAN model produces a balanced distribution with respect to the target attribute. The de-biased GAN model can then be used for sampling purposes or directly used as a generative backbone model in downstream applications.

n-dimensional image dataset $\mathcal{I} \subseteq \mathbb{R}^n$, GANs attempt to learn such a distribution $P(\mathcal{I}) = P_{\text{data}}(\mathcal{I})$. Thus, a well-trained generator is a mapping function $\mathcal{G} : \mathcal{Z} \to \mathcal{I}$, where $\mathcal{Z} \subseteq \mathbb{R}^m$ denotes the m-dimensional latent space, usually assumed to be a Gaussian distribution. Moreover, we can sample latent codes $\mathbf{z}$ and use the trained model to generate a realistic dataset $D = \{\mathcal{G}(\mathbf{z}_i)\}_{i=1}^{N}$ of N generated images belonging to the distribution $P(\mathcal{I}) \approx P_{\text{data}}(\mathcal{I})$.

Assuming that real and generated images contain k semantic attributes $a_1, a_2, ..., a_k$, a well-trained GAN learns any bias inherent in the original data distribution $P_{\text{data}}(\mathcal{I})$ with respect to the semantic attributes. In our work, we are interested in finding both the marginal distribution of the individual semantic attributes $P(a_i)$ and the joint distributions of the attribute pairs $P(a_i, a_j)$ of the generated dataset D. To measure generation bias, we generate N random images with pre-trained StyleGAN2 trained on the FFHQ dataset, and use 40 pre-trained binary attribute classifiers [15] to assign labels to each image such that $a_i = 1$ if the image contains the attribute a_i, and $a_i = 0$ otherwise.

3.3 Identifying Channels that Control Certain Attributes

For a target attribute a_t such as *eyeglasses*, we first propose a simple approach that identifies a single style channel $s_{i,j}$ responsible for controlling the target attribute, where layer and channel indices are denoted by i and j, respectively. We assume that there is a binary classifier C_{a_t} corresponding to the target attribute, such as pre-trained CelebA binary classifiers [15]. The identified style channel $s_{i,j}$ is then used for debiasing the GAN model with respect to single (Sect. 3.4) and multiple attributes (Sect. 3.5).

To identify $s_{i,j}$, we first generate N random noise vectors to obtain their style codes using StyleGAN2. Given an arbitrary style code $\mathbf{s}$, we generate two perturbed style codes by adding and subtracting a value of c at the corresponding index i and channel j. This process is repeated for N randomly generated style codes, and each perturbed style code is forward propagated through the StyleGAN2 generator to synthesize images. Finally, we identify $s_{i,j}$ corresponding to the target attribute by selecting the style channel for which the perturbation causes the highest average change in classification score over the batch of N images:

$$\arg\max_{i,j} \frac{\sum_{k=1}^{N} |C_{a_t}(\mathcal{G}(\mathbf{s} - \Delta s_{i,j})) - C_{a_t}(\mathcal{G}(\mathbf{s} + \Delta s_{i,j}))|}{N} \tag{1}$$

where $\Delta s_{i,j}$ represents c as the perturbation value, k denotes the index of the generated image, and $\mathcal{G}$ denotes the generator of StyleGAN2. In other words, we repeat the same process for each channel of the style codes and leave the values of the other style channels unchanged. In our experiments, we use the perturbation value $c = 10$ and $N = 128$.

3.4   Debiasing Single Attributes

Once we have identified a style channel $s_{i,j}$ that controls the target attribute a_t, we can perturb the value of the channel to increase or decrease the representation of the target attribute in the generated output. In our work, we use this observation to edit the parameters of a pre-trained StyleGAN2 model that can be used to generate balanced outputs with respect to the target attribute a_t.

To this end, we introduce additional bias tensors, which we call *fairstyle tensors*, into the GAN model (see Fig. 2). These tensors are added to the StyleGAN2 convolution modulations on a channel-wise manner. More specifically, for a fairstyle tensor, $\mathbf{b}$, we set $\mathbf{b}_{i,j} = c$ and $\mathbf{b}_{m,n} = 0$, where $m, n \neq i, j$, and c is initialized to 0. In other words, the values inside the fairstyle tensors are set to zero except for the channel indices i, j that correspond to the target attribute.

We then iteratively generate a batch of $N = 128$ latent codes and compute their updated style vectors. Given an arbitrary style vector $\mathbf{s}$, we then compute the updated vector $\mathbf{s}' = \mathbf{s} + \mathbf{b}$. We forward propagate these style vectors to generate a batch of images and compute the distribution of the target attribute using an attribute classifier. Our goal is to optimize fairstyle tensor $\mathbf{b}$ such that the images generated using the updated GAN model have a fair distribution with respect to the target attribute a_t. Similar to [30], we use the Kullback-Leibler divergence between the class distribution of a_t and a uniform distribution to compute a fairness loss value $\mathcal{L}_{\text{fair}}$, formulated as follows:

$$\mathcal{L}_{\text{fair}} = KL(P_D(a_t) \; || \; \mathcal{U}(a_t)) \tag{2}$$

where P_D denotes the class probability distributions and $\mathcal{U}$ denotes the uniform distribution. We used a one-dimensional gradient descent for optimizing fairstyle tensors $\mathbf{b}$. The updated GAN model with the optimized fairstyle tensors can then be used to generate images with a balanced distribution with respect to the target attribute.

3.5   Debiasing Multiple Attributes

While our first method is effective at debiasing the GAN model with respect to a single attribute such as *eyeglasses*, it does not allow for the joint debiasing of multiple attributes such as *gender and eyeglasses*. Therefore, we propose to extend our method to multiple attributes. Let a_{t_1} and a_{t_2} represent attributes that we want to jointly debias, such as *gender* and *eyeglasses*. Let s_{i_1,j_1} and s_{i_2,j_2} represent the target style channels identified by the method in Sect. 3.3 for attributes a_{t_1} and a_{t_2}, respectively. Similar to our first method, we iteratively generate $N = 128$ random noise vectors and their corresponding style codes. Given an arbitrary style code $\mathbf{s}$, we then compute the fairstyle tensor for the corresponding channels as follows:

$$
\begin{aligned}
\mathbf{b}_{i_1,j_1} &= x_2 \times \tfrac{\mathbf{s}_{i_2,j_2} - \bar{\mathbf{s}}_{i_2,j_2}}{\hat{\sigma}_{\mathbf{s}_{i_2,j_2}}} + y_2 \\
\mathbf{b}_{i_2,j_2} &= x_1 \times \tfrac{\mathbf{s}_{i_1,j_1} - \bar{\mathbf{s}}_{i_1,j_1}}{\hat{\sigma}_{\mathbf{s}_{i_1,j_1}}} + y_1
\end{aligned}
\tag{3}
$$

where x_1, y_1, x_2, y_2 are learned parameters initialized at 0 and optimized using gradient descent over a batch of N images, and $\bar{s}_{i,j}$, $\hat{\sigma}_{s_{i,j}}$ denote the mean and standard deviation for a given target style channel $s_{i,j}$ calculated as follows:

$$
\bar{\mathbf{s}}_{i,j} = \frac{1}{N} \sum_{k=1}^{N} s_{i,j}
\tag{4}
$$

$$
\hat{\sigma}_{\mathbf{s}_{i,j}}^2 = \frac{1}{N-1} \sum_{k=1}^{N} (\mathbf{s}_{i,j} - \bar{\mathbf{s}}_{i,j})^2
\tag{5}
$$

Similar to our first method, we use KL divergence as a loss function between the joint class distribution of attributes a_{t_1}, a_{t_2} and a uniform distribution. After optimizing the fairstyle tensor, we use the GAN model to produce a balanced distribution of images with respect to the target attributes.

Our method can also be extended to support joint debiasing for more than two attributes. Let the number of attributes for which we want to jointly debias our model be M and assume that we have identified a style channel $s_{i,j}$ for each target attribute. In this case, each corresponding channel of the fairstyle tensor is updated as follows:

$$
\mathbf{b}_{i_m,j_m} = \sum_{k=1,k\neq m}^{M} \left(x_{m_k} \times \frac{\mathbf{s}_{i_k,j_k} - \bar{\mathbf{s}}_{i_k,j_k}}{\hat{\sigma}_{\mathbf{s}_{i_k,j_k}}} + y_{m_k} \right)
\tag{6}
$$

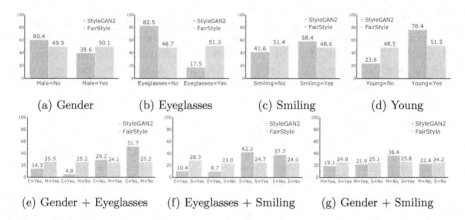

(a) Gender   (b) Eyeglasses   (c) Smiling   (d) Young

(e) Gender + Eyeglasses   (f) Eyeglasses + Smiling   (g) Gender + Smiling

Fig. 3. Distribution of single and joint attributes before and after debiasing StyleGAN2 model with our methods.

We note that Eq. 6 is simply a generalized version of Eq. 3 where each fairstyle tensor channel for a target depends on the other target channels. In this case, the number of resulting subclasses is equal to M^2 and the number of parameters to be learned is equal to $2 \times M \times (M - 1)$.

3.6   Debiasing Attributes with Text-Based Directions

The first two methods debias the GAN model with single or multiple channels, where the channels responsible for the desired attributes were identified using pre-trained attribute classifiers. However, the complexity of the attributes is limited by the availability of the classifiers. To debias even more complex attributes such as 'a black person' or 'an asian person', we debias style channels with text-based directions using CLIP. We use StyleMC [17], a text-guided image generation and manipulation framework, to identify the top style channels that control the attributes described in the input text.

In addition to the text-based directions, we also replace the attribute classifier with a CLIP-based one, since binary classifiers are not available for more complex attributes. In this case, we label images by comparing their CLIP-based distances, D_{CLIP}, with a text prompt a_t describing our target attribute and with another text prompt $a_{t_{neg}}$ negating the attribute (e.g., 'the photo of a person with curly hair' vs. 'the photo of a person with straight hair') as follows:

$$
\mathcal{C}_{a_t} = \begin{cases} 1, & \text{if } D_{\text{CLIP}}(\mathcal{G}(\mathbf{s}), a_t) < D_{\text{CLIP}}(\mathcal{G}(\mathbf{s}), a_{t_{neg}}). \\ 0, & \text{otherwise.} \end{cases} \tag{7}
$$

where $\mathbf{s}$ is an arbitrary style code, D_{CLIP} is the cosine distance between CLIP embeddings of the generated image and the text prompt a_t or $a_{t_{neg}}$, and $\mathcal{C}_{a_t}$ is the binary label assigned based on whichever text prompt (a_t or $a_{t_{neg}}$) achieves the shortest CLIP distance from the input image. We note that the negative text prompt $a_{t_{neg}}$, as in the example above, may be biased and exclude certain groups, such as *'the photo of a black person'*.

With an effective approach to assign classification scores to generated images, we identify a direction s_{a_t} consisting of one or more style channels using [17]. We use the same debiasing approach as our first method by replacing $\mathbf{b}$ with αs_{a_t}, where α is a learned manipulation strength parameter initialized as 0. Similarly, we use the binary attribute scores $\mathcal{C}_{a_t}$ calculated with CLIP to compute the fairness loss $\mathcal{L}_{\text{fair}}$ and optimize the *fairstyle tensors*.

4 Experiments

In this section, we explain our experimental setup and evaluate the proposed methods using StyleGAN2 trained on the FFHQ dataset. Furthermore, we show that our methods effectively debias StyleGAN2 without requiring model training or affecting the quality of generation. Next, we compare our methods to FairGen [30] and StyleFlow [1] methods.

4.1 Experimental Setup

For the first two methods, we identify a layer and a style channel for the *gender, eyeglasses, smiling* and *age* attributes and use them in our single or multiple attribute debiasing methods as described in Sect. 3.4 and Sect. 3.5. For the third method, described in Sect. 3.6, we experiment with a variety of simple and complex attributes such as *'a person with eyeglasses'*, *'a smiling person'*, *'a black person'*, *'an asian person'* using [17]. We generate and label 1000 images to compute the mean and std statistics for our second method.

For our experiments, we use the official pre-trained StyleGAN2 models and binary attribute classifiers pre-trained with the CelebA-HQ dataset[1]. The architecture of the binary classifiers is described in Appendix A. To identify attribute-relevant style channels, we exclude s_{tRGB} layers from the style channel search since they cause entangled manipulations [38]. Following [17], we also exclude the style channels of the last four blocks from the search, as they represent very fine-grained features.

For the comparison with FairGen, we use the pre-trained GMM models[2] and we had to limit our comparison to the available pre-trained models in Table 1. We used the StyleFlow's official implementation[3] to uniformly sample latent codes from each attribute group. Although StyleFlow is not intended for fairness, we use it for conditional sampling similar to [30]. In StyleFlow, we had to limit our comparisons to the available attributes *gender, smiling, eyeglasses* and *age* and their multiple attributes *age and eyeglasses, age and gender, gender and eyeglasses*. We exclude the comparison for *racial attributes* for both methods because no pre-trained models were available for these attributes and the training

---

[1] https://github.com/NVlabs/stylegan2.

[2] https://github.com/genforce/fairgen.

[3] https://github.com/RameenAbdal/StyleFlow.

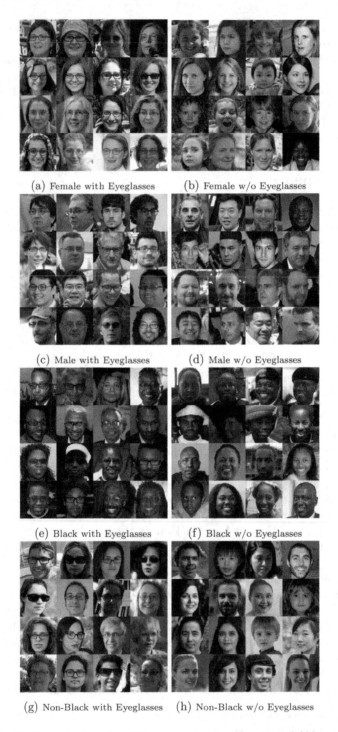

(a) Female with Eyeglasses   (b) Female w/o Eyeglasses

(c) Male with Eyeglasses   (d) Male w/o Eyeglasses

(e) Black with Eyeglasses   (f) Black w/o Eyeglasses

(g) Non-Black with Eyeglasses   (h) Non-Black w/o Eyeglasses

Fig. 4. Qualitative results for fair image generation in GANs with **Gender+Eyeglasses** and **Black+Eyeglasses** attributes.

code was not available to train new ones. We run all experiments, including comparisons, on same server using a single GeForce GTX Titan X GPU (see Appendix D for runtime analysis).

4.2 Fairness Analysis

To assess the fairness of the generated images, we report the KL divergence between the marginal or joint distribution of the generated images with respect to the target attributes and a uniform distribution (see Eq. 2). Our goal is to obtain a distribution with respect to one or more attributes that closely resembles a uniform distribution in order to achieve a fair distribution. To this end, we generate 10,000 images for each of our methods as well as for the pre-trained StyleGAN2 model, FFHQ dataset, FairGen and StyleFlow.

We start with our first method to debias a single target attribute, and present marginal distribution of the datasets generated with our method and the pre-trained StyleGAN2 in Fig. 3 (a-d). As can be seen in the figure, our first method can successfully debias attributes and achieves almost perfectly balanced datasets for the attributes *gender, eyeglasses, age* and *smiling*. Next, we use our second method to debias *gender and eyeglasses, eyeglasses and smiling* and *gender and smiling* attributes. As can be seen in Fig. 3 (e-g), our second method is very effective at debiasing even extremely imbalanced distributions as in the case of the *gender and eyeglasses* attributes, and can achieve a significant balance.

We then measure the KL divergence between the distribution of generated datasets and a uniform distribution, and provide a comprehensive comparative analysis with the FFHQ training dataset, pre-trained StyleGAN2, FairGen, and StyleFlow. We debias single attributes for *eyeglasses, age, smiling, gender* and joint attributes for the Age+Gender, Age+Eyeglasses, and Gender+Eyeglasses (see Table 1). As can be seen in the table, our method outperforms StyleFlow, Fairgen and the pre-trained StyleGAN model on all attributes and achieves KL divergence values that are very close to uniform distribution in all single-attribute debiasing experiments. We note that FairGen requires training separate GMM models for each attribute and sampling input latents while our method directly edits the GAN model, which can be used for sampling images like Fair-Gen, or in any downstream application.

We also perform additional single-attribute debiasing experiments for the highly biased attributes *black, asian,* and *white*. Since the CelebA classifiers did not cover these attributes, we used our CLIP-based method to debias the StyleGAN2 model for the *black, asian,* and *white* attributes. Additionally, we provide performance comparisons between our CLIP-based classifier and binary classifiers for existing attributes in Appendix E. We present the results of this experiment in Table 2. As can be seen in the table, our method achieves a distribution that is very close to a uniform distribution, and effectively produces unbiased datasets with respect to the racial attributes.

Table 1. KL Divergence between a uniform distribution and the distribution of images generated with our method, StyleFlow and FairGen. FFHQ and StyleGAN2 are included for comparison purposes.

Method	Age+Gender	Age+Glasses	Gender+Glasses	
FFHQ	0.2456	0.3546	0.2421	
StyleGAN2	0.2794	0.3836	0.2495	
StyleFlow	0.2141	0.1620	0.1214	
FairGen	3.73×10^{-2}	3.30×10^{-2}	1.85×10^{-3}	
FairStyle	2.57×10^{-2}	1.57×10^{-2}	2.41×10^{-4}	
	Glasses	Age	Smiling	Gender
FFHQ	0.186	0.091	0.005	0.015
StyleGAN2	0.180	0.109	0.011	0.018
StyleFlow	0.061	3.98×10^{-4}	0.045	0.023
FairGen	7.07×10^{-4}	1.77×10^{-3}	1.80×10^{-5}	4.21×10^{-4}
FairStyle	0	1.80×10^{-7}	8×10^{-8}	3.20×10^{-7}

4.3 Qualitative Results

We use our methods to debias StyleGAN2 for multiple attributes and show the generated images in Fig. 1 and Fig. 4. As can be seen in the figures, our multi-attribute debiasing method generates balanced images for the attributes *gender with eyeglasses* (Fig. 4 (a-d)), and our CLIP-based method generates balanced images for the attributes *gender and black* (Fig. 1 (a-d)) and attributes *black and eyeglasses* (Fig. 4) (e-h)).

4.4 Generation Quality

We note that a fair generative model should not compromise on generation quality to maintain its usefulness. To ensure that our methods generate high quality and diverse images, we report the Fréchet Inception Distance (FID) between sets of $10K$ images generated by the debiased StyleGAN2 model produced by our method and by the pre-trained StyleGAN2 model. Unlike our method, FairGen and StyleFlow do not edit the GAN model, but rely on subsampling latent vectors from GMM or normalizing flows models. Therefore, we exclude them from the FID experiments.

To test image quality after debiasing the GAN model, we use the attribute pairs *gender and eyeglasses, race and gender* and *race and eyeglasses* to compute the FID scores of the debiased datasets. While the pre-trained StyleGAN2 model achieves a FID score of 14.11, our method achieves fairly similar FID score of 14.72 (a lower FID score is better). Note that a small increase in FID scores is expected as the distribution of generated images is shifted for debiasing compared to the real images from the training data. However, we note that the

Table 2. KL Divergence between a uniform distribution and the distribution of images generated by our text-based method to debias the *black*, *asian*, and *white* attributes. FFHQ and StyleGAN2 are included for comparison purposes.

Method	Black	Asian	White
FFHQ	0.576	0.279	0.042
StyleGAN2	0.603	0.319	0.057
FairStyle	8.00×10^{-6}	7.20×10^{-7}	2×10^{-6}

increase in FID score is negligible and the debiased GAN model still generates high quality images (see Fig. 1 and Fig. 4).

5   Limitations and Broader Impact

While our proposed method is effective in debiasing GAN models, it requires pre-trained attribute classifiers for style code optimization. We note that the debiasing process can be affected by biases in these classifiers, a problem that also occurs in the competing methods. This is especially important when debiasing attributes that are known to be biased, such as racial attributes like *black* or *asian*.

6   Conclusion

Generative models are only as fair as the data sets on which they are trained. In this work, we attempt to address this problem and propose three novel methods for debiasing a pre-trained StyleGAN2 model to allow fairer data generation with respect to a single or multiple target attributes. Unlike previous work that requires training a separate model for each target attribute or subsampling from the latent space to generate debiased datasets, our method restricts the debiasing process to the style space of StyleGAN2 and directly edits the GAN model for fast and stable fair data generation. In our experiments, we have shown that our method is not only effective in debiasing, but also does not affect the generation quality. We believe that our method is not only useful for generating fairer data, but also our debiased models can serve as a fairer framework for various applications built on StyleGAN2. Our method is currently applicable to style-based architectures such as StyleGAN2 since it directly benefits from stylespace. However, we consider extending our method to other architectures such as BigGAN as future work.

Acknowledgments. This publication has been produced benefiting from the 2232 International Fellowship for Outstanding Researchers Program of TUBITAK (Project No: 118c321).

References

1. Abdal, R., Zhu, P., Mitra, N.J., Wonka, P.: StyleFlow: attribute-conditioned exploration of StyleGan-generated images using conditional continuous normalizing flows. arXiv preprint arXiv:2008.02401 (2021)
2. Agarwal, A., Beygelzimer, A., Dudík, M., Langford, J., Wallach, H.M.: A reductions approach to fair classification. arXiv preprint arXiv:1803.02453 (2018)
3. Azadi, S., Olsson, C., Darrell, T., Goodfellow, I.J., Odena, A.: Discriminator rejection sampling. arXiv preprint arXiv:1810.06758 (2019)
4. Bau, D., Liu, S., Wang, T., Zhu, J.Y., Torralba, A.: Rewriting a deep generative model. arXiv preprint arXiv:2007.15646 (2020)
5. Brock, A., Donahue, J., Simonyan, K.: Large scale GAN training for high fidelity natural image synthesis. CoRR abs/1809.11096, arXiv preprint arXiv:1809.11096 (2018)
6. Buolamwini, J., Gebru, T.: Gender shades: intersectional accuracy disparities in commercial gender classification. In: FAT (2018)
7. Feldman, M.: Computational fairness: preventing machine-learned discrimination. Ph.D. thesis, Haverford College (2015)
8. Goetschalckx, L., Andonian, A., Oliva, A., Isola, P.: GANalyze: toward visual definitions of cognitive image properties. In: Proceedings of the IEEE/CVF International Conference on Computer Vision, pp. 5744–5753 (2019)
9. Goodfellow, I., et al.: Generative adversarial nets. In: Ghahramani, Z., Welling, M., Cortes, C., Lawrence, N.D., Weinberger, K.Q. (eds.) Advances in Neural Information Processing Systems, vol. 27, pp. 2672–2680. Curran Associates, Inc. (2014). https://papers.nips.cc/paper/5423-generative-adversarial-nets.pdf
10. Grover, A., Choi, K., Shu, R., Ermon, S.: Fair generative modeling via weak supervision. In: ICML (2020)
11. Grover, A., et al.: Bias correction of learned generative models using likelihood-free importance weighting. In: DGS@ICLR (2019)
12. Hardt, M., Price, E., Srebro, N.: Equality of opportunity in supervised learning. In: NIPS (2016)
13. Härkönen, E., Hertzmann, A., Lehtinen, J., Paris, S.: GANSpace: discovering interpretable GAN controls. arXiv preprint arXiv:2004.02546 (2020)
14. Jahanian, A., Chai, L., Isola, P.: On the steerability of generative adversarial networks. arXiv preprint arXiv:1907.07171 (2019)
15. Karras, T., Laine, S., Aila, T.: A style-based generator architecture for generative adversarial networks. CoRR abs/1812.04948. arXiv preprint arxiv:1812.04948 (2018)
16. Karras, T., Laine, S., Aittala, M., Hellsten, J., Lehtinen, J., Aila, T.: Analyzing and improving the image quality of StyleGAN. In: 2020 IEEE/CVF Conference on Computer Vision and Pattern Recognition (CVPR), pp. 8107–8116 (2020)
17. Kocasari, U., Dirik, A., Tiftikci, M., Yanardag, P.: StyleMC: multi-channel based fast text-guided image generation and manipulation. In: 2022 IEEE/CVF Winter Conference on Applications of Computer Vision (WACV), pp. 3441–3450 (2022)
18. Lang, O., et al.: Explaining in style: training a GAN to explain a classifier in stylespace. arXiv preprint arxiv:2104.13369 (2021)
19. Li, S., et al.: Single image deraining: a comprehensive benchmark analysis (2019)
20. Liu, Z., Luo, P., Wang, X., Tang, X.: Deep learning face attributes in the wild. In: 2015 IEEE International Conference on Computer Vision (ICCV), pp. 3730–3738 (2015)

21. Louizos, C., Swersky, K., Li, Y., Welling, M., Zemel, R.S.: The variational fair autoencoder. In: CoRR abs/1511.00830 (2016)
22. McDuff, D., Ma, S., Song, Y., Kapoor, A.: Characterizing bias in classifiers using generative models. arXiv preprint arXiv:1906.11891 (2019)
23. Oneto, L., Chiappa, S.: Fairness in machine learning. arXiv preprint arXiv:2012.15816 (2020)
24. Patashnik, O., Wu, Z., Shechtman, E., Cohen-Or, D., Lischinski, D.: StyleCLIP: text-driven manipulation of styleGAN imagery. arXiv preprint arXiv:2103.17249 (2021)
25. Radford, A., et al.: Learning transferable visual models from natural language supervision. arXiv preprint arXiv:2103.00020 (2021)
26. Ramaswamy, V.V., Kim, S.S.Y., Russakovsky, O.: Fair attribute classification through latent space de-biasing. In: 21 IEEE/CVF Conference on Computer Vision and Pattern Recognition (CVPR), pp. 9297–9306 (2021)
27. Shen, Y., Yang, C., Tang, X., Zhou, B.: InterFaceGAN: interpreting the disentangled face representation learned by GANS. In: Transactions on Pattern Analysis and Machine Intelligence (2020)
28. Shen, Y., Zhou, B.: Closed-form factorization of latent semantics in GANs. arXiv preprint arXiv:2007.06600 (2020)
29. Sun, W., Chen, Z.: Learned image downscaling for upscaling using content adaptive resampler. IEEE Trans. Image Process. **29**, 4027–4040 (2020). https://doi.org/10.1109/tip.2020.2970248
30. Tan, S., Shen, Y., Zhou, B.: Improving the fairness of deep generative models without retraining. arXiv preprint arXiv:2012.04842 2020)
31. Tanaka, A.: Discriminator optimal transport. In: NeurIPS (2019)
32. Tanielian, U., Issenhuth, T., Dohmatob, E., Mary, J.: Learning disconnected manifolds: a no GANs land. arXiv preprint arXiv:2006.04596 2020)
33. Voynov, A., Babenko, A.: Unsupervised discovery of interpretable directions in the GAN latent space. In: International Conference on Machine Learning, pp. 9786–9796. PMLR (2020)
34. Wang, T., Yang, X., Xu, K., Chen, S., Zhang, Q., Lau, R.: Spatial attentive single-image deraining with a high quality real rain dataset (2019)
35. Wang, T.C., Liu, M.Y., Zhu, J.Y., Tao, A., Kautz, J., Catanzaro, B.: High-resolution image synthesis and semantic manipulation with conditional GANs (2017)
36. Wold, S., Esbensen, K., Geladi, P.: Principal component analysis. Chemom. Intell. Lab. Syst. **2**(1–3), 37–52 (1987)
37. Woodworth, B.E., Gunasekar, S., Ohannessian, M.I., Srebro, N.: Learning non-discriminatory predictors. arXiv preprint arXiv:1702.06081 (2017)
38. Wu, Z., Lischinski, D., Shechtman, E.: StyleSpace analysis: disentangled controls for styleGAN image generation. arXiv preprint arXiv:2011.12799 (2020)
39. Yüksel, O.K., Simsar, E., Er, E.G., Yanardag, P.: LatentCLR: a contrastive learning approach for unsupervised discovery of interpretable directions. arXiv preprint arXiv:2104.00820 (2021)
40. Zafar, M.B., Valera, I., Gomez-Rodriguez, M., Gummadi, K.P.: Fairness constraints: mechanisms for fair classification. In: AISTATS (2017)
41. Zemel, R.S., Wu, L.Y., Swersky, K., Pitassi, T., Dwork, C.: Learning fair representations. In: ICML (2013)

42. Zhang, H., et al.: StackGAN++: realistic image synthesis with stacked generative adversarial networks. CoRR abs/1710.10916, arXiv preprint arXiv:1710.10916 (2017)
43. Zhu, J., Park, T., Isola, P., Efros, A.A.: Unpaired image-to-image translation using cycle-consistent adversarial networks. CoRR abs/1703.10593, arXiv preprint arXiv:1703.10593 (2017)

Distilling the Undistillable: Learning from a Nasty Teacher

Surgan Jandial[1]([✉]), Yash Khasbage[2], Arghya Pal[3],
Vineeth N. Balasubramanian[2], and Balaji Krishnamurthy[1]

[1] Adobe MDSR Labs, Bangalore, India
jandialsurgan@gmail.com
[2] Indian Institute of Technology, Hyderabad, Sangareddy, India
[3] Department of Psychiatry and Radiology, Harvard University, Cambridge, USA

Abstract. The inadvertent stealing of private/sensitive information using Knowledge Distillation (KD) has been getting significant attention recently and has guided subsequent defense efforts considering its critical nature. Recent work *Nasty Teacher* proposed to develop teachers which can not be distilled or imitated by models attacking it. However, the promise of confidentiality offered by a nasty teacher is not well studied, and as a further step to strengthen against such loopholes, we attempt to bypass its defense and steal (or extract) information in its presence successfully. Specifically, we analyze *Nasty Teacher* from two different directions and subsequently leverage them carefully to develop simple yet efficient methodologies, named as *HTC* and *SCM*, which increase the learning from Nasty Teacher by upto 68.63% on standard datasets. Additionally, we also explore an improvised defense method based on our insights of stealing. Our detailed set of experiments and ablations on diverse models/settings demonstrate the efficacy of our approach.

Keywords: Knowledge distillation · Model stealing · Privacy

1 Introduction

Knowledge Distillation utilizes the outputs of a pre-trained model (i.e. teacher) to train a generally smaller model (i.e. student). Typically, KD methods are used to compress models that are wide, deep and require significant computational resources and pose challenges to model deployment. Over the years, KD methods have seen success in various settings beyond model compression including few-shot learning [29], continual learning [6], and adversarial robustness [11], to name a few – highlighting its importance in training DNN models. However, recently, there has been a growing concern of misusing KD methods as a means to steal the implicit model knowledge of a teacher model that could be proprietary and confidential to an organization. KD methods provide an inadvertent pathway for leak of intellectual property that could potentially be a threat for science and society. Surprisingly, the importance of defending against such KD-based stealing was only recently explored in [19,22], making this a timely and important topic.

S. Avidan et al. (Eds.): ECCV 2022, LNCS 13673, pp. 587–603, 2022.
https://doi.org/10.1007/978-3-031-19778-9_34

In particular, [22] recently proposed a defense mechanism to protect such KD-based stealing of intellectual property using a training strategy called the 'Nasty Teacher'. This strategy attempts to transform the original teacher into a model that is *'undistillable'*, i.e., any student model that attempts to learn from such a teacher gets significantly degraded performance. This method maximally disturbs incorrect class logits (a significant source of model knowledge), which produces confusing outputs devoid of clear, meaningful information. This method showed promising results in defending against such KD-based stealing from DNN models. However, any security-related technology development requires simultaneous progress of both attacks and defenses for sturdy progress of the field, and eventually lead to the development of robust models. In this work, we seek to test the extent of the defense obtained by the 'Nasty Teacher' [22], and show that it is possible to recover model knowledge despite this defense using the logit outputs of such a teacher. Subsequently, we leverage the garnered insights and propose a simple yet effective defense strategy, which significantly improves defense against KD-based stealing.

To this end, we ask two key questions: (i) can we transform the outputs of the Nasty Teacher to reduce the extent of confusion, and thus be able to steal despite is defense? and (ii) can we transform the outputs of the Nasty Teacher to recover hidden essential relationships between the class logits? To answer these two questions, we propose two approaches – High-Temperature Composition (HTC) which systematically reduces confusion in the logits and Sequence of Contrastive Model (SCM) which systematically recovers relationships between the logits. These approaches result in performance improvement of KD, thereby highlighting the continued vulnerability of DNN models to KD-based stealing. Because of their generic formulation and simplicity, we believe our proposed ideas could apply well to similar approaches that may be developed in future along the same lines as the Nasty Teacher. To summarize, this work analyzes key attributes of output scores (which capture the strength and clarity of model knowledge) that could stimulate knowledge stealing and thereby leverages those to strengthen defenses against such attacks too. Our key contributions are summarized as follows:

- We draw attention to the recently identified vulnerability of KD methods in model-stealing, and analyze the first defense method in this direction, i.e. Nasty Teacher, from two perspectives: (i) reducing the extent of confusion in the class logit outputs; and (ii) extracting essential relationship information from the class logit outputs. We develop two simple yet effective strategies – High Temperature Composition (HTC) and Sequence of Contrastive Model (SCM) – which can undo the defense of the Nasty Teacher, pointing to the need for better defenses in this domain.
- Secondly, we leverage our obtained insights and propose an extension of Nasty Teacher, which outperforms the earlier defense under similar settings.
- We conduct exhaustive experiments and ablation studies on standard benchmark datasets and models to demonstrate the effectiveness of our approaches.

We hope that our efforts in this work will provide important insights and encourage further investigation on a critical problem with DNN models in contemporary times where privacy and confidentiality are increasingly valued.

2   Related Work

We discuss prior work both from perspectives of Knowledge Distillation (KD) as well as its use in model-stealing below.

Knowledge Distillation: KD methods transfer knowledge from a larger network (referred to as *teacher*) to a smaller network (referred to as *student*) by enforcing students to match the teacher's output. With seminal works [4,14] laying the foundation, KD has gained wide popularity in recent years. The initial techniques for KD mainly focused on distilling knowledge from logits or probabilities. This idea got further extended to distilling features in [28,31,36,40], and many others. In all such methods, KD is used to improve the performance of the student model in various settings. More detailed surveys on KD can be found in [12,21,35]. Our focus in this work, however, is on recent works [19,22,37], which have discussed how KD can unintentionally expose threats to Intellectual Property (IP) and private content of the underlying DNN models and data, thereby motivating a new, important direction in KD methods.

Model Stealing and KD: Model stealing involves stealing any information from a DNN model that is desired to be inaccessible to an adversary/end-user. Such stealing can happen in multiple ways: *(1) Model Extraction as a Black Box.* An adversary could query existing model-based software, and with just its outputs clones the knowledge into a model of their own; *(2) Using Data Inputs.* An adversary may potentially access similar/same data as the victim, which can be used to extract knowledge/IP; or *Using Model Architecture/Parameters.* An adversary may attempt to extract critical model information – such as the architecture type or the entire model file – through unintentional leaks, academic publications or other means. There have been a few disparate efforts in the past to protect against model/IP stealing in different contexts such as watermark-based methods [34,41], passport-based methods [8,42], dataset inference [25], and so on. These methods focused on verifying ownership, while other methods such as [15,17] focused on defending against few model extraction attacks. However, the focus of these efforts was different from the one discussed herein. In this work, we specifically explore the recently highlighted problem of KD-based model stealing [19,22]. As noted in [19,22], most existing verification and defense methods do not address KD-based stealing, leaving this rather critical problem vulnerable. Our work helps analyze the first defense for KD-based stealing [22], identifies loopholes using simple strategies and also leverages them to propose a newer defense to this problem. We believe our findings will accelerate further efforts in this important space. The work closest to ours is one that has been recently published – Skeptical Student [19] – which probes the confidentiality of [22] by appropriately designing the student (or hacker) architecture. Our approach in this work is different, and focuses on mechanisms of student training, without changing the architecture.[1]

3   Learning from a Nasty Teacher

3.1   Background

Knowledge Distillation (KD): KD methods train a smaller student network, θ_s, with the outputs of a typically large pre-trained teacher network, θ_t alongside the ground-truth labels. Given an input image $\mathbf{x}$, the output logits of student given by $\mathbf{z}_s = \theta_s(\mathbf{x})$ and teacher logits given by $\mathbf{z}_t = \theta_t(\mathbf{x})$, a temperature parameter τ is used to soften the logits and obtain a transformed output probability vector using the softmax function:

$$\mathbf{y}_s = softmax(\mathbf{z}_s/\tau), \mathbf{y}_t = softmax(\mathbf{z}_t/\tau) \tag{1}$$

where $\mathbf{y}_s$ and $\mathbf{y}_t$ are the new output probability vectors of the student and teacher, respectively. The final loss function used to train the student model is given by:

$$\mathcal{L} = \alpha \cdot \lambda \cdot KL(y_s, y_t) + (1 - \alpha) \cdot \mathcal{L}_{CE} \tag{2}$$

where KL stands for Kullback-Leibler divergence, ($\mathcal{L}_{CE}$) represents standard cross-entropy loss, and λ, α are two hyperparameters to control the importance of the loss function terms ($\lambda = \tau^2$ generally).

KD-Based Stealing: Given a stealer (or student) model, denoted by θ_s, and a victim (or teacher) θ_t, the stealer is said to succeed in stealing knowledge using KD if by using the input-output information of the victim, it can grasp some additional knowledge which is not accessible in the victim's absence. As stated in [22], this phenomenon can be measured in terms of difference in maximum accuracy of stealer with and without stealing from victim. Formally, stealing is said to happen if:

$$Acc_w(KD(\theta_s, \theta_t)) > Acc_{wo}(\theta_s) \tag{3}$$

where the left expression refers to the accuracy with stealing, and the right one refers to accuracy without stealing.

Defense Against KD Based Stealing: Following [22], we consider a method M as defense, if it degrades the student's tendency (or accuracy) of stealing. Formally, considering the accuracy of stealer without defense M as $Acc_w(KD(\theta_s, \theta_t))$ and with defense as $Acc_{wm}(KD(M(\theta_t, \theta_t)))$, M is said to be a defense if:

$$Acc_{wm}(KD(M(\theta_s, \theta_t))) < Acc_w(KD(\theta_s, \theta_t)) \tag{4}$$

---

[1] Code available at https://github.com/surgan12/NastyAttacks.

Nasty Teacher (NT) [22]: The Nasty Teacher methodology transforms the original model to a model which has accuracy as high as the original model (to ensure model usability) but whose output distribution (or logits) significantly camouflages the meaningful information.

Formally, given a teacher model θ_t, they output a nasty teacher model θ_n trained by minimizing cross-entropy loss $\mathcal{L}_{CE}$ with target labels y (to ensure high accuracy) and also by maximizing KL-Divergence $\mathcal{L}_{KL}$ with the outputs of the original teacher (to maximally contrast or disturb from the original and create a confusing distribution). This can be written as:

$$\mathcal{L}_n(\mathbf{x}, y) = \mathcal{L}_{ce}(\theta_n(\mathbf{x}), y) - \omega \cdot \tau_A^2 \cdot \mathcal{L}_{KL}(\theta_n(\mathbf{x}), \theta_t(\mathbf{x})) \qquad (5)$$

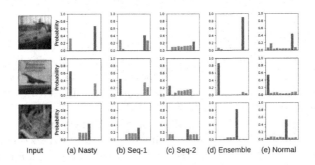

Fig. 1. Softmax Outputs of: (a) Nasty Teacher; (b) Seq-1 (Intermediate model S^i in Sect. 3.4); (c) Seq-2 (Similar to Seq-1); (d) Ensemble of Seq-1 and Seq-2 as used in SCM; and (e) Normal Teacher. Note that the class output distribution of the ensemble is similar to the original (normal) teacher. Maroon = Target class; Orange = other classes.

where ω is a weighting parameter, and τ_A^2 is a temperature parameter. Figure 1(a) provides a visual illustration of Nasty Teacher's outputs after softmax. We see that when compared to a normal teacher model in Fig. 1(e), it maintains correct class assignments but significantly changes the semantic information contained in the class distribution.

3.2 Feasibility of KD Based Stealing

As discussed earlier, standard KD techniques [12, 14, 21, 35] learn well with just the outputs of the teacher and hence are well-suited for stealing models released as APIs, MLaaS, so on (known as the black-box setting). However, it is also true that the performance of KD methods relies on factors such as training data, architecture choice and the amount of information revealed in the outputs. Thus, one might argue that we can permanently restrict attackers' access to these and prevent KD-based stealing attacks. We now discuss each of these and illustrate the feasibility of KD-based attacks. **(1) Restricting Access to Training Data:** While developers try their best to protect such IP assets, as discussed by [19], there can continue to be numerous reasons for concern: (i) The developers might have bought the data from a vendor who can potentially sell it to others; (ii) Intentionally or not, there is a distinct possibility for data leaks; (iii) Many datasets are either similar to or subsets of large-scale public datasets (ImageNet [32], BDD100k [38], so on), which can be effectively used as proxies; or (iv) Model inversion techniques can be used to recover training data from a pre-trained model [3,16,30,37,43] both in white-box and black box settings. Such methods [16], in fact, do not even require the soft outputs, just the hard predicted label from the model suffices. Thus, as these methods evolve, we can only expect an adversary to become capable of obtaining training data of sufficient quantity and quality to allow such KD-based stealing. **(2) Restricting Access to Architecture:** While developers may not reveal the architecture information completely, common development practices still pose concerns for safety: (i) Most applications simply utilize architectures from existing model hubs [1,2], sometimes even with the same pre-trained weights (transfer learning), which narrow down the options an adversary needs to try; (ii) Availability of additional tools such as AutoML [10,27], Neural Architecture Search (NAS) [7,20] can help attackers search for architectures that match a specific criteria. When combined with the increasingly available compute power (in terms of TPUs, GPUs), this can make models significantly vulnerable to attacks; (iii) With advancements in KD methods, it has been shown that knowledge can be distilled from any architecture to the other: [9] shows distillation with same capacity networks, [39] shows distillation from even poorly trained networks, and so on. Besides, KD has also witnessed techniques that require no data information and still achieve distillation (i.e. data-free distillation [5,37]). Hence, more opportunities for an attacker to carry out KD-based stealing. **(3) Releasing Incomplete or Randomly Noised Teacher Outputs:** The degree of exposition (i.e. the number of classes revealed) and the clarity of scores (i.e. ease of understanding and inferring from scores) play a vital role in ensuring the quality of knowledge transfer. Hence, one might argue that releasing only top-K class scores can help contain attackers; however, such an approach is infeasible in many use cases where it is necessary to fetch the entire score map. One might also consider adding random noise to make teacher outputs undistillable. This approach generally lowers model performance but also make its failure tracking difficult.

The above discussion motivates the need to develop fundamentally sound strategies to protect against stealing. To this end, we analyze "Nasty Teacher" [22] from two different directions and subsequently leverage insights from KD literature to propose simple yet effective approaches to show that it is still vulnerable to knowledge stealing. We name our attack methods as: *"High Temperature Composition (HTC)"* and *"Sequence of Contrastive Models (SCM)"*, and describe them below. We explain our methods using the Nasty Teacher as the pivot, primarily because it is the only known KD-stealing defense method at this time. Our strategies however are general, and can be applied to any KD based stealing method.

3.3   High Temperature Composition: HTC

Motivation: Nasty Teacher Creates Confusing Signals. In Fig. 1, we observe that the original teacher θ_t emulates a single-peak distribution and consistently has low scores for incorrect classes. Now, because the Nasty Teacher is trained to contrast with the original teacher, it produces high scores for few incorrect classes, and thus results in a multi-peak distribution (see Fig 1b). In particular, a few incorrect classes score almost as high as the correct class while other incorrect classes score almost a zero, which, as discussed in [22] introduces confusion in the outputs. We attribute this confusion to two key aspects: (i) some low-scoring incorrect classes getting ignored, and (ii) some high-scoring incorrect classes behaving as importantly as the correct class. Fig 2c shows a visualization of this observation. Since the student model is now forced to learn these incorrect peaks as equally important as the correct class, it gets a false signal and diverges while training.

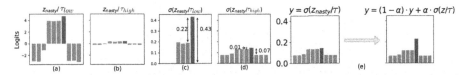

Fig. 2. The effect of temperature in HTC. We demonstrate the logits and probabilities at low temperature (as generally used in KD) and high temperature (as used in HTC). **(a)** Logits at low temperature $\tau_{low} = 4$, **(b)** Logits at high temperature $\tau_{high} = 50$, **(c)** Probabilities at τ_{low}, **(d)** Probabilities at τ_{high}, **(e)** Composing with one-hot to increase the peak.

Proposition. *Transform the output to reduce the degree of confusion in them.*

Method. We hypothesize that distillation from defenses such as Nasty Teacher can be improved by increasing the relative importance of low-scoring incorrect classes and including their presence in the output. Increasing the importance of low-scoring incorrect classes makes the high-scoring incorrect classes lesser important, thus reducing confusion. We note that this idea can be used generically, even independent of the Nasty Teacher's defense. To this end, we first soften the teacher's outputs with a high temperature τ ($\tau > 50$ in our case). Figure 2b shows how this reduces the relative disparity among the scores and brings them closer, thus helping reduce confusion. From the softmax outputs in Fig. 2d, we further see that this not only allows the other incorrect classes to be viewed in the output but also gives rise to relationships (or variations) which were earlier not visible. Formally, the above operation can be written as:

$$\mathbf{y}_{nasty} = softmax(\mathbf{z}_{nasty}/\tau) \tag{6}$$

Although we get a much more informative output, the above transformation does also reduce the relative peak of the correct class, which for distillation may not be ideal. We overcome this by using a convex combination of $\mathbf{y}_{nasty}$ with the one-hot target vector to obtain the final output $\mathbf{y}_{net}$, which makes this strategy more meaningful (see Fig. 2)):

$$\mathbf{y}_{net} = (1 - \alpha) \cdot \mathbf{y} + \alpha \cdot \mathbf{y}_{nasty} \tag{7}$$

In the above discussion, we propose to create our own training targets which satisfy the two properties to learn despite the Nasty Teacher's defense: (i) has a high peak for the correct class; and (ii) has the rich semantic class score information. Finally, to learn from this teacher and match its distributions, we minimize the cross-entropy lpss between student probabilities ($\mathbf{s} = softmax(\mathbf{z}_{student})$) and HTC teacher ($\mathbf{y}_{net}$) targets as:

$$\mathcal{L}_{\mathcal{HTC}} = -\sum_i \mathbf{y}_{net,i} \cdot \log \mathbf{s}_i$$

Combining the above with Eq. 7, $\mathcal{L}_{CE}$ as cross-entropy loss and $\mathcal{L}_{KL}$ as KL-Divergence, we can now write the above as:

$$\mathcal{L}_{\mathcal{HTC}} = -\sum_i ((1-\alpha) \cdot \mathbf{y}_i + \alpha \cdot \mathbf{y}_{nasty,i}) \log \mathbf{s}_i$$

$$= -(1-\alpha) \cdot \sum_i \mathbf{y}_i \cdot \log \mathbf{s}_i - \alpha \cdot \sum_i \mathbf{y}_{nasty,i} \cdot \log \mathbf{s}_i$$

$$= (1-\alpha) \cdot \mathcal{L}_{CE}(\mathbf{s}, \mathbf{y}) + \alpha \cdot \mathcal{L}_{CE}(\mathbf{s}, \mathbf{y}_{nasty}) \tag{8}$$

$$\mathcal{L}_{\mathcal{HTC}} = (1-\alpha) \cdot \mathcal{L}_{CE}(\mathbf{s}, \mathbf{y}) + \alpha \cdot m \cdot \mathcal{L}_{KL}(\mathbf{s}, \mathbf{y}_{nasty}) \tag{9}$$

In Eq. 9, we see that $\mathcal{L}_{CE}$ is replaced with $\mathcal{L}_{KL}$. Here, we use the fact that cross-entropy loss and KL-divergence differ by a term $\sum_i \mathbf{y}_{nasty,i} \log \mathbf{y}_{nasty,i}$, which remains a constant for student gradient computation because of fixed teacher outputs $\mathbf{y}_{nasty}$. $\mathcal{L}_{\mathcal{HTC}}$ is thus a KD-loss similar to what was discussed in Sect. 3.1. To adjust the extent of knowledge transfer, we finally re-weight the KL-divergence term with a hyperparameter multiplier m. Conceptually, m does not make a difference to the idea, but we observe this to be useful while training. Figure 3a provides a visualization for this approach.

3.4   Sequence of Contrastive Models: SCM

Motivation: Nasty Hides Essential Information. As Nasty Teacher selectively causes some incorrect classes to exhibit peaks while inhibiting scores for others, it hides certain inter-class relationships to protect against KD-based attacks.

Proposition. *Transform the output to extract/recover the essential class relationships or possibly the entire original teacher distribution*

Method. To begin with, we ask the question - what would happen if we used Eq. 5 as is with the given nasty teacher θ_n? We would expect to see a model with accuracy as high as the teacher but with presence of class distribution peaks different from it. If we perform this operation for "k" such sequential steps, we can expect to obtain "k" potentially different output distributions. Building on this thought, we introduce a Sequential Contrastive Training strategy, wherein we form a sequence of "k" contrastive models by training each model to contrast

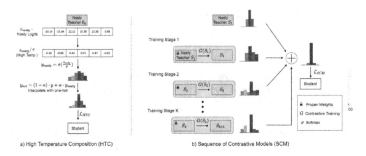

a) High Temperature Composition (HTC)   b) Sequence of Contrastive Models (SCM)

Fig. 3. *Illustration of our Methods*: High Temperature Composition (HTC) and Sequence of Contrastive Models (SCM). *HTC* learns from Nasty Teacher (NT) outputs by reducing their confusion, while *SCM* learns by extracting semantic information from them.

with the model just before it. Formally, taking the nasty teacher θ_n as the starting point of the sequence, G as the method for generating the next contrastive item in the sequence, which in our approach is the same as the one described in Eq. 5, the sequence S^k with k as the sequence length can be written as:

$$
S^k = \begin{cases} S^i = \theta_n & i = 1 \\ S^i = G(S^{i-1}) & 1 < i \leq k \end{cases} \tag{10}
$$

Thus, while maximising KL-divergence between models, each model learns a different probability distribution and has its own unique set of confusing class relationships. We then take an ensemble of their outputs, which is denoted as $\mathbf{z}_{ens}$ and use this alongside the ground truth labels y to train the student (or stealer) model, i.e.

$$
\mathcal{L}_{SCM} = (1 - \alpha) \cdot \mathcal{L}_{CE}(softmax(\mathbf{z}_s), \mathbf{y})
$$
$$
+ \alpha \cdot m \cdot \mathcal{L}_{KL}(softmax(\mathbf{z}_s/\tau), softmax(\mathbf{z}_{ens}/\tau)) \tag{11}
$$

where hyperparameters m, α, τ have the same meaning as in Eq. 9. The core intuition behind SCM is that a relationship may be important in its own distribution but only the essential relationships will be important across distributions. Therefore, by taking the ensemble, we not only capture such relationships but also obtain a distribution closer to the original teacher. This idea is visualized in Fig. 1 where (b) and (c) represent two successive checkpoints in the sequence, and (d) represents their ensemble. It can be clearly noted that different items in the sequence consistently output diversity in class relationships, and further, their ensemble illustrates a class distribution closer to the original teacher (Fig. 1e).

4 Experiments and Results

4.1 Experimental Setup

For all the experiments, we follow the same models and training configurations as used in the code provided by [22]².

Datasets and Network Baselines: For datasets, we use CIFAR-10 (C10), CIFAR-100 (C100) and TinyImageNet (TIN) datasets in our evaluation. For teacher (or victim) networks, we use ResNet18 [13] for CIFAR-10, both Resnet18 and ResNet50 for CIFAR-100 and TinyImageNet. For student (or stealer) networks, we use MobileNetv2 [33], ShuffleNetV2 [23], and Plain CNNs [26] in CIFAR-10 and CIFAR-100 and MobileNetV2, ShuffleNetV2 in TinyImageNet. For baselines, Vanilla in Table 1 refers to the cross entropy training, *Normal KD/Nasty KD* refer to the distillation (or stealing) with original/nasty teacher, *Skeptical* refers to the recent work [19], and *HTC, SCM* refers to our approaches.

Training Baselines: We follow the parameter choice from [22]. For generating Nasty Teacher in Eq. 5, τ_A is set to 4 for CIFAR-10 and 20 for CIFAR-100/TinyImageNet, correspondingly ω to 0.04, 0.005, 0.01 for CIFAR-10, CIFAR-100, TinyImageNet respectively. For both Nasty KD and Normal KD, (α, τ) parameters of distillation in Eq. 2 are set to (0.9, 4) in plain CNNs and (0.9, 20) in MobileNetV2, ShuffleNetV2. Plain CNNs are optimized with Adam [18] (LR=1e–3) for 100 epochs while MobileNetV2, ShuffleNetV2 are optimized with SGD (momentum=0.9, weight decay=5e–4, initial LR=0.1) for 160 epochs with LR decay of 10 at epoch [80, 120] in CIFAR-10 and for 200 epochs with LR decay of 5 at epoch [60, 120, 160] in CIFAR-100. Training settings in TinyImageNet are same as used in CIFAR-100. Moreover, all the experiments use batch size of 128 with standard image augmentations.

Training HTC and SCM: For both HTC and SCM, we search m in {1, 5, 10, 50}, τ in {4, 20, 50, 100}, α in {0.1,....0.9}. For TinyImageNet, we include $\tau = 200$ also in the earlier set of τ. While any number of sequence models can conceptually be chosen for SCM , our experiments only leverage a max. of 4 such Sequence Contrastive models. Note, for all these we choose the search space rather intuitively and finally present their impact in Sect. 4.3.

4.2 Quantitative Results

We report the results in Table 1 and clearly observe the degradation of student performance while learning from Nasty teacher. Subsequently, our approaches: HTC and SCM increase learning from Nasty by upto 58.75% in CIFAR-10, 68.63% in CIFAR-100 and 60.16% in TinyImageNet. We significantly outperform

---

² https://github.com/VITA-Group/Nasty-Teacher.

the recent state of the art Skeptical [19] and unlike them we also consistently outperform the Vanilla training. Moreover, many times we achieve very close performances and other few times even better performance than Normal-Teacher (i.e. stealing from unprotected victim model), see the † marked cells in Table 1. Further, we combine our training methods HTC and SCM with the novel stealing architecture Skeptical Student [19] and report improvements in Table 1.

Table 1. *Accuracy (higher is better)* of HTC and SCM against baselines. **bold** represents best performance, underline the second best in learning from Nasty Teacher. † *represents instances that even outperform the Normal KD. Abbreviations* – Tch: Teacher, Stu: Student, Skep: Skeptical [19], Res50: ResNet50, Res18: ResNet18, Mob: MobileNetV2, Shuf : ShuffleNetV2.

Dataset	Tch.	Stu.	Vanilla	Normal KD	Nasty KD	Skep. (NeurIPS'21)	HTC	SCM	Skep. +HTC	Skep. +SCM
C10	Res18	CNN	86.31	87.83	82.27	86.71	<u>87.38</u>	**87.85**	87.17	87.04
		Mob	89.58	89.30	31.73	90.53	90.03†	<u>90.48</u>†	91.45†	**91.55†**
		Shuf	91.03	91.17	79.73	91.34	91.61†	91.93†	92.45†	**92.76†**
C100	Res18	CNN	58.38	62.35	58.62	58.38	<u>61.21</u>	**61.31**	59.64	59.17
		Mob	68.90	72.75	3.15	66.89	71.01	71.06	<u>71.48</u>	**71.74**
		Shuf	71.43	74.43	63.67	70.00	74.04	**75.23†**	73.78	<u>74.23</u>
C100	Res50	CNN	58.38	61.84	58.93	59.15	**61.24**	<u>59.58</u>	59.48	59.17
		Mob	68.90	72.22	3.03	66.65	70.49	**71.66**	<u>71.54</u>	71.16
		Shuf	71.43	73.91	62.8	70.02	72.37	73.25	<u>73.60</u>	**74.73†**
TIN	Res18	Mob	55.69	61.00	0.85	47.37	56.28	**61.01†**	<u>59.05</u>	58.88
		Shuf	60.30	63.45	23.78	54.78	60.46	62.09	**63.05**	<u>62.28</u>
TIN	Res50	Mob	55.89	57.84	1.10	48.21	56.00	**59.46†**	58.56†	<u>58.88†</u>
		Shuf	60.30	62.02	24.27	56.08	60.80	61.55	**63.14†**	<u>61.92</u>

Table 2. Analysing hyperparameter choice for SCM.

	Vanilla	Nasty KD	Ours
CNN	58.38	58.62	**61.25**
ShuffleNetV2	71.43	63.67	**72.71**

(a) Effect of architecture choice.

	2	3	4
CNN	60.99	61.24	**61.31**
ShuffleNetV2	74.45	74.24	**75.23**

(b) Effect of sequence length.

4.3   Ablation Studies

Choice of τ, m in HTC: HTC (Sect 3.3) depends on softening temperature (τ) which adjusts the optimal representation, and multiplier m which adjusts the optimal weight to transfer this knowledge. Thus, we now study each of these parameters separately. We also note that α primarily controls the ground truth signal, hence, we omit varying α here and set it to 0.9. We vary the τ as 10, 20, 50, 100 with $m = 50$ on ShuffleNetV2 and present results in Fig. 4 (a),(b) to demonstrate the effect of setting temperature to an optimal higher value. We then vary m keeping the τ at 50 to observe the motivation of its careful selection in 4(d).

Choice of Architecture and k in SCM : Given a Nasty Teacher, we currently use the same architecture type to generate $S^1, S^2, ..S^k$. However, we now explore if SCM generalizes to different architecture choices in

Table 3. KL-Divergence scores of a given model (col 1) with the original teacher.

	CIFAR10 ResNet18	CIFAR100 ResNet18	CIFAR100 ResNet50
Nasty teacher	0.4446	14.6363	10.4892
SCM ensemble	**0.2471**	**5.8398**	**5.3165**

Table 2(a). Rather than obtaining seq. items as ResNet18 $\rightarrow$ ResNet18 i.e. $S^i{}_{ResNet18} = G(S^{i-1}{}_{ResNet18})$, we hereby do $S^i{}_{ShuffleNetV2} = G(S^{i-1}{}_{ResNet18})$, and finally ensemble generated ShuffleNetV2 (S^2) and original ResNet18 (S^1) to train the students (or stealers). Table 2 further shows that even with different architecture, SCM can extract information from Nasty Teacher. Moving ahead, we now ablate on *sequence length k*. From Table 2(b), we observe improvement in performance as we increase number of sequence items. This can be intuitively linked to getting better estimate of essential relationships with more number of models, hence improved distillation.

Similarity of SCM and Original Teacher: As with SCM we seek to potentially recover the original teacher distribution, thus in addition to the visualization we present in 1 we hereby conduct this study to quantitatively estimates the closeness of the SCM ensemble and normal teacher. We use KL-Divergence as our metric and present results in Table 3. It can can be clearly seen that compared to Nasty Teacher, SCM ensemble consistently results in low KL-Divergence, thereby lending support to our motivation in recovering original teacher.

4.4   Limited and No Data Setting

In this section, we consider settings to learn from the nasty teacher by using only a part of the data. Specifically, we experiment three settings and for the sake of simplicity use HTC to investigate learning from nasty under these settings.

No Label Available: Here, we consider no access to the labels for data used in Sect. 4.1. Table 5 includes the results against this setting.

Limited Data Available: Here, we evaluate the learning by varying the percent of data used [10%, 30%, 50%, 70%, 90%]. From Fig. 4(c), we observe to better extract knowledge in all data-subset fractions. Specifically, performance difference becomes even more notable when very low fraction is used (like in 10% setting, we perform approx. 15% better than Nasty Teacher). In addition, we also observe that we always remains significantly closer to the original teacher.

Table 4. No data available results for CIFAR10.

Network	Nasty	HTC
CNN	16.38	**26.03**
MobileNetV2	41.79	**52.96**
ShuffleNetV2	70.04	**76.29**

Table 5. No label available results. Using images without their ground truth.

Dataset	Network	Nasty	HTC
CIFAR-10	CNN	82.64	**87.48**
CIFAR-100	Shufflenetv2	64.41	**74.17**

No Data Available: Here, we consider the setting where no data is available. More precisely, we take the existing data-free distillation method [5], and add our method to it. Table 4 demonstrates consistent improvement while learning from nasty in this setting.

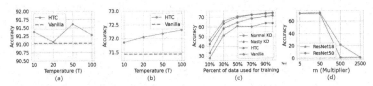

Fig. 4. Effect of Temperature: **(a)** C10, Student : ShuffleNetV2, Teacher : ResNet18 and **(b)** C100, Student : ShuffleNetV2, Teacher : ResNet50. **(c)** Effect of percentage of data. **(d)** Effect of multiplier m.

4.5   Leveraging SCM for an Improved Defense

Previously, we discuss the vulnerabilities of Nasty Teacher [22]. We now discuss this section in regards to improve "Nasty Teacher" defense.

Nasty Teacher derives its efficacy from the peaks created for the incorrect classes (Fig. 1). Along the lines that each in-correct peak adds to the confusion while learning, we hypothesize that the number of incorrect peaks in the output distribution affects the effectiveness of the defense. In general, more number of peaks can be correlated with the increased confusion, hence a better defense. However, in case of Nasty we often see the number of peaks to be not many in comparison to the total number of classes (see Fig. 1(a) for illustration), thereby creating a chance to improve Nasty's defense via increasing the number of in-correct

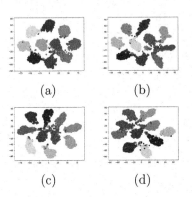

Fig. 5. t-SNE plots of features before FC layers for SCM on CIFAR-10. Model: ResNet-18, **a)** Normal Teacher **b)** Nasty Teacher **c)** Seq-1 **d)** Seq-2

peaks. In lieu of this observation, we propose to use our previously proposed Sequence of Contrastive Model Training for an improved defense. As model obtained with each SCM's step displays diverse set of peaks, we expect them to exhibit more number of peaks, largely because they were trained in a way to eventually contrast from nasty teacher (i.e. low number of peaks). Figure 1 illustrates this via columns (b),(c) where Seq-1/Seq-2 to have more number of peaks than Nasty Teacher. Thus, we choose one of these intermediate sequence models ($S^1, S^2...S^k$) for teacher and further show our results (denoted by **Ours**) in Table 6. For ease of our exploration, we typically test out with first or second model from our sequence in Sect. 3.4 as our defense teacher. Though our model incurs a small drop in accuracy ($< 2\%$), the significant improvement (sometimes, as much as 10%) it produces while defending makes it attractive for application.

Diving deep into the results, one may consider this degradation in KD related to the decrease in accuracy. We now evaluate this dimension for a better understanding. Specifically, we obtain a model with an accuracy similar to ours by training a Nasty Teacher (refer Sect. 3.1) followed by early stopping it at the desired accuracy. We dub this approach Nasty KD ES (Early Stopped) and include the results in Table 6. We observe that for a similar accuracy Nasty KD ES has a significantly poor defense against **our method**, and in some cases it even defends poorly compared to original Nasty KD. Moreover, we visualize the features of intermediate sequence models in Fig. 5 t-SNE [24] plots and infer the intermediates i.e. Seq-1 and Seq-2 to possess a similar class separation as the normal teacher Fig. 5(a) while maintaining the desired defense.

Table 6. Results of our defense, Nasty KD and Nasty KD ES. Training hyperparameters are same as discussed in Sect. 4.1.

CIFAR-10 ResNet18	Normal teacher (Acc = 95.09)	Nasty KD (Acc = 94.28)	Nasty KD ES (Acc = 93.02)	Ours (Acc = 92.99)
CNN	85.99	<u>82.27</u>	84.62	**80.13**
MobileNetV2	89.58	31.73	<u>28.58</u>	**22.12**
ShuffleNetV2	91.03	<u>79.73</u>	87.81	**73.23**
CIFAR-100 ResNet50	Normal teacher (Acc = 77.96)	Nasty KD (Acc = 77.4)	Nasty KD ES (Acc = 76.2)	Ours (Acc = 75.44)
CNN	58.38	58.93	<u>58.45</u>	**54.26**
MobileNetV2	71.43	3.03	<u>2.16</u>	**1.4**
ShuffleNetV2	68.90	63.16	<u>62.95</u>	**54.00**

5   Conclusion

In this work, we focus on the threat of KD-based model stealing; specifically, the recent work Nasty Teacher [22] which proposes a defense against such stealing.

We study [22] from two different directions and systematically show that we can still extract knowledge from Nasty Teacher with our approaches: HTC and SCM. Extensive experiments demonstrate our efficacy to extract knowledge from Nasty. Leveraging the insights we gain in our approaches, we finally also discuss an extension of Nasty Teacher that serves as a better defense. Concretely, we highlight a few dimensions that affect the defense against KD-based stealing to facilitate subsequent efforts in this direction. As our future work, we intend to improvise the existing defense and simultaneously explore such stealing in a relatively white-box setting, wherein the goal will be to defend even if the adversary gets hold of the model features/parameters.

Acknowledgements.. This work was partly supported by the Department of Science and Technology, India through the DST ICPS Data Science Cluster program. We also thank the anonymous reviewers for their valuable feedback in improving the presentation of this paper.

References

1. Pytorch model hub (2022). Accessed 8 Mar 2022. http://pytorch.org/hub/
2. Tensorflow model hub (2022). Accessed 8 Mar 2022. http://www.tensorflow.org/hub
3. Aïvodji, U., Gambs, S., Ther, T.: Gamin: an adversarial approach to black-box model inversion. ArXiv (2019)
4. Bucilua, C., Caruana, R., Niculescu-Mizil, A.: Model compression. In: Proceedings of the 12th ACM SIGKDD International Conference on Knowledge Discovery and Data Mining, KDD 2006, pp. 535–541. Association for Computing Machinery (2006)
5. Chen, H., et al.: Dafl: data-free learning of student networks. In: ICCV (2019)
6. Delange, M., et al.: A continual learning survey: defying forgetting in classification tasks. IEEE Trans. Pattern Anal. Mach. Intell. **44**, 3366–3385 (2021)
7. Elsken, T., Metzen, J.H., Hutter, F.: Simple and efficient architecture search for convolutional neural networks (2018)
8. Fan, L., Ng, K.W., Chan, C.S.: Rethinking deep neural network ownership verification: embedding passports to defeat ambiguity attacks. Adv. Neural Inf. Process. Syst. **32** (2019)
9. Furlanello, T., Lipton, Z.C., Tschannen, M., Itti, L., Anandkumar, A.: Born-again neural networks. In: International Conference on Machine Learning, ICML 2018, vol. 80, pp. 1602–1611 (2018)
10. Gaudel, R., Sebag, M.: Feature selection as a one-player game, ICML 2010, pp. 359–366. Omnipress, Madison (2010)
11. Goldblum, M., Fowl, L., Feizi, S., Goldstein, T.: Adversarially robust distillation. In: Proceedings of the AAAI Conference on Artificial Intelligence, vol. 34, no. 04, pp. 3996–4003 (2020)
12. Gou, J., Yu, B., Maybank, S.J., Tao, D.: Knowledge distillation: a survey. Int. J. Comput. Vision **129**(6), 1789–1819 (2021)
13. He, K., Zhang, X., Ren, S., Sun, J.: Deep residual learning for image recognition. In: 2016 IEEE Conference on Computer Vision and Pattern Recognition (CVPR), pp. 770–778 (2016)

14. Hinton, G., Vinyals, O., Dean, J.: Distilling the knowledge in a neural network. In: NIPS Deep Learning and Representation Learning Workshop (2015)
15. Juuti, M., Szyller, S., Dmitrenko, A., Marchal, S., Asokan, N.: Prada: protecting against dnn model stealing attacks. In: 2019 IEEE European Symposium on Security and Privacy (EuroS&P), pp. 512–527 (2019)
16. Kahla, M., Chen, S., Just, H.A., Jia, R.: Label-only model inversion attacks via boundary repulsion (To Appear CVPR 2022)
17. Kariyappa, S., Qureshi, M.K.: Defending against model stealing attacks with adaptive misinformation. In: Proceedings of the IEEE/CVF Conference on Computer Vision and Pattern Recognition (CVPR) (2020)
18. Kingma, D.P., Ba, J.: Adam: a method for stochastic optimization. In: Bengio, Y., LeCun, Y. (eds.) 3rd International Conference on Learning Representations, ICLR 2015, San Diego, CA, USA, 7–9 May 2015, Conference Track Proceedings (2015)
19. Kundu, S., Sun, Q., FU, Y., Pedram, M., Beerel, P.A.: Analyzing the confidentiality of undistillable teachers in knowledge distillation. In: 35th Neural Information Processing Systems (2021)
20. Liu, H., Simonyan, K., Yang, Y.: DARTS: differentiable architecture search. In: International Conference on Learning Representations (2019)
21. Liu, Y., Zhang, W., Wang, J., Wang, J.: Data-free knowledge transfer: a survey (2021)
22. Ma, H., Chen, T., Hu, T.K., You, C., Xie, X., Wang, Z.: Undistillable: making a nasty teacher that cannot teach students. In: International Conference on Learning Representations (2021)
23. Ma, N., Zhang, X., Zheng, H.T., Sun, J.: Shufflenet v2: practical guidelines for efficient cnn architecture design. In: Proceedings of the European Conference on Computer Vision (ECCV) (2018)
24. van der Maaten, L., Hinton, G.: Visualizing data using t-SNE. J. Mach. Learn. Res. **9**, 2579–2605 (2008)
25. Maini, P., Yaghini, M., Papernot, N.: Dataset inference: ownership resolution in machine learning. In: International Conference on Learning Representations (2021)
26. Mirzadeh, S., Farajtabar, M., Li, A., Levine, N., Matsukawa, A., Ghasemzadeh, H.: Improved knowledge distillation via teacher assistant. In: Proceedings of the AAAI Conference on Artificial Intelligence, vol. 34, 5191–5198 (2020)
27. Nargesian, F., Samulowitz, H., Khurana, U., Khalil, E.B., Turaga, D.: Learning feature engineering for classification. In: Proceedings of the 26th International Joint Conference on Artificial Intelligence, IJCAI 2017, pp. 2529–2535. AAAI Press (2017)
28. Park, W., Kim, D., Lu, Y., Cho, M.: Relational knowledge distillation. In: Proceedings of the IEEE Conference on Computer Vision and Pattern Recognition, pp. 3967–3976 (2019)
29. Rajasegaran, J., Khan, S., Hayat, M., Khan, F.S., Shah, M.: Self-supervised knowledge distillation for few-shot learning. https://arxiv.org/abs/2006.09785 (2020)
30. Razzhigaev, A., Kireev, K., Kaziakhmedov, E., Tursynbek, N., Petiushko, A.: Black-box face recovery from identity features. In: Bartoli, A., Fusiello, A. (eds.) ECCV 2020. LNCS, vol. 12539, pp. 462–475. Springer, Cham (2020). https://doi.org/10.1007/978-3-030-68238-5_34
31. Romero, A., Ballas, N., Kahou, S.E., Chassang, A., Gatta, C., Bengio, Y.: Fitnets: hints for thin deep nets. In: Bengio, Y., LeCun, Y. (eds.) International Conference on Learning Representations, ICLR 2015

32. Russakovsky, O., et al.: ImageNet Large scale visual recognition challenge. Int. J. Comput. Vision **115**(3), 211–252 (2015). https://doi.org/10.1007/s11263-015-0816-y

33. Sandler, M., Howard, A.G., Zhu, M., Zhmoginov, A., Chen, L.C.: Mobilenetv 2: inverted residuals and linear bottlenecks. In: 2018 IEEE/CVF Conference on Computer Vision and Pattern Recognition, pp. 4510–4520 (2018)

34. Uchida, Y., Nagai, Y., Sakazawa, S., Satoh, S.: Embedding watermarks into deep neural networks. In: Proceedings of the 2017 ACM on International Conference on Multimedia Retrieval, pp. 269–277 (2017)

35. Wang, L., Yoon, K.: Knowledge distillation and student-teacher learning for visual intelligence: a review and new outlooks. IEEE Trans. Pattern Anal. Mach. Intell. (01) (2021)

36. Yim, J., Joo, D., Bae, J., Kim, J.: A gift from knowledge distillation: Fast optimization, network minimization and transfer learning. In: 2017 IEEE Conference on Computer Vision and Pattern Recognition (CVPR), pp. 7130–7138 (2017)

37. Yin, H., et al.: Dreaming to distill: data-free knowledge transfer via deepinversion. In: Proceedings of the IEEE/CVF Conference on Computer Vision and Pattern Recognition (CVPR) (2020)

38. Yu, F., et al.: Bdd100k: a diverse driving dataset for heterogeneous multitask learning. In: IEEE/CVF Conference on Computer Vision and Pattern Recognition (CVPR) (2020)

39. Yuan, L., Tay, F.E., Li, G., Wang, T., Feng, J.: Revisiting knowledge distillation via label smoothing regularization. In: Proceedings of the IEEE/CVF Conference on Computer Vision and Pattern Recognition, pp. 3903–3911 (2020)

40. Zagoruyko, S., Komodakis, N.: Paying more attention to attention: improving the performance of convolutional neural networks via attention transfer. In: International Conference on Learning Representations, ICLR 2017 (2017)

41. Zhang, J., et al.: Model watermarking for image processing networks. In: Proceedings of the AAAI Conference on Artificial Intelligence, vol. 34, no. 07, pp. 12805–12812 (2020)

42. Zhang, J., Chen, D., Liao, J., Zhang, W., Hua, G., Yu, N.: Passport-aware normalization for deep model protection. Adv. Neural Inf. Process. Syst. (NeurIPS) (2020)

43. Zhang, Y., Jia, R., Pei, H., Wang, W., Li, B., Song, D.: The secret revealer: generative model-inversion attacks against deep neural networks. In: Proceedings of the IEEE/CVF Conference on Computer Vision and Pattern Recognition (CVPR) (2020)

SOS! Self-supervised Learning over Sets of Handled Objects in Egocentric Action Recognition

Victor Escorcia[✉], Ricardo Guerrero, Xiatian Zhu, and Brais Martinez

Samsung AI Center Cambridge, Cambridge, UK
{v.castillo,r.guerrero,brais.a}@samsung.com

Abstract. Learning an egocentric action recognition model from video data is challenging due to distractors in the background, *e.g.*, irrelevant objects. Further integrating object information into an action model is hence beneficial. Existing methods often leverage a generic object detector to identify and represent the objects in the scene. However, several important issues remain. Object class annotations of good quality for the target domain (dataset) are still required for learning good object representation. Moreover, previous methods deeply couple existing action models with object representations, and thus need to retrain them jointly, leading to costly and inflexible integration. To overcome both limitations, we introduce **S**elf-Supervised Learning **O**ver **S**ets (SOS), an approach to pre-train a generic Objects In Contact (OIC) representation model from video object regions detected by an off-the-shelf hand-object contact detector. Instead of augmenting object regions individually as in conventional self-supervised learning, we view the action process as a means of natural data transformations with unique spatiotemporal continuity and exploit the inherent relationships among per-video object sets. Extensive experiments on two datasets, EPIC-KITCHENS-100 and EGTEA, show that our OIC significantly boosts the performance of multiple state-of-the-art video classification models.

Keywords: Handled objects · Egocentric action recognition · Self-supervised pre-training over sets · Long-tail setup

1 Introduction

Egocentric videos recorded by wearable cameras give a unique perspective on human behaviors and the scene context [9,32,44]. Existing action recognition methods, typically developed for third-person video understanding, focus on learning from the whole video frames [4,6,15,28,34,51,60]. Unlike third-person videos where actions often take place in dramatically different background scenes

Supplementary Information The online version contains supplementary material available at https://doi.org/10.1007/978-3-031-19778-9_35.

Fig. 1. Handled objects are vital for determining actions in egocentric videos. However, most action classification models learn directly from video frames (left). This paper puts manipulated objects (right) at the forefront *without* the need for expensive and tedious fine-grained object annotations.

(e.g., swimming in a pool, cycling on the road) [6,45], egocentric videos are often collected at a specific scene (e.g., a kitchen) with similar background shared across different human actions (e.g., cutting onion and washing knife) and cluttered with distractors (e.g., a knife on the countertop). These distinctive characteristics bring extra challenges for most existing action models *without a fine-grained understanding of spatiotemporal dynamics and context.*

Recent works have incorporated information from other modalities, such as audio [28,29], narration language [3,27], and eye gaze [31], to overcome these challenges in the video action model. This is motivated by their complementary information and the modality-specific nature of distractors. Object information is a powerful complement to prior video action models [12,13,52,56]. While a video model represents the sequence as a whole, combining foreground and context, object detectors exploit bounding box annotations to explicitly model each object, separately from the others and background.

Our work falls in this line of research with a crucial difference. We consider that bounding box annotation is costly and unsuited for *long-tail* open-vocabulary object distributions across the scenes, e.g., a kitchen setting. Large-scale annotations are thus seldom possible in most cases. We tackle this issue by capitalizing an *off-the-shelf hand-object contact detector* to localize class-agnostic object regions in the video. Crucially, we introduce a novel self-supervised approach to learning a specialized representation of the detected object regions without resorting to object-level labels. Our key idea is to leverage the spatiotemporal continuity in videos as *a native context constraint* for exploiting the inherent relationships among the set of detected object regions per video. Intuitively, all the handled object regions play respective roles during an action, and they collectively provide a potentially useful context clue for learning a suitable object representation (e.g., the "pan" and "spoon" while mixing - see Fig. 1). With our class agnostic self-supervised learning, there is also a potential that the natural action class imbalance problem would be simultaneously alleviated – a typical yet understudied problem in video understanding. We term our self-supervised pre-training **S**elf-**S**upervised Learning **O**ver **S**ets (SOS). After pre-training, we transfer the specialized representation of detected objects to a target task, e.g., video classification. For this purpose, we employ an Objects in Contact (OIC) network and further fine-tune the entire representation with *weak* video-level labels. Once trained, our OIC can be flexibly integrated with existing video classification models, further boosting their performance.

We make three **contributions** in this paper. (**1**) We investigate the merits of learning a representation of handled objects for egocentric action recognition, easy to integrate over multiple state-of-the-art video action models without the need for expensive fine-grained region-level labeling on the target dataset. (**2**) To that end, we leverage an off-the-shelf hand-object contact detector to generate class-agnostic object regions and introduce a novel set self-supervised learning approach, SOS, to learn a specialized representation of object regions. SOS exploits the inherent relation (e.g., temporal continuity and concurrence) among handled objects per video to mine the underlying action context clue by treating all the objects collectively as a set. (**3**) Experiments on two egocentric video datasets showcase that our OIC, aided with our SOS pre-training, complements multiple existing video classification networks and yields state-of-the-art results in video classification. Moreover, we demonstrate the benefit of SOS for dealing with the realistic long-tail setup in videos. (Sec. 4.3).

2 Related Work

Egocentric Action Recognition. Egocentric action recognition has made significant advances in recent years, thanks to the introduction of ever-larger video benchmarks [9,10,32]. Early efforts were focused on adapting representative generic video models [15,34,51,60]. Later on, a variety of dimensions were investigated. For example, Kazakos et al. [28] combined multi-modal information (e.g., optical flow, audio) within a range of temporal offsets. Bertasius et al. [3] leveraged the language-based semantic context to supervise the learning of active object detection. Li et al. [30] investigated the pre-training of a video encoder for mitigating the domain gap from the common pre-trained video datasets (e.g., Kinetics [6]). Sudhakaran et al. [46] designed an LSTM-based Long-Short Term Attention model to locate relevant spatial parts (e.g., active objects) with temporally smooth attention. Similarly, Yan et al. [57] proposed an Interactive Prototype Learning (IPL) model for better learning active object representations by interaction with different motion patterns. Instead, Li et al. [31,32] and Liu et al. [35] used human gaze to guide the attention of deep models to interacting regions. Similar to ours, object detection has been previously exploited to improve action recognition. Indeed, early work already identified explicit hand detection as an informative queue for action recognition [1]. More recently, Wang et al. [54] exploited object regions and their spatiotemporal relations to enhance video representation learning. Similar to ours, Baradel et al. [2] devised an architecture with a video branch and an object branch. However, their approach requires object-level annotations and has no mechanism to identify foreground/active objects, thus being vulnerable to distractors. Wu et al. [56] used an attentive mechanism and incorporated long-term temporal context. Wang et al. [52] proposed a model for egocentric action recognition that relies on a complex attentive mechanism to sieve out distractors. Unlike prior work, our method does not assume fine-grained object-level annotations from the target dataset, hence being scalable in practical applications. Critically, their object representation is tightly coupled with an action model with the need for joint training. In contrast, we learn an independent object representation model enabling to flexibly benefit from off-the-shelf action models in a decoupled post-training manner.

Hand-Object Interaction (HOI). While generic Human-Object Interaction is a widely-studied topic [16,22,33,40], recent works have shown that it is possible to train large-scale domain-agnostic hand and hand-object contact detectors [37,43]. As face detection models, these models can be deployed without domain-specific retraining and still maintain reasonable effectiveness. We apply one such off-the-shelf hand-object contact model without retraining in our work [43].

Self-supervised Learning. There has been a recent surge in self-supervised learning (SSL) for learning generic feature representation models from large-scale datasets without labels [5,7,8,18,20,48]. Inspired by this trend, we introduce a novel application of exiting SSL techniques to learn a representation specific for handled objects. A direct application of an SSL algorithm to our problem does not produce optimal results. We propose two important modifications: firstly, instead of following a classic fine-tuning from domain-agnostic pre-training, e.g. over ImageNet, our method leverages on-domain SSL for solving the domain shift problem with model pre-training. To this end we use a domain-agnostic SSL model as means of pre-training, followed by domain-specific SSL training [41]. Secondly, existing SSL methods focus on single images, using two different augmentations to obtain two copies of an image. Instead, in the presence of video, sampling different timestamps and locations can create more natural and effective augmentations [39]. Inspired by this insight, we propose a variant of SwAV that operates on sets of image regions extracted from a video sequence.

Long-Tail Learning in Video. Real-world egocentric actions are typically class-imbalanced [9,10,32]. Despite extensive works in image domains [11,23, 25,26,36,58], class imbalance is still less studied in video tasks [59]. Inspired by the intriguing finding that SSL learns a suitable representation with class-imbalance scenarios [58], we evaluate if the insights also apply to videos. Unlike [58] images, video data is more complex due to the extra temporal dimension and the structured nature of action labels (*i.e.*, defined as a tuple of two imbalanced label distributions, verb, and noun) and only access to video-level supervision. This paper contributes to the first study of the relationship between SSL and long-tailed learning in egocentric video understanding.

3   Method

We aim to learn a generic object-in-contact (OIC) model for improving the performance of existing egocentric action models in a plug-and-play manner.

Overview. Given a video V and an off-the-shelf hand-object contact detector model [43], we obtain a set of object regions that likely contain objects manipulated by the hands. Let $\mathcal{B} = \{B_i\}_{i=1:M}$ denote the set of M object regions in the video. We have an object region encoder f_B so that $y_B^i = f_B(V, B_i; \theta_B)$. To that

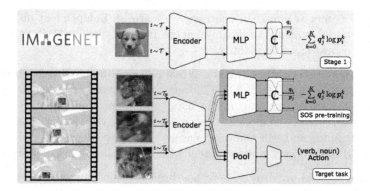

Fig. 2. Overview of the proposed self-supervised learning over sets (SOS) approach for pre-training a specialized objects in contact (OIC) representation model. Taking as input object regions extracted by an off-the-shelf hand-object contact detector in videos, we formulate a two-staged pre-training strategy. The *first* stage consists of generic self-supervision learning (e.g. ImageNet). In the *second* stage, we exploit self-supervised learning on per-video object sets using actions as the natural transformations with spatiotemporal continuity. Given a target task, we further fine-tune the representation through *video-level* action labels.

end, we propose a simple yet effective approach termed, **S**elf-**S**upervised Learning **O**ver **S**ets (SOS), to train θ_B in two steps: **(I)** First, a large-scale self-supervised learning model is used for pre-training. **(II)** Followed by, an on-domain self-supervised learning stage yielding a specialized representation better suited for the task of interest. Given a target task, standard discriminative fine-tuning is followed, using the video-level labels and standard cross-entropy as supervision. An overview of our SOS is depicted in Fig. 2.

3.1 Self-supervised Object Representation Learning from Video Object Regions

Object representations are typically learned as part of the standard object detector training pipeline [52]. However, we do not assume the availability of object-level annotations. Instead, we learn the object representation in an unsupervised manner using class-agnostic regions from the hand-object contact detector [43].

Stage I: Model pre-training. There is a lack of standard large-scale datasets for model pre-training in the egocentric video so that one could use the widely used ImageNet [42] supervised pre-trained weights for model initialization. This gives rise to an inevitable domain shift challenge for object representation learning due to the intrinsic discrepancy in data distribution. To overcome these domain shift challenges, we leverage the more domain-generic self-supervised learning (SSL) strategy for model pre-training [5,7,8,18,20,50]. In practice, due to the relatively small size of the target dataset, it is key to start with an SSL model trained on ImageNet for model initialization. In general, any existing SSL

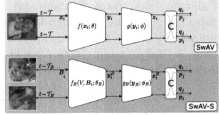

Fig. 3. Overview of the proposed SwAV-S. Schematically outlining the differences w.r.t.the standard SwAV [5] for image regions, and our self-supervised pre-training approach using videos and leveraging actions as natural transformations.

method is applicable. Based on preliminary experiments, we select the recent state-of-the-art model SwAV [5] (Fig. 3 top - Stage I).

Stage II: On-domain Self-supervised Learning Over Sets, SOS. The key challenge is how to capitalize the unlabeled object regions. Motivated by the results of [41], we perform on-domain SSL to specialize the object region encoder f_B to better represent the regions in the target domain, egocentric videos.

The promising pre-training recipe from [41] ignores a crucial piece of information from our problem definition, object regions extracted from a single video are *not* independent but *collectively* correlated due to the ongoing action. Inspired by this consideration, we introduce the notion of actions as natural data transformation exploiting the unique spatiotemporal continuity of videos and the inherent relations among a collection of objects per video. We argue that statistically predominant inter-object relationships (*e.g.*, temporal continuity and concurrence) provide a strong self-supervisory signal for learning a specialized object representation suitable for action recognition.

We consider each video V as a training sample and treat the *set construction process from all regions in the video* $\mathcal{B}$ as *a spatiotemporal transformation process*, subject to the structural variations of the performed action in the video (*i.e.*, elastic, geometrical or ambient changes that objects undergo through space and time). This is conceptually reminiscent of and complements the standard image augmentation process (e.g., cropping, flipping, jittering). Interestingly, under this perspective, our approach fits exactly on recent top-of-the-line self-supervised frameworks such as contrasting learning, clustering, instance similarity, and decorrelated representation, to name a few [5,7,8,18,20]. Without loss of generality, we present our Self-supervised Learning Over Sets approach (SOS) on top of the SwAV formulation due to their state-of-the-art results. Yet, we anticipate that our SOS could be extended to other frameworks [7,8,18,20].

SwAV Review. SwAV [5] aims to learn a feature representation that matches different views of the same image. Specifically, the representation of one of these views is used to compute a code q, which is then predicted from the code of another view. Formally, given an image x, two corresponding views x_1 and x_2 are created by applying a random transformation $t \in \mathcal{T}$, where $\mathcal{T}$ is the set of all considered transformations (typically these are synthetic, such as random crops, color jittering, Gaussian blurring, and flipping, etc.). Corresponding feature vectors $z_i = g(f(x_i; \theta); \phi)$ are generated and projected into the unit sphere, where $z_i \in \mathbb{R}^d$, f represents a backbone network with parameters θ and g a projection head with parameters ϕ. SwAV can be seen as an online clustering method, where the cluster centroids are defined by a set of learnable prototypes $c_i \in C^{K \times d}$, which are used as a linear mapping function to compute each view's code $q_i = z_i^\top C$. The objective is to predict a view's code q_i from the other view's features z_j, and the problem is formulated via cross-entropy minimization as:

$$L(z_1, z_2) = \ell(q_1, z_2) + \ell(q_2, z_1) \tag{1}$$

where the first term is

$$\ell(q_1, z_2) = -\sum_{k=0}^{K} q_1^k \log p_2^k , \tag{2}$$

where q_1 represents the prototype likelihood or soft cluster assignment of x_1, p_2^k represents the prediction of q_1 as the softmax of $z_2^\top c_k / \tau$ and τ is a temperature parameter. Additionally, q_1^k comes from Q, which normalizes all q in a mini-batch (or queue) using the Sinkhorn-Knopp algorithm. The second term of Eq. (1) is similarly defined. In practice, SwAV uses more than two views per image. More specifically, the concept of multi-crop is introduced, where crops taken as part of the augmentation strategy can be either global or local concepts of an image. Furthermore, the problem is formulated in such a way that prototype code q assignments are only done on global views, while predictions p are done using both local and global views.

Our SwAV-S. To better exploit unlabeled object regions from videos, we introduce a set structure into SwAV's formulation, resulting in a new SSL variant dubbed as *SwAV-S*. Specifically, we sample a subset of object regions from $\mathcal{B}' = \{B_i\}_{i=1:N}, \mathcal{B}' \subset \mathcal{B}$ from each video. Then, each region undergoes an independent image transformation and is treated as one view of V to be predicted (or contrasted) from another region of the same set. This set of regions are encoded, generating embedding vectors $\{z_i = g_B(f_B(V, B_i; \theta_B); \phi_B)\}_{i=1:N}$, where f_B and g_B represent a non-linear encoder function and projection head, respectively.

In contrastive learning design, we make a couple of important differences against the original SwAV. (1) At each training iteration, we sample $N > 2$ object regions $\{B_i\}_{i=1:N}$ from a video sequence V. (2) We only consider global views, which allows the expansion of terms in Eq. (1) to N, effectively treating all object regions as a set as follows:

$$L = \frac{-1}{N^2 - N} \sum_{i}^{N} \sum_{j \neq i}^{N} \sum_{k=0}^{K} q_i^k \log \left(\frac{\exp\left(\frac{1}{\tau} z_j^\top c_k\right)}{\sum_{k'} \exp\left(\frac{1}{\tau} z_j^\top c_{k'}\right)} \right) \tag{3}$$

where (i, j) indexes the pairs of regions from a video.

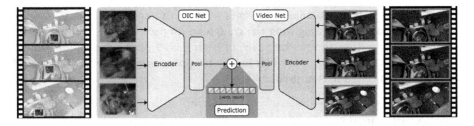

Fig. 4. Our OIC model can complement any existing video classification network, Video Net. While most existing classification networks consume the entire video frames, ours OIC only takes object regions. Their predictions are then late fused.

Discussion. While our approach shares some high-level ideas w.r.t. earlier SSL algorithms [55], SOS relies on (1) different assumptions (*e.g.*, do not require an explicit graph of relations among patches or tracking), (2) different aims (integrating object representations for action recognition), and (3) specific methodology (self-supervised learning over sets). All in all, our approach revives this line of research with a refreshing perspective and using leveraging recent insights.

3.2   Target Task Fine Tuning: OIC Net and Model Fusion

Following the typical transfer learning of SSL pipelines, The pre-trained enhanced object region encoder θ_B serves as initialization for the OIC encoder f_B addressing the target task (*cf.* Fig. 4 - OIC Net). In our case, the target task corresponds to supervised video classification using object patches.

Given a set of object regions $\mathcal{B}$ per video, we feed them through the OIC encoder, followed by a pooling module aggregating the information from all the cohort to obtain the classification logits of interest $l = h(f_B(V, \mathcal{B}; \theta)) \in \mathbb{R}^{|\mathcal{Y}|}$, where $|\mathcal{Y}|$ corresponds to the size of the label space. Note that we only have access to weak video-level supervision. We apply the standard cross-entropy loss between the logits and the video-level label to optimize the network parameters.

Class Imbalanced Fine-Tuning. To complement our SOS pre-training for tackling the class imbalance issue, we adopt the recent logit adjustment method [36] with the key idea is to impose the class distribution prior of the training data through logit regulation. For training, we optimize a logit adjustment cross-entropy loss, $L_{la} = -\log \frac{e^{f_y + \tau \log \pi_y}}{\sum_{y' \in \mathcal{y}} e^{f_{y'} + \tau \log \pi_{y'}}}$ with π_y the frequency of class y on the training set (i.e., the class prior), and τ the temperature. In our case, we impose this adjustment to the noun and verb branches separately, so their imbalance can be remedied according to their respective distribution priors.

Model Fusion. Once trained as discussed above, our OIC model can be integrated with any existing action models [4,15,34] as depicted in Fig. 4. For simplicity and flexibility, we use a weighted late-fusion of video predictions as:

$$l = \alpha_{\text{OIC}} l_{\text{OIC}} + \alpha_i l_i, \tag{4}$$

where l_{OCI}, l_i are the classification logits of our OIC and any existing model; and $\alpha_{\mathrm{OCI}}, \alpha_i$ are scalars weighting the confidence of each model. In practice, we set $\alpha_{\mathrm{OCI}}, \alpha_i$ based on the performance of each model on a pilot validation set (*e.g.*, 30% of the training set). The fusion is applied separately in the case of verb and noun-based action prediction.

4   Experiments

Datasets. We evaluate our method on two standard egocentric video datasets in the domain of kitchen environments. **EPIC-KITCHENS-100** [10] is a large-scale egocentric action recognition dataset with more than 90,000 action video clips extracted from 100 h of videos in kitchen environments. It captures a wide variety of daily activities in kitchens. The dataset is labeled using 97 verb, and 300 noun classes and their combinations define different action classes. Please refer to the **supplementary material** for results in the test server, and additional details, among others. **EGTEA** [32] is another popular egocentric video dataset consisting of 10,321 video clips annotated with 19 verb classes, 51 noun classes, and 106 action classes.

Performance Metrics. We adhere to the standard action recognition protocol [10,32,53]. Specifically, each model predicts the verb and the noun using two classification heads, and we report accuracy rates of verb, noun, and action (*i.e.* verb and noun tuple) as performance metric. For EPIC-KITCHENS-100, we report the top-k accuracy over different sets of instances. For EGTEA, we adopt the mean class accuracy on the three train/test splits.

Implementation Details. We use an off-the-shelf hand-object contact detector to extract candidate regions of interest where it is likely to find hands and manipulated objects [43]. We only consider the object regions and select those with a confidence threshold greater than 0.01 non-filtered by the typical non-maxima suppression operation of object detector pipelines [16]. Each region of interest is cropped from the original frame size and resized such that the resolution of each object region is 112×112. During training, we enable the center and size jittering as data augmentation. The jittering is proportional to the size of the region of interest and sampled from a uniform distribution $[1, 1.25)$. For each frame, we consider three regions at most. At test time, we retained the most confident detected regions. Yet, we sampled object regions irrespective of the confidence score during training for data augmentation purposes.

Our OIC network uses a 2D-CNN backbone, ResNet-50 [21], to encode each object region. Its Pool block corresponds to an integrated classifier followed by a aggregation module, the video prediction is done by classifying each object region independently, and then aggregating all the object predictions with a parameterless Mean pooling operation. We use the standard frame sampling [51], and modestly consider 8 frames per video. In contrast to prior art [4], we did not resort on additional test-time data augmentations (*e.g.* multi-crop/views) per video. Thus, the performance of our model could improve further.

Fig. 5. Qualitative Results. The green bounding boxes represent automatically detected object regions being manipulated. The left examples are corrected by our method, while the right two examples either error were maintained or flipped. (Color figure online)

During the on-domain SOS self-supervised pre-training (Stage II), we sample sets of size $N = 8$ objects per video, and apply the standard set of photometric and geometric data augmentation (*e.g.*, color jittering and cropping *cf.* [5] for more details) independently per element. We resort to single-machine training with a batch size of 256 over 400 epochs and used the default optimization hyperparameters [5]. We initialize the CNN backbone of OIC from an off-the-shelf self-supervised pre-trained network on ImageNet [5] (*i.e.*, Stage I pre-training). During the target task stage, we tune the whole OIC network end-to-end for video classification. We train with SGD using an initial learning rate of 0.02 and momentum 0.9 with a batch size of 64 videos. We decay the learning rate by a factor of 0.1 after 20 epochs. We implemented our approach in Pytorch [38], PytorchLightning [14] and the NUMFocus stack [19, 49].

4.1 Evaluation on EPIC-KITCHENS-100

Qualitative Analysis. Figure 5 depicts qualitative results, each quadrant depicts three frames from a particular video with its associated object regions, ground truth labels, and the predictions made by TSM as well as OURS (*i.e.*, TSM+OIC). Correctly predicted verbs and nouns are highlighted as green, while incorrectly predicted as red. We observe that OIC network provides additional context to guide predictions correctly. Figure 5 (bottom left) depicts an example where the noun of interest is mainly out of view during the duration of clip (only visible at the very beginning and at the end), hence the verb is also implicitly also not visible. Nevertheless, including the OIC module allows this information to be correctly captured and preserved. Similarly, Fig. 5 (top right) shows that TSM alone makes somewhat nonsensical prediction of "fill, tap", while ours predicts "wash, bowl" which is arguably visually and semantically closer to the ground truth "fill, bowl", after all filling a bowl looks much like washing a bowl. However, both TSM and ours still struggle with visually confusing noun classes, as shown in Fig. 5 (bottom right). Although both models correctly predict the verb "pour-in", they both confuse the white water kettle with a jug of milk. Perhaps surprisingly, we appreciate that TSM often struggles with seemingly simple cases (noun and verb clearly visible and executed), as shown in Fig. 5 (top left), while the inclusion of OIC greatly alleviates this problem.

Table 1. Results on the validation set of EPIC-KITCHENS-100 [10]. Modality: V=Visual; F=Optical flow. [†]: Results computed with the model weights released by the authors of [4,10]. TTDA: Test-time data-augmentation (*e.g.*, multi-crop). Underlined numbers correspond to best results across the board. Bold numbers highlight the best between a proxy model and proxy + ours. All in all, our model yields state-of-the-art results and it is versatile as improved four strong action classification models.

Modality	Method	TTDA	Overall						Unseen participants			Tail classes		
			Top-1			Top-5			Top-1			Top-1		
			Verb	Noun	Action	Verb	Noun	Action	Verb	Noun	Action	Verb	Noun	Action
V	TSM[†] [34]	✗	63.0	47.3	35.6	88.9	74.2	57.2	**54.6**	37.1	26.3	35.9	26.7	18.1
V	+ OIC	✗	**64.0**	**52.3**	**39.0**	**90.2**	**78.4**	**61.6**	53.1	**40.3**	**27.2**	**36.2**	**29.9**	**20.5**
V	SlowFast[†] [15]	✗	65.6	50.0	38.5	**90.0**	75.6	58.7	**56.7**	41.6	30.0	36.3	23.3	18.7
V	+OIC	✗	**66.5**	**53.5**	**40.9**	89.6	**77.8**	**61.8**	56.6	**43.6**	**31.1**	**37.6**	**27.3**	**20.3**
V	X-ViT[†] [4]	✗	62.9	49.1	37.7	87.5	73.8	57.1	54.4	41.7	30.5	35.7	28.0	19.42
V	+OIC	✗	**64.7**	**54.6**	**40.9**	**91.0**	**79.3**	**62.8**	**54.6**	**43.8**	**31.2**	**37.0**	**31.1**	**21.2**
V	X-ViT [4][†]	✓	68.7	56.4	44.3	90.4	79.4	64.5	57.8	47.4	34.9	38.2	31.8	22.4
V	+OIC	✓	<u>**69.3**</u>	<u>**57.9**</u>	<u>**45.7**</u>	**91.2**	<u>**81.1**</u>	<u>**66.2**</u>	**57.9**	<u>**49.3**</u>	<u>**36.3**</u>	<u>**38.6**</u>	<u>**33.1**</u>	<u>**23.7**</u>
V+F	TSM[†] [34]	✗	67.9	49.1	38.4	91.0	74.9	60.7	58.5	39.2	29.3	36.8	22.5	17.7
V+F	+OIC	✗	**68.4**	**53.7**	**41.8**	<u>**91.4**</u>	**78.7**	**64.0**	<u>**58.7**</u>	**42.7**	**30.8**	**37.1**	**26.7**	**20.1**
V+F	IPL(I3D) [53]	✗	67.82	50.87	39.87	–	–	–	–	–	–	–	–	–
V+F	IPL(R2+1D) [53]	✗	68.61	51.24	40.98	–	–	–	–	–	–	–	–	–

Baselines. For extensive comparative evaluation, we consider a variety of state-of-the-art action recognition models including (1) top CNN action models: TSM [34], and SlowFast [15] designed for generic action recognition tasks with varying architectural design for spatio-temporal representation learning, (2) a recent vision transformer: X-ViT [4] with superior cost-effective formulation for spatio-temporal attention learning, and (3) the latest egocentric action model: IPL [53] designed to learn superior active object representation subject to human motion cues. We test the effective of our OIC in improving several above methods with the proposed fusion method.

Results Analysis. We report the action recognition results in Table 1. We have the following observations: (**1**) The performance of CNN action models, SlowFast and TSM, are similar to the recently introduced X-ViT without heavy test-time data augmentation. (**2**) Importantly, our OIC further improves SlowFast(V), TSM(V+F) and X-ViT by 2.4%, 3.4%, and 3.2% on overall action accuracy, respectively. Without using computationally expensive optical flow, TSM still benefits from OIC at a similar scale. These results verify the versatility and consistent usefulness of our OIC in enhancing prior art models. As expected, the improvement is mainly achieved in noun recognition. This evidence indicates that generic action recognition methods are limited in modeling the handled objects from cluttered backgrounds and scenes. This is exactly the motivation for learning our OIC model. (**3**) We also observe that our OIC clearly improves the accuracy scores on unseen participants and tail classes. This implies that exploiting our OIC could help reduce the negative impact of domain shift (seen vs. unseen participants in this case) and mitigate the overwhelming effect from head classes to tail classes, concurrently. (**4**) Along with TSM, our method also

Table 2. Comparison against state of the art in EGTEA [32]. Modality: V=Visual; F=Optical flow; G=Gaze. *: Results are taken from [31].

Modality	Method	Split 1	Split 2	Split 3	Avg
V	TSM [34]	61.2	61.2	59.6	60.7
V	TSM+**OIC**	**62.0**	**61.9**	**60.0**	**61.3**
V+F	I3D* [6]	55.8	53.1	53.6	54.2
V+F	Ego-RNN-2S* [47]	52.4	50.1	49.1	50.5
V+F	LSTA-2S* [46]	53.0	-	-	-
V+F	MutualCtx-2S* [24]	55.7	-	-	-
V+F	Prob-ATT [31]	56.5	53.5	53.6	54.5
V+F	I3D+IPL [53]	60.2	59.0	57.9	59.1
V+F+G	I3D* [6]	53.7	50.3	49.6	51.2
V+F+G	Prob-ATT [31]	57.2	53.8	54.1	55.0

clearly outperforms the latest egocentric action model IPL designed to learn better active object representations. This indicates that without explicit region detection, the CNN model is less effective in isolating the active objects from the scenes. (5) The recent X-ViT model lifts the performance of CNN using additional test-time data augmentation (*i.e.*, averaging the results from 3 crops per video). It is worth noting that even after triplicating the computational budget, our computationally modest OIC representation stills provides a further gain of 1.4% on overall actions to this model. ***Computational complexity and runtime.*** In a 1080Ti GPU, TSM and XViT run in 12 and 66 msec. respectively, while the OIC module runs in 10.7 msec. The OIC complexity is 26 GFLOPs while XViT is much larger, 285 GFLOPs. OIC is comparatively efficient.

4.2 Evaluation on EGTEA

Baselines. Compared to EPIC-KITCHENS-100, EGTEA uniquely features eye gaze tracking information. We compare our method with the following alternatives: (1) I3D [6]: A two-stream I3D with joint training of RGB and optical flow, (2) I3D+Gaze: Instead of average pooling, the ground truth human gaze is leveraged to pool the features from the last conv layer, (3) Ego-RNN-2S [47] and LSTA-2S [46]: two recurrent networks with soft attention, (4) MutualCtx-2S [24]: A gaze-enhanced action model trained by alternating between gaze estimation and action recognition, (5) Prob-ATT [31]: A state-of-the-art joint gaze estimation and action recognition model featured with a stochastic gaze distribution formulation, (6) TSM [34]: A recent strong action recognition model with efficient temporal shift operation between nearby frames for motion modeling, (7) IPL [53]: A recent state-of-the-art egocentric action model as discussed earlier. We combine our OIC with TSM in evaluating this dataset.

Results Analysis. Table 2 reports the results. We observed that: **(1)** using gaze modality does not guarantee superior results; For example, without gaze IPL still achieves better results than Prob-ATT using gaze. This suggests that video data alone already provide rich information and the key is how to learn and extract discriminative action information with proper model design. The way to leverage the gaze data is also equally critical. **(2)** Similarly, the computationally expensive optical flow is not the highest performance promise, as indicated by the excellent performance with TSM using only 2D video frames as input. **(3)** Importantly, our OIC again further improves the performance of TSM consistently over all the splits, suggesting the generic efficacy of our method on a second test scenario.

4.3   SOS and Long-Tail Learning

Here we present a rigorous assessment on the role of our SOS pre-training for dealing with class-imbalance distributions in videos. ***Dataset and metrics.*** We perform the study in the validation set of EPIC-KITCHENS-100 using the standard metrics for evaluating long-tail learning algorithms [11], class-balanced average accuracy for verb, noun and action. Concretely, each video is weighted by the inverse of the number of instances of its corresponding label. Note that we retain the tail classes definition from [10], but the metrics reported in this section differ from those in Table 1. ***Baselines.*** We consider our OIC network aided (or not) with our SOS pre-training and using (or not) the long-tail (LT) loss of [36] during the target task fine-tuning. We also report of single-crop X-ViT [4], using the pre-trained weights of the authors, and our fused model.

Table 3. Long-tail results (accuracy) on the validation set of EPIC-KITCHENS-100, showcasing the impact of SOS for dealing with class-imbalance distributions. Refer to text for details about the metric.

	Method	SOS	LT loss [36]	Overall			Tail classes		
				Verb	Noun	Action	Verb	Noun	Action
A	**OIC**	✗	✗	18.2	21.1	8.7	13.2	11.9	6.1
B	**OIC**	✗	✓	27.5	25.0	8.1	25.4	19.9	7.1
C	**OIC**	✓	✗	20.8	25.0	**10.8**	15.9	16.7	8.6
D	**OIC**	✓	✓	<u>**30.3**</u>	**28.0**	9.4	<u>**28.6**</u>	**23.4**	8.7
E	X-ViT	✗	✗	22.1	25.9	12.8	15.9	17.8	9.5
F	X-ViT + **OIC**	✓	✓	**30.2**	<u>**31.8**</u>	<u>**15.2**</u>	25.2	<u>**24.9**</u>	<u>**12.8**</u>

Results Analysis. Table 3 reports the results. We observed that: **(1)** Our SOS pre-training indeed helps for dealing with class-imbalanced scenarios. It naturally improves noun and action classes the most, by +3.9% and +2.1% overall classes respectively (row **C** v.s. **A**). Note that aiding OIC with SOS (**C**) significantly reduced the gap between the X-ViT (**E**) and our plain OIC (**A**). **(2)** SOS is complementary to the state-of-the-art LT learning approach. SOS and the LT loss [36] yields the best results for the OIC model, except for overall action classes where SOS pre-training achieves the best result. The relatively minor setback evidences the relevance of studying LT and SSL pre-training within the context of structured labels such as actions in videos. **(3)** Our fused model (**F**) , X-ViT with OIC aided with SOS and the LT loss [36], achieves the state-of-the-art on LT accuracy for noun and action by a large margin.

Overall, we have validated the relevance and complementary of SOS for dealing with long-tail learning scenarios in egocentric action recognition.

4.4   Ablation Study

As prior art [53], we validate the major components of our approach on EPIC-KITCHENS-100 using the corresponding evaluation protocol [10].

Off-the-Shelf Self-supervised Encoder. We study the impact of using off-the-shelf supervised [38] vs. self-supervised [5] encoders for representing handled objects in the target dataset. Both encoders were trained in ImageNet [42], and serve as initialization for our OIC backbone. Table 4 row **A** and **B** report the results of supervised and self-supervised encoders, respectively. Self-supervised initialization improves the performance w.r.t. supervised initialization in noun by 1.3% and action by 0.5% without degrading verb performance. These results echo the relevance and popularity of self-supervised pre-training [17] in the domain of egocentric visual perception, which has been relatively under-explored.

Table 4. Ablation of different components of our approach on EPIC-KITCHENS-100. Rows **A–D** report the top-1 accuracy Verb, Noun, and Action of the OIC model by itself (*i.e.*, without video network fusion) for *overall* and *tail* instances [10]. OD: On-Domain pre-training in target dataset, EPIC-KITCHENS-100.

	Method	OD	Overall			Tail classes		
			Verb	Noun	Action	Verb	Noun	Action
A	Supervised pre-training	✗	49.3	44.5	27.4	32.0	23.6	14.8
B	SwAV	✗	49.2	45.8	27.9	31.2	21.2	14.0
C	SwAV	✓	49.9	47.0	28.7	30.6	23.1	14.6
D	SwAV-S	✓	**51.5**	**48.5**	**30.2**	**32.4**	**25.6**	**16.4**

Impact of Self-supervised Adaptation. We gauge the impact of adopting the off-the-shelf self-supervised representation to the domain of interest, manipulated object regions in EPIC-KITCHENS-100. For this purpose, we employ the standard SwAV loss (Eq. (1)) during the Stage II pre-training, (*cf.* Fig. 2). We use the original set of data augmentations and optimization hyper-parameters as in [5]. Table 4 row **C** reports the results of the self-supervised domain adaptation with SwAV loss over individual object regions (Fig. 3 - top). Adapting the representation helps to boost the predictive power for verb, noun and action by 0.7%, 1.2% and 0.8% w.r.t. no domain adaptation Table 4 row **B**.

Relevance of SOS. We validate the impact of SwAV-S (*i.e.*, our incarnation of SOS), which treats actions as a natural self-supervised transformation. For this purpose, we employ the SwAV-S loss (Eq. (3)) during the Stage II pre-training (see Fig. 2). We kept the same set of hyper-parameters as SwAV. Table 4 row **D** reports the results of SwAV-S. We observe the best performance across the board and a more significant boost w.r.t. on-domain SwAV (Table 4 row **C**) by 1.6% for verb, 1.5% for noun and 1.5% for action. This result validates the benefit of our novel approach for self-supervised domain adaptation.

5   Conclusions

We presented a novel approach, Self-supervised Learning Over Sets (SOS), for learning an object representation suitable for egocentric action recognition without needing object-level annotations. SOS exploits the temporal consistency and concurrence relations among a set of handled objects as a self-supervisory signal. Experiments show that prior state-of-the-art video models consistently benefit from our object representation, with improved ability to tackle the challenging long-tail setup.

References

1. Bambach, S., Lee, S., Crandall, D.J., Yu, C.: Lending a hand: detecting hands and recognizing activities in complex egocentric interactions. In: ICCV (2015)
2. Baradel, F., Neverova, N., Wolf, C., Mille, J., Mori, G.: Object level visual reasoning in videos. In: ECCV (2018)
3. Bertasius, G., Torresani, L.: COBE: contextualized object embeddings from narrated instructional video. In: NeurIPS (2020)
4. Bulat, A., Perez-Rua, J.M., Sudhakaran, S., Martinez, B., Tzimiropoulos, G.: Space-time mixing attention for video transformer. In: NeurIPS (2021)
5. Caron, M., Misra, I., Mairal, J., Goyal, P., Bojanowski, P., Joulin, A.: Unsupervised learning of visual features by contrasting cluster assignments. In: NeurIPS (2020)
6. Carreira, J., Zisserman, A.: Quo vadis, action recognition? a new model and the kinetics dataset. In: CVPR (2017)
7. Chen, T., Kornblith, S., Norouzi, M., Hinton, G.: A simple framework for contrastive learning of visual representations. In: ICML (2020)
8. Chen, X., He, K.: Exploring simple Siamese representation learning. In: CVPR (2021)
9. Damen, D., et al.: Scaling egocentric vision: the epic-kitchens dataset. In: ECCV (2018)
10. Damen, D., et al.: Rescaling egocentric vision: collection pipeline and challenges for epic-kitchens-100. In: IJCV (2021)
11. Dong, Q., Gong, S., Zhu, X.: Imbalanced deep learning by minority class incremental rectification. IEEE TPAMI **41**(6), 1367–1381 (2018)
12. Escorcia, V., Carlos Niebles, J.: Spatio-temporal human-object interactions for action recognition in videos. In: ICCVW, June 2013
13. Escorcia, V., Soldan, M., Sivic, J., Ghanem, B., Russell, B.C.: Temporal localization of moments in video collections with natural language. CoRR abs/1907.12763 (2019). arXiv:1907.12763

14. Falcon, W.: Pytorch lightning. https://github.com/PytorchLightning/pytorch-lightning (2019)
15. Feichtenhofer, C., Fan, H., Malik, J., He, K.: SlowFast networks for video recognition. In: ICCV (2019)
16. Gkioxari, G., Girshick, R., Dollár, P., He, K.: Detecting and recognizing human-object interactions. In: CVPR (2018)
17. Goyal, P., et al.: Self-supervised pretraining of visual features in the wild. CoRR (2021). arXiv:2103.01988
18. Grill, J.B., et al.: Bootstrap your own latent: a new approach to self-supervised learning. In: NeurIPS (2020)
19. Harris, C.R., et al.: Array programming with NumPy. Nature **585**(7825), 357–362 (2020)
20. He, K., Fan, H., Wu, Y., Xie, S., Girshick, R.: Momentum contrast for unsupervised visual representation learning. In: CVPR (2020)
21. He, K., Zhang, X., Ren, S., Sun, J.: Deep residual learning for image recognition. In: CVPR (2016)
22. Hou, Z., Peng, X., Qiao, Y., Tao, D.: Visual compositional learning for human-object interaction detection. In: ECCV (2020)
23. Huang, C., Li, Y., Loy, C.C., Tang, X.: Learning deep representation for imbalanced classification. In: CVPR, pp. 5375–5384 (2016)
24. Huang, Y., Cai, M., Li, Z., Lu, F., Sato, Y.: Mutual context network for jointly estimating egocentric gaze and action. IEEE TIP **29**, 7795–7806 (2020)
25. Kang, B., Li, Y., Xie, S., Yuan, Z., Feng, J.: Exploring balanced feature spaces for representation learning. In: ICLR (2021)
26. Kang, B., et al.: Decoupling representation and classifier for long-tailed recognition. In: ICLR (2020)
27. Kazakos, E., Huh, J., Nagrani, A., Zisserman, A., Damen, D.: With a little help from my temporal context: multimodal egocentric action recognition. In: BMVC (2021)
28. Kazakos, E., Nagrani, A., Zisserman, A., Damen, D.: Epic-fusion: audio-visual temporal binding for egocentric action recognition. In: ICCV (2019)
29. Kazakos, E., Nagrani, A., Zisserman, A., Damen, D.: Slow-fast auditory streams for audio recognition. In: ICASSP (2021)
30. Li, Y., Nagarajan, T., Xiong, B., Grauman, K.: Ego-Exo: Transferring visual representations from third-person to first-person videos. In: CVPR (2021)
31. Li, Y., Liu, M., Rehg, J.: In the eye of the beholder: gaze and actions in first person video. IEEE TPAMI (2021)
32. Li, Y., Liu, M., Rehg, J.M.: In the eye of beholder: Joint learning of gaze and actions in first person video. In: ECCV (2018)
33. Li, Y.L., Liu, X., Wu, X., Li, Y., Lu, C.: Hoi analysis: Integrating and decomposing human-object interaction. In: NeurIPS (2020)
34. Lin, J., Gan, C., Han, S.: Temporal shift module for efficient video understanding. In: ICCV (2019)
35. Liu, M., Tang, S., Li, Y., Rehg, J.M.: Forecasting human-object interaction: joint prediction of motor attention and actions in first person video. In: ECCV (2020)
36. Menon, A.K., Jayasumana, S., Rawat, A.S., Jain, H., Veit, A., Kumar, S.: Long-tail learning via logit adjustment. In: ICLR (2021)
37. Narasimhaswamy, S., Nguyen, T., Hoai, M.: Detecting hands and recognizing physical contact in the wild. In: NeurIPS (2020)

38. Paszke, A., et al.: PyTorch: an imperative style, high-performance deep learning library. In: Wallach, H., Larochelle, H., Beygelzimer, A., d' Alché-Buc, F., Fox, E., Garnett, R. (eds.) NIPS, pp. 8024–8035 (2019). https://papers.neurips.cc/paper/9015-pytorch-an-imperative-style-high-performance-deep-learning-library.pdf

39. Purushwalkam, S., Gupta, A.: Demystifying contrastive self-supervised learning: invariances, augmentations and dataset biases. In: NeurIPS (2020)

40. Qi, S., Wang, W., Jia, B., Shen, J., Zhu, S.: Learning human-object interactions by graph parsing neural networks. In: ECCV (2018)

41. Reed, C.J., et al.: Self-supervised pretraining improves self-supervised pretraining. arXiv:2103.12718 (2021)

42. Russakovsky, O., et al.: ImageNet large scale visual recognition challenge. IJCV **115**(3), 211–252 (2015)

43. Shan, D., Geng, J., Shu, M., Fouhey, D.F.: Understanding human hands in contact at internet scale. In: CVPR (2020)

44. Sigurdsson, G.A., Gupta, A., Schmid, C., Farhadi, A., Alahari, K.: Actor and observer: joint modeling of first and third-person videos. In: CVPR (2018)

45. Soomro, K., Zamir, A.R., Shah, M.: Ucf101: a dataset of 101 human actions classes from videos in the wild. arXiv preprint arXiv:1212.0402 (2012)

46. Sudhakaran, S., Escalera, S., Lanz, O.: LSTA: long short-term attention for egocentric action recognition. In: CVPR (2019)

47. Sudhakaran, S., Lanz, O.: Attention is all we need: nailing down object-centric attention for egocentric activity recognition. In: BMVC (2018)

48. Sun, C., Nagrani, A., Tian, Y., Schmid, C.: Composable augmentation encoding for video representation learning. In: ICCV (2021)

49. Umesh, P.: Image processing in python. CSI Commun. **23** (2012)

50. Vondrick, C., Shrivastava, A., Fathi, A., Guadarrama, S., Murphy, K.: Tracking emerges by colorizing videos. In: ECCV (2018)

51. Wang, L., et al.: Temporal segment networks for action recognition in videos. IEEE TPAMI **41**(11), 2740–2755 (2018)

52. Wang, X., Wu, Y., Zhu, L., Yang, Y.: Symbiotic attention with privileged information for egocentric action recognition. In: AAAI (2020)

53. Wang, X., Zhu, L., Wang, H., Yang, Y.: Interactive prototype learning for egocentric action recognition. In: ICCV (2021)

54. Wang, X., Gupta, A.: Videos as space-time region graphs. In: ECCV (2018)

55. Wang, X., He, K., Gupta, A.: Transitive invariance for self-supervised visual representation learning. In: ICCV (2017)

56. Wu, C.Y., Feichtenhofer, C., Fan, H., He, K., Krahenbuhl, P., Girshick, R.: Long-term feature banks for detailed video understanding. In: CVPR (2019)

57. Yan, R., Xie, L., Shu, X., Tang, J.: Interactive fusion of multi-level features for compositional activity recognition. arXiv:2012.05689 (2020)

58. Yang, Y., Xu, Z.: Rethinking the value of labels for improving class-imbalanced learning. NeurIPS **33**, 19290–19301 (2020)

59. Zhang, X., et al.: VideoLT: large-scale long-tailed video recognition. In: ICCV, pp. 7960–7969 (2021)

60. Zhou, B., Andonian, A., Oliva, A., Torralba, A.: Temporal relational reasoning in videos. In: ECCV (2018)

Egocentric Activity Recognition and Localization on a 3D Map

Miao Liu[1(✉)], Lingni Ma[5], Kiran Somasundaram[5], Yin Li[2],
Kristen Grauman[3,4], James M. Rehg[1], and Chao Li[5]

[1] Georgia Institute of Technology, Atlanta, USA
mliu328@gatech.edu
[2] University of Wisconsin-Madison, Madison, USA
[3] The University of Texas at Austin, Austin, USA
[4] Meta AI, New York, USA
[5] Meta Reality Labs, Menlo Park, USA

Abstract. Given a video captured from a first person perspective and the environment context of where the video is recorded, can we recognize what the person is doing and identify where the action occurs in the 3D space? We address this challenging problem of jointly recognizing and localizing actions of a mobile user on a known 3D map from egocentric videos. To this end, we propose a novel deep probabilistic model. Our model takes the inputs of a Hierarchical Volumetric Representation (HVR) of the 3D environment and an egocentric video, infers the 3D action location as a latent variable, and recognizes the action based on the video and contextual cues surrounding its potential locations. To evaluate our model, we conduct extensive experiments on the subset of Ego4D dataset, in which both human naturalistic actions and photo-realistic 3D environment reconstructions are captured. Our method demonstrates strong results on both action recognition and 3D action localization across seen and unseen environments. We believe our work points to an exciting research direction in the intersection of egocentric vision, and 3D scene understanding.

Keywords: Egocentric vision · Activity recognition · 3d scene understanding

1 Introduction

Egocentric vision has emerged as a promising paradigm for understanding human activities in a mobile setting. Its defining characteristic is the continuous capture

---

M. Liu—This work was primarily done during an internship at Meta Reality Labs.

Supplementary Information The online version contains supplementary material available at https://doi.org/10.1007/978-3-031-19778-9_36.

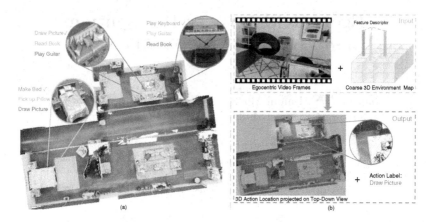

Fig. 1. (a) The activities of daily life take place in a 3D environment, and the semantic and spatial properties of the environment are powerful cues for activity recognition. (b) *Our Proposed Task*: Given an input egocentric video sequence and a 3D volumetric representation of the environment (carrying both semantic and geometric information), our goal is to detect and localize activities, by jointly predicting the action label and location on the 3D map where it occurred.

of first-person visual experience. In particular, egocentric videos implicitly and naturally connect the camera wearer's activities to the relevant 3D spatial context, such as the surrounding objects and their 3D layout. While this observation has been true since the beginning of egocentric vision, it is only recently that 3D scene models that can capture this context have become readily available, due to advances in 3D scanners [57] and Augmented Reality (AR) headsets [22]. Figure 1 (a) gives an example of a 3D scan of a subject's apartment in which the 3D layout of the furniture and appliances is known *a priori*. Given an egocentric video, our goal is to leverage this 3D map to reason about the camera wearer's activities and the 3D locations in which they are performed, *eg* drawing a picture while sitting on the sofa. Such a capability could enable future context-sensitive applications in AR and Human-Robot Interaction (HRI).

This paper addresses the following research question: *How can we design vision models to exploit the prior knowledge of a known 3D environment for recognizing and localizing egocentric activities?* This question has not been tackled by existing works on egocentric action and activity recognition [23,29,31,34,36, 41,43,67]. Prior works have used limited contextual cues for egocentric video analysis, such as a 2D ground plane [46] or a topological map [38], and have focused on understanding the functions of an environment, such as the common locations at which activities occur. In contrast, this work introduces the new task of the *joint recognition and 3D localization of egocentric activities given trimmed videos and a coarsely-annotated 3D environment map*. We provide a visual illustration of our problem setting in Fig. 1 (b).

Two major challenges arise in our task. First, standard architectures for egocentric activity recognition are not designed to incorporate 3D scene context, requiring a new design of action recognition models and associated 3D scene representations. Second, the exact ground truth for the locations of actions in a 3D scene that is the size of an entire apartment is difficult to obtain, due to ambiguities in 2D to 3D registration. As a remedy, we leverage camera registration using structure-from-motion that yields "noisy" locations, which requires the model to address the uncertainty in action locations during training.

To address the challenge of leveraging context in recognition, we develop a Hierarchical Volumetric Representation (HVR) to describe the semantic and geometric information of the 3D environment map (see Fig. 2 (a) and Sec 3.1 for explanation). We further present a novel deep model that takes egocentric videos and our proposed 3D environment HVR as inputs, and outputs the 3D action locations and the activity classes. Our model consists of two branches. The *environment branch* makes use of a 3D convolutional network to extract global environmental features from HVR. Similarly, the *video branch* uses a 3D convolutional network to extract visual features from the input video. The environmental and visual features are further combined to estimate the 3D activity location, supervised by the results of camera registration. Moreover, we tackle the second challenge of noisy localization by using stochastic units to account for uncertainty. The predicted 3D activity location, in the form of a probabilistic distribution, is then used as a 3D attention map to select local environmental features relevant to the action. Finally, these local features are further fused with video features for recognition.

Our method is trained and evaluated on the recent, freely-available Ego4D dataset [13], which contains naturalistic egocentric videos and photo-realistic 3D scene reconstructions along with 3D static object annotations. We demonstrate strong results on action recognition and 3D action localization. Specifically, our model outperforms a strong baseline of 2D video-based action recognition methods by 4.2% in mean class accuracy, and beats baselines on 3D action localization by 9.3% in F1 score. Furthermore, we demonstrate that our method can generalize to unseen environments not present in the training set yet with known 3D maps and object labels. We believe this work provides a useful foundation for egocentric video understanding in a 3D scene context

2   Related Work

We first discuss the most relevant works on egocentric vision, and then review several previous efforts on human-scene interaction and 3D scene representation.

Egocentric Vision. There is a rich set of literature aiming at egocentric activity understanding. Prior works have made great progress in recognizing and anticipating egocentric actions based on 2D videos [10,24,31,34,36,41,43,52,67], and predicting gaze and locomotion [18,28,29,39,40,42,51,55,64]. Far fewer works have considered environmental factors and spatial grounding of egocentric activity. Guan et al. [14] and Rhinehart et al. [47] jointly considered trajectory forecasting and egocentric activity anticipation with online inverse reinforcement learning. The most relevant works to ours are recent efforts on learning affordances for egocentric action understanding [38,46]. Nagarajan et al. [38] introduced a topological map environment representation for long-term activity forecasting and affordance prediction. Rhinehart et al. [46] considered a novel problem of learning "Action Maps" from egocentric videos. However, methods that use ground plane representations of the environment [46] or environmental functionality as the context [38] may lack the specificity provided by 3D proximity. In contrast to these prior efforts, our focus is on exploiting the geometric and semantic information in the HVR map to address our novel task of joint egocentric action recognition and 3D localization.

Human-Scene Interaction. Human-scene constraints have been proven to be effective in estimating human body model [16,65,66]. The most relevant prior works focus on understanding environment affordance. Grabner et al. [12] predict object functionality by hallucinating an actor interacting with the scene. A similar idea was also explored in [20,21]. Koppula et al. [25] leveraged RGB-D videos to jointly recognize human activities and estimate objects affordances. Savva et al. [49] predicted action heat maps that highlight the likelihood of an action in the scene by partitioning 3D scenes into disjoint sets of segments and learning a segment dictionary. Gupta et al. [15] presented a human-centric scene representation for predicting the afforded human body poses. Delaitre et al. [5,8] introduced a statistical descriptor of person-object interactions for object recognition and human body pose prediction. Fang et al. [7] proposed to learn object affordances from demonstrative videos. Nagarajan et al. [37] proposed to use backward attention to approximate the interaction hotspots of future action. Those previous efforts were limited to the analysis of environment functionality [5,8,20,21], constrained human action and body pose [49], or hand-object interaction on 2D image plane [7,37]. In contrast, we are the first to utilize the rich geometric and semantic information of the 3D scene for naturalistic human activity recognition and 3D localization.

3D Scene Representation. Many recent works explored various 3D representations for 3D vision tasks, including 3D object detection [3,63,68] and embodied visual navigation [11,17,27]. Deep models have been developed for point clouds [44,45,60,61] with great success in object recognition, semantic segmentation, and sceneflow estimation. However, using point clouds to describe a large-scale 3D scene will result in high computational and memory cost [68]. To address this challenge, many approaches used rasterized point clouds in a 3D voxel grid, with each voxel represented by either handcrafted features [6,53,54,58] or learning-based features [68]. Signed-Distanced value and Chamfer Distance between 3D scene and 3D human body have also been used to enforce more plausible human-scene contact [16,33,65,66]. Building on this prior works, we utilize a 3D Hierarchical Volumetric Representation (HVR) that encodes the geometric and semantic context of a 3D scene for egocentric activity understanding.

3   Method

We denote a trimmed input egocentric video as $x = (x^1, ..., x^t)$ with frames x^t indexed by time t. In addition, we assume a global 3D environment prior e,

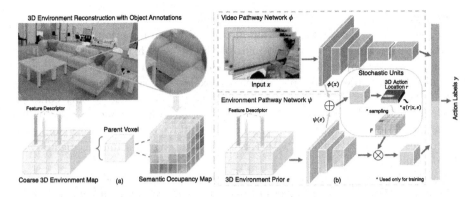

Fig. 2. (a) Hierarchical Volumetric Representation (HVR). We rasterize the semantic 3D environment mesh into two levels of 3D voxels. Each parent voxel corresponds to a possible action location, while the children voxels compose a semantic occupancy map that describes their parent voxel. (b) Overview of our model. Our model takes video clips x and the associated 3D environment representation e as inputs. We adopt an I3D backbone network ϕ to extract video features and a 3D convolutional network ψ to extract the global environment features. We then make use of stochastic units to generate sampled action location $\tilde{r}$ for selecting local 3D environment features for action recognition. Note that $\otimes$ represents weighted average pooling, while $\oplus$ denotes concatenation along channel dimension.

associated each with input video, is available at both training and inference time. e is environment specific, eg the 3D map of an apartment. Our goal is to jointly predict the action category y of x and the action location r on the 3D map. r is parameterized as a 3D saliency map, where the value of $r(w, d, h)$ represents the likelihood of action clip x happening in spatial location w, d, h. For tractability, we associate the entire activity with a specific 3D location and do not model location change over the course of an activity. This is a valid assumption for the activities we address, such as sitting down, playing keyboards, etc. r thereby defines a proper probabilistic distribution in 3D space.

In this section, we first introduce our proposed joint model of action recognition and 3D localization, leveraging a 3D representation of the environment. We then describe key components of our model, training and inference schema, as well as our network architecture.

3.1   Joint Modeling with the 3D Environment Representation

3D Environment Representation. We seek to design a representation that not only encodes the 3D geometric and semantic information of the 3D environment, but is also effective for 3D action localization and recognition.

To this end, we introduce a Hierarchical Volumetric Representation (HVR) of the 3D environment. We provide an illustration of our method in Fig. 2(a). We assume the 3D environment reconstruction with object labels is given in advance as a 3D mesh (see Sect. 4 for details). We first divide the 3D mesh into $X \times Y \times Z$ parent voxels, that define all possible action locations. We then divide each parent voxel into multiple voxels at a fixed resolution M and further assign an object label to each child voxel based on the object annotation. Specifically, the object label of each child voxel is determined by the majority vote of the vertices that lie inside that child voxel. Note that we only consider static objects of the entire environments and treat empty space as a specially-designated "object" category. Therefore, the child voxels compose a semantic occupancy map that encodes both the 3D geometry and semantic meaning of the parent voxel.

We further vectorize the semantic occupancy map and use the resulting vector as a feature descriptor of the parent voxel. The 3D environment representation e can then be represented as a 4D tensor, with dimension $X \times Y \times Z \times (M^3)$. Note that higher resolution M can better approximate the 3D shape of the environment. Our proposed HVR is thus a compact and flexible environment representation that jointly considers the 3D action location candidates, geometric and semantic information of the 3D environment.

Joint Learning of Action Category and Action Location. We present an overview of our model in Fig. 2(b). Specifically, we adopt a two-pathway network architecture. The video pathway extracts video features with an I3D backbone network $\phi(x)$, while the environment pathway extracts the global 3D environment features with a 3D convolutional network $\psi(e)$. Visual and environmental features are jointly considered for predicting the 3D action location r. We then adopt stochastic units to generate sampled action $\tilde{r}$ for selecting the local environment features relevant to the actions. Local environment features and video features are further fused together for activity recognition.

Our key idea is to utilize the 3D environment representation e for jointly modeling the action label y and 3D action location r of video clip x. We consider the action location r as a probabilistic variable, and model the action label y given input video x and environment representation e using a latent variable model. Therefore, the conditional probability $p(y|x, e)$ is given by:

$$p(y|x, e) = \int_r p(y|r, x, e)p(r|x, e)dr. \tag{1}$$

Notably, our proposed joint model has two key components. First, $p(r|x, e)$ models the 3D action location r from video input x and the 3D environment representation e. Second, $p(y|r, x, e)$ utilizes r to select a region of interest (ROI) from the environment representation e, and combines selected environment features with the video features from x for action classification. During training, our model receives the ground truth 3D action location and action label as supervisory signals. At inference time, our model jointly predicts both the 3D action location r and action label y. We now provide additional technical details in modeling $p(r|x, e)$ and $p(y|r, x, e)$.

3.2   3D Action Localization

We first introduce our 3D action localization module, defined by the conditional probability $p(r|x,e)$. Given the video pathway features $\phi(x)$ and the environment pathway features $\psi(e)$, we learn a mapping function to predict location r, which is defined on a 3D grid of candidate action locations. Note that the 3D grid is defined globally over the 3D environment scan. The mapping function is composed of 3D convolution operations with parameters w_r and a softmax function. Thus, $p(r|x,e)$ is given by:

$$p(r|x,e) = softmax(w_r^T(\phi(x) \oplus \psi(e))), \tag{2}$$

where $\oplus$ denotes concatenation along the channel dimension. Therefore, the resulting action location r is a proper probabilistic distribution normalized in 3D space, and $r(w,d,h)$ can be considered as the expectation of video clip x happening in the spatial location (w,d,h) of the 3D environment.

In practice, we do not have access to the precise ground truth 3D action location and must rely on camera registration results as a proxy. Using a categorical distribution for $p(r|x,e)$ thus models the ambiguity of 2D to 3D registration. We follow [30,32] to adopt stochastic units in our model. Specifically, we follow the Gumbel-Softmax and reparameterization trick from [19,35] to adopt the following differentiable sampling mechanism:

$$\tilde{r}_{w,d,h} \sim \frac{\exp((\log r_{w,d,h} + G_{w,d,h})/\theta)}{\sum_{w,d,h} \exp((\log r_{w,d,h} + G_{w,d,h})/\theta)}, \tag{3}$$

where G is a Gumbel Distribution for sampling from a discrete distribution. This Gumbel-Softmax trick produces a "soft" sample that allows the gradients propagation to video pathway network ϕ and environment pathway network ψ. θ is the temperature parameter that controls the shape of the soft sample distribution. We set $\theta = 2$ for our model. Notably, the expectation of sampled 3D action location $E[\tilde{r}]$ can be modeled by the distribution $p(r|x,e)$ using Eq. 2.

3.3   Action Recognition with Environment Prior

Our model further models $p(y|r,x,e)$ with a mapping function $f(\tilde{r},x,e)$ that jointly considers action location r, video input x and 3D environment representation e for action recognition. Formally, the conditional probability $p(y|r,x,e)$ can be modeled as:

$$p(y|r,x,e) = f(\tilde{r},x,e) = softmax(w_p^T \Sigma(\phi(x) \oplus (\tilde{r} \otimes \psi(e)))), \tag{4}$$

where $\oplus$ denotes concatenation along channel dimension, and $\otimes$ denotes the element-wise multiplication. Specifically, our method uses the sampled action location $\tilde{r}$ for selectively aggregating environment features $\psi(e)$ and combines the aggregated environment features with video features $\phi(x)$ for action recognition. Σ denotes the average pooling operation that maps 3D feature to 2D feature, and w_p denotes the parameters of the linear classifier that maps feature vector to action prediction logits.

3.4   Training and Inference

We now present our training and inference schema. At training time, we assume a prior distribution of action location $q(r|x, e)$ is given as a supervisory signal. $q(r|x, e)$ is obtained by registering the egocentric camera into the 3D environment (see more details in Sect. 4). Note that we factorize $p(r|x, e)$ as latent variables, and based on the Evidence Lower Bound (ELBO), the resulting deep latent variable model has the following loss function:

$$\mathcal{L} = -\sum_r \log p(y|r, x, e) + KL[p(r|x, e)||q(r|x, e)], \tag{5}$$

where the first term is the cross entropy loss for action classification and the second term is the KL-Divergence that matches the predicted 3D action location distribution $p(r|x, e)$ to the prior distribution $q(r|x, e)$. During training, a single 3D action location sample $\tilde{r}$ for each input within the mini-batch will be drawn.

Theoretically, our model should sample $\tilde{r}$ from the same input multiple times and take average of the predictions at inference time. To avoid such dense sampling for high dimensional video input, we choose to directly plug in the deterministic action location r in Eq. 4. Note that the recognition function f is composed of a linear mapping function and a softmax function, and therefore is convex. Further, $\tilde{r}$ is sampled from the probabilistic distribution of 3D action location r, similar to the formulation in [29, 32], r is thus the expectation of $\tilde{r}$. By Jensen's Inequality, we have:

$$E[f(\tilde{r}, x, e)] \geq f(E[\tilde{r}], x, e) = f(r, x, e). \tag{6}$$

That being said, $f(r, x, e)$ provides an empirical lower bound of $E[f(\tilde{r}, x, e)]$, and therefore provides a valid approximation of dense sampling.

3.5   Network Architecture

For the video pathway, we adopt the I3D-Res50 network [2,59] pre-trained on Kinetics as the backbone. For the environment pathway, we make use of a lightweight network (denoted as EnvNet), which has four 3D convolutional operations. The video features from the 3rd convolutional block of I3D-Res50 and the environment features after the 2nd 3D convolutional operation in EnvNet are concatenated for 3D action location prediction. We then use 3D max pooling operations to match the size of action location map to the size of the feature map of the 4th convolution of EnvNet for the weighted pooling in Eq. 2. More implementation details can be found in our supplement.

4   Experiments and Results

4.1   Dataset and Benchmarks

Datasets. Note that existing egocentric video datasets (EGTEA [30], and EPIC-Kitchens [4] etc.) did not explicitly capture the 3D environment. We follow [46] to run ORB-SLAM on EGTEA and EPIC-Kitchens. However, less than 30% of frames can be registered, and the quality of the reconstructed point cloud is unsatisfactory. Our empirical finding is that existing visual SfM methods can not address the naturalistic egocentric videos. In contrast, the newly-developed Ego4D [13] dataset has a subset that includes egocentric videos, high-quality 3D environment reconstructions, and 3D static objects annotation.

The subset captures 34 different indoor activities from 3 real-world living rooms, resulting in 6868 action clips. Similar to [4], we consider both *seen* and *unseen* environment splits. In the seen environment split, each environment is seen in both training and testing sets (5163 instances for training, and 1705 instances for testing). In the unseen split, all sequences from the same environment are either in training or testing (4392 instances for training, and 2476 instances for testing). As discussed in [13], the photo-realistic 3D reconstruction of the environment is obtained from the state-of-the-art dense reconstruction system [56]. Furthermore, the static 3D object meshes are annotated by painting an semantic label over the mesh polygons. The annotation includes 35 object categories plus a background class label. It is worthy noting that the static object annotations can be automated with the state-of-the-art 3D object detection algorithms.

Prior Distribution of 3D Activity Location. To obtain the ground truth of the activity location for each trimmed activity video clip, we first register the egocentric camera in the 3D environment using a RANSAC based feature matching method. Specifically, we first build a base map from the monochrome camera streams for 3D environment reconstruction using Structure from Motion [9,50]. The pre-built base map is a dense point cloud associated with 3D feature points. We then estimate the camera pose of the video frame using active search [48]. Note that registering the 2D egocentric video frames in a 3D environment is fundamentally challenging, due to the drastic head rotation, featureless surfaces, and changing illumination. Therefore, we only consider the key frame camera registration, where enough inliers were matched with RANSAC. As introduced in Sect. 3, the action location is defined as a probabilistic distribution in 3D space. Thus, we map the key frame camera location into the index of the 3D action location tensor, with its value representing the likelihood of the given action happening in the corresponding parent voxel. To account for the uncertainty of 2D to 3D camera registration, we further enforce a Guassian distribution to generate the final 3D action location ground truth.

Evaluation Metrics. For all experiments, we We follow [4,30] to evaluate the performance of both action recognition using both Mean Class Accuracy and Top-1 Accuracy. As for 3D Action Localizatio, we consider 3D action localization as binary classification over the regular 3D grids. Therefore, we report the Precision, Recall, and F1 score on a downsampled 3D heatmap ($\times 4$ in X, Y direction, and $\times 2$ in Z direction) as in [29].

Table 1. Comparison with other forms of environment context. Our Hierarchical Volumetric Representation (HVR) outperforms other methods by a significant margin on both action recognition and 3D action localization. The best results are highlighted with **boldface**, and the second-best results are underlined.

Method	Action Recognition		3D Action Localization		
	Mean Cls Acc	Top-1 Acc	Prec	Recall	F1
I3D-Res50	37.48	55.15	8.14	<u>38.73</u>	13.45
I3D+Obj	37.66	55.11	10.04	35.08	15.61
I3D+2DGround	38.69	55.37	10.88	36.19	16.73
I3D+SemVoxel	39.23	<u>56.07</u>	11.26	**38.77**	<u>17.45</u>
I3D+Affordance	<u>39.95</u>	55.82	<u>11.55</u>	35.35	17.41
Ours(HVR)	**41.64**	**56.94**	**16.71**	35.55	**22.73**

4.2   Action Understanding in Seen Environments

Our method is the first to utilize the 3D environment information for egocentric action recognition and 3D localization. Previous works have considered various environment contexts for other tasks, including 3D object detection, affordance prediction etc. Therefore, we adapt previous proposed contextual cues into our proposed joint model and design the following strong baselines (see supplementary material for the details of baseline models):

- **I3D-Res50** refers to the backbone network from [59]. We also use the network feature from I3D-Res50 for 3D action localization by adopting the KL loss.
- **I3D+Obj** uses object detection results from a pre-trained object detector [62] as contextual cues as in [10]. This representation is essentially an object-centric feature that describes the attended environment (*ie* where the camera wearer is facing towards), therefore 3D action location can not used for selecting surrounding environment features.
- **I3D+2DGround** projects the object information from the 3D environment to 2D ground plane. A similar representation is also considered in [46]. Note that the predicted 3D action location will also be projected to 2D ground plane to select local environment features.
- **I3D+SemVoxel** is inspired by [68], where we use the semantic probabilistic distribution of all the vertices within each voxel as a feature descriptor. Therefore, the resulting environment representation is a 4D tensor with dimension $X \times Y \times Z \times C$, where X, Y, Z represent the spatial dimension, and C denotes the number of object labels from the 3D environment mesh annotation introduced in Sect. 4.
- **I3D+Affordance** follows [38] to use the afforded action distribution as feature descriptor for each voxel. The resulting representation is a 4D tensor with dimension $X \times Y \times Z \times N$, where N denotes the number of action classes. The afforded action distribution is derived from the training set.

Table 2. Ablation study for the 3D representation. We present the results of our method that adopts different semantic occupancy map resolution M.

Method	Action Recognition		3D Action Localization		
	Mean Cls Acc	Top-1 Acc	Prec	Recall	F1
I3D-Res50	37.48	55.15	8.14	38.73	13.45
I3D+SemVoxel	39.23	56.07	11.26	38.77	17.45
Ours ($M = 2$)	39.04	56.26	12.19	36.82	18.32
Ours ($M = 4$)	**41.64**	**56.94**	**16.71**	35.55	22.73
Ours ($M = 8$)	40.06	56.04	16.13	**39.84**	**22.96**

Results. Our results on the seen environment split is listed in Table 1. Our method outperforms I3D-Res50 baseline by a large margin (4.2%/1.8% on Mean Cls Acc/Top1 Acc) on action recognition. We attribute this significant performance gain to explicitly modeling the 3D environment context. As for 3D action localization, our method outperforms I3D-50 by 9.3% – a relative improvement of **69%**. Notably, predicting the 3D action location based on video sequence alone is erroneous. Our method, on the other hand, explicitly models the 3D environment factor and thus improves the performance of 3D action localization. In subsequent sections, we will show that the performance improvement does not simply come from additional input modalities of 3D environment, but attributes to a careful design of 3D representation and probabilistic joint modeling.

Comparison on Environment Representation. We now compare HVR with other forms of environment representation. As shown in Table 1, I3D+Obj has minor improvement on the over all performance, while I3D+2DGround, I3D+SemVoxel and I3D+Affordance can improve the performance of action recognition and 3D localization by a notable margin. Those results suggest that the environment context (even in 2D space) plays an important role in egocentric action understanding. More importantly, our method outperforms all previous methods by at least 1.7% for action recognition and 5.3% for 3D action localization. *These results suggest that our proposed HVR is superior to a 2D ground plane representation,* and demonstrates that using the semantic occupancy map as the environment descriptor can better facilitate egocentric understanding.

4.3   Ablation Studies

We now present detailed ablation studies of our method on seen split. To begin with, we analyze the role of semantic and geometric information in our hierarchical volumetric representation (HVR). We then present an experiment to verify whether fine-grained environment context is necessary for egocentric action understanding. Furthermore, we show the benefits of probabilistic joint modeling of action and 3D action location.

Semantic Meaning and 3D Geometry. The semantic occupancy map carries both geometric and semantic information of the local environment. To show how each component contributes to the performance boost, we compare Ours with I3D+SemVoxel, where only semantic meaning is considered, in Table 2. Ours outperforms I3D+SemVoxel by a notable margin for action recognition and a large margin for 3D localization. These results suggest that semantic occupancy map is more expressive than only semantic information for action understanding, yet it has smaller impact on action recognition than 3D action localization.

Granularity of 3D Information. We further show what level of 3D environment granularity is needed for egocentric action understanding. By the definition of occupancy map, increasing the resolution M of children voxels will approximate the actual 3D shape of the environment. Therefore, we report results of our method with different occupancy map resolution in Table 2. Not surprisingly, low occupancy map resolution lags behind Ours for action recognition by 2.6% ↓ and 3D action localization by 4.4% ↓, which again shows the necessity of incorporating the 3D geometric cues. Another interesting observation is that higher resolution can slightly increase the 3D action localization accuracy by 0.2%, yet decreases the performance on action recognition by 1.6% ↓. These results suggest that fine-grained 3D shape of the environment is not necessary for action recognition. In fact, higher resolution will dramatically increase the feature dimension of the environment representation, and thereby incurs more barriers to the network.

Table 3. Ablation study for joint modeling of action category and 3D action location. Our proposed probabilistic joint modeling can consistently benefit the performance on action recognition and 3D action localization

Method	Action Recognition		3D Action Localization		
	Mean Cls Acc	Top-1 Acc	Prec	Recall	F1
I3D-Res50	37.48	55.15	8.14	**38.73**	13.45
I3D+GlobalEnv	35.99	54.93	8.82	36.40	14.20
I3D+DetEnv	39.37	55.88	14.11	32.66	19.71
Ours	**41.64**	**56.94**	**16.71**	35.55	**22.73**

Joint Learning of Action and 3D Location. We denote a baseline model that directly fuses global environment features, extracted by the same 3D convolutional network from our method, with video features for activity reasoning as I3D+GlobalEnv. The results are presented in Table 3. I3D+GlobalEnv decreases the performance of I3D-Res50 backbone network by 1.5% ↓ /0.2% ↓ for action recognition and has marginal improvement for 3D action localization (+0.8%). We speculate that this is because only 3 types of scene reconstruction available for training may lead to overfitting. In contrast, our method makes use of the learned 3D action location to select interesting environment features associated with the action. As the action location varies among different input videos, our method can utilize the 3D environment context without running into the pitfall of overfitting, and therefore outperforms I3D+GlobalEnv by 5.7%/2.0% for action recognition and 8.5% for 3D action localization.

Probabilistic Modeling of 3D Action Location. As introduced in Sect. 4, considerable uncertainty lies in the prior distribution of 3D action location, due to the challenging artifact of 2D to 3D camera registration. To verify that the probabilistic modeling can account for the uncertainty of 3D action location ground truth, we compare our method with a deterministic version of our model, denoted as DetEnv. DetEnv adopts the same inputs and network architecture as our method, except for the differentiable sampling with Gumbel-Softmax Trick. As shown in Table 3, Ours outperforms DetEnv by 2.3% for action recognition and 3.0% for 3D action localization. These results demonstrate the benefits of the stochastic units adopted in our method.

Remarks. To summarize, our key finding is that both 3D geometric and semantic contexts convey important information for action recognition and 3D localization. Another important take home is that egocentric understanding only requires a sparse encoding of geometric information. Moreover, without a careful model design, the 3D environment representation has minor improvement on (or even decreases) the overall performance as reported in Table 3.

Table 4. Experimental results on unseen environment split. Our model show the capacity of better generalizing to an unseen environment with known 3D map. The best results are highlighted with **boldface**, and the second-best results are underlined.

Method	Action Recognition		3D Action Localization		
	Mean Cls Acc	Top-1 Acc	Prec	Recall	F1
I3D-Res50	29.24	52.22	6.20	45.14	10.90
I3D+2DObject	29.91	53.05	6.31	42.22	10.98
I3D+2DGround	30.06	53.87	6.95	41.27	11.90
I3D+SemVoxel	30.19	53.37	7.03	43.55	12.11
Ours	**31.55**	**55.33**	**7.50**	44.97	**12.86**

4.4 Generalization to Novel Environment

We further present experiment results on the unseen environment split in Table 4. Our model outperforms all baselines by a notable margin on both action recognition and 3D action localization. Note that the affordance map requires the observation of action instances on the 3D spatial location and thus cannot be applied on the unseen split. These results suggest that explicitly modeling the 3D environment context can improve the generalization ability to unseen environments with known 3D maps. However, the performance gap is smaller in comparison to the performance boost on seen split. We speculate that this is because we only have two different types of environments for training and therefore the risk of overfitting on unseen split is further exemplified.

4.5 Discussion

Fig. 3. Visualization of predicted 3D action location (projected on top-down view of the reconstructed 3D scene) and action labels (captions above the video frames). We present both successful and failure examples. We also show the "zoom-in" spatial region of the action location to help readers to better interpret our action localization results.

Visualization of Action Location. We visualize our results on seen environment split. Specifically, we project the 3D saliency map of action location on the top-down view of the 3D environments. As shown in Fig. 3, our model can effectively localize the coarse action location and thereby select the region of interest from the global environment features for action recognition. By examining the failure cases, we found that the model may run into the failure modes when the video features are not sufficiently discriminative (*ie* when the camera wearer is standing close to a white wall.)

Limitation and Future Work. One limitation of our method is the requirement of high-quality 3D reconstruction with object annotations. However, we conjecture that 3D object detection algorithms [68], semantic structure from motion [26] and 3D scene graphs [1] can be used to replace the human annotation, since our current volumetric representation only adopts a low resolution semantic occupancy map as environment descriptor. We plan to explore this direction as our future work. Another limitation is the potential error in 2D to 3D camera registration, as discussed in Sect. 4. Currently, only camera poses from key video frames can be robustly estimated. Our method thus does not model the location shift within the same action. We argue that camera registration can be drastically improved with the help of additional sensors (*eg* IMU or depth camera). Incorporating those sensors into egocentric capturing setting is an exciting future direction. In addition, our method did not consider the camera orientation. We will leave this for future efforts.

5   Conclusion

We introduced a deep model that makes use of egocentric videos and a 3D map to address the novel task of joint action recognition and 3D localization. Our key insight is that the 3D geometric and semantic context of the surrounding environment provides critical information that complements video features for action understanding. The key innovation of our model is to characterize the 3D action location as a latent variable, which is used to select the surrounding local environment features for action recognition. Our model demonstrated impressive results on seen and unseen environments when evaluated on the newly released Ego4D dataset [13]. We believe our work provides a critical first step towards understanding actions in the context of a 3D environment, and points to exciting future directions in connecting egocentric vision and 3D scene understanding for AR and HRI.

Acknowledgments. Portions of this project were supported in part by a gift from Facebook.

References

1. Armeni, I., et al.: 3D scene graph: a structure for unified semantics, 3D space, and camera. In: ICCV (2019)
2. Carreira, J., Zisserman, A.: Quo Vadis, action recognition? a new model and the kinetics dataset. In: CVPR (2017)
3. Chen, X., Ma, H., Wan, J., Li, B., Xia, T.: Multi-view 3D object detection network for autonomous driving. In: CVPR (2017)
4. Damen, D., et al.: The epic-kitchens dataset: collection, challenges and baselines. IEEE Computer Architecture Letters (01) (2020)
5. Delaitre, V., Fouhey, D.F., Laptev, I., Sivic, J., Gupta, A., Efros, A.A.: Scene semantics from long-term observation of people. In: Fitzgibbon, A., Lazebnik, S., Perona, P., Sato, Y., Schmid, C. (eds.) ECCV 2012. LNCS, vol. 7577, pp. 284–298. Springer, Heidelberg (2012). https://doi.org/10.1007/978-3-642-33783-3_21
6. Engelcke, M., Rao, D., Wang, D.Z., Tong, C.H., Posner, I.: Vote3Deep: fast object detection in 3D point clouds using efficient convolutional neural networks. In: ICRA (2017)
7. Fang, K., Wu, T.L., Yang, D., Savarese, S., Lim, J.J.: Demo2Vec: reasoning object affordances from online videos. In: CVPR (2018)
8. Fouhey, D.F., Delaitre, V., Gupta, A., Efros, A.A., Laptev, I., Sivic, J.: People watching: human actions as a cue for single view geometry. IJCV (2014)
9. Frahm, J.-M., et al.: Building Rome on a cloudless day. In: Daniilidis, K., Maragos, P., Paragios, N. (eds.) ECCV 2010. LNCS, vol. 6314, pp. 368–381. Springer, Heidelberg (2010). https://doi.org/10.1007/978-3-642-15561-1_27
10. Furnari, A., Farinella, G.M.: What would you expect? anticipating egocentric actions with rolling-unrolling LSTMs and modality attention. In: ICCV (2019)

11. Gordon, D., Kadian, A., Parikh, D., Hoffman, J., Batra, D.: SplitNet: Sim2Sim and Task2Task transfer for embodied visual navigation. In: ICCV (2019)
12. Grabner, H., Gall, J., Van Gool, L.: What makes a chair a chair? In: CVPR (2011)
13. Grauman, K., et al.: Ego4D: around the world in 3,000 hours of egocentric video. arXiv preprint arXiv:2110.07058 (2021)
14. Guan, J., Yuan, Y., Kitani, K.M., Rhinehart, N.: Generative hybrid representations for activity forecasting with no-regret learning. In: CVPR (2020)
15. Gupta, A., Satkin, S., Efros, A.A., Hebert, M.: From 3D scene geometry to human workspace. In: CVPR (2011)
16. Hassan, M., Choutas, V., Tzionas, D., Black, M.J.: Resolving 3D human pose ambiguities with 3D scene constraints. In: ICCV (2019)
17. Henriques, J.F., Vedaldi, A.: Mapnet: An allocentric spatial memory for mapping environments. In: CVPR (2018)
18. Huang, Y., Cai, M., Li, Z., Sato, Y.: Predicting gaze in egocentric video by learning task-dependent attention transition. In: Ferrari, V., Hebert, M., Sminchisescu, C., Weiss, Y. (eds.) ECCV 2018. LNCS, vol. 11208, pp. 789–804. Springer, Cham (2018). https://doi.org/10.1007/978-3-030-01225-0_46
19. Jang, E., Gu, S., Poole, B.: Categorical reparameterization with gumbel-softmax. In: ICLR (2017)
20. Jiang, Y., Koppula, H., Saxena, A.: Hallucinated humans as the hidden context for labeling 3D scenes. In: CVPR (2013)
21. Jiang, Y., Lim, M., Saxena, A.: Learning object arrangements in 3D scenes using human context. In: ICML (2012)
22. Karthika, S., Praveena, P., GokilaMani, M.: Hololens. Int. J. Comput. Sci. Mobile Comput. 6(2), 41–50 (2017)
23. Kazakos, E., Nagrani, A., Zisserman, A., Damen, D.: EPIC-Fusion: audio-visual temporal binding for egocentric action recognition. In: ICCV (2019)
24. Ke, Q., Fritz, M., Schiele, B.: Time-conditioned action anticipation in one shot. In: CVPR (2019)
25. Koppula, H.S., Gupta, R., Saxena, A.: Learning human activities and object affordances from RGB-D videos. Int. J. Robot. Res. 32(8), 951–970 (2013)
26. Kundu, A., Li, Y., Dellaert, F., Li, F., Rehg, J.M.: Joint semantic segmentation and 3D reconstruction from monocular video. In: Fleet, D., Pajdla, T., Schiele, B., Tuytelaars, T. (eds.) ECCV 2014. LNCS, vol. 8694, pp. 703–718. Springer, Cham (2014). https://doi.org/10.1007/978-3-319-10599-4_45
27. Li, J., et al.: Unsupervised reinforcement learning of transferable meta-skills for embodied navigation. In: CVPR (2020)
28. Li, Y., Fathi, A., Rehg, J.M.: Learning to predict gaze in egocentric video. In: ICCV (2013)
29. Li, Y., Liu, M., Rehg, J.M.: In the eye of beholder: joint learning of gaze and actions in first person video. In: Ferrari, V., Hebert, M., Sminchisescu, C., Weiss, Y. (eds.) ECCV 2018. LNCS, vol. 11209, pp. 639–655. Springer, Cham (2018). https://doi.org/10.1007/978-3-030-01228-1_38
30. Li, Y., Liu, M., Rehg, J.M.: In the eye of the beholder: gaze and actions in first person video. TPAMI (2021)
31. Li, Y., Ye, Z., Rehg, J.M.: Delving into egocentric actions. In: CVPR (2015)
32. Liu, M., Tang, S., Li, Y., Rehg, J.M.: Forecasting human-object interaction: joint prediction of motor attention and actions in first person video. In: Vedaldi, A., Bischof, H., Brox, T., Frahm, J.M. (eds.) Computer Vision - ECCV 2020, pp. 704–721. Springer International Publishing, Cham (2020)

33. Liu, M., Yang, D., Zhang, Y., Cui, Z., Rehg, J.M., Tang, S.: 4D human body capture from egocentric video via 3D scene grounding. 3DV (2021)
34. Ma, M., Fan, H., Kitani, K.M.: Going deeper into first-person activity recognition. In: CVPR (2016)
35. Maddison, C.J., Mnih, A., Teh, Y.W.: The concrete distribution: a continuous relaxation of discrete random variables. In: ICLR (2017)
36. Moltisanti, D., Wray, M., Mayol-Cuevas, W., Damen, D.: Trespassing the boundaries: labeling temporal bounds for object interactions in egocentric video. In: ICCV (2017)
37. Nagarajan, T., Feichtenhofer, C., Grauman, K.: Grounded human-object interaction hotspots from video. In: ICCV (2019)
38. Nagarajan, T., Li, Y., Feichtenhofer, C., Grauman, K.: EGO-TOPO: environment affordances from egocentric video. In: CVPR (2020)
39. Ng, E., Xiang, D., Joo, H., Grauman, K.: You2Me: inferring body pose in egocentric video via first and second person interactions. In: CVPR (2020)
40. Park, H., Jain, E., Sheikh, Y.: 3D social saliency from head-mounted cameras. In: NeurIPS (2012)
41. Pirsiavash, H., Ramanan, D.: Detecting activities of daily living in first-person camera views. In: CVPR (2012)
42. Poleg, Y., Arora, C., Peleg, S.: Head motion signatures from egocentric videos. In: ACCV (2014)
43. Poleg, Y., Arora, C., Peleg, S.: Temporal segmentation of egocentric videos. In: CVPR (2014)
44. Qi, C.R., Su, H., Mo, K., Guibas, L.J.: PointNet: deep learning on point sets for 3D classification and segmentation. In: CVPR (2017)
45. Qi, C.R., Yi, L., Su, H., Guibas, L.J.: PointNet++: deep hierarchical feature learning on point sets in a metric space. In: NeurIPS (2017)
46. Rhinehart, N., Kitani, K.M.: Learning action maps of large environments via first-person vision. In: CVPR (2016)
47. Rhinehart, N., Kitani, K.M.: First-person activity forecasting with online inverse reinforcement learning. In: ICCV (2017)
48. Sattler, T., Leibe, B., Kobbelt, L.: Improving image-based localization by active correspondence search. In: Fitzgibbon, A., Lazebnik, S., Perona, P., Sato, Y., Schmid, C. (eds.) ECCV 2012. LNCS, vol. 7572, pp. 752–765. Springer, Heidelberg (2012). https://doi.org/10.1007/978-3-642-33718-5_54
49. Savva, M., Chang, A.X., Hanrahan, P., Fisher, M., Nießner, M.: SceneGrok: inferring action maps in 3D environments. In: TOG (2014)
50. Schönberger, J.L., Frahm, J.M.: Structure-from-motion revisited. In: CVPR (2016)
51. Serra, G., Camurri, M., Baraldi, L., Benedetti, M., Cucchiara, R.: Hand segmentation for gesture recognition in ego-vision. In: Proceedings of the 3rd ACM International Workshop on Interactive Multimedia on Mobile & Portable Devices, pp. 31–36 (2013)
52. Shen, Y., Ni, B., Li, Z., Zhuang, N.: Egocentric activity prediction via event modulated attention. In: Ferrari, V., Hebert, M., Sminchisescu, C., Weiss, Y. (eds.) ECCV 2018. LNCS, vol. 11206, pp. 202–217. Springer, Cham (2018). https://doi.org/10.1007/978-3-030-01216-8_13
53. Song, S., Xiao, J.: Sliding shapes for 3D object detection in depth images. In: Fleet, D., Pajdla, T., Schiele, B., Tuytelaars, T. (eds.) ECCV 2014. LNCS, vol. 8694, pp. 634–651. Springer, Cham (2014). https://doi.org/10.1007/978-3-319-10599-4_41
54. Song, S., Xiao, J.: Deep sliding shapes for amodal 3D object detection in RGB-D images. In: CVPR (2016)

55. Soo Park, H., Hwang, J.J., Niu, Y., Shi, J.: Egocentric future localization. In: CVPR (2016)
56. Straub, J., et al.: The Replica dataset: a digital replica of indoor spaces. arXiv preprint arXiv:1906.05797 (2019)
57. Sulaiman, M.Z., Aziz, M.N.A., Bakar, M.H.A., Halili, N.A., Azuddin, M.A.: Matterport: virtual tour as a new marketing approach in real estate business during pandemic COVID-19. In: Proceedings of the International Conference of Innovation in Media and Visual Design (IMDES 2020). Atlantis Press, pp. 221–226 (2020)
58. Wang, D.Z., Posner, I.: Voting for voting in online point cloud object detection. In: TSS (2015)
59. Wang, X., Girshick, R., Gupta, A., He, K.: Non-local neural networks. In: CVPR (2018)
60. Wu, W., Qi, Z., Fuxin, L.: PointConv: deep convolutional networks on 3D point clouds. In: CVPR (2019)
61. Wu, W., Wang, Z.Y., Li, Z., Liu, W., Fuxin, L.: PointPWC-Net: cost volume on point clouds for (self-)supervised scene flow estimation. In: Vedaldi, A., Bischof, H., Brox, T., Frahm, J.-M. (eds.) ECCV 2020. LNCS, vol. 12350, pp. 88–107. Springer, Cham (2020). https://doi.org/10.1007/978-3-030-58558-7_6
62. Wu, Y., Kirillov, A., Massa, F., Lo, W.Y., Girshick, R.: Detectron2. https://github.com/facebookresearch/detectron2 (2019)
63. Yang, B., Luo, W., Urtasun, R.: PIXOR: real-time 3D object detection from point clouds. In: CVPR (2018)
64. Zhang, M., Teck Ma, K., Hwee Lim, J., Zhao, Q., Feng, J.: Deep future gaze: gaze anticipation on egocentric videos using adversarial networks. In: CVPR (2017)
65. Zhang, S., Zhang, Y., Ma, Q., Black, M.J., Tang, S.: PLACE: Proximity learning of articulation and contact in 3D environments. In: 3DV (2020)
66. Zhang, Y., Hassan, M., Neumann, H., Black, M.J., Tang, S.: Generating 3D people in scenes without people. In: CVPR (2020)
67. Zhou, Y., Ni, B., Hong, R., Yang, X., Tian, Q.: Cascaded interactional targeting network for egocentric video analysis. In: CVPR (2016)
68. Zhou, Y., Tuzel, O.: VoxelNet: end-to-end learning for point cloud based 3D object detection. In: CVPR (2018)

Generative Adversarial Network for Future Hand Segmentation from Egocentric Video

Wenqi Jia$^{(\boxtimes)}$, Miao Liu, and James M. Rehg

Georgia Institute of Technology, Atlanta, USA
wenqi.jia@gatech.edu

Abstract. We introduce the novel problem of anticipating a time series of future hand masks from egocentric video. A key challenge is to model the stochasticity of future head motions, which globally impact the head-worn camera video analysis. To this end, we propose a novel deep generative model – EgoGAN. Our model first utilizes a 3D Fully Convolutional Network to learn a spatio-temporal video representation for pixel-wise visual anticipation. It then generates future head motion using the Generative Adversarial Network (GAN), and predicts the future hand masks based on both the encoded video representation and the generated future head motion. We evaluate our method on both the EPIC-Kitchens and the EGTEA Gaze+ datasets. We conduct detailed ablation studies to validate the design choices of our approach. Furthermore, we compare our method with previous state-of-the-art methods on future image segmentation and provide extensive analysis to show that our method can more accurately predict future hand masks. Project page: https://vjwq.github.io/EgoGAN/.

Keywords: Egocentric vision · Hand segmentation · Visual anticipantation

1 Introduction

The egocentric vision paradigm provides an ideal vehicle for studying the relationship between visual anticipation and intentional motor behaviors, as head-worn cameras can capture both human visual experience and related sensory-motor signals. While prior works have recently addressed action anticipation in an egocentric setting [11,13,24,32,49], the problem of forecasting the detailed shape of hand movements in egocentric video remains unexplored. This is a significant deficit because many everyday motor behaviors cannot be easily categorized into specific action classes and yet play an important role in preparing and

---

W. Jia and M. Liu—Equal contribution.

Supplementary Information The online version contains supplementary material available at https://doi.org/10.1007/978-3-031-19778-9_37.

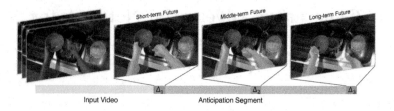

Fig. 1. *Future hand segmentation task*: Given an input egocentric video, our goal is to predict a time series of future hand masks in the anticipation video segment. Δ_1, Δ_2, and Δ_3 represent the short-term, middle-term, and long-term time points in the anticipation segment, respectively. The entanglement between drastic head motion and non-rigid hand movements poses a significant technical barrier in computer vision. Here, we visualize our forecasting results on this challenging task (best viewed in color).

executing our routine activities. Such a general prediction capability could enable new applications in Augmented Reality (AR) and robotics, such as monitoring for safety in dangerous environments such as construction sites, or facilitating human-robot collaboration via improved anticipation.

To bridge this gap, this paper introduces a novel task of forecasting the detailed representation of future hand movements in egocentric video. Specifically, given an egocentric video, we seek to predict the hand masks of future video frames at three time points defined as short-term, middle-term, and long-term future (see Fig. 1 for a visual illustration of our problem setting). This task is extremely challenging for two reasons: 1) hands are deformable and capable of fast movement, and 2) head and hand motion are entangled in the egocentric video. Addressing these challenges requires the ability to 1) address the inherent uncertainty in anticipating the no-rigid hand movements, and 2) explicitly model the coordination between head and hand [42].

We attack the unique challenges of hand segmentation prediction by introducing a novel deep model – *EgoGAN*. Our model adopts a 3D Fully Convolutional Network (3DFCN) as the backbone to learn spatio-temporal video features. We then utilize the Generative Adversarial Network (GAN) to aid pixel-wise visual anticipation. Instead of using GAN to directly generate future video frame pixels from egocentric videos as in [67], our key insight is to use the GAN to model an underlying distribution of possible future head motion. The adopted generative adversarial training schema can account for the uncertainty of future hand movements anticipation. In addition, the generated future head motion provides ancillary cues that complement video features for anticipating complex egocentric hand movements. Our end-to-end trainable EgoGAN model uses future hand masks as supervisory signals to train the segmentation network and estimated sparse optical flow maps from head motions to train the Generator and the Discriminator. At inference time, our model predicts a time series of future hand masks based *only* on the egocentric video frame inputs.

To demonstrate the benefits of our proposed EgoGAN, we evaluate our model on two egocentric video datasets: EPIC-Kitchens 55 [5] and EGTEA Gaze+ [28].

We first conduct detailed ablation studies to validate our model design, and then compare our approach to the state-of-the-art methods on future image segmentation, demonstrating consistent performance gains on both datasets. We further provide visualizations to show the effect of our method. In summary, our paper makes following contributions:

- We introduce a novel problem of predicting a time series of future hand masks from egocentric videos.
- We propose a novel deep generative model – EgoGAN, that hallucinates future head motions and further predicts future hand masks. To the best of our knowledge, we are the first to use a GAN to generate egocentric motion cues for visual anticipation.
- We conduct comprehensive experiments on two benchmark egocentric video datasets: EPIC-Kitchens 55 [5] and EGTEA Gaze+ [29]. Our model achieves 1.3% performance improvements on EPIC-Kitchens and 0.7% on EGTEA in average F1 score. We also provide visualizations of our results and additional discussion of our method.

2   Related Work

We first review the most relevant works on egocentric vision. We then discuss previous literature on future image segmentation. Furthermore, we describe the related efforts on developing generative models for visual anticipation.

Hands in Egocentric Vision. Previous efforts on egocentric vision addressed a variety interesting problems, including action analysis [8,11,24,28,31,32,38,44, 45,53] and social interaction understanding [7,52,63,65], etc. Here, we focus on discussing prior works on learning hand representations from egocentric videos. The most relevant work is from Liu et al. [32], where they factorized the future hand positions a latent attentional representation for action anticipation without considering the head motion. Similarly, Dessalene et al. [6] focused on predicting the hand-object interaction region of an action. Fathi et al. [9] utilized hand-eye coordination to design a probabilistic model for gaze estimation. Li et al. [30] showed how the motion patterns of the hands can be utilized for egocentric action recognition. Ma et al. [36] made use of a hand segmentation network to predict hand masks for localizing the object of interest and further recognizing the action. Shen et al. [49] proposed to use hand mask and gaze fixation as additional cues for action anticipation. Rather than anticipating the hand movements, these previous works mainly use egocentric hand movements as an additional modality or intermediate representation for egocentric action understanding. Recently, Cai et al. [1] proposed a Bayesian-based domain adaptation framework for hand segmentation on egocentric video frames. In contrast, we address the novel task of predicting pixel-wise hand masks, which captures the fine-grained details of future hand movements.

Future Segmentation. A rich set of literature addressed the related but vastly different task of video segmentation [3,39,54,62,64]. We refer to a recent survey [60] for a thorough discussion on this topic. Note that previous works on video segmentation seek to track the instance masks within the video segment, and therefore do not apply to the anticipation setting, where the information of future video frames is not accessible for making an inference. Fewer works address the more relevant topic of future image semantic segmentation. Luc et al. [35] first investigated the problem of semantic segmentation of future video frames and further extended their work to future instance segmentation [34]. Nabavi et al. [46] utilized the ConvLSTM network to model the temporal correlations of video sequences for future semantic segmentation. Jin et al. [22] proposed to anticipate the future optical flow and future scene segmentation jointly. Recently, Chiu et al. [4] introduced a teacher-student knowledge distillation model for predicting the future semantic segmentation based on preceding video frames. Building on these prior works, we propose the first model to address the future segmentation problem under the challenging egocentric setting. It is worth noting that previous methods recursively predict future segmentation, in which the current anticipation result is used as the input for predicting the segmentation of the next time step. In contrast, we use a 3D Fully Convolutional Network (3DFCN) to predict a time series of future hand masks in one shot. In Sect. 4.3, we show that the 3DFCN can effectively capture the spatio-temporal video features for pixel-wise visual anticipation in an end-to-end fashion. We also compare our EgoGAN model to those relevant works and demonstrate a clear performance improvement.

Generative Models for Visual Anticipation. Tremendous efforts have been made in action anticipation [11,12,16,23–25,32,47,53,56] and generative adversarial networks [14,15,21,37,40,66]. Here we mainly discuss previous investigations on forecasting the human body motions using generative models. Fragkiadaki et al. [10] proposed to use a recurrent network for predicting and generating the human body poses and dynamics from videos. A similar idea was also explored in [17]. Walker et al. [58] utilized Variational Autoencoders (VAE) for predicting the dense trajectories of video pixels. They further leveraged human body poses as an intermediate feature for generating future video frames with a Generative Adversarial Network (GAN) [59]. Gupta et al. [18] explored a GAN-based model for forecasting human trajectories. Zhang et al. [68,69] developed a Conditional Variational Autoencoder to generate human body meshes and motions in 3D scenes. Despite the success in forecasting body motion, the use of GANs was largely understudied in egocentric vision. Zhang et al. [67] used a GAN to generate future video frames and further predict future gaze fixation. Though GAN has the capability of addressing the uncertainty of data distribution, using GANs to directly forecast pixels in video [55] remains a challenge, especially when there exists drastic background motion in the egocentric videos [67]. In contrast, our method adopts the adversarial training mechanism to model the underlying distribution of possible future head motion, and thereby captures the drastic change of scene context in egocentric video. In the ablation study, we show that our approach outperforms a baseline model that uses GAN to directly predict future hand masks.

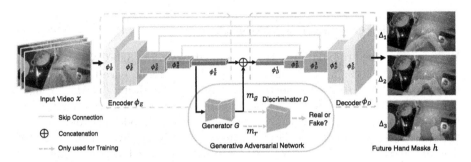

Fig. 2. *Overview of our proposed EgoGAN model.* Our model takes egocentric video frames as the inputs, and outputs future hand masks at different time steps. It is composed of a **3D Fully Convolutional Network (3DFCN)** and a **Generative Adversarial Network (GAN)**. The Encoder Network ϕ_E in the **3DFCN** extracts video features from the input frames, and is then separated into two branches: (1) encoded feature $\phi_E(x)$ is fed into the **Generator (G)** in **GAN** for generating fake future head motion m_g, and a **Discriminator (D)** is trained to distinguish the generated future head motion from the real ones; (2) m_g is concatenated to $\phi_E(x)$ and the concatenated tensor are then fed into the Decoder Network ϕ_D in **3DFCN**. Finally, the encoder features are further combined with corresponding decoder features using skip connections for future hand mask prediction.

3   Method

Given an input egocentric video $x = \{x^1, ..., x^t\}$, where x^t is the video frame indexed by time t, our goal is to predict a time series of future hand masks $h = \{h^{t+\Delta_1}, h^{t+\Delta_2}, h^{t+\Delta_3}\}$. As illustrated in Fig. 1, we consider hand segmentation as a binary classification problem: the value of $h^i(x, y)$ can be viewed as the probability of spatial position (x, y) being a hand pixel at time step i, where $i \in \{t + \Delta_1, t + \Delta_2, t + \Delta_3\}$. Δ_1, Δ_2, and Δ_3 represent the time steps for short-term, middle-term, and long-term future segmentation, respectively. This three-steps-ahead visual anticipation setting is also used in previous works on future image segmentation [35,46].

We now present an overview of our **EgoGAN** model in Fig. 2. We make use of a 3D Fully Convolutional Network (3DFCN) ϕ as the backbone model for future hand segmentation. The 3DFCN is composed of a 3D convolutional encoder ϕ_E and a 3D deconvolutional decoder ϕ_D. We further adopt a Generative Adversarial Network (GAN) for learning future head motions. Specifically, a Generator network (G), composed of 3D convolutional operations, is used to generate future head motion m_g based on the encoded video feature $\phi_E(x)$. A

Discriminator Network (D) is trained to distinguish the fake future head motions m_g from real future head motions m_r. Finally, ϕ_D combines m_g and $\phi_E(x)$ for predicting future hand masks. In the following sections, we detail each key component of our model.

3.1 3D Fully Convolutional Network

We first introduce the 3D Fully Convolutional Network (3DFCN) backbone in our method. We use an I3D model [61] as the backbone encoder network ϕ_E for learning spatio-temporal video representations. Following [19,51], ϕ_E has 5 convolutional blocks, thereby producing video features at different spatial and temporal resolutions. Following [33], we construct the decoder network ϕ_D symmetric to ϕ_E. Therefore, ϕ_D is also composed of 5 deconvolution layers. We denote the encoder and decoder video features from the ith convolutional block as $\phi_E^i(x)$ and $\phi_D^i(x)$, respectively (See Fig. 2 for the index naming of ϕ_E and ϕ_D). The features of each decoder layer are combined with the features from the corresponding encoder block with skip connections and are then fed into the next layer. Formally, we have:

$$\phi_D^{i+1}(x) = deconv(\phi_D^i(x) + \phi_E^{6-i}(x)), \tag{1}$$

where $i \in \{1, 2, 3, 4\}$. We design our decoder so that ϕ_D^i produces a feature map with the same tensor size as $\phi_E^{6-i}(x)$. The deconvolution operation is implemented with 3D transposed convolution. Note that the last deconvolution layer of ϕ_D produces a tensor of the same size as the input video ($T \times W \times H$). We further apply a 3D convolutional operation with a kernel size of $k \times 1 \times 1$ to predict the future hand mask tensor h with size $3 \times W \times H$, where each temporal slice corresponds to the predicted hand masks of the short-term, middle-term, and long-term future video frames. We describe the details of our network architecture in the supplementary materials.

3.2 Generative Adversarial Network

The key to our approach is to use the Generative Adversarial Network (GAN) to hallucinate the future head motions for future hand mask segmentation. Our design choice stems from the observation that head motion causes drastic changes in the active object cues and background scene context captured in the egocentric videos, and this motion is closely related to hand movements. Therefore, we seek to explicitly encode the future head motion cues for hand motion anticipation. Moreover, visual anticipation has intrinsic ambiguity – similar current observations may correspond to different future outcomes. This observation motivates us to use the adversarial training scheme to account for the inherent uncertainty of future representation. In this section, we introduce the egocentric head motion representation. We then describe the design choice and learning objective of the GAN in our method.

Egocentric Head Motion Representation. In the egocentric setting, head motion is implicitly incorporated in the video itself. Thus, we follow [27] to use the sparsely sampled optical flow to represent the egocentric head motion. As mentioned before, the real future head motion is denoted as m_r, and is only available for training.

Generator Network and Discriminator Network. The generator network (G) takes video feature $\phi_E(x)$ as inputs and generates future head motions $m_g = G(\phi_E(x))$. Following [21,57,59,67], G does not take any noise variables as additional inputs. This is because the $\phi_E(x)$ is a latent representation that incorporates the noisy signals of visual anticipation. G is composed of multiple 3D convolutional operations and a nonlinearity function, and is trained to produce a realistic m_g that is difficult to distinguish from m_r for an adversarially-trained discriminator network (D). D takes future head motion samples as inputs and determines whether the input sample is real or fake. It is composed of 3D convolutional operations and a sigmoid function for binary classification, and is trained to classify the input sample as either real or generated.

Learning Objective of GAN. We now formally define the objective function of the GAN in our method. The objective function for training the discriminator network is given by:

$$\mathcal{L}_d = \mathcal{L}_{ce}(D(m_r), 1) + \mathcal{L}_{ce}(D(m_g), 0), \tag{2}$$

where $\mathcal{L}_{ce}$ is the standard cross-entropy loss for binary classification. The generator loss $\mathcal{L}_g$ can be formulated as:

$$\mathcal{L}_g = \mathcal{L}_{ce}(D(m_g), 1) + \lambda |m_g - m_r|. \tag{3}$$

Here, we follow [41] to adopt a traditional L1 distance loss that encourages the generated sample to be visually consistent with the real sample, while λ denotes the weight to balance the two loss terms.

3.3 Full Model of EgoGAN

We now summarize the full architecture of our proposed EgoGAN model. The main idea is to explicitly model the underlying distribution of possible future head motion m_g with the GAN, and use m_g as additional cues to facilitate future hand mask segmentation from the video representations of the encoder network. Specifically, the video feature from the last encoder block $\phi_E^5(x)$ and generated future head motions m_g are concatenated and fed into the first layer of the decoder as inputs. Therefore, we have:

$$\phi_D^1(x) = deconv(\phi_E^5(x) \oplus m_g). \tag{4}$$

Hence, the decoder network jointly considers $\phi_E(x)$ and m_g for predicting future hand masks h.

Training and Inference. We use the binary cross-entropy loss to train the 3DFCN encoder and decoder:

$$\mathcal{L}_{seg} = \mathcal{L}_{ce}(\phi_D(\phi_E(x), m_g), \hat{h}), \tag{5}$$

where $\hat{h}$ denotes the ground truth of future hand masks. We adopt the standard adversarial training pipeline in [14], where G and D are trained to play against each other. Therefore, we let the gradients alternatively flow through D, and then G. Moreover, we freeze the encoder weights during the gradient step on G and D, and freeze the generator weights during the gradient step on the 3DFCN to isolate their training processes from each other.

Note that our model does not need the real future head motion as additional inputs at inference time. Instead, our model can generate future head motion and further predict future hand masks based on only raw video frames.

3.4   Implementation Details

Network Architecture. We adopt an I3D-Res50 model [2,61] that is pre-trained on Kinetics as the backbone encoder network. It is composed of five 3D convolutional blocks, connecting with a symmetrical decoder network that contains five 3D deconvolutional layers. As for the GAN network, the generator network takes the video features from the 5th block of the encoder network as inputs and produces a low-resolution future head motion flow map as output. The discriminator network serves as a binary classifier to supervise the quality of the output of the generator. Our model is implemented in PyTorch and will be made publicly available.

Training Schema. As discussed in the previous section, the gradients step separately for 3D Fully Convolutional Network (3DFCN), Generator (G), and Discriminator (D). The 3DFCN model is trained using an SGD optimizer with momentum of 0.9. The initial learning rate is 0.1 with cosine decay. We set weight decay to 1e–4 and enable batch norm [20]. G and D are trained using the Adam Optimizer with momentum parameters $\beta_1 = 0.5$, $\beta_2 = 0.999$ and a initial learning rate of 0.01 with cosine decay. Our model was trained for 70 epochs with batch size 16 on 4 GPUs, and synchronized batch normalization was enabled.

Data Processing. We downsampled all video frames to a height of 256 while preserving the original aspect ratio. For training, we applied several data augmentation techniques, including random flipping, rotation, cropping, and color jittering to avoid overfitting. Our model takes an input of 8 frames (temporally sampled by 8) with a resolution of 224×224. We use the TV-L1 algorithm [43] to compute the optical flow, and sparsely sample from the computed flow map to approximate the head motion as discussed in Sect. 3.2. Therefore, the head motion is represented as a sparse flow map spatially downsampled by 32. At inference time, our model takes the downsampled videos with the original aspect ratio as inputs, and predicts the future hand masks.

4   Experiments

4.1   Dataset and Metrics

Dataset. We make use of two egocentric video benchmark datasets: EPIC-Kitchens 55 [5] and EGTEA Gaze+ [29]. For the EPIC-Kitchens dataset, we set $\delta_{1,2,3} = \{1, 15, 30\}$, which corresponds to a long-term anticipation time of 1.0 s. As for the EGTEA dataset, we set $\Delta_{1,2,3} = \{1, 6, 12\}$, which corresponds to an anticipation time of 0.5 s, because EGTEA has a smaller angle of view in comparison with the EPIC-Kitchens. The same anticipation time setup is also adopted in [32]. To encourage our model to capture the meaningful preparation and planning process of daily actions, we segment the data so that the long-term future frame is chosen right before the beginning of each trimmed action segment annotated in EPIC-Kitchens and EGTEA. We use the train/val split provided by [11] for EPIC-Kitchens 55 and the train/test split1 from EGTEA. We remove the instances where hands are not captured within the anticipation segment, which results in 11,935/2,746 (train/val) samples on EPIC-Kitchens, and 4,042/991 (train/test) samples on EGTEA.

Hand Mask Ground Truth. For the EPIC-Kitchens dataset, we use the domain adaption method introduced in [1] to generate the ground truth hand masks. [1] has empirically verified the quality of generated hand masks. As for the EGTEA dataset, we train a 2D FCN model for frame-level hand segmentation using the provided hand mask annotation. As discussed in [26], the FCN model can generalize well on the entire dataset. We thus use the inference results on the anticipation video frames as the ground truth of future hand masks.

Metrics. As discussed in Sect. 3, we consider future hand segmentation as a pixel-wise binary classification problem. Previous future image segmentation works [4,22] use pixel accuracy and mIoU as evaluation metrics. However, pixel accuracy does not penalize the false-negative prediction of the long-tailed distribution, and mIoU can not properly evaluate the shape of the predicted masks for binary segmentation. Therefore, we follow [28,32] to report Precision and Recall values together with their corresponding F1 scores.

4.2   Model Ablations and Analysis

To validate our model design, we conduct experiments on ablations and variations in our model. Specifically, we investigate how the egocentric head motion cues facilitate future hand segmentation and demonstrate the benefits of using the GAN for modeling future head motion. We also show how modeling the future gaze as attentional representation affects the future hand segmentation performance.

Table 1. *Analysis of variations in our approach.* We conduct detailed ablation studies to validate our model design, and further show the results of variations of our method to demonstrate the benefits of using the GAN for modeling future head motion. *: HeadDir takes future head motions as additional input modalities at inference time, which in fact violates the future anticipation setting (See more discussion in Sect. 4.2). The best results are highlighted with **boldface**.

(a) Experimental Results on EPIC-Kitchens Dataset

Method	EPIC-Kitchens (Precision/ Recall/ F1 Score)		
	Short-term	Middle-term	Long-term
Future gaze	N/A	N/A	N/A
HeadDir*	70.55/ 71.33/ 70.94	43.15/ 53.66/ 47.83	30.51/ 49.60/ 37.78
3DFCN (w/o GAN, w/o Head)	69.51/ 70.81/ 70.15	42.51/ 51.66/ 46.64	29.88/ 47.46/ 36.67
HeadReg (w/o GAN, w/ Head)	70.46/ 70.25/ 70.36	41.41/ 52.55/ 46.32	29.22/ 48.50/ 36.47
DirectGan (w/ GAN, w/o Head)	69.12/ **71.60**/ 70.34	43.83/ 51.32/ 47.28	30.76/ 47.48/ 37.33
EgoGAN (w/ GAN, w/ Head)	**70.89**/ 71.24/ **71.07**	**43.79/ 53.23/ 48.05**	**31.39/ 48.57/ 38.14**

(b) Experimental Results on EGTEA Gaze+ Dataset

Method	EGTEA (Precision/ Recall/ F1 Score)		
	Short-term	Middle-term	Long-term
Future gaze	45.17/ 59.94/ 51.51	38.63/ 64.02/ 48.19	35.71/ 63.78/ 45.78
HeadDir*	44.58/ 63.87/ 52.51	41.29/ 60.65/ 49.13	39.36/ 59.02/ 47.23
3DFCN (w/o GAN, w/o Head)	43.62/ **61.69**/ 51.11	40.25/ 58.93/ 47.83	37.83/ 58.32/ 45.89
HeadReg (w/o GAN, w/ Head)	43.54/ 61.03/ 50.82	**41.31**/ 55.24/ 47.27	36.87/ 58.23/ 45.15
DirectGan (w/ GAN, w/o Head)	43.78/ 61.33/ 51.09	38.38/ **63.81**/ 47.93	35.53/ **63.41**/ 45.54
EgoGAN (w/ GAN, w/ Head)	**44.91**/ 61.48/ **51.91**	41.10/ 59.90/ **48.75**	**38.16**/ 59.88/ **46.61**

Benefits of Encoding Future Head Motions. As a starting point, we compare the model that uses only the 3D Fully Convolutional Network (denoted as *3DFCN*) with the model that directly takes future head motion as an additional input modality (denoted as *HeadDir*). HeadDir shares the same backbone network as 3DFCN, but requires the future head motions for making an inference and therefore violates the future anticipation setting, where the model can not use any information from the anticipation video segment for making an inference. HeadDir quantifies the performance improvement when the egocentric head motion cues are explicitly encoded into the model in a two-stream structure [50]. The experimental results are summarized in Table 1. Compared to 3DFCN, HeadDir achieves a large performance gain on EPIC-Kitchens (+0.8%/1.2/1.1% in F1 score for short/middle/long term anticipation), and reaches (+1.4%/1.3%/1.3%) on EGTEA.

Our method, on the other hand, consistently outperforms 3DFCN on both EPIC-Kitchens(+0.9%/1.5%/1.8%) and EGTEA (+0.8%/0.9%/0.7%). More importantly, our method improves HeadDir by +0.1%/0.2%/0.4% on EPIC-Kitchens. This result suggests that the GAN from our model does not simply learn to predict a future head motion flow map; instead, it models the underlying distribution of possible future head motion and thus improves the future hand anticipation accuracy by addressing the inherent uncertainty of visual forecasting. It is to be observed that our model slightly lags behind HeadDir (0.6%/0.4%/0.6% ↓) on EGTEA, because EGTEA has fewer samples to train our deep generative model. And we also re-emphasize that our method does not use any additional inputs at inference time as in HeadDir.

The Effect of GAN. To further show the benefits of using the GAN for learning future head motions, we consider a baseline model – *HeadReg*, that uses a regression network to predict future head motions with only L1 distance in Eq. 3. Note that the regression network is implemented the same way as the generator network from EgoGAN. As shown in Table 1, without using an adversarial training mechanism in our approach, HeadReg lags behind our model by 0.7%/1.7%/1.7% ↓ and 1.1%/1.5%/1.5% ↓ in F1 score for short/middle/long term anticipation on EPIC-Kitchens and EGTEA, respectively. These results support our claim that the GAN can address the stochastic nature of representation and thereby outperforms HeadReg by a notable margin on the future hand segmentation task.

Video Pixel Generation vs. Head Motion Generation. We denote another baseline model that directly uses a GAN for anticipating future hand masks, as *DirectGan*. This model is composed of the 3DFCN backbone network that generates the future hand masks, and a discriminator network that classifies whether the given hand masks are real or not. The results are presented in Table 1. Importantly, the adversarial training schema in DirectGan slightly decreases the performance of 3DFCN model on EGTEA, and has minor improvement on EPIC-Kitchens. We speculate that this is because directly using a GAN for predicting future hand masks cannot effectively capture the drastic change of scene context in egocentric video. In contrast, our model uses a GAN to explicitly model the head-hand coordination in the egocentric video thereby being capable of more accurately forecasting egocentric hand masks.

Future Head Motion vs. Future Gaze. Furthermore, we present experimental results on how modeling future gaze fixation affects future hand segmentation. Note that the gaze tracking data is only available for the EGTEA dataset. Specifically, we make use of a GAN to model the probabilistic distribution of future gaze fixation. Instead of concatenating future gaze with encoded video features as in Eq. 4, we follow [28] to use gaze distribution as a saliency map to select important spatio-temporal video features with element-wise multiplication. As shown in Table 1, the resulting future gaze model slightly outperforms the baseline 3DFCN model, yet lags behind our model that uses head motion as the key representation (0.7%/0.6%/0.6% ↓ in F1 score on EGTEA). Previous work [27] suggested that eye-head-hand coordination is important for egocentric gaze estimation, while our results further show that exploiting the eye-head-hand coordination is also beneficial for pixel-wise egocentric visual anticipation. Moreover, future head motion potentially plays a more important role than future gaze fixation on our fine-grained hand forecasting task.

Analysis on Ablation Studies. To help interpret the performance improvement of our method, we consider a baseline 3DFCN model that uses dense I3D-Res101 as the encoder network. Importantly, with 50 more layers, the I3D-Res101 backbone can only improve the model performance by +0.1%/0.3%/0.3% on EPIC-Kitchens and +0.7%/0.4%/0.5% on EGTEA. As shown in Table 1, our model has a larger performance improvement than switching to a dense encoder network. In supplementary material, we also present additional results of our model using the I3D-Res101 backbone and further demonstrate our method is a robust approach that can generalize to different backbone networks.

4.3   Comparison to State-of-the-Art Methods

We are the first to address the challenging problem of future hand segmentation from the egocentric video. We note that another branch of prior work considered the related problem of future image segmentation [3,39,54,62,64], track instances masks over time, and therefore can not be used to address the future segmentation problem where the future video frames are not available as inputs for the tracking model. Therefore, we adapt previous state-of-the-art future image segmentation methods to our problem setting and consider the following strong baselines (additional discussion of the baseline choices can be found in the supplementary material):

Table 2. *Comparison with previous state-of-the-art methods on future image segmentation.* Our results consistently outperform the second-best results (across all methods) by +1.3% on EPIC-Kitchens and +0.7% on EGTEA in average F1 score. *: We re-implement the model to take raw video frames as inputs as our method (See more discussion in Sect. 4.3). The best results are highlighted with **boldface**, and the second-best results are underlined.

(a) Experimental Results on EPIC-Kitchens Dataset

Method	Epic-Kitchens (Precision/ Recall/ F1 Score)		
	Short-term	Middle-term	Long-term
X2X [35]	68.69/ 69.35/ 69.02	40.81/ 50.61/ 45.18	28.14/ 45.76/ 34.85
ConvLSTM [46]	69.02/ 69.44/ 69.22	42.72 /51.78/ 46.82	30.01/ 48.01/ 36.94
FlowTrans [22]	69.38/ 69.70 /69.54	42.90/ 52.02/ 47.02	30.19/ 47.56/ 36.94
EgoGAN (Ours)	**70.89/ 71.24/ 71.07**	**43.79/ 53.23/ 48.05**	**31.39/ 48.57/ 38.14**

(b) Experimental Results on EGTEA Gaze+ Dataset

Method	EGTEA (Precision/ Recall/ F1 Score)		
	Short-term	Middle-term	Long-term
X2X [35]	42.96/ 59.32/ 49.84	38.70/ 59.89/ 47.01	36.55/ 59.67/ 45.33
ConvLSTM [46]	44.55/ 59.43/ 50.93	38.28/ **63.54**/ 47.78	36.58/ 62.04/ 46.03
FlowTrans [22]	44.22/ 61.36/ 51.40	40.38/ 58.62/ 47.82	35.04/ **64.34**/ 45.37
EgoGAN (Ours)	**44.91/ 61.48/ 51.91**	**41.10**/ 59.90/ **48.75**	**38.16**/ 59.88/ **46.61**

- X2X [35] proposes a recursive method that uses the anticipated mask at time step $t + 1$ as an input to predict the future masks at time step $t + 2$, and so forth.
- FlowTrans [22] jointly predicts the masks and optical flow at time step $t + 1$ and recursively predicts the future masks with preceding flow and masks.
- ConvLSTM [46] uses a Convolutional LSTM to model the temporal relationships of image features, and uses both the sequence of image features and the output of the ConvLSTM module for future image segmentation.

It is worth noting that the baseline methods [22, 35, 46] adopt a weaker backbone network than ours. To show that the performance gain of our method does not come from a stronger video feature encoder, we re-implement the above methods with the same I3D-Res50 backbone network as ours. Moreover, both FlowTrans and ConvLSTM assume accurate semantic segmentation of observable video frames is available as input, but our model seeks to forecast future hand segmentation using only raw video frames, and thus is a more challenging and practical setting. In addition, accurate semantic segmentation results on egocentric video frames are difficult to obtain due to the domain gap and lack of training data. Therefore, for a fair comparison, we implement the ConvLSTM and FlowTrans models to take the same input as our method. In our supplementary materials, we show that using the segmentation results from the pre-trained segmentation network as inputs will compromise the performance of FlowTrans and ConvLSTM.

The experimental results are summarized in Table 2. Among all baseline methods, FlowTrans achieves the best performance for short-term anticipation. However, it is less effective for long-term anticipation, due to the error accumulation of predicted future optical flow. ConvLSTM can better capture the long-term temporal relationship and thereby achieving the best baseline performance for long-term anticipation. Instead of encoding the temporal connection with recursive prediction, we found that the 3D deconvolution operation is effective for capturing the temporal correlation of anticipation video segments, and in doing so, it helps capture the future hand masks in one shot. More importantly, our method outperforms previous best results (underlined in Table 2) by +1.5%/1.0%/1.2% and +0.5%/0.9%/0.6% in F1 score for short/middle/long term hand mask anticipation on EPIC-Kitchens and EGTEA, respectively. Once again, these results demonstrate the benefits of explicitly modeling future head motion with a GAN.

4.4   Discussion

Visualization. We visualize the results from both our method *EgoGAN* and the best baseline *FlowTrans* on EPIC-Kitchens in Fig. 3. Even though our proposed problem of future hand segmentation from egocentric video poses a formidable challenge in computer vision, our method can more accurately predict the hand region of future frames compared to FlowTrans, together with capturing the hand shape and poses. Notably, as the uncertainty increases with the anticipation

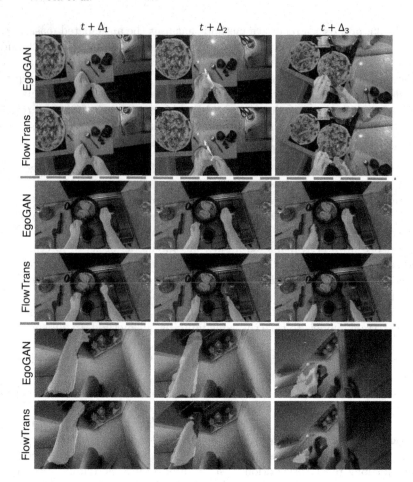

Fig. 3. *Visualization of our results.* From left to right, each column presents the future hand segmentation results of short-term $(t + \Delta_1)$, middle-term $(t + \Delta_2)$, and long-term $(t + \Delta_3)$ time steps from the EPIC-Kitchens dataset. Predictions from our method *EgoGAN* and the best baseline *FlowTrans* are presented in each sample. (See more discussion in Sect. 4.4)

time, our model may produce blurry predictions, yet can still robustly localize the hand region. The video demo in our supplementary material also suggests that our approach can produce satisfying results even when there are drastic hand and head movements. We conjecture that our model can better forecast the scene context change driven by head motion, and thereby more accurately predicts future hand masks.

Remarks. To summarize, our quantitative results indicate that future head motion carries important information for future hand movements. We show that explicitly modeling the underlying distribution of possible future hand movements with a GAN enables the model to predict the future hand masks more accurately. Another important takeaway is that our method is more effective than directly using a GAN for predicting future hand masks, as reported in Table 1. Furthermore, our visualizations demonstrate that our method can effectively predict future hand masks.

Limitations and Future Work. We also point out the limitations of our method. Since the hand mask ground truth does not differentiate left and right hands, our method cannot make separate predictions for the left and right hands. Recent work [48] does have the capability of localizing left and right hand bounding boxes separately during human-object interaction, and we plan to explore this direction in our future work on visual anticipation. In addition, our work does not explicitly exploit the action and object features for future hand prediction and will leave this for our future efforts. Nonetheless, our work investigates a novel and important problem in egocentric vision, and offers insight into visual anticipation and video pixel generation.

5   Conclusion

In this paper, we introduce the novel task of predicting a time series of future hand masks from egocentric videos. We present a novel deep generative model EgoGAN to address our proposed problem. The key innovation of our method is to use a GAN module that explicitly models the underlying distribution of possible future head motion for a more accurate prediction of future hand masks. We demonstrate the benefits of our method on two egocentric benchmark datasets, EGTEA Gaze+ and EPIC-Kitchens 55. We believe our work provides an essential step for visual anticipation as well as video pixel generation, and points to new research directions in the egocentric video.

Acknowledgments. Portions of this project were supported in part by a gift from Facebook. We thank Fiona Ryan for the valuable feedback.

References

1. Cai, M., Lu, F., Sato, Y.: Generalizing hand segmentation in egocentric videos with uncertainty-guided model adaptation. In: CVPR (2020)
2. Carreira, J., Zisserman, A.: Quo vadis, action recognition? a new model and the kinetics dataset. In: CVPR (2017)
3. Chandra, S., Couprie, C., Kokkinos, I.: Deep spatio-temporal random fields for efficient video segmentation. In: CVPR (2018)
4. Chiu, H.K., Adeli, E., Niebles, J.C.: Segmenting the future. In: ICRA-L (2020)

5. Damen, D., et al.: Scaling egocentric vision: the dataset. In: Ferrari, V., Hebert, M., Sminchisescu, C., Weiss, Y. (eds.) ECCV 2018. LNCS, vol. 11208, pp. 753–771. Springer, Cham (2018). https://doi.org/10.1007/978-3-030-01225-0_44

6. Dessalene, E., Devaraj, C., Maynord, M., Fermuller, C., Aloimonos, Y.: Forecasting action through contact representations from first person video. TPAMI (2021)

7. Fathi, A., Hodgins, J.K., Rehg, J.M.: Social interactions: a first-person perspective. In: CVPR (2012)

8. Fathi, A., Farhadi, A., Rehg, J.M.: Understanding egocentric activities. In: ICCV (2011)

9. Fathi, A., Li, Y., Rehg, J.M.: Learning to recognize daily actions using gaze. In: Fitzgibbon, A., Lazebnik, S., Perona, P., Sato, Y., Schmid, C. (eds.) ECCV 2012. LNCS, vol. 7572, pp. 314–327. Springer, Heidelberg (2012). https://doi.org/10. 1007/978-3-642-33718-5_23

10. Fragkiadaki, K., Levine, S., Felsen, P., Malik, J.: Recurrent network models for human dynamics. In: ICCV (2015)

11. Furnari, A., Farinella, G.M.: What would you expect? anticipating egocentric actions with rolling-unrolling lstms and modality attention. In: ICCV (2019)

12. Gao, J., Yang, Z., Nevatia, R.: Red: reinforced encoder-decoder networks for action anticipation. In: BMVC (2017)

13. Girdhar, R., Grauman, K.: Anticipative video transformer. In: ICCV (2021)

14. Goodfellow, I., et al.: Generative adversarial nets. In: NeurIPS (2014)

15. Gregor, K., Danihelka, I., Graves, A., Rezende, D., Wierstra, D.: Draw: a recurrent neural network for image generation. In: International Conference on Machine Learning, pp. 1462–1471. PMLR (2015)

16. Guan, J., Yuan, Y., Kitani, K.M., Rhinehart, N.: Generative hybrid representations for activity forecasting with no-regret learning. In: CVPR (2020)

17. Gui, L.-Y., Wang, Y.-X., Liang, X., Moura, J.M.F.: Adversarial geometry-aware human motion prediction. In: Ferrari, V., Hebert, M., Sminchisescu, C., Weiss, Y. (eds.) ECCV 2018. LNCS, vol. 11208, pp. 823–842. Springer, Cham (2018). https://doi.org/10.1007/978-3-030-01225-0_48

18. Gupta, A., Johnson, J., Fei-Fei, L., Savarese, S., Alahi, A.: Social gan: socially acceptable trajectories with generative adversarial networks. In: CVPR (2018)

19. He, K., Zhang, X., Ren, S., Sun, J.: Deep residual learning for image recognition. In: CVPR (2016)

20. Ioffe, S., Szegedy, C.: Batch normalization: accelerating deep network training by reducing internal covariate shift. In: ICML (2015)

21. Isola, P., Zhu, J.Y., Zhou, T., Efros, A.A.: Image-to-image translation with conditional adversarial networks. In: CVPR (2017)

22. Jin, X., et al.: Predicting scene parsing and motion dynamics in the future. In: NeurIPS (2017)

23. Kataoka, H., Miyashita, Y., Hayashi, M., Iwata, K., Satoh, Y.: Recognition of transitional action for short-term action prediction using discriminative temporal cnn feature. In: BMVC (2016)

24. Ke, Q., Fritz, M., Schiele, B.: Time-conditioned action anticipation in one shot. In: CVPR (2019)

25. Kitani, K.M., Ziebart, B.D., Bagnell, J.A., Hebert, M.: Activity forecasting. In: Fitzgibbon, A., Lazebnik, S., Perona, P., Sato, Y., Schmid, C. (eds.) ECCV 2012. LNCS, vol. 7575, pp. 201–214. Springer, Heidelberg (2012). https://doi.org/10. 1007/978-3-642-33765-9_15

26. Li, Y.: Learning embodied models of actions from first person video. Ph.D. thesis, Georgia Institute of Technology (2017)

27. Li, Y., Fathi, A., Rehg, J.M.: Learning to predict gaze in egocentric video. In: ICCV (2013)
28. Li, Y., Liu, M., Rehg, J.M.: In the eye of beholder: joint learning of gaze and actions in first person video. In: Ferrari, V., Hebert, M., Sminchisescu, C., Weiss, Y. (eds.) ECCV 2018. LNCS, vol. 11209, pp. 639–655. Springer, Cham (2018). https://doi.org/10.1007/978-3-030-01228-1_38
29. Li, Y., Liu, M., Rehg, J.M.: In the eye of the beholder: gaze and actions in first person video. TPAMI (2021)
30. Li, Y., Ye, Z., Rehg, J.M.: Delving into egocentric actions. In: CVPR (2015)
31. Liu, M., et al.: Egocentric activity recognition and localization on a 3D map. arXiv preprint arXiv:2105.09544 (2021)
32. Liu, M., Tang, S., Li, Y., Rehg, J.M.: Forecasting human-object interaction: joint prediction of motor attention and actions in first person video. In: Vedaldi, A., Bischof, H., Brox, T., Frahm, J.-M. (eds.) ECCV 2020. LNCS, vol. 12346, pp. 704–721. Springer, Cham (2020). https://doi.org/10.1007/978-3-030-58452-8_41
33. Long, J., Shelhamer, E., Darrell, T.: Fully convolutional networks for semantic segmentation. In: CVPR (2015)
34. Luc, P., Couprie, C., LeCun, Y., Verbeek, J.: Predicting future instance segmentation by forecasting convolutional features. In: Ferrari, V., Hebert, M., Sminchisescu, C., Weiss, Y. (eds.) ECCV 2018. LNCS, vol. 11213, pp. 593–608. Springer, Cham (2018). https://doi.org/10.1007/978-3-030-01240-3_36
35. Luc, P., Neverova, N., Couprie, C., Verbeek, J., LeCun, Y.: Predicting deeper into the future of semantic segmentation. In: ICCV (2017)
36. Ma, M., Fan, H., Kitani, K.M.: Going deeper into first-person activity recognition. In: CVPR (2016)
37. Mirza, M., Osindero, S.: Conditional generative adversarial nets. arXiv preprint arXiv:1411.1784 (2014)
38. Moltisanti, D., Wray, M., Mayol-Cuevas, W., Damen, D.: Trespassing the boundaries: labeling temporal bounds for object interactions in egocentric video. In: ICCV (2017)
39. Nilsson, D., Sminchisescu, C.: Semantic video segmentation by gated recurrent flow propagation. In: CVPR (2018)
40. Odena, A., Olah, C., Shlens, J.: Conditional image synthesis with auxiliary classifier gans. In: ICML (2017)
41. Pathak, D., Krahenbuhl, P., Donahue, J., Darrell, T., Efros, A.A.: Context encoders: feature learning by inpainting. In: CVPR (2016)
42. Pelz, J., Hayhoe, M., Loeber, R.: The coordination of eye, head, and hand movements in a natural task. Exp. Brain Res. 139(3), 266–277 (2001)
43. Pérez, J.S., Meinhardt-Llopis, E., Facciolo, G.: TV-L1 optical flow estimation. In: IPOL (2013)
44. Poleg, Y., Arora, C., Peleg, S.: Temporal segmentation of egocentric videos. In: CVPR (2014)
45. Poleg, Y., Ephrat, A., Peleg, S., Arora, C.: Compact CNN for indexing egocentric videos. In: WACV (2016)
46. Rochan, M., et al.: Future semantic segmentation with convolutional lstm. In: BMVC (2018)
47. Rodriguez, C., Fernando, B., Li, H.: Action anticipation by predicting future dynamic images. In: Leal-Taixé, L., Roth, S. (eds.) ECCV 2018. LNCS, vol. 11131, pp. 89–105. Springer, Cham (2019). https://doi.org/10.1007/978-3-030-11015-4_10
48. Shan, D., Geng, J., Shu, M., Fouhey, D.: Understanding human hands in contact at internet scale. In: CVPR (2020)

49. Shen, Y., Ni, B., Li, Z., Zhuang, N.: Egocentric activity prediction via event modulated attention. In: Ferrari, V., Hebert, M., Sminchisescu, C., Weiss, Y. (eds.) ECCV 2018. LNCS, vol. 11206, pp. 202–217. Springer, Cham (2018). https://doi.org/10.1007/978-3-030-01216-8_13
50. Simonyan, K., Zisserman, A.: Two-stream convolutional networks for action recognition in videos. In: NeurIPS (2014)
51. Simonyan, K., Zisserman, A.: Very deep convolutional networks for large-scale image recognition. In: ICLR (2015)
52. Soo Park, H., Shi, J.: Social saliency prediction. In: CVPR (2015)
53. Soran, B., Farhadi, A., Shapiro, L.: Generating notifications for missing actions: Don't forget to turn the lights off! In: ICCV (2015)
54. Tsai, Y.H., Yang, M.H., Black, M.J.: Video segmentation via object flow. In: CVPR (2016)
55. Tulyakov, S., Liu, M.Y., Yang, X., Kautz, J.: Mocogan: decomposing motion and content for video generation. In: CVPR (2018)
56. Vondrick, C., Pirsiavash, H., Torralba, A.: Anticipating visual representations from unlabeled video. In: CVPR (2016)
57. Vondrick, C., Pirsiavash, H., Torralba, A.: Generating videos with scene dynamics. In: NeurIPS (2016)
58. Walker, J., Doersch, C., Gupta, A., Hebert, M.: An uncertain future: forecasting from static images using variational autoencoders. In: Leibe, B., Matas, J., Sebe, N., Welling, M. (eds.) ECCV 2016. LNCS, vol. 9911, pp. 835–851. Springer, Cham (2016). https://doi.org/10.1007/978-3-319-46478-7_51
59. Walker, J., Marino, K., Gupta, A., Hebert, M.: The pose knows: video forecasting by generating pose futures. In: ICCV (2017)
60. Wang, W., Zhou, T., Porikli, F., Crandall, D., Van Gool, L.: A survey on deep learning technique for video segmentation. arXiv preprint arXiv:2107.01153 (2021)
61. Wang, X., Girshick, R., Gupta, A., He, K.: Non-local neural networks. In: CVPR (2018)
62. Xu, Y.S., Fu, T.J., Yang, H.K., Lee, C.Y.: Dynamic video segmentation network. In: CVPR (2018)
63. Yagi, T., Mangalam, K., Yonetani, R., Sato, Y.: Future person localization in first-person videos. In: CVPR (2018)
64. Yang, L., Fan, Y., Xu, N.: Video instance segmentation. In: ICCV (2019)
65. Yonetani, R., Kitani, K.M., Sato, Y.: Recognizing micro-actions and reactions from paired egocentric videos. In: CVPR (2016)
66. Zhang, H., et al.: Stackgan: text to photo-realistic image synthesis with stacked generative adversarial networks. In: ICCV (2017)
67. Zhang, M., Teck Ma, K., Hwee Lim, J., Zhao, Q., Feng, J.: Deep future gaze: gaze anticipation on egocentric videos using adversarial networks. In: CVPR (2017)
68. Zhang, Y., Black, M.J., Tang, S.: We are more than our joints: predicting how 3D bodies move. In: CVPR (2021)
69. Zhang, Y., Hassan, M., Neumann, H., Black, M.J., Tang, S.: Generating 3D people in scenes without people. In: CVPR (2020)

My View is the Best View: Procedure Learning from Egocentric Videos

Siddhant Bansal[1]([envelope]), Chetan Arora[2], and C. V. Jawahar[1]

[1] Center for Visual Information Technology, IIIT, Hyderabad, India
siddhant.bansal@research.iiit.ac.in
[2] Indian Institute of Technology, Delhi, India

Abstract. Procedure learning involves identifying the key-steps and determining their logical order to perform a task. Existing approaches commonly use third-person videos for learning the procedure, making the manipulated object small in appearance and often occluded by the actor, leading to significant errors. In contrast, we observe that videos obtained from first-person (egocentric) wearable cameras provide an unobstructed and clear view of the action. However, procedure learning from egocentric videos is challenging because (a) the camera view undergoes extreme changes due to the wearer's head motion, and (b) the presence of unrelated frames due to the unconstrained nature of the videos. Due to this, current state-of-the-art methods' assumptions that the actions occur at approximately the same time and are of the same duration, do not hold. Instead, we propose to use the signal provided by the temporal correspondences between key-steps across videos. To this end, we present a novel self-supervised Correspond and Cut (CnC) framework for procedure learning. CnC identifies and utilizes the temporal correspondences between the key-steps across multiple videos to learn the procedure. Our experiments show that CnC outperforms the state-of-the-art on the benchmark ProceL and CrossTask datasets by 5.2% and 6.3%, respectively. Furthermore, for procedure learning using egocentric videos, we propose the EgoProceL dataset consisting of 62 hours of videos captured by 130 subjects performing 16 tasks. The source code and the dataset are available on the project page https://sid2697.github.io/egoprocel/.

1 Introduction

Imagine showing an autonomous agent how to prepare a sandwich, and it learns the steps required for it! Motivated by this vision, our work focuses on developing a framework that allows an agent to identify the steps required to perform a task and their order after observing multiple visual demonstrations by experts. Given a set of instructional videos for the same task, procedure learning [18,

---

Supplementary Information The online version contains supplementary material available at https://doi.org/10.1007/978-3-031-19778-9_38.

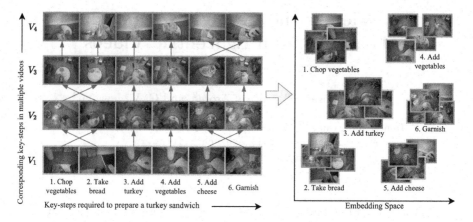

Fig. 1. The left-hand side figure shows six key-steps required to prepare a turkey sandwich [47] across four egocentric videos. The arrows among the videos highlight the change in the ordering of corresponding key-steps. This work utilizes these correspondences and aims to learn an embedding space where the corresponding key-steps have similar embeddings (right-hand side figure). To this end, we propose CnC which learns the embedding space and utilizes it to localize the key-steps and identify their ordering.

19, 63] broadly consists of two steps, (a) assigning all the frames to the K key-steps (including the background), and (b) discovering the logical ordering of the key-steps required to perform the task. Procedure learning differs from action segmentation as it aims to *jointly* segment common key-steps (actions required to accomplish a task, as shown in Fig. 1) across a given set of videos. In contrast, action segmentation aims to identify actions (unrelated to their relevance to accomplishing a task) from a *single* video. Furthermore, procedure learning deals with additional or missing key-steps and background actions unrelated to the task and identifies an ordering of the key-steps.

Existing instructional videos datasets [2, 19, 33, 38, 51, 67, 77, 79] majorly consist of third-person videos. Here, the camera is kept far from the expert, to avoid interference in the actual task. Due to this, the manipulated objects are typically small or sometimes invisible. Additionally, third-person videos can be captured from various positions, leading to wide variations in the camera viewpoints for the same task [11]. Further, most datasets comprise videos scraped from the internet (YouTube) [19, 33, 51, 67, 79], which are noisy and have large irrelevant segments. In contrast, egocentric cameras are typically harnessed to the subject's head and have a standardized location. They provide a clearer view of the executed task, including the manipulated objects. As a result, recent works have introduced datasets consisting of egocentric videos [9, 24, 32, 47, 57, 64], which have proven helpful for various tasks [23, 31, 46, 54, 65].

Motivated by the advantages of egocentric videos over third-person videos, we propose an egocentric videos dataset for procedure learning: EgoProceL. EgoProceL consists of 62 hours of egocentric videos of 16 tasks ranging from making a salmon sandwich to assembling a Personal Computer (PC), thereby ensuring diversity of tasks and facilitating generalizable methods. However, egocentric videos come with their own set of challenges. For example, the camera view undergoes extreme movements due to the wearer's head motion, introducing frames unrelated to the activity and unavailability of the actor's pose [65].

To overcome the challenges and learn the procedure from egocentric videos, we propose utilizing the signal provided by temporal correspondences across videos. As shown in Fig. 1, critical moments like putting a slice of turkey on the bread while preparing a turkey sandwich are present across all the videos. To exploit the signal provided by such temporal correspondences, we propose a self-supervised, three-stage, Correspond and Cut (CnC) framework for procedure learning. The first stage of the CnC uses the proposed self-supervised TC3I loss to learn an embedding space such that the same key-steps across the videos have similar embeddings (Fig. 1). The second stage consists of the proposed ProCut Module (PCM). PCM performs clustering on the learned embeddings and assigns each frame to a key-step. The final stage of CnC creates a key-step sequence for each video and infers relevant ordering to perform the task.

Current works mostly use frame-wise metrics to evaluate the models developed for procedure learning [18,19,40,63,70]. While these metrics evaluate the procedure reasonably well compared to simply calculating the accuracy, they do not suit datasets with significant class imbalance. Furthermore, procedure learning datasets consist of significant background frames [79]. Hence, a model assigning all the frames to the background might achieve high scores. We propose to solve this problem by calculating the scores via the contribution of each key-step, leading to lower scores when models assign most of the frames to the background. Further, when comparing with the previous works, (a) we use CnC on standard third-person benchmark datasets [19,79] and (b) employ existing metrics to evaluate. We show that CnC outperforms the state-of-the-art techniques for procedure learning (Table 2).

Contributions: The major contributions of our work are:

- To facilitate procedure learning from egocentric videos, we create the Ego-ProceLdataset. The dataset consists of 62 hours of videos captured by 130 subjects performing 16 tasks.
- We propose CnC, which utilizes the proposed TC3I loss and PCM to identify the key-steps and their ordering required to perform a task.
- We investigate the usefulness of egocentric videos over third-person videos for procedure learning. We observe an average improvement of 2.7% in the F1-Score when using egocentric videos instead of third-person videos.
- The EgoProceLdataset and the code written for this work are released on http://cvit.iiit.ac.in/research/projects/cvit-projects/egoprocel (mirror link).

2   Related Works

We aim to perform procedure learning in a self-supervised fashion, unlike previous works [53,61,77], which assume the availability of mapping between video frames and key-steps. Also, different from weakly supervised approaches [3, 7, 13, 30, 44, 45, 59, 60, 79], we neither use the number of key-steps required to perform the task nor an ordered or unordered list, as it requires viewing the videos or defining heuristics, leading to scalability issues [18, 19]. Additionally, learning various procedures requires numerous videos and annotating all the videos would consume considerable resources. Motivated by this, we create CnC as a self-supervised framework for procedure learning to create a scalable and efficient solution.

Multimodal Procedure Learning: Another class of methods work with multimodal data, like narrated text and videos [2, 10, 14, 22, 50, 62, 63, 76, 78]. These works use Automatic Speech Recognition (ASR) to obtain the text, which is not perfect. Due to this, the output needs to be manually cleaned, which is not scalable. Additionally, such methods assume an alignment between the text and videos [2, 50, 76], which might not be accurate for most cases [18, 19]. Instead, we use only the visual modality as an input to the framework. Due to this, we eliminate the need to obtain narrations that might be inaccurate and make our framework scalable.

Learning Key-Step Ordering: Current works do not capture different key-step ordering to perform the same task. They either assume a strict ordering [19, 40, 70] or do not predict the order [18, 63]. However, we observe that subjects perform the same task in multiple ways (Fig. 1), motivating us to capture different ways to accomplish the task. Therefore, the final stage of CnC aims to create a key-step order for each video and infer the relevant ordering to perform the task.

Representation Learning for Procedure Learning: Existing works on procedure learning employ various ways to create frame-wise features. To learn the representation space, Kukleva *et al.* [40] use relative timestamps of frames, and Vidal *et al.* [70] predict the representation and timestamps of the future frames. On the other hand, Elhamifar *et al.* either use the latent states obtained from an HMM [19] or discover and utilize attention features from individual frames [18]. However, these methods do not exploit the signal provided by temporal correspondences, which is crucial for procedure learning, as we show in this work.

Self-supervised Representation Learning: Learning a representation space without annotations saves substantial time and energy when creating deep learning solutions. Motivated by this, recent works explore various pretext tasks to generate supervision signals for training deep learning architectures [6, 28, 68, 69, 73]. A few pretext tasks for learning image representations include image colourization [41, 42], object counting [48, 55], solving jigsaw puzzles [5, 36], predicting image rotations [20, 37], and reconstructing input images [29] from noise [71]. Pretext tasks for learning video representations include predicting future frames [1, 12, 26, 35, 66, 72], using temporal order and coherence as labels [21, 34, 43, 52, 75], and predicting the arrow of time [74].

Video representation learning methods mentioned above employ a single video. However, we want to identify similar key-steps in multiple videos for

Table 1. Comparison of datasets for Procedure Learning. The average number of key-steps and video length for EgoProceLare the highest, highlighting the complexity of the procedures included in EgoProceL

Dataset	Egocentric view	Manually created	Avg. key-steps	Avg. video length (sec)	#tasks
Breakfast [38]	✗	✓	5.1	137.5	10
Inria [2]	✗	✗	7.1	178.8	5
ProceL [18]	✗	✗	8.3	251.5	12
CrossTask [79]	✗	✗	7.4	297	18
EgoProceL (ours)	✓	✓	**8.7**	**769.2**	16

procedure learning. To this end, we build upon existing video alignment techniques [16,27] and devise a loss function that works well for procedure learning. Note that procedure learning aims to find key-steps across a given set of videos; hence, it differs from video alignment.

3 EgoProceL: Egocentric Video Dataset for Procedure Learning

The EgoProceLdataset focuses on the key-steps required to perform a task instead of every action in the video. To construct EgoProceL, we take two approaches: (a) identifying publicly available datasets that we annotate for key-steps; (b) recording new tasks to expand the range of tasks. We follow the following criteria to shortlist from the public datasets: (1) The task should require multiple key-steps to perform. For example, preparing a sandwich involves a minimum of four key-steps [11]. (2) Videos of the same task must contain a similar set of key-steps. However, the order of the key-steps can differ. (3) To compare the performance of CnC in egocentric and third-person views, we require a dataset with recordings of the same task in both views. (4) We prefer longer videos with sparse key-steps to generate practical solutions.

We select CMU-MMAC [11], EGTEA Gaze+ [47], MECCANO [58], and EPIC-Tents [32] based on the above criteria. CMU-MMAC contains recordings of subjects performing the same task from one egocentric and four third-person views. Therefore, by using it, we compare the performance of CnC between egocentric and third-person views. Though these four datasets include a diverse range of tasks, they do not contain tasks where the subject works in a constrained environment and deals with small objects (*e.g.*, screws). To alleviate this, we include manually recorded videos of assembling and disassembling a Personal Computer (PC). This addition makes the dataset diverse and challenging in terms of variability in the size of objects involved and the complexity of key-steps (*e.g.*, fixing the motherboard requires fastening nine screws).

EgoProceL contains videos and key-step annotations for multiple tasks from CMU-MMAC [11] and EGTEA Gaze+ [47] and individual tasks like toy-bike assembly [58], tent assembly [32], PC assembly, and PC disassembly. EgoProceLconsists of 62 hours of annotated egocentric videos, including 16 tasks with an

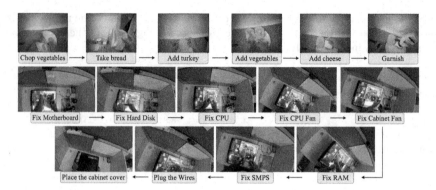

Fig. 2. Key-step annotations for making turkey sandwich [47] and assembling a PC.

average duration of 13 minutes. To annotate the videos for key-steps, we create a list of key-steps for each task, *e.g.*, assembling a PC requires 'Fix motherboard', 'Fix hard disk', ..., 'Place the cabinet cover'. We use ELAN [17] to annotate each video by marking the start and end location during which the key-step occurs.

Along with various procedure learning tasks, EgoProceL is appropriate for understanding hand-object interaction, action forecasting and recognition, and a shared study of videos and text. Figure 2 shows some example annotations and Table 1 compares EgoProceL with existing datasets. We also considered a few other datasets that did not satisfy the requirements mentioned above [9,64]. The reasons for their non-inclusion are given in the supplementary.

4 Correspond and Cut Framework for Procedure Learning

Humans often follow the same steps to perform any particular task, though the order of steps might be different. This work proposes a methodology which, given a set of videos of humans performing a task, learns similar embeddings across videos for the key-steps required to complete a task. Once we have the embeddings, learning a procedure reduces to clustering the embeddings for localizing the key-steps among all the videos. To learn the embeddings, we exploit temporal correspondences between the videos of the same task. For that purpose, we train a representation learning network using the proposed TC3I loss. TC3I builds on top of existing temporal video alignment methods [16,27]. After learning the embeddings, we use PCM, shown in Fig. 3, to cluster and localize the underlying key-steps. PCM models the clustering problem as a multi-label graph cut problem and solves it to localize the key-steps. Once we localize the key-steps using PCM, we use the frame's relative location in a video to generate the key-step ordering for each video.

Notation. CnC takes in $V = \{V_i : i \in \mathbb{N}, 1 \leq i \leq n\}$ untrimmed videos of the same task, where n is the total number of videos. Each of the n videos can have a

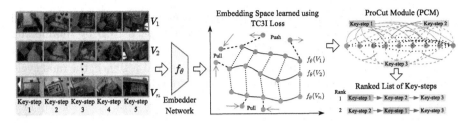

Fig. 3. Correspond and Cut (CnC) framework for Procedure Learning. CnC takes in multiple videos from the same task and passes them through the embedder network trained using the proposed TC3I loss. The goal of the embedder network is to learn similar embeddings for corresponding key-steps from multiple videos and for temporally close frames. The ProCut Module (PCM) localizes the key-steps required for performing the task. PCM converts the clustering problem to a multi-label graph cut problem solved using the Alpha Expansion algorithm [4]. The output provides the assignment of frames to the respective key-steps and their ordering.

different number of frames. We denote the embedding function used to generate the frame-level embeddings as f_θ, which is a neural network with parameters θ. A video V_k with m frames is denoted as $V_k = \{f_k^1, f_k^2, \ldots, f_k^m\}$ and the video's frame-level embeddings are denoted as $f_\theta(V_k) = \{v_k^1, v_k^2, \ldots, v_k^m\}$. We assume K key-steps in a task, where K is a hyper-parameter.

4.1   Learning the Embeddings Using the TC3I Loss

We aim to learn similar embeddings for the frames with comparable semantic information across different temporal locations from multiple videos. For that purpose, we use Temporal Cycle Consistency (TCC) [16] to find correspondences across time in videos.

Consider two videos V_1 and V_2, with lengths p and q, respectively. To check if a point v_1^i in V_1 is cycle consistent, its nearest neighbour $v_2^j = \arg\min_{v_2 \in V_2} \|v_1^i - v_2\|$ is calculated in V_2. Then the process is repeated for v_2^j in V_1 to get $v_1^k = \arg\min_{v_1 \in V_1} \|v_2^j - v_1\|$. If $i = k$, then the point is considered cycle consistent. An acceptable embedding space consists of a maximum number of cycle-consistent points for a pair of sequences. Specifically, for a point v_1^i in V_1, we determine its soft nearest neighbor $\widetilde{v}_2$ in V_2 by using the softmax function as follows:

$$\widetilde{v}_2 = \sum_j \alpha_j v_2^j, \quad \text{where} \quad \alpha_j = \frac{e^{-\|v_1^i - v_2^j\|^2}}{\sum_k e^{-\|v_1^i - v_2^k\|^2}}. \tag{1}$$

Here α_j signifies the *similarity* between v_1^i and individual $v_2^j \in V_2$. Once we have the soft nearest neighbor, a similarity vector β_1^i is calculated. β defines the proximity between $\widetilde{v}_2$ and each frame $v_1^k \in V_1$ as:

$$\beta_1^i[k] = \frac{e^{-\|\widetilde{v}_2 - v_1^k\|^2}}{\sum_j e^{-\|\widetilde{v}_2 - v_1^j\|^2}}. \tag{2}$$

As β is a discrete distribution of similarities over time, it peaks around the ith time index. To avoid this, a Gaussian prior is applied to β by minimizing the normalized squared distance $\frac{|i-\mu|^2}{\sigma^2}$ as the objective. By applying additional variance regularization, β is enforced to be peaky around i. Hence, the final cycle consistency loss between videos V_1 and V_2, corresponding to i^{th} frame of V_1 is:

$$L(V_1, V_2, v_1^i) = \frac{|i-\mu|^2}{\sigma^2} + \lambda \log(\sigma). \qquad (3)$$

Here, $\mu_i = \sum_k \beta_1^i[k] \times k$ and $\sigma_i^2 = \sum_k \beta_1^i[k] \times (k-\mu_i)^2$, and λ is the regularization weight. Formulating TCC in this way ensures the model is not heavily penalized when it cycles back to close-by frames.

We observe that there are many repetitive frames in egocentric videos because of which cycle consistency loss often loops back to similar but temporally far-away frames. To alleviate the issue, we utilize the Contrastive-Inverse Difference Moment (C-IDM) loss [27] (a modified form of Inverse Difference Moment [8]) for applying temporal regularization on each video. The C-IDM loss between the two frames i and j of a video V_1 is computed as:

$$I(V_1, i, j) = (1 - \mathcal{N}(i, j))\,\gamma(i, j) \max\left(0, \zeta - d(i, j)\right) + \mathcal{N}(i, j)\frac{d(i, j)}{\gamma(i, j)}. \qquad (4)$$

Here, $\gamma(i, j) = (i - j)^2 + 1$, $d(i, j)$ is the Euclidean distance between $f_\theta(v_1^i)$, and $f_\theta(v_1^j)$, ζ is the margin parameter, and $\mathcal{N}$ is the neighborhood function such that, $\mathcal{N}(i, j) = 1$ if $|i - j| \leq \sigma$, and 0 otherwise. Here, σ is the window size for separating temporally far away frames. The C-IDM loss encourages the embeddings of the temporally close frames to be similar and the embeddings of temporally far frames to be dissimilar. The final loss combines both TCC and C-IDM (referred to as TC3I loss from now on):

$$\text{TC3I}(V_1, V_2) = \sum_{i \in V_1} L(V_1, V_2, v_1^i) + \sum_{j \in V_2} L(V_1, V_2, v_2^j)$$
$$+ \xi \sum_{i \in V_1} \sum_{j \in V_1} I(V_1, i, j) + \xi \sum_{i \in V_2} \sum_{j \in V_2} I(V_2, i, j). \qquad (5)$$

Here, ξ is a regularization parameter.

4.2   Localizing the Key-Steps Using the ProCut Module

Once we learn the embeddings, we aim to localize the key-steps required for performing the task. Kukleva et al. [40] localize the key-steps by generating K clusters of embeddings using the K-Means algorithm [49]. However, they need to assume a fixed order of key-steps to assign frames to the key-steps. Instead, we propose a novel ProCut Module (PCM) for the purpose. PCM converts the clustering problem to a multi-label graph cut problem [25], as described below.

Let $G = \langle V, E \rangle$ be a graph consisting of a set of nodes V and a set of directed edges E connecting them. The node set V consists of K terminal nodes representing the key-steps, and non-terminal nodes (equal to the number of frames)

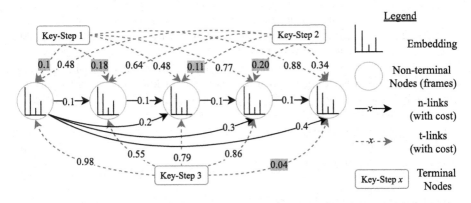

Fig. 4. ProCut Module (PCM). Non-terminal nodes in the graph represent the embeddings of the frames. Terminal nodes represent the key-steps required to perform the task. The terminal and non-terminal nodes are connected using the t-links. Non-terminal nodes are connected using the n-links. The numbers inscribed in arrows represent the cost of using the respective link. Costs highlighted in green represent the lowest cost to assign a frame to the key-step. For brevity, n-links are shown only for the first non-terminal node. Diagram best viewed in colour. (Colour figure online)

representing the embeddings of the frames generated using the Embedder network. There are two kinds of edges in the graph: *t-links* connecting non-terminal nodes to the terminal nodes, and *n-links* connecting two non-terminal nodes.

We use the Fuzzy C-Means algorithm [15] to assign a cost to the *t-links*. The algorithm performs soft clustering and calculates the probability of a frame belonging to each cluster. We subtract the probability value from 1 to obtain the cost of assigning a frame to each cluster. The cost value for the *n-links* is assigned based on the temporal distance between the nodes. For example, if the nodes are temporally closer (*e.g.*, nodes at positions 1 and 2 in Fig. 4), the cost of assigning the same label to them is lower, otherwise (*e.g.*, for nodes at positions 1 and 5 in Fig. 4), the cost is high. After creating the graph G, we use α-Expansion [4] to find the minimum cost cut. We use the discovered cut to assign frames to K labels. As shown in Fig. 4, the lowest costs (highlighted in green) result in assigning the first and second frames to key-step 1, the third and fourth frames to key-step 2, and the last to key-step 3.

4.3 Determining Order of the Key-Steps

When it comes to determining the ordering of the key-steps, it makes sense to allow each video to have a distinct key-step ordering as there can be multiple ways to perform a task. However, current works either use a fixed order of key-steps to decode all the videos [19,40,70] or do not predict the ordering [18,63]. One of the advantages of using CnC to determine the key-step is that it allows each video to have its independent order of the key-steps.

To infer the sequential order of key-steps, we calculate the normalized time for each frame v_i^n in video V_i consisting of p frames as $T(v_i^n) = \frac{n}{p}$ [40,70]. Then we calculate the time instant for each cluster as the average normalized for frames assigned to it. The clusters are then arranged in increasing order of the average time, providing us with the sequence of key-steps used to perform the task in a video. Once we have key-step order for all the videos of the same task, we generate their ranked list based on the number of times the subjects followed a particular order. The order followed the most ends up being at the top of the ranked list. Doing this enables us to determine different sequential orders of key-steps to accomplish a task.

4.4   Implementation Details

We use ResNet-50 [28] as our backbone network to extract the features. Motivated by [16], for training the Embedder network, we use a pair of training videos at a time, select frames at random within the videos and optimize the proposed TC3I loss until convergence. The features are extracted from the *Conv4c* layer and a stack of c context frames features is created along the temporal dimension. We reshape our input video frames to 224×224. To aggregate the temporal information, we pass the combined features through two 3D convolutional layers followed by a 3D global max pooling layer, two fully-connected layers, and a linear projection layer to output the embeddings of dimension 128. We set the value of K to 7 and compare the performance of CnC with the other values of K in Table 6. Furthermore, for all our experiments, we follow the task-specific settings laid out in [18]. We use PyTorch [56] for all our experiments.

5   Experiments

5.1   Evaluation

Current works compute framewise F1-Score and IoU scores for key-step localization [18,19,40,63,70]. The F1-Score is a harmonic mean of precision and recall scores. For calculating recall, the ratio between the number of frames having correct key-steps prediction and the number of ground truth key-step frames across all the key-steps of a video is calculated. For precision, the denominator is the number of frames assigned to the key-steps. For calculations, the one-to-one mapping between the ground truth and prediction is generated using the Hungarian algorithm [39] following [2,18,19,40,63]. However, these metrics tend to assign high scores to models that assign most frames to a single cluster, as the key-step with most frames matches with the background frame's label in the ground truth. Furthermore, for untrimmed procedure learning videos, most of the frames are background, resulting in high scores.

Shen *et al.* [63] attempt to solve this problem by analyzing the MoF score, but as pointed out in [40], MoF is not always suitable for an imbalanced dataset. Instead, we propose calculating the framewise scores for each key-step separately and then taking the mean of the scores over all the key-steps. This penalises the cases when there is a large performance difference for different key-step, *e.g.*, when all the frames get assigned to a single key-step. Upon following this protocol, the scores for all the methods decrease. This paper presents the results generated using the proposed evaluation protocol unless otherwise mentioned.

Table 2. Procedure Learning from Third-person Videos. Comparison between state-of-the-art methods and CnC on benchmark third-person video datasets [19,79]. Our method outperforms all the techniques using videos only (in F-Score). It even manages to give at par performance compared to the techniques using multi-modal input. **P**, **R**, and **F** represent precision, recall, and F-score respectively

	Input modality	ProceL [19]			CrossTask [79]		
		P	**R**	**F**	**P**	**R**	**F**
Uniform	Video	12.4	9.4	10.3	8.7	9.8	9.0
Alayrc *et al.* [2]	Video + Narrations	12.3	3.7	5.5	6.8	3.4	4.5
Kukleva *et al.* [40]	Video	11.7	30.2	16.4	9.8	35.9	15.3
Elhamifar *et al.* [18]	Video	9.5	26.7	14.0	10.1	**41.6**	16.3
Fried *et al.* [22]	Video	–	–	–	–	28.8	–
Shen *et al.* [63]	Video + Narrations	16.5	**31.8**	21.1	15.2	35.5	21.0
CnC (*ours*)	Video	**20.7**	22.6	**21.6**	**22.8**	22.5	**22.6**

5.2 Procedure Learning from Third-Person Videos

To test the generalizability of CnCon third-person videos and to ensure a fair comparison with existing methods [2,18,22,40,63], we perform experiments on third-person procedure learning benchmark datasets: ProceL [19] and CrossTask [79]. We obtain the results of previous works from [63]. Note that here we use the evaluation protocol employed by the previous works [18,19,40,63]. As seen in Table 2, CnC outperforms other methods (in terms of the F-Score) utilizing only videos as the input modality. Further, with only video as the input modality, CnC even manages to perform at par with multi-modal methods. Previous works have used different forms of self-supervision. For example, [18] use the pseudo-labels provided by subset selection and [40] utilize the relative timestamps of video frames. Instead, the comparison in Table 2 shows that the signal provided by corresponding frames is superior for the task of procedure learning.

5.3 Procedure Learning Results from Egocentric Videos

Baselines. We consider three baseline methods:

1. **Random.** Here we predict the labels by randomly sampling predictions from a uniform distribution with K values representing K key-steps.

2. **TC3I + HC.** Instead of PCM, we use the K-Means algorithm and generate K clusters from the representation space.
3. **TC3I + SS.** Here, instead of PCM, we use subset selection for the key-step assignment. The algorithm takes in the frame's embeddings and M (hyper-parameter) latent states obtained using K-Means [49]. It then selects a subset S (of size K) of the states as key-steps and finds the frames' assignments. We use the greedy algorithm used in [18] to perform subset selection. Refer to the supplementary material for the hyper-parameter values.

Table 3. Procedure Learning Results obtained on EgoProceL. Here, CnC performs the best, highlighting the effectiveness of the TC3I loss and PCM

| | EgoProceL | | | | | | | | | | | |
| | CMU-MMAC | | EGTEA G. | | MECCANO | | EPIC-Tents | | PC assembly | | PC Disas. | |
	F1	IoU	F1	IoU	F1	IoU	F1	IoU	F1	IoU	F1	IoU
Random	15.7	5.9	15.3	4.6	13.4	5.3	14.1	6.5	15.1	7.2	15.3	7.1
TC3I + HC	19.2	9.0	20.8	7.9	16.6	**8.0**	15.4	7.8	21.7	11.0	24.9	14.1
TC3I + SS	19.7	8.9	20.4	7.9	16.3	7.8	15.9	7.8	24.8	11.9	23.6	14.0
CnC	**22.7**	**11.1**	**21.7**	**9.5**	**18.1**	7.8	**17.2**	**8.3**	**25.1**	**12.8**	**27.0**	**14.8**

Table 3 summarises the results obtained on EgoProceL using the baselines and proposed CnC. CnC performs higher than all the three baselines. This is due to (a) the ability of the TC3I loss to learn the representation space where similar key-steps lie close without enforcing any ordering or temporal constraints. Moreover, TC3I adds temporal coherency to the learned representations by adopting the C-IDM loss [27] (Fig. 5). (b) PCM gains a comprehensive view of the problem by considering the cost of assigning each frame belonging to every key-step and its temporal relationship with the other frames. CnC performs better on long sequences as the TC3I loss compensates by searching for corresponding frames in the entire length of the videos, making it possible to learn a reasonable representation space despite the length of the videos. Further, the results in Table 3 show that PCM is superior for key-frame clustering and assignment along with TC3I as it results in the highest F-Score and IoU on EgoProceL. The gain in performance is because PCM considers the cost of assigning each frame to every key-step and its temporal relationship with the other frames (Fig. 5). This allows PCM to gain a comprehensive view of the problem compared to HC, which does not consider the cost of each frame belonging to other key-steps and SS, which has lower generalisation power [18].

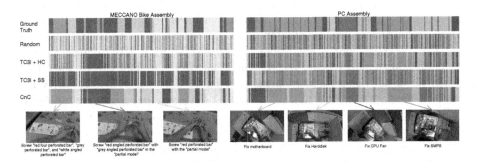

Fig. 5. Qualitative results for MECCANO and PC Assembly highlight the effectiveness of CnC. Additionally, PCM outperforms HC and SS when clustering the key-steps. Furthermore, due to the TC3I loss, CnC correctly identifies the key-steps that are short (fix a hard disk in PC Assembly). The gray segments denote the background.

5.4 Egocentric vs. Third-Person Videos

Here, we compare the results obtained after training CnC on multiple views from CMU-MMAC [11]. As seen in Table 4, the frame-wise F1-Score and IoU scores are the highest for the egocentric view. This is because egocentric videos offer lower occlusion by the expert's body and provide higher visibility of hand-object interactions. This highlights one of the central hypotheses of this paper: the effectiveness of using egocentric videos over third-person videos for procedure learning. Also, we observe

Table 4. Egocentric vs. Third-person results. We use different views from [11] for comparison. We obtain better results using CnC on egocentric videos highlighting their effectiveness. **P**, **R**, and **F** denote precision, recall, and F-score respectively

View	P	R	F	IoU
TP (Top)	17.4	18.4	17.9	8.1
TP (Back)	18.8	21.5	20.0	8.5
TP (LHS)	21.2	22.7	21.8	9.7
TP (RHS)	19.8	21.7	20.6	8.7
Egocentric	**21.6**	**24.4**	**22.7**	**11.1**

that the results vary for third-person videos due to the camera placement. This increases one variable when creating data for procedure learning. Alternatively, egocentric videos use head-mounted cameras, eliminating uncertainty.

5.5 Ablation Study

Here, we quantitatively evaluate our design choices. Due to space constraints, results for [11] and [47] are provided here, and the rest are in the supplementary.

Effectiveness of the TC3I Loss: Here, we replace the TC3I loss in CnC with TCC [16], LAV [27], and a combination of LAV and TCC [27] to study the efficacy of the proposed TC3I loss. TC3I loss in Table 5 obtains the highest F-Score and IoU. As observed in our initial set of experiments, TCC loss lacks temporal coherency due to which temporally close frames do not lie close in the learned representation space, resulting in lower results when compared to TC3I and LAV, which account for temporal coherency using the C-IDM loss. For LAV + TCC, our observations are consistent with [27] because there is no performance gain when directly combining LAV and TCC losses since LAV works on L2-normalised embeddings, whereas TCC does not [27]. The LAV loss performs better than TCC and LAV + TCC; however, the results are not better than TC3I because the Soft-DTW used in LAV accounts for global alignment. However, LAV does not focus on the per-frame features [27], which is beneficial when looking for similar key-steps in different videos. The TC3I loss overcomes these issues by focusing on correspondences in multiple videos at frame level and adding temporal coherency by adopting the C-IDM loss.

Table 5. Effectiveness of the TC3I loss. TC3I loss outperforms other losses as it focuses on corresponding frames and employs C-IDM for temporal coherency

Experiment	CMU-MMAC [11]			EGTEA Gaze+ [47]		
	Precision	F-Score	IoU	Precision	F-Score	IoU
TCC + PCM	18.5	19.7	9.5	17.5	19.7	8.8
LAV + TCC + PCM	18.8	19.7	9.0	16.4	18.6	7.5
LAV + PCM	20.6	21.1	9.4	17.4	19.1	8.0
TC3I + PCM (CnC)	**21.6**	**22.7**	**11.1**	**19.6**	**21.7**	**9.5**

Selecting the Value of K: Table 6 contains results of CnC and the baselines as the function of K. Additionally, it features the results after replacing PCM with HC and SS as the function of K. Here, key observations are: (a) CnC performs the best when $K = 7$, (b) the results do not change significantly for CnC as K increases. However, we observe a decline in the results for HC and SS as K increases, highlighting the effectiveness of PCM for key-step localisation.

Table 6. Selecting K. Results with various values of K. Numbers in bold are highest in the respective row, and underlined numbers are highest in the respective column

Experiment	CMU-MMAC [11]				EGTEA Gaze+ [47]			
	$K=7$	$K=10$	$K=12$	$K=15$	$K=7$	$K=10$	$K=12$	$K=15$
Random	**15.7**	12.7	11.6	10.4	**15.4**	12.3	11.4	10.4
TC3I + HC	**19.2**	17.4	16.3	16.8	**20.8**	17.8	16.7	17.3
TC3I + SS	**19.7**	17.3	17.0	15.7	**20.4**	17.8	16.7	16.8
CnC	**<u>22.7</u>**	<u>19.1</u>	<u>20.4</u>	<u>20.1</u>	**<u>21.7</u>**	<u>19.9</u>	<u>19.9</u>	<u>19.9</u>

6 Conclusion

Learning procedures from the visual demonstration of a task by an expert, is an important step in scaling the learning capabilities of autonomous agents. Unlike current state-of-the-art techniques, instead of third-person videos, we have proposed procedure learning from first-person viewpoint. Given the unavailability of the datasets for the purpose, we proposed the EgoProceLcontaining egocentric videos for procedure learning. We also proposed a new technique, CnC, for procedure learning from egocentric videos that utilize the proposed TC3I loss to learn an embedding space in a self-supervised fashion. Finally, we employ PCM to identify the key-steps. Our results demonstrate the superiority of using the egocentric view and the effectiveness of the proposed technique for procedure learning.

Acknowledgements. The work was supported in part by the Department of Science and Technology, Government of India, under DST/ICPS/Data-Science project ID T-138. We acknowledge Pravin Nagar and Sagar Verma for sharing the PC Assembly and Disassembly videos recorded at IIIT Delhi. We also acknowledge Jehlum Vitasta Pandit and Astha Bansal for their help with annotating a portion of EgoProceL.

References

1. Ahsan, U., Sun, C., Essa, I.: DiscrimNet: semi-supervised action recognition from videos using generative adversarial networks. In: Computer Vision and Pattern Recognition Workshops (CVPRW) 'Women in Computer Vision (WiCV)' (2018)
2. Alayrac, J.B., Bojanowski, P., Agrawal, N., Laptev, I., Sivic, J., Lacoste-Julien, S.: Unsupervised learning from narrated instruction videos. In: Computer Vision and Pattern Recognition (CVPR) (2016)
3. Bojanowski, P., et al.: Weakly supervised action labeling in videos under ordering constraints. In: Fleet, D., Pajdla, T., Schiele, B., Tuytelaars, T. (eds.) ECCV 2014. LNCS, vol. 8693, pp. 628–643. Springer, Cham (2014). https://doi.org/10.1007/978-3-319-10602-1_41
4. Boykov, Y., Veksler, O., Zabih, R.: Fast approximate energy minimization via graph cuts. IEEE Trans. Pattern Anal. Mach. Intell. (2001)
5. Carlucci, F.M., D'Innocente, A., Bucci, S., Caputo, B., Tommasi, T.: Domain generalization by solving Jigsaw puzzles. In: Computer Vision and Pattern Recognition (CVPR) (2019)
6. Carreira, J., Zisserman, A.: Quo Vadis, action recognition? A new model and the kinetics dataset. In: Computer Vision and Pattern Recognition (CVPR) (2017)
7. Chang, C.Y., Huang, D.A., Sui, Y., Fei-Fei, L., Niebles, J.C.: D3TW: discriminative differentiable dynamic time warping for weakly supervised action alignment and segmentation. In: Computer Vision and Pattern Recognition (CVPR) (2019)
8. Conners, R.W., Harlow, C.A.: A theoretical comparison of texture algorithms. IEEE Trans. Pattern Anal. Mach. Intell. (1980)
9. Damen, D., et al.: Scaling egocentric vision: the EPIC-KITCHENS dataset. In: Ferrari, V., Hebert, M., Sminchisescu, C., Weiss, Y. (eds.) ECCV 2018. LNCS, vol. 11208, pp. 753–771. Springer, Cham (2018). https://doi.org/10.1007/978-3-030-01225-0_44

10. Damen, D., Leelasawassuk, T., Haines, O., Calway, A., Mayol-Cuevas, W.: You-Do, I-Learn: discovering task relevant objects and their modes of interaction from multi-user egocentric video. In: British Machine Vision Conference (BMVC) (2014)

11. De La Torre, F., et al.: Guide to the Carnegie Mellon University Multimodal Activity (CMU-MMAC) database. In: Robotics Institute (2008)

12. Diba, A., Sharma, V., Gool, L., Stiefelhagen, R.: DynamoNet: dynamic action and motion network. In: International Conference on Computer Vision (ICCV) (2019)

13. Ding, L., Xu, C.: Weakly-supervised action segmentation with iterative soft boundary assignment. In: Computer Vision and Pattern Recognition (CVPR) (2018)

14. Doughty, H., Laptev, I., Mayol-Cuevas, W., Damen, D.: Action modifiers: learning from adverbs in instructional videos. In: Computer Vision and Pattern Recognition (CVPR) (2020)

15. Dunn, J.C.: A fuzzy relative of the ISODATA process and its use in detecting compact well-separated clusters. J. Cybern. (1973)

16. Dwibedi, D., Aytar, Y., Tompson, J., Sermanet, P., Zisserman, A.: Temporal cycle-consistency learning. In: Computer Vision and Pattern Recognition (CVPR) (2019)

17. ELAN (Version 6.0) [Computer software] (2020). Nijmegen: Max Planck Institute for Psycholinguistics, The Language Archive: https://archive.mpi.nl/tla/elan

18. Elhamifar, E., Huynh, D.: Self-supervised multi-task procedure learning from instructional videos. In: Vedaldi, A., Bischof, H., Brox, T., Frahm, J.-M. (eds.) ECCV 2020. LNCS, vol. 12362, pp. 557–573. Springer, Cham (2020). https://doi.org/10.1007/978-3-030-58520-4_33

19. Elhamifar, E., Naing, Z.: Unsupervised procedure learning via joint dynamic summarization. In: International Conference on Computer Vision (ICCV) (2019)

20. Feng, Z., Xu, C., Tao, D.: Self-supervised representation learning by rotation feature decoupling. In: Computer Vision and Pattern Recognition (CVPR) (2019)

21. Fernando, B., Bilen, H., Gavves, E., Gould, S.: Self-supervised video representation learning with odd-one-out networks. In: Computer Vision and Pattern Recognition (CVPR) (2017)

22. Fried, D., Alayrac, J.B., Blunsom, P., Dyer, C., Clark, S., Nematzadeh, A.: Learning to segment actions from observation and narration. In: Association for Computational Linguistics (ACL) (2020)

23. Furnari, A., Farinella, G.: Rolling-unrolling LSTMs for action anticipation from first-person video. IEEE Trans. Pattern Anal. Mach. Intell. (2020)

24. Grauman, K., et al.: Ego4D: around the world in 3,000 hours of egocentric video. In: Computer Vision and Pattern Recognition (CVPR) (2022)

25. Greig, D., Porteous, B., Seheult, A.: Exact maximum a posteriori estimation for binary images. J. Roy. Stat. Soc. Ser. B-Methodol. (1989)

26. Han, T., Xie, W., Zisserman, A.: Video representation learning by dense predictive coding. In: Workshop on Large Scale Holistic Video Understanding, ICCV (2019)

27. Haresh, S., et al.: Learning by aligning videos in time. In: Computer Vision and Pattern Recognition (CVPR) (2021)

28. He, K., Zhang, X., Ren, S., Sun, J.: Deep residual learning for image recognition. In: Computer Vision and Pattern Recognition (CVPR) (2016)

29. Hinton, G.E., Zemel, R.S.: Autoencoders, minimum description length and helmholtz free energy. In: Neural Information Processing Systems (1993)

30. Huang, D.-A., Fei-Fei, L., Niebles, J.C.: Connectionist temporal modeling for weakly supervised action labeling. In: Leibe, B., Matas, J., Sebe, N., Welling, M. (eds.) ECCV 2016. LNCS, vol. 9908, pp. 137–153. Springer, Cham (2016). https://doi.org/10.1007/978-3-319-46493-0_9

31. Huang, Y., Cai, M., Li, Z., Sato, Y.: Predicting gaze in egocentric video by learning task-dependent attention transition. In: Ferrari, V., Hebert, M., Sminchisescu, C., Weiss, Y. (eds.) ECCV 2018. LNCS, vol. 11208, pp. 789–804. Springer, Cham (2018). https://doi.org/10.1007/978-3-030-01225-0_46

32. Jang, Y., Sullivan, B., Ludwig, C., Gilchrist, I., Damen, D., Mayol-Cuevas, W.: EPIC-tent: an egocentric video dataset for camping tent assembly. In: International Conference on Computer Vision (ICCV) Workshops (2019)

33. Ji, L., et al.: Learning temporal video procedure segmentation from an automatically collected large dataset. In: Proceedings of the IEEE/CVF Winter Conference on Applications of Computer Vision (WACV) (2022)

34. Choi, J., Sharma, G., Schulter, S., Huang, J.-B.: Shuffle and attend: video domain adaptation. In: Vedaldi, A., Bischof, H., Brox, T., Frahm, J.-M. (eds.) ECCV 2020. LNCS, vol. 12357, pp. 678–695. Springer, Cham (2020). https://doi.org/10.1007/978-3-030-58610-2_40

35. Kim, D., Cho, D., Kweon, I.S.: Self-supervised video representation learning with space-time cubic puzzles. In: AAAI Conference on Artificial Intelligence (2019)

36. Kim, D., Cho, D., Yoo, D., Kweon, I.S.: Learning image representations by completing damaged Jigsaw puzzles. In: Winter Conference on Applications of Computer Vision (WACV) (2018)

37. Komodakis, N., Gidaris, S.: Unsupervised representation learning by predicting image rotations. In: International Conference on Learning Representations (ICLR) (2018)

38. Kuehne, H., Arslan, A.B., Serre, T.: The language of actions: recovering the syntax and semantics of goal-directed human activities. In: Computer Vision and Pattern Recognition (CVPR) (2016)

39. Kuhn, H.W.: The Hungarian method for the assignment problem. Naval Res. Logist. Q. (1955)

40. Kukleva, A., Kuehne, H., Sener, F., Gall, J.: Unsupervised learning of action classes with continuous temporal embedding. In: Computer Vision and Pattern Recognition (CVPR) (2019)

41. Larsson, G., Maire, M., Shakhnarovich, G.: Colorization as a proxy task for visual understanding. In: Computer Vision and Pattern Recognition (CVPR) (2017)

42. Larsson, G., Maire, M., Shakhnarovich, G.: Learning representations for automatic colorization. In: Leibe, B., Matas, J., Sebe, N., Welling, M. (eds.) ECCV 2016. LNCS, vol. 9908, pp. 577–593. Springer, Cham (2016). https://doi.org/10.1007/978-3-319-46493-0_35

43. Lee, H.Y., Huang, J.B., Singh, M.K., Yang, M.H.: Unsupervised representation learning by sorting sequences. In: International Conference on Computer Vision (ICCV) (2017)

44. Li, J., Lei, P., Todorovic, S.: Weakly supervised energy-based learning for action segmentation. In: International Conference on Computer Vision (ICCV) (2019)

45. Li, J., Todorovic, S.: Set-constrained viterbi for set-supervised action segmentation. In: Computer Vision and Pattern Recognition (CVPR) (2020)

46. Li, Y., Fathi, A., Rehg, J.M.: Learning to predict gaze in egocentric video. In: International Conference on Computer Vision (ICCV) (2013)

47. Li, Y., Liu, M., Rehg, J.M.: In the eye of beholder: joint learning of gaze and actions in first person video. In: Ferrari, V., Hebert, M., Sminchisescu, C., Weiss, Y. (eds.) ECCV 2018. LNCS, vol. 11209, pp. 639–655. Springer, Cham (2018). https://doi.org/10.1007/978-3-030-01228-1_38

48. Liu, X., van de Weijer, J., Bagdanov, A.D.: Leveraging unlabeled data for crowd counting by learning to rank. In: Computer Vision and Pattern Recognition (CVPR) (2018)
49. Lloyd, S.: Least squares quantization in PCM. IEEE Trans. Inf. Theory (1982)
50. Malmaud, J., Huang, J., Rathod, V., Johnston, N., Rabinovich, A., Murphy, K.: What's Cookin'? Interpreting cooking videos using text. speech and vision. In: HLT-NAACL (2015)
51. Miech, A., Zhukov, D., Alayrac, J.B., Tapaswi, M., Laptev, I., Sivic, J.: HowTo100M: learning a text-video embedding by watching hundred million narrated video clips. In: International Conference on Computer Vision (ICCV) (2019)
52. Misra, I., Zitnick, C.L., Hebert, M.: Shuffle and learn: unsupervised learning using temporal order verification. In: Leibe, B., Matas, J., Sebe, N., Welling, M. (eds.) ECCV 2016. LNCS, vol. 9905, pp. 527–544. Springer, Cham (2016). https://doi.org/10.1007/978-3-319-46448-0_32
53. Naing, Z., Elhamifar, E.: Procedure completion by learning from partial summaries. In: British Machine Vision Conference (BMVC) (2020)
54. Ng, E., Xiang, D., Joo, H., Grauman, K.: You2Me: inferring body pose in egocentric video via first and second person interactions. In: Computer Vision and Pattern Recognition (CVPR) (2020)
55. Noroozi, M., Pirsiavash, H., Favaro, P.: Representation learning by learning to count. In: International Conference on Computer Vision (ICCV) (2017)
56. Paszke, A., et al.: PyTorch: an imperative style, high-performance deep learning library. In: Neural Information Processing Systems (2019)
57. Pirsiavash, H., Ramanan, D.: Detecting activities of daily living in first-person camera views. In: Computer Vision and Pattern Recognition (CVPR) (2012)
58. Ragusa, F., Furnari, A., Livatino, S., Farinella, G.M.: The MECCANO dataset: understanding human-object interactions from egocentric videos in an industrial-like domain. In: Winter Conference on Applications of Computer Vision (WACV), pp. 1569–1578 (2021)
59. Richard, A., Kuehne, H., Gall, J.: Action sets: weakly supervised action segmentation without ordering constraints. In: Computer Vision and Pattern Recognition (CVPR) (2018)
60. Richard, A., Kuehne, H., Iqbal, A., Gall, J.: NeuralNetwork-viterbi: a framework for weakly supervised video learning. In: Computer Vision and Pattern Recognition (CVPR) (2018)
61. Sener, F., Yao, A.: Zero-shot anticipation for instructional activities. In: International Conference on Computer Vision (ICCV) (2019)
62. Sener, O., Zamir, A.R., Savarese, S., Saxena, A.: Unsupervised semantic parsing of video collections. In: International Conference on Computer Vision (ICCV) (2015)
63. Shen, Y., Wang, L., Elhamifar, E.: Learning To segment actions from visual and language instructions via differentiable weak sequence alignment. In: Computer Vision and Pattern Recognition (CVPR) (2021)
64. Sigurdsson, G.A., Gupta, A., Schmid, C., Farhadi, A., Alahari, K.: Actor and observer: joint modeling of first and third-person videos. In: Computer Vision and Pattern Recognition (CVPR) (2018)
65. Singh, S., Arora, C., Jawahar, C.V.: First person action recognition using deep learned descriptors. In: Computer Vision and Pattern Recognition (CVPR) (2016)
66. Srivastava, N., Mansimov, E., Salakhutdinov, R.: Unsupervised learning of video representations using LSTMs. In: International Conference on Machine Learning (ICML) (2015)

67. Tang, Y., et al.: COIN: a large-scale dataset for comprehensive instructional video analysis. In: Computer Vision and Pattern Recognition (CVPR) (2019)

68. Tran, D., Bourdev, L.D., Fergus, R., Torresani, L., Paluri, M.: Learning spatiotemporal features with 3d convolutional networks. In: International Conference on Computer Vision (ICCV) (2015)

69. Tran, D., Wang, H., Torresani, L., Ray, J., LeCun, Y., Paluri, M.: A closer look at spatiotemporal convolutions for action recognition. In: Computer Vision and Pattern Recognition (CVPR) (2018)

70. VidalMata, R.G., Scheirer, W.J., Kukleva, A., Cox, D., Kuehne, H.: Joint visual-temporal embedding for unsupervised learning of actions in untrimmed sequences. In: Proceedings of the IEEE/CVF Winter Conference on Applications of Computer Vision (WACV) (2021)

71. Vincent, P., Larochelle, H., Bengio, Y., Manzagol, P.A.: Extracting and composing robust features with denoising autoencoders. In: International Conference on Machine Learning (ICML) (2008)

72. Vondrick, C., Pirsiavash, H., Torralba, A.: Generating videos with scene dynamics. In: Neural Information Processing Systems (2016)

73. Wang, X., Girshick, R.B., Gupta, A., He, K.: Non-local neural networks. In: Computer Vision and Pattern Recognition (CVPR) (2018)

74. Wei, D., Lim, o., Zisserman, A., Freeman, W.T.: Learning and using the arrow of time. In: Computer Vision and Pattern Recognition (CVPR) (2018)

75. Xu, D., Xiao, J., Zhao, Z., Shao, J., Xie, D., Zhuang, Y.: Self-supervised spatiotemporal learning via video clip order prediction. In: Computer Vision and Pattern Recognition (CVPR) (2019)

76. Yu, S.I., Jiang, L., Hauptmann, A.: Instructional videos for unsupervised harvesting and learning of action examples. In: ACM International Conference on Multimedia (2014)

77. Zhou, L., Xu, C., Corso, J.J.: Towards automatic learning of procedures from web instructional videos. In: AAAI Conference on Artificial Intelligence (2018)

78. Zhukov, D., Alayrac, J.-B., Laptev, I., Sivic, J.: Learning actionness via long-range temporal order verification. In: Vedaldi, A., Bischof, H., Brox, T., Frahm, J.-M. (eds.) ECCV 2020. LNCS, vol. 12374, pp. 470–487. Springer, Cham (2020). https://doi.org/10.1007/978-3-030-58526-6_28

79. Zhukov, D., Alayrac, J.B., Cinbis, R.G., Fouhey, D., Laptev, I., Sivic, J.: Cross-task weakly supervised learning from instructional videos. In: Computer Vision and Pattern Recognition (CVPR) (2019)

GIMO: Gaze-Informed Human Motion Prediction in Context

Yang Zheng[1,2], Yanchao Yang[1(✉)], Kaichun Mo[1], Jiaman Li[1], Tao Yu[2],
Yebin Liu[2], C. Karen Liu[1], and Leonidas J. Guibas[1]

[1] Stanford University, Stanford, USA
yanchaoy@cs.stanford.edu
[2] Tsinghua University, Beijing, China

Abstract. Predicting human motion is critical for assistive robots and
AR/VR applications, where the interaction with humans needs to be safe
and comfortable. Meanwhile, an accurate prediction depends on understanding both the scene context and human intentions. Even though
many works study scene-aware human motion prediction, the latter is
largely underexplored due to the lack of ego-centric views that disclose
human intent and the limited diversity in motion and scenes. To reduce
the gap, we propose a large-scale human motion dataset that delivers
high-quality body pose sequences, scene scans, as well as ego-centric
views with the eye gaze that serves as a surrogate for inferring human
intent. By employing inertial sensors for motion capture, our data collection is not tied to specific scenes, which further boosts the motion
dynamics observed from our subjects. We perform an extensive study of
the benefits of leveraging the eye gaze for ego-centric human motion prediction with various state-of-the-art architectures. Moreover, to realize
the full potential of the gaze, we propose a novel network architecture
that enables bidirectional communication between the gaze and motion
branches. Our network achieves the top performance in human motion
prediction on the proposed dataset, thanks to the intent information
from eye gaze and the denoised gaze feature modulated by the motion.
Code and data can be found at https://github.com/y-zheng18/GIMO.

1 Introduction

A large portion of the human brain cortex is devoted to processing visual signals
collected by the optic nerve, and over half of the nerve fibers carry information
from the fovea that is responsible for sharp central vision. When modulated
through foveal fixation, or equivalently, *eye gaze,* important sensory input of
fine details perceived with the fovea can inform future actions of the human
agent [8,42]. As shown in Fig. 1, a human agent intending to perform two tasks
entails distinctive gaze patterns, even though the first few moves are not very

---

Supplementary Information The online version contains supplementary material
available at https://doi.org/10.1007/978-3-031-19778-9_39.

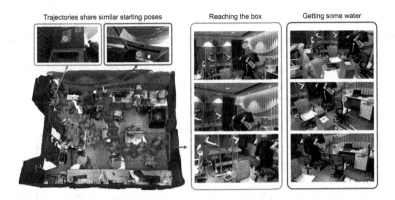

Fig. 1. Human motion driven by different intents look similar at the beginning. However, the scanning patterns of the eye gaze (red dots) during the starting phase are pretty distinctive, which suggests that we can leverage eye gaze to reduce uncertainties when predicting future body movements. (Color figure online)

distinguishable. Hence, it is beneficial to employ eye gaze when making human motion predictions in the 3D scene, which is of great importance for human-machine interactions [1,6]. For example, a human agent wearing an AR/VR headset may approach a chair to sit on it or grab a cup on the table behind it. If the latter is true, we may want the headset to send a warning for collision avoidance based on the forecasted future. To resolve ambiguities for reliable human motion prediction, there is an increasing interest in leveraging eye gaze as it highly correlates to the user intent that motivates the consequent actions.

The key to understanding the role of gaze and how it can effectively inform human motion prediction lies in two folds. First, it is critical to have a dataset with high-quality 3D body pose annotations and corresponding eye gaze. Besides data quality, the 3D scene and motion dynamics should be diverse to enable meaningful learning and evaluation of the gain when eye gaze is incorporated. Second, it is crucial to have a network architecture that can efficiently utilize *sparse* eye gaze during predictions given the multi-modal setting (e.g., gaze, human motion and scene geometry) and the fact that *not* every single gaze is of the *same* significance regarding the agent's intent (e.g., one may get distracted by a salient object in the scene that has nothing to do with the task at hand).

However, most existing human motion datasets *do not* support evaluating the effect of eye gaze due to the lack of ego-centric data annotated with both gaze and 3D body pose within the same scene. Recently, there are a few datasets proposed on ego-centric social interaction and object manipulation where gaze and the viewer's 3D poses are available. Nevertheless, they are not suitable for ego-centric human motion prediction since the diversity of scenes and the variation in motion dynamics are very limited. To validate the benefits of eye gaze in *human motion prediction*, we propose a large-scale ego-centric dataset, which contains the scene context, eye gaze, and accurate 3D body poses of the human actors. By employing an advanced motion capture system based on Inertial Measurement Units (IMUs), we can collect 3D pose data with high fidelity and avoid the limits of conventional multi-camera systems. For example, the actor can walk through any environment without performing a cumbersome setup of motion capture devices. Moreover, accurate poses can be recorded without any 2D-3D lifting, which could induce errors due to occlusions and noise in the detection. These advantages enable the actors to perform various long-horizon activities in a diverse set of daily living environments.

In order to check the effectiveness of eye gaze in improving human motion prediction, we perform an extensive study with multiple state-of-the-art architectures. However, we note that gaze and motion could both be inherently ambiguous in forecasting future movements. For example, the gaze may be allocated to a TV monitor while walking towards the dining table. In this case, the actor may simply follow the momentum, thus rendering the eye gaze uninformative about the body motion. To fully utilize the potential of eye gaze, we propose a novel architecture that manifests cross-modal attention such that *not only* future motion can benefit from the eye gaze, *but also* the significance of gaze in predicting the future can be reinforced by the observed motion. With eye gaze, better human motion predictions are observed across various architectures. Furthermore, the proposed architecture achieves top performance measured under different criteria, verifying the effectiveness of our bidirectional fusion scheme.

In summary, we make the following contributions. First, we provide a large-scale human motion dataset that enables investigating the benefits of eye gaze under diverse scenes and motion dynamics. Second, we propose a novel architecture with a bidirectional multi-modal fusion that better suits gaze-informed human motion prediction through mutual disambiguation between motion and gaze. Finally, we validate the usefulness of eye gaze for human motion prediction with multiple architectures and verify the effectiveness of the proposed architecture by showing top performance on the proposed benchmark.

2   Related Work

Datasets for Human Motions. Human motion modeling is a long-standing problem and is extensively explored with high-quality motion capture datasets, ranging from small-scale CMU Graphics Lab Motion Capture Database [5] to large-scale ones like AMASS [31]. Human3.6M [13] captures high-quality motions using a multi-view camera system and serves as a standard benchmark for motion prediction and 3D pose estimation. While these datasets provide adequate data to learn motion dynamics, the constraints from the 3D environment are usually not included. Later, more datasets containing the 3D scene are proposed, and scene-aware motion prediction can be studied using GTA-1M dataset [4]. PROX [11] includes both 3D scene and human interaction motions which can be used to explore scene-aware motion generation [51] task and the problem of placing human to the scene [60,62]. As the data is always collected with a human agent, ego-centric videos are provided in EgoPose [54,55], Kinpoly [30] and HPS [9] to study how the motion estimation and prediction can benefit from these ego-centric observations. Moreover, social interaction is considered in

You2Me [36] and EgoBody [57]. However, existing datasets do not contain diverse 3D scenes and human motions with intentions, we collect a large-scale dataset for gaze-guided human motion prediction, and it consists of high-quality human motions, 3D scene, ego-centric video and corresponding eye gaze information.

Human Motion Prediction. RNNs have proven successful in modeling human motion dynamics [3,7,27,34,61]. [32] proposes an attention-based model to guide the future prediction with motion history. To effectively exploit both spatial and temporal dependencies in human pose sequences, ST-Transformer [2] designs a spatial temporal transformer architecture to model the human motions. Pose Transformers [35] investigates a non-autoregressive formulation using transformer model and shows superior performance in terms of both efficiency and accuracy. As human motions are tightly correlated with the scene context, scene-aware motion prediction is also actively studied [4,10,63]. A three-stage pipeline is established to predict long-term human motions conditioned on the scene context [4]. SAMP [10] further includes object geometry to estimate interaction positions and orientations, and generates motions following a calculated collision-free trajectory. Besides the scene constraints, other modalities such as gaze and music also provide clues for future motion prediction. Transformer [48] is applied to generate dance movements conditioned on music [24,25,47]. MoGaze [21] verifies the effectiveness of eye gaze information for motion prediction with an RNN model in a full-body manipulation scenario. Our work aims to predict long-term future motions with both 3D scene and gaze constraints. We differ from existing motion prediction works, as their focus is the dense motion predictions, while we are predicting long-term sparse motions to understand human intentions.

Human Motion Estimation. 3D pose estimation is extensively studied in third-person view images or videos [12,18–20,29,43,56,58]. VIBE [18] propose a sequential model to estimate human poses and shapes from videos, along with a motion discriminator to constrain the predictions in a plausible motion manifold. TCMR [12] explicitly enforces the neural nets to leverage past and future frames to eliminate jitters in predictions. Motion priors are founded effective in improving the temporal smoothness and tackling the occlusion issues [23,40,59]. More attentions are received in ego-centric pose estimation recently. Pose estimation from images captured using a fish eye camera is explored in [41,44,45,50,53]. [15] deploy a chest-mounted camera and predict motions based on an implicit motion graph. Following the chest-mounted camera setting, You2Me [36] introduces the motions of the visible second person as an additional signal to constrain the motion estimation of the camera wearer. [30,54,55] explores motion estimation and prediction with head-mounted front-facing camera. In this work, we are addressing the ego-centric motion prediction task where past motions are given. Our proposed dataset can benefit the ego-centric motion estimation problem.

3   GIMO Dataset: Gaze and Motion with Scene Context

Human motion is affected by the scene, which provides physical constraints and the agent's psychological demand that drives body movements. To have a

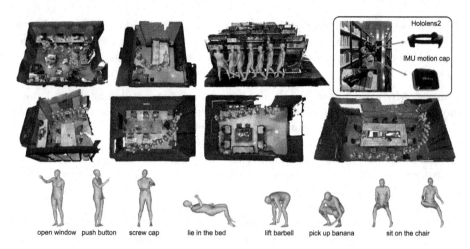

Fig. 2. We collect human motion data in various indoor environments (1st, 2nd rows), allowing the human subject to perform a diverse range of daily activities exhibiting rich dynamics (bottom). Top-right: motion and gaze capture devices.

concrete assessment of the benefits induced by eye gaze, we need both ego-centric views, and 3D body poses of the agent. Particularly, they should be temporally synchronized and spatially aligned within the 3D scenes. Current datasets for human motion prediction are either collected in a virtual environment risking being unrealistic or captured by an array of cameras with limited scene diversity and motion dynamics. Moreover, eye gaze is usually not available.

Therefore, we propose a real-world large-scale dataset that provides high-quality human motions, ego-centric views with eye gaze, as well as 3D environments. Next, we describe our data collection pipeline.

3.1   Hardware Setup

We employ a commercialized IMU-based motion capture system to record high-quality 3D body poses of the human agent, whose eye gaze in 3D is detected using an AR device mounted on the head. The 3D scenes are scanned by a smartphone equipped with lidar sensors (please see Fig. 2, top-right).

Motion Capture. To capture daily activities in various indoor environments, we resort to motion capture from IMU signals following HPS [9]. While HPS only provides SMPL [28] models with body movements, we take advantage of an advanced commercial product[1] which can record at 96 fps 3D body and hand joint movement of the subject. To obtain the full-body pose and hand gesture of the subject, we apply SMPL-X [37] model to fit the recorded IMU signals from multiple joints. Compared to human motion datasets like PROX [11], where the 3D body pose is estimated from monocular RGB videos, the pose obtained using

---

[1] https://noitom.com/perception-neuron-series.

Table 1. Statistics of existing and our datasets. * means virtual 3D scenes, e.g., from game engine [4] or CAD models [10]. *Ego* denotes egocentric images are available, and *Intent* indicates whether the motions have clear intentions, e.g., fetching a book.

Dataset	Frame	Sub	3D scene	Ego	Gaze	3rd-person	Human pose from	Parametric model	Intent	Task
EGTEA Gaze+ [26]	2419k	32		✓	✓				✓	Action recognition
TIA [52]	330k	-		✓	✓				✓	Attention prediction
Human3.6M [13]	3600k	11				✓	Marker-based			Pose estimation
TNT15 [49]	13k	4				✓	RGB+IMU			Pose estimation
3DPW [33]	51k	7				✓	RGB+IMU	SMPL		Pose estimation
Panoptic [16]	297k	180+				✓	Multi-RGB			Pose estimation
TotalCapture [17]	1,900k	5				✓	Multi-RGB	Frank		Pose estimation
HPS [9]	300k	7	✓	✓			IMU	SMPL		Pose estimation
EgoBody [57]	153k	20	✓	✓	✓	✓	Multi-RGB-D	SMPL-X		Pose estimation
EgoMoCap [30]	148k	3		✓			Marker-based			Pose estimation
PROX [11], [62]	100k	20	✓			✓	RGB	SMPL-X		Human generation
GTA-IM [4]	1000k		✓*			✓	Game engine			Motion prediction
SAMP [10]		1	✓*				Marker-based	SMPL-X	✓	Motion prediction
GIMO (ours)	129k	11	✓	✓	✓		IMU	SMPL-X	✓	Motion prediction

the above procedure is free from estimation errors caused by noisy detection and occlusions. Fitting parametric human body models for poses from multi-view RGB(D) streams or with marker-based systems is also commonly used to collect human motion data [13,17,57], however, our pipeline requires much less effort in presetting the environment; thus, we can collect human motion data in any indoor scene. These characteristics endow us with the capability to ensure the diversity of the scene and motion dynamics in our dataset.

Gaze Capture. Following [57], we use Hololens2[2] and its Research Mode API [46] to capture the 3D eye gaze. It also records ego-centric video at 30 fps in 760×428 resolution, long-throw depth streams at 1–5 fps in 512×512, and 6D poses of the head-mounted camera. The 3D scene is reconstructed through TSDF fusion given the recorded depth, which is used for the subsequent global alignment. The eye gaze is recorded as a 3D point in the coordinate system of the headset.

3D Scene Acquisition. To obtain high-quality 3D geometry of the scene (the reconstructed TSDF result from Hololens2 is usually noisy), we use an iPhone13 Pro Max equipped with LiDAR sensors to scan the environment through 3D Scanner APP[3]. The output mesh contains about 500k vertices and photorealistic texture, providing sufficient details to infer the affordance of the scene. The data collection process involving human agents and the alignment of different coordinate frames to the scanned meshes are described in the following.

3.2 Data Collection with Human in Action

One distinct feature of our dataset is that it captures long-term motions with clear intentions. Different from prior datasets for motion estimation purposes where the subjects are performing random actions such as jumping and waving

---

[2] https://www.microsoft.com/en-us/hololens.

[3] https://apps.apple.com/us/app/3d-scanner-app/id1419913995.

hands, we aim at collecting motion trajectories with semantic meaning, e.g., walk to open the door. Thus, we focus on collecting data from various daily activities in indoor scenes. The full statistics of our dataset are listed in Table 1.

Table 2. Activities performed by our subjects.

Category	Activities
Resting Interacting with objects	Sitting or laying on objects Touching, holding, stepping on, reaching to objects
Changing the state of objects	Opening, pushing, transferring, throwing, picking up, lifting, connecting, screwing, grabbing, swapping objects

To this end, we recruit 11 university students (4 female and 7 male) and ask them to perform the activities defined in Table 2. The subjects are instructed to start from a distant location to the goal object and then move to the destination to act. Therefore, long-term motion with clear intention can be obtained. Especially, the collection progress includes the following steps: (i) the subject wears the head-mounted Hololens2, the IMU-based motion capture clothes, and gloves, where calibration is performed to set up the motion capture system; (ii) the subject chooses the action from the activities in Table 2 according to the affordance of the scene; (iii) the 3D scene is scanned; (iv) the subject starts to carry out the planned activities in the scene while data are collected; (v) the scene is reset for the following subjects to perform their activities. Note, if the subject changes the scene geometry, we reset the objects to their original states to avoid rescanning the whole environment.

As a result, our dataset contains 129k ego-centric images, 11 subjects, and 217 motion trajectories in 19 scenes, manifesting enough capacity and diversity for gaze-informed human motion prediction. As illustrated in Fig. 2, the motions are smooth and convey clear semantic intentions.

3.3   Data Preparation

Synchronization. Given compatibility issues, it is difficult to synchronize the motion capture system with Hololens2 without modifying their commercialized software. Instead, we use a hand gesture that can be observed in the ego-centric view as a starting signal. Once the pose and ego-centric image of the hand gesture are aligned, the rest frames can be synchronized according to the timestamps.

Parametric Model Fitting. To obtain the 3D body pose and shape of the subject, we fit SMPL-X [37] model to the 3D joints (23 body joints, 15 left-hand joints, and 15 right-hand joints), which are computed from the recorded IMU signals by the provided commercial software. In addition, the 6D head pose is used to determine the head position and orientation of the SMPL-X model.

Alignment. The Hololens2 coordinate system and the fitted SMPL-X models need to align with the high-quality 3D scene scans. The former is aligned through ICP between the TSDF fusion result of the depth recorded by Hololens2 and the 3D scene. The SMPL-X motion sequence is first transformed to the Hololens2

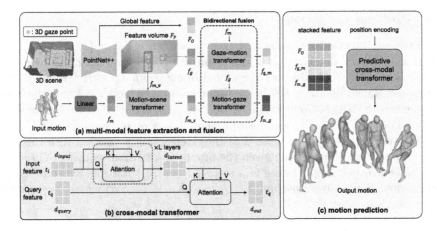

Fig. 3. Our gaze-informed human motion prediction architecture. Multi-modal features, i.e., gaze feature, human motion feature, and global scene feature, are extracted and then fused through the proposed *bidirectional* fusion scheme (a). The fused features are then stacked into a holistic representation and used for future motion prediction (c). The cross-modal transformer component [14] is illustrated in (b). Please refer to Sect. 4 for more details.

coordinate system via human annotations, i.e., the start and end shapes of the human body are scanned by Hololens2 and visible in the TSDF reconstruction, which serves as anchor shapes for aligning the fitted models. The pose can then be aligned to the 3D scene using the global transformation obtained from the previous ICP alignment between the scene scans. Our dataset is named GIMO, and we describe our method for gaze-informed motion prediction in the following.

4   Gaze-Informed Human Motion Prediction

Gaze conveys relevant information about the subject's intent, which can be used to enhance long-horizon human motion prediction. On the other hand, past motions [2,4], ego-centric views [10,55], or 3D context [10,51] could provide helpful constraints on human motion, yet, the prediction is still challenging and suffers from uncertainties in the future. Here, we aim at gaze-informed long-term human motion prediction. Specifically, given the past motion, 3D scene, and 3D eye gaze as inputs, we study how they can be integrated to resolve the ambiguities in future motion and generate intention-aware motion predictions.

To fully utilize the geometry information provided by the 3D scene and intention clues from past motions and gaze, we propose a novel framework with a bidirectional fusion scheme that facilitates the communication between different modalities. As shown in Fig. 3, we use PointNet++ [39] as the encoding backbone to extract per-point features of the 3D scene, followed by several cross-modal transformers to transcend information from multi-modality embeddings.

4.1 Problem Definition

We represent a motion sample as a parametric sequence $X_{i:j} = \{x_i, x_{i+1}, \cdots, x_j\}$ where $x_k = (t_k, r_k, h_k, \beta_k, p_k)$ is a pose frame at time k. Here $t \in R^3$ is the global translation, $r \in SO(3)$ denotes the global orientation, $h_k \in R^{32}$ refers to the body pose embedding, $\beta \in R^{10}$ is the shape parameter, and $p \in R^{24}$ is the hand pose, where SMPL-X body mesh $M = \mathcal{M}(t_k, r_k, h_k, \beta_k, p_k)$ can be obtained using VPoser [37]. The 3D scene is represented as a point cloud $S \in R^{n \times 3}$, and the 3D gaze point $g \in R^3$ is defined as the intersection points between the gaze direction and the scene. Thus, given the inputs of a motion sequence $X_{1:t}$ along with the corresponding 3D gaze $G_{1:t} = \{g_1, g_2, \cdots, g_t\}$ and the 3D scene S, we aim to predict the future motion $X_{t:t+T} = \Phi(X_{1:t}, G_{1:t}, S|\theta)$ where θ represents the network parameters.

4.2 Multi-modal Feature Extraction

Instead of extracting the multi-modal embeddings independently [25], we propose a novel scheme to integrate the motion, gaze, and scene features. The gist is to let the motion and gaze features communicate to each other, so their uncertainties regarding the future can be mutually decreased, resulting in more effective utilization of the gaze information.

Scene Feature Extraction. To learn the constraints from the 3D scene and guide the network to pay attention to local geometric structures, we apply Point-Net++ to extract both global and local scene features. Specially, we obtain the per-point feature map and a global descriptor of the scene as follows:

$$F_P, F_o = \Phi_{scene}(S|\theta_s) \tag{1}$$

where $S \in R^{n \times 3}$ is the input point cloud, $F_P \in R^{n \times d_p}$ is the per-point d_p dimensional feature map, and $F_o \in R^{d_o}$ is the global descriptor of the scene. Given the per-point feature F_P, the feature of an arbitrary point e can be computed through the inversed distance weighted interpolation [39]:

$$F_{P|e} = \frac{\sum_{i=1}^{n_e} w_i F_{P|p_i}}{\sum_{i=1}^{n_e} w_i}, w_i = \frac{1}{||p_i - e||_2} \tag{2}$$

where $\{p_1, p_2, \cdots, p_{n_e}\}$ are the nearest neighbors of e in the scene point cloud.

Gaze Feature Extraction. We query the gaze point feature f_g from the per-point scene feature map F_P according to Eq. 2, i.e., $f_g = F_{P|g}$. Thus, the interpolated gaze feature contains relevant scene information that provides cues to infer the subject's intention.

Motion Feature Extraction. A linear layer is used to extract the motion embedding f_m from the input motion parameter x. To endow the embedding awareness of the 3D scene, we further query the scene features of the SMPL-X vertices using Eq. 2. These SMPL-X per-vertex features are then fed to Point-Net [38] to get the ambient scene context feature f_{m_v} of the current motion pose:

$$f_{m\_v} = PointNet(\{F_{P|v}, v \in \mathcal{M}(x)\}) \tag{3}$$

where $\mathcal{M}(x)$ is the SMPL-X vertex set with motion parameter x.

4.3   Attention-Aware Multi-modal Feature Fusion

Given the multi-modal nature of the gaze, scene, and motion, an efficient feature fusion module is necessary to leverage the information from different modalities. Instead of directly concatenating the features [25], we propose a more effective scheme by deploying a cross-modal transformer [14] to fuse the gaze, motion, and scene features (Fig. 3). We explain our design in the following.

Cross-Modal Transformer. The cross-modal transformer [14] is used to capture the correlations between input embedding sequences and to establish communications between the multi-modal information. It is largely based on attention mechanism [48]. An attention function [14] maps a query and key-value pairs to an output as:

$$Attention(Q, K, V) = softmax(\frac{QK^T}{\sqrt{d_K}})V, Q = qW_q, K = kW_k, V = vW_v \tag{4}$$

where $q \in R^{l_q \times d_q}$, $k \in R^{l_{kv} \times d_k}$, $v \in R^{l_{kv} \times d_v}$ are input query, key and value vectors, and $W_q \in R^{d_q \times d_K}$, $W_k \in R^{d_k \times d_K}$, $W_q \in R^{d_v \times d_V}$ embed the inputs. Here d denotes the dimension of the input vector and l is the sequence length.

As shown in Fig. 3(b), the cross-modal transformer is built on a stack of attention layers, which maps a t_i-length input into a t_q-length output by querying a t_q-length feature:

$$\phi_{out} = cross\_trans(\phi_{query}, \phi_{input}) \tag{5}$$

It is proved to be efficient in processing multi-modal signals, e.g., text, & audio.

Motion Feature Fusion. The motion feature should be aware of the 3D scene context and the subject's intention inferred from the gaze information, so that it can guide the prediction network to generate more reasonable motion trajectories (e.g., free from penetration and collision) and accurate estimations of the ending position or pose of the subject. For this purpose, we first use the scene context feature f_{m_v} acquired from the ambient 3D environment (Eq. 3) as the query to update the motion feature f_m through a motion-scene transformer:

$$f_{m\_s} = cross\_trans(f_{m\_v}, f_m) \tag{6}$$

Thus, the output motion embedding f_{m_s} is expected to be aware of the 3D scene. We then feed f_{m_s} to the next motion-gaze transformer where the gaze feature f_g is the query input:

$$f_{m\_g} = cross\_trans(f_g, f_{m\_s}) \tag{7}$$

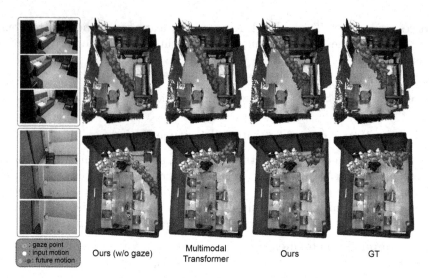

Fig. 4. Qualitative results. Top row: results on a known scene from the training set. Bottom row: results in a new environment. We compare our method with Multimodal-Net [25] and ours without gaze. Please zoom in for details.

The final motion embedding f_{m_g} is expected to integrate both the 3D scene information and the intention clues from the gaze features.

Gaze Feature Fusion. While gaze can help generate intention-aware motion features, the motion could also provide informative guidance to mitigate the randomness of gaze since not every gaze point reveals meaningful user intent. Therefore, we treat the gaze embedding in a bidirectional manner, i.e., the motion embedding f_m is also used as the query to update the gaze features such that the network can learn which gaze features contribute more to the future motion:

$$f_{g\_m} = cross\_trans(f_m, f_g) \tag{8}$$

The bidirectionally fused multi-modal features are then composed into holistic temporal representations of the input to perform human motion prediction. As illustrated in Fig. 3(c), the updated gaze feature f_{g_m}, motion feature f_{m_g} and the global scene feature F_O are used to predict the future motion by:

$$X_{t:t+T} = cross\_trans(h_{position}, cat(f_{g\_m}, f_{m\_g}, F_O)_{1:t}) \tag{9}$$

where cat denotes the concatenation operation, and $h_{position}$ is the latent vector that contains temporal positional encodings for the output [14]. We verify the effectiveness of our design in utilizing gaze information through experiments.

5   Experiments

In this part, we explain our experimental setup and results. Our goal is to examine the following questions:

1. Does gaze help disambiguate human motion prediction?
2. How do state-of-the-art methods perform on our dataset?
3. What is the contribution of each part of our design to the final performance? Overall, is the proposed architecture effective?

5.1 Experimental Setup

In our experiments, we predict the future motion in 5 s from 3 s input, where the first 3 s of a trajectory is just about to start an activity in our dataset, and in the next 5 s the trajectory proceeds to finish the activity. We set the motion frame rate to 2 fps, i.e., 6 pose input and 10 pose output. Since we aim to explore the effect of gaze in disambiguating motion prediction, high-frequency motion is not necessary. Note that once the waypoints are predicted, a full motion sequence with high fps can be easily generated [51].

Baselines. We implement several state-of-the-art motion prediction and generation baselines including ST-Transformer [2] and an RNN network [22] for full motion prediction from the past motion input, and MultimodalNet [25] based on transformer for motion synthesis from multi-modal data (i.e., gaze, motion, and the 3D scene feature in our experiments). We build our pipeline by incorporating 6 cross-modal transformer layers [14]. L1 loss between the predicted motion and the ground truth is used to train the network. More details about the network architecture and training are available in the supplementary material.

Table 3. Destination accuracy. We report the global translation and orientation error and mean per-joint position error (*MPJPE*).

Method	Known scenes			New scenes		
	Trans	Ori	MPJPE	Trans	Ori	MPJPE
ST-Transformer [2]	0.587	0.864	279.9	0.516	0.682	236.8
RNN [22]	0.538	0.822	272.5	0.547	0.894	230.4
MultimodalNet [25]	0.442	0.699	260.0	0.389	0.658	236.0
RNN+gaze [21]	0.389	0.882	264.2	0.345	0.611	230.0
MultimodalNet+gaze [25]	0.316	0.743	266.6	0.300	0.583	**204.9**
Ours (w/o gaze)	0.393	0.656	262.1	0.389	0.709	228.7
Ours (pointnet)	0.310	0.659	240.6	0.394	0.563	234.5
Ours (vanilla)	0.353	0.739	249.0	0.365	0.602	220.4
Ours	**0.245**	**0.579**	**237.8**	**0.280**	**0.556**	209.0

Table 4. Path errors of the predicted motions.

Method	Known scenes			New scenes		
	Trans	Ori	MPJPE	Trans	Ori	MPJPE
ST-Transformer [2]	0.329	0.503	201.4	0.339	0.537	201.7
RNN [22]	0.308	0.476	195.2	0.324	0.495	180.3
MultimodalNet [25]	0.273	0.383	190.0	0.294	0.425	177.0
RNN+gaze [21]	0.235	0.457	190.1	0.278	**0.288**	182.6
MultimodalNet+gaze [25]	0.246	0.424	193.1	**0.250**	0.374	183.7
Ours (w/o gaze)	0.305	0.412	180.1	0.315	0.403	182.5
Ours (pointnet)	0.218	0.360	180.5	0.267	0.403	184.5
Ours (vanilla)	0.238	0.399	182.7	0.286	0.348	180.3
Ours	**0.213**	**0.340**	**177.1**	0.261	0.322	**160.3**

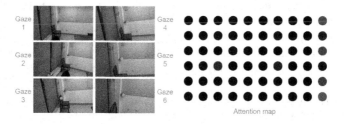

Fig. 5. The attention map of the 6 input gaze for the 10 output motion. The gaze influences the ending output most (brighter means larger weight), indicating that the gaze features reveal the subject's final goals.

5.2   Evaluation

To evaluate, we divide the 217 trajectories of our dataset into 180 trajectories for training and 37 for testing. The 37 motions consist of 27 trajectories (different from the training ones) performed in known scenes from the training set and 10 in 2 new environments scanned only for evaluation purposes.

Evaluation Metrics. We employ the destination error and the path error as our evaluation metrics. The destination error refers to the global translation, rotation error and the mean per-joint position error (MPJPE) [13] of the last pose in the predicted motion. The destination pose contains essential information about the subject's goal, which is our experiments' primary focus. The path error is computed as the mean error of the predicted poses in 5s [4]. We treat the global translation and rotation error as the $l1$ distance between the predicted SMPL-X translation and orientation parameter with the ground truth [51].

Quantitative Evaluation. As shown in Table 3 and Table 4, while the state-of-the-art methods based on spatio-temporal transformer [2] suffer from ambiguities since the prediction is simply from the past motion, a simple RNN method with motion and gaze input [21] can significantly reduce the ambiguity, indicating the effectiveness of gaze in guiding the prediction of motion. Our method achieves promising results in predicting reasonable future motion with small destination and translation errors. Compared to MultimodalNet [25] built on the vanilla transformers [47], our method outperforms in recognizing the subject's intent from the gaze and thus predicts more accurate destination poses.

Qualitative Evaluation. Figure 4 shows that in a "going to sit" activity performed in one scene from the training set (top row), our method manages to generate accurate destination poses, i.e., sitting on the sofa. In the new environment, the subject first grabs a blackboard eraser and then starts wiping. While all the methods generate walking actions, ours without gaze input fails to predict the correct motion. When given gaze, results from MultimodalNet [25] and our method both reach out the hand and try to grab something. Our prediction successfully arrives at the destination point where the eraser lies; however, the results of MultimodalNet [25] reach out to the wrong place. More visualizations and failure cases are included in the supplementary material.

5.3   Ablation Study

In this part, we aim to answer question 3 by finding the factors that contribute to the superior performance of our method.

Variant 1: Gaze. We evaluate the baseline's performance with and without gaze input to explore how gaze could influence the motion prediction results. As clearly demonstrated in Table 3 and Table 4, the RNN network [21] and the MultimodalNet [25] both gain significant accuracy improvement given gaze inputs. Figure 4 shows that without gaze, our method is confused about the future destination. To find more intuitions about the role of gaze in motion prediction, we visualize the attention weights of gaze feature query over the motion feature as depicted in Fig. 5. Interestingly, we find the gaze feature does influence the ending poses in the predicted motion, implying that the gaze can serve as a strong indicator of the destination of a motion, which reveals the user's intent.

Variant 2: PointNet++ for Scene Feature Query. We propose to use PointNet++ [39] to extract the per-point feature of the scene such that the gaze feature and scene-aware motion feature can be obtained (Sect. 4.2). We replace it with PointNet to extract the global scene feature and use a linear layer to get the gaze feature. Results in Table 3 and Table 4 demonstrate that the variant can act well on scenes from the training set, but lose its competitiveness when generalized to new environments with different 3D structures.

Variant 3: Cross-Modal Transformer. The cross-modal transformer architecture proves to be effective in bridging multi-modal information [14]. We replace it with the vanilla transformer [48] as used in [25]. Results in Table 3 and Table 4 (*Ours (vanilla)*) demonstrate the loss of accuracy compared to the full design. Note that the path error of the variant on the new scenes is even larger than the results without gaze input, indicating that the vanilla transformer might not be efficient enough to capture the correlations between multi-modal inputs.

6   Discussion and Future Work

We present the GIMO dataset, a real-world dataset with ego-centric images, 3D gazes, 3D scene context, and ground-truth human motions. With the collected dataset, we define a new task, i.e., gaze-informed human motion prediction, and further contribute a novel framework to minimize the ambiguities in motion prediction by leveraging eye gaze to infer the subject's potential intention. While our method only relies on 3D inputs, future work can incorporate visual information from ego-centric images to further improve accuracy. Besides the proposed task and framework, our dataset can benefit various applications, e.g., intention-aware motion synthesis and gaze-guided ego-centric pose estimation. We believe our work opens not only new directions for motion prediction but also has foreseeable impacts on ego-centric vision topics.

Acknowledgments. The authors are supported by a grant from the Stanford HAI Institute, a Vannevar Bush Faculty Fellowship, a gift from the Amazon Research Awards program, the NSFC grant No. 62125107, and No. 62171255. Also, Toyota Research Institute provided funds to support this work.

References

1. Admoni, H., Scassellati, B.: Social eye gaze in human-robot interaction: a review. J. Hum.-Robot Interact. **6**(1), 25–63 (2017)
2. Aksan, E., Kaufmann, M., Cao, P., Hilliges, O.: A spatio-temporal transformer for 3D human motion prediction. In: 2021 International Conference on 3D Vision (3DV), pp. 565–574. IEEE (2021)
3. Aksan, E., Kaufmann, M., Hilliges, O.: Structured prediction helps 3D human motion modelling. In: Proceedings of the IEEE/CVF International Conference on Computer Vision, pp. 7144–7153 (2019)
4. Cao, Z., Gao, H., Mangalam, K., Cai, Q.-Z., Vo, M., Malik, J.: Long-term human motion prediction with scene context. In: Vedaldi, A., Bischof, H., Brox, T., Frahm, J.-M. (eds.) ECCV 2020. LNCS, vol. 12346, pp. 387–404. Springer, Cham (2020). https://doi.org/10.1007/978-3-030-58452-8_23
5. CMU Graphics Lab (2000). http://mocap.cs.cmu.edu/
6. Duarte, N.F., Raković, M., Tasevski, J., Coco, M.I., Billard, A., Santos-Victor, J.: Action anticipation: reading the intentions of humans and robots. IEEE Robot. Autom. Lett. **3**(4), 4132–4139 (2018)
7. Fragkiadaki, K., Levine, S., Felsen, P., Malik, J.: Recurrent network models for human dynamics. In: Proceedings of the IEEE International Conference on Computer Vision, pp. 4346–4354 (2015)

8. Gottlieb, J., Oudeyer, P.Y., Lopes, M., Baranes, A.: Information-seeking, curiosity, and attention: computational and neural mechanisms. Trends Cogn. Sci. **17**(11), 585–593 (2013)

9. Guzov, V., Mir, A., Sattler, T., Pons-Moll, G.: Human poseitioning system (HPS): 3D human pose estimation and self-localization in large scenes from body-mounted sensors. In: Proceedings of the IEEE/CVF Conference on Computer Vision and Pattern Recognition, pp. 4318–4329 (2021)

10. Hassan, M., et al.: Stochastic scene-aware motion prediction. In: Proceedings of the IEEE/CVF International Conference on Computer Vision, pp. 11374–11384 (2021)

11. Hassan, M., Choutas, V., Tzionas, D., Black, M.J.: Resolving 3D human pose ambiguities with 3D scene constraints. In: Proceedings of the IEEE/CVF International Conference on Computer Vision, pp. 2282–2292 (2019)

12. Hossain, M.R.I., Little, J.J.: Exploiting temporal information for 3D human pose estimation. In: Proceedings of the European Conference on Computer Vision (ECCV), pp. 68–84 (2018)

13. Ionescu, C., Papava, D., Olaru, V., Sminchisescu, C.: Human3. 6m: large scale datasets and predictive methods for 3D human sensing in natural environments. IEEE Trans. Pattern Anal. Mach. Intell. **36**(7), 1325–1339 (2013)

14. Jaegle, A., et al.: Perceiver IO: a general architecture for structured inputs & outputs. arXiv preprint arXiv:2107.14795 (2021)

15. Jiang, H., Grauman, K.: Seeing invisible poses: estimating 3D body pose from egocentric video. In: 2017 IEEE Conference on Computer Vision and Pattern Recognition (CVPR), pp. 3501–3509. IEEE (2017)

16. Joo, H., et al.: Panoptic studio: a massively multiview system for social motion capture. In: Proceedings of the IEEE International Conference on Computer Vision, pp. 3334–3342 (2015)

17. Joo, H., Simon, T., Sheikh, Y.: Total capture: a 3D deformation model for tracking faces, hands, and bodies. In: Proceedings of the IEEE Conference on Computer Vision and Pattern Recognition, pp. 8320–8329 (2018)

18. Kocabas, M., Athanasiou, N., Black, M.J.: Vibe: video inference for human body pose and shape estimation. In: Proceedings of the IEEE Conference on Computer Vision and Pattern Recognition, pp. 5253–5263 (2020)

19. Kocabas, M., Huang, C.H.P., Hilliges, O., Black, M.J.: Pare: part attention regressor for 3D human body estimation. In: Proceedings of the IEEE/CVF International Conference on Computer Vision, pp. 11127–11137 (2021)

20. Kolotouros, N., Pavlakos, G., Black, M.J., Daniilidis, K.: Learning to reconstruct 3D human pose and shape via model-fitting in the loop. In: Proceedings of the IEEE International Conference on Computer Vision, pp. 2252–2261 (2019)

21. Kratzer, P., Bihlmaier, S., Midlagajni, N.B., Prakash, R., Toussaint, M., Mainprice, J.: Mogaze: a dataset of full-body motions that includes workspace geometry and eye-gaze. IEEE Robot. Autom. Lett. **6**(2), 367–373 (2020)

22. Kratzer, P., Toussaint, M., Mainprice, J.: Prediction of human full-body movements with motion optimization and recurrent neural networks. In: 2020 ICRA, pp. 1792–1798 (2020)

23. Li, J., et al.: Task-generic hierarchical human motion prior using VAEs. In: 2021 International Conference on 3D Vision (3DV), pp. 771–781. IEEE (2021)

24. Li, J., et al.: Learning to generate diverse dance motions with transformer. arXiv preprint arXiv:2008.08171 (2020)

25. Li, R., Yang, S., Ross, D.A., Kanazawa, A.: AI choreographer: music conditioned 3D dance generation with AIST++. In: Proceedings of the IEEE/CVF International Conference on Computer Vision, pp. 13401–13412 (2021)
26. Li, Y., Liu, M., Rehg, J.: In the eye of the beholder: gaze and actions in first person video. IEEE Trans. Pattern Anal. Mach. Intell. (2021)
27. Li, Z., Zhou, Y., Xiao, S., He, C., Huang, Z., Li, H.: Auto-conditioned recurrent networks for extended complex human motion synthesis. arXiv preprint arXiv:1707.05363 (2017)
28. Loper, M., Mahmood, N., Romero, J., Pons-Moll, G., Black, M.J.: SMPL: a skinned multi-person linear model. ACM Trans. Graph. (TOG) **34**(6), 1–16 (2015)
29. Luo, Z., Golestaneh, S.A., Kitani, K.M.: 3D human motion estimation via motion compression and refinement. In: Proceedings of the Asian Conference on Computer Vision (2020)
30. Luo, Z., Hachiuma, R., Yuan, Y., Kitani, K.: Dynamics-regulated kinematic policy for egocentric pose estimation. In: Advances in Neural Information Processing Systems, vol. 34 (2021)
31. Mahmood, N., Ghorbani, N., Troje, N.F., Pons-Moll, G., Black, M.J.: Amass: archive of motion capture as surface shapes. In: Proceedings of the IEEE/CVF International Conference on Computer Vision, pp. 5442–5451 (2019)
32. Mao, W., Liu, M., Salzmann, M.: History repeats itself: human motion prediction via motion attention. In: Vedaldi, A., Bischof, H., Brox, T., Frahm, J.-M. (eds.) ECCV 2020. LNCS, vol. 12359, pp. 474–489. Springer, Cham (2020). https://doi.org/10.1007/978-3-030-58568-6_28
33. von Marcard, T., Henschel, R., Black, M.J., Rosenhahn, B., Pons-Moll, G.: Recovering accurate 3D human pose in the wild using IMUs and a moving camera. In: Proceedings of the European Conference on Computer Vision (ECCV), pp. 601–617 (2018)
34. Martinez, J., Black, M.J., Romero, J.: On human motion prediction using recurrent neural networks. In: Proceedings of the IEEE Conference on Computer Vision and Pattern Recognition, pp. 2891–2900 (2017)
35. Martínez-González, A., Villamizar, M., Odobez, J.M.: Pose transformers (POTR): human motion prediction with non-autoregressive transformers. In: Proceedings of the IEEE/CVF International Conference on Computer Vision, pp. 2276–2284 (2021)
36. Ng, E., Xiang, D., Joo, H., Grauman, K.: You2me: inferring body pose in egocentric video via first and second person interactions. In: Proceedings of the IEEE/CVF Conference on Computer Vision and Pattern Recognition, pp. 9890–9900 (2020)
37. Pavlakos, G., et al.: Expressive body capture: 3D hands, face, and body from a single image. In: Proceedings of the IEEE/CVF Conference on Computer Vision and Pattern Recognition, pp. 10975–10985 (2019)
38. Qi, C.R., Su, H., Mo, K., Guibas, L.J.: Pointnet: deep learning on point sets for 3D classification and segmentation. In: Proceedings of the IEEE Conference on Computer Vision and Pattern Recognition, pp. 652–660 (2017)
39. Qi, C.R., Yi, L., Su, H., Guibas, L.J.: Pointnet++: deep hierarchical feature learning on point sets in a metric space. In: Advances in Neural Information Processing Systems, vol. 30 (2017)
40. Rempe, D., Birdal, T., Hertzmann, A., Yang, J., Sridhar, S., Guibas, L.J.: Humor: 3D human motion model for robust pose estimation. In: Proceedings of the IEEE/CVF International Conference on Computer Vision, pp. 11488–11499 (2021)
41. Rhodin, H., et al.: Egocap: egocentric marker-less motion capture with two fisheye cameras. ACM Trans. Graph. (TOG) **35**(6), 1–11 (2016)

42. Tatler, B.W., Hayhoe, M.M., Land, M.F., Ballard, D.H.: Eye guidance in natural vision: reinterpreting salience. J. Vis. **11**(5) (2011)

43. Tian, Y., Zhang, H., Liu, Y., Wang, l.: Recovering 3D human mesh from monocular images: a survey. arXiv preprint arXiv:2203.01923 (2022)

44. Tome, D., et al.: Selfpose: 3D egocentric pose estimation from a headset mounted camera. arXiv preprint arXiv:2011.01519 (2020)

45. Tome, D., Peluse, P., Agapito, L., Badino, H.: xR-EgoPose: egocentric 3D human pose from an HMD camera. In: Proceedings of the IEEE/CVF International Conference on Computer Vision, pp. 7728–7738 (2019)

46. Ungureanu, D., et al.: Hololens 2 research mode as a tool for computer vision research. arXiv preprint arXiv:2008.11239 (2020)

47. Valle-Pérez, G., Henter, G.E., Beskow, J., Holzapfel, A., Oudeyer, P.Y., Alexanderson, S.: Transflower: probabilistic autoregressive dance generation with multimodal attention. ACM Trans. Graph. (TOG) **40**(6), 1–14 (2021)

48. Vaswani, A., et al.: Attention is all you need. In: Advances in Neural Information Processing Systems, vol. 30 (2017)

49. Von Marcard, T., Pons-Moll, G., Rosenhahn, B.: Human pose estimation from video and IMUs. IEEE Trans. Pattern Anal. Mach. Intell. **38**(8), 1533–1547 (2016)

50. Wang, J., Liu, L., Xu, W., Sarkar, K., Theobalt, C.: Estimating egocentric 3D human pose in global space. In: Proceedings of the IEEE/CVF International Conference on Computer Vision, pp. 11500–11509 (2021)

51. Wang, J., Xu, H., Xu, J., Liu, S., Wang, X.: Synthesizing long-term 3D human motion and interaction in 3D scenes. In: Proceedings of the IEEE/CVF Conference on Computer Vision and Pattern Recognition, pp. 9401–9411 (2021)

52. Wei, P., Liu, Y., Shu, T., Zheng, N., Zhu, S.C.: Where and why are they looking? Jointly inferring human attention and intentions in complex tasks. In: Proceedings of the IEEE Conference on Computer Vision and Pattern Recognition, pp. 6801–6809 (2018)

53. Xu, W., et al.: Mo2cap2: real-time mobile 3D motion capture with a cap-mounted fisheye camera. IEEE Trans. Visual Comput. Graphics **25**(5), 2093–2101 (2019)

54. Yuan, Y., Kitani, K.: 3D ego-pose estimation via imitation learning. In: Proceedings of the European Conference on Computer Vision (ECCV), pp. 735–750 (2018)

55. Yuan, Y., Kitani, K.: Ego-pose estimation and forecasting as real-time PD control. In: Proceedings of the IEEE/CVF International Conference on Computer Vision, pp. 10082–10092 (2019)

56. Zhang, H., et al.: PyMAF: 3D human pose and shape regression with pyramidal mesh alignment feedback loop. In: Proceedings of the IEEE/CVF International Conference on Computer Vision (2021)

57. Zhang, S., et al.: Egobody: human body shape, motion and social interactions from head-mounted devices. arXiv preprint arXiv:2112.07642 (2021)

58. Zhang, S., Zhang, Y., Bogo, F., Marc, P., Tang, S.: Learning motion priors for 4D human body capture in 3d scenes. In: International Conference on Computer Vision (ICCV), October 2021

59. Zhang, S., Zhang, Y., Bogo, F., Pollefeys, M., Tang, S.: Learning motion priors for 4D human body capture in 3D scenes. In: Proceedings of the IEEE/CVF International Conference on Computer Vision, pp. 11343–11353 (2021)

60. Zhang, S., Zhang, Y., Ma, Q., Black, M.J., Tang, S.: Place: proximity learning of articulation and contact in 3D environments. In: 2020 International Conference on 3D Vision (3DV), pp. 642–651. IEEE (2020)

61. Zhang, Y., Black, M.J., Tang, S.: We are more than our joints: predicting how 3D bodies move. In: Proceedings of the IEEE/CVF Conference on Computer Vision and Pattern Recognition, pp. 3372–3382 (2021)
62. Zhang, Y., Hassan, M., Neumann, H., Black, M.J., Tang, S.: Generating 3D people in scenes without people. In: Proceedings of the IEEE/CVF Conference on Computer Vision and Pattern Recognition, pp. 6194–6204 (2020)
63. Zhang, Y., Tang, S.: The wanderings of odysseus in 3D scenes. In: Proceedings of the IEEE/CVF Conference on Computer Vision and Pattern Recognition, pp. 20481–20491 (2022)

Image-Based CLIP-Guided Essence Transfer

Hila Chefer[1]([⊠]), Sagie Benaim[2], Roni Paiss[1], and Lior Wolf[1]

[1] Tel Aviv University, Tel Aviv, Israel
hilachefer@mail.tau.ac.il
[2] University of Copenhagen, Copenhagen, Denmark

Fig. 1. Results of our method on various targets and sources. The first row presents the target images to extract the essence from, the middle row shows the sources to transfer the essence to, and bottom row presents the results of our method.

Abstract. We make the distinction between (i) style transfer, in which a source image is manipulated to match the textures and colors of a target image, and (ii) essence transfer, in which one edits the source image to include high-level semantic attributes from the target. Crucially, the semantic attributes that constitute the essence of an image may differ from image to image. Our blending operator combines the powerful StyleGAN generator and the semantic encoder of CLIP in a novel way that is simultaneously additive in both latent spaces, resulting in a mechanism that guarantees both identity preservation and high-level feature transfer without relying on a facial recognition network. We present two variants of our method. The first is based on optimization, while the second fine-tunes an existing inversion encoder to perform essence extraction. Through extensive experiments, we demonstrate the superiority of our methods for essence transfer over existing methods for style transfer, domain adaptation, and text-based semantic editing. Our code is available at: https://github.com/hila-chefer/TargetCLIP.

Supplementary Information The online version contains supplementary material available at https://doi.org/10.1007/978-3-031-19778-9_40.

1   Introduction

Style transfer, which typically refers to rendering the content of an image in the style of a different image, is a highly researched task in computer vision and computer graphics [5, 6, 10, 12, 16, 19, 28, 32, 33, 35, 44]. This work explores a related task, which we refer to as *essence transfer*. The essence of an image is defined to be the set of attributes that appear in the high-level textual description of the image. Our blending involves borrowing semantic features from a "target" image I_t and transferring them to a "source" image I_s, thus creating an output image $I_{s,t}$. We find that "essence" features capture properties such as skin complexion or texture, as do traditional style transfer methods, but also semantic elements such as gender, age, and unique facial attributes, when considering faces (Fig. 1).

A rigorous definition of our goal is elusive, as the set of features defined as the essence may change from image to image, so we adopt a pragmatic approach. It has been shown [11, 36] that latent spaces of high-level vision networks, (i.e., involving capabilities such as image understanding [48]) are additive. Ergo, subtracting the representation of two inputs yields a meaningful shift between the inputs encoding the difference between the two. Our method transforms source images I_s conditioned on a target image I_t. It forces the learned transformation to be doubly additive: once in the latent space of the generator, and once in the latent space of the understanding engine. Out of all possible ways of transforming a source image I_s according to a target image I_t, we obtain, for every I_t a transformation that is based on a constant shift over all I_s in the generator space and leads to a constant difference in the high-level description of the image.

For the generator network, we employ the powerful StyleGAN [23] generator. Additivity in the latent space of StyleGAN was demonstrated in [15, 43, 49], for linearly interpolating different images along semantic directions, as well as for the manipulation of semantic attributes ([36] for example). For the image recognition engine, we employ the CLIP network [39], which has shown impressive zero-shot capabilities across multiple domains such as image classification [39] and adaptation of generated images [11]. It was also shown to behave additively [11, 36]. Since CLIP was trained in a contrastive manner, using textual descriptions, different images with the same high-level textual description are expected to receive a high similarity score, as their textual descriptions will be nearly identical. This allows our method to enforce consistency based on the semantic properties of the image, rather than pixel-level similarity.

We propose a method based on two loss terms. The first term ensures that the transformed image is semantically similar to the target image I_t in the latent space of CLIP. The second term links the constant shift in the latent space of the generator to a constant shift in the latent space of CLIP, leading to a semantically consistent edit that is independent of the identity of the source I_s. We propose two methods for essence transfer. The first is based on per target optimization, while the second fine-tunes an inversion encoder to perform essence transfer. While an optimization-based approach is more accurate in capturing the relevant semantic properties, our encoder version only requires a forward pass on the target image to produce the target-specific (source-agnostic) essence vector, which defines the essence transfer operator for that image. We compare our method with state of the art style transfer and semantic editing methods and show that our novel double-additive formulation is necessary to successfully perform essence transfer. Finally, we decode to text the learned directions, demonstrating that the semantic edits we employ correspond to the attributes of the target image.

2   Related Work

Style Transfer. Our work most closely relates to style transfer [10,16,25,28,32, 33,44]. Unlike [12,18,20], we derive style from CLIP [39], a recently proposed method for the semantic association of text and images. In this space, two images are close, or similar, to each other if their textual association is close. Such similarity may consider unique style elements, such as texture or complexion. It may also consider semantic elements, such as gender and facial attributes. We argue that this notion of style, which we use here, is more general. CLIP has been used in several recent works to enable the fine-tuning of StyleGAN for domain adaptation [11,52] with impressive results, yet, as we show, the existing style transfer and domain adaptation methods fall short on the task of essence transfer, focusing usually on colors, textures and domain shifts, and can suffer from severe identity loss.

Image Manipulation. Our work is also related to recent image manipulation works based on a pre-trained generator [7,15,36,45]. One set of works typically manipulates an image based on finding a set of possibly disentangled and semantic directions [43,49]. These works typically borrow the semantic meaning from the generator itself. A recent work called StyleCLIP [36] showed the remarkable ability to borrow the semantic meaning from the CLIP space, and inspired many additional works to use CLIP for semantic editing and domain adaptation [2,11,52]. Our method uses CLIP in a similar manner to that presented in [36]. However, unlike our method, StyleCLIP considers text-driven manipulations, thus it is limited by what can be described in words, and the knowledge obtained by CLIP.

GAN Inversion. GAN inversion aims to extract a latent vector z that corresponds to a target image I, i.e. z holds that $G(z) = I$, where G is the generator. Most inversion methods can be split into two types; optimization-based methods [1, 4,8,13,29,51,53], which employ an optimization process to find a latent z such that $G(z)$ is closest to a specific target image I, and encoders [3,14,21,24,34,37, 38,47,50] which are trained to extract a latent z for any input image I. Most methods for StyleGAN inversion focus on the $\mathcal{W}, \mathcal{W}+$ latent spaces. The $\mathcal{W}$ space is more editable, yet suffers from degraded expressiveness [1], therefore $\mathcal{W}+$ has been adopted for inversion. We employ the e4e encoder [47] since it mitigates the distortion-editability trade-off by training an encoder in the $\mathcal{W}+$ latent space while encouraging the result to be close to the $\mathcal{W}$ space.

3   Assumptions and Problem Formulation

We now provide a formal definition of the essence transfer task, and an overview of the proposed method for any generator G and semantic encoder C.

We define the essence of an image I as the set of semantic features that constitute the high-level textual description of the image. The method employs four input components: (i) A generator G, which, given a vector z, generates an image $G(z)$, (ii) An image recognition engine C, which, given an image I, provides a latent representation of its high-level textual description, $C(I)$, in some latent space, (iii) A target image I_t, from which the essence is extracted, and (iv) A set of source images S, which are used to provide the statistics of images for which the method is applied. For clarity, we define S as a set of z vectors in a latent space of G, and each source image as $G(z)$.

Given these four inputs, our goal is to provide a generator H such that the image $H(z)$ transfers the high-level textual features of a target image I_t to the source image $I_s = G(z)$. If one wishes to transform an image I_s rather than a vector z using H, the image can be converted to a latent z using an inversion method [40,41,47]. We note that our formulation does not require, at any stage, the inversion of I_t. On the generator side, linearity is expressed by:

$$H(z) = G(z + b) \tag{1}$$

for some shift vector b, in the latent space of G. Linearity in the latent space of the image recognition engine is expressed as:

$$\forall z \in S \quad d = C(H(z)) - C(G(z)), \tag{2}$$

for some fixed d. Put differently, modifying any vector z in G's latent space with b induces a constant semantic change in the latent space of C. This property is what is referred to as a "global semantic direction" by Patashnik et al. [36]. However, our method goes about obtaining said global direction differently. The source-agnostic behavior is obtained by minimizing the following over H and d:

$$\sum_{z \in S} dist(C(H(z)) - C(G(z)), d), \tag{3}$$

where $dist(\cdot, \cdot)$ calculates the distance between two vectors in the latent space of the semantic encoder C. For example, CLIP uses cosine similarity to estimate vector similarities.

Equivalently, to obtain H, we can minimize the following over H:

$$\sum_{z1,z2 \in S} dist\left(C(H(z_1)) - C(G(z_1)), C(H(z_2)) - C(G(z_2))\right). \tag{4}$$

So far, we defined the problem of learning a pair of semantic directions b, d, in two different latent spaces, such that (b, d) match. We wish to add a constraint that ties the shifts to I_t. To this end, we wish to maximize similarity in the semantic space provided by the recognition engine C between I_t and the generated images $H(z)$. That is, we wish to minimize the sum of distances $\sum_{z \in S} dist(C(H(z)), C(I_t))$.

4   Method

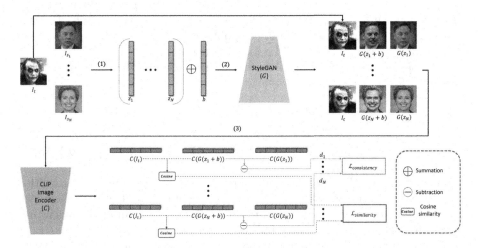

Fig. 2. An illustration of our loss calculation flow. Step (1) inverts the source images to obtain their latents $z_1, ..., z_N$, and adds the proposed essence vector b. In step (2), the StyleGAN generator decodes the source latents $z_1, ..., z_N$ and the manipulations $z_1 + b, ..., z_N + b$ to images. Step (3) encodes the sources ($G(z_1), ..., G(z_N)$), manipulations ($G(z_1+b), .., G(z_N+b)$), and target (I_t) with CLIP. $\mathcal{L}_{consistency}$ demands that semantic changes be identical for $z_1, .., z_N$. $\mathcal{L}_{similarity}$ ensures that $G(z_1 + b), ..., G(z_N + b)$ are semantically similar to I_t.

We now define our method, based on the formulation in Sect. 3. Note that in accordance with the training process of CLIP, we employ cosine similarity to estimate semantic similarity between two images. $\sum_{z \in S} dist(C(H(z)), C(I_t))$ becomes the following loss term, applied over a batch of source images, S:

$$\mathcal{L}_{similarity} = \frac{1}{N} \left(\sum_{z \in S} 1 - \frac{C(I_t) \cdot C(G(z + b))}{\|C(I_t)\|_2 \|C(G(z + b))\|_2} \right), \quad (5)$$

where $N = |S|$ is the batch size, and $z_1, .., z_N \in \mathcal{W}+$. The similarity loss estimates the semantic similarity between the image encodings of the target image and the manipulated images. By setting $N = 1$, this loss becomes identical to the semantic loss employed by other semantic editing methods based on CLIP [36].

The second concept we enforce is consistency. The goal of essence transfer is to modify the source image using a collection of semantic attributes that encapsulates the essence of the target image. These attributes are independent of the source image. We demand that the semantic edits induced by the direction b in the latent space of G be consistent across the source images, using CLIP's latent space. This is expressed in Eq. 4 above and translates to the following loss:

$$\mathcal{L}_{consistency} = \frac{1}{\binom{N}{2}} \left(\sum_{i_{src_1}, i_{src_2} \in I_s} 1 - \frac{\Delta i_{src_1} \cdot \Delta i_{src_2}}{\|\Delta i_{src_1}\|_2 \|\Delta i_{src_2}\|_2} \right) \quad (6)$$

where $\Delta i_{src} = C(G(i_{src} + b)) - C(G(i_{src}))$, as annotated in Eq. 2 as d, and, as before, N is the batch size. $\mathcal{L}_{consistency}$ guarantees that the direction encapsulated in b produces semantic edits that are identical across a batch of source images S. Figure 2 illustrates the steps of obtaining $\mathcal{L}_{similarity}, \mathcal{L}_{consistency}$ from a batch of sources $I_{s_1}, ..., I_{s_N}$ and a target image I_t.

The optimization problem solved during training in order to recover H, as defined in Eq. 1, is given as:

$$b^* = \arg\min \mathcal{L}_{similarity} + \lambda_{consistency}\mathcal{L}_{consistency} + \lambda_{L_2} \|b\|_2, \qquad (7)$$

where $\lambda_{consistency}, \lambda_{L_2}$ are hyperparameters. We use the same hyperparameter values in all our experiments and all our methods: $\lambda_{consistency} = 0.5, \lambda_{L_2} = 0.003$.

In contrast to other methods [36], ours does not rely on any face recognition models for preventing identity loss. In order to maintain the identity of the source images $I_1, ..., I_N$ we employ a standard L_2 regularization to limit the magnitude of the effect that b has on source images.

Restating Eq. 1, after obtaining the essence vector b^* for a target image I_t, manipulating a source image I_s is done as follows:

$$I_{s,t} = G(z_s + b^*), \qquad (8)$$

where z_s is the latent that corresponds to the source image I_s, which can be obtained by inverting the image I_s. Thus, we simply add the essence vector b^* to the latent representing the source image.

Essence Optimization. The first method we propose is a simple optimization process of finding an essence vector b^* that minimizes the objective in Eq. 7. Unlike other optimization-based methods for semantic editing, our method is more stable in the sense that the same set of hyperparameters can be applied for each target, and no target-specific tuning is required. The implementation employs the Adam optimizer [26] for 1000 iterations with a learning rate of 0.2. Due to resource limitations, we use only $N = 4$ images for our double additivity losses (Eq. 5, 6). For difficult edits, i.e. edits containing unconventional or extreme semantic attributes such as blue skin, we found it beneficial to initialize the direction b in the optimization process to be the inversion of the target produced with the e4e encoder. This can be attributed intuitively to the fact that the inversion of the target contains, among other identity-specific attributes, the semantic attributes that constitute the high-level textual description of the image, i.e. its essence. Therefore, initializing the direction b to be the inversion of the target steers the optimization toward semantic properties that are related to the target image.

Essence Encoder. For our second method, we fine-tune a pre-trained e4e encoder [47] over the pSp framework [40] to output the essence vector b^* of the input image instead of its inversion. Since the encoder is pre-trained for inversion, the initial output for each image I_t contains, among other features, the semantic features that comprise its essence. The goal of the fine-tuning process is to shift the weights of the encoder such that the output for each image I_t

Fig. 3. Examples of using our optimization-based method. Output images preserve the identity of the sources, while borrowing the semantic essence of the targets.

will be the semantic parts of the inversion that correspond to the essence vector. This fine-tuning is performed on a small dataset of 200 random images from the CelebA-HQ dataset [31], and evaluated on 50 random images from the CelebA-HQ test set. We use a learning rate of $1e - 4$ for 3000 iterations, with a batch size of 1 target image and $N = 5$ source images for our double additivity losses (Eq. 5, 6). The objective and its hyperparameters are identical to the ones used for the optimization-based method (Eq. 7). Unlike other methods that train an encoder or a generator for each target text or image, such as [11,36], our encoder is fine-tuned once and can accommodate *any* target after the fine-tuning. Other methods require training for each target text or image from scratch, which takes at least a few minutes and in some cases hours, while our inference time per target is just a few seconds.

5   Experiments

We present qualitative and quantitative results that demonstrate the advantage of our method for the task of essence transfer over the most recent methods for style transfer and domain adaptation. For a complete evaluation, we make an effort to be inclusive and compare also with methods that have somewhat different goals, i.e. text-based image editing methods.

Qualitative Results. Figure 3, Fig. 4 contain results of our optimization-based method and encoder-based method, using a wide variety of target and source images. All source images were inverted with e4e [47], and were not part of the training batch of sources used for optimization. The manipulation of the sources with the essence vector was done as detailed in Eq. 8. We present different choices of sources and targets in Fig. 3 and Fig. 4, in order to demonstrate the diversity of

Fig. 4. Examples of using our essence encoder on various targets and sources. Output images preserve the identity of the sources while borrowing the semantic essence of the targets.

both our methods. For completeness, the complementary versions of the figures, in which the sources and targets in Fig. 3 are edited with the encoder, and the sources and targets in Fig. 4 are edited with the optimizer, are also presented in the supplementary material.

As can be seen, our essence transfer results display the most notable semantic attributes of the target. For example, when using Doc Brown as target (first row in Fig. 3), the signature wild, white hair is transferred from the target to all sources, as are the wide open eyes. Our methods also preserve the identity of the sources well, despite training with only $N = 4$ ($N = 5$) images to enforce semantic consistency for our optimization (encoder) method. Additionally, the semantic edits are consistent across all sources, demonstrating that our method is indeed able to produce source-agnostic essence vectors.

Quantitative Results. Our experiments use as sources a set of 68 images inverted with e4e. For each target image I_t and source image I_s we use our methods and the baseline methods to edit the source according to the target and produce $I_{s,t}$. We then evaluate the quality of the produced edits for each method. Since there are many works involving style transfer and domain adaptation, we focus on the most recent state of the art, including unpublished works. We focus on works that are applicable to our use-case, i.e., methods that are able to perform one-shot editing. Our baselines include BlendGAN [30] and JoJoGAN [6] for face stylization, StyleGAN-NADA [11] and Mind The Gap (MTG) [52] for domain adaptation, and as a CLIP-aided text-based image editing method, we include StyleCLIP's [36] global directions method. We note that since the Style-CLIP method is text-based, it can only be used in manipulations where the target is a well-known character. Despite its inherent limitation, we also present this comparison for completeness, since the global directions method resembles

Table 1. Quantitative comparison with baselines. The StyleCLIP baseline can only be applied to well-known characters (celebrities test), and Mind the Gap provides no public code at this time, thus can only be applied to the celebrities test (see main text). Results that indicate identity loss of the source are marked in orange; results that indicate that no semantic attributes were transferred are marked in red.

| | | Quality | Identity scores | | Semantic scores | |
		FID ($\downarrow$)	Source ($\uparrow$)	Target ($\downarrow$)	BLIP ($\uparrow$)	CLIP ($\uparrow$)
Celebrities test	StyleGAN-NADA [11]	215.7 ± 26.1	23.0 ± 4.7	33.0 ± 7.1	**84.5 ± 3.6**	**94.0 ± 1.3**
	Mind The Gap [52]	180.4 ± 19.3	27.2 ± 5.6	39.4 ± 8.1	75.8 ± 5.6	75.4 ± 7.0
	JoJoGAN [6]	186.1 ± 12.7	36.0 ± 6.1	50.7 ± 6.9	72.6 ± 7.3	71.8 ± 6.2
	BlendGAN [30]	177.8 ± 12.6	37.6 ± 6.5	**5.2 ± 7.7**	60.8 ± 6.2	58.4 ± 5.2
	StyleCLIP [36]	166.9 ± 9.0	**70.7 ± 26.0**	6.2 ± 6.8	54.8 ± 6.6	55.7 ± 5.0
	Our encoder	188.7 ± 23.2	39.0 ± 6.5	31.9 ± 5.7	69.0 ± 6.0	72.6 ± 5.5
	Our optimization	**163.6 ± 16.7**	43.5 ± 6.8	17.0 ± 6.6	66.9 ± 6.0	74.4 ± 3.2
FFHQ test	StyleGAN-NADA [11]	220.2 ± 41.8	24.1 ± 5.5	28.3 ± 9.2	**81.1 ± 4.2**	**91.0 ± 3.2**
	JoJoGAN [6]	175.2 ± 15.2	42.3 ± 4.0	41.7 ± 11.4	76.0 ± 6.0	67.1 ± 7.4
	BlendGAN [30]	175.1 ± 14.5	37.6 ± 5.3	**2.4 ± 6.0**	64.4 ± 6.7	54.7 ± 7.8
	Our encoder	175.6 ± 23.5	42.5 ± 5.5	30.8 ± 6.9	72.8 ± 4.9	66.7 ± 6.1
	Our optimization	**161.1 ± 17.2**	**45.2 ± 8.6**	17.0 ± 7.2	74.1 ± 4.9	74.8 ± 5.8

ours in that it outputs a target-dependent and source-agnostic direction in the StyleGAN $\mathcal{S}$ space to perform a manipulation according to an input textual description. Since our methods strive to transfer the features of the high-level textual description of the target, we find this comparison to be relevant as well.

The goal of essence transfer is twofold. First, we wish to transfer the semantic properties that constitute the high-level textual description from a target image I_t to a source image I_s. Second, we wish to maintain the identity of I_s as much as possible. We therefore suggest two types of metrics to evaluate the quality of a proposed essence transfer result, $I_{s,t}$. The first type employs the ArcFace [9] network for face recognition to ensure that the manipulation maintains the identity of I_s as much as possible, while avoiding an identity shift towards I_t, i.e. we calculate:

$$\text{ID-score}_{source}(I_{s,t}) = \langle R(I_s), R(I_{s,t}) \rangle, \quad \text{ID-score}_{target}(I_{s,t}) = \langle R(I_t), R(I_{s,t}) \rangle,$$

where R denotes a pre-trained ArcFace face recognition representation, and $\langle \cdot, \cdot \rangle$ computes cosine similarity. Since neither of our methods uses face recognition in the training process, this metric faithfully measures how well our manipulations preserve the source identity. Intuitively, since we add semantic features from the target, we shift the identity of the source to some extent. For example, modifying the gender of the source induces an inherent change in one of the identity attributes of the source. The combination of scores ID-score$_{source}$, ID-score$_{target}$ reveals whether the manipulation was able to remain close to the identity of the source or shifted toward the identity of the target. A successful essence transfer is expected to maintain a *high* ID-score$_{source}$ score, and a *low* ID-score$_{target}$

score, indicating that the manipulation's identity fits the source better than the target.

Next, to estimate the semantic quality of the manipulation, we use the latent spaces of BLIP [27] and CLIP [39], as follows:

$$\text{Semantic-score}(I_{s,t}) = \langle C(I_t), C(I_{s,t}) \rangle,$$

where C notates a pre-trained BLIP or CLIP image encoder, and $\langle \cdot, \cdot \rangle$ computes cosine similarity. Since our method, as well as most baselines [11,36,52], use the latent space of CLIP in the training process, BLIP provides an important alternative for estimating the semantic similarity between the target image I_t and the manipulation $I_{s,t}$. For each target I_t, the overall identity scores and semantic scores are calculated as an average of the scores for all source images. The aggregated scores for the models are calculated as an average of the score for each target, i.e. we average the results across the sources for each target, and then average across the targets to obtain the model's final score. We also present the standard deviations as an indication of the method's consistency.

Additionally, in accordance with previous works on style transfer, we present the Fréchet inception distance (FID) [17] as implemented in [42] to estimate the quality of the manipulations, which is calculated as follows:

$$\text{FID-score}(I_{s_1,t}, ..., I_{s_{68},t}) = \text{FID}(\{I_{s_1,t}, ..., I_{s_{68},t}\}, \{I_1, ..., I_{7,000}\}),$$

where $\{I_{s_1,t}, ..., I_{s_{68},t}\}$ are the manipulations of the sources induced by the target t, and $\{I_1, ..., I_{7,000}\}$ is a set of $7,000$ randomly chosen images from the FFHQ [22] dataset, which provides the background distribution of natural faces. Since some of our baselines are trained to adapt the domain of the target, we calculate the FID score only for the targets describing a human face, in order to avoid biasing the results against these baselines. Note that this calculation produces a relatively high FID score for all methods, since the produced dataset $\{I_{s_1,t}, ..., I_{s_{68},t}\}$ is inherently limited in its diversity, due to the fact that all images share semantic properties transferred from t, leading to a shift from the distribution of unedited faces, which are more diverse. However, methods that suffer from mode collapse or overfitting are expected to achieve a much higher (lower is better) score than those that preserve the original identity of the source images, since identity preservation will lead to greater diversity among the results.

We present two experiments. For the first, we construct a comparison in a setting that is more similar to the setting the baselines were trained for, i.e. we construct a dataset of 31 images of celebrity faces with notable or extreme semantic properties, such as unusual hair colors and styles, beards, glasses, as well as a variety of ages, genders, and ethnicities, and also out-of-domain animated characters (see the supplementary material for all examples used in this experiment). For the text-based baseline, we employ the same course of action as in the StyleCLIP paper, where the textual prompt for the manipulation is of the form "an image of {*name of target*}". Our second experiment involves targets with less extreme semantic features. We use the first 50 images of the FFHQ [22]

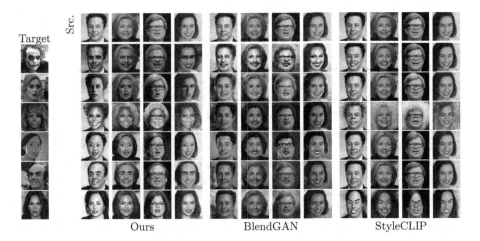

Fig. 5. Comparison to methods that only partially transfer the semantic properties. First three rows are manipulations with our optimizer, and the last three are with our encoder.

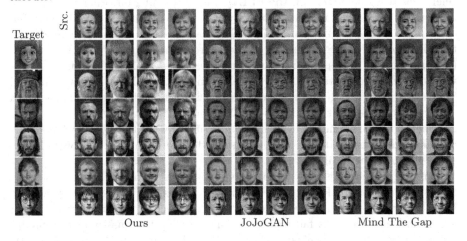

Fig. 6. Comparison to methods that suffer from high loss of source identity. First three rows are manipulations with our optimizer, and last three with our encoder.

dataset as targets, and the same 68 source images as before. Since our targets are no longer well-known characters, the baseline for text-based image editing is no longer applicable. Additionally, for the Mind The Gap baseline [52], no official code was released- although the authors kindly provided results for the first experiment, but not the second one - therefore this baseline is not presented in our second experiment.

Table 1 presents the results of both our experiments. We divide the methods into three types. (i) Methods that demonstrate underfitting, i.e., fail to transfer the essence of the target. These methods perform very well on the identity metrics and very poorly on the semantic metrics. As can be seen in Table 1, both BlendGAN and the StyleCLIP demonstrate this phenomenon. Marked in red in the tables are the similarity scores for the methods by BLIP and CLIP. Both are significantly lower than the semantic scores of the other methods. See Fig. 5 for examples of this case from our first experiment. BlendGAN focuses on modifying almost only the colors, and StyleCLIP either hardly changes the semantic properties or distorts the sources. (ii) methods that demonstrate over-fitting, i.e. methods that suffer from identity preservation issues. These methods transfer most or all of the semantic features of the target, and eliminate the source identity in the process or create a blended identity of source and target. This results in very high semantic compatibility scores, but on the other hand, a failure in identity preservation. As can be expected, the methods designed for domain adaptation, i.e., StyleGAN-NADA and Mind The Gap fall in this category, as does JoJoGAN. The values marked in orange in Table 1 demonstrate that both StyleGAN-NADA and Mind The Gap obtain very low source identity scores (significantly lower than the other methods), while JoJoGAN receives the highest (lower is better) target identity score in both experiments (50.7% on the celebrities test and 41.7% on the FFHQ test, surpassing all other baselines by more than 10%). This indicates that StyleGAN-NADA and Mind The Gap fall short on identity preservation, while JoJoGAN results in an image derived from the identity of the target instead of the source. For example, the Ariel target (first row in Fig. 6) demonstrates that the baselines result in a unified identity with the semantic features of the target. Similarly, the Keanu Reeves and Ed Sheeran targets (fourth and fifth rows in Fig. 6) result in blended identities with the baselines. We omit StyleGAN-NADA from Fig. 6 for brevity, as the other two methods scored higher in terms of identity preservation. The full compar-ison, as well as comparisons from our second experiment can be found in the supplementary material.

Lastly, (iii) methods that successfully transfer the semantic properties of the target (have high BLIP and CLIP similarity scores) while also preserving the identity of the source more than the target (i.e., ID-score$_{source}$ > ID-score$_{target}$), which both our methods fall under. When analyzing the quality of the manip-ulated images, our optimization-based method scores the best overall FID score in both experiments by a significant margin, indicating that it is able to produce high-quality manipulations. In addition, our optimization demon-strates a very low (lower is better) target identity score, suggesting that our essence transfer does not borrow from the identity of the target in order to obtain the semantic changes. While our encoder preserves the identity quality (ID-score$_{source}$ > ID-score$_{target}$), notice that it achieves a higher target identity score, indicating that our encoder is not as successful as our optimizer in identity preservation. This can be attributed to two facts. First, our encoder is based on a pre-trained inversion encoder that encapsulates the target identity by design. Second, while our optimizer learns an essence vector for each target, the encoder is only fine-tuned on a small set of images and is not optimized for each target at inference time.

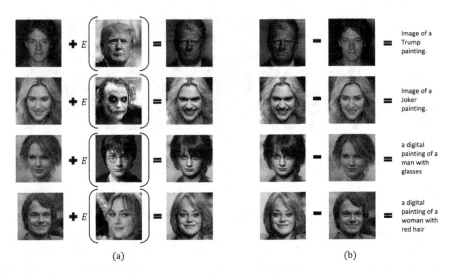

(a)   (b)

Fig. 7. Examples of essence decoding. (a) presents the targets, sources, and manipulation results, with E representing the essence extraction, i.e. we add the essence of the right image to the left image, and (b) demonstrates the decoding of the essence vectors for each example.

Essence Interpretability. To demonstrate that our methods indeed produce essence vectors that correspond to the semantic attributes of the target image I_t, we present results of decoding the essence vectors to text. We observe semantic differences by applying a decoder on the vector $d = C(I_{s,t}) - C(I_s)$ where C represents the semantic image encoder of CLIP or BLIP, i.e. we decode the difference between the source image after and before the manipulation. Figure 7 shows examples for four different edits and their interpretations. The Donald Trump and the Joker edits (first and second row of Fig. 7) were performed with our optimization-based method, encoded with CLIP, and decoded with [46], and the rest were performed using our encoder approach and encoded/decoded with BLIP. As can be seen, the textual interpretations of each direction correspond well to the semantic properties of the targets, and for the Donald Trump and Joker edits, the directions are decoded as Trump and the Joker, demonstrating the ability of our method to capture essential semantic features of the targets used. For targets with less distinct semantic properties, the decoding shows that the apparent gender is transferred along with other significant semantic properties such as hair color and eye glasses. See the supplementary material for more examples of essence interpretability using decoding.

Limitations of the Encoder-Based Approach. Unlike the optimizer, the encoder is not re-trained for each target. This results in an accuracy-runtime trade-off, i.e., while the encoder produces an essence vector in a few seconds, in some cases - where the target contains unconventional semantic properties - it produces a result that does not encapsulate all the semantic attributes one would expect to

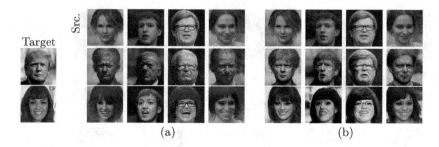

Fig. 8. A comparison between our optimizer (a), and encoder (b).

be included in the essence. In contrast, since the optimization is performed from scratch for each target, it takes longer (a few minutes) to produce the result, but it is more accurate. Figure 8 presents two examples of such challenging targets, where the optimization-based method is superior to the encoder. For Donald Trump (first row in Fig. 8), optimization results in an essence that includes all notable semantic properties- the wrinkles, lips, and unique hair color - while the result of the encoder fails to capture the unique attributes with the same accuracy. Similarly, for Katy Perry (second row in Fig. 8), optimization captures the unconventional hair color, while the encoder fails to do so. As evident from Table 1, while both the encoder and optimizer receive high semantic scores, the optimizer allows for results with higher quality (lower FID, lower target ID score).

Ablation Study. We refer the reader to the supplementary material for an ablation study that examines the impact of each loss term of our method.

6   Conclusions

We define a novel task referred to as essence transfer. Unlike style transfer or domain adaptation, essence transfer draws semantic features that correspond to the high-level textual description of an image. Essence transfer is particularly challenging since the set of attributes that constitute the high-level description may differ from image to image. We propose an optimizer and an encoder, both based on double-additivity in the latent spaces of StyleGAN and CLIP, and measure our method against state of the art methods adapted from style transfer and domain adaptation. Our extensive experiments demonstrate that our novel formulation is significantly preferable to the baselines in terms of identity preservation, the quality of the produced images, and the identification of the essential attributes of an image.

Acknowledgment. This project has received funding from the European Research Council (ERC) under the European Unions Horizon 2020 research and innovation programme (grant ERC CoG 725974).

References

1. Abdal, R., Qin, Y., Wonka, P.: Image2StyleGAN: how to embed images into the StyleGAN latent space? In: 2019 IEEE/CVF International Conference on Computer Vision (ICCV), pp. 4431–4440 (2019)
2. Abdal, R., Zhu, P., Femiani, J.C., Mitra, N.J., Wonka, P.: Clip2StyleGAN: unsupervised extraction of StyleGAN edit directions. ArXiv abs/2112.05219 (2021)
3. Alaluf, Y., Patashnik, O., Cohen-Or, D.: ReStyle: a residual-based StyleGAN encoder via iterative refinement. In: 2021 IEEE/CVF International Conference on Computer Vision (ICCV), pp. 6691–6700 (2021)
4. Bau, D., et al.: Semantic photo manipulation with a generative image prior. ACM Trans. Graph. (TOG) **38**, 1–11 (2019)
5. Bousmalis, K., Silberman, N., Dohan, D., Erhan, D., Krishnan, D.: Unsupervised pixel-level domain adaptation with generative adversarial networks. In: 2017 IEEE Conference on Computer Vision and Pattern Recognition (CVPR), pp. 95–104 (2017)
6. Chong, M.J., Forsyth, D.: JoJoGAN: one shot face stylization. ArXiv 2112.11641 (2021)
7. Collins, E., Bala, R., Price, B., Susstrunk, S.: Editing in style: uncovering the local semantics of GANs. In: CVPR, pp. 5771–5780 (2020)
8. Creswell, A., Bharath, A.A.: Inverting the generator of a generative adversarial network. IEEE Trans. Neural Netw. Learn. Syst. **30**, 1967–1974 (2019)
9. Deng, J., Guo, J., Zafeiriou, S.: ArcFace: additive angular margin loss for deep face recognition. In: 2019 IEEE/CVF Conference on Computer Vision and Pattern Recognition (CVPR), pp. 4685–4694 (2019)
10. Efros, A.A., Leung, T.K.: Texture synthesis by non-parametric sampling. In: Proceedings of the Seventh IEEE International Conference on Computer Vision, Kerkyra, Greece, vol. 2, pp. 1033–1038 (1999).https://doi.org/10.1109/ICCV.1999.790383
11. Gal, R., Patashnik, O., Maron, H., Chechik, G., Cohen-Or, D.: StyleGAN-NADA: clip-guided domain adaptation of image generators (2021)
12. Gatys, L.A., Ecker, A.S., Bethge, M.: Image style transfer using convolutional neural networks. In: The IEEE Conference on Computer Vision and Pattern Recognition (CVPR), June 2016
13. Gu, J., Shen, Y., Zhou, B.: Image processing using multi-code GAN prior. In: 2020 IEEE/CVF Conference on Computer Vision and Pattern Recognition (CVPR), pp. 3009–3018 (2020)
14. Guan, S., Tai, Y., Ni, B., Zhu, F., Huang, F., Yang, X.: Collaborative learning for faster StyleGAN embedding. ArXiv abs/2007.01758 (2020)
15. Härkönen, E., Hertzmann, A., Lehtinen, J., Paris, S.: Ganspace: discovering interpretable gan controls. arXiv preprint arXiv:2004.02546 (2020)
16. Hertzmann, A., Jacobs, C.E., Oliver, N., Curless, B., Salesin, D.H.: Image analogies. In: Proceedings of the 28th Annual Conference on Computer Graphics and Interactive Techniques. Association for Computing Machinery, New York (2001). https://doi.org/10.1145/383259.383295
17. Heusel, M., Ramsauer, H., Unterthiner, T., Nessler, B., Hochreiter, S.: GANs trained by a two time-scale update rule converge to a local nash equilibrium. In: Proceedings of the 31st International Conference on Neural Information Processing Systems, NIPS 2017, pp. 6629–6640. Curran Associates Inc., Red Hook (2017)

18. Huang, X., Belongie, S.: Arbitrary style transfer in real-time with adaptive instance normalization. In: 2017 IEEE International Conference on Computer Vision (ICCV), Venice, Italy, pp. 1510–1519 (2017). https://doi.org/10.1109/ICCV.2017.167

19. Huang, X., Belongie, S.J.: Arbitrary style transfer in real-time with adaptive instance normalization. In: 2017 IEEE International Conference on Computer Vision (ICCV), pp. 1510–1519 (2017)

20. Johnson, J., Alahi, A., Fei-Fei, L.: Perceptual losses for real-time style transfer and super-resolution. In: Leibe, B., Matas, J., Sebe, N., Welling, M. (eds.) ECCV 2016. LNCS, vol. 9906, pp. 694–711. Springer, Cham (2016). https://doi.org/10.1007/978-3-319-46475-6_43

21. Kang, K., Kim, S., Cho, S.: GAN inversion for out-of-range images with geometric transformations. In: 2021 IEEE/CVF International Conference on Computer Vision (ICCV), pp. 13921–13929 (2021)

22. Karras, T., Laine, S., Aila, T.: A style-based generator architecture for generative adversarial networks. In: 2019 IEEE/CVF Conference on Computer Vision and Pattern Recognition (CVPR), pp. 4396–4405 (2019)

23. Karras, T., Laine, S., Aittala, M., Hellsten, J., Lehtinen, J., Aila, T.: Analyzing and improving the image quality of StyleGAN. In: CVPR, pp. 8110–8119 (2020)

24. Kim, H., Choi, Y., Kim, J., Yoo, S., Uh, Y.: Exploiting spatial dimensions of latent in GAN for real-time image editing. In: 2021 IEEE/CVF Conference on Computer Vision and Pattern Recognition (CVPR), pp. 852–861 (2021)

25. Kim, S.S.Y., Kolkin, N., Salavon, J., Shakhnarovich, G.: Deformable style transfer. In: Vedaldi, A., Bischof, H., Brox, T., Frahm, J.-M. (eds.) ECCV 2020. LNCS, vol. 12371, pp. 246–261. Springer, Cham (2020). https://doi.org/10.1007/978-3-030-58574-7_15

26. Kingma, D.P., Ba, J.: Adam: a method for stochastic optimization. CoRR abs/1412.6980 (2015)

27. Li, J., Li, D., Xiong, C., Hoi, S.: BLIP: bootstrapping language-image pre-training for unified vision-language understanding and generation (2022)

28. Li, Y., Fang, C., Yang, J., Wang, Z., Lu, X., Yang, M.H.: Universal style transfer via feature transforms. In: Proceedings of the 31st International Conference on Neural Information Processing Systems, NIPS 2017, pp. 385–395. Curran Associates Inc., Red Hook (2017)

29. Lipton, Z.C., Tripathi, S.: Precise recovery of latent vectors from generative adversarial networks. ArXiv abs/1702.04782 (2017)

30. Liu, M., Li, Q., Qin, Z., Zhang, G., Wan, P., Zheng, W.: BlendGAN: implicitly GAN blending for arbitrary stylized face generation. In: Advances in Neural Information Processing Systems (2021)

31. Liu, Z., Luo, P., Wang, X., Tang, X.: Deep learning face attributes in the wild. In: Proceedings of International Conference on Computer Vision (ICCV), December 2015

32. Luan, F., Paris, S., Shechtman, E., Bala, K.: Deep photo style transfer. In: 2017 IEEE Conference on Computer Vision and Pattern Recognition (CVPR), Honolulu, USA, pp. 6997–7005 (2017). https://doi.org/10.1109/CVPR.2017.740

33. Luan, F., Paris, S., Shechtman, E., Bala, K.: Deep painterly harmonization. Comput. Graph. Forum 37(4), 95–106 (2018). https://doi.org/10.1111/cgf.13478

34. Luo, J., Xu, Y., Tang, C., Lv, J.: Learning inverse mapping by autoencoder based generative adversarial nets. In: Liu, D., Xie, S., Li, Y., Zhao, D., El-Alfy, E.S. (eds.) Neural Information Processing. ICONIP 2017. LNCS, vol. 10635, pp. 207–216. Springer, Cham (2017). https://doi.org/10.1007/978-3-319-70096-0_22

35. Ojha, U., et al.: Few-shot image generation via cross-domain correspondence. In: 2021 IEEE/CVF Conference on Computer Vision and Pattern Recognition (CVPR), pp. 10738–10747 (2021)
36. Patashnik, O., Wu, Z., Shechtman, E., Cohen-Or, D., Lischinski, D.: StyleClip: text-driven manipulation of StyleGAN imagery. In: Proceedings of the IEEE/CVF International Conference on Computer Vision, pp. 2085–2094 (2021)
37. Perarnau, G., van de Weijer, J., Raducanu, B., Álvarez, J.M.: Invertible conditional GANs for image editing. ArXiv abs/1611.06355 (2016)
38. Pidhorskyi, S., Adjeroh, D.A., Doretto, G.: Adversarial latent autoencoders. In: 2020 IEEE/CVF Conference on Computer Vision and Pattern Recognition (CVPR), pp. 14092–14101 (2020)
39. Radford, A., Kim, J.W., Hallacy, C., et al.: Learning transferable visual models from natural language supervision. arXiv preprint arXiv:2103.00020 (2021)
40. Richardson, E., et al.: Encoding in style: a StyleGAN encoder for image-to-image translation. In: IEEE/CVF Conference on Computer Vision and Pattern Recognition (CVPR), June 2021
41. Roich, D., Mokady, R., Bermano, A.H., Cohen-Or, D.: Pivotal tuning for latent-based editing of real images. arXiv preprint arXiv:2106.05744 (2021)
42. Seitzer, M.: PyTorch-FID: FID Score for PyTorch, August 2020. github.com/mseitzer/pytorch-fid. Version 0.2.1
43. Shen, Y., Zhou, B.: Closed-form factorization of latent semantics in GANs. In: Proceedings of the IEEE/CVF Conference on Computer Vision and Pattern Recognition, pp. 1532–1540 (2021)
44. Sunkavalli, K., Johnson, M.K., Matusik, W., Pfister, H.: Multi-scale image harmonization. ACM Trans. Graph. **29**(4) (2010). https://doi.org/10.1145/1778765.1778862
45. Tewari, A., et al.: StyleRig: rigging StyleGAN for 3d control over portrait images. In: CVPR (2020)
46. Tewel, Y., Shalev, Y., Schwartz, I., Wolf, L.: Zero-shot image-to-text generation for visual-semantic arithmetic. In: CVPR (2021)
47. Tov, O., Alaluf, Y., Nitzan, Y., Patashnik, O., Cohen-Or, D.: Designing an encoder for stylegan image manipulation. arXiv preprint arXiv:2102.02766 (2021)
48. Ullman, S.: High-Level Vision: Object Recognition and Visual Cognition. MIT Press, Cambridge (2000)
49. Voynov, A., Babenko, A.: Unsupervised discovery of interpretable directions in the GAN latent space. In: International Conference on Machine Learning, pp. 9786–9796. PMLR (2020)
50. Wang, T., Zhang, Y., Fan, Y., Wang, J., Chen, Q.: High-fidelity GAN inversion for image attribute editing. ArXiv abs/2109.06590 (2021)
51. Zhu, J.-Y., Krähenbühl, P., Shechtman, E., Efros, A.A.: Generative visual manipulation on the natural image manifold. In: Leibe, B., Matas, J., Sebe, N., Welling, M. (eds.) ECCV 2016. LNCS, vol. 9909, pp. 597–613. Springer, Cham (2016). https://doi.org/10.1007/978-3-319-46454-1_36
52. Zhu, P., Abdal, R., Femiani, J.C., Wonka, P.: Mind the gap: domain gap control for single shot domain adaptation for generative adversarial networks. ArXiv:2110.08398 (2021)
53. Zhu, P., Abdal, R., Qin, Y., Wonka, P.: Improved StyleGAN embedding: where are the good latents? ArXiv abs/2012.09036 (2020)

Detecting and Recovering Sequential DeepFake Manipulation

Rui Shao(i), Tianxing Wu(i), and Ziwei Liu(✉)(i)

S-Lab, Nanyang Technological University, Singapore, Singapore
{rui.shao,twu012,ziwei.liu}@ntu.edu.sg
https://rshaojimmy.github.io/Projects/SeqDeepFake

Abstract. Since photorealistic faces can be readily generated by facial manipulation technologies nowadays, potential malicious abuse of these technologies has drawn great concerns. Numerous deepfake detection methods are thus proposed. However, existing methods only focus on detecting *one-step* facial manipulation. As the emergence of easy-accessible facial editing applications, people can easily manipulate facial components using *multi-step* operations in a sequential manner. This new threat requires us to detect a sequence of facial manipulations, which is vital for both detecting deepfake media and recovering original faces afterwards. Motivated by this observation, we emphasize the need and propose a novel research problem called Detecting Sequential DeepFake Manipulation (**Seq-DeepFake**). Unlike the existing deepfake detection task only demanding a binary label prediction, detecting Seq-DeepFake manipulation requires correctly predicting a sequential vector of facial manipulation operations. To support a large-scale investigation, we construct the first Seq-DeepFake dataset, where face images are manipulated sequentially with corresponding annotations of sequential facial manipulation vectors. Based on this new dataset, we cast detecting Seq-DeepFake manipulation as a specific image-to-sequence (*e.g.* image captioning) task and propose a concise yet effective Seq-DeepFake Transformer (**SeqFakeFormer**). Moreover, we build a comprehensive benchmark and set up rigorous evaluation protocols and metrics for this new research problem. Extensive experiments demonstrate the effectiveness of SeqFakeFormer. Several valuable observations are also revealed to facilitate future research in broader deepfake detection problems.

Keywords: DeepFake detection · Sequential facial manipulation

1 Introduction

In recent years, hyper-realistic face images can be generated by deep generative models which are visually extremely indistinguishable from real images. Meanwhile, the significant improvement for image synthesis brings security concerns

Supplementary Information The online version contains supplementary material available at https://doi.org/10.1007/978-3-031-19778-9_41.

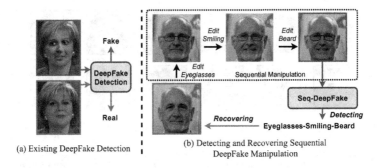

Fig. 1. Comparison between (a) existing deepfake detection and (b) proposed detecting and recovering sequential deepfake manipulation.

on potential malicious abuse of these techniques that produce misinformation and fabrication, which is known as *deepfake*. To address this security issue, various deepfake detection methods have been proposed to detect such forged faces. As illustrated in Fig. 1 (a), given the manipulated face image generated by face swap algorithm [33] and the original face image, the existing deepfake detection task requires the model to predict the correct binary labels (Real/Fake).

With the increasing popularity of easy-accessible facial editing applications, such as YouCam Makeup [2], FaceTune2 [1], and YouCam Perfect [3], it is convenient for people to edit face images in daily life. Compared to existing deepfake techniques mainly carrying out *one-step* facial manipulation [14,33], we can now easily manipulate face images using *multi-step* operations in a *sequential* manner. As shown in Fig. 1 (b), the original image can be manipulated by adding eyeglasses, making a bigger smile and removing beard sequentially. This expands the scope of existing deepfake problem by adding sequential manipulation information and poses a new challenge for current *one-step* deepfake detection methods. This observation motivates us to introduce a new research problem—Detecting Sequential Deepfake Manipulation (**Seq-Deepfake**). We summarize several key differences between detecting Seq-Deepfake and the existing deepfake detection: 1) rather than only predicting binary labels (Real/Fake), detecting Seq-Deepfake aims to detect sequences of facial manipulations with diverse sequence lengths. For example, the model is required to predict a 3-length sequence as 'Eyeglasses-Smiling-Beard' for the manipulated image as shown in Fig. 1 (b). 2) As illustrated in Fig. 1 (b), beyond pure forgery detection, we can further **recover** the original faces (refer to Sect. 5.4 of Experiments) based on the detected sequences of facial manipulation in Seq-Deepfake. This greatly enriches the benefits of detecting Seq-Deepfake manipulation.

To facilitate the study of detecting Seq-Deepfake, this paper contributes the first Seq-Deepfake dataset. Figure 2 shows some samples in Seq-Deepfake dataset. From Fig. 2, it can be seen that one face image can be sequentially manipulated with different number of steps (from minimum 1 step to maximum 5 steps), which leads to facial manipulation sequences with diverse lengths. It is extremely

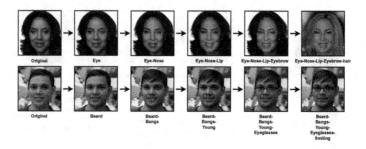

Fig. 2. Illustration of sequential facial manipulation. Two types of facial manipulation approaches are considered, *i.e.* facial components manipulation [19] in the first row and facial attributes manipulation [16] in the second row.

difficult to distinguish the original and manipulated face images, and even harder to figure out the exact manipulation sequences. To make our study more comprehensive, we consider two different facial manipulation techniques, facial components manipulation [19] and facial attributes manipulation [16], which are displayed in the first and second row, respectively in Fig. 2.

Most current facial manipulation applications are built based on Generative Adversarial Network (GAN). It is well known that the semantic latent space learned by GAN is difficult to be perfectly disentangled [21,42]. We argue that this defect is likely to leave some spatial as well as sequential manipulation traces unveiling sequential facial manipulations. Based on this observation, to detect such two types of manipulations traces, we cast detecting Seq-Deepfake as a specific image-to-sequence (*e.g.* image captioning) task and thus propose a concise yet effective Seq-DeepFake Transformer (**SeqFakeFormer**). Two key parts are devised in SeqFakeFormer: **Spatial Relation Extraction** and **Sequential Relation Modeling with Spatially Enhanced Cross-attention**. Given a manipulated image, to adaptively capture subtle spatial manipulation regions, SeqFakeFormer feeds the image into a deep convolutional neural network (CNN) to learn its feature maps. Then we extract the relation of spatial manipulations captured in feature maps using the self-attention modules of transformer encoder, obtaining features of spatial relation, i.e. spatial manipulation traces. After that, the decoder of SeqFakeFormer models the sequential relation of extracted features of spatial relation via cross-attention modules in an autoregressive mechanism, contributing to the detection of sequential manipulation traces, and thus detecting the facial manipulation sequences. To enable more effective cross-attention given limited annotations of facial manipulation sequences in Seq-DeepFake, SeqFakeFormer further integrates a Spatially Enhanced Cross-Attention (SECA) module in the decoder. This module enriches the spatial information of annotations of manipulation sequences by learning a spatial weight map. After fusing the spatial weight map with the cross-attention map, a spatially enhanced cross-attention can be achieved.

Main contributions of our paper can be summarized as follows:

- We introduce a new research problem named Detecting Sequential Deepfake Manipulation (**Seq-DeepFake**), with the objective of detecting sequences of facial manipulations, which expands the scope and poses a new challenge for deepfake detection.
- We contribute the Sequential Deepfake Dataset with sequential manipulated face images using two different facial manipulation techniques. Corresponding annotations of manipulation sequences are provided.
- We propose a powerful Seq-DeepFake Transformer (**SeqFakeFormer**). A comprehensive benchmark is built and rigorous evaluation protocols and metrics are designed for this novel research problem. Extensive quantitative and qualitative experiments demonstrate its superiority.

2 Related Work

Deepfake Detection. Nowadays, security of facial information [29] is threaten by physical attacks [26,34–37,39,41,51] and digital attacks [32,38,40,49]. This paper focuses on detecting one of the digital attacks, *deepfake*. Current deepfake detection methods can be roughly categorized into spatial-based and frequency-based deepfake detection. The majority of spatial-based deepfake detection methods focus on capturing visual cues from spatial domain. Face X-ray [23] is proposed to detect the blending boundary left in the face forgery process as visual cues for real/fake detection. A multi-attentional deepfake detection network is proposed in [52] to integrate low-level textural features and high-level semantic features. Zhu *et al.* [55] introduce 3D decomposition into forgery detection and propose a two-stream network to fuse decomposed features for detection. Pair-wise self-consistency learning (PCL) [53] is introduced to detect inconsistency of source features within the manipulated images. Inconsistencies in semantically high-level mouth movements are captured in [12] by fine-tuning a temporal network pretrained on lipreading. On the other hand, some methods pay attention to the frequency domain for detecting spectrum artifacts. There exist distinct spectrum distributions and characteristics between real and fake images in the high-frequency part of Discrete Fourier Transform (DFT) [8,9]. Qian *et al.* [31] propose a F^3-Net to learn local frequency statistics based on Discrete Cosine Transform (DCT) to mine forgery. Liu *et al.* [25] present a Spatial-Phase Shallow Learning method to fuse spatial image and phase spectrum for the up-sampling artifacts detection. A two-stream model is devised in [28] to model the correlation between extracted high-frequency features and regular RGB features to learn generalizable features. A frequency-aware discriminative feature learning framework [22] is introduced to integrate metric learning and adaptive frequency features learning for face forgery detection.

So far, several deepfake datasets have been released to public, such as Face-Forensics++ [33], Celeb-DF [24], Deepfake Detection Challenge (DFDC) [7], and DeeperForensics-1.0 (DF1.0) [15]. However, only binary labels are provided in most of existing deepfake datasets, and thus most of the above works are trained to carry out binary classification, which results in performance saturation and poor generalization.

Fig. 3. Illustration of Seq-Deepfake dataset. Samples of Seq-Deepfake are provided with annotations of manipulation sequences. We also show sequence length distribution.

Facial Editing. Several methods have been proposed for editing facial components (*i.e.* eye, nose, month). Lee *et al.* [20] present a geometry-oriented face manipulation network MaskGAN for diverse and interactive face manipulation guided by semantic masks annotations. A semantic region-adaptive normalization (SEAN) [54] is proposed to facilitate manipulating face images by encoding images into the per-region style codes conditioned on segmentation masks. StyleMapGAN [19] introduces explicit spatial dimensions to the latent space and manipulates facial components by blending the latent spaces between reference and original faces. Moreover, some works target editing specific facial attributes such as age progression [50], and smile generation [48]. Some recent works discover semantically meaningful directions in the latent space of a pretrained GAN so as to carry out facial attributes editing by moving the latent code along these directions [42–45,56]. InterFaceGAN [42,43] tries to disentangle attribute representations in the latent space of GANs by searching a hyperplane, of which a normal vector is used as the editing direction. Fine-grained facial attributes editing is achieved by [16] through searching a curving trajectory with respect to attribute landscapes in the latent space of GANs.

3   Sequential Deepfake Dataset

To support the novel research problem, we generate a large-scale Sequential Deepfake (Seq-Deepfake) dataset consisting of sequential manipulated face images based on two representative facial manipulation techniques, facial components manipulation [19] and facial attributes manipulation [16]. Unlike most of existing deepfake datasets [14,33] only providing binary labels, the proposed dataset contains annotations of manipulation sequences with diverse sequence lengths. Details of generation pipelines based on the two facial manipulation techniques are as follows.

Sequential Facial Components Manipulation. We adopt the StyleMap-GAN proposed in [19] for facial components manipulation. Facial components manipulation is carried out based on original images from CelebA-HQ [17,27] and corresponding facial component masks from CelebAMask-HQ [20] dataset. Facial components manipulation aims to transplant some facial components of a reference image to an original image with respect to a mask that indicates the components to be manipulated. Specifically, we project the original image and the reference image through the encoder of StyleMapGAN to obtain stylemaps, which are intermediate latent spaces with spatial dimensions. Then, the facial components manipulation is carried out by blending the stylemaps extracted from reference and original faces based on facial component masks. Due to the inevitable appearance of degraded images in the generation process, we adopt the Generated Image Quality Assessment (GIQA) algorithm [11] to quantitatively evaluate the quality of each generated image and then filter out some low-quality ones based on the pre-defined threshold. Figure 3 (a) shows some samples with corresponding annotations of sequential facial components manipulation. Through this data generation pipeline, we can finally generate 35,166 manipulated face images annotated with 28 types of manipulation sequences in different lengths (including original). As illustrated in Fig. 3 (a), the proportions of 1–5 different lengths of manipulation sequences are: 20.48%, 20.06%, 18.62%, 20.88%, 19.96%.

Sequential Facial Attributes Manipulation. Unlike facial components manipulation methods that swap certain local parts from a reference image to an original image, facial attributes manipulation approaches directly change specific attributes on the original face image without any reference images. To take this manipulation type into consideration, we utilize the fine-grained facial editing method proposed by [16]. This method aims to learn a location-specific semantic field for each editing type on the training set, then edit this attribute of interest on the given face image to a user-defined degree by stepping forward or backward on the learned curve in latent space. Based on this idea, we further generate face images with sequential facial attributes manipulation by performing the editing process in a sequential manner. Specifically, we first sample latent codes from the StyleGAN trained on FFHQ dataset [18] to generate original images. Then according to pre-defined attribute sequences, we progressively manipulate each attribute on the original face to another randomly chosen degree using the above method. After generating the final manipulation results, we also perform GIQA algorithm to filter out low-quality samples. Using this pipeline, we generate 49,920 face images with 26 manipulation sequence types, with the length of each sequence ranging from 1 to 5, as shown in Fig. 3 (b).

4   Our Approach

4.1   Motivation

Most current facial manipulation applications are constructed using algorithms of Generative Adversarial Network (GAN). However, it is a well known fact that due to imperfect semantic disentanglement in the latent space of GAN [21,42],

Eye-Nose   Nose-Eye   Bangs-Smiling   Smiling-Bangs
(a) Facial components manipulation   (b) Facial attributes manipulation

Fig. 4. Effect of different sequential order for facial manipulation. Switching the sequential order of manipulations between (a) eye and nose and (b) bangs and smiling results in different facial manipulations.

manipulating one facial component or attribute is likely to affect the others. As shown in the first row of Fig. 2, manipulating the nose in the step of 'Eye-Nose' simultaneously results in some little modification on the eye and mouth components compared to the former step 'Eye', which alters the overall **spatial relation** among facial components. We can thus discover some **spatial manipulation traces** from the spatial relation. Furthermore, as illustrated in Fig. 4, switching the sequential order of manipulations (*e.g.,* manipulation order between eye and nose in (a) and bangs and smiling in (b) in Fig. 4) causes different facial manipulation results (*e.g.,* distinct gazes in (a) and distinct amount of bangs in (b) in Fig. 4), which indicates that when changing the sequential order of manipulations, the above overall spatial relation of facial components altered by manipulations will also be changed. This means there exists sequential information from spatial relation that reflects the sequential order of manipulations, which corresponds to the facial manipulation sequence. That is, we can extract the spatial relation among facial components to unveil the **spatial manipulation traces** and model their **sequential relation** to detect the facial manipulation sequence. We thus regard the sequential relation as **sequential manipulation traces**.

4.2   Overview

Based on the above observation, we cast detecting Seq-Deepfake manipulation as a specific image-to-sequence task, where inputs are manipulated/original images and outputs are facial manipulation sequences. Three challenges will be encountered when addressing the task. 1) From Figs. 2 and 3, it can be seen that distinguishing original faces and sequential manipulated faces is extremely hard. Besides, with respect to different people, differences in face contour cause diverse manipulation regions for the same type of facial components/attributes manipulation. Thus, given indistinguishable and diverse facial manipulations, how to adaptively capture subtle manipulation regions and model their spatial relation accurately is quite challenging. 2) Based on the spatial relation of manipulated components/attributes, how to precisely model their sequential relation so as to detect the sequential facial manipulation is another challenge. 3) Compared to normal image-to-sequence task (*e.g.* image captions), the annotations of manipulation sequences are much shorter and thus less informative in our task.

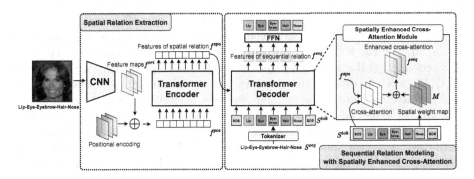

Fig. 5. Overview of proposed Seq-DeepFake Transformer (**SeqFakeFormer**). We first feed the face image into a CNN to learn features of spatial manipulation regions, and extract their spatial relation via self-attention modules in the encoder. Then sequential relation based on features of spatial relation is modeled to detect the sequential facial manipulation. A spatial enhanced cross-attention module is integrated into the decoder, contributing to a more effective cross-attention.

Therefore, how to effectively learn the sequential information of facial manipulations given limited annotations of manipulation sequences should also be considered.

To cope with the above three challenges, as shown in Fig. 5, we propose a Seq-DeepFake Transformer (**SeqFakeFormer**), which is composed of two key parts: **Spatial Relation Extraction, Sequential Relation Modeling with Spatially Enhanced Cross-attention**. To capture spatial manipulation traces, features of subtle manipulation regions are first adaptively captured by a CNN and their spatial relation are extracted via self-attention modules in the transformer encoder. After that, we capture sequential manipulation traces by modeling sequential relation based on features of spatial relation through cross-attention modules deployed in the decoder with an auto-regressive mechanism. To achieve more effective cross-attention given limited annotations of manipulation sequences, a spatially enhanced cross-attention module is devised to generate different spatial weight maps for corresponding manipulations to carry out cross-attention. In the following subsections, we describe all components in detail.

4.3   Spatial Relation Extraction

To adaptively capture subtle and various facial manipulation regions, we exploit a CNN to learn feature maps of the input image. Given an input image $x \in \mathbb{R}^{3 \times H' \times W'}$, we first feed it into a CNN [13] to extract its visual feature maps $f^{ori} = \text{CNN}(x)$, $f^{ori} \in \mathbb{R}^{C \times H \times W}$, where H', W', and H, W are the height and width of the input image and its corresponding feature maps, respectively. C is the number of channels of feature maps.

Since the transformer architecture is permutation-invariant, we supplement original visual features maps f^{ori} with fixed positional encodings [4,30], resulting in feature maps denoted as f^{pos}. Since transformer encoder accepts a sequence as input, we reshape the spatial dimensions of f^{pos} to one dimension, generating reshaped features $f^{pos} \in \mathbb{R}^{C \times HW}$. After feeding into the transformer encoder, f^{pos} conducts self-attention by generating the key, query, and value features K, Q, V so as to extract the relations among all spatial positions. Through this self-attention operation on CNN features, spatial relation of manipulation regions are exploited and thus spatial manipulation traces can be extracted. To further facilitate spatial relation extraction, this paper adopts multi-head self-attention which splits features f^{pos} into multiple groups along the channel dimension. The multi-head normalized attention based on dot-product is as follows:

$$f_i^{spa} = \text{Softmax}(K_i^T Q_i / \sqrt{d}) V_i, f^{spa} = \text{Concat}(f_1^{spa}, ..., f_D^{spa}) \tag{1}$$

where K_i, Q_i, V_i denote the i-th group of the key, query, and value features, d is dimension of queries and keys, and total D groups are generated. We then concatenate all the groups to form the features of spatial relation f^{spa} as the output of encoder.

4.4 Sequential Relation Modeling with Spatially Enhanced Cross-attention

Given features of spatial relation f^{spa} extracted from the encoder, we propose to model the sequential relation among them to detect the facial manipulation sequences. To this end, we carry out cross-attention between features of spatial relation f^{spa} and corresponding annotations of manipulation sequences in an auto-regressive manner. To achieve this, we send original annotations of manipulation sequences $S^{ori} \in R^{C \times N}$ (e.g., N=5 in Fig. 5 before a Tokenizer) into a Tokenizer, where we transform each manipulation in the sequence into one token and insert Start of Sentence (SOS) and End of Sentence (EOS) tokens into the beginning and end of sequence. After that, we obtain tokenized manipulation sequences $S^{tok} \in R^{C \times (N+2)}$ to be cross-attended with features of spatial relation f^{spa}. With the auto-regressive mechanism, the decoding process of facial manipulation sequence in the transformer decoder (aided by cross-attention) is triggered by SOS token and will be automatically stopped once the EOS token is predicted. In this way, we can predict facial manipulation sequences with adaptive lengths.

Normally, cross-attention between tokenized sequences S^{tok} and features of spatial relation f^{spa} should be performed directly. However, as mentioned above, compared to the normal image-to-sequence task, annotations of manipulation sequences are much shorter and thus less informative (S^{tok} only has $(N+2)$-length and maximum of N is 5). To effectively cross-attend features of spatial relation with limited annotations of manipulation sequences, inspired by [10], we propose a sequential relation modeling with spatially enhanced cross-attention. We argue that each manipulation in S^{tok} corresponds to one specific facial component/attribute which has a strong prior of spatial regions, thus we can enrich the information of manipulation sequences guided by this prior. To this end, we generate the spatial weight map for each manipulation by dynamically predicting the spatial center and scale of each manipulation component/attribute in annotations of manipulation sequences as follows:

$$t_h, t_w = \text{sigmoid}(\text{MLP}(S^{tok})), r_h, r_w = \text{FC}(S^{tok}) \tag{2}$$

where t_h, t_w and r_h, r_w are estimated 2-dimensional coordinates corresponding to spatial centers and scales of specific manipulations in the sequences, respectively. Then the Gaussian-shape spatial weight map can be generated as:

$$M(h, w) = \exp\left(-\frac{(h - t_h)^2}{\lambda r_h^2} - \frac{(w - t_w)^2}{\lambda r_w^2}\right) \tag{3}$$

where $(h, w) \in [0, H] \times [0, W]$ are 2-dimensional coordinates of the spatial weight map M, and λ is a hyper-parameter to modulate the bandwidth of the Gaussian-shape distribution. From Eq. 3, it can be seen that spatial weight map M can assign higher importance to spatial regions closer to the centers and lower weights to locations farther from the centers. Moreover, as analyzed before, since diverse manipulation regions are presented for different people, the above dynamically learned scales can further tune the height/width ratios of spatial weight map based on each manipulation, contributing to a more adaptive spatial weight map. Based on this idea, we can enhance the cross-attention between features of spatial relation and annotations of manipulation sequences with generated spatial weight map M as follows:

$$S = \text{FC}(S^{tok}), K, V = \text{FC}(f^{spa}),$$
$$f_i^{seq} = \text{Softmax}(K_i^T Q_i \sqrt{d} + logM)V_i, \tag{4}$$
$$f^{seq} = \text{Concat}(f_1^{seq}, ..., f_D^{seq})$$

where FC denotes a single fully-connected layer, and f_i^{seq} denotes features of sequential relation. The cross-attention of the i-th head is further element-wise added with logarithm of spatial weight map M, which contributes to spatially enhanced cross-attention. Furthermore, to model the sequential relation of facial manipulation, the auto-regressive mechanism is integrated into the above cross-attention process. This is implemented by masking out (setting to $-\infty$) all values in the input of the Softmax function in Eq. 4 which correspond to illegal connections. Through concatenation of features of sequential relation from all cross-attention heads, we can obtain the final features of sequential relation f^{seq} as the output of decoder.

The features of sequential relation are then fed into a Fast Forward Network (FFN) and transformed to a class score for each manipulation. Finally, we jointly train the CNN, transformer encoder and decoder by minimizing the cross-entropy loss between each class score and corresponding annotation of manipulation in the sequence.

5   Experiments

5.1   Experimental Setup

Baseline Methods. The most straightforward solution for detecting Seq-Deepfake manipulation is to regard it as a multi-label classification problem [46]. It treats all manipulations in the sequences as independent classes and classifies the manipulated images into multiple manipulation classes. Specifically, we design a simple multi-label classification network (denoted as **Multi-Cls**) as one of the baselines. We use ResNet-34 [13] and ResNet-50 [13] pre-trained on ImageNet [6] dataset as backbones for the multi-label classification network, which is concatenated with N classification heads ($N = 5$). Moreover, we study a more complex transformer structure **DETR** [5] modified for our problem. To examine the performance of existing deepfake detection methods for our research problem, we compare three state-of-the-art deepfake detection methods, a Dilated Residual Network variant (**DRN**) [47], a two-stream network (**Two-Stream**) [28], and a multi-attentional deepfake detection (**MA**) [52]. More details of baseline methods can be found in **Supplementary Material**.

Evaluation Metrics. We propose two evaluation metrics for this new task.

- **Fixed Accuracy (Fixed-Acc):** Given prediction with fixed N-length ($N = 5$) by above baselines, as in the training process, the first type of evaluation pads 'no manipulation' class into the annotated manipulation sequences and compares each manipulation class in the predicted sequences with its corresponding annotation to calculate the evaluation accuracy.
- **Adaptive Accuracy (Adaptive-Acc):** Since the proposed method exploits sequential information to detect facial manipulation sequences based on the auto-regressive mechanism, predictions will be automatically stopped once predicting the EOS token. Thus, the proposed method can detect facial manipulation sequences with adaptive lengths. To conduct the evaluation in this scenario, the second type of evaluation is devised, which compares predicted manipulations and corresponding annotations within the maximum steps of manipulations ($N \leq 5$) between them. This makes the evaluation focus more on accuracy of manipulations.

More details of two evaluation metrics can be found in **Supplementary Material**.

5.2   Benchmark for Seq-Deepfake

We tabulate the first benchmark for detecting sequential facial manipulation based on facial components manipulation and facial attributes manipulation in Tables 1 to 3. We note that, both baselines and the proposed method obtains much higher performance under evaluation metric Fixed-Acc than Adaptive-Acc. This validates that detecting sequential facial manipulation with adaptive lengths is much harder than its simplified version with fixed length. It can be

Table 1. Accuracy of detecting Seq-Deepfake based on sequential facial components manipulation

Methods	ResNet-34		ResNet-50	
	Fixed-Acc	Adaptive-Acc	Fixed-Acc	Adaptive-Acc
Multi-Cls	69.66	50.54	69.65	50.57
DETR [5]	69.87	50.63	69.75	49.84
Ours	**72.13**	**54.80**	**72.65**	**55.30**

Table 2. Accuracy of detecting Seq-Deepfake based on sequential facial attributes manipulation

Methods	ResNet-34		ResNet-50	
	Fixed-Acc	Adaptive-Acc	Fixed-Acc	Adaptive-Acc
Multi-Cls	66.99	46.68	66.66	46.00
DETR [5]	67.93	48.15	67.62	47.99
Ours	**67.99**	**48.32**	**68.86**	**49.63**

observed from Tables 1 and 2, that the proposed SeqFakeFormer obtains the best performance of detecting facial manipulation sequences compared to all considered baselines in both facial components manipulation and facial attributes manipulation. In addition, SeqFakeFormer also performs better than other baselines with both CNNs (ResNet-34 and ResNet-50), indicating the compatibility of the proposed method with different feature extractors. Specifically, the proposed method has achieved about 3–4% improvement in facial components sequential manipulation and 1–2% improvement in facial attributes sequential manipulation under two evaluation metrics. In particular, there exists a larger performance gap between SeqFakeFormer and other baselines under evaluation metric Adaptive-Acc than Fixed-Acc, which demonstrates that the effectiveness of the proposed method is more significant in the harder case. Moreover, we tabulate the comparison between three SOTA deepfake detection methods and our method in Table 3. SeqFakeFormer also outperforms all SOTA deepfake detection methods in both manipulation types. Since all the baselines treat detecting Seq-Deepfake as a multi-label classification problem, only spatial information of manipulated images are extracted. In contrast, SeqFakeFormer is capable of exploiting both spatial and sequential manipulation traces and thus more useful sequential information can be modeled, which is the key to enhance the performance of Seq-Deepfake Detection.

5.3   Ablation Study

In this sub-section we investigate the impact of two key components in SeqFake-Former, auto-regressive mechanism and Spatially Enhanced Cross-Attention module (SECA), to the overall performance. The considered components and

Table 3. Accuracy of detecting Seq-Deepfake compared to deepfake detection methods

Methods	Face components manipulation		Face attributes manipulation	
	Fixed-Acc	Adaptive-Acc	Fixed-Acc	Adaptive-Acc
DRN [47]	66.06	45.79	64.42	43.20
MA [52]	71.31	52.94	67.58	47.48
Two-Stream [28]	71.92	53.89	66.77	46.38
Ours	**72.65**	**55.30**	**68.86**	**49.63**

Table 4. Ablation study of detecting Seq-Deepfake based on sequential facial components manipulation

Components		ResNet-34		ResNet-50	
Auto-regressive	SECA	Fixed-Acc	Adaptive-Acc	Fixed-Acc	Adaptive-Acc
✗	✗	70.64	52.19	71.22	53.43
✗	✔	70.77	51.71	70.99	52.66
✔	✗	71.88	53.84	72.18	54.64
✔	✔	**72.13**	**54.80**	**72.65**	**55.30**

the corresponding results obtained for each case are tabulated Tables 4 and 5. As evident from Tables 4 and 5, removing either auto-regressive mechanism or SECA will degrade the overall performance. This validates that auto-regressive mechanism facilitates the sequential relation modeling and SECA benefits the cross-attention. These components complement each other to produce better performance for detecting Seq-Deepfake.

5.4 Face Recovery

After detecting facial manipulation sequences, we are able to perform more challenging tasks, like recovering the original face from the manipulated face image. Specifically, we formulate the Face Recovery task as: given a sequentially manipulated face image, reverse the manipulation process to get an image as close as possible to the original image. For example, in the facial attributes manipulation case, given an image generated by sequential manipulations on different attributes on the original face, we want to recover the original image. In fact, this task can be seen as an inverse sequential facial attribute manipulation problem, which can be effectively solved by the data generation pipeline described in Sect. 3 in an inverse manner. Specifically, as can be observed in Fig. 6, once we detect the correct facial manipulation sequence, i.e. correct manipulations ordered with correct manipulation steps, we can recover original face by performing face attribute manipulation based on the inverse order of detected facial manipulation sequence (process with green arrow). Comparatively, recovering the face image with wrongly ordered manipulation sequences may encounter dif-

Table 5. Ablation study of detecting Seq-Deepfake based on sequential facial attributes manipulation

Components		ResNet-34		ResNet-50	
Auto-regressive	SECA	Fixed-Acc	Adaptive-Acc	Fixed-Acc	Adaptive-Acc
✗	✗	66.98	45.87	68.14	48.49
✗	✔	67.36	47.22	68.77	49.54
✔	✗	66.70	46.56	68.17	48.81
✔	✔	**67.99**	**48.32**	**68.86**	**49.63**

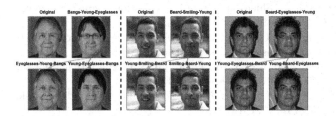

Fig. 6. Face recovery based on correct and wrong facial manipulation sequences.

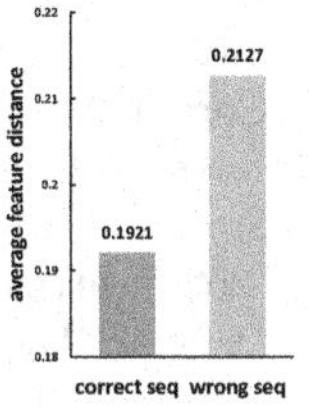

Fig. 7. Identity preservation.

ferent problems, such as incomplete recovery of age, smile, glasses, etc. (process with red arrow). Figure 7 evaluates the results using identity preservation metrics as in [16], where smaller feature distance means identity is better preserved. The average feature distance between randomly selected 100 original faces and recovered faces using correct manipulation sequences is clearly smaller than that of the wrongly ordered sequence, indicating that the identity can be better recovered with correct manipulation sequence. Based on the above analysis and experiments, we prove that the detection of facial manipulation sequences is highly useful for face recovery, and we hope it can be applied to more meaningful tasks in the future.

6   Conclusion

This paper studies a novel research problem – Detecting Sequential DeepFake Manipulation, aiming to detect a sequential vector of multi-step facial manipulation operations. We also introduce the first Seq-DeepFake dataset to provide sequentially manipulated face images. Supported by this new dataset, we cast detecting Seq-DeepFake manipulation as a specific image-to-sequence task and propose a Seq-DeepFake Transformer (SeqFakeFormer). Two modules, Spatial Relation Extraction and Sequential Relation Modeling with Spatially Enhanced Cross-Attention, are integrated into SeqFakeFormer, complementing each other. Extensive experimental results demonstrate the superiority of SeqFakeFormer and valuable observations pave the way for future research in broader deepfake detection.

Acknowledgements. This work is supported by NTU NAP, MOE AcRF Tier 2 (T2EP20221-0033), and under the RIE2020 Industry Alignment Fund - Industry Collaboration Projects (IAF-ICP) Funding Initiative, as well as cash and in-kind contribution from the industry partner(s). Ziwei Liu is the corresponding author.

References

1. https://apps.apple.com/us/app/facetune2-editor-by-lightricks/id1149994032
2. https://apps.apple.com/us/app/youcam-makeup-selfie-editor/id863844475
3. https://apps.apple.com/us/app/youcam-perfect-photo-editor/id768469908
4. Bello, I., Zoph, B., Vaswani, A., Shlens, J., Le, Q.V.: Attention augmented convolutional networks. In: CVPR (2019)
5. Carion, N., Massa, F., Synnaeve, G., Usunier, N., Kirillov, A., Zagoruyko, S.: End-to-end object detection with transformers. In: Vedaldi, A., Bischof, H., Brox, T., Frahm, J.-M. (eds.) ECCV 2020. LNCS, vol. 12346, pp. 213–229. Springer, Cham (2020). https://doi.org/10.1007/978-3-030-58452-8_13
6. Deng, J., Dong, W., Socher, R., Li, L.J., Li, K., Fei-Fei, L.: ImageNet: a large-scale hierarchical image database. In: CVPR (2009)
7. Dolhansky, B., Howes, R., Pflaum, B., Baram, N., Ferrer, C.C.: The deepfake detection challenge (DFDC) preview dataset. arXiv preprint arXiv:1910.08854 (2019)
8. Durall, R., Keuper, M., Pfreundt, F.J., Keuper, J.: Unmasking deepfakes with simple features. arXiv preprint arXiv:1911.00686 (2019)
9. Dzanic, T., Shah, K., Witherden, F.: Fourier spectrum discrepancies in deep network generated images. In: NeurIPS (2020)
10. Gao, P., Zheng, M., Wang, X., Dai, J., Li, H.: Fast convergence of DETR with spatially modulated co-attention. In: CVPR (2021)
11. Gu, S., Bao, J., Chen, D., Wen, F.: GIQA: generated image quality assessment. In: Vedaldi, A., Bischof, H., Brox, T., Frahm, J.-M. (eds.) ECCV 2020. LNCS, vol. 12356, pp. 369–385. Springer, Cham (2020). https://doi.org/10.1007/978-3-030-58621-8_22
12. Haliassos, A., Vougioukas, K., Petridis, S., Pantic, M.: Lips don't lie: a generalisable and robust approach to face forgery detection. In: CVPR (2021)
13. He, K., Zhang, X., Ren, S., Sun, J.: Deep residual learning for image recognition. In: CVPR (2016)
14. He, Y., et al.: ForgeryNet: a versatile benchmark for comprehensive forgery analysis. In: CVPR (2021)
15. Jiang, L., Li, R., Wu, W., Qian, C., Loy, C.C.: DeeperForensics-1.0: a large-scale dataset for real-world face forgery detection. In: CVPR (2020)
16. Jiang, Y., Huang, Z., Pan, X., Loy, C.C., Liu, Z.: Talk-to-edit: fine-grained facial editing via dialog. In: ICCV (2021)
17. Karras, T., Aila, T., Laine, S., Lehtinen, J.: Progressive growing of GANs for improved quality, stability, and variation. In: ICLR (2018)
18. Karras, T., Laine, S., Aila, T.: A style-based generator architecture for generative adversarial networks. In: CVPR (2019)
19. Kim, H., Choi, Y., Kim, J., Yoo, S., Uh, Y.: Exploiting spatial dimensions of latent in GAN for real-time image editing. In: CVPR (2021)
20. Lee, C.H., Liu, Z., Wu, L., Luo, P.: MaskGAN: towards diverse and interactive facial image manipulation. In: CVPR (2020)

21. Lee, W., Kim, D., Hong, S., Lee, H.: High-fidelity synthesis with disentangled representation. In: Vedaldi, A., Bischof, H., Brox, T., Frahm, J.-M. (eds.) ECCV 2020. LNCS, vol. 12371, pp. 157–174. Springer, Cham (2020). https://doi.org/10.1007/978-3-030-58574-7_10
22. Li, J., Xie, H., Li, J., Wang, Z., Zhang, Y.: Frequency-aware discriminative feature learning supervised by single-center loss for face forgery detection. In: CVPR (2021)
23. Li, L., et al.: Face x-ray for more general face forgery detection. In: CVPR (2020)
24. Li, Y., Yang, X., Sun, P., Qi, H., Lyu, S.: Celeb-DF: a large-scale challenging dataset for deepfake forensics. In: CVPR (2020)
25. Liu, H., et al.: Spatial-phase shallow learning: rethinking face forgery detection in frequency domain. In: CVPR (2021)
26. Liu, S.-Q., Lan, X., Yuen, P.C.: Remote photoplethysmography correspondence feature for 3D mask face presentation attack detection. In: Ferrari, V., Hebert, M., Sminchisescu, C., Weiss, Y. (eds.) ECCV 2018. LNCS, vol. 11220, pp. 577–594. Springer, Cham (2018). https://doi.org/10.1007/978-3-030-01270-0_34
27. Liu, Z., Luo, P., Wang, X., Tang, X.: Deep learning face attributes in the wild. In: CVPR (2015)
28. Luo, Y., Zhang, Y., Yan, J., Liu, W.: Generalizing face forgery detection with high-frequency features. In: CVPR (2021)
29. Pang, M., Wang, B., Huang, S., Cheung, Y.M., Wen, B.: A unified framework for bidirectional prototype learning from contaminated faces across heterogeneous domains. IEEE Trans. Inf. Forensics Secur. **17**, 1544–1557 (2022)
30. Parmar, N., et al.: Image transformer. In: ICML (2018)
31. Qian, Y., Yin, G., Sheng, L., Chen, Z., Shao, J.: Thinking in frequency: face forgery detection by mining frequency-aware clues. In: Vedaldi, A., Bischof, H., Brox, T., Frahm, J.-M. (eds.) ECCV 2020. LNCS, vol. 12357, pp. 86–103. Springer, Cham (2020). https://doi.org/10.1007/978-3-030-58610-2_6
32. Qiu, H., Xiao, C., Yang, L., Yan, X., Lee, H., Li, B.: SemanticAdv: generating adversarial examples via attribute-conditioned image editing. In: Vedaldi, A., Bischof, H., Brox, T., Frahm, J.-M. (eds.) ECCV 2020. LNCS, vol. 12359, pp. 19–37. Springer, Cham (2020). https://doi.org/10.1007/978-3-030-58568-6_2
33. Rossler, A., Cozzolino, D., Verdoliva, L., Riess, C., Thies, J., Nießner, M.: Faceforensics++: learning to detect manipulated facial images. In: CVPR (2019)
34. Shao, R., Lan, X., Li, J., Yuen, P.C.: Multi-adversarial discriminative deep domain generalization for face presentation attack detection. In: CVPR (2019)
35. Shao, R., Lan, X., Yuen, P.C.: Deep convolutional dynamic texture learning with adaptive channel-discriminability for 3D mask face anti-spoofing. In: IJCB (2017)
36. Shao, R., Lan, X., Yuen, P.C.: Joint discriminative learning of deep dynamic textures for 3D mask face anti-spoofing. IEEE Trans. Inf. Forensics Secur. **14**(4), 923–938 (2018)
37. Shao, R., Lan, X., Yuen, P.C.: Regularized fine-grained meta face anti-spoofing. In: AAAI (2020)
38. Shao, R., Perera, P., Yuen, P.C., Patel, V.M.: Open-set adversarial defense. In: Vedaldi, A., Bischof, H., Brox, T., Frahm, J.-M. (eds.) ECCV 2020. LNCS, vol. 12362, pp. 682–698. Springer, Cham (2020). https://doi.org/10.1007/978-3-030-58520-4_40
39. Shao, R., Perera, P., Yuen, P.C., Patel, V.M.: Federated generalized face presentation attack detection. IEEE Trans. Neural Netw. Learn. Syst. (2022)
40. Shao, R., Perera, P., Yuen, P.C., Patel, V.M.: Open-set adversarial defense with clean-adversarial mutual learning. Int. J. Comput. Vision **130**(4), 1070–1087 (2022)

41. Shao, R., Zhang, B., Yuen, P.C., Patel, V.M.: Federated test-time adaptive face presentation attack detection with dual-phase privacy preservation. In: FG (2021)
42. Shen, Y., Gu, J., Tang, X., Zhou, B.: Interpreting the latent space of gans for semantic face editing. In: CVPR (2020)
43. Shen, Y., Yang, C., Tang, X., Zhou, B.: InterfaceGAN: interpreting the disentangled face representation learned by GANs. TMPAMI (2020)
44. Shen, Y., Zhou, B.: Closed-form factorization of latent semantics in GANs. In: CVPR (2021)
45. Voynov, A., Babenko, A.: Unsupervised discovery of interpretable directions in the GAN latent space. In: ICML (2020)
46. Wang, H., Liu, W., Bocchieri, A., Li, Y.: Can multi-label classification networks know what they don't know? In: NeurIPS (2021)
47. Wang, S.Y., Wang, O., Owens, A., Zhang, R., Efros, A.A.: Detecting photoshopped faces by scripting photoshop. In: CVPR (2019)
48. Wang, W., Alameda-Pineda, X., Xu, D., Fua, P., Ricci, E., Sebe, N.: Every smile is unique: landmark-guided diverse smile generation. In: CVPR (2018)
49. Xiao, Z., et al.: Improving transferability of adversarial patches on face recognition with generative models. In: CVPR (2021)
50. Yang, H., Huang, D., Wang, Y., Jain, A.K.: Learning face age progression: a pyramid architecture of GANs. In: CVPR (2018)
51. Yu, Z., et al.: Searching central difference convolutional networks for face anti-spoofing. In: CVPR (2020)
52. Zhao, H., Zhou, W., Chen, D., Wei, T., Zhang, W., Yu, N.: Multi-attentional deepfake detection. In: CVPR (2021)
53. Zhao, T., Xu, X., Xu, M., Ding, H., Xiong, Y., Xia, W.: Learning self-consistency for deepfake detection. In: ICCV (2021)
54. Zhu, P., Abdal, R., Qin, Y., Wonka, P.: Sean: image synthesis with semantic region-adaptive normalization. In: CVPR (2020)
55. Zhu, X., Wang, H., Fei, H., Lei, Z., Li, S.Z.: Face forgery detection by 3D decomposition. In: CVPR (2021)
56. Zhuang, P., Koyejo, O., Schwing, A.G.: Enjoy your editing: Controllable GANs for image editing via latent space navigation. In: ICLR (2021)

Self-supervised Sparse Representation for Video Anomaly Detection

Jhih-Ciang Wu[1,2], He-Yen Hsieh[1], Ding-Jie Chen[1], Chiou-Shann Fuh[2], and Tyng-Luh Liu[1(✉)]

[1] Institute of Information Science, Academia Sinica, Taipei, Taiwan
liutyng@iis.sinica.edu.tw
[2] National Taiwan University, Taipei, Taiwan

Abstract. Video anomaly detection (VAD) aims at localizing *unexpected* actions or activities in a video sequence. Existing mainstream VAD techniques are based on either the one-class formulation, which assumes all training data are *normal*, or weakly-supervised, which requires only video-level normal/anomaly labels. To establish a unified approach to solving the two VAD settings, we introduce a *self-supervised sparse representation* (S3R) framework that models the concept of anomaly at feature level by exploring the synergy between dictionary-based representation and self-supervised learning. With the learned dictionary, S3R facilitates two coupled modules, *en-Normal* and *de-Normal*, to reconstruct snippet-level features and filter out normal-event features. The self-supervised techniques also enable generating samples of pseudo normal/anomaly to train the anomaly detector. We demonstrate with extensive experiments that S3R achieves new state-of-the-art performances on popular benchmark datasets for both one-class and weakly-supervised VAD tasks. Our code is publicly available at https://github.com/louisYen/S3R.

Keywords: Sparse representation · Video anomaly detection

1 Introduction

These days surveillance/security cameras are ubiquitously deployed in various public places, such as factories, offices, shopping malls, and intersections. To strengthen public safety, it is constructive to automatically detect abnormal events such as accidents, illegal activities, or crimes. In practice, abnormal events are rare and diverse in nature; manually identifying abnormal events is laborious and time-consuming, especially for long-duration video sequences. To facilitate

---

J.-C. Wu and H.-Y. Hsieh—Both authors contributed equally to this work.

Supplementary Information The online version contains supplementary material available at https://doi.org/10.1007/978-3-031-19778-9_42.

S. Avidan et al. (Eds.): ECCV 2022, LNCS 13673, pp. 729–745, 2022.
https://doi.org/10.1007/978-3-031-19778-9_42

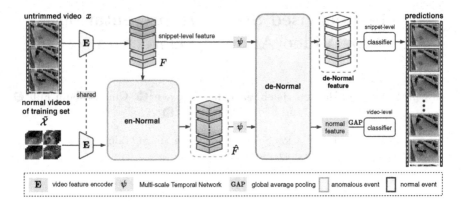

Fig. 1. The proposed S3R framework couples dictionary learning with self-supervised techniques to model the concept of feature-level anomaly. First, a feature extractor **E** represents each untrimmed video x as the snippet-level feature F, and all the normal training videos $\tilde{\mathcal{X}}$ are collected to build the task-specific dictionary. Next, the en-Normal module employs F and the dictionary to reconstruct the feature $\hat{F}$. Then, the de-Normal module explores F and $\hat{F}$ differences to filter out the normal-event patterns. Finally, the filtered features are ready to discriminate the normal and anomalous events of the snippet-level and video-level features.

recognizing the varied anomalies, developing intelligent computer vision algorithms, i.e., video anomaly detection (VAD) systems, is a pressing need.

Recent efforts to tackle the VAD task can be categorized into unsupervised and weakly-supervised techniques, depending on the annotations or assumptions about the training video sequences. The unsupervised VAD scenario, which we instead refer to as one-class VAD, assumes that only anomaly-free videos are available for training. The widely adopted approaches to discriminating normal and anomalous patterns are embedding-space learning or data reconstructing. The weakly-supervised VAD assumes that video-level normal/anomaly labels are given for training. Compared to the unsupervised VAD, obtaining such video-level labels requires more human effort but could achieve significant performance gains. A popular strategy to tackle weakly-supervised VAD is the inclusion of multiple instance learning (MIL). Specifically, an MIL-based weakly-supervised VAD algorithm treats each video and snippet as the bag and instance respectively, and the annotation for each bag, indicating whether a bag contains at least one anomalous instance, is known in the training stage.

In dealing with a VAD task, exhaustively modeling all possible scenarios of abnormal events is infeasible. Our method casts VAD as an out-of-distribution problem. A video clip that cannot be well reconstructed or explained by the normal-event dictionary is supposed to involve abnormal events. To realize such an idea, we develop the self-supervised sparse representation (S3R) framework to model the concept of feature-level anomaly by generalizing a dictionary-based representation with self-supervised techniques. We further infuse the MIL strategy into the proposed S3R to form a unified reconstruction-based method for effectively solving both unsupervised VAD and weakly-supervised VAD tasks.

In sum, S3R learns a normal-event dictionary for generating two opposite network modules, i.e., en-Normal and de-Normal, to reconstruct snippet-level features and filter out the normal-event features. These two modules complement each other and enable the processed features to be better discriminated by our snippet-level and video-level anomaly classifiers. With the aid of self-supervised techniques, we can generate more pseudo anomaly data concerning a specific dictionary to optimize the anomaly detector training. Since all samples in inference are unseen from the training stage, S3R indeed can adequately distinguish between unseen normal and unseen anomalous snippets.

We validate the usefulness of S3R by conducting experiments on both one-class and weakly-supervised VAD tasks, which include model evaluations on three popular datasets, i.e., ShanghaiTech, UCF-Crime, and XD-Violence. We also ablate each module within S3R to evaluate their effectiveness. To our knowledge, S3R is the first unified framework that can be applied to both one-class and weakly-supervised VAD task. We highlight the main contributions as follows.

- We introduce a novel self-supervised sparse representation (S3R) framework for modeling and generating the feature-level anomalies through the (offline) learned dictionary and self-supervised learning. Our experimental results support the advantage of such a strategy in addressing the VAD task.
- We propose two coupled modules, en-Normal and de-Normal, leading to a unified framework for tackling both one-class and weakly-supervised tasks.
- Our method achieves significant performance gains over other state-of-the-art on one-class and weakly-supervised video anomaly detection tasks.

2 Related Work

2.1 Anomaly Detection

Anomaly detection aims to discover the irregular pattern with subtle or significant differences to the normal data. With the remarkable progression for deep neural networks, several types of research on anomaly detection are prospering. Ruff et al. [29] used the simulated image-based dataset and tackled it in the one-class framework in the early periods due to the absence of the corresponding data. The one-class anomaly detection intends to determine whether the test image belongs to the said class or not. Following the development of one-class anomaly detection, the industrial dataset named MVTec AD [2], which with pixel-level annotation for the manufacturing inspection, is proposed. The purpose of anomaly detection using MVTec AD focuses on image-level anomaly classification or pixel-level anomaly localization. Various works handle MVTec using different manners such as knowledge distillation [3], self-supervised learning [18], and meta-learning [45].

Another more challenging anomaly detection leverages temporal information, known as video anomaly detection, searching for unexpected actions or illegal activities in a video clip. Specifically, it is demanding to estimate whole anomalous patterns for all types of anomaly detection in real-world applications. Therefore, the approaches for numerous types of anomaly detection are usually completed in an unsupervised manner, assuming that only access normal data during training while it has been unsuitably termed as the unsupervised VAD. Several works engage in one-class VAD from different perspectives. For instance, Liu et al. [20] took VAD as a video prediction framework and measured the anomaly score based on the gap between the ground-truth the predicted future frame. Another work [21] proposed a multi-level memory-augmented autoencoder with skip connection conditioned on reconstructed optical flow. Moreover, several approaches [11,15] embedded a pre-trained object detector into the model and used motion cues to deal with VAD. Recently, the VAD with weak supervision [34] that contains video-level labels in the training stage shows noticeable progress. It is considerable and trades the human annotations off against performance. Several approaches have evident improvement compared to unsupervised VAD. For example, RTFM [36] uses feature magnitude with the multi-scale temporal scenario from the video to select the top-k snippets and determine whether it belongs to an abnormal video or not. MSL [19] proposes multi-sequence learning and designs the exclusive ranking loss to select the most anomalous sequence. In contrast to previous works, we introduce an architecture with flexibility to deal with one-class and weakly-supervised VAD together.

2.2   Video Feature Extractors

Recently, neural network-based models have achieved a substantial performance boost for tackling the action recognition task and serve as powerful video feature extractors to obtain robust representations in downstream tasks. These popular models fall into two major categories of two-stream networks [9,32,41] and 3D networks [5,28,37,47]. The two-stream network exploits RGB images and stacked optical flow clues separately to generate appearance and motion features. The 3D networks directly employ raw video volumes to learn spatio-temporal representations. In this paper, we follow current efforts on VAD and employ the latter style as the video feature extractor, i.e. I3D, to encode untrimmed video and acquire snippet-level representation F.

2.3   Self-supervised Sparse Dictionary Learning

The goal of dictionary learning is to find a linear combination using the elements in a dictionary and keep the sparsity of the weights as possible at the same time. With the optimization for dictionary learning, the redundant atoms are filtered out, and pivot ones are preserved [1]. Cong et al. [8] proposed sparse reconstruction cost over a dictionary to estimate the anomaly score for local and global abnormal events in the testing stage. Lu et al. [22] adopted this strategy to encode normal event patterns in the surveillance video and boost the running time speed by constraint the sparsity coefficient. Luo et al. [23] proposed temporally-coherent sparse coding accompanying a stacked recurrent neural network to speed up the time of the testing phase. In contrast to the most of former works focusing on acceleration, we explore the capability of sparse representation learning and optimize all features obtained from the video feature extractor to formulate the universal dictionary D_U and task-specific dictionary D_T. Notably, since the most standard video feature extractors such as C3D or I3D are pre-trained on Kinetics-400 [16], we formulate the D_U and D_T using Kinetics-400 and the target dataset, respectively. The resulting dictionaries are then employed to feature reconstruction and pseudo label generation.

Self-supervised learning aims to increase the labels without manual annotation. [10] Some recent works deal with VAD adopt this strategy by generating pseudo labels. For example, Pang et al. [26] proposed formulating the ordinal regression as a pretext task. The model initially learns anomaly scores for pseudo normal and anomaly-free frames and applies the pseudo label to an end-to-end detector. Feng et al. [10] proposed to train a generator via MIL and predict the pseudo label for the segments of anomalous videos and address VAD in the self-training scheme. In this paper, we introduce pseudo label generation to deal with VAD. By comparison, we generate video-level pseudo labels in latent representation space with non-parametric sparse dictionary learning.

3 Our Method

Learning to carry out video anomaly detection is often cast in two different settings. The first is a one-class formulation that the provided training data include only the video samples describing the underlying normal activities. Despite that the one-class scenario has explicitly assumed the training data are all from the normal category, it has been unsuitably termed as the *unsupervised* VAD task in most previous works [12,35,43]. Departing from the anomaly-free assumption, the other popular setting is called the *weakly-supervised* VAD task. In this case, video samples in the training set are categorized by their video-level label into normal (label 0) and anomaly (label 1); however, the frame-level labels are not available to precisely locate exact segments of abnormal activities. For the ease of presentation, we hereafter refer to the two settings of video anomaly detection as oVAD ("o" for one-class) and wVAD ("w" for weakly-supervised).

We aim at developing a unified reconstruction-based method that can be effectively applied to solve both oVAD and wVAD tasks. To this end, we consider establishing a dictionary learning approach, coupling with self-supervised techniques, to model the concept of *anomaly* at the feature level, no matter which of the two VAD settings we are exploring. In the following sections, we will first elaborate our method for tackling the oVAD task as the problem is more challenging due to the lack of anomaly samples in the training data, and then explain how our method is also applicable to solving the wVAD task.

3.1 Sparse Representation for oVAD

One-class VAD assumes that only anomaly-free videos are accessible in the training set $\mathcal{X} = \{\mathbf{x}_i\}$. Now given an untrimmed frame-level video $\mathbf{x} \in \mathcal{X}$, we decompose $\mathbf{x}$ into the snippet-level video sequence $\mathcal{V} = \{\mathbf{v}_t\}_{t=1}^T$ of T snippets, where each snippet $\mathbf{v}_t$ comprises 16 consecutive frames. We follow previous work [6,10,19,36] to adopt a pre-trained I3D network [5] as the default feature extractor $\mathbf{E}$ to each snippet-level video $\mathcal{V}$, resulting in snippet-level representations $F = \{\mathbf{f}_t\}_{t=1}^T$, where $\mathbf{f}_t \in \mathbb{R}^C$ stands for each encoded snippet feature.

The dictionary learning [17,25] presumes an overcomplete basis, and prefers a sparse representation to succinctly explain a given sample. With the training set $\mathcal{X}$, whose video samples are anomaly-free, we are motivated to learn its corresponding dictionary D of N atoms. More specifically, we apply dictionary learning technique to each representation $F = \mathbf{E}(x) \in \mathbb{R}^{T \times C}$ and optimize as

$$\underset{D, \{\mathbf{w}_t\}}{\arg\min} \sum_{\mathbf{x} \in \mathcal{X}} \sum_{t=1}^T \left(\|\mathbf{f}_t - D\mathbf{w}_t\|^2 + \lambda \|\mathbf{w}_t\|_0 \right), \qquad (1)$$

where $D \in \mathbb{R}^{C \times N}$ is the resulting VAD dictionary, and $\mathbf{w}_t \in \mathbb{R}^N$ is the coefficient vector constrained by the sparsity prior. Since the derivation of D is specific to the training dataset $\mathcal{X}$, we will use the notation D_T to emphasize that the underlying dictionary from (1) is *task-specific*.

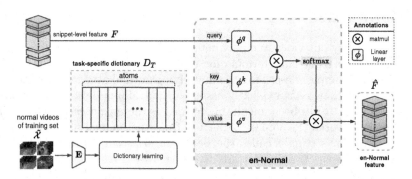

Fig. 2. The pipeline for en-Normal. This module takes the snippet-level feature F and task-specific dictionary D_T to reconstruct feature $\hat{F}$ via an attention mechanism.

3.2   A Dictionary with Two Modules

With the learned task-specific dictionary D_T from (1), we can design two opposite network components: the *en-Normal* and *de-Normal* modules. Given a snippet-level feature F, the former is used to obtain its reconstructed normal-event feature, while, on the contrary, the latter is applied to filter out the normal-event feature. The two modules complement each other and are central to our approach to anomaly video detection.

en-Normal Module. With the learned task-specific dictionary D_T, we design a dictionary-based attention module to better correlate the snippet-level feature F and the resulting D_T, leading to the corresponding normal-event feature $\hat{F}$. That is, since D_T is assumed to span the feature space of all normal-event patterns, we use the attention mechanism [38,42] to reweigh snippet-level input feature F with respect to D_T to obtain its reconstructed normal-event feature $\hat{F}$. In particular, we employ linear embeddings ϕ to project F and D_T. The attention is computed in the embedding space and defined as

$$\hat{F} = \text{softmax}\left(\phi^q(F)\phi^k(D_T)^\mathsf{T}\right)\phi^v(D_T),\tag{2}$$

where ϕ^q, ϕ^k, and ϕ^v separately represent linear functions to derive *query*, *key*, and *value* embeddings as in [38,42]. Thus, we adaptively involves normal-event patterns from the dictionary D_T based on F to reconstruct normal feature $\hat{F}$. Figure 2 depicts how the normal-event feature $\hat{F}$ is obtained from an input feature F and D_T.

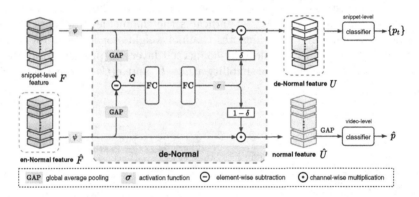

Fig. 3. The illustration of the de-Normal module. This module takes the channel-wise difference between F and $\hat{F}$ to form the cross-video semantics S. Then, the channel scale δ is derived to depress S for describing normal events.

de-Normal Module. Opposite to the previous design, the de-Normal module aims to depress the normal-event patterns within the input video feature. Thus, patterns related to normal events are expected to be filtered out, and the remaining can be used to infer whether the input video includes anomalous events or not. In practice, given the snippet-level feature $F \in \mathbb{R}^{T \times C}$ and the reconstructed normal feature $\hat{F} \in \mathbb{R}^{T \times C}$, we first explore the temporal dependency via the multi-scale temporal network (MTN) [36] and retrieve the enhanced features as $\psi(F) \in \mathbb{R}^{T \times C}$ and $\psi(\hat{F}) \in \mathbb{R}^{T \times C}$, where ψ denotes the MTN operation. Next, we employ the *global average pooling* (denoted as $g(\cdot)$) temporally to collect global events, where each channel includes normal or anomalous semantics. We express the retrieved cross-video semantics of $g(\psi(F)), g(\psi(\hat{F})) \in \mathbb{R}^C$ as $S \in \mathbb{R}^C$ which is formulated as their channel-wise difference,

$$S = g(\psi(F)) - g(\psi(\hat{F})), \tag{3}$$

Notice that the cross-video semantics S from (3) remove the normal-event semantic channels. Hence, the cross-video semantics S is able to depress semantic features for describing those normal events. To further keep the anomalous-event channels of cross-video semantics and simultaneous depress normal-event channels, we employ SENet-style [14] operations to explore the channel-wise relationship and derive the corresponding channel scales for depressing normal event within the input video representation as

$$\delta = \sigma(\text{MLP}(S)) \tag{4}$$

$$U = \delta \odot F, \quad \hat{U} = (1 - \delta) \odot \hat{F} \tag{5}$$

where MLP comprises two fully-connected layers to probe the channel-wise relationship, σ denotes the *sigmoid* activation, and $\odot$ means the channel-wise multiplication. The scale vector $\delta \in \mathbb{R}^c$ indicates the channel-level weights to keep anomalous events, while $1 - \delta$ denotes channel weights for focusing on normal events. Finally, we use multiple fully-connected layers to predict snippet-level $P = \{p_t\}$ and video-level $\hat{p}$ probability using U and $g(\hat{U})$, respectively. (See Fig. 3.)

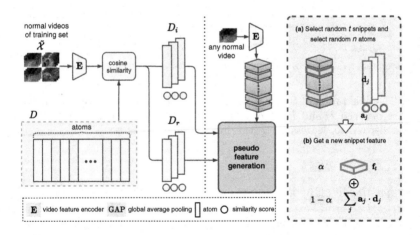

Fig. 4. Pseudo feature generation. A learned dictionary D is first divided into two equal-size dictionaries involving irrelevant atoms D_i and relevant atoms D_r. Then, randomly selected atoms are fused to generate the new snippet features.

3.3 Dictionary-Based Self-supervised Learning

We have described how to learn a task-specific dictionary D_T from anomaly-free training data, and use it to establish two useful modules for achieving video anomaly detection. However, as illustrated in Fig. 1, the overall training of the proposed model has implicitly assumed the availability of training data comprising anomaly events (*i.e.*, of label 1). Whereas the oVAD setting does not provide training data other than anomaly-free, we propose effective self-supervised techniques to generate *pseudo anomaly* data with respect to a given dictionary D. Assume now we are given a training set $\tilde{\mathcal{X}}$, the steps to generate a pseudo anomaly video based on D are listed below.

1. Collect all normal videos in $\tilde{\mathcal{X}}$ to form the training set $\mathcal{X}$. (This step is for the consideration of wVAD; otherwise, we already have $\mathcal{X} = \tilde{\mathcal{X}}$.)
2. For each atom in D, compute its averaged cosine similarity to $\mathcal{X}$, and obtain a ranking list according to their similarity scores in ascending order.
3. Divide D into two equal-size dictionaries, $D = D_i \cup D_r$, where D_i includes those *irrelevant* atoms from the first half of the ranking list, and D_r comprises the remaining *relevant* atoms. The self-supervised scheme uses D_i to generate pseudo anomaly features and D_r for pseudo normal features.
4. By sampling from $\mathcal{X}$, a normal video with representations $F = \{\mathbf{f}_t\}_{t=1}^{T}$, we create an anomalous video by replacing its $2 \times t$ snippets as follows:
   (a) We randomly select t snippets from F. For each snippet, we randomly select n atoms $\{\mathbf{d}_j\}_{j=1}^{n}$ from D_i as pseudo anomalous candidates.
   (b) We further apply the weighted fusion to get a new snippet feature $\hat{\mathbf{f}}_t = \alpha\mathbf{f}_t + (1-\alpha)\sum_j \mathbf{a}_j \cdot \mathbf{d}_j$, where $\mathbf{a}_j$ denotes the weight vector. (We set $\alpha = 0.01$ for pseudo anomaly, and 0.5 for pseudo normal.)
   (c) Repeat 4-(a) and 4-(b) steps for replacing the other t snippets with pseudo normal features from relevant atoms of D_r.
5. The process of creating a pseudo anomaly video is completed.

In our study, we have considered two reasonable choices of D. The first is simply the task-specific dictionary D_T, and the second is a task-independent *universal dictionary* D_U, which is optimized via (1) over the Kinetics-400 [16] dataset. Notice that in learning D_U, we do not need any label information, and instead consider D_U as a general dictionary to account for a rich variety of activities. The steps of pseudo anomaly generation are illustrated in Fig. 4.

3.4 S3R: A Unified VAD Framework

To show the proposed self-supervised sparse representation (S3R) is indeed a unified framework for solving both the oVAD and wVAD problems, we are left to justify that our method works equally well for the weakly-supervised scenario. Assume that we are given the training dataset $\tilde{\mathcal{X}}$ for solving the wVAD task. We can readily collect those anomaly-free videos (with label 0) to form the dataset $\mathcal{X}$ and obtain the corresponding dictionary D_T from (1). Then all other procedures remain the same as before except that we now have the choice to decide whether the technique to generate pseudo anomaly data is employed or not.

Our network is end-to-end trained and built upon RTFM [36] with respect to the following multi-task objective/loss:

$$\mathcal{L} = \mathcal{L}_{sep} + \gamma \mathcal{L}_{cls}, \tag{6}$$

where $\mathcal{L}_{sep}$ measures the separability of normal and anomalous videos, and $\mathcal{L}_{cls}$ optimizes the snippet-level and video-level classifiers. The weight γ balances the two loss terms and is set to 0.001. In addition, we have

$$\mathcal{L}_{sep} = \sum_k \left(\left| m - \|U^+ = \{u_t^+\}_k\|_2 \right| + \|U^- = \{u_t^-\}_k\|_2 \right), \tag{7}$$

where m is the adopted margin ($m = 100$ in our experiments) and $\|\cdot\|_2$ represents the ℓ_2-norm operation. We denote $U^+ = \{u_t^+\}_k$ and $U^- = \{u_t^-\}_k$ as the top-k feature magnitude of U when $y = 0$ and $y = 1$, respectively. Finally, $\mathcal{L}_{cls}$ is the binary logistic regression loss defined by

$$\mathcal{L}_{cls} = BCE(P = \{p_t\}_k, y) + BCE(\hat{p}, y), \tag{8}$$

where $P = \{p_t\}_k$ denotes the top-k snippet probabilities based on the feature magnitude of U as in RTFM (k is set to 3). Following [34], we also adopt temporal smoothness and sparsity regularization in our implementation. Please refer to [36] for the details of training the MIL model.

4 Experiments

4.1 Dataset and Metric

We evaluate our S3R against SOTA methods on three datasets: ShanghaiTech [20], UCF-Crime [34], and XD-Violence [46]. Notably, ShanghaiTech is used for one-class and the others are for weakly-supervised VAD primitively. To facilitate the evaluation for both settings, we choose the existing variants or follow the previous procedure to create corresponding types of supervision for VAD. Specifically, Zhong et al. [49] transferred ShanghaiTech to weak supervision VAD by reorganizing the dataset. Sun et al. [35] collects all normal training videos as the training set and remains the same in the testing set in UCF-Crime to perform oVAD. We use the same criteria as the former one to obtain an one-class version XD-Violence. We briefly state the composition of each dataset in the following and report details in the form of a table in supplementary material.

ShanghaiTech. The ShanghaiTech contains 437 videos from 13 scenes of campus surveillance. The original one-class version comprises 330 regular videos and 107 irregular videos, carrying 130 abnormal events for training and testing, respectively. After reorganization, it retains 238/199 videos that cover all 13 scenes for training/testing in the weakly-supervised setting.

Table 1. Comparison of frame-level AUC performance for VAD on ShanghaiTech. We present the current SOTA with the corresponding feature and published year. S3R* and S3R† indicate using D_U to generate pseudo labels and reconstruct features, respectively. TSN$_{flow}$ and I3D$_{flow}$ represent only access flow, and I3D$_{f2}$ means access to both frame and flow.

oVAD				wVAD			
Method	Feature	Year	AUC (%)	Method	Feature	Year	AUC (%)
Conv-AE [13]	–	2016	60.85	Sultani *et al.* [34]	I3D	2018	85.33
Stacked-RNN [23]	–	2017	68.00	GCN-Anomaly [49]	C3D	2019	76.44
Frame-Pred [20]	–	2018	73.40	GCN-Anomaly [49]	TSN$_{flow}$	2019	84.13
Mem-AE [12]	–	2019	71.20	GCN-Anomaly [49]	TSN	2019	84.44
MNAD [27]	–	2020	70.50	AR-Net [39]	I3D$_{flow}$	2020	82.34
VEC [48]	–	2020	74.80	AR-Net [39]	I3D	2020	85.38
STC Graph [35]	–	2020	74.70	AR-Net [39]	I3D$_{f2}$	2020	91.24
CAC [44]	–	2020	79.30	MIST [10]	C3D	2021	93.13
AMMC [4]	–	2020	73.70	MIST [10]	I3D	2021	94.83
HF2-VAD [21]	–	2021	76.20	RTFM [36]	C3D	2021	91.51
ROADMAP [43]	–	2021	76.60	RTFM [36]	I3D	2021	97.21
SVD-GAN [30]	–	2021	78.42	MSL [19]	C3D	2022	94.81
BDPN [7]	–	2022	78.10	MSL [19]	I3D	2022	96.08
S3R	I3D	2022	79.89	S3R	I3D	2022	**97.48**
S3R*	I3D	2022	**80.47**	S3R†	I3D	2022	97.47

UCF-Crime. The UCF-Crime has 1900 surveillance videos covering 13 real-world anomalous classes such as robbery, explosion, and road accident. Compared to ShanghaiTech, which nearly includes pedestrian activities in the university, the scenes in this dataset are more diverse and more complex. The number of videos for training/testing is 1610/290 in incipient weakly-supervised requirement and reduce the number of training to 800 by discarding anomalous videos for the unsupervised assumption.

XD-Violence. The XD-Violence is the latest and the most large-scale dataset, which involves 4754 untrimmed videos together with audio signals. The sources of scenery are various, including surveillance, movies, dashcam, games, etc. The videos number for one-class and weakly-supervised scenarios are 3954/800 and 2049/800, respectively. To measure the effectiveness of our model fairly, we use the same features as previous works that access video only.

Metric. For evaluating the model performance in VAD, we calculate the Area Under Curve (AUC), a conventional threshold-independent metric used for earlier works. We follow [46] for evaluating the XD-Violence experiment and use the same Average Precision (AP) metric to compare the performance.

4.2   Implementation Details

For a fair comparison, we adopt the I3D network [5] pre-trained on Kinetics-400 [16] as [6,10,19,36] for the video feature extraction. During training, we train our S3R through Adam optimizer with a batch size of 64 for 50 epochs on all dataset, and sample each video with 32 snippets via the linear interpolation, *i.e.* $T = 32$. Furthermore, we randomly sample 32 normal and 32 anomalous videos to form a mini-batch under wVAD and oVAD settings. Notably, we establish anomalous videos when training through a dictionary for the oVAD setting , *e.g.* D_T or D_U, as mentioned in Sect. 3.3. Following the previous work [36], our S3R uses the learning rate of 0.001 for ShanghaiTech and UCF-Crime, and 0.0001 for XD-Violence.

Table 2. Comparison of frame-level AUC performance for VAD on UCF-Crime. S3R* and S3R† indicate using D_U to generate pseudo labels and reconstruct features, respectively.

oVAD				wVAD			
Method	Feature	Year	AUC (%)	Method	Feature	Year	AUC (%)
SVM Baseline	–		50.00	Sultani *et al.* [34]	I3D	2018	77.92
Conv-AE [13]	–	2016	50.60	GCN-Anomaly [49]	TSN	2019	82.12
S-SVDD [33]	–	2018	58.50	MIST [10]	I3D	2021	82.30
Lu *et al.* [22]	C3D	2013	65.51	Wu *et al.* [46]	I3D	2020	82.44
BODS [40]	I3D	2019	68.26	RTFM [36]	I3D	2021	84.30
GODS [40]	I3D	2019	70.46	Chang *et al.* [6]	I3D	2021	84.62
STC Graph [35]	RPN	2020	72.70	MSL [19]	I3D	2022	85.30
S3R	I3D	2022	77.15	S3R	I3D	2022	**85.99**
S3R*	I3D	2022	**79.58**	S3R†	I3D	2022	85.00

4.3   Results of oVAD

Previous methods [4,7,12,13,20–23,27,30,31,33,35,40,43,44,48] deal with VAD in the one-class setup. The left part in Table 1, 2 and 3 show the comparison results of the oVAD on the corresponding dataset. We provide a variant S3R* that adopts the universal dictionary D_U for pseudo label generation. As seen in Table 1, 2 and 3, our model outperforms the other state-of-the-art models for all benchmarks. Our model achieves new art on ShanghaiTech, UCF-Crime, XD-Violence, improving around 1.2%, 6.9% and 2.7%, respectively.

4.4   Results of wVAD

We consider VAD approaches under weakly-supervised fashions in recent year, including [6,10,19,34,36,39,46,49]. The right part in Table 1, 2 and 3 show the comparison results of the weakly-supervised VAD on the corresponding dataset.

Table 3. Comparison of AP performance on XD-Violence. S3R* and S3R† indicate using D_U to generate pseudo labels and reconstruct features, respectively.

oVAD				wVAD			
Method	Feature	Year	AUC (%)	Method	Feature	Year	AP (%)
–	–	–	–	Sultani *et al.* [34]	I3D	2018	75.68
SVM Baseline	–	–	50.78	Wu *et al.* [46]	I3D	2020	75.41
OCSVM [31]	–	1999	27.25	RTFM [36]	I3D	2021	77.81
Conv-AE [13]	–	2016	30.77	MSL [19]	I3D	2022	78.28
S3R	I3D	2022	51.64	S3R	I3D	2022	**80.26**
S3R*	I3D	2022	**53.52**	S3R†	I3D	2022	79.54

The feature column without emphasis shows that the extractor accesses the frame solely. In particular, we report the AP scores that utilize video but discard audio for proper comparison on XD-Violence.We provide a variant S3R† that adopts the universal dictionary D_U for the en-Normal. As seen in Table 1, 2 and 3, our model outperforms the other state-of-the-art models for all datasets. Our model achieves new art on all benchmarks, improving around 0.3%, 0.7% and 2%, respectively.

4.5   Ablation Study

To verify the effectiveness of each module in the S3R, we consider four configurations for the model deal with wVAD, *i.e.*, baseline without de-Normal and dictionary, S3R with de-Normal using $\tilde{\mathcal{X}}_{avg}$, D_U or D_T, respectively. Table 4 shows the ablation study on these configurations. All the models are end-to-end trained and under the same remaining configuration. Precisely, the baseline model is similar to RTFM since we adopt MTN and also build an MIL-based model. Consequently, the AUC of baseline does not perform much of a difference to RTFM. The second configuration employs de-Normal without any dictionary but uses the averaged feature of all normal training videos. The configuration shows the benefit and effectiveness of the proposed de-Normal module, which significantly improves AUC on ShanghaiTech and UCF-Crime. The last two configurations ablate our full model by utilizing the different dictionaries. Particularly, S3R using the task-specific dictionary obtains the best score with a broad margin on UCF-Crime.

Another ablation exploits the composition of the pseudo label. As shown in Table 5, we generate pseudo normal and pseudo anomaly by referring to several ratios. Notably, the snippets and atoms are selected according to their mutual similarity rather than the hand-crafted annotations [24]. The ratio for anomaly and normal is 25%, *i.e.*, $T/4$ snippets are replaced, which obtains the best score in our framework.

Table 6 ablates the channel reduction rate for en-Normal and de-Normal modules on the ShanghaiTech dataset under the oVAD setting, respectively. The first row shows different rates of the embedding layers, *i.e.* ϕ^q and ϕ^k. With the 25% reduction rate, we obtain the best performance of 80.47 in AUC. As the reduction rate increases or decreases, the performance drops at least 2.59% in AUC. The second row ablates the channel reduction of MLP in (4) for the de-Normal module. With the 25% rate, we get the worst performance of 66.14% in AUC. Using the rate of 6.25%, we improve the performance by 14.33% AUC.

Table 4. Ablation study on *S3R's modules* tackling wVAD task with AUC metric and AUC's improvement against the baseline on ShanghaiTech and UCF-Crime.

Configuration		ShanghaiTech		UCF-Crime	
de-Normal	en-Normal	AUC (%)	improvement	AUC (%)	Improvement
–	–	96.97	–	83.42	–
✓	$\tilde{X}_{avg}$	97.28	↑ 0.77	84.19	↑ 0.77
✓	D_U	97.47	↑ 0.19	85.00	↑ 0.81
✓	D_T	**97.48**	↑ 0.20	**85.99**	↑ 1.80

Table 5. Ablation study on *snippet ratio* tackling oVAD task with AUC metric on ShanghaiTech. A and N represent the ratio of anomaly and normal, respectively.

Ratio (A / N)	25% 25%	25% 0%	25% 50%	25% 12.5%	50% 25%	12.5% 25%
AUC (%)	**80.47**	79.59	79.18	76.46	78.02	60.43

Table 6. Ablation study on *channel reduction rate* in en-Normal module (2) and de-Normal module (4) tackling oVAD task with AUC metric on ShanghaiTech.

Channel reduction rate	50%	25%	12.5%	6.25%	3.125%
en-Normal (embedding layers ϕ^q, ϕ^k in (2))	70.38	**80.47**	77.88	76.01	73.36
de-Normal (MLP in (4))	72.73	66.14	70.31	**80.47**	68.77

5   Conclusion

We establish a self-supervised sparse representation framework, a unified model for simultaneously tackling both oVAD and wVAD tasks. At the core of S3R is to model the feature-level anomaly through the offline trained dictionary and self-supervised learning. Our design results in two opposite modules. The first module, en-Normal, is in charge of reconstructing normal-event features, while the second one, de-Normal, filters out the normal-event feature. By using the self-supervised techniques, we are able to further generate the pseudo anomaly/normal data concerning the learned dictionary to guide the training of our anomaly detector. The extensive experiments on three public benchmarks show that S3R consistently surpasses state-of-the-art oVAD and wVAD methods, demonstrating that our unified reconstruction-based framework effectively solves both one-class and weakly-supervised video anomaly detection tasks.

Acknowledgements. This work was supported in part by the MOST grants 110-2634-F-007-027, 110-2221-E-001-017 and 111-2221-E-001-015 of Taiwan. We are grateful to National Center for High-performance Computing for providing computational resources and facilities.

References

1. Barlow, H.B.: Single units and sensation: a neuron doctrine for perceptual psychology? Perception **1**(4), 371–394 (1972)
2. Bergmann, P., Fauser, M., Sattlegger, D., Steger, C.: MVTec AD - a comprehensive real-world dataset for unsupervised anomaly detection. In: CVPR, pp. 9592–9600 (2019)
3. Bergmann, P., Fauser, M., Sattlegger, D., Steger, C.: Uninformed students: student-teacher anomaly detection with discriminative latent embeddings. In: CVPR, pp. 4183–4192 (2020)
4. Cai, R., Zhang, H., Liu, W., Gao, S., Hao, Z.: Appearance-motion memory consistency network for video anomaly detection. In: AAAI, pp. 938–946 (2021)
5. Carreira, J., Zisserman, A.: Quo vadis, action recognition? A new model and the kinetics dataset. In: CVPR, pp. 4724–4733 (2017)
6. Chang, S., Li, Y., Shen, J.S., Feng, J., Zhou, Z.: Contrastive attention for video anomaly detection. IEEE Trans. Multimedia **24**, 4067–4076 (2021)
7. Chen, C., et al.: Comprehensive regularization in a bi-directional predictive network for video anomaly detection. In: AAAI (2022)
8. Cong, Y., Yuan, J., Liu, J.: Sparse reconstruction cost for abnormal event detection. In: CVPR, pp. 3449–3456 (2011)
9. Feichtenhofer, C., Pinz, A., Zisserman, A.: Convolutional two-stream network fusion for video action recognition. In: CVPR, pp. 1933–1941 (2016)
10. Feng, J.C., Hong, F.T., Zheng, W.S.: Mist: multiple instance self-training framework for video anomaly detection. In: CVPR, pp. 14009–14018 (2021)
11. Georgescu, M.I., Barbalau, A., Ionescu, R.T., Khan, F.S., Popescu, M., Shah, M.: Anomaly detection in video via self-supervised and multi-task learning. In: CVPR, pp. 12742–12752 (2021)
12. Gong, D., et al.: Memorizing normality to detect anomaly: memory-augmented deep autoencoder for unsupervised anomaly detection. In: ICCV, pp. 1705–1714 (2019)
13. Hasan, M., Choi, J., Neumann, J., Roy-Chowdhury, A.K., Davis, L.S.: Learning temporal regularity in video sequences. In: CVPR, pp. 733–742 (2016)
14. Hu, J., Shen, L., Sun, G.: Squeeze-and-excitation networks. In: CVPR, pp. 7132–7141 (2018)

15. Ionescu, R.T., Khan, F.S., Georgescu, M.I., Shao, L.: Object-centric auto-encoders and dummy anomalies for abnormal event detection in video. In: CVPR, pp. 7842–7851 (2019)
16. Kay, W., et al.: The kinetics human action video dataset. arXiv preprint arXiv:1705.06950 (2017)
17. Kreutz-Delgado, K., Murray, J.F., Rao, B.D., Engan, K., Lee, T.W., Sejnowski, T.J.: Dictionary learning algorithms for sparse representation. Neural Comput. **15**(2), 349–396 (2003)
18. Li, C.L., Sohn, K., Yoon, J., Pfister, T.: CutPaste: self-supervised learning for anomaly detection and localization. In: CVPR, pp. 9664–9674 (2021)
19. Li, S., Liu, F., Jiao, L.: Self-training multi-sequence learning with transformer for weakly supervised video anomaly detection. In: AAAI (2022)
20. Liu, W., Luo, W., Lian, D., Gao, S.: Future frame prediction for anomaly detection-a new baseline. In: CVPR, pp. 6536–6545 (2018)
21. Liu, Z., Nie, Y., Long, C., Zhang, Q., Li, G.: A hybrid video anomaly detection framework via memory-augmented flow reconstruction and flow-guided frame prediction. In: ICCV, pp. 13588–13597 (2021)
22. Lu, C., Shi, J., Jia, J.: Abnormal event detection at 150 fps in MATLAB. In: ICCV, pp. 2720–2727 (2013)
23. Luo, W., Liu, W., Gao, S.: A revisit of sparse coding based anomaly detection in stacked rnn framework. In: ICCV, pp. 341–349 (2017)
24. Lv, H., Zhou, C., Cui, Z., Xu, C., Li, Y., Yang, J.: Localizing anomalies from weakly-labeled videos. IEEE Trans. Image Process. **30**, 4505–4515 (2021)
25. Mairal, J., Bach, F., Ponce, J., Sapiro, G.: Online dictionary learning for sparse coding. In: ICML, pp. 689–696 (2009)
26. Pang, G., Yan, C., Shen, C., Hengel, A.V.D., Bai, X.: Self-trained deep ordinal regression for end-to-end video anomaly detection. In: CVPR, pp. 12173–12182 (2020)
27. Park, H., Noh, J., Ham, B.: Learning memory-guided normality for anomaly detection. In: CVPR, pp. 14372–14381 (2020)
28. Qiu, Z., Yao, T., Mei, T.: Learning spatio-temporal representation with pseudo-3d residual networks. In: ICCV, pp. 5534–5542 (2017)
29. Ruff, L., et al.: Deep one-class classification. In: ICML, pp. 4393–4402 (2018)
30. Samuel, D.J., Cuzzolin, F.: SVD-GAN for real-time unsupervised video anomaly detection. In: BMVC (2021)
31. Schölkopf, B., Williamson, R.C., Smola, A.J., Shawe-Taylor, J., Platt, J.C.: Support vector method for novelty detection. In: NIPS, pp. 582–588 (1999)
32. Simonyan, K., Zisserman, A.: Two-stream convolutional networks for action recognition in videos. In: NIPS, pp. 568–576 (2014)
33. Sohrab, F., Raitoharju, J., Gabbouj, M., Iosifidis, A.: Subspace support vector data description. In: ICPR, pp. 722–727 (2018)
34. Sultani, W., Chen, C., Shah, M.: Real-world anomaly detection in surveillance videos. In: CVPR, pp. 6479–6488 (2018)
35. Sun, C., Jia, Y., Hu, Y., Wu, Y.: Scene-aware context reasoning for unsupervised abnormal event detection in videos. In: ACMMM, pp. 184–192 (2020)
36. Tian, Y., Pang, G., Chen, Y., Singh, R., Verjans, J.W., Carneiro, G.: Weakly-supervised video anomaly detection with robust temporal feature magnitude learning. In: ICCV, pp. 4975–4986 (2021)
37. Tran, D., Bourdev, L.D., Fergus, R., Torresani, L., Paluri, M.: Learning spatiotemporal features with 3d convolutional networks. In: ICCV, pp. 4489–4497 (2015)

38. Vaswani, A., et al.: Attention is all you need. In: NIPS, pp. 5998–6008 (2017)
39. Wan, B., Fang, Y., Xia, X., Mei, J.: Weakly supervised video anomaly detection via center-guided discriminative learning. In: ICME, pp. 1–6 (2020)
40. Wang, J., Cherian, A.: Gods: generalized one-class discriminative subspaces for anomaly detection. In: ICCV, pp. 8201–8211 (2019)
41. Wang, L., Xiong, Y., Wang, Z., Qiao, Y., Lin, D., Tang, X., Gool, L.V.: Temporal segment networks: towards good practices for deep action recognition. In: ECCV, pp. 20–36 (2016)
42. Wang, X., Girshick, R.B., Gupta, A., He, K.: Non-local neural networks. In: CVPR, pp. 7794–7803 (2018)
43. Wang, X., et al.: Robust unsupervised video anomaly detection by multipath frame prediction. IEEE Trans. Neural Netw. Learn. Syst. **33**(6), 2301–2312 (2021)
44. Wang, Z., Zou, Y., Zhang, Z.: Cluster attention contrast for video anomaly detection. In: ACMMM, pp. 2463–2471 (2020)
45. Wu, J.C., Chen, D.J., Fuh, C.S., Liu, T.L.: Learning unsupervised metaformer for anomaly detection. In: ICCV, pp. 4369–4378 (2021)
46. Wu, P., et al.: Not only look, but also listen: learning multimodal violence detection under weak supervision. In: ECCV, pp. 322–339 (2020)
47. Xu, H., Das, A., Saenko, K.: R-C3D: region convolutional 3d network for temporal activity detection. In: ICCV, pp. 5794–5803 (2017)
48. Yu, G., et al.: Cloze test helps: effective video anomaly detection via learning to complete video events. In: ACMMM, pp. 583–591 (2020)
49. Zhong, J.X., Li, N., Kong, W., Liu, S., Li, T.H., Li, G.: Graph convolutional label noise cleaner: train a plug-and-play action classifier for anomaly detection. In: CVPR, pp. 1237–1246 (2019)

Author Index

Printed in the United States
by Baker & Taylor Publisher Services